Microsoft BackOffice™ 2

Joe Greene, et al.

SAMS
PUBLISHING

201 West 103rd Street
Indianapolis, IN 46290

UNLEASHED

International Standard Book Number: 0-672-30816-9

Library of Congress Catalog Card Number: 96-67199

99 98 97 96   4   3   2   1

Interpretation of the printing code: the rightmost double-digit number is the year of the book's printing; the rightmost single-digit, the number of the book's printing. For example, a printing code of 96-1 shows that the first printing of the book occurred in 1996.

Composed in AGaramond and MCPdigital by Macmillan Computer Publishing

Printed in the United States of America

Publisher and President   *Richard K. Swadley*

Publishing Team Leader   *Rosemarie Graham*

Managing Editor   *Cindy Morrow*

Director of Marketing   *John Pierce*

Assistant Marketing Managers   *Kristina Perry, Rachel Wolfe*

Acquisitions Editor
Corrine Wire

Development Editor
Todd Bumbalough

Software Development Specialist
John Warriner

Production Editor
Nancy Albright

Copy Editors
David Bradford, Cheri Clark
Keith Davenport

Indexer
John Hulse

Technical Reviewers
Robert L. Bogue, Blake Hall,
Kelly Held

Editorial Coordinator
Katie Wise

Technical Edit Coordinator
Lorraine Schaffer

Resource Coordinator
Deborah Frisby

Editorial Assistants
Carol Ackerman, Andi Richter,
Rhonda Tinch-Mize

Cover Designer
Tim Amrhein

Book Designer
Gary Adair

Copy Writer
Peter Fuller

Production Team Supervisor
Brad Chinn

Production
Debra Bolhuis, Jeanne Clark,
Kevin Cliburn, Jason Hand,
Daniel Harris, Chris
Livengood, Casey Price, Shawn
Ring, Laura Robbins, Janet
Seib, Ian Smith, Mark Walchle

Overview

Contents

Part V SQL Server

28 SQL Server 6.5 Overview   689

Part VII SNA Server

Acknowledgments

Some people might think that authors just sit down at our PCs, write these books completely from memory, then just have them bound and published. These people are wrong. There are a large number of people who work to take our words and ideas and put them in a final published form that has correct grammar, spelling, and technical content. This book all started with our acquisitions editor Corrine Wire who managed to find people who were qualified to write on the wide variety of extremely technical topics that you see in this book. After we wrote our original drafts, we received many good suggestions and corrections from the technical editor Todd Bumbalough, and also the technical reviewers Blake Hall, Kelly Held, and Robert L. Bogue. Production editor Nancy Albright worked to bring all of the details together and correct us when our presentation started to lack clarity and readability. Finally, I would like to thank all the people whose names I do not even know who worked to prepare graphics, lay the pages out, and actually produce the book. **Joe Greene**

I would like to express my gratitude to Larry Ketchersid for his support and encouragement. I want to thank my wife Ritu for her patience, care, and help during the long hours I spent working on this book. I could not have finished this effort without her help. I am thankful to my friends Mahender and Divya for their constant encouragement. I would also like to thank my acquisitions editor Corrine Wire for giving me this wonderful opportunity. **Vipul Minocha**

Dedications

I would like to dedicate this book to my wife Vicki and our child who is on the way for their patience and support during this and all of the other book projects that I have worked on.

—Joe Greene

I would like to dedicate my effort to the two most important people in my life—my parents.

—Vipul Minocha

I wish to dedicate my section of this book in memory of my loyal pet Rottweiler, Lady CRC Omega, who passed away during the writing of Chapter 21. CRC was my faithful companion during many late-night writing sessions. I also want to extend an affectionate thank-you to my wife, Sheri, for her loving support and encourgement throughout this project.

—Gregory H. Dodge

About the Authors

Joe Greene has been working with computers for over 20 years now. He has worked with some of the best, leading-edge technologies for the past 10 years in various computer consulting, planning, and development roles. Much of his work involves databases and system development, which is how he started to work with Windows NT, developing a multimedia database running on a Windows NT Server. He has worked with most of the popular operating systems over the last decade, but now focuses primarily on Windows NT and Windows 95. For fun, he occasionally works with release versions of software before he installs the next beta version and tries to make it work. He lives in Pittsburgh with his wife and soon-to-be child. He is the author of the *Oracle DBA Survival Guide* and is a contributing author for *Oracle Unleashed* and *Windows NT Server 4.0 Unleashed*, all from Sams Publishing.

Gregory H. Dodge has worked in a computer consulting capacity for the last six years. While earning a Bachelor of Science degree in Management Information Systems from the University of South Florida, Greg worked in the End User Support division of IBM, where he provided technical assistance on various software packages. He then joined National Data Products in 1991 and became its first Microsoft Certified Systems Engineer. He is presently a Senior Systems Engineer for Dataflex Corporation, specializing in Windows NT Architecture and Design, with an emphasis on Microsoft Exchange. He has been involved with Exchange since the beta 1 release and is currently supporting several "First Look" customers as they migrate from MS Mail to Exchange.

Vipul Minocha works in the Platform Infrastructure Group of Compaq Computer Corporation. He has over six years of experience working with Sybase and Microsoft SQL Server. He has taught classes and made presentations on various SQL Server topics. He presented a paper in October 1995 at the Sybase International European Conference. His areas of interests are database design, performance, and tuning.

John W. Fronckowiak is president and founder of IDC Consulting, Inc., which specializes in Internet/intranet consulting, application development, and network consulting. He is currently employed by Academic Medicine Services, Inc., which is affiliated with the School of Medicine at the State University of New York at Buffalo. He is also a computer science graduate student at the State University of New York at Buffalo. John lives in East Amherst, New York with his wife Diane and their cat Eiffel. John can be reached via e-mail at john@buffnet.net or his Web page http://www.buffnet.net/~john, or by phone at 716-689-6286.

Arthur Knowles is president and founder of Knowles Consulting, a firm specializing in systems integration, training, and software development. Art is a Microsoft Certified Systems Engineer. His specialties include Microsoft Windows NT Server, Windows NT Workstation, SQL Server, Systems Management Server, Windows 95, and Windows for Workgroups. Art is the author of *Internet Information Server 2 Unleashed* and *Microsoft BackOffice Administrator's*

Survival Guide, Second Edition, and has served as a contributing author to several books, including *Designing and Implementing Microsoft Internet Information Server 2, Windows 3.1 Configuration Secrets, Windows NT Unleashed,* and *Mastering Windows 95.* He is the forum manager of the Portable Computers Forum on the Microsoft Network. You can reach Art on the Internet at webmaster@nt-guru.com or on his Web site at http://www.nt-guru.com.

Richard Neff is a Microsoft Certified Professional, certified as a Systems Engineer with elective exams in Microsoft Mail and Systems Management Server (SMS). He is also a Product Specialist in Microsoft Excel 5.0 and Microsoft Word for Windows 2.0/6.0. He has a B.S. in Computer Science from VMI and has worked with personal computers for over 15 years. He is a contributing author to the books *Windows NT 4.0 Installation and Configuration Handbook* and *Windows NT 4.0 Advanced Technical Reference,* both published by Que Publishing. He currently writes a column called Unleashing Windows for the electronic magazine *ChipNet* found on America Online (keyword: Chipnet) or on the World Wide Web. He has formed his own computer consulting company, Network Technologies Group, which specializes in Novell NetWare, Microsoft Windows NT, and Microsoft BackOffice solutions. Network Technologies Group is located in Blacksburg, Virginia, and also has a Web site at http://www.bnt.com/~netech/. He can be reached by e-mail at RickNeff on America Online (rickneff@AOL.COM over the Internet) or at 70761,3615 on CompuServe (70761.3615@COMPUSERVE.COM).

Ahsan Farooqi is a Microsoft Certified Trainer (MCT) and a Microsoft Certified Systems Engineer (MCSE), as well as a CAN-3, CAN-4, CNE3, and CNE4. Ahsan has been working in the field for about six years and has been training for the last three. He was the lead in development of the entire client-server and networking program for a training division of CHUBB Computer Services of Chubb & Sons. Ahsan has written many student and instructor manuals in addition to this book. He specializes in Novell and NT BackOffices, including NT Server, SQL Server, and SMS Server. Ahsan is the president of his own company, Farrisons Enterprise USA Inc. Ahsan can be reached via e-mail at A_Farooqi@msn.com. Look for www.Farrisons.com, coming shortly.

Martin Larsson is a software developer from Norway. He specializes in Windows and Web programming. He is currently involved in several projects for some of the largest banks in Norway using Borland Delphi. When he's not hacking away, searching for the ultimate Windows API function, he's probably out sailing in the rain, with his love and some red wine.

Paul Thomsen is the SMS Columnist for *BackOffice Magazine* and a frequent contributor to SMS-related articles. He is also a Personal Computing Integration Specialist for the Ontario Ministry of Natural Resources and teaches Microsoft and Digital Equipment courses in Southeast Asia for Global Consulting Networks. Previously, Paul was a technical specialist and programmer for 15 years, 10 of those in large end-user organizations in government and in the health industry. Paul lives at his home, fronting Chemong Lake in Peterborough, Ontario, with his wife Janet and golden retriever Kaila.

William Robert Stanek (`director@tvp.com`) is a leading Internet technology expert and a working professional who directs an Internet startup company called The Virtual Press (`http://tvp.com/` and mirror site `http://www.tvpress.com/`). As a publisher and writer with over 10 years experience on networks, William brings a solid voice of experience on the Internet and electronic publishing to his many projects. He has been involved in the commercial Internet community since 1991 and was first introduced to Internet e-mail in 1988 when he worked for the government. His years of practical experience are backed by an M.S. in Information Systems and a B.S. in computer science. In addition to writing best-sellers, such as Sams.net's *Web Publishing Unleashed* and *Microsoft FrontPage Unleashed*, William advises corporate clients and develops hot new Web sites.

Diane Andrews is a Windows consultant with Fountainhead Software, Inc. in Seattle, Washington. Under contract with Microsoft, she is currently a software test engineer for the Microsoft Exchange Forms Designer. In addition, Diane does technical writing for user documentation and enjoys VB programming. She can be reached via e-mail at `DianeAndrews@FountainheadSoftware.com`.

Rick Andrews is a Windows consultant with Fountainhead Software, Inc. in Seattle, Washington. Under contract with Microsoft, he was the Visual Basic technical lead/developer for the Microsoft Exchange Forms Designer. In addition, Rick is the developer of the Visual Basic Setup Toolkit for Microsoft. He can be reached via e-mail at `RickAndrews@FountainheadSoftware.com`.

Stephen Gutknecht is a Microsoft Certified Systems Engineer (MCSE) with a deployment and support background. He has worked for more than 10 years with Microsoft and IBM products, including the first release of OS/2 and Microsoft's Windows NT and BackOffice products. Stephen has focused on Microsoft Exchange messaging product support and training. For the past eighteen months, he was the lead support engineer for a Microsoft Authorized Support Center. In that role, he is certified by Microsoft's PSS organization as a Windows NT escalation engineer. Most recently, he is a Microsoft product support endorsed trainer for Exchange Server, one of only a few outside Microsoft. He is currently a Principal Consultant at Software Spectrum, Inc., working at its Bellevue, Washington, office. Stephen has previously worked as both author and technical editor on several OS/2-related books, including *Maximizing OS/2* and several editions of *Inside OS/2*.

Tell Us What You Think!

As a reader, you are the most important critic and commentator of our books. We value your opinion and want to know what we're doing right, what we could do better, what areas you'd like to see us publish in, and any other words of wisdom you're willing to pass our way. You can help us make strong books that meet your needs and give you the computer guidance you require.

Do you have access to CompuServe or the World Wide Web? Then check out our CompuServe forum by typing **GO SAMS** at any prompt. If you prefer the World Wide Web, check out our site at http://www.mcp.com.

> **NOTE**
>
> If you have a technical question about this book, call the technical support line at (800) 571-5840, ext. 3668.

As the team leader of the group that created this book, I welcome your comments. You can fax, e-mail, or write me directly to let me know what you did or didn't like about this book—as well as what we can do to make our books stronger. Here's the information:

FAX: 317/581-4669

E-mail: enterprise_mgr@sams.mcp.com

Mail: Rosemarie Graham
         Comments Department
         Sams Publishing
         201 W. 103rd Street
         Indianapolis, IN 46290

Introduction

by Joe Greene

Most of us have worked with a variety of electronic mail and database systems during our careers. In this book, we challenge you to consider the components in the Microsoft BackOffice family. This integrated environment provides most of the core services that you would want when designing a network server. This product family has the advantage of being implemented as a single architecture. This leads to tight integration between components and use of common administrative tools.

There are a number of other, more business-oriented reasons to seriously consider these products. Microsoft is devoting considerable effort to this product family. With all its development talent and experience, Microsoft is capable of turning out quite a bit of software. Many industry analysts who measure sales of the Windows NT Server environment also show Microsoft making great strides in this arena and project that it may soon lead this market. It is always easier to sell your services for a popular environment than for one which is slowly dying out.

This book is not designed for the beginner who wants to use the Web browser or mail reader that came with the operating system. It is designed for more experienced computer support staff members who are responsible for designing, programming, or maintaining one or more servers that run BackOffice components. It does not replace the Microsoft online documentation. Instead, it tries to provide both the background material to understand how a BackOffice component functions and the hands-on experience needed to make it work well.

To accomplish these ambitious goals, this book is divided into the following major sections:

- Introduction to BackOffice
- Windows NT Server
- Internet Information Server
- Exchange Server and Mail
- SQL Server
- Systems Management Server
- SNA Server
- Integrating BackOffice
- Finishing Touches

The goal is to provide you with both a broad overview of BackOffice and the details that you will need to implement an effective BackOffice information environment.

Part I, "Introduction to BackOffice," provides a broad overview of the technologies and architecture associated with BackOffice. It is a good place to start when you are trying to see what all the components of BackOffice are and how they fit together. Key topics in this part include the overall BackOffice architecture, security environment, monitoring environment, and administrative environment. The Internet and intranets are also covered to give you an appreciation for these networked computer environments, their protocols, and standard services.

With the general overview of BackOffice completed, Part II, "Windows NT Server," deals with the first product in the BackOffice family. Windows NT Server is the basis for the BackOffice family. The other servers are optimized toward only one operating system—Windows NT. They also use a number of operating system components, such as the monitoring and administrative tools. Therefore, a BackOffice administrator is actually an extension of a Windows NT systems administrator. This part covers planning, installation, administration, tuning, and integration with other computer environments.

With all the groundwork laid, Part III, "Internet Information Server," covers the first BackOffice product that you may want to implement in your environment. The Internet Information Server (IIS) is actually bundled with the Windows NT Server operating system. It provides three key servers for Internet and intranet environments: a World Wide Web (WWW) server, a File Transfer Protocol (FTP) server, and a Gopher server (which enables you to search for information on the Net). The chapters in this part cover setting up an IIS installation and the basics of administration.

Part IV, "Exchange Server and Mail," introduces two products designed to accomplish the same basic goal. Microsoft has marketed an electronic mail server product for a number of years known as Microsoft Mail. As the need to provide larger electronic mail installations grew, Microsoft rebuilt its electronic mail system into a much more robust system known as Microsoft Exchange Server (which strongly resembles a modern database management system). The chapters in this part of the book cover both Microsoft Mail and Exchange Server from the configuration, interfacing, tuning, and client setup perspectives. The emphasis is on Exchange Server, which is the current product that fits well into the overall BackOffice environment.

Part V, "SQL Server," covers Microsoft SQL Server. SQL, or Structured Query Language, is an international standard for accessing relational database management systems. Microsoft SQL Server is the large-scale, server-based database management system. It is designed to store the neatly ordered bits of information that are currently stored in databases, such as accounting records, personnel records, and so forth. It is being extended to handle more disorganized forms of information, such as images and audio data. Part V is devoted to discussing installation, administration, tuning, and application building in the SQL Server environment.

Part VI, "Systems Management Server," discusses a new product in the BackOffice family that is designed to solve the problems associated with a large number of distributed computers located on a local or wide area network. The Systems Management Server enables information systems personnel to capture the configuration of these distributed workstations, see what is happening on these workstations, and even distribute software automatically. Part VI covers installation and use of this product in a modern network environment.

Part VII, "SNA Server," covers a topic that is very important in some environments, but is never used in other environments. Organizations that have important data located on IBM mainframes and AS/400 computers usually need an efficient means to access that information from other computers on the network. The SNA Server product provides the gateway between the proprietary protocols in the IBM environment (SNA, SAA, LU6.2, and a whole bunch of other acronyms that have grown up in the big blue world) and the protocols that are more common in local area network (LAN) environments, such as NetBEUI, IPX/SPX, and TCP/IP.

Part VIII, "Integrating BackOffice," contains the chapters that should appeal most to developers and integrators. It covers an important concept in the design of the BackOffice family. Microsoft realized that no matter how much time it spent building a flexible product family, it could not anticipate every requirement in every organization in the world. To deal with this, it built a series of tools and programming interfaces that enable you to use the BackOffice family as the basis for applications that you develop locally. Part VIII covers the most popular interfaces and also those that have only recently come into being to support Internet/intranet needs.

Part IX, "Finishing Touches," wraps up the book. The BackOffice logo requirements are presented, which enable you to advertise that applications that you develop are compatible with BackOffice. Part IX also covers some resources that you may want to use to get more information on BackOffice and also get updated files. The final chapter enables me to get out my crystal ball and provide a few guesses as to where BackOffice is heading.

Learning about BackOffice and the related technologies may seem like trying to drink from a fire hose. Microsoft has not stopped its development efforts. There are already beta test versions of products such as merchant servers and search engines that will take their places in the BackOffice product family soon enough. For developers, Microsoft is turning out application programming interfaces far more quickly than any one developer can master them. This book will make your task of keeping up with this flood of information just a little easier.

Conventions Used in This Book

This book uses the following conventions:

- Words that you enter appear in regular text in `monospace bold`.
- Placeholders (words that stand for what you actually type) appear in *`italic monospace`*.

PART

I

Introduction to BackOffice

Microsoft BackOffice as an Intranet/ Internet Server Suite

by Joe Greene

IN THIS CHAPTER

CHAPTER 1

Why mention "Intranet/Internet Server Suite" in the title of the first chapter of a book? Some might argue that the Internet is the hottest topic in the computer industry these days and that everyone wants to jump on the bandwagon to help sell computers, software packages, and, of course, books. Actually, there is a justification for this mention of the Internet and intranets—they are about the only thing that you can get Microsoft executives (and those of most other big computer firms) to talk about these days. Going beyond mere talk, these network technologies are where a high percentage of the development talent is allocated. The result is that whether you like or want to link to the Internet, you will find many of its technologies and standards creeping into the computers and operating systems that you will be buying in the future.

BackOffice was a product line conceived well before the Internet craze that has seemed to dominate the industry recently. Why try to confuse a discussion of electronic mail and database management systems with the Internet? The two worlds—the client-server local area network (LAN) environment and the Internet—are surprisingly compatible, trying to accomplish very similar goals, and they actually need one another to continue their evolution. Microsoft and other vendors have realized this and devoted a lot of effort to adapt their products to work in this brave new world.

This may not be obvious to all observers. They could argue that Microsoft is making billions delivering operating systems and desktop applications. There are many examples of software firms that have destroyed themselves when they go on a binge of buying other companies or try to expand their product lines to cover every application imaginable. They could also argue that the Internet has grown up quite nicely, powered largely by UNIX workstations and servers using technologies developed by governments and universities. This "free-thinking" culture would seem incompatible with the hard-nosed business application environment found in the large software development firms.

One of the most interesting explanations of how these two worlds are, and should be, merging is in *Microsoft's Intranet Strategy Whitepaper,* published by Microsoft in June 1996. For those of you who already have access to the Internet, you can find this paper on the Microsoft World Wide Web site (www.microsoft.com). The key focus of many information system projects today is to provide access to information. This is not just the neatly structured information that you would find in a relational database management system. It includes information stored in the form of a published document or even complex data such as an image or full-motion video. The problem faced by many information systems professionals these days is to integrate the many dissimilar forms of information that relate to a given business and provide tools that enable people to access all the types of data that they need to get their job done.

How hard can this challenge be? We have standard electronic file formats to hold audio, video, and graphic files. Word processors have been around for decades that can store text and even text/graphic documents. Database management systems have also been around for decades that can store neatly organized data, such as the columns in an accounting general ledger. The challenge lies in providing a single, simple interface to *all* this data at the same time. A related need is the capability of storing this information so that it can be accessed quickly, easily, and securely.

The "front" office tools made by Microsoft, Netscape, and all the other players in the desktop software arena provide the user with the door into the network. There are a lot of good people working in this field, and they are turning out some good front-end tools. However, front-end tools are not enough. There needs to be the back-end, server-based tools that provide access to the information. The purpose of BackOffice is to provide the places to store the information that these users are seeking.

By the way, if you want to ignore the intranet/Internet concepts and build just basic, client-server applications, BackOffice will do that job. It will also provide you with basic electronic mail. The SNA server will provide access to mainframes and their data using traditional IBM protocols. Systems Management Server fills important needs in traditional LANs for client configuration and support. However, you may want to take a look at the Internet extensions that are being built into the BackOffice products. The millions of Internet users around the world could be very wrong and we will some day find out that the World Wide Web and other Internet interfaces are really useless, but I doubt it. It seems much more likely that people will continue to clamor for this interface to their information stores, and you will be asked to build systems that have to support these interfaces. BackOffice will be waiting for you when these needs arise.

BackOffice Positioning in the Market

BackOffice is an ambitious undertaking, even by Microsoft standards. It encompasses every-thing from a server operating system (Windows NT) to a suite of specialized server applications. Behind the scenes, Microsoft has spent quite a bit of time working with various standards bodies to get their standards adopted (or even get any standard adopted) to enable them to build a suite of products that can work in a wide variety of environments and with a wide range of other software products. Each of the applications in BackOffice is a technically complex undertaking in itself. Microsoft is trying to offer a full-featured product in each of these areas that can be extended from LANs, through intranets, and even through the Internet itself.

It's useful to look at a little history to figure out how server suites are going to evolve. Just a few short years ago, WordPerfect and Lotus 123 were dominant products in the desktop industry. There were a few other products that were roughly comparable in terms of features, but the majority of users were sticking with the two products that they were all used to. This made sense because people were not as PC-savvy as they are today, and it did not make sense to force these people to learn new products when there was no discriminator to cause organizations to make a switch.

Then along came the Windows operation system. Actually, it sort of evolved rather than sud-denly appearing. The first couple of versions were received without any great enthusiasm. With version 3 of Windows, Microsoft finally had a product that started to generate enthusiasm among buyers. The standard interface and application standards (that is, the menu structures looking similar) enabled you to use many Windows applications after having spent the time to learn the basic user interface of the first one. Microsoft bet heavily on this new user interface and designed a series of Windows-based products. At the same time, the desktop product leaders stuck with their DOS-based products, taking a more cautious approach to building Windows versions of their tools.

Eventually, however, almost everyone was coming out with Windows-based products. It was getting more difficult to find DOS-based products that offered the full feature set of a "modern" application. It was actually easier to develop Windows applications than DOS applications, because the Windows environment provided many more services to the applications than DOS. For example, in DOS you had to build printer drivers to handle the hundreds of different printers that are available on the market. In Windows, you relied on the operating system to provide the printer drivers and you wrote to a standard interface. It was not particularly easy to learn the new environment that had so many more user interface and services options that you had to learn, but once you learned the environment, it was much easier to develop applications that were better than anything you could have dreamed of doing under DOS.

With its Windows-based products, Microsoft started to pull even with the other office automation software product vendors in terms of sales. Microsoft led in sales of Windows-based products, and the old leaders had the advantage in sales of DOS-based products. Windows itself continued to evolve and provide new capabilities, chiefly in the areas of network support and application integration in the form of Object Linking and Embedding (OLE). These technologies met a need that many users were asking for, because they enabled desktop applications to work with one another. For example, you could easily share data between your spreadsheet and word processor. You could link to a standard financial model stored as a spreadsheet located on the server. This enabled you to have a very tightly integrated environment on your desktop rather than hoping that you had the right filters or import routines for your DOS applications.

Microsoft took the high ground in this area when it came out with its Microsoft Office suite, a combination of spreadsheet, word processor, and presentation graphics package with a few integration tools and common components. This integrated package, wherein the tools worked together and used the much easier and finally reliable Windows environment, finally offered users the incentive that was needed to make them change from their old tools. These tools have become the standard in many businesses. Even the old office automation desktop leaders saw the wisdom of the suite concept and integrated their products into suites in the Windows environment.

Many in the computer industry would argue that Microsoft is an evil empire destroying the true pioneers and little companies with its magnificent marketing machine. They usually go on about there being some magical hidden interfaces to the operating system that enable Microsoft to write its applications in a small fraction of the time that it would take others to do it.

I often find this save-the-little-guys attitude somewhat difficult to understand. To me, computer applications are nothing but a bunch of ones and zeros. I just want tools that get the job done. Microsoft has, over the years, seen some great market opportunities to provide the products that people really want. The Windows environment and the Microsoft Office tools helped me get that job done, so I bought them. Remember, it is not like Microsoft can get sloppy. If it does, companies like Oracle and Netscape will gobble it up for lunch.

With this history in hand, let's consider the current computer environment. There are established server vendors who have been leading their fields for quite some time (Novell and the various UNIX vendors). A new technology has recently broken through that has the potential to revolutionize the server environment—the Internet, especially the World Wide Web. Users also want a single interface to the server world, much as they have a single interface in their desktop world. Many would prefer the same interface to both the desktop and the servers.

The next major evolution in computer environments will come on the server side. It will not just be a server upgrade. Instead, Microsoft and other vendors are correct in their vision of a fused information environment where your desktop computer is a gateway to a vast array of information. It will no longer be your problem to know where things are. There will be simple tools and search engines that enable you to say what information you want. The desktop tools, operating system, network, and servers will then do what it takes to get that information to you in the format that you prefer. Figure 1.1 is my rendition of this brave new world. Hey, integration was a big-win theme in the desktop computer environment. Imagine what it could do for a world-wide information network.

FIGURE 1.1.
Integrated information environment.

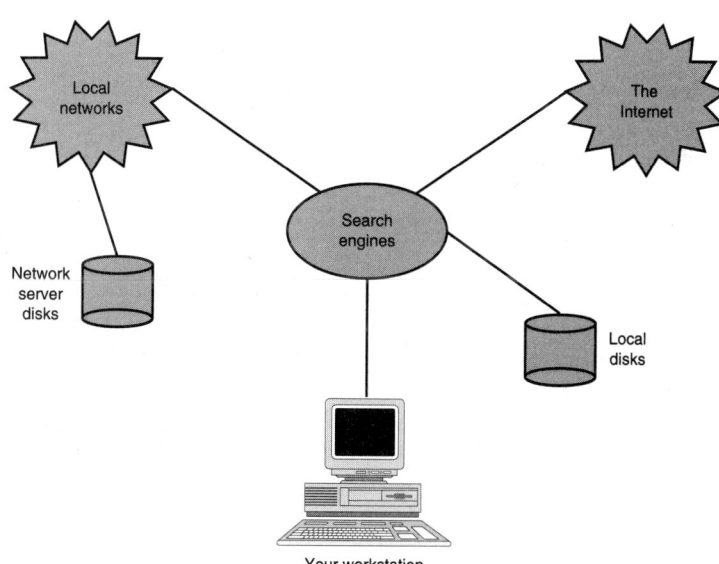

There are several means to accomplish these integration goals. The UNIX world is all about collages. The operating system and most of the applications in the UNIX environment are composed of a number of different programs that work together to accomplish all the goals of the system. Here, you would find a number of different vendors making the various Internet and communications packages that work separately to get the job done as opposed to a single product family produced by the operating system vendor. Many business information systems shops have had some difficulty with this model, because you have to deal with smaller vendors whose support varies from great to poor. You also have to learn each of the products individually and provide support staff for each of them. This raises support costs, and if you choose one of the smaller vendors, you may not be able to provide the level of support for the product that your internal customers are used to. Complicating the support picture for these product vendors are the differences between the many vendors of the UNIX operating system. The various flavors of UNIX are close, but not identical.

Microsoft has taken an integrated environment approach, hoping to appeal to businesses that are looking for that integrated solution. It has simplified its support picture to target on operating systems that are built to function optimally for the integrated suite of applications. Microsoft has also looked for opportunities to share tools between the applications in this suite. For example, you have the need to monitor the performance of databases and mail systems just as you have to monitor the performance of the operating system. Microsoft has extended the operating system's Performance Monitor tool to accommodate the needs of SQL Server and Exchange Server so that you do not need to learn different tools for performance monitoring (and, by the way, not waste time writing the same application over and over). Microsoft even extended this concept to enable you to interface your locally developed applications into the monitoring environment so that you can monitor everything from one application. You will find this integration and programmatic interfaces in many locations in the Windows NT and BackOffice environments.

That covers the integration strategy for BackOffice, but what services does BackOffice provide? That is evolving as this book is being written—there are immediate plans to double the number of products in the BackOffice family. Some of these products also may become part of the operating system itself and not be sold separately. Remember when you had to purchase networking software separately from your operating system? Modern operating systems such as Windows 95 and Windows NT come with the most common forms of networking built into the operating system. You can count on the continued evolution of the BackOffice and Windows NT Server operating system for some time to come.

However, it is important to consider what is currently in the BackOffice environment to get an appreciation of where this product family is targeted in the marketplace. Here is a list of key functions of the BackOffice family (see Figure 1.2):

■ A server operating system that provides the basic file storage, peripheral handling, and network transmission capabilities for the product suite.

■ An intranet/Internet server suite to provide the basic functions of a World Wide Web server and a File Transfer Protocol server. There is also a Gopher server to facilitate looking for information that is not available through standard Web services.

■ A relational database management system that can handle the storage and retrieval of organized collections of data common to most business environments.

■ An electronic mail system to handle basic messaging functions facilitating communication between users and between applications. This package can be extended to serve as groupware (software designed to facilitate collaboration by exchanging messages in more of a dialog format and also supporting forms for data collection and display).

■ A connectivity solution for legacy mainframe environments. This package acknowledges that there is a lot of data on IBM mainframes and AS/400 computers that run in their own network environments. This package provides the bridge into those environments.

■ A management solution for computers on the network. This product enables you to control inventory, update software, and provide better help desk support.

FIGURE 1.2.

Functions of the current BackOffice family.

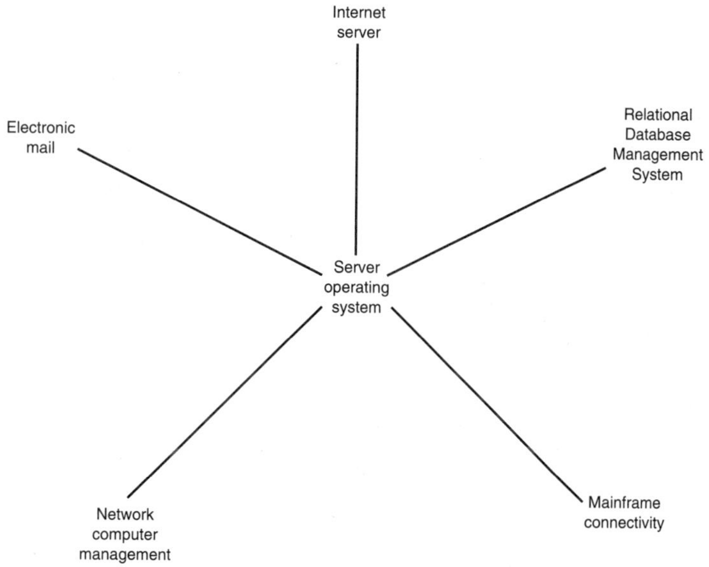

As mentioned earlier, Microsoft is already working to extend the functions of this product family. Key components of this expansion include the following:

■ An Internet proxy server that provides controlled access to the Internet

■ An Internet merchant server to provide support for retail operations over the Internet and intranets

- A media server that enables you to have real-time access to audio and video information stored electronically on a server

- A catalog server that provides access services for large published information collections

Remember, these products are very much market-driven. There are a number of vendors out there, such as Netscape and Oracle, that are pushing their own visions of the future. They have substantial talent and will probably put some products on the market that you have not yet dreamed of, but will want in your future information systems environments. Microsoft, being market-driven, may well adopt some of these technologies as it did with the Java scripting language and the entire World Wide Web concept, both of which were developed by groups outside of Microsoft. If things did not change in the computer field, everyone could become an expert and that would depress all our salaries.

BackOffice and Intranets

Here is a bold statement: an intranet is a logical evolution of the LAN. Microsoft has defined an intranet as "the application of Internet technologies on internal corporate networks" (*Microsoft's Intranet Strategy Whitepaper*). Perhaps it is simply borrowing some really good ideas from someone else when it makes sense. Let's explore some of the background related to intranets so that you can appreciate how the BackOffice components are designed to support the intranet in addition to traditional LAN environments.

Actually, Chapter 7, "Windows NT Server Overview," explores intranets in more detail, but this chapter clarifies the positioning of an intranet. This will help you understand many of the decisions that Microsoft made when designing the various components of BackOffice.

Many years ago, Sun Microsystems stated that the network is the computer. Earlier operating systems were designed before the days of modern computer networks. The large IBM mainframe and minicomputers that evolved in the '70s and '80s were designed to support a network of relatively "dumb" terminals, whose only function was to display the characters and graphics that were sent to them and send the keystrokes that were made by the user to the central computer. All the brains of the operation were centralized in the big host computer.

There are a few practical problems with this architecture. The components of a given computer have certain capacity limits of how much information they can process. It would cost much more than twice as much to build a processor that was twice as fast as its predecessor, if it were possible at all with a given technology. Therefore, the larger computer environments became extremely expensive when compared with the smaller workstations that were entering the marketplace in the '80s.

Users on these workstations, however, suffered from a lack of ability to share information (which was easy on the mainframe because everyone was using the same computer). The solution to this problem came with several computer networking technologies that have been developed to enable computers to communicate with one another on a peer-to-peer basis. The peer-to-peer networking emphasizes sharing of information among equals. In client-server networking, the server tends to have the information and the client and server share the processing load. This is in contrast to older host-based systems where the central computer had all the information and performed all the processing, and the terminals were really too stupid to bother with. These modern network technologies have evolved into a fairly advanced state over the years and are now an effective, reliable, and fast means of communications between workstations, servers, and even the central computers such as mainframes.

There are a number of network technologies that you may run across. New technologies are being created and some older ones are dying out. Chapter 9, "Planning a Server," covers some of these technologies in a little more detail. For now, let's take a broad look at two categories of computer networks—the local area network (LAN) and the wide area network (WAN). This is a big simplification, but it is good enough for this introductory discussion.

A LAN consists of a two or more computers, some wiring, network interface cards (NICs), and network concentrators. There are a few additional complexities, but, again, this is good enough for now. Figure 1.3 illustrates this basic conceptual system. The network interface cards enable the computers to transmit the appropriate signals to the computer network and receive information destined for them. The network concentrators are electronic devices into which you plug the wires running to the various computers. They electronically join the signals from the computers and therefore make network transmissions possible.

FIGURE 1.3.

Simplified view of the local area network.

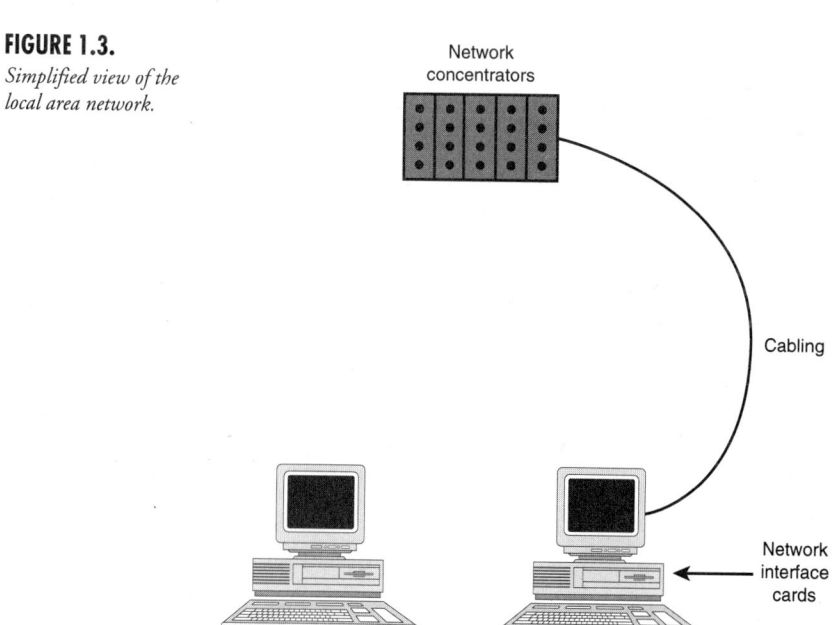

Network concentrators

Cabling

Network interface cards

Workstations

Although it was great to get everyone at a particular location connected, there was more that needed to be done. The WAN came into being to enable individuals at several locations to communicate with each other. A wide area network starts with local area networks at the various locations. A device known as a *router* is attached to some communications equipment to transmit signals between networks. Figure 1.4 illustrates this very simplified view of wide area networks. The other key component in a WAN is the communications lines between the two facilities. In a LAN, you travel over relatively short distances and can therefore use a higher transmission capacity cable than would be economically feasible for most wide area networks. This is the key issue for almost everyone except the network professionals when it comes to distinguishing between LANs and WANs.

FIGURE 1.4.

Simplified view of the wide area network.

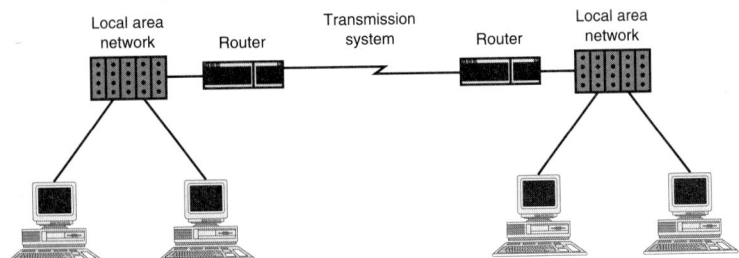

Some of you may be a little bored right now with this simplified introduction to networks, especially if you are the network expert at your location. However, if you are from a non-network environment and are being thrust into the BackOffice environment, you need to be indoctrinated in the technology and terminology.

One of the hottest discussion topics in the computer arena today is the Internet. Many BackOffice components have been designed to work in an Internet environment, so I want to discuss this subject briefly for those who have not had the pleasure of working on the "Net" yet.

The Internet was started by the United States government to support research projects in the Department of Defense. Research dollars were provided to determine the most effective way to link computers over a wide area. It took a lot of work to come up with the hardware, transmission protocols, and simple services that formed the beginning of the Internet. The basis of this network was the Transmission Control Protocol and Internet Protocol (TCP/IP), which enabled everyone to talk to one another. Several government agencies implemented these types of wide area networks, as did many universities and other members of the academic community. The users of these networks began to develop new add-ons to the basic technology. Much of the work came in the form of services that went beyond transmission of data to the beginnings of true information services that enabled you to find and access the data that you needed.

These networks began to connect to each other, and new networks came into being that were connected to this collection of networks. This is what is now known as the Internet. It is actually a collection of networks that is very loosely governed by its users. Much of the communications technology that ties the various networks together is funded by governments, but more commercial users are tapping into this backbone to get the information they need to run their businesses.

This network connection view—the Internet transmission system of the Internet—is actually only half the picture. The other view lies in the information technologies that it provides. For a while, people were thrilled with the idea of being able to log on to remote computers and transfer files to and from them.

Fortunately, however, these computer types became impatient with trying to find other sites that contained the information that they wanted, coordinating accounts and passwords and all these other headaches. Early attempts were focused on cataloging information and providing search capabilities to these catalogs. That was better than it was before, but not perfect. The next major advance came with the implementation of the World Wide Web. This technology enabled you to display text and graphics. Most important however, it implemented the concept of hypertext links wherein you could click on a line of text that was underlined (or a picture) and be taken magically to another computer that contained the information described by this link. Although the various other services of the Internet are important and heavily used, it was this Web technology that has led to the explosion in the use of the Internet by computers running a wide range of operating systems and locations around the world.

Suppose you are about to install or upgrade a local area network. You could build your own information repositories and data search tools. You could buy tools from a favorite vendor that implements that vendor's proprietary tool set and communications protocols. On the other hand, you could buy a series of tools that are designed to work with the millions of computers available. These protocols and products have been tested to work on a wide variety of platforms and are the result of thousands of users and developers trying to achieve better presentation formats. If you choose this option, welcome to the world of intranets.

One of the best things about intranets is that you have the option of connecting to the Internet. Perhaps you trust only a few users to get out to the Internet (fearing the rest will spend their days surfing the Web). Perhaps you want to have one set of tools to let your users access data in Poland and the data in your office. Finally, you may not want them to access the Internet at all (at least today). The good news about intranet tools is that you can install them today and provide as much Internet access as you feel comfortable with and still have the option to expand that access in the future.

Key BackOffice Technologies

There are a few underlying technologies that support BackOffice that you may never see directly, but should know about. How many of you actually turn on network monitoring equipment to determine which protocols your system is using? Probably not that many. That is perhaps the best feature of these technologies—they work without a lot of user intervention.

What technologies do I mean? An amazing amount of work has gone into developing the Windows and Windows NT environment. The key technologies to focus on for this discussion are the following:

- Network communications
- The Windows application programming interface
- Specialized Microsoft application programming interfaces
- The Windows graphical user interface standards
- The Windows NT security environment
- The Windows NT administrative environment
- Compatibility products
- Object linking and embedding and COM
- ActiveX

The capability of connecting to most of the common network technologies in use today (except for SNA, which is covered by SNA Server) is built directly into the Windows NT operating system for all applications to use. This makes it easy for you to adapt this operating system for use in a number of environments, ranging from the UNIX world (TCP/IP-based networking) to the Novell environment (which is based on the IPX/SPX protocols). More importantly, you do not need to worry about protocols when it comes to installing the various BackOffice applications (or even when developing your own applications). That is a job for the operating system. The operating system networking subsystem is also smart enough to figure out whether there is a common protocol with which to talk to another computer and then set up communications based on that protocol.

This established Windows application programming interface (API) enables you to run the vast majority of applications that were designed under Windows and Windows 95 on the Windows NT operating system. With the substantial number of applications that are commercially available in this environment, this can be a significant benefit. It also means that there is a fairly large pool of programmers who understand how to build applications in the Windows NT operating system environment that can be used to interface with BackOffice. Try to find a reasonably priced programmer who works in a highly-specialized environment such as the SAP Financials package.

The Windows API provides you with the basic constructs for interacting with the operating system itself. However, how do you interact with the other BackOffice applications if you want to build extensions yourself? Microsoft provides a number of specialty APIs that are designed to interface with the BackOffice family. For example, the Message API (or MAPI) is used to build the capability of sending electronic mail messages to Exchange Server from your applications. The ISAPI (Internet Server API) is used to interface your applications, such as databases to BackOffice's Web server.

Another point that is just as important as an ease-of-use technology that is built into BackOffice (as well as most major Windows applications) is the Windows graphical user interface standards. These are published by Microsoft to provide standards for navigation to various functions within an application and other "look and feel" properties. This is the key to allowing users to pick up new applications quickly. It comes from the fact that the basic features are all in the same place, and all the user has to learn about is the features that are specific to the new application (such as how do you set up the properties of a particular electronic mail service).

Next on the list of enabling technologies for BackOffice is the Windows NT security environment. In the old days, programmers had to devote a lot of time building complex security schemes into each application because the operating systems were not very secure and there was no way to access their security systems. Windows NT was designed with a fair degree of security built into it (it is C2-certified by the United States government). It also provides mechanisms for applications to query the operating system to determine the security privileges of the current user. BackOffice has been built to make extensive use of Windows NT security. This greatly simplifies the implementation of BackOffice servers.

Just as important to the administrators of the BackOffice tools as the security environment is the administrative environment. Although there are certain functions that are unique to a given server (such as shutting down the Web server) and that require separate control consoles, the standard Windows NT administrative tools are used whenever possible. Thus, when you set up users for the operating system, you are also setting them up for access to BackOffice components. When the BackOffice applications need more information than is provided with the standard operating system account (as is the case with user profile for electronic mail use in Exchange Server), a dialog pops up to get that additional information when you are creating the user account with User Manager.

Another key technology from the Windows NT operating system that is beneficial to BackOffice is the compatibility products that enable NT to communicate with a wide variety of servers and clients. Although the SNA Server, which enables you to talk to IBM mainframes and AS/400 computers, is sold as a separate product, many of these compatibility products are built directly into the Windows NT operating system. This includes compatibility with the large world of UNIX workstations and servers. It also includes compatibility with the largest installed base of LAN servers that are based on Novell Netware. Finally, there is even compatibility with the Apple Macintosh network environment. This provides a lot of connectivity for the BackOffice suite without having to add any nonoperating system components.

There are several more-technical enabling technologies for BackOffice, including Object Linking and Embedding (OLE) and its parent the Common Object Model (COM). These are actually some relatively complex internal technologies; however, they have a simple goal. Imagine the capability of running functions from your spreadsheet while working in your word processor. If your applications are OLE-compliant, this is just what you can do. This technology is being extended to enable you to call functions from within applications that are running on other computers on the network. This technology is used heavily within Microsoft products, although you may not be able to see it working directly.

The final key technology on which the BackOffice suite is based is relatively new (Spring of 1996). It is referred to as ActiveX and it is actually a series of components that deal with presenting various forms of media to the users. The first thing that you may notice is the vastly improved video playback capabilities of the NT 4.0 and later operating systems. This may not apply immediately to most of the servers, but it probably will. One current implementation of ActiveX is in the area of the Web clients that are serviced by the Internet Information Server. The latest Web browsers enable you to transmit videos to your users for display within the Web browser.

You will probably see these technologies directly only on rare occasions or if you are a programmer. However, you should understand that they are there supporting you. They make your job as an administrator, developer, or even user much easier. The good news is that this ends the sections in this chapter that provide background material related to BackOffice. The final sections deal with BackOffice itself to give you an overview of what lies ahead.

Current BackOffice Components

This basic overview covers the BackOffice family as it existed in July 1996. The next section discusses some of the products that have been announced for this family. Figure 1.5 shows the current BackOffice product suite. As you can see, the Windows NT Server operating system is the basis for all of these products. The Internet Information Server is actually bundled as part of the operating system, although you have the option of installing it. The rest of the products are purchased separately, although some depend on other members of the BackOffice family (such as SMS being based on SQL Server).

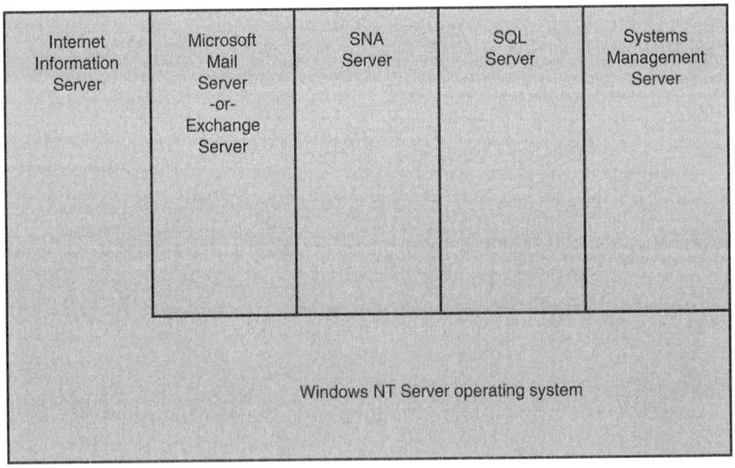

FIGURE 1.5.

Current BackOffice suite.

Internet Information Server	Microsoft Mail Server -or- Exchange Server	SNA Server	SQL Server	Systems Management Server

Windows NT Server operating system

First, let's look at the Windows NT Server and what it brings to the table. It is a full-featured operating system, and is designed not only to support the file server and print server roles typical of Novell Netware servers, but also to be an applications server much like a UNIX server. It is also very much a network operating system, with most of the network connectivity built directly into the operating system itself, not as an afterthought as in Windows 3.1. Part II, "Windows NT Server," covers this topic in more detail.

Figure 1.6 shows the basic functions provided by the Windows NT Server Operating system, which include the following:

- The environment in which the applications function
- Interaction of the users with the applications
- Interaction of the applications with one another
- Connection to other computers through various forms of networking, including local area networks and modems
- A security system controlling user access
- Administrative and monitoring tools

FIGURE 1.6.
Basic functions of the Windows NT Server operating system.

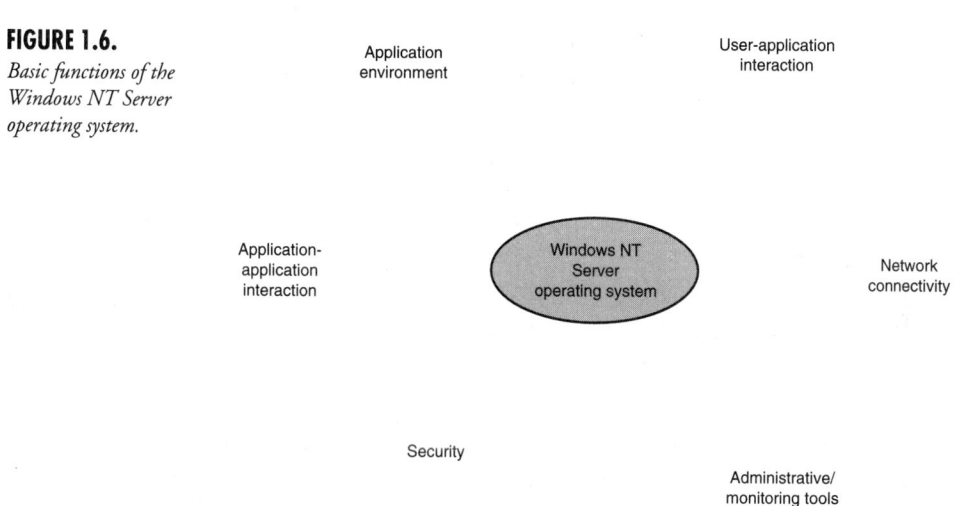

Microsoft Mail Server is a part of many BackOffice installations. It is the latest evolution of the original electronic mail system and has been around for a number of years. Mail Server is somewhat similar to Lotus cc:Mail, because it functions with a series of data files located on a shared network drive. These files are accessed by client software that is run on each of the client workstations. It has the blessing of simplicity in the older environments where sharing network drives and printers was about all network operating systems could do. Part IV, "Exchange Server and Mail," covers Microsoft Mail in more detail.

Figure 1.7 shows the functions of Microsoft Mail Server, which include the following:

- Sending and receiving mail with other users
- Sharing information through public folders that are, in effect, bulletin boards containing information to be shared by a project team
- Connecting with other, external mail systems (that is, cc:Mail) through the use of gateway products

FIGURE 1.7.

Basic functions of Microsoft Mail Server.

Send and
receive mail

Public
folders

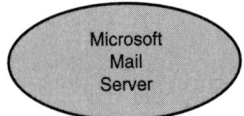

External
mail
connections

Next on the list of products in the current BackOffice environment is the Exchange Server product. Some may have questioned my calling Mail Server the latest evolution of Microsoft's original mail system when Exchange Server has actually just come on the market and is much newer than Mail Server. Perhaps it is just a matter of terminology, but I consider Exchange Server to be more of a revolution as opposed to an evolution in mail products for Microsoft. Instead of relying on simple file sharing, it relies on more sophisticated interprocess client-server communications to interact with clients. Its architecture closely resembles that of a database management system. Part IV also discusses Exchange Server in more detail.

Figure 1.8 illustrates the basic functions of Microsoft Exchange Server, which include the following:

- Sending and receiving mail with other users
- Sharing information through public folders, which are, in effect, bulletin boards containing information to be shared by a project team
- Providing programmatic interfaces that enable developers to build mail capabilities into the applications that they develop; this includes providing mail services to Microsoft applications such as Internet Information Server

■ Providing excellent connectivity to Internet mail systems

■ Connecting with other, external mail systems (that is, cc:Mail) through the use of gateway products

FIGURE 1.8.

Basic functions of Microsoft Exchange Server.

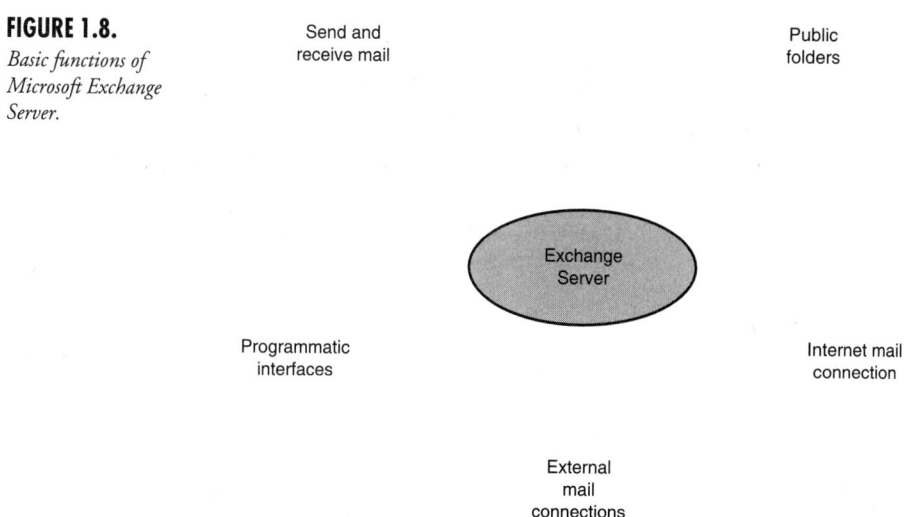

Send and
receive mail

Public
folders

Exchange
Server

Programmatic
interfaces

Internet mail
connection

External
mail
connections

The Internet Information Server (IIS) provides the World Wide Web, File Transfer Protocol, and Gopher capabilities in the BackOffice family. In an interesting move, Microsoft decided to include IIS as part of the Windows NT Server operating system, although you do have the option of whether to install IIS. This probably reflects a general trend to make Internet/intranet as easy as access to your local hard disk drive. The IIS components function as separate Windows NT services that rarely require any attention, but seem to get the job done. They access information stored in directories on the hard disks of your server. Part III, "Internet Information Server," covers IIS in more detail.

Figure 1.9 illustrates the basic functions of the Internet Information Server, which include the following:

■ Enabling users on the network to access World Wide Web documents (and applications) that are stored on this server

■ Providing an enhanced File Transfer Protocol server that enables users to upload and download files from this server, which are located in directories specifically designated for this purpose

■ Providing a tool that enables users to locate information stored on the network that they may be interested in

■ Providing management services that enable administrators to control access and monitor loading to these services, which may allow general Internet users access to your server

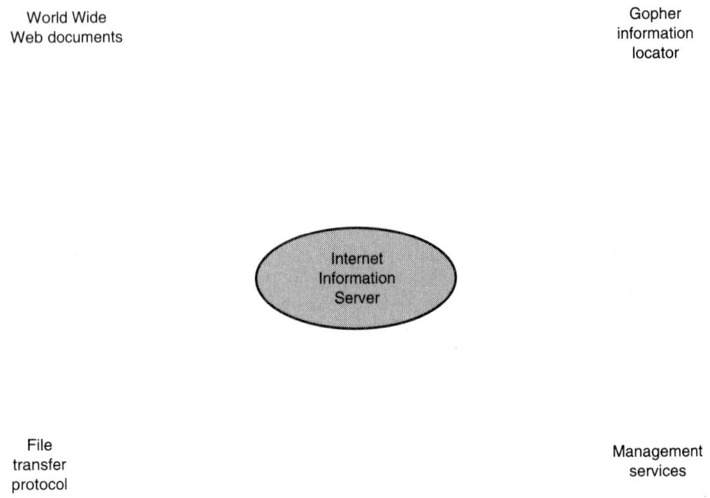

FIGURE 1.9.

*Basic functions of the
Internet Information
Server.*

World Wide
Web documents

Gopher
information
locator

Internet
Information
Server

File
transfer
protocol

Management
services

Many of the servers in the BackOffice family are designed for a wide variety of uses in a large number of environments. The SNA Server, on the other hand, is a specialist. Its main function in life is to connect local area network (intranet) environments to IBM mainframe and AS/400 environments. Many locations that have both these environments rely on IBM mainframe terminal connections (separate wires running to cards and software in the PC that turn highly intelligent personal computers into really dumb terminals) or use network utilities such as telnet and FTP to connect to the mainframe (which often is difficult for the mainframe that was not designed for this type of processing environment). Part VII, "SNA Server," covers this server in more detail.

Figure 1.10 illustrates the basic services provided by the SNA Server, which include the following:

- Enabling access to files stored on the mainframe
- Providing terminal connectivity to enable users to run jobs

FIGURE 1.10.

*Basic functions of the
SNA Server.*

Mainframe
AS/400 terminal
connection

Mainframe
AS/400 file
transfer

SNA
Server

The next-to-last product in the current BackOffice suite is Microsoft's server database management system, known as SQL Server. It is a fairly traditional relational database management system. The primary architecture for databases built using SQL Server uses the client-server model. In this model, a process on your local PC communicates requests to, and receives responses from, a process on the server. The server processes, then updates, the data files and takes care of other administrative tasks. This server is discussed in more detail in Part V, "SQL Server."

Figure 1.11 illustrates the basic services provided by SQL Server, which include the following:

- Storing organized collections of data into tables
- Responding to queries and data updates sent by users
- Executing software stored within the database
- Providing utilities for performance monitoring and administration

FIGURE 1.11.

Basic functions of SQL Server.

Store organized data

Query and update service

SQL Server

Stored procedures

Monitoring and administration

The final product in the current BackOffice suite is relatively new. Systems Management Server supports the need of information systems organizations to support large numbers of client workstations distributed on a network. Often, support costs make up a very high percentage of the total costs of a network of computers. Systems Management Server is designed to support the most common and time-consuming support functions.

Figure 1.12 shows the basic services provided by Systems Management Server, which include the following:

- Client workstation hardware and software inventory
- Automated software installation from servers to client workstations

■ Remote system troubleshooting, including the capability of controlling that workstation remotely

■ Network application management

FIGURE 1.12.

Basic functions of Systems Management Server.

Hardware/
software
inventory

Remote
system
support

Systems
Management
Server

Automated
software
installation

Network
application
management

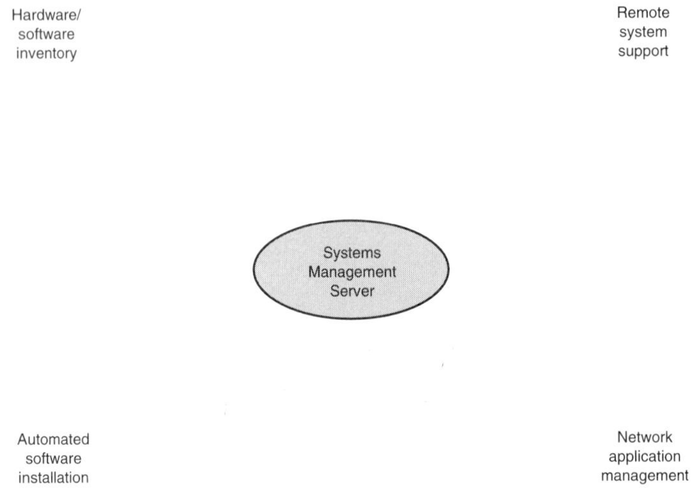

The current BackOffice components work together to provide the more common services needed by users and developers. Someday, some of these services may be bundled into the base operating system itself (just as network interfaces used to be purchased as add-ons to the operating system and Internet Information Server is currently bundled with the Windows NT Server operating system). The key theme that integrates the various BackOffice components is that they are common components and applications that run on servers or that provide the foundation for other server applications. They are built strictly for the Windows NT operating system, and they extend its capabilities.

Planned BackOffice Components

Microsoft BackOffice is currently a fairly complete and powerful system to support most server-based needs. However, time marches on and BackOffice has to keep pace with it. Because of various trends in the industry and Microsoft's goal of extending the capabilities of smaller, PC-based servers into the realm traditionally occupied by UNIX servers and even larger computers, there is already a series of powerful extensions to the BackOffice family that will make it even more powerful. These will move fairly quickly through the beta testing process and may be available for download from the Microsoft World Wide Web page if they are still in beta while you are reading this.

The first is Microsoft's proxy server, which is code-named *catapult*. The term "proxy server" may seem somewhat confusing for those of you who do not work in the network and security

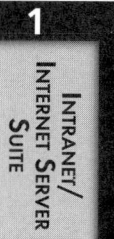

fields. It is a key component in the Microsoft networking strategy, however, because it solves at least some of the security problems associated with connecting your precious little network to larger networks, especially the Internet. You do not want any of those famous Internet hackers getting into your computers and doing mischievous or even damaging deeds. The proxy server acts as a traffic cop for network traffic, enabling the signals from the right workstations using the right protocols to pass while blocking other signals.

The next product is Microsoft's Merchant Server. Again, the terminology here seems to be somewhat imprecise. Databases have been serving merchants for years. This server is designed to provide some features that enable businesses to conduct business transactions while transmitting their signals over the Internet. This can be a scary thought. Imagine what it could be like if someone could listen in, get the credit card number that you are transmitting, and start ordering things with that number over the telephone. The Merchant Server provides support and programming interfaces for encryption, payment, order caching, and address information. It is designed to be easily linked to product information and order databases and also interfaces to legacy order processing systems.

The next new component to the BackOffice family is a media server designed to enable the distribution of audio and video over future computer networks. Current cable companies distribute a large number of video channels over their networks. The general concepts of storing digital video and audio information are fairly well understood. The real challenge is the building of computer networks that can support the enormous demands of a large number of video transmissions. With the media server product, Microsoft hopes to be ready in this market when the network world catches up to the dreams of the user community for media transmission over computer networks.

The final component of interest is Microsoft's Viper product. It is designed to better support the needs of online transaction processing. Business transactions have been processed online for a number of years, and most of them have gone quite smoothly. This product is designed to implement many of the algorithms that developers currently have to write to ensure that the transaction has completed successfully before the remote computer tells the user that it has completed. This requires some sophistication as distributed databases and complex computer networking schemes are implemented.

One final note on the subject of additions to BackOffice—expect even more changes. Microsoft is a market-driven company. The Internet and intranet worlds are evolving rapidly. There are a number of very bright people working at Microsoft and other places to make this environment better. As new ideas and standards come up, you can expect Microsoft to adapt its product suite to meet the consumer's demands. One small example of a new, unexpected product that went into beta testing during the week of this writing was a small tool that helped users move Web pages that have been authored locally to their servers. This is a really great idea to help automate the process of building and testing Web pages. It may even become a built-in feature of future Web page authoring tools and Web servers. Yes, sometimes watching technology evolve can be really fun.

Integrating BackOffice Components with Each Other

Much of the work involved with integrating the various components of Microsoft BackOffice has already been done by Microsoft. For example, the Systems Management Server is built to use the SQL Server database. All these components (with the exception of the older Microsoft Mail Server product) are built into the common architecture, administrative, and security schemes of the Windows NT operating system. Your main challenge is learning how to use these components together to your best advantage. The chapters in the rest of this book go into more detail on these products and prepare you to use them to their fullest capability. After that, it is up to you.

Integrating BackOffice with Your Applications

Perhaps you are a really talented programmer. There is no software algorithm that is beyond your abilities. You can even write your own operating system, given enough time and budget. However, the real world rarely has enough time and budget available. Therefore, one of the key design features of BackOffice offers you the ability to have its functions accessed by other programs. This can save you a lot of time. Why write complex message handling applications when you can simply interface your code to Exchange Server? Why write a series of complex data selection and update algorithms going against custom-designed files when you can use SQL Server for those tasks and instead concentrate on the user interface and business logic portions of the application? Part VIII, "Integrating BackOffice," discusses the programmatic interfaces to the various BackOffice components that you can use to save yourself a lot of work and produce better applications (remember, Microsoft has more programmers working on its BackOffice components than most of you have in your entire company).

Summary

This chapter provided you with a brief introduction to BackOffice. The remaining chapters are devoted to the details that you will need to set up, administer, and use BackOffice to your best advantage. It is a powerful suite of products that can be purchased as needed to meet your local needs. Feel free to skip over those sections that are not applicable to you. For example, I do not have the slightest idea as to how SNA Server functions (don't worry, the author who wrote those sections does). I am nowhere near a mainframe environment and do not want to complicate my job any further. However, the SNA Server could be the most important section for administrators who have the task of linking their local area networks to the mainframe. You may have no interest in the SQL Server section (perhaps your organization has standardized on Oracle as the database management system). Therefore, you can skip the sections that are not applicable to you, and the authors promise not to get offended if you skip the chapters that we slaved over for so many hours.

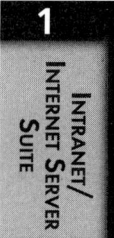

Before we get into the details of each of the products, it seems appropriate to cover some common ground that is applicable to all the products in the BackOffice family. The rest of this first section of the book is devoted to covering these common topics. Chapter 2, "Integrated Architecture," presents the overall architecture of the BackOffice family to give you an idea of the components that are shared by all family members. Chapter 3, "Security Environment," discusses the security environment and how it can be used to control access to the services of BackOffice. Chapter 4, "Monitoring Environment," discusses the monitoring tools that you can use to see how well your system is performing and areas where it might need a little help. Chapter 5, "Administrative Environment," covers the tools that help the administrators set up and keep the BackOffice environment running smoothly. As stated earlier, Chapter 6, "Intranets," discusses the subject of intranets, which are like the Internet, but have a number of advantages that you might want to exploit. So, without any further ado, on with the rest of the book.

Integrated Architecture

by Joe Greene

IN THIS CHAPTER

Applications depend on their operating system for a number of services, such as access to memory, disk storage, and the network. They can also depend on one another for services, as in the case of Systems Management Server, which uses SQL Server to maintain its data. With the exception of the elder member of the BackOffice family (Microsoft Mail Server), the components are designed to run under only one operating system (Windows NT). This may be a problem for locations that would want to use BackOffice tools, but have standardized on another operating system, such as one of the many variants of UNIX that are available. However, it does have the advantage of enabling the BackOffice component developers to optimize their products for this single operating system and utilize its best features (such as Windows NT services) to provide better functionality.

This chapter presents this basic architecture for your consideration. This is one of the few computer environments where, once you understand the basics of the operating system, you actually have a good understanding of how the various components are designed. In most cases, you have to learn the design philosophies, administrative philosophies, and user interface philosophies of a number of different vendors to run an application server. BackOffice simplifies this learning task, because some taskmaster at Microsoft has forced all the programmers (many probably against their will) to use a common design architecture. This lack of artistic creativity on the part of the hundreds of programmers who worked on BackOffice gives you a great advantage when you actually have to use the products and just want to know where the menu option or button to stop the background processes is located.

This chapter begins with an overview of the generic Windows NT architecture and then adds a discussion of how BackOffice fits into this architecture. However, I wanted to add a few more topics that go beyond the pure technical, behind-the-scenes features of Windows NT to cover some of the other component technologies that come into play when working with BackOffice applications. First, you look at the Windows interface. This may be obvious to some of you, but not everyone has spent years in the PC environment. This is actually a good technology to be familiar with because Microsoft follows its style conventions when designing its products. The next discussion covers some advanced technologies that Microsoft uses behind the scenes to enable applications to work together. These technologies are built into the operating system itself or are available as add-ons from the Microsoft World Wide Web site. The next three sections explore the security, monitoring, and administration tools provided in Windows NT. Rounding off this chapter are sections on the application programming interfaces that programmers can use to interface local applications with its services and a closing discussion on other forms of integration.

Overview of the Integrated Architecture

When Microsoft chose to label its new server and workstation operating system Windows NT, they ran the risk that many people would think it was just another upgraded version of their DOS/Windows product family. The good news is that while it can still run most DOS and

Windows applications, it is a completely new operating system when you look under the hood. Although it was quite a challenge for the development team to write almost everything from scratch, it has a number of advantages. It was probably the only way that certain design goals could be achieved.

What is the Windows NT operating system? The following are some of its highlights:

■ *32-bit foundation.* This sounds like a discussion of registers and all those other internals that you do not have time to deal with. This is important to you because the larger the size of the processor bus, the fewer games operating system developers have to play to reference large arrays of data. When operating systems are not playing games swapping between pages of memory, they have more time to perform useful work for the end-users; it also reduces the complexity, and therefore the number of problems, of the operating system itself.

> **NOTE**
>
> The 32-bit architecture provides a vast improvement in stability and multiprocessing capabilities.

■ *Built-in networking.* Many years ago, Sun Microsystems came out with the concept that the network was the computer (meaning that your total processing capability was actually made up of a number of computers working together connected by a network of some type). However, networking was not around when most operating systems were being designed (including UNIX on which Sun's Solaris is based). Therefore, much like Microsoft Windows 3.1, you have to use add-on packages to get networking support for these operating systems. However, networking was already a hot topic when Windows NT was being conceived, and it was decided that network support was to be built directly into the operating system itself. This has a number of performance advantages and reliability improvements, including that the operating system is tolerant of the communications issues that arise when your applications depend on files that you might have to wait to access over busy networks.

■ *Compatibility with other major operating systems.* Perhaps you do not care who writes the operating system or makes the hardware—you just want to get your job done. People who think this way will really like the fact that Windows NT was designed to provide file sharing, print sharing, and application-to-application interfaces with most of the popular operating systems available. These interfaces include links to UNIX, Macintosh, and even Microsoft's arch rival for the PC server operating system market: Novell NetWare. This can be especially helpful in environments where you cannot just shut everything down for a year or so to covert all data and applications to run in a new environment.

- *Multiple hardware architectures.* The Intel-based microprocessor world is, by far, the largest computer market in terms of the number of processors sold per year. However, this computer chip family was optimized for a certain type of computations (those done by average office automation users, for example). There are other computer architectures that are designed for different types of processing. The major alternatives to Intel processors (which are referred to as complex instruction set computers) are those that use reduced instruction sets (simply the complexity of an individual computation so that you can do more computations per second). The NT operating system functions on a number of these other chip families, most notably the very fast DEC Alpha architecture, the MIPS architecture, and the PowerPC architecture.

- *Symmetric multiprocessor support.* The industry spends millions trying to make the individual computer chip faster. It is a challenging problem where there are worries about how far an electron can travel at nearly the speed of light in the time it takes to execute a single instruction. An alternative to this really high-tech work that can speed up the processing capacity of a computer is to put more computer chips to work on the tasks that your computer is being asked to perform. Windows NT is designed from scratch to support multiple computer processors. Currently, it works well with four chips in most architectures, but the latest releases are pushing the number of processors that it can effectively use much higher.

- *Preemptive multitasking.* These are two big words that operating system types throw around all of the time. I am not sure how many end-users really appreciate what these words mean to them (they were IBM's OS/2 operating system's main claim to fame, and not many people purchased that operating system). Multitasking means that the operating system can work on multiple jobs at the same time, keeping straight the data areas, input/output requests, and so forth. The preemptive part means that the operating system does not just give every process a fixed number of seconds, and you have to wait until it is your turn again to get processing time. Instead, you can designate certain processes (such as critical operating systems or network components) as being more important than others, and they can therefore get attention when they need it, stealing the time that would normally be given to a low-priority process.

- *Capability of running most Windows applications.* Finally, although the design team was free to rewrite the operating system itself without having the legacy of the old code contained in MS-DOS and Windows, it would have been foolish to ignore the large product base of Windows products that is available on the market. Many IBM salespeople have argued that OS/2 was vastly superior to MS Windows as an operating system, but their arguments usually fell on deaf ears. Instead, people listened to Microsoft proponents who extolled the virtues of having thousands of applications that would run on the Windows operating system and the huge number of hardware components that were supported by the operating system. Windows NT does a good job of running well-behaved Windows applications. There are a number of applications that cheated a little bit (that is, used memory areas in nonstandard ways to make the application just a little faster and therefore more competitive). Windows NT did not attempt to handle all these older applications, but I have had quite a bit of luck running most Windows applications.

Microsoft's Design Goals

Before going on with a discussion of the Windows NT architecture, it is interesting to consider Microsoft's stated design goals when it built this operating system. This was really Microsoft's second attempt at a server operating system. In the early days, it was partnered with IBM on the earlier versions of OS/2 (before the 2.0 release of OS/2). For a number of reasons, the two decided to go their separate ways; IBM kept the OS/2 name, and Microsoft chose to sell its product under the new name of Windows NT. The stated goals for this operating system were the following:

- Compatible with the Windows interface, applications, existing file systems, and popular network environments
- Portable to a number of hardware platforms
- Scaleable to multiple processors (up to 32 processors in its current release, although 4 is generally considered to be the practical limit)
- Security built directly into the architecture that meets the requirements for C2 rating by the United States government
- Distributed processing capabilities to enable connectivity to different host computer and client-server environments
- Reliable and robust design that prevents applications from causing problems with one another and with the operating system itself
- Localization to support multiple languages and countries around the world
- Extensible to add future modules (such as the BackOffice servers) to extend the operating system

When you look at these goals, you find that they are echoed in the design of the BackOffice products other than just Windows NT itself. This ensures that the other BackOffice servers will stay in synch with the operating system itself. It also extends its marketability, especially in multinational companies.

The Windows NT Architecture

Discussions of computer architectures can get into some really nasty details about the protocols used to signal between the various subsystems and other such stuff. My goal here is not to teach you enough information that you could rewrite the operating system from scratch given a good C++ compiler. Instead, my focus is to provide you with just enough information that you feel comfortable with the operating system, its services, and how the various BackOffice components interface with the architecture to make a working system. If you are interested in the details of the operating system, there are a number of technical papers on the Web, on the Microsoft TechNet CD-ROM, and also in print in the Windows NT Resource Kit from Microsoft.

Another question is whether this discussion covers Windows NT 3.51 or Windows NT 4.0. The basic answer is "yes." You learn about the architecture of Windows NT 3.51 and then some of the upgrades in the NT 4.0 product. Actually, if you understand the basics of NT 3.51, you have a really good handle on the architecture under NT 4.0. There were a number of technology upgrades; however, they tend to be things such as a change to the graphical user interface (to look more like the Windows 95 interface) and greatly improved utilities rather than fundamental changes to the underlying architecture. The major improvements are with the addition of several high-performance graphics technologies that enable applications to go through a thinner layer of processing to access the capabilities of high-performance graphics cards more directly.

A simple starting point for this discussion is the three-layer model shown in Figure 2.1. At the top of this hierarchy are the applications with which we are all familiar. They are the user mode applications that include the BackOffice components, our word processors, and almost everything else that we interact with directly. Beneath this are the kernel mode services. The kernel of an operating system is its central processing logic and can be thought of as the heart of the operating system. The final layer is the hardware on which Windows NT is implemented. This is an important component that Windows NT has to adapt to, because it must support a number of different hardware platforms.

FIGURE 2.1.

Three layers of the Windows NT architecture.

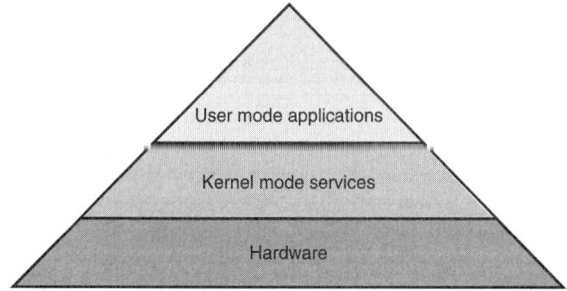

User mode applications

Kernel mode services

Hardware

User Mode Applications

Let's look at each of these layers in a little more detail, starting with the user mode applications, because they are probably the simplest and most intuitive ones to deal with. Figure 2.2 shows a more detailed drawing of the user mode applications of most interest for these purposes. The system has at its heart the Win32 subsystem. Recall that Windows NT was a 32-bit operating system (as opposed to Windows 3.1, which uses smaller, 16-bit addresses). The early

Intel chips (the 8086 and 80286) supported only 16-bit words, so operating systems had difficulty referencing large amounts of memory and using the most complicated instructions. However, the newer chips, such as the Intel 80486 and Pentium processors, support 32-bit instructions and memory referencing, which enables them to use a more complex operating system effectively. The Win32 subsystem is responsible for executing all the 32-bit applications that are on the market today.

FIGURE 2.2.

User mode applications.

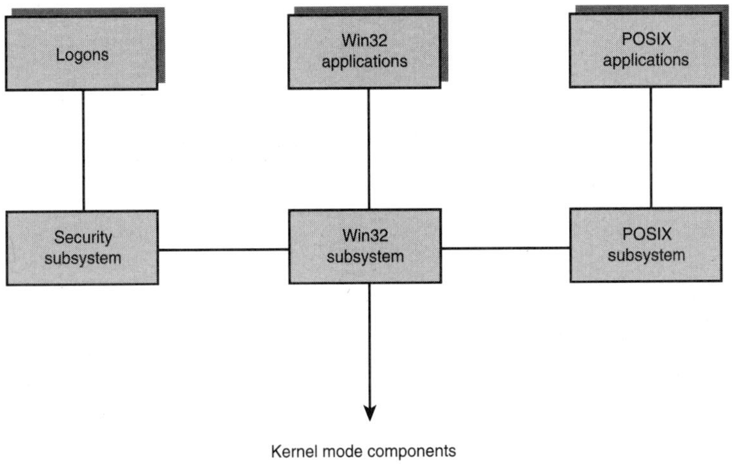

Kernel mode components

There are actually more 32-bit applications than you might imagine. Windows 95 is a 32-bit (mostly) operating system that executes 32-bit code. I have had relatively good luck getting Windows 95 applications to work well under Windows NT. Because this is a BackOffice book, I also have to mention that BackOffice is a 32-bit application suite that is specifically designed to take advantage of the new capabilities (that is, use of common memory areas for speed in such applications as Exchange Server and SQL Server).

The next component in the user mode application area is the Windows on Win32 (WOW) Virtual DOS Machine (VDM) shown in Figure 2.3. You may also hear a reference to WOW when talking about this technology. A lot of Windows NT references do not even show this component on the basic architecture chart. Perhaps they want to stress the sexier components in the architecture, such as 32-bit processing or the capability of running OS/2 applications. I have run across a number of good old 16-bit DOS and Windows applications that are still out there, however, and form important components in some users' architectures. Therefore, let's look at the VDM here.

The basic concept is simple. You simulate a 16-bit DOS environment within the Windows NT operating system. This is nice because it isolates the relatively ill-behaved DOS applications to a separate space, thereby preventing them from getting near the more sensitive parts of the operating system. Remember, DOS was a relatively simple operating system, which did not provide a lot of services to the application developers. Therefore, these creative folks made up their own services and worked hard on tricks to increase performance. However, problems arose when multiple application and driver vendors tried to use the same tricks and they conflicted with one another (often crashing the operating system).

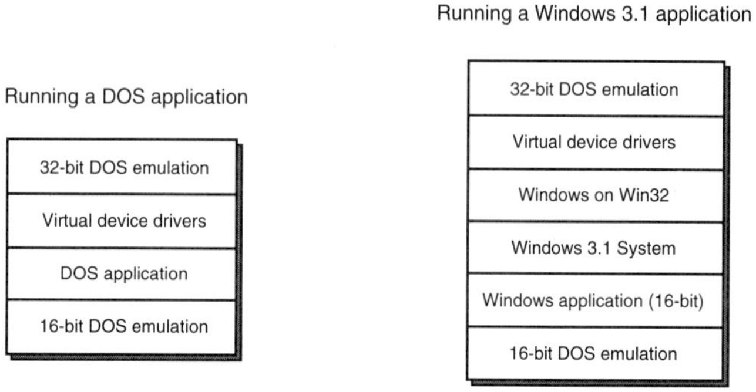

FIGURE 2.3.

Windows NT's virtual DOS machine.

Running a Windows 3.1 application

Running a DOS application

| 32-bit DOS emulation |
| Virtual device drivers |
| DOS application |
| 16-bit DOS emulation |

| 32-bit DOS emulation |
| Virtual device drivers |
| Windows on Win32 |
| Windows 3.1 System |
| Windows application (16-bit) |
| 16-bit DOS emulation |

This explains why not all Windows 3.1 applications run under Windows NT. There are some vendors who had a job to do and did things that were outside the boundaries of the operating system. The Windows NT designers could not simulate ways to handle all these possible tricks. Therefore, although well-behaved Windows 3.1 applications will run without problems, other 16-bit applications may not run at all. Your job is to know which ones work (or perhaps just upgrade your application suite to all newer 32-bit applications).

The next set of applications in the user mode that are of interest to us are the OS/2 and POSIX subsystems. The OS/2 subsystem is designed to run applications written for the OS/2 operating system. Remember, Windows NT started out from the same project work as OS/2, and compatibility was a logical choice at the time. Today, however, there are many more Win32 applications on the market than there are OS/2 applications. The POSIX subsystem derives from the UNIX world. POSIX is the United States government standard for interaction with an operating system (both programmatic and command-line) and is based on UNIX. It is required in many government contracts and can be a selling point if you are supporting one of these contracts. Anyway, this subsystem enables applications that are written to the POSIX standard to interact with the Windows NT operating system.

The final subsystem of interest in the user mode is the security subsystem. You learn more details of the Windows NT security model in Chapter 3, "Security Environment." The key to gain from this discussion is that the security subsystem exists in the user mode, far away from the kernel and operating system internals. It interacts with the security components in the operating system in a controlled (and secure) manner to control user access to information via the logon process.

Kernel Mode Components

The heart of the Windows NT operating system is the kernel and other components that provide the basic operating system services to the users. Figure 2.4 shows these basic components. The isolation of these key system processes from general user processes enables Windows NT to achieve a higher degree of stability than its predecessors. Of course, if you have a problem with any of these processes, your system is in deep trouble and you would get the dreaded blue screen (which indicates a system crashed—I have always found it to be associated with an incomplete installation of Windows NT or a failure in key hardware components such as the system memory).

FIGURE 2.4.

Kernel mode components.

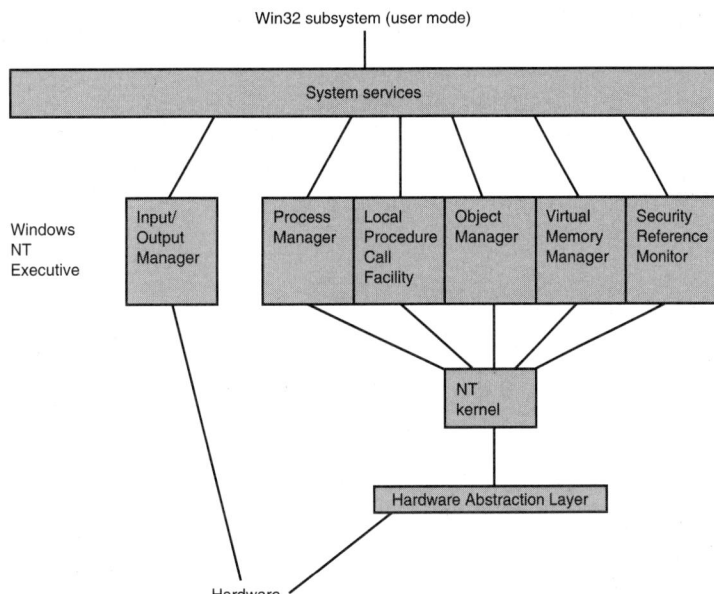

The system services component is a layer that provides the connection between the user mode subsystems and the other components in the kernel mode. Its main function is to route requests and responses correctly. It is usually drawn to be a relatively thin box to show that it is not a complicated layer and that it does not provide a lot of overhead to the applications.

The next component of interest is the Input/Output (I/O) Manager (see Figure 2.5). At the lowest level of the I/O Manager, you have a series of device drivers that function to take a standard series of operations (an interface to the higher-level drivers) and turn them into the detailed set of signals that it takes to get a particular device (that is, a CR-563 CD-ROM drive) to do the job. This is an excellent design feature, because you can isolate the details of how a particular device works in a single software component that has a defined interface to the rest of the operating system. Above the device drivers, you have network drivers (specific to a networking environment), file systems (which control how the data is stored on the device), and cache managers (because most peripheral devices are much slower than the processors to which they are attached).

FIGURE 2.5.

Components of the Input/Output Manager.

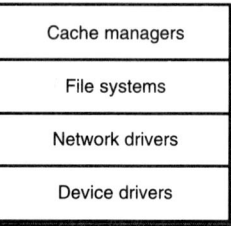

| Cache managers |
| File systems |
| Network drivers |
| Device drivers |

Another important concept is the input/output queue. In a multitasking system, a number of applications could want to access a particular device (for example, your C: driver) at the same time. You need a mechanism to control who gets the device first and track which jobs are waiting to get access. That is the purpose of the queue (a word rarely used in American English, except in computer circles). The I/O Manager is also responsible for maintaining these queues. Actually, when you get to Chapter 12, "Windows NT Performance Tuning," you will find that the length of this queue is a good overall measure of how well the system is keeping up with its I/O demands.

The final subject that needs to be discussed related to the I/O Manager is the difference between synchronous and asynchronous I/O (see Figure 2.6). Quite simply, synchronous I/O means that the application makes a request for an input/output operation and then waits for the result before proceeding further. This is necessary when you are loading the next statement that you plan to execute off a disk drive (you cannot execute it until after you load it). There are other types of operations where you do not need to wait around for the operation to complete. Suppose, for example, that you want to save some partial results of your calculations to disk. Why wait for this operation to complete? Instead, you can just tell the operating system's I/O Manager what to write and then go on about your business, trusting that the I/O Manager will get the job done for you. This is referred to as asynchronous I/O. It is used a lot by the operating system and other applications that have been designed in an environment where every ounce of performance is worth the effort.

The next component in the Windows NT Executive is the Process Manager. This is the component that creates and destroys the various processes that may be running on your system. It can be thought of as the key component that enables Windows NT to be a multitasking operating system. Typically, applications are comprised of a single process, although there are applications that actually start up multiple processes that coordinate their activities to get the job done. A key Windows NT design feature is that a process has its own physical memory areas and other system resources that are separated from those of all other processes. This helps to prevent a single poorly written application from taking down the entire system (I definitely like this idea).

FIGURE 2.6.

Synchronous and asynchronous I/O.

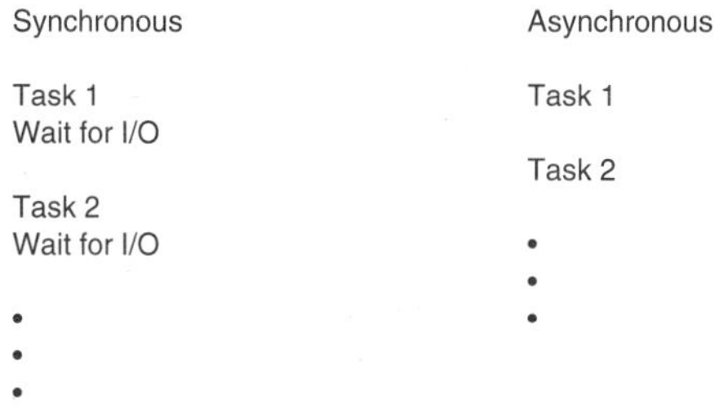

Synchronous	Asynchronous
Task 1	Task 1
Wait for I/O	
	Task 2
Task 2	
Wait for I/O	•
	•
•	•
•	
•	

Having multiple processes is a good start for an operating system, but you can do a little better, especially on computers where you have multiple central processing units installed. Many computer tasks can be broken down into components that can function in either a parallel (each doing its own work) or serial (one task's output is the other task's input) fashion. It can be thought of as an assembly line within an application. Anyway, if your application can be broken down into this series of tasks, it might be nice to assign different tasks to different central processing units to get the job done more rapidly. In the Windows NT (actually, Win32) environment, these little tasks are referred to as threads. Application processes are written in Win32 to spawn multiple threads. If there are multiple processors available, threads can be assigned (scheduled) to processors as needed to complete the tasks at hand.

The next component in the Executive is the Local Procedure Call facility. It is interesting to note that Microsoft has set up a client-server architecture within the Windows NT operating system. The user applications and the Windows NT environment subsystems communicate with one another through a set of standardized messages. Most of these calls are made when an API is called. The Local Procedure Call facility serves as the traffic cop for these messages.

The Local Procedure Call facility is especially interesting for its client-server nature. Many applications are going to a client-server architecture to improve performance by leveling the processing load and enabling individual components to become more specialized. The use of this architecture within the operating system has the advantages of client-server computer environments, which are based on multiple computers on some form of network. It also minimizes the chief disadvantage of client-server architectures in that the network traffic bottlenecks are not noticeable when communications are taking place over the high-speed internal buses and use internal memory structures within one computer.

The next component is the Object Manager. Object-oriented technology had just started to come into its own when Windows NT was under construction. Therefore, you will see some object-oriented concepts creeping into the operating system along with its associated terminology. An object can be thought of as a combination of information and actions that can be associated with that object. For example, if you are working on medical records for a patient, you might consider the patient object to be a collection of data (his blood pressure since being admitted, his classification by his doctors, and even whether he has insurance and a good record for paying his bills). Associated with that collection of data is a series of actions that you could take on the patient—discharge him, take out his gall bladder, and so forth. Depending on the state of the patient, some actions may not be applicable (that is, you would not want to perform a heart transplant action if the doctors have diagnosed a broken toe). Anyway, that is the crude basics behind objects. With this understanding (perhaps you already knew far more than I do about the subject), I can discuss Windows NT objects and how the Object Manager deals with them.

Objects within Windows NT are things such as processes, threads, ports, files, directories, and a number of other things associated with the internal functioning of the operating system. You can have multiple instances of an object (you may have the Windows NT performance monitoring tools open in three different windows on your desktop monitoring three different sets of parameters). Object Manager's job is to keep track of what objects are out there, how the operating system refers to them, when they are being used, and so forth. Just looking at the process example alone, you can see how important it is to keep track of what is going on with your operating system and how to control access to those resources.

Next on the list of Windows NT Executive components is the Virtual Memory Manager. Virtual memory is a concept that is common to most modern operating systems. It comes from the fact that random access memory (RAM) is relatively expensive and disk storage space is relatively cheap (I never would have believed—even a few short years ago—that I could own a home computer with several gigabytes of disk storage). Operating systems have real troubles when they run out of places to put data, instructions, and other critical processing information (they usually crash). Because it is unlikely that you will have the money to buy so much RAM that you could never run out, operating systems have designated certain places on their disk drives to store overflow information that cannot fit into RAM (see Figure 2.7).

This wonderful convenience comes with a price, of course. Central processing units access instructions and data that are located in memory, not directly on disk drives. Therefore, you have to develop a process that transfers overflow information from memory to disk and then brings it back again when it is needed for processing. Transfers to and from disk drives are many orders of magnitude slower than the transfers between RAM and the central processing unit. Therefore, if your system is swapping information to and from virtual memory, your performance usually degrades substantially. Operating system vendors have been studying this problem for some time and do have a few tricks that they implement to minimize this performance impact. They track which components are frequently used (for example, the instructions within a given subroutine that is being iterated through for a long-running application) and those that are not. When it comes time to transfer information virtual memory, the less frequently used information is transferred to disk. (These tricks help somewhat, but in the performance tuning section, I will get on my soapbox about how you have to work extremely hard to minimize swapping if you want to get the optimal performance out of your system.)

FIGURE 2.7.

Basic concepts behind virtual memory.

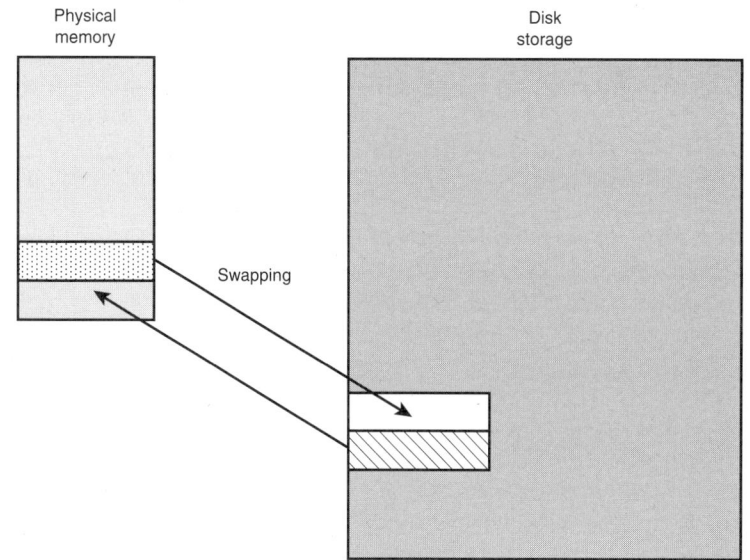

The last item in the Windows NT Executive is the Security Reference Monitor. It is certainly not that security is a trivial consideration in an operating system or that Windows NT is in any way lax on security. In fact, it is one of the few commercial operating systems that has been rated at the C level by the United States government. You can get a publication known as the "orange book" to see what all this means, but you get the general idea—it has a much higher security rating than the vast majority of operating systems that are out there on the market today.

Where does the Security Reference Monitor fit in to this security picture? Basically, it uses its privileged position within the Windows NT Executive to ensure that privileges are correct before access is given to operating system resources such as disk files or printers. It receives the request for validation of user ID and password when the user first logs on and checks this against the list of valid domain or server accounts. Then it sends a notification to the requesting process as to whether this login in permitted or not. In domains, it also sends a security key to the requesting workstation that allows this workstation to access resources without going through the server. When it comes time to access a resource, the request is routed through the Security Reference Monitor on the computer that owns the resource. The request is validated against the privilege assignments for that resource when compared with the security key associated with that user ID or password.

The Security Reference Monitor also takes the results of its privilege authentication efforts to generate information for the auditing records kept by the operating system. These audit trails enable administrators and security types to see what has been happening from an access point of view to look for warning signals (like hundreds of invalid login attempts spaced only seconds apart, which is probably a sign of hacking) and also see general trends (how many users are logging in at a given hour of the day).

Working through the Windows NT kernel components shown in Figure 2.4, you come to the kernel itself. It is the heart of the Windows NT operating system and provides most of the central coordination involved with keeping the computing work going. You can think of it as the component that tells the central processing unit which tasks to perform. It is also the component that is designed to split work between multiple processors, if your computer has them. The basic units of assignment for processing are the threads that were discussed earlier.

You can tell some of the influences of the VMS architecture in Windows NT when you see the 32 priority levels that are available for threads under NT. The really high-priority items are reserved for real-time events, which are typically tied to a fixed schedule (such as a timer for a critical system process going off). The lower-priority (variable) items still need to get completed, but only when there are no high-priority threads waiting for service. The kernel is always in memory and runs on multiple processors.

There are two basic types of objects that the kernel deals with. The first is used to cause actions (dispatch), to keep all activities of the system flowing in the proper order. The second type is used to control the kernel itself, but it does not cause dispatches. Key examples of this type are the interrupts that are used by devices to indicate that they are ready for service.

Before you leave the kernel, remember this. First, the best type of kernel is the one that you never see. In older flavors of UNIX, you often had to adjust kernel settings to improve the performance of your system. This was very risky. On most operating systems, if the kernel is not adjusted properly, you are in real trouble. You often get the whole system crashing at seemingly random intervals and other confusing behavior. The good news about Windows NT is that Microsoft has put some algorithms in that let the kernel tune itself for the most part. When everything is working properly and your system is just churning away, life is good.

The final component is the Hardware Abstraction Layer. This is a really neat concept. One of the greatest blessings of modern computer architectures is that you have such a wide range of choices to find components that meet your needs. The bad news is that because there are so many choices, selecting the right products and implementing them correctly can be a nightmare. There are dozens of different PC motherboards out there and that covers only the Intel-based architectures. It does not even begin to deal with the details of DEC Alpha, MIPS, PowerPC, or the other architectures.

The Hardware Abstraction Layer is designed to keep the rest of the operating system manageable. It takes the unique requirements of a given type of hardware system and translates them into a standard set of interfaces to the other components in the operating system. In that sense, it is similar to the device drivers in the I/O Manager. Examples of problems that it deals with are how to send signals to various different processors in multiprocessor systems. The Hardware Abstraction Layer is called by various device drivers to deal with the wide variety of I/O architectures available (SCSI, PCI, IDE, and so forth). It does this while trying to keep itself to a relatively thin layer, thus improving performance of the operating system.

This concludes my brief introduction to the key components of the Windows NT operating system that operate in the kernel mode area. They are truly the guts of the operating system, and you will be using them every time you access NT. The good news is that they function fairly well without your intervention. It is interesting to study their highly modular design to understand how the Windows NT operating system adapts to a wide range of hardware platforms.

Hardware Components

Unlike many other computer systems, Microsoft does not supply most of the hardware along with the operating systems. Yes, it does dabble in mice, keyboards, and a few things like that, but for the most part, you integrate hardware systems from many hundreds of vendors. The Intel world offers the widest range of vendors, and this makes the price and performance competition most intense in this environment. The other hardware environments tend to be more limited in terms of the number of vendors offering products, which reduces the hardware integration options. Magazines and the Internet are the best places to keep up with the latest advances in this technology.

There are a few additional points regarding the hardware architecture for Windows NT. The first point—that I cannot stress enough—is that you have to look at the hardware compatibility list for Windows NT before you buy the products. Windows NT developers have never tried to build drivers for every imaginable piece of hardware. Not all the hardware vendors who are looking to build cheap, home PC products have devoted the effort that it takes to build NT drivers; instead, they focused on Windows and Windows 95 drivers. You must also be very explicit. You need to check that the model X external disk drive from vendor Y is on the list. It does not help if there are disk drives from vendor Y on the list unless it is a model X external disk drive.

A second point is that you should really ensure that your hardware is completely set up before you try to install Windows NT. Windows 95 is a great tool to use to ensure that your configuration is correct. It has been designed to be easy for the very casual home user. There are a large number of Wizards, which seek out hardware configuration information and work to resolve conflicts. The classic examples of this are the interrupts and input/output memory addresses for add-in cards on an Intel-based computer. This can be quite tricky, because there are only 16 interrupts and you can use almost all of them if you have a PC with a sound card, CD-ROM drive, and network card. (I have one machine that uses all the interrupts; there are none available for future expansion.) Windows NT, on the other hand, is typically installed on higher-end workstations. Although you can resolve problems with Windows NT installed, the relatively long boot and reinstallation process with Windows NT can make this a slow process (if something goes terribly awry). Therefore, unless you have bought an integrated hardware platform that has all the conflicts already resolved and the interrupt/memory/version information documented for all the peripherals, you might want to solve these problems with a simpler operating system first and then install Windows NT on top of this configuration.

> **TIP**
>
> You can save a lot of time when installing the operating system if you ensure that the hardware is set up correctly and free of any conflicts (try loading Windows 95 on the machine to help debug hardware conflicts).

The final point is that your hardware configuration strongly affects your performance. This may seem obvious to most people, but I want to emphasize it here in the context of a BackOffice server. Most PC hardware has been designed for simple desktop computers. Its performance is good enough to keep up with the needs of your average users running their word processors. These products were not designed for a large PC server that is running a mail server with dozens of users attached to it, along with a World Wide Web server and dozens of other users who are just sharing files with one another via the server. Therefore, you have to be more concerned with getting higher-performance components in the PC market when you are picking out a server. Most workstation configurations will actually work as a server (assuming you have enough memory and disk space), but they will soon overload if you have more than a few users. What is enough? That is the subject of the performance monitoring and tuning chapters: Chapters 4, "Monitoring Environment," and 13, "NT Integration with NetWare and UNIX."

NT 4.0 Versus NT 3.51

How has the architecture changed for Windows NT 4.0 from that of Windows NT 3.51? The folks at Microsoft put a lot of effort into version 4.0 and it looks radically different. However, as a tribute to the original architectural design, the architecture did not change for this release very much. Instead, Microsoft made modifications to a few of the subsystems and implemented a new graphical user interface and its associated application programming interfaces.

The biggest and most noticeable change is that Windows NT 4.0 now sports the graphical user interface first introduced in Windows 95. Figure 2.8 shows the graphical user interface that Windows users have grown accustomed to over the years. You deal with the operating system through a shell known as the Program Manager. There are a number of common tools to manipulate files (File Manager) and performance system configuration functions (Control Panel). The applications run inside windows (areas on the screen with borders and control buttons), which are customized to the needs of the application.

Next the Windows 95 and Windows NT 4.0 graphical user interface steps up, which is shown in Figure 2.9. First, why change something that has sold millions of copies? The folks at Microsoft were quite careful about this process and got user interface experts to run experiments on people to see what functions of the graphical user interface were most intuitive and productive for the users. A few of the things that they implemented based on this study were the desktop, new tools for finding files, and increased use of the right mouse button and property pages.

FIGURE 2.8.

Traditional Windows graphical user interface.

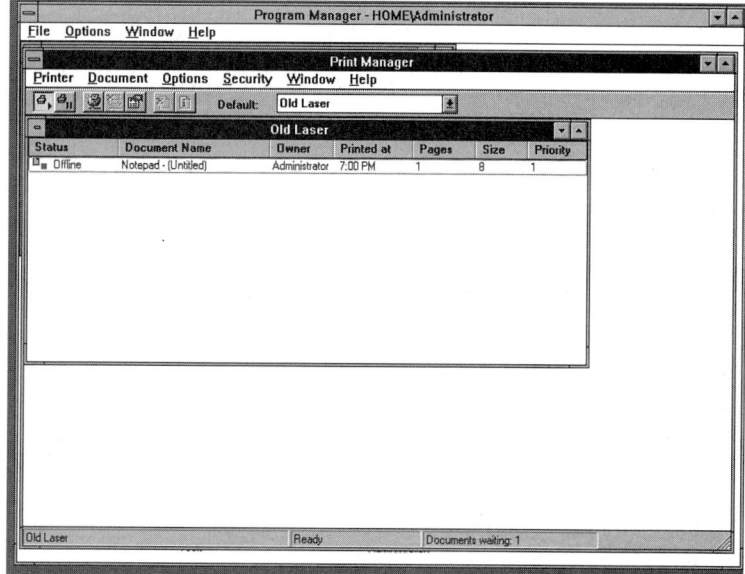

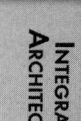

FIGURE 2.9.

The Windows 95 and Windows NT 4.0 graphical user interface.

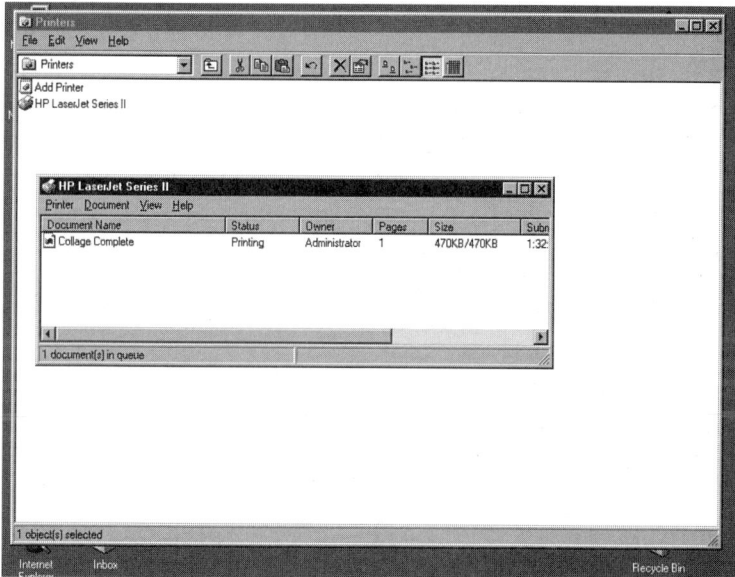

The desktop is probably the first thing you notice when entering Windows NT 4.0. Instead of being trapped inside the Program Manager application for processing support, you have a desktop that consumes the entire screen. You can access pretty much any application by creating a shortcut to that application and placing it on the desktop. It makes it easy to customize your environment to your personal taste. Each user ID also has its own environmental settings so that users can determine the look and feel of their environments.

The file location tools are also a big change in the NT 4.0 interface. You have My Computer, Network Neighborhood, and Explorer to work with as opposed to File Manager (which is also there in case you want to stick to stone knives and bear clubs). These tools enable you to navigate files located on your network as easily as you can find them on your local hard disk drive. You have a number of options for display and navigation. There is a heavy emphasis on drag-and-drop for copying or moving files. (I found that after learning and using these new tools, I have real trouble going back to File Manager on those servers that I work with that are still running NT 3.51.)

There is also increased use of the right mouse button and property pages. The right mouse button under Windows 3.51 is a rarely used feature, even though most users sit with fingers poised over both of the buttons on a traditional two-button PC mouse. The graphical user interface designers concluded that it was easier to teach people to use the second button on a mouse to call up menus that it was to have them move the mouse to the top of the screen and then find a function in a pull-down menu. Therefore, they implemented pop-up menus that are activated by right-clicking on an object (such as a desktop shortcut or a file). The most used features from this pop-up menu are the properties pages (see Figure 2.10 for an example). This is a series of one or more dialog boxes that have tabs at the top or side to help you locate a particular piece of information. Instead of looking for a setup or configuration utility located somewhere in the same directory as your application or actually running the application and looking for options or settings menu selections, you point your mouse at the application, right-click, select Properties from the pop-up menu, and then set the properties to suit your needs. It takes some getting used to but, once again, after learning this new environment, I hate going back to the old one.

FIGURE 2.10.

Properties pages.

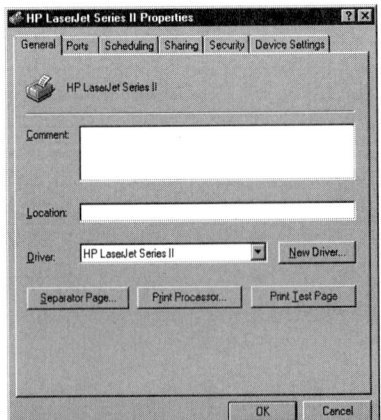

A few of the Windows NT utilities and services have changed their names and functions. Highlights of these changes include the following:

- Printer setup has been configured with a wizard to take you through the setup process by asking you a series of relatively simple questions.

- RAS dial-out has been changed in name and functionality to match the Network Neighborhood functionality of Windows 95 (find it under My Computer). This is a much easier interface for dial-out.

- The 4.0 User Manager can perform the setup functions of several other tools in the 3.51 environment. It is now your one-stop place to perform all the administration tasks associated with a user.

- Major improvements have been made to the graphics subsystems (starting with beta 2 of the Windows NT 4.0 product) that support things such as video and animation. Beware, though, that this will cause a substantial change in device drivers and applications that access advanced video functions (such as the ActiveMovie player).

In conclusion, even though the two versions of the operating system look radically different, they are architecturally the same. There have been substantial changes, especially to the user interface functionality, but the modular nature of the architecture accommodates these changes well. By now, you should have an appreciation for the basis of the operating system. If you are searching for more details, check out the Windows NT Resource Kit, articles on the Microsoft TechNet CD-ROM, or the Microsoft Web page (www.microsoft.com).

BackOffice Architecture

As stated earlier, BackOffice is designed for the Windows NT environment. Therefore, it is safe to say that the BackOffice architecture is the Windows NT architecture. However, that is not the complete picture. How do the BackOffice components interface with Windows NT to get their jobs done? The simple answer is that they are Win32 applications (the 32-bit Windows application programming interface was used to build these applications). Most of these applications are implemented as services with multiple threads.

Let's take a moment to look at the concept of a service. The standard definition goes something like "services provide system functions." That never seemed to be enough for me. A service should be a specific type of application that is started and run by the operating system. Whereas normal applications that you are running are terminated when you log off the Windows NT computer, sessions are started and stopped by a Control Panel utility and run whether anyone is logged in to the system or not. They can be configured so that they start up automatically upon system startup. You can even write batch files that start and stop services as needed. The key is that services depend only on the operating system, rather than any single user logged in to the system.

This is very useful for most BackOffice components. You would hate to have to leave your workstation logged in to a special privileged account all the time, especially if your server is located in your office environment as opposed to a protected data center. You want your mail server or Web server operating around the clock ready to service user requests as they come in. Windows NT is not like the mainframe environment where you might shut down time sharing operations after normal business hours to begin batch processing. You can access it even when you are working into the wee hours of the morning.

Another important feature is that most services are implemented so that they can be accessed through application programming interfaces. You want a means for your client workstations to access the central mail server or Web server to transfer information. This also is important for client-server database communications. It is especially important to Microsoft's goal of having an extensible architecture where BackOffice components can work together and users can build their local applications so that they can interface to BackOffice.

It is important to emphasize that BackOffice is dependent on the Windows NT architecture. In the DOS world, the operating system did not do all that much for you other than provide a way of executing applications. Operating systems such as Windows NT provide advanced services, such as network connectivity, printer drivers, and even fonts that your application can access. Therefore, BackOffice components enable you to focus on the job at hand (for example, processing electronic mail messages) rather than worrying about the low-level services. Microsoft tends to make its programmers use the operating systems services more than many other companies who think that they know better ways to get the job done. Therefore, you need to be aware of the services provided in the Windows NT operating system to fully control the BackOffice suite.

The Windows Interface

Another fundamental standard that defines the BackOffice environment is the Windows interface. Although it is not always observed by every vendor out there, it is followed well enough to enable you to pick up the operation of almost all Windows applications in a relatively short period of time. There are a couple of levels of this interface to look at in this chapter:

- Basic interface of applications to the operating system
- Use of common components by applications
- Graphical user interface standards

The first function, providing the basic interface of applications to the operating system, has been around since the earliest operating systems. The key here is that there is a wider range of services that are provided by the operating system. This application programming interface is quite extensive and growing. There is also another important set of interfaces in the BackOffice architecture—those of the BackOffice components themselves. This can become quite a challenge when you consider the number of new APIs that are coming out. Some months, there are several new APIs that are released. This is good, because software components are beginning to work together more and use one another for services, thereby making each application simpler. However, it can be a lot to keep straight as a programmer.

Some of the new technologies that Microsoft is coming out with create other interfaces between applications and the operating system. One that is particular interesting is the Component Object Model (COM), which includes Object Linking and Embedding (OLE). There are a lot of technical details to these technologies, but the key to focus on is that they provide ways in which you can access specific functions within another application if that application has been written to enable this to happen. You can, for example, call up a fully functional set of spreadsheet calls in the middle of your word processing document. They are not just for display purposes. You can actually alter the data and formulas to produce the desired results. You will soon see some of this technology in the basic user interface wherein Web browsing technology will be incorporated into windows in the explorer tools.

Another key that you should be aware of in the Windows NT environment is the use of common components by multiple applications. The primary means for doing this is the dynamic link library (DLL). Here, you have a stored series of functions that any application can call. The DLL files are located either in your current working directory or in your file search path. A common example is that in a subdirectory of Windows NT main directory (\winnt\system32), you find a number of application and operating system DLLs, and this directory is in your search path by default.

This DLL concept sounds nice—and in most cases it is. It saves programmers from having to code every function in every application from scratch. They can call DLLs that have been tested and are therefore fairly reliable. The disadvantage to this concept is that a number of vendors feel that it is necessary to have updated versions of commonly used windows DLLs to make their application work better. This can sometimes cause problems with other applications that cannot work with these updated DLLs. You should keep an eye out for this when applications start acting "funny" soon after you install a new application.

The final point is that there are graphical user interface (GUI) standards for the windows interface. The windows API is a collection of basic, low-level functions that are supported by the operating system (such things as windows that are fixed size, windows that can be resized, and so forth). The individual developers could assemble these components in any number of ways to build an application. Although this might be a great victory for individual creativity, it would be difficult for users who had to adapt to a different way of thinking when working in each new application.

To solve this problem, Microsoft has published official graphical user interface standards. For example, if you have a print function for your application and use a pull-down menu system, the print command is normally located under the File pull-down menu. Help is also an option on pull-down menus and is located to the far right. These and hundreds of other little standards help users find things quickly and are an important part of the application environment.

The good news is that Microsoft has worked hard in recent product releases to ensure compliance with standards, which makes your job easier in administration and user support.

The complication in this scheme is that the graphical user interface standards for Windows 95 and Windows NT 4.0 have changed in response to the changes in the basic navigation algorithms that are used. It is not as bad as you might think. You may click on folders and now have shortcuts on your desktop to access applications. You also will probably start using your right mouse button to call up properties pages for applications. Once you get used to these new concepts, you will probably even like the new interface better (most people that I have met do after they have had time to get used to it). The good news is that many of the application GUI standards remain the same. For example, Print is still located under the File menu in applications. There is an updated publication for the GUI standards for the Windows 95 interface that is published by Microsoft (if you have access to the Internet, look under the Microsoft Press section of the www.microsoft.com Web page for the latest version numbers, prices, and so forth).

This section was just a brief introduction to some of the important concepts of the Windows interface and how it relates to the BackOffice application. Purists may argue that architectures should only include discussions of the main functional components along with detailed specifications of the message formats used to communicate between the components. Perhaps that would be good for a Windows NT operating system internals book. However, this book is focused on BackOffice, the way you access the BackOffice tools, and how they relate to the operating system. You should be feeling pretty comfortable with basic operating system concepts by now and ready to take on a few of the newer technologies used to make Windows NT and BackOffice work even better than before.

Advanced Windows Technologies

The good news is that the folks at Microsoft rarely rest on their laurels when it comes to their technologies. It can be a real challenge to keep up with all the APIs, technologies, and add-ons that they keep throwing at us month after month. This section covers a brief introduction to some of the technologies that BackOffice is (or will soon be) using that have recently been introduced as add-ons or new components to Windows NT.

There are entire books devoted to each of the technologies that are emerging in the Windows environment. This section focuses on three key items that may be of interest to general BackOffice users. The chapters in Part VIII, "Integrating BackOffice," cover these and other technologies in more detail. The three technologies important to discuss in this architectural section are the following:

■ Distributed Component Object Model (DCOM)

■ ActiveX

■ Nashville

Let's start with DCOM. Recall the previous discussion about the basics of COM/OLE and how it could be used to enable applications to access functions within other applications. This provides a good way to get functionality without having to write the application yourself. The next logical extension of this concept is to apply its principles across the local area network as shown in Figure 2.11. Under this scenario, you could access application functions from an application located on the server. Why implement another standard when there are already methods of accessing client-server data? The answer lies in the fact that the DCOM architecture enables you to access a wide range of functions within a wide range of applications. The existing standard protocols are designed mostly for information transfer, not for using functions from applications on other machines.

FIGURE 2.11.

*Basic COM and
DCOM concepts.*

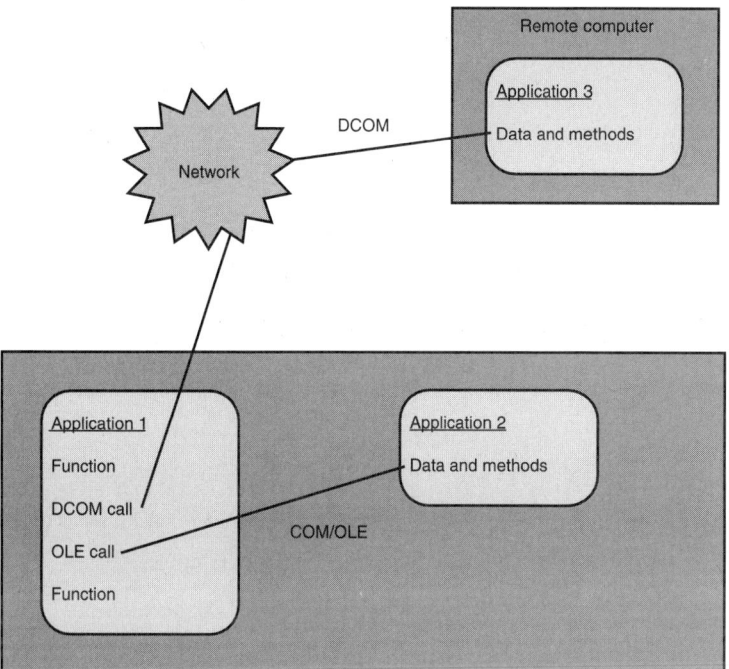

ActiveX technologies also enhance the modular nature of the operating system and serve to help simplify your locally written applications. Basically, ActiveX applications are modules that you can download from the network and call to perform specified functions. Examples of functions that can be performed by ActiveX components include playing MPEG videos or viewing a document prepared in Adobe Acrobat format. These can be much more than simple functions. In the case of the Acrobat viewer, it is a relatively complex view-and-print environment for authored documents (including text, graphics, and other information).

There is one particularly interesting concept for ActiveX components as they apply to Web pages. Imagine that you are on a Web page that has content that requires a specific ActiveX component in order to view it as shown in Figure 2.12. The HTML code can contain data that tells the browser that you are using the unique ID number of the ActiveX component that is needed. Your browser will check to see whether you have that component, and if not, you can download it and then run it. There are technologies involved with these components to validate that you got the correct component (for example, it is not something that calls itself the Acrobat viewer, but is actually a virus written by some hacker). This technology is still in its early days and is focused on Web uses, but it could well be extended to any number of operating system needs. Only time will tell.

FIGURE 2.12.

ActiveX components.

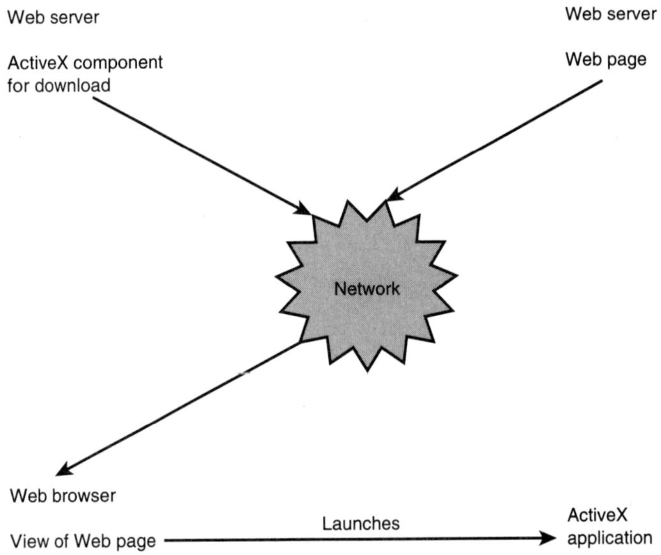

The final technology is generally classified under the development code name from Microsoft of Nashville. It is a revision to the Windows 95 and Windows NT 4.0 user interface that integrates Web browsing directly into the desktop environment. Microsoft is still working out the final details, but the prototypes that I have seen make accessing information located on a Web site (either intranet or Internet) as easy from the desktop as it is to access local hard disk drives or shared network drives on current networks. It also enables you to use the current browser and search interfaces to move around between information sources.

Integrated Security

It's time to look a little closer at integrated security of the Windows NT operating system. Chapter 3 covers security in more detail, but for now let's check the following points related to security:

- Security is part of the operating system itself.
- Security is designed around a single login.
- Security is applied to all sharable resources.
- Security can be applied to individual disk files.
- Applications can access operating system security features.
- BackOffice uses Windows NT security quite heavily.

The first key feature of Windows NT security is that it is part of the operating system itself. In many environments, such as mainframes, you purchase add-on packages from IBM or other vendors that perform the security checking beyond the very rudimentary features of the operating system. The good news is that this provides some competition in the market. The bad news is that because it is an add-on, there are many more ways to get around the security system, and the security systems have to be more complex to deal with these holes in the operating system. There are interfaces from the security systems of Windows NT that enable you to use third-party security packages or even make one of your own (in your spare time). However, because the checking is integral to all operating system operations, it is much harder to bypass.

The next good feature of Windows NT security is that it is based on a single login model. I have worked in environments where you had to set up users with logins on the Novell servers, each of the UNIX servers, and on the local computers (for password protection on the screen savers). Although all the user IDs were the same (for example, jgreene), the passwords had to be synchronized manually by the users (that is, using passwd on UNIX, using control panel to alter the local screen saver password, and running the Novell password utilities). These accounts had different expiration times, so it became easy for users to forget to change some of the passwords, forget which ones were which, and then have to call the system administrators to get their accounts straightened out. There were also always the loud complaints about having to reenter a password every time a user moved to a new server or logged in to a new database.

In Windows NT networks, you basically get a single login ID for access to all resources when you are set up in a domain (more on domains versus workgroups in the next chapter). You log in once (when you log in to your Windows NT or 95 workstation) and then continue to access resources on other machines in the domain based on the privileges that are associated with this one account. The operating systems coordinate who you are and what your access rights are for you, behind the scenes. In this fashion, you only have one account to maintain and one password to remember.

Another good feature of Windows NT security is the fact that it is applied at the operating system level to all sharable resources. These resources include such things as directories and printers. As part of the process of telling Windows NT that you wish to make these resources available to other users on the network, you specify which users or groups have access rights. You can also specify, as in the case of shared directories, what level of access rights a user has.

For example, I could declare that one person is limited to read-only access to a particular directory whereas another can read and write data to this directory.

Security can also be extended to the individual file and directory level if you have implemented the NT File System (NTFS) on your disk drives (covered in detail in Chapter 10, "Setting Up Windows NT"). The DOS operating system used a scheme for storing data on disk drives known as the File Access Table (FAT) system. This was starting in the early days long before the reliability and security concerns for computers were as high as they are today. This system worked fairly well, but it was designed in an era wherein you wanted to keep things simple to work on the less-powerful computers of the day.

When designing Windows NT, however, it was decided that a more complicated and powerful data storage scheme was needed for those users who wanted to implement features such as file level security. The design team came up with NTFS. Windows NT users have the option of choosing between FAT (which provides compatibility with DOS partitions on your PC) and NTFS (which offers advanced features such as file/folder level security). I tend to run servers using NTFS for security (people cannot reboot the server using a DOS disk and access data from an NTFS hard drive) and FAT for workstations that have both Windows 95 and Windows NT partitions.

Another good feature of Windows NT security is that it has APIs that enable you to query the security system from within your applications. The earliest PC-based applications had almost no security. If you could get to the PC, you had full access to its information. Early Windows-based PC applications tended to implement their own security scheme within the applications. Each one used its own user ID and password scheme or something similar. Some were obviously better than others.

Windows NT makes life a lot simpler for the users. Again, when the operating system does more for programmers, they have more time to focus on the business needs of the application, rather than focusing on building network drivers, print drivers, and security schemes into their applications. Because you have already gone through the validation process to get to the operating system, why not just ask the operating system who the individual is in some secure way (so that hackers cannot intervene)? You can then validate the user's access privileges and get on with the main business of the application.

BackOffice makes excellent use of Windows NT security. With the exception of Microsoft Mail Server, which dates from an earlier, simpler time, the components of BackOffice make calls to the operating system security system to see who the user is and then determine what their privileges are within the application. When additional information about the user is required, it is integrated with the basic Windows NT tools. For example, when you are running Microsoft Exchange Server, it requires more information about the user than the operating system collects (address information, signatures for messages, mail options, and so forth). When you create a user with User Manager on NT, you get a second screen that enables you to fill in the Exchange Server parameters immediately after you complete the basic operating system user information screen.

Integrated Monitoring

One of the keys to being able to manage a system is being able to see what is going on with that system. Windows NT provides a good set of monitoring tools for this purpose. These monitoring tools provide the following basic services:

■ Record events of interest that have occurred on the system.

■ Audit the occurrence of certain activities that may involve security problems or be used for statistical analyses later.

■ Monitor usage of system resources and overall load on the system.

Chapter 4 covers these topics in more detail, but basically these operating system tools provide interfaces so that application information can be recorded in addition to the operating system information. For example, the Event Viewer tool, which is used to see events of interest on your system, can also record events from your locally written applications. This saves you from having to write your own log display tools, maintenance tools, and so forth.

BackOffice products were designed to make heavy use of the integrated monitoring tools. Figure 2.13 shows the Event Viewer with some SQL Server and Exchange Server information recorded. This principle of integration applies to performance monitoring as well, which is useful because very few other applications come with the capability of seeing what is happening inside the application from a performance standpoint. You know that things are slow, but what is causing the problems? With the monitors built into BackOffice components that integrate with NT's Performance Monitor tool, you can get the data you need to help solve problems.

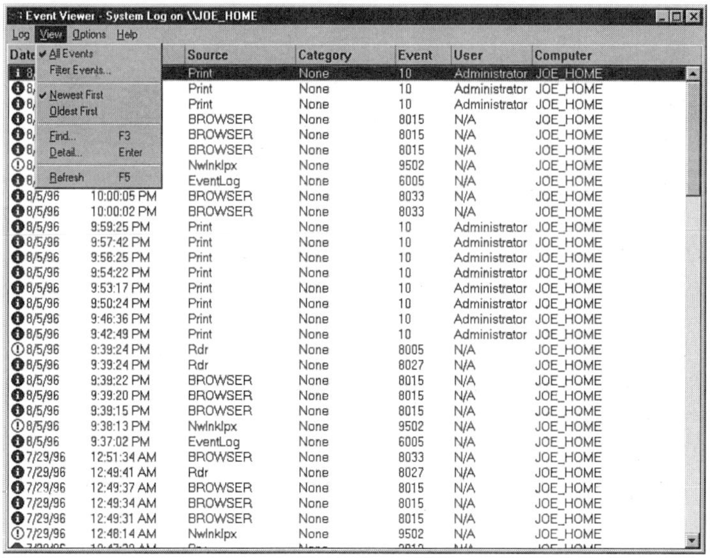

FIGURE 2.13.

BackOffice component using Event Viewer tool.

Integrated Administration

Recall the virtues of interfacing applications with the Windows NT security system pointed out earlier in this chapter. Recall also that the basic administration tools can be used to capture additional information needed by your applications, as is the case for Exchange Server. When you build extensions to BackOffice components locally (as is discussed in Part VIII of this book), you need to keep integrated administration in mind. Many programmers have the tendency to code things the way they always have. If they need additional information about a user for the application, they build a menu pick into the application menu system or provide a property page that has to be edited for that user. You may find it easier to deal with, as an administrator, if the programmers take a little time to learn the techniques for interfacing with NT's administrative environment rather than building another administrator application that the system administrator will have to run after creating the user's account.

Summary

This chapter provides a basic introduction to the Windows NT and BackOffice architectures. There are papers and entire books available on this subject. You can look in the Windows NT Resource Kit, TechNet CD-ROM, or visit the Microsoft Web page for more information. However, the goal here is to give you a basic overview of the operating system that is good enough for the BackOffice administrator and/or user. Sams Publishing offers another book in the Unleashed series that also goes into more detail: *Windows NT 4.0 Server Unleashed.*

Here are the more important themes related to the architecture:

- BackOffice is built to function in a Windows NT environment and is tightly integrated into the Windows NT architecture.

- BackOffice is a series of 32-bit applications that provide higher performance and stability than older, 16-bit applications.

- Networking support is built directly into the operating system and architecture. It is not an "add-on."

- There are compatibility features that enable you to interface to computers running other major operating systems, including Novell, UNIX, and IBM mainframes.

- Windows NT and BackOffice run on multiple different hardware architectures, including Intel, DEC Alpha, MIPS, and PowerPC.

- There is built-in support for computers that have multiple processors built into them.

- The Windows NT and BackOffice components are extensible, enabling developers to use their services and develop local applications that work tightly with the operating system services and BackOffice.

■ The security system is tightly integrated into the operating system itself and is not a separately purchased package.

■ You need to be careful when selecting hardware components to ensure that they are on the Windows NT compatibility list (that is, they have tested device drivers for Windows NT).

■ Extra care needs to be taken when selecting server hardware components to ensure that they have enough performance to meet your needs. This is especially true of Intel-based systems, wherein many components such as disk drives are designed for small user desktop workstations and not PCs running multiple BackOffice servers supporting a large number of users.

In the next several chapters, you go into a little more detail about the various major environments within BackOffice. Chapter 3 covers the security environment. As stated before, Chapter 4 discusses the monitoring environment. Finally, Chapter 5, "Administrative Environment," reviews administration in a little more detail.

2

INTEGRATED
ARCHITECTURE

Security Environment

by Joe Greene

CHAPTER 3

The previous chapter covered the basics of the Windows NT and BackOffice architectures. This and the next several chapters explore some of the major portions of this architecture in more detail. This chapter is devoted to the security environment. Some of you may not be interested in security at all. Perhaps you think that information should be accessible to everyone or something like that. Others of you may live and breathe security. It may be the most important decision when designing new systems in your super-classified environment. Whatever your philosophy about security, there is at least some minimal level of security implemented in the most basic BackOffice installations, so you need to know about this topic to make your system work.

This chapter is somewhat of a balancing act—enough information to understand the security environment, but no excessive information about the internal mechanisms and so forth.

General Computer Security Concepts

There are entire books on computer security out there and this is not one of them. Instead, this is a reasonable introduction to make sure that you are ready when you look into the implementation of security in BackOffice. The following general security concepts are important for the discussions in the rest of this chapter:

- System access
- Resource access
- Client-server access model
- Application security
- Viruses
- Hacking

The first layer of computer security that you will typically deal with is the system access layer. Figure 3.1 shows how the various security concepts fit together. You could say that if people can't access a system that they should not have access to, you have a relatively safe system. Typically, this form of security is implemented with a user ID and password combination that gives some assurance that the person requesting access to the system is really the person who has access to the system.

Another major component in providing access security is limiting who has access to the system and from where they have this access. Both of these concepts can really help increase your overall security. Perhaps you are one of those poor administrators who has to enable access to your server from anyone connected to your internal network, the Internet, and a large dial-in modem pool. You have no way to limit access and will have to rely on some of the other concepts discussed later in this chapter. However, if you do have the ability to control your access, you may want to limit the users who have access to your system (that is, not give out user IDs to people who are unlikely to use the system). Access to the computer system is what makes it actually useful, of course, so instead you may just want to limit where the users have access to your computer from. You may want to enable users to transfer information to and from disk drives only when they are connected from certain workstations that are in public areas and therefore would be less comfortable about doing mass downloads of corporate data or playing around to set up a virus.

FIGURE 3.1.

Interaction of various security concepts.

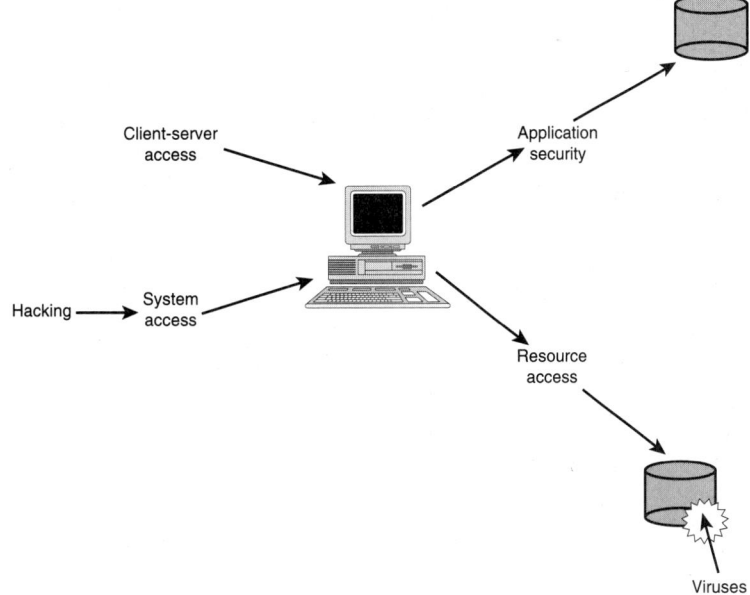

Let's spend a few moments on the user IDs and passwords that will be used to control access. User IDs control very little. They get sent with electronic mail messages, and most organizations have standards that enable you to determine user IDs just by knowing users' names (for example, jgreene). The password, then, is the place where most of the security is enforced. In the early days, people could enter anything (or nothing) for their passwords. Some places enable very simple patterns (such as 12345), and others issue policies requiring relatively complex passwords. An example of a relatively complex password is one that is assigned by a random generator that links two short words together (for example, treedogs). Modern operating systems enable you to enforce policies that keep users from choosing relatively simple passwords (or none at all). A nice feature of Windows NT is that the administrator can choose to install the password security policies or let the users do whatever they want, as is appropriate for a given environment.

Before you leave the topic of system access, you should know about a few things that are coming on the horizon (or are already here for some frontline organizations). User IDs and passwords can be compromised or hacked. There is no way a system can provide security if users write their passwords on sticky notes and attach them to the computers. Some places need more security than user IDs and passwords can provide, and they are looking to advanced technologies to help them. Among the more promising technologies for the near term are access cards and voice recognition. Access cards have been around for some time, but they are reaching the point where they are moving out of the deeply classified world and into the "real" world. The basic concept behind this is that you use a card reader attached to your computer that either sends an identification code (indicating that the computer is being used by a user with a valid key card) or actually scrambles the signals for transmission and descrambles at the other end of the transmission. Voice interfaces are some interesting technologies that are starting to be supported in the standard Windows API set. You could speak your name and have your voice pattern recognized against a master pattern stored when your account was created. I have a package that I played with that uses speech recognition to navigate through the Windows menu system (for example, saying "Excel" launches the Excel spreadsheet application). You can't say that there is a shortage of fun technologies that are being worked on today that will probably be standard equipment in the not too distant future.

The next general security topic is resource access. The term "resource" is used to describe anything on a computer that a user would want to access. Example of resources include disk directories, disk files, printers, or even applications that are running. You start thinking about limiting access to resources when you have a number of different groups accessing a single computer. Taking a BackOffice example, you would want to enable BackOffice and Windows NT system administrators to access various administrative and monitoring programs that you would prefer to restrict from the regular system users. You might also want to restrict sensitive personnel information (such as performance appraisal results and salaries) from all users except those in the personnel department and management.

The first task in the process of restricting access is identifying the various resources on a computer system. You could, for example, make each file a separate resource and go through a process of granting, on a user-by-user basis, access to that file. This would consume quite a bit of time. With another system, you group files into directories and then grant access to the directories based on access needs. Still other schemes might function on a whole disk or multiple disk basis.

The next task would be to actually perform the access grants. This also could be quite a time-consuming process on large systems. Most security schemes give permissions to users based on their jobs or the group in which they function (that is, payroll clerks can access financial information, and human resources types can access the personnel system data). Most operating systems mimic this real world organization by enabling system administrators to define groups of users and then associate individual users with the appropriate groups. They can then grant privileges to groups. You can still grant privileges to individual users, but you would do this only if you absolutely had to.

The third concept in relationship to security is the client-server model for computer system access. Figure 3.2 contrasts the client-server and host terminal methodologies. The host terminal access method matches the concepts discussed previously for system access. You identify yourself to the system and then go to either a command prompt or a graphical user interface to perform some processing. However, many modern computer environments are designed to enable you to be logged on to one computer yet access resources that are located on another computer. These resources that are accessed would include databases, directories that are shared, and even remote printers.

FIGURE 3.2.
Client-server and host terminal access models.

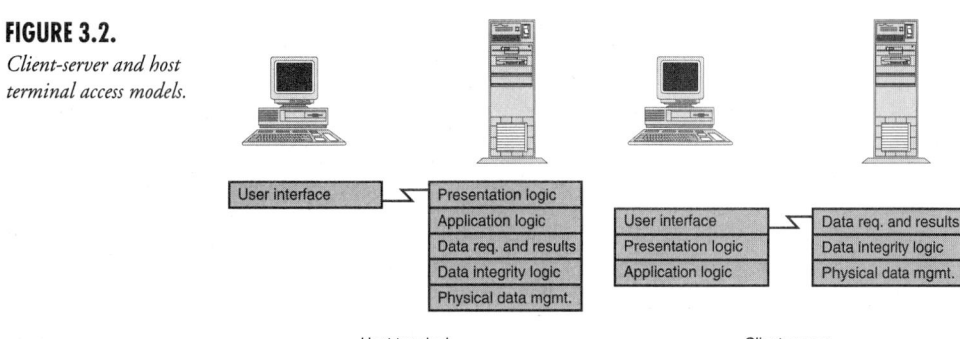

This presents a few additional challenges for a security system. First, because you have not formally logged on to the host computer system, you need to be authenticated on a request-by-request basis. There are a couple of ways that the server can approach validating your access rights. First, it could just ask you to supply your user ID and password each time you want some information from it. Although this would technically work, it would be an extreme burden on users who are frequently accessing resources on other computers. A second approach would be that you would be asked to identify yourself the first time you tried to access that host computer and it would then permit you to continue to access its resources until you log off the system. The final basic approach would be to enable you to log on to the entire network of computers once and then get access to any resources to which you are entitled based on a security token that you are given upon that first login.

There is one complication to this client-server world (yes, there are almost always complications). Some resources that you wish to access are controlled by the operating system itself (shared directories or printers). Other resources are under the control of applications that are running on the server that have implemented their own security schemes. A classic example of this would be an Oracle database management system that is running on your server. To provide additional speed, the communications protocols have been set up to route signals for the database directly from the TCP/IP communications processes to the Oracle utilities. There is no operating system security involved with this process (you could, of course, limit the TCP/IP transmissions or cut off signals to the database). This was originally designed for operating systems that had little security and a lot of overhead. Today, however, it means that you may have to implement security within your application packages if they are connected directly to the communications services of the operating system. Note that BackOffice components are designed to utilize the security mechanisms of the operating system, which is good news for the poor overworked administrators.

Application security is the next security concept, and it fits in nicely with the last discussion on the client-server access model. I know a lot of developers who have been implementing security within their applications for so many years that they automatically do it when they build a new application. That worked well in the client-server model on operating systems where security varied in quality and was not usually that good. Today however, you have large groups of programmers making operating systems secure. They have more time to build in security, and when implemented at the operating system level, it is usually faster.

There are reasons to consider using application security instead of or in addition to operating system security. If your application is to run on a large number of platforms and you want to provide a consistent administration interface, application security is probably the way to go. There is a price, however. When you use application security, someone has to go into the administrative programs you write after having learned your rules for granting privileges and then maintain user accounts. It is easiest on those who have to do the administration if you could access the operating system security mechanisms to validate who the user requesting the information is and then determine the appropriate access rights.

Now for a truly disgusting topic. Yes, computer viruses annoy me no end. Computers can be used for so many good purposes. They can make your work easier and get you home a little earlier each day (unless you have one of those bosses who expands the workload to ensure that he gets a 10-hour day out of everyone no matter what!). Some computers run critical applications that can affect safety of personnel. Yet there are some really sick people out there who get great joy out of writing software programs that harass or damage other people's computers. Worse yet, the virus problem causes information system types to have to spend time trying to look out for and combat viruses. Companies spend money on virus software and then lack money to upgrade all those old 80286 computers that are sitting on people's desks.

Viruses are a reality, and you have to think about protecting your machines from programs that come in and destroy data for the fun of it just as much as you have to protect that data from corruption by a disgruntled employee. Security mechanisms can be quite useful in preventing viruses. Most viruses are designed to access special operating system functions to do their damage (for example, destroy tables containing the list of files on a disk drive). If the operating system is enforcing tight security, viruses have fewer holes to get through. The account auditing tools can also detect common signs of viruses and warn the administrator of suspicious activities.

Hacking is a topic closely related to viruses. For the purposes of this discussion, hackers are described as people trying to get access to resources that they are not entitled to access. Just as there are folks out there working into the wee hours of the morning writing computer viruses, there are those folks who spend their nights trying to hack into other people's computers. Some have made it a symbol of a computer counterculture to say what computers they have been able to break into. If it were just bragging rights, it might be tolerable. However, it often goes way beyond access for the sake of access. Imagine the value of your critical business plans or even source code for your new product release. Suppose someone could get into your computer and provide this information to competitors. Of course, while in your computer, the hacker could also wipe out your hard disks or any number of other annoying tactics.

There are a number of security mechanisms that can come into play to minimize the risk of hackers. First, the login mechanisms can be set to disable accounts that have had too many failed logins in a row (a sign of a hacker trying to guess passwords by trying the user ID, 12345, and so forth). Another useful tool is to have the auditing mechanisms record data about failed logins so that the administrator can detect patterns of suspicious activity. If the security system requires users to pick nontrivial passwords and change them on a routine basis, that can really hurt the hacker's efforts.

With an apology to the security experts in the audience who may have found this discussion too basic, the rest of you should appreciate the basics of computer security at this point. This will prepare you for the next section where you consider some alternative security schemes. This will set the stage for the following section, in which you explore the security schemes implemented in Windows NT and BackOffice.

Alternative Security Architectures

Why discuss alternative security architectures when all you really need to know is the one that is implemented for BackOffice? My goal is to give you an appreciation of the alternatives that the Microsoft team had to choose from when they implemented NT and BackOffice. This will also enable you to appreciate the relative strengths and implications of the strategy Microsoft has chosen. First, you get a quick overview, with a list of pros and cons for each strategy, that will lead you into the BackOffice-specific discussions.

A Bit of History

In ancient times (or actually not all that many years ago), computer applications consisted of card decks that were processed by card readers and enormous computer complexes that were only a fraction as powerful as the computers that most grade school students play with today. The only resource that you accessed was the computer itself. The security scheme consisted of a job control card that identified you as a user and maybe even required a password. Actually, I believe the job control card was less a security mechanism than a means to ensure that the data center could properly bill the users for services (it cost a fortune back then). Your application had to contain all the software and data that your program was going to work with. Although this allowed a very simple security scheme, it made application programming a tedious task (imagine having a punch card for every transaction that occurred to your general ledger so that you could run a simple report).

Computer types of that era recognized that this was not a very productive environment (and hated to see adults crying when they dropped their decks of computer cards and watched them scatter over the floor). Storage technologies were soon developed that enabled users to store large (for the time) data sets on magnetic disk drives. This freed users from needing to store all their data in card decks but created the operating system problem of having to control access to information. You would not, for example, want university students to have access to the databases that contained their grades (talk about grade inflation).

One of the early schemes involved creating levels of users (somewhat analogous to groups, but with a hierarchy that enabled people at the top to access anything). You could access information based on your level of access (administrators could get everything and undergraduate users could not even access the disk storage systems). This was a good start, but then you got into conflicts when the scheduling people did not want the professors to see their information and everyone became concerned about personnel and financial information access. The good news was that as financial information started to be stored on computers, money started to become available to fund development (they were real systems and not toys for the engineers).

Computers continued to evolve and they started to get more resources attached to them. In addition to disk drives, there were printers, plotters, and tape drives. Because paying for the computers was a big concern in this era, wherein a machine that was still much dumber than today's common PC cost millions of dollars, I always sensed that money was more of a concern in most of the places where I worked than was some philosophical concern about controlling access to information. There were prehistoric hackers back then who managed to figure ways around the security system and store files that were too large for their disk packs on someone else's disk packs. However, for the most part, the basic login ID, password, and resource access privilege scheme as a security system was in place and functioning.

This worked fine for most university and business organizations. They got away with limiting who had access to the system. Back then, only a few people were enabled to run jobs and they were supposedly trusted individuals. The masses were limited to reading printouts prepared by the data center. However, this was not good enough for many government agencies around the world. The military and intelligence communities needed to store and process large volumes of information. The computer was the only tool that could manage this information overload. When large numbers of people started to need access to data, it became important to be able to closely control who had access to individual files as opposed to merely just controlling access to the computer itself. Some other issues such as auditing to determine who actually did access information in the past also became important.

These needs led governments to pour a lot of money into research on computer operating systems, network architectures, and security systems. This work was split between universities, laboratories, and private companies who tried a number of different concepts to see what would work best. It started as a series of add-on packages that you could install on your computer to increase its security level. The bad news was that these add-on packages often disabled a number of your applications, which were performing basic operations that the security package deemed to be illegal. So you wound up rewriting applications and going through other changes. Many organizations also changed security systems one or more times as the products that they started with went out of business, or evolved into a new scheme that could do more or one that used less system resources to provide security.

Part of this funding also helped to develop more advanced computer networks to link computers. This enabled users to access multiple computers, which contained different bits of information that were needed to get their work done. The peer-to-peer networks (all computers are treated as equals regardless of their speed ratings or amount of disk storage) and even the beginnings of client-server computing came into being. The bad news was that these networking alternatives created new security problems that had to be solved as you tried to control access to shared disk drive information without having the advantages of a controlled login on a terminal that was on a controlled terminal network. Some of the problems with network security are still being worked on today, although most operating systems can now handle this world well, if not with perfection.

Another interesting development is the newer operating systems that have come into being. DEC's VMS operating system was probably one of the first commercial operating systems written after the days of card decks. It had a lot of terminal and resource security built directly into the operating system itself, as opposed to security being a separate, add-on package. It also was one of the first major operating systems to assimilate networking technologies that were evolving from some of the research mentioned earlier. UNIX came into its own at about the same time, and it quickly supported minimal security and networking (although networking was a later add-on, the highly modular nature of UNIX enabled it to be assimilated quickly). UNIX never really picked up heavily on the security theme until the government started to use it, but there are now some UNIX systems that have relatively high security ratings (although this often required a complete rewrite of the UNIX kernel and other major components to make it look like traditional UNIX but have security built into its heart).

Finally, there are operating systems such as Novell NetWare, IBM OS/2, and Windows NT that have come about in the modern era of networked computers, intelligent workstations, and nonbatch operating systems. They have the advantage of being built from the ground up for this new world. They have also been optimized for distributed processing, where you have a large number of smaller computers as opposed to one giant computer with a number of clients. From a security point of view, these operating systems have the advantage of being built during an era wherein the standard level of security was much higher than when IBM started building mainframes. Therefore, the designers put more security features into the basic architecture, which usually results in a higher level of security and less overhead.

Security Models

With that brief discussion of history aside, let's look at the more common security models. Figure 3.3 illustrates these basic alternatives. One important point to keep in mind is that each of these alternatives has advantages and disadvantages. For example, if every computer had a security system that was complex and secure enough for the CIA or NSA, the only person who would be able to log on to your home computer would probably be one of your kids (they are so much better at computers than many adults that I know). That would not be very useful and is just not needed for most home PCs.

FIGURE 3.3.

Alternative security models.

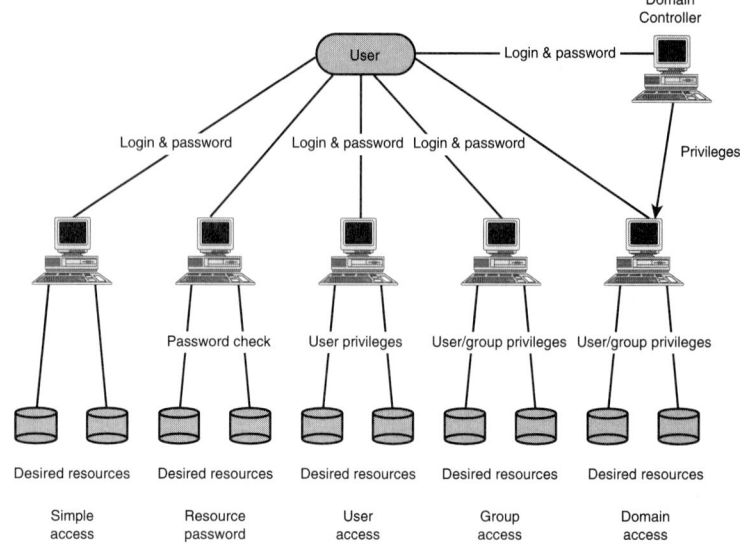

The first model is simple access, which is used in the typical PC environment. You have a user ID and password (maybe) to access the system. Once you are at the login prompt (in the DOS case) or the graphical user interface (Windows) you have full control over everything on the system. Unless someone has encrypted files or done some other special application security features, you have full access to all data and other resources. This model is the simplest to deal with when you have a truly "personal" computer where there is one person who uses it and has full access to all its resources.

The next model is resource password security, in which you assign a password to each resource. For example, you have a shared accounting data directory on which you put the password of IRS and a shared engineering data directory on which you put the password of EINSTEIN. This is also fairly simple to initially configure and, assuming that you do not choose dreadfully simple passwords such as the ones in the example, it can work fairly well. The problems with this system typically occur when individuals leave the group for which the data was created (or get fired). In this case, you may want to consider changing the password to ensure that the data is not viewed by these former group members. If you have an organization that has a reasonable turnover rate, this can cause a lot of headaches because you have to change the passwords, as do your users.

The third model is user access security. In this model, you identify yourself as a user to the computer that has the resource that you want by entering your user ID and password as it is recorded on that computer. The system administrator for that particular computer has created an account for you. That administrator then assigns access rights to your account that determine what you have access to. If you leave the company or your job changes, all the administrator has to do is either cancel your account or change your resource access rights.

An extension of the user access security scheme is the group access security scheme. Because most access rights are given to a number of people who work in the same group or even have the same job, it is logical to teach the computer about these groups and assign access rights to the group as a whole. Then all the administrator has to do is create a user account, then assign it to the appropriate group or groups. The administrator can always assign unique rights to an individual if there is something specific about this individual—for example, the person is the database administrator in the development group and therefore needs access not only to the software directories, but also needs special privileges to access the controlling utilities for the database management system.

The schemes proposed so far work for individual computers or even small groups of computers. However, in the world of distributed computer resources where you replace a single large computer with many smaller servers, it could be a nightmare to perform administration on dozens or even hundreds of computers. The basic goal therefore would be to provide a single point for user administration and have all computers access this security information. Microsoft refers to this arrangement as domain access security. There are other vendors who implement the same general concept. You effectively have a login ID, password, and group accesses that are recognized by all computers on the network. The administrator has only to adjust your group structure in one location and you acquire the appropriate rights on any computer that is participating in the domain.

The Windows NT Security Architecture

Recall that Windows NT supports a domain security model. However, you can configure your systems into what Microsoft refers to as a workgroup configuration. This model is basically the group access security scheme discussed in the last section. The workgroup concept came along first. It started about the time Microsoft extended the basic Windows 3.1 operating system to provide native support for computer networking with the Windows for Workgroups product. Before this point, most networking was done through add-on software drivers that enabled the computers to use network cards to access data on servers (most of which were running Novell NetWare).

There were a few problems with the older operating systems providing network support. The Windows 3.1 operating system could support additional memory above its original 640K limit, but it was not easy. There were some software components that could be loaded into what was referred to as upper memory (actually there were several regions), but there were others that insisted on being loaded into that precious first 640K. This became a problem because they often had to load network drivers into the lower memory regions and that meant they could not run certain applications that demanded a lot of memory in the lower region.

Workgroups

Microsoft improved the memory management features of the operating system and polished off all of the hooks needed to ensure that the operating system and the network linked together well. It started with a simple peer-to-peer model because it did not have a strong presence in the server operating system market at that time. It appealed to small groups of users who wanted to share Bill's printer with everyone and let all the word processors use the large disk drive in Tom's machine to store large files. It was very simple to administer and ran on the resource password security model—Tom could put a password on his disk drive that users had to enter in order to get access to it or he could just leave it without a password.

With Windows NT Server, Microsoft had a product that could seriously compete within the server market. Unlike the Windows for Workgroups product, it also had an operating system that had reasonable security and therefore could use more sophisticated security schemes. Therefore, Microsoft extended the workgroup concept to enable users to have login IDs and passwords on the NT servers. If you could supply the correct login ID and password, you were then given access to resources based on the permission grants made by the system administrator for the server. The administrator had the choice of making the resource access grants based on login IDs or by group memberships.

Domains

This workgroup scheme was good enough to meet the needs of almost all computer networks of the day. However, things were growing rapidly in the area of PC servers. Larger numbers of users were accessing larger number of servers. To accommodate these needs, Microsoft implemented its domain architecture. Figure 3.4 shows the differences between domains and workgroups. The domain is a concept that applies to both workstations and servers. The key is that you have to have at least one Windows NT server to have domain.

The central security focus in a domain is a Windows NT server that has been configured to run as a domain controller. You have to be careful when setting up your servers because you cannot switch a server that was configured to run as a workgroup server to run as a domain server. You basically get the pleasure of reinstalling the operating system and rebuilding all your configuration and access data. It is not an easy task, so if you think that you might want to move into the domain architecture, it is best to start out that way before you get too much invested in your current configuration.

> **NOTE**
>
> If you might want to move to a domain architecture, it is best to configure your network as a domain from the start.

FIGURE 3.4.

Workgroups versus domains.

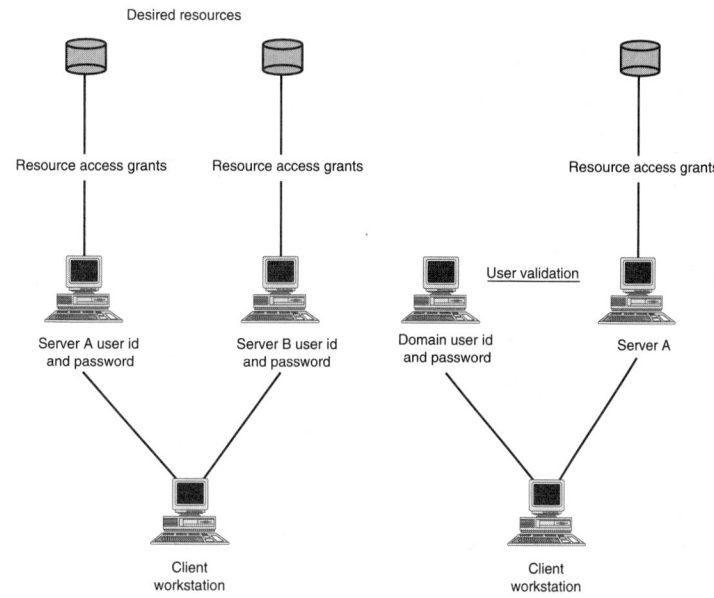

Another point to consider in the planning process is that because this domain controller is the key to all security access information within your little network, what can you do when the domain controller runs into a hardware problem and is shut down? Microsoft has considered this and devised the concept of primary and backup domain controllers. You have one primary domain controller that is the ultimate authority on who has what security access rights. You have the option of implementing one or more backup domain controllers. These computers actually serve two functions. First, they can take over and validate security access information when the primary domain controller is not available. Second, they can also service security information requests from users, thereby reducing the load on the primary domain controllers.

You build a domain network by installing the Windows NT Server operating system on one of your computers with the primary domain controller option specified. (You learn more about installing the Windows NT Server operating system in Chapter 11, "Windows NT Administration.") Once you have this primary domain controller configured, you can install backup domain controllers. You install the Windows NT Server operating system on these machines and select the backup domain controller option. You will be prompted for the name of the domain that this backup domain controller is to join. You will need to supply a valid, domain administrator user ID and password as registered on the primary domain controller. Once you are validated as a domain administrator, the two servers exchange security databases and encrypted security keys with one another. This is all transparent to you at this point. All you see

3

SECURITY ENVIRONMENT

is that once you have completed the server installation process, you can run the administrative tools on the new backup domain controller and see all the same security information that you could see on the primary domain controller.

> **NOTE**
>
> When you perform security administration tasks on a domain, you are making changes that are replicated on all domain controllers within that domain. You do not have to update the other domain controllers manually. If one of the controllers is down while you are making the administrative changes, the other controllers will provide any updates that have occurred during the downtime to the restarted controller when it starts up.

Imagine that you could write a program that would send out requests to the domain controller and record them, and then you could look through the data that is sent back to figure out how Microsoft encodes all that security access information. That would enable you to figure out, using your user ID, how to hack into other, more privileged accounts. The folks at Microsoft thought of this. Basically, before your computer gets any real security information sent to it, you need to have it join the domain. You join a domain by setting up the network configuration showing you as a member of the domain. To create an account for your computer in that domain, you need to have someone with domain administrator privileges log on to the system. This also assures that you are running a trustworthy operating system (such as Windows NT) that isolates security information from user processes.

Your next question might be which is better—domains or workgroups? I started with workgroups and became quite comfortable with them. They were what I was used to from the Windows for Workgroups world and being in a development environment, I hated the idea of having to keep the servers up to ensure that security information is available. However, one fine day when I was first installing some remote administration tools, I found out that these tools worked only when you were using the domain architecture. That made sense because you need to have a good handle on who is trying to modify user security information, and the secure protocols used in the domain world were probably a good idea.

About a month later, when I tried to install either SMS or Exchange Server, I got a similar error message saying that I had to be a domain in order to install that product. I guess that there is very little that can be done with simple workgroup configurations to provide the kind of security that many users are now demanding for their business applications. From these experiences, I got the basic message. Many of the future business applications that I will run across under Windows NT will be using the advanced security features of domains.

It was quite maddening at first. I tried time and again to get my workgroup server upgraded to a domain server. Finally, I bought a couple of reference books and found that this was not possible. I had to reinstall my server. This also meant that I had to reinstall my Oracle database and a few other things that I wanted on that server. However, once I did this I was surprised to find out how easy it was to administer a domain. I had a little learning to do with regard to adding computers to the domain and a few other areas (which are presented in Chapter 11 and also in Chapter 12, "Windows NT Performance Tuning"). All in all though, I have actually come to prefer domains, because I have one set of user IDs and passwords for all my servers. I then only have to go to the individual servers to set up access rights to resources (and I almost always grant resource privileges by group).

The following are the advantages of working with domains:

- They are easier to maintain for large groups of servers.
- They are required for many BackOffice products.

The following are the advantages of working with workgroups:

- They are simplest for networks with a single server.
- They save the time involved with network login requests to the domain server.

Domain Trust Relationships

Why stop here with the concept of domains? With the way computer networks continue to expand, it is not too difficult to imagine a world where you have access to all computers in your organization to which you need access. One solution might be to create really large domains that cover all locations and groups. Although this would be theoretically possible, there are some practical concerns that must be dealt with. The tight integration of domain controllers needed to enable backups to take over and also share some of the load with the primary controller can cause a problem when you have a large number of controllers spread out over a large area. This is compounded by the fact that almost all wide area networks have much less communications transmission capacity than the local area networks. You would not typically want to bog down the WAN with a lot of user security transmissions.

Another practical concern is service. Users generally like to have access to someone at their location (or at least in their time zone) to get help when problems come up. It would be difficult for many of these users to accept a system where they had to contact some central office (perhaps located on the other side of the world) to get routine account maintenance services. Therefore, local control over computer security will be around in many organizations for some time to come.

To solve this problem of very large networks, Microsoft chose another methodology. It has built its domain security systems to be able to trust the judgment of other domains when it comes to validation of user identity and group privileges. These trust relationships are relatively straightforward. You tell one domain that it should trust the security validations of another domain. Note that the trust relationship is a one-way street. If you tell domain A to trust domain B, it does not mean that domain B will trust domain A. If the controller in domain B validates the user though, domain A will accept that validation and provide access to any of the groups to which that user has been assigned.

Another key point in this architecture is that trust relationships need to be made by domain administrators in both domains. An administrator from domain A cannot just say that domain B is to be trusted. Domain B is not configured to provide validation information to domain A until the domain B administrator says that it is possible to let domain A trust domain B. Once both administrators agree to this one-way trust relationship, the validation information can be transmitted.

This could actually lead to some very big holes in security. Imagine, for example, that all domain administrators use the default roles for domain administrators and users. Would you really want someone from another domain that you trust coming in and acting as an administrator for your domain just because that person is an administrator for the other domain? Not really. Microsoft has implemented the concepts of local groups and global groups. All the groups that you find in your normal domain environment are local groups who have meaning only within the domain. Feel free to create local groups to meet your needs; you do not have to coordinate your group names with everyone in the organization.

Instead, interdomain access rights are defined by membership in global groups. You create global groups the same way that you create local groups; however, you specify the global option. This name is coordinated with the groups that trust you and that you trust. When you add a user to one of these global groups, that information is passed to the other domains when they do a security validation of that user. They then can assign the appropriate access rights to these global groups that are appropriate for visitors in their domains.

One final point related to domains: the trust relationships are point-to-point and not hierarchical. Figure 3.5 illustrates the difference between these two concepts. Suppose that domain A trusts domain B. You also know that domain B trusts domain C. This does not mean that group A trusts domain C. You do not inherit trust relationships from groups that you trust.

FIGURE 3.5.

Trust relationships.

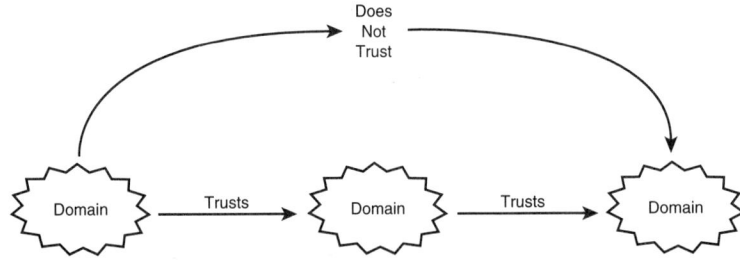

NOTE

Trust relationships are point-to-point, not hierarchical.

There is, of course, a lot more that could be said about the Windows NT security scheme. If you want additional information, I suggest *Windows NT 4.0 Server Unleashed* from Sams Publishing, the Microsoft Windows NT Resource Kit, or the Microsoft TechNet CD-ROM. The following is a summary of the security architecture in which Windows NT and the BackOffice components operate:

- It is a relatively secure environment. It has been rated at the C2 level by the United States government, which is much higher than the vast majority of operating systems available. You only achieve this level of security if you enable the security options that will be discussed in the section on user administration in the next chapter.

- Most of the security work is done behind the scenes from the user perspective. The user supplies one login ID and password and is provided with access to all resources that are approved by the system administrator. There are no extra actions required on the user's part to establish security relationships with different resources.

- The domain environment makes it much easier to administer privileges on networks that consist of a fair number of computers.

- As you will see in the next chapter, the administrator is provided with a convenient graphical interface to the utilities that control security accesses. This makes the job much easier.

Integration of BackOffice with Windows NT Security

I have some good news for you. Once you learn to work with Windows NT security, you have almost all the knowledge that you need to work with the security systems of most BackOffice components. The key here is the capability of these applications (and others developed for the Windows NT network environment) of making calls to the operating system to ask for validation of a user ID and password combination. This is perhaps one of the most useful integration features between other BackOffice components and Windows NT.

The first advantage achieved by using Windows NT security, as opposed to all BackOffice developers making their own security, is that it provides better security. Not only do operating system developers have more time to work on a comprehensive security scheme than most application developers, they have the advantage of being able to access internal structures that are protected by the operating system from access by regular programs. As mentioned earlier, Windows NT security also has the blessing that administrators have to learn only one interface to the security system, which reduces the burden of maintaining user accounts. In this environment, access to a database or electronic mail system is just like access to any other server resource.

A key advantage for users is that they see access to system resources via a single login. Users get quite annoyed when they have a large number of different accounts—one for each server, another for each database, and so forth. If the user IDs and passwords are not coordinated with one another, the users usually wind up forgetting their passwords for one or more systems; then the administrator has to intervene to reset the passwords. It also reduces the risk that they will have to write down all their accounts and passwords on sticky notes that are posted on their computers (some people will still write their single user IDs and passwords on such notes, but there is nothing we can do about them).

The best news about this integration is that it is almost transparent to you. For example, when you add a new user to Microsoft Exchange Server, the only way that you notice it is that you get a really detailed property page after you create the user account. It can be somewhat confusing the first time that you see it (especially if you have just performed an operating system upgrade), because all it says is Server in its title bar. It does not say NT Server, Exchange Server, or SQL Server. As it turns out, it is actually the detailed information (office address, telephone numbers, and all those e-mail preferences, such as whether a return receipt is desired) that is associated with an Exchange Server account. Once you have that figured out, you fill out the details desired in your organization and click on the correct button, and the account is created in both NT Server and Exchange Server.

Using the Security Environment to Your Advantage

No, I am not going to disclose a bunch of secrets gleaned from hacker bulletin boards that will let you access information that you should not have access to. Instead, let's look at how you, as an administrator or developer, can set things up so that you derive productivity benefits from the operating system security system. It is a powerful system with defined interfaces. If you choose to take advantage of this powerful environment, you can make your job much easier.

The first suggestion that I have for those organizations where you write local applications is to use the Windows NT security system if you have to do any access validation at all. The API for this interface is defined. If the user is actually on a local computer or is logged in to a domain, you can use the login ID and then map application-specific privileges to this login ID rather than building your own login system. You can also work to interface special data collection mechanisms to the basic User Manager interface in much the same manner Microsoft does for Exchange Server. As an administrator, you do not want to run a separate package to set people up for a user's application in addition to the setup that you go through for operating system or domain accounts.

Spend a little time doing some group planning before you set up your systems. Once you have a large number of users in your system, it can be quite time-consuming if you have to change your groups and then grant all the new privileges. Chapter 10, "Setting Up Windows NT," presents some of the basic planning processes for a server. You can actually build schemes with a hierarchy of privileges that can simplify your later administrative tasks. See Figure 3.6, for example. Here, you have a base set of privileges that you give to all users (such as access to the shared printers and the company-wide information directories). You then add specific groups to capture people with similar privileges. For example, all accounting clerks have a certain set of accesses to update the books, but the accounting manager has a special monthly report directory. Only the manager can write to it, but the rest of the department can read it. If you spend a little time talking to your users and thinking about your organizational structure, you can probably come up with a pretty good scheme to match your needs.

FIGURE 3.6.

Hierarchy of group privileges.

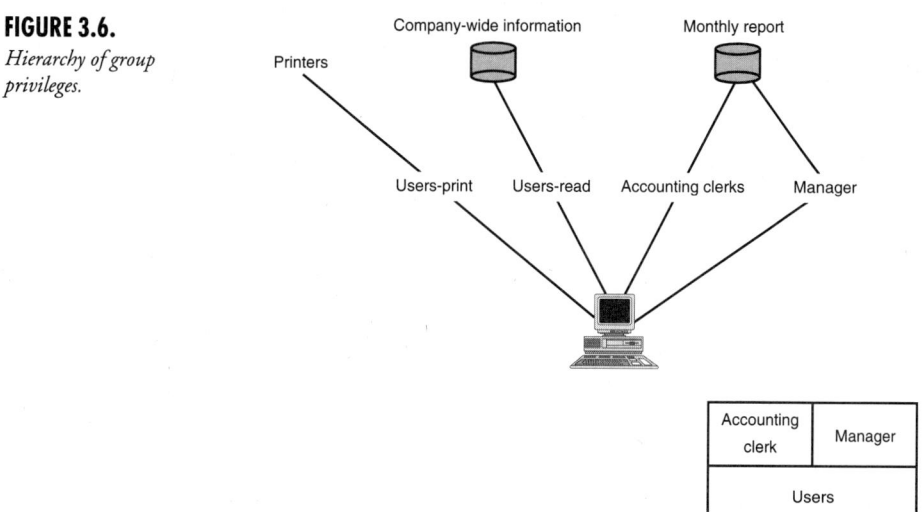

The application log is especially recommended for application developers (and system administrators who have input into the application development process), an interface of Event Viewer to which applications can write. (Event Viewer is covered in the next chapter as one of the administrative tools of interest to system administrators.)

The only time that I have seen the application log used is when a BackOffice product writes to it. I have not loaded any non-Microsoft commercial applications that have been set up for this function, but I am sure that they are out there. I have seen locally written applications use this log and it works quite well. The basic concept is easy and it took the group of programmers that I work with less than an hour to figure out how to use this interface. Best of all, once your applications learn to write to this tool, you no longer have to worry about building your own message log viewer or log file cleanup routines. Microsoft provides them for you with Event Viewer.

What kind of messages can you write to Event Viewer? Generally, short text is used as opposed to long dissertations. However, I have seen some fairly complicated messages that dump the status of internal application variables and other such data. The key is that you can record what your application needs. There are several different types of events—informational, warning, and general processing. You can record as little or as much as you want. The only thing that you have to keep in mind when designing your messages is that you might have to read through this log some day when a problem comes up. You do not want to have to wade through a lot of garbage to get to the important stuff.

Summary

The goal of this chapter was to give you a general understanding of the security environment in which your BackOffice applications will be hosted. You should also be comfortable with the concepts of workgroups and domains. Finally, you should have an appreciation of how tightly BackOffice security is coupled with the Windows NT Server security environment.

You may feel a little empty at this point when it comes to security. Although this chapter discusses security system concepts, it does not present anything practical about how to perform even the simple task of creating a user account. Don't worry, that is what the next couple of chapters are about. With the basics under your belt, you are ready to plunge into the more practical subjects of tools and techniques. Chapter 4, "Monitoring Environment," covers the monitoring environment that you will use to keep track of Windows NT and other BackOffice components from both a performance and security auditing point of view. Chapter 5, "Administrative Environment," presents the administrative tools that you will be using to set up accounts and perform all the other functions that are needed to keep a server functioning happily. Remember, when this book discusses these Windows NT Server tools, it is talking about the tools you will be using for other BackOffice components as well. Many of the BackOffice components have their own little control applications, but they use the Windows NT tools for most common administrative functions. I have only run the Exchange Server administrative application a handful of times, and that was mostly to figure out whether there were advanced options that I could play with to improve performance.

Monitoring Environment

by Joe Greene

IN THIS CHAPTER

CHAPTER 4

Integrated architectures and security environments are a good foundation on which to build systems. So far, so good. Now it is time to leave the theoretical and architectural worlds behind and start talking about the actual implementation of the BackOffice family. The first topic in this chapter should be close to the hearts of administrators and systems support staff. It deals with the tools that are available to monitor the BackOffice family during operation to see how it is performing.

A good starting point is a clarification of what tools are being discussed in this chapter. Are you going to learn the tools that monitor the operating system, Windows NT? Does this chapter cover the tools needed to monitor SQL Server? How about Exchange Server, SNA Server, SMS, and IIS? The answer to these questions is yes, but there is a really neat catch. You are going to look at only the set of tools that is built into the Windows NT operating system. The neat catch is that when you learn the NT tools, you also learn the tools for BackOffice, because the folks at Microsoft were kind enough to make their developers use the NT tools for the various BackOffice components.

This is good in a number of ways. It is good for Microsoft because they do not have to pay people to develop, test, and support a number of different monitoring tools. That obviously saves them some money and enables them to use programmers elsewhere to develop useful features that are specific to the various BackOffice components. It is also very good for those of us who use the monitoring tools in the field. Learning one set of monitoring tools is much easier than having to learn how Exchange Server developers thought and then learn how the SMS people approached the issue. The support staff of most systems that I have run across have more than enough to do already, so every bit of time savings is generally appreciated.

What functions do monitoring tools perform for you? It generally depends on who you are talking to. Security types say that the main functions of monitoring tools are to capture who has access to the various types of data and validate these accesses against the standard list of security privileges. Users, on the other hand, are generally interested in having their huge database queries complete within a fraction of a second. Therefore, you are usually under some pressure to monitor performance of the system and see what you can do to improve it. Finally, because software and hardware are imperfect, it is sometimes useful to have tools that record messages from the various hardware and software components to see what they are doing. This can often take the form of the last words from a dying process that try to capture what caused the problem.

Where do monitoring tools fit into the duties of BackOffice support staff? I tend to think of them as part of the first-aid kit for the operating system and other BackOffice components. You typically do not use them every day. You typically do not use them a lot. However, when the system is crashing and users are desperate to get their work done, these are the essential tools that help you determine what the problem is and what you need to do to fix it. Therefore, it is wise to become comfortable with the various tools, what each one can do for you, and which bits of information provided by these tools are most useful when you have a particular problem.

This chapter begins with an overview of some of the general monitoring concepts that you should consider when getting acquainted with your monitoring tools. Next, you look at the tools that are provided by Windows NT for monitoring your operating system and BackOffice components. An overview of the parameters that can be monitored and which are most useful in common situations is followed by several sample monitoring plans for your consideration when you plan for your own installations. You explore the integration of BackOffice with Windows NT monitoring tools next. This chapter wraps up with a discussion on how your developers can integrate their applications into the NT/BackOffice monitoring environment.

General Monitoring Concepts

Before you jump into the details of the monitoring tools that are provided in Windows NT and BackOffice, let's look at a few of the design considerations and functional requirements of a good set of monitoring tools. This will enable you to better understand the way things have been set up in NT and reduce the amount of time that it will take for you to learn the environment. The first concept to be covered is *parameter*. Basically, it is something that can be measured. Examples of computer parameters could include disk space used or abnormal termination of a particular application (which I hope you won't observe very often).

There are an enormous number of parameters of a computer and its operation. Some are not very useful (the color of the metal on the inside of the computer's cover, for example). Others are useful at planning time, but after that are seldom used (the size of the computer case, for example). This chapter focuses on those parameters that are important to computer operations— and therefore are of interest to BackOffice and NT administrators.

After eliminating the parameters that do not deal with computer operations, you still have a large number of parameters that can be measured or observed. These measurements can include usage (how much of a disk drive is currently filled with data), activity (number of reads and writes to a particular disk drive per second), or other quantities (such as an internal application error occurring). It seems appropriate to break these parameters down into categories so that they can be studied in more detail. For purposes of this discussion, the operational parameters of the system are divided into three categories:

- *Hardware parameters* relate to the physical pieces of equipment in your computer, such as the central processing unit (CPU) or disk drives.
- *Operating system parameters* relate to tunable portions of the operating system.
- *Application parameters* are specific to the individual applications.

These parameters form a hierarchy, as shown in Figure 4.1. The key item to remember is that you need to have all parts of this hierarchy working together to get the performance that you want. For example, you can have the best operating system and applications in the world, but there are fixed limits as to the number of computations an 80286 processor can complete in a given period of time. Therefore, it is important to be able to understand what is going on at all levels to achieve the performance (and reliability) that you need.

FIGURE 4.1.

Hierarchy for performance and monitoring.

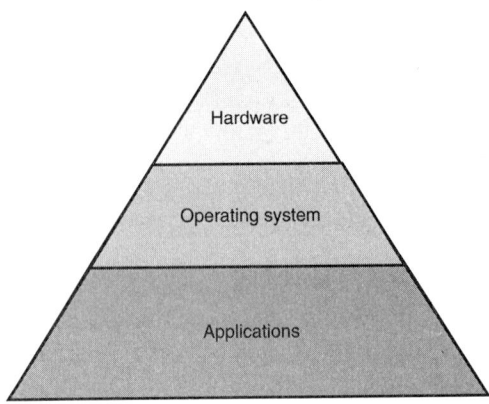

The first set of parameters, hardware items, typically falls into the areas of capacity (megabytes of disk storage), performance (number of bytes transferred per second to a given disk drive), and events (such as an error when trying to read from a disk drive). They also can be divided according to hardware components. The three big items monitored on most computer systems are the CPU, disk drives, and physical memory. Of course, you may be interested in the transfer capacity to a CD-ROM drive at certain times, so you also need to be able to monitor the less commonly used parameters.

The next set of parameters relate to the operating system. If operating systems were fixed entities that performed the same for all computer systems and applications, you probably would not need to be concerned with this category of parameters, because they would map directly to the performance parameters of the hardware. However, operating system designers are quite clever and work hard to enable their creations to adapt to different hardware configurations and application needs. For example, if you put additional memory into a Windows NT system, it will reconfigure itself to use that additional memory to speed up application processing. You also may want to intervene to adjust various operating system parameters to adapt to special needs of your application (complex numerical models of the interaction of galaxies with one another have different needs than those of a word processor).

The final set of parameters relate to the applications that are running on the computer. This could liberally be thought of as all software that did not come as part of the operating system distribution media. This is often the most difficult area to deal with from a monitoring point of view, because many developers record little about the execution of their application other than fatal error messages. It is also one of the more pleasant design features of BackOffice tools, because this set tends to record a substantial amount of information (startup, shutdown, and even processing levels). The more data that you have about critical application parameters, the better you will be able to support those applications and keep performance levels high.

One thing that you have to be careful about is the volume of data that you monitor. As you will learn throughout the rest of this section, Windows NT is designed to enable you to select the parameters that will be monitored instead of recording every scrap of information that is available to it. The good news is that you can see the status of important parameters right away, without having to wade through a mountain of numbers. The bad news is that you have to figure out which of the hundreds of parameters available are important to you. Later sections in this chapter cover the list of parameters and preparation of monitoring plans.

Another factor in the monitoring process is the utility of the numbers themselves. Suppose I told you that a disk drive has had 100M of data transferred to it since the operating system was started up and its counters reset. What exactly does that tell you? Actually, it tells you very little. If the operating system had just been started a few minutes ago, this could be a sign that this is a heavily loaded (and perhaps overloaded) disk drive. If the operating system was last started up a month ago, it could be a very normal number. The point is that to have true utility, numbers need to be expressed in terms that are useful (bytes read per second) for the particular parameter measured and also provide a reasonable graduation of time over which the data was taken (what was the average over the last minute as opposed to the average over the last six months). A particularly useful unit of measurement is a percentage of total capacity. For example, knowing the number of instructions processed per second by the CPU is nice, but being told that the CPU is operating at 20 percent of its processing capacity is much more useful.

The next consideration when you are trying to monitor the operations and performance of your system is the presentation format of the data. A few dozen screens with a few hundred numbers each is generally difficult for mere human beings to wade through. However, a graph that has a line showing how the disk throughput varied over the last day and another one showing CPU utilization are easy formats for administrators to review. Other parameters, such as the log of problems with the operating system, do not lend themselves to graphical formats. However, Windows NT uses time-ordered lists of errors and uses icons and filters to enable you to sort out the problem messages from the normal routine. The key to remember is that you need to be familiar with the various display formats of the monitoring utilities so that you can select the one that is most useful to you on a given task.

Now you have a set of data regarding only those parameters that are truly important to you. A logical question at this point is to ask when a given parameter being monitored is cause for concern. That is actually quite a tricky question in many cases. Some parameters are easy to understand and have fixed capacity values. For example, a disk drive will store a certain number of megabytes and no more. CPU utilization is another example in which if you see that your CPU is running at 100 percent utilization and all your other parameters are well within their limits, it may be time to get a faster CPU.

The problem comes when you try to measure performance of a large number of the parameters in your system. For example, you find that a disk drive is transferring 10M per second to your system. Is that too high or absolutely normal? It depends on the type of disk drive, the type of disk drive controller, and the type of transfers involved. (Do they cause the heads of the disk drive to have to keep moving around or is it one long sequential read?) With all these variables, it is almost impossible to come up with an absolute set of numbers that can be used to interpret the numbers that are coming from your monitoring efforts.

The only practical solution for many parameters is to just observe the values for the parameters and the performance of the system. Take a set of numbers when the system is lightly loaded and everything is working well. Then try taking numbers at higher load levels and observe the performance of your applications. If everything is functioning well and the users are happy, that number of 10M-per-second data transfer to a disk drive must be okay. Save this data for problem times. Then, when you monitor your system, you may find that the disk drive is transferring 12M per second and that the queue of requests for that disk drive is very high. This is your indicator that the drive has reached capacity. You can store this number for future reference to help you avoid problems with this and similar disk drives.

Another important point about the monitoring process is that it should not bias any data that you are receiving. This can be tricky on a computer where monitoring a large number of parameters can take up a lot of CPU time and disk transfer capacity. The good news is that you have a fairly fine level of control over the number of parameters and where you are storing your data. You just need to keep this in the back of your mind before you start logging every event that is happening to your computer.

That is probably enough discussion on the basics of monitoring. These are some of the general monitoring considerations that you need to think about and that do not fit in with the discussion of this tool or that pull-down menu. To close out this section, let's look at a brief presentation of another way of classifying parameters that matches well with the tools that are provided in Windows NT:

- *Events* are records of discrete event occurrences. They usually do not have a value associated with them. Instead, they contain a text message, such as the fact that the browser service started successfully or that a print job from a certain user was completed.

- *Performance parameters* are records of performance or utilization measurements. They almost always have numbers associated with them that can be graphed and compared with other measurements.

- *Auditing records* are similar to event monitoring, but they tend to focus on actions taken by users and applications. They are typically used for security and other such applications. An example of this would be recording the fact that a specific user used a particular system administrator privilege.

Windows NT Monitoring Tools

With this general discussion completed, it is time to move on to the specific tools and parameters that you will use in Windows NT to measure the performance of your BackOffice system. This section focuses on the tools that are available to you. Its goal is to cover the basics of how to set up and use these tools for common monitoring tasks. The next sections review the various parameters and what they mean.

As mentioned in the last section, Windows NT provides three basic tools to enable you to monitor activities on your system. These tools are used for monitoring both Windows NT operating system activities and the activities internal to most of the BackOffice tools. Figure 4.2 shows these tools and their basic functions.

FIGURE 4.2.
Windows NT performance monitoring tools.

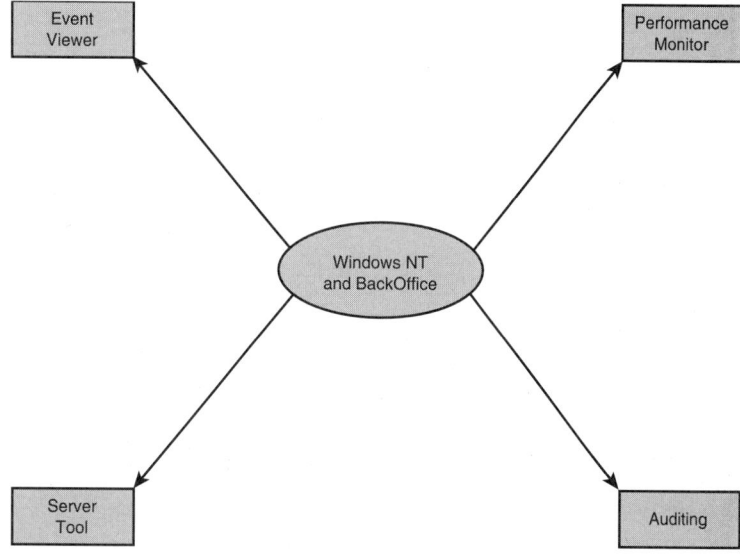

The first tool that you need is the Performance Monitor. Its main task is to measure performance parameters for both the operating system and the hardware. It has been extended to be able to present performance parameters for most of the BackOffice applications. You also have the option of using it to capture performance information for your applications. It provides a number of display formats and data capture options to enable you to see the data in the way that makes the most sense to you.

The second tool in the Windows NT monitoring tool kit is the Event Viewer. Its goal is to provide a means of displaying records of activities that have occurred on the system. There are several different logs (security, application, and system events) that can be displayed. There are also a number of display formats.

The next Windows NT monitoring tool is the auditing record. The good news is that the auditing data is presented in a tool with which you will soon be familiar—the Event Viewer. The only trick is that you have to set your options using another tool, the User Manager.

The final monitoring tool is the Server application, which can be found on Control Panel. Although it does not produce fancy graphics, it is the best source for finding out things such as who is connected to the system and what resources they are sharing. There is not much to discuss about this tool, because it is relatively simple; however, that is part of its charm. The key points are that this is a tightly integrated monitoring environment and there are only a few simple tools to learn.

4

MONITORING
ENVIRONMENT

Performance Monitor

Figure 4.3 shows my favorite Performance Monitor view—the line graph. Performance Monitor is a flexible tool that presents data in a number of different formats. It is also very graphically oriented and easy to get used to. The basic interface for this tool has the following characteristics:

- Across the top of the windows is the standard Windows menu bar. It enables you to access all your basic processing options.

- Just below the menu is a toolbar that enables you to pick the most commonly used functions with a single menu click. The first set of four buttons enables you to select the type of display that you want to view: chart view, alert view, log view, or report. The next three buttons enable you to add, modify, or delete a particular counter from your list via a pop-up dialog box. The next button enables you to take a picture of the parameters data at the current moment. The next-to-last button enables you to write a comment to the log file at a particular time that might help you to remember what was going on later when you are reviewing the log. The final button displays the Display Options dialog box to enable you to set the environment to your liking.

- The rest of the display is used to display the actual performance data itself. As mentioned earlier, there are four display formats. Each of these formats is covered in the next sections of this chapter.

FIGURE 4.3.

Performance Monitor's line graph interface.

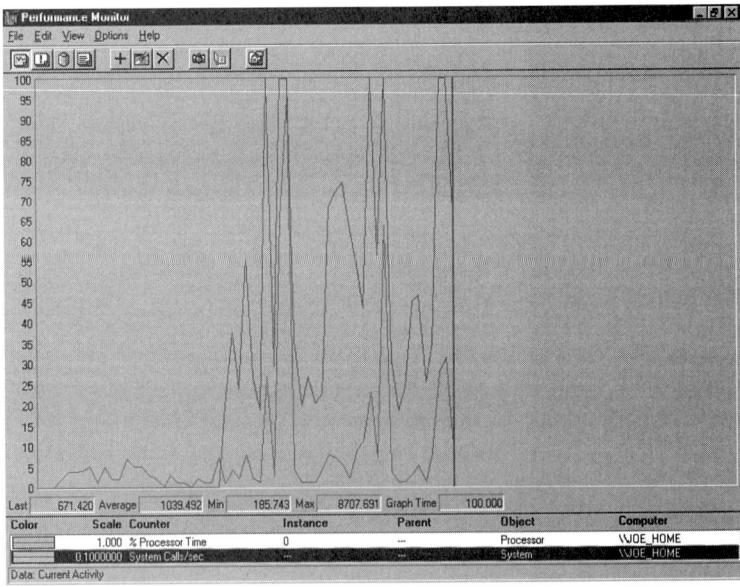

Before getting into the specifics of the various displays in Performance Monitor, let's look at an option that might be useful to some of you. Many people are comfortable with only one window opened up to the full size of the monitor at a time. Those of you who are comfortable with several windows or toolbars being open on your desktop at a given time, however, can use a few control keys to minimize the Performance Monitor display and keep it open for your review at all times.

Figure 4.4 shows a Performance Monitor graph of SPU process time use in a nice, graph-only window. How do you accomplish this? First, set up the Performance Monitor graph that you want to see (the details of this process are shown in a few paragraphs). To trim the windows, press the following keys: Control+M (which toggles the menu on and off), Control+S (which toggles the status line on and off), and Control+T (which toggles the toolbar on and off). You can also use Control+P to set up Performance Monitor so that it stays on top of all the other windows on your desktop. In summary, set up the graph that you want and then press a few control keys to customize the display to suit your tastes.

The best thing about Performance Manager is that it is installed when you install Windows NT. You do not have to go through any additional steps to get the software on your system. When you start Performance Monitor, you will notice that it is not doing anything. There are no monitoring parameters selected, so it is just sitting there waiting for you to instruct it on what you want done. This makes sense, because there are so many different parameters and monitoring needs that Microsoft could not even begin to guess what it was that you needed by default.

FIGURE 4.4.

Trimmed Performance Monitor window.

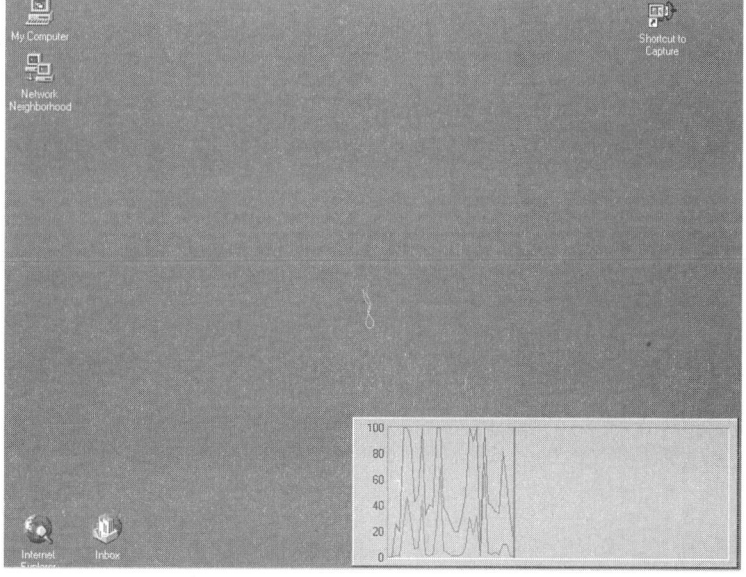

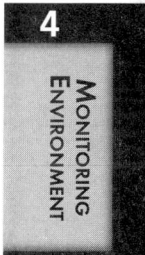

Your first task is to set the options, counters (monitored parameters), and instances (for monitored objects such as disk drives, you have to tell it which disk drive you are interested in when you have more than one) for the monitoring task at hand. This is a relatively easy task. Click on the plus sign icon in the toolbar to add the counters for the parameters that you need to monitor. Performance Monitor displays the Add to Chart dialog box that is shown in Figure 4.5. The following are the options that you specify on this dialog:

FIGURE 4.5.

Add to Chart dialog box.

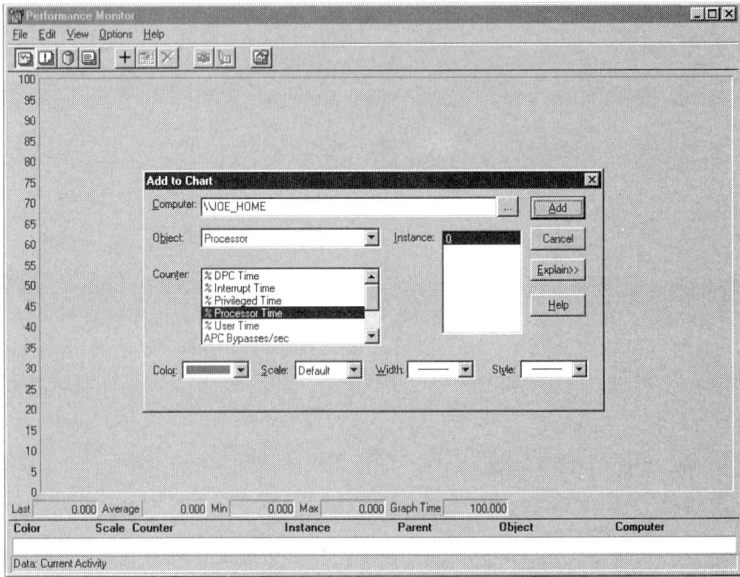

- The Computer box enables you to select the computer for which you want the monitoring to occur. Performance Monitor is running on your current computer, but it can collect and display statistics for any Windows NT computer on your network. You can even get a version of Performance Monitor for Windows 95 that enables you to monitor remote NT Servers from a Windows 95 computer. The selection box at the right enables you to search the network for a list of computers that you can monitor (using the standard computer name that you put in when you installed that computer). You can, of course, type in the computer name at the prompt using the standard double-backslash notation (for example, **MASTER_SERVER**).

- The Object drop-down listbox enables you to select the objects (that is, physical disk drives or CPU) that you wish to monitor. The object selected determines the values that are available in the Counter and Instance scrollable listboxes.

- The Counter scrollable listbox enables you to select which of the various counters (parameters) is applicable to the selected object that you wish to monitor. You can select multiple counters for a given object.

■ The Instance scrollable listbox enables you to choose which particular object for the selected object type that you wish to monitor. In most instances, there is only one instance of the object (that is, systems with only one CPU or one set of random access memory). However, there are cases, such as multiple physical and logical disk drives, that are common.

■ The Add button enables you to add the monitoring Computer, Object, Counter, and Instance configurations specified to be added to the parameters being monitored in your current instance of the Performance Monitor application. You can have multiple instances of Performance Monitor running on your computer to monitor the performance of different computers or different parameters on a single computer.

■ The Explain button is for those of you who do not have the time to become intimately familiar with all the various counters. It displays some additional text at the bottom of the dialog box. It is not the most detailed explanation of the subject matter, but it is helpful.

■ The Cancel button enables you to close out the Add to Chart dialog box.

The same basic Add to dialog box is used for all the views (chart, alert, log, and report). This reduces the number of user interfaces that you have to learn to work with. The last word in the title bar changes to show the type of view that you are working with (Add to Chart, Add to Log). You will also notice the color, scale, width, and style controls at the bottom of the dialog box. Performance Monitor automatically cycles through a predefined set of color and line patterns as you add counters. However, those of you with finer artistic tastes may want to take matters into your own hands and specifically set the patterns on your graphs. These buttons enable you to accomplish this task.

The Chart View in Performance Monitor

The chart view is my personal favorite for displaying performance data. I have a science and engineering background, so I have gotten quite used to following lines across the page. There are a few considerations that you should keep in mind when you are setting up a chart view. The first is that the chart view is best suited for viewing numeric data that varies over time. It is not that great when you are looking for a rare occurrence (a spike in CPU utilization, for example), because the data on the chart view is routinely overwritten with new data. Therefore, you may want to use the alert view to catch rare events.

Another important chart consideration is avoiding excessively busy graphs. The human eye can follow a few lines as they vary over time, but it can be very confusing if you have a large number of lines moving all over the screen (see Figure 4.6). This graph illustrates several points. First, you probably find it difficult to distinguish which line is associated with a given counter. Very few people can follow a large number of lines, especially if they intersect (it is okay to have a few more lines if some are at the top of the graph and the others are at the bottom).

> **TIP**
>
> You can solve the problem of excessive graph complexity simply by starting up multiple instances of Performance Monitor with several, less-busy graphs running at the same time.

Another consideration that most people might forget is that Microsoft uses color well to help you distinguish the lines. It is easier to differentiate the green line from the red line, especially when they intersect. However, you may have difficulty presenting your wonderful color charts to a boss who is color-blind. If you do not have access to a wonderful color printer, the charts that make so much sense to you when you look at them on your color screen may be impossible to read in black and white off your laser printer. The line pattern can be used to compensate for this somewhat; however, if you have to present them to others, you may want to keep the complexity of the charts down (see Figure 4.6).

FIGURE 4.6.

A busy Performance Monitor chart.

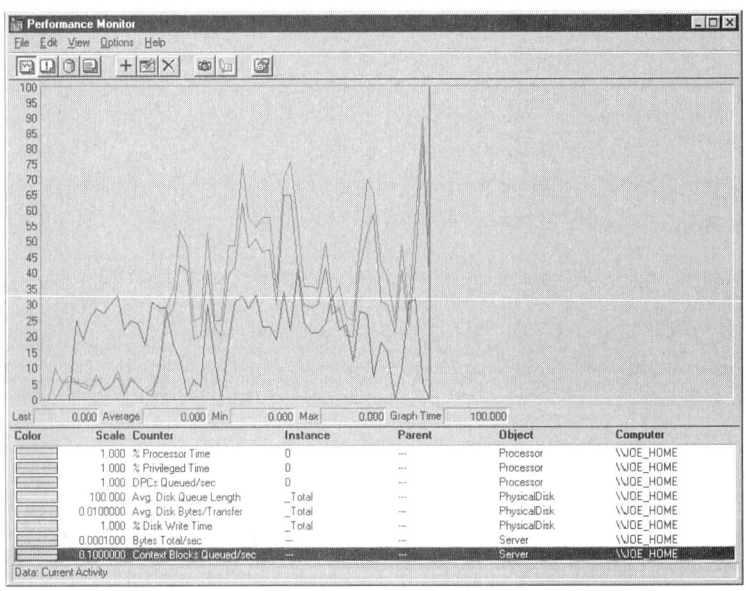

Perhaps you are a displaced graphical artist. You spend a lot of time customizing the counters, colors, patterns, and other chart settings to get that perfect graphical display of the key parameters of your system. It would be annoying to have to go through this every time you start Performance Monitor. On the File menu, you have the option of saving your chart settings as shown in Figure 4.7. You also have the option of saving your charts, option menu selections, and so forth using the Save Workspace menu option. The goal of these menu picks is to let you build up a series of Performance Monitor charts, alerts, and so forth that provide you with key system information. You can do this while everything is going along smoothly and you have a little spare time. Then, when everything is crashing down around your feet, you can call up the appropriate monitors to determine the true problems quickly. Put this on your list of things to do.

FIGURE 4.7.

Saving Performance Monitor settings to a file.

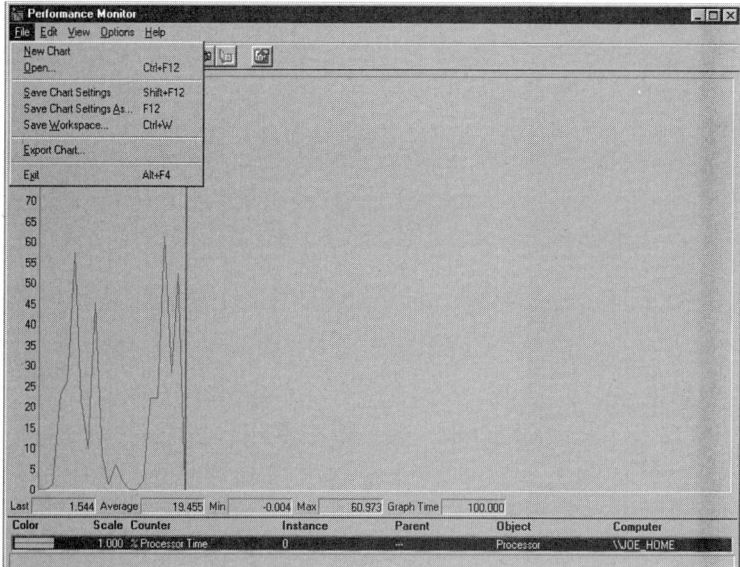

If you have ever done business application development, you have probably come to appreciate the diverse formatting and display demands of different users of the system. I have seen people argue for hours over the exact point size for the font used on reports and what the exact wording of the heading should be. Microsoft deals with this fact of life by providing you several options for presenting this data. These controls enable you to set the details about how the data on the chart is presented and collected. The Chart Options dialog box enables you to set the following presentation options (see Figure 4.8):

- The Legend checkbox enables you to specify whether you want to use part of the display space to show a legend. The legend shows a sample section of a particular line (for example, the green one) and associates with a specified computer, object, counter, and instance. I recommend keeping this option activated unless the contents of a particular graph are really obvious.

- The Value Bar checkbox controls whether the Last, Average, Minimum, Maximum, and Graph Time data displays are presented beneath the chart itself, as is shown in Figure 4.8.

- The Vertical Grid checkbox controls whether vertical lines are drawn in the middle of the graph to help you see the value of a given data point.

- The Horizontal Grid checkbox controls whether horizontal lines are drawn in the middle of the graph to help you see the time that corresponds to a given data point.

- The Vertical Labels checkbox controls whether the scale of values for the vertical label is displayed.

- The Gallery option contains radio buttons to select either Graph (a line graph where all the data points are represented as dots connected together with a line) or Histogram (a bar chart where each data point is represented as a vertical bar whose height corresponds to the value being measured).

- The Vertical Maximum edit box enables you to control whether you display the whole range of values possible, as determined by Windows NT (0 to 100 percent), or whether you want to focus on a narrower range where the interesting data lies (0 to 50 percent). This can be useful in situations where you want to see finer variations in data that is confined to a narrower range.

- The Update Time section enables you to specify whether you want Periodic Update or Manual Update. Periodic Update is the default in which Performance Monitor collects a data point for the parameters being monitored at the interval (in seconds) specified in the edit box. Manual Update collects data for all the parameters being monitored when you select the Update Now selection from the Options menu, when you click the toolbar item that looks like a camera, or when you press Control+U.

FIGURE 4.8.

Chart Options dialog box.

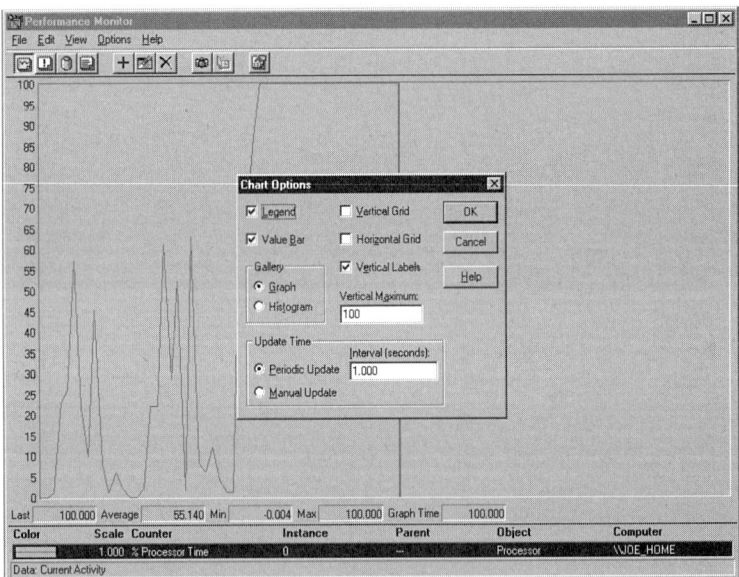

In summary, the chart view in Performance Monitor provides an impressive array of data presentation options. You are probably uncertain as to which options suit your tastes from this brief discussion. There is no substitute for actually sitting down and trying out the options. As mentioned earlier, it is beneficial to figure out the key parameters and charting options that you like when you have time to work with the system. So far, however, you have seen only one of the four views of data provided by Performance Monitor. The good news is that although the format of the displays differs between these views, user interface is very similar so you should be able to adapt quickly to the other three presentation formats.

The Alert View in Performance Monitor

The next Performance Monitor view is the alert view (see Figure 4.9). The basic concept behind this display is quite simple. Suppose you want to monitor several parameters on several servers to detect any problems. You are not interested in the many hours of normal, within-limits data that would be generated on these servers. Instead, you want to know only when action is required on your part. The alert view enables you to tell the system to write an entry into the log whenever a parameter on a given system exceeds the value that you specify. The computer then takes on the task of sorting through the data that is collected at routine intervals and writing the values that meet your criteria.

FIGURE 4.9.

Alert Log display.

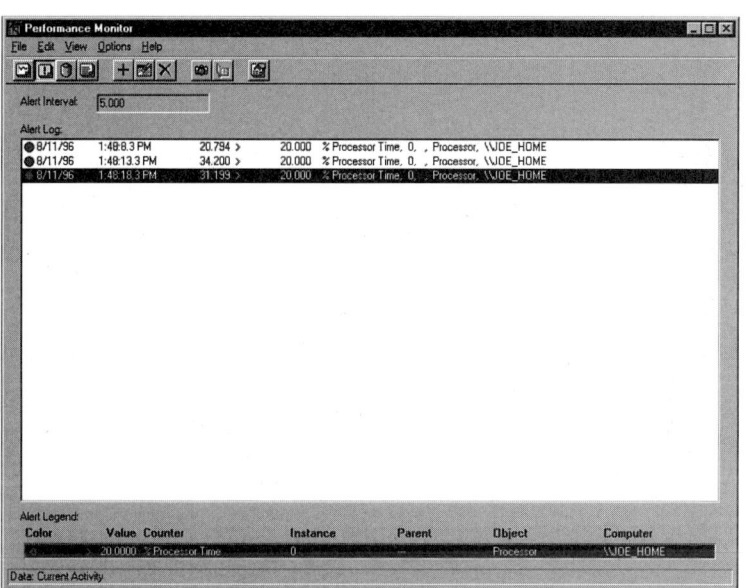

To set up monitoring using the alert view, you first select this view from the toolbar (the icon has a log book with an exclamation mark on it). You add the systems, objects, counters, and instances that are of interest to you using the Add to Alert dialog box, which is very similar to the Add to Chart dialog box discussed previously (see Figure 4.10). The key data element that you want to enter on this panel is at the bottom of the screen. The Alert If control enables you to specify when the alert record is written. You can specify that you are interested in values that are either under or over the number that you specify.

FIGURE 4.10.

Add to Alert dialog box.

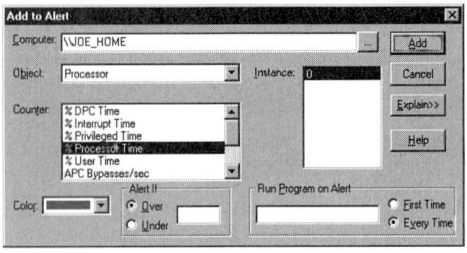

An interesting option that can be used to provide highly automated systems is the Run Program on Alert control. You have already defined a condition that will trigger activity based on the built-in monitoring utilities in Windows NT. This control enables you to run a specified program when this limit value is reached. You could, for example, run a program that clears out temporary log files when a certain disk drive starts to get too full. Another option is to activate a mail utility to send you mail or a telephony utility that pages you with a coded message. You have the option of running this program every time the alert condition is reached or only the first time that you run across this condition (depending on how you want to implement your administrative programs).

The alert view is a very useful option when you want to run your monitoring on a continuous basis over long periods of time. It collects only that data that is of interest to you. It gives you a quick summary of what occurred and when. This makes it ideally suited to running over long periods of time, trying to catch when problem conditions arise. You can even run a specified program when the alert condition is reached that either tries to fix the problem or at least notifies you that the problem was detected. You still have to make time on a routine basis to read the data, but at least you avoid having to sort through large volumes of data to find the interesting events.

The Log View in Performance Monitor

The next view provided by Performance Monitor is the log view. The principle behind this view is simple. You write all the data to a log file instead of displaying it on the screen in a chart or scanning it for out-of-limits parameters as with the alert view. Later, you open this log file using Performance Monitor and either view the results or export the results to a data file that can be imported into spreadsheets such as Microsoft Excel or Lotus for further processing. You can even write your own software applications to read these files and massage the data.

The log view is relatively simple to work with. First, you need to specify the computer, objects, counters, and instances that you wish to monitor using the Add to Log menu or toolbar options. Next, you need to specify the file that is going to contain the logging data and how often the data points are to be collected. You have to be careful because collecting data for even a few counters with a relatively frequent sampling interval can add up to a fair amount of disk space when running over several days or weeks. Figure 4.11 shows the Log Options dialog box.

FIGURE 4.11.
Log Options dialog box.

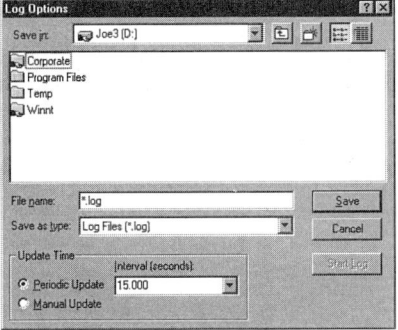

The Log Options dialog box contains the standard file selection controls. You can add data to an existing file or create a new file. You may want to consider locating all your log files (from all applications) in a separate directory so that it is easy to find them and also easy to purge them when they are no longer needed. I have run across systems where log files have been capturing data without anyone even knowing that they are there leading to log files that are many tens of megabytes in size. Once you have specified the filename, the only other real decision is the update interval. You need to be careful to pick an interval that captures problems that occur (daily averages will not show peak usage at certain hours of the day) but does not overload you with data that has to be processed (as a 1-second average might). For reference purposes, if you choose a 10-second interval, you will generate over 8,600 data points per counter selected per day. Then click the Start Log button to begin data capture. You need to keep Performance Monitor running to continue to collect data to this log file.

If you wish to collect performance data in an automated fashion without keeping a particular computer logged in at all times, you can use scripts to start and stop the Performance Monitoring logging. This is actually useful, because you can pick different monitoring profiles for different periods of the day. You may not want to collect a lot of data at night when no one is logged in to the system. You may also want to collect more detailed data between 8 and 9 a.m. when you experience very slow response times.

Automated performance monitoring is accomplished using an interesting little utility in the Windows NT Resource Kit. This datalog.exe utility enables you to capture performance data using a Performance Monitor settings file. You can customize your data collection to various parts of your processing cycle using multiple settings files. You turn this service on and off using the **at** scheduling utility of Windows NT (similar to **cron** on UNIX). The following starts the monitoring utility at 8 a.m. and stops it at 11:59 a.m. (the Windows NT Resource Kit provides more details about this and other interesting utilities):

```
c:\> at 8:00 "monitor START"
c:\> at 11:59 "monitor STOP"
```

4

MONITORING
ENVIRONMENT

The Report View in Performance Monitor

The final view provided by Performance monitor is the report view. It functions, once again, according to a very simple concept. You specify a set of counters that you want to monitor, and Performance Monitor gives you a screen that lists the parameter and the value observed in the last time interval. Figure 4.12 shows the report view's display. This is one view where manual data collection can be especially useful. Imagine a situation where everything is running fine on your system until you start up an application. You may want to collect a set of performance data manually when the application is not running to a report (which you save for later reference). You then start up the offending application and capture a new set of data to see what the problems are.

FIGURE 4.12.

Report view in Performance Monitor.

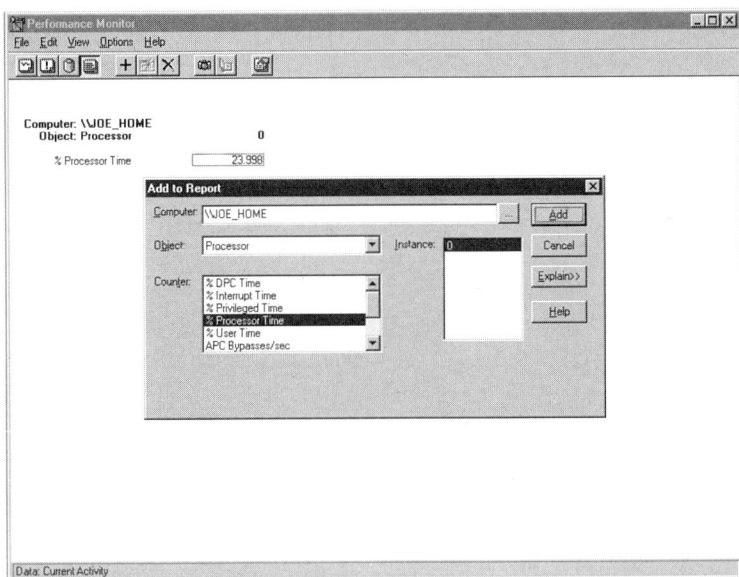

Selection Data Sources in Performance Monitor

Each of the views in Performance Monitor is suited to a specific set of monitoring problems and also different users' tastes. There is one especially interesting feature in Performance Monitor that has become available with Windows NT 4.0 (although you could download the files from the Internet for Windows 3.51 several months before 4.0 was available). This modified version of Performance Monitor enables you to monitor the performance of remote NT computers almost as easily as if you were monitoring your local machine. There is even a version for Windows 95 that lets you monitor remote NT (but not Windows 95) computers. This can be really convenient when you have a series of servers and workstations scattered around the building or in a data center, but your desk is in a traditional office area. The remote-capable version of Performance Monitor is actually part of a series of remote administration tools that enable you to manage user accounts and a number of other functions remotely. Many functions that involve sensitive activities (such as adding user accounts) require that you be a member of a Windows Domain, but that is not especially difficult to set up.

A lot more could be written about performance monitoring and the Windows NT Performance Monitoring tool. It is a flexible tool that can be extended by application developers to meet additional needs. It is relatively easy to set up. It can be customized to suit your individual needs and tastes. Best of all, it comes as part of the Windows NT operating system, so there are no additional software packages to purchase and install.

Auditing

Auditing information is actually displayed using the Event Viewer tool that is discussed in the next section. I have intentionally split auditing into a separate section for several reasons. First, auditing is typically associated with the gathering of information for future review. This includes such things as user access to sensitive information and logging in as a privileged (administrative) user and performing security maintenance tasks. The other reason is to bring out the auditing configuration tools, which are separate from the Event Viewer display.

Auditing is typically viewed by computer people as a defense against hackers and others who are trying to get at data and resources that they are not allowed to access. Although it is true that you do have to waste a lot of your precious time putting up a defense against these less-than-desirable individuals, auditing can be used for other, more beneficial purposes. One of the most difficult problem-solving tasks on a computer is to figure out why an application crashed or started performing poorly and then started to perform well at a later time. Usually, by the time you get your other monitoring tools started up, the problem has already gone away or the system has restarted. If you have a good audit trail, you can look at what was happening on the system just before the crash or slowdown to see what the possible causes of the problem were.

Let's start this discussion of auditing by exploring the three areas on which Windows NT auditing provides information:

- Operating system events
- System security events
- Application events

The first area is the operating system events. Microsoft has trained Windows NT to write a number of useful bits of information that can be viewed using Event Viewer. This information includes the following types of system events:

- Services that fail to start
- Hardware conflicts detected
- Start of key services, such as the Event Viewer
- Print jobs completed
- Anonymous login requests, such as those from the World Wide Web

- Disks nearing or completely out of space
- Access requests to the CD-ROM drive where there is no CD in the drive

The second area that NT monitors captures data related to system security events, such as the following:

- Activation of Remote Access Server (RAS) processes
- Use of special privileges by users
- User login and logout
- Failed logins
- Access to certain objects (for example, the auditing setup)
- Policy changes
- System shutdown and restart
- User and group management activities

The final, and most expandable, area of monitoring under Windows NT is the capability of capturing events from within applications on the system, including those of the BackOffice applications. The developers of these programs have to insert code to make their applications write event data to the log. The good news is that the developers of BackOffice have written a fair amount of this event logging code, and therefore you get a good picture of what is happening in your BackOffice applications when reviewing the Event Log. The following are some examples of audited application events:

- Setting up BackOffice applications, such as Exchange Server
- Starting up BackOffice applications
- Events from your locally developed applications that might indicate that there are problems or suspicious activities going on

The one auditing tool that is not located within the Event Viewer is contained as a menu selection within the User Manager tool. Although system and application logging is a pretty straightforward application, the security logging mechanisms need finer control to accommodate the wide variety of environments available. If you audited everything imaginable in security, your log file would be so large that you would have to write an application just to filter out the events that might possibly be of interest (which would not be all that difficult, actually). However, some groups that I work with do not even want to waste the disk space for security auditing because everyone has full access to all resources, and therefore these records have no meaning (small software development environments can be fun in this regard).

You can set security auditing policies from within User Manager using the Policies menu's Audit option. The Audit option displays the Audit Policy dialog shown in Figure 4.13. The radio buttons are important, because they make the basic selection as to whether you perform any of these detailed security auditing functions. If you select to perform these security auditing actions, you are given two basic choices for auditing. The first column of checkboxes enables you to audit when users perform the functions listed successfully (such as logging on with the correct user ID and password). The second column of checkboxes enables you to audit when users fail when trying to perform a function. You can greatly reduce the number of events recorded if you look only for failures. This catches hackers or people trying to access a resource for which they lack permission. However, if you are trying to gather statistics on usage or logging all (legal) access to a resource, you use the first column's checkboxes. Of course, if you really want a lot of information, you can audit both successes and failures.

FIGURE 4.13.

Audit Policy dialog box.

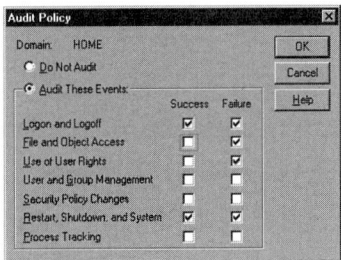

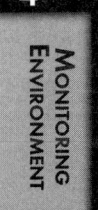

Splitting the security auditing features into these seven categories enables you to pick the items that meet your needs and ignore the others, which can also reduce the number of log file entries you have to review. The categories you have to choose from are as follows:

- *Logon and Logoff.*
- *File and Object Access.* This shows when a given user reads or changes a particular object (for example, read a file or print to a printer.) This can be very detailed, but it works only for NTFS file systems that have access rights (FAT is a pretty open storage mechanism designed for nonsecure DOS environments).
- *Use of User Rights.* This refers to rights that have been granted to a user or group (for example, performing system administrative functions with a personal NT account).
- *User and Group Management.* This catches when someone alters the privileges of another account or creates an account to perform some bad activities and then deletes it. It can also detect unauthorized password changes.
- *Security Policy Changes.* This is another area where the whole security picture of your system can be changed, and therefore it is a common audit function.
- *Restart, Shutdown, and System.* This can be useful for recording downtime and determining when serious problems such as power outages occurred.
- *Process Tracking.* This captures some very detailed information, such as process activation and indirect object access.

Event Viewer

With all the general discussion of auditing out of the way, let's look at the tool that you use to get at that wealth of event information that NT is collecting for you. The first key concept to grasp with the Event Viewer is that this one interface displays all three types of Windows NT audit records: system events, security events, and application events. You select which of these event types is displayed using the Log menu. The Event Viewer remembers the type of log you were looking at the last time you used this utility and displays this same log type when you next start it. To determine which log is displayed at any given time, you simply look at the title. The title contains two useful bits of information. First is the type of auditing performed. The other is the machine whose audit log is being displayed. Once of the nice features for administrators who are in charge of multiple systems is the capability of selecting various Windows NT computers for which you want to display the audit log. Of course, you have to have the appropriate trust relationships established with these machines, but it is worth it if you have several systems to keep track of.

Although these columns provide useful summary information, they are not everything you would want or need to solve a really nasty problem. They are useful to scan through quickly to see whether you have any real problems or whether your log is just full of routine information messages and expected conditions. To get the full details about a particular event that catches your interest, double-click on that event. When you do, you see a detailed display dialog, as shown in Figure 4.14.

FIGURE 4.14.

Event Detail
dialog box.

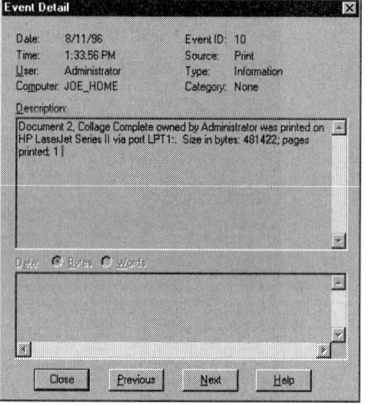

This dialog echoes the information contained on the summary display, along with several other useful bits of information. The exact details depend somewhat on the event encountered. For example, in Figure 4.14 where I intentionally typed in a bad password, you can see a text description of the reason and even the logon authentication package used. Some events display data in the bottom text area that can give you clues as to the state and activities that were occurring to cause the event. I always like to screen-print messages that I might have to take action on (or copy them down if screen printing is too much of a problem).

The next log to review is the security log, which is shown in Figure 4.15. Again, you see the same basic columns as in the system log. You get detailed information about a particular event by double-clicking on it just as in the system log. The key differences for this log are the icons that you see at the left edge of the display, the use of the Category field, and the fact that the User column is often the most important bit of information displayed.

FIGURE 4.15.

Security Log.

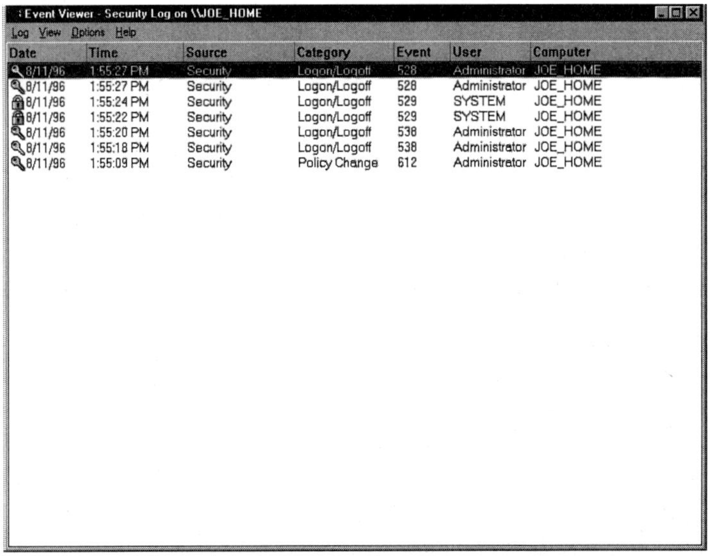

The two icons you typically see are a key (indicating success, which could be bad in the case of hackers accessing something they shouldn't have) and a lock (indicating that the system stopped a user from doing something). It is normal to see a few failures now and then (for example, I have so many passwords that I have trouble keeping them all straight). You are really looking for several failures occurring in a short period of time, which might indicate hacking. You can also scan through the Category list for events that are of interest to you (for example, logon/logoff events). Finally, the User column can help you zero in on the activities of a particular user that you might be watching.

One thing I considered a bit strange with the Event Viewer display was the fact that it does not enable you to sort on any of the categories in the multicolumn listbox display by simply clicking the column heading (such as Category). You can find this type of control on the My Computer utility on your desktop. This makes it really easy to sort the list by user, for example, and see who is being naughty and nice. You do have some of this functionality by using the Filter option on the View menu. This gives you a dialog that enables you to focus on a particular category, user, and so forth (see Figure 4.16). You have to be somewhat careful because you don't see events that don't match your input criteria but might be important to you (use the Clear button on the Filter dialog to view all events). This is an interesting technique to keep in your inventory when you have to audit a large number of events.

4

MONITORING
ENVIRONMENT

FIGURE 4.16.

Event Viewer Filter
dialog box.

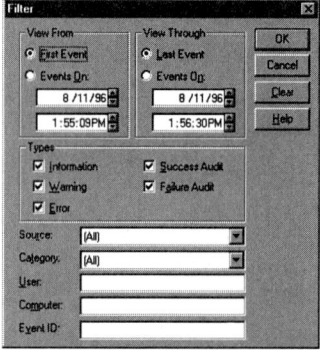

The final log is the application log, shown in Figure 4.17. This is perhaps the least-exploited log in its basic form. About the only applications I have loaded that make good use of this log are the Microsoft BackOffice applications, and even they could make greater use of it. I like the concept of being able to record application events in one central point rather than dozens of different log files scattered all over the system. (I have had to deal with these files before, and they can be a bit of a pain.) The software development kits from Microsoft enable programmers to interface to these audit files. You might want to consider this if you have any input into the application development at your facility.

FIGURE 4.17.

Event Viewer
Application Log.

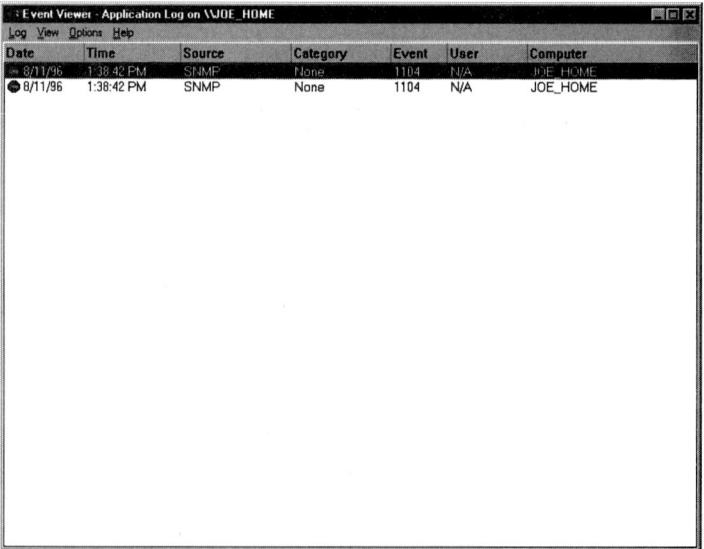

The best way to get used to these logs is to run your system for a while and review the events that get recorded. You should be especially sensitive to the icons displayed on the far left side of the list of events, because these help you sort out the problems from the routine items. The next issue you have to deal with is controlling the event log itself. The control over the size of the data and time it is retained is set using the Log Settings option of the Log menu (see Figure 4.18).

FIGURE 4.18.

Event Log Settings dialog box.

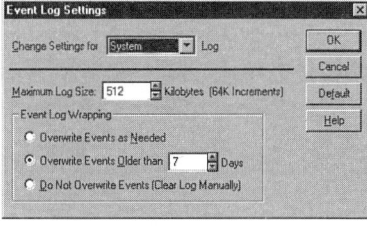

You set each of the log record sizes separately as controlled by the drop-down listbox. First, you set the maximum size of the log. Basically, I accept the default and adjust it only if I am retaining information for too long or too short a period. The next feature you set here is the one that controls the Windows NT auditing log self-cleaning feature. I really like this because I have seen some huge log files that someone (like me) forgot to clean out. Your options are to overwrite as needed, to overwrite events only if they are more than a certain number of days old, or to never overwrite (to clear the log manually). Remember: you have to set this up for each of the three logs used by NT's auditing (system, security, and application).

One final set of controls you have in the Event Viewer tool is shown in Figure 4.19. You have already learned about the All Events and Filter Events options. This menu also gives you the option of displaying the events from earliest to latest or latest to earliest. The Find dialog looks similar to the Filter dialog, but instead of limiting what is displayed, it takes you to the records that meet your input criteria. The Detail option is similar to double-clicking on a particular event. Finally, Refresh updates the display with any new events.

FIGURE 4.19.

Event Viewer's View menu.

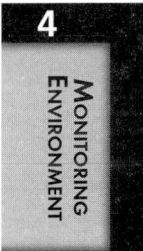

As you can see, you can set up a lot with NT auditing and Event Viewer. The interface that controls and reviews the auditing information is also a clean and simple one. Your steps in setting up auditing on an NT Server should include the following:

1. Determine the factors that affect your auditing needs.

2. Develop an audit plan.

3. Use Event Viewer's Event Log Settings dialog to control the amount of information retained in each of the logs.

4. Use the User Manager's Audit Policy dialog to control which security auditing features are implemented on your system.

5. Make time to review the logs using Event Viewer (often the biggest challenge related to auditing).

The Server Control Panel Tool

So far, you have explored the traditional monitoring tools that most people would consider. There are graphs that show system utilization in Performance Monitor and all the traditional auditing in the Event Viewer. There is one more standard Windows NT tool. Under the Control Panel, there is a little tool titled Server (not to be confused with the little tool in Control Panel titled Services). Figure 4.20 shows the Server window.

FIGURE 4.20.

The Server tool under Control Panel.

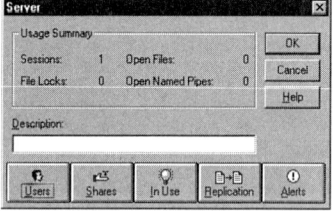

The Server tool is a place to check several parameters quickly that impact system operations and performance without setting up formal Performance Monitor counters. The items that you can use for monitoring are the following:

■ *The number of users who currently have sessions on your server.* You can click the Users button to get a list of these users. If you have an intermittent problem, it might be useful to see who is always logged on when the problem occurs. You can then explore what that user is doing that might be causing the problem. This sounds tedious, but it may be the only way to figure out those problems that crop up and then disappear before you have time to set up formal monitoring routines.

■ *The number of files that are locked.* Certain applications are very interested in maintaining data integrity. They therefore lock up their data files while a thread is in the process of updating that file. The problem is that other user applications that need to access those files might be stuck waiting for the first application to release the data file. This period of being stuck seems the same to an end-user as a grossly overloaded CPU—it is just time sitting there looking at the hourglass cursor.

■ *The other indicators.* These might be interesting in certain cases. You might want to explore them when you get some time.

Third-Party Monitoring Tools

The discussion so far emphasized the monitoring capabilities that are provided by Microsoft with Windows NT. As with almost everything in the computer industry, there are a number of third-party products that are also targeted at monitoring the Windows NT environment. I am hesitant to take on a detailed discussion of these products for several reasons. First, the tools that I have described have the advantage of coming with Windows NT. You do not have to study the alternatives, purchase them separately, or install them. Second, it is difficult enough to keep up with all the revisions that are going on in the Windows NT/BackOffice environment without trying to track new features and releases of third-party monitoring tools. You should know that these tools exist, however, and may be exactly what you want to meet some of your special needs.

Parameters that Can Be Monitored

Actually, a complete listing of all the counters that are associated with a given Windows NT/BackOffice system would probably fill an entire chapter—and it would probably go out of date fairly quickly as new revisions of NT and the BackOffice components are released. There is just no substitute for getting into Performance Monitor, Event Viewer, and the User Manager Audit Policies windows and trying out the various configurations. To pique your interest in Performance Monitor, here are the objects that I found on my Windows NT 4.0 server installation and the number of counters that are associated with these objects:

■ Browser (21)

■ Cache (27)

■ IP (17)

■ Logical Disk (21)

■ Memory (27)

■ NetBEUI (39)

■ NetBEUI Resource (3)

■ Network Interface (17)

■ NWLink IPX (39)

■ NWLink NetBIOS (39)

■ NWLink SPX (39)

- Objects (Events, Mutexes, Processes, Sections, Semaphores, and Threads)
- Paging File (2)
- Physical Disk 19)
- Process (18)
- Processor (10)
- RAS Port (17)
- RAS Total (18)
- Redirector (37)
- Server (26)
- Server Work Queue (17)
- System (24)
- TCP (9)
- Thread (12)

As you can see, there are a large number of parameters that can be monitored. In reality, there are only a few that are important to most administrators. The short list of items to consider include the following:

- Processor: percent processor time
- Memory: pages/second
- Physical disks: percent time
- Physical disks: queue length
- Server: bytes total/second

BackOffice Integration with NT Monitoring

Remember: the various BackOffice tools do not come with monitoring utilities. Instead, Microsoft has integrated the monitoring services of these applications with those of the host operating system, Windows NT. You use the standard Windows NT tools, such as Performance Monitor and Event Viewer, to check on the activity within your BackOffice applications. The one BackOffice component that is not tightly integrated into this architecture is sort of the grandfather of the BackOffice family—Microsoft Mail. However, its heir apparent, Exchange Server, is very tightly integrated into the Windows NT monitoring environment.

This tight integration gives you even more incentive to become familiar with the Windows NT monitoring tools. You have the advantage of having to learn only one set of tools to aid in your administration of a number of tools. The best time to become familiar with these tools and build settings files is when everything is running well. That way, all you have to do is call up your standard Exchange Server Performance Monitor settings file to see what might be going wrong.

Extending Windows NT Monitoring for Applications

You can interface your locally developed applications with the Windows NT monitoring environment. Microsoft has published the specifications for this interface, and a number of development tools vendors have built object classes, subroutines, and so forth that enable you to write records to the event log or set up a Performance Monitor counter. You should check with your development tool documentation to see what these classes, methods, and so forth are.

Summary

Windows NT provides a fairly robust set of monitoring utilities as part of the basic operating system itself. You can examine various performance factors and review logs of events that have occurred both within the operating system and your application software. BackOffice products are especially well-integrated into this environment and use standard Windows NT tools for monitoring purposes. You can even extend this monitoring environment to locally developed applications. This integration theme continues in the next chapter where you explore the Windows NT administrative environment.

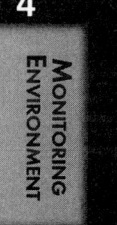

4

MONITORING
ENVIRONMENT

Administrative Environment

by Joe Greene

IN THIS CHAPTER

If you are a system or BackOffice server administrator, the topics in this chapter should be near and dear to your heart. This chapter describes the environment—the tools and services—that you use to keep things running on your server. It covers topics from the mundane (adding user accounts) to the excessively exciting (diagnosing problems that have brought down one of your critical applications). It also focuses on the tools as opposed to the actual techniques. Although it covers the User Manager tool, it does not discuss the planning and use of this tool when adding a user who needs, for example, access to the NT operating system and Exchange Server. That information is specific to the individual BackOffice servers with which you are working. You can find this type of information in the chapters on administering those individual components.

The chapter begins with an introduction to system administration. Although some of you may have been doing system administration, there are others who are new to the task. It also seems that there are a number of different definitions of what a system administrator is and does.

Next, you look at an overview of the Windows NT administrative environment, a fairly powerful and nicely integrated environment. Although you may not think that you are going to need to use a particular tool, you might when a particularly nasty problem comes up or someone else is on vacation and you have to fill in.

The third section of this chapter covers the central topic—the tools. By this point, you should be ready to understand what the tools are trying to accomplish. You explore the basics of how to use the tools; the individual strategies for each individual BackOffice server are covered in the appropriate section of the book.

The next section covers some of the specific tools that are unique to the individual BackOffice servers. Although you do not use these tools a lot, you should understand that they are there and have a basic understanding of what they do. They integrate well into the overall BackOffice environment and do not duplicate the functions of the basic Windows NT tools. If you are used to traditional application administration tools that relied on command files or something like that, you will really like these graphical tools.

The final section in this chapter covers the concepts of how you can use the standard Windows NT administration tools to control your applications. Microsoft has gone a long way to provide a tightly integrated environment. It would be a shame if you developed local applications that broke that integration and forced your poor administrators to have to learn how to use another set of tools. The Microsoft tools may not be perfect, but they are better than almost all the locally developed tools for application administration. Remember, Microsoft can prorate the costs of building these tools over the many thousands of copies of Windows NT that are sold as opposed to having to build them each time for an application used by 20 people.

The Windows NT 4.0 environment has significant improvements in the administration portions of the operating system. It is not just the more convenient and graphically more appealing changes made to the graphical user interface. It is also not the hidden internal changes that come in 4.0, such as improvements in the graphics device drivers (which were major). The changes to user administration must have been made by people who actually served as system administrators. They increased the functionality of the User Manager tool, for example. It is now a one-stop place to go when you want to perform almost all user setup and permissions functions. This section of the chapter uses the new 4.0 administration tools and notes wherever there are differences in the 3.51 products.

Overview of System Administration

What is system administration? I have come across a lot of answers to this question during my consulting travels. Part of this derives from individual managers' preferences as to how they want to arrange their departments. Part of it comes from the amount of work there is for various positions that results in the combining of two jobs into one person. It also often derives from the individual skill sets of the people doing the work. I have seen many different combinations (some of which I will never understand).

There was actually a document published by IBM in the early days of its mainframe computers that listed suggested staffing for the data center. Many organizations adopted these standards. You can still see its effects on some current organization charts (where there are small systems and database groups that are separated, and they still have a relatively large operations staff). It would be interesting in this era of more for less to see the huge number of people that it used to take to run those early computers that were not as powerful as some of the larger PC servers that are available now.

Here are some suggestions of jobs that I either have seen or can conceive of having as a systems administrator under Windows NT:

- Install and upgrade the operating system.
- Install and upgrade all major software components (that is, the BackOffice servers).
- Monitor and maintain performance levels of the system.
- Design upgrades to the operating system and software components.
- Build system scripts and utilities to perform special tasks.
- Serve as database administrator.
- Serve as electronic mail system administrator.
- Serve as administrator for the SNA server and SMS server.
- Serve as an application developer for locally produced applications.
- Serve as an application developer for commercially released applications.
- Serve as the system security administrator.
- Provide hardware support for your organization.
- Serve as network administrator, cable technician, and so forth.
- Provide support to users with questions ranging from the operating system to how to change the font on their word processors.

- Work at a job in one of the business units (that is, engineer or accountant) and be a system administrator for the department server as a collateral duty.

- Serve as system administrator for a number of other operating systems, such as UNIX or NetWare.

These and any number of other tasks can fill up your job jar as a systems administrator. One of the most difficult tasks for most computer support types is getting a reasonable list of tasks so that they have time to get the work done properly. This is a difficult job, even when you have experience in the area. There are so many factors that come into play that you need to consider. Here are a few of them:

- *How much time do you have to spend on user support?* This can vary from just a little—if you are working with a bunch of computer types who would rather fix it themselves than ask for help—to a lot—if you have a bunch of users who have never touched a PC until the company took away the terminals they had been using for decades. Err on the conservative side if you have to support a large number of users who are new to the environment.

- *How often does your organization perform upgrades or system installations?* If you will be required to have nothing but the latest and greatest on all servers, you had better allocate some time for installations (which are often the longest and most complicated single evolution that you will have to perform). Better still, get enough time to test the new product installations on a test server first. That way you will not be finding bugs and problems with your system configuration in the middle of the night on your most critical production server.

- *How many servers and users are you going to be asked to support?* It is true that you can perform many tasks more quickly the second time you do them, but you still have to spend some time waiting for all that software to be offloaded from the CD and the setup procedure to complete all the system configuration updates (unless, of course, you are using SMS). This is especially important if your job scope is growing rapidly (that is, the organization is downsizing on a department-by-department basis to Windows NT servers from some host platform).

- *How much time do you need to spend keeping up with current technologies?* Remember, you are just a few years away from becoming one of the dinosaurs that people in the current PC world joke about when they talk about mainframes and old, proprietary minicomputer systems. I never have enough time to keep up on technologies. Microsoft, for example, puts out a number of new products on its Web site each month for evaluation. They release new application programming interfaces almost as quickly. Keeping up with technology can be a full-time job, and if you are required to be the technology expert, you will need time to keep up.

■ *How much time will your other assigned duties take up?* I work part-time as a systems administrator while developing applications and serving as a database administrator. I like it much better that way because I am constantly learning new things in a number of areas. It has meant that I have to control my natural impulse to volunteer to do some systems administration tasks that would be nice, but not nice enough to cause me to defer some of my other work.

■ *How much of an administrative or supervisory role will you be asked to play?* Some systems administrators have to allocate a fair amount of time for paperwork or supervising and training other staff members.

■ *How important is it for you to learn the new environment thoroughly?* Be selfish for a moment. Perhaps you are getting into NT and BackOffice because you read all those articles about how it is a hot technology and poised to gain market share rapidly. You see in our industry that people who have hot skills that are in short supply can command very nice salaries. Perhaps you want to allocate time for yourself to become an expert in the technology so that when your organization converts over to NT, you are the system administration manager, or even go out and start your own highly successful consulting practice. If you want to become an expert on these technologies, you have to leave yourself some time to study and keep up. I know that I never have enough time to learn even a small fraction of the things that I want to learn.

It's a good idea to work with your management to make your job description both reasonable and enjoyable. These thoughts may make sense to you, but they may not all be the best ones to present to management when you are trying to justify what you think your job description should be (leave off the one about you starting a successful consulting practice, for example). Computer types might get a lot further in their arguments if they presented their rationale in terms of business goals. They often have these in the back of their minds, but they never quite express them. Therefore, here is a list of goals and thoughts that you may want to consider for your system, tailored to what might be reasonable for a Windows NT environment:

■ *Ensure less than 30 minutes of downtime per month on production servers during normal business hours.* This is a great thought when you are asking for uninterruptible power supplies or a test server. The amount of downtime varies by organization. I have much more in the way of downtime on development servers because we are always trying new server products and testing server software that is developed locally.

■ *Provide a cost-effective computing environment.* This is a good justification for trips to visit vendors and trade shows. It also justifies magazine subscriptions and other such resources.

■ *Ensure adequate time for customer service.* This is a way to remind management politely that if you want them to provide user support, they cannot give you eight hours of other work to do per day. Many managers assume that each call is 30 seconds and that can solve everything. They do not account for the calls that cause you to spend days tracking down a problem.

■ *Ensure that there is adequate time to meet a stated goal.* This is another polite way to remind management in organizations that have aggressive growth or system replacement plans that you have to allocate time for installing new systems, designing the configurations, pulling cables, and so forth.

> **TIP**
>
> One of the greatest hindrances to having adequate service from computer support organizations is that they are too busy fighting fires to do any planning. Without planning, they are guaranteed to face more crises in the future. The core technologists are among the most overloaded in this group, and this further impedes user support and general administrative efficiency.

Windows NT Administrative Environment

With the generalities out of the way, it is time to move on to the Windows NT administrative environment. You may be anxious to move right into the tools so that you can figure out how to set the callback number for a particular user in remote access. However, before you start going through the tools, you should review the things that you can control as an administrator. Once you have this, you can then worry about which checkbox on which tab dialog box you use to configure a particular function.

What are the things over which an administrator in the BackOffice environment has control? My list of the things that I consider to be most important includes the following:

■ *User account setup.* This will be the primary focus of this section, because Windows NT is a user-focused environment, as opposed to batch job processing environments on mainframes.

■ *Access rights to system resources.* This will also be a major focus of this section, because the complete administrative picture for users' accounts is a combination of who they are and what resources they have access to.

■ *Usage of system resources by various groups.* The administrator can control this, but only indirectly. You can alter user rights based on the results of performance monitoring and auditing. This will be discussed in the various performance tuning chapters, such as Chapter 13, "NT Integration with NetWare and UNIX," which covers Windows NT performance tuning.

■ *Configuration parameters for the operating system.* This is a tricky task in which the system administrator alters some of the settings that are used by the operating system to allocate its resources internally. This is another topic that will be addressed in Chapter 13, because you should never consider altering system tuning parameters if you have not made a thorough analysis of the performance problems that you may be experiencing.

■ *Special configuration parameters for specific applications.* Vendors provide special tuning parameters that enable you to adapt their applications to a wide range of environments. You obviously need to have more system resources and configure your internal structures differently if you are running a 10G database, as opposed to a little 10M information store.

■ *Activation or deactivation of system services.* Most of the BackOffice components are implemented as services in the Windows NT environment (that is, they run in the background on the system, as opposed to running in the foreground on a console somewhere). You have the ability to control when these processes are turned on, which can be a useful technique for leveling the processing load on your system.

There are three key components, generic across the BackOffice environment, that make up the majority of the work performed in system administration. The first of these is maintaining the user environment. This is a combination of the user's account, password, group associations, resource privileges, and a few other parameters that can be used to ensure that the users have the accesses they need (and no more). The second is the controls that the administrator has over the background processes (services) that are running on the server.

The third is tuning parameters, and that discussion is deferred to Chapter 12, "Windows NT Performance Tuning," Chapter 25, "Exchange Server Performance Tuning and Scaling," Chapter 31, "SQL Server Monitoring and Tuning," and Chapter 41, "Optimizing SNA Server." It takes a lot of background material to understand these concepts and it is not that common a system administration task (which reflects well on the BackOffice suite).

Attributes of a User

It would be extremely difficult for you to control user accounts properly if you did not know the various things over which you have control. This section discusses the components in the *overall user environment.* The environment is similar between Windows NT 3.51 and 4.0. The major advantage of NT 4.0 is that it centralizes the administration of the user into the User Manager tool, as opposed to scattering them over a couple of tools as is done in NT 3.51. The following is a simple summary list of control features:

■ User account and password
■ User group membership
■ Account policies
■ User rights
■ User profile
■ User home directory
■ User login script
■ User login times

- User login capabilities
- Remote Access Service capabilities
- Access to applications

If you want to get fancy, you can find more to tweak, but from my experience, this is the set that will serve you in the vast majority of cases. The preceding items interact with one another to help you accomplish your goals. Each item is incomplete by itself and requires the other items to control the user's interactions with resources properly. The rest of this section provides an overview of each of the tools that you will need to understand in order to become a full-fledged Windows NT system administrator.

Login IDs, Passwords, and Groups

The first user attribute topic is the user login ID and password. The concepts actually are relatively simple and resemble those on most other operating systems. This is the first instance of how the various properties of the user environment will interact, however. Many security types set limitations on the passwords that are selected, in order to make them difficult to guess. The rule of thumb usually is "at least seven characters long." Even if you, as the administrator, create the user login ID and password following this rule, what will stop the users from using the password change utilities to choose a password such as 12345? To prevent this, you need to use the policy features of Windows NT.

The *group feature* is a powerful tool in the user administration process, and the key is that resource accesses can be given to either individuals or groups. When given to groups, a user who is made a member of that group automatically inherits all the privileges of the group itself. This enables you to quickly give users the privileges they need to complete their jobs. Another advantage of this is that you can choose the group names to be meaningful to you. This enables you to quickly scroll through the list of groups and determine which groups are appropriate for a new user.

Account Policies, Rights, and Profiles

The *account policy feature* is not always used by NT administrators, but can be quite powerful. The user policy under Windows NT sets up facets of the user operating environment other than the group privileges related to what the user is allowed to do on the system. This is where you set up the system to ensure that the password is complex and secure enough for your organization's security needs. Some of the features controlled by the user profile include the following:

- *Password length.* You set the minimum number of characters that constitute an allowable password.
- *Password age.* This determines the number of days until the system requires users to change their passwords.

■ *Password history.* The operating system can keep track of previously entered passwords to prevent duplication and use of easy passwords.

■ *Account lockout on failed login attempts.* This locks out the account from logon if there are the specified number of failed logon attempts in a row.

Closely related policies made by the system administrator are *user rights.* These focus primarily on what the user is allowed to do with the operating system. This is discussed in detail in the User Rights section, but for now you should have a feel for a few of the functions of the User Rights tool:

■ *Accessing computers from the network.* Users need this to share resources via the network.

■ *Adding computers to the domain.* This privilege allows administrators to sign on to local computers and allows them to join the domain.

■ *Backing up files.* This allows users to perform backups.

■ *Logging on locally to this computer.* This allows users to log on using the local keyboard and monitor.

A closely related user control feature is the *user profile.* This feature specifies the available program groups. It also controls whether the Run command is allowed on the File menu. You can create a number of profiles and assign them to various users.

There used to be some confusion over having to work with multiple tools that were needed to set up the profile of operation for a given user. The good news about Windows NT 4.0 is that Microsoft has consolidated almost all the user setup controls in the User Manager tool. When you call up the properties screen for a given user under User Manager, you will find a button labeled Profile, which discusses many of the features discussed in the next couple of paragraphs. Some enhanced fine tuning over the user's working environment can be made using the System Policy Editor on the Administrative Tools menu. You get to control some low-level details, such as which wallpaper graphic will be displayed as the desktop for a given user. The System Policy Editor allows you to assign a policy to a given user or group. These profiles are not enforced when the user accesses resources from other workstations running Windows 95, DOS, and so forth.

Home Directories, Login Scripts, Login Time, and Login Capabilities

The next control feature of the user environment is the *home directory.* You have the option of specifying a directory that the user will access by default for all save operations that are directly controlled by the operating system. If you open a DOS prompt, for example, the home directory is the default. Note, however, that many applications (such as Microsoft Word) have their own Settings panels in which they set up the default storage and retrieval directories for their files.

Another useful environmental control feature is the *login script*. Suppose that there is an action you want performed every time the user logs in, but you cannot find any operating system setting to accomplish your goal. An alternative is to create a batch file (or an executable program) that performs the action you want and then specify that file or program to be the login script for a given set of users. This also is a nice alternative in environments in which you want to force the users into a menu program or perhaps even just a single application when they log in. In these cases, you can enhance security and usability by not allowing the users to get to the desktop and have the full power of the Windows NT operating system.

Rounding out the list of environmental control features, you come to the capability of controlling when a user can log in to the system. A major security concern in some organizations is that a user could come in after hours and access the system in an illegal manner. Other environments might contain large batch jobs or have system maintenance activities that occur during specified periods. If these maintenance activities require that all users be logged off, it would be helpful to have a utility that keeps disallowed users from logging in during these periods. Windows NT provides such a utility in the User Manager tool that gives you a control over the hours that users can access the system.

Remote Access

You use the RAS administrative utilities to specify whether a given user has access to RAS. You also can implement additional security by requiring a callback to a specified number when a user dials into your system. This way, the only way someone can hack in, using one of your user's IDs, is to call from the user's house (add breaking and entering to the computer hacking crimes). Remote access to computer resources such as data files and electronic mail is a wonderful convenience; however, it can also be a major security hole. Anyone with a modem and telephone connection can dial up your server (assuming that they know the telephone number) and gain access to your network, bypassing all the physical security controls of your building. You need to consider the impact of security against productivity when implementing RAS dial-in.

An interesting note for version 4.0 of NT is that RAS security is now integrated into the User Manager tool. In version 3.51, you set up the properties of your user (with the exception of remote access) using the User Manager tool. You then had to use the RAS Admin tool to grant dial-in privileges (which were defaulted to prevent remote access). Although you can still use the RAS Admin tool to set up dial-in privileges, the User Properties page enables you to set up dial-in permissions for the section user from within User Manager.

User Environment

Finally, the user environment is rounded out by rights and privileges set up for the applications provided on your server. Depending on the application, rights and privileges might simply enhance the environmental parameters you set up for the users as the Windows NT administrator, or they might form a complete environment of their own. If you are using a client-server architecture to access information on a Windows NT Oracle database, for example, the database will provide all security and control the user environment. In many cases, users do not even need an operating system account to access the database.

Control of Services

There are several parameters associated with services over which the administrator has control. Here are the two key parameters:

- *Whether the service is running.* You can use the Services tool under Control Panel to start or stop any service on the system. Some applications have a series of services that make up the application, and you may have to be aware of the hierarchy so that you can start or stop the services in the correct order.

- *Whether the service starts automatically at system startup.* You have the option of designating that certain services are to be started manually. This allows you to control load on your system. Most of the services that you run will be configured for automatic startup when the system starts.

Windows NT Administrative Tools

The tools that are at your disposal to help you get your job done are fairly impressive, even by modern operating system standards. They are well-integrated. They also have the advantage of a graphical user interface and a unified architecture and approach to administration. The screens shown here reflect NT 4.0. I have made notes where there are significant differences between 3.51 and 4.0. The tools that I will be covering in this section are the following:

- User Manager
- Remote Access Admin
- Windows Explorer
- Printer control tool

Windows NT Server's User Manager Tool

The main tool that enables you to control your users is User Manager, which is available on the Administrative Tools menu. User Manager has one of two titles, depending on whether you are using a server, a workstation in a domain, or a workstation in a workgroup. The server always uses the User Manager for Domain tools (even when you are in a workgroup). The workstation uses User Manager (without the Domains) when you are in a workgroup, but can use User Manager for Domains (loaded from the NT Resource Kit or as a part of NT 4.0) if it is in a domain. In the domain environment, the updates are sent to the domain controllers rather than the local security database.

My first impression of the administrative environment in Windows NT 3.5 was based on the Control Panel mind-set. When you have a function that you want to perform, you build a small application to perform the function and slap it into a program group with the other administrative tools. I am impressed with the trend in Windows NT 4.0, and especially in the User Manager tool, toward building integrated tools. The User Manager tool sets almost all the administrative properties for a user. It even integrates with Microsoft Exchange Server (their electronic mail system in BackOffice) to bring up properties pages to configure the person's electronic mail account when you add a new user to the operating system. With all the power built into User Manager, I like to place a shortcut to the application on my desktop so that I have ready access to it.

Most of the tools in Windows NT 4.0 seem determined to use an explorer-like tree control somewhere in their display. User Manager is one exception to this rule (at least for now). Its interface adheres to the basic premise of a relatively clean interface that provides access to all the necessary control features using pull-down menus and simple controls, such as double-clicking. Figure 5.1 shows the basic User Manager display. Note that if you are not part of a domain, you do not get the Logon To, Hours, and Account options.

FIGURE 5.1.

User Manager for Domains display.

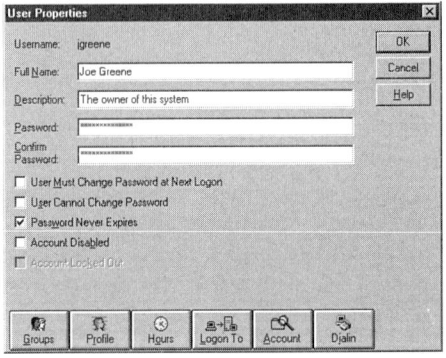

This review of User Manager begins by going through the key pull-down menu items that you will be using, beginning with the User menu. Here, you will see a couple of clues that say you are using a Windows NT 4.0 server, which gives you the User Manager for Domains utility. The clues are that there are menu picks to add a New Global Group and Select Domain. These menu picks typically display a dialog box that enables you to fill in the details of the action you are taking or prompts you to confirm that you really want to do what you asked for (such as delete a user). The actions on these menus are taken for the user that is highlighted, in the case of copy, delete, rename, and properties. The remaining items, such as New User, by their very definition, imply that you should see a dialog box to create a new item or perform an action, such as select domain.

The next menu is the Policies menu. (The View menu was skipped because it is pretty much what you expect—it controls the way in which items are sorted in the display and provides an option to refresh the lists.) The Policies menu provides you with access to most of the user environmental parameters that do not involve resource access discussed in the last section. It also includes a function that enables you to set your Trust Relationships.

Groups in User Manager

Now it is time to go over some of the functions that are activated by these menus. The first function enables you to add or modify groups. You can add a new group by choosing either New Local Group or New Global Group from the User menu. To modify an existing group, highlight the group and choose Properties from the User menu or double-click the group name. Figure 5.2 shows the panel that appears when you modify the properties of an existing group. The only difference you will see when adding a new group is that you are allowed to enter the group name; otherwise, the panels are identical.

FIGURE 5.2.

Global Group
Properties dialog box
under User Manager.

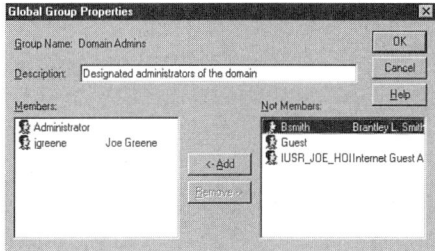

The Group Properties pane is very simple to work with. You have the group name, a text description to help you out in the future, and two sets of lists. The first list shows the users who are members of the group. The second list shows the users who are not members of the group. To move users between the members and nonmembers categories, use the Add or Remove buttons.

User Properties in User Manager

The User Properties panel is shown in Figure 5.3. It enables administrators to add or modify the basic login properties of a user and, therefore, is one of the most commonly used tools in User Manager. As you can see, it is a simple panel that enables you to enter the user name (when adding users, this becomes a noneditable field when modifying the properties of an existing user), full name, description of the user, and two fields that enable the administrator to modify the user's password. In addition, the checkboxes control the following features:

- *Whether users must change their passwords next time they log in.* This feature is useful when you create all accounts with some neutral or even a null password and then want to force the users to choose passwords of their own when they log on.

- *Whether users are prevented from changing their passwords.* This reduces instances of users forgetting their passwords and making you reset them.

- *Whether passwords expire.* This overrides the password aging functionality, which is described in the Policies section.

■ *Whether accounts are disabled.* You may want to disable users' accounts when they go on vacation or leave the company. With those accounts disabled, you then have time to go through those users' data files and transfer them to other users who may need them.

■ *Whether users accounts have been locked out.* A lockout typically occurs when someone fails to supply the correct password after a number of tries and no automatic reset time interval is specified for this account. A locked-out account can be an indication of hacking, or merely an indication of a forgetful user. This is a good security feature in environments in which you have to be careful of hackers.

FIGURE 5.3.

User Properties page of User Manager.

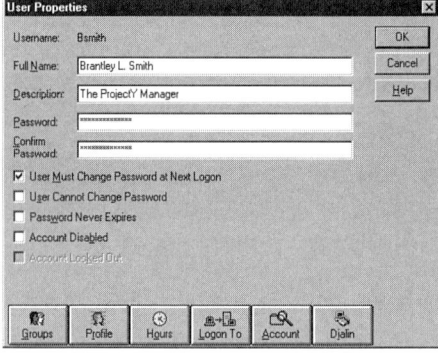

Group Memberships in User Manager

At the bottom of the User Properties page are important buttons with which you need to become familiar. These buttons access dialog boxes that enable you to set many of the other environmental parameters for the user's account.

The first of these properties is the group affiliation of the user. Figure 5.4 shows the Group Memberships dialog box. As you can see, it provides you with two lists: one showing the groups to which the user belongs, and one that shows the groups to which the user does not belong. The Add and Remove buttons enable you to move a group from one list to the other.

FIGURE 5.4.

Group Memberships dialog box of User Manager.

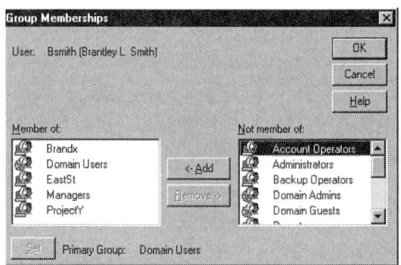

User Environment Profile in User Manager

The User Environment Profile is activated by the Profile button. Figure 5.5 shows the panel that appears. Be careful not to confuse this button with the User Profile Editor that is provided in the Administrative Tools Start Menu group. The Profile button enables you to select the user profile file (as edited by the User Profile Editor) that applies to this user. It also enables you to specify a login script that runs every time the user logs on to the system or domain. At the bottom of this panel are fields that enable you to specify the home directory the operating system will use as a default for those times when the applications do not provide their own fully qualified path.

FIGURE 5.5.

User Environment Profile panel of User Manager.

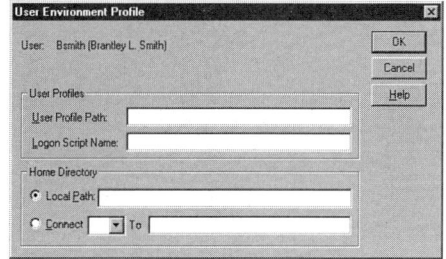

Logon Hours in User Manager

Continuing on with the user environmental parameters that are controlled from the buttons on the bottom of the User Properties page, you come to the Logon Hours panel (see Figure 5.6). To set the hours of operation, using your mouse, highlight the range of hours you want to work with and then click on the allow or disallow buttons. The sections with the blue lines through the middle are the allowed hours of operation. The sections that are black are the hours in which the user is not allowed to log on. The key here is that these are the hours when the system will allow the login (connection) process to occur. It does not automatically log off users who are on the system if they are still on the system after the allowed hours.

FIGURE 5.6.

Logon Hours panel of User Manager.

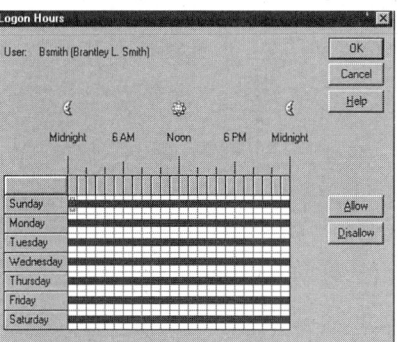

Workstations Allowed in User Manager

Another useful feature on the User Properties page is the capability of restricting workstations from which a particular user is allowed to log in. Figure 5.7 shows the basic data entry panel, which is a very simple interface. You can allow the user to log on from all workstations in the domain or you can specify the list of workstations from which the user can log on. This is helpful in operational environments where users should be at a specific console when performing certain critical tasks. You should ensure that people can log in to enough workstations to ensure system access in the event of hardware or network failures.

FIGURE 5.7.

Logon Workstations panel of User Manager.

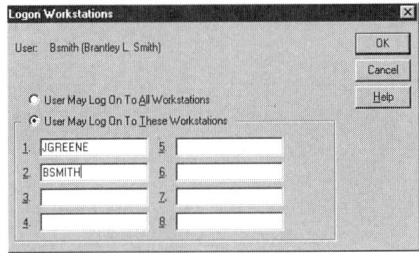

Account Parameters in User Manager

The next dialog box that you can access from the buttons at the bottom of the User Properties page controls certain parameters related to the user's account (see Figure 5.8). The first parameter controls when the user's account expires. This usually is implemented as a safeguard to prevent you from forgetting to disable the accounts of contractors or permanent employees when they leave. I tend not to use this parameter, but there are some environments in which this parameter might be mandatory (such as access to a computer that requires a security clearance to be updated at regular intervals so that access is not denied). The other parameter enables you to specify whether this is a Global Account (which is the normal account that you create) or a local account for users from nontrusted domains.

FIGURE 5.8.

Account Information panel of User Manager.

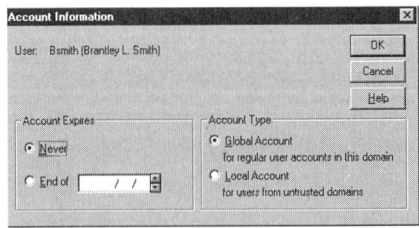

Dialin in User Manager

The Dialin button in User Manager enables you to set up permissions for the user to utilize the remote access facilities to dial into your Windows NT 4.0 server. You used to have to run the Remote Access Admin utility to set up this important user account property under NT 3.51. Whichever version you are using, the basic functions are the same. Figure 5.9 shows the properties that can be set with this panel. The first checkbox indicates whether the user will be allowed to use his or her account to dial into this RAS server. The next three buttons determine whether the server will call the user back to complete the connection. The Set By Caller button can be used to save long distance phone charges to individuals who are working from home or are on the road (hotels really mark up phone calls). The Preset To button and edit box enable you to indicate that the only way that certain users can connect is if the system dials them back at a specified number. This can be used to increase security because you program in only the users' home numbers to prevent a hacker from being able to use a compromised account ID and password via the telephone (unless they also break into a user's house, that is).

FIGURE 5.9.

Dialin Information panel of User Manager.

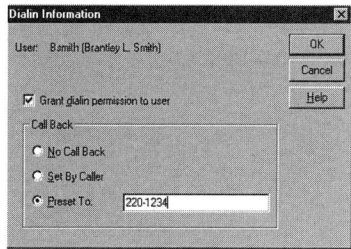

Policies

This section provides a review of the attributes of the user environment that are controlled from the Policies pull-down menu, where you set the global policies for your domain or server as a whole, as opposed to the properties that you set for individual users. The first of these properties pages is the Account Policy page (see Figure 5.10). Most of the features you see in this figure determine whether you are going to implement those complex security features that Microsoft had to put into Windows NT to receive C2 security certification. The good news is that you can turn them all off, turn them all on, or select the features that will be operational, based on your needs.

FIGURE 5.10.

Account Policy dialog box of User Manager.

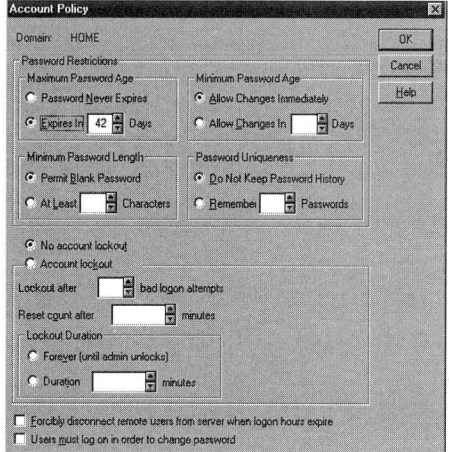

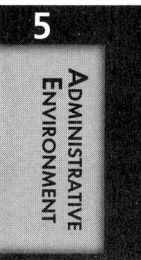

User Rights

The User Rights Policy editor facilitates granting users and groups the ability to perform certain sensitive system functions. Figure 5.11 shows the dialog box that appears. You need to select the function that you wish to grant or revoke privileges on and then use the add or remove buttons to add or remove users or groups from this privilege. The following list discusses the privileges you can control with the User Rights Policy dialog box:

■ *Access this computer from network.*

This is the basic use of Windows NT servers—to share files, printers, and so on. You might, however, build a database system on which users do not need to access anything except the database, using the database communications processes.

■ *Add workstations to domain.*

This is an important domain administrative function, because it controls who can make a workstation a trusted member of the domain.

■ *Backup files and directories.*

This gives the user access to the utilities and files to create a backup tape.

■ *Change the system time.*

This is a relatively minor function in terms of use, but it can have some serious security impacts (such as users altering file timestamps to hide illegal activity).

■ *Force a shutdown from a remote system.*

This is a useful feature when you want to perform a shutdown from a desktop workstation.

■ *Load and unload device drivers.*

This privilege enables you to reconfigure the devices attached to your system (such as CD-ROM drives and printers). You probably do not want all those who perform operational tasks to have this level of access, due to the possibility that they could damage your system.

■ *Log on locally.*

This enables you to log on to the system from the keyboard and monitor attached to the system. A good way to radically increase your security level is to keep all users off the console except for the administrators.

■ *Manage auditing and security log.*

Some systems may prefer to have separate security administrators who have system privileges, but who do not get involved with backups or device driver changes.

■ *Restore files and directories.*

This is the opposite of the backup privilege. You may want to restrict this somewhat more than backups, because although it usually is not harmful to have someone create extra backup tapes, it can be disastrous if someone overwrites all the current disk files with old files.

■ *Shut down the system.*

This is the privilege with which you log in to the console and perform a system shutdown.

■ *Take ownership of files or other objects.*

Windows NT enables users to own files. This privilege enables you to take ownership of files owned by other users (which is needed to delete user files for which you do not have access).

FIGURE 5.11.

User Rights Policy dialog box of User Manager.

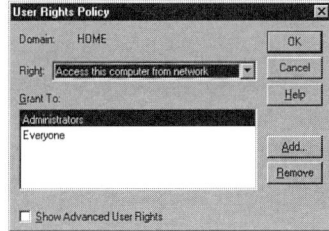

Auditing

The final policy editor that you will work with sets up the events to be audited by your system. Chapter 4, "Monitoring Environment," discusses auditing in greater detail. For now, look at Figure 5.12. As you can see, you have the option of disabling auditing (you still have the basic security and system event monitoring provided by Event Viewer) or activating only the pieces that interest you.

Before activating any of these menu choices, you need to think about the times per day the event you are going to audit occurs. For example, although security policy changes are rare (and also extremely important from a security point of view), use of user rights occurs many times per minute. Each time the event occurs, you will have a record written to the audit trail that you have to review (this also takes up space on your hard disk drives). It is a balancing act of getting enough information without creating more information than you can review or store.

FIGURE 5.12.

Audit Policy dialog box of User Manager.

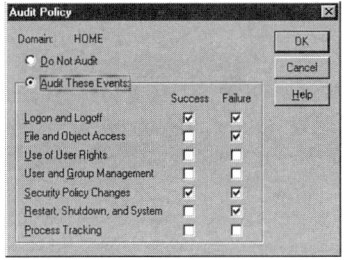

Trust Relationships

The Trust Relationships dialog box enables you to say that you trust another domain or that you permit another domain to trust you (see Figure 5.13). Remember that both sides must agree to a trust relationship (I trust you and you allow me to trust you) before anything happens with it. You should be sure that you are comfortable with the implications of trust relationships and discuss the setup with the other domain administrators before you set up trust relationships. The key to a successful multiple domain configuration is having an agreed-to plan before the network is implemented.

FIGURE 5.13.

Trust Relationships dialog box of User Manager.

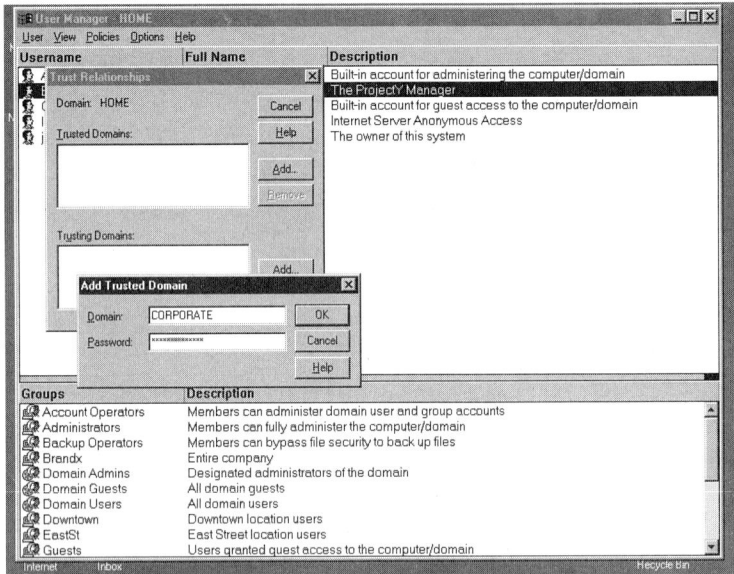

Other User Manager Panels

There are a few other minor panels that you can find on the User Manager display, but the ones discussed in this section are the ones that you need to get your day-to-day job done. Before moving on, there are a few topics to clean up. First are the following groups, created by default when you set up a Windows NT 4.0 server:

- Account Operators
- Administrators
- Backup Operators
- Domain Admins (domains only)
- Domain Guests (domains only)
- Domain Users (domains only
- Guests

- Print Operators
- Replicators
- Server Operators
- Users

Predefined Accounts

You also will have the following accounts set up for you:

- Administrator (with full system privileges and a password you set during the installation process)
- Guest (an account that has very little in the way of privileges, but is a tool to allow casual access to your server by users who do not have their own accounts)

Windows NT Server's System Policy Editor

Almost all the properties of a user's environment are set by the User Manager tool. Microsoft has continued to enhance this feature so that it is a complete tool for administrators. The System Policy Editor (which is not yet integrated into User Manager) enables you to set a series of parameters that relate to the appearance of the user's desktop, which operating system functions (Control Panel, for example) they are allowed to access, and other very fine controls over user activity (see Figure 5.14). If you are running servers exclusively using a client-server architecture, you probably will not use the System Policy Editor often, because your users will access the server through the network for shared resources (see Figure 5.14). If you have a number of users who actually work on NT workstations, you might want to take the time to become familiar with the functionality that this editor enables you to control on your user accounts.

Remote Access Service (RAS) Administration

The Remote Access Service (RAS) monitoring and configuration tool is accessed from the Administrative Tools menu. Its purpose is to control the service that monitors your modems for dial-in requests. It also enables you to specify which users are allowed to access the modems, although the User Manager tool can also be used in NT 4.0 to set up user access to RAS. Another key change in NT 4.0 is that the dial-out utilities are no long called RAS. Instead, they are located under the Dial-Up Networking tool in the Accessories menu or in the My Computer display. The Remote Access Admin tool has a simple display that shows you the status of the RAS server on the computer that you have selected, as shown in Figure 5.15. Note that you can control and monitor the RAS services on another computer by choosing the Server menu, Select Domain, or Server option.

The first task you might want to accomplish is to start or stop the RAS, which might be necessary to run other communication packages that will not run as long as your modem is dedicated to listening for incoming calls to RAS. The start and stop functions are located on the

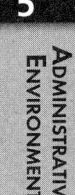

Server menu, along with a pause (which means don't take calls, but don't shut down the server or free up the modem). An interesting thing to note is that you can select the domain and server you are administering when you are in a domain environment. This is another example of how Microsoft is integrating remote administration into its basic tools, as opposed to building separate remote access tools. (Just wait until you see the next version of the operating system and applications that Microsoft will use to integrate Web access.)

You can also set user access permissions for RAS using the RAS Admin tool. This option functions exactly like the panel in User Manager. I personally prefer to work within the User Manager environment so that I can quickly see all the factors related to a particular user's account. However, there may be situations when you are in the RAS Admin tool and you want to check out a particular user's setup. This panel will let you do that.

FIGURE 5.14.

System Policy Editor.

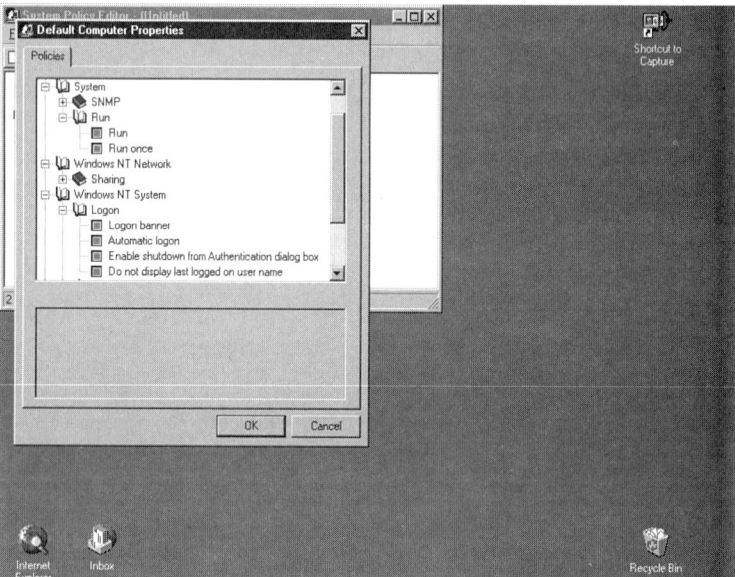

FIGURE 5.15.

Remote Access Admin display.

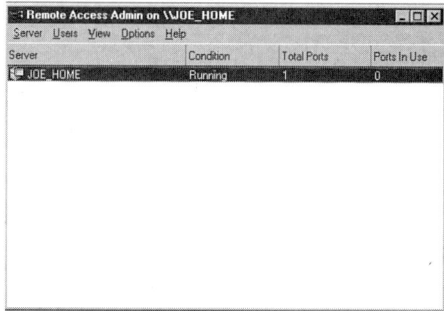

There is one final topic left in my RAS discussion. Suppose that you see the lights on your modem and know that someone has dialed in. How do you find out who logged in? The Active Users menu item on the Users menu shows you who is connected, to which server the user is connected, and when that user's connection started (see Figure 5.16). The buttons at the right of the display enable you to get more information on the user account, send that user a message, (such as "the system is going down in 10 minutes"), or even disconnect the user.

FIGURE 5.16.

Remote Access Users display.

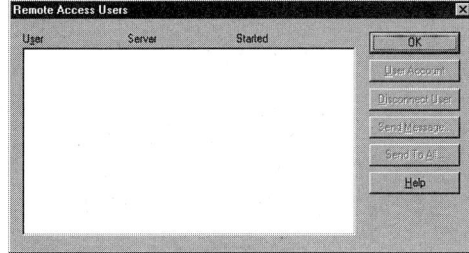

Resource Access Grants

So far, we have classified users into groups and set environmental parameters for them. However, they still have next to nothing in terms of shared network resources unless they are connected to their local machines. The other half of the user administration picture is the access grants to resources. This actually is quite simple under the new Windows NT 4.0 interface. For example, to grant a user access to a directory, you follow a simple two-step process. First, you select the directory that is to be shared using Explorer or My Computer tools and create a share name for it (see Figure 5.17). The easiest way to create a share name is to highlight the directory of interest and then right-click your mouse and select the sharing option from the pop-up menu that appears.

FIGURE 5.17.

Creating a share name for a folder.

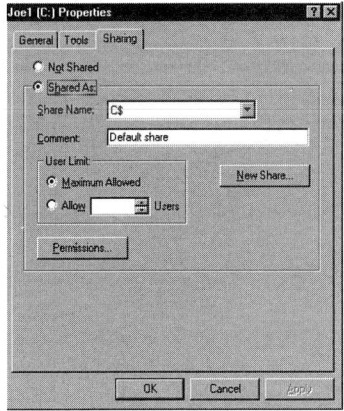

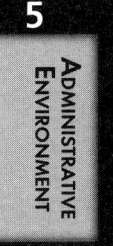

5

ADMINISTRATIVE
ENVIRONMENT

Step two in this process is to select the permissions button on the Sharing tab dialog and fill in the Permissions dialog box (see Figure 5.18). This functions like most of the other administrative control tools. To delete permissions, highlight that user and click the Remove button. To add permissions, click the Add button, select first the user or group to give the permission to, and then choose the type of access permission. For files, the permissions are Full Control, which allows directory modification, Read, which allows users to look but not touch, No Change, which allows them to look but not change, and No Access, which does not allow them even to look at the list of files. Note that you may have to give permissions to the appropriate users or groups through the Security Properties page under the given files or directories if you have implemented file-level security restrictions on some of your directories or files under NTFS.

FIGURE 5.18.

Access Through Share
Permissions dialog box.

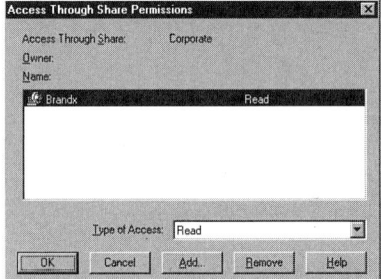

The concepts in the preceding paragraph apply to printers also. You select the Printers option of the Settings selection on the Start menu and then highlight the printer with which you want to work. Specify the share name under the Sharing tab of the tab dialogs that are presented to you when you right-click on that printer and select the Sharing menu option. You control who has access to the printer on the security tab dialog. The enhanced NT 4.0 printer setup options provide the fine degree of printer control that is provided by mainframes and minicomputer systems, which is pretty impressive for a little PC-based server.

Starting and Stopping Processes

To control whether a particular service is running and also to set the startup parameters for that service, you use the Services tool under the Windows NT Control Panel (see Figure 5.19). To start or stop a service, select the service from the list and click on the start or stop buttons. To control whether and how the user starts up, you select the startup button, which brings up the dialog box shown to the right of the Services dialog box in Figure 5.19. As mentioned earlier, almost all your major services will be set to start automatically when the operating system starts.

This concludes the basic discussion of the administrative tool set for the BackOffice environment. Not all the many options that are available have been covered, and this chapter hasn't gone into any of the details as to what values you would want to pick when setting up a given user. The setup configurations needed to allow users to work with a given application are shown for each of the BackOffice applications later in this book.

FIGURE 5.19.

Service tool from Control Panel.

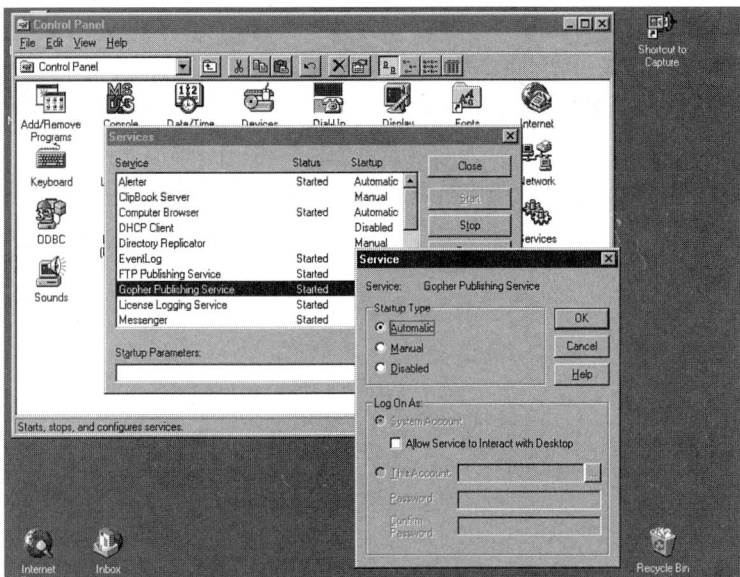

NOTE

To pick up some of the finer points of using the tools (working with the View menu to improve the display appearance, for example), try out the other options and see what they can do for you.

BackOffice Administrative Tools

As you can see, Windows NT provides a pretty comprehensive set of administrative tools. These tools meet all the general administrative needs of most applications. However, there are always a few specific functions (such as setting parameters that control how the application is performing) that you need application-specific administrative tools to handle. I use these tools rarely, and the basic tools such as User Manager meet almost all my routine administrative needs.

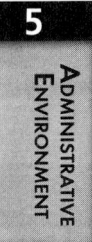

Extending Windows NT Administrative Environment for Applications

> **NOTE**
>
> Recall that the tools that are mentioned previously and the Windows NT security/administrative environment are accessible through API calls for applications that you develop. You can use the tools that are already in place to help configure security within your application. This can make life much easier for the poor, suffering system administrator and the developers.

Summary

There are still a few details about the administrative environment that need to be worked out to make you a proficient administrator on the individual components of BackOffice. There are chapters that cover the administration of each of these tools later. They will make a lot more sense to you after you have read the introductions to the individual products. However, the basic Windows NT administrative tool set provides a comprehensive and easy-to-use tool set that will meet most of your needs.

Intranets

by Joe Greene

IN THIS CHAPTER

CHAPTER 6

Many of you may be getting a little impatient to actually start installing software and tweaking buttons on configuration dialog boxes. You have bravely read your way through five introductory chapters that provided some material that you may have already known. I know how you feel. I often install the software and then read the instructions when I run into a problem. However, I believe that this introductory material is needed for those individuals who are converting to BackOffice from other computer environments. Many mainframe types are experts on SNA, but may never have seen the protocols and nonbatch operating system concepts that have been presented in this section. Even the Novell folks are probably not used to the wide array of built-in services and protocols that you find in the baseline Windows NT Server environment (there is a reason that NT is gaining market share so rapidly).

This chapter lays the final set of groundwork before you jump into the first of the BackOffice products (the Windows NT Server operating system). In this chapter, you learn a little background material on intranets. This is a relatively new term in the computer industry and it's worthwhile not only to go over the product sets, but also to cover the pros and cons of this configuration. Because the term is so new, it is useful to fix the meaning of it as it will be used in this book. It is not really that strange a concept and can make building an effective in-house network really simple.

An intranet is a network that provides service within an organization that utilizes Internet technologies. There are probably more elegant and precise definitions, but this one should suit your purposes for this book. By this definition, you can qualify yourself as an intranet if you install any of the following components on one of your servers for use by general users on your network:

- A World Wide Web server
- An FTP server
- An electronic mail system that interfaces with other mail systems using Internet standard protocols
- A Domain Name Server
- A telnet server
- A gopher server
- A newsgroup server

This may seem like a relatively simple process, but it shows an underlying philosophical shift that you need to be aware of. Basically, when you set up an intranet, you are moving away from proprietary vendor product suites into a more open product environment. If your intranet products adhere to standards, you have the option of switching out a poorly performing product for one that provides better performance. You also open up your options later on if you decide to expand onto the Internet or even provide simple point-to-point links to other organizations that you work with. It will likely be easier to find organizations that support Internet transmission standards than to find those that support the particular version of proprietary electronic mail that you might have chosen.

For those of you who are moving seriously into the Windows NT environment, you also need to consider Microsoft's stated product directions. They are not only pushing the Internet, they are also stressing the intranet concept. They have a large number of products in place to support this environment and a number of others that are slated for delivery in the not-too-distant future. They have even built World Wide Web page interfaces directly into their word processing package. There is no doubt that Microsoft is serious about this concept.

Another advantage that you should consider if you use Microsoft operating systems on your workstations (that is, almost all PC users) is that Microsoft is bundling tools that interface to the Internet into their operating systems or common utility packages such as the Microsoft Plus! product. To support organizations, this means that you will have a built-in client available to you that supports Internet mail systems and even Web browsers. If you want to use proprietary electronic mail systems or other tools to distribute multimedia information, you have to allocate time to install and support these third-party packages.

Intranet Versus Internet

There are a few other differences between the Internet and intranets that you should consider. The following are the most important:

- Higher bandwidth on the intranet
- Better security on the intranet
- Fewer users on the intranet
- A more homogenous environment on the intranet
- Better network monitoring on the intranet

The Internet backbone uses communications lines that have very high transmission capabilities. This bandwidth is divided among the millions of Internet users, which means that you do not have any guarantee that the bandwidth will be available to you when you need it. The lines that connect your network to the Internet also tend to be much slower than the main Internet backbone (transmission companies charge for the distance of the connection and the speed of the connection). Figure 6.1 illustrates these basic issues.

This higher bandwidth allows you to implement technologies that are not quite ready for the main Internet yet. A prime example is digital video transmission from a media server. This would be a very slow process on the main Internet. However, it could be possible on a moderately loaded local intranet—especially if you implemented 100 Mbps (megabits per second) networks, which are becoming readily available. Other multimedia and bandwidth-intensive transfers are also a possibility using the intranet.

FIGURE 6.1.

Bandwidth consider-ations for intranets and the Internet.

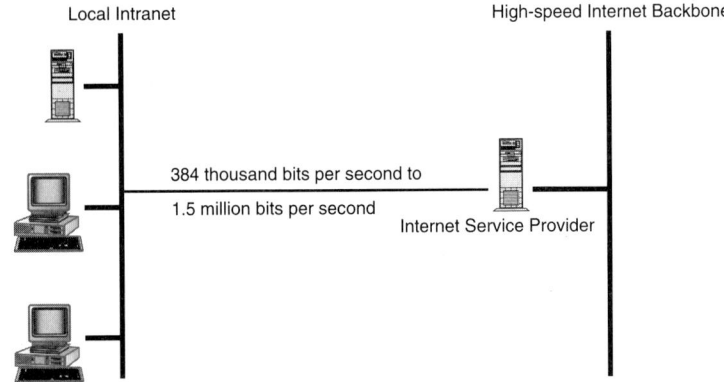

FIGURE 6.1.

Local Intranet   High-speed Internet Backbone

384 thousand bits per second to

1.5 million bits per second

Internet Service Provider

10/16/100 million bits per second

The next advantage that intranets have over the Internet is security (see Figure 6.2). Perhaps you are not ready to jump into that wild world of the Internet where there are all those hackers, viruses, and scary people. You can isolate your Internet transmissions with a firewall and provide only controlled access to the Internet. On the safe side of the firewall, you can implement an intranet environment that contains sensitive information that you would not want to have available to outsiders. The key is that when you have this higher level of security, you have the option of implementing a number of systems that you may not be comfortable implementing in the Internet world.

FIGURE 6.2.

Security advantages of intranets.

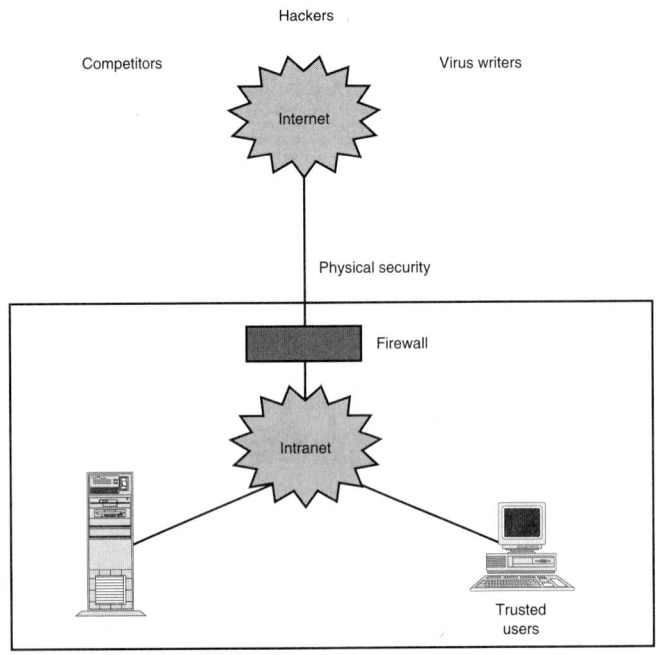

Hackers

Competitors   Virus writers

Internet

Physical security

Firewall

Intranet

Trusted users

6

Another advantage of the intranet is that you will be serving fewer users. A very real concern for those who put interesting content on the Internet is that everyone will want to get at it. There are a number of fairly powerful servers that have been dragged to their knees when someone puts some content out there that everyone wants. These popular users are often asked to find another server by the system administrator. Therefore, you may want to make your first use of this technology an intranet so that you can get comfortable with the basic concepts of administration. You also can implement better applications and make more detailed content available when you have fewer users.

The fourth advantage of intranets over the Internet is that you will probably have a more homogenous user environment to deal with. Your corporate standards will probably limit you to one or two Web browsers, a common electronic mail package, and so forth. It can take quite some time if you are trying to support users who are using a wide variety of applications to access your Web site. For example, how do you help users access your FTP site when they are using a tool that you have never even heard of? This is especially critical on Web pages, because different browsers support different HTML Web page extensions. On an intranet, you can design your Web pages for the browsers that your users will have on their computers.

The final advantage is that you have better network monitoring with an intranet. Because the Internet is maintained by other people, you are never sure whether your problems are a result of something that you did or something in the Internet that is beyond your control. The key to exploiting this advantage is to learn to use the network monitoring tools provided as a part of Windows NT Server. Chapter 4, "Monitoring Environment," covered the basics of these tools.

You should consider these advantages when you are planning an intranet. My goal in pointing them out was to raise your awareness that an intranet is not some form of poor man's Internet. It actually has several advantages over the Internet (okay, the Internet wins when it comes to connectivity to the rest of the world) that you can exploit.

NOTE

You can build applications for an intranet that the Internet is just not ready to handle at this time.

Intranets Versus LAN

A few years ago, local area networks were the hot new technology. Today, they are the old tradition that is probably going to be replaced by the newer intranet technology. These differences need to be considered when you are evaluating implementing or revising your network configuration. Here are the top factors that need to be considered:

- Effectiveness of current product suite
- Cost of conversion

- Expandability
- Capability of supporting new products
- Need for standards
- Leading versus bleeding edge

The first question that you should consider with regard to intranets versus LANs is how good is your current LAN product suite. The decision to consider new products such as those of an intranet is much easier if your current products are just not doing the job. Now that people are starting to use electronic mail systems and other such products, the tools that met their needs in the beginning often seem inadequate. Compare the features of your current tools against those of the newer products to see whether there are some key features that your users want that are missing in your current products.

Another important consideration is the cost of conversion. You should try to estimate the cost of upgrading your current products. You can then compare that with the cost of purchasing intranet products. Another important consideration that is often ignored is the labor and training time required for the conversion. You may have to spend a lot of time getting ready to install and support the new products. Conversely, many upgrades to current products also require quite a bit of time as vendors upgrade their architecture substantially in order to support the more complex features that users are demanding.

The third consideration is expandability. Many LAN products were built in the days of small workgroups of users. This worked fine for a while, but eventually people started to ask about connectivity to other departments. Now the entire organization is wired together into a LAN environment. Not only has the use of these systems grown as users have come to see their advantages, but cost considerations come into play because it is easier and less expensive to maintain a few larger servers than it is to maintain a large number of smaller servers. Many LAN applications (such as Microsoft Mail) were designed to support smaller groups of users, and they lack the architecture to take on the larger number of users that are typical of servers today. These products may need to be replaced in your environment with intranet products that have been designed to support larger user volumes.

You should also consider the cost of supporting LAN applications as opposed to that of supporting intranet applications. Recall that you can usually save money by reducing the number of servers in your environment. This tends to favor the more scalable intranet products. However, there are costs to retrain people in a new product suite. If the newer product suite is better engineered, you can actually save costs if the interface is more intuitive and there are fewer bugs that you have to help users get through.

The fifth consideration for intranet products is your need to support product standards. Some products interface grudgingly to the Internet. However, intranet products use the Internet protocols and therefore go smoothly onto the Internet. If you foresee having to exchange information with others who are already using standard Internet-based products, this may lead you to adopt intranet-based products over traditional LAN products.

A final consideration is whether you want to be on the leading edge or the bleeding edge. Some organizations have to be at the forefront of technology. If your company is into interactive multimedia applications, you will probably have a tough time implementing your products in a DOS environment. However, it is tough if you just want to get your basic administrative processing work done if you are constantly fussing with new, experimental technologies. Most of the products in the intranet product suite implemented by Microsoft have been around for a number of years and are fairly well tested. They are leading edge, but also production grade.

> **TIP**
>
> You may want to be a little more cautious about implementing some of the bleeding edge technologies, such as Internet phone.

Setting Up an Intranet

This section takes you through the process of setting up an intranet. It happens to be the first intranet that I set up so it is a real-world example. Let me set the stage for you. There is a group of software developers. We have a couple of servers running Windows NT Server configured in the workgroup configuration. The main goal is to implement a set of tools that enables developers to communicate with one another and share resources. They have a fair amount of experience as users of the Internet and are therefore comfortable with many of these tools.

The first thing that we tried to come up with was a list of functional requirements. There was not enough time to conduct a formal study, but the list of requirements that seemed reasonable included the following:

- Electronic mail to send messages
- Group scheduling to coordinate calendars
- An area where developers can store information that others might need to read
- A common repository for source code with version control
- Areas where project team members can load software for transfer to other developers

The first requirement that I came across was the electronic mail system. Because the developers did a lot of work under Windows 95 and Windows NT and the corporate standard LAN-based electronic mail system had problems in these environments, we selected Microsoft Exchange Server. It provided us with a standard interface to expand onto the Internet when the time came and also met all of our needs in the short term. The Exchange client was frequently used by developers who had accounts with their own Internet service providers.

The next requirement focused around group scheduling. There is no real intranet tool for group scheduling, so we used the LAN-based product Schedule Plus. It interfaces to Microsoft Exchange well for transmitting meeting requests, and it was good enough for our relatively simple needs.

The next requirement was a more interesting one to satisfy. We needed a place to store information (specifications, project schedules, and so forth) where everyone could access it. This could have been done with a simple shared folder or some public folders in Exchanger Server. The solution that we chose was to implement an Internet Information Server. The reasons that we chose this solution included the following:

- We had developers who were basically familiar with Web pages and wanted to learn more. They were probably about as comfortable with making Web pages as they were with word processors and project scheduling tools. It also helped develop those individuals who will probably be developing Web-based applications in the near future.

- Common directories and group folders did not provide us with easy access mechanisms to find the information that we were interested in. Even with the longer Windows 95/NT filenames, we still had to figure out what the person decided to call the document by reading down the list. The Web pages enabled us to implement a hierarchy and use explorer formats, frames, and other techniques to make it easy to find information.

- Internet Information Server is licensed with the operating system; Exchange Server licenses are priced separately. We might have had to purchase additional Exchange Server licenses if everyone was using it all the time.

- Many users did not have all the tools needed to view our information in its native format. The key examples were the project schedules that were prepared in Microsoft Project. Only a few team leaders had this software on their systems. Therefore, it was easiest for everyone concerned if we displayed the project schedule on the screen, did a screen capture, and stored the resulting image in GIF format for display on a Web page.

The next task at hand was to provide a source code version control system. Again, there are no Internet standard protocols related to software version control, so we picked a traditional LAN-based product. This is another example where you will not find intranet products to meet all your needs. The network environment that you construct will most likely be a mixture of LAN technologies and technologies that have their origin on the Internet.

The final requirement is that we needed a place where programmers could upload and download files to and from the server for others to access. Examples of this would be new software modules or executables for testing. Figure 6.3 shows this sample intranet. We could have set up an FTP server area for them to work with. We could have made a series of folders under the main FTP server root directory for the various types of files that needed to be stored. Although this would have worked well, we chose instead to use the standard Windows networking utilities to share folders.

FIGURE 6.3.

Sample intranet implementation.

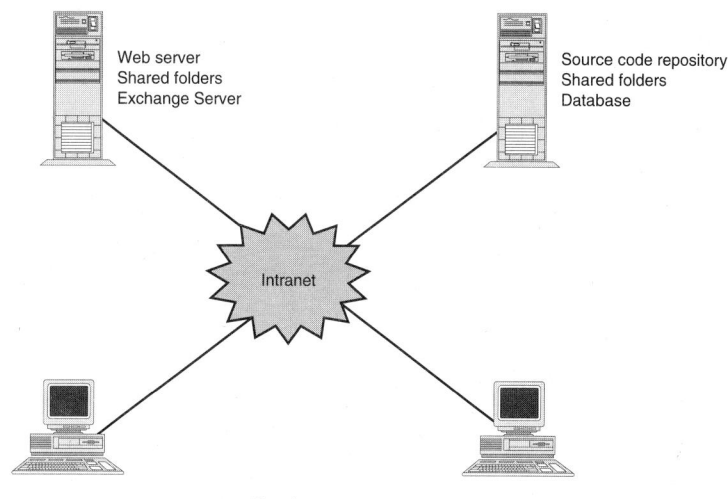

Web server
Shared folders
Exchange Server

Source code repository
Shared folders
Database

Intranet

Developers

This may seem like heresy in a chapter that is devoted to intranets. Am I truly saying that FTP has no place in the world and that only Windows network shared directories are acceptable? Not at all. I am saying that for this particular installation, the shared folder concept made the most sense. We came to this conclusion based on the following reasons:

- Everyone was already comfortable with Windows network shared directories and had been using them for many months. Although most people knew the basics of FTP, it was not their most comfortable product suite.

- The only FTP package that we had was the traditional DOS command-line version. This was a pain for people who were used to drop-and-drag and all the other Windows user-interface techniques. We did not think that this would get a very good reception.

- We had no need to communicate with workstations that were not running Windows NT or Windows 95. They all had the standard Windows file sharing utilities built into their operating systems.

This little example of an intranet installation should give you some food for thought. As you can see, even people who write books about BackOffice and sing the praises of intranets occasionally fall back and use conventional LAN tools when it makes sense to do so. The key is to take just a few moments to write down your user's needs and match them against the alternative products.

Services for an Intranet

This section provides you with a basic mapping between the services that you might want to implement on your intranet and the products in the BackOffice family. You can find each of these products discussed in more detail in upcoming sections, but this section can be your cross-reference of function versus product. These are the most common functions used on an intranet/LAN:

- Electronic mail
- Shared information repositories
- Common file storage area
- Newsgroups
- Databases

The electronic mail function is handled by Exchange Server in the BackOffice family. This product supports the standard Internet mail protocols and also a few of the Microsoft formats. There are, of course, a number of third-party products from Lotus and smaller companies that perform the same function but are not as integrated into the BackOffice environment as Exchange Server. You also have the choice of installing the older Microsoft Mail product. This lacks the scalability of Exchange Server and may not be supported in the distant future. One note, Exchange Server will force you to enter into a domain configuration as opposed to a workgroup.

When it comes to storing shared information you have basically four options. First, you can use shared folders on your server and tell people to browse these folders using File Manager, Network Neighborhood, or Explorer. This will work, but it is more of a challenge to figure out what the person who wrote the file would call it. The second option is to use public folders within Exchange Server. You can make a series of topical folders and access them using your standard mail client. The third option is to set up an FTP server and allow users to use FTP utilities to upload and download files. This is not as convenient as Windows-based shared folders, but it can be accessed by a wide variety of client workstations. The final option is to put up a Web server. This may take a little bit more learning, but it is an interface that you can extend to meet a wide range of future needs.

For simple file storage, you have the same three options as for shared information. For this purpose, using shared folders is probably the simplest solution. An FTP server still has appeal if you wish to make your files available to people who use a wide variety of operating systems. Finally, a Web site for this file storage is not that bad an option if the list of files does not change that often. It is still an easy paradigm to work with, but it can be a pain if you have to keep updating your Web pages that link to the files.

Newsgroups is another feature that many intranet users desire. Right now, Exchange Server is being modified to accommodate downloading newsgroup information. It should be out by the end of 1996 or so. This will complete the list of major Internet services that BackOffice can provide.

Finally, a traditional LAN application is that of the database management system. The usage is simple. You build a database and some access/reporting software and deliver it as a package to your users. The LAN mindset works and there is no need for any Internet stuff. You can continue to do things the traditional way. However, Microsoft and other major vendors are working to enable you to access a database with a combination of a Web browser (for display of information) and a series of miniapplications that are downloaded from the server (for business logic and processing). There are already some impressive sites that provide some relatively complex database access. This may become a trend in the future to help minimize the complexity of the distributed computer resources on a network by downloading simpler applications only when they are needed.

Security Environment of an Intranet

You may notice that you are not logging in to the host computer when you access a Web page. This is because you are actually accessing the system through a specially designed Web user account, which usually has full read permissions in the Web pages directory. If you wish to control access to certain portions of the Web page, you are going to have to get a user ID and password combination from the user and have it validated before you continue with further processing.

Another feature that is often used is anonymous FTP. This data is made available to a default account that is set up for the FTP server. This makes it easy for you to provide a number of people with access to the data without granting explicit access rights to them. If you use this feature and want to have some data restricted to only certain users, you need to set up subdirectories under that main directory that have access control permissions set accordingly (and use the NTFS file system).

Be aware of these common holes that were designed to promote better access to information at a slight cost in security. They can be dealt with rather easily if you know that they are there. You just need to decide whether you can live with the security implications in return for the ease of access to that data. Your decision may have to be on a server-by-server, application-by-application basis.

Summary

This chapter provided an introduction to the subject of intranets. Most of the computer industry seems to be stressing intranets almost as heavily as they stress the Internet. This means that you will see a wealth of products in the near future that are based on this technology. This chapter presents some of the pros and cons associated with intranets to help you decide which environment best fits your situation.

II

PART

IN THIS PART

Windows NT Server

Windows NT Server Overview

by Joe Greene

CHAPTER 7

You can buy Windows NT Server without buying any of the other components in the BackOffice family. Therefore, some might argue that the operating system is a separate product from the suite of tools used to provide server-based applications to the end-users. However, there are a number of reasons why the components of the BackOffice family are a tightly integrated suite:

- All the components of the BackOffice family, with the exception of Microsoft Mail Server, are designed to work only under the Windows NT Server environment.

- One key server (Internet Information Server) is already being bundled as a part of the Windows NT Server operating system. It is possible that some of the products that are currently being offered as separate components today may someday be integrated into the base Windows NT Server operating system. Remember, networking was once an add-on component to operating systems, yet today it is part of the baseline package.

- Microsoft has coupled the various components of the BackOffice family to the Windows NT Server operating system more tightly than almost any other commercial applications designed to run in the Windows NT environment. The BackOffice applications do not just run in the Windows NT environment, they use its services (that is, security and event logging) as part of their basic functions. Microsoft has referred to this as a "no-compromise architecture" for the Internet Information Server product, where you can take advantage of all the special features of Windows NT, because they do not have to be able to run under any other operating system.

- BackOffice components are designed to work with and depend on one another in much the same manner that they depend on the Windows NT Server operating system. For example, the Systems Management Server is designed to depend on the services of SQL Server. It cannot run under Foxbase or Oracle.

- Finally, they are designed from a marketing perspective to form a complete server environment for the users. The components in BackOffice were not randomly chosen. They are designed to fill each of the major functions that people are demanding from their network servers. You have the operating system, database, Web server, and mail server. You even have some imaginative applications, such as a network configuration management tool (Systems Management Server) and gateway to the mainframe world (SNA Server), which are not currently the rage in the typical PC server environment. Microsoft sees a need for them, however, and hopes that these products take off. There are components coming down the line, such as the Internet merchant server product, that Microsoft is betting people will want to have as the ever-changing computer environment evolves.

This chapter is the high-level overview that describes what role the Windows NT Server plays in the BackOffice environment. Along the way, you will look at functions that Windows NT Server provides to the users whether or not there are other BackOffice components installed. There is an impressive number of services built into the baseline NT operating system. It is a rich environment that you can configure to meet a wide variety of needs.

By the end of this chapter, you will be ready to appreciate the rich environment that this operating system provides. When you understand how all the pieces fit together, you will be in a much better position to go through the installation and planning chapters that follow. Once you start working with the system day-to-day, you may not get the chance to step back and see the other options that you have available to you.

A Little History

There was no Windows NT version 1.0 and no Windows NT version 2.0. It all started with Windows NT version 3.0. Why start with version 3? The answer lies in the fact that Windows NT was not the first server/workstation operating system on which Microsoft worked.

In the days when IBM and Microsoft were allowed to and wanted to cooperate with one another on operating systems (which had gone on since the earliest days of the DOS operating system), they decided that they needed a product that would be a more powerful big brother to the DOS/Windows family of computers that were dominating the market. Computers based on the PC were growing in power at a very rapid pace, but the DOS/Windows architecture had been designed in an earlier, simpler era. It did not have the robust framework to support larger, memory-intensive applications. It could not evolve into a system that was capable of performing multiple tasks at the same time. Basically, although it was dominating the market and making money hand over fist, people could see that it was not going to last forever and that maybe it was time to plan for its successor.

That successor was intended to be the OS/2 operating system. It was a rather straightforward succession path, as shown in Figure 7.1. You would start with the desire to maintain the ability to run at least most of the thousands of DOS and Windows applications that were available on the market. The rest of the operating system was up for rewrite, and this rewrite was substantial. It was not a complete revision just for the sake of revision. There were some substantial changes that had taken place in the computer environment that made the old architecture seem archaic:

- Intel had started to produce 32-bit microprocessors as opposed to the earlier 16-bit microprocessors. This meant that the operating system was moving data around in chunks that were double the size of the previous architecture, in addition to performing more computations per second. The key element of the 32-bit architecture was the fact that you could reference much more memory with a single instruction than you could with the old 16-bit words. Because memory is many orders of magnitude faster to access than disk drives, this allowed developers to put huge applications in memory and perform amazing feats with blinding speed. When you can write an application like that, people will buy it.

- People, most of whom instinctively want more of everything, began to think of ways that they could run multiple jobs on their computers at the same time. Why not work on a word processing document while you are generating the data needed for a report or performing some other task? Computer processors were reaching the point where they had enough power to run multiple jobs. All that was lacking was an operating system that could support multitasking.

■ Many developers were reaching the point where they wanted to be able to perform multiple tasks at the same time. One way to make your application look faster is to use an idle CPU cycle to preload and calculate information that will be needed in the near future. A multitasking operating system enabled developers to perform some of these tasks while the display was waiting for a response from the user.

■ The DOS/Windows environment was powerful for its day, but it did not provide a lot of services at the operating system level. It did not include integrated networking and other features that we have come to expect as standard. DOS, for example, did not even provide printer drivers at the operating system level, which meant that application developers had to write drivers for every printer that their users might possibly want to use. This was actually quite a problem. Because the operating system was not doing the job, developers had to think up ways to get the job done. They all came up with their own creative ideas on ways to extend the basic operating system. The problem was that the solution that your networking vendor chose might eat up too much memory to enable you to run your word processor (whose vendor required at least 540K of base memory).

■ Microsoft wanted to be able to expand its operating system to a variety of hardware platforms, such as those based on a RISC architecture.

FIGURE 7.1.

OS/2 as the successor to DOS and Windows.

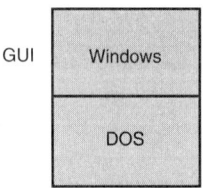
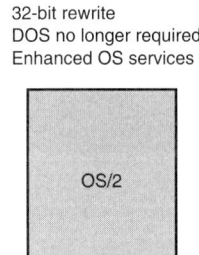

In summary, a new operating system was needed. Dusting off DOS and Windows would not be enough. IBM and Microsoft set off down the path of building an operating system for the future. Future is a key word here. When you look at the design of OS/2 and Windows NT, there is a lot of extensibility built in—ways in which you can interface new modules in the future to meet changing needs. It appears that the two companies did not want to be put into the position of doing another complete rewrite in the near future to meet the ever-increasing needs of users.

The OS/2 operating system was born after several years of work. Although it was technically fascinating, it was not a rousing market leader. Common complaints included such things as it was too slow, it took too much memory, it did not run a particular DOS or Windows application, there was not a device driver for my graphics card, and so forth. Many of the big industry leaders such as Lotus were pledging to produce products for this environment, but it suffered from a lack of software that took advantage of its advanced features, and the power of PCs was not quite enough to keep up with its demands.

About this time, Microsoft and IBM decided to go their separate ways when it came to operating system development, one of the more significant events in computer history. They agreed to share source code for a brief period, but they soon started to work hard to make their operating systems distinctive from one another to gain market share. There were now two paths to choose from in the evolution of computer operating systems (see Figure 7.2).

FIGURE 7.2.

Divergence of OS/2 and Windows NT operating systems.

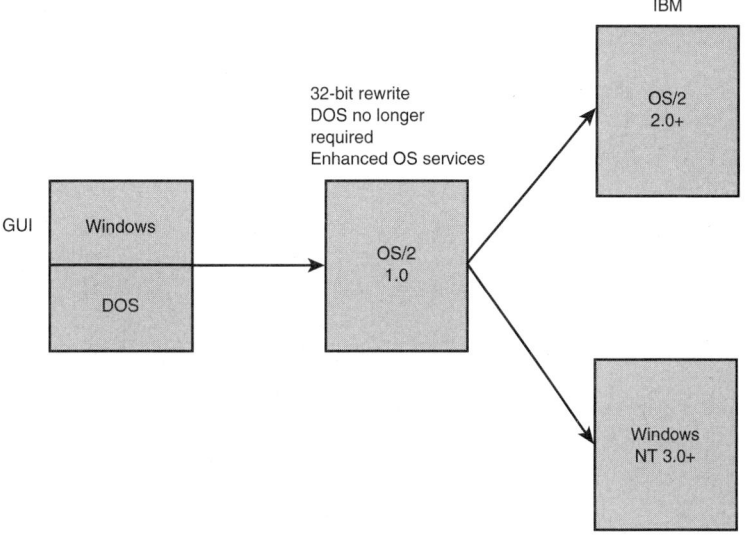

IBM pushed on with OS/2 version 2 and later operating systems. Microsoft did a bit of reengineering and came out with the Windows NT operating system that, as mentioned earlier, started with version 3. Neither of these products set the world on fire. Everyone wanted more powerful operating systems, but the prices for memory, disk drives, and the top-of-the-line processors that were needed to run these operating systems were too much for most users. It would actually be several years until these two operating systems became stable enough, the prices for hardware dropped, and the performance of hardware increased to the point where they became attractive.

To their credit, both IBM and Microsoft continued to believe in their products and the vision that some day the 32-bit operating system would be the choice of every consumer. IBM came out with a number of versions of OS/2 intended for both the workstation and the server. Microsoft refined Windows NT in the 3.50 and 3.51 releases and defined versions for the workstation and the server. With the release of version 3.51, Windows NT had finally come of age at a time when the computer industry was ready for it.

There were a couple of other industry factors that contributed to Windows NT breaking out from being an interesting product to a productive operating system. The first was the fact that Novell had a bit of a lag between releases in major upgrades to its network server operating system. In the computer industry, a year can be an eternity, so people were more open to considering NT and OS/2 products than they would have been a few years earlier. A second factor came from the high-end server market as many UNIX vendors continued to lag in their ability to agree on operating system and graphical user interface standards. This led to a real lack of common business applications that were based on the more powerful operating systems in the UNIX world, because vendors could not afford to build and support different versions of their products that matched each UNIX operating system vendor.

NT Server 3.51 finally started to gain significant market share. If you believe the industry predictors, it is set to become the dominant PC server operating system in a few years. With the NT Server 4.0 product, Microsoft continues to position powerful features into the product (such as the inclusion of a Web server with the basic operating system) and also refine existing features. It has a number of the other server operating system vendors concerned—probably with good reason.

Services Provided by Windows NT Server

The Windows NT operating system has a number of really interesting technical features, and its history is entertaining. However, in the end, you have to ask what a product can do for you today. That is the focus of this section. Unlike earlier operating systems, which merely provided a basic framework to enable you to execute applications, the Windows NT environment is rich with services that are provided by the operating system. This frees developers from having to write basic functionality and instead concentrate on the particular functions that are unique to their applications.

This rich operating system functionality also helps promote standardization. One of the key problems with DOS and Windows was that every application developer made up its own rules for how they were going to implement functions such as memory management. They often conflicted with one another, and this led to all sorts of integration headaches. With Windows NT, most of these headaches have gone away (although you still might have trouble finding a driver for a printer that sold only 50 units and that was discontinued three years ago).

What are these services that are provided by the Windows NT operating system that help applications so much? A list of all of these features would be quite long. The following are those that are most important to general users, administrators, and, of course, BackOffice users (see Figure 7.3):

- File system management
- Integrated networking
- Print services
- Common fonts
- Products that support compatibility with other environments
- Security services
- Common network services
- Administrative tools
- Application interfaces

FIGURE 7.3.

Important services provided by the Windows NT server.

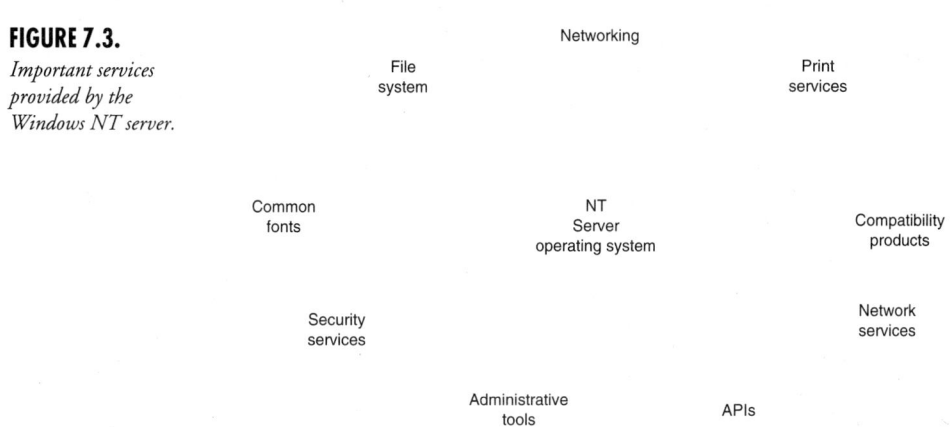

The first is file system management. The heart of most computer operating systems is still stored in files located on magnetic and optical disk drives. Without these files, there is no operating system. There are also no applications without these files. Perhaps you load your applications from a server, but they are still probably stored on a disk drive on that other computer. Therefore, the operating system's capability of managing files is an important part of its overall usefulness. Windows NT supports a number of different file systems and provides the capability of performing most of the common file creation and maintenance services. The architecture also enables NT to support new file systems as they are developed.

The next key service provided by the NT operating system to its client applications and users is its integrated networking. Windows NT was one of the first popular operating systems to build networking into its core. UNIX and VMS added networking features to their base operating system and even bundled these products with the operating system. Windows NT was designed from the start to support networking. This shows, because it is almost getting to the point where it is as easy to access information stored on a shared disk drive in another computer as it is to access information on your own disk drive. It is not as fast, but that is a problem for the network design engineers to work on.

Another key feature of the operating system is its print services. We are not yet a paperless office environment, and there is a lot of printing going on every day. One of my criticisms of the DOS environment was that you had to get printer drivers (which varied in quality from vendor to vendor) for your printers for each application that you ran. Windows NT takes responsibility for providing device drivers to your printers. Applications write to a neutral printer API that is translated by the Windows NT device drivers into the commands that are appropriate for your particular printer. NT extends this basic service by providing utilities for controlling your printer queue and printing to printers that are attached to other computers or the network itself.

One feature that is not really a major service, but is important, is the common fonts that are provided in Windows NT. People are now no longer content with the ability to get some text on the screen or on a printout. They want to make their presentation look good and appealing to the reader. The bar has been raised in terms of what the market will accept. Having the common fonts of Windows NT is a major factor that allows you to achieve this "what you see is what your user will get" environment. All vendors access a common set of fonts that are provided as part of the operating system. The True Type fonts are designed to ensure that your presentation will look the same when printed out as it does on the screen. I spent many hours in the DOS world editing documents so that they looked bad on the screen but looked great when printed out.

One area in which NT clearly excels over its competition is in the area of compatibility products. Perhaps you have a unified computer environment that runs only one operating system and one set of application software. If so, you are rare in this world. The more common scenario is that you have one environment, your central computer organization has another, and several of the other departments have their own. You have to live and work with these people, and they are not likely to convert over to your standards. Windows NT provides a number of services that enable you to communicate over the network, exchange information, and even execute applications on computers that are running most of the common operating systems in use today.

An important service for most users is security. This topic is covered extensively in Chapter 3, "Security Environment." Windows NT has a sound, C2-rated security foundation that does not intervene except when necessary in your applications. It is relatively easy to administer, especially if you use applications such as those in BackOffice that are designed to work with the basic security tools provided by the operating system.

An extension of the idea of providing basic networking as part of the operating system is a series of common network services that Windows NT provides. It is not enough to be able to send a signal to a remote computer. You have to make it easy to interact with that computer to get productive work done. Windows NT provides a number of utilities that provide directory lookup services (Domain Name Servers, for example) that help you convert easy-to-remember addresses into the numerical addresses that computers like. There are also tools that perform services such as converting Windows NT print jobs into a format that will print on other computers (the UNIX print services via LPR/LPD, for example).

Administrative tools are also an important service provided by the operating system itself. People who worked on administrating early versions of UNIX remember having to know the location and format of several dozen text files that were scattered throughout the system. You had to edit these to control the system and perform routine administrative functions. Windows NT provides a series of convenient, graphical tools that enable you to control the system with a minimal amount of effort. This is not an insignificant service provided by the operating system (because a computer is useless to a new user until he or she has an account with the appropriate privileges).

I call another important function performed by the operating system *application interfaces.* One of the key selling points of Windows, and now Windows NT, is the fact that there is a rich set of commands that developers can access to perform functions such as building windows on the screen with a pull-down menu. This application-centric view has carried the Windows family well over the years; there have been a number of operating systems that have claimed technical and theoretical superiority, but never caught on because there were not many applications that let the users get their work done. The number of APIs continues to grow every year as more functionality gets built in (the Messaging API that lets you send electronic mail directly from your locally developed application, for example).

This list is not complete or detailed, but it is good enough to start to build an appreciation for what Windows NT does for you. You will go over some of the more important subjects in a little more detail in the sections that follow. By now though, you should see that Windows NT does a lot more work for you than the earlier operating systems, such as Windows, would ever be capable of doing. Perhaps that will make it a little easier next time you have to go out and buy a server with more memory and disk space than you ever thought would fit inside a PC.

Differences Between NT Server and Workstation

You may have noticed that there are actually two products that bear the Windows NT name. This section contrasts these two products. This will give you an appreciation of how the NT Server product is optimized for its tasks. It will also explain why you might not want to try and save money by purchasing the Windows NT Workstation product and trying to run it as a server.

A good first question would be, Why have two versions of Windows NT? Both perform the task of running the computer and allowing applications to access system capabilities. Remember, having standards is important. It is easy to imagine that Microsoft could save money by having to produce and support only one product instead of two.

The Workstation-Server combination is actually designed to meet these goals. Most of the core operating system code is the same between these two products. Microsoft has examined what each of the two types of platforms is typically asked to do and allocated extra tools to the environment that needs them. In a sense, you can think of NT Server as NT Workstation with a bunch of added features. It is a little more than that, but it does keep those of you who just want the basic workstation functionality from having to pay for software that only servers use. Let's look at these differences in a little more detail.

The first version of NT is Windows NT Workstation. It is less expensive and takes up less in the way of disk space and memory. This was a very important consideration that actually delayed the acceptance of Windows NT until Microsoft was able to reduce the requirements for the NT Workstation product and hardware vendors were able to lower the price of memory and disk drives. It is now at the point where the additional functionality of NT is worth the additional cost.

Of course, you do not want to purchase a number of the wonderful services that were described in the previous section for every computer on your network. Perhaps you can get away with a single computer acting as the gateway to Novell servers in another department. You also may not want all your users to set up their own World Wide Web servers. One should do the job nicely because you would let them have their own home pages on this machine. Many services are needed on both platforms (both have to print and work with file systems, for example). Microsoft has tried to match the services provided in Workstation to some common baseline of services desired in the industry. You are able to add additional services (a Web server), but you have to pay additional costs.

A final key difference that distinguishes the Workstation product is the way the operating system is tuned. Workstations, by their definition, are the interface points of users to the computer world. Users tend to be very impatient and want the operating system to respond to them instantaneously, if not sooner. Servers, on the other hand, have a main function of servicing requests from other users on the network and background processes, such as database management systems that are running on that server. They can be tuned to listen a little bit less to the console and a little bit more to the background processes.

With the contrasts provided by the preceding paragraphs, let's look at the Windows NT Server product. It is designed to be more responsive to background and network requests than those of the user at its keyboard. It also has a number of special products that are intended for servers that come bundled with it and that are not bundled with the workstation product. Finally, it will ask you to provide a more capable and expensive computer to make it work properly. This has been the case since PC servers were first introduced. If you want more in the way of capabilities, you have to have a bigger box. There are a number of other contrasts that could be drawn between the two products; however, there is other material to be covered. Figure 7.4 summarizes these key differences between the Workstation and Server products.

FIGURE 7.4.

Key differences between the NT Server and the Workstation.

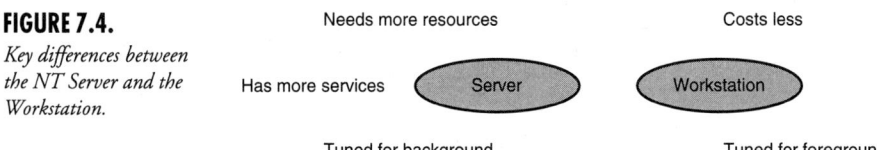

Needs more resources

Costs less

Has more services   Server   Workstation

Tuned for background   Tuned for foreground

File System

Recall that you need the operating system to properly handle file systems that are used to store data on disk drives. Is that enough so that you can get on to the next topic? Not quite. What is important to discuss is the file system options that Windows NT provides services for so that you understand what you can do with your system.

The basic file system that has been supported on PCs since the dawn of time (or at least since DOS was created) is the File Access Table (FAT) file system. It has been used for floppy disks and hard disks. Even UNIX-based computers and Macintoshes have been trained to read this type of file system, which is a sign of how popular it has become. It is relatively simple in its structure, which was necessary back in the days when you had only 360K of storage space available on those 5.25-inch disks.

FAT has had a long life (at least for the computer industry) and provides a reasonable level of service. However, it has its limitations. First, it is not very robust. Space is not allocated to provide check-sums and other techniques that can help you recover information if there is a problem with the media. A number of products, such as Norton Disk Doctor, were created to help you recover when the operating system lost track of file segments and other things such as that, but even they could not fix every problem.

Another feature that you might want, especially when moving into the server environment, is the ability to control access to individual files. The FAT system just puts the files out there. It does not have any space to say who owns the file system. It does not have any constructs to enable you to say which users or groups are permitted to read or write to it. About the only feature that FAT supports is the capability of designating a file as read-only. Of course, it is easy for anyone to reset that read-only attribute, so not even that is guaranteed.

In the early days of OS/2 when IBM and Microsoft were working together, they came up with the High Performance File System (HPFS) to address some of these needs. It permitted security and ownership. After IBM and Microsoft separated their development efforts, Microsoft continued to support HPFS, but decided to come out with its own file system that could do some additional things: the NT File System (NTFS). An important point to consider, by the way, is that Microsoft will be dropping support for HPFS in version 4 of the NT operating system. I guess that there were not all that many NT users using HPFS and very few dual boot NT and OS/2 servers, so they did not want to waste the effort maintaining support for HPFS.

NOTE

NTFS provides support for file-level ownership and security access control.

So far, you have seen three ways of storing information on a disk that is supported by the Windows NT operating system. Although there are a number of other file systems out there that Microsoft could have supported, there is one key file system that almost every computer will be supporting in the future (especially those with NT). That format is the one used for CD-ROMs. There are some special considerations for these read-only devices that have led the industry to come up with a separate means of storing information that is actually an international standard (you can read the same CD on PCs, Macintoshes, and UNIX boxes). Actually there are a few different file formats that are used for CDs (Kodak photo CDs have one format, audio CDs have another). The good news is that NT supports most of the common formats for you (I am listening to an audio CD on my PC while writing this chapter).

One other feature of the operating system that is important to applications is the capability of finding, loading, executing, and saving files. Obviously, the programmers have to decide what they want to do and manipulate the data as appropriate. However, Windows NT will do a lot of the work involved when a program asks to save a file. It will figure out which segments are to be written to, update the directory, and so forth. This saves a lot of work for the individual applications and also provides good standardization for data storage. When combined with some fairly sophisticated disk administration utilities and support for a variety of disk hardware options (including such technologies as RAID), Windows NT provides excellent data storage mechanisms.

Integrated Networking

If you listen to some of the industry "experts," the PC is going the way of the dinosaurs. Instead, we will commit ourselves to use servers owned by other people and we will have very simple display devices in our homes and at work. I do not subscribe to this theory, but I will concede that the network is an increasingly important source of information for modern PC environments. One of the things that impressed me most about Windows NT when I first started using it was the almost seamless integration of network data access and services with the base operating system.

I had been working with network data transfers for years in the UNIX and VMS environments. These operating systems had a number of add-on components that provided file transfer and printing services that were bundled with later versions of those operating systems. They were functional and got the job done. What they lacked was a convenient (that is, GUI) interface that resembled that of the local file management tools. For example, the File Transfer Protocol (FTP) got the job done, but you had to run a separate utility, use its set of commands, and then go back to the operating system prompt to look at the contents of this file or execute it.

With NT 3.51, you had the ability to use the same File Manager tool that you used for all your other file work to share and access shared drives over the network. Once you mapped a drive letter to a network drive, the only way that you could tell the difference functionally was the icon that was used to represent the disk drive and, usually, the speed at which you could access information. This interface has been improved even further in NT 4.0 with the Network Neighborhood and Explorer tools that let you access shared information with or without formally mapping the drive. You can double-click on the file to run or display it. You can drop and drag the file to perform copy and move operations just as on a local drive. The network file handling capabilities are almost seamless.

Another strong feature of the Windows NT environment that usually is only of interest to developers and administrators is the applications' capability of communicating with one another over the network. This is the basis of the whole client-server architecture. You have a number of computers, each performing specific functions that coordinate their activities to get the job done. There are a number of technical details that Windows NT provides to make it easy for applications to talk to one another (Windows sockets, for example). NT supports most of the common communications techniques and is even pushing some advanced technologies, such as Distributed Common Object Model (DCOM), to provide the same type of cooperation found in current OLE applications.

The server version of NT also supports a number of utilities that make working in the network environment easier. For example, you can have services such as DHCP, which automatically provide network addresses to the computers on your network to save you from having to go to each machine. There are also tools to help you look up common addresses and provide your applications with the information needed to make these connections. NT provides most of the commonly used services for the TCP/IP and Microsoft networking environments.

Printing Services

Windows NT provides a number of print services to the user. Many NT users may not appreciate everything NT is doing for them because these tasks are done in a manner that is fairly transparent to the user. About the only time the users get involved is when they send the job and if they get a message box indicating that the printer is out of paper or offline. That is one of the charms about an NT printer, but not its only one.

What printing functions does NT provide for you? The first one that you might not think about is print queue management. Your powerful PC can generate printer data at a rate that is much higher than the printer is capable of processing. In the old days, the application would sit and wait, feeding the printer at whatever rate the printer wanted. This worked, but you had a lot of dead time when you could not run other applications while this was going on. Windows implemented the concept of the print queue (a sort of background process) and Windows NT has enhanced the concept. The basics of print queues are shown in Figure 7.5.

FIGURE 7.5.

Print queues.

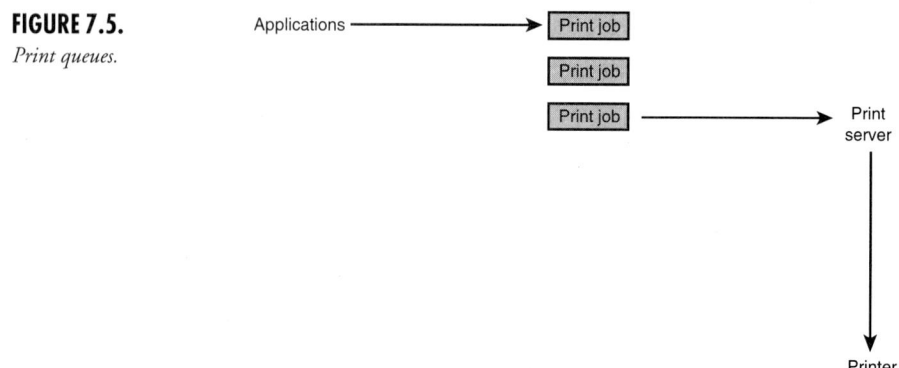

The general concept of a print queue is simple. Take the information from the application at whatever rate the application can sustain and store it in a file on disk. You then have a background process reading the files that are in the print queue and sending them to the printer at whatever rate the printer can handle. This division of labor simplifies the requirements on applications that no longer have to be sensitive to printer needs and capabilities. Windows NT provides a fairly sophisticated queuing system that enables you to send print jobs not only to your favorite local printer, but also to printers located on other computers running Microsoft operating systems, UNIX computers, Macintosh computers, and even printers that are directly attached to the network. NT takes care of all the little details associated with the different standards and protocols associated with the different computer environments.

A final important function of the Windows NT operating system with regard to printing relates to the tools that are used to control and set up the printers. Let's look at control first. You may send a job to the printer that is stuck or perhaps you specified an option that is not supported by your printer and that printer is spitting out dozens of pages of garbage. Windows NT provides a simple printer control utility with the traditional graphical user interface that enables you to pause the printer output, cancel print jobs, and so forth (see Figure 7.6). You are not always able to stop a printer from printing by canceling a print job. Modern printers have substantial amounts of memory, which can store a lot of pages of garbage that get printed even after you kill the print job (you usually have to turn the printer on and off to clear the memory).

Another important tool is the one that enables you to set up the properties of your printer (see Figure 7.7). Just as modern computers have grown in complexity, adding more features, bells, and whistles, printers have also grown up. You now have options to select the page orientation, which paper tray is used, and even what color to use. Because Windows NT provides the print services to the user, it needs a utility to specify the type of printer and which capabilities of that printer you have selected (did you buy the extra paper tray, for example). The Windows NT 4.0 interface for printer setup shown in Figure 7.7 is an easy way to set these properties. You can do the same work in NT 3.51 and earlier, but I was really impressed with the layout and functionality of the 4.0 tools.

FIGURE 7.6.

The Windows NT printer control utility.

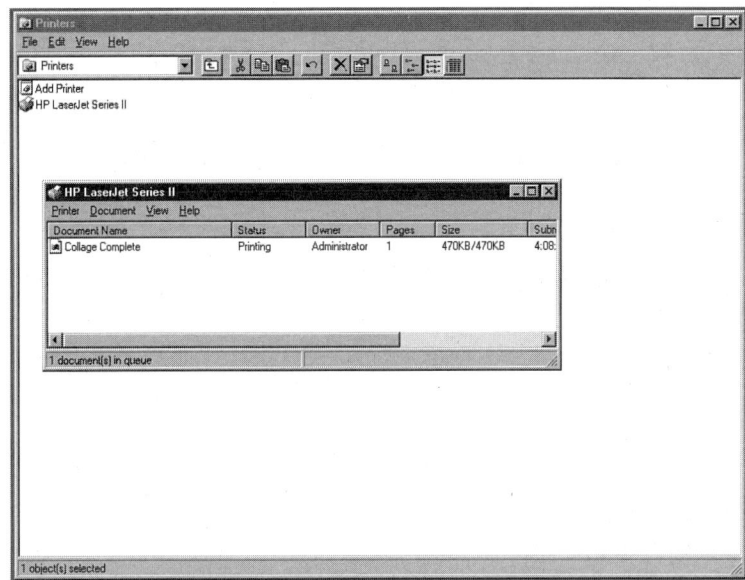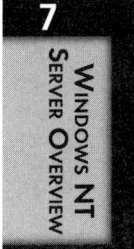

NOTE

NT 4.0 provides some fairly sophisticated printer control tools.

FIGURE 7.7.

Printer setup.

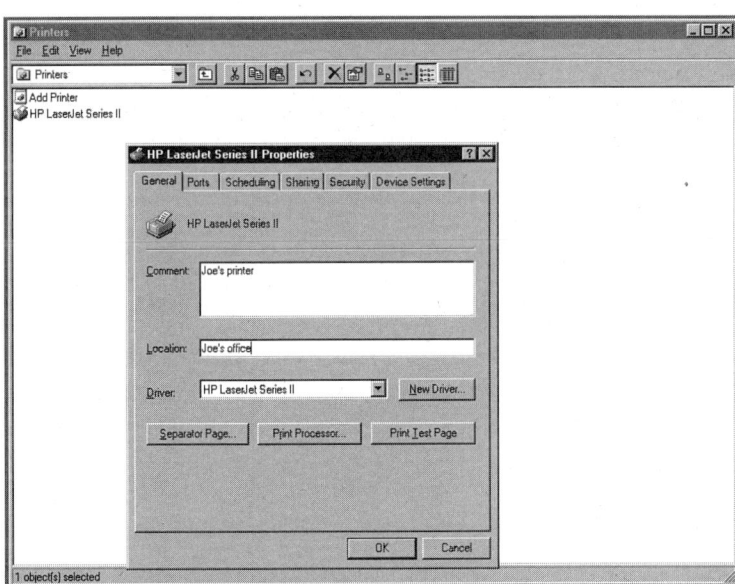

The good news, once again, is that once you or your administrator set up the properties of a printer and share it to the network, it is really easy for users to attach to that printer and just use it. They will probably never appreciate all the technical details that are going on behind the scenes to transfer the print job through the network to the appropriate server and from there through the print queue to the printer itself. They will be blissfully unaware of the command set used by that printer to tell it to print the job sideways. All they know is that they select the printer and click on the print icon on their application toolbar.

Compatibility Options

When Microsoft first entered the server operating system market, it was the outsider. The other servers were established and had all the resources (printers, for example) connected to them. To help ease its way into the server market, Microsoft devoted a lot of attention to building capabilities into NT to enable it to work with these other environments. This goes way behind the capability of transmitting a signal over a common protocol (as with TCP/IP). They engineered capabilities to deal with the native file management systems, printing tools, and other utilities found in these environments. Even today, when NT has a reasonable and growing market share, it is nice to be able to interface with other groups in an almost seamless manner.

> **NOTE**
>
> NT's capability of integrating into a wide range of computer environments is one of its strongest points.

Let's take the Novell environment as one example. When you choose the IPX/SPX protocol set (which is the native environment of Novell NetWare networks), you have the option of adding services for NetWare. On the server side, you can add a gateway product that enables the server to attach to Novell drives and then make the contents of these drives available to its clients on the Microsoft network. You can also add the basic workstation services, which enable you to use your standard File Manager, Network Neighborhood, and other tools to browse shared Novell drives in the same manner that you work with shared NT drives. The printer sharing works the same way. The NetWare servers and shared resources appear on the same lists as those of the Microsoft resources.

The UNIX world has its own set of protocols and utilities just as NetWare does. Microsoft has included these utilities in their native formats to enable users to share files and printers with members of the UNIX world. The good news is that these utilities are fairly well standardized across the UNIX world (unlike some of their components). You therefore have a good chance of being able to communicate with servers from a wide range of vendors. The key utilities from this world include the File Transfer Protocol (NT can act as a server listening for requests and a client making the requests), telnet (which enables NT computers to log on to UNIX servers), and printing (via the LPR/LPD protocols). These tools are not as convenient as those for Novell networks, but they get the job done and match up well with the UNIX and Internet standards.

The Macintosh world is still very important to many organizations. Apple was fairly healthy and having good sales when NT was being born, so Microsoft put in a reasonable support package for the Mac world. These services include file sharing and printer sharing. These are the main services provided by Macintosh networks. As with all the compatibility options mentioned previously, the nice thing is that if you do not have Macintosh computers, you do not have to waste disk space or server processing capacity to load this compatibility option.

The final compatibility option is the one that costs extra. Yes, many vendors figure that if you have the money to pay for a mainframe, you can pay extra for connectivity software. Perhaps that is not the only reason, but the fact is that SNA Server is one of the BackOffice components discussed later in this book and it is not bundled with Windows NT. It provides some very powerful capabilities related to terminal emulation, file transfer, and job execution in that mainframe world. It also takes into account the fact that good connections to the mainframe are limited. SNA Server lets you funnel your mainframe requirements through the SNA Server product to make more efficient use of that big blue computer.

There are a number of other interesting features that help you integrate NT computers into your existing computer environment. (There are so many topics to cover and so little time to cover them.) Take a look at Figure 7.8, which shows the conceptual picture of how all the various compatibility features work together to enable you to integrate NT into diverse network and computer environments. Most of these tools work well, and some are almost invisible to the user once the system is configured.

FIGURE 7.8.
Windows NT compatibility features.

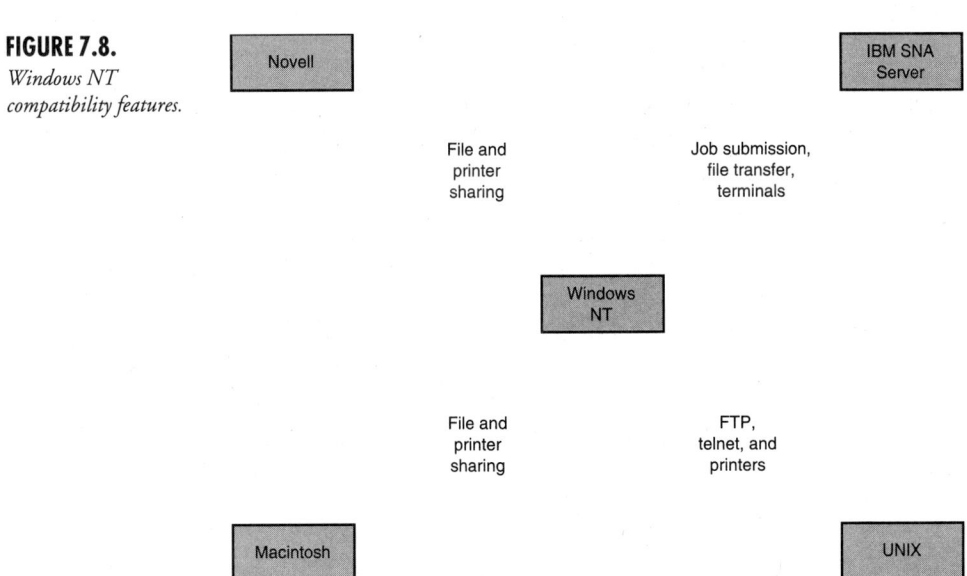

The Registry

One feature that was not mentioned on the previous main list of services, but that should be covered in this chapter, is the registry. One of the major configuration problems with the old Windows environment was the number of configuration files that were available. The idea behind these configuration (or INI) files was basically good. There were a number of ways of setting up and using a given application. I may want to have the ruler turned on in my word processor, whereas you despise the ruler. Because it would be impractical to compile dozens of different versions of the software to match each combination of settings that might be possible, vendors started using configuration files to capture local preferences set using the options or settings menu pick that they built into their interface.

Worse than the number of files was the fact that they were scattered all over the disk drives. Being limited to eight characters for filenames, they also might even conflict between applications. You had to know on an application-by-application basis what the configuration files were, what their formats were, and where they stuck the stupid file. You also had to deal with the fact that a number of initialization files might be interacting with one another. The list of files that could be affecting you included (but was not limited to) the following:

- autoexec.bat
- config.sys
- win.ini
- system.ini
- Application initialization files
- Parameters set in the batch files that were used to start the application

It was also less efficient to read all these values from common text files. It takes some time and training for a computer to learn to read the file, line-by-line, figure out what parameter was being set, and then read the value located several columns away (translating text characters into numbers, and so forth). It was also somewhat risky because you had a lot of people who thought they knew what they were doing (notice the key word "thought"), who would go into these files and start tweaking values all around and then complain when the application stopped working. Just ask a tech support person—these configuration files were a source of many a trouble call.

Microsoft's solution to this problem was to use a database-like structure to store all the initialization settings for all the applications and the operating system itself. Better still, they enabled you to build settings for individual users. Because NT is a multiuser operating system, I would not want to use the settings that you prefer for a word processor. I had no choice when we had to share the initialization file, but now I get my own registry key. Several of the older configuration files (for example, win.ini) are provided for those applications that have not been modified for the newer Windows 95/NT architecture.

The registry is a tree view with multiple sections, keys, and parameters. You still face problems with people who have access to the registry and go in to mess up things. The good news is that you have just one place to look for the messed-up values. The capability of having named branches on the tree enables you to locate the appropriate set of values. One word of caution: you can seriously harm your system if you make incorrect changes to the registry (you can delete services, and so forth). Be sure that you know what you are doing before you start editing the registry. Windows NT does provide a graphical tool to interact with the registry known as `regedt32`. Figure 7.9 shows the basic registry editor display.

FIGURE 7.9.

Registry Editor.

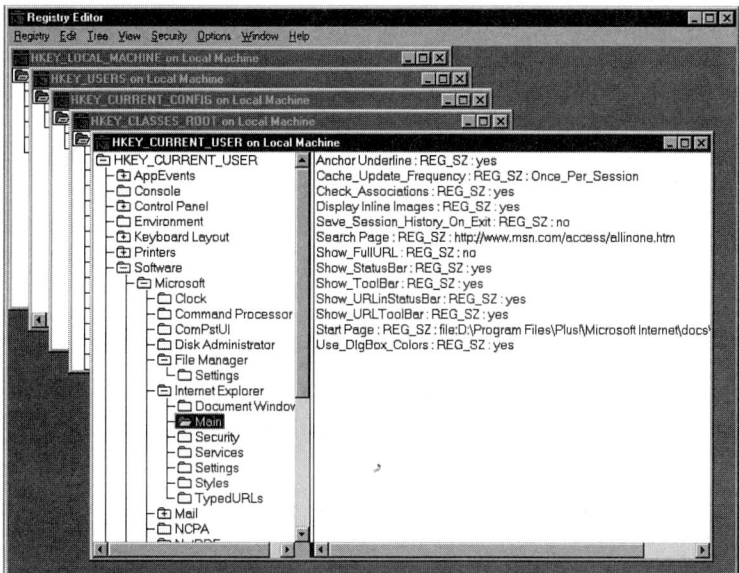

Versions 3.51 and 4.0

Computer vendors normally use the first digit in their product numbers (the 3 in 3.51, for example) to designate major releases of their products. Because it looks so different from the previous version, it was appropriate to designate Windows NT 4.0 as a major release of the product. In working with this product, I find that they have done a lot—not just on the look of the user interface, but on making it easier to use.

What does this new release encompass? A lot of work was put into the product, and I'm sure that there are many behind-the-scenes items that took more work. However, my list of the highlights of NT 4.0 when compared with NT 3.51 includes the following:

- The user interface is changed to match that used in Windows 95. The first thing that is noticeable is that you now use the entire desktop as your workspace. You are no longer confined to the Window or functionality provided by Program Manager. You also have a toolbar across the bottom of the screen that enables you to use the mouse to switch between applications that are running quickly. The interface also uses a number of pop-up menus that are activated by right-clicking the mouse on the object of interest. This menu calls up a number of functions, including the properties page, which is a tabbed dialog that enables you to set all the properties without popping up a sequence of simple dialog boxes.

- The Internet Information Server is bundled as part of the NT 4.0 Server operating system. This product provides you with a World Wide Web server, an enhanced File Transfer Protocol (FTP) server, and a Gopher server (used, in the days before the Web and its search engine services, to locate information that is stored on the Internet). As mentioned earlier in this book, the fact that this product is bundled as part of the base NT Server operating system gives you a clue as to the amount of emphasis that Microsoft is placing on Internet-related products in its future plans.

- Much of the graphics display system is rewritten, (which caused vendors to make substantial changes to their device drivers). These changes are designed to enable use of many capabilities first seen in Windows 95 for video, animation, and games. The goal was to leverage these tools, many of which are designed to help support activation of Web pages and similar initiatives. The goal was to ensure that Windows NT had at least the same capabilities as other operating systems.

- Almost all the user administrative functions are centralized within the User Manager tool. In 3.51, you had to use a number of tools including the RAS Admin tool to configure all the settings related to a user's account.

- A number of the tools in Control Panel are improved to provide you with a more extensive, yet easy-to-use, system configuration capability. Significant improvements in this area include using tab dialog boxes for property settings and wizards to walk administrators through the process of creating new objects.

- The dial-out modem software is modified to match more closely the Dial-Up Networking features of Windows 95 (they even changed the name to Dial-Up Networking). Now, Remote Access Service (RAS) is used for dial-in processing, and Dial-Up Networking is used for outgoing calls.

- You have a recycle bin that is used to collect files that you delete. You have the option of restoring them if you make a mistake. You also have the option of emptying the recycle bin, which permanently removes the files from your system.

- You can place shortcuts to applications directly on your desktop. You can also create folders on your desktops that map to data directories, hold shortcuts, or even hold applications that you can open.

- A World Wide Web browser is bundled with the operating system. This tool is used to enable you to surf the Web, looking at sites that contain information of interest to you. As a point of reference, the Web browser technology is being integrated into the basic user interface of the next release of NT.

There are a lot of good changes in NT 4.0. Many users have tested it and say it is faster; some others complain that it is a little slower for some of their applications. The good news is that although it does not look very much like the NT 3.51 product, it still has the same basic architecture and functions. It is just a little easier to work with for administrators and users. Other than the look and feel, I tend to think of it as an evolution in the Windows product line, rather than a revolution.

Summary

This chapter covered a lot of material. Its goal was to provide you with an overview of a rather complex operating system, emphasizing its strengths. This chapter covered all the Windows NT Server features, which is quite a challenge in this limited space. It did not cover the details of any given feature, because that discussion fills an entire book (check out *Windows NT Server 4.0 Unleashed* from Sams Publishing). Here are a few summary thoughts on the operating system:

■ It combines the power of a server with the ease-of-use of a GUI-based personal computer.

■ It integrates the network directly into its environment and makes accessing network resources almost as easy as accessing local resources.

■ It has a reasonable level of security that is not intrusive into the business of the average user.

■ It has a powerful set of utilities that enables it to work with a wide variety of operating system environments, including Novell NetWare, UNIX, and Macintosh.

■ The two versions of the product, Workstation and Server, enable you to load and pay for what you need. At their cores, the two products are almost identical.

Computer Network Overview

by Joe Greene

IN THIS CHAPTER

CHAPTER

This chapter focuses on providing an overview of computer networking as it is implemented on Windows NT. As mentioned in the last chapter, networking is an important built-in feature that Windows NT provides both for itself and for other BackOffice components. Because all BackOffice components are extremely dependent on networking, this is a very important feature. Because there are so many different types of networks that are common in modern business environments, it is important to understand all the options that Windows NT provides so that you are ready at implementation time.

This is also an important topic to get under your belt before you begin the server planning exercise in the next chapter. Many of the decisions that you will have to make are relatively straightforward (do you need a database management system or a Web server, for example). The network decisions that you will be asked to make are a little tougher. For example, the decision on whether to install a particular network protocol or service depends on your application plans or the needs of another dependent network service. Therefore, you need to be at least familiar with the ideas of computer networks, if not comfortable with them.

PC-Based Local Area Networks

PC-based local area networks grew up somewhat differently than their mainframe, minicomputer, and larger server cousins, and this has some effect on where they are today. The earliest PC networks were built to share expensive resources, such as printers, with one another. They also provided the capability of sharing files. They were not asked to perform cooperative processing between applications or provide convenient directory services.

Based on these rather simple needs, many early networking standards evolved. NetBEUI was among these early standards. It is important to consider when it was designed when we look at these utilities today and note their limitations when it comes to modern uses. For example, NetBEUI is a somewhat limited and problematic protocol to use if you are implementing client-server database connections. It was never designed for that purpose. It also is not designed for routing between networks.

Functions Required of a Network

This section challenges you to think about what you are asking a network to do for you. Although this list could go on for pages and you might think up some unique needs that you have come across, here is a list to start you off:

- Provide a means to transfer information between computers.
- Provide a way of finding out the addresses of the other computers on the network, to enable people to use easy-to-remember ways of addressing these computers.
- Provide support tools that help administrators build and configure these networks.

- Provide support tools that monitor the status of the network.

- Provide a means of isolating traffic flow between networks that have been connected together by passing only that information that the receiving network absolutely requires.

- Provide tools that enable you to control the processing of other computers.

I'm sure that you can come up with some additions to this list. However, it should get you started thinking of the functions of a network. The designers of Windows NT and networking in general have thought through this list and come up with a number of products and standards that can be used to meet these needs. As with many things in the computer industry, you are blessed with a wealth of alternatives, and the challenge comes down to determining which alternative to choose. The section after next discusses these options to help you with your decisions.

Interfacing Applications to a Network

Before you get into the network details (at least the level of details that you can get into in a single chapter), let's explore how applications interface to the network. If the NT networking utilities provided service only for Windows NT, they would be of little use. To leverage their investment in networking technology to the large number of applications that are available, Microsoft has published a number of standard APIs that enable developers to use the services of the network. The most common use of networks by applications is accessing the file and print services that are provided by the operating system. However, there are an increasing number of applications that use more sophisticated interfaces that transmit data between programs or even use functions of applications that are running on one computer directly in an application that is running on a different computer. The key from an administrator's point of view is understanding which of the many forms of interface were used in your applications (for example, SQL*Net from Oracle, which interfaces directly to the TCP/IP, IPX/SPX, and NetBEUI protocols) and what that requires from you in terms of support.

Networks Supported by Windows NT

Let's start by going over what makes up Windows NT's integrated networking. Previous chapters have covered some of the technologies at the technology level (such as NetWare services and FTP). This section is devoted to presenting an integrated picture of the networking components and how they fit together. Perhaps the easiest way to start this task is with a picture (see Figure 8.1).

FIGURE 8.1.

*Windows NT
networking overview.*

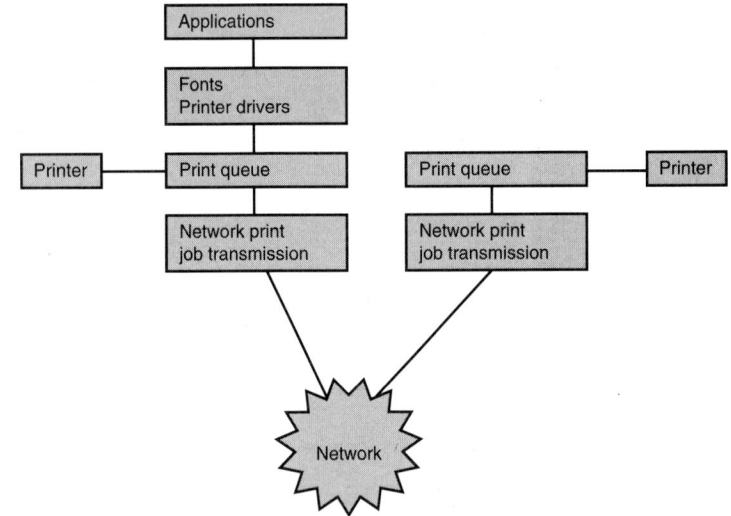

You need to understand these components and how they fit together before you can start configuring your network. The basic goal is to get data from a user application (such as Explorer or a client-server database application that you develop locally) to the networking wire running out of your machine. For purposes of this discussion, I divided the networking hierarchy into three components:

■ *Services and programs.* This layer is a series of services that handle the high-level functions that users and applications require. Examples of services are File and Print Sharing for Microsoft Networks. Windows NT Server also has some services that run in the background and are available whenever they are started (even if no one is logged in to the server console). Examples of these services include the FTP server or the remote procedure call server. Finally, there are a series of applications that are run in the foreground that provide specific networking services, such as checking to see whether other TCP/IP computers are available (Ping) or logging into a remote computer (Telnet).

■ *Protocol.* This is the language and format of the communication signals. This really gets into some dirty, gut-level communications parameters, but for the purposes of most system administrators, all you have to worry about is that you are using the same protocol on all machines with which you want to communicate. You should be careful with NT, which enables multiple protocols to be available at a given time, to ensure that you have the appropriate protocols for all the applications and remote machines supported by your NT server.

■ *Adapter.* This is the device that connects the logical signals that you formed in the protocol portion of the hierarchy to the physical wires (or electromagnetic emissions, because there are some wireless networks out there) that connect your computer to other computers. Windows NT considers a modem to be a network adapter (although it also provides additional control panel icons to set it up completely), and you also have to set up protocols and services for the modems.

Standards Implemented in Windows NT

The key to connecting workstations together for network communications is standards. Of course, the industry has a number of players who think that they are, by definition, the standard. (I am not just talking about Microsoft.) Therefore, your ability to connect to other workstations is limited by the standards that your computer supports. Fortunately, Windows NT supports a wide range of computers through its built-in networking protocols and services. Because almost everyone is building operating systems that connect to the Internet, TCP/IP is the most common communications protocol in use today, and Windows NT supports it as part of the standard delivery (no extra products or options to buy).

Therefore, before you go into the actual configuration procedures for Windows NT networking, it might be helpful to review the list of options that you have that relate to network standards. These standards include not only the protocols that you will use to configure your network, but also several interface standards that will enable applications that you purchase to interface with the NT networking services to communicate with remote systems:

■ TCP/IP protocol for communications with the Internet and UNIX worlds.

■ NetBEUI protocol for communications with traditional Microsoft networks, such as those under Windows for Workgroups.

■ IPX and SPX protocols, which enable communications with Novell NetWare networks using their own language (not a gateway or interpreter).

■ Remote Access Services (a Microsoft standard) enables you to dial in from compatible Microsoft remote computers to your server and from your server to other Microsoft remote computers (such as Windows NT and Windows 95).

■ The Telnet program enables you to connect to remote servers (such as UNIX computers) that have a Telnet server active. You effectively become a terminal on that computer through this program.

■ FTP services enable other workstations that have FTP to connect to your workstation and your computer to connect to other FTP servers.

■ Remote procedure calls (RPCs) enable you to execute programs on other computers that support RPCs.

■ Named Pipes enables you to connect two Windows applications to communicate.

■ Open Database Connection (ODBC) enables client-server applications to communicate with databases for queries and results.

■ Object Linking and Embedding (OLE) enables applications to communicate with and use one another in a cooperative fashion. OLE can be used for simple functions, such as embedding a spreadsheet in the middle of a document, or complex functions, such as communications between a client application and a database server.

Working with the standards listed are dozens of other lower-level items, such as the Ethernet and token ring transmission standards associated with a given network card. However, for purposes of this discussion, the preceding list can be thought of as a basic laundry list of services that you would install under Windows NT networking. These standards make it easy to integrate Windows NT servers and workstations into existing networks. This is especially true of the Netware connectivity and TCP/IP (hence UNIX) connectivity components. You might still have to work out the details of the connection, but it is a good start to know that communication is possible and relatively easy in the NT environment.

Common Networking Protocols

Many of the acronyms in this chapter end in the letter P, which usually stands for protocol. I like to think of a protocol as an agreed-upon standard that ensures that I can communicate my information with others. This section focuses on a specific set of protocols that determine who can receive your signals on the network. These transmission protocols set standards that enable computers on the network to determine whether the packets are intended for them and then determine what should be done with the information.

There are entire books devoted to the details of these protocols from Sams, and the Windows NT Networking Guide in the resource kit provides more detailed discussions on protocols. I have chosen to focus this section on providing an overview of these protocols that covers the information that a system administrator (not a network engineer) would want to see:

- An overview of the history of the protocol
- The basics of how the protocol transmits signals
- A discussion of the pros and cons of this protocol

TCP/IP

Let's start with a discussion of TCP/IP. What is it that makes TCP/IP an important protocol for today's system administrators? It is the protocol that drives the Internet, for one thing. It is also a protocol that can be routed (signals sent only to those network segments that need them as opposed to being broadcast throughout the entire network), which keeps overall network traffic loads down. It is also a robust protocol that incorporates transmission reliability features and a capability of interfacing applications to sockets for specialized forms of communications (that is, FTP or client-server database communications).

The TCP/IP protocol was originally developed by the United States military and it was soon adopted by universities and other government agencies as a standard. A large boost came when the Berkeley UNIX world started to emphasize networking and adopted TCP/IP as its standard. Over the years, the Internet, and its protocol suite, have developed a sort of life of its own. There are working groups composed of industry experts and concerned users who are working to evolve the standards to meet the new requirements that are ahead. An example of this is the work being done to address the issue of the rapid expansion of the Internet, how additional addresses can be made available, and how to improve traffic routing.

Recall that the acronym TCP/IP stands for Transmission Control Protocol and Internet Protocol. My rough distinction between these two is that TCP handles the details of the message, and IP provides an easy-to-use route address for each computer. There are a number of other standard supporting protocols that are grouped into the TCP/IP family in common practice. Examples of this include Ping to see whether a remote server is responding to the network or FTP to transfer files between computers.

From the system administrator's point of view, the pros and cons of this protocol include the following:

- It is the most accepted protocol in the world. Almost all major computer operating systems support this protocol. A huge suite of software (from Internet Web browsers to client-server database tools) is built to use this protocol.

- It is robust enough to support demanding communications. For example, it is extremely difficult to get reliability and performance for client-server database communications in the Oracle database management system using NetBEUI, but things work very smoothly under TCP/IP.

- You can route TCP/IP, thereby segmenting your network into segments that carry only the traffic that is applicable to their users. With a well-defined set of application-specific interfaces (sockets), you can control what type of traffic is allowed on a network segment. This is one of the keys to security devices such as firewalls.

- It is a multipurpose transmission protocol. Therefore, it is not optimized to simple file and printer sharing services, although it gets the job done.

- It requires a fair amount of configuration work to get everyone talking to one another. You absolutely need a plan and control mechanisms before you implement a TCP/IP network.

NetBEUI

NetBEUI sort of falls at the other end of the spectrum in terms of standardization and robustness. Windows NT uses the NetBEUI Frame (NBF) protocol, which is an extension of the old NetBIOS Extended User Interface (NetBEUI) protocol. IBM introduced NetBEUI in 1985 to support its PC network communications. It was intended to be simple and optimized for simple network functions, such as printing and file sharing, which are common to PC networks. NBF's main enhancement is that it enables you to have more than the 254 sessions that are permitted under NetBEUI.

When NetBEUI was invented, this seemed a very reasonable limit for local area networks. A more telling limitation is the fact that NetBEUI was not designed to provide reliable connectionless communications. The Windows NT Networking Guide provides an interesting discussion of this topic, but it basically means that it does not get a confirmation that the message has made it to the sender. This is not a big problem for a print job (if you do not get your printout, you resend it), but it could be a severe problem for a large financial database transaction sent over the network.

The summary of pros and cons of NetBEUI, as viewed by systems administrators, include the following:

■ It cannot be routed. Therefore, you cannot segment your network without losing the capability of communicating between certain computers or using another protocol such as TCP/IP.

■ It is small and efficient for the tasks that it was designed to accomplish. Most of your basic workgroup and small domain processing fits into this category.

■ It is supported on a wide range of Microsoft and IBM PC operating systems (which make up the majority of computers installed today).

■ It is not robust enough to handle demanding messaging needs such as client-server database transactions.

■ It is really simple to configure and would be a good choice for a small, simple local area network.

IPX/SPX

IPX/SPX is the protocol suite that forms the basis for the majority of Novell NetWare installations that are available today. Novell has recently provided you with the option of using TCP/IP for your Novell network. Recall that IPX stands for Internetwork Packet Exchange. It is designed to have a low overhead and is optimized for local area networks. SPX (Sequenced Packet Exchange) functions like NetBIOS for IPX/SPX networks. It is connection-oriented (both sides talk to one another about the transmissions they are making).

As with the previous two protocols, there are books on the subject that can take you into the details of the packets, addressing, and so forth. However, the key points to take away from this chapter about IPX/SPX are the following:

■ It is the most common way to interface with Novell NetWare networks.

■ It is a routable protocol.

■ It is a fairly robust protocol and able to handle some more demanding network applications.

■ It is small and efficient for the types of communications it was designed for (file and print sharing).

■ It is simple to configure.

Choosing Your NT Networking Environment

As with most Windows NT components that are integrated with the operating system, networking is configured using the Control Panel, which can be accessed with the My Computer desktop icon or from the settings option of the start menu. As you can see in Figure 8.2, there are a number of Control Panel icons that relate to networking: FTP server, modems, ODBC, services, and the one that we are interested in for this chapter—Network. This icon is the key to setting up your networking functionality, and you need to complete this setup before you can set up the other functions.

FIGURE 8.2.

Windows NT Control Panel and Network icon.

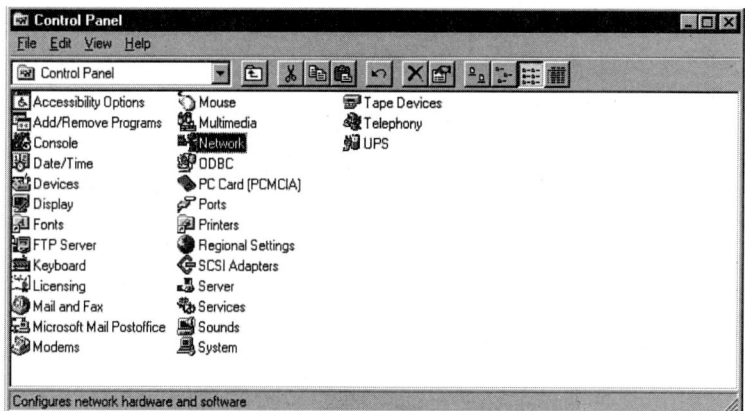

When you double-click on the network icon, you are presented with the new Windows NT 4.0 setup panel (see Figure 8.3). Based on my observations of Windows NT 4.0 and Windows 95, Microsoft seems to be moving heavily toward the tabbed dialog interface for configuring items, so it would be useful for you to get comfortable with this interface. It is relatively simple to work with; there are a number of tabs across the top, each of which corresponds to a data entry or display panel with which you need to work. The items that are being configured are listed in a window similar to the one showing network adapters in Figure 8.3. The plus sign indicates that if you click the icon, you will get an expanded list of items that are associated with the item that you just clicked (an expanding list). Finally, there are a series of buttons (such as Add and Remove) that enable you to perform the allowable actions on the list.

The tabs correspond to the items in the hierarchy discussed earlier in this chapter. In this case, you build your network from the bottom up, starting with the adapters. Next, you select the protocols and then the services. To connect all this, use the Bindings tab dialog. Finally, an identification tab enables you to specify how your computer is identified on a Microsoft network. Each of these tabs builds on the others to form the complete network picture, so you have to work with all of them to set up your network.

8

COMPUTER
NETWORK
OVERVIEW

FIGURE 8.3.

Network setup panel.

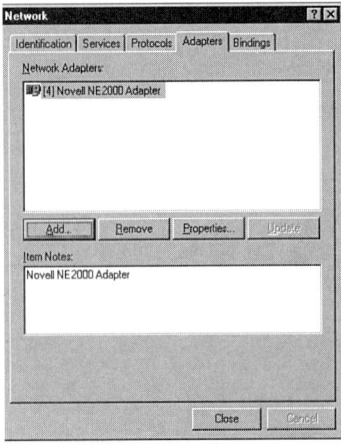

When you set up networking, you are probably going to have to reboot your computer after you finish entering the new settings. This is because networking is tightly integrated into the operating system itself. At the end of the setup, you will receive a prompt that asks whether you want to reboot the system now. I like to choose a time when I can do the reboot immediately after my work so that I can check to see whether everything went okay. (A little mistake could deactivate your client-server database connection, for example.) As another example, if I clicked the wrong button (Yes) when prompted for the reboot, the system would shut down and restart. Therefore, I do not do this work on a production server during production hours. Users of a network-based computer system get really sensitive when their server is down unexpectedly.

One of the features that some people were hoping for in Windows NT 4.0 was what Microsoft and others refer to as Plug and Play. Unfortunately, that will not be completed in this release. Under Windows 95, the system has a reasonable chance of recognizing the existence and type for a large number of cards and peripherals that you might connect to your system. It will then take you through a series of wizards to set things up correctly (you hope). It is not perfect, but it makes life much easier when it works.

Network Adapter Setup

Under the 4.0 version of Windows NT, you still have to manually tell the operating system what components you have installed. Therefore, you start the networking section with the network adapters. You might be thinking that Windows NT 4.0 is more like Windows 95. Even though modems are part of networking under Windows NT, they do not show up as a network adapter the way they do under Windows 95. However, you will find bindings to the RAS wrappers later in the network setup, so RAS is not a totally separate subsystem.

Let's look at the options in the Adapters tab on the Network Setup panel (refer to Figure 8.3). As you can see, it lists my network adapter. It lists multiple network adapters and enables you to configure each of them individually. If you add a new adapter to your system, you click the Add button on the Adapters tab of the Network Setup panel. NT then presents you with a list of adapters that it supports (that are distributed on the Windows NT operating system CD) and enables you to choose one of them, as shown in Figure 8.4. This list is not very long when compared with that of Windows 95, for example, so it is important to check that your adapter is supported by Windows NT *before* you buy it. If it is not one of the ones that Microsoft provides drivers for on the NT operating system CD, you can use the Have Disk button to enable NT to read a disk or CD drive that contains drivers given to you by the manufacturer.

FIGURE 8.4.

Select Network Adapter dialog box.

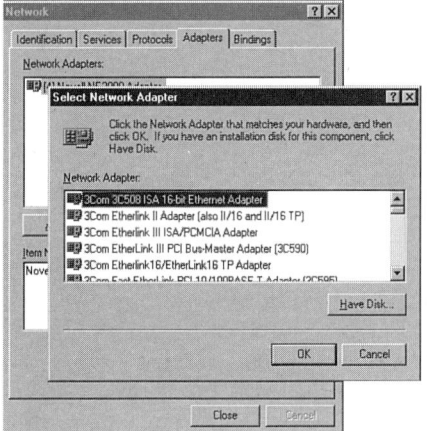

Once you select the adapter that you are going to use, you need to configure it. Here is where all that hardware stuff can be a challenge for an operating system type who just wants to get things up and running quickly. The various adapter manufacturers have different ways to configure an adapter. Some use jumpers located on the card itself, others use software utilities that will enable you to set it up programmatically. Whatever the method, you may have quite a challenge in front of you to select settings for this network card that do not conflict with other hardware components that you might have installed, such as serial ports, drives, or sound systems.

There are two key addresses that you need to worry about when setting up an Intel-based machine, which is the most popular platform for NT by far. The first address is known as the IRQ level, which is also referred to as the interrupt number. It is one of 16 addresses that are available to get the attention of the operating system at the hardware level. You may think that 16 is a lot of addresses, but the machine that I am typing on has all 16 addresses used up between network cards, modems, a sound card, and the motherboard itself (which takes up 4 or more addresses before you put the first card on the system). The next address is usually referred to as the I/O port address. It is a section of the memory of your computer that is used for transferring data from the various installed cards and components.

When you buy workstations based on the MIPS or Alpha architectures, they usually have fixed addresses for their various components, and your task is to figure out what these standard addresses are and just use them. The unfortunate part of the Intel world is that the operating system fixes a couple of addresses for such things as the system clock and then throws the rest up for grabs—with only some suggestions as to what should be used for what purpose. To make matters more complex, certain peripheral devices support only a few of the many possible combinations of IRQ and I/O port addresses. You need to have this worked out before you start working on your server or schedule plenty of time to try out all the possible combinations. Finally, don't feel bad if it takes a while. I have found several machines that, no matter what combinations we tried, we could not make certain components work. We had to replace them with others that were more compatible with the other components in the system.

NOTE

The NT Diagnostics tool on the Administrative Tools menu can provide some insight into the resources in use by your computer.

Let's return to the actual configuration task itself. You will be asked to set the addresses and possibly some additional configuration parameters for the adapter that you have chosen. You may choose poorly and be informed that your networking services did not start up because of some addressing conflict. Your task is to then adjust the settings of your adapter card, both through its jumper settings or setup utility and through the Network Setup panel. On the Network Setup panel, you select the Adapters tab and then choose the Configure button. You are presented with a panel similar to Figure 8.5, which enables you to alter the settings.

FIGURE 8.5.

Network adapter configuration settings.

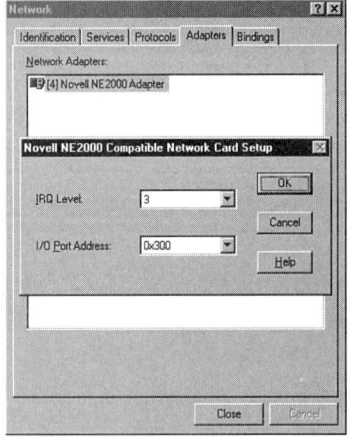

Perhaps you have gathered from the tone of my writings that this can be a very frustrating part of setting up a system. I can always tell those in my group who are setting up the hardware on a computer system, because they stare intently and furiously at the monitor—or yell at their systems (I dread the day when they yell back). There are a few tips that may help when you are trying to get through the installation and configuration of hardware:

- Keep all your hardware manuals and read them.

- Look at the boards that have jumpers and record what their settings are.

- Make a chart that shows the addresses used by your various system components so that you can figure out what is available.

- If you are really stuck and comfortable with Windows 95, try installing Windows 95 on this machine first to see whether the setup wizards in Windows 95 can figure out a workable combination of settings for the hardware in your machine.

After that, you're working a puzzle to see whether you can get all the pieces to fit together.

Network Protocol Setup

The next step in configuring your network is to decide which protocols you need to support. Usually, you will have these dictated to you by corporate standards, places you need to connect to, and so forth. There are a few general suggestions for you to consider when deciding:

- If you might be using the Internet, you need to load TCP/IP.

- If you are going to be doing a lot of client-server database work, you should seriously consider using TCP/IP or IPX, not NetBEUI.

- If you need just a simple Microsoft network, NetBEUI is probably the easiest protocol to set up.

- If you are going to be coexisting with Novell NetWare systems, the IPX/SPX protocol is needed.

To set up protocols in your system, you will use the Protocols tab on the Network Setup panel (see Figure 8.6). The nice thing that you will notice is that it looks very similar to the previous Adapters tab. That is the real benefit to this common interface for properties settings. Basically, you have to add protocols from the list of available protocols (you can even add protocols from third-party manufacturer disks, but I have never had to use more than what is provided on the NT distribution CD). The complexity comes in when you configure the protocols. NetBEUI is relatively simple to configure and IPX/SPX usually works with the minimal default settings (see Figure 8.6). However, TCP/IP usually requires some work to get running properly.

FIGURE 8.6.

Protocol setup.

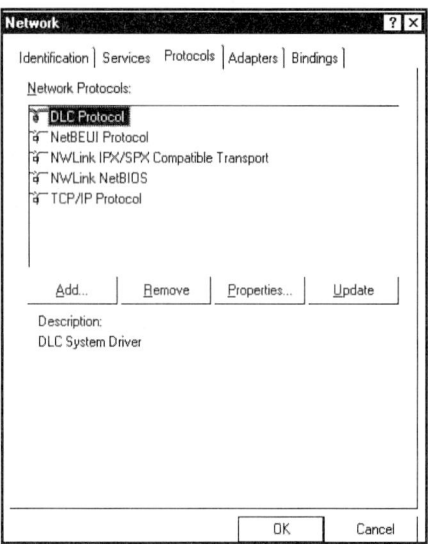

The reason that TCP/IP is so complex to set up comes from some of its ambitious design goals. It connects millions of computers worldwide through a logical network made up of many thousands of other networks. To make this all work together, software and hardware vendors have built up a scheme started by the United States military that enables you to map the hardware address (the ethernet address, which is a set of hexadecimal numbers assigned by the network card manufacturer) to a set of numbers that correspond to your organization (the Internet address or IP address). Therefore, the first key to remember is that an IP address is your key to getting on the Internet, and therefore all the TCP/IP software is designed to work with this address (even if you do not plan on surfing the Internet).

Figure 8.7 shows you the panel that will pop up when you configure TCP/IP. It is far more complex than the protocol setup panel and also requires that you understand a little about the fundamentals of TCP/IP systems before you can answer all the questions. There are a number of considerations that you use in making your decision, but here are a few of the more common ones:

- IP addresses are made up of a series of four numbers (bytes often referred to as octets) ranging between 0 and 255 that are separated by periods (such as 123.123.123.123).

- If you are on an isolated network that you do not intend to connect to the Internet, you can make up your own addresses (by convention, you should use addresses in the 10.*x*.*x*.*x* range). Keep all the addresses that you want to communicate with one another starting with the same first number.

■ If you are on a network connected to the Internet, you have to have someone (usually in the network group) who parcels out official addresses. Otherwise, they are coordinated by someone responsible for your local network.

■ The subnet mask parameter is designed to help you ignore addresses that are not of concern to you (outside of your group, and therefore the responsibility of a gateway if you have one). The subnet mask is a bit pattern comparison (255 in one of the digits means that the address incoming has to match, and 0 means let everything in this digit pass). For example, 255.0.0.0 as a subnet mask means pass everything that has the same first number as my address and reject everything else.

■ Gateways are computers or network devices that enable you to communicate outside your local network to the bigger world. When you define a gateway (or multiple gateways), TCP/IP traffic that is outside your subnet mask is routed to the gateway(s) to see whether they can resolve the address and transmit the information to the remote computer. You may actually go through a series of gateways when transmitting to distant computers.

■ Domain name servers are computers that enable you to use text names instead of IP addresses to describe remote computers. These are officially assigned names that are coordinated through the various Internet agencies and reflect the purpose and country in which the computer is located. (For example, aol.com references America Online; com identifies it as a commercial organization, and the lack of a country suffix indicates that it is in the United States.) Windows NT can act as a domain name server or use it to translate IP names for your users. You can have primary and backup name servers in case one of these computers is unavailable.

■ WINS stands for Windows Internet Naming Service, which enables you to enter the IP addresses for your local computers and have other computers use these central lookup tables to translate a name into an address. This product now works with DNS to resolve names on networks with both local and larger scopes. Again, NT can act as a WINS server or use its services.

■ The routing tab determines whether your workstation will forward packets it receives that are intended for other TCP/IP computers that it can communicate with (that is, act as a router). This can be useful if you have multiple networks and want to use one of your servers to forward traffic and connect the two networks, but transmit only those packets that need to cross between the networks.

Suppose that you want to keep things simple and get a basic TCP/IP network up and running. You do not plan on getting on the Internet. What I usually do is specify an explicit set of IP addresses similar to those shown in Figure 8.7 (the 10.*x.x.x* family is reserved for internal assignments). I set the simple subnet mask of 255.0.0.0. I then set up a special file used by most TCP/IP configurations known as the hosts file (which is a local file that resolves names to addresses similar to the WINS and DNS servers).

8

COMPUTER
NETWORK
OVERVIEW

FIGURE 8.7.

Configuring the
TCP/IP protocol.

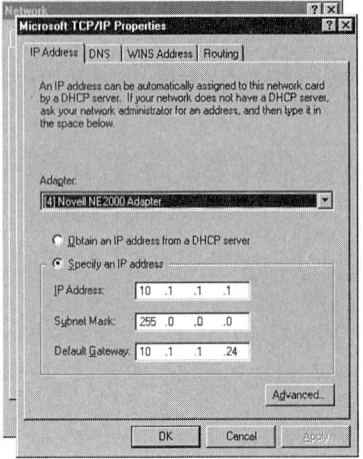

Let's look at a sample hosts file. It is a simple mapping between an IP address and a name that is easier for people to type. As you can see, it would be impossible to maintain this table for the millions of people on the Internet, but it works well in small workgroups. You need to place this file under your Windows NT directory in the system32\drivers\etc subdirectory. (Mine is in d:\winnt35\system32\drivers\etc because I upgraded to 4.0 from 3.51.) This file should also be distributed to all clients so that they can work with these easy names:

```
# *****************************************
#
# File:       hosts
# Purpose:    Capture TCP/IP Configuration
#
# Revisions:
#
# 9/1/96      File created (Joe Greene)
#
# *****************************************

127.0.0.1           localhost jbgreene
193.9.12.13         BIG_SERVER
193.9.12.45         SMALL_SERVER

# *****************************************
# END OF FILE
# *****************************************
```

There are a lot of additional considerations with TCP/IP networking. The key to remember is that every computer that is running on a TCP/IP network at a given time should have a unique IP address. When this type of network is set up correctly, it runs well and provides you with connectivity and service that is hard to beat.

NOTE

You can run into severe addressing problems if you do not get a unique, officially assigned IP address and you connect to the Internet. Your Internet Service Provider should be able to help you to contact the correct addressing authority.

Network Services Setup

So far, you have laid the foundation for networking, but you do not have much that is useful to the end-user. For those of you who labored hours to set up a working IRQ setting on your network card, this may not seem fair. However, now you get to install the services that will enable your network to be used by the end-users to get things done. I have found the services to be relatively simple to set up and configure once the networking basics are out of the way. You start with the Services tab of the Network setup panel (see Figure 8.8).

FIGURE 8.8.

Network Services setup.

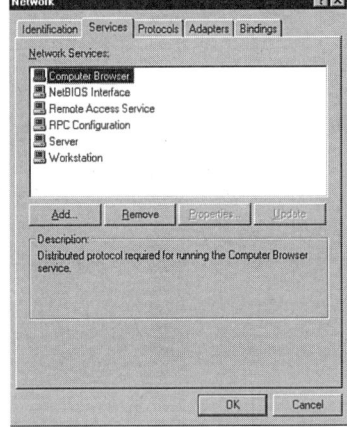

To add to the services that you have installed, choose the Add button. It gives you a list of available services and the option of adding additional services from separate CDs or disks (the magic Have Disk button). The most difficult task is understanding what services are available to you (and there is quite a list of services that come off the operating system CD):

■ Computer Browser enables you to see a list of computers that are available on the network.

■ NetBIOS Interface is the basic interface to the Network Basic Internal Operating System.

- Server enables your machine to act as a network server.

- Workstation provides the services that you will need when using your server as a workstation.

- BOOTP Relay Agent was the predecessor of DHCP. Use it if you already have such a network; otherwise, stick with the newer DHCP service. (You never know when they'll drop support on older products.)

- FTP Server enables your computer to provide access to its files to other computers using the file transfer protocol common to UNIX and other computers.

- Gateway (and Client) Services for Netware is your door into the world of Novell NetWare, providing you with file sharing, print sharing, and other common Novell services.

- Microsoft DHCP Server, the dynamic host configuration protocol, enables your computer to act as a master repository for IP addresses so that you do not have to assign them manually to each computer.

- Microsoft DNS Server enables your computer to act as a TCP/IP domain name server.

- Microsoft TCP/IP Printing enables your computer to use UNIX TCP/IP print job transfer services (LPR/LPD).

- Network Monitor Agent enables your computer to perform basic monitoring on the network.

- Network Monitor Tools and Agent provides tools to enable your computer to monitor the network via the Simple Network Monitoring Protocol (SNMP).

- Remote Access Service is the modem interface under Windows NT that enables you to dial in to the server.

- Remoteboot Service enables your server to serve as the boot drive for remote computers with compatible remote boot software.

- RIP for Internet Protocol enables your computer to route TCP/IP traffic between segments on your network (that is, act as a router).

- RIP for NWLink IPX/SPC Compatible Transport enables your computer to determine routes for IPX/SPX (Novell) traffic on your network.

- RPC Configuration enables you to execute remote procedure calls (a standard way of executing jobs on other computers in the UNIX world).

- RPC Support for Banyan enables you to execute jobs on computers using Banyan networks.

- SAP (Service Advertising Protocol) Agent enables remote computers to determine the network access points on your computer.

- Services for Macintosh provides you with a gateway into the world of Macintosh AppleTalk networks.

■ Simple TCP/IP Services provides you with the basic services that you need to participate in a TCP/IP network (many other services require this service before they can start).

■ SNMP Services enables your server to provide basic operational information on load, availability, and so on, using the Simple Network Monitoring Services protocols that can be read by a number of monitoring packages.

■ Windows Internet Name Service enables your server to resolve IP addresses for clients on your network.

Many of these services are just installed. There are no configuration chores that you have to perform on them. Those that do require some form of configuration are presented with a panel similar to Figure 8.9 that is specific to that particular service.

FIGURE 8.9.

Remote Access Setup panel.

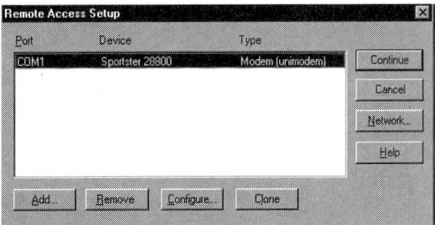

As you can see, there is a wide range of services available under Windows NT. The key to something that is implemented as a service is that it will be a background process that is in continuous operation once started, which usually occurs at system startup. Therefore, it is available even though there are no users logged in at the console and running programs. They are essential to Windows NT Server 4 being able to serve clients on the network.

Network Identification Setup

After the long discussion of options when setting up TCP/IP networking and the many services available under NT server, it is refreshing to see a relatively simple tab on the Network setup panel—the Identification tab (see Figure 8.10). This tab sets what other computers on the Microsoft network will see when they are looking for computers. The key components are Computer Name, which is just a unique identifier for the computer that should make sense to everyone else in your workgroup or domain. The next box for workgroups is your workgroup name. (You are asked to identify your domain if you chose the Domain option when setting up your Microsoft network.) The workgroup and domain names are names made up by administrators to refer to a particular group of computers. In the domain environment, it has special meaning in that you can teach domains to trust one another and grant privileges to members of other domains. If you are looking for a more detailed discussion of domains and workgroups, the Windows NT Networking Guide in the resource kit provides some good material.

FIGURE 8.10.

Network Identification.

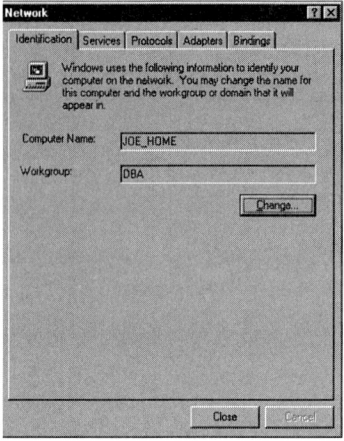

Network Bindings Setup

So far, you have explored the various options that are available when you set up networks. Now consider the possibility of setting up multiple network adapters and remote access services that use different sets of protocols and services, and perhaps even different configuration parameters for those protocols and services. It may seem like an unusual setup to some, but I have run across several examples of this being needed. A classic example is a server acting as a gateway between two network segments. You may have Novell and TCP/IP machines on one side, which your network administrator has assigned the IP address range of 123.123.1.*xxx*. The other network segment might have Microsoft networking (NetBEUI) and TCP/IP clients, but they use the IP address range of 123.123.2.*xxx*. In this manner, you can isolate and balance network traffic between different network segments. You use the adapter configuration tab to set up the IP addresses for the two adapters, but you then have to use the Binding tab (see Figure 8.11) to configure which protocols went where.

There are three ways to sort the list of bindings. The one that you choose depends on how you think of things and what problem you are working on. As you can see in Figure 8.11, I have linked the TCP/IP protocol to my network card and the Remote Access Server. If I wanted to remove this connectivity or add in additional connectivity, I would use the Enable and Disable buttons. Be careful where you are when you start disabling bindings. The key is knowing what protocols, services, and adapters depend on one another to ensure that you do not disable other things that you want when you disable a particular binding.

FIGURE 8.11.

Network Bindings.

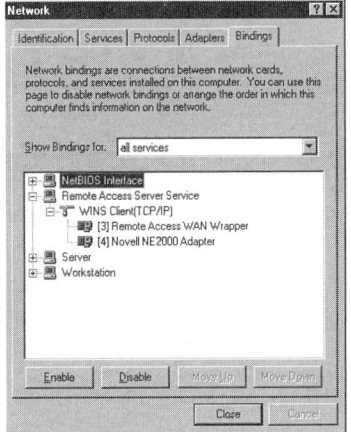

Remote Access Service (RAS)

Under Windows 95, dial-up networking (the modems) is considered an integral part of networking and is set up pretty much the way you set up any other adapter. Of course, the modems have their own property pages that take into account the unique setup parameters of a modem (all the bit settings and whether you have to display a terminal screen before and after dialing a number). Windows NT 4 server has not quite embraced this philosophy yet. Although you do bind the network wrappers (between the computers connected with the modem to computers connected via your network cards) using the network setup panel, you do most of your other work setting up these connections using the Modem option on Control Panel. The actual modem connections and privilege setup (who can dial in, for example) is set up through the Remote Access Administration utility accessible from the Startup Menu, Programs selection, and Remote Access Service selection (see Figure 8.12).

The first thing that you need to set up RAS is to have a modem properly configured. This might involve some of the same painstaking work described previously for network adapters (such as getting drivers loaded for your modem and resolving IRQ/memory addresses). Figure 8.13 shows you the basic modem setup screen. You have to add a modem type that is supported by Windows NT 4 (again, see the hardware compatibility list or get an NT 4 driver from the modem vendor). You then have to identify a communications port to which that modem is mapped (yet another address when dealing with serial communications devices on Intel PCs).

FIGURE 8.12.

Accessing the Remote Access service utilities.

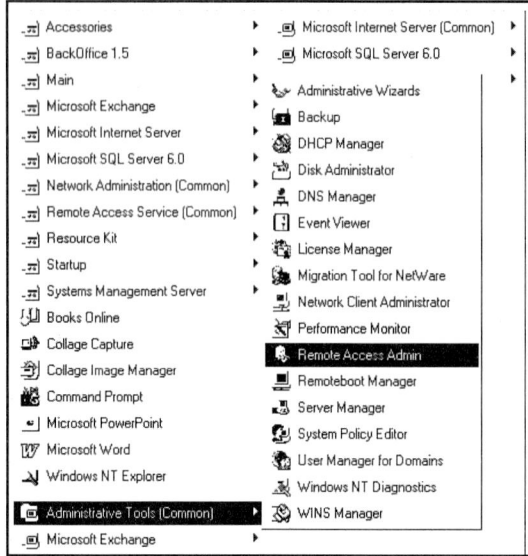

FIGURE 8.13.

Modems configuration panel.

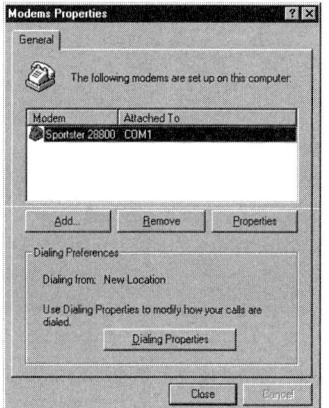

Once you have your basic modem set up, you may have two additional panels to set up. The Properties button gets into the communications details (see Figure 8.14) associated with the modem and its connection (speed, speaker volume, and all those bit settings common to modem communications take the defaults whenever you can on these items). The Dialing Properties button enables you to set up the details of dialing, such as whether you need to dial 9 to get an outside line.

Once your modem is set up, you are ready to use the Remote Access Admin utility that is located in the Remote Access Service program group on Windows NT 3.51 and the Administrative Tools Startup Menu group under Windows NT 4.0. This utility is based on a pull-down menu system that enables you to perform the following useful services:

- Start or stop your remote access service (such as stop picking up incoming calls). Note that you might need to do this to allow other applications to access your modem because RAS tends to monopolize the modem even when it is not actively processing a call.

- Grant permission to users to dial in from remote locations.

- Show users who are currently connected to RAS.

FIGURE 8.14.

Modems Properties panel.

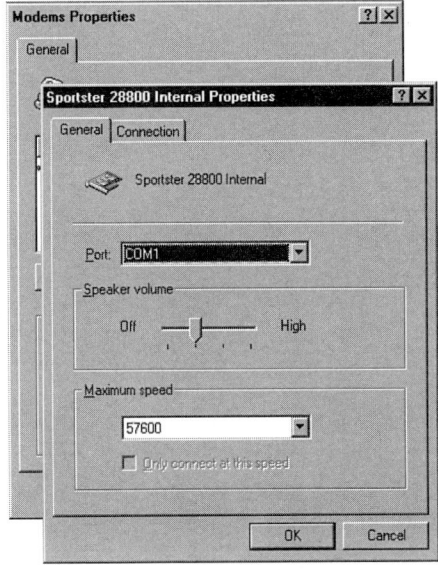

With the number of people who are accessing networks from remote locations (other groups that you work with or *road warriors* who travel a lot), RAS connectivity and modem pools are an important part of the Windows NT networking architecture. After having set up similar functions under UNIX and earlier versions of Novell, the RAS configuration is relatively simple and very reliable. I have set up my home PC to dial in to the server and perform functions ranging from simple file transfers from my work PC to interacting with client-server databases using ODBC. If you have a modem, take some time to learn how to use it as a remote administrator. It could save you a trip to work in the middle of the night when your server has a few problems.

Useful Networking Utilities

One of the challenges with working and providing services in a network environment is that most users see only the end result. For example, they install new client-server applications on their PCs and complain that they can't access the database that is on your server. What is the problem? (I can't tell you how many error messages read something like, "I couldn't talk to the server.") Recall that the many layers and bindings involved have to be set up correctly on both ends to make communications happen. You also have to worry about logon IDs and passwords being set and used correctly to provide access to resources that are password-protected.

With all the things that can go wrong, I like to follow some basic checks from the client end to troubleshoot problems.

If anyone has trouble accessing the server, you can try it from your workstation using the My Computer icon or File Manager. (Note that File Manager and Explorer enable you to enter explicit network paths that may be available, but somehow the network browsing function does not detect when you look at the available nodes.) You can also use the NET VIEW command at the command prompt (NET VIEW \\joe, for example). This proves the server is up and accepting at least NetBEUI communications.

If you are troubleshooting a TCP/IP link from the user workstation, go to the DOS prompt and type ping followed by the IP address of the server. If this works, you can try the ping command with the name to see whether your problem lies in the name resolution process. Together, these utilities test the basics of TCP/IP networking on the server.

The tools that are available depend to a high degree on your environment. However, if you keep the fundamental principles in mind and start testing the various types of communications from the lower levels (such as ping and File Manager) and then work your way up in the chain (such as ODBC connections or trying to access a shared directory using the user's logon ID and password), you can usually spot the problem. If all else fails, try doing the same things using the user's logon ID from a similar workstation in the same area and see whether that clears up the problem.

Summary

This chapter covered a lot of information in a short span of pages. It showed you the broad range of networking functions that are built in to the Windows NT operating system. Coming from older environments where everything costs extra, it is impressive to look at this list of standard features. These features are made available to your applications, especially the network-dependent BackOffice suite, to enable them to accomplish their objectives.

Planning a Server

by Joe Greene

IN THIS CHAPTER

CHAPTER 9

The preceding chapters have laid some groundwork of both the BackOffice family and the Windows NT environment. It's now time to get into the actual implementation of the BackOffice family of tools on your servers. What I am suggesting in this chapter is that you spend some time planning your server before you begin the implementation process. I have found that it usually saves time to do some planning up front.

Overview of Server Planning

Server planning is a process that is somewhat dependent on the preferences of the person who is doing the analysis and the standard methods employed in a given organization. For example, government agencies usually prefer formal written analysis documentation and recommendations that follow a standard outline format. In the business world, many companies prefer interactive briefing slides that enable you to present the concepts to management for approval. What I stress here is not the delivery format, but the tools and techniques that you should consider when conducting an analysis for your server.

In Figure 9.1, I summarized the basic process that I recommend as a baseline on to which you can add local preferences. It merges information gained during requirements gathering with technical requirements of the software components and budgeting to form the basis of an analysis. It also builds directly into the process the concepts of expansion planning. An important concept is that of revisiting the plan on a routine basis. With the current pace of changes in the computer industry, few plans are good for more than a year or so.

FIGURE 9.1.

Basic requirements analysis process.

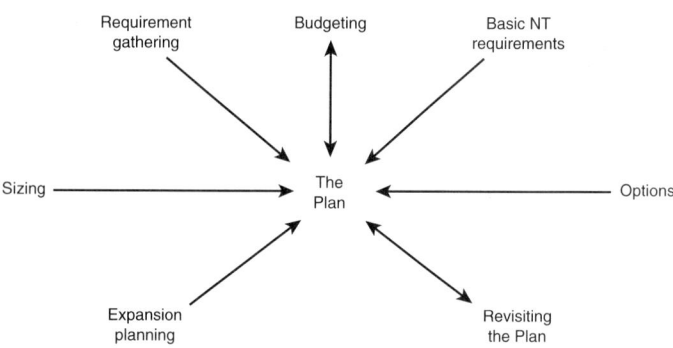

Some other processes and techniques that you might want to consider during your planning process include the following:

- *Preliminary analyses to reserve funds.* Sometimes the beginning of the entire planning process is a quick analysis that is used to justify funding requests. There are no detailed user requirements analyses, just a general mission statement and rough cost.

- *Preparation and approval of engineering and program change documentation.* In formal organizations and government contracts, you may have to go through quite a process to get your equipment ordered.

■ *Involvement from outside consultants.* Some organizations listen to outsiders better than they do their own people. In these cases, it is sometimes important to get a consultant to perform portions of the needs analysis or concur with your recommendations.

■ *Team formation and analysis.* Some organizations form teams or committees to study everything and make recommendations. In these cases, you have to go through the process of forming the group, making assignments of tasks and then fusing together the various opinions into a unified recommendation.

There are a number of other options that could pop up. Although I could not think of or document all of them, I think that what I have listed previously is a good start. It gives you an idea of what is involved with the process and lets me get on to my next several topics that provide you with a few thoughts on the steps in the planning process.

Requirements Gathering

It's always risky to start out assuming that you understand everything that is needed with regard to a computer system. Perhaps you are in such close contact with your users and have already discussed the subject so many times that you already know their opinions. However, if you are not in a small group where you have a lot of direct communication with all your users, you might want to consider taking some time to gather your requirements. Some techniques that can be useful in this process include the following:

■ *Brain storming sessions.* These usually take the form of meetings where you invite users and other players to come in and present ideas. The key concept of brain storming is that you do not criticize ideas or try to take each of the ideas to the detailed design stage. Instead, you just let people express their opinions and write them down for further analysis. It may seem like a somewhat chaotic technique, but some of the most interesting and amazing ideas come out when people start to loosen up and think freely.

■ *Guided analysis sessions.* Many organizations have more formal processes used to rapidly build useful designs for systems such as software applications. There are a number of terms for this process, such as joint application development (JAD). The key here is that there are trained facilitators who go through a formal, tested process to get information out of the key players and use that information to fuse a design that can be implemented. It may take some time to adapt your process to system designs, but it is something that you might want to at least consider.

■ *Open request for suggestions.* Perhaps you do not have time for formal sessions. Perhaps your users are scattered so far across the building or even across the world that it is impractical for you to convene a meeting with them. One solution might be to use existing technology and send out either a memo or an electronic mail message asking them for their input on the requirements for the new server. It is not as personal as a meeting, but at least it gives them a chance for input.

- *Group design sessions.* Another technique that you might consider in the design process would be group design sessions. More limited than guided analysis sessions and more focused on analysis and results than brain storming sessions, these meetings can bring together the key technical, managerial, and even financial players to work though various alternatives to nail down the requirements for the system and maybe even work out the parts list for the order. It is a good technique when you have to get players in from a number of groups within the information systems community such as the network group, the operations group, and so on.

- *Iterative designs.* The final technique that I want to throw out for your consideration is that of the iterative design. Some people want to sit down and, in one massive session of brain power, nail down all the details and produce a design that is absolutely perfect. Others have trouble getting anyone to provide you with input because they are just too busy or have a meeting or some other distraction. A technique that can be useful in these cases is to just make up a design with what input you have and send it out for people to review. You have to balance statements that you are looking for help and advice with statements that say that this design will become final and the system will be ordered if no comments are received by a certain date.

One feature of the requirements gathering process that I want to stress is that of making the users and other technical support groups feel as if they are part of the process and have input on the alternatives being discussed. People tend to be resistant to change. This feeling is heightened if they feel something is being shoved down their throats—something they didn't help plan. Motivational theory types talk about things such as feelings of ownership and having others buy in to a play. It could be a small representative sample of people from different groups. All I know is that I get a lot more help and fewer complaints from users when they have at least had representation in the planning process.

Basic NT Requirements

There are some requirements that you have to factor into the system planning process that users and even other technical support groups cannot help you with. Those requirements are levied from Microsoft and other vendors when they design their products. Here are a few tips on collecting these requirements and factoring them into your planning process:

- *Web pages.* Back in ancient times (which was actually just a few years ago), I prided myself on the collection of vendor literature that I maintained. I religiously gathered and filed the information that I gathered from conferences and vendor briefings. I sent in a lot of vendor literature requests from magazines to get data on products that might be of use in the future. While I still keep some of this information, there is a much better source today. Most computer vendors (and even other companies) have built World Wide Web servers that contain a wealth of up-to-date product literature. The better sites go beyond salesman talk to provide detailed technical specifications, white papers on their technical architectures, and other such information. It has the benefits of being an on-demand system (you do not have to collect it until you need it) and also being much more current than a paper document (that you might have had for six months or so—an eternity in the computer world).

■ *Technical specification sheets.* Many vendors put out sales literature that uses a lot of terms such as better, strong, and faster. They talk about how they can work with a wide variety of products in a wide variety of computer environments. While this may be interesting literature that contains impressive art work and color coordination, you cannot do any design work on a new NT server unless you have technical specifications. You have to look for the little detail such as how much memory is required when running the product in the NT operating system, exactly which versions of the operating system and supporting products will work with this product, and so on. With some vendors, you have to get down into some low-level details to find things such as the fact that their product is certified to run under NT 3.51, but if you install NT 4.0 all bets are off.

■ *Hardware compatibility list.* Microsoft does a lot of testing with products to ensure that they will work properly in the NT environment. Remember that for a device to work on NT, there has to be a compatible device driver for it. You could trust hardware salesmen who are trying to make a commission when they tell you that their printers work wonderfully with NT, but I tend to feel better when a third party comes in, performs a structured test, and then tells me whether or not the product is compatible. Microsoft does test products and certify which ones it considers compatible with Windows NT. They publish these results routinely. The best place to get hold of this information is on the Microsoft Web site (start at www.microsoft.com and follow the links to the Windows NT product and find the hardware compatibility list). The latest version is always up there, and it is a reasonably lengthy download. I cannot stress enough that you have to ensure that a device is NT compatible. There are a number of PC hardware vendors who have targeted the DOS/Windows/Windows 95 market and have not bothered to write drivers for Windows NT.

■ *Check into all products.* It is the little things that often get you in the technical planning process. I would recommend that you be as thorough as possible and check out every product that you plan on putting into the environment. If you have a magnificent system and all of the software that you need, but you have chosen a CD-ROM drive that is not supported by Windows NT, you will not even be able to load your operating system.

■ *Know which requirements are additive.* When vendors list requirements, they often give numbers for amount of memory in the system and amount of disk space. You have to be careful to know which of these specifications are additive and which ones are just totals. For example, if you buy a database management system for NT, you will usually see a specification of, say, 24M of RAM. This is a total requirement that covers the needs of the database and the operating system. It does not cover memory needs of an electronic mail server such as Exchange Server, for example. It's best to ask a lot of questions when reviewing this material in order to save yourself from running into problems later.

9

PLANNING A SERVER

- *Look for references and real-world configurations that are similar to the one you are proposing.* When all is said and done, vendor literature can be confusing. It is almost always targeted to helping the vendor make a sale. One of the things that makes me feel better is when I can see a real-world system configuration that resembles the system that I am planning. If you can talk to its administrators and users to find out what they like and what they would change, you get the benefit of hands-on experience. On any complicated system design, you may want to try to get your vendor to provide you with a reference or show you one of their systems that is similar to the one on which you are working.

- *Prototype a system whenever possible.* One technique that can be useful if you have a few extra resources lying around is prototyping. Here you would get loaner hardware, software, or both from vendors and actually build a miniature version of the proposed system. You not only get the benefits of verifying that all of the annoying things such as version numbers and parameter files get worked out in advance, you also get experience on the installation process before you have to do it for real. I always feel better if I have had the time to build a prototype before placing a large order. Many vendors are very cooperative on this process, especially if you are placing a fairly large order or could be useful as a reference to them.

Budgeting

Now is the time to get serious. People can be easygoing when it comes to talking about requirements. However, when it comes time to pay for them, they often start to ask the serious questions and look for hard answers. Because budgeting processes often involve management styles and organizational cultural issues, I cannot guess all of the hoops that you might be asked to jump through. What I can offer are a few suggestions that you might consider when preparing to go through this process:

- Prepare a list of alternatives and costs.
- Structure whole alternative solutions (for example, the high, medium, and low cost alternatives).
- Link all purchases to customer/user requirements (it provides justifications up front and documentation in case the decisions are questioned later).
- Document the vendor selection process work that you have done.
- Give people rough estimates early on and then continue to refine those estimates.
- Always start out with conservative estimates and then start cutting costs.
- Always factor in some safety margin.
- Always factor in budget for growth.
- Do not forget to consider costs, such as training (user training, support staff training, conferences, and so forth) and outside consultants if you need them.
- Ensure that you have a budget for local staff time, even if it not charged directly.

Sizing—Metrics and Advice

When I discuss performance tuning in Chapter 12, "Windows NT Performance Tuning," you will see that one of the most difficult topics in performance tuning is knowing when a particular resource is overloaded. The same can be applied to your sizing analysis. How do you know the number of users that a particular computer can support when running Exchange Server and SMS? My solutions to this problem include the following:

- Prototyping can be quite useful to check performance on the actual architecture with which you are working. Remember to factor in some stress tests where you run a large number of jobs at the same time to try and simulate a production environment. Also, you can find tools on the Web or supplied with vendor products that are used to simulate higher loads on their products.

- Check with any fellow system administrators who are running similar systems. Remember that they have to have a somewhat similar configuration to make their advice more meaningful.

- Post a question on an Internet newsgroup to see whether they have some opinions on the subject. You have to look closely at the response to make sure that the sender knows what he or she is talking about, is working with a similar configuration, and is not a vendor trying to sell you something.

- Look at vendor literature for other client configurations. They will often include success stories from clients who have previously purchased their products. You can look at their configurations and compare their loads with your loads. Often you can even call the reference to get questions answered.

Considering All of the Options

One of the things that I cannot stress enough is that you should work hard to consider all of the options when planning a system. This not only includes purchased products, but options selected with the NT operating system itself such as which network protocols you want to use. It is much easier to make these changes when everything is still on paper, as opposed to having a production server that needs to have some changes made. Some of the changes that you might want to make could involve serious amounts of work. For example, if you want to convert an NT server from a workgroup server to a domain controller (either primary or backup) you have to reinstall the operating system. You cannot just load some magical domain configuration file and reboot. Heck, it is hard enough to get time on production servers to perform even minor maintenance. Major upgrades like this are often almost impossible to schedule.

Preparing a Plan

Eventually the talk will subside, and it will come time to actually prepare a plan. This plan takes a number of different forms from a set of notes that you make to yourself, a purchase order, a written plan document, or even a set of briefing slides for management. Whatever the form it takes, there are a few principles that I recommend you follow when you write the plan:

- Do not start with a list of what is to be purchased unless you anticipate absolutely no questions. It is usually best to start with business requirements to get agreement on what is to be accomplished. You can then move through the process that you used to prepare the design, alternatives that were considered, and then the final recommendation.

- Have backup slides or appendixes that provide alternatives if you anticipate that people will be asking for them.

- Have someone else who has both at least a rough user and technical understanding similar to your own review the plan before you publish or brief it.

- Use a format that your organization is used to. If you come up with a new presentation format, people may be concentrating on trying to figure out where the information is as opposed to listening to your ideas.

- Get to the point and avoid long discussions. You can lose people's attention. If you really want to put in detailed analyses, consider using appendixes or backup slides.

- Consider coordinating your presentation while it is still in draft form with key users, managers from the various groups being supported, or even other technical staff. It is much easier to make changes early on than when you are in the final design review.

Expansion Planning

I know of very few places where the computer processing requirements are stagnant. Technology marches on, prices continue to fall and users continue to want more. Many places double the power of their computer complex every couple of years. Some places experience almost meteoric growth and their computer staff is tasked to keep up with it. What I would argue here is that you should plan for growth as part of your basic plan for a system even if the users did not state it in their requirements to you. A few of my thoughts on the subject follow:

- As a rule of thumb, plan a system that can at least double in capacity for such things as disk storage, memory, and so on. The cost of having a few extra slots on the motherboard is small compared to the cost and labor involved with swapping out the entire box for a new one six months down the line.

- Consider purchasing computers that support multiple CPUs. Windows NT supports multiprocessor configurations. Although we have proven techniques to double disk storage and memory in a system, we usually wind up replacing the entire box when the processor capacity is exceeded. A system that can take a second processor chip is a good expansion alternative for NT.

■ In the PC world, purchase computers that allow you to replace the CPU with the newer, faster models that will be coming out. The Zero Insertion Force (ZIF) socket is a standard that allows you to easily change computer chips.

■ Always consider banking requirements when planning out memory configurations. Electronics engineers usually design memory slots such that they are arranged in pairs that must contain chips of similar size and speed. Therefore, you may not be able to build a 24M configuration from three 8M memory modules. You may have to use two 8M modules and two 4M modules, which may take up all your memory slots. If you wanted to upgrade to 32M, you would have to throw out (or give to another user) the two 4M modules and replace them with two 8M modules.

■ Consider building test configurations that match those of your users in terms of hardware and software. You can use these workstations to ensure that the configurations will support the new hardware and software that you plan on deploying in your organization.

Revisiting Your Plan

Plans do not last forever. With all of the new technologies and industry directions that are changing almost every day, it is impossible to construct a plan that will endure. It is useful then to actually include as part of your plan a step to review it in the future on a routine basis to make sure it is keeping up with requirements and technologies. This may not be acceptable in some organizations. Some managers may rather foolishly conclude that you are just not capable of planning properly and that is why you want to change your plan on a routine basis. Others, however, will understand that this is an evolutionary process and appreciate this step.

Perhaps it is not possible to present plan revisions as "changes." So sell your plan as a short term implementation to get to a given state. In Chapter 13, "NT Integration with NetWare and UNIX," you explore performance tuning and how this is a continuous process in which you keep up with demand. Perhaps that will be a more acceptable means of presenting the reality that computer needs change very rapidly.

Summary

This chapter was not designed to cover all the things that might affect you when planning out an NT installation. There are so many factors that are unique to your organization, and only you could guess what they are. Also, it cannot be a single product checklist because these products are changing at a rapid pace and you need to make your analysis based on the current information. I recommend that you get Web access, because the Web is one of the most useful tools that I have come across to get current information about the computer industry.

This chapter presented some overall considerations based on my experience. Although my points may be obvious to some of you who have experienced planning out systems, I find that there are a lot of people who get thrust into the role of planning a system who have never done this task before. Few get formal training on this process in universities or on the job.

Setting Up Windows NT

by Joe Greene

IN THIS CHAPTER

Windows NT is a very robust operating system. I have found that it will give many wonderful hours of service with minimal attention, once you have it set up properly. This chapter is devoted to that tricky subject of getting NT installed and configured properly. Don't get me wrong; we are not talking about magic or dumb luck here. We are talking about engineering discipline and basic problem-solving skills. It often takes patience, as you have to try multiple combinations and wait many minutes in between tries as your server reboots itself so that you can see the results of your actions. Eventually, you will have experience, which can help you to avoid most of the more common problems.

Some of you may feel disgruntled. Why should it be so hard to install an operating system? Why can't Microsoft make it so that it is easy? The complexity lies in the wide variety of products in the PC world. Everywhere you look there are a number of computer vendors out there making every product imaginable. They do a lot of good things to push technology forward and keep prices down. However, sometimes their innovations call for some changes requiring alterations to the operating-system device drivers that interface them to the operating system.

Although change can be good, it does pose a problem for those of us who are just trying to get and keep our computers operational. These vendors usually come out with drivers for the mass-produced operating systems such as Windows 3.1 or Windows 95. However, these vendors have not always come out with Windows NT drivers. Part of this is due to the fact that Windows NT has never had the millions of users that Windows 3.1 or Windows 95 has. The other part came from the fact that the Windows NT drivers are somewhat different from the Windows 3.1 drivers that vendors were used to and had programmed with.

The recent rise in Windows NT popularity may help to ease this lack-of-drivers problem. However, in the near term, you have to deal with the fact that Windows NT does not have drivers for every imaginable device that you may install in your computer. So how do you get around this? The answer comes in the form of the hardware-compatibility list provided on the Microsoft Web page and some sound planning. This chapter is devoted to a final review of the plans that you have made and then takes you through the installation process.

Ensuring that Everything Is Ready

The key to a successful installation is having a sound plan. You probably have guessed my feelings on choosing compatible hardware (yes, I have mentioned it many times so far). There are also a few other things that you should consider when you look at your plans that will help you along the way. This section is devoted to providing a final checklist and an example of an installation plan for your consideration. The topics that I thought to include are as follows:

- The hardware list
- The software list
- The basic security configuration
- Network configuration
- Shared resources
- Users and groups
- The installation procedure chosen
- The checklist

Let me start off with the hardware list. You already know to verify that there are software drivers for the version of Windows NT that you are working with for all of your hardware devices. A general suggestion when configuring a server is to stick with the more common hardware items, especially in the server environment. You do not typically have the large number of servers that you do with workstations. Therefore, saving a few hundred dollars by picking out less commonly used components for a server will not save you all that much money. However, it could cost you a lot of time and money when it comes to getting these uncommon components to work with the Windows NT server. You do not have to be extravagant and only choose the most expensive components. Just try to pick parts that are very common in the NT server environment (for example, Adaptec SCSI controllers and US Robotics modems) if you can at all justify the costs. Honestly, I am not working as a representative for the bigger, more expensive product vendors. I am just relaying my experiences with trying to integrate no-name products into an NT-based server.

The next task in front of you is to develop your software list. This list is composed of the optional Windows NT components (for example, the Internet Information Server), other BackOffice products (such as Exchange Server), and third-party products that will be installed on your server. You will have to choose which disk drives to install the products on. This can be a significant factor in overall system performance—for example, splitting indexes and tables on different disk drives can provide significant performance improvements for database management systems—so you need to consider this carefully in consultation with other administrators (especially the database administrator) and perhaps even users. This list should reflect options that are to be selected with the products and also the order in which the products need to be installed.

Your next big decision (and this is a big one) is the security configuration of your new server. As I mentioned earlier, you cannot just switch between a workgroup server and a domain server. You would have to reinstall the operating system and do a lot of configuration work to get yourself back to a working system. The factors in favor of choosing the domain environment are easier maintenance, if you have a number of servers, and also the fact that many BackOffice components are prodding you in the direction of domains. It could also be important to choose the domain architecture if you want to use some of the remote-administration tools that are available for Windows 95 and Windows NT workstations (one of which might be located on your desk and thereby save you from having to do all of your work in the computer room).

Your next decision is what your network configuration will be. This includes the basics as to which protocols you will be loading and how each of these protocols is configured. If you are using TCP/IP, you will have to obtain a list of legal IP addresses for your network. If you are planning to be connected to the Internet, you will have to obtain an official set of IP addresses from an NIC. If you are just using a local network, then you or your network-operations staff will have to decide on the list of addresses. It can cause a number of strange conflicts if you have two PCs that are trying to use the same IP address, so spend some time sorting this out up front. Also, you have to decide on the optional network services (WINS servers, DHCP servers, and so on) that you will be installing on your computer.

Next, you should plan out which resources you will be sharing with your user community. This starts with the list of resources and which share name they are going to be using. Typical shared resources include directories (whose names change to "folders" under NT 4.0), printers, Remote Access Service permissions, and access to other applications (such as an Oracle or SQL Server database). You should also spend some time now deciding which groups and users will be allowed to access these shared resources, the hours of their availability, and so on.

Your next task is to decide what your user and group structure will be. It can start with a simple mapping of the groups. You can build on this with a more detailed explanation showing what the resource access privileges of the groups are. It is important to take some time up front to think this process out. It can be a challenge to change the group structures around after the fact; your users usually will have to log off and log back on to gain access to new group privileges, so this can be a pain if you are in a busy production environment. Getting your naming conventions (for example, your building designation or which department you work in as being part of the name) documented before implementing your network is much easier than after the fact.

A big task in the installation procedure is choosing how you will install NT. In the next section, I will present the various alternatives for installing Windows NT. Although you have the one basic idea that the Windows NT software is on a CD-ROM and you want to put it on your hard disk drive, there are several different ways of accomplishing this task. The method that you choose depends on which format you received the NT system in and the starting configuration of your server.

Finally, I would argue that it is useful in most cases to build a simple checklist of tasks and options before you begin the actual installation process. This does not have to be fancy or even word processed (although I type faster than I write so I would typically use a word processor). It should be a means that can jog your memory to ensure that all of the details are taken care of. It is also a form of discipline to ensure that you think of everything in enough detail to put it down on paper (some people think that they know what to do until they actually have to do it or write it down). So what would I consider a checklist to be? Figure 10.1 shows a sample checklist that I would consider a basic starting point (you can get fancier and more detailed, but this is a good beginning).

These are some of the basics to be considered before performing a general NT Server installation. In the installation chapters for the other BackOffice components, you will find additional pointers and planning steps that you will want to incorporate into this server installation plan for servers that contain these components. Third-party products (such as Oracle databases) also have their own installation needs, which must be factored into plans for their servers. The key point that I cannot stress enough is that you need to do a little planning up front to ensure that you have enough space on all of your disk drives, you have arranged data directories to meet your user needs and optimize performance, and a host of other issues. It can be very difficult to change the configuration of a server after it is turned over to the users.

Basic Installation Procedure

This section actually has two purposes. I first want to go over the alternative installation procedures that are available to you with NT Server. The different paths have advantages and disadvantages, so you should be aware of what you are doing. The next topic is the installation of Windows NT Server 4.0 using one of these scenarios. Will this be the exact scenario for you? Probably not exactly. Your exact path will vary slightly depending on the version of NT that you are installing and the configuration of your machine (both hardware and the network/optional products that you select). However, it gets across the basic ideas and will be useful when you perform your own installations. The chapters that have led up to this chapter were designed to prepare you to answer the questions that will come up (for example, which network protocols to use) in your specific installations.

FIGURE 10.1.

*Sample installation
checklist.*

Server Name: MAIL_CTR
Operating System: NT Server 4.0 Release
Planned Installation: 10 August 1996

Hardware: Micron P133 Tower
                        64M RAM
                        2 2G Seagate SCSI disk drives
                        Adaptec AHA-2940 SCSI controller
                        4X Micron SCSI CD-ROM drive
                        US Robotics Sportster 28.8 external modem (COM 1)
                        NEC Multisync 2V monitor

Software: Windows NT Server 4.0 Release
                        Microsoft Exchange Server 2.0
                        Internet Information Server 4.0

Security Configuration: Backup domain controller, MAIN_OFF domain

Shared Resources: HP4SI_MKTG (HP Laserjet 4SI in Marketing)

Users: Everyone in domain from existing domain list

Groups: Existing groups from domain list

Installation Process: Install from DOS without NT disks

Checklist:

___ Ensure DOS boot disk boots server and can access CD drive.

___ Boot with DOS disk.

___ Partition hard disks as follows:

        C: 500M
        D: 1500M
        E: 2000M

___ Format the logical disk drives.

___ Run winnt.exe from i386 directory on CD.

___ Complete installation option questions as specified above with the
     following parameters:

        Network name: MAIL_CTR
        IP address: 001.002.003.004
        Domain: MAIN_OFF
        IPX Frame Type: 802.3
        Windows NT Folder: c:\winnt
        IIS products: Web server only
        WWWRoot: d:\wwwroot

___ Verify ability to access CD-ROM drive after installation completed.

___ Verify ability to transfer files from the SNA_GATE server to verify
     network access.

___ Map connection to Marketing printer.

___ Install Exchange Server per installation procedure provided by the
     mail administrator.

___ Verify ability to add mail accounts using User Manager.

___ Have mail administrator review set up.

___ Load Web pages and other content provided by marketing.

___ Make server available for production.

Installation Procedure Options

So what are these installation options that you will be faced with? You may ask, "Why isn't being a system administrator ever simple?" Actually, the installation options are not all that bad, and they depend on two key factors: which installation media you received and the current condition of your server. Windows NT comes on CD-ROM media. Microsoft has given up on the idea of trying to distribute a huge box of disks that contain all of the contents of this rather robust operating system. It is not practical and I, for one, would not have the patience to change all of those disks. You can get a CD-ROM drive for a reasonable price these days, and it is worth it when you perform a massive installation such as NT. The only question is whether you received a set of disks with your distribution. If you received only the CD, then you will want to make a set of disks so that you can boot your server from these NT disks in case you run into any problems.

The second variable that will determine your choice of installation procedures is the current state of your server. If you are starting out with a blank computer, you will need to start from a boot disk, format the hard disks, and then install the operating system. If, however, you are upgrading an existing NT Server installation, all you want to do is install the new software. A slight variation on this theme would be a complete reinstallation of the operating system, which is required when you convert a workgroup server to a domain controller.

Figure 10.2 shows the installation options that I will be discussing. You might be able to think up some other scenarios, but the basic ones that I will be covering are the following:

- Installation from DOS without NT disks
- Installation from DOS with NT disks
- Complete reinstallation of Windows NT Server
- Upgrade from a previous release of Windows NT Server

Installation from DOS Without NT Disks

The first option, installation from DOS without NT disks, covers the situation in which you have a new server with empty hard disk drives.

To install from DOS without NT disks:

1. Prepare and check the DOS boot disk.
2. Boot the computer in DOS.
3. Partition and format the fixed disk drives.
4. Prepare the Windows NT boot disks.
5. Uncompress and load the NT files from the CD to the fixed disk.
6. Boot under Windows NT and the installation operating system.
7. Reboot under Windows NT for the final configuration.

FIGURE 10.2.

Windows NT Server installation options.

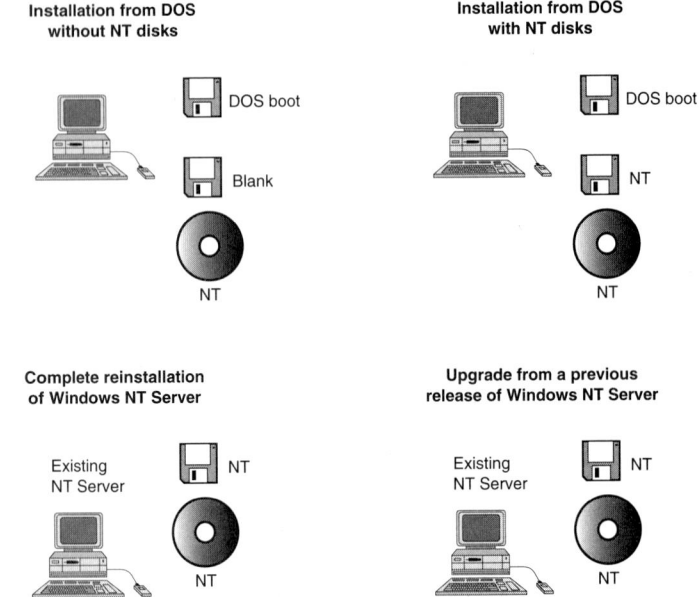

The first task that you might be faced with is preparing a bootable DOS disk that has CD-ROM support. This can be a bit tricky if you received the machine with Windows 95 or NT Workstation installed. Because these operating systems have their own CD-ROM drivers, you do not load the old CD-ROM drivers using the autoexec.bat file (which you could use to determine the interrupt settings and device-driver files you would need for your boot disk). Anyway, you can usually find all of the device drivers and put together a disk that can boot and access the CD-ROM. Test this disk thoroughly for its ability to access the CD drive before you begin the installation procedure. There are also a couple of key DOS utilities that I like to put on these boot disks:

- fdisk
- format
- edit
- attrib

Perhaps I am living in the past, but I like to have one of these boot disks for my computers. They boot a really simple operating system that I can use to access the computer. There is one complication, though. These DOS disks do not have drivers to read NTFS partitions. For this, you will need NT-based disks, which you have either received as part of your installation package or can make from your CD. Most of the box sets that I have received contain the disks, whereas distributions such as those of the Microsoft Developer Network usually contain only the CD.

Anyway, after you have the computer booted into DOS mode, you have to set up your disk partitions (using fdisk) and format your drives, if this has not already been completed by the manufacturer. This basic process prepares the drives to receive data. Note that these disks are formatted with the FAT file system. You will be given the option of upgrading from FAT to NTFS later in the installation process. When the drives are ready to receive data, you have to complete the following steps:

1. Prepare disks that can be used to boot the NT operating system.
2. Unload the operating system files from the CD-ROM to the fixed disk drive.
3. Boot under Windows NT, install the operating system files, and configure NT for operation.
4. Reboot under Windows NT and complete a few final configuration tasks.

All of these tasks are kicked off by running the winnt.exe file that is located in the appropriate directory on the Windows NT Server CD-ROM (\i386 for the Intel-based PCs). The first task is to prepare the disks that can be used to boot the NT operating system. This is not absolutely necessary for the installation process. You can use the command line winnt -b, which will install the boot files from the operating system directly to the fixed disk drive. However, if you ever run into problems with your fixed disk drives, you will want to have a set of bootable NT disks available to enable you to repair your operating-system installation. Of course, you may have a set of these disk provided to you by Microsoft, in which case you would use the Installation From DOS with NT Disks described in the next section. By the way, you can get a list of all the options available from the winnt.exe program by typing winnt /? at the command line.

The next task is to unload the operating-system installation files from the CD-ROM to the hard disk drive. These files are stored on the CD in a compressed format. Therefore, it takes a while for the computer to copy the files to the hard disk drive and uncompress them. This will make the next step go a little bit faster, but it can still take quite some time, especially for Windows NT 4.0. These files are copied to a temporary holding directory that is usually titled something like WIN_NT.~LS.

The third task is to reboot the system under the Windows NT operating system (at least the subset used for Windows NT installation). When you are running NT (either as loaded from disks or from your hard disk drive), you will be given a series of panels that let you select from a number of installation options. Key items in this configuration step include specifying where you wish to locate Windows NT and whether you want to use FAT or NTFS file systems (see the File System section in Chapter 7, "Windows NT Server Overview," for more information). After you have specified all of the options and have loaded, you will be asked to reboot the system for final configuration work.

The final task after this reboot is to perform a few more configuration options. Many of these options are prepared by *wizards*, which are software routines that examine your system to determine the hardware that is installed or other configuration options that make sense. This wizard

10

SETTING UP
WINDOWS NT

is not as detailed or extensive as the Windows 95 installation script, but it is getting close. After this process is completed, you will be asked to reboot the system once again. After you complete this reboot, however, you should have a functioning Windows NT operating system ready for all of the postinstallation configuration work such as adding users and loading applications.

A few notes on this process are in order. Loading NT from DOS may seem like a rather primitive process, especially when you can just boot from the disks provided by Microsoft (if you have them). It has the advantage of being the start-from-zero approach—which is needed if you lack boot disks or if you need to partition and format your hard disk drives. This is also the process you may want to use if the computer already has Microsoft Windows installed on it.

A final note on this installation process: the software that Microsoft provides with Windows NT enables you to start multiple operating systems on the same computer. This is an interesting "free" piece of software that is most often useful in the workstation environment. For example, you may want to run either Windows NT or Windows 3.1, depending on the task that you need to perform. Anyway, this software provides you with a menu upon startup that lets you select which operating system (or version of an operating system when you have multiple versions on the same system) you wish to run. It has a countdown that automatically loads the default operating system you designate after a specified period of time (useful when you are recovering from power outages or automatically reboot your system). The following is a sample of the boot.ini file (a hidden file located on your C:\ drive in the root directory) that is used to control this process:

```
 [boot loader]
timeout=5
default=c:\
[operating systems]
C:\="Microsoft Windows 95"
multi(0)disk(0)rdisk(1)partition(1)\WINNT="Windows NT Server Version 4.00"
multi(0)disk(0)rdisk(1)partition(1)\WINNT="Windows NT Server Version 4.00 [VGA
mode]" /basevideo /sos
```

Installation from DOS with NT Disks

This process is similar to the one already described, but you use the NT boot disks that came with your CD or that you made for a previous installation of NT Server. The key difference here is that if you have the Microsoft distribution disks, you do not have to make boot disks. This can save a bit of time as you have to wait while the disks are formatted and then loaded to nearly full capacity. The Microsoft-supplied disks enable you to load software from the CD to the hard disk, whereas the disks you make from the CD assume that this process has already been completed.

Upgrade from a Previous Release of Windows NT Server

If you have a previous version of Windows NT installed on your computer, you can save some time during the installation process. You can run the winnt32.exe file that is found in the appropriate installation directory on your Windows NT Server CD (for example, \i386). This executable enables you to make boot disks and load software from the CD to the hard disk drive at the same time.

The actual decision about whether to upgrade or to overwrite an existing installation is made after you reboot the computer and choose the directory in which to load NT. Windows NT scans the directory to see if there is an existing Windows NT installation in that directory. If there is, you will be given the option of upgrading this installation or performing a new installation. I have run into problems when trying to use this upgrade process to revert to a previous version of NT. In these cases, I have had to wipe out the directory and perform a fresh installation. However, I have had good luck on the upgrade process.

The key difference between upgrades and fresh installations is whether the configuration information stored in the registry and other locations is preserved. This is very important because most applications need their configuration parameters to function properly. It can take quite a bit of time to reinstall all of your dependent applications. I would always use the upgrade option whenever possible. You may want to try out the upgrade on a development or test server to verify that the benefits outweigh the costs of the upgrade.

Complete Reinstallation of Windows NT Server

This process is basically similar to the one described in the previous section. Again, the key difference is that you wipe out the registry on a reinstallation and therefore lose all of your application settings. This may be necessary in cases where you have a really messed-up registry that you cannot seem to reset. It is also necessary to convert a workgroup server to a domain controller. It is a serious operation that can take quite a bit of time, especially if you are running a number of BackOffice and third-party applications on your server.

Details on the Installation from DOS Without NT Disks

What I want to do next is cover a sample installation process for Windows NT Server. I have chosen to cover the installation from DOS without NT disks. It is a superset of the steps that you would have to perform on most of the other installation paths. I have also chosen the NT 4.0 process because that is the current version on the market, even though there are still a lot of 3.51 users. The installation process is fairly similar; if you understand one, you will understand the basics of the other. Once again, you will find that the screens you receive will be based on the options you select and the configuration of your system. That is one of the great things about the installation-wizard concept. Windows NT senses which equipment you have in your system and presents you with only the screens that are necessary. It also presents additional screens based on previous options selected rather than displaying them all of the time. The bottom line is that if you get a screen as part of the Windows NT installation process, you probably need to review what it is telling you (in the case where NT has sensed something and wants a confirmation) or enter some data.

10

SETTING UP WINDOWS NT

The first phase that you need to go through involves the preparation of your system to load NT. You can think of it as starting in the planning processes described in the last chapter and the beginning of this chapter. It also includes setting up the hardware if your system has not been completely assembled at the factory. It may also involve partitioning and formatting your hard disk drives if the factory did not take care of this task or you are not fond of the way that the factory has set things up. In either case, the end result of this phase is that you have a working computer with disk drives that are ready to receive the NT operating-system files.

To prepare your system to load NT:

1. Plan the installation.

2. Assemble the hardware.

3. Prepare disk drives.

The next phase in the installation process is the DOS-based installation process (see Figure 10.3). You now need to insert the Windows NT Server CD into your CD-ROM drive and run the winnt.exe program. The first screen that you get asks you where the Windows NT distribution files are located. Even though you ran the winnt.exe program from the CD drive, you have to put in its path again (for example, e:\i386 for Intel-based PCs that use E:\ as their CD drive). In this DOS-based portion of installation, you hit either the F3 function key (if you want to exit the installation procedure) or Enter (to continue to the next screen).

FIGURE 10.3.

The DOS-based portion of the installation process.

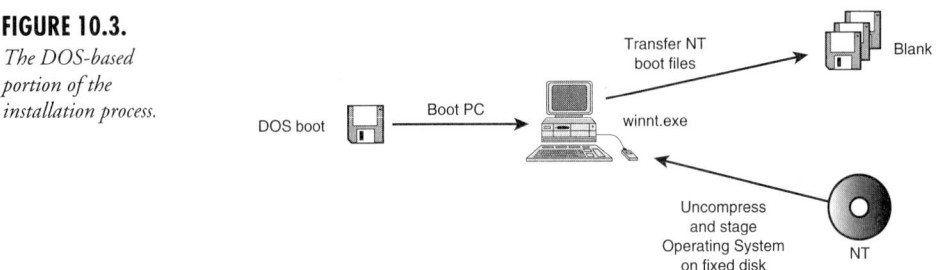

Next you will see a series of three screens that ask you to insert the three disks you will be using to boot your Windows NT system in the next phase. These disks need to be completely empty and formatted. You will get an error message if you try to use disks that already have some data on them. These disks are to be labeled as follows:

- Windows NT Server Setup Disk #3
- Windows NT Server Setup Disk #2
- Windows NT Server Setup Boot Disk

One of the neat things that Microsoft did when designing this portion of the installation process was to write the disks in reverse order. This causes you to make the setup boot disk last. Thus, you have the first disk that will be used when you reboot the system in the drive at the end of the disk-creation process. I guess the little things impress someone like me.

After you have created that last disk and pressed Enter to continue, you are taken to a screen that shows you the progress as you copy files from the CD to your fixed disk drive. This process may seem as if it takes a long time, especially with version 4 of NT (which has so much more to it). What the system is doing is taking the compressed files from the CD, uncompressing them, and then placing them in a temporary directory on the server's fixed disk. This will make the later installation work go much more quickly, so try to be patient. Also, I have found that the percent indicator does not move in a linear fashion. It seems to move more quickly at the beginning of the process than at the end. Apparently the files at the end of the distribution take longer to uncompress than those at the beginning.

At the end of this installation, you get another screen that tells you to ensure that the boot disk is in drive A:\ and press Enter to restart your computer. This is the first reboot that you will go through in your installation. It also marks the dividing line between the DOS-based portion of installation and that conducted under the Windows NT environment (see Figure 10.4). This is a key point in the installation process. After you leave this point, you will be dependent on NT device drivers and not those that existed in your previous DOS and/or Windows environment. I have had several cases where I did not have a working driver for NT for a network card or CD-ROM drive and lost functionality for these components after this point.

FIGURE 10.4.

The NT-based software installation process.

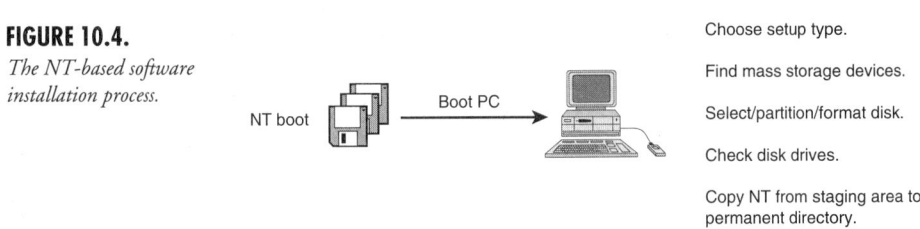

Choose setup type.

Find mass storage devices.

Select/partition/format disk.

Check disk drives.

Copy NT from staging area to permanent directory.

After you reboot your system, Windows NT will start loading from the setup boot disk. When the system is done with that disk, you will be prompted to insert Setup disk #2. It will continue to load for a while. During this time, it will load the Windows NT Executive, the hardware abstraction layer, and some of the device drivers. You are then presented with the blue startup screen you will soon become familiar with. This is a text-based screen that indicates NT is starting up. It will indicate the version and build of NT being loaded for your reference.

After NT is running (at least in the limited form loaded from disks), you are given a welcome screen. Here you can choose between express and custom setup. I typically choose the express setup because it still gives a fair degree of control during this process and is quicker. Anyway, you can press Enter to continue with express setup or c to perform a custom setup.

The next screen indicates that NT is searching for mass storage devices. This is primarily focused on SCSI controllers/drives and CD-ROM drives. If you have standard IDE fixed disk drives, they will not show up on this list, but you will have access to them. I guess Microsoft just assumes that you will have IDE fixed disk drives, so they are not treated as anything special. Next, you are given a list of these devices for your review, and you can add devices if need be. Otherwise, you can press Enter to continue on with the process.

The next screen shows you the disk partitions available for Windows NT installation. You can adjust these partitions and select the one that has adequate space. I usually want to put NT on a partition that has at least 200–300M free. It may not take all of that space now, but operating systems continue to grow in size. Also, some less sophisticated applications install themselves on the same disk drive as the operating system without giving you the option to move them. If you run out of space on the operating-system drive, you can run into some really nasty problems as the operating system tries to allocate temporary or log files and cannot.

Your next decision is whether to leave the file system intact or convert it to the NTFS file system. FAT was designed in a simpler era. There are certain things, such as having file ownership and access permissions, that can be done only under NTFS. Also, it would be easy for some nefarious person to boot your computer with a DOS disk and access any information that you have on FAT drives. Finally, FAT drives are somewhat more sensitive to being corrupted than NTFS drives. I typically use NTFS for server drives. If you choose to convert the file system to NTFS, it will take a little bit of time for this conversion to take place.

Your next choice is the name of the directory that will contain Windows NT. If you are trying to perform an upgrade, you will want to ensure that you specify the name of the current Windows NT operating-system directory. Otherwise, you can accept the defaults or pick a name that suits your taste. I typically accept the defaults.

At the next step, NT performs an "exhaustive" check of the drives. It actually does not take that long. After this check is completed, NT will copy the files from the temporary staging directory to the permanent NT operating-system directory. When this is completed, you are presented with a screen informing you that this portion of the installation process is completed. You will be prompted to reboot your computer.

You are now ready to enter the final installation phase (see Figure 10.5). In this phase, you will set up the detailed hardware- and software-configuration parameters that your operating system will use. This is where you choose which protocols to use, what your security environment will be, and all of those other choices that you have been waiting to set ever since you wrote up your installation checklist.

FIGURE 10.5.

The final NT configuration process.

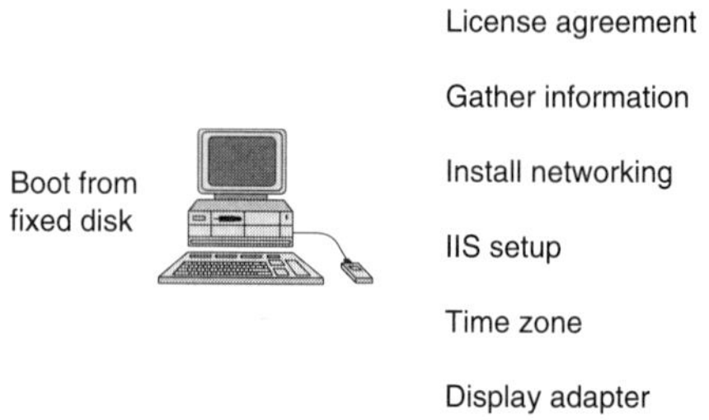

Boot from fixed disk

License agreement

Gather information

Install networking

IIS setup

Time zone

Display adapter

The first screen that you are presented with is designed to satisfy all of the lawyers in the crowd. Yes, to continue with the installation process, you have to agree to the Microsoft license agreement that says you will not pirate software or use the operating system in ways that violate this agreement. After you select yes, the operating system copies a few more files to your disk drive.

When this is completed, you start the setup wizard. This is similar to the Windows 95 wizard concept in that the software looks at your configuration and previous responses and presents you with a series of questions (with a fair amount of explanatory text) that guide you through the installation process. The first step in this process displays the stages of the installation process:

- Gathering information about your computer
- Installing Windows NT Networking
- Finishing Setup

One of the nice features about these wizards is that you have Next and Previous buttons. When you run into a problem, you can usually go back one or more screens and reset some options to try and solve that problem. For example, when you get to the screen that prompts you for an IP address and you realize that you do not have one, you can go back and deselect TCP/IP networking to avoid getting the IP address screen (which you cannot leave unless you put an address in). You can then get the address after you complete the installation and add TCP/IP using Control Panel.

The information-gathering section presents screens that ask for the following information:

- *Name and organization.* This is relatively straightforward. Note that this is the licensee's name (that is, you) as opposed to the name by which the computer will be known on the network. The network name will be entered later on.

- *Licensing option purchased.* There are two basic options. The first enables you to buy a certain number of concurrent connections to your server. This is the easiest to maintain and the most common. The other option is to purchase a license for each remote computer out there that will be accessing resources on the server. Note that this means accessing file- and printer-sharing resources and not things such as the Internet Information Server or client-server database access to an Oracle database. Check the appropriate radio button based on what you have purchased.

- *Computer name.* This is the name by which your computer will call itself internal to the operating system. Your domain name and network name will be specified later.

- *Server role.* Here you make that critical decision as to whether you will be a primary domain controller, a backup domain controller, or a standalone server. You cannot change a workgroup server to a domain server without reinstalling the operating system, so make your choice wisely.

10

SETTING UP WINDOWS NT

■ *Administrator account password.* Here you type in and confirm the password that will be applied to the Administrator account, which is the basic account that you will be accessing to create your other accounts. Write it down or choose something that you are sure to remember (Windows NT security is pretty efficient, you know).

■ *Floating-point workaround.* Some older Pentium-based computers have a slight problem with their floating-point processors. If you run a specific series of calculations in the right order, you will get a slight error. I typically do not enable this workaround (where Microsoft basically performs these calculations in the operating system as opposed to the floating-point processor) because I really want the speed of the floating-point processor and do not see much likelihood that I will run into this problem.

■ *Create emergency repair disk.* This option enables you to store key operating-system configuration information on a disk that you can use in conjunction with the startup disks to recover your operating system in the event of a major problem. This will almost always recover the system, and I recommend having it around. It does not take long to create.

■ *Select components.* This list enables you to pick the multimedia and graphics components of the operating system that you will be installing. You still have other panels from which to select major operating-system components, such as networking tools or Internet Information Server.

The next phase determines your Windows NT networking configuration. Although you could have a standalone Windows NT server, I'm not sure why you would do this. The typical server configuration has you connected to a local area network and/or telephone network. To set up networking, you will go through the following sequence (note that the exact list of panels is strongly dependent on the options that you select in previous panels, but this gives you the general idea):

■ *Network connection options.* Here you get to indicate whether you are connected to a network via a network interface card or use a modem and the remote access service. Check the appropriate boxes.

■ *Install Internet Information Server.* This screen merely lets you indicate whether you are going to install IIS. The exact IIS options will be specified later on. This information is used to predetermine certain future networking options (you must have TCP/IP if you are going to use IIS).

■ *Search for network adapters.* One of the blessings of these wizards is that you can click the search button and have Windows NT interrogate your modem card to try and figure out which type of card you are using. This makes the rest of the setup process much easier. If you are using an unusual card, you still have the option of supplying your own driver and specifying the card name manually.

■ *Select protocols.* Windows NT supports three protocols in its basic networking—NetBEUI, TCP/IP, and IPX/SPX. The other protocols you might want to use can get loaded later as optional services. Here you have to pick which ones you wish to use on your network.

■ *Select network services.* Here you can select the basic and advanced networking services that you wish to install. The typical default list includes IIS, RAS, remote procedure calls, NetBIOS interface, workstation, and server.

■ *Ready to install screen.* This screen is just a last chance for you to go back and change your settings before the installation process begins.

■ *Network card setup.* If you have a network card selected, you will be given a screen that is appropriate to that network card. Here you will select configuration parameters such as the interrupt and input/output memory address.

■ *Use DHCP.* If you are loading TCP/IP and have a dynamic host configuration protocol server to give out TCP/IP addresses, you should indicate this on this panel. Otherwise, you will be asked to supply a specific IP address that is entered into this server's basic TCP/IP protocol configuration.

■ *Add modem dialog.* If you have selected network access via RAS at the beginning of the network-setup phase, you will be prompted to select your modem. If you do not have a modem set up, you can select to have Windows NT search for the modem and set it up for you. If you are using a common modem, this is the easiest way to configure it—and it even goes through and tests the connection for you.

■ *Verify modem type.* If you told NT to find your modem for you, you will be prompted to verify that NT found the modem correctly.

■ *Modem location.* Here you will be asked to enter in your area code, whether you have to dial a number (usually 9) to get an outside line, and whether you are using pulse or tone dialing.

■ *Modem setup configuration.* This is another of those last screens in a section of the setup wizard that gives you one last chance to verify your configuration is correct before moving to the next step.

■ *RAS setup screen.* Here you verify which device you wish to use for RAS. Although this may be obvious in single-modem systems, there are folks who are more fortunate and have to make a choice.

■ *RAS list of protocols.* Here you select the protocols that will be used for RAS. This does not necessarily have to be the same as the protocols used for your network card.

■ *RAS TCP/IP setup.* Here you indicate whether a person dialing in with TCP/IP has access to the server or can use the server to access the entire network. You also select whether to use DHCP or provide a static pool of addresses to anyone dialing in and

10

SETTING UP
WINDOWS NT

requesting a IP address. Remember that you have to have a means of ensuring that any IP address that is used is unique on your network (you see some really strange and nasty problems if you have two computers trying to use the same IP address).

■ *RAS IPX access.* This lets you specify whether a user dialing in with IPX/SPX can access only the server or has access to the entire network. You can also specify a Novell network number, but I have never had to set this option. Contact your Novell administrator to see if this is needed in your case.

■ *TCP/IP properties page.* This lets you specify the TCP/IP configuration for your system. You have a series of tab dialog boxes similar to those shown in Figure 10.6. Here you specify the IP address of your network card (or cards) and which of the optional TCP/IP services you might be using (for example, WINS).

FIGURE 10.6.

TCP/IP Properties page.

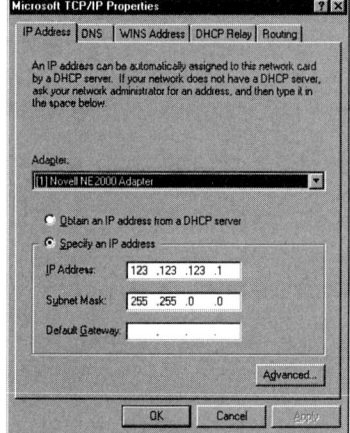

■ *Server setup page.* Here you see the bindings for the services.

■ *Network startup screen.* This is just a screen to let you know that the network is about to be started. Click next to start the network.

■ *Computer name and domain screen.* Here you specify the computer name as it will be known on the network and what your domain or workgroup is to be called. Note that you may have a different alias set up in the TCP/IP host files, DNS, or WINS servers that are used on your network for TCP/IP access. I, however, recommend keeping the name the same in all network environments unless you have a good reason not to (I get confused easily).

This completes the network setup phase. Your final phase is referred to as finishing setup. You have just a few more details to clean up before you can start your new server. The steps in this phase are also determined by the options that you have previously selected. Typically they include the following:

- *Internet Information Server setup options.* Here you indicate which of the IIS components that you wish to install—Internet Service Manager, WWW Service, Gopher Service, FTP Service, ODBC Drivers, Administration and Help Files, and Samples.

- *Publishing directories for the IIS services specified.* Here you indicate where the information that is provided by the IIS services resides. This is analogous to specifying share names for shared-network directories.

- *ODBC driver selection.* If you chose to install ODBC drivers, you will be asked to choose which one to install (currently the list contains a driver only for SQL Server, so the choice is not difficult).

- *Date, time, and time zone.* You tell the computer where it is located and what the current date and time are. You should look at this closely because there is no guarantee that the computer manufacturer is in the same time zone that you are, and PC clocks do lose/gain time.

- *Display adapter.* The system tries to figure out what type of display adapter you are using and gives you the option of setting up the properties and testing correct functionality. If it does not find your adapter, you have the option of manually selecting the adapter and supplying an alternative device driver.

After this, Windows performs a number of steps including copying more files, updating shortcuts, removing the temporary installation files, and saving its configuration. The configuration save can take quite a bit of time and may appear to be stuck at certain points. Give it a liberal amount of time before you conclude that there is a problem. It just takes time, and you are at a very sensitive juncture here. You are almost ready to start up, but you need to save all of the settings that you have just entered.

Finally, you will be prompted to restart your computer. This reboot should take you to a working Windows NT server. There are still a few steps left that will be discussed in the next couple of sections, but your NT installation is complete. Now might be a good time to consider taking a system backup. You may encounter problems installing other BackOffice components or third-party products. It may be useful to return to this known working configuration if problems get really bad.

Issues and Things to Watch Out For

There are a number of problems that you can encounter and things that you need to keep in mind while installing Windows NT. I want to mention a few of the ones that come to mind based on my experience:

- Make sure that you choose products on the hardware compatibility list if at all possible. If you are sure that a particular component that is not on the list will work, you can try it, but there is no guarantee that future releases of NT will work with it. Device problems due to unusual devices have been the biggest problem I have had working with NT.

■ Always save your work at every logical stopping point. Always back up the entire system before upgrading. Back up the system after the operating-system installation and after every major server is installed. Update your emergency repair disk when you make significant changes to the registry (new applications, configuration changes, and so forth).

■ Become familiar with vendor-support options, especially those provided on the Web and FTP servers. You may need to download device drivers for various cards or other peripherals to make these products work with NT.

■ Ensure that you leave plenty of time for the installation. This is not a DOS/Windows 3.1 installation. It usually takes one or two hours just to get the operating system installed and configured. This is not the type of operation that you can rush.

Postinstallation Configuration

After you have completed your installation, there are still a number of tasks that need to be accomplished. You have to create user accounts, shared directories, and all of the other things that are needed to make this server useful to your user community. This can often take a lot of time (especially if there are a lot of user accounts). Therefore, you also need to factor this time into your schedule.

Another demanding task can be installing the other BackOffice components and any third-party applications that will be running on this server. Each of these will have its own installation procedure. They may also require a fair amount of configuration work. It is usually best to complete the installation of these products before you create user accounts. That way, if they interface with Windows NT's security system, you can provide access to these applications for your users when you create the accounts as opposed to after the fact.

Verifying Successful Installation

I would also argue that you should spend a reasonable amount of time verifying that everything is functioning well with your new server. Think of this as taking your server for a test drive before you let your users go at it. I recommend that you test the functions in detail (for example, try to copy a file located on a remote server rather than just bringing up Network Neighborhood to see if you see any remote computers). This can take some time, but it is easier to make the time now rather than after you have turned the system over to the users and it is in production.

Summary

This chapter has covered the Windows NT Server installation process. It is a rather complicated process that has a number of options to it. The exact set of screens varies with the version that you install and the configuration options that you select. However, the basic process follows one of several defined paths that are based on the current condition of your server and the media you have received. The key to being able to work through this process for your particular situation is a good general knowledge of the operating system and a plan that you work out in advance based on your reading of the installation notes and understanding your user's needs.

10

SETTING UP
WINDOWS NT

Windows NT Administration

by Joe Greene

IN THIS CHAPTER

CHAPTER 11

Now that your Windows NT Server is up and functioning perfectly, it is time to get into the topic of administration. I like to think of this chapter as the "care and feeding" of your new server. It requires a number of skills that go above and beyond those needed for the installation process (for example, time management). This chapter also covers those subjects that take a fully functional operating system and turn it into a productive server environment.

I have taken a divide-and-conquer approach in this chapter. After presenting an overview discussion of system administration, I go into each of the specialty areas. You may or may not use some of these specialty areas. For example, remote access to your server may be completely forbidden by your local security policies, or it may be the sole reason that this particular server was installed. Also, there are so many possible uses for your server (and therefore so many possible administrative topics) that I had to limit my discussion to those that I thought were most likely to be needed by a wide range of administrators. Also, the administration of each of the other BackOffice components is discussed in a chapter located in the appropriate section of the book.

The topics that I chose for this chapter include the following:

- Overview of NT administration
- User administration
- Backup and recovery
- RAS administration
- Managing shared resources
- Auditing
- Performance tuning
- Client-server environment administration
- Administration for server-based applications
- Other administrative tasks

Overview of NT Administration

Ongoing system administration can be as much of a challenge as the initial server installation. It is not usually as much of a technical challenge. After you have all of those drivers working, things tend to stay working well (at least until the next upgrade). However, I find that it is usually harder to get the time to keep up with user accounts and disk-drive utilization than it is to allocate that day or two it takes for the special project of installing a new server. Also, it can be quite a challenge to find the time to perform system maintenance after it goes into production. Most users, I have found, become quite dependent on their computer systems and do not want to live without them for a few hours while you rearrange files on disks or perform hardware upgrades. Most administrators do not like the idea of having to work in the middle of the night (in addition to their normal work day) to get these maintenance tasks accomplished.

So there are challenges to system administration that go far beyond the standard technical competencies. You have to work to solve these problems based on your individual situation. What I can do in this chapter is offer discussions on the technical Windows NT tasks that the administrator needs to perform to keep servers working properly. These tasks are actually a combination of technical knowledge, planning, and policy making that comes together to form a workable system of doing business.

The unfortunate thing is that I cannot offer one simple task list and schedule for every administrator. Windows NT is a flexible operating system that is designed to meet a number of needs and work in a number of environments. I have sketched out just a few ideas on environments in Figure 11.1. You need to keep in mind the overall system goals when you are planning your administrative routine. For example, security may be a trivial concern or a matter of national security for your server. Also, certain production environments cannot ever lose a scrap of data, whereas other environments would prefer to avoid losing data but cannot afford mirrored disk drives or other reliability-enhancement technologies.

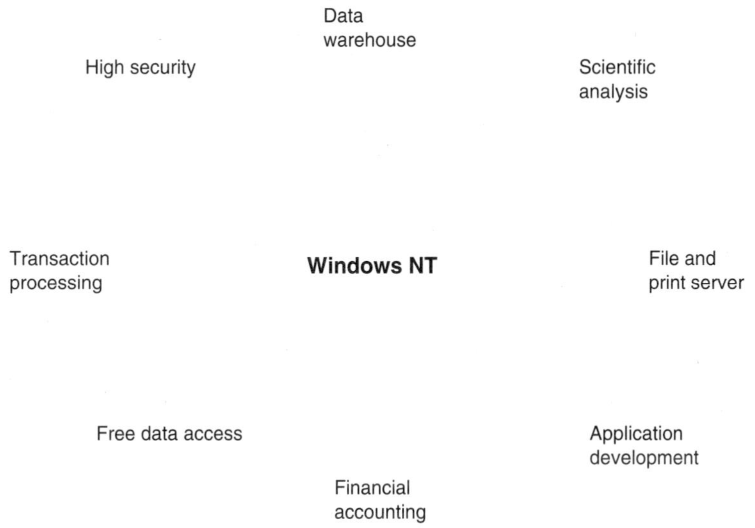

FIGURE 11.1.
Different administrative environments.

High security

Data warehouse

Scientific analysis

Transaction processing

Windows NT

File and print server

Free data access

Application development

Financial accounting

Ideally, some of the administrative requirements were factored into the overall system design. This usually happens when you have experienced system administrators participating in the overall system design. However, you may find that others have designed a system lacking, for example, a tape drive (or have installed a very low-capacity tape drive on a server with a lot of disk storage in order to save money). At any rate, you have to review your environment against your administrative needs. Sometimes you have to adapt your administrative procedures (for example, back up data to writable CD drives) or adapt your system configuration (get that high-capacity tape drive) to enable you to accomplish your goals. Ideally, you have had the chance to read this chapter and plan out your administrative tasks before the system configuration was completed. If not, perhaps you have some additional budget for the little extras that you think of while reading this chapter.

As I go through the tasks, you will note a large number of things that need to get done, and it may seem overwhelming. This is especially true if you are just a part-time NT administrator who has another main job (engineer, for example) that is supposed to be your primary focus in life. There are two components that you have to balance to fit your administrative tasks within the available time. The first is that you have to select which tasks you are going to perform. Some things may not be that important in your environment, and therefore you may not have to perform them. Perhaps there is another person or group who will do that job for you. The other option, though, would be not to completely ignore a given task, but to alter how often you do it. For example, if you are working on a system that has plenty of disk space and the users do not use the system for a lot of data storage (that is, they are accessing some relatively small Web pages that do not grow radically over time), you might perform capacity-planning tasks only every six months or even annually. The key here is to ensure that everyone understands what they are getting when it comes to service so that they do not get upset if they have to wait for something to get done. Another key is that if other people or groups are performing some of the common administrative tasks, it is important to ensure that both your users and those other people are clear as to the assignments.

Chapter 5, "Administrative Environment," went over most of the tools that will be used to accomplish the tasks discussed in this chapter. Please refer to that chapter if you wish to refresh yourself on the details such as which pull-down menu enables you to activate a particular needed function. This chapter focuses more on figuring out what needs to get done. You can then use the tools provided in Windows NT to actually get the job done.

One final note about tools and tasks. You may choose to extend the tools provided with Windows NT, or you may wish to use alternative management tool sets. There are a number of third-party vendors who provide management tools for Windows. The tools that come with the operating system are fairly complete and work well. I have, on occasion, automated certain repetitive tasks with a series of batch files. I will discuss this later in this chapter, but the basic concept is that you can build scripts that use the basic NT tools in a fixed combination. They can be run either from the command line or through tools such as the Remote Command Server provided in the Windows NT Resource Kit. Again, I have a section on scripting coming up in just a little bit.

Why spend a long time in the overview section? There are a number of practical tasks to discuss in the sections that follow. That is where you will find the real value in this section. I inserted this section merely to focus your attention on a few issues that you should keep in mind as you are working through the following sections.

User Administration

User administration is one of the strengths of the Windows NT operating system, especially under version 4.0. It is easy to work with, and you have a powerful, graphical tool in the User Manager tool (see Figure 11.2) to get the job done. Version 4.0 is an improvement on the 3.51

release in that Microsoft has enabled you to access those few user administration functions (for example, remote access setup for users) from the User Manager tool. It is now pretty much the one place you have to go and the one tool you have to learn to keep your user accounts properly configured.

FIGURE 11.2.

The User Manager tool.

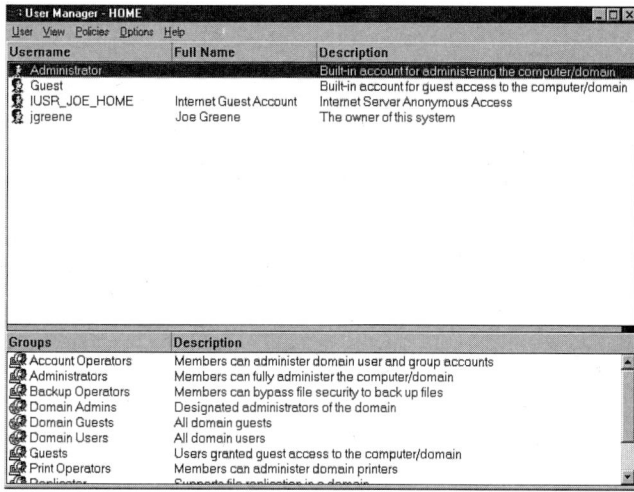

The first issue that you have to deal with regarding user administration was actually decided for you when you installed your Windows NT Server operating system. That issue is whether you are operating as part of a workgroup or domain. Again, I recommend the domain option for BackOffice users because several products (for example, Exchange Server) are configured to work only in the domain environment. It does not cost extra to be a domain as opposed to a workgroup (both sets of software come as part of NT), and your clients can deal with both systems of government equally well. The key is that the domain environment has a number of security enhancements that BackOffice developers wanted to take advantage of when implementing their products. Their decision can force you to make your decisions towards domains also.

So what does this domain environment mean to the average overworked system administrator out there in the field? If you have more than one server, it means that it will usually reduce the amount of work you have to do. It also means that if you are used to workgroups, you will have to spend a little bit of time learning about and getting used to the domain environment. It took me only a day or so to adapt to this environment, so you should have little trouble doing it. The only real recommendation that I would put forward is to have a backup domain controller if at all possible. This ensures that people can log on to the network even if your primary domain controller is down for maintenance.

In line with this, I always recommend at least a basic Uninterruptible Power Supply (UPS) for your servers. There are expensive ones that can keep you going for days in the event of a power failure, but you can also get some very simple units good enough to keep your system from going down in the event of short outages (such as those that are common with lightning strikes). Windows NT does a number of fancy things with disk drives and memory to improve performance. It may take you some time to recover if your system goes down with even a brief power outage and NT has to clean up the files that it was working with when the power went out. These basic units sell for under $100, although you might consider a bigger unit if you want to remain operational during extended power outages. Remember to consider UPS devices for your network equipment also. (I have seen servers that are functioning well, but no one can get to them without a network.)

Your decision on domain versus workgroup will determine whether you have to create user accounts on each server (workgroup) or create one account for each user that is valid throughout the domain. The domain security system is really quite good. Do not decide to use workgroups just because you feel someone will hack their way through NT security and access information they are not supposed to on a server if they have an account that is valid on it. NT gains a lot of security by enabling you to prevent people from having access to the command line or main GUI interface on the remote computer. Instead, you have resources accessed through common utilities that enforce security.

If you have decided on the domain architecture, you next need to consider setting up trust relationships between domains. If you do not have connectivity to other domains, you can skip this step. However, if there are other domains, you should at least consider setting up a global group on your computer that matches those set up from the other domains. Again, you have to coordinate the trust relationships with the other domain administrators, because a two-way permission grant is needed to make a trust relationship work. After you have the trust relationships and global groups set up, you have a way to control access by these outsiders into the resources of your system.

The next issue that you have to deal with is establishing your user groups. Unless you are working on an extremely small server, it is impractical to grant all accesses on a user-by-user basis. It becomes even more difficult to try and remove selective accesses if the user changes jobs. What you must plan out now is which groups make sense for your environment. This comes from an analysis of who will be given access to different types of information. You look for patterns in this permission scheme (for example, every user has access to some things, all accountants have access to others), and you make a group to represent each of these patterns. You can make changes to group membership easily over time, but changing your group structure can be quite time-consuming later on. It is worth a little extra effort up front to at least get close to the ultimate group structure for your environment. Also, note that grouping applies just as much to workgroups as it does to domains. If you use workgroups, it might be a whole lot easier for you to at least keep your group names straight across your various servers. It would be a real pain to have to remember that a group is called HR on one server and HumanRes on another.

An important point to keep in mind is that you can still give individual permission grants on top of this group structure. The group structure is designed to make the bulk of your permission grants easier. It is all right if you have a few special users who need special privileges that are granted on an individual basis. For example, say you have a large number of users who need access to a common corporate-policies directory. You could grant read access to the general users group and then assign all users to that group. They all have access to that directory for read purposes. Someone has to maintain that directory, though. Perhaps you have two people in human resources who are allowed to change policies. You can give change permissions to these two accounts individually, and you are done.

One thing that can be useful in larger systems is a map of your groups to hang up on your wall. I have included Figure 11.3 to stimulate your thoughts. You can arrange groups from top to bottom, in order of who has the most privileges, and from left to right, corresponding to your various departments. You could also pick another arrangement scheme that matches your own way of thinking. The key is that having this map, even if it is hand-drawn on the back of an old printout, can help you see the security scheme in a visual format. It also comes in handy when you are on vacation and someone has to fill in for you who does not instinctively understand the way you think.

FIGURE 11.3.

A sample of group mapping.

Users

Human Resources

Managers

Domain Administrators

You now have buckets in which to place your users. What does that mean to them? Actually, very little until you start sharing some resources on the network that they want to have access to. They rarely appreciate computers for their technical or artistic merit. You now need to come up with some names for your resources. I have seen a number of different resources and system-naming conventions, ranging from planets visited by the original "Star Trek" television series to detailed naming conventions that show location, equipment version, and other technical details. The key is having names that convey what the resource is and give the user enough information to actually use it.

First, a few thoughts on conveying what the resource is as part of the name. In small shops, in which everyone knows that the only printer is an HP Laserjet 3si, you can come up with a simple, cute name that everyone can remember. However, if you have a vast network of printers (some color, some duplex, and so on), it can be difficult for people to remember that Babel is the duplex and Deneb is the color printer. Therefore, you might want to come up with names such as Duplex or Color. If you have a network with multiple printers on each floor, you might consider adding a floor or department designator to the name (for example, 3Color or MktgColor). Remember, they do not have to type in a long resource name under the NT environment. Instead, they pick the resource from a list of resources. You can go a little bit longer with the resource name unless you have some old DOS workstations (where the share-name limit is eight characters). Otherwise, you are free to convey much more information to your users.

Just as it was useful to have a map of your user groups, it is useful to keep a map or list of your resources (named according to the standards that you planned out in Chapter 9, "Planning a Server"). It should contain a few more details that you, as the administrator, may want to keep track of. Figure 11.4 shows a sample for a relatively simple installation. You may want to divide the resources up on a floor-by-floor (or location-by-location) basis if you have larger installations. The key is that you have some documentation on your resources that goes beyond the share name, which can help you and your group provide better administration. If you like, you could even write up a formal configuration document for each server.

FIGURE 11.4.

A sample resource diagram.

Laserjet_4SI

Color_Printer

Corp_Policies

HR_Shared

Dev_Shared

The final step is mapping access privileges for resources to groups and users. This could be a very generous scheme, for those places that believe everyone should have access to knowledge, or a very stingy scheme, in places where data security is important. You will have to decide what those rules are, but I thought that I would leave you with Figure 11.5 as an example of a tool that can help you to keep these access grants straight.

FIGURE 11.5.

A resource access table.

	Users	Human Resources	Managers	Domain Administrators
Laserjet_4SI	Print	Print	Print	Print
Color_Printer		Print		Print
Corp_Policies	Read	Change	Read	Full Control
HR_Shared		Change		Full Control
Dev_Shared	Read		Change	Full Control

So much for theories of user management. An example of this process for a mythical small group of users might be useful. This small group needs to access several common directories and one of two printers (based on their location). They have not wanted the printer in the other location to be available to users ever since the day one user sent a huge print job to the wrong location when a manager wanted to get out a big proposal.

You have configured all workstations to be members of the BrandX domain. Your analysis indicates the need for the following groups:

- BrandX—A general group for the whole company. You did not want to use the generic user group supplied with NT because you were unsure which resource grants may be made by installation scripts of purchased software packages.

- EastSt—A group for all users at the East Street office.

- Downtown—A group for all users at the downtown office.

- Managers—A special group for managers who have access to financial information not available to other employees.

- Personnel—A special group for personnel administrators who have access to a small employee database with sensitive information.

- ProjectY—A special group for people working on the new ProjectY team. Unlike other groups who are paper-based, the ProjectY team wants to try to share information electronically.

You add these groups to your domain configuration using the User Manager tool, as shown in Figure 11.6. Obviously, larger networks would have a larger number of groups. Typical reasons to classify employees into various groups include projects worked on, job title within the company, or group that you work in. The scheme presented here reflects a knowledge of the organization of BrandX and what the Windows NT servers are going to be used for.

FIGURE 11.6.

User groups in the BrandX example.

	BrandX	EastSt	Downtown	Managers	Personnel	ProjectY	Admin
East_Color		Print					
East_HP3SI		Print					
Down_HP4M			Print				
Managers				Change			Full Control
HR	Read				Change		Full Control
Corporate	Read				Change		Full Control
ProjectY						Change	Full Control
IS_Info	Read						Full Control

Your next step is to map the resources that will be shared on your domain. This is probably easier for computer types to deal with than the organizational structure issues. Although it is sometimes a challenge to get users to describe how they plan to use information or even which information they plan on storing, you should be aware of the hardware and shared directories on your servers. Also, because it should take an administrator to share server resources, that means you will stay in the loop. In light of this, the following is a list of shared resources for the mythical BrandX example:

- East_Color—A color printer at the East Street location.

- East_HP3SI—A Hewlett-Packard Laserjet 3SI high-capacity printer at the East Street location.

- Down_HP4M—A Hewlett-Packard Laserjet 4M printer at the downtown location.

- Managers—A shared directory of data that only managers can look at.

- HR—A shared directory of personnel information that only people in the Human Resources department (at both locations) can look at.

- Corporate—A general bulletin board for corporate information.

- ProjectY—The shared data directory for ProjectY team members.

- IS_Info—A directory in which you put information about the information system architecture at your location, services available, and so on, to help you communicate with your users.

I'm sure that you can imagine a dozen other possibilities, but this is enough to illustrate my point. What you have to do next, after you have made up the names, is to actually share the resources. Again, you would use a tool such as File Manager or Windows Explorer to share directories on the network and Print Manager or Printers on Control Panel to share printers. Figure 11.7 shows a sample sharing of the Corporate directory on the network.

FIGURE 11.7.

A sample directory sharing.

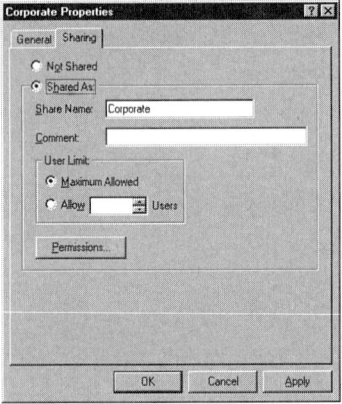

Figure 11.8 is an example of a more detailed chart of shared resources. The users care only that they have to find a shared directory or printer with a certain name. You, however, often need to know a few more details. You might want to draw such a chart (even by hand) for yourself.

FIGURE 11.8.

A sample shared resources chart.

\\server1\corporate
d:\corporate
d: = 500M
Read to all

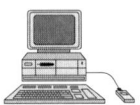

\\server2\HP4SI
HP Laserjet 4SI
Top tray = letterhead
Bottom tray = letter-sized paper
No envelope feeder
Attached to LPT1

An important task when sharing resources is to designate who has access to those resources (groups and individuals). This is controlled by selecting the permissions button on the panel that you are using to share the resource (printer or directory/folder). Figure 11.9 shows a typical sharing display panel. What you have to do for this resource is add a series of users or groups to the list of those that have the access. You also have to designate the type of access (read only, changes allowed, or full control are the most common ones) for file systems. After this is completed and you have exited from this panel, the users and groups designated will have access to those resources. It does not take a server reboot for these changes to take effect.

FIGURE 11.9.

A typical resource-sharing panel.

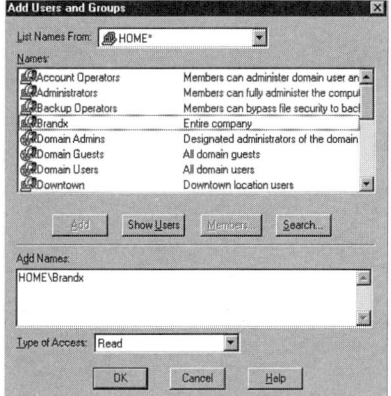

Your final task is to create user accounts and assign the appropriate group privileges to the users. Figure 11.10 shows the easy-to-deal-with user interface in Windows NT 4.0. To create a user, you select add user, type in the basic information (as shown in Figure 11.10), and then add group privileges for the user by selecting the groups button. This will give you the groups display shown in Figure 11.11. For this example, I have added user Bsmith who works at the East Street location of BrandX and is the manager of the ProjectY team. After you have completed this display, you can exit. One small note: if you add or remove group privileges from a user who is currently logged on to the system, that user will have to log out and log back in again for the privilege changes to take effect.

FIGURE 11.10.

Adding a sample user.

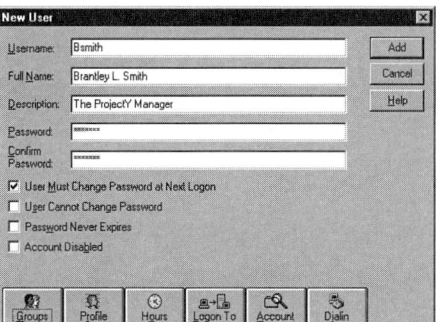

FIGURE 11.11.

*Sample group
associations.*

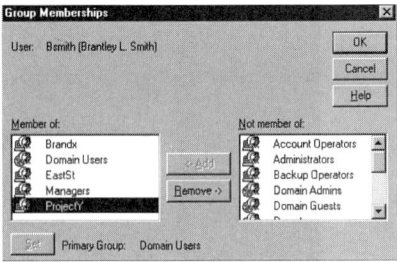

Hopefully this section has given you a feel for the basic user-management process under Windows NT. You may have to go through additional steps for various BackOffice and third-party applications. The section on client-server user administration later in this chapter will speak to some common third-party application needs. Also, there are chapters on administration in the sections on each of the BackOffice components that will cover the tricks needed to make these applications work well for the users. There is much more that could be said about user administration (there are several chapters on the subject in various NT books, such as *Windows NT Server 4.0 Unleashed* from Sams Publishing), but there are other topics we need to cover.

Backup and Recovery

A topic very near to my heart is backup and recovery. I cannot tell you about all of the really big mistakes and disasters I have seen as an administrator that turned out to be not that big a deal due to the existence of good backups. It has saved me so many times that I do not consider this to be an option on a server—it is a baseline feature. I have actually written long lectures on the subject of why backups are great, but I will spare you that discussion in this book.

I hope you got a backup device with your server when you were making that initial configuration. If not, why not go out and order one? There are a number of tape and disk drives that can be used for backup with NT (see the Hardware Compatibility List on the Microsoft Web page or TechNet CD to be sure) that vary in capacity and, of course, cost. You should find one that matches your needs and budget.

Let's say that you have a tape drive that is just right for your particular needs. You have it installed and it works just fine. The question now is, what do you do with it? There are a lot of backup utilities and scenarios out there that you need to consider. I want to take just a few moments to bring up some of the factors that you might want to consider for your system.

The first choice, after choosing your hardware, is the backup utilities that you will use. Windows NT provides a really convenient backup utility that I have always used (see Figure 11.12) on the NT boxes that I have cared for. It has an easy-to-use interface and works with all of the common tape drives that I have used. You can even write scripts to automate the backup process, as I will discuss in the scripting section towards the end of this chapter.

11

FIGURE 11.12.

*The Windows NT
backup utility.*

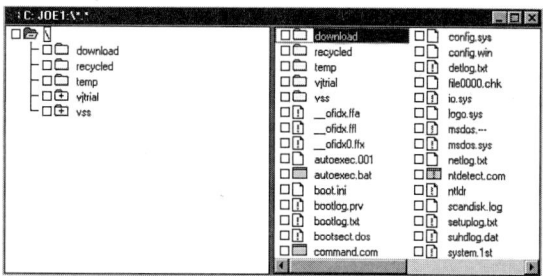

However, there are third-party backup utilities that you may want to consider. Several of the larger tape-drive manufacturers have written their own backup tools. They perform additional functions such as automating the backup process similar to my scripts. Others may be more closely tied to the particular hardware and be able to access some of their advanced features. If your tape drive comes with some of these other backup utilities, you may want to take a look at them. This is especially true if you standardize on a single tape-drive family for your entire organization. The only time the non-Microsoft tools become a problem is if you have a number of them on different servers that you have to learn and maintain.

You may want to consider a number of different backup schemes for your server. You may also implement a combination of these backup schemes to ensure that you are doing the best that you can given your system needs. The basic schemes that you should be aware of include the following:

- *Full backups.* This concept is simple; back up every file on the system. On NT boxes, you have to make sure you have a backup of the data in the registry also (this data is treated somewhat specially by NT—for good reason, because this is the heart of your control system).

- *Incremental backups.* In this case, you back up only files that have changed since the last backup was taken. Therefore, to restore your system configuration, you would have to restore from a full backup and then apply all of the incremental changes from the time of the last full backup to the time that the system failure occurred.

- *Partial backups.* Finally, you may need to back up only certain portions of the system. The partial backup enables you to back up those items that are needed while not taking the time or using the tape capacity for a full backup.

Let me throw out an example of how these schemes can be mixed. Imagine you have a server with only two disk drives. Drive C:\ contains the operating system and applications that have been loaded. Drive D:\ contains all of the user data. You have a tape drive that is not big enough to back up both drives at once. Your solution might be to do a complete system backup whenever you install or upgrade a software package on your system. You then perform nightly backups of only the D:\ drive. If drive C:\ fails, you restore from the last complete backup. If drive D:\ fails, you restore from that backup. You have to be careful to ensure that your applications do not write critical log or configuration files on the C:\ directory, but if need be you can just add these files to your nightly partial backup of the D:\ drive. Finally, you might perform an incremental backup at noon to ensure that you do not lose data from the morning's processing run if you were to have a failure in the afternoon.

An important point to consider when backing up applications is whether or not they have to be stopped for the backup to be useful. Many applications, such as older versions of the Oracle database and Exchange Server, require that you stop them before completing the backup to ensure that you have a time-consistent data set in your backup. Imagine that you are backing up a large Oracle database that is receiving a stream of transactions. It takes a finite amount of time to back up the various data files. Therefore, a table in the last data file that you back up may contain a number of changes not reflected in a key table that is related to the first table, but is physically stored in the first data file that was backed up. As you can see, this could cause a great deal of confusion with the database and lead to useless backups. Many of these applications have options in which you can back up the system while the database is running, but you have to ensure that you set the right options and always test that these procedures are working correctly by verifying that a restore of the data is usable.

A final point is that many Windows NT installations may not have evening-shift operators to perform backups. Because it is difficult to get system time and perhaps even shut down applications during the business day, administrators have trouble backing their systems up during the day. Now, for those of you who actually like 16-hour days, it is not a problem. You simply do the backup at midnight, right before you go home. The rest of us need to consider building scripts to automate the backup process. The section on scripting shows you a few simple backup scripts. I build a script to perform the backup that I want (I have one to perform a partial backup, and another to back up the rest of the system) that I store on the system and then run using the AT utility described under scripting. My only responsibilities after this are to ensure that there is a tape in the drive before I go home and check that the backup completed successfully in the morning.

RAS Administration

The next administrative area for users who allow people to dial in to their computer systems via the telephone lines is the Remote Access Service (RAS) administration. In the Windows NT setup process, you would have configured in the details of what type of modem that you have and what its settings are. You would also have to configure the network protocols that you are going to use and whether users who dial in can access just the computer that has the modem or the entire network.

With that configuration being taken care of as part of the setup process, it is time to let users actually start using the dial-in service. The first thing that you have to do is grant access to the users of the dial-in services. Under Windows NT 4.0, you are able to use either the RAS Admin tool or the User Manager tool, both of which are located under the Administrative Utilities menu. Under 3.51, you have only the option of using RAS Admin. Figure 11.13 shows the RAS options panel under NT 4.0.

FIGURE 11.13.

The Remote Administration Access setup.

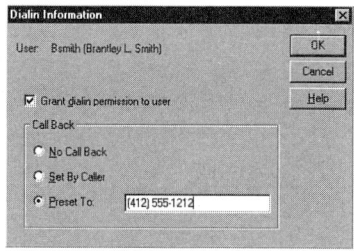

There is one key option after you have indicated that you want to allow a user to use the dial-in services. You have to indicate whether the user has direct access to the system, an optional call back, or a mandatory call back. The optional call back enables you to save employees telephone charges if they dial in and work from home. The mandatory dial-back feature is a security option that enables you to control which remote telephones (that is, the known home phones of your employees) can access your server.

The nicest feature about RAS is that it is fairly automatic and easy to set up. When users dial in to the server and network, they use the same interface as when they are on the local network and have the same privileges as they would otherwise. You do not have to set up special dial-in privileges. If you want to limit access for people coming in through RAS, you can create special, limited-access accounts and assign them limited access privileges (that is, read to only nonsensitive directories).

Auditing

Another routine task for many system administrators is auditing. Auditing is a form of monitoring that is focused on what people and applications have done (as opposed to performance monitoring, which is focused on the usage of system resources and speed). It is nicely integrated with the rest of the Windows NT environment in that you find the logged events using the same Event Viewer tool you use for other forms of monitoring—for example, application events and routine system messages such as those generated at startup.

Auditing has a number of different flavors under Windows NT. Some examples of things that might be interesting to you include the following:

- Someone trying multiple times to log into several of the accounts on your system (hackers?)
- A service that is routinely failing to start up when it is supposed to or stopping in an unplanned manner
- Someone trying to use privileged system functions (those that you normally restrict to yourself)
- A person logging on or off the system at unusual hours

- The number of people logging on or off the system at various hours, to determine the number of users you are supporting at different times of the day or days of the week

- A person using a sensitive right (such as administrator privileges) that has been granted to him or her

- Certain files or other resources (objects) being accessed by various individuals

Certain people view auditing strictly as something designed to detect and potentially stop hackers and other security risks. Certainly that is the focus of several classified government agencies, and rightly so. Audit trails that are carefully reviewed can enable people to detect new ways users are probing the information in a computer that have never been used before. Hackers are just like virus writers—they sit up all night thinking of new ways to hack.

However, I would like you to also consider a broader use for auditing that might interest even those of you who implicitly trust everyone who has access to your server. The first audit records were not written by people trying to stop Internet hackers. Instead, they were people dealing with early computers that just halted in the middle of executing a program. Because there were no fancy computer monitors back in that era (or any monitors, for that matter), people had little idea where their program halted. After many frustrating attempts to solve problems by trial and error, people started to record progress that was being made in their applications to output devices such as printers (or paper tape). When applications crashed, they simply traced the progress through these checkpoints to determine where the problems occurred.

As operating systems grew and become more capable, the auditing capabilities were built into the operating system. This is especially important for multiuser operating systems, where you need to know who caused the problem and what they were doing at the time to prevent it from happening again. Eventually, auditing was expanded beyond the "finding who caused the crash" stage to provide additional helpful information. It became a tool to record usage of the computer and its various resources. It was also extended to perform the security-monitoring tasks mentioned earlier.

A general-purpose operating system distributed to a large number of users now has to support a wide range of auditing. It has to cover the security angle to meet the needs of those super-secret environments, but also provide usage metering for people concerned with efficiently using their resources and planning for the future. Others might be concerned with only a light level of security (for example, who is using system administrator privileges). Windows NT has to meet this wide range of challenges and also enable the users to pick from various forms of auditing to suit their individual needs.

Let me discuss auditing as it is implemented under Windows NT. I like the way Windows NT implements auditing for the following reasons:

- It integrates all the various forms of auditing (operating system events, security events, and application events) into a single system for review and monitoring. It can be difficult to find time to review your log files, and having all the information in one place displayed by one user interface makes life much easier.

■ It is highly automated, with a fair level of basic information recorded automatically using the default system installation procedures.

■ It is highly customizable, enabling you to pick exactly what you want and need based on your environment.

■ You can interface applications that you develop locally with the auditing subsystem, thereby extending auditing to meet specialized needs, or integrate all your auditing activity into a single system.

■ It is self-cleaning. I have gone into several computer systems where people have used up many tens of megabytes of disk space with logs that they never even knew existed (database and middleware log files, for example). These logs were so large that no one would ever bother to go through them (although UNIX does have utilities that let you see only the last *x* lines in the file).

For smaller server environments, it is often difficult to get a lot of formal training on your operating systems. What basic training you do get does not emphasize the finer features of the operating system, such as auditing. Therefore, I thought it would be useful to go over the auditing options that are available to you. The first set of events that are audited deal with operating system events:

■ Services that fail to start

■ Hardware conflicts detected

■ Start of key services such as the Event Viewer

■ Print jobs completed

■ Anonymous login requests such as WWW

■ Disks nearing or completely out of space

■ Access requests to the CD-ROM drive when there is no CD in the drive

The second area you can monitor involves system-security events such as these:

■ Activation of remote access server (RAS) processes

■ Use of special privileges by the users

■ User logon and logoff

■ Failed logins

■ Access to certain objects (for example, the auditing setup)

■ Policy changes

■ System shutdown and restart

■ User- and group-management activities

Finally, the most expandable area involves Windows NT's capability to audit events within applications on the system:

- Setting up BackOffice applications such as Exchange Server or SQL Server
- Starting up BackOffice components
- Other events that you build into your applications or system scripts using the Software Development Kit (SDK) routines

Because the first thing you would want to do if you were trying to do something illegal is cover your trail, the auditing information in Windows NT is fairly well-protected inside the operating system (it doesn't have even the old, relatively obvious auditing registry keys you had in NT 3.51). The bad guys can't just delete a file and be done with it. You can, however, make a copy of the current log file to save error conditions or document unauthorized activity. This is especially important when you use the automatic overwrite features in the Windows NT auditing system.

Now that I have covered the "what to do" discussion of auditing, it is time for the "how to do it" discussion. The truly practical among you can rejoice that I am now leaving the theory world and getting down to business. A good place to start would be what I consider to be the heart of auditing under Windows NT—the Event Viewer. You access the Event Viewer through the Start menu, as shown in Figure 11.14.

FIGURE 11.14.

*Accessing the Event
Viewer.*

The system-audit events are pretty clear as to what you would want to record (you almost always want to know if your serial port has an interrupt conflict). The same goes for application events, because you would have to add them to your applications to get anything to go in there other than a few of the BackOffice products that are currently using this portion of the auditing system. However, the security-logging mechanisms need finer control to accommodate the wide variety of environments that are out there. If you were to audit everything imaginable in security, your log file would be so large that you would have to write an application just to filter out the events that might possibly be of interest (which would not be all that difficult, actually). However, some groups that I work with do not even want to waste the disk space for

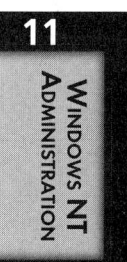
security auditing because everyone has full access to all resources and therefore these records have no meaning (small software development environments can be fun in this regard).

NT's auditing system accommodates this wide range of needs through the User Manager utility. This is another of the administrative tools that are available to you (refer back to Figure 11.14). I guess it was a toss-up as to whether to put all auditing controls in the Event Viewer or to put all the features involved with user security in the User Manager. Microsoft chose the latter option. To access the controls for security auditing, choose the Audit option from the Policies menu in User Manager (see Figure 11.15).

FIGURE 11.15.

Selecting the Audit option in User Manager.

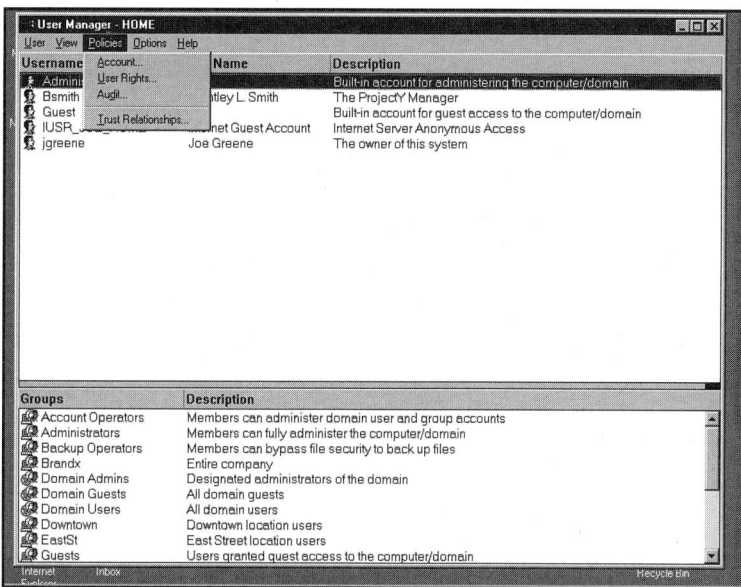

The Audit option displays the Audit Policy dialog shown in Figure 11.16. The radio buttons are important because they make the basic selection as to whether you perform any of these detailed security-auditing functions. If you select to perform these security-auditing actions, you are given two basic choices for auditing. The first column of checkboxes enables you to audit when users perform the functions listed successfully (such as logging on with the correct user ID and password). The second column of checkboxes enables you to audit when users fail when trying to perform a function. You can greatly reduce the number of events recorded if you look only for failures. This catches hackers or people trying to access a resource for which they lack permission. However, if you are trying to gather statistics on usage or logging all (legal) access to a resource, you would want to use the first column's checkboxes. Of course, if you really want a lot of information, you can audit both successes and failures.

FIGURE 11.16.

The Audit Policy dialog box.

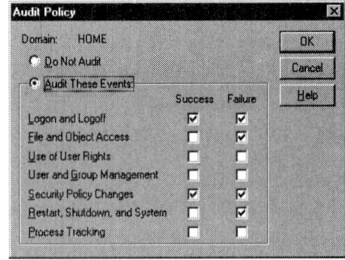

Splitting the security-auditing features into these seven categories enables you to pick the items that meet your needs and ignore the others, which can also reduce the number of log-file entries you have to review. The categories you have to choose from are as follows:

- *Logon and Logoff.* You can choose to record all events or only those such as failures which might indicate problems.

- *File and Object Access.* This can be very detailed, but it works only for NTFS file systems that have access rights (FAT is a pretty open storage mechanism designed for nonsecure DOS environments).

- *Use of User Rights.* This refers to rights that have been granted to a user or group (for example, performing system-administrative functions with a personal NT account).

- *User and Group Management.* This catches when someone alters the privileges of another account or creates an account to perform some bad activities and then deletes it.

- *Security Policy Changes.* This is another area in which the whole security picture of your system can be changed and therefore is a common audit function.

- *Restart, Shutdown, and System.* This can be useful for recording down time and determining when serious problems such as power outages occurred.

- *Process Tracking.* This captures some very detailed information such as process activation and indirect object access.

As you can see, you can set up a lot with NT auditing. The interface that controls and reviews the auditing information is also a clean and simple one. The challenge often is to make the time to review the log. In summary, your steps in setting up auditing on an NT Server should include the following:

1. Determine the factors that affect your auditing needs.
2. Develop an audit plan.
3. Use Event Viewer's Event Log Settings dialog to control the amount of information retained in each of the logs.
4. Use the User Manager's Audit Policy dialog to control which security-auditing features are implemented on your system.

Performance Tuning

We live in a world in which everyone wants you to do more with fewer resources. System administrators in charge of a Windows NT server are no exception to this rule. As a matter of fact, they often feel more pressure in this regard because a lot of NT servers were designed to replace much larger computer systems to help the organization save money. These organizations often forget about the increased load placed on computer systems when users actually start to use the newer, more convenient applications. Therefore, it is in the best interest of administrators to understand performance tuning.

I like the subject of performance tuning so much, I decided to devote all of Chapter 13, "NT Integration with NetWare and UNIX," to the subject. It is a somewhat challenging discipline in that you have to really understand how your hardware, operating system, and applications are interacting to affect your overall performance. You also have to deal with the concept of the bottle neck. What this means is that you can have tons of resources on your system, but if you are shy of just one little resource it can drag down system performance severely. After Chapter 13, you should be able to understand enough of the basics to track down your performance problems and get the best amount of performance possible for your resources (sometimes you have to tell your boss that the best-tuned 60MHz Pentium cannot be made to outperform a multimillion-dollar Cray computer).

Before leaving this chapter, though, I wanted to give you a basic understanding of the two key concepts that relate to performance management. The first of these is that of resources on your system. What this discipline involves is breaking down the hardware, operating system, and applications into logical components that affect performance. Examples of the more commonly used resources include central processing units, physical memory, and disk capacity. These fundamental resources are broken down into things that can actually be measured that affect performance. Examples of this include the number of bytes that are transferred per second to a specific disk drive, or the number of processes that are waiting to access a particular disk drive. These are the things you measure when you are conducting performance monitoring that will tell you when your system is having a problem.

The other key concept that I want to discuss related to performance monitoring is the capacity of the various system resources. This is very difficult to measure in absolute terms. It often depends on a number of factors, such as how your system is being used, which model of disk drive is installed, and so on. With the exception of a few parameters (for example, CPU capacity) that have absolute numbers (which can be provided by the vendors), you are often left to measure the performance of your system when everything is working properly to provide a baseline for comparison when your system starts to exhibit performance problems. Absolute numbers would be nice, but there are just too many variables between all existing installations to make such numbers readily available.

Presented here are a few key concepts related to performance tuning, to be considered along with the overall administrative picture. Windows NT is described as a self-tuning operating system. This means that the operating system works to adjust its internal system parameters to get the most that it can out of given resources. However, it does not mean that you can expect to have good performance if all of your commonly used files are on a single disk drive and it happens to be the slowest drive on your system. Chapter 13 goes into this subject in more detail.

Client-Server Environment Administration

The BackOffice family of products integrates quite nicely into the Windows NT security and administration scheme. There are products out there that do not fit into this scheme, so I want to make sure that you are aware of these cases. The most difficult to control as a system administrator are those applications that access your server via client-server applications. The basic concept of many of these applications is that you have a server application that is accessed via a direct connection from the client via Windows Sockets or some other mechanism, as shown in Figure 11.17. You have to have server permission to start your database (this example shows an Oracle database on your NT server), but all access to that database is controlled internally to the database. You can shut down the access mechanism (in this case the SQL*Net communications service that runs under NT), but you cannot monitor and control the users who are using this communications channel.

FIGURE 11.17.

An example of client-server access for Oracle.

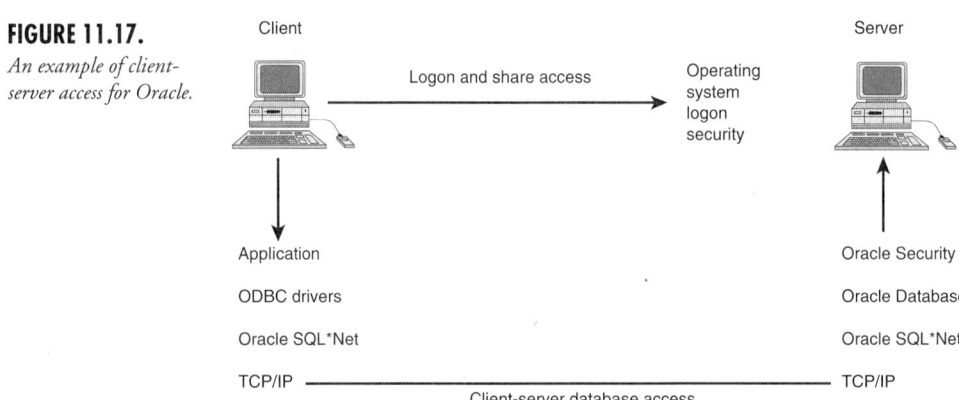

This is a valid access mode, and it works quite well for most such applications. However, there are a few things that you as the system administrator need to consider:

- ■ The administrator for that client-server application has to be responsible for user-account management.

- ■ It is very difficult to troubleshoot problems within the application for the system administrator. Although you can identify that the performance problem with the system is, say, a particular disk drive being overloaded, you have no idea why the application is using that disk or what you can do to remedy the situation.

■ Access to the rest of your system is controlled by the server that is accessed via the client serve mechanisms. Therefore, you have to trust these applications to prevent illegal access to your system.

One point to note before leaving this section is that one of the BackOffice products can be configured to enable general access to your computer bypassing user ID and password validation. Before you get too nervous, remember that access through this tool is limited to those directories you designate. The tool is the Internet Information Server product. The World Wide Web service is designed to enable anyone on the network who can find the Web server to access specified Web pages. As a matter of fact, you have to do some pretty fancy page design to restrict access to certain Web pages. The other tool is the File Transfer Protocol service when configured to allow anonymous FTP access. Again, in the case in which you enable anonymous FTP, you are trying to let anyone from the general population access the data you place in the FTP directories. The key with these two products is understanding that the general public can access the specified directories and making sure that you do not put any sensitive information in them.

Administration for Server-Based Applications

One topic that an administrator has to consider in light of the client-server discussion above is the fact that many other, purely server-based applications may also need special attention. Classic examples of this are applications that require certain batch jobs to be run every so often, or applications producing log files that need to be cleaned out on a routine basis. This book cannot anticipate all of the possibilities. Instead, I recommend that you check for this every time a new application is loaded on your server and put it into your task list.

Other Administrative Tasks

Just as a reminder, here are a few other tasks that you need to factor time into your schedule for as an administrator. I will break these other tasks down into four general areas:

■ Upgrades
■ Customer support
■ Keeping your skills up-to-date
■ Problem solving

In some ways, upgrades to operating systems or other BackOffice components can be trickier than installations on a new system. For example, let's say that you really mess up when installing a new server. You can generally start from scratch. You may have trouble making deadlines, but no one has lost any data. On an upgrade, though, the system is in production. You usually get only a limited time window to perform the upgrade, and you also have live user data that must be preserved. The pressure is on. A few suggestions that I always try to follow when performing upgrades include the following:

- Always, always, always perform a complete backup before starting the upgrade. Do not forget to back up the registry as well as the rest of the system data. Assume that the worst will happen and all of the hard disk drives will be reformatted during the upgrade process and that you will have to rebuild everything from scratch (very unlikely, but I like to err on the conservative side).

- If possible, test the upgrade procedure on a test server. This way you can work out any of the bugs while users are working away on the production system. After you have the procedure down, you can then try it out in production.

- Make sure that you know who to call for technical support if you run into a problem. You might want to have the numbers at hand before you start. You should also consider the hours of availability of this support (if you upgrade in the middle of the night, for example, you might not have support available until 9 a.m. the next day, which is when you promised to return the system to the users).

- If the upgrade procedure is nontrivial, consider writing out the steps in a checklist for yourself while reading the manuals. A simple checklist is easier to follow than the manual, and you can check off the steps as you go. This can be especially useful if you are doing a number of systems and you cannot remember whether you did a particular step on this system or not.

Another task system administrators generally need to allocate some time for is customer support. There are many forms of customer support, such as adding user accounts, but what I want to focus on here is all of those calls where users have questions about how to do something or are having problems with something. No matter how good the system documentation is, these calls are going to come up and you will have to make the time to deal with them. Perhaps you have a help desk to field the initial calls, but some are usually going to be beyond the help-desk level and filter down to you.

Another thing you need to make time for as an administrator is keeping your level of knowledge up-to-date. If you were an experienced OS/2 version 1 administrator who did not update his skills, you would be pretty useless in today's market. The computer industry changes quickly. You need to make time to keep up on these changes, or else you will be unable to give the right advice and keep your systems up-to-date. There are some antiquated systems that are running fine out there, but all computers eventually get retired. Hopefully the system administrator will not get retired with the computer.

One final thought: problem solving is a major job for most administrators. The time required for user administration and backup has decreased. The good news is that Windows NT servers are very reliable once set up. I spend very little time tweaking them, and that is pretty impressive considering that I work in an ever-changing development environment. However, hardware fails and software has problems. The only thing I can offer is that you need to learn as much as you can about your system before the problems start and combine that knowledge with a logical problem-solving methodology to figure out the problem. Some of the discussions on monitoring in Chapter 13 might be useful when you are trying to figure out exactly where the problem lies.

Scripting

I want to throw this section in here even though many of you will not want to batch files (sometimes called scripts for ex-UNIX types) to automate system functions. I typically try to build a script for any repetitive task I have to perform that requires a fair amount of time at the keyboard and requires me to issue a number of operating-system commands (as opposed to those long-running jobs that are kicked off by running a single command). Batch files enable you to perform a number of routine system functions. Batch-file programs take the commands that you enter at the DOS command line and store them in an ASCII text file, which usually ends with the BAT or CMD extension. You then can execute these files from the command line. You usually can put together batch files quickly, making it easy for you to automate common administrative tasks. You may even want to create a directory of your common scripts that has some form of protection (ownership and access privileges for only administrators, for example).

Although you can use a local command prompt or remote procedure call to execute these scripts on an as-needed basis, there is a more interesting use for your administrative batch files. The best form of remote processing is that taking place automatically, without your involvement. To accomplish this, create a script and store it in a batch file. The following is a portion of a script that would stop an Oracle database, stop its services, and perform a backup of the C:\ drive:

```
net stop "OracleServiceORCL" >> c:\scripts\backup.log
ntbackup backup c: /d"Daily Backup" /b /l"C:\daily_bk.log" /tape:0
net start "OracleServiceORCL" >> c:\scripts\backup.log
```

Using the preceding code, you have saved the complete listing of the script in a file called BACKUP.BAT, which is located in the protected C:\SCRIPTS directory. Suppose that you also want to perform your nightly backups at 2 a.m. every morning of the week. (Hopefully, someone else will come in and change the tape that is in the tape drive on weekends.) To schedule a job to run at a time you specify (either once or on a recurring basis), use the at command. In this command, you specify the time and then the script to run. It is similar in concept to the UNIX cron utility. To set up your backups, at the DOS command prompt, type the following:

```
at 2:00 "c:\scripts\backup.bat"
```

The graphical administrative tools provided in Windows NT are easier to deal with than batch programs. Batch files, however, provide a tool that enables you to perform tasks that graphical tools cannot. You can use batch programs rather than GUI tools to more easily meet special needs or perform simple tasks. For example, I have a simple batch file on my computer at work that copies the contents of my six data-holding directories to my directory on the server drive about an hour before the nightly backup kicks off. This way, my workstation (which lacks a tape drive) has its user data backed up nightly. Although I could set up the server to back up my local hard disk through the network as part of its backup job, I like to do it this way because if I mess up a file, all I need to do is copy it from my server, without restoring from tape.

You might be surprised at the number of NT command-line applications that enable you to specify a remote computer name for execution. One of the biggest is probably the `shutdown` command. You use the UNC name for the computer to specify which computer is to be shut down. An example of this command (for shutdown and reboot) is the following:

```
shutdown \\joe /R
```

You might want to consider these concepts when it comes time to automate some of your routine tasks. I want to mention, before leaving this section, the Remote Command Server and Executable program found on the Windows NT Resource Kit from Microsoft. You load and start this service on the server of interest. Then you load the `Rcmd.exe` program into the system directory of a client workstation (like the one located on your desk in your office). You can then send commands to the server via the Rcmd utility. All you have to do is specify the command name (for example, `c:\scripts\backup.bat`) and the server name as parameters to this command and you get a window in which you are executing a program using the CPU and other resources of the remote computer while displaying the results on your computer. You could take this to higher levels and set up a rather nice remote-administration system going beyond the remote-administration tools provided as part of Windows NT.

Summary

This chapter has covered a rather broad topic that is very important to system administrators. It involves a series of skills and tools that are used to keep the NT operating system functioning. I will go into the performance-tuning topic in more detail in the next chapter. I separated this out because it goes beyond routine administration and gets into some low-level details. Many Windows NT administrators do not have to worry about tuning. They have sufficient resources and their user demands are reasonable. Others, however, will have to crawl inside the guts of their system using performance-monitoring tools to help squeeze some additional performance out of a disk drive or perhaps justify the procurement of additional disk-storage space.

Windows NT Performance Tuning

by Joe Greene

IN THIS CHAPTER

CHAPTER 12

More for less. The watchwords of modern corporations. This chapter is devoted to the concept of getting as much performance as possible from your computer. Over the past several decades, one trend is clear: applications continue to demand more processing capacity, more memory, and more disk space as time progresses. Be cheerful—this trend helps keep the computer gurus employed.

The downside of this trend is that you have to be ready for the increased load that your users will be putting on your server and deal with performance problems that come up. Perhaps one of the features you liked when you first read about Windows NT was that line in the marketing materials about Windows NT being a self-tuning operating system. Yes, it is true that Windows NT takes much better care of itself than systems such as VMS and UNIX. Especially in older versions of UNIX, many of the parameters were poorly documented (if at all). The whole system could be brought to its knees if one of these parameters was not adjusted properly for the load applied to your specific system.

Having hired some of the folks who designed one of the best of the previous generation of operating systems (VMS, which was revolutionary for its day), Microsoft tried to take a logical scheme for allocating resources and make it one better with algorithms that help divert resources to where they are most needed. Windows NT does an admirable job (especially considering that it has not been out for that many years) at getting the most out of your existing computer systems running NT. However, there are a few real-world considerations that you need to factor in against your joy at having a self-tuning operating system:

- Your hardware has real limits. You can get only so much processing out of a 486/66 computer, no matter how well tuned it is. The same applies to all your disk drives, memory areas, and other hardware items.

- You can configure your system poorly so that no amount of automated tuning will help. An example of this would be a file server that has ten disk drives, only one of which contains information of interest to the users and is therefore the one that bears all the load for data transfer operations.

- You can have bad applications that either you write or you buy from a vendor. A relatively simple function (such as a device driver or financial database) can put a huge load on the system. You might not have much control over this as the system administrator, but you might want to coach your developers, or influence your users who are purchasing applications, to choose applications that match your available processing capacity.

- Your server can be limited by the loading and performance of your network. Many experienced computer systems professionals still find all those wires, concentrators, and protocols to be a dark mystery. However, that mystery has a significant impact on the overall performance of client-server applications and network operating system services (such as file sharing and printing). Therefore, you need to be conversant on what the capabilities of these networks are and when they are affecting your performance.

This chapter is devoted to arming you with the knowledge of when you need to intervene to help keep your system running at peak performance. This process starts with an introduction to the components of your hardware and operating system that relate to performance. It then introduces the monitoring tools that are used to help you figure out if your system is operating well and, if not, where the problems lie. Next, this chapter covers the various steps that can be taken to alleviate common problems. Finally, there is a discussion of capacity planning, which helps you ensure that you have the resources you need before you need them.

One final note is that there are entire books devoted to this topic (that is, in the resource kit). The goal of this chapter is not to capture all the wisdom of these large volumes in a matter of a few pages. Instead, my goal is to present material that helps you understand the basics of the tuning, optimization, and capacity-planning processes. That, combined with an understanding of the most common problems, will equip you to handle the vast majority of NT Server installations out there. Finally, don't forget that not all the tuning responsibility lies at the operating system administrator level. Applications, especially complex databases and three-tier client-server applications, can humble the most powerful computer systems if they are not tuned properly. Therefore, system tuning might involve obtaining support from database administrators or application administrators to ensure that their applications are making efficient use of your system resources.

The Basics of Performance Monitoring

This section is the starting point for the performance management discussions. My goal is to cover the typical hardware and software found on Intel-based servers running Windows NT. These concepts can easily be extended to the other hardware platforms on which NT runs.

The first challenge when working in the PC server world is the number of vendors out there. This is good when it comes to keeping pressure on the vendors to innovate and offer products at a reasonable price. However, it does complicate things for administrators who have to keep up with these innovations and keep the systems running. It is not just a matter of dealing with the different transfer rates of different types of hard disk drives. It involves having disk drives that have completely different data transfer architectures and capabilities. The industry is committed to ensuring that you don't get bored with a lack of new technologies to keep up on.

Intel-Based PC Architecture

What is the Intel-based PC architecture? Figure 12.1 presents a sample of such an architecture. It starts with a processor chip made by Intel or one of the companies that produces chips compatible with those made by Intel (Cyrix, AMD, and so on). This chip dictates several things about the architecture; it defines the interface between the processor chip, cache memory, and main random access memory. Intel numbers its chips with numbers ending in 86 (such as 80386 and 80486), although the later generations have been marketed by fancier names, such as Pentium. Whatever you call them, they define the hardware standard for Intel-based PCs and drive how Microsoft builds the versions of Windows NT that are designed to run on these processors. For purposes of this discussion, all the internals of these Central Processing Unit (CPU) chips are skipped, because they don't contain anything related to tuning you need to worry about. Two of your most precious resources are connected to the processor chip by the highest-speed bus in your computer (which is 32 bits wide in the processors that run Windows NT 4.0). The first of these resources is the random access memory (RAM). This is the main memory in your computer, which enables you to hold the instructions that make up the programs you want to execute. The next resource, the second-level cache, is designed to make things a little faster. Conceptually, it is similar to random access memory, although it is faster. The goal is that if the operating system and processor guess correctly as to which is the next instruction or data element that needs to be retrieved and draws it into this cache, you can speed up the operation of the computer. It becomes important to you when purchasing systems that talk about cache in the specifications. Typically, computers that have more cache for the same processor speed operate slightly faster.

FIGURE 12.1.

Typical Intel-based PC architecture.

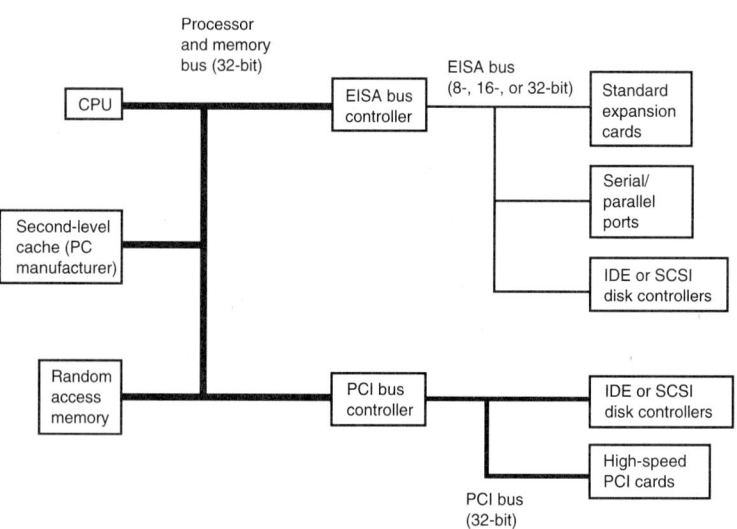

Because Windows NT operates on a variety of computer platforms, there is one thing related to the central processing units that needs to be discussed. A computer in the Intel 80×86 family of computers is known as a complex instruction set computer (CISC). This means that each instruction actually performs relatively complex tasks. This is in contrast to the reduced instruction set computers (RISC), such as the DEC Alpha, which process relatively simple tasks with each instruction. This becomes important when you consider the processing speed ratings that computer makers always throw at you. RISC computers almost always have higher speed ratings than CISC computers that perform the same amount of useful processing per unit of time. Because the Intel family continues to evolve, later generations of Intel processors usually outperform older processors that have similar speed ratings, assuming that the operating system is designed to take advantage of these features. Windows NT is one of the few operating systems in the PC world that exploits many of the advanced features of recent Intel chips such as the Pentium.

So far, this chapter has discussed the three main components (CPU, cache, and RAM) that are attached to the processor's wonderful, high-speed data transfer bus. To keep this bus available for the important transfers between memory and the CPU, lower-importance communications are split off onto other buses within the computer. This was not the case in the early PC days. What happened here is that the slow stream of data from the various peripherals impeded the communications of the more critical components. Designers learned from this and placed these other devices on their own buses.

Many of the modern PCs that you would be considering for server configuration actually have two different types of supporting data transfer bus. The EISA (Enhanced Industry Standard Architecture) bus has been around for a while. Because of this, the majority of expansion cards on the market today support this architecture. It comes in two flavors: one uses an 8-bit or 16-bit wide data transfer bus, and the other uses a 32-bit wide data transfer bus. This architecture was designed when processors and peripheral devices were much slower than they are today.

In recent years there have been several attempts to specify a new standard data transfer bus for the industry. The one that seems to be assuming this role is the PCI bus. This bus uses 32-bit wide data transfer rates. Some other technical design considerations also enable it to transfer data at much higher rates than the older EISA bus. What this means to you is that if your server has a PCI bus and you can find a peripheral (such as a SCSI disk drive controller card) that supports this structure, you get higher levels of performance. Be aware, though, that most of these cards cost more than their EISA counterparts. In addition, some peripherals cannot use the higher performance capabilities of the PCI bus (floppy disk drives). Most of the servers I have configured recently have a mix of EISA and PCI slots. You typically guard the PCI slots for needs such as 100Mbps network cards that need the speed of the PCI bus.

Suppose you have a processor chip that executes the instructions that allow the computer to process information. You have two forms of high-speed data and instruction storage in the RAM and cache that have a direct line to the CPU. You then have controllers that link the high-speed processor and memory bus to slower peripherals. The lower-speed data transfer buses come in several different flavors. The key is that you have to match the data transfer bus used in your machine with the type of card you want to add to your machine.

Now that you are comfortable with those basic concepts, there are a few other wrinkles you should be aware of before you jump in and start measuring your system performance in preparation for a tuning run. Some of the cards you attach to the EISA, PCI, or other lower-speed data transfer buses are actually controllers for a tertiary bus in the computer. The most common example of this is hard disk drive controllers. Of course, there are several different standards for these controllers (SCSI, Fast-Wide SCSI, IDE, and others) that you have to get used to and that offer different performance characteristics. Let's look at a few of these so that you understand some of the differences.

IDE stands for Integrated Drive Electronics, which simply means that many of the logic circuits are on the drive itself and therefore provide a smarter drive that burdens the system less and is capable of supporting higher transfer rates than the older drives (MFM, RLL, and ESDI). These controllers can typically support two drives, which are referred to as master and slave (if one is a boot drive, it is typically the master). They are typically slower than SCSI controllers and support fewer drives per controller. The IDE drive is by far the most popular drive architecture in today's PCs.

SCSI stands for Small Computer System Interface and was first commonly used in the UNIX world. As such, it was designed for a slightly higher transfer speed and also supported more devices (typically seven peripherals on a single controller). You can usually have multiple SCSI controllers in a system if you have really big disk needs. SCSI components cost a bit more, and the device drivers are harder to come by, but many administrators prefer a SCSI bus for servers. You can also buy SCSI tape drives (my favorite is the 4mm DAT tape drive), optical drives, and a few other peripherals, such as scanners. The SCSI bus is an architecture designed for the more demanding data transfer requirements that used to occur only in UNIX workstations and servers, but today are being levied on Windows NT Servers.

Now that you are getting somewhat comfortable with SCSI, you should be aware that it comes in several flavors. All those people out there who want to do more with computers each year keep driving vendors to bring out hardware and software that does more. The good news about SCSI is that there is a standard specification, and thus you can almost always get SCSI devices from different vendors to work together. However, SCSI was designed for a kinder, gentler world several years ago, and it is time to push forward. Because the SCSI specification limits the technology that can be brought to bear on the performance needs of the users, vendors had to come up with newer forms of the SCSI standard. The most common version of this is fast-wide SCSI. It uses a data transfer bus that is twice as wide as the original and can generally perform at twice the data transfer rate of basic SCSI. These controllers often enable you to install up to 15 peripherals on the SCSI bus. Be ready for a SCSI-3 standard. It might be the solution when PC servers running NT need large disk farms that have very high data transfer rates (everyone keeps pushing video and other demanding applications).

Other components also have their standards. Modems are often referred to as Hayes or US Robotics compatible. For the most part, however, these devices do their own thing, and it typically has a lesser impact on the performance of the computer system. One area that does have an impact on the system performance is the video subsystem. Several graphics cards take high-level graphics commands and work the display details out on the graphics card itself using on-board processors and special high-speed graphics memory. NT can be set up to interface directly with these cards at a high level, or it can be asked to work out the display details using the main CPU, which increases the load on the system.

For those of you who have already exceeded your limits on hardware-related information, be brave. There is only one more hardware topic to discuss before moving on to the software world. The final topic is the components themselves. Memory chips have speed ratings, but because the data transfer rate is synchronized by the processor bus, all you have to worry about is that your memory chips are good enough for the clock speed of your computer. The performance effects that are most commonly considered are those associated with disk drives. You might have a fast bus, but if the disk drive is slow, your overall data transfer rate is reduced. Therefore, if you have a system that needs a lot of performance, you need to check out the performance characteristics of your peripherals as well.

Computer systems are a collection of hardware components that interact to perform the tasks assigned to them. Figure 12.2 shows a hierarchy of these components. These levels need to act together to perform services for the user, such as accessing data on a hard disk drive. Each of these components can be purchased from several vendors. Each of these products has varying levels of price and performance. The difficulty is finding that correct blend of price and performance to meet your needs.

FIGURE 12.2.

Hierarchy of hardware components.

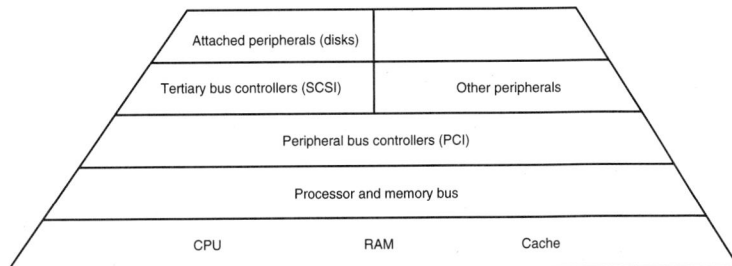

The Operating System and Its Interaction with Hardware

This section addresses the operating system and how it interacts with all this hardware. Chapter 2, "Integrated Architecture," provides a more detailed discussion of the NT architecture. Think of the way you set up a new computer. Typically, you set up all the hardware first and then you install your operating system. If your hardware doesn't work (the machine is dead), it really doesn't matter what the operating system can do. This is a good way to think of the interaction of the operating system with the hardware. The operating system is designed to interface with the various hardware devices to perform some useful processing.

The first interface between the operating system and your computer is pretty well defined by Intel (or your hardware vendor, such as DEC) and Microsoft. The operating system contains a lot of compiled software that is written in the native language of the CPU and related processors (a bunch of 1s and 0s). The low-level interface to the computer chips is segregated into a small set of code that is specific to the particular computer chip used (this helps NT port between Intel, DEC Alpha, and other host platforms).

Each of the other hardware devices (expansion cards, SCSI controllers, and disk drives) responds to a series of 1s and 0s. The challenge here is that different devices use a different set of codes to control their devices. For example, you would transmit a specific binary number to eject the tape on a four millimeter DAT tape drive and another binary number to eject a CD-ROM from its drive. Walking through any major computer store and seeing the huge variety of hardware available gives me a headache just thinking about all the possibilities for controlling commands.

In the old DOS world, each application was pretty much on its own and had to worry about what codes were sent to each of the peripherals. That made the lives of the people who wrote DOS easier, but created great headaches for application developers. Realizing this problem, Windows (before Windows 95 and Windows NT) introduced the concept of device drivers. This enabled you to write your application to a standard interface with the operating system (part of the application programming interface, or API, for that operating system). It was then the operating system's job to translate what you wanted to have done into the appropriate low-level codes specific to a particular piece of hardware. The section of the operating system that took care of these duties was the device driver (sometimes referred to as printer drivers for printers).

It is now no longer your problem to deal with the hardware details as an application designer. You have a few other things to think about, though. Because different hardware devices have different capabilities (for example, some printers can handle graphics and others are text-only), the device driver has to be able to signal the applications when it is asked to do something that the attached device cannot handle. Because these device drivers are bits of software, some are better written than others. Some of these device drivers can get very complex and might have bugs in them. This leads to upgrades and fixes to device drivers that you have to keep up on. Finally, although Windows NT comes with a wide variety of device drivers (both Microsoft and the peripheral vendors want to make it easy for you to attach their products to your Windows NT machine), other devices might not have drivers on the NT distribution disks. New hardware or hardware from smaller vendors requires device driver disks (or CDs) for you to work with them. An excellent source of the latest device drivers is the Internet Web pages provided by Microsoft and most computer equipment vendors. The key to remember here is that you need to have a Windows NT–compatible (not Windows 3.1 or Windows 95) device driver for all peripherals that you will be attaching to your NT system. If you are in doubt as to whether a peripheral is supported under NT, contact the peripheral vendor or look at the NT Hardware Compatibility List on the Microsoft Web page (www.microsoft.com or CD-ROMs if you lack Web access).

Now that you have eliminated the low-level interfaces to all that hardware, you have a basis on which you can build operating system services that help applications run under Windows NT. Using the same logic that drove the developers to build device drivers, there came to be several common functions that almost every application uses. Microsoft has always been sensitive to the fact that you want a lot of great applications to run on your operating system so that it is useful to people and they will buy it. Rather than have the application developers spend a lot of time writing this code for every application, Microsoft engineers decided to build this functionality into the operating system itself. Examples of some of these services include print queue processing (killing print jobs and keeping track of which job is to be sent to the printer next) and TCP/IP networking drivers. This actually has the side benefit of enabling Microsoft engineers who are specialists in these components and the operating system itself to write these services and drivers. This usually results in more powerful and efficient processes than would be written by your typical application programmer, who has to worry about the screen layout and all those reports that Accounting wants to have done by Friday.

Finally, at the top of the processing hierarchy are the end-user applications themselves. One could consider a computer as next to useless if it lacks applications that help people get their jobs done. Remember, UNIX talks about its openness, Macintosh talks about its superior interface that has existed for several years, and the OS/2 folks usually talk about the technical superiority of the internals of their operating system. All Microsoft has going for it is a few thousand killer applications that people like. One thing you have to remember as a system administrator, now that you are at the top of the performance hierarchy, is that you still have the opportunity to snatch defeat from the jaws of victory. You can have the best hardware, the best device drivers, and the most perfectly tuned Windows NT system in the world, but if your applications are poorly written, your users will suffer from poor system performance.

Figure 12.3 provides a summary of what this chapter has covered so far in a convenient, graphical form. Obviously, this drawing does not depict the interaction of all the components. The operating system interfaces with the CPU, and some peripherals actually interact with one another. What it does show is that several components need to work together to provide good performance as seen by the end-users. This can be a complex job, but fortunately Windows NT provides you with the tools that help you manage this more easily than most other server operating systems. That is the subject of the rest of this chapter.

FIGURE 12.3.

Hierarchy of hardware and software components.

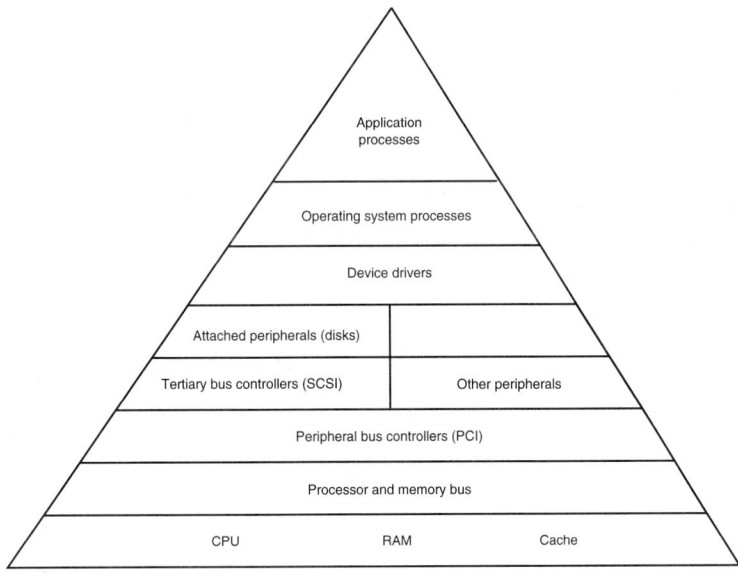

Determining Normal Efficiency Levels

You might be wondering how to figure out all the options and how to have any idea whether this complex array of components is functioning at normal efficiency. There are articles that go through the theory behind components and try to calculate values for various configurations. However, because hardware technology continues to march on, and any configuration you might read about is quite possibly out of date by the time you read it, many prefer a more empirical approach.

Unlike most other operating systems, Windows NT is designed to handle most of the details of the interaction of its components. You can control a few things, but I wouldn't recommend it unless you have a really unusual situation and a really serious need. You might do things that the designers never intended. Therefore, I start by accepting my hardware and operating system configuration. From there, I look for metrics that measure the overall performance of the resources that typically have problems and that I have some form of control over. For purposes of this chapter, I treat the vast complexity of computers running Windows NT as having five components that can be monitored and tuned:

- CPU processing capacity
- Random access memory and virtual memory capacity
- Input/output capacity
- Network transmission capacity
- Application efficiency

CPU Processing Capacity

The first component specifies the amount of processing work that the central processing unit of your computer can handle in a given period of time. Although this might depend on the clock speed, the type of instruction set it processes, the efficiency with which the operating system uses the CPU's resources, and any number of other factors, I want to take it as a simple limit that is fixed for a given CPU and operating system. You should be aware that different CPUs exhibit different processing capacities based on the type of work presented to them. Some computers handle integer and text processing efficiently, whereas others are designed as numeric computation machines that handle complex floating-point (with decimals) calculations. Although this is fixed for a given family of processor (such as the Intel Pentium), you might want to consider this when you are selecting your hardware architecture.

RAM and Virtual Memory Capacity

The next component is RAM and virtual memory. Applications designers know that RAM can be read quickly and has a direct connection to the CPU through the processor and memory bus. They are under pressure to make their applications do more and, of course, respond more quickly to the user's commands. Therefore, they continue to find new ways to put more information (data, application components, and so on) into memory, where it can be gotten much more quickly than if it were stuck on a hard disk drive or a floppy disk. Gone are the days of my first PC, which I thought was impressive with 256K of memory. Modern NT Servers usually start at 24M of RAM and go up from there.

With Windows NT and most other operating systems, you actually have two types of memory to deal with. RAM corresponds to chips physically inside your machine that store information. Early computer operating systems generated errors (or halted completely) when they ran out of physical memory. To get around this problem, operating system developers started to use virtual memory. Virtual memory combines the physical memory in the RAM chips with some storage space on one or more disk drives to simulate an environment that has much more memory than you could afford if you had to buy RAM chips. These operating systems have special operating system processes that figure out what sections of physical memory are less likely to be needed (usually by a combination of memory area attributes and a least recently used algorithm) and then transfer this data from RAM to the page file on disk that contains the swapped-out sections of memory. If the swapped-out data is needed again, the operating system processes transfer it back into RAM for processing. Obviously, because disk transfers are much slower than RAM transfers and you might be in a position of having to swap something out to make room and then transfer data into RAM, this can significantly slow down applications that are trying to perform useful work for your users.

Some use of virtual memory is harmless. Some operating system components are loaded and rarely used. Some applications have sections of memory that get loaded but are never used. The problem occurs when the system becomes so memory-bound that it has to swap something out, then swap something in before it can do any processing for the users. Several memory areas are designated as "do not swap" to the operating system; these cause you to have even less space for applications than you might think. If you are using a modern database management system such as SQL Server or Oracle, be ready to have large sections of memory taken up in shared memory pools. Databases use memory areas to store transactions that are pending, record entries to their log file for later transfer to disk, and cache records that have been retrieved on the hope that they will be the next ones asked for by the users. They are probably the most demanding applications on most servers.

Input/Output Capacity

The next component to discuss is the input/output capacity of the computer. For today at least, you can simplify this to be the input/output capacity of your disk drives and controllers. Someday, not too long from now, you might be worrying about saturating your PCI bus with complex audio/video traffic. However, for now, let's concentrate on disk drives. Typically, three components are involved with getting data from the high-capacity disk drives to the RAM memory where the CPU can use it. The first is the secondary data transfer bus controller, usually a PCI or EISA controller. The next is the actual disk drive controller, which is most often an IDE controller, with more reasonably priced SCSI showing up as time progresses. Finally, there is the disk drive itself. I discuss ways to measure the overall transfer capacity of the disk drive systems as if they were individual drives directly connected to the processor bus. This simplification treats the controllers and drives as a single entity and makes measurement and management easier. You still need to keep in the back of your mind the possibility that you might saturate the capacity of your disk drive controller even though you have not saturated the capacity of any of the individual disk drives attached to it.

Network Transmission Capacity

An important component in many Windows NT Servers is the network transmission capabilities. Windows NT Server is a network-based computing environment. This is basically data input and output using a card similar to those used to attach disk drives, right? I separated my discussion of network I/O from other I/O for several reasons. First, the technologies are completely different and you have to get used to a different set of terminology. You usually have to deal with a different group of engineers when trying to resolve problems. Second, unless you are also the network administrator, you typically do not completely own the network transmission system. Instead, you are just one of many users of the network. This means that you have to determine whether you are the cause of the network bottleneck or if you are merely the victim of it. Finally, you end up using a different set of monitoring utilities when dealing with networks.

Network cards are an often overlooked component in a server. The networking world is somewhat deceptive because it quotes transmission rates for the type of network you are using (for example, 10 million bits per second on Ethernet). This might lead you to think that it doesn't matter which network interface card you choose because the transmission rate is fixed anyway. Unfortunately, that is not the case. If you ran different network cards through performance tests, you would find that some are much more capable than others at getting information onto and off of a particular computer. Because most network cards on the market are designed for workstations that individually have relatively light network loads, you might have to look around to find a network interface card that is designed to meet the much more demanding need of a server that is continuously responding to network requests from several workstations.

Application Efficiency

Finally, I want to reemphasize the idea of application efficiency as an important part of overall performance. Perhaps this is because I come from the perspective of the database administrator, where you continuously run across developers who are complaining that "the database is too slow." I can't tell you how many times I have looked at their software only to find things such as if they want 10 numbers, they put the program in a loop and make 10 calls to the database over a heavily loaded network, as opposed to one call that brings back all the data at once. Perhaps they are issuing queries without using the indexes that are designed to make such queries run faster. By changing a few words around in the query, they could take a 30-minute query and turn it into a 10-second query. (I'm not kidding—I saw this done on a large data warehouse many times.) Unfortunately, this is one of those things that requires experience and common sense. You have to judge whether the application is taking a long time because it is really complex (for example, a fluid flow computation with a system that has 10,000 degrees of freedom) or because it is poorly tuned (developers want to retrieve 10 simple numbers and it is taking 30 seconds). Of course, you need to be certain before you point the finger at someone else. That is what the Performance Monitoring Utilities section is all about. It gives you scientific data to show that you are doing your job properly before you ask for more equipment or tell people to rewrite their applications.

In this section, I have tried to give an overview of how the hardware, software, and operating system interact to give an overall level of computer service to the users. The difficulty in this process is that a huge variety of hardware components, device drivers, and applications all come together to affect the performance of your Windows NT Server. I don't believe it is worthwhile to calculate out numbers that indicate the capacity of your system. Instead, I believe in measuring certain key performance indicators that are tracked by Windows NT. Over time, you will develop a baseline of what numbers are associated with good system performance and what are associated with poor performance. I have also simplified the vast array of components in the system to a list of five key components that you will want to routinely monitor. These are the ones that will cause your most common problems.

Data Gathering

One of the more interesting things about coming to Windows NT after having worked on several other types of server platforms is the fact that several useful, graphical administrative tools come as part of the operating system itself. Although UNIX and other such operating systems come with tools that can get the job done if you are fluent in them, they are neither friendly nor powerful. My main focus in this section is the built-in utility known as Performance Monitor. This tool enables you to monitor most of the operating system performance parameters that you could possibly be interested in. It supports a flexible, real-time interface and also enables you to store data in a log file for future retrieval and review.

However, before I get too far into the tools used to measure performance, a few topics related to monitoring need to be covered. Although you could put your ear to your computer's cabinet to see if you hear the disk drives clicking a lot, it is much easier if the operating system and hardware work together to measure activities of interest for you. Windows NT can monitor all the critical activities of your system and then some. Your job is to wade through all the possible things that can be monitored to determine which ones are most likely to give you the information you need.

Activity Measurement

How does Windows NT measure activities of interest? The first concept you have to get used to is that of an object. Examples of objects in Windows NT performance would be the (central) processor or logical disk drives. Associated with each of these objects is a series of counters. Each of these counters measures a different activity for that object, such as bytes total per second and bytes read per second. That brings me to a good point about counters. To be useful, counters have to measure something that is useful for indicating a load on the system. For example, six million bytes read does not tell you very much. If it were six million bytes per second, that would be a significant load. If it were six million bytes read since the system was last rebooted two months ago, it would be insignificant. Therefore, most of your counters that show activity are usually rated per second or as a percentage of total capacity or usage (as in percent processor time devoted to user tasks). A few items, such as number of items in a queue, have meaning in and of themselves (keeping the queue small is generally a good idea).

Another important concept when working with counters is that you have to measure them over an appropriate time interval. A graph showing every instant in time would produce an enormous amount of data very quickly. To control this, measurement programs such as Performance Monitor average the values over an amount of time you specify. You have to be somewhat careful when you specify the time interval. For example, if you average the data over a day, you can see long-term trends on the increase in usage of your system when you compare the various days. However, you would not notice the fact that the system is on its knees from 8 a.m. to 9 a.m. and from 1 p.m. to 2 p.m. This is what your users will notice; therefore, you need to be able to measure over a more reasonable interval, such as several minutes. I'll show you later how to turn monitoring on and off automatically so that you aren't collecting a lot of relatively useless data when no one is using your server.

Another important point about monitoring is that you need to monitor the system without influencing the data. For example, imagine setting up several dozen instances of Performance Monitor to measure all the parameters that could possibly be needed for later analysis using a time interval of one second and logging all this information to a single disk drive. The data you collected by this process would be heavily influenced by the load placed on the system to collect, process, and store the information related to monitoring. Your counters for the number of processes running, threads, and data transfer to that logging disk might actually reflect only the load of the monitoring application and not show any data about the use of the system by other applications.

A final term you need to get comfortable with that relates to Windows NT performance monitoring is that of an instance. Most of the objects monitored by Performance Monitor have multiple instances. An example of this is when you try to monitor the logical disk object: the system needs to know which of your logical disks (such as the C drive) you want to monitor. As you see later, Performance Monitor provides you with a list of available instances for the objects that have them.

In summary, monitoring under Windows NT is provided by a built-in, graphical utility known as Performance Monitor. This tool monitors many different types of objects (for example, processors). Each object has several possible attributes that might need to be measured. Windows NT refers to these attributes of the objects as counters (for example, percent processor time). Finally, there are more than one of many of the objects in your system. When there are multiple items of a given object, you need to tell Performance Monitor which instance of that object you want to have measured and for which of the counters. Figure 12.4 illustrates these concepts.

FIGURE 12.4.

Performance Monitor terminology.

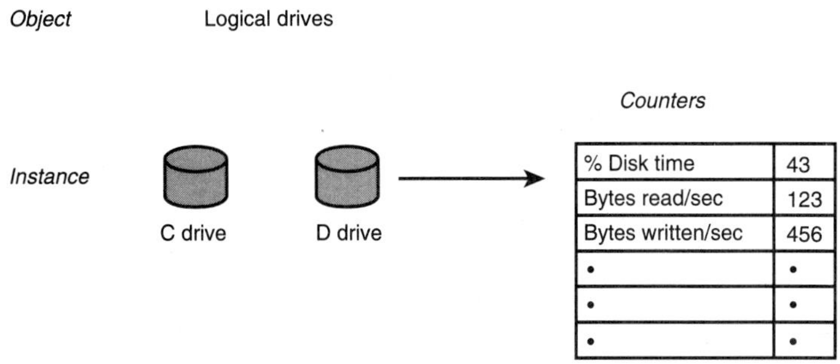

Activities that Can Be Monitored

As I alluded to earlier in my discussion, Windows NT provides you with a large number of counters from which to select. I found the following objects, with the number of counters associated with them in parentheses:

- Browser (21)
- Cache (27)
- IP (17)
- Logical Disk (21)
- Memory (27)
- NetBEUI (39)
- NetBEUI Resource (3)
- Network Interface (17)
- NWLink IPX (39)
- NWLink NetBIOS (39)
- NWLink SPX (39)
- Objects (Events, Mutexes, Processes, Sections, Semaphores, and Threads)
- Paging File (2)
- Physical Disk 19)
- Process (18)
- Processor (10)
- RAS Port (17)
- RAS Total (18)
- Redirector (37)
- Server (26)
- Server Work Queue (17)
- System (24)

- TCP (9)
- Thread (12)

Much as the Event Log can be used by applications to give you one place to look at for things that have happened (information and problems) on your system, applications can be interfaced with Performance Monitor to give you one place to look for performance information. One of the things I found useful is that the monitoring options appear on the list of objects only when you have the appropriate applications running. The five Performance Monitor objects associated with SQL Server, for example, and the nine Performance Monitor objects associated with Exchange Server are listed only when you have those servers running. This does not prevent you from running Performance Monitor in multiple windows to monitor things one at a time. It does enable you to put the usage data for an application on the same graph as critical operating system parameters to see how the application is interacting with the operating system. Think of it as being able to put the blame on a particular application for bringing your server to its knees.

This brings me to my first bit of advice related to using the Performance Monitor built into Windows NT: Try it out. It can monitor numerous things, but the interface is fairly simple. It is not like the Registry Editor, where you are doing something risky. You might waste a little time playing with this utility when everything is going well on your system. Being comfortable with selecting the various counters and graphical options could pay you back in the future when things are not going well and you are under pressure to solve the problems quickly.

With all this performance theory and terminology out of the way, it is time to actually look at Performance Monitor and see how it can be used to get you the data you need. Figure 12.5 shows you how to access Performance Monitor in the Start menu hierarchy. As you can see, it is conveniently located with all the other administrative tools that you will come to depend upon to keep your server going.

FIGURE 12.5.

Accessing Performance Monitor.

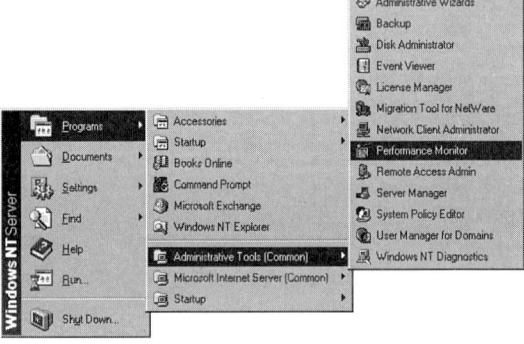

Performance Monitor

What does Performance Monitor do for you? Figure 12.6 shows my favorite means of displaying data: the line graph. It is a flexible utility that has other ways to capture data, but for now you can learn a lot about the tool using this format. Following is a description of the basic interface:

- Across the top is a traditional Windows menu bar that enables you to access all your basic processing options.

- Underneath the menu is a toolbar that enables you to pick the most commonly used options with a single mouse click. The first four buttons enable you to select the type of display to be presented: chart view, alert view, log view, and report view. The next three buttons enable you to add, modify, or delete a particular counter from your list via a pop-up dialog box. The next button enables you to take a snapshot of performance data (for when you are not collecting data at predefined intervals). The next-to-last button enables you to write a comment (bookmark) to the log file at a particular time that might help jog your memory later when you are reviewing the data. The final button displays the Display Options dialog to enable you to set things up to your liking.

- The majority of the display is consumed with the display of performance data. You will learn about the various display formats shortly.

FIGURE 12.6.

Performance Monitor's basic interface.

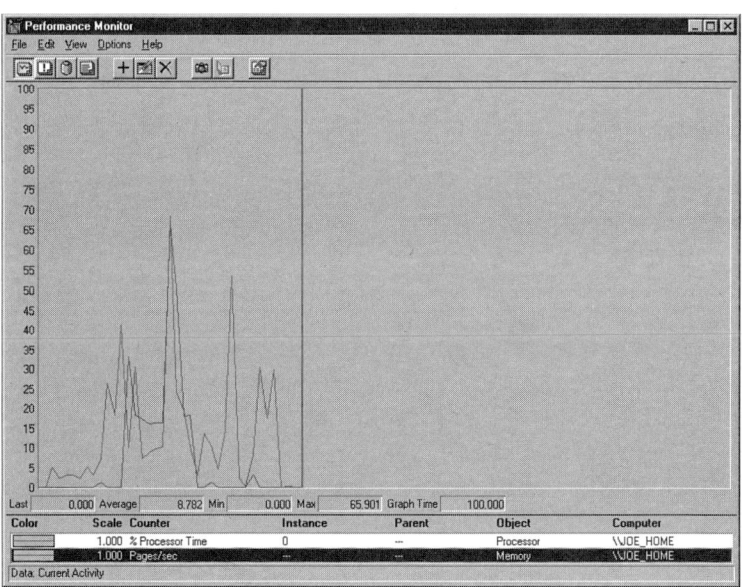

Before leaving the basics of the Performance Monitor display, let's look at a few options that might appeal to some of you. Those of you who are comfortable with several windows or toolbars being open on your desktop at a given time so you can see everything that is happening can use a few control keys to minimize the Performance Monitor display. Figure 12.7 shows a Performance Monitor graph of CPU processor time use in a nice, graph-only window. To do this, I hit the following keys: Ctrl+M (toggles the menu on and off), Ctrl+S (toggles the status line on and off), and Ctrl+T (toggles the toolbar on and off). You can hit Ctrl+P to toggle a setting that keeps the Performance Monitor display on top of other windows on your desktop. All you have to do is set up Performance Monitor to monitor the items you want, trim off the menu, toolbar, and status window, then size the window and move it to where you want it.

FIGURE 12.7.

Trimmed Performance Monitor window.

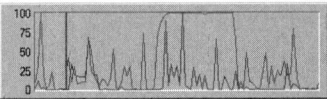

When you first start Performance Monitor, you notice that it is not doing anything. With the large number of monitoring options, Microsoft was not willing to be presumptuous and assume which counters should be monitored by default. Therefore, you have to go in and add the options, counters, and instances you want to get the system going. It is not at all difficult to accomplish this task. The first thing you do is click on the plus sign icon on the toolbar. You are presented with the Add to Chart dialog box, shown in Figure 12.8. From here, all you have to do is select the options you want:

FIGURE 12.8.

The Add to Chart dialog box.

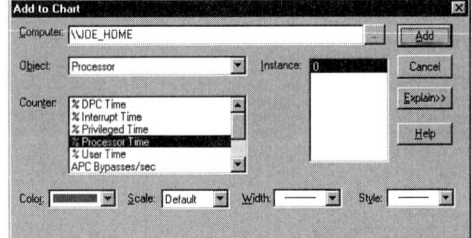

- ■ *Computer.* This box enables you to select which computer you want to monitor. This is a really nice feature because it lets you sit at your desk and use your terminal to monitor the world (at least that part of the world to which you have privileges). The selection box at the right helps you locate the computers that are available for you to monitor, or you can do it the old-fashioned way by typing a double backslash followed by the computer name.

- ■ *Object.* This is a drop-down listbox that enables you to select which object you want to monitor. The object selected drives the legal values that are displayed in the next two controls.

- *Counter.* This is a scrollable list that enables you to choose which of the counters associated with your selected object you want to monitor.

- *Instance.* To the right of the Object and Counter controls is a scrollable list of the instances of the object you have selected (which disk drive).

- *Add.* To add the specified object counter instance you have entered to the list of counters monitored, click on the Add button.

- *Explain.* To get a more detailed explanation of the counter you are selecting, click on the Explain button and you get some text at the bottom of the dialog box (see Figure 12.9). This text could be a little more detailed and easy to understand, but it can be useful in certain circumstances.

FIGURE 12.9.

The Add to Chart dialog box with the Explain option selected.

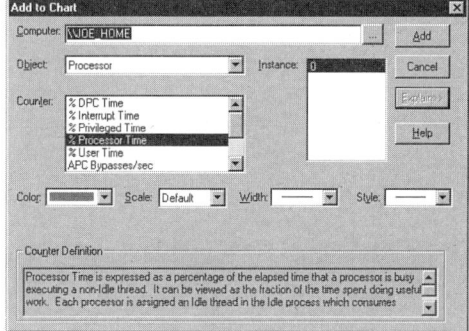

- *Cancel.* When you are finished, click on the Cancel button before you click on the Add button, or click on Done after you click on the Add button. This takes you back to the main display so that you can see what is happening.

  You should note that this same dialog box is used for all the types of monitoring (chart, alert, log, and report) that are supported by Performance Monitor. The last word in the title bar changes to correspond to the display option with which you are working.

- Finally, you see Color, Scale, Width, and Style controls at the bottom of this dialog box. Performance Monitor automatically cycles through a predefined color and line pattern list as you add different counters, but you might want to take control of this decision to suit your artistic sense. These buttons let you do that.

Considerations for Charts

There are a few considerations for laying out this chart. So far I have presented relatively simple graphs to illustrate my points. However, now consider Figure 12.10, which I intentionally made complex to illustrate a few new points. First, you might find it hard to distinguish which line corresponds to which counter. There are several lines, and they are all crossing one another.

Very few people, even those comfortable with graph reading, can follow more than a few lines. You might want to keep this in mind when you take your wonderful charts before management to prove a point. You also might find it especially difficult to read the graphs presented here, because Microsoft uses different colors and patterns for the lines to help you pick out which line corresponds to which data element. Although there are shading differences between the various colors and there is the line pattern, you might want to keep the number of lines on your graph especially small if you are presenting it in black and white.

FIGURE 12.10.

A complex Performance Monitor chart.

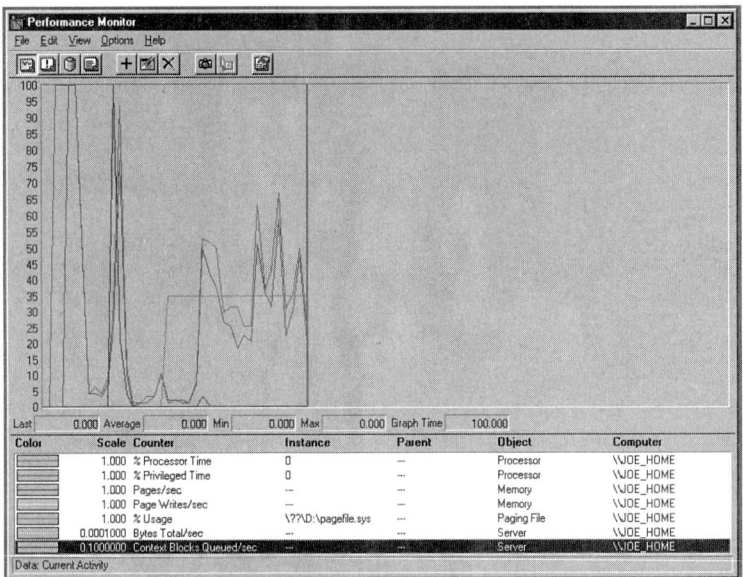

It can take some time to customize this display with the counters you want to monitor, the display options, and the colors that appeal to your sense of beauty. It would be a real pain if you had to go through this process each time you wanted to start up Performance Monitor. Microsoft has provided the Save Chart Settings option under the File menu in Performance Monitor (see Figure 12.11) for you to save your settings for the chart. You can also save all the settings for your charts, option menu selections, and so forth in a workspace file using the Save Workspace menu option. These features can be quite powerful. You can actually create a series of Performance Monitor settings files in advance when everything is working well. You can even record data for these key parameters that correspond to times when the system is working well. Then, when a crisis comes up, you can quickly set up to run performance charts that can be compared with the values for the system when it was running well. This up-front preparation can really pay off when everyone is running around screaming at you, so you might want to put it on your list of things to do.

FIGURE 12.11.

Saving Performance Monitor settings to a file.

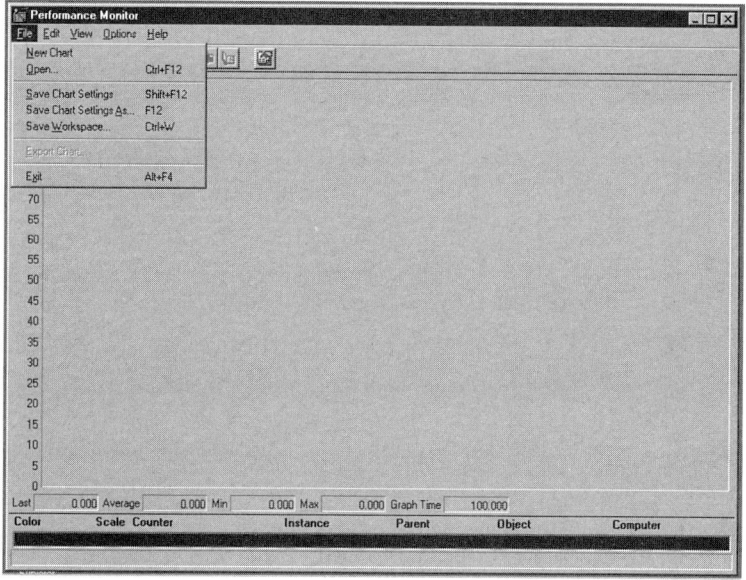

If you develop applications in addition to administering an NT system, you are probably aware that report generation and presentation utilities are the ones that generate the most debate and interest in the user community. You can get away with a wide variety of data entry forms, as long as they are functional and efficient. However, when it comes to reports and presentation utilities, you will have users arguing with each other about which columns to put on the report, what order the columns have to be displayed in, and sometimes how you calculate the values in the columns. I have seen people go at it for hours arguing about such little details as the font used and what the heading of the document should be. You are in the position of being the consumer of a data presentation utility (Performance Monitor), and Microsoft knows that everyone has slightly different tastes. Therefore, the company has provided you with several options for presenting the data. Not only are there basic format options such as alert reports versus the graphical charts I have been discussing, but they even let you get into the details as to how the data on a chart is collected and presented. The Chart Options dialog box is shown in Figure 12.12.

FIGURE 12.12.

The Chart Options dialog box.

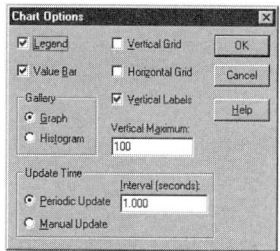

This dialog box enables you to set the following presentation options:

- ■ *Legend.* This checkbox enables you to specify whether to take up part of the screen display with a legend (the section where you match a line color and pattern to a specified computer, object, counter, and instance). Unless this is absolutely obvious to anyone walking up to the display, I recommend keeping the legend available at all times.

- ■ *Value Bar.* This checkbox controls whether the Last, Average, Minimum, Maximum, and Graph Time data displays are presented just below the graph itself (refer to Figure 12.12, which has this option selected).

- ■ *Vertical Grid.* This checkbox controls whether vertical lines are drawn in the middle of the graph to help you see what the values of a given data point are. (Both horizontal and vertical lines were selected for the graph displayed in Figure 12.12.)

- ■ *Horizontal Grid.* This checkbox controls whether horizontal lines are drawn in the middle of the graph to help you see what the times corresponding to a given data point are.

- ■ *Vertical Labels.* This checkbox controls whether the scale of values for the vertical line is displayed.

- ■ *Gallery.* This option contains radio buttons to select either Graph (a line graph where all the data points are represented as dots connected together with a line) or Histogram (a bar chart where each data point is represented as a vertical bar whose height corresponds to the value being measured).

- ■ *Vertical Maximum.* This edit box enables you to control whether you display the whole range of values possible as determined by NT (0 to 100 percent) or you focus on a narrower range of data (such as 0 to 50 percent). This can be useful in situations where you want to see finer variations in data that is confined to a narrower range.

- ■ *Update Time.* This section enables you to specify whether you want Periodic Update or Manual Update. Periodic Update is the default, in which Performance Monitor automatically collects a data point for the parameters being monitored at the interval (in seconds) specified in the edit box. Manual Update collects data manually, by clicking on the Performance Monitor toolbar item that looks like a camera, by selecting the Options menu and Update Now, or by pressing Ctrl+U.

By now you should be impressed with the wide array of charting options Performance Monitor provides. You are probably a little uncertain as to which of the many options you will want to use in your environment. I give my list of favorite counters to monitor later in this section. Also, as I mentioned before, there is no substitute for sitting down and actually playing with Performance Monitor to get comfortable with it and see how you like the environment to be set up. Let's take a look at the other data collection and presentation options provided by Performance Monitor. You have so far experienced only one of the four possible presentation formats. The good news is that although the format of the displays is different, the thinking behind how you set things up is the same, so you should be able to adapt quickly to the other three presentation formats.

The Alert View in Performance Monitor

Figure 12.13 presents the next display option Performance Monitor provides: the alert view. The concept behind this is really quite simple. Imagine that you want to keep an eye on several parameters on several servers to detect any problems that come up. The problem with the chart view is that the vertical line keeps overwriting the values so that you see a fixed time interval and lose historical information. You probably don't want to have to sit in front of your terminal 24 hours a day waiting for a problem value to show up on your chart, either. Later, I explain the log view, which enables you capture each piece of data and save it in a file for future reference. If you want to have a fairly reasonable time interval that enables you to detect response time problems for your users (for example, 60 seconds), however, you will generate a mountain of data in a relatively short period of time.

FIGURE 12.13.

The Alert Log display.

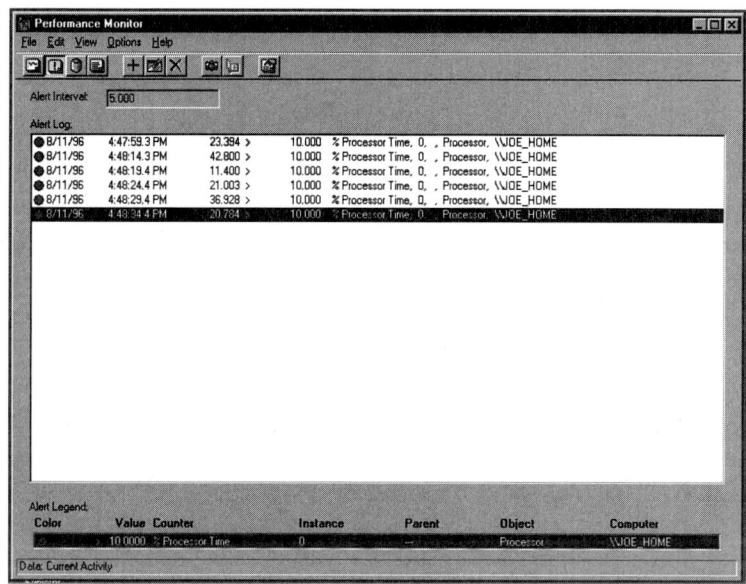

When you look at the data that would be captured in a Performance Monitor log file, the one thing that hits you is that the vast majority of the data collected is of no interest to you. It shows times when the system is performing well and there are no problems. Disk drives are relatively inexpensive these days, so it isn't that much of a burden to store the data. However, your time is valuable, and it would take you quite some time to wade through all the numbers to find those that might indicate problems. People are generally not very good at reading through long lists of numbers containing different types of data to find certain values. Computers, on the other hand, are quite good at this task. The alert view combines savings on disk space and the task of sorting through values that are of no interest into one utility. It enables you to record data only when the values reach certain critical values that you tell Performance Monitor are of interest to you.

To set up monitoring with the alert view in Performance Monitor, you first select this view from the toolbar (the icon with the log book with an exclamation mark on it). Next, you click on the plus sign icon to add counters to be monitored. The Add to Alert dialog box you get (see Figure 12.14) has the basic controls that you used to specify the counters under the graph view (Computer, Object, Counter, and Instance). The key data that is needed to make the alert view work is entered at the bottom of the screen. The Alert If control enables you to specify when the alert record is written. You specify whether you are interested in values that are either under or over the value you enter in the edit box. The Run Program on Alert control gives you the option to run a program when these out-of-range values are encountered. You can specify whether this program is to be run every time the alert condition is encountered or only the first time it is encountered.

FIGURE 12.14.

The Add to Alert dialog box.

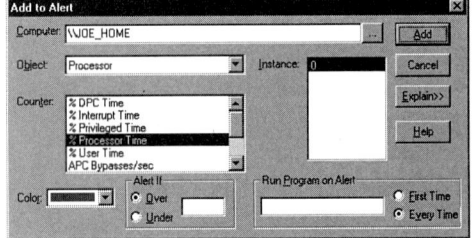

The alert view can be really useful if you want to run it over a long period of time (or continuously whenever the server is running). It collects only data that is of interest to you. You can specify values that indicate both extremely high load and extremely low load. You can even kick off a program to take corrective action or enable more detailed monitoring when you run across an unusual condition. You still have to make time to view the data, but at least you get to avoid reading anything but potentially interesting events.

The Log View in Performance Monitor

The next view provided by Performance Monitor is the log view. The principle behind this is simple—you write all the data to a log file. Later, you can open this log file using Performance Monitor and view the results or export the results to a data file that can be imported into a spreadsheet like Microsoft Excel for further processing, or you could even write your own program to read this file and massage the data. The log view is relatively simple to work with. First, you need to specify the parameters that you want to log using the plus sign toolbar icon. Next, you have to specify the file that is to contain the logging data and how often the data points are to be collected. Figure 12.15 shows the Log Options dialog box, which captures this information.

FIGURE 12.15.

*The Log Options
dialog box.*

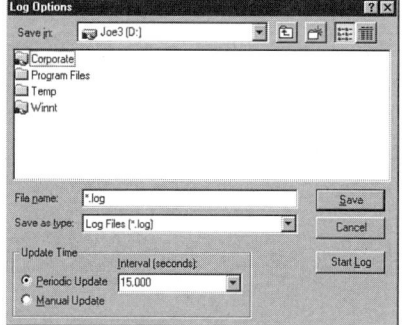

The Log Options dialog box contains your standard file selection controls. You can add to an existing file or make up a new filename. You can even keep all your log files in a separate directory (or on a network drive) so that it is easy to find them. Once you have specified the filename, your only other real decision is the update interval. Again, you have to be careful, because if you choose a 10-second interval, you will generate over 8,600 data points per counter selected per day. Finally, you click on the Start Log button to get the process going. The Log Options dialog is also used to stop the logging process. Note that you need to keep Performance Monitor running to continue to collect data to this log file. I will show you later how to run Performance Monitor as a service in background.

The Report View in Performance Monitor

The report view is actually a very simple concept, as is shown in Figure 12.16. You specify a set of counters that you want to monitor, and it gives you a screen that lists the parameter and the value observed in the last interval. This is one view where manual data collection could be useful. Imagine a situation where you have an application turned off and everything is running fine. You collect a set of values for this normal time and save them to disk. You can then start up the application that seems to be causing the problem and capture a new set of data to see what the differences are. This is yet another tool to add to your arsenal for those times when problems arise.

FIGURE 12.16.

*The Add to Report
dialog box.*

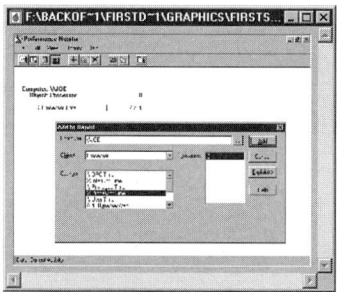

Selecting the Data Source in Performance Monitor

There is one more interesting feature of Performance Monitor before moving on. Performance Monitor has lots of nice display capabilities built into its graph view. However, the log option is useful for collecting data over a long period of time when you can't sit at your terminal and review the graphs before they are overwritten. A menu selection on the Options menu helps you with this situation. The Data From option brings up a dialog box (see Figure 12.17) that enables you to select what you are graphing. The formal setting is to graph current activity (the counters that you have currently selected to monitor). You have the option of selecting one of the log files you built to be the subject of the graph for later review.

FIGURE 12.17.

The Data From dialog box.

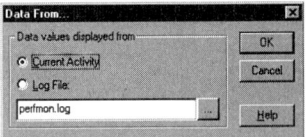

So far you have explored the four views Performance Monitor provides that can be used to display data in different formats. One of these views should be what makes the most sense for you when you need to review data. You also learned how to set these monitors up and alter their display to your taste. You need to remember that if you set up to monitor a certain set of parameters in one view, these settings do not carry over to the other views. (For example, if you are monitoring logical disk transfer rates in the graph view, it does not mean that you can access this data and settings from within the report view.)

Unfortunately, your newfound knowledge of how to analyze the source of a Windows NT performance problem is not enough. You also need to know how to pinpoint the problem and fix it to get performance back up to standard. Armed with the magnificent array of data you collected from Performance Monitor, you should be able to have the system back to peak efficiency in a matter of minutes. Although you are well on the way to returning your system to health, you might still have a few hurdles to jump over along the way:

- Problems can tend to hide one another. For example, you might have a disk drive that is being used excessively. Unless you check all your indications and think the problem through carefully, you might miss the fact that this particular problem was caused by a high degree of paging that is occurring to a drive that also contains most of your database files. This is really indicative of a problem with both memory and the way you have your disk drives laid out. Therefore, it is always wise to check all the information available to you.

- You must also know what is running on your system when problems are observed in order to know what to adjust. This can be tough on systems that are processing a large number of users and a variety of applications. Just knowing that a disk drive is overloaded is not enough. You have to know which application is causing the problem so that you know what adjustments to make. (It could take a long time if you moved files around one by one until you found the one that reduced the load to acceptable values.)

■ There are differing opinions as to what is satisfactory response time. People who are used to working with simple PC applications usually consider instantaneous response time to be at least adequate. If you are searching for data in a database that contains a few hundred gigabytes of information, you have to be a little more tolerant as to how long it takes to search the data for your query. This is something that should be agreed to by your organization, preferably before the applications are built, so that you can obtain adequate processing resources. It can make the administrator's job extremely difficult if you have to spend all your time chasing after performance problems that you can do nothing about because users' expectations are unreasonable.

■ You also have to be sensitive to the cost/performance trade-offs that have to be made. Although extra speed is a good idea in any system, it might not be worth devoting your efforts for several months to cut a second or two off user response time on a particular application. Most administrators have plenty of other work to do. Another trade-off that has to be made is whether it is cheaper to spend $400 on an extra 8M of RAM or have a contractor come in at $50 per hour and spend a month tuning the system (at a cost of around $8,000). Technical people are often not trained to think about these considerations, but they probably should be.

■ Finally, you should sometimes consider nontechnical solutions to your problems before you buy equipment or spend a lot of your time on tuning. One of the classic loading problems on servers is the fact that they experience peak loads for the first hour of the business day and the first hour after lunch. This is relatively easy to explain, because most people come in, get their coffee, and log onto the e-mail system to check their mail. The same thing happens after lunch, and possibly just before the end of the business day (which also might experience peak printing loads as everyone finishes off what they have been working on and prints it before they go home). Sometimes an e-mail (or memo) to your users explaining the situation and offering them greatly improved response times if they alter their habits a little can be enough to solve the problem without any drastic measures or purchases.

A Starting Set of Counters

There are many possible things you can look at and several tools you can use. Many of these counters are designed for very special situations and yield little useful information about 99 percent of the servers that are actually in operation. My next task is to present what I would consider to be a good set of counters to monitor to give you a feel for the overall health of your system. If one of these counters starts to indicate a potential problem, you can call into play the other counters related to this object to track down the specifics of the problem.

Recall from the earlier discussion that numerous hardware and software systems on your computer can be simplified into four basic areas: CPU, memory, input/output (primarily hard disk drives), and networking. Based on this model, I offer the following counters as a starting point for your monitoring efforts:

■ *Processor: percent processor time.* If your processor is running continuously at near 100 percent load, you are probably nearing the limit of processing capacity for your computer. If you have multiprocessor systems, remember to look at the loads on all the processor instances. It might turn out that your system and applications are beating up on one processor while the rest remain idle (one of the areas Windows NT is working upon is splitting the load across multiple processors). Remember that processing naturally comes in surges (an application waits for a while for data to load from disk, then suddenly starts off in a burst of activity), so you have to consider the load measured over a reasonable period (10 seconds or more).

■ *Memory: pages/second.* Some paging between physical and virtual memory is normal and happens even in periods of light loading. You have to be sensitive about when this paging becomes higher than normal and your system is spending all its time transferring information between the paging files and physical memory instead of servicing user processing needs. A number of 5 or less in this category is generally considered to be acceptable, but it varies between systems.

■ *Physical disks: percent time.* Applications tend to like to have all their files located together so they can be found and segregated from the files created by other applications. This leads to a problem: when an application is running, especially when it is supporting multiple users, it tends to place a high load on the disk drive where the file is located, whereas other disk drives might be sitting idle. Because disk drives are one of the slowest components in most applications, this is an area where you can build up a bottleneck where applications sit and wait for data transfers for one user to be completed before the other users can access their data. In databases, this is usually the single biggest tuning activity that can improve performance. General wisdom usually states that if a drive has over 90 percent disk time, it is very busy and might be a candidate for a bit of load reduction. If you have a number of users contending for a busy disk, you might notice performance degradations at the 70 percent disk time level.

■ *Physical disks: queue length.* Another important indicator designed to catch the fact that several user processes are sitting idle while waiting to be granted access to a disk drive is the queue length. A good rule of thumb is that if the queue length is greater than two, you should be investigating ways to lighten the load on this disk drive.

■ *Server: bytes total/second.* The final component you need to keep an eye on is network transmissions. This is a tough one because there are so many monitors for each of the different protocols. Perhaps this is a sign that very few people truly understand networking to the point where they are one with the network and instantly know of problems. The server total-bits-per-second counter provides a good overall picture of when the network and/or network interface card is struggling to keep up with the load. Anything near the rated sustained limit for the type of network that you are using (3 million bits per second for Ethernet and either 4 or 16 million bits per second for token ring) is an indication that the network itself is overloaded. This can be somewhat deceptive because you might be connected to a local network that can transmit signals at the speeds listed earlier, but you might be connected to other local networks by lines as slow as 56 thousand bits per second that might be your true bottleneck. Finally, your network might be within its rated transmission capacity, but your network card might not be. This varies between cards, so you have to get a feeling for the limit of your particular system.

These rules of thumb are fine for the industry in general, but they do not reflect the unique characteristics of your particular configuration. You really need to run your performance monitoring utilities when your system is running well to get a baseline as to what counter values are associated with normal performance. This is especially important for some of the counters that are not in the preceding list; it is difficult to prescribe a rule of thumb for them because they are very dependent on your hardware. For example, a fast disk drive on a fast controller and bus can read many more bytes per second than a slow disk drive on a slower controller. It might be helpful to run Performance Monitor with several of these other counters that make sense to you and write down what the normal values are.

You can take the preceding discussion one step further and use a utility found in the Resource Kit to simulate loads on your system to determine what counter values correspond to the limits of your system. This utility is relatively simple to operate. Your goal is to start with a moderate load and increase the load until performance is seriously affected. You record the values of the counters of interest as you increase the load and then mark those that correspond to the effective maximum values. This takes time, and you do not want to impact your users; however, if you are running a particularly large or demanding NT environment, you might want to have this data to ensure that you line up resources long before the system reaches its limits.

One final point is that each application has a slightly different effect on the system. Databases, for example, tend to stress memory utilization, input/output capabilities, and the system's capability to process simple (integer) calculations. Scientific and engineering applications tend to emphasize raw computing power, especially calculations that involve floating-point arithmetic. It is useful for you to have an understanding of what each of the applications on your server does so that you can get a feel for which of the applications and therefore which of the users might be causing your load to increase. Remember, a disk queue counter tells you that a certain disk drive is overloaded. However, it is your job to figure out which applications and users are placing that load on the drive and to determine a way to improve its performance.

Time-Based Data Collection

Finally, you do not have to collect performance data all the time. In many organizations, you find very little processing during the evening or night hours. Why waste disk space collecting data from numerous counters when you know they are probably close to zero? The answer to this is a neat little utility included in the Windows NT Resource Kit that enables you to start performance monitoring in the background using settings files that you have previously saved to disk. You can configure multiple settings files to take averages every minute during the normal work day and collect averages every half-hour at night when you are running fairly long batch processing jobs whose load varies little over time. The service to accomplish this function is datalog.exe. You turn this on and off at various times using the command-line (and batch file) utility of NT and the monitor.exe command-line utility. The following example starts the monitoring utility at 8:00 and stops it at 11:59 (the morning data run):

```
at 8:00 "monitor START"
at 11:59 "monitor STOP"
```

The Resource Kit provides more details about using the automated monitoring service. You still have to look at the log files to see what is happening with your system, but at least you don't have to be around to start and stop the monitoring process. It also has the convenience of enablng you to build and check out settings files interactively using Performance Monitor. This feature, combined with all the other monitoring functions discussed earlier, gives you a really powerful set of tools to track what is going on with your NT system.

Common Bottlenecks

This theory was all good and unfortunately necessary to ensure that everyone was up to speed on the basics of system performance. Now, let's look at the more common problems that you will run across in Windows NT and BackOffice systems. This would be the first place to start when you have a performance problem and have collected a good series of data to help you pinpoint the cause. You may have some really unusual problem, but I would not chase after unusual solutions until you have eliminated these more common problem sources.

CPU capacity problems is the first area to consider. This is an area where you have to be somewhat careful in your analysis. Adding an extra disk drive is becoming a relatively insignificant expense that will probably be needed in the future anyway, with the growth in data storage needs and application sizes. However, you are talking serious expense and effort to upgrade to a higher capacity CPU in most cases. Some servers have the capability of just plugging in additional processors, but most do not. Therefore, you better be absolutely sure you have exhausted all other possibilities before you bring up buying a new CPU as a solution. Some things to consider when you think you might have a CPU problem include the following:

■ Is the load placed on the CPU reasonable for the applications that are being run? This might be tough to assess for individuals who are not experienced in the computer industry. However, if you have a 150MHz Pentium processor that is being overloaded by running an e-mail system for 10 users, I would say that you have a problem with the application or other tuning parameters; this is not a load that would typically require a more powerful processor.

■ Do you have any new or uncommon hardware devices in your computer? A poorly written device driver can waste a lot of CPU time and weigh down the processor. You can check to see whether the vendor has seen this problem before and possibly has an updated device driver that is kinder to the CPU.

■ Do you have monitoring data from your capacity planning efforts (which I discuss later) that backs up your claim that the users' demands have grown to the point where a new processor is needed? Have any new applications been loaded on the system that might need tuning or be the cause of the problem that forces you to upgrade the CPU?

The next area of concern is memory. One of the main complaints PC users have about Windows NT is that it demands what seems to them to be a large amount of memory. As I discussed earlier, accessing information stored in memory is so much faster than accessing data located on disk drives that operating system and application designers will likely continue to write software that requires greater memory to perform more complex tasks and produce reasonable response times. Another point to remember is that many Windows NT self-tuning activities are centered around allocating memory space to help improve system performance. A few thoughts related to memory problems include the following:

■ Are your applications that use shared memory areas properly tuned? An Oracle database can be tuned by the DBA to use only a few megabytes of memory or almost a hundred megabytes (I did that once on a very large data warehouse). You should check to see that these applications are properly tuned (neither too much nor too little memory used) before you go out and purchase memory. It is also useful to check whether you have any unnecessary services running. With all these automated installation utilities, it is hard to remember whether you have cleared out old application services when new ones are installed. It doesn't hurt to scan through the list of services in the Control Panel just to be sure.

■ What is the configuration of your memory expansion slots? Typically you have a relatively small number of memory expansion slots in a computer. Hardware vendors often tie pairs of these memory slots together and require you to install the chips in this bank (as they call it) in matched pairs. If you are expecting to continue to expand the use of your server and its memory requirements, you might want to consider getting slightly larger memory chips now so that you don't have to remove older, smaller chips in the future to make room for chips that are large enough to support your needs.

Next on the list of problem areas are input/output problems related to disk drives. Working with a lot of database systems, I find this to be the most common problem. The good news is that with current disk drive capacities and prices, it is also one of the easiest to solve. Almost all the servers I have worked with have their disk requirements grow every year, so it isn't much of a risk that you will never use additional disk capacity. The risk you take is that you will spend extra money this year on a disk drive that has half the capacity and twice the cost of next year's model. Some considerations when you have a disk input/output problem include the following:

- One of the easiest solutions to an overworked disk situation in a system with multiple disk drives is to move files around to balance the load. The basic process is to figure out which files are accessed frequently (or accessed at the same time by a given application) and put them on separate disk drives. The biggest tuning recommendation for an Oracle database that is performing poorly due to input/output is to place the tables and indexes on separate disk drives. You have to be sensitive to how the disk drives are connected together when you are doing this. You can split the load between several disk drives so that each disk drive is well below its data transfer capacity, but you might run into problems when you exceed the transfer capacity of the disk controller card to which these drives are attached. On very large disk farms with multiple levels of disk controllers, someone has to balance the load across controllers (and controllers of controllers) in addition to worrying about the load on individual disk drives.

- You will run into situations where your application load or other factors will not enable you to split the load across several disk drives (for example, all the input/output activity is centered around a single file). In this case, you might have to consider buying faster disk drives and controllers (such as fast-wide SCSI or even electrostatic disk drives) to handle these busy files and reallocate the other disk drives to other purposes (such as holding all the performance data you are going to have to log onto this heavily loaded system). You could also implement disk striping to split single data files across multiple disk drives.

- Depending on which of the NT file systems (FAT, NTFS, and so on) you have used on a given disk drive, you might run into a problem known as fragmentation. Back at the dawn of time in the computer world, all data in a file had to be located in a set of contiguous blocks on a disk drive. People had a lot of problems dealing with this as they tried to write applications such as word processors, where they would write a little bit on one document, do some other things, and then write a little bit more. The disk blocks at the end of the word processing document would get filled by other work, and it would take a lot of rearrangement of files to make space for the new, larger document. The solution to this was to allow files to be split into multiple sections on the disk drive with file access utilities that are smart enough to put all the pieces together when the user accessed the file. This can be a problem in many file systems when you consider the fact that the disk drives can transmit data much more quickly than they can move the mechanical arms to which the heads read and write data. Therefore, a file that is scattered all over the disk drive (known as a fragmented file) is much slower to access than one on which all the data is located in one chunk. There is some debate over whether NTFS suffers from fragmentation, but there are utilities that can defragment different types of file systems, such as Executive Software with its Diskkeeper product.

■ An interesting situation relates to the fact that disk services have a lower priority than printing services. If you are really daring, you can go into the registry under the `service\lanman\server\parameters` key and raise the priority of the server from its default priority of 1 to 2 (add `ThreadPriority` of type `DWORD` with a value of 2).

■ An alternative that is supported on many different types of disk drives enables you to scatter a single file across multiple disk drives. You can rely on either hardware or software to let you tie together sections of several disk drives and treat them as if they were a single logical disk drive. In a two-disk pair, for example, the first logical block would be on the first physical disk drive; the second logical block would be on the second physical disk drive; the third logical block would be on the third disk drive; and so on. This technique, known as striping, is actually just one form of a technology known as RAID (redundant arrays of inexpensive disks) that can be used to improve performance and reliability.

The final area in which you might encounter problems is the network. I have always found this to be a much tougher area to troubleshoot, because I do not own it all. Even the network administrators can have troubles because servers or workstations can cause the problems as often as a basic lack of network capacity or failed equipment. One of the keys to being able to troubleshoot a network effectively is to have a drawing of how things are laid out. This is difficult because it changes regularly and most people do not have access to these drawings, if anyone has even bothered to make one. A few thoughts on the area of network problem-solving are as follows:

■ The best hope for quick and efficient solutions for network problems is to isolate the problem to a particular section of the network or even a particular machine. This often involves going around to friends on the various network segments and seeing how their systems are performing. Perhaps you have some of the advanced network monitoring technologies that will help you in this process. One of the most common problems on a wide area network is the limited transmission capacities of the links to remote sites. Although these network links might not be your problem to solve, you are often the first one to hear about it ("Why is your server so slow today?") and you have to come up with some data to prove that it is not your problem and that someone else has to solve the problem.

■ If the problem is actually with your server, you might try to reduce the number of network protocols that have to be monitored by the server. It is easy to just check every protocol when installing the server so that you don't have to worry about it in the future, but this can become a burden later.

- You might also want to see what is causing the traffic load. You can do this by looking for patterns or shutting down applications briefly to see whether this reduces network traffic. You might find that it is an application that could be rewritten (if developed locally) to be more efficient or done away with (for example, users chatting on the Internet or using a stock ticker application).

- You might also want to rearrange the binding order for the various protocols to emphasize those that are more important (for example, TCP/IP for those database transactions that everyone wants to speed up) at the cost of increasing response time for those services that need speed less (the print jobs where the printout can always get to the printer faster than the user can).

- If all else fails, talk to network experts and see if they can recommend a network card that has better throughput than your current card. There is a wide variation in performance, with most PC cards designed for the relatively simple transmission requirements of workstations, not the more demanding needs of servers. It is less expensive than replacing your network with a faster network or altering the topology to provide better routing.

That is probably sufficient for this introductory discussion of performance problem-solving. Try not to feel overwhelmed if this is your first introduction to the subject. It is a rather complex art that comes easier as you get some experience. It is not easy, and there are people who specialize in solving the more complex problems. It is often a challenge just to keep up with all the available technology options. Windows NT will probably also continue to evolve to meet some of the new challenges that are out there, including Internet/intranet access and multimedia initiatives such as PC video. It could almost be a full-time job just to keep up with all the application programming interfaces that Microsoft releases to developers these days.

A Self-Tuning Operating System

As I mentioned earlier, Windows NT is a self-tuning operating system—within limits. Don't get me wrong. Having worked with UNIX, I appreciate all the self-tuning that Windows NT does for you. Just don't think that NT can tune itself on a 486/33 to support thousands of users. With that caveat out of the way, I want to explore some of the things that Windows NT does to keep itself in tune for you and how you can affect this process. Once you understand what NT is doing to help itself, you will be in a better position to interpret monitoring results and therefore know when your intervention is required.

First, there are several things you do not want Windows NT to try to do for you. Moving files between disks to level the load might cause certain applications to fail when they cannot find their files. That is something you have to do for yourself. You also don't want NT to decide whether background services that have not been used for a while should be shut down. You might have users who need to use those services and applications and who cannot start the services automatically if they are currently shut down.

There are also some things Windows NT cannot do. It cannot change the jumper settings on your expansion cards and disk drives to reconfigure your system to be more efficient. It cannot rearrange cabling. Thankfully, it also cannot issue a purchase order to buy additional memory or CPU upgrades. Basically anything that requires human hands is still beyond the reach of Windows NT self-tuning.

So what does Windows NT have control over? Basically, it boils down to how Windows NT uses memory to improve its performance. There are several games it plays to try to hold the information you will probably want to work with next in memory. To do this, it sets aside memory areas for disk caches and other needs. It also tries to adapt itself to your demonstrated processing needs. When changes in your needs are detected, it reallocates memory to try to best meet your needs. This is why you almost always find almost all your system memory used on a Windows NT Server even when you are not especially busy. Windows NT senses that there is a lot of memory available and it tries to apply it to best meet your anticipated needs rather than just having it sit around unused.

Another thing Windows NT can do automatically for you is adjust its virtual memory space. If your existing page file space (pagefile.sys) is not large enough to handle your needs, it can go after other space that is available on your disks to get additional temporary paging space. The downside of this is that the new page file space is probably not located next to the default page files on disk. Therefore, when you are writing to or reading from these page files, you will probably have extra delays as the heads on the disk drive move between the various files. Although disk drive transmission rates are relatively slow when it comes to paging, the physical movement of the arms that hold the heads is even slower, so it should be avoided whenever possible. You might also want to consider multiple page files on separate disk drives (or even separate disk controllers) to spread the load between disk drives.

Although I'm sure that self-tuning is the topic of many of the white papers available on the Microsoft Web page or Technet CD, the previous page is good enough for these purposes. Although I spent only a page on the subject, do not underestimate the power of self-tuning. In UNIX, if you had to go in to tune the kernel, you were faced with a series of parameters that were ill-documented and had strange, unexpected effects on one another. I have more than once done more harm than good when changing UNIX kernel parameters to get applications such as databases going. However, self-tuning is not a magic silver bullet that solves all your problems. The next section starts the discussion of how you can tell when your system is having problems that self-tuning cannot solve and how to identify what the specific problem is.

Capacity Planning

Some people spend their entire lives reacting to what others are doing to them. Others prefer to be the ones making the plans and causing others to react to what they are doing. When you get a call from a user saying that the system is out of disk space or it takes 10 minutes to execute a simple database transaction, you are put in the position of reacting to external problems. This tends to be a high-pressure situation where you have to work quickly to restore service. If you have to purchase equipment, you might have great problems getting a purchase order through your procurement system in less than a decade (government employees are allowed to laugh at that last comment). You might get called in the middle of the night to come in and solve the problem, and you might have to stay at work for 36 hours straight. This is not a fun situation.

Although these reactive situations cannot always be avoided (and some people actually seem to prefer crisis management), I prefer to avoid them whenever possible. The best way to avoid crises is to keep a close eye on things on a routine basis and try your best to plan for the future. All the performance monitoring techniques presented in this chapter can be run at almost any time. You could be running some basic performance monitoring jobs right now. The key to planning is some solid data that shows trends over a significant period of time combined with information on any changes planned in the environment.

This process has been the subject of entire books. There are several detailed, scientific methodologies for calculating out resource needs and performance requirements. For the purposes of this book, I just want to present a few basic concepts that I have found useful and that can be applied with a minimal amount of effort by administrators who take care of small workgroup servers or large data centers of servers:

- If your program to track performance and capacity requirements takes too much time to complete, you are probably going to have trouble keeping up with it. I would recommend automating the data collection using Performance Monitor log files either started with the at command or run as a service. Make it one of your routine tasks to collect averages or maximum/minimum values from these log files and place them in a spreadsheet, database, or log book. Although minimizing the time required to collect statistics is a worthy goal, you should never find out about a problem that has been occurring for days that your monitoring program did not detect.

- You should present this data to management, users, and so forth on a routine basis. People tend to react poorly if you suddenly tell them that they need to buy some new disk drives next month (which is the end of the fiscal year and all the budget for such things is already spent). You might want to tie your capacity planning into the budgeting cycle for your organization.

- I like to use a spreadsheet to store the data so that I can easily construct a graph showing load over time. People tend to get lost in a long series of numbers but can easily see that line of disk utilization progressing relentlessly toward its limits.

Knowing what has happened and using it as a prediction for the future is often not enough. For example, based on past trends, you might have enough processor capacity to last for two years. However, you also know that your development group is developing five new applications for your server that are to be rolled out this summer. You need to find a way to estimate (even a rough estimate is better than none at all) the impact of these planned changes on your growth curves to determine when you will run out of a critical component in server performance.

Factoring in Application Planning to Performance

If your Windows NT server is just used to share files that are located in shared folders and also share a few printers, the discussion so far will probably cover all of your performance issues. However, Windows NT is also an application server (there would not be a book on BackOffice if it weren't an application server). Therefore, you need to consider the performance of your applications in addition to those of the operating system itself when forming an overall performance picture. This effort requires a knowledge of the functions of the application. Here are some questions that you might want to consider:

- What files does it use and where are these files located ("hot" files)?
- What network loads and types of transmissions are required for the application?
- What processing patterns are there for the application (for example, everyone checks electronic mail first thing in the morning and right after lunch)?
- What types of computation does the application perform?
- Are there any Performance Monitor counters (as there are for many BackOffice tools) that can be used to determine application specific problems?
- Are there any activities recorded in the event log by the application that can be used to determine the status of the application?

Keep these factors in mind as you learn more about the BackOffice components that you will be using in the sections that follow. The key to performance management is knowing what is going on with your system. Once you have a good handle on how your application is installed (which disk drives and so forth), and what it is doing, you can apply this knowledge to the observed symptoms (a particular disk drive is terribly overloaded, for example) to determine a solution. It is not always easy, but that's the challenge of it all.

Summary

This chapter has covered the rather deep and broad subject of performance management. It started with a good bit of theory for those who are not fully up on the details of a computer's architecture. It then focused attention on the tools that can be used to determine what is going on from a performance standpoint within Windows NT. This data can be compared against common problems or the processing requirements of your application to determine the appropriate solution. Along the way, I threw in a few words about proactive capacity planning, which will help you avoid the truly serious disasters that can occur with system performance.

NT Integration with NetWare and UNIX

by Joe Greene

IN THIS CHAPTER

CHAPTER

13

One of the most unusual features of Windows NT is its built-in capability of integrating with computers that run different operating systems. Those familiar with the UNIX world may point out that UNIX had a series of utilities that are fairly standard across the various product families that enable you to communicate with other UNIX computers or computers that have these standard UNIX protocols. There are two areas where the integration found in NT is radically different from this standard communications protocol approach:

- The level of integration is much deeper. It involves the capability of logging on to these remote systems and treating the remote resources exactly as Microsoft network resources are treated. For example, the only way that you can tell which network a printer is connected to is if you look at the top of your tree view when you select that printer. The complex details of communicating with radically different systems is well hidden from the users.

- The baseline Windows NT package comes with the integration utilities for UNIX, NetWare, and Macintosh environments built in. Although you can often find add-on packages for other computer environments that allow integration, Windows NT provides it as part of your basic cost. The only major environment that is an add-on is the IBM mainframe and AS/400 connectivity provided by the SNA Server in BackOffice.

This chapter covers the integration of Windows NT with the two major environments that you are likely to encounter in corporate networks: Novell NetWare and the various flavors of UNIX. My goal is to provide an overview of the connectivity techniques. I also point out some architectural and integration considerations that you may have to consider. I treat each of these environments separately because the tool sets are different.

Reasons for Integrating with NetWare and UNIX

Why bother integrating with NetWare? Microsoft can take on and beat any competitor, right? Well, the current outlook for Windows NT is quite bright if you read all of the trade journals. It has a family of operating systems that run the same applications from large servers to small desktop workstations. Its operating systems run on a wide variety of hardware platforms from those using powerful Reduced Instruction Set Computer (RISC) technology to the common Intel PC. So why cooperate with Novell?

First, Novell still has the largest market share in the PC server world. Its lead was larger just a few years ago when NT was being introduced. It was advantageous for those early sales personnel who were trying to get organizations to try this new product to be able to say that you could integrate these new servers with your existing servers without taking any great risk. Also, there are many environments that have to integrate with other computer environments over which the first set of administrators have no control. They may stay with NetWare until the end of time, and it is your job to interface with them.

Although NetWare integration was Microsoft's way to enter into the PC server market smoothly, its UNIX integration strategy was aimed at letting them enter into the "real" server market with equal ease. Although there are still some shops that have and love their mainframes, most of the shops that were downsizing when NT was first introduced had adopted UNIX servers as their computer platform. Unlike NetWare, which focuses its main efforts on file and printer sharing, NT also possesses a reasonable computer processing environment. Therefore NT was also designed to compete with the smaller UNIX boxes that were on the market. With recent advances in PC technology and the support for Windows NT provided on the DEC Alpha boxes, Windows NT can now be used by some of the largest and most powerful computers on the market.

Of course, there are die-hard Macintosh users out there who may feel offended by the fact that I am not including Macintosh integration in this chapter. My excuse for not doing this is that in BackOffice, I am focusing on the Windows NT Server product. The Macintosh integration was always more focused towards allowing Windows NT workstations to access Macintosh resources and vice versa. The Apple product line never really had a large server product that was a target for Windows NT Server.

So there are a number of good reasons why Windows NT has built in so many integration capabilities for dealing with the UNIX and NetWare environments. Although much of it may have been strategic positioning on the part of corporate giants, it has some good side effects for users and administrators. It enables us to use expensive resources that are currently attached to these other networks. It also enables users on these systems to access a number of NT resources, thereby helping us to justify our resources. Finally, for administrators, it enables us to form a unified computer environment (see Figure 13.1) that is easier to maintain and administer.

13

NT INTEGRATION
WITH NETWARE
AND UNIX

FIGURE 13.1.

*Integrated computer
environment.*

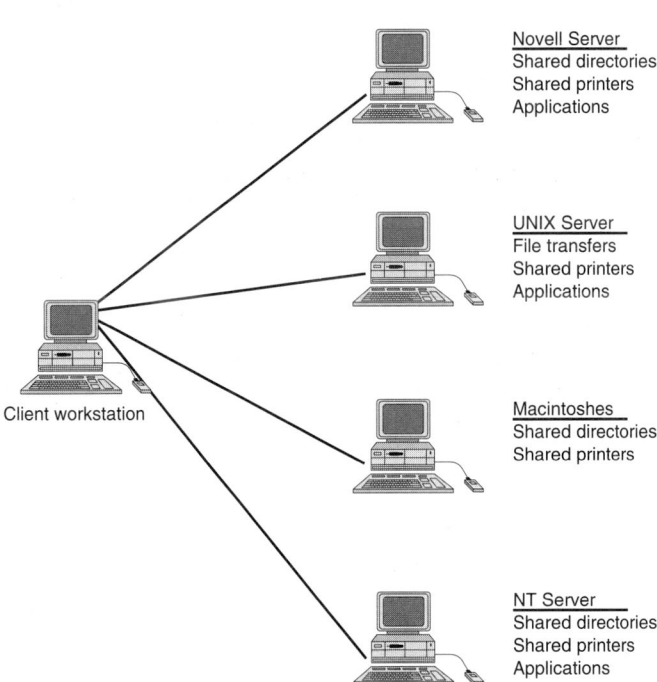

Client workstation

Novell Server
Shared directories
Shared printers
Applications

UNIX Server
File transfers
Shared printers
Applications

Macintoshes
Shared directories
Shared printers

NT Server
Shared directories
Shared printers
Applications

NetWare Integration Considerations

The good news about integration with the Novell NetWare product family is that it is almost mindless. If it were totally mindless, this would be a really short section. However, there are a few things that you need to consider when getting up your interface with the NetWare world. The considerations that I want to talk about in this section follow:

- Gateway or individual workstation access
- Protocols
- Frame types
- Sensitivity to NetBEUI

The first topic that I want to cover is the basic architecture of your Novell connection. Microsoft Windows NT provides you with two basic options for connecting to the Novell world as shown in Figure 13.2. The first option lets you share the Novell resources on your server and then share those shared resources with members of your network. This may be desirable if you have different local area network segments that you have to deal with. Perhaps you wish to isolate your NT network traffic from the Novell network traffic. You could accomplish this by putting two network cards in your server, one attached to each network. The Gateway service would be installed as an option under Windows NT networking (the Network icon under Control Panel). You would then access the desired Novell resources and share them back to the user community. You have to coordinate a gateway user ID and password with the Novell administrator to make this connection work.

FIGURE 13.2.

Novell gateway versus direct connections.

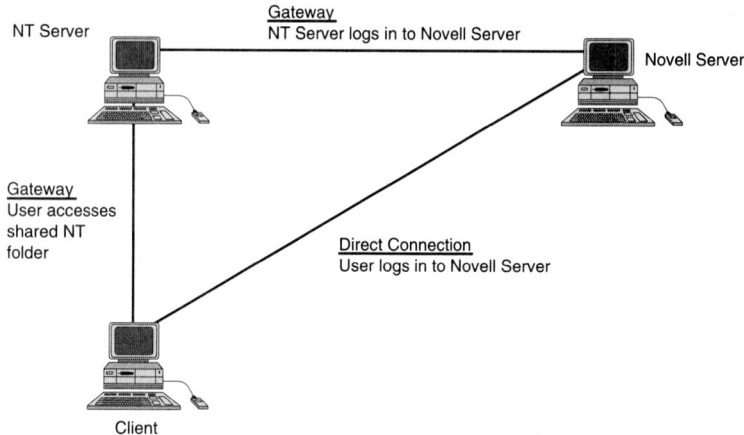

The other option that you have for workstations running Windows NT and Windows 95 is to simply connect directly from those resources to the Novell server. This direct connection is the simplest connection to set up. It does require that each of your users have accounts on both the Novell server and therefore both you and the Novell administrator (which could also be you) have to establish the appropriate groups and privilege sets. It does minimize network traffic in that you do not have to transfer all requests to the NT server and then out to the workstation requesting the information.

The next issue that you have to deal with is the communications protocol. The Novell world grew up with its own protocol set known as IPX/SPX. Back then, there was not a universally accepted local area network protocol set. The early network protocols were somewhat limited in their capabilities to be routed and perform more complex functions. The TCP/IP protocol set was being developed, but it was rather complex for the early PC computer networks at the time. It probably would have been too demanding on early PCs. Therefore, Novell came up with its own suite that works well.

However, it is not the industry or Microsoft standard. The industry (that is, the Internet) favors the TCP/IP suite. The Microsoft network world grew up with the NetBEUI protocol. The NetBEUI protocol set works well for simpler functions, but it cannot be routed nor does it support tasks such as client-server database access well. For purposes of our discussion here, it also does not work with Novell servers. Novell is offering increased support for TCP/IP in its products, but the bulk of NetWare installations use IPX/SPX. Therefore, if you want to play in the Novell server world, you pretty much have to adopt the IPX/SPX protocol set. Complaining about this protocol is pretty much like complaining about SNA in the mainframe world—it doesn't do you much good.

It's easy to use IPX/SPX under Windows NT and Windows 95. As a matter of fact, it is usually one of the default protocols that you will see in your installation process. Once you select the protocol, all you have to make sure of is that you pick the appropriate service (gateway or NetWare link). This protocol cooperates well on Microsoft networks and I have not seen it cause any problems for the other protocols selected.

You may have to adjust some of the settings for the IPX/SPX protocol occasionally—for example, one setup parameter for the IPX/SPX protocol that I have observed some sensitivity to in the NetWare world is its frame type parameter. The frame is a construct that wraps around the content of your message to facilitate transmission across the network. It is one of those details that is normally reserved for network design types. However, I have noticed several Novell networks that used the 802.3 (ethernet) frame type that could not communicate well with NT workstations that used the default setting for frame type (auto detect). We had to switch the setting under the IPX/SPX protocol on the Network utility on Control Panel (see Figure 13.3) to have a frame type of 802.3 and everything worked well. Be aware that you may have to adjust some of the advanced settings to allow your workstations and servers running Windows NT to be compatible with other devices on your network.

FIGURE 13.3.

Setting the frame type for IPX/SPX.

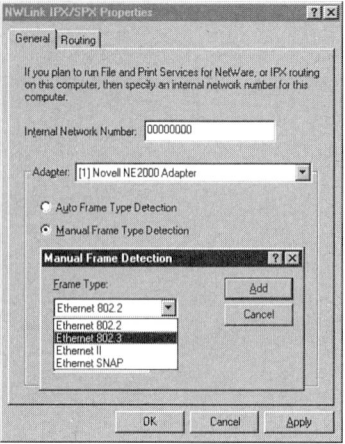

The final little note that I can offer you is that I have seen some Novell networks that are really sensitive to the presence of the NetBEUI protocol on which many Microsoft networks run. We had a network that was working quite well with NetBEUI and NetWare co-existing, and then they performed an upgrade of the Novell network. We started using a new network card in the server and a few other network changes, but we could not even get our machines to talk to one another. Our solution, achieved by trial and error, was to eliminate the NetBEUI protocol from our network. It was easier than getting the Novell folks to change and Microsoft networks will work well as long as they have just one common protocol (IPX/SPX). Although this was not an elegant solution, it did minimize the amount of work that was needed, and we were able to get everything done without changing our hardware or implementing complex software solutions. (The joys of a flexible, modern operating system.)

I thought I would end this section with a few other miscellaneous thoughts to consider:

- You might want to work with the Novell administrators to establish common group names and other similar integration issues. Who knows, you may have to take over Novell users one day if your company likes NT a lot.

- A common response center is helpful where you have both NetWare and NT working together. You can try and explain to users until you are blue in the face which resources are yours and which ones are supplied by the Novell people, but they will still come to you if you are their primary caregiver.

- You might want to set up with the Novell administrator to have the utilities and permissions to monitor one another's systems. For example, if a print job intended for a Novell printer appears to be stuck, it would be helpful if you could run the Novell printer control utility to see what is going on.

File Sharing with NetWare

Once you have gone through the initial setup and resolved any problems (which are actually quite rare, I was just lucky to run across the ones that I describe previously), it is actually easy to access NetWare file resources. Windows NT and Windows 95 appear to the Novell servers just like traditional NetWare clients. They play all the games by Novell rules.

You are somewhat limited in that you cannot share resources using Novell except on the server. They do not share workstation directories as we can under NT. However, you have whatever access privileges that your Novell logon ID commands when you attach to one of their servers. The privileges include all of our favorites such as read-only, change, and full-access.

So what do users see when they try to access a Novell shared directory resource? Well, they see their traditional File Manager, Network Neighborhood, or Windows Explorer display. If they have set themselves up for NetWare networking, they will have another option at the root of their directory trees that lets them access resources on the Novell network. There are no visual differences for the user when accessing Novell shared directories. You have to know what the resource is called and on which server it is located. If you were not paying too much attention when you first started down the directory hierarchy, you might not even notice that you are on Novell networks (unless you see a lot of share names such as system, volume1, and so on, which are traditional on Novell servers).

There are a few considerations with Novell file sharing that you should keep in mind:

- The network segments on which the Novell servers reside could be much busier than your segments.

- You may have lower bandwidth connectivity to remote Novell sites. This could make transfers to these locations take longer than those you would experience on your network.

- The Novell administrator may enforce different password conventions such as aging, complexity, and so on. You may want to coordinate these conventions so that users can have a single password and user ID that works both for the Novell networks and the Microsoft networks.

Print Sharing with NetWare

A good reason to interface with the Novell world, especially when NT is new in the environment, is to get access to all those expensive printers that are located on the Novell network and scattered around the building. The great thing about Novell printer access is that it, again, tries to give the user exactly the same interface as they are used to when accessing Windows NT network resources. There are a few printer connectivity options that you might want to be aware of in the NetWare environment. Figure 13.4 shows the three basic configurations.

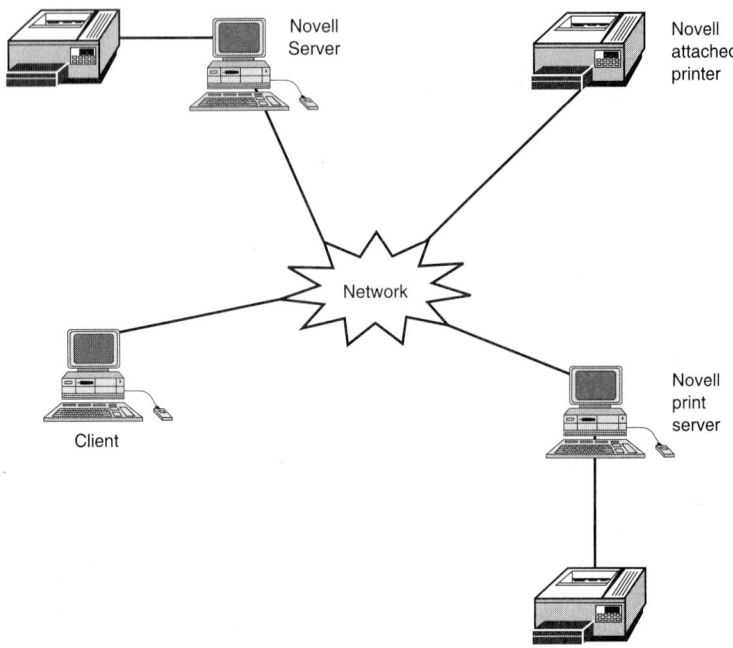

FIGURE 13.4.

Basic NetWare printer configurations.

The first configuration is where the printer is connected through a traditional printer cable to the Novell server. The Novell server provides the printer queue that sequences the print jobs. This print server process has a control utility (printcon) that can be used by people with the appropriate accesses to start and stop the queue, to remove jobs from the queue, and so on. It is not as convenient as the NT printer control utilities, but it accomplishes a similar function and gets the job done.

The second Novell printer configuration uses a printer queue on the Novell server and a printer that is attached directly to the local area network. This is similar to network attached printers under NT. The key is that you have to access the printer controls for the server that is maintaining the print queue in order to control printing on this printer. This configuration allows a lot of flexibility for placing printers throughout your building.

The final configuration is a step back to the early days when network connected printers were either too expensive or just not available. It uses a PC (usually an older model) that acts like a miniature Novell server by running a print spooling process. This process runs under DOS as opposed to the real Novell server operating system. It gets the job done and was an option to get printers to remote parts of the building that were far away from the servers.

With this introduction behind us, all I have left to say is that connecting to NetWare printers is just like connecting to Microsoft network printers. You go under the printers option in Control Panel and select the option to add a printer. Follow through the setup wizard panels, selecting a network printer as opposed to a local printer. When you browse the network to find your printer, you will see the Novell printers (assuming that you have set yourself up for Novell networking and logged in to the Novell network at start up). Select the one that you want and complete the driver specification panel that specifies the type of printer that you will be using. After that, it will appear as a valid printer in your list of printers and you may even forget to which network it is attached.

UNIX Integration Considerations

The integration of Microsoft networks with UNIX is not quite as easy as integration with NetWare. That is not to say that it is difficult either. It is just that many of the ease-of-access paradigms that exist in the NetWare and NT worlds were just never used in the UNIX world. There, you still access disks in much more of a static link fashion. They do not advertise the services that they provide in the same way that PC network servers do. However, there are ways of getting at their data and computing resources. You can co-exist quite well in the UNIX world.

Figure 13.5 shows some of the basic techniques that I want to discuss with regard to integration with the UNIX environment. There are four basic connectivity utilities that are provided under Windows NT:

- Telnet terminal connections
- File transfer protocol
- LPR/LPD printing
- Remote procedure calls

FIGURE 13.5.

NT integration with the UNIX environment.

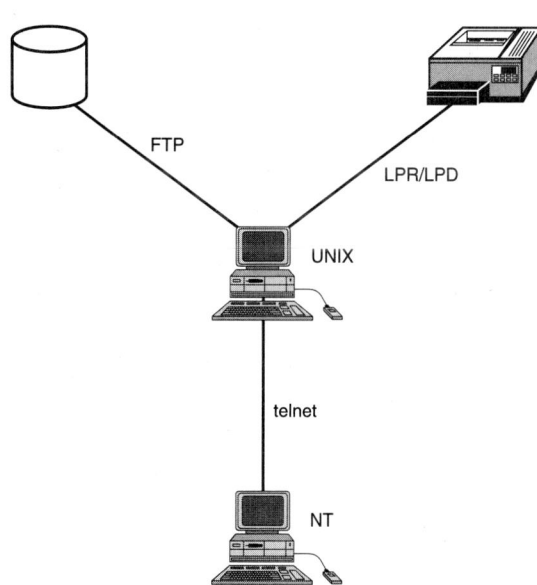

There is one important file sharing tool from the UNIX world that is not supported in the basic Windows NT package. UNIX has its own version of directory sharing known as the Network File System or NFS. Originated by Sun Microsystems, it is supported by almost all the popular UNIX systems that are out there, although some still require you to purchase it as a separate product from the operating system. In the NT world, there are NFS products available from third-party vendors, but not currently from Microsoft.

I am hesitant to recommend any one NFS vendor in the Windows NT world. They are still relatively young products, although they are often ports of packages that have existed for some time in other computer environments. New products tend to leapfrog one another in terms of performance and capabilities. Therefore, I would recommend that you check out the products that are currently on the market if you need to use NFS. With the ready access to the Web, it is easy to look up product information and you can often download trial versions of products for in-house testing.

The first issue to address when working with UNIX integration is that of the protocols used. In terms of the basic communications protocol, that is almost always TCP/IP when dealing with the UNIX world, where the wide range of protocols that are found in the PC world are not supported. Also, many people in the field feel that they have a better foundation by working only with a protocol that is a vendor-neutral international standard. That's OK; NT works well with TCP/IP so you can adapt to the needs of the UNIX world.

There are a series of higher level functional protocols that you will be dealing with for connectivity. These include telnet, FTP, LPR/LPD, and RPC. How's that for a series of acronyms? The key is now in knowing the internal details of how messages are built using these protocols. That is what the software and network engineers get paid to do. All you have to know is what they can do for you and when you want to use them. Anyway, let me give you the basic translation of these protocols.

- Telnet is a basic protocol for terminal emulation across a network to log on to a remote computer's command line.
- FTP stands for File Transfer Protocol. It is a standard that enables you to send (put) and receive (get) files to and from a remote computer via the network.
- LPR/LPD stands for Line Printer Requestor/Line Printer Daemon. It is a pair of protocols that lets the requester transmit jobs to the print server.
- RPC stands for remote procedure call. It is the UNIX tool for starting a job on another computer similar to the remote command server in the Windows NT Resource Kit.

Another integration concept that you need to master is that of the server process and the client process. UNIX boxes have been multiprocessing since their creation. They tend to think of computing as having a large series of specialist processes running at the same time to split up the workload. When you look at a UNIX system that has almost no users logged in to it, you will still find dozens of processes running. These processes were often designed separately by different design teams and have little knowledge of one another. This is in contrast to Windows NT's integrated approach to the operating system. Anyway, you will find that most of these utilities are designed to have both a server process that allows other computers to access your resources and a client process that enables you to access the resources of other computers. The key is that the remote server is a separate process in the operating system that must be running for you to complete your connection. Figure 13.6 illustrates this basic concept.

FIGURE 13.6.

Server and client processes for UNIX networking services.

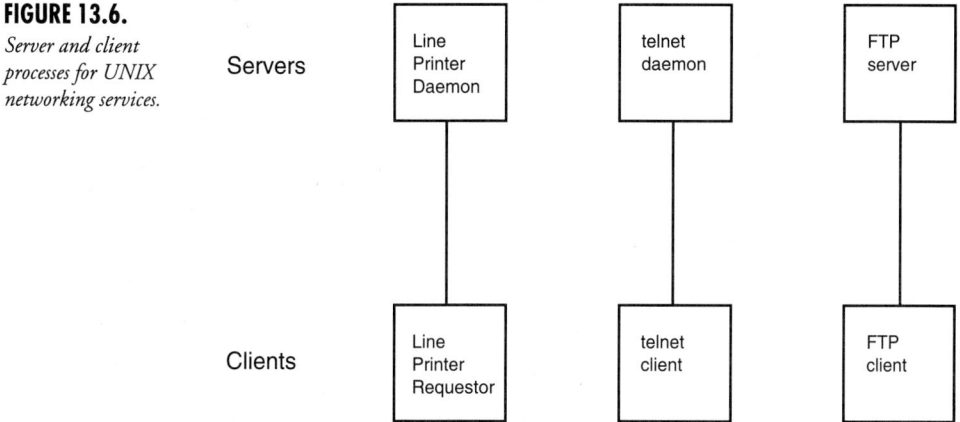

File Sharing with UNIX

Your basic tool for file sharing between UNIX and Windows NT is the File Transfer Protocol. It is a simple command-line utility where you specify the IP address or alias for the server to which you want to connect. You then can issue one or more of the following commands to interact with the remote file system:

- `ascii`—this instructs to send only characters that are in the ASCII character set, performing any translations as needed. This deals with the fact that operating systems have different internal representations for characters (EBCDIC for IBM mainframes, for example) and a neutral standard is needed for communications. This will transfer text files, but it will not transfer binary, executable files.

- `bell`—toggles on and off the bell sound for those of us who like to keep things nice and quiet.

- `binary`—the opposite of ASCII. This sends the internal binary representation of characters over the telnet session. It usually requires a compatible computer and operating system on the other end for the files to be understandable.

- `cd`—changes the remote directory to the directory specified by this command. It allows you to move around as you would in the DOS/Windows file system with the exception that UNIX systems use forward slashes as opposed to backslashes in their directory hierarchy (`/usr/bin` as opposed to `c:\winnt\system32`, for example).

- ■ delete—enables you to delete the single file specified in this command from the remote system.
- ■ dir—lists the directory on the remote computer. This is not normal FTP, but is provided for the DOS/Windows types who are used to this command.
- ■ disconnect—terminates your FTP session with the remote computer.
- ■ get—transfers the single file specified from the remote computer to your local computer.
- ■ help—provides a list of commands. You can enter help plus one of these commands to get a very brief description of the command.
- ■ lcd—changes your local directory (the computer at which you are sitting) to the directory specified.
- ■ ls—provides a listing of files in the directory specified on the remote computer. If no directory is specified, you will get the list of files in the current directory on the remote computer.
- ■ mdelete—deletes multiple files on the remote computer that match the criteria specified (*.txt, for example).
- ■ mget—transfers multiple files from the remote computer to the local computer that match the criteria specified.
- ■ mkdir—creates a new directory with the name specified on the remote computer.
- ■ mput—transfers multiple files from the local computer to the remote computer that match the criteria specified.
- ■ open—connects the user to the remote computer specified. You will be prompted for your user ID and password.
- ■ prompt—many FTP commands are designed to ask you whether you really want to take certain actions (in a multiple file copy, for example, you would be asked about each file). This command toggles the prompting on and off for these commands.
- ■ put—sends the single file specified to the remote system.
- ■ pwd—lists on the screen the current working directory on the remote system.
- ■ quit—terminates the FTP client process.
- ■ rename—enables you to change the name of the file specified on the remote server to a new value.
- ■ rmdir—deletes the directory specified on the remote server.
- ■ verbose—many FTP commands can give you short and to the point feedback or tell you about all of the details. This commands toggles the detailed discussions on and off.

Let me give you a brief example of an FTP session. Here I connect to a remote server, show you the basic directory listing command, show the basic directory listing command with the long option, and then download one of the files from the server to my local directory (by the way, UNIX is case-sensitive, and lowercase is much more commanding than uppercase in commands and filenames):

```
c:\ ftp unix1 jgreene/hithere
Connected to unix1.
220 unix1.
User (unix1:none)):jgreene
Password:
230 jgreene user logged in
ftp> ls
200 PORT command successful.
150 Opening ASCII mode data connection for file list.
SQLNET.ORA
TNSNAMES.ORA
226 Transfer complete.
26 bytes received in 0.06 seconds (0.43 Kbytes/sec)
ftp> ls -l
200 PORT command successful.
150 Opening ASCII mode data connection for /bin/ls.
09-28-95  05:56AM                  116 SQLNET.ORA
06-19-96  04:55PM                 1831 TNSNAMES.ORA
226 Transfer complete.
104 bytes received in 0.05 seconds (2.08 Kbytes/sec)
ftp> get sqlnet.ora
200 PORT command successful.
150 Opening ASCII mode data connection for sqlnet.ora(116 bytes).
226 Transfer complete.
116 bytes received in 0.27 seconds (0.43 Kbytes/sec)
ftp>
```

Some key points to remember about FTP:

The server has to be running the FTP server process for you to be able to connect to it.

IIS provides an upgraded version of the basic FTP server provided with NT. Think of this as a more rugged version that is designed to handle the potentially large loads of an Internet-connected and very popular server.

The FTP tools think like engineers and computer network types. They require you to know a set of aliases or IP addresses. There is no simple advertising service that lets you pick from a list of available computers. This would be a very long list for computers connected to the Internet (probably in the hundreds of thousands, if not millions), so I guess that it is just not practical in this case.

There are a number of third-party FTP tools (such as those from Delrina as part of their CommSuite product) that enable you to have a graphical version of FTP. Some of us grew up with the command line, but others might find it to be a bit of a step backwards.

Print Sharing with UNIX

Printers can be expensive resources on your computer networks. You have to scatter them throughout the building to make them close to the users. You may also have to provide a number of specialty printers such as color printers, large size plotters, and duplex printers. The UNIX utilities to connect to a remote printer are rather simple. You have the line printer requester who sends out the jobs and the line printer daemon who receives the job and transfers them to the appropriate local print queue.

To identify a printer on the remote system, you need to specify both the remote system alias or IP address and then the name of the remote print queue. In Windows NT, you also have to install the TCP/IP printing option. It is provided with the basic Windows NT distribution, but it is not one of the default products installed. Anyway, it is a relatively simple system to configure. You also have all your normal Windows NT printer access (it becomes a shared printer on your server that NT people access like any other shared printer).

Distributed Processing with UNIX

The UNIX standard for distributed processing is the Remote Procedure Call (RPC). Again, the format is relatively simple in that you specify the name of the remote server along with the procedure to execute. For this function to work, you need to have the Remote Procedure Call server running on the remote machine. This is not heavily used in my experience, but you should be aware of it when you plan to start processes on other machines that support RPC.

Summary

This chapter has gone over the basics of connecting to the Novell NetWare and UNIX environments. It did not cover all the possible options that you might use based on your individual situations. Instead, it focused on the issues that you will need to think about and the various options that are available to you. The interesting feature is that most of this connectivity to other vendor's environments is provided as part of the basic Windows NT operating system. There are third-party products that try to improve on this baseline which you may investigate as time permits.

## CHAPTER 14

BackOffice and Windows NT

by Joe Greene

IN THIS CHAPTER

Now that you have learned several of the topics related to the Windows NT Server operating system, let's link this to the other BackOffice products. This chapter takes the operating system's point of view. Specifically, what are the other BackOffice servers demanding of the operating system and what problems are they causing? The remaining sections of this book cover the individual BackOffice servers and will take their point of view when they discuss what the NT operating system is providing for them.

Design Integration Goals

This is a good place to review the integration goals that are part of the BackOffice design. This will set the stage for the discussions on the impacts that the various BackOffice components have on the NT operating system and its servers. The following is my short list of NT design features and goals that are important in the context of this chapter:

- Built-in networking
- File and printer sharing
- Application server support
- Common security model
- Client-server architecture
- Common administrative tools
- Common monitoring tools
- Cooperation between applications.

The first of these topics is the built-in networking. The Windows NT operating system provides networking utilities as a basic part of its functionality (see Figure 14.1). It is a rich networking environment that provides connectivity to a wide range of Microsoft and non-Microsoft computing environments. This permits a high degree of integration in a variety of computer environments that is standardized as part of the operating systems. Applications can take advantage of these networking services through standard interfaces without having to write their own networking interface code.

The second NT design feature that affects its applications is the built-in file and printer sharing services (see Figure 14.2). This goes beyond pure network communication and moves into the realm of higher-level networking services where you exchange information, not just communications signals. These standards allow applications to dispose print jobs to a standard location (a local print queue) and then have the operating system worry about how to get the actual printing accomplished. The file sharing standards provide a standard interface to determine all the files that are available to the user, both those on the network and on local storage devices. This frees the applications from worrying about the details of file systems, network transports, and so on. The Universal Naming Convention (UNC) provides a standard means for referencing files in the format of \\server_name\share_name.

FIGURE 14.1.
Built-in networking.

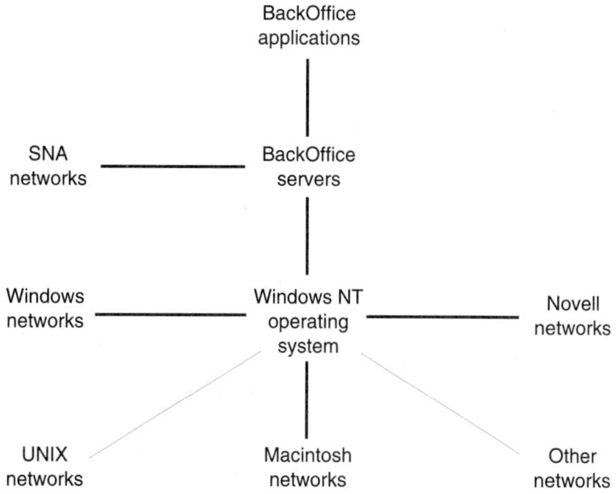

FIGURE 14.2.
Built-in file and printer sharing services.

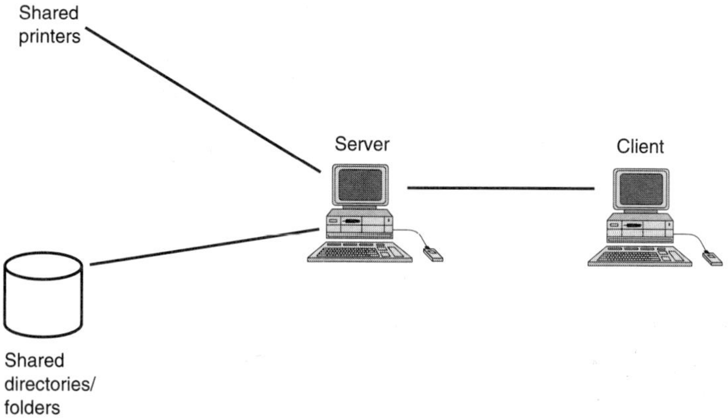

14

BACKOFFICE AND WINDOWS NT

The third function provided by Windows NT that is used by applications designed for this environment is the ability to act as an efficient application server. Although many earlier PC server operating systems were designed almost entirely to perform the file and print server roles, Windows NT is actually an efficient place to run applications. For applications to run properly in the Windows NT environment, they must be designed for the Windows 32-bit application programming interface (API). In addition, there are a number of additional APIs that Microsoft has come out with to enhance this programming environment. Many of the BackOffice applications have their own APIs (MAPI, for example, that allows programs to send electronic mail to Exchange Server).

The next feature of BackOffice that is designed to be common is the security model. This model features a single login ID and password for use at both the operating system level and within applications. The operating system provides capabilities for applications to verify the security privileges assigned to users. The key to this environment, though, is that applications use the basic security features of the operating system, providing extensions if needed, as opposed to implementing their own security systems.

A common set of administrative tools is another key element of the BackOffice environment. The basic tool set has been designed to be extended for individual application needs through a series of APIs. This alleviates the needs for each application to build its own administrative screens. It also guarantees that administrators only have to learn one way of doing business, which can save them a lot of time.

The common set of performance monitoring tools is another hallmark of the Windows NT and BackOffice environments. The Performance Monitor tool provides a very flexible and graphical means of viewing performance data from both the operating system and the application levels. All your applications have to be designed to track and report counters that are applicable to their internal processing to the Performance Monitor interface. You no longer have to worry about designing the graphs or reports because that is provided by Performance Monitor.

A final design feature that marks the BackOffice family is that each member has the capability to work with one another. This goes against many designers' first instincts in that they could, for example, write a database management system that is more optimized to their particular needs. What this would mean though is that there would be additional database administrative work and that administrators would have to learn a new set of tools and have a separate entity to maintain. It also means that a lot of the programming resources would be devoted to rebuilding these common functions as opposed to focusing on the main functions of the application on that they are working. BackOffice has taken the position of using other components in the BackOffice architecture when it makes sense.

The integration of components to work together should continue in the future. Many of the new BackOffice servers, such as the Merchant Server, will probably be dependent on both the Internet Information Server and SQL Server products. With the ISAPI interface, databases and IIS will continue to be more tightly integrated as Web sites add dynamic, database-driven content to their current static Web pages. There are a number of complex applications that are coming down the road, and they will need the services of the existing foundation components.

With these design goals in mind, let's move on to how the various BackOffice components affect the Windows NT Server operating system. It is important for system administrators to understand these impacts to ensure that they have adequate resources to cover their needs. It also helps during performance monitoring and tuning to enable you to better understand the numbers that you see. Systems are really sensitive beasts. You can have a large amount of resources in your system-memory, CPU, and disk drives. However, if you have just one component that is overloaded (for example, one of your many disk drives seems to receive almost all the data requests and cannot keep up with demand), system performance and user response time can degrade rapidly.

Implications for NT of Microsoft Mail

Microsoft Mail is the grandfather of the BackOffice family. This product evolved in the era wherein file and print sharing was about all you got from your servers. Therefore, it is not a sophisticated client server application that takes advantage of the advanced capabilities of the Windows NT platform as an application server. Instead, it merely uses the server as a place to store files that the users will need to access to exchange electronic mail.

Figure 14.3 is a graph for the Microsoft Mail product, showing the resource implications of the BackOffice products on the NT server. The various major server performance and processing components are shaded to show the relative demands of the various BackOffice components. Nonshaded areas show little or no load, and the two shades of gray show increasing loads.

FIGURE 14.3.

Effect of Microsoft Mail on a server.

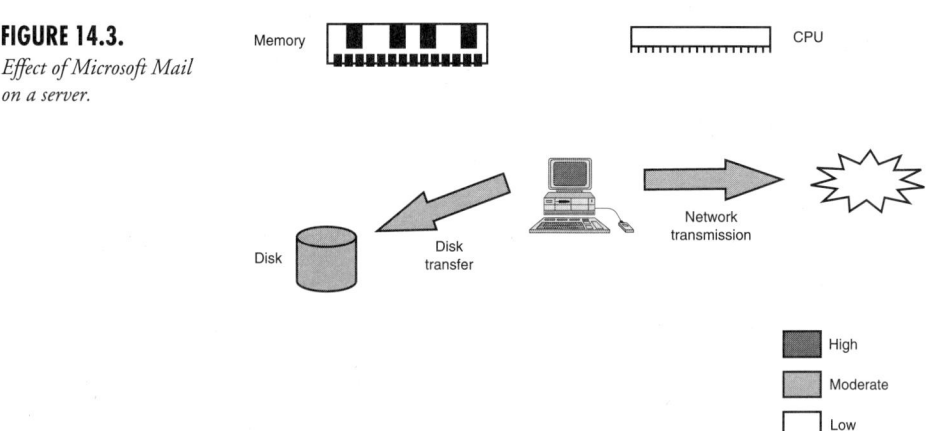

The typical Microsoft Mail installation has the following effect on a server:

- *Disk storage capacity.* The major impact of a larger mail installation is the disk usage for the message and perhaps schedule files that are stored on the server. One way to minimize this effect on the server is to have your users keep their personal folders on their local disk drive (an option under their MS Mail client). You also need to keep after people to read their mail frequently and delete mail that they do not need any longer. There are some people who would record their entire corporate history using saved copies of their electronic mail messages.

- *Disk input/output capacity.* Another factor that you have to deal with in Microsoft Mail is that all the data is stored on a single disk drive. That means that all the data transfer traffic is focused on that drive and you could overload the capacity of the drive. Solutions to this problem on busy mail servers include choosing a drive that has little activity other than the mail system and ensuring that you have one of your faster drives allocated to this purpose.

- *CPU processing capacity.* Microsoft Mail is a relatively insignificant load on the CPU. Again, it is designed for the relatively simple file sharing environment that was used several years ago and not the more demanding application server environment of today.

- *Memory utilization.* Again, because Microsoft Mail is based around simple file sharing, it uses very little system memory (one of the few products that you can find these days that can honestly make that claim).

- *Network input/output capacity.* Depending on the volume and size of the mail messages, Microsoft Mail can cause a reasonable amount of network loading. This is especially true if there are a large number of public folders that have large group documents in them for review. Otherwise though, its network load is usually quite moderate.

One of the features of mail system utilization that you commonly see is that it is subject to very strong peaks during the business day. The typical game plan is that everyone checks e-mail first thing in the morning, just after lunch, and just before going home. Surrounding these peaks are periods of relative calm. It does mean that you will have to design your server to provide adequate response times during the peak periods as opposed to using just a daily average loading in your design calculations.

Implications for NT of Exchange Server

The son of Microsoft Mail and the product that Microsoft plans to use in future versions of BackOffice is Exchange Server. It is a radically different design concept than that used in Microsoft Mail. It is designed specifically to take advantage of the application server capabilities of Windows NT in a client-server environment. Actually, it strongly resembles a client-server database management system in a number of ways (transaction logs, background processes servicing memory areas, and so forth). This was no accident. There were a number of design goals that required this type of architecture including:

- Capability of scaling up to support larger numbers of users on a single server

- Mechanisms to ensure that electronic mail transactions are recorded and can be recovered in the event of a disk or system failure

- Capability of supporting backups while the system is available for user processing

- Capability of being extended to support groupware (applications that facilitate communications among a group of users who are working in a common area)

- Capability of being extended to support forms-based applications that interface with electronic mail

- Capability of interfacing to a wide variety of external mail systems created by other vendors

Based on this different architecture compared with Microsoft Mail, you expect a somewhat different set of effects on your server. Figure 14.4 illustrates the effects of Exchange Server on Windows NT, which are as follows:

FIGURE 14.4.

Effect of Exchange Server on a server.

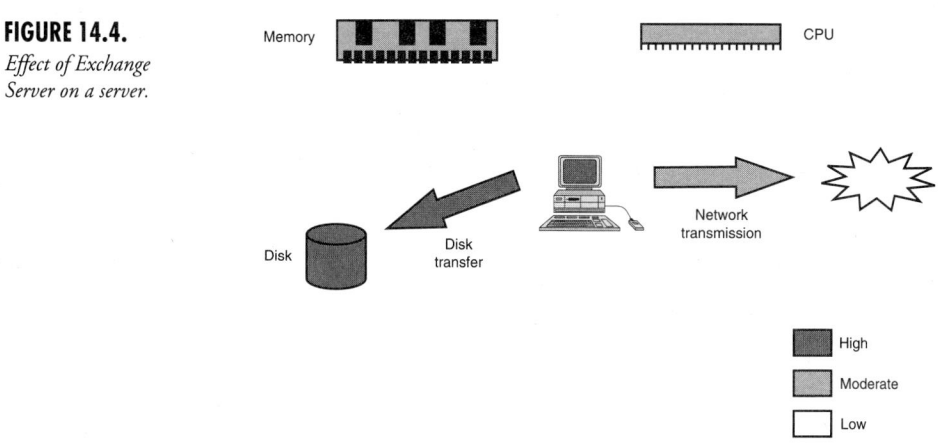

- *Disk storage capacity.* Disk storage can vary from moderate to heavy depending on the number and size of messages transmitted. As more people become comfortable with attaching documents and other materials to messages, the size of the average message will grow substantially. Because Exchange Server uses logging and some other transaction recording mechanisms for reliability and speed, there will be a moderate increase in the amount of disk storage needed when compared with Microsoft Mail. This can be offset by enforcing policies that users keep their personal folders on their local hard disk drives.

- *Disk input/output capacity.* This can vary from moderate to heavy, again depending on the number and size of messages transmitted. You may get a much heavier traffic volume if you set up your system to interface with Internet mail systems or implement the Newsgroup server technology in the next release of Exchange Server. The good news is that Exchange Server has automatic utilities that are designed to analyze your system configuration and determine the best locations for the Exchange Server files.

- *CPU processing capacity.* There will typically be a moderate load on the CPU by Exchange Server. The fact that there are multiple threads running in the background to service requests from the user and store data on the disk drives makes this much more of a load than Microsoft Mail while relying basically on file sharing. If you implement groupware applications, this load may tend to increase.

- *Memory utilization.* Exchange server puts a moderate load on memory as it runs. Memory equates to speed, so servers typically will use as much memory as is reasonable for a given server.

■ *Network input/output capacity.* This will again vary according to the amount and size of traffic from this server. If you link to external mail systems, you may double the load for transmissions that are first received by Exchange Server and then are transmitted to the users.

I want to leave you with a few final comments on the effects of Exchange Server on your system. First, much as in my discussion of Microsoft Mail, Exchange Server is often subject to high peak usage periods. Typical examples of these peak periods are first thing in the morning, after lunch and just before everyone goes home. This can be somewhat minimized if you have client workstations that have enough memory to enable you to run the Exchange clients minimized on the users' desktops at all times. People can easily send mail when they think up an idea and their recipients get the mail soon thereafter as opposed to whenever they next log in to the mail system.

Another subject that will soon come to the forefront is the Internet newsgroup server technology. If you choose to allow your users to access Internet newsgroups from your server, you will have to pay special attention to system loading. First, there are an enormous number of newsgroups that are out there. Many of these newsgroups receive hundreds of messages per day. There are also newsgroups that contain large binary files (most often images, many of which you may not want to display in a professional office environment) that take up huge amounts of disk space. You have to select the newsgroups that you carry carefully to ensure that the load on your system is reasonable. This includes considering the transfer capacity of your network card (remember, many PC network cards are designed to be cost competitive and therefore do not always have high transfer rates). It also includes considering how many files and how long you store these files. One feature that I have seen a number of Internet service providers have trouble keeping up with is the newsgroups (even on DEC Alpha servers)—just a word of caution to keep a close eye on things for a while as users try this new service and see how useful it can be.

In summary, Exchange Server is a very useful tool that can have a serious performance impact on your server computer. This comes from a combination of factors. First, it addresses one of the primary needs of users—to communicate ideas with each other. It adds to this the ability to attach a wide variety of documents and files, which means it serves as an effective transfer mechanism using an interface with which the users are already familiar (sending electronic mail). Finally, it does this all in a rather friendly manner for the users. This ease of use and powerful functionality means that users will use it. This is good, but also means that the server administrator has to keep an eye on disk space utilization, network transfer needs, and server processing capabilities.

Implications for NT of SQL Server

SQL Server is the next member of the BackOffice family to consider here. Similar to Exchange Server, it is a true server application as opposed to being merely a database that allows users to share data files that are stored on a shared network directory (dBase or Microsoft Access files, for example). As with Exchange Server, SQL Server has extended the processing capabilities of early PC databases to provide the power and functionality of database management systems that have been developed for larger computer systems ranging from mainframes to UNIX servers. Along with this additional power comes additional loading for the server, and that is what this section is all about.

The following are the additional functions that distinguish SQL Server from the smaller PC-based databases that many of you are familiar with. With SQL Server, you can do the following:

- Handle large numbers of users
- Coordinate data changes from multiple users
- Provide good performance and response times in a client server environment
- Integrate with the Windows NT operating system and its security features
- Provide flexibility in its configuration for differing hardware environments
- Provide strong recovery and security features for mission-critical databases
- Have the capability to distribute the processing load between the client and the server (for example, the capability to execute data processing routines on the server in the form of stored procedures)

To accomplish these additional tasks, SQL Server has a number of design features that are different from common PC-based applications. The following are some of the more important design considerations:

- SQL Server makes heavy use of shared memory areas to buffer transactions and data for rapid access by the users.
- SQL Server uses a number of background threads to service the memory areas in the form of writes to the data files and other clean up functions.
- SQL Server is tightly coupled with Windows NT networking to allow remote users to rapidly access the SQL Server data by using the installed networking protocols.
- SQL Server implements log files and temporary storage constructs that increase the amount of data storage and traffic, but provide that increased scalability and reliability.
- SQL Server provides the ability to store software in the database in the form of stored procedures. These procedures can be called by clients and are executed on the server. This can reduce network traffic (that is, the data does not have to be transmitted to the client and processed and then have the results transmitted back to the server). However, it increases the processing load on the server.

14

BACKOFFICE AND
WINDOWS NT

Based on this design, the effects on your server of this database management system are shown in Figure 14.5.

■ *Disk storage capacity.* Database management systems can be the heaviest users of disk storage space on a server computer. Of course, the exact nature of the database will determine the storage space required. For example, a small accounting database will take up much less space than a large corporate data warehouse. SQL Server does implement some duplicative data storage mechanisms such as log files, but these are routinely cleaned out on a well-maintained system.

■ *Disk input/output capacity.* Depending on the nature of your transactions and queries, your input/output systems can be strained. For example, if you have a query that requires most of the database be read to calculate a series of number, you will have to transfer most of the contents of that database from disk into memory. Query-intensive databases are good candidates for high-performance input/output systems such as those provided with fast/wide SCSI busses. Other databases, such as those designed to capture online transactions, may require only a small set of data be read or written per minute. These are good issues to explore when you are planning to put up a server designed to support a SQL Server database.

■ *CPU processing capacity.* Once again, this depends on the nature of your database. If you have a large number of stored procedures, you will probably place a fair amount of strain on your CPU. If you perform a lot of calculations in the database (for example, you calculate sums of a series of purchase prices and return only the summation to the client workstation), then you will also experience a significant amount of CPU processing load. However, if all you do is enter data in and get it out in the exact format that it was put in, you will probably have a more moderate CPU utilization. Remember, though, that there are a number of background processes keeping the database management system running that will be adding to the CPU load in addition to those of your user interaction processes.

■ *Memory utilization.* Database management systems thrive on memory. A programmer can access data that is in memory in a small fraction of the time that it takes to access data stored on a disk drive. Because one of the key criteria in selecting a database management system is speed and therefore processing volume, database management system designers have spent quite a bit of time working on ways to increase performance, and this usually involves memory in one way or another. Bigger databases consume more memory, but they all consume much greater sections of memory than those of you who are used to simple file servers or PC-based applications will be used to. Expect the memory requirements for even moderate databases to be in the ten megabyte region (in addition to the space consumed by the operating system). I have seen databases consuming hundreds of megabytes of memory on servers with large transactions that support large numbers of users.

■ *Network input/output capacity.* SQL Server is a client-server database management system. This means that very few users actually use the server console to run applications. Instead, everyone is using the network to communicate with the database. Depending on the nature of the transaction (do you want just a single summary number, or do you really want to pull down thousands of complete records from the server to your workstation), the network loads can vary from moderate to quite heavy. Again, you should work to understand the nature of the data transfers when you are planning out your server so that you can ensure that you have adequate network transfer capacity.

FIGURE 14.5.
Effect of SQL Server on a server.

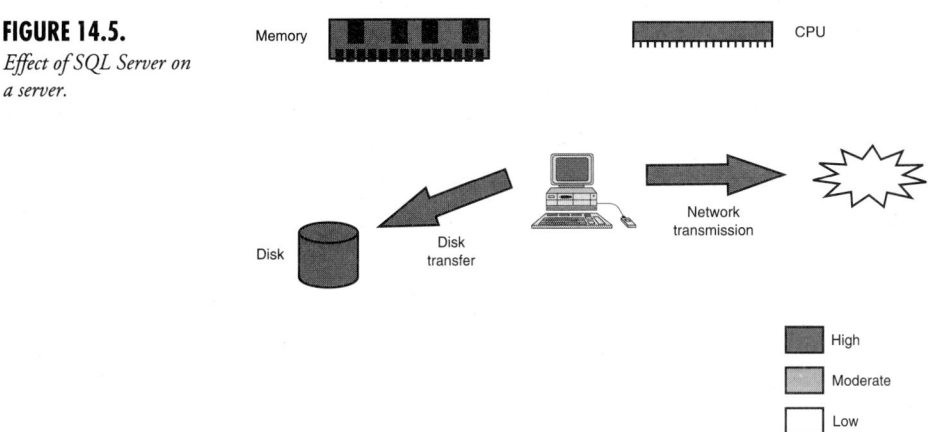

I can't leave this section without giving you a few parting remarks. The first is that you really need to take tuning to heart on SQL Server installations. Even if you are not overloading your system in large scale terms (for example, your CPU is at 100-percent capacity all day long), you can often do a lot to reduce user response times which helps them with their productivity. It can often be as simple as spreading out the various database files across several disk drives to balance the load more evenly.

The next item that you need to keep an eye on during the design process is the use of stored procedures. These can be wonderful tools to increase application performance. It is a time-consuming process to take the data from the server's disk drives, transfer it over the network, and then process it on the remote workstation. It is much easier if you can eliminate a lot of the network traffic. Also, you have much greater control over software that is stored in a central, secure location compared with software that is distributed to every workstation in your organization. However, in most cases, there is more processing capacity and memory in the many user workstations than there is on the relatively few servers. If you are going to be asked to support a lot of stored procedures, make sure that you are given adequate processing capacity.

14

BACKOFFICE AND
WINDOWS NT

Another feature of most database systems is that you can have wide variances in the processing load. Often there are massive update jobs that can take up the entire processing capacity of the system. Some downloads may require that users are not permitted to access the system during the course of the download for consistency purposes. Finally, you have to be really careful about the queries that users issue. I have seen poorly formed queries that had to be terminated after an hour of processing that could be tuned to take less than 30 seconds. If you have developers writing new reports or users forming their own queries in ad-hoc reports, make sure that they are at least moderately qualified in the Structured Query Language (or are only using a controlled set of tables and views which are efficient). If they issue a demanding query, it can severely degrade performance for all the users for quite some time.

Finally, you will probably need to get into a real capacity planning mindset when you work with databases. I can think of only a handful of databases that I have run across that do not grow rapidly. When you first install the system, it may get a moderate amount of use. People are not familiar with the system capabilities and use it only when they have to. Soon however, if your application design is good, people will find new ways to use the system to look up information. Your usage will start to grow in both amount of processing and amount of information stored. Therefore, you need to keep an eye on usage trends (data storage, temporary storage, and so forth) over time so that you can identify when additional capacity is needed long before your system becomes overloaded. You may also want to ensure that your backup subsystem is up to storing this additional information according to your backup schedule.

Implications for NT of Internet Information Server

The Internet Information Server is a relatively new application in the BackOffice family. It started out as a downloadable add-on to NT 3.51 in the spring of 1996. It became a built-in feature with the release of Windows NT Server 4.0. It also represents the first real gateway for NT computers to the enormous world of computer users that is out there. Oh yes, Microsoft has been working for years to increase SQL Server's abilities to handle large numbers of users (hundreds). The domain architecture is designed to enable you to use a single security architecture for access to resources even if you have many thousands of users scattered across the world on your wide area network. These examples are small change compared with the millions of users who are out there on the Internet.

You may only want to use Internet Information Server for your local area network or perhaps your corporate network. That is OK. Internet Information Server will meet your needs and get the job done. From a performance standpoint, it will probably resemble a file server in terms of loading unless you implement a number of the ActiveServer components to shift processing load to your server. Remember, static HTML pages are really just another form of document. True, if you want to have a "good looking" Web page, you will probably include more graphics and art work than you would typically include in a business memorandum done on your word processor.

If you are a site on the Internet, however, your load can go straight through the roof. There are a number of search engines on the Internet that you can register with, or one of your users can register you by themselves. Once you start appearing in these searches, any number of people can log into your site and start downloading your information. Perhaps, as in the case of a marketing-based Web page, this is good news for your company. However, it can be a significant problem for the system administrator. When you were designing the system, everyone told you that there would be some moderate usage level. Now that the equipment is in place, everyone wants to access your page. Therefore, you have to carefully consider the effect of number of users on your server and have some contingencies (for example, the capability to add another processor or upgrade the disk drives or network cards).

Although it is difficult to state the effects of Internet Information Server on its host computer given the wide variation in number of users and content, I decided to give you my best estimate in Figure 14.6. These effects break down as follows:

- *Disk storage capacity.* This is driven strictly by the content of your Web. If you have a large number of pages, or especially if you have a large number of graphics, you can consume quite a bit of disk space.

- *Disk input/output capacity.* This is driven by a combination of your content (simple pages or complex pieces of art, for example) and the number of visitors that you are servicing. Although this is typically not a big consideration except in the larger Web servers, you should at least consider its impact. You may, for example, want to place the Web and FTP pages on a drive that has little other activity. Try to avoid drives that support busy databases or other such tasks.

- *CPU processing capacity.* Processing Web and FTP queries is relatively simple for a computer. However, the latest extension and rage in the Internet world is active Web pages. Typically this involves executing applications (such as those written in the Java programming language) or running animations and other active controls. Although these are typically executed on the client, Microsoft has built a number of constructs into its server that enable you to run the applications on the server. Such things as security checks and certain application processing need to be tightly controlled, and this is much easier to do on the server. Therefore, if your developers are building a lot of Web applications that do things such as interface with your server databases or perform a lot of server-based processing, you will need to keep an eye on CPU utilization.

- *Memory utilization.* Typical Web and FTP servers are not really intense on the memory capabilities of a server. This, of course, grows as you add server-based Web applications or provide interfaces to databases located on your server.

- *Network input/output capacity.* This can be one of the more severe limitations for many servers asked to perform Internet services. Many PC network cards are not designed to meet the very high performance standards that an Internet connection may demand. This is especially true if you become a popular server. Microsoft, for example, had over 30,000 people download its new Internet Explorer 3.0 product during the first six hours that it was available. What makes that even more impressive is the fact that the file took almost an hour for most people with normal modems to download and that the product was not made available until midnight in the Pacific time zone of the United States (three in the morning, that is, for those of us in the East). Even Microsoft had difficulty handling this volume with multiple download servers scattered throughout several locations. Perhaps you will not achieve this level of popularity, but it does show that you can run into some severe peaks in usage, especially if you have great content.

FIGURE 14.6.

Effect of Internet Information Server on a server.

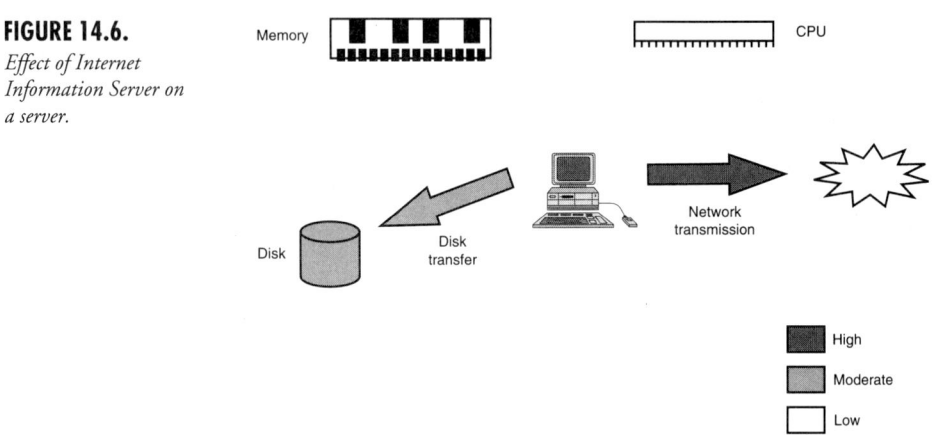

Another effect that you should consider when implementing an Internet/intranet server is the security effect. Although it is true that Web server can only access files in a given directory tree (unless you build server-side Web applications that do otherwise), the access is pretty much there for all. You have to go out of your way to implement some form of security, and this is really a relatively new discipline. Therefore, you should carefully consider your content before you make it available on a Web server, especially one that is accessible from the Internet (where all your competitors are located).

Another point to consider is that your usage patterns for an Internet-based server are controlled by the outside world and not your organization's normal work hours. If you have a site that appeals to regular consumers, much of your activity may occur during the evening hours when people are home to surf the Web. In other cases, you may even be subject to traffic at all hours of the day (that is, your site becomes popular around the world). This can have effects on other system activities such as shutting databases down in the middle of the night for backup. Night in your time zone is the middle of the business day somewhere in the world.

A good impact issue to address here is how do you handle the situation where your server faces overloading from the millions of people on the Internet who are anxious to see what you have? You could just unplug the Internet connection when you see the server load going through the ceiling. However, that would form a bad impression. You could just stop the Web server service, but again that would lead to a bad impression. One of the easiest techniques to deal with that I have run across on the Web is swapping the pages around to control load. Remember a Web page is nothing more than an ASCII file written in HTML format. If the Web page has a hot spot that lets you download a file, then the user can perform that action. However, if the page does not contain these high-load features, then the users will not be able to put as much of a load on the system. You could design a multimillion-dollar system that swaps in less demanding Web pages in place of those that are overloading your system. Of course, you could also just type up a quick batch file that uses the DOS copy command to move files from a staging directory of content to the actual Web server directory. I am not much for elegance, so I tend to choose the old batch file route. You can even put a message on these less capable pages as to when the download services will be available.

Finally, a Web/FTP server can become quite a maintenance task. As you will learn in the next section, it is blissfully simple to set up the Internet Information Server product. A child can do it with ease. However, that is just the beginning of the maintenance process. Web pages are getting to be a form of art. They are a combination of text, graphics, software programs, and other active components that are used to make an impression on your visitors. As such, people from the CEO on down will have opinions as to the message that you are trying to get across with your Web site. These opinions turn into a lot of work—updating the pages and building active controls and miniature applications. Perhaps this is the responsibility of someone else. If it is not, it could turn into quite a task. Major vendors in the computer industry such as Microsoft and Oracle redesign the look, feel, and content of their Web pages every couple of days. They even do major look-and-feel changes every couple of months. Make sure you clarify who is going to do this work before you get involved with having a Web server on your computer.

Implications for NT of Systems Management Server

Another newcomer to the BackOffice family is the Systems Management Server. This is a powerful tool for managing that vast sea of computers that are sitting on your user's desks. It can also help keep all your servers up to date and functioning at maximum efficiency. As with every wonderful thing that computers can do, there is also an effect on the computers themselves.

To quickly review, here are some of the major functions of the Systems Management Server:

- Automated client computer hardware and software inventory collection and storage
- Automated client computer software installation
- General help desk support functions

The help desk support functions are important and interesting, but usually have little effect on the server. The other two functions, on the other hand, can have a substantial impact on your server as shown in Figure 14.7. These effects include the following:

- *Disk storage capacity.* The impact of Systems Management Server on your disk storage capacity can vary from a little to a lot, depending on how you are using the system. If you are just keeping an inventory of the equipment on your network, the impact on disk storage is not too high. If you are performing automated software installations and you are one of the many shops that supports almost every computer software package known to mankind, then you may have to allocate a bit more storage for the applications that you will be distributing.

- *Disk input/output capacity.* If you are performing a mass upgrade of a number of computer systems out on your network, the disk input/output capacity of your system could be a significant factor. In these cases, it would be wise to invest in a higher transfer capacity disk storage system (fast/wide SCSI, for example) to improve your transfer capabilities.

- *CPU processing capacity.* The scripts associated with Systems Management Server will require some processing, but this is not typically the most significant impact of this system.

- *Memory utilization.* This is similar to the CPU processing capacity in that it is not typically the most significant impact of Systems Management Server. However, because you will also have a SQL Server database running to support many Systems Management Server functions, you could have significant memory utilization from the SQL Server services.

- *Network input/output capacity.* This can be a significant impact of Systems Management Server, especially if you are using it to distribute large updates to a number of client computers. Again, if you see this as a significant function of your server, you may want to invest in a higher-capacity network interface card to prevent this from becoming a bottleneck in your software distribution process. You may also want to consider linking your servers with a higher capacity network (such as a 100Mbps Ethernet backbone) to improve transmission capabilities.

One of the interesting design features built into Systems Management Server is the capability of distributing software in a hierarchical fashion as shown in Figure 14.8. This scheme is especially useful in limiting network transmissions in a network that includes some form of routing (for example, there are network devices that transmit signals from one side to the other if the signals are intended for a computer on the other side thereby eliminating unnecessary signals from your network segment). In this scheme, your master server sends out the changes and orders to a number of other servers. These servers then send the upgrades to their clients. You could implement a number of such tiers to control upgrades for a large organization.

FIGURE 14.7.

Effect of Systems Management Server on a server.

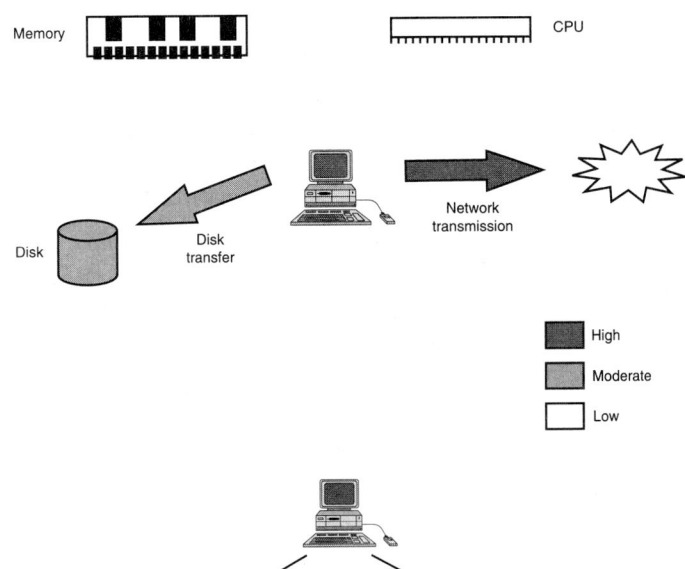

FIGURE 14.8.

Hierarchical software distribution scheme.

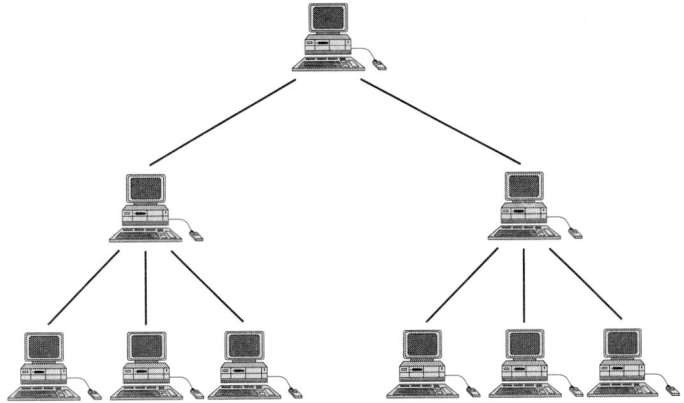

One of the keys to controlling the effect of Systems Management Server on your systems is scheduling. These transfers can be large and may tie up the client computers while they are receiving their upgrades. A large upgrade can cause a large amount of network traffic that can interfere with other processing activities. It is usually best to schedule upgrades to occur automatically during off hours (at night, for example). This will require you to train your people to leave their PCs powered on and logged off at night. It may also mean a few headaches for you in that you will probably want to check how things are going during the time that you would normally be sleeping or surfing the Internet.

A final, positive, effect that Systems Management Server provides for your network is license security. Many companies are worried about violating software licensing agreements. There are so many computers out there, and many have replaced previous computers that had software licenses that you think were transferred to the new machine. There probably have also been a number of upgrades to previous licenses, and so on. Systems Management Server provides a central database to help keep track of the licenses. The best feature is the one that lets you audit your network to see what is actually in use. This task would take up quite a bit of time if you had to send someone out to find every computer on your network and look at the applications.

14

BACKOFFICE AND WINDOWS NT

Implications for NT of SNA Server

The SNA Server is not designed to perform a lot of local area network processing. Instead, it is designed to act as a gateway from the local area network to the IBM mainframe and AS/400 world. Mainframe types might be comfortable with this type of connection. They feel comfortable with terms such as channel attached and the like. Those from the PC world might find some of these terms to be a bit alien. There should also be a healthy amount of concern when you attach your server to a computer that is as big as most mainframes. Mainframes are designed to process huge volumes of information and spit the data out in the form of enormous reports and data files. The client server world is designed to have the user ask a specific question and receive a response on an as-needed basis. Most networks were not designed to handle large batch jobs that produce thousand page printouts (in which a user might look up a few numbers of interest). If not controlled properly, users could saturate your server and network with jobs that were never intended for the local area network environment.

Here are the potential effects of SNA Server (see Figure 14.9):

- *Disk storage capacity.* There is nothing about SNA Server itself that places any significant disk loads on your NT Server. However, many mainframe users are used to running big batch jobs that produce big flat files with data in them. They tend to like to leave these jobs out on the network so that they can be quickly accessed when needed. If they choose to transfer these data files down to a shared drive on your server, it could start to take up a lot of disk space in a hurry.

- *Disk input/output capacity.* Typically, SNA Server is not disk intensive unless your users transfer a lot of data between the mainframe and your server.

- *CPU processing capacity.* This is typically relatively moderate for computers running SNA Server. There is some translation and routing work to be done, but the majority of the work is done on the mainframe (such as running batch jobs) and the workstations (providing the user interface).

- *Memory utilization.* This is also relatively moderate for computers running SNA Server.

- *Network input/output capacity.* This is an area where you could run into problems depending on how your users plan to use their SNA Server connection. Although the typical mainframe terminal has a very low speed connection to the mainframe itself, there are a large number of them. Also, data files on the mainframe can get quite large, and this can be a large network burden if your users need to send and receive a lot of files with the mainframe. This data also tends to come all at one time, typically at the end of a batch job.

FIGURE 14.9.

Effect of SNA Server on a server.

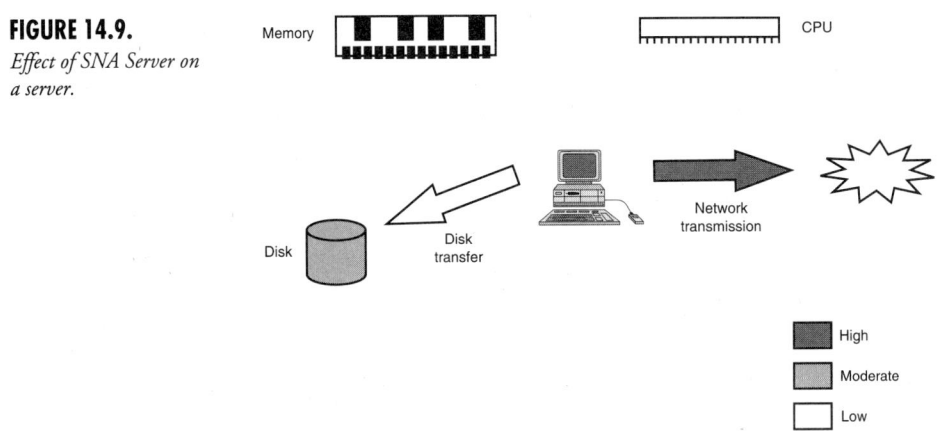

One of the most important variables in the load placed on your NT server by SNA Server is the type of connection used to communicate with the IBM mainframe or AS/400. There are a number of means of hooking into the mainframe that vary from extremely high speeds (right into the main communications bus, for example) to relatively slow speeds (that are used for common mainframe terminals, for example). The data transfer needs of your users need to be coordinated with the mainframe systems staff to ensure that you have an adequate transfer capability based on the number of users and the size of the data transfers. This will affect your choice of interface technologies in your server. These options are discussed in more detail in the SNA Server section.

Working to Keep the Environment Integrated

One of the most impressive features of BackOffice is the tight integration between the products. They are good at using the standard security and administrative features provided by the Windows NT operating system. This integration (see Figure 14.10) reduces the administrative burdens, improves security, and reduces the number of interfaces that you have to learn. You have the opportunity to mess things up and slip back into old habits, however, so let's look at how you can keep the Windows NT and BackOffice environment working together.

The first challenge to your integrated environment will often come from your local application developers. They have grown up using operating systems that had little or no security. What security and administrative features the operating system did provide were not accessible to developers. Therefore, most developers are used to developing their own security systems and administrative systems for every application. Although this may work, they typically do not have enough control over the functions of the operating system to have a fully bullet proof security system. It also means that you have to go through a number of additional administrative steps (such as creating user IDs and passwords for the operating system and the database management system).

FIGURE 14.10.

*Integrated BackOffice
environment.*

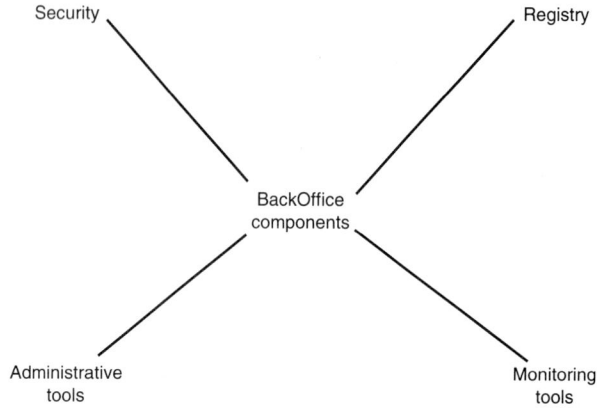

There is no easy way to enforce this. Your developers and management may feel it necessary to use a commercial product that cannot interface with the NT security and administrative system. However, if you do have a choice, always recommend a product that can interface with the operating system utilities. You should lobby with local application developers to use the operating system tools rather than build their own.

The registry is a specific operating system feature that you should use for locally developed applications. This is a centralized repository where all the initialization data is stored. Earlier versions of the Windows operating system used a number of ini files to store this information. They were scattered all over the hard disk (some in the applications directory, others in the Windows directory). The registry enables you to store the data in a system "database" of information that has values both for individual users and the system as a whole. This is much easier to troubleshoot and maintain than the scattered collection of files, so at least try to lobby for its use with your developers.

A final subject to consider is keeping up with all the new tools and features that come out for Windows NT. There are some environments where the vendors tell you not to apply a patch unless you absolutely need it (if your system has crashed, for example). One common flavor of UNIX had hundreds of patches out there including almost one major patch to the operating system kernel itself on an almost weekly basis. In this environment, you never were sure where you stood or whether you could run a new product on your system.

Windows NT and BackOffice are somewhat different. It is a good idea in this case to keep up with the service packs and upgrades to these products. Because these products are so tightly coupled with one another, you may often find that you need to have the latest service pack for the operating system installed in order to load a new version of a BackOffice component. A nice feature of the service packs is that a later service pack includes all the changes of the earlier service pack plus the new changes. This makes it easy to keep up to date. Best of all, most of these upgrades can be found on the Microsoft Web page making it very easy to keep up to date (you no longer have the excuse that the vendor never sent you the upgrade disks).

Summary

This chapter has covered a lot of ground. My goal was to cover how the various components of BackOffice affected the Windows NT operating system and computer systems on which they are running. These interactions often depend on the exact uses to which you are putting the components in your particular environment. You have to be careful, therefore, when planning out a new server to ensure that you have adequate capacity.

The effects of the BackOffice components on your server can be generalized as follows:

- Microsoft Mail tends to be a relatively light load on the server for a given number of users. Designed for file server environments, its major impact is on the disk storage and network transmission systems.

- Exchange Server is a more complicated environment in that it is a true server application. It benefits from its use of server memory and processing capabilities. It also uses additional disk storage to record log files to increase reliability. It could be an extremely heavy disk storage space user if you implement the newsgroup server technologies that are being integrated into this product.

- SQL Server is another true server application that provides the full spectrum of relational database management system services to your environment. As such, it can be a heavy user of disk storage, disk data transfer, CPU, and even network transmission capabilities on your server.

- Internet Information Server typically affects the network transmission and disk storage capacities of the server. If you implement some of the ActiveServer or dynamic Web page technologies that Microsoft makes available, you could put significant processing and memory loads on your system.

- Systems Management Server typically affects the disk storage and network transmission capabilities of your system. However, because it is based on SQL Server, you could get significant memory and CPU usage if you perform a large number of transactions and queries.

- SNA Server typically affects the network transmission capabilities of the server. This depends on the type of network connection that you implement into the mainframe environment.

This chapter ended with a few words on keeping the BackOffice environment integrated. There are a number of benefits for administrators and users alike that are derived from the integrated environment. You must remain vigilant, however, when integrating new products to try to use the operating system services as opposed to application specific tools. This is especially true of locally developed applications where you have (you hope!) some input into the development process.

14

BACKOFFICE AND
WINDOWS NT

PART

III

IN THIS PART

Internet Information Server

Internet Information Server Overview

by Joe Greene

IN THIS CHAPTER

So far, this book has presented an overview of the BackOffice family and its architecture. Then you delved into the basis of the BackOffice family—the Windows NT Server operating system. This chapter begins your exploration of the individual BackOffice components. There are two reasons for choosing the Internet Information Server as the first of these discussions. First, it is bundled with Windows NT Server. You do not have to purchase it separately, and that makes it really easy to implement even when faced with a limited budget. Second, with all the push on Internet and intranet services, this may well be the cornerstone of information processing systems of the future.

This topic is also fun to discuss. DOS made desktop computing possible for those who were willing to learn a little about computers, command lines, and running applications. Windows, on the other hand, made desktop computing friendly enough for the average person to use at home and at work. The early Internet tools made worldwide exchange of information within the reach of computer professionals who were willing to worry about protocols, IP addresses of computers of interest, and other such details. However, the Web and operating systems that are Internet-friendly have put information from across the globe within the reach of mere mortals. The Internet Information Server (IIS) is Microsoft's answer to the server side of this technology.

This is the overview chapter for the IIS. It is designed to be an easy introduction to a topic that may not be obvious to all BackOffice administrators out there. Many may come from the Novell environment, where their tasks to date have been providing file and printer sharing services to their users. Others may come from minicomputer and large server environments where they ran databases and other applications, but did not have connections to the Internet.

Functions of an Internet Server

What is an Internet server? My definition goes something like "a computer that is used to provide information services using the protocols and tools popularized on the Internet." Actually, many of the "Internet servers" will be providing services to users on an intranet and not even have connectivity to the actual Internet. The need for quality information services is just as important in the Internet and intranet environments.

I like to differentiate between what I call the physical and functional definitions of the Internet. The physical definition of the Internet is a series of computer networks that have been connected to one another and share the common TCP/IP protocol set. Figure 15.1 depicts this vision of the Internet. A lot of technology and standards are used to make the Internet work in countries that speak many different languages and have a wide variety of internal communications systems. Imagine the thousands of wires that are transmitting data across the globe at speeds that were unimaginable just ten years ago.

The key to the whole computer network is the TCP/IP protocol. It provides a link that is rarely found in other transmission systems. For example, there are dozens of different formats used to transmit television signals around the world. Your television set would probably not work, except in a few other countries, without a converter. Telephone systems suffer from similar problems, although long distance networks have defined interfaces that enable transmission between these dissimilar systems.

FIGURE 15.1.

Physical definition of the Internet.

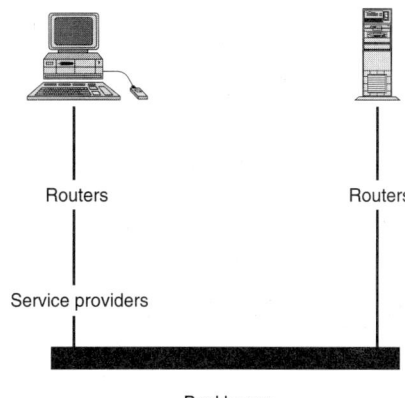

The computer world was wise enough to pick a common transmission protocol. There are protocols that are more theoretically elegant and that might be faster. There is something to be said for being able to communicate with almost everyone, however. The goal of this protocol is to provide a means of addressing a packet of information and sending it out across a network that speaks the protocol. The network will take care of the details to ensure that it gets to its destination, assuming that the address is reachable. This is much like the system for conventional mail. You are responsible for putting the correct address on the envelope, and the post office is responsible for figuring out which plane to put it on and then which delivery truck is needed to get the letter to the recipient.

There are a number of different transmission technologies that TCP/IP can use to get from here to there. It can go over conventional telephone lines using modem transmission protocols. It can be transferred via both Ethernet and token-ring local area networks. Finally, it can use a number of high-speed networks such as ATM and FDDI. Assuming that the network engineers have connected the wires and configured the communications devices properly, all you need to know is the correct address to which to send it.

Therefore, in this physical view of the Internet, all you have to do is have the network engineers give you a connection to the Internet. Perhaps you do not have such a staff of wiring experts working for you. You can still connect to the Internet using a dial-up connection to an Internet Service Provider (ISP). These places make it really easy to get your Internet connections, and many even support dedicated lines connecting into their systems. Windows NT is very supportive of Internet connectivity and makes it easy to use dial-up networking or network interface cards to access TCP/IP networks.

This is not a book on wiring or network devices. Not every location is ready to connect to the Internet in spite of a number of reasonable security solutions that are on the market today to keep out those evil hackers that everyone reads about. There is another view of the Internet that you should consider even if you are just running a small local area network. I call this the functional view of the Internet (see Figure 15.2).

FIGURE 15.2.

Functional view of the Internet.

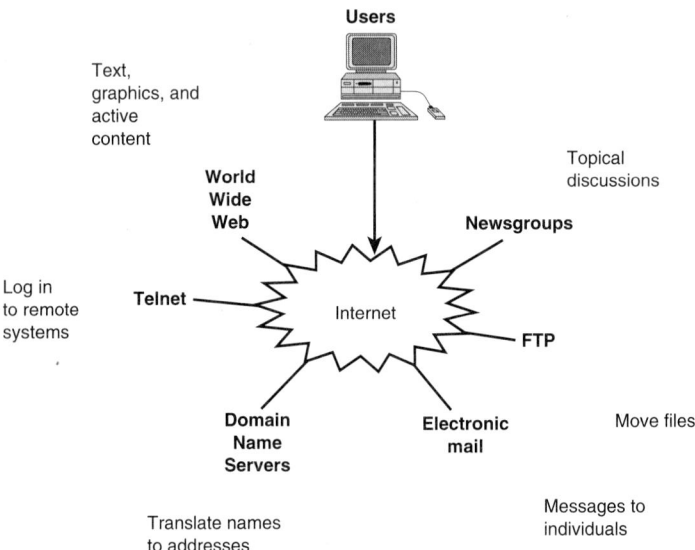

The functional view of the Internet is based on the fact that there are a number of tools and protocols that have developed for the Internet. It is actually a very interesting test bed for application development. With the rapid and free access to information and products that are provided by the Internet, it perhaps most closely approaches an environment of pure capitalism than any other market known to mankind. Although it is true that many of these products have been distributed free, the key is that the "buyer" has free access to a number of products and can switch at will. It is not like the traditional mainframe environment where you have a limited selection of vendors and an all-powerful information systems organization that decides what products you will be able to use.

This environment has bred a lot of half-baked products that were designed for the pure technologist. They were command-line interfaces for people who loved to type at the keyboard throughout the night and were proud that they could remember arcane command sequences. For a long time, the Internet remained a haven for these pure technologists. Then along came some scientists who just wanted to use the Internet to exchange data and other information. Most of their organizations had the Internet connection, but these people were experts in their respective fields and may or may not have been computer experts. To accommodate this, they developed the technologies that have grown into our current World Wide Web.

The World Wide Web is the key to acceptance of the Internet in the broader world. I first used the Internet for some work I did for NASA many years ago; I was comfortable with FTP, telnet, and other such tools because I worked in the UNIX world. However, many of my colleagues were not comfortable with these tools and I often wound up having to perform downloads for them. There were still too many addresses and commands to remember. You had to remember these commands and addresses every time you wanted to access the information.

The Web, on the other hand, is based on authored pages that contain their own unique content (text and graphics), but also contain links that lead you to other parts of the Web. This is a key, because you can have some folks who are more comfortable with addresses and finding things on the Web-built pages with links. The people who do not want to get into the computer details only need to be able to find the pages that contain all these links and use them to find what they want. Such was born the art of "surfing" the Web.

The Web is not everything on the Internet from a functional point of view. Developers have built convenient interfaces to the traditional Internet tools, such as FTP and telnet, that enable regular users to be able to use these tools effectively. The Web pages also have the capability of linking to FTP sites and downloading their files. In that sense, many of the old protocols are still being used for what they are good at even by the newer, more convenient interfaces. My short list of major functional tools on the Web from a business perspective currently includes the following:

- *The World Wide Web.* A tool set that enables you to display text, graphics, audio, video, animations, and even applications within a standard document display window. Figure 15.3 shows a sample Web page that you should be familiar with if you do a lot of BackOffice work.

FIGURE 15.3.

Sample Web page
(www.microsoft.com).

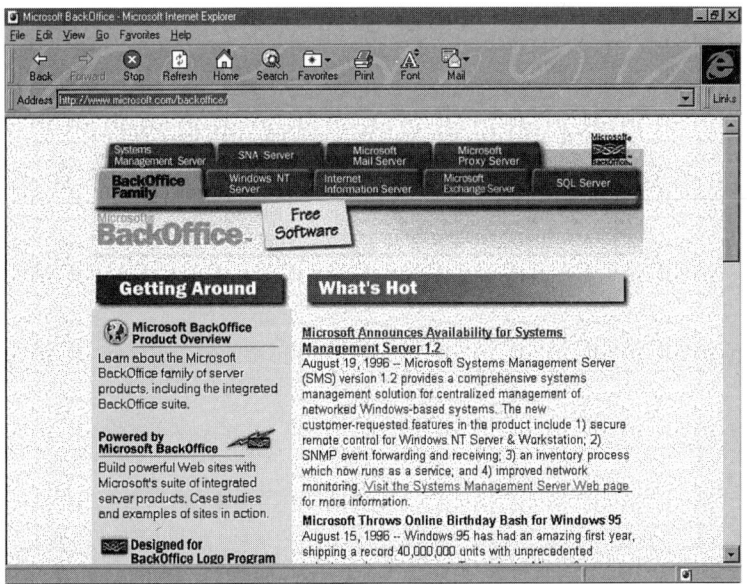

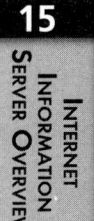

■ *Internet newsgroups.* A tool set that enables you to post and read articles on a wide range of subjects. Figure 15.4 shows a sample newsgroup article.

FIGURE 15.4.

Sample newsgroup article.

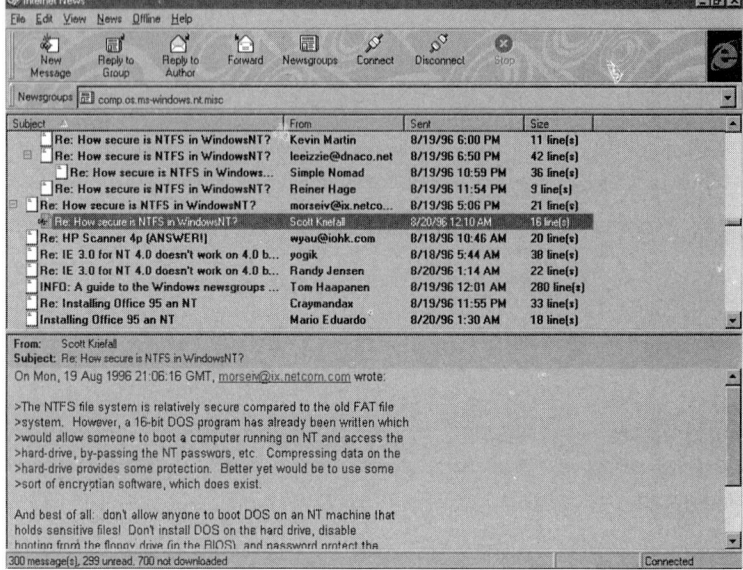

■ *File Transfer Protocol.* A tool set that enables you to move files between two computers.

■ *Telnet.* A tool set that enables you to log on to a remote computer.

■ *Domain Name Server.* A utility that enables you to enter a convenient text name that can be cross-referenced to the numerical address of a computer on the Internet.

■ *Internet mail.* This is actually a set of tools and a number of protocols that are used to send messages, often with attachments, over the Internet.

There are also a number of products that are not exactly related to the business world. An example of these would be the Internet Relay Chat (IRC) tools. These tools enable users to type messages to one another in a live, roundtable discussion format. There is even an Internet telephone protocol setup that enables you to talk to one another using voices over the Internet. There are people working right now to bring out even more of these enhanced services. Which ones will take hold is anyone's guess. There are some who say that telephone companies are in big trouble when people can use the Internet to place a voice call around the world for the price of a connection to the Internet (about $25 per month in my neighborhood).

Today's Internet is impressive, but tomorrow's will probably make us wonder how we survived with such a primitive tool. Microsoft currently has three products in some form of beta release that will greatly enhance its ability to provide Internet services. Major thrusts of current development include secure commerce protocols that will enable you to conduct your business over the Internet. You will look through a catalog on the World Wide Web and place your order in a secure format without having to call the vendor's 800 number and listen to elevator music for a half an hour. (Could this be the end of elevator music?)

Microsoft's Goals for IIS

Where does Internet Information Server (IIS) fit into this picture? Several of the functions mentioned in the last section are already being accomplished by other components in the BackOffice family. For example, the domain name server functionality is now part of Windows NT Server itself. The Internet mail function also is a central component in the Exchange Server and operating system mail client software produced by Microsoft. IIS, therefore, does not have to worry about any of these functions.

It is also important to remember that IIS is focused on the server side of the Internet world. There are a number of tools that are placed on the client to help it access the various Internet services. Microsoft has products to meet most of these needs, and more tools are on the way all of the time. IIS is designed to provide services in the two key areas of the Internet in terms of information access—the World Wide Web and File Transfer Protocol. They added support for Gopher servers, although this is not an intensely popular service on the Internet or intranets these days.

Another goal of IIS was the capability of supporting an intranet as well as the Internet. A lot of this capability comes from choosing an operating system that runs on a wide variety of computer platforms, including the relatively inexpensive Intel-based PCs. This, combined with the pricing for IIS, makes it a cost-competitive solution for even small organizations who wish to set up an intranet. The fact that many of the client tools are bundled as part of their operating systems or available for free downloading from this Internet increases the attractiveness of the intranet solution.

Another goal of the IIS product is to form the basis that will enable future product development. Many technologies can be based around the World Wide Web. It is a good communications and navigation tool for a wide range of information. Examples of products that Microsoft plans to build around the Web include the merchant server and media server. With the development tools and application programming interfaces that are available, it will be relatively easy for companies to develop their own applications based on Web technologies and link to BackOffice and third-party servers.

Another interesting use of Internet Information Server is its part in the product suite that Microsoft is putting together for ISPs. These organizations offer connectivity to the Internet as a service to their clients. Most of them offer a wide range of Internet services, including Web access, newsgroups, mail, and domain name servers. Microsoft has bundled the products in the BackOffice family in a platform that is optimized toward the needs of the ISP. This package has some attractive costs when compared with the larger UNIX installations that are

15

**INTERNET
INFORMATION
SERVER OVERVIEW**

common today, where the ISP has to integrate a number of third-party Internet tools to form a complete Internet environment for its customers. This bundle for ISPs is often referred to by its code name of Normandy.

Services Provided by IIS

Internet Information Server provides three basic services to users:

■ World Wide Web server
■ File Transfer Protocol server
■ Gopher server

This may not seem like a lot of services. Remember, however, that several Internet-related services, such as the Domain Name Server and all the communications protocols, are already bundled with Windows NT Server. Several more are available for downloading or are included as part of the Windows NT Resource Kit—for example, a telnet server. Others, such as electronic mail, are already provided by other components in the BackOffice family. As this book is being written, a newsgroup server is in beta testing for addition to a future release of Exchange. Taken together, they form a complete Internet server environment (see Figure 15.5).

FIGURE 15.5.

Internet server environment provided by BackOffice.

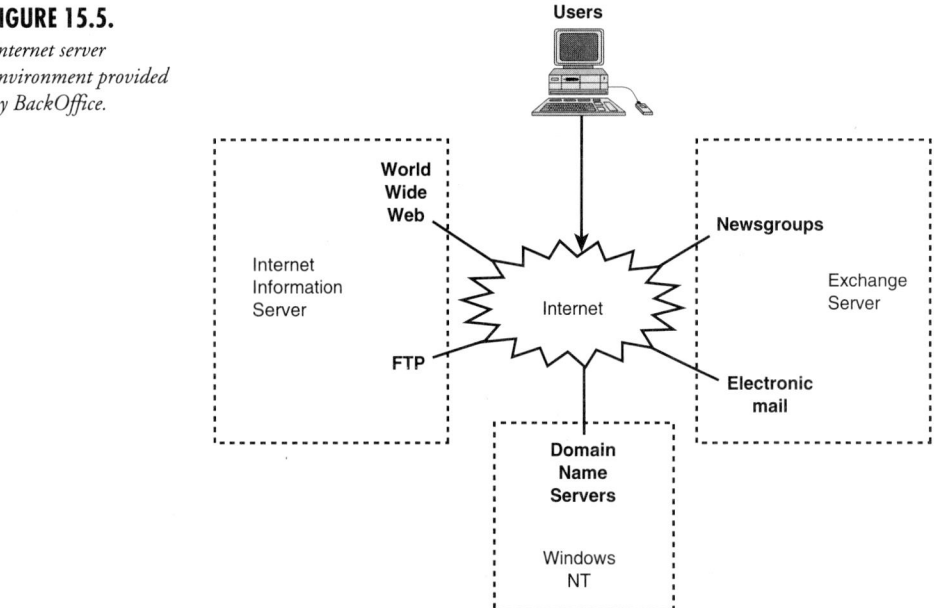

World Wide Web Servers

The first service provided by the Internet Information Server is perhaps the most popular one—a World Wide Web server. It is all the rage and all users want to try their hand at authoring Web pages. The basic concepts behind a Web server are actually quite simple (see Figure 15.6). You designate a directory as the Web server's root directory. You then place a series of content files in this directory and subdirectories underneath this directory. These content files include documents that are ASCII text files containing text to be displayed, along with a series of formatting controls that are coded using the standards for the Hypertext Markup Language (HTML). Here are some of the common examples of HTML formatting controls:

- Links to other Web pages.
- Links to graphics files that are to be displayed as part of the page.
- Formatting controls that determine the font, size, and color of the text being displayed.
- Tags that identify the page (that is, give it a name that is displayed in the header of your Web browser).
- Sections that contain programs that are written in other languages, such as Microsoft Basic Script, Java, or the Common Gateway Interface (CGI).
- Extended formatting tags that cause special visual effects to be displayed, such as marquee displays, sounds, and even movies. The programs that control these special effects are written using such tools as Java or Microsoft's ActiveX.
- Links to files that are to be downloaded or even executed on the recipient's PC. Some good examples of this are the many downloads available on the Microsoft Web page.
- Formatting extensions, such as frames, that enable you to have multiple "windows" of information active on your screen.

FIGURE 15.6.

Basic concepts behind a Web server.

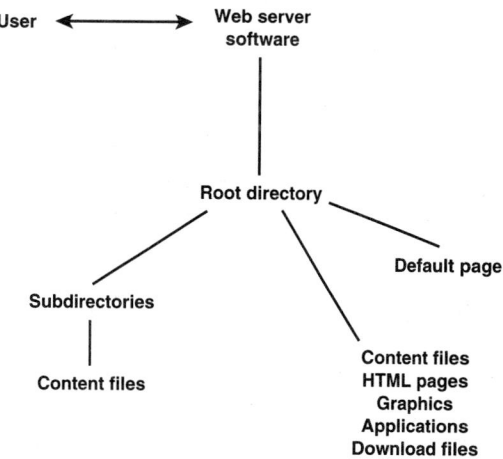

15

INTERNET
INFORMATION
SERVER OVERVIEW

One of the challenges of being a Webmaster is ensuring that your content is compatible with a wide range of common browsers that are available. This can be quite a challenge because vendors are working hard to outdo one another and wow the general public. It was a happy day when most of the big vendors in the Web field got together and agreed to work through the World Wide Web consortium. You may want to check out `http://www.w3.ora/pub/www` for more information on their activities. It is something to consider when your authors are designing their content.

In its basic form, a Web server functions very much like a traditional file server—you have content that people access through a standard series of utilities. Many Web sites provide useful functions and never go beyond this model. However, Microsoft and other vendors are starting to push what they refer to as active or dynamic Web sites, and this changes the picture somewhat. If you want additional information on these topics, you can refer to books such as the *CGI Developer's Guide* or *Teach Yourself Java in 21 Days,* both from Sams Publishing.

An active Web site is one where there are Web software processes being run. These may be simple scripts written in the traditional Web programming language (CGI) that collect a little data from users who visit the page or that count the number of users who have visited the site. These are really simple applications and usually do not put any kind of stress on the host computer. Users have taken these basic concepts and extended them to build entire applications that run off Web technologies, however.

- The first extension is the use of programming languages, such as Java, to run small applications of either the client or the server that interact with the user, perform computations, or display information in a more creative fashion (animations, for example). Although most of this work is currently focused on the client side, there are a number of application components that are best implemented on the server side (for example, issues dealing with commerce where you are concerned about security).

- Another extension is the use of database management systems to dynamically build the content of the Web pages. A Web page that is written to contain text and graphics may be fine for a brochure that describes the technical features of a new product, but what about pricing information or product availability? Many of the data elements that are involved with commerce or even news are dynamic, and it would be almost impossible to keep this information up-to-date using static authoring tools. (Have you seen what ESPN has done on the Web at `http://espnet.sportszone.com` to provide up-to-the-minute scores and sports news?) Databases are good at tracking information, and programs can be written that take data from the databases and translate it into the ASCII text that is needed to display it in HTML format.

- A final area that you might consider is the use of commercial servers that are designed to meet specific needs. The Microsoft merchant server product is an example of a tool that interfaces with a Web server, a database, and even external communications systems to provide the functions needed for Internet commerce. You might consider this to be just a combination of the previous two options, but I see one key difference.

Rather than building the product, you just go out and buy it. Because internal development time is limited, you will probably see a growing number of shrink-wrapped applications that tie into Web servers.

The key for the system administrator of active Web sites is to realize that these active components are going to be placing processing and memory demands on the server. They are no worse than those of other applications. If you are connected to the Internet, however, you could be subject to huge surges in volume if your site becomes popular. There have been many creative sites that have become inundated with traffic to the point where they have actually been removed from the server to prevent server overload.

FTP Servers

The concept behind an FTP server is also relatively simple. You have a directory on your server that you make available to users who access your FTP site. Unlike the Web, the FTP service has been designed with security in mind so you can validate user access. However, you also have the option of allowing anonymous connections, which will give anyone access to the site. The main maintenance task is keeping the directories fresh with content and creating user access accounts if you are enforcing security.

FIGURE 15.7.

Basic concepts behind an FTP server.

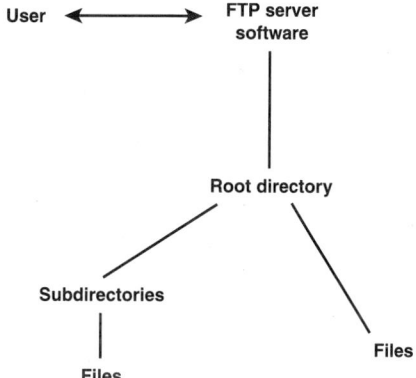

There are no advanced FTP concepts such as Active FTP. It is a simple service that gets its job done efficiently. It can be a very fast means to download a file (much faster than transferring the information via Web services) and can work with Web servers to take care of the file download tasks. You may wonder what the differences are between the Internet Information Server FTP Server and the FTP Server that comes as part of Windows NT. The key differences lie in the scalability and security areas. They function exactly the same and the clients will not even notice the difference. The IIS version, however, is a bigger, more robust package that will be needed if you try to service a large number of users accessing your site from the Internet.

Gopher Servers

Gopher servers provide an alternative information search medium for non-Web servers. They are not very sophisticated when you compare them to the Web, and you actually have to search to find other Gopher servers to get information from. There are some users who use this as the basis of their processing, so Microsoft included it in this package. I have only installed it for test purposes and do not see this service lasting long when the Web is available.

Summary

I have intentionally kept this chapter short in order to get right into the next couple of chapters. There, you explore using IIS. It is hard to go into too much theoretical detail, because the IIS packages are actually quite simple conceptually. Perhaps that is part of their popularity. The main points to take away from this chapter are that Microsoft has decided to bundle three key servers into IIS and sell them as part of the Windows NT Server operating system. The three key services are: the World Wide Web server, the FTP server, and the Gopher server.

Setting Up IIS

by Joe Greene

IN THIS CHAPTER

With many products, there are a lot of tips and tricks that you can pass on regarding setup. There are a lot of places where you can go wrong and do things that you will regret later. Sometimes you are actually placing a fair amount of data at risk during the upgrade process and have to perform a set of careful backups before you even begin the upgrade process. This is not one of those products. The Internet Information Server is actually a part of the BackOffice installation process, and if you are not paying careful attention on the three screens or so that select this option and configure the product, you might not even notice that you have installed it.

It's tough to argue with this situation. There are enough things that really require your attention. With all of this said, you may be wondering what you're going to learn in this chapter. There are a few things to look at that will ensure that you understand what your options are and that you get the best performance out of your Internet services.

Overview of the Setup Process

You have two basic starting points for setting up Internet Information Server. You can choose it as part of the NT 4.0 installation process, or you can add it as a network component after you have installed NT 4.0 or 3.51 (although IIS does not come as part of the NT 3.51 distribution). The basic process is the same in both cases. The key to this process is planning a few details up front and then plugging them into the appropriate boxes on the installation screens:

1. Plan the IIS configuration.
2. Prepare the system for installation.
3. Run the setup program.
4. Configure the installed servers.
5. Install the content for the servers.

The first step in the installation process involves planning your IIS configuration. Here, you have to decide which of the IIS components you are going to install and in which directories you will be storing your content for the IIS servers. These are the components from which you will be choosing when you install IIS:

- Internet service manager
- World Wide Web service
- Gopher service
- FTP service
- ODBC drivers and administration
- Help and sample files
- Microsoft Internet Explorer

As to your choice of directories for IIS, you have a few things to consider when making these decisions. First, you will have greater security for your server if you locate these relatively open directories on a partition that is formatted using NTFS. NTFS will even enable you to set security down at the directory and individual file levels if you want to ensure that certain portions of your Web site or FTP site are limited to a certain set of users. Another important consideration is balancing your input/output load for the disk drives. If your IIS site becomes popular, you will probably want to locate your files on drives that are used only lightly for other purposes.

Your next step is to prepare your system for installation. For this discussion, I will assume that you have worked out the details of getting NT Server installed and have worked out device drivers and so forth. There are a few other preparation steps that you should consider before you start the installation:

- You must install the TCP/IP protocol. Although many other NT network functions are designed to be protocol-independent, these Internet services are not. As part of this, you have to obtain an IP address or have a Dynamic Host Configuration Protocol (DHCP) server provide you with an address.

- If you are going to be connected to the Internet, you have to arrange the connectivity with your Internet Service Provider or whatever networking staff takes care of these details. These details include a registered IP address and a domain name by which you will be identified to remote computers using the Domain Name System (DNS).

- If you plan to provide services to the Internet community, you may want to look into the transmission capacity of your network card. A popular site can generate a lot of traffic that is beyond the capabilities of many of the network cards on the market, especially in the PC world.

- You may want to publish the IP address for this new server in one of the name lookup services that are available. The Windows Internet Names Service (WINS), Domain Name Service (DNS, which you can run under NT 4.0), or hosts files enable you to associate an easy to remember name (www.Microsoft.com, for example) with one of those long IP addresses. It is your call; however, I have found that people are really getting used to this convenience and might balk at typing the old IP addresses to connect to your server.

- You may also want to review the general security configuration of your server before installing IIS. An example of a good security measure is using NTFS on the drives to restrict access for the anonymous FTP and generic Web account to only the appropriate directories. You may also want to check your passwords to ensure that they have a reasonable complexity.

- You may also want to see whether you need to implement advanced security features, such as firewalls, proxy servers, and so forth, to keep your system safe—especially if you are letting users from the Internet in.

- You may want to use a dedicated network adapter for Internet services and bind only the network components that are needed for IIS on to this card.

The third step in the overall setup process is to run the IIS setup program. That will be covered in a little more detail in just a few sections. It should only take a couple of minutes if you have everything planned out and set up for this process. You go through a few screens that ask simple questions and you are done.

The next step in the setup process is to configure your servers. To allow IIS to adapt to a number of different environments ranging from small intranet servers to large Internet sites, Microsoft has built a number of configuration options that you can set as needed. They are relatively straightforward and, unlike tuning UNIX kernels, you are really not going to cause any great problems if it takes you a while to get the settings just right. An entire section later in this chapter is devoted to going through these settings.

The final step in the installation process is to add your content to the servers that you have installed. All these sites come with some very boring default Web pages and so forth. The key here is that you are ready to create the environment of each of your servers. It is a relatively simple authoring process using tools such as Microsoft FrontPage or one of its competitors. FTP sites are easy to build because all you have to do is set up directories and copy in the files (you might also want to set up some file access permissions if the need arises). Your site will be judged by the value of its content, so this is where you should really put your main emphasis.

System Requirements

The following are the installation requirements:

- A computer running the NT Server version 4.0 operating system.
- Adequate memory for the NT Server version 4.0 operating system. These applications are similar to file sharing on a local network and are therefore not memory-intensive unless you are planning to build a lot of server-based Web applications.
- Adequate disk storage space for the planned content of the Web pages, FTP server, and/or Gopher server.
- CD-ROM drive for installation.
- TCP/IP protocol installed.
- Unique IP address. Official domain name is optional.
- Network adapter card.

Installation Procedure

Typically, you will set up Internet Information Server as part of your Windows NT Server installation. You merely select the checkbox labeled Install Microsoft Internet Information Server when you are selecting network components during installation. If you did not install IIS at that time, however, you can install it by running the inetstp.exe file that is in the \inetsrv directory on the Windows NT Server CD-ROM. Either way, the basic installation steps are the same.

If you run IIS setup after NT Server installation, the first screen that you will see is your typical welcome screen for IIS. I suppose that this is just a tradition, and it also ensures that you are running the right installation process. Click the OK button to get to the real business at hand.

The first real task in the installation process is selecting which of the components of IIS to install. If you have carefully made your plans as described earlier in this section, you already know the answers to these questions. You will probably always want to install the Internet Service Manager, Help and Sample Files, and Microsoft Internet Explorer. The Internet Service Manager is your main tool for controlling the server processes related to IIS and enables you to configure all the details described in the next section. The Help and Sample Files do not take up that much space and provide useful templates when you are making your own Web pages. It is somewhat interesting that the help for IIS is actually in the form of a Web page, as shown in Figure 16.1. Finally, the Microsoft Internet Explorer will be useful when you want to test your Web server installations, and it also enables you to read the help files.

FIGURE 16.1.

Help for Internet Information Server.

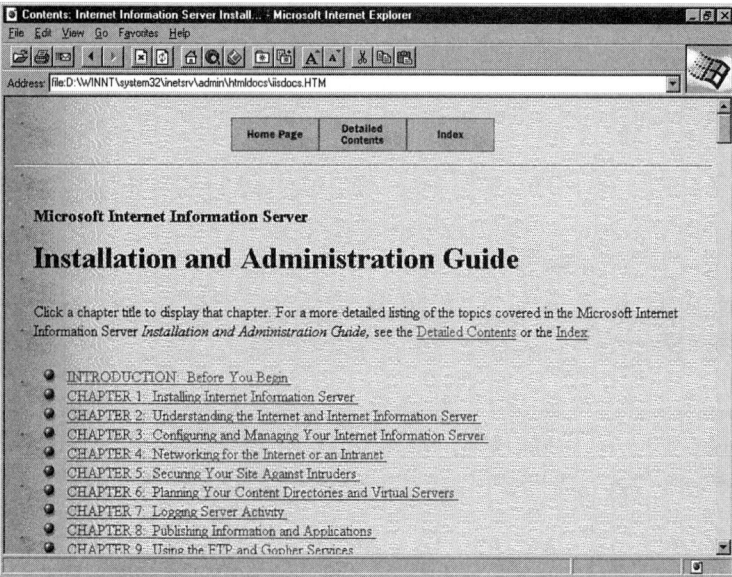

The ODBC drivers and administration section provides you with the capability of interfacing your Web server with a database. The current drivers supported in this option enable you to connect to Microsoft SQL Server. However, there are drivers available that enable you to connect to a number of common relational database management systems, such as Oracle. Note that in addition to installing the drivers, you need to configure a data source (a link to a specific database) using the ODBC tool that is located under Control Panel.

You also have to choose the directory in which you want the Internet Information Server software to be loaded. I would typically accept the default, because the IIS software usually takes up a relatively small amount of disk space, with content taking up the majority of the space. You can use the change button if you want. It will bring up a dialog that enables you to select a directory on your system in the traditional windows fashion. Once you click on OK, you will go to the next screen.

The next screen enables you to specify the publishing directories (that is, the location of your contents) for your servers. Note that you have the option of entering multiple directories (potentially on multiple disk drives) during the configuration process described in the next section. You specify the first directory for each of the servers. You will be prompted to create the service directories if they do not already exist.

The final general purpose setup task is to create the account that will be used for generic access to your IIS system. This account name has the format IUSR_*computername* where *computername* is the network name that you have set up for your computer. I call my test server tester, so the generic Internet account name is IUSR_TESTER. Almost all the access through the Web on the Internet uses a generic account such as this to provide access to the system. You will be asked to enter a password and confirm it. Once you complete the information and click on OK, the system will copy the Internet Information Server files from the CD to your hard disk drive. If you chose to install ODBC drivers, you will be prompted for which ones to install in another dialog box.

Finally, setup displays a completion dialog box. This is designed to let you know that everything has been done and you are ready to use IIS. All you have to do is to select the OK button. You now have a running Internet server.

Configuration After Setup Is Complete

Although your Internet server is now functional, there are a number of options that you might want to set to customize it for your needs. Many of these options are just personalization features. You can enter custom greetings that are displayed when users access your FTP server. Others are related to configuring your servers to the expected load sizes. They enable you to protect your server from having too many connections from the network and thereby causing an overload of your server. This section will go through the various configuration utilities that are available to you for Internet Information Server. These utilities are accessed through the Microsoft Internet Server startup menu shown in Figure 16.2.

There are a number of tools here that you might need to use. The first of these tools is the Internet Information Server Setup utility that is shown in Figure 16.3. This enables you to add or remove IIS components. You have the option of performing a complete reinstallation of the product. Finally, you can also remove the product from your system. Note that this affects the IIS software itself. If you wish to remove the content directories, you have to do that manually.

FIGURE 16.2.

Location of the Internet Information Server controls.

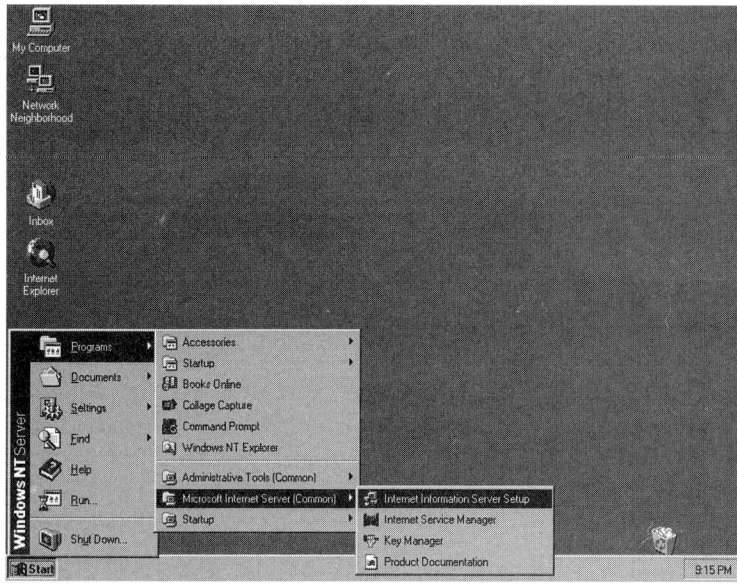

FIGURE 16.3.

Internet Information Server Setup utility.

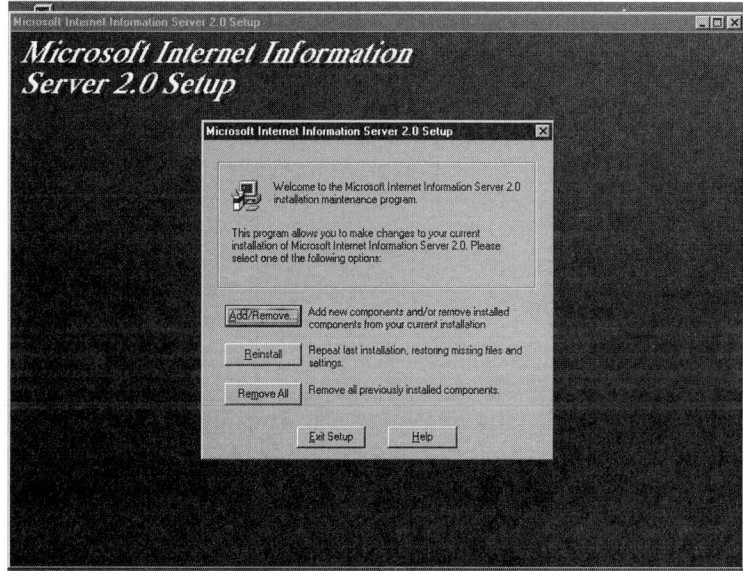

The next tool is probably the one that you will use most often when working to administer IIS. Figure 16.4 shows the basic display for the Internet Service Manager. This tool is used to both configure the properties of the servers and to control whether the servers are running. The basic display shows you the servers that you have installed and whether their services are currently running.

FIGURE 16.4.

*Internet Service
Manager display.*

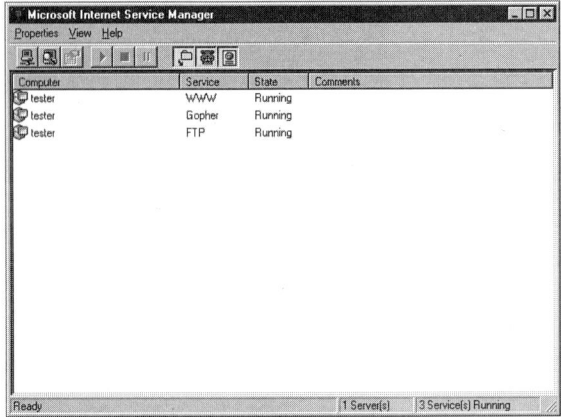

The first task that you might want to perform using the Internet Service Manager is to connect to a server. By default, you will be connected to the Internet Information Server that is running on the computer on which you are working. You have the option through the connect icon or the File, Open menu selections of connecting to a remote IIS instance. Type the name of the computer in the Connect To Server dialog box, shown in Figure 16.5.

FIGURE 16.5.

*Connect To Server
dialog box.*

Your next task might be to start or stop one of the servers. To do this, highlight the server of interest with your mouse and use the toolbar buttons just as you would a VCR. The one that looks like a VCR stop button stops the instance, and the one that looks like a VCR play button starts it. Because most of these servers are based on answering requests that come in over the network, the shutdown and startup processes do not take very long.

Each of the servers also has a series of configuration options that you might want to set. The interface to set up these configurations is activated by clicking the right mouse button over the server of interest and then selecting the properties option from the menu that pops up. All configuration options are set using a series of tab dialog box properties sheets, as has become common with the Windows NT 4.0/Windows 95 interface. Figure 16.6 shows the properties pages that come up for the Web server.

The first tab dialog that you might want to work with contains the basic settings for the WWW service. Key elements of this dialog box are the following:

■ *Timeout.* Determines the maximum amount of time that will be spent waiting for a remote computer to respond before it gives up.

FIGURE 16.6.

WWW Service Properties page for the Web server.

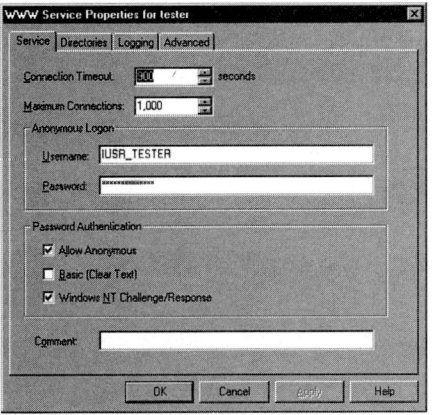

- *Maximum connections.* Determines the maximum number of connections that the system will respond to on the Web. It is a tool that helps you prevent Web users from overloading your server.

- *Anonymous logon.* The user ID and password that would be used for traditional network browsers to access your system.

- *Password authentication.* Allow Anonymous enables the logon ID specified in the previous bullet point. Basic (Clear Text) is the normal means of passing authentication information over the Internet. Windows NT Challenge/Response enables you to use standard Windows NT security mechanisms to establish the identity of the user requesting access to the Web.

The next page in this Properties tab dialog set controls the directories that contain the content for the Web. Figure 16.7 shows this dialog. As you can see, you are allowed to enter one or more directories that contain content. This is interesting because you can link directories together that appear to the user to be on the root level of the Web server or in a number of subdirectories under the root level of the Web server. The directory structure that appears to the Web user does not necessarily have any relation to that of the directories as they exist on your hard disk drives. This is a powerful means of controlling your structure and balancing your disk loads. Another important feature here is that you get to set the default document for your Web server. This is the HTML document that is displayed when a user enters your server name in the address box, but does not specify a specific page. Default.htm is the default here, but you might want to change it to index.htm or index.html, which is what you may have authored for most of the other Web servers that are available. There is also a checkbox that disables directory browsing (which is just what it sounds like). You can expose entire file systems to unwanted eyes, not just the directories of your Web server.

> **TIP**
>
> Unless you can think of a good reason why users need to have directory browsing capabilities, I would recommend disabling it.

FIGURE 16.7.

*Web Directories
dialog box.*

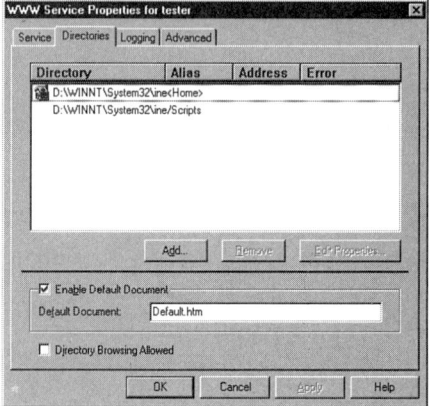

The next properties that you might want to set up for your new Web server are logging properties, as shown in Figure 16.8. You will probably want to keep logs showing activity on your Web for later analysis. You have two options for logging. The basic option is to use system text files to record activity. You can have these files started on a regular basis (daily, for example). This log cycling prevents you from having to look through a single very large file to find a particular date. You could also store this information in a database that you connect to using ODBC. The advantage of using the database is that you can use report writing and other analytical tools to provide reports off your logging data.

FIGURE 16.8.

*Logging Properties
dialog box.*

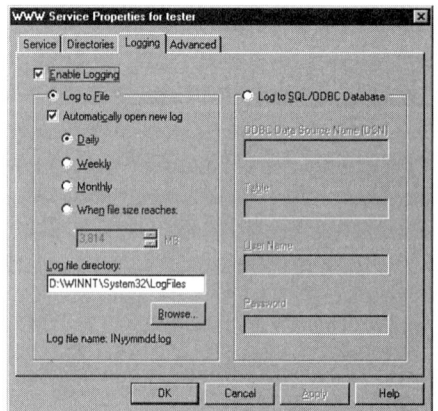

The final properties page for the Web server enables you to place some finer controls over the access provided to your server. Figure 16.9 shows the Advanced dialog. Here you can grant free access to your Web server (which is the default), or you can grant or deny access to a specific list of computers (by IP address) that you enter. This way you can control access only to your group or filter out groups of IP addresses that belong to competitors or other people that you want to keep out. Finally, you can use this screen to set a limit on the maximum data transfer rate that would be devoted to all your IIS needs. This is another tool to prevent the popularity of your Web site from dragging your server to its knees.

FIGURE 16.9.

Advanced dialog box.

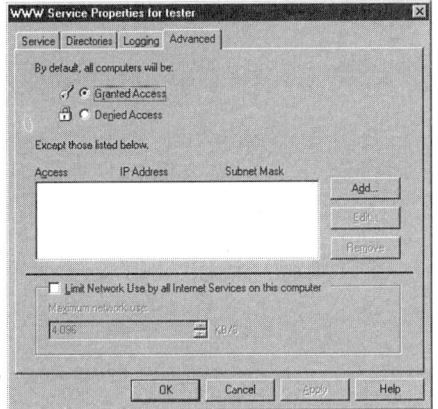

The tab dialog boxes that enable you to set properties for the other two IIS servers are generally similar to those used for the Web server. Let's look at those that have some significant differences. The only dialog that has a significant difference for the Gopher server is the Service dialog box, which is shown in Figure 16.10. The key difference here is that you have both an anonymous logon account and a service administrator (which is by default the system administrator account but does not have to be). Remember, if you have used the NTFS file system, you can set access permissions for files and directories in the Gopher directories to control access to information based on the logon account used to access the server (that is, anonymous logons get most of the material, but some sensitive stuff is restricted to users whom you specify).

There are two properties pages for the FTP server that merit some comments. Figure 16.11 shows the Service Properties page for the FTP Server. Much like the Gopher server, you have the option of setting accounts for both the administrator and anonymous user. Remember that you do not have to allow anonymous access if you do not want to. Note that your electronic mail address is provided for the administrator. Many FTP utilities are designed to enable users to communicate with the administrators of the FTP servers, much like a send mail to tag is used on a Web page.

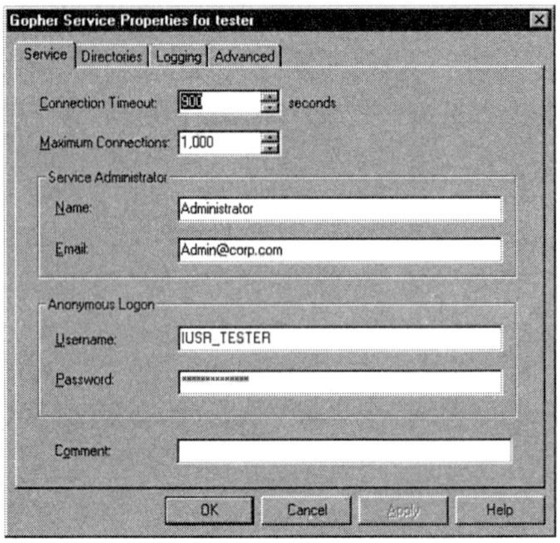

FIGURE 16.10.

*Gopher Service
Properties page.*

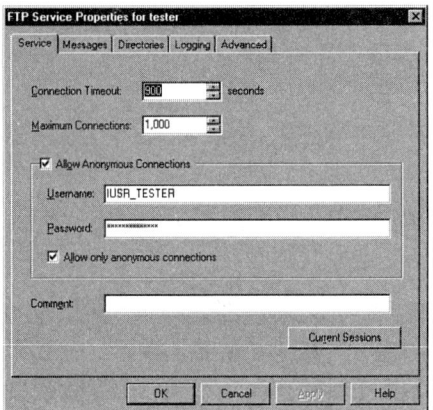

FIGURE 16.11.

*FTP Service Properties
page.*

The second properties page of interest for the FTP server is the Messages properties page. Figure 16.12 shows you this page. You enter three different types of messages for your users. The first is the message with which they will be greeted when they first connect to the FTP site. The second message will be presented to them when they choose to quit from your site. The third message will be displayed when there are already too many users connected to your FTP site (as determined by the maximum number of connections properties that you have set on the previous properties page). Some people spend a great deal of time creating messages that comply with regulations and disclaimers. Others do not have any messages at all. This is about your only vehicle to communicate with your FTP clients.

The next utility that you might want to access related to IIS is relatively new. Figure 16.13 shows the Key Manager Utility. This is a utility that enables you to use the Secure Sockets Layer (SSL) standard to provide secure Web data transmissions over the network. You have to have a machine on the other side that supports this protocol. The Key Manager enables you to identify who you are through a key issued by a certification authority. You use the Key Manager to generate a request file that you can send to the certification authority. This authority will send you a certificate (which is a long string of cryptographic key numbers) that will identify you and enable you to use SSL. Once you receive the certificate, you can activate that security on one or more specific Web directories (that is, you do not have to do your entire site). If you activate this security, only clients who have SSL certificates can use the specified Web directories. You can use Internet Service Manager to enable or disable SSL security.

FIGURE 16.12.

FTP Messages Properties page.

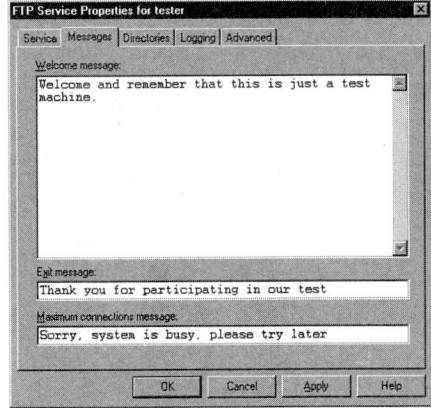

FIGURE 16.13.

Key Manager utility.

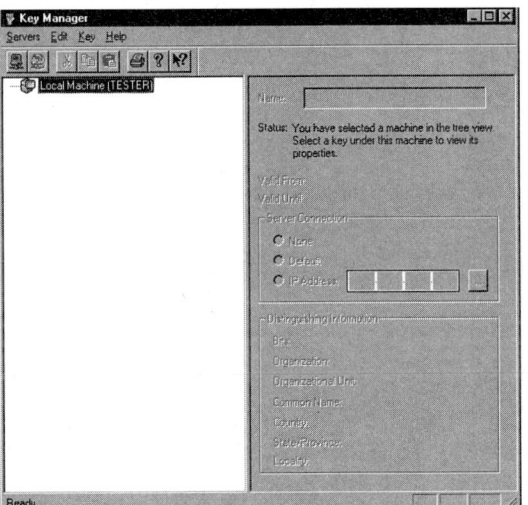

A final tool that can be useful when setting up your Web site is the Services tool located under Control Panel (see Figure 16.14). There are two basic tasks that you perform here. The first is starting or stopping the services associated with the specific Internet services from here just as you would under the Internet Service Manager. You can also start and stop these processes from the DOS command line using the net start *servicename* command. This can come in handy when you want to control Internet servers using batch files and the at utility. The second property that you control using the Services tool is whether the service is started automatically or manually. You usually start your Internet servers automatically on system startup, but you do not have to do this.

FIGURE 16.14.

Services tool under Control Panel.

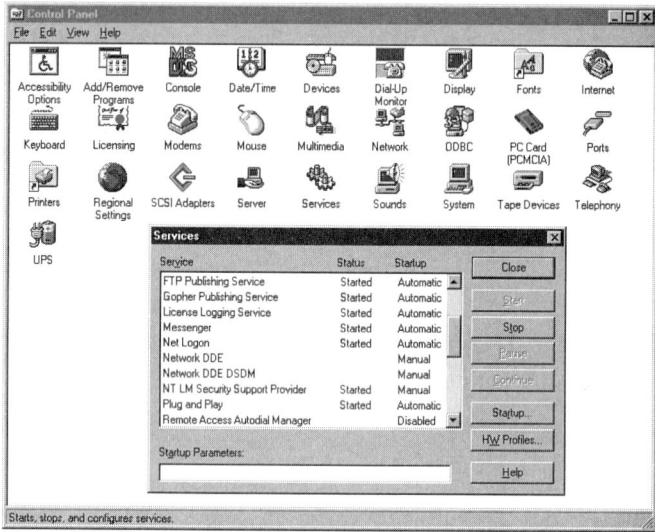

There are actually quite a number of options that you can set related to your IIS servers. A good question at this point would be what settings should you use for your installation? Unfortunately, that depends on the capacity of your system, the other functions that your server is asked to perform, and the types of access that you are providing. Start with the default settings provided for all the security and tuning parameters. Then monitor your system as discussed in Chapter 12, "Windows NT Performance Tuning," to see whether you have performance issues. If your server is being overloaded, you can start lowering the tuning parameters until you are working within the capacity of your system. It would be nice if I could display a chart that gave you an easy answer, but there are too many performance variables that interact with one another to make any such chart meaningful.

Planning for Content

So far, you have explored the operating system services and tools that are used to run your Internet servers. In spite of all the screens discussed, IIS is actually a relatively simple product to set up and keep going from a system administrator perspective. I have had working Web servers where I just ran the setup utility and never touched any of the configuration options. This light load on the system administration side can free you up to do something that is far more interesting—develop your server content.

FTP and Gopher servers are really just collections of files (although Gopher supports links and a few more advanced concepts). You will typically only concern yourself with building a hierarchy of directories so that it is easy for people to find the files in which they are interested. You should probably consider keeping the amount of files in any given directory to a reasonable number (under 50), because it can be a real pain to scroll through a directory with hundreds of files trying to find the one that you want. Other than that, all I can suggest is that you build a hierarchy of directories that will make sense to your intended audience (how they would think of classifying things).

The Web is an entirely different animal. It can be as simple as a single default Web page with just a little bit of text, or it can be a complex system of HTML pages, graphics, animations, sounds, applications, and even databases. In order to set up the directories and options that will be needed to support the content that you will be providing, a little content planning is needed. You really need to draw a picture of the pages that you will want to present and any associated applications, graphics, and so forth. Some Web authoring tools, such as FrontPage, have an Explorer view that enables you to see the links between pages (see Figure 16.15). Once you have this picture, you can start planning your Web directories, estimating sizes, and so forth.

FIGURE 16.15.

FrontPage Explorer.

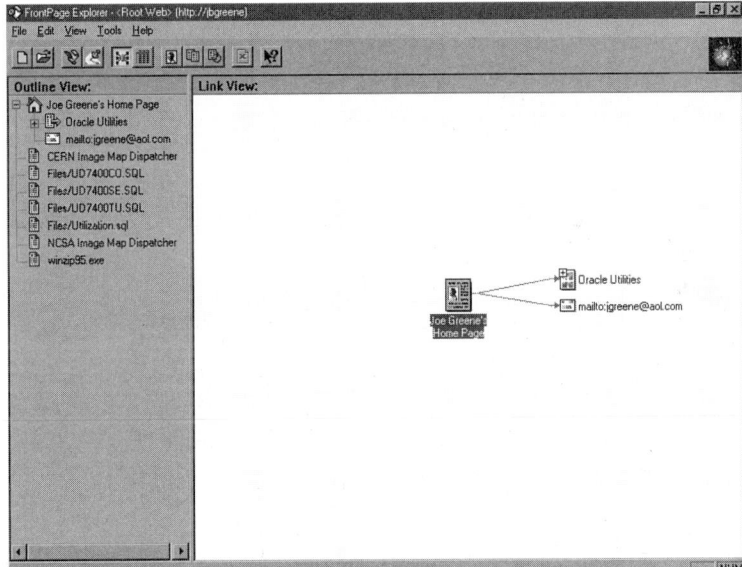

Verifying a Successful Installation

Although I have found the IIS installation process to be completely reliable and easy, the only way to know for sure is to test the system. To do this, you need to have some content in the appropriate directories for your Internet servers and have the servers themselves running. You should then use the appropriate tools from both the server itself and some client workstations to verify that you can work with the content files. Cruise through a series of Web pages and actually upload/download files from FTP to make sure that all the security permissions are set properly, links defined correctly, and so forth. It is always better if *you* find the problems rather than having your users find them.

Issues and Cautions

Before finishing this chapter, here are some ideas to consider when working with IIS:

- Different Web servers and authoring tools use different extensions for Web pages. Depending on whether they are trying to accommodate the old DOS 8.3 naming convention, they will typically use either an htm or an html extension. You need to be sensitive to this when specifying links and URLs.

- Many Web servers use a default page of index.html. You can configure the name of the default Web page in IIS, but it will usually be default.htm. You may have to change this if you have a whole Web system authored for another Web server that you want to bring up under IIS.

- If you want to secure some files, but not others, from specific groups of users under the IIS content directories, you have to places these files on NTFS drives. The traditional FAT file system has no security mechanisms built into it.

- If you are connected to the Internet or even a large intranet, you really need to pay attention to performance monitoring as outlined in Chapter 12. I have seen a number of sites get swamped when they contain popular Web sites. I have even seen the administrators kick the more popular sites off their systems to keep the load level reasonable.

- If you are going to allow uploads to your system, you might want to consider implementing an automated virus scanning system. It is really easy to spread computer infections with a popular file transfer site.

- Massive file downloads can be the greatest burden on many Internet sites. It may take a while for a Web page with graphics to display on a screen, but I have seen file downloads that can take up to an hour. You may want to control the number of file downloads or the times that they are permitted by automatically swapping in Web pages that restrict downloads during busy periods. If you want to get really clever, you can cause these swapping programs to be run automatically when you exceed a certain limit using the NT Performance Monitor.

Finally, if you want any real security, you have to get familiar with SSL and some of the new standards that are just coming into commercial reality. If your transmissions are not secure, you are setting yourself up for all kinds of trouble. Be aware, though, that these wonderful security mechanisms place restrictions on access to your pages (that is, the client has to have these mechanisms installed to access your information).

Summary

This chapter presented the installation and configuration options for the Internet Information Server product. It is actually quite simple to get working. You have a number of tuning and personalization options that you can set. The default settings work quite well in the vast majority of situations, so tuning is needed only if you have a particularly large or popular site.

Web Server Administration

by Joe Greene

IN THIS CHAPTER

This chapter covers some of the highlights of Web server administration. This is a topic that can—and has—filled entire books. I will not replicate all that detailed information in this chapter. Rather, I cover a few thoughts that you might want to consider when starting out.

Overview of Concerns

A Web server is an amazing tool. It can enable you to present a wide range of information in some fascinating formats. You can provide text, graphics, video, audio, animations, and even applications to your users. You can link to other Web servers located anywhere on the Internet to access their capabilities. The standard protocols enable you to present your information to users with UNIX workstations, PCs, and even Macintoshes without any great problem. It may seem as if you are limited only by the amount of time you have to spend working with this system and your creativity.

There are a number of issues that have to be dealt with when it comes to Web server administration, however. Those of you used to formal application environments may find the Web site a little loose in terms of its structure and control. As with any young technology, there seem to be so many changes swirling about. You probably have a number of questions about when and how to implement these changes. Here are a few issues that seem most challenging to me:

- Control of content updates
- Keeping content organized and up to date
- HTML extensions
- Use of active server
- Use of active client
- Security of server
- Limiting load on your system

The first is control over content updates. Your NT Server will have one or more directories that contain the content that is provided to the user community. You need to put some thought into controlling who is allowed to update your content and how they are going to accomplish this. One solution that I have implemented is to make a root Web directory that is shared using standard Windows NT directory sharing. I limit access to this root directory to a few Web masters who are experienced in the subject and who are responsible for the overall content of the system. Other users and project teams also want access to Web resources, however. I have shared several of the subdirectories under the root Web directory and given access grants to the appropriate NT user groups. Figure 17.1 illustrates my example.

This may not be the perfect solution for your needs. You might, for example, need to provide FTP capabilities to allow users of UNIX workstations to upload new content. You might need to have a much tighter control scheme, where authors put updates into a staging directory.

This directory is then reviewed by the Webmaster (such an interesting term—everyone else is an administrator, but these people are masters). If the content passes muster, it is transferred by the Webmaster to the appropriate directories on the Web. You might consider adapting your software building procedures to Web content if you need to have some form of control.

FIGURE 17.1.

Sample shared directories for Web content.

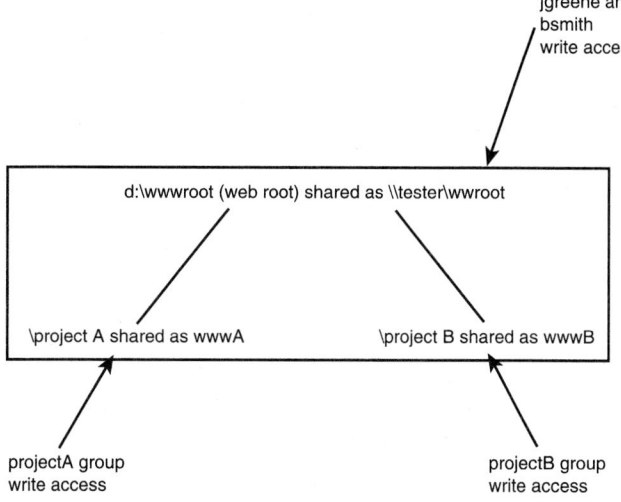

jgreene and bsmith write access

d:\wwwroot (web root) shared as \\tester\wwroot

\project A shared as wwwA   \project B shared as wwwB

projectA group write access

projectB group write access

A related topic that you need to think about is how you will keep your content organized and up-to-date. Web sites are a loose collection of files whose links are determined by the internal content of the Web pages. Although there are some explorer tools that let you see the structure of a Web site graphically (for example, FrontPage, as shown in Figure 17.2), for the most part you have to know the content well enough to keep the site running.

There are several issues related to organizing content. The first is ensuring that you have all the needed files. A tool such as the FrontPage Explorer shown in the figure can help with this somewhat. In the end, however, you wind up testing your pages to make sure that you can exercise all the links and that all the graphics display. It can be tricky, especially if you link to external sites, which can move or disappear without any warning.

The second content organization issue is whether you need to keep previous versions around and store a backup copy of the files. Authors can spend quite a bit of time on some pages and graphics. What happens if you have an author who names a graphics file or Web page with the same name that another author used? If you copy the files into the Web root directory, you have just wiped out the old content. One solution is to use a version control system such as SourceSafe, which keeps old versions of the files. Another might be to divide the Web into a series of subdirectories that keep content from different project teams or authors in separate folders. This minimizes the chance that files will be overwritten.

FIGURE 17.2.

FrontPage Explorer tool.

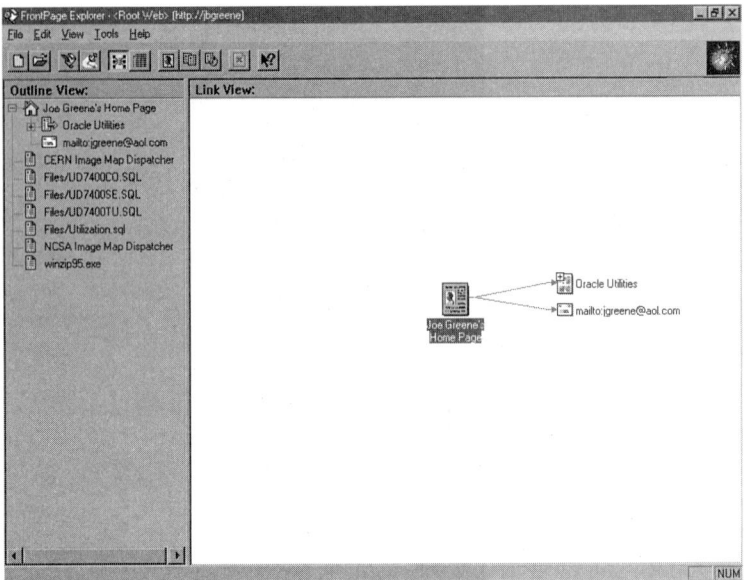

Another issue to deal with on your Web site is the idea of HTML extensions. The original HTML specification was great for its day, but the moment the Web became popular, a lot of bright people starting thinking up ways to improve things. Different Web browser vendors adapted one or more extensions to the basic HTML specification. It became difficult because authors often required users to have a specific browser to visit their Web sites, due to the extensions that they were using. This defeated the purpose of the HTML standards. The major vendors got together under the auspices of the World Wide Web Consortium, and they are working on an updated HTML standard and some other standards that will bring the feature sets back under some standard control. Until then though, you may run into sites that require some extension, such as frames, that your browser may lack. You need to consider this when you are setting up your Web site, because you will want authors building to some standard level of HTML to ensure that your clients can actually read the wonderful pages that are written.

Another issue that is creeping up in the Web world is that of active servers. This is sort of a marketing term that embraces a wide range of technologies. It is designed to cover those technologies that enable the server to make decisions based on user responses, algorithms input by developers, or even the content of a database that controls the HTML Web page content sent out to the users. This ranges from a very simple technique of sensing the type of browser that the user is working with and adjusting your content to match the capabilities of that browser to complex systems that draw information and send updates to large databases, such as those used in Internet commerce. You need to think seriously about which of these features might be used on your site, because it will greatly impact the processing and memory loads on your server. My recommendation is not to implement these features unless you have tried them out in a test environment and can be sure that the load is within the capacity of your Web server.

Just as you need to be conscious of which of the HTML extensions you are using in your Web pages, you need to think about the active client features that you are implementing. Similar to active servers, active content is a term that embraces a range of technologies that download software to the client workstations. This downloaded software is executed on those client workstations and controls the information that is displayed to the user. Examples of this technology are the JAVA programming language and the ActiveX technologies from Microsoft. You need to be sensitive as to which technologies you are using, because the client computer needs to be able to execute them. For example, you need a JAVA interpreter to run JAVA applications, and ActiveX clients do not work on all browsers and operating systems. Make sure that your target audience is capable of taking advantage of any active client features that you implement.

Because most Web sites are concerned with distributing information as opposed to collecting it, you have fewer worries than you would on an FTP site, for example. You do have some concerns about the information that you are distributing, however. Many companies are sensitive about prices and new product information. If you are connected to the Internet, your competitors could surf into your Web site and gather information that you really wanted to give only to your customers. You might want to consider having a group of people get together to determine what is considered appropriate information to give out on the Web server and what information should be restricted (for example, only users who have logged in using valid Windows NT logons would have access to a subdirectory on the Web site that has NTFS file permissions set to allow only specific groups access). You learn about security in more detail later in this chapter.

The final topic that you might have to deal with is limiting the load placed on your server. Chapter 16, "Setting Up IIS," covered a number of the properties pages for the Web server product. With these pages, you can control the data transfer capacity that was devoted to IIS and also the maximum number of current connections. If you feel that you might be inundated (or have already been overloaded), you might want to set down these values until you reach a happy medium between user service and server capacity.

Accounts

Chapter 16 also covered the default Web user account, which allows anonymous access. You also learned that you have the option to use clear text user IDs or the Windows challenge/response mechanisms if you make users log on with their own accounts. If you have a Web page that is designed to allow everyone in the world to access all its content, the anonymous access account will serve your needs. This section explored some of the user account-related topics between a Web server and system administrator who is supporting Internet Information Server.

Windows NT is an operating system that bases all accesses on a logon ID and password. All activity on the system is associated with a logon ID. In the case of the Web server, the users have the option of passing in their user ID and password. This is not commonly the case. Almost all access on the current Web is accomplished by users who do not pass any identification. The

Web servers are designed so that when they do not receive a logon ID, they will try to use a special logon ID that is designed for anonymous access. In the case of Internet Information Server, that anonymous ID is IUSR_*computername.*

> **NOTE**
>
> Most access to Internet Information Server and other Web servers is through anonymous user IDs. These allow anyone on the network to access (but not write to) the content of the Web pages.

How does this anonymous access scheme fit into the NT security scheme? When users do pass a logon ID and password, IIS will attempt logon to the NT Server as those people. When those people try to access files, their personal and group security privileges will be used to make the decision to grant or deny the access. If there is not a logon ID and password associated with the user and anonymous logon is permitted in IIS, IIS takes on the identify of IUSR_*computername,* and the privileges of that user ID is used to make the decision to grant or deny access.

The IUSR_*computername* account is typically not a very powerful account on your system—for good reason. The only system privilege that it needs is the capability of logging on locally to the computer on which IIS is running. This is because the IIS process seems to be a local user to the operating system. The only group membership that this account will have is that of the guest group. Therefore, you should make sure that you have not granted any special privileges to members of that guest group.

When initially created, IUSR_*computername* has a randomly generated password. You can change this password to something else, but it should be relatively hard to guess. Because the IUSR_*computername* account does not have access to network resources by default, even if the password is compromised, users cannot use this account to access some of your directories. I avoid granting this user any access privileges (for example, the ability to transfer content into the Web directories for maintenance purposes). Instead, I grant these privileges to real users who are functioning in the authoring capacity. I leave the IUSR_*computername* account a stripped-down user ID that has full read access to my Web directories, but no other capabilities.

Speaking of user accounts, when you are an Internet or intranet server, you have attracted attention to yourself. Your domain name or IP address is now public knowledge. Everyone knows about you and that you have some interesting content. Because you now have so much attention, you should consider looking at the other accounts on your system for security. For example, if you use IIS, you will have an account with a logon ID of administrator. You will also have a few other accounts, such as guest. If you have null or easy passwords on these accounts, you have left a security hole right where a hacker would first try to penetrate your system. You should review your overall security policy to see whether your passwords are secure enough.

A few other recommendations include looking at who has access to resources. One of the safest Web servers is one where the Internet connection comes into one network card, and IIS and its protocols are the only ones that are bound to that network card. You use another network card to provide access to the server from your local area network. You would have a few more network services available on this card that would allow you to transfer files, and so forth.

Other things that you should watch out for include checking what policies have been set for your system. Do a lot of people have accesses beyond the basic user level, such as those provided by the domain administrator role? If you can keep down the privileges of users on this server, even if someone hacks into one of their accounts, they would not be able to do damage. Of course, it would be ideal to have an Internet server that had no functions other than IIS; then you would not really need to have many user accounts (only the administrator and those people involved with maintaining IIS and its content).

One final account issue to consider is where is the IUSR_*computername* account created? If you are running IIS on a primary or backup domain controller, the account is created for the domain. If you are running IIS on other NT computers, the account is created on the local machine. This is not a particular concern unless you have granted a lot of privileges in your domain to everyone or guest.

Content Maintenance

Your approach to content maintenance will vary according to the complexity of your Web site. Basically, I would recommend keeping the complexity down to the minimum level needed to get the job done. If you need to distribute information across multiple disk drives or even multiple servers, however, IIS does have those capabilities. There are three basic configuration options that you need to consider (see Figure 17.3).

FIGURE 17.3.
Basic Web site configuration options.

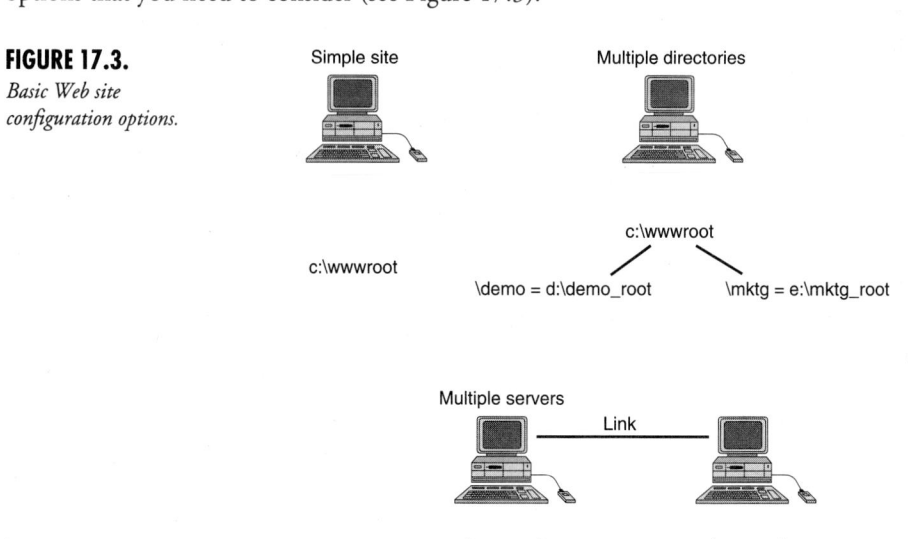

Simple site

c:\wwwroot

Multiple directories

c:\wwwroot
\demo = d:\demo_root   \mktg = e:\mktg_root

Multiple servers

Link

c:\wwwroot   c:\wwwroot

The first option is your simple site where everything resides under the single root directory. You can put subdirectories under this main directory. To access content in a subdirectory, add the subdirectory name after the domain name. For example, to access the file joe.htm in the users subdirectory under the main root directory of a Web server whose domain name is www.orange.com, you enter an address of http://www.orange.com/users/joe.htm. You can use subdirectories to segregate different types of content (all graphics in one directory and all executable CGI or JAVA scripts in another). You could also use subdirectories to allow different individuals to contribute content. In this case, you might have three project teams that have their own Web pages. You keep control of the master Web pages that are located in the root directory and create a share name that only you have write access to. You then create share names for the project Web subdirectories and grant access to the appropriate project team members for these directories.

The second option is to create multiple directories located on different parts of your hard disk system. For example, if you have a really large Web site, you might have to spread the contents across several disk drives just to fit within disk capacity or to balance the data transfer loads between drives. This is also relatively simple. In IIS, you use the Directories Properties page for the Web server in the Internet Service Manager shown in Figure 17.4. You can add directories to this list and give them aliases. An alias makes a directory located anywhere on your system look as though it were a subdirectory of the root directory. In the example given in the last paragraph, you could have the users subdirectory on the d: drive and the Web root directory on the c: drive. You would set up the d:\users directory to have an alias of /users. To access the joe.htm page, you would type http://www.orange.com/users/joe.htm, as you would in the case shown previously. You can even use shared directories on other computers located in your domain, although this could present a network performance problem if you have to do a lot of transfers. To use a network drive, just use the UNC name (that is, \\tester\Web_pages for the tester server's Web_pages shared directory). Note that you cannot use redirected drive designations to access shared drives on another server for IIS (that is, if you shared \\tester\Web_pages as your f: drive, you could not use f:\ in IIS; you would have to use \\tester\Web_pages instead). This concept is referred to as creating virtual directories.

The third basic configuration option is to use multiple servers that are running IIS. This concept is simple once you are comfortable with the concept of links. You have a main Web page on your primary server that has the registered domain name. When users want to go to another page, you use a link to reference them to that page. They are not responsible for understanding the details of the connection; they merely click on the text that you have provided or the right section of a picture. You usually have this link pointing to another page on your current server; however, there is nothing stopping you from making this a link to another server in your computer complex that is running IIS. This machine could even have a different connection line to the Internet to balance traffic loads. If you are into a little programming, you might even write scripts that could help you determine which of many identical machines to send the user to in order to balance the load.

FIGURE 17.4.

Configuring directories for a Web server.

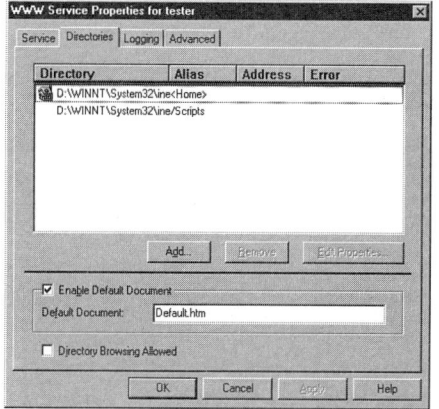

Another concept that you should be aware of is that of the virtual server. You have one physical computer running IIS. You have registered a number of different domain names for that computer (and therefore have a number of IP addresses), however. Windows NT enables you to add multiple IP addresses to a single network card, and you can also use multiple network cards. Each of these virtual servers can have its own home directory and default page. Therefore, you could set up a marketing.*yourcompany*.com and a techsupport.*yourcompany*.com that are both located on the same server. One would start off with a page designed by marketing and the other with the technical support page.

One thing to note is that you set a default filename for your system in IIS setup. This means that if someone types your domain name, they will automatically load the filename that has this default filename located in your Web root directory. However, this default filename applies to all directories within your Web. Therefore, if someone types www.oracle.com/users, IIS tries to load a file that has the default filename but was located in the /users subdirectory or directory referenced by that alias. This is a useful technique to save users from typing. Remember, they are getting used to point and click—they may have forgotten *how* to type.

Traffic Volume Control and Management

Let's look at your options for traffic control on your Web server. You usually have very little control over the demand. Users will access the site when they want it and if you have great content, they may come in droves. Your control is basically over the supply side of the equation. Here are a few tricks that can help you control how much information you are supplying and therefore how much load is being placed on your poor server:

■ The most obvious controls are those supplied in the property pages for the Web server under the Internet Service Manager tool. You get to set the number of sessions and also the maximum data transfer rate to be devoted to IIS purposes.

- You can also alter the content that is available to your users. You might, for example, have different versions of your main Web pages. Each might link to a different set of Web pages and contents. If your server becomes too heavily loaded, you might substitute pages that have fewer downloads or use lower resolution graphics. It is as simple as using the DOS copy command.

- You can extend the technique of the previous bullet to automate the content change process. You could use the Windows NT AT utility to schedule automatic changes in content. Perhaps you want to make more content available at night when it will have less impact on your other users and then switch back to the less-demanding content during normal work hours. Again, all you need are some batch files, the alternate content pages, and the AT job scheduling utility.

One thing that you might consider about content is the use of a version control system and backups. It is easy to make mistakes and overwrite Web pages (there are going to be a lot of default.htm or index.htm pages out there). If you do not keep backup copies or use a version control system such as SourceSafe, you may not be able to recover content that you overwrite. If you have a fair amount of content or spend a lot of time and money making truly artistic Web pages, it might be worth your while to implement such as system.

Security Options

Here are some other security recommendations that you might want to consider for your Web site:

- Microsoft recommends using NTFS for Web sites because that is the file system that enables you to set directory and file access restrictions.

- Microsoft recommends that you set your permissions as follows for directories in your IIS system: content directories, read only; programs, read and execute; and databases, read and write.

- You may want to allow auditing on your system to see whether people are accessing information that they should not be. In this case, you want to record both successful and unsuccessful access to this information. Note that this auditing will mean extra work for your server and could affect performance if you are near your processing capacity limits.

- Run only the services that are necessary on your IIS server. If you are not using a service such as RAS, don't make it available and complicate your security picture.

- Double-check the access permissions on all your network shares. A lot of them come with default access of full access to everyone.

If you need additional security, consider using the Secure Sockets Layer (SSL) authentication scheme. You send away for a key that gives you a unique ID for your computer (see the Key Manager discussion in Chapter 16). This ID enables you to identify yourself for encrypted transmissions over the Internet. This would, for example, enable you to send financial information, such as credit card numbers, without worrying about who would see it.

Protection from Hackers

If you have an FTP server that allows uploads, you may want to check out what has been placed on your server every now and then. Some people like to use servers for purposes for which they were not intended. You have to be the judge as to what content is appropriate. You also need to be concerned that your server is being used as an incubator for computer viruses. I suggest that you monitor things routinely to see what has been placed on your machine. You could automate the process by running a script that searches for files that have extensions that are not within the intended purpose of your server (look for all jpg or gif files if your server was not intended to store pictures, for example). Just a thought—some places might blame the administrator for content that was placed on there by unknown users.

There are a couple of other things to remember. The first is that you can install just the Internet Service Manager on a computer. A good use for this type of installation would be to put Internet Service Manager on your desktop computer and use it to control all your Web servers from the comfort of your desk. To do this, you use the connect option as discussed in Chapter 16. You need to have a domain set up to make all the security accesses work properly, but you will probably be moving to a domain anyway, so why not start now.

Another point is the value of scripts, mail, and the AT utility. It seems that most administrators get very busy and are called off on other projects soon after they get a new system working. They rarely get the time to go back and review their systems in the manner that they had originally intended. If you spend a little time up front building some batch files (or other programming tools if you are so inclined) that you set up to run routinely and send you the results by electronic mail, you will be able to keep up with the status of your system with relatively little pain. Just make sure that you include the script building as part of the basic project.

Summary

This chapter covered some food for thought on the subject of being a Web administrator. There are entire books devoted to this subject if you are really getting into maintaining large sites. Although there are some features that you might find in other Web server products, IIS has most of the important features and is combined with the easy-to-use Windows NT operating system. This provides you with a lot of capabilities for automating your system. All you have to do is be careful to ensure that you have a good security setup and that you control the traffic so that your server can provide good response times.

Internet/Intranet Security

by John Fronckowiak

IN THIS CHAPTER

CHAPTER 18

Security is the cornerstone of any successful computer system. Placing a system on the Internet or a corporate intranet can make system resources available to illegitimate as well as legitimate users. System security is always a balancing act of providing ease of access and usefulness to the legitimate users, while preventing access by the illegitimate users, which always involves a compromise. The most secure computer system is one that functions in isolation; placing a system on an Internet/intranet involves by definition placing the system on a network of hundreds or, in the case of the Internet, millions of other computer systems and users. Hackers are continually learning about potential security holes that exist in Internet sites and ways to exploit them. It's almost impossible to completely secure an Internet/intranet server, but there are a number of measures that can be taken to decrease the risks involved. The most important steps that can be taken to ensure the most effective security for an Internet/intranet site are taking the necessary steps from the start of implementation and continually staying informed regarding potential risks.

Because businesses are setting up Internet and intranet sites in record numbers, ensuring the security of corporate systems is becoming increasingly important. An Internet Web server can provide access to corporate information to Internet users worldwide, whereas an intranet Web Server provides access to corporate data within a corporation. Although the security implications in the setup of an Internet server are slightly different from an intranet server, they are based on a few basic concepts: proper placement of the Web server, simplifying operations, and proper administration.

The Internet Information Server (IIS) and Windows NT provide a number of mechanisms to help ensure security:

- Windows NT Event Logging system is integrated with the IIS to help track usage and avoid potential problems.
- Windows NT Security, which has been granted C2 compliance rating by the United States National Security Agency, can provide secure access to files by requesting a username and password from clients before access is granted.
- The capability of setting up user accounts and directory permissions can help protect important data from unauthorized access.
- Internet Information Server can use Secure Sockets Layer (SSL) when transferring data between the client and server. SSL provides a mechanism to encrypt the transmissions between the client and server, a mechanism to provide secure logons to the server, and mechanisms to verify message integrity.

Why You Need Security

When a computer system is connected to the Internet, it is open to numerous routes for potential attack by hackers, viruses, unauthorized internal users, and competitors, just to name a few. A server connected to the Internet can be accessible to millions of potential users, many of which may not have your best interests at heart. An intranet server can be just as vulnerable to attack from authorized users attempting to access unauthorized information. It may be even easier for an authorized user to exploit backdoors (undocumented methods used to access a host system) or unnoticed security holes.

Hackers who gain unauthorized access to the Windows NT administration account can cause a great deal of damage. They can execute programs, move, copy, or delete files, or access sensitive corporate data without ever leaving a trace. A hacker can attempt to crack an administrator's password by running applications that repeatedly generate login attempts by guessing random passwords until successful, or simply guess the administrator's password because it is too common (for example, ADMIN). For this reason, it is extremely important to change the administrator's password often, and to keep it complex so that it cannot be guessed easily. A password is the first line in defense of a system, and since the administrator, and any other user with administrative privileges, has the greatest system rights, it is of utmost importance to protect these accounts.

Here are some recommendations to follow when choosing a password:

- Don't use the login name as the password.
- Don't use your name or nickname, or your spouse's, children's, or friend's name.
- Don't use the server name.
- Don't use your birthday or social security number.
- Don't use a single word that may appear in a dictionary (a common hacking technique is to use a dictionary of words for passwords when attempting to break into an account).
- Don't use a repeated series of the same number or letter—for example, AAAAA or 11111.
- Don't write your password down.
- Do use numbers and alphabetic characters (upper- and lowercase) in your password.

Even proper passwords and user privileges may not be enough to prevent unauthorized access to sensitive information by an internal intranet user. An internal user may be able to gain access to restricted data by accessing an unsecured network workstation with administrative capabilities. From that workstation, users could access unauthorized data or change their own system privileges. It is important to educate users to practice due diligence in protecting their workstations from attack. Users logged into the network should *not* leave their workstations unattended, especially if those users have administrative privileges. All servers should be located in a secure area with only authorized personnel granted access.

There are a number of high-tech mechanisms to help ensure system security. It is important to remember, though, that an effective security strategy begins internally. A system that takes all the appropriate measures to ensure proper file and directory protections, sets up a firewall and proxy server, and employs packet filtering can still be vulnerable to a low-tech attack of someone guessing the administrator's password or gaining access to an unsecured workstation.

Windows NT and the IIS

When planning security for the IIS and Windows NT Server, there are some major considerations to account for:

- Use of the NTFS file system is the only way to protect access to files on a user-by-user, file-by-file basis.

- Use the integrated Windows NT Event Logging and the IIS to track unauthorized access and detect security holes.

- Use IP filtering to prevent internal network users from accessing unauthorized sites, and to block users and groups from unauthorized sites from accessing your server.

- Use the Administrator account properly. Be sure to set up an account with limited authority to test new applications and prevent viruses. Because an account with administrative privileges can access system files and directories, a potential virus could be easily spread throughout the system from these accounts.

How the IIS Applies Security

The IIS applies security using the following process:

1. The IIS receives a request for data.
2. The IIS verifies that the IP is permitted; if not, access is denied.
3. The IIS verifies that the user is permitted; if not, access is denied.
4. The IIS verifies that IIS permissions will allow access; if not, access is denied.
5. The IIS verifies that NTFS file system permission allows access to the requested file; if not, access is denied.
6. If all of these conditions are met, access is granted.

Placing Your Server

The most secure server is one that is locked up in isolation. Unfortunately, an isolated server is virtually unusable. A system that offers unrestricted access to its information can be the easiest to use, but obviously is totally insecure. A continual balance between security and usability must be maintained. Physical and communications barriers can be constructed to help prevent unauthorized system access.

A physical barrier is easy to construct. A server should be placed in an environment where only authorized personnel have access. A communications barrier can be erected by utilizing firewalls, proxy servers, and packet filtering.

Firewalls

A firewall is a computer system that bridges a trusted and untrusted network by examining incoming and outgoing packets and filtering out unwanted data. A firewall can prevent unauthorized external users from accessing the local area network (LAN) and can restrict how internal users access the Internet. A firewall can also be utilized to keep internal users from accessing internal servers to which they have no rights. A firewall can filter data based on an IP address so that only certain IP addresses can pass through the firewall. A firewall can also filter traffic based on a port number. Web servers usually use port 80; to prevent internal users from accessing external Web sites, a firewall could block access to port 80.

Proxy Server

When a request is made to a remote system and packets are exchanged, these packets can disseminate unwanted information about your server and network configuration, such as its IP addresses. A firewall alone cannot prevent this information from being released. A proxy server runs on the firewall host. It operates on a store-and-forward mechanism. Instead of each individual user connecting directly to outside Internet resources, a proxy server directs all requests and responses through itself. When a request is made to an external Internet resource, the proxy server examines the request and communicates with the remote system to satisfy the request. The only system the outside world "sees" is the proxy server.

Some proxy servers can cache often accessed external information to help speed up future requests. A proxy server can also log client requests, which can be useful to track and detect attacks against your server. The downside of running a proxy server is that it can degrade system performance, especially database queries.

Packet Filters

A packet filter examines all packets that pass in and out of the network, and can prevent packets from passing through that do not conform to the configurable rules that are defined. A packet filter can filter packets based upon several criteria:

- The protocol that the packet belongs to (TCP, UDP, and so forth)
- The originating address
- The destination address
- The port number of the destination resource (see Table 18.1 for port numbers of common services)
- The packet direction, out to the Internet or into the local network

18

INTERNET/
INTRANET SECURITY

Table 18.1. Common service port numbers.

Service	Port Number
HTTP	80
DNS (Domain Name Service)	53
Telnet	23
FTP	20 and 21
RIP (Routing Information Protocol)	520
SMTP (Simple Mail Transfer Protocol)	25

The IIS can provide packet filtering of a specific IP address. To set up IP address filtering in the IIS, open the Service Manager applications and double-click on the server to configure. Click on the Granted Access button or the Denied Access button. If the Granted Access button is selected, you can specify which IP addresses you want to restrict. If you choose Denied Access, you can specify the IP addresses you want to allow. Click on the Add button to specify these exceptions. Click on Single Computer and specify the IP address you want to create an exception for, or click on Group Of Computers and enter the IP address and subnet mask to create an exception for a group of computers.

Network Protection Strategies

There are a number of measures that must be taken to help ensure the security of your IIS.

Allowing Anonymous Access

During the setup of the IIS, the user account IUSR_*computername* is created for anonymous access. If the computer name is IDCSERVER, the anonymous access account is IUSR_IDCSERVR. By default, all client requests to the IIS use this account. IIS clients are logged into the server using the IUSR_*computername* account. The IUSR_*computername* is only allowed to log on locally. The IUSR_*computername* is also added to the Guest group, if any changes have been made to the guest group, they will also apply to the IUSR_*computername* account. The Guest group privileges should be reviewed to assure their appropriateness to the IUSR_*computername* account. If remote access is allowed only through the IUSR_*computername* account, remote users will have the only permissions assigned to that account, which can help prevent hackers from gaining access to the server.

Requiring Usernames and Passwords

The IIS can also allow authenticated client access, which requires a valid Windows NT username and password to access system resources. The basic authentication mechanism provided by the IIS does not encrypt the username and password; they are simply encoded using UUEncode.

They can easily be decoded by anyone who can intercept packets transferred over your network.

The WWW Service of the IIS supports the Windows NT Challenge/Response encrypted password transmission mechanism. The Challenge/Response mode can be configured by double-clicking on a specific service in the Service Manager application. On the Service tab, the Password Authentication mode can be selected. The only Web browser client that supports Windows NT authentication is the Microsoft Internet Explorer for Windows 95.

Both authentication mechanisms, basic and Windows NT–authenticated, allow access only when a valid username and password is supplied. Both IUSR_*computername* and authenticated access can be enabled at the same time.

Other Network Services

A thorough review of all services being run on the IIS system should be conducted to ensure the highest level of security. With a fewer number of services running on the system, the risk of an administration problem causing an exploitable hole is reduced. Using the Service applet in the Control Panel, review all the services that are currently enabled and running.

Using the Bindings option on the Network applet in the Control Panel, verify the services bound to the adapter connected to the Internet. The FTP Server services included with Windows NT Server should also be disabled. The FTP services in the IIS should be used instead.

LAN Internet Server Connections

There are a number of different ways the IIS system can be connected to the LAN and the Internet. Isolating the IIS system from the LAN offers the most security. Multiple adapters in a single IIS system running different protocols offers a high degree of security. A router with packet filtering can offer various levels of security depending on the model. Multiple adapters in a single IIS system, where each adapter is connected to a separate network can also offer a high degree of security, when routing is disabled. Each of the IIS system connection strategies offers different levels of security and usability. You need to choose the model that works best in your organization.

Isolation

In the isolated configuration of the IIS system (see Figure 18.1), the IIS system is connected to a network separate from the LAN. To achieve the highest level of security, users connected to the LAN can be connected to the Internet through a firewall. The disadvantage of this configuration is that users who need to access the IIS system servers to update files or Web pages need to connect to one of the workstations connected to the IIS system network.

FIGURE 18.1.
Isolated IIS system configuration.

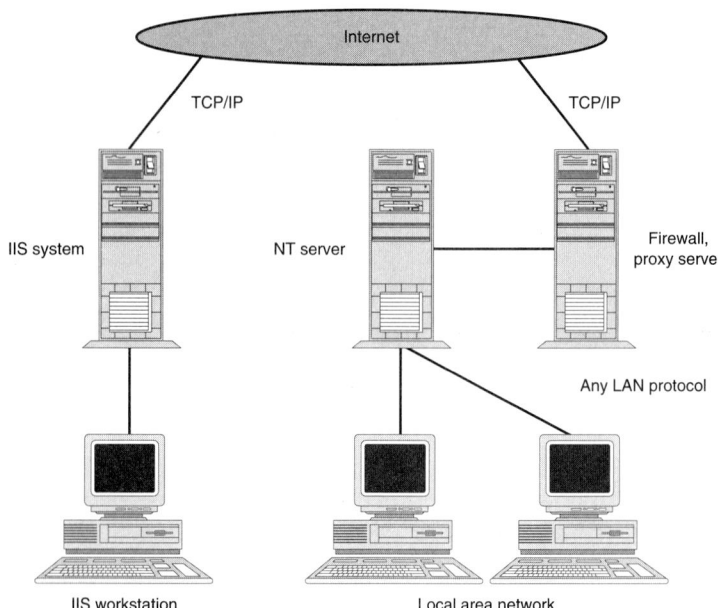

Multiple Network Adapters Running Different Protocols

With multiple adapters in a single IIS system running different protocols (see Figure 18.2), each adapter in the IIS system runs a different network protocol isolating the LAN and Internet traffic from each other. The LAN can run any networking protocol supported by NT Server (except for TCP/IP); the Internet is connected using the standard TCP/IP protocol. This configuration addresses the main disadvantage of the isolated configuration, because users who need to update files for access by the IIS can do so from their own workstations. The disadvantage of this configuration is that LAN users do not have access to the Internet. As long as the adapter cards are not configured for protocol conversion, this configuration offers a high degree of security. When setting up this configuration, it is important to ensure that the adapter card connected to the Internet is bound only to the TCP/IP protocol, and the adapter connected to the LAN is bound only to that protocol. Check the adapter bindings from the Network applet in the Control Panel.

Router Packet Filtering

There are a number of commercially available routers that can perform packet filtering (see Figure 18.3). These routers can be configured to filter packets according to predefined specifications. Some of these routers can offer proxy services along with packet filtering. Packet filtering is not as secure as multiple adapters with different protocols in a single IIS system.

FIGURE 18.2.
Multiple adapters with different protocols in a single IIS system configuration.

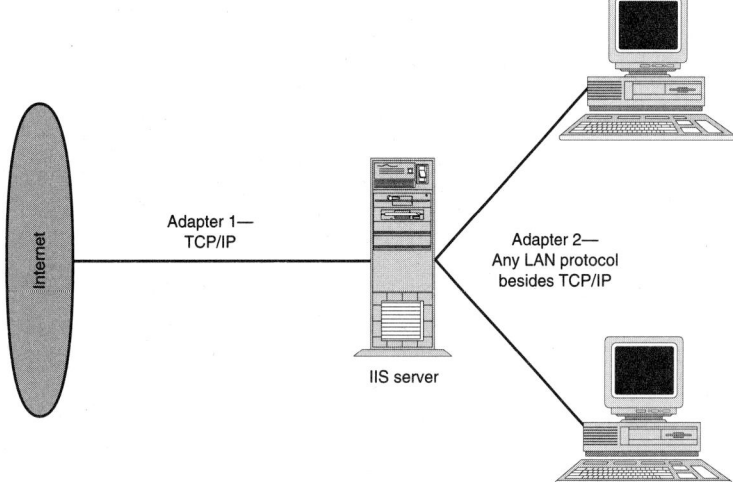

FIGURE 18.3.
Router packet filtering configuration.

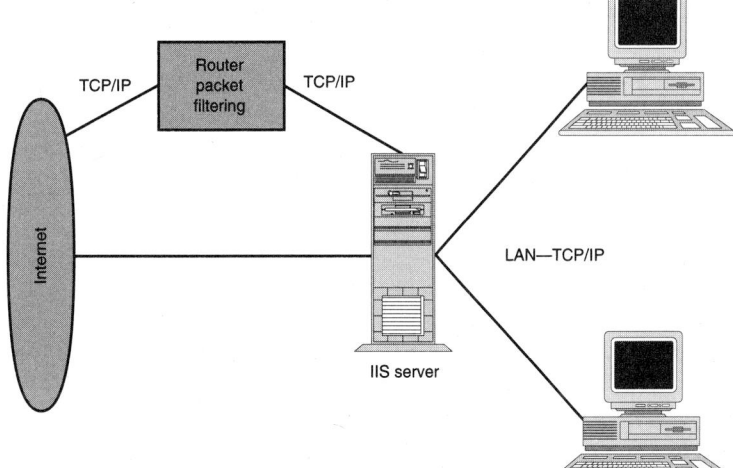

Multiple Network Adapters Attached to Different Networks

With the multiple network adapters in an IIS system attached to different networks, each adapter can run the same protocol, but with routing disabled, the network traffic can be isolated (see Figure 18.4). Each adapter card can run the TCP/IP protocol, with each adapter being assigned its own IP address. The main advantage to this configuration is that LAN clients could use the TCP/IP protocol, allowing access by internal users to IIS resources. To set up this configuration, IP forwarding must be disabled for each network adapter. This can be done from the TCP/IP configuration dialog box by clicking on the Advanced button and then disabling the Enable IP Routing option.

FIGURE 18.4.

Multiple network adapters attached to different networks configuration.

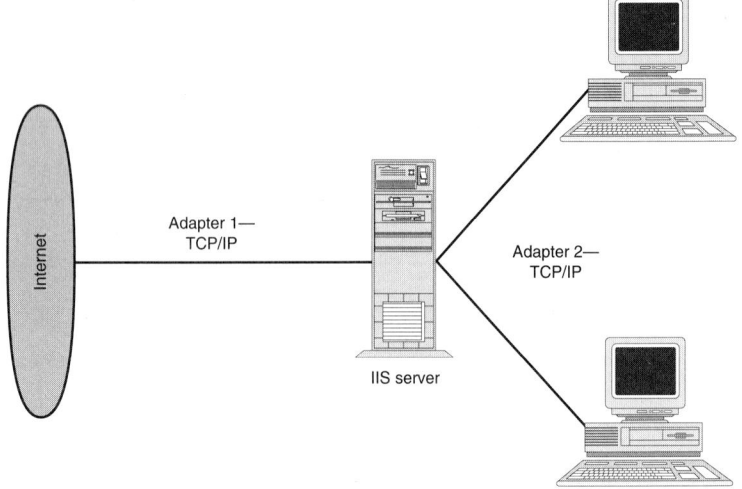

Security Administration

The IIS can be configured to log the activity of the Web server. This information can be used to monitor the server, along with information provided by the Windows NT Performance Monitor, and Windows NT Auditing. This information can be used to track who site users are, when peak access times occur, and which services receive the most access.

Logging

The IIS can be configured to log activity. Log files can be created as standard text files or as part of SQL/ODBC databases. To configure logging in the IIS, open the Services Manager, then double-click on the server for which you want to enable logging. The Properties dialog box will be displayed. Click on the Logging tab of the dialog box. Click on the Enable Logging checkbox to turn on logging. Choose the Log to File or the Log to SQL/ODBC Database option. If logging to a file, click on the Automatically Open New Log checkbox to create a new log file every specified period. A new log file can be created on a daily, weekly, or monthly basis, or when the log file reaches a certain size, by selecting the appropriate radio button. Enter the name of the log file directory in the corresponding edit box. It's advisable to specify a secure directory in which to create the log file. The log file is named based on the following specifications:

Log Filename	Logging parameters.
SLOG.LOG	When the Automatically Open New Log option is not enabled.
S*nnn*.LOG	When the File Size Reaches option is enabled. The *nnn* is incremented sequentially each time a new log file is created.
M*mddyy*.LOG	When one of the Daily, Weekly, or Monthly options is selected. *Mm* specifies the month, *dd* specifies the day, and *yy* specifies the year.

If the Log to SQL/ODBC Database option is selected, you can log information to a SQL database. It works best if Microsoft SQL Server version 6.0 or greater is installed. The Data Source Name (DSN) specifies the name of the database defined with a device for SQL Server or the filename of the database for Microsoft Access. Table 18.2 specifies the name of the database table the logging information will be appended to. Username and Password specifies the name and password of the user account required to log in to the database.

The information in Table 18.2 is logged by the IIS system. This field definition information should be used to create the database table for logging.

Table 18.2. Log file field names and descriptions.

Field Name	Description	Data Type	Length
ClientHost	Client IP address	Character	50
Username	Client user name if specified	Character	50
LogDate	Date of access	Character	12
LogTime	Time of access	Character	12
Service	Service accessed	Character	20
Machine	Name of the server accessed	Character	20
ServerIP	IP address of the server (a server can have multiple IP addresses)	Character	50
ProcessingTime	Time to process request in milliseconds	Integer	Not Applicable
BytesRecvd	Bytes received from the client	Integer	Not Applicable
BytesSent	Bytes sent to the client	Integer	Not Applicable
ServiceStatus	Service status code	Integer	Not Applicable
Win32Status	Windows NT status code	Integer	Not Applicable
Operation	Name of the operation	Character	200
Target	Target of the operation	Character	200
Parameters	Operation parameters	Character	200

The Service field identifies which service was accessed, W3SVC indicates the Web Service, MSFTPSVC indicates the FTP Service, and the GopherSVC indicates the Gopher Service. The Services status codes can be of different levels: 200-level codes indicate *n* operations successful, 300-level codes indicate data has been moved to another site, 400-level codes indicate client errors, and 500-level codes indicate server errors.

Text-based log files can be imported into Microsoft Excel or Microsoft Access for further analysis. IIS log files can also be converted to one of two other formats using the convlog utility. The log files can be converted to European Microsoft Windows NT Academic Centre (EMAC) format, or to Common Log File Format. These formats can be used by a number of different log analysis formats. The convlog utility is located in the \INTERSRV\ADMIN directory, and accepts the following command-line syntax:

```
convlog -s[f¦g¦w] -t [emwac¦ncsa[:GMTOffset]¦none] -o [output directory]
[ccc]-f [temp file directory] -n[m[cachesize]¦i] -h LogFileName
```

The -s parameter specifies which services log entries should be converted to: f for FTP, g for Gopher, or w for Web entries. The -t parameter specifies the target conversion format, emwac or ncsa for Common Log File format. The -o parameter specifies the output directory. The second -t parameter specifies the temporary file directory. The -n parameter specifies whether to convert IP addresses to domain names. The default I option is not to perform this conversion. The m option specifies the IP conversion, the default cache size is 5000 bytes. The -h parameter displays help. The LogFileName specifies the name of the log file to be converted.

Windows NT Performance Monitoring

The Windows NT Performance Monitor can track processes and services running on a Windows NT Server. There are a number of different counters that can be used to track the IIS on a dynamic basis. The Performance Monitor can also create alerts, logs, and reports, which can be effective tools in dynamic security management. The Performance Monitor can track information for HTTPD Services (in Table 18.3) and for the IIS Global Object (in Table 18.4).

Table 18.3. HTTPD counters.

Counter	Description
Bytes Rec/Sec	Rate of bytes received by the HTTP Server
Bytes Sent/Sec	Rate of bytes sent by the HTTP Server
Bytes Total/Sec	Total rate of bytes transferred by the HTTP Server
CGI Requests	Number of Common Gateway Interface (CGI) requests
Connection Attempts	Number of connection attempts made to the HTTP Server
Connections/Sec	Rate of connection attempts made to the HTTP Server
Current Anonymous Users	Number of anonymous users connected to the HTTP Server

Counter	Description
Current CGI Requests	Current number of CGI requests being processed by the HTTP Server
Current Connections	Current number of simultaneous connections to the HTTP Server
Current ISAPI Extension Requests	Current number of simultaneous extension requests being processed by the HTTP Server
Files Received	Number of files received by the HTTP Server
Files Sent	Number of files sent by the HTTP Server
Files Total	Total number of files sent and received by the HTTP Server
Get Requests	Number of HTTP requests using the GET method
Head Requests	Number of HTTP requests using the HEAD method
ISAPI Extension Requests	Number of requests made using the ISAPI Extensions
Logon Attempts	Number of logon attempts to the HTTP Server
Maximum Anonymous Users	Maximum number of simultaneous anonymous users connected to the HTTP Server
Maximum CGI Requests	Maximum number of simultaneous CGI requests to the HTTP Server
Maximum Connections	Maximum number of simultaneous connections to the HTTP Server
Maximum ISAPI Extension Requests	Maximum number of simultaneous ISAPI extension requests to the HTTP Server
Maximum Nonanonymous Users	Maximum number of simultaneous nonanonymous connections to the HTTP Server
Not Found Errors	Number of requests to the HTTP Server that could not be satisfied
Other Requests Methods	Number of requests that weren't GET, POST, or HEAD; can include PUT, DELETE, and LINK.
Post Requests	Number of POST requests to the HTTP Server
Total Anonymous Users	Total number of anonymous users connected to the HTTP Server
Total Nonanonymous Users	Total number of nonanonymous users connected to the HTTP Server

Table 18.4. IIS global object counters.

Counter	Description
Cache Flushes	Number of times the memory cache has been expired because of a file or directory change
Cache Hits	Number of times a request was found in cache
Cache Hits %	Ratio of cache hits to misses
Cache Misses	Number of requests that weren't found in cache
Cache Size	Maximum size of the shared HTTPD, Gopher, and FTP cache
Cache Used	Current size of the cache being used
Cached File Handles	Number of file handles being cached
Current Async I/O Requests Blocked	Current number of Async I/O requests that have been blocked
Directory Listings	Number of directory listings cached by the IIS
Measure Bandwidth Of Async I/O	Average asynchronous I/O per minute
Objects	Number of cached objects cached by all of the IIS
Total Async I/O Requests Allowed	Total number of Async I/O requests allowed
Total Async I/O Requests Blocked	Total number of Async I/O requests blocked
Total Async I/O Requests Rejected	Total number of Async I/O requests blocked

Windows NT Auditing

Windows NT Auditing can track events performed by authorized and unauthorized users. The Windows NT Event Viewer can be used to filter and view these audited events. When auditing is enabled, performance will be decreased and large amounts of disk space can be utilized quickly. Two types of auditing can be tracked:

- User Account Auditing tracks and logs user-level security events.
- File System Auditing tracks and logs file system events.

User Account Auditing Setup

To configure User Account Auditing, from the User Manager for Domains utility, choose Audit on the Policies menu, then click on the Audit These Events button. Selecting the following options to track these events:

- Logon and Logoff tracks when a user logged on, off, or connected to the server.

- File and Object Access tracks when a user accesses a file, directory, or printer that has been set for auditing.
- Use of User Rights tracks when a user exercises a user right.
- User and Group Management tracks when a user account is created or changed.
- Security Policy Changes tracks when a change was made to User Rights, Audit, or Trust Relationship policies.
- Restart, Shutdown, and System tracks when a user restarts the system, a user shuts down the system, or an event occurs that affects system security, respectively.
- Process Tracking tracks events such as program activation and exits.

These events can then be filtered and viewed using the Windows NT Event Viewer.

File System Auditing Setup

To ensure the highest level of security for your file system, it should be placed on an NT File System (NTFS) partition. NTFS can control file access on a file-by-file, user-by-user basis. If there is a conflict between NTFS files permissions and IIS settings, the stricter of the two settings will be utilized.

To configure Windows NTFS auditing, from the File Manager, select the Security menu option, then choose the Auditing option. Add the user or group account you want to enable auditing for by clicking on the Add button. The following success or failure of the following events can be audited: Read, Write, Execute, Delete, Change Permission, and Take Ownership. These events can then be filtered and viewed using the Windows NT Event Viewer.

Secure Sockets Layer

The IIS provides Secure Sockets Layer (SSL) to ensure secure communications by using data encryption. An IIS that is enabled with SSL can send and receive data across the Internet to an SSL-enabled client and ensure that it remains private.

SSL operates as a layer between the TCP/IP network protocol and the HTTP applications. Server authentication, encryption, and data integrity are provided through SSL utilization. Data integrity ensures that data that has been transmitted has not been altered. Encryption ensures the privacy of the data transferred. SSL provides RSA-compliant encryption. Authentication ensures the client side that its data is sent to the correct server, and that the server is secured. SSL is an important component of protecting financial transactions over the Internet.

To enable SSL on the IIS, follow these steps:

1. Change the current directory to C:\INETSERV\SERVER (or to the directory where the IIS was installed).
2. Use the KEYGEN.EXE utility to create the key pair KEYPAIR.KEY and certificate request REQUEST.REQ files.

3. A fully distinguished name for the server must be specified using the following variables:

   C = A two-letter ISO Country code (US, CA, FR, AU, UK).

   S = State or province (New York, Maine, Washington). Do not abbreviate.

   L = Locality (Buffalo, Portland, Redmond).

   O = Organization (preferably the ISO-registered top-level organization or company name).

   CN = Common Name (the domain of the server—for example, `www.microsoft.com`).

4. If the KEYGEN utility is used more than once, it will return an error 80. You must be sure to delete existing KEYPAIR.KEY and REQUEST.REQ files.

5. Run the KEYGEN application. The command line to generate the file pair for the marketing department of IDC Consulting, Inc. in Buffalo, New York uses the following command line (replace *Password* with your appropriate password choice):

```
KEYGEN {Password} KEYPAIR.KEY REQUEST.REQ C=US,S=NEW YORK, L=BUFFALO,
O=IDC CONSULTING, OU=MARKETING, CN=www.idcconsult.com
```

6. Edit the REQUEST.REQ file, and enter the command line used to create the REQUEST.REQ file; be sure to remove the password from the command line. E-mail the REQUEST.REQ file to the appropriate certification organization. Verisign, Inc. is a widely known certification agency. It may be contacted on the Web at `http://www.verisign.com`.

7. Once all the appropriate documentation and authorization steps have been taken by the certifying agency, an e-mail response will probably be returned containing a signed certificate from the certification authority. Save this message to a file (CERTIF.TXT, for example).

8. Use the SETKEY.EXE utility to install the signed certificate. The SETKEY.EXE utility is in the C:\INETSERV\SERVER (or the directory where the IIS was installed).

9. Run the SETKEY utility using the following example command line (the password must be the same password as specified in step 5):

```
SETKEY {Password} KEYPAIR.KEY CERTIF.TXT {IP Address}
```

NOTE

If an IP Address is not specified, the certificate will be applied to all virtual servers supported by the IIS that are configured to utilize the SSL channel.

10. Activate SSL on the IIS. Start the Internet Service Manager, and double-click on the server you would like to configure for SSL. On the Service properties page, select the Windows NT Challenge/Response to enable secured HTTP authentication. On the Directory properties page, double-click on the directory that will require secure

connections. Microsoft recommends that separate content directories be used for secure and public content. If the directory is not listed, click on the Add button and fill out the dialog box to add the directory.

11. Back up the KEYPAIR.KEY file to a floppy disk and remove it from the server, in case it is required in the future. It is important to also remember the password utilized in steps 5 and 9.

NetBIOS Security

NetBIOS is the Windows-based file and print sharing protocol, and is used by Windows NT Browser, Messenger, and Net Logon services. The NetBIOS protocol maps unique computer and services names. The NetBIOS protocol can be used over the TCP/IP protocol, providing NetBIOS client access over a Wide Area Network (WAN). Using the NetBIOS protocol over TCP/IP when a computer is connected to the Internet can be a potential security risk. An unauthorized user could impersonate an authorized user, issue a NET VIEW command to view resources, and issue the NET USE command to attach to those resources, gaining access to the server's file system. There are some steps that can be taken to reduce the potential security risk of NetBIOS over TCP/IP:

■ As described previously, install two network adapters using different protocols—one adapter running TCP/IP and the other the NetBIOS protocol. On the adapter card bound to the TCP/IP protocol, remove the NetBIOS, Workstation, and Server bindings. On the adapter card bound to the NetBEUI protocol, bind the NetBIOS, Workstation, and Server.

■ Disable the UDP/TCP ports 137, 138, and 139, on your router. These ports are used by the NetBIOS over TCP/IP protocol.

Service Message Block (SMB) Security

Microsoft's proprietary Service Message Block (SMB) handles file and printing requests, no matter which network protocol stack is used. SMB fulfills the OSI presentation layer functionality, but it operates in the application layer as a software module. SMB is a core component of Microsoft Networking and installed by default whenever Microsoft Networking is installed.

> **WARNING**
>
> By default, a Guest account is created when the NT Server is installed. The Guest account is configured with a blank password. When a server with the Guest account enabled is connected to the Internet, it is possible for anyone to connect to the server, log in as Guest, and cause problems with the shared resources or even the registry, utilizing the SMB functionality. For this reason, it is imperative that any server connected to the Internet *disable the Guest account.*

Java Security

With the introduction of the Java programming language to the Internet, a new set of system security concerns has been introduced. Java applets are retrieved from the Internet just like any other Web Page. Once the Java applet has been retrieved, the Java interpreter in the Web browser executes the applet. In theory, the Java interpreter should enforce security restrictions, limiting an applet's behavior. A number of different security problems have been uncovered in the Netscape Navigator and Internet Explorer. Although there have not been widespread reports of Java applets that attack a system, there is still reason for concern. It is possible to execute Java applets that send back sensitive data from your system to another server. It is also possible to execute a Java application that monitors your Web browsing session and sends back details to another server—all without leaving any trace that these applets were run. It is important to educate users on the potential security risks of Java applications. In Netscape Navigator 2.0, Java can be disabled through the Options, Security Preferences dialog box.

ActiveX Security

With the release of Microsoft's Internet Explorer version 3.0, ActiveX controls were introduced. ActiveX controls can be developed using tools native to the Windows Operating System, producing applets that can run much quicker than Java applets. Although the Java programming language has built-in security restrictions, the ActiveX specification does not. There are no restrictions on what an ActiveX applet can do. ActiveX is based on Object Linking and Embedding (OLE) technology. Although OLE linked files to an external application, ActiveX creates an applet within an existing document.

Without any built-in security restriction, the potential for abuse by an ActiveX applet is quite large. To counter these effects, Microsoft has presented a solution based on digital signatures. Using a digital signature, the creator of an ActiveX applet signs the applet with a private key. When an ActiveX applet is downloaded, the digital signature is checked against a public key to verify its authenticity. If the applet has been tampered with, the authenticity check will fail. Although digital signatures are new technology, they have been in use for quite some time in e-mail with the Pretty Good Privacy (PGP) shareware application.

A number of concerns must be addressed before digital signature technology can be effective with ActiveX applications: digital signatures need to be more effectively integrated with existing applications, digital signatures do not ensure that the applet does not contain a virus or malicious code, and end-users must decide whose digital signatures they will trust.

Catapult Proxy Server

With the release of Windows NT Server version 4.0, Microsoft will be releasing a new proxy server (which is currently in beta testing) named Catapult. Catapult will become another member of the Microsoft BackOffice family of applications. Catapult provides the following features:

- Support for all Internet protocols, including HTTP, FP, RealAudio, VDOLive, IRC, and news and mail.
- Capability of filtering and replicating Web pages for corporations and Internet Service Providers.
- Support for IPX/SPX transport.
- Capability of Web browsers running on any operating system of accessing Internet sites through Catapult.
- Proactive caching of frequently accessed information. Catapult can automatically refresh cached copies of frequently accessed information based on heuristics of usage.
- Support over dial-up lines.
- Capability of granting or denying inbound or outbound connections based on user, service, port, or IP domains. Specific sites can also be blocked.
- Mechanisms to interconnect branch offices by using the Internet and encrypted transmissions.
- Tight integration with Windows NT Server, including Event Logging, Performance Monitor, and User Manager.
- Support for ISAPI (Internet Server API), which allows extension such as customized logging, authentications, and access control.
- Filtering of packets that do not originate from an internal user.
- Support Policy Domain Name filtering, which creates a list of domain that users can or cannot access.
- User-level permissions, which control which users can and cannot access Internet resources.
- Remote management capabilities.
- Support for Secure Sockets Layer (SSL) and Private Communication Technology (PCT) protocols.
- Integration with other BackOffice components, including SQL Server and Exchange Server.

To set up and configure a Catapult proxy server, two network adapters are required. One adapter is attached to the LAN, and the other is connected to the Internet. The network card attached to the LAN utilizes Remote Procedure Calls (RPC) to transmit Internet requests and responses over the network. The LAN can utilize the TCP/IP, IPX/SPX, NetBEUI, or other protocols. The Internet-connected adapter must utilize the TCP/IP protocol. Catapult manages communications between the LAN and the Internet.

To configure the Catapult services, IP routing between the LAN and the Internet must be disabled. This prevents Internet packets from reaching the LAN, so unauthorized Internet users cannot gain access to the LAN. Routing can be disabled by accessing Advanced Options from Network applet in the Control Panel.

Clients on the LAN must also be configured to direct their Internet requests through the Catapult server. The Gateway applet in the control panel enables users to specify which gateway to use for Internet access.

Stay Informed—Stay Secure

Potential intruders to your systems stay well-informed regarding potential security holes. To maximize the security of your system, it is essential that you stay just as informed. There are a number of Internet Web sites available to keep up-to-date on current security issues and IIS updates, including the following:

- Microsoft: `http://www.microsoft.com`
- Netscape: `http://www.netscape.com`
- JavaSoft Web Site: `http://www.javasoft.com/java.sun.com/sfaq/index.html`
- Verisign: `http://www.verisign.com/netscape/`
- World Wide Web Security FAQ:
  `http://www-genome.wi.mit.ed/WWW/faqs/www-security-faq.html`
- Computer Emergency Response Team: `http://www.cert.com`
- Computer Incident Advisory Capability site: `http://ciac.llnl.gov/`
- National Computer Security Association: `http://www.ncsa.com`
- NT Security Issues: `http://www.somarsoft.com/security.htm`
- Yahoo!: `http://www.yahoo.com/Computers_and_Internet/Security_and_Encryption`
- World Wide Web Consortium: `http://www.w3.org`

Summary

The threat of a security breach from the outside is, in all likelihood, very low. Data is more likely to be lost due to a natural disaster or internal theft by a trusted user. This does not mean that security issues should be overlooked. Internet/intranet security with the IIS should be given its due diligence. It is always best to take the necessary security precautions in a proactive manner. It is impossible to make a networked system completely secure. Increased security almost always comes at the cost of usability. This compromise must continually be evaluated to ensure safety and usability.

Introducing FrontPage

by William Robert Stanek

Whether you plan to set up a corporate intranet or create a site on the World Wide Web, FrontPage should be your application of choice. With this easy-to-use toolkit, anyone can create and manage a world-class Web site. This chapter introduces the applications that are a part of the FrontPage toolkit and provides a quick tour that should help you get started.

Quick Setup and Installation

Before installing FrontPage, you should quit all other applications running on your desktop. This ensures that there are no conflicts for files FrontPage must update on your system.

Installing FrontPage from CD-ROM or floppy disk is easy. The first step is to select Run from the Windows 95/NT Start menu. Then, as shown in Figure 19.1, enter the directory path to the FrontPage setup program on your CD-ROM or floppy drive, such as

```
E:\Setup.exe
```

In the example, `E:` is the location of the CD-ROM drive and `Setup.exe` is the name of the file you want to run. If your CD-ROM is on the D drive, you would type the following to run the setup program:

```
D:\Setup.exe
```

FIGURE 19.1.

Running the setup program.

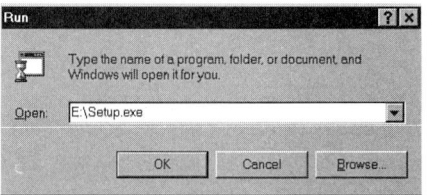

When you start the FrontPage setup program, you will see the Welcome dialog box (see Figure 19.2). Most dialog boxes used in FrontPage contain buttons you can use to obtain help, make selections, or exit the program. The Help button accesses the online help. The Cancel button exits the program. To move to the previous or next phase of the setup process, use the Back or Next buttons. When you have completed the setup process, you can click on the Finish button, and the setup program will start installing FrontPage on your system. You should click on the Next button to continue.

FIGURE 19.2.

The first step in the setup program.

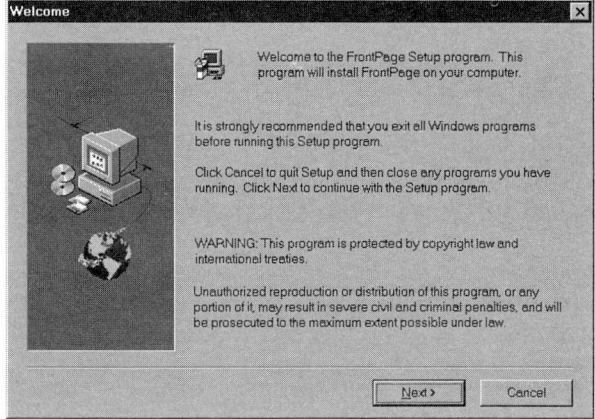

You will need about 9M of free space to install FrontPage and the FrontPage server extensions. By default, the Setup program installs FrontPage on the C drive in a folder called Microsoft FrontPage under the `Program Files` directory. To change the default, click on the Browse button, shown in Figure 19.3. This opens a dialog box that lets you specify a new folder and path for the base installation. When you are satisfied with the path, click on the Next button.

FIGURE 19.3.

Determining the location of FrontPage on your file system.

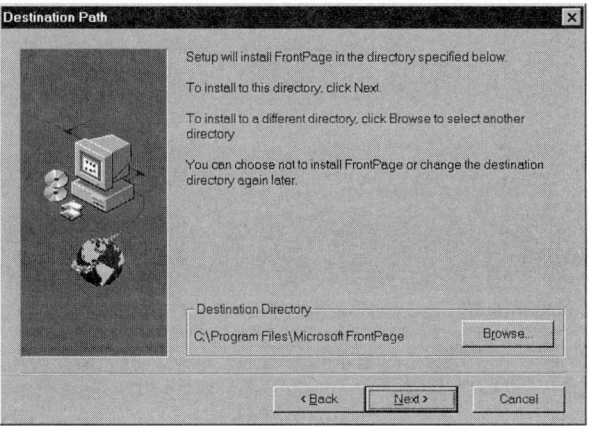

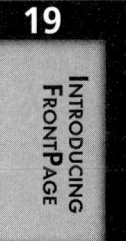

As shown in Figure 19.4, FrontPage allows you to select one of two types of installation: typical and custom. The typical installation installs everything most users will need including the Client Software, the Personal Web Server, and the FrontPage Server Extensions. The custom installation allows you to select the components you would like to install. The client software includes the FrontPage Explorer and the FrontPage Editor. The Personal Web Server is the server you will use to provide services for just about everything you do in FrontPage. The FrontPage server extensions are used with external Web servers, such as your Internet Service Provider's (ISP) UNIX-based Web server.

FIGURE 19.4.

Selecting the type of installation.

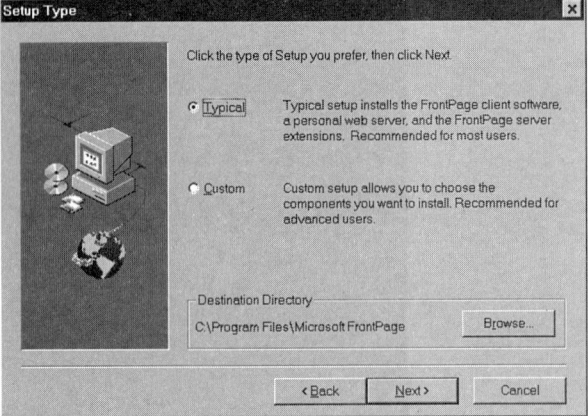

> ### TIP
>
> FrontPage makes extensive use of both the client and the server software. The only components you might not need are the server extensions. Unless you are sure you will not need to use an external Web server, you really should install all the components.

Because most users will need all the components, you will probably want to use the typical installation option. However, the typical installation assumes that you have enough space on your hard drive for the installation. If you want to check the space on your hard drive, you should select the custom installation option and possibly change the destination directory.

When you select custom installation and click on the Next button, you will see the setup page shown in Figure 19.5. Not only can you select the FrontPage components you would like to install from this page, you can also see the disk space you need and the amount of free space on your hard drive.

FIGURE 19.5.

Custom installation lets you see all the components and disk space.

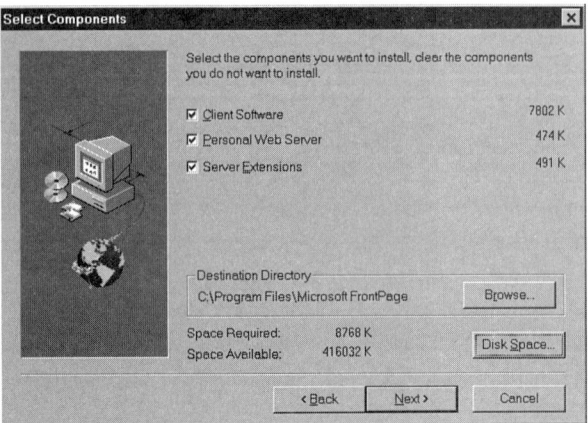

If you choose to install the Personal Web Server, the next setup page lets you specify a directory for the server executables (see Figure 19.6). Keep in mind, this same directory is used to store all the files and documents you create or import into FrontPage. By default, the server directory is

```
C:\FrontPage Webs
```

> ### TIP
>
> Creating content for your Web site is easy with FrontPage. It is also easy to get caught up in the content creation process and quickly eat up several megabytes of disk space. For this reason, I recommend using a drive with 2 to 5M of free disk space if you plan to create a small to moderately sized Web site. This disk space requirement is in addition to the 9M of free space you will need for the base installation.

FIGURE 19.6.

Determining the location of the Personal Web Server and content.

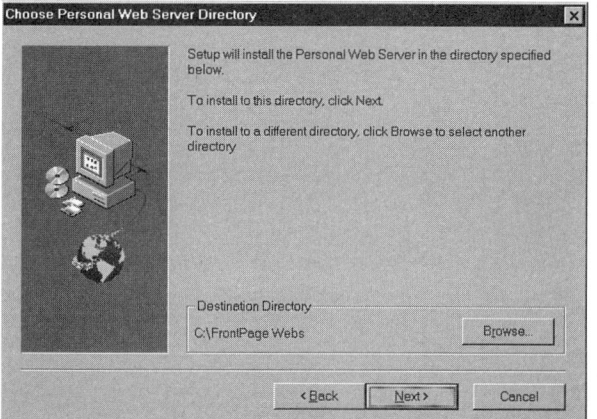

After you select a server directory or decide to accept the default, click on the Next button (see Figure 19.7). You can now choose a name for the folder that will hold the program icons.

> ### TIP
>
> The name of the folder is not as important as remembering where the folder is located. This folder holds the icons used to start the FrontPage Editor, the FrontPage Explorer, the Personal Web Server, and other tools provided with the installation.
>
> You will need to run the FrontPage Editor, the FrontPage Explorer, and the Personal Web Server just about every time you want to create, manage, or edit Web files. Thus, most users will want to move the entire folder onto the desktop after the installation, which

provides easy access to all the programs you will need for publishing. If you use your computer exclusively or mostly for Web publishing, you can also move the FrontPage Editor, the FrontPage Explorer, and the Personal Web Server to the Startup folder, which ensures the applications are started every time you turn on your computer.

FIGURE 19.7.

Selecting a folder name for the FrontPage installation.

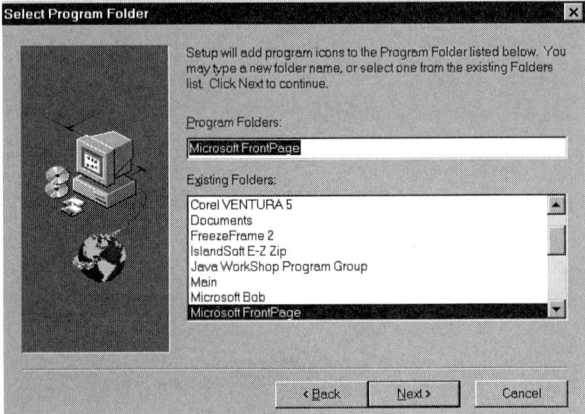

After you enter a folder name, the Setup program is ready to begin the installation process. When you click on the Next button, you will be able to review the current settings for the installation (see Figure 19.8). If you are not satisfied with any settings, click on the Back button. Otherwise, click on the Next button, and the setup program will begin copying files to your hard drive.

FIGURE 19.8.

Reviewing the installation settings before starting to copy files.

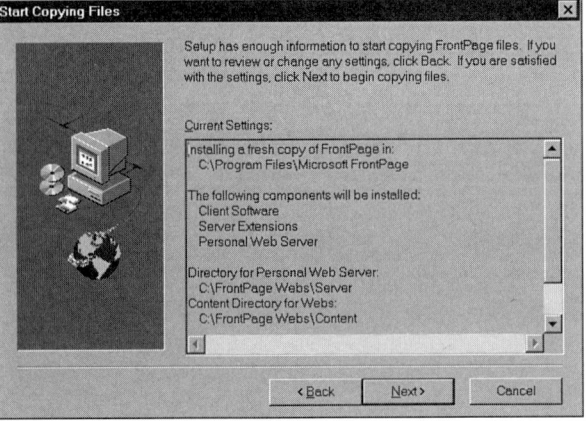

Before setup completes, you will need to set up an account for the server administrator. FrontPage will prompt you for this information automatically.

Another name for the server administrator is the Webmaster. The Webmaster is the person who controls access to the server and also is responsible for administering the server. As shown in Figure 19.9, you need to enter a user name and password for the server administrator. You will also need to re-enter the password in the Confirm password field. Remember the user name and password you enter. You need them to verify your user name and password each time you restart the FrontPage Explorer.

> **TIP**
>
> To protect the security of your Web, you should use a secure password. I recommend using a password that is at least six characters long that includes numbers and wild card characters, such as !, @, #, $, and ?.

FIGURE 19.9.

Setting a user name and password for the server administrator.

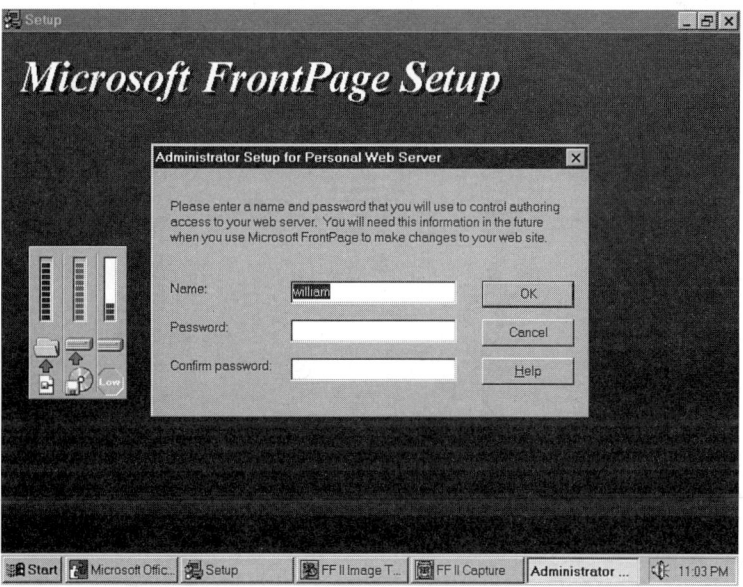

When setup completes successfully, you will have the option of starting the FrontPage Explorer (see Figure 19.10). The explorer lets you create new Webs. Usually, you will want to start the FrontPage Explorer immediately. You can click on the Finish button to complete the setup process.

FIGURE 19.10.

A successful installation.

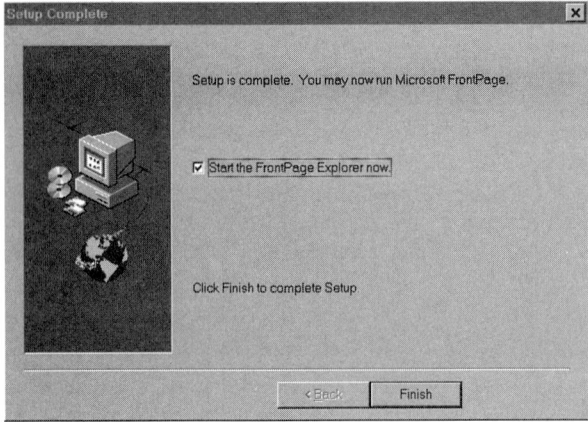

After the Explorer starts, FrontPage will try to determine the IP address and host name of your system, and you will see the dialog box shown in Figure 19.11. FrontPage uses a tool that checks for a Transmission Control Protocol/Internet Protocol (TCP/IP) connection to a network.

FIGURE 19.11.

FrontPage checks your IP address and host name automatically.

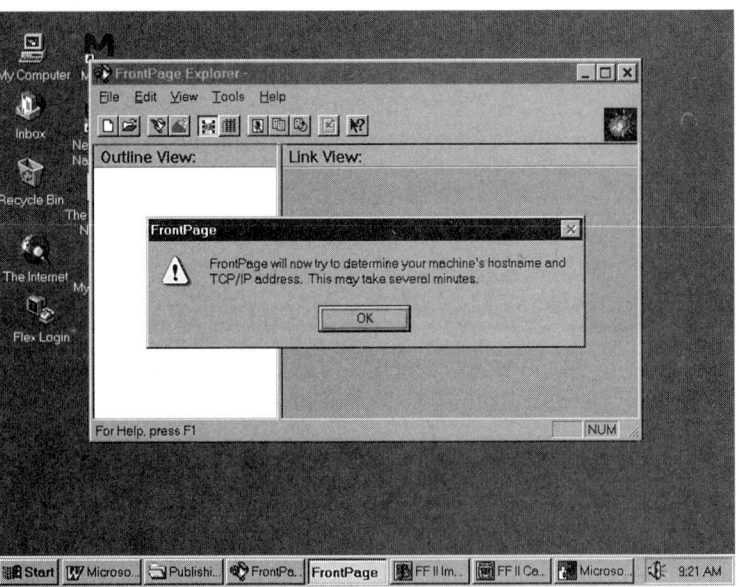

If you are connected to a network and your system has an IP address and host name, FrontPage should return accurate results. If you are not connected to a network but use a TCP/IP dialer to access the Internet, as most Web publishers do, FrontPage might return inaccurate results. For example, on my system FrontPage returned my login name with my ISP instead of a valid server name. Don't worry, the next section looks briefly at configuring your new Web server.

Configuring Your New Web Server

If you have browsed the Web, you know how Hypertext Markup Language (HTML) documents are served to your browser. The browser is a client application. When you access a file with a client, the client contacts a server and requests a uniform resource locator (URL), such as http://www.mcp.com/. The Web server gets the referenced file and passes it to the client. The client displays the file in its viewing window.

In FrontPage, there are two client applications: the FrontPage Explorer and the FrontPage Viewer. Both applications depend on a server to retrieve files for them. The server included in FrontPage is the Personal Web Server. FrontPage also includes two tools for configuring and testing the server: the Server Administrator and the FrontPage TCP/IP Test.

This section is designed to get you started with server administration and testing so you can use FrontPage. You can use one of two basic setups to do this. The first basic setup is for anyone using a computer physically connected to the corporate network or to the Internet and who does not want to test FrontPage locally before publishing documents. The second setup is for anyone using a computer not physically connected to a network. If you will use the second setup, jump forward to the section, Configuring and Testing Your Non-Networked System.

Configuring and Testing Your Networked System

To configure and test your server using the networking techniques discussed in this section, you must be using a computer physically connected to the corporate network or to the Internet. This means your computer has a numeric IP address and a host name. If your system is connected or you plan to connect to the Internet, you must also have registered your IP address and host name with the InterNIC.

> **NOTE**
>
> When you are done reading this section you can skip the section, Configuring and Testing Your Non-Networked System.

When you installed FrontPage, the TCP/IP Test probably returned valid results. You can test the results using the TCP/IP Test tool included with FrontPage. After you start the test tool, you will see a dialog box similar to the one shown in Figure 19.12.

FIGURE 19.12.
The TCP/IP Test tool at startup.

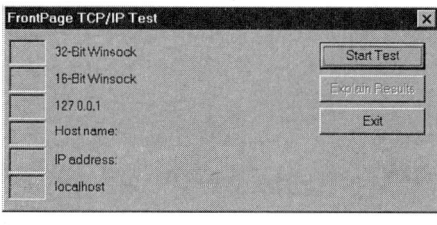

To have FrontPage automatically test your TCP/IP connection, click on the Start Test button. It takes a few minutes for the test tool to check your connection. When the test finishes, you will see information similar to that shown in Figure 19.13. To see a detailed explanation that relates to your system, click on the Explain Results button.

NOTE

When you click on the Start Test button, the test tool might launch your Internet dialer, and you will see a dialog box prompting you for user name and password information. If this happens, you are not on a network or do not have a dedicated connection to the Internet. You should skip this section and read the next section in this chapter. Although you can enter the login name and password you use to connect to your Internet or commercial service provider's Web server and follow the steps you would normally take to login, you probably will not be able to use the results returned by the TCP/IP Test tool.

FIGURE 19.13.

The TCP/IP Test tool returns results.

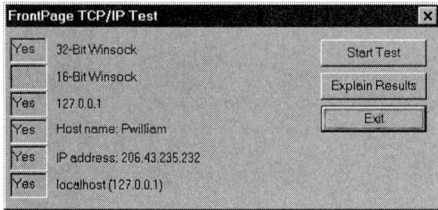

As you can see from Figure 19.13, FrontPage tests to see whether your system uses a 16-bit or 32-bit Winsock. The Winsock is used in network communications. Next, FrontPage checks to see whether the local loopback host 127.0.0.1 is usable on your system. On most networked systems, 127.0.0.1 is the IP address listed in the /etc/hosts file for the local host. You will use the local host when you want to test your Web or publish documents for testing purposes.

The next three tests determine your system's host name, IP address, and local loopback address. The final test ensures that if your local host is different from the standard 127.0.0.1, you will know about it. You should write down this information if you do not already know it.

Now that you know key server information, you can start the Personal Web Server and the FrontPage Explorer. In the FrontPage Explorer, select New Web from the File menu. This opens the New Web dialog box, shown in Figure 19.14. You will use this dialog box to create new Webs.

For now, create a Web based on the Normal Web by double-clicking on the words Normal Web. The Explorer will prompt you with the dialog box shown in Figure 19.15. You should verify the server name or IP address in the Web Server field, then select a name for your Web and enter it in the Web Name field.

FIGURE 19.14.
Selecting a new Web template.

CAUTION

If you use your system's host name or IP address, anything you publish in FrontPage will be available to anyone accessing your Web server. To start, you might want to publish files only locally, which means only someone logged in to the Web server will be able to access the files. To publish files locally, enter the IP address of the local host, such as 127.0.0.1. Because FrontPage allows you to use multiple host names and IP addresses, you can enter the valid host name or IP address when you decide to publish materials for others to access.

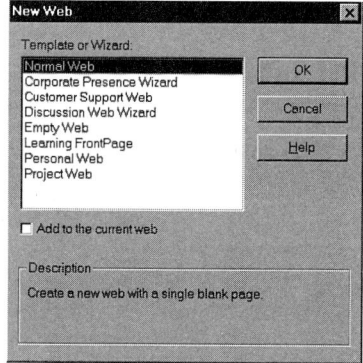

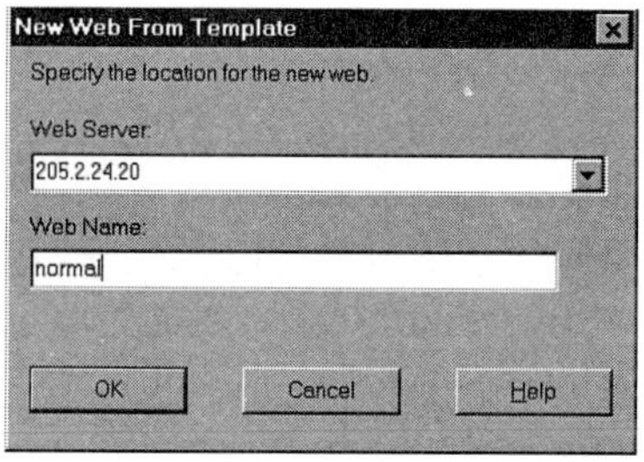

FIGURE 19.15.
Creating a new Web for testing purposes.

After entering this information, FrontPage will create your Web and load the related pages into the FrontPage Explorer. If you have not identified yourself to FrontPage by entering your user name and password, the FrontPage Explorer will display a dialog box that asks you to enter that information. Whenever you create Webs, you will probably want to use the account you created for the system administrator.

In the FrontPage Explorer, double-click on the Normal Page icon in the Link View window. If your Web is working normally, the FrontPage Explorer should contact the Personal Web Server, which in turn starts the FrontPage Editor with the normal page loaded for editing. If the FrontPage Editor does not start, re-read this section and ensure that you have followed the instructions. Remember, both the FrontPage Explorer and the Personal Web Server should have been running on your system before you tried to access the normal page in your new Web.

Configuring and Testing Your Non-Networked System

If your system is not physically connected to a network and you do not have a dedicated connection to the Internet, FrontPage can create a pseudonetworked environment for you. This pseudonetworked environment works only on your local system.

When you installed FrontPage, the TCP/IP test probably returned results you will not want to use. Primarily this is because FrontPage thinks you have a dedicated connection to the Internet and you do not. The first step in testing the server is to start the Personal Web Server and the FrontPage Explorer. In the FrontPage Explorer, select New Web from the File menu. This opens the New Web dialog box shown in Figure 19.16. You will use this dialog box to create new Webs.

FIGURE 19.16.

Selecting a new Web template.

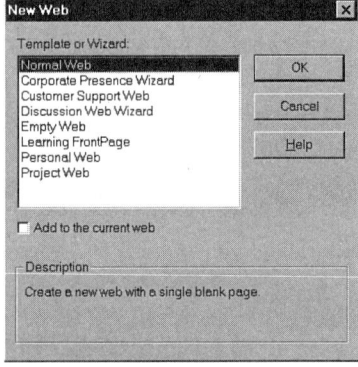

For now, create a Web based on the Normal Web by double-clicking on the words Normal Web. The Explorer will prompt you with the dialog box shown in Figure 19.17. The server name entered in the Web Server field is probably the user name you used to log in to your Internet or commercial service provider's Web server. Delete the server name and enter the IP address 127.0.0.1. This IP address is for the local loopback, and it allows you to set up a pseudonetwork on your system. All requests to the local loopback are served directly by the Personal Web Server.

CAUTION

If you do not change the server name, it is possible that the only time you have access to your server is when you are connected to the Internet. Although it might seem that you are publishing files on the Internet or commercial service provider's Web server, you are actually using the local loopback. Because of this, it is better to use the local loopback directly. You can do this by specifying the IP address of 127.0.0.1, as shown in Figure 19.17. Keep in mind that when you use the local host your files are only available on the local system, and you must transfer the files to a public server for the files to be available for others to access.

FIGURE 19.17.

Change the IP address so it points to the local host.

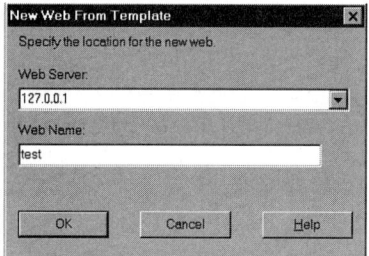

The next field you need to fill in is the name of your Web. After entering the server and Web information, FrontPage will create your Web and load the related pages into the FrontPage Explorer. If you have not identified yourself to FrontPage by entering your user name and password, the FrontPage Explorer will display a dialog box that asks you to enter your user name and password. Whenever you create Webs, you will probably want to use the account you created for the system administrator.

In the FrontPage Explorer, double-click on the Normal Page icon shown in the Link View window. If your Web is working normally, the FrontPage Explorer should contact the Personal Web Server, which in turn starts the FrontPage Editor with the normal page loaded for editing. If the FrontPage Editor does not start, re-read this section and ensure that you have followed the instructions. Remember, both the FrontPage Explorer and the Personal Web Server should have been running on your system before you tried to access the normal page in your new Web.

FrontPage Quick Tour

FrontPage publishing relies on three tools: the FrontPage Explorer, the FrontPage Editor, and the Personal Web Server. This section looks at these tools as they relate to the two most basic FrontPage publishing concepts: pages and Webs.

Creating and Manipulating Pages with the FrontPage Editor

Pages are HTML documents that can contain references to images, sound, and even video files. You view pages in the FrontPage Editor. Because the FrontPage Editor is a what-you-see-is-what-you-get (WYSIWYG) editor, your HTML documents look the same in the FrontPage

Editor as they do in most Web browsers, which means all document formatting and inline images are displayed just as they should be. Most pages are a part of a specific Web.

Figure 19.18 shows the FrontPage Editor with a page for editing. Just as you can open multiple documents in most word processors, you can open multiple documents in the FrontPage Editor. In fact, for all practical purposes there is no limit on the number of documents you can have open at one time.

FIGURE 19.18.

Viewing a page in the FrontPage Editor.

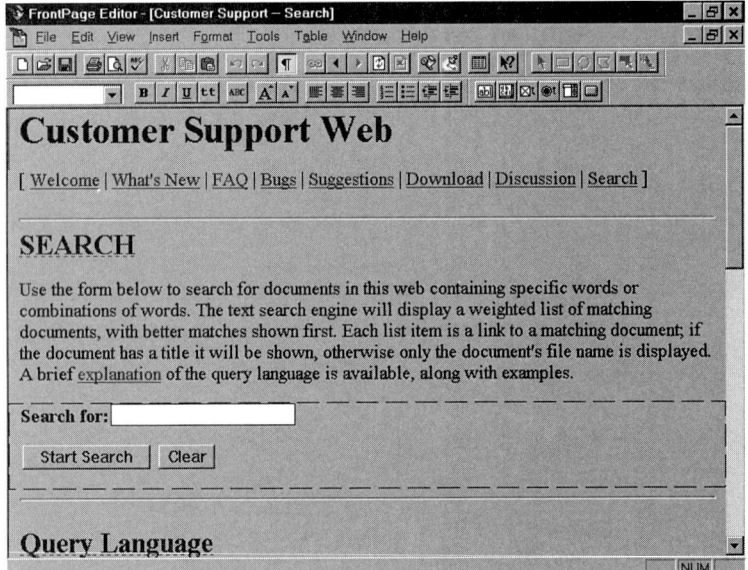

Creating and Manipulating Webs with the FrontPage Explorer

Webs are collections of pages and their related image, sound, and video files. You will use the FrontPage Explorer to create new Webs, to access existing Webs, and to set the current Web for editing. Setting the current Web is important.

When you save a new page, it generally becomes part of the current Web. When you open pages in the FrontPage Editor, you generally open them from the current Web. At any given time, you can have only one open Web, which is always considered to be the current Web.

Figure 19.19 shows the FrontPage Explorer with a sample Web. As you can see from the figure, the Explorer provides an overview of your Web. You can use this information to quickly examine the layout of any Web and to access any pages for editing.

FIGURE 19.19.
Viewing a Web in the
FrontPage Explorer.

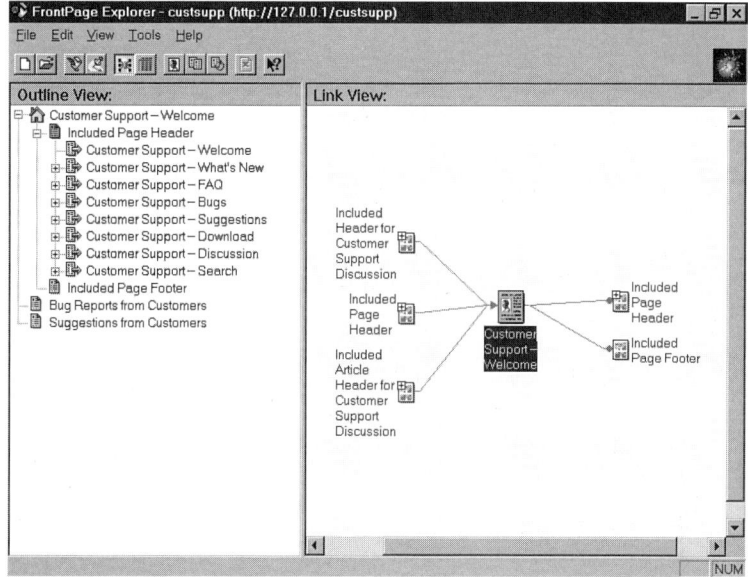

Personal Web Server

Without the Personal Web Server running, you cannot manipulate or access Webs because the Personal Web Server is the mechanism that retrieves pages from the current Web and saves pages to the current Web. Whenever you use FrontPage, you should start the Personal Web Server along with the FrontPage Explorer and the FrontPage Editor. Otherwise, when you use a FrontPage function that uses the Personal Web Server, you might see an error dialog box similar to the one shown in Figure 19.20.

> **NOTE**
>
> Port 80 is the port normally used for the Hypertext Transfer Protocol (HTTP). You will see the error depicted in Figure 19.20 if you incorrectly set up the server, changed the port setting to a port that cannot be used, or if the server is not running. Thus, if the server is running and you get this error, check your server configuration.

FIGURE 19.20.
This error indicates
that the server cannot
be accessed.

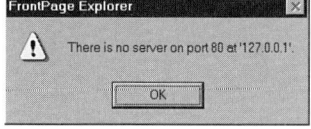

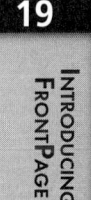

19

INTRODUCING
FRONTPAGE

FrontPage Features

Beyond pages and Webs, you should learn about three additional FrontPage publishing concepts: templates, wizards, and WebBots. These are important concepts to understand, especially because you will find references to them throughout this book.

What Are Templates?

When you create a page or a Web in FrontPage, you will usually base the page or Web on a template. FrontPage includes dozens of templates designed to make content creation a snap. You will find two types of templates in FrontPage: page templates and Web templates.

A page template is an outline for a specific type of page, such as a home page or a customer survey page. A Web template contains outlines for a specific set of pages, such as all the pages that relate to a business-oriented Web site. Usually, templates for Webs and pages contain guidelines that make development easier. Just as there are very basic templates, such as the normal page template, there are also very advanced templates, such as the template for a customer support Web.

What Are Wizards?

Some pages and Webs you create in FrontPage are very complex. To ensure that anyone can create these complex pages and Webs without any problems, FrontPage includes powerful tools called wizards. Wizards help you automatically generate content. All you have to do is start the wizard and follow the prompts. As with templates, FrontPage includes two types of wizards: page wizards and Web wizards.

You can use page wizards to create documents with fill-out forms and frames. Forms allow you to collect information from the reader. Frames allow you to display documents with multiple windows displayed in a single viewing area. A page wizard will also help you create a home page.

You can use Web wizards to create entire Webs with dozens of pages. FrontPage includes two powerful Web wizards: the Corporate Presence Wizard and the Discussion Web Wizard. Using the Corporate Presence Wizard, you can create a site that is designed to help you establish a presence on the Web. Using the Discussion Web Wizard, you can create a Web with multiple discussion groups that company employees and customers alike can use to discuss topics of interest.

What Are WebBots?

In FrontPage, you will find more than a dozen WebBots. Another name for a WebBot is simply a bot. Each bot can be thought of as a program that runs when needed. Bots automate complex administration processes and eliminate the need to write your own scripts or add complicated HTML commands.

Before FrontPage introduced WebBots, administration of world-class Web sites was the realm of those who earned the name Webmaster by being the best at what they did. Great Webmasters know how to create scripts that process the input of forms; can insert headers, footers, and images into documents at any time using programs they created; can change colors used in backgrounds, links, and text using UNIX tools such as Sed and Auk; and much more. With a WebBot you can collect the results from forms, automatically add navigation bars, create pages with full text searches, allow registered users to access key areas of your Web, and do just about anything else that once only a skilled Webmaster could do.

WebBots are great for most publishing tasks. However, they cannot do advanced follow-on processing of input from forms, and they cannot help you generate content based on the type of the user's browser. Therefore, in a some instances, you might have to use a custom script.

Summary

After reading this chapter, FrontPage should be installed successfully on your system. This chapter teaches you about key FrontPage publishing tools and concepts. You will use the FrontPage Explorer, the FrontPage Editor, and the Personal Web Server whenever you create and edit files in FrontPage.

IV
PART

Exchange Server and Mail

Exchange Server and Mail Overview

by Gregory Dodge

IN THIS CHAPTER

CHAPTER 20

Deep within each of us is the need to communicate. From the earliest cave drawings to today's electronic messages, humans have demonstrated the need to share their thoughts with each other. Although we have replaced stone tools and pigments with keyboards and bytes, the need to express our ideas in writing has remained constant.

In this chapter you will learn about the history of messaging standards and their impact on Microsoft Exchange. You will examine the different messaging standards, such as SMTP, X.400, and X.500, and how they came about. Then the discussion picks up where Microsoft entered the game with MS Mail, and you will read about the transition to Exchange. This section should be helpful for those administrators using MS Mail today. The success of any messaging system depends on how well it can "play with others," so an explanation of the different connectors and gateways is needed. Good directory management is crucial to any enterprise messaging system, so you will learn about Exchange's directory services. And last, but not least, is a discussion of the groupware, electronic forms, and scheduling features found within Exchange.

Industry requirements and competitive pressures demand that a messaging system's primary focus be on the timely, reliable transfer of messages from sender to recipient. Customer requirements for groupware functionality demand the system go beyond the traditional messaging services and provide features that support collaboration and coordination of information among users. This situation creates many challenges for both the application developer and the support professionals responsible for implementation and maintenance.

Microsoft Exchange may have arrived on the scene four years later than initially promised, but after reading this section, you will see why the product was worth the wait. Building a robust client-server messaging system with integrated groupware and standards-based gateway services is a major accomplishment. The needs of this powerful multiuser messaging system were a perfect match for the Windows NT platform, which brings Exchange Server the horsepower, security, and scaleability it needs to support large enterprise organizations. This overview of the different messaging standards and their relationship to Exchange is necessary to properly convey the rest of the concepts in this section.

The History of Messaging Standards and Architecture

Picture yourself as a typical end-user in the 1970s attempting to communicate with other employees in your organization. You would be sitting at a "dumb" terminal attached to a proprietary time-sharing host computer using text-based editors to send "messages" to your intended recipients. Although the process was frustrating at times, your messages could be sent to and received by any other person connected to the local host. Now let's say that you wanted to send a message to your customer on a different proprietary host two states away. This was virtually impossible at the time because no real standards for interchange of electronic mail between dissimilar systems were available.

The Timeline of Messaging

In the early 1970s the Department of Defense commissioned a research project to create a communications network that could survive nuclear attack. This brought about the creation of the ARPANET (Advanced Research Projects Agency Network), which used packet-switching technology to ensure that there was no single point of failure. Although ARPANET and its offspring, the Internet, were a good solution for connecting government installations and universities, corporations were not initially allowed to "connect up" for commercial purposes.

In 1972 Ray Tomlinson of BBN (Bolt Beranek and Newman, Inc.) created "e-mail" to send messages over distributed networks such as ARPANET. In 1972 more than 100 researchers at the University of Wisconsin were sending e-mail over THEORYNET using UUCP (UNIX to UNIX Copy). Finally, in the early 1980s messaging standards solidified with the adoption of TCP/IP as the standard protocol, with RFCs (Request for Comments) #821 and #822 defining the format and delivery method for messages. This began the process of establishing and enhancing messaging standards, most of which we still use today.

Refer to Figure 20.1 for the major events in the evolution of messaging.

FIGURE 20.1.

The timeline of messaging standards.

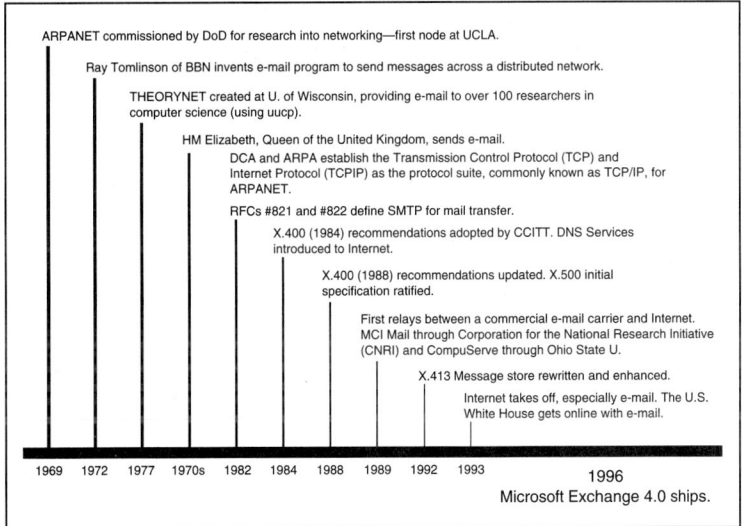

The Need for Standards

Throughout the 1970s and 1980s, companies realized that host-based messaging was good for supporting the needs of the organization, but not flexible enough to communicate externally. Around this time other proprietary LAN file-sharing based systems were developed by software vendors to support the demands of the new corporate personal computers. These new systems were also limited in their capability to communicate with other systems outside the local network or workgroup. This produced problems for many enterprise-level companies that had various proprietary host and LAN-based systems that could not talk to each other, even within the same organization.

Many of the software vendors developed gateway products to link to external systems, but they were also proprietary in nature and did not solve the underlying problem of interoperability. Fierce competition among the various software vendors created some de facto standards, but seamless message transfer between dissimilar systems was still not possible. The industry realized that messaging standards were needed to allow for the exchange of messages among a large number of highly dispersed users on dissimilar systems.

This situation allowed organizations such as the International Telegraph Union (ITU) (formerly the International Consultative Committee on Telephony and Telegraphy, or CCITT) and International Standards Organization (ISO) to develop the X.400 recommendation for messaging, and the X.500 recommendation for directory services. Because X.400 and X.500 were created by communication service providers for their proprietary networks, they did not necessarily meet the needs of the growing Internet. This problem prompted the IETF (Internet Engineering Task Force) to enhance the earlier RFCs #821 and #822 by adding such services as MIME, PGP, RECIPT, PEM, and NOTARY. This leads to a discussion of the various messaging standards.

Messaging Standards for the Internet

The journey Internet messaging standards have taken from the inception of the ARPANET to the Internet of today has been an interesting one. Electronic mail and the transports that carry it have changed drastically, with various groups and individuals adding RFCs to upgrade and enhance mail features. Due to the culture of the Internet, these messaging standards are uniquely tailored for simplicity and ease of use. Here is a list of the most prevalent Internet messaging standards:

- RFC 821 describes the commands and arguments passed between hosts to transfer a mail message. The Simple Mail Transfer Protocol (SMTP) is defined by this specification.

- RFC 822 defines the syntax for text messages, split into the envelope and unstructured message contents. The message contents are concatenated with no boundaries for different body types or attachments. Nontext attachments are usually handled by UUENCODE encryption by the sender, and UUDECODE decryption by the recipient, stored as a message body part.

- RFC 1521 (Multipurpose Internet Mail Extensions, or MIME) defines the format of the actual message body parts and specifies the methods to tag each part for identification. Message body parts can be different kinds of data, such as sound and video rich-text.

- RFC 1154 defines the message format used by the Microsoft Mail Gateway to SMTP. Nontext attachments are encoded with UUENCODE after the first body part, with the extra message header X-MS-Attachment defining the various properties of the attachments.

- RFC 1327 is a proposal for a series of mappings to be used to allow X.400 and SMTP systems to exchange mail messages without the use of a gateway.

- RFC 1725 POP3 (Post Office Protocol 3) is a standard by which an Internet mail server allows clients to connect directly via TCP/IP to send, retrieve, and delete mail.

The messaging protocols utilized by the Internet are very basic in design, but they serve the needs of millions of users every day. With the advent of Domain Name Services (DNS), messages can be routed to the intended recipient via a structured naming convention to map to a physical address. Unfortunately, the Internet messaging standards are lacking in a few crucial services, such as read receipt, delivery receipt, and guaranteed message delivery. Future enhancements should allow for better mapping of message fields, as well more structured definitions of service requests.

X.400 and X.500

As the emerging Internet messaging standards were gaining support in the early 1980s, the United Nations group CCITT was addressing the needs of worldwide telephone systems and public data networks. The CCITT realized the need to create a robust standard for international computer-based message handling. This lead to the initial X.400 (1984) recommendation to allow electronic mail users to exchange messages regardless of the system they are on. Although X.400 gained very strong support from many parties, this first attempt at a standard fell short of solving all the messaging issues.

In 1988 the recommendations were refined and updated to meet the ever-changing needs of message handling systems (MHS), establishing the X.400 (1988) specification. It defined new guidelines for security, directory services, distribution lists, extended mapping, and the definition of the message store. Since the 1988 specification the combined efforts of the ITU (Formerly CCITT) and ISO have overhauled the X.413 message store, and when this specification is officially published later this year it should take X.400 into the next century.

While the CCITT was working on the X.400 (1984) specifications, the need for an extensible directory service became apparent. The directory is required to maintain information about all the various objects within an organization, such as people, distribution lists, message transfer agents (MTA), mail messages, and organizational units. This lead to the X.500 directory recommendation's adoption in 1988; unfortunately, it was not able to meet all the requirements of true directory services. Further work by the ITU/ISO refined the specification to extend directory services to meet these challenges.

From MS Mail to Exchange

Microsoft Mail first came on the scene in the late 1980s. It was derived from a product named Network Courier. Microsoft Mail had some distinct features of a LAN-file-sharing-based architecture, such as GUI client software, post office message stores, message transfer agents, store-and-forward message routing, and directory synchronization. Often referred to as client-server-less architecture, the active processes for mail transfer are located in the client software and external message transfer agents. Imagine if you had to drive to the post office every time you wanted to send or receive letters, with no mailman to deliver the letters to your mailbox, with your intended recipients having to do the same at their post offices. This process allowed for simple and easy messaging for small, locally connected workgroups, but it presented many challenges for administrators in large enterprise organizations.

In 1990 Microsoft began work on its next-generation messaging system, Exchange Server, code-named "touchdown." The product team for Exchange realized that a complete departure from the architecture of MS Mail was needed to build a competitive product. Utilizing client-server architecture and the X.400/X.500 messaging recommendations, the team members set out to build a scaleable, reliable, interoperable enterprise messaging product. Naturally, they had to be sure to provide for backward compatibility with the MS Mail environment to allow for easier migration. Around the same time, the Internet was gaining popularity with Microsoft's customers, so they had to ensure that Exchange could work with Internet protocols.

MS Mail and Exchange have different architectures, which means there are differences in the messaging components that make up each system. These messaging components can be divided into six parts:

- Client software
- Administration tools
- Server message store
- Message transfer agents
- Directory services
- Gateways

Client Software

The client software for MS Mail is based on the MAPI (Messaging Application Programming Interface) specification and is designed to use transport-specific service provider drivers to access various mail systems. Support for simple MAPI and CMC (Common Mail Calls) allow it to work across various platforms, such as Windows 16-bit, Windows 32-bit OS/2 Presentation Manager, and Macintosh. Messages are retrieved from the Shared File System (SFS) post office and moved to the user's appropriate MMF (Microsoft Mail File format) file located either locally or on the server. Messages are moved by the client software to and from the post office, without the assistance of any process running on the server. The user interface is GUI-based (except for DOS); it provides panes for viewing the tree of folders on the left and the contents of each folder on the right. Figure 20.2 shows an example of the MS Mail client interface.

FIGURE 20.2.

The MS Mail client interface.

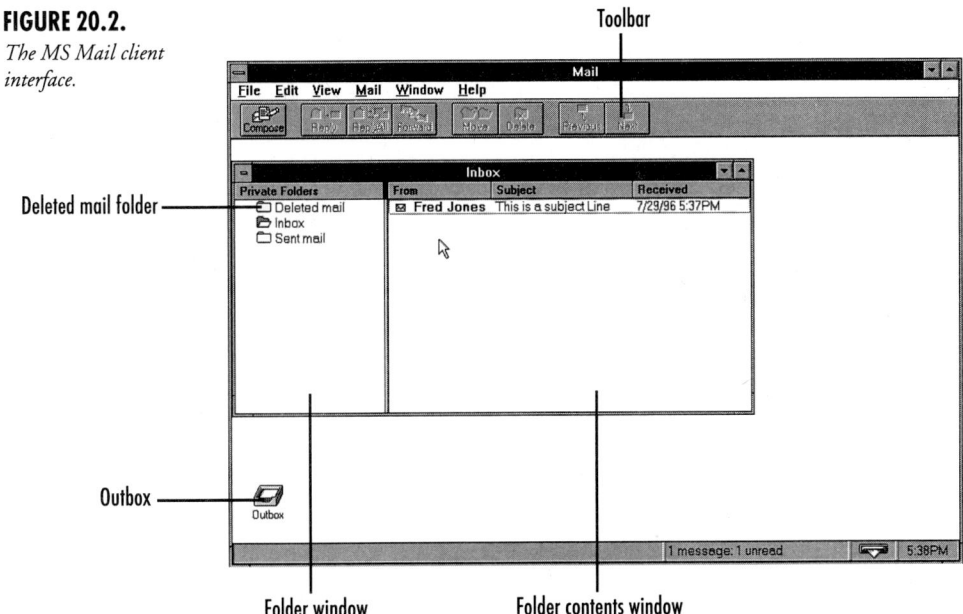

Microsoft Exchange Client is also built on an enhanced MAPI specification, but it supports dynamic simultaneous connections to various service-provider drivers, while storing messages in a universal inbox message store. The Exchange Client has the same look and feel on the following environments:

- Microsoft Windows 3.1
- Microsoft Windows for Workgroups
- Apple Macintosh System 7
- MS-DOS
- Microsoft Windows NT (Intel, MIPS, and Alpha)
- Microsoft Windows 95

The Exchange Client establishes a synchronous RPC (Remote Procedure Call) connection to the Exchange Server over any number of network protocols, not using any SFS access methods. The mail messages are moved from the server to a server-based or local message store. Because Exchange uses the client-server architecture, both the server and the client can initiate two-way mail transfer. The client software is GUI-based (except for DOS) and has folder and folder-contents viewing panes similar to MS Mail's. The main difference in the interface is in the hierarchical view of message stores and folders in the left pane. Figure 20.3 shows an example of the Exchange Client interface.

FIGURE 20.3.

The Exchange Client interface.

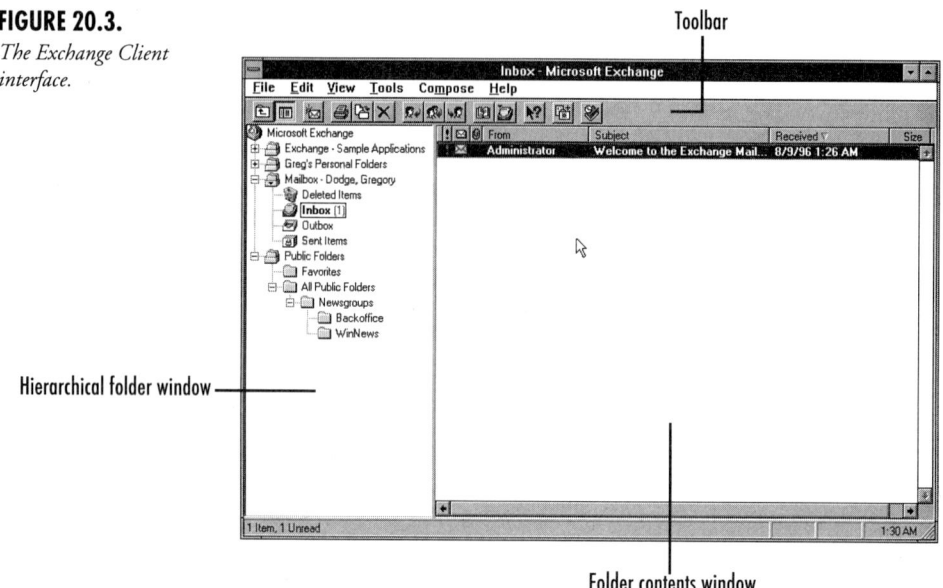

Folder contents window

Administration Tools

The Administration program for Microsoft Mail is DOS-based and requires a redirected drive letter to the post office that needs to be administered. From this interface, administrators can add, modify, and delete user mailboxes, external post offices, and change system options. The menus within this program are not generally considered intuitive and take time to get used to. Remote users' settings and gateways are also administered from this program and provide the administrator with simple tools for checking message queues and configuration. The import/export utility is command line-driven and is used to maintain address lists for the local and externally defined post offices.

The Exchange server administration program is GUI-based and leverages the client-server architecture by making connections to servers over RPCs. From this interface, an administrator can manage the entire enterprise, consisting of many servers at different locations. Every object within the X.400 schema database is accessible for doing maintenance and configuration, with an emphasis on being able to see the entire system from one view. The bulk import/export utility is integrated to enable easy creation and manipulation of mailboxes. This program will run only on computers running NT, so administrators must plan accordingly to make sure they have appropriate hardware on administrative workstations. Other administrative tasks are performed by using the various administrative tools, such as Server Manager and Event Viewer.

This tight integration with NT makes this program much more usable and enables a single-seat view of the entire Exchange messaging system.

Server Message Store

Microsoft Mail utilizes a courier-derived database that clients access through their network operating system redirector as an SFS. This message store is the repository for undelivered user mail, user message stores (server-based), outbound inter-post office messages, folders, address lists, and server configuration files. Because the MS Mail message store is proprietary, it does not adhere to any widely adopted messaging standard.

The Exchange Server message stores, split into public and private, are vastly different from the SFS stores of MS Mail. Because the database underneath the Exchange information store is based upon a fully relational transactional 24X7 database technology, the clients do not need to make a redirected drive connection. The private message store contains all the user messages and uses pointers to a single instance of a message to reduce the storage needed when there are multiple recipients. The public message store contains the public folders, electronic forms, documents, and messages stored in those folders. Currently, the maximum size of any message store is 16G, but the next version will increase the size to 16T essentially removing that limitation.

Message Transfer Agents

Microsoft Mail uses external MTAs for inter-post office message transfer, and they can operate over X.25-, modem-, LAN-, or WAN-based connections. For direct connections via a drive letter, networking software is necessary for each type of network operating system to which a post office connection needs to be made. MTAs come in three flavors: DOS, OS/2 MMTA, and Windows NT MMTA, with each type capitalizing on the strengths of the operating system on which it runs. The asynchronous MTA is also used to support remote mail clients via modem, or message transfer between post offices.

In contrast, the MTA for Exchange Server conforms to the X.413 (1988) specification for a message transfer agent. It can operate over the following OSI transports:

- TP0/X.25
- TP4/(CLNP)
- TP0/RFC 1006 to TCP/IP

The Exchange MTA can be used to connect different Exchange sites, or to connect an Exchange site to another system running either the 1984 or the 1988 X.400 specifications. For asynchronous connections, Exchange uses the Dynamic RAS Connector, which utilizes the remote access services built into Windows NT. Exchange also includes an MS Mail–compatible NT MMTA so that it can interoperate with MS Mail systems. The Exchange MTA also has the capability to act as a relay MTA, to help it seamlessly send and receive messages to other X.400 systems. Another robust feature of the MTA is the capability of acting as a PRMD-to-PRMD (private management domain) MTA, eliminating the need to connect to a public X.400 service.

Directory Services

Microsoft Mail has a simple directory synchronization (dirsync) protocol that depends on a single post office to act as the master repository for directory updates. The dirsync process has four transaction processing cycles:

- *T0.* This is the time when a user mailbox or group is created, modified, or deleted. Transactions are stored in the file reqtrans.glb on the post office and can happen at any time.

- *T1.* This is the time when the requester post offices process and send a list of the T0 transactions to the dirsync server via a special message called dispatch mail.

- *T2.* This is the time when all the T0 transactions sent by the T1 process are compiled by the dirsync server. The updates from each post office are grouped into update lists to be sent as dispatch mail to all the appropriate requester post offices.

- *T3.* This is the time when the dispatch mail is received and imported by all the requester post offices. Then the process to rebuild the global address list (GAL) runs to complete the dirsync process.

The directory synchronization process for MS Mail is very structured and easy to follow, but it lacks features such as fault tolerance and decentralized server processes necessary for enterprise systems.

Exchange's Directory Service is built to handle the very large number of objects necessary in an enterprise or worldwide system. Because its Directory Service is built on many of the recommendations of X.500, directory exchanges should be possible with other systems based upon X.500 standards. The directory update process is automatic within a site, and delta changes can be periodically sent and received with other sites or foreign X.400 systems. The Directory Service is also a transactional database, with transaction logging for roll-forward, roll-back restoration capabilities. Exchange Server also includes MS Mail–compatible directory server and requester processes to allow MS Mail to participate in a much more robust directory-management process.

Gateways

Microsoft Mail 3.x Enterprise server edition does not ship with any of the most common gateways, with the exception of the AT&T mail gateway. Microsoft has written gateways from MS Mail to X.400, SMTP (RFC 1154), Fax, MHS (Novell), MCI, 3COM, PROFS, and various proprietary networks such as CompuServe and AT&T. A gateway for MS Mail has two components: the access component and the gateway program. The gateway access component is loaded on the gateway post office, and all downstream post offices, to provide the address space and mailbags for collecting mail to the foreign mail system. The gateway program interfaces with the foreign system to exchange mail. The gateway can also be used for directory synchronization of addresses to and from the foreign system. Many third-party gateways are also available to various systems.

> **NOTE**
>
> Most of the gateways for MS Mail use File Format API (FFAPI) messages to and from the foreign system. FFAPI defines the format of tags and data within the text messages that are exchanged between the two gateway programs. The Exchange AppleTalk MTA uses FFAPI to transfer messages to MS Mail for AppleTalk networks.

Microsoft Exchange has connectors for Microsoft Mail, X.400 (1984 and 1988), and the Internet (via SMTP). The term *connectors* is used rather than *gateways* because they can be used to connect Exchange sites for mail transfer as well as directory exchange. These connectors are built into the Enterprise edition and are options for the standard edition. Other third-party gateways and connectors are available to link Exchange to legacy mail systems, such as DEC All-in-one, PROFS, MHS, and CC-Mail. Microsoft Mail post offices can utilize these connectors through gateway access components that route through the Exchange shadow post office. Later in this chapter, you can find a more detailed analysis of the connectors and gateways available in Exchange.

Exchange Messaging Architecture

As mentioned in previous sections, compatibility with current messaging standards is critical to the success of any messaging system in today's competitive market. Many messaging vendors have attempted to introduce proprietary messaging solutions with the hope that they will be adopted by the industry as a standard. This is probably due to the development time and effort that goes into bringing a messaging product to market. More recently, many vendors have adopted the posture of creating messaging products that have their architectures based on commonly adopted industry standards. This allows them to spend most of their development efforts on creating a competitive product that meets the needs of their customers, instead of trying to develop new standards that will not be able to interoperate with other systems.

20

EXCHANGE SERVER AND MAIL OVERVIEW

Microsoft Exchange was built from the ground up, utilizing standards such as X.400, X.500, SMTP, and MAPI to create an enterprise-level messaging system. The architecture of Exchange is deeply rooted in these standards and takes advantage of Windows NT Server to ensure a powerful, robust, and scaleable messaging system. The various components that make up the Exchange Server architecture were designed to be mutually independent processes that communicate with each other through internal APIs. To understand the messaging architecture of Exchange Server, you must take a look at its components:

- The System Attendant
- The Information Stores
- The Directory Services
- The MTA/Connectors

Figure 20.4 shows a diagram of the core components of Exchange Server.

FIGURE 20.4.

The core components that make up Exchange Server.

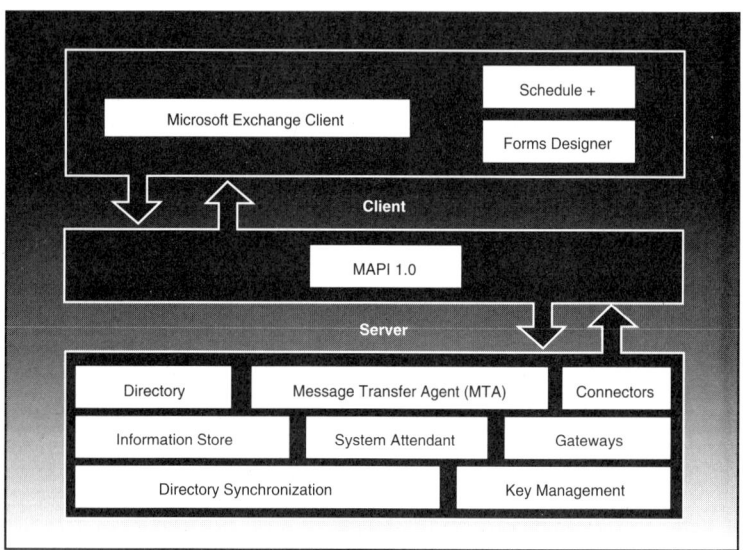

These components make up the core services of Exchange Server. The Exchange Server administration program is used to manage these services, as well as Windows NT administration tools such as Server Manager and Event Viewer. The flexibility of these components running as services can be appreciated only by those of you who spend hours administering current mail systems. For instance, you can perform a manual directory synchronization with users still logged onto the system without their knowing. This capability should help those mail administrators out there get home much earlier. Figure 20.5 shows the relationship of these services.

FIGURE 20.5.

The Exchange Server component relationships.

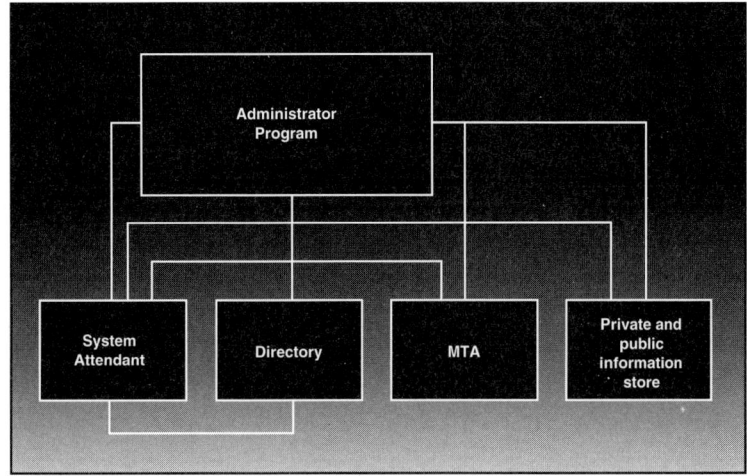

These services work together to perform the following tasks:

- Monitor the state of server services and the links between them.
- Maintain the objects in the directory database for the organization and its sites.
- Control user and system access to directory objects and message stores.
- Provide users with a single point of access to manage, send, and receive messages.
- Receive, deliver, transfer, and route messages to the intended recipients.
- Keep all the servers within and outside the site up-to-date on directory changes.
- Monitor the replication process and take steps to resolve any conflicts.
- Perform general housekeeping tasks assigned by the administrator.

To help explain the roles of the various components that make up Exchange, let's assume that you are about to take your annual vacation. You are planning to drive your car across country to your secluded mountain cabin, which should take about a week. Along the way you receive help from various sources that assist you in getting to your destination. This example will be used in explaining the roles of the various Exchange Server components.

The System Attendant

The Microsoft Exchange System Attendant is the janitor of the Exchange Server. It carries out the tasks that the other services need not be burdened with, such as monitoring, logging, and general housekeeping. Do not discount the importance of this service, because it will help you keep tabs on the health of your entire organization. As you begin to work with Exchange, you will come to realize that the System Attendant is your friend and should be treated as such. The System Attendant performs the following functions:

- Works with the monitoring tools to determine the status of all the server services running within a site or the organization
- Performs the dirty work for a link monitor, sending and receiving the poll messages used to test the status of a connection between sites, servers, or other systems outside the organization
- Builds the system routing tables for a site on a scheduled basis
- Generates e-mail addresses when new users are added or imported into the site
- Maintains the tracking and system logs for the site

In the trip example, the System Attendant would be your travel agent. When you first came in to the travel office to plan your trip, the agent created a new customer account for you and wrote down your home address. Your agent would calculate the best route to your cabin and keep track of you as your trip progressed. Unlike a standard travel agent, the agent would have already driven the route to your cabin to make sure it was valid. If anyone needed to get in touch with you while you were driving, your agent would have a log of your current location and where you had been.

The Information Stores

Have you ever had a hard time finding a reliable place to stay when traveling? So have some of the messages sent on other e-mail platforms; they've gotten lost or stranded within the system. On the other hand, the Exchange Information Store is a reliable place for any message to stay. This is due to the transactional logging capabilities of the jet database engine underneath the Information Store component. A space-saving feature of the Information Store is the single instance of any message object, with pointers assigned to the message recipients. These features allow for better message storage and retrieval in heavy load environments.

Two different Information Stores are included: the public and the private. The private Information Store is the repository for all the user's messages, attachments, electronic forms, enhanced data types (sound, video, and such), and documents. The public message store contains public folders with the associated messages and electronic forms that can be replicated throughout the organization. Both the public and the private Information Stores are accessed and maintained through the Information Store service component, but they are stored as separate databases on the physical disks. Both message stores also have the following responsibilities:

- Monitoring storage limits established by the administrators, and notifying users when they are nearing or have exceeded their limits
- Enforcing mailbox and folder security to prevent unauthorized access to messaging resources
- Interfacing with the backup/restore engine to save copies of the Information Store, even when users are in the system

■ Monitoring age limits for the Information Store, removing anything that has been deemed "outdated" by the administrators

■ Monitoring the replication of public folder data, according to a predetermined schedule, to keep folder information updated within the organization

Very strict NT-based security prevents any user from accessing objects in either message store to which they do not have permission. The security properties of each mailbox and folder in the Information Store are contained within the Exchange directory as an object permissions property. Any service such as the MTA or Directory Service cannot access the Information Store databases directly, but must pass all requests on the Information Store service.

In the vacation road-trip example, the Information Stores are the hotel desk clerks who check you in and out of each hotel along the way. They record your name, keep a log of your stay, and issue you the key to your hotel room. When you stay in a hotel, you have a private room that only you can stay in (but you can delegate it to others), and you have public areas where you can talk with other guests or catch up on some reading. The desk clerks would report back to your travel agent with the logs concerning your stay and would make sure that you check out at the predetermined time.

The Directory Services

One of the most important components of the Exchange Server messaging system is the directory services. The DS (Directory Service) and the DX (Directory Exchange) are responsible for managing many thousands of different X.500 standard objects contained within the directory schema. The Exchange directory contains information on all the objects within an organization, such as local and custom recipients, public folders, servers, MTA configuration, and distribution lists. The directory agents are responsible for keeping the directory up-to-date within the organization, and they also exchange directory information with external systems such as MS Mail.

The Exchange directory is queried by users and system components to access information on the objects stored in the directory schema. A user might click the Properties button to get another user's location and telephone number, whereas an MTA service might query the directory to find the distinctive name of a recipient for a message. Neither users nor system components can access the directory database directly, and they must make requests to the Directory Service for any information on a directory object.

> **NOTE**
>
> The current version of Exchange uses the standard X.500 database object schema but does not support object queries or modifications by way of the Directory Access Protocol (DAP) or the Directory Service Protocol (DSP). Future versions of the Directory Service probably will support these access methods as the Exchange product matures.

The Directory Service Agent (DSA) and the Directory Synchronization Agent (DXA) perform different tasks relating to the Exchange directory. The DSA is responsible for replicating the directory databases between servers within the site and other configured sites to ensure that the directory is consistent within the Exchange organization. The DXA synchronizes the directory with MS Mail 3.x and compatible systems by acting as either an MS Mail directory synchronization server or requester. As you can tell, the DSA and DXA are critical for maintaining up-to-date global address lists within Exchange and external systems. A more in-depth discussion of the directory services is found in the section Directory Management, later in this chapter.

As you continue driving to your cabin in the mountains, the directory services act as your phone book and atlas to provide you with information as you need it. You might need the phone number of the next hotel you are staying at to guarantee your reservation. Or you might need to consult your atlas for information about roads and points of interest ahead. The directory services ensure that the information in your phone book and atlas is current, and you can get updated copies of them from gas stations along the way.

The Message Transfer Agent

The Message Transfer Agent within Exchange is the workhorse of the Exchange messaging architecture. It is primarily responsible for moving large volumes of messages from point A to point B by the quickest and least costly route. Assigning routing costs to the different connectors allows the MTA to find alternative routes if a connection is down, or to load balance across two connections with the same cost. The MTA can also be configured for message tracking to allow administrators to trace the route of messages between any number of recipients.

The Exchange MTA has the following core messaging components available for its use in transferring messages: Site Connector, Dynamic RAS Connector, Internet Mail Connector, Microsoft Mail Connector, and X.400 (1984 and 1988) Connector. The method by which the MTA selects a connector for message delivery is based on the recipient type (SMTP, X.400, and so on), the entries in the Gateway Address Routing Table (GWART), and the associated costs for each connector stored in the GWART. Because Exchange is built on the X.400 standard, the MTA is fully integrated with this connector. Each connector available to the Exchange MTA is discussed in greater length in the following section, Connectors and Gateways.

The Exchange MTA is always with you as you are driving to your cabin, because it is your automobile. Also assume that you have a "smart" car with a Global Positioning System (GPS) connected directly to your atlas, or Directory Service. Your car would already know your route, because the travel agent put it in the directory, and you would receive frequent updates from your travel agent about the road conditions ahead. Your car could alert you to change to different highways on the recommendations of your travel agent and could determine the route that would get you the best gas mileage.

You have now reached your cabin, and you settle down for a good night's sleep after all that driving. You recollect that your trip was made easier with the help of your travel agent (System Attendant), the hotel desk clerks (Information Stores), your phone book and atlas (Directory Service), and your faithful "smart" automobile (MTA). You now can sleep soundly with the knowledge that these things will be available to assist you in getting back home at the end of your vacation.

Connectors and Gateways

A system's capability to interchange messages with other systems is only as good as the service components assigned to talk to those other systems. Exchange includes connectors for the most widely used protocols and messaging standards, as well as those specific to internal Exchange messaging. A messaging system must also be able to provide solid internal routing of messages within the organization. In the following text, you will read about each of the five connectors available in Exchange Server:

- Site Connector
- Dynamic RAS Connector
- Microsoft Mail Connector
- Internet Mail Connector
- X.400 Connector

Site Connector

The Site Connector component of Exchange was designed to be the easiest connector to set up and administer, while also being the most efficient way to move messages between sites in an organization. During configuration, the Site Connector asks the administrator whether to automatically set up directory synchronization between the sites and automatically configure the other site (if selected). This does not mean that you should always choose this connector to link your sites, because the requirements introduce some limitations. If you are considering using the Site Connector over a WAN, it is recommended that you use network sniffing and monitoring software to determine the effect it will have on WAN connectivity.

These are the benefits of using Site Connector:

- It is the easiest to configure because it uses RPCs; no transport configuration is needed.
- It is the most efficient message transfer because any one server in site A can transfer the message directly to any server in site B.

- It can be configured as a bridgehead server for the remote site, or it can establish a many-to-many relationship to remote servers.
- There is no need to schedule connections; message transfer is instantaneous.
- Messages do not need to be translated; they are sent in native form.
- It can take advantage of a high-speed backbone.
- Public folder replication can be almost instantaneous.

These are the drawbacks of using Site Connector:

- It requires RPC connectivity between sites.
- It cannot schedule connection times.
- It cannot control the message size sent through the connector.
- It requires high-speed network access, at least 64K net *available* bandwidth to work efficiently.
- It requires both Exchange sites to run under the same security context, unless you use the override feature.

Dynamic RAS Connector

The Dynamic RAS Connector is actually a modified Site Connector, tuned to work with the RAS service over asynchronous modem connections. You must set up the RAS connectors at both sites individually and must also manually configure directory synchronization between sites. This connector is the most inexpensive way to connect two sites that have limited or nonexistent WAN communications.

These are the benefits of using Dynamic RAS Connector:

- It offers an inexpensive solution when a WAN is not present.
- It can schedule connect times and MTA parameters.
- Messages are not converted from their native format.
- It is a good solution for branch offices.

These are the drawbacks of using Dynamic RAS Connector:

- Message volume is limited by the speed of the connection.
- It can actually cost more per month than a WAN link if used for long distance.
- Asynchronous communications can be unreliable.
- It requires more complex route tuning if many sites are involved.

> **TIP**
>
> The Dynamic RAS Connector is an inexpensive way to provide backup routes between sites. For the cost of a modem and a phone line, you gain the ability to transfer mail if your WAN links go down. Just be sure to increase the cost of this connector so that it will not be used when all is working correctly. You can also add a link monitor action to start the RAS service on the determination that a link to another site has been broken. Thus, you'll give your boss the impression that you have taken care of the e-mail system when you were actually putting for a birdie on the 17th hole.

Microsoft Mail Connector

The Microsoft Mail Connector component of Exchange is designed specifically to connect to systems running MS Mail for PC Networks version 3.x and MS Mail for AppleTalk Networks version 3.1. Those of you who are administering MS Mail networks today will find that the configuration and administration of this connector are very straightforward. Those of you who have had an MS Mail network "dumped" in your lap, or who are unfamiliar with how MS Mail works, should read on.

The MS Mail Connector is composed of four services:

- Microsoft Mail Interchange (MSMI)
- MS Mail Connector ("shadow" post office)
- MS Mail AppleTalk MTA (ATMTA) with associated Macintosh Gateway extensions
- LAN and asynchronous MMTA services

The MSMI is responsible for transferring and converting messages to and from the Exchange Server MTA and the connector shadow post office. This process involves conversion of MS Mail native messages into Exchange message format, and vice versa. The MSMI can be considered the core service for connections to MS Mail systems, because without its services the files would have to remain in their native formats, and the recipient would have to convert the message locally. The MSMI also makes it possible to have Exchange leverage existing gateways that are available only on MS Mail, and it allows MS Mail to use the Exchange Server for SMTP, X.400, and ATMTA gateway access.

The MS Mail Connector post office, or shadow post office, provides just enough of the MS Mail database structure to allow for mail transfer to and from native MS Mail post offices. It also allows gateway traffic to be routed through this post office and provides the MSMI and ATMTA with the appropriate directories for message transfer. The post office directories can be found on the share named `maildat$` on your Exchange Server, but you do not need to perform routine maintenance on this post office.

CAUTION

Even though the Exchange MS Mail connector shadow post office seems to have all the directories of an MS Mail database, do not be tempted to create users or run any of the MS Mail–specific utilities against this post office unless instructed by product support. One exception is that you can install gateway access components on this shadow post office.

The AppleTalk MTA service and its associated Macintosh native gateway extension make up the gateway from Exchange to MS Mail for AppleTalk networks. The gateway components use FFAPI to communicate between the two systems, converting the messages to and from their appropriate native format. The two systems exchange messages by placing them in the \macgate\store\pctomac and \macgate\store\mactopc directories on the connector post office and picking up messages from their respective directory. Another program, the Directory Exchange Requester (DER), is similar to the directory requester from the MS Mail connection gateway product, except that it is compatible with the Exchange dirsync message format and can filter addresses based on their network/post office names.

NOTE

Exchange Server 4.0 shipped with version 3.1a of the Macintosh gateway extension, which can cause problems in certain situations. You can replace this version with the newer version 3.1d gateway extension located on your MS Mail for AppleTalk Networks version 3.1d server disks.

To facilitate mail transfer from the connector shadow post office to MS Mail 3.x native post offices, the Microsoft Mail Connector has the capability to create and configure instances of external MMTAs. This means that you can replace your existing DOS, OS/2, or NT MMTA external instances with a more versatile Exchange version. These Exchange MMTAs can communicate with MS Mail post offices via LAN, WAN, X.25, and modem connections. The configuration of the external MMTA services is done via MS Mail connector MTA property page, eliminating the need for editing the external.ini on your post offices. Use of this MMTA requires you to reconfigure your routing on existing post offices to allow messages to be transferred "Direct via DOS drive" to the Exchange network/post office, but it proves to be more reliable in the long run. This routing change and MMTA configuration is also necessary before you begin any migration from MS Mail to Exchange so that migrated users will still receive mail addressed to their old post office addresses.

Internet Mail Connector

Of all the connectors available on Exchange Server, the Internet Mail Connector (IMC) is the one most of you need to configure as soon as you get your Exchange Server installed. It provides connectivity to the Internet and UNIX sendmail or POP3 mail servers using the specifications in RFC #821 and RFC #822. The IMC operates as a smart mail host, and it allows for message attachments to be sent and received in either UUENCODE or MIME format.

I know that if you are a current MS Mail 3.0a SMTP gateway administrator, you will want to get your existing MS Mail post offices changed over to use the IMC immediately. This change will enable your MS Mail users to send and receive MIME-encoded attachments seamlessly, without any change at their desktop. The steps necessary to perform this conversion are outlined in Chapter 24, "Interfacing with Other Mail Systems."

Because the IMC is a connector, it can be used to connect one or more Exchange sites and allow for directory replication and message transfer over the Internet or private network. Even though the X.400 Connector is a better choice for directory replication, this type of configuration is possible. The IMC also has the following features:

- The capability of sending and receiving rich-text messages, configurable by the administrator and the users

- The capability of configuring one server IMC for inbound traffic and another server IMC for outbound traffic, to load balance on mail systems with a high volume of SMTP mail

- Configuration of default attachment encoding methods and interoperability parameters—this feature also can be set on a per-domain basis

- The capability of sending encrypted messages between Exchange sites if keyserver is installed

> **TIP**
>
> By default, the Exchange IMC is configured to allow rich-text messages to be sent over the Internet. This creates an attachment, winmail.dat, that contains the rich-text formatting codes and any file attachments. To disable this option for default connections, use the interoperability button in the IMC general properties page and set the Send rich-text setting to never. You can then configure rich-text capabilities on a per-domain basis for messaging systems with the appropriate support.

X.400 Connector

The X.400 Connector for Exchange is tightly integrated with the Exchange MTA, which is compatible with the 1988 X.400 MTA specification. Because Exchange is built on X.400 messaging recommendations, very little conversion is needed to transfer mail to other X.400 systems. Currently, Exchange X.400 connections are supported on the following OSI transports:

- TP0/X.25
- TP4/(CLNP)
- TP0/RFC 1006 to TCP/IP

The X.400 Connector supports many of the standard textual message body parts, such as International IA5, T.61 (Teletex), ISO 6937, and ISO 8857-1. This support ensures that mail addressed from foreign-language messaging systems will have most characters kept in a displayable format. The X.400 Connector also supports file attachments using the following binary body parts:

- BP9 provides support for embedding and forwarding messages based on the X.400 standard.
- BP14 (1984 specification) provides support for simple transport of binary attachments.
- BP15 provides support for the 1988 X.400 standard for sending attachments.
- File Transfer Body Part (1992 specification) includes file name, size, properties, and other information.
- Other X.400 body parts not listed above are converted to MAPI binary attachments.

When you define a connection to another message handling system via the X.400 Connector, you can specify the properties for the body part conversion and the version of X.400 (1984 or 1988) to use for that connection. This step ensures that your X.400 Connector can communicate and transfer mail and attachments to most X.400 message handling systems.

The X.400 Connector can also be used to connect two Exchange Server sites, giving the administrators a higher level of control over the behavior of the MTA than with other connectors. They can schedule times for activity, control message size, and assign cost routing and be used for directory replication between sites. Directory replication can only occur over the X.400 Connector when the connected site property page is correctly defined. You can even connect Exchange Server to an MS Mail network over X.400, given that the MS Mail system has the X.400 gateway installed and running.

Directory Management

As mentioned earlier in this chapter, Exchange implements the directory structure recommendations specified in X.500 but does not support the X.500 directory access recommendations in the current version 4.0 release. The Exchange Server Directory Service stores all the objects defined by the X.500 object classes in an X.500 schema and tracks each object's attributes and relationships to other objects. The Exchange directory does differ from the X.500 recommendation in the directory names of the objects in the schema. Table 20.1 shows how those names map to the X.500 name space.

Table 20.1. Exchange Server to X.500 name space mappings.

Exchange Server	*X.500 Name Space*
Country	Country
Organization	Organization
Site Name	Organizational Unit
Exchange Server Recipient Container	Common Name
Exchange Server Recipient	Common Name

The Exchange Server also adds object classes not found in X.500 to the Directory Service to support objects such as customizable fields, alternative recipients, additional phone numbers, and organizational chart data. Information from other databases within the organization can be used to populate the directory, enriching the value of the directory as a central repository of company information.

Directory Service Agent

The Directory Service Agent must keep tabs on the status of all the objects within the X.500 schema. Any changes to the local directory database must be copied to all the other servers within the same site immediately. Additionally, these changes must be propagated throughout the entire organization at the next scheduled replication time with any connected sites. The DSA is also responsible for interfacing with the backup/restore process to allow online backup of the directory database.

Any and all inquiries to the directory database must pass through the DSA to keep the integrity of the database intact. The DSA constantly monitors the status of the directory database, and it performs recovery if necessary in the case of corruption or loss of power to the system. Future versions of Exchange will provide support for services such as Directory Access Protocol and Directory Service Protocol to allow for other systems to query and modify the directory objects. Another up-and-coming directory access method, Lightweight Directory Access Protocol (LDAP), will allow various "light" e-mail clients and Web browsers to query for information in the Exchange X.500 directory.

Directory Synchronization Agent

The Directory Synchronization Agent (DXA) is responsible for the MS Mail–compatible directory synchronization process. This allows the Exchange Server to function as either a directory synchronization server or a requester utilizing the Microsoft Mail version 3.2 for PC Networks directory synchronization protocol to exchange directory updates with other systems. This allows companies to add extra capacity to their current MS Mail dirsync process and gain control over which addresses are sent to which post offices. The capability of the DXA to act as both a dirsync server and a requester will help alleviate some of the problems for large implementations of MS Mail in enterprise environments.

Groupware, E-Forms, and Scheduling

The first time I heard the word *groupware,* I pictured a group of users all huddled around a PC fighting for control of the keyboard. I have since seen the light, and I now understand that groupware is generally defined as "The management and sharing of information to allow a group to be more productive, allowing for collaboration and coordination of resources within the group." Although this definition might be a little lacking in specifics, it should get the general point across.

Exchange Server integrates many aspects of groupware, with support for discussion threading applications, group scheduling, data replication, electronic forms, e-mail, information repositories, and information-tracking databases. This discussion touches on the three most important features that allow Exchange Server to provide groupware functionality, allowing users and administrators to build customized solutions for the ever-changing business environment.

Public Folders

A public folder can be many different things to many different people. It can be a repository for documentation on a soon-to-be-released product, with technical writers checking in and checking out the different chapters of the various manuals. It can also be a threaded discussion database that allows users to openly discuss their viewpoints on new ideas from upper management for new products. Or it can be a forms library for Human Resources, enabling users to compose items, such as vacation requests, that would be automatically routed to their manager for approval. As you can see, public folders are extensible directory objects that can contain various types of information and that can be available throughout the organization through the replication process.

Next, you'll examine a simple example of a public folder that solves a simple business need. I know that many of you currently subscribe to at least a few Internet mailing lists. If you are unable to check your e-mail for even a few days, you are greeted by multiple messages from the previous days all mixed in with your normal allotment of messages from your manager and coworkers. Wouldn't it be nice if you could have those messages stored in a folder to enable you to browse them at your leisure? Setting up a public folder to perform this function is easier than you think.

First, log on to an Exchange Client and access the public folders from the tree view. Create a new public folder, being sure to set the default permission to Create to allow for new messages to be put in the folder. You can set up any custom views at this time. Then find out the SMTP address of the folder by adding the folder to your personal address book, and then view the e-mail Addresses tab from the properties of the folder. Next, send mail to the listserver address subscribing the SMTP address of the public folder. Typically, you can do this with the command `subscribe list email-address` for most lists. Some listservers require the subscription to come from the person subscribing, so you must send mail "on behalf" of the folder. To do this, compose a message and select the From selection on the View menu, and enter the SMTP address of the public folder. After the folder is subscribed, you should start to see messages accumulating in the folder. Other users should also be able to browse the folder. This technique is much more efficient than having numerous individuals subscribing to the list individually. If you need more detailed instructions than are provided here, go to Microsoft's Web site in the Exchange product section at http://www.microsoft.com/exchange.

Electronic Forms

Electronic forms are based on the Visual Basic 4.0 language. You can create them by using the Electronic Forms Designer (EFD) included on the Exchange Client CD-ROM. I suggest that you take a look at the sample applications Microsoft has provided. You can find them on the `samples` share located on your Exchange server. The versatility of the applications created with EFD can be utilized for many different business solutions.

The discussion folders included in the sample applications are one example of a collaborative application. The customer-tracking application is an example of an information-tracking application for managing client data. I think that the chess application is just plain fun, and it shows what you can do with a crack programming staff. Creating custom forms and applications with EFD is a snap, with an intuitive user interface that one can learn in very little time. Administrators should not be wary of their users' getting their hands on EFD, because EFD can enable them to create their own applications to solve various business needs. You should control the deployment of these applications, though, and you might want to set the proper permissions on the root folder to control the creation of public folders. I suggest that you set up a folder where users can submit new applications for review before placing them into production.

20

EXCHANGE SERVER
AND MAIL
OVERVIEW

> **CAUTION**
>
> The EFD application creates native VB 4.0 source code just before you compile and load the application into the Exchange Server. You can extend the functionality of this code by adding your own functions or procedures, such as database queries to a SQL Server. But after you have edited the source code, the EFD will be unable to open and modify that application. If you are comfortable with the VB 4.0 language, I say happy coding. If you are more comfortable with EFD, look for third-party add-ons to extend your applications.

Group Scheduling

The Microsoft Exchange Client includes a copy of Schedule Plus 7.0 for group scheduling, contact management, and project tracking. The Schedule Plus client is optimized for both remote and local access, working primarily from the local file with two-way replication of updates to the Exchange Server private store. Users can view each other's schedule files (assuming that they have the proper permissions), invite others to meetings, schedule resources such as conference rooms, and send messages—all from the Schedule Plus client.

The functionality of Schedule Plus can easily be extended using Electronic Forms Designer to create "schedule-sensitive" applications. One such example that's included with the sample applications is used to notify others of vacation or sick time. This example application demonstrates how EFD applications can be extended to interface with MAPI-based applications to promote collaborative efforts by users. All the data you need in order to create a project management application is contained within the Exchange Client. It is your job to create that application and put it to work in your organization.

Summary

Throughout the evolution of messaging systems, the industry has realized the need for reliable standards to allow for interoperability among systems. This realization is demonstrated by the efforts of the ITU and ISO to create the X.400 and X.500 recommendations for messaging systems. Members of the Internet community also recognized that they needed standards for exchanging messages, which prompted them to cooperatively develop the SMTP standard that we still use today. Many messaging vendors have attempted to create their own de facto standards, but have realized that their customers want messaging systems that can seamlessly communicate with other systems.

Microsoft brought these lessons to the drawing table, and decided to develop a new messaging system that embraces these widely adopted standards. Exchange Server was designed to capitalize on the strengths of the client-server architecture built into Windows NT to address the needs of large organizations. Although the product took much longer to develop than expected, the final result is a robust, secure, and scaleable messaging system built on an X.400 engine with X.500 directory services.

The Exchange Server includes connectors that allow it to exchange messages with SMTP, X.400, MS Mail, and other third-party systems. Future enhancements to Exchange will allow other systems to query and modify the X.500 directory objects contained within the database schema. With such a robust directory database, you can expect future products to utilize this information to extend their own functionality.

The success of any messaging system is also tied to user acceptance of the client components. The redesigned user interface of Exchange Client, and its cross-platform conformity, are winning over new users every day. The Exchange Client and Server use MAPI to communicate over Remote Procedure Calls to reduce LAN traffic and enhance remote connectivity. The groupware features built into Exchange allow organizations to build customized applications to promote user collaboration, and to distribute business information throughout the enterprise.

The next chapter takes you through the process of planning, testing, and implementing an Exchange Server messaging solution in your organization. Key topics include a discussion on naming conventions, server hardware planning, site planning, connector selection, installation tips, and post-installation testing.

Installing Exchange Server and Mail

by Gregory Dodge

IN THIS CHAPTER

CHAPTER 21

One of the most challenging steps of any major undertaking is the planning process that precedes the actual implementation. Just think of all the planning that took place before the first stone was laid for the Great Wall of China. Installing an Exchange Messaging system also requires a very structured planning cycle, with many decisions that must be made before you even crack the shrink-wrap.

Exchange Server is a very flexible, powerful, and robust enterprise messaging system. It can also be very unforgiving, ineffective, and unhealthy if improperly designed and deployed. Determining the hardware and software requirements for Exchange in your environment is the first step. This task requires you to document what your current mail system looks like and the messaging load it is currently managing. A careful analysis of your network operating system infrastructure, and the physical network it runs on, is necessary to properly design a routing topology. Because Exchange uses X.400/X.500 naming conventions, you must plan your naming conventions carefully.

The installation of the Exchange Server software is a very straightforward process, assuming that you are working from a solid deployment plan. This chapter describes some of the most common installation problems and how to get around them. Some pre- and post-installation guidelines are also discussed in this chapter. Although tuning the Exchange Server is not covered in this chapter, some references to general optimization guidelines are offered. After you have the server installed, testing and verifying full functionality will ensure that you won't be uttering that famous four-letter word, "oops!"

System Requirements

Software vendors are known for publishing the most basic system requirements for their software. Sure, their product might install, and even run, on the systems specifications recommended on the back of the box. But these requirements usually will not meet the needs of the typical user community. Microsoft is guilty of doing this with many of its products, and Exchange is no exception.

The specific system requirements for running their software in your environment can be determined only by properly establishing your organization's needs and expectations. Remember, Exchange and NT are scaleable to the hardware they are running on, so plan for at least one year of growth in the system. What I see at many new installations of Exchange is that users tend to "exercise" the new system in their learning process. I had one gentleman who decided to back up his entire hard drive to a public folder. Other than taking a long time and eating hard drive space for lunch, it seemed to work fine for him. The system administrators were furious about what this user did, but could you blame him?

Hardware and Software

Microsoft Exchange Server currently comes in two flavors, Enterprise edition and Standard edition. The Enterprise edition includes all the available connectors, such as the Internet Mail Connector (IMC), X.400 connector, MS Mail Connector, Site Connector, and Dynamic RAS Connector. The standard edition includes the MS Mail Connector only, with the other connectors being optional components. The system requirements for both editions should be the same because the overall system requirements are based on what services you are running.

The hardware and software requirements for the Exchange Server and Client are published as shown here:

Server

- For Intel and compatible systems:
    - System with a 486/66 or faster microprocessor (Intel Pentium 90 recommended)
    - 24M of memory (32M recommended)
    - 250M of available hard-disk space (500M recommended)
- For RISC-based systems:
    - System with MIPS R4x00 or Alpha AXP processor
    - 32M of memory (48M recommended)
    - 300M of available hard-disk space (500M recommended)
- Windows NT Server version 3.51 (with service pack #4) or later
- CD-ROM drive
- $3^1/_2$ inch Macintosh disk drive for Microsoft Mail Connector for AppleTalk

Clients

- For Microsoft Windows version 3.1, Windows for Workgroups version 3.11, and Windows 95:
    - 8M of memory (12M recommended); with Forms Designer, 12M of memory (16M recommended)
    - 12–22M of available hard-disk space
- For Microsoft Windows NT version 3.51 on Intel-based systems:
    - 16M of memory (20M recommended); with Forms Designer, 20M of memory (24M recommended)
    - 12–22M of available hard-disk space

- For Microsoft Windows NT version 3.51 on RISC-based systems:
    - 20M of memory (24M recommended)
    - 15–22M of available hard-disk space
- For MS-DOS version 5.0 or later:
    - 1M of memory (460K of free conventional memory)
    - 2–3M of available hard-disk space

As you look over this list, you are probably wondering, *How do I figure out what the requirements are for my system?* You might also be asking yourself that notorious question, *How many users can that machine support if I buy it?* Both questions require you to be much more involved in answering the necessary questions to come to a meaningful conclusion. This section does not cover tuning, because that topic is covered in Chapter 25, "Exchange Server Performance Tuning and Scaling."

Generally, I suggest that you start with an Exchange server that has no less than the following specifications:

- Pentium, Alpha, or MIPS machine with dual processor option or SMP (Symmetric Multiprocessing) capabilities
- 64M of RAM minimum, with larger systems having 128M or more
- Fast network card(s), such as 100Tx, FDDI, or 100VG
- 1G Mirrored Fast/Wide system drive, 500M–1G dedicated drive for transaction logs, and 4–16G of hardware RAID5 array for information store databases
- 4X speed CD-ROM or higher
- PCI or EISA bus with a fast backplane (no ISA bus machines or ISA cards recommended)

TIP

I know that I am jumping the gun when it comes to tuning, but there is a reason for the dedicated transaction log drive. If you disable circular logging for the IS (Information Store) service and routinely back up at night, you should get excellent performance from a dedicated log drive with large numbers of concurrent users. Formatting the log drive with the FAT file system also gives a measurable performance gain, but only if the logging drive is less than 1G.

You might look over these requirements and think they are overkill for your little 50-user LAN. Well, think ahead to when it will be a 250-user LAN with many critical business processes running on the system. The server will probably be working with large voice and imaging files, exchanging live data to an Internet/intranet, and managing large numbers of public folders. My motto is "Plan for the worst, and you will never be disappointed." If you are really worried about justifying such a system now, just have your boss take a look at the performance available from current desktops.

The actual memory requirements for your server can be higher if it is providing these additional Windows NT services:

- Domain controller services, such as a primary or backup domain controller
- Remote Access Services (RAS)
- Application services such as SQL Server, SMS, or SNA Server
- DHCP and/or WINS
- File and/or printer sharing
- Network Traffic services such as Multi-Protocol Router (MPR) or catapult proxy server
- Third-party products for such things as faxing, paging, or imaging

You should include the additional memory requirements of these services to determine the actual amount of RAM your system requires. You can calculate the general requirements of each of the previously listed services by referring to Microsoft technote #Q139100, available in the Microsoft knowledge base. Also, as a general rule, try not to run other application services such as SQL Server or SMS on your exchange box, because they will compete for similar resources and could produce undesired application bottlenecks.

Network Connectivity

Have you taken a long hard look at your network lately? This is one of the areas most system administrators overlook when establishing the needs for a new system. Exchange Server uses a more efficient means of connectivity, termed RPC (Remote Procedure Calls), to communicate from a server to other servers and clients. This means that it generates less network traffic than SFS-based mail systems, but it does require a higher level of available bandwidth in certain situations.

The amount of available network bandwidth needed is different for each connectivity option available in Exchange. The term *available bandwidth* refers to the amount of network bandwidth available to Exchange after all other network requirements are met. For instance, you might have a very fast T1 connection to one of your locations. If the accounting system is utilizing 80–90 percent of that connection's bandwidth, you would have only 150–300K of available bandwidth for Exchange to use. Refer to Table 21.1 to determine the minimum network bandwidth needs for the different connectivity options for Exchange.

Table 21.1. Available bandwidth requirements for each connectivity option.

Connectivity Option	Available Bandwidth	Network Options
Intra Site	High-speed 1.5M or higher	T1 and T3 leased lines 10M or higher LAN
Site Connector	256K or higher	T1 and T3 leased lines Frame Relay 256K
Dynamic RAS Connector	Asynchronous 14.4–28.8 baud	Modem X.25 ISDN
Internet Mail Connector	Asynchronous 14.4–28.8 baud	Modem X.25 ISDN leased line
X.400 Connector	128–256K	X.25 ISDN T1 and T3 leased lines

As you can see, the available network bandwidth determines which connectivity options you should use to connect servers or Exchange sites. These requirements are for general message delivery and do not include any of the additional Exchange services. These are the other services that will affect your selection of a network connectivity option:

- Directory replication
- Public folder replication
- Value-added services such as fax or paging
- Site administration
- Windows NT security
- Protocols utilized

Chapter 25 covers recommendations for tuning the Exchange Server system to allow for faster network access. It also describes how to design and modify your network to provide support for the services beyond standard messaging. Understanding how the various components of Exchange will impact your network allows for modifications prior to any implementation. A proactive network analysis lowers the possibilities of unexpected network problems—and helps keep your blood pressure lower.

Network Operating System

Most critics of Exchange Server claim that it was designed and optimized exclusively for Windows NT Server networks. This is true only in the fact that the server runs solely on the Windows NT platform. Exchange supports many other Network Operating System (NOS) clients, only requiring the appropriate protocols to be loaded at the client. The default protocol support included with the Exchange Client is for

- Local RPC (protocol independent)
- TCP/IP Winsock 1.*x*
- IPX/SPX
- NetBIOS
- Named Pipes (transport independent)
- Banyan VINES Protocols

Exchange includes tailored conversion and protocol support for Novell Networks, allowing it to support NetWare native clients. Novell userid extraction tools allow you to get lists of users from your Novell servers and use the lists to create NT userids and Exchange mailboxes with the bulk import utility. The SAP agent, a service included in Windows NT Server, is required to allow the Exchange Server to register itself for access by the Novell clients. Native NetWare clients require the most recent updates to the client ODI support drivers, and it is recommended that you plan accordingly for your deployment.

> **TIP**
>
> If you are planning to install an Exchange Server in a completely Novell environment, you can make use of a few tools to make the job of account management easier on you and your users. The Directory Service Manager for NetWare (DSMN) keeps the user group and account information replicated between the NT domain and Novell 3.*x* servers. This allows for a single userid and password for each NetWare client, with the added benefit of bringing a robust directory service to the Novell 3.*x* environment.

End-users of these other NOSs will be required to log on to the NT domain when starting the Exchange Client. This additional logon is needed to properly authenticate users from NT for secure access to their mailboxes. This is also necessary if you are not able to keep the passwords synchronized between the NT domain and the NOS your clients are logging onto. Many users are already familiar with separate passwords for their e-mail, so this should not be a major problem.

Planning and Considerations

The amount of time you spend planning for your Exchange implementation is inversely proportional to the amount of time you'll spend for actual implementation. The more proactive planning time your organization does before installation, the less reactive "down" time will be needed during the implementation phase. Many very important decisions are made in this planning stage, requiring approval from management and acceptance by the user community. Remember, it is better to have other people in the boat with you to bail if the boat takes on water.

When planning for your Exchange implementation, take into account the reasons your company has decided to implement Exchange. You might be converting from an existing system that is not meeting the company's needs, or installing your company's first messaging system. In both instances, not truly knowing why you are proceeding with the Exchange installation can spell trouble for the implementation phase. Write these reasons on poster board and display them prominently at every related meeting to keep things in perspective.

> **CAUTION**
>
> In life, there is perception and then there is reality; they are mutually exclusive. If your management is proposing Exchange as the fix for all your messaging problems, be very apprehensive. Many managers and support professionals perceive all the problems with e-mail and messaging to be caused by the current system. In reality, most of these difficulties are actually related to network issues, desktop resources, improper design, unrealistic expectations, or other non-messaging problems. The planning process should expose these obstacles so that they can be corrected before your Exchange implementation.

Establishing Your Corporate Needs

Humans have very basic needs such as food, water, and shelter. Corporations also have basic messaging needs such as composition, delivery, and storage of messages. A corporation's extended messaging needs can be divided into those of the users, those of the support professionals, and those of managers.

Determining the end-user's needs might be the most challenging part of the planning stage. You must determine the different applications and services the users must have, such as public folders, e-mail, scheduling, and electronic forms. Establishing how each of these services will be used can help model the resource requirements for the servers. The best way to establish the end-users' needs is to involve the users in the pilot project, allowing them to provide feedback by using the survey form from the Exchange sample applications.

Support professionals' messaging needs are not focused on the fluff, but are deeply rooted in the manageability and stability of the system. They want to make sure that the user's needs are fulfilled, and at the same time keep their beepers quiet. They are looking for proactive analysis tools to alert them to system problems, as well as good reactive tools to assist in repairing those problems. You should plan for a dedicated system to run the link and server monitors, and be sure to have the support tools and resource kit installed on all servers and administrative machines.

The messaging needs of management can be directly linked to those of the users and support professionals. The management wants to make sure that their users get value from the system and that the support professionals are able to keep it running. Their goals are also tied to the strategic technological direction of the company, such as directory services or Internet commerce. Unfortunately management will sometimes include company politics in their requirements, so be careful not to allow your messaging system design to be shaped by politics.

Network Planning

To properly visualize and modify the physical network topology, you must first develop a working map of the company's geographical locations. From this map, place the various links, link speeds, link utilization, and percentage of uptime for each location and the connections between them. You can use software packages that have been specifically designed to help you with this task, or if you are currently using network management software, this information is at your fingertips. Take this map to your Exchange kickoff meeting, and have everyone involved validate its accuracy.

After you have a working network topology map everyone agrees on, add the messaging data from your current system. Give it to your e-mail administrators, and have them overlay it with the following information from your current system, or estimates if you don't currently have a system:

- Message routing topology
- Number of mailboxes for each messaging server
- Average number of messages per day at the same location
- Average number of messages per day between different locations
- Average message size per day per route
- Average number of messages transferred by gateways

Your map might be getting pretty crowded by this time, so you will need to be creative with the way the information is presented. You might also be dreading the time necessary to develop this map, but it will definitely pay off in the long run. From this map you can get a better picture of how your messaging system looks today and correctly plan for servers and connectors to match the underlying network needs.

> **TIP**
>
> Most messaging systems have a "fingerprint" that can be used to track message statistics. Figure out specific network traffic patterns or packet signatures with network sniffing software for messages sent, received, and transferred out for each post office. Set up a sniffer to monitor each post office with filters for these fingerprints, and you will soon have all the data you need. The Microsoft Network Monitor software included in Windows NT Server 4.0 or SMS 1.x can easily perform this function.

Domain Planning

Because Exchange depends solely on NT domains to grant secure access to messaging resources, planning for your domain topology is a very important step. Regardless of whether you have a current domain topology or are looking at implementing one, Exchange will interact under the same set of guidelines. NT domain security is used to grant permissions to messaging resources for users, administrators, and service accounts. The various connectors have specific security requirements, and allow you to override the security information used for that connection.

Simply put, an NT domain is a grouping of one or more servers that share common security, policy, and account databases. Servers can be Primary Domain Controllers (PDCs), Backup Domain Controllers (BDCs), or member servers in the domain. Trust relationships allow domains to communicate with each other to utilize accounts from another domain. Microsoft defines the four basic domain models as single, master, multiple master, and full trust. For our purposes, I will examine only how Exchange works within the single domain model and the master domain model. The multiple master and full trust models are variants of the single and master domain models, and you should avoid them if possible due to their complexity and many design challenges.

Exchange's interaction with the single domain model is the easiest to explain but the most challenging when it comes to multiple site topology design. Exchange servers are members of the single account domain, and all permissions for messaging resources are assigned to accounts and groups in the domain. The Exchange servers can be PDCs, BDCs, or servers in the domain, depending on your user authentication needs. This domain model is good for organizations with fewer than 10,000 users that have a limited number of locations across WAN links. Figure 21.1 shows an example of a single domain model with two Exchange sites.

FIGURE 21.1.

Exchange sites in a single domain model.

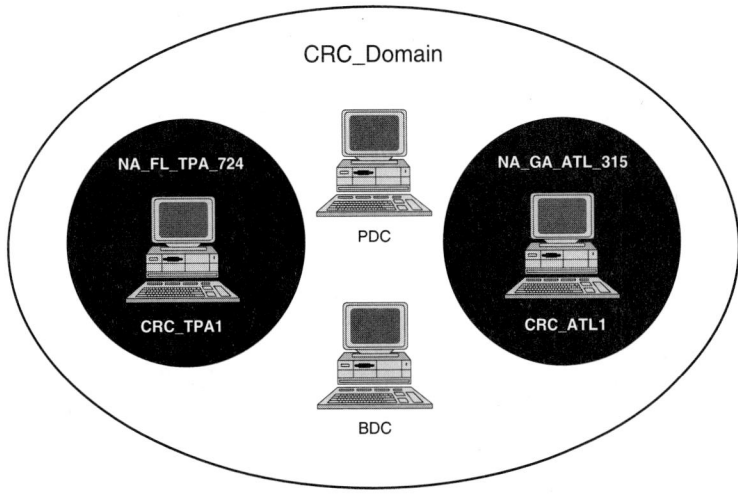

The master domain model is a better choice for organizations with fewer than 40,000 users at multiple locations separated by WAN links. Exchange servers are located in the resource domains with permissions being assigned to accounts and groups in the master user account domain (MUD). The separation of accounts and resources at the domain level adds granularity in administration of Exchange servers and sites. The Exchange servers are usually PDCs or BDCs in the resource domain, reducing the overhead involved in replicating the changes normally associated with a Master User Domain (MUD). BDCs for the MUD should be located at each location separated by a WAN link to provide user authentication services should the PDC go down. Figure 21.2 shows an example of a master domain model with two Exchange sites.

Larger organizations can use variants or hybrids of the different domain models to tailor their domain topology to suit their needs. In Windows NT 3.51, Microsoft suggests that you not exceed 40,000 users in a single domain, but future versions of NT (4.0) have performance enhancements to overcome this design restriction. If your organization is fairly large (more than 10,000 users) and widely distributed, it is suggested that you break out your domain planning and Exchange implementation into separate projects. Using this technique, you can focus on designing the best domain topology for your organization, and then utilize the flexibility available in Exchange to operate under that topology.

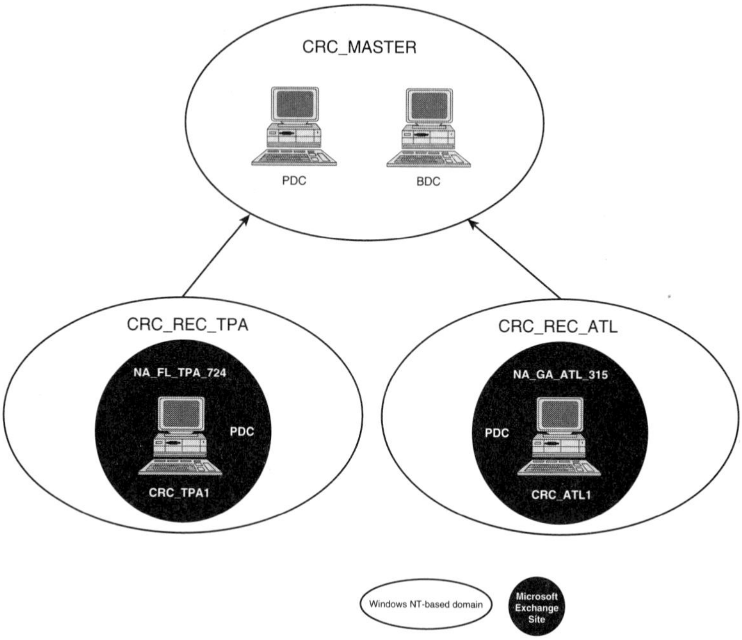

FIGURE 21.2.

*Exchange sites in a
master domain model.*

CRC_MASTER

PDC   BDC

CRC_REC_TPA

NA_FL_TPA_724

PDC

CRC_TPA1

CRC_REC_ATL

NA_GA_ATL_315

PDC

CRC_ATL1

Windows NT-based domain

Microsoft Exchange Site

CAUTION

Even though Microsoft suggests that one Exchange service account be used for all Exchange servers in the sites, I highly recommend that you not do this. If one of your site administrators accidentally resets the service account password or locks the service account out, all the Exchange services throughout your organization will suddenly stop. I suggest that you live with the added complexity of separate service accounts for each site and utilize the security override feature on the various connectors for inter-site connectivity that crosses domain boundaries.

Site Topology Planning

In planning your Exchange sites, you are not required to map to your domain topology. Site planning is based on factors that are independent of the requirements of domain design. Defining the number of sites and the site boundaries is more dependent on your company's messaging requirements, and how messaging resources are affected by your network topology. For you to properly plan your Exchange site topology, the following requirements must be met within a single site:

- Synchronous RPC connectivity between all servers
- Continuous network connectivity
- Same security context for service accounts
- High-speed available network bandwidth

Your site planning will also include other factors such as administration, performance, link costs, data replication, and the structure of the organization. For example, you might want to create separate sites for two distinct corporate divisions at one physical location to allow for separate administration and different SMTP e-mail domain names. On the other hand, you might want to plan for sites based on geographic location and assign servers to the different organizational units for administration of messaging resources.

You cannot fully determine the number of sites your organization needs until other planning steps are completed. You will probably change the number and location of sites many times throughout the planning process as you discover additional requirements. Because it is very time-consuming and nearly impossible to change site names after installation, the site planning process should run parallel with the entire planning process. You should begin to add proposed site configurations to your organizational topology map as early as possible, because this step will help the team visualize the message routing and site relationships within the organization.

Establishing Naming Conventions

Are your current naming conventions loosely based on cartoon characters or popular names for dogs? How many servers on your network have the same name because that name "sounded good"? This section is specifically targeted at your organization, because these unstructured naming conventions will create many problems if used in your Exchange messaging system. Determining meaningful names for the objects in the Exchange directory will help users and administrators find the messaging resources they need. Establishing naming conventions that are not affected by the ever-changing business environment will also minimize the need to frequently rebuild resources.

Because Exchange is built on an X.400 engine with X.500 directory services, your naming conventions should follow the recommendations of these standards. The X.208 recommendation defines characters that are "printable string types," and the Exchange directory objects conform to this standard. Table 21.2 lists the allowable characters according to the X.208 recommendation, "Abstract Syntax Notation One" (ASN.1).

Table 21.2. The X.208 recommendation of allowable printable string types.

Characters	Printable String Type
A, B, . . . , Z	Capital letters
a, b, . . . , z	Small letters
0, 1, . . . , 9	Digits
(space)	Space
'	Apostrophe
(	Left parenthesis
)	Right parenthesis
+	Plus sign
,	Comma
-	Hyphen
.	Full stop
/	Solidus
:	Colon
=	Equals sign
?	Question mark

The two most important names you must plan for before installing your first Exchange Server are the Organization and Site names. The Organization name should embrace the name of the entire company, must be unique, and cannot be changed. Site names should be related to the site's location, building name, or a user-identifiable code. Site names must also be unique and cannot be changed without a complete reinstall of all servers within the site. Even though these names can be up to 64 characters in length, you might want to limit them to 10 or fewer characters for interoperability with external legacy systems.

Windows NT naming standards define the allowable characters for the NT computer name. Because Exchange uses the NT computer name as the Exchange Server name, you should use meaningful computer names for your servers. You cannot change the Exchange Server name without reinstalling, so use server names that are related to the site. Windows NT Server names are limited to 15 characters, and they *cannot* contain the following characters:

- Bullet — A round bullet character
- Currency sign — $
- Broken vertical bar — ¦
- Section sign — §
- Paragraph sign — ¶
- Space — A space (for login script support)

Installing Exchange Server and Mail

CHAPTER **21**

451

21

INSTALLING
EXCHANGE SERVER
AND MAIL

Each object in the directory has a distinguished name, which is a concatenation of the organization name, site name, recipient container, and recipient mailbox. An example of a distinguished name for a user would be o=Dataflex/ou=Clearwater/cn=Exchange Recipients/ cn=GDodge. This name can also be abbreviated by removing the labels for the naming components such as the o= and cn=. Each object also has a valid X.400 address that allows for interoperability with other X.400-based systems.

Because every organization will want to connect Exchange to the Internet, you should consider the limitations of SMTP-based systems. You can use alphanumeric characters such as upper- and lowercase letters *a* through *z*, the numbers 0 through 9, and hyphens. The Internet address generator will use these restrictions to generate appropriate SMTP-type addresses for all exchange recipients, and you should plan appropriately in your naming conventions.

Server Planning

When your boss asks you to estimate the number of servers needed in order for your organization to implement Exchange, keep a very straight face and answer, "Without the appropriate planning, I estimate we need one server for every twenty users." After your boss regains his or her composure, explain that the worst-case ratio of users to server is 20 to 1 when imaging applications are used. You should then explain that a proper analysis of the user's messaging needs can help to determine the optimal size and number of servers for your organization.

Planning your organization's server requirements is more of an art than a science. You need to be aware of the current messaging, scheduling, and groupware needs of your users, and you should be able to determine these needs well into the future. You also need to be up-to-date on current and future hardware designs, as you might be asked to predict the direction the hardware industry is taking. Determining the number of servers in a site, and the primary roles of each server, requires good visualization techniques.

These are the factors you should consider for planning server hardware requirements:

- System memory is used to cache the directory for user object queries, transferring data to and from users and the message stores and maintaining connection information for each user.
- The system CPUs process requests for data from users, gateways, and system processes according to the NT multiprocessing model.
- Network adapter cards handle all traffic from servers to users and between MTAs.
- The disk subsystem provides storage capacity for system files, the directory database, and the information stores.
- The system's backplane handles all aggregate intercomponent data transfer and is determined by the bus and expansion slot architecture.

Two schools of thought exist regarding planning for the size and number of servers. One method is to purchase many inexpensive servers and distribute them throughout the organization; the other is to acquire a few expensive high-performance servers with one for each site. I suggest that you tailor your hardware resources with a combination of both, depending on the specific needs of each site. Select hardware that can be easily upgraded over time, giving you the flexibility of adding resources as your messaging system grows.

Inter-Site Connectivity

Planning your site topology involves the selection of connectors to facilitate mail transfer, directory replication, and public folder replication between your sites. These selections will also determine how messaging data will route throughout your organization based on the cost associated with the various message types. These are the connector options that can be used to link sites together:

- Site Connector
- Dynamic RAS Connector
- X.400 Connector
- Internet Mail Connector

Site Connector is the easiest connector to configure, but the most demanding on network bandwidth. When using the Site Connector, plan for net *available* bandwidth between the sites to be no less than 64K, and it must support permanent synchronous RPC connections. Servers in the sites using this connector have a many-to-many relationship, which means that message transfer is from the source server directly to the destination server with no additional hops. Message transfer and replication are fast and efficient, assuming that the network is capable of supporting this type of connection. Connections cannot be scheduled or controlled because servers are continuously connecting as needed.

Dynamic RAS Connector connects sites via asynchronous modem, X.25, or ISDN connections, and it is limited in the amount of data the pipe can handle. This connector is best used for organizations that do not have an established WAN, and need to provide site connectivity for many remote locations. Routing should be designed to have a hub site that all remote sites connect to, with messages and replication happening at scheduled connect times. This connector is also a good solution for planning backup connections for WAN or network outages.

The X.400 Connector is the most versatile of the connector options, and it allows a higher degree of control over the routing structure and message transfer properties. Bridgehead servers are configured at each site, and redundant routes for load balancing and fault tolerance can be established by assigning costs to each connection. If you are planning to utilize a public X.400 network backbone, this option only requires that the appropriate network transports be loaded for each MTA. Connections can be scheduled and message size controlled through this connector, giving you flexibility in planning how Exchange will utilize network bandwidth.

The Internet Mail Connector can also fit into your plan for connecting sites, but you should use it with caution due to its limitations. Connections can be scheduled and message size controlled, but data is transferred in plain-text format and has to be converted to and from Exchange native format and SMTP between the sites. This option fits best into your routing plans as a higher-cost backup route in case another connector or route fails. You might also decide to use the IMC to connect your sites over the Internet, but we all know how dangerous and unreliable the Internet can be when it comes to your mission-critical business data. Who would you call when the Internet is down?

External Connectivity

Exchange connectivity to external systems is very robust, supporting connections to MS Mail 3.*x* post offices, X.400 native systems, and SMTP-based systems. Exchange can also connect to other systems through MS Mail gateways, enabling you to leverage existing connections that might not be available in a native Exchange connection. You should plan to install these external connections only at sites that have direct connectivity to these systems. This method will enable you to develop a routing topology that allows all Exchange sites to utilize these connections, eliminating the need to install the connectors at each site.

In the MS Mail environment, the Microsoft Mail Connector uses a "shadow" post office and Exchange MMTAs to link to existing post offices. Your plan for connectivity to MS Mail should also include switching to the directory synchronization server built into Exchange to produce a more robust global address list. You can also set up Exchange to be both a dirsync server and a requester, creating a tiered design to the MS Mail dirsync structure and thus solving many problems for large organizations. If you have MS Mail AppleTalk networks, the AppleTalk MTA and gateway component should replace existing 1.0 or 3.2 connection gateways to MS Mail.

TIP

If you need to provide connectivity between existing MS Mail for PC Networks and MS Mail for AppleTalk networks, Exchange is your answer. When it's configured, you can replicate the AppleTalk mailbox addresses to the MS Mail 3.x post offices without installing the gateway access component. Because each custom recipient for the Macintosh addresses contains a valid network/post office/mailbox (10/10/10) e-mail address, users on the MS Mail 3.x post offices can mail to these addresses, and Exchange will route them to the appropriate AppleTalk server through the MS Mail AppleTalk MTA.

Connections to legacy X.400 systems are made through the built-in X.400 Connector. If your routing plan calls for the use of X.400 Connectors to link sites, you can leverage this backbone for message transfer to external systems. Bridgehead servers can be configured at one site or multiple sites to provide the lowest-cost routing to external systems. You should plan for at least one X.400 Connector for every external ADMD and determine whether you want those connectors to act as relay MTAs. This portion of your planning should be straightforward, and it will easily provide the level of service your messaging system requires.

The Internet Mail Connector will fit into any organization's plan to provide mail connectivity with the Internet or local SMTP hosts. The number of IMCs needed for your organization will depend on your current network connections to the Internet and the message volume you expect to support. You can use two Exchange Servers configured with IMCs to load-balance your SMTP mail, or you can configure one to handle outbound traffic and the other to handle the inbound traffic to divide the load. You even have the option of allocating an IMC for each site and configuring it to only queue SMTP mail for that site for eventual delivery to a site that has an active IMC with Internet connectivity.

TIP

To use the IMC to transfer mail to a dial-up connection at an Internet Service Provider (ISP), you need to use the RASDIAL.EXE program and a custom batch file. You first must make arrangements with your ISP to hold mail at that server and to dial up at predetermined times for mail transfer. Also, your IMC should be configured to forward all mail to a specific IP address, the address of your ISP's mail server.

Configure a RAS phone book entry for scripted logon to your ISP, and test the connection. Then create the batch file imcdial.bat, with the following format:

```
@echo off
:top
rasdial RAS Phonebook Entry name here
net start msexchangeimc
REM Use sleep command from NT resource kit to stay connected for XX minutes
sleep 30
net stop msexchangeimc
rasdial /disconnect
REM Use sleep command to wait for XX minutes
sleep 60
goto top
```

Save the file in the \exchsrvr\bin directory, and create an icon in your StartUp group that points to this file. If you do not want to log on to your Exchange Server every time you want to start this process, use the Windows NT resource kit utilities INSTSRV.EXE and SRVANY.EXE to create a service to run this process. Be sure to assign the Exchange service account to your newly created service in Control Panel so that it has the proper rights. If you have installed service pack #2 on your Exchange servers, you can select the RAS connection to use in the IMC properties page. This eliminates the need for the batch file, but you should still test the RAS connection first.

Installation Procedure, Step-by-Step

Now that you have a well-defined plan for implementation of your Exchange messaging system, it's time to examine the process of installing the server software. This section begins with the assumption that you have successfully installed Windows NT Server Version 3.51 on your system and applied service pack #4 from the Exchange CD-ROM. The computer name of your NT Server should follow the naming convention you decided on in the planning process, and the appropriate amount of system resources such as RAM and hard disks should already be configured. The installation steps for Exchange Server are as given here:

1. Run the program SETUP.EXE from the directory \setup*platform* on the CD-ROM, in which *platform* refers to I386, Alpha, or MIPS. See Figure 21.3 for the directory contents on the Exchange CD-ROM.

2. Click on OK at the welcome screen shown in Figure 21.4. This is the start of phase 1 in the install process.

3. You are presented with the different installation types pictured in Figure 21.5. The installation types install the following components:

   ■ Typical: Installs the Exchange Server and Administrator

   ■ Complete/Custom: Installs the Exchange Server, Administrator, and all connectors

   ■ Minimum: Installs only the Exchange Server

   It is suggested that you always select the Complete/Custom type.

FIGURE 21.3.

*Directory contents of
the Exchange
CD-ROM.*

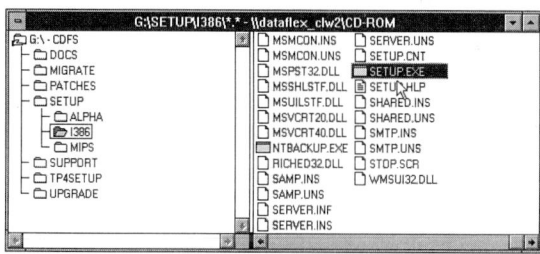

FIGURE 21.4.

*The Exchange Server
Setup welcome screen.*

FIGURE 21.5.

*Exchange Server
installation types.*

4. If you click on the Change Directory button, you can specify the drive and directory to install the Exchange components in. See Figure 21.6 for this selection.

FIGURE 21.6.

*The Change Directory
selection.*

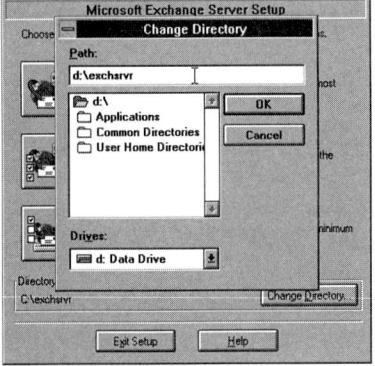

Confirm creation of the new directory by clicking on OK.

5. Because you should have selected Complete/Custom, you should see the options list pictured in Figure 21.7. Select the options you want to install.

6. If you click on the Change Option button while the Exchange Server selection is highlighted, you can choose which connectors and sample applications to install, as shown in Figure 21.8. Click on OK when you are done with your selections.

7. Click on OK from the Complete/Custom options list to proceed to phase 2 of the install.

8. The screen shown in Figure 21.9 prompts you to join an existing site or create a new site.

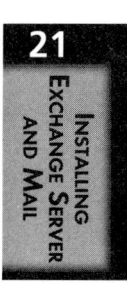

FIGURE 21.7.

*Complete/Custom
options list.*

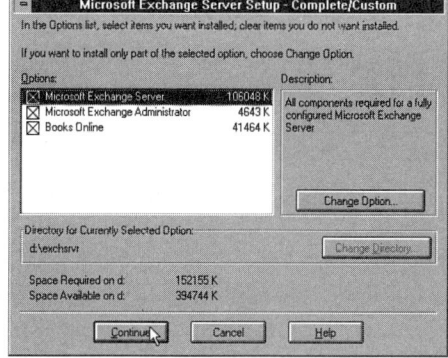

FIGURE 21.8.

*Exchange Server
options list.*

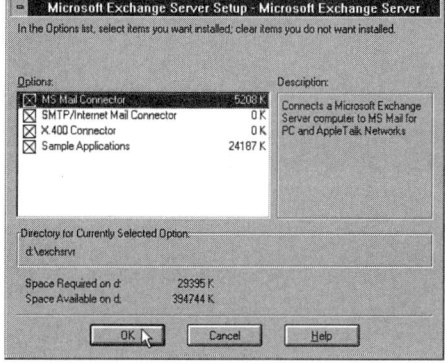

FIGURE 21.9.

*Organization and site
information.*

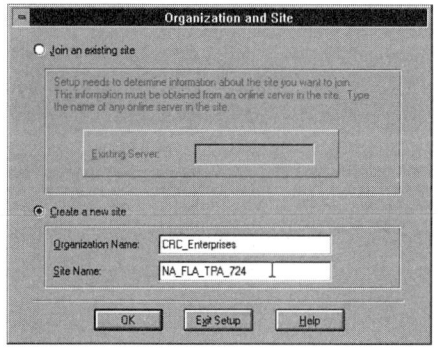

9. If this is your first server in a site, you should choose to create a new site. The Organization and Site information are automatically filled in from the registry, but you should override this information with the names you established in the planning stage. After you click on OK, you are prompted to confirm the creation of a new site, as shown in Figure 21.10.

FIGURE 21.10.

Confirmation of the creation of a new site.

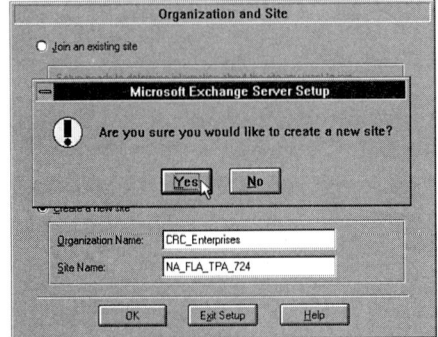

10. When you choose to create a new site, the next step is to select the service account the Exchange services will run under. Click on the Browse button and select an account you created in your planning sessions. You then need to supply the password for the account to continue, as shown in Figure 21.11. You might receive a message stating that the account has been granted the Log on as a Service and Restore Files and Directories rights if this is the first Exchange Server to use this service account in the current domain.

FIGURE 21.11.

Selecting the Site Service Account for the Exchange services.

11. If you are adding a server to an existing site, you need to select to join an existing site and enter the server name of an Exchange Server in that site, as pictured in Figure 21.12. You then need to confirm that you want to join the organization and site listed for the server, as shown in Figure 21.13.

FIGURE 21.12.

Joining an existing site via an existing server name.

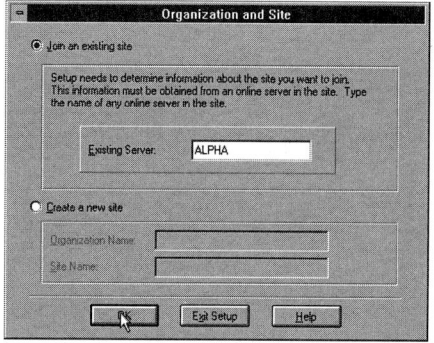

FIGURE 21.13.

Confirmation to join an existing organization and site.

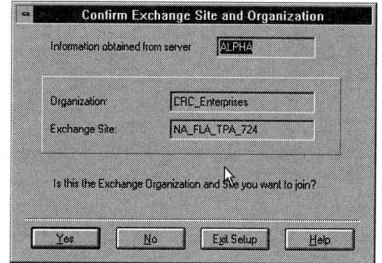

12. The install process now begins phase 3, which carries out the following actions:

- Records setup settings to the registry
- Creates the setup log file
- Copies the files and creates the script for an uninstall
- Configures Exchange registry keys
- Launches Exchange services
- Configures the directory
- Installs the connectors
- Creates the shares on the Exchange Server
- Replicates the directory (for a new server in an existing site)
- Creates program manager items

13. The phase 3 portion of the install ends at the screen shown in Figure 21.14. I suggest that you skip the optimizer for now, because it is covered in a following section, Configuration Tasks After Setup Is Complete. Click on the Exit Setup button to complete your Exchange Server install.

FIGURE 21.14.

Exchange Server Setup complete dialog box.

You have now successfully installed an Exchange Server, unless you experienced problems during the install. If setup failed or you received any weird messages, you should find an answer in the next section. If the setup still fails after you have gone through that section, verify that you have met all the requirements outlined earlier in this chapter. If you are still having problems, it is time to get on the phone with Microsoft Product Support Services (PSS), or contact your Microsoft solution provider.

Issues and Possible Obstacles

The actual install process for Exchange seems fairly easy until you encounter an error that halts or ends the setup process. The installation process can bring up a few known problems, but these have easy workarounds. If you experience a problem on your first try at an installation, then I say try, try again.

If you attempt to install Exchange on a version of NT later than 3.51 (NT 4.0), you might experience many setup errors concerning files that cannot be copied because they are open. You might also see this error message if you are running any mail-aware applications in the background during the install. In both instances note the name and location of the file, and click the Ignore button. After the install is complete, verify that the file on your local hard drive is newer than the one on the CD-ROM, and copy it from the CD-ROM if necessary.

Another problem can arise if you select a group for the service account when prompted during the install. The setup process should not let you do this, and it is a known bug. You need to manually assign the proper service account to all the Exchange services in the control panel, as well as the appropriate permissions in the Exchange administrator.

If you receive the message The service did not start due to a logon failure, you might have typed the service account password incorrectly. It is more likely that you left the checkbox for "User must change password at next logon" checked when you created the account in User Manager for Domains, and it needs to be unchecked. You might also see this message if your account replication pulse has not completed and you are installing from a BDC. Wait a few minutes for the user database to replicate, or use the server manager to force a replication immediately.

In very rare instances, immediately on starting setup you might receive an error message advising you that you do not have the "teletex" code page installed from service pack #4, even though service pack #4 is installed. This is because the file C_20261.NLS was not properly registered as a language support module when service pack #4 updated the system. You should copy this file to the %systemroot%\system32 directory of the NT Server and add the file value to the registry for the key \HKLM\System\Current Control Set\Control\NLS. Setup should continue correctly after doing this procedure.

Configuration Tasks After Setup Is Complete

Immediately after finishing the setup, you will want to run the Exchange Performance Optimizer in verbose mode. To run it in verbose mode, modify the properties of the icon for the optimizer, and add the -v option to the command line. The performance optimizer is a straightforward procedure that analyzes the system resources of your server, asks you some pertinent questions about the role of the server, and tests the hard-drive access speeds for performance-tuning purposes. You should run the Exchange performance optimizer any time you modify hardware resources or your organizational needs change. You can override the file locations to better match where you want specific components to be stored.

Now that your Exchange Server is installed and tuned, it is ready for configuration of the various system components. This task includes, but is not limited to, the following actions:

- Configuring the various connectors to link sites
- Configuring directory replication between the various sites
- Disabling circular logging for the Information Store
- Setting up nightly backups of the DS and IS
- Setting up and configuring the MS Mail Connector for 3.*x* post office connectivity
- Configuring the directory synchronization server and each MS Mail 3.*x* post office
- Configuring an Exchange Server to act as a directory synchronization requester to an existing MS Mail dirsync server
- Configuring the IMC for Internet or SMTP connectivity
- Configuring the X.400 Connector to external systems
- Establishing the site addressing for SMTP and X.400 address spaces
- Importing or configuring replication of foreign addresses from other systems

When you are satisfied that the system components you defined in your planning process are properly configured, you can start moving actual users to the system. At this point, I highly recommend that you expand your pilot to include additional users outside the initial pilot, which will allow you to really exercise the system.

Your deployment plan should be well-defined by this time. You should begin to test-migrate groups of users to document the conversion process. Train the people who will be responsible for the actual desktop deployment, because they need to be comfortable with the process. The more you test at this stage, the smoother your deployment will be.

Verifying Successful Installation

The best way to verify that the system is installed correctly is to let the users tear into it. Users have the uncanny ability to discover those configuration issues you did not identify in your planning sessions. They have a vested interest in being involved in testing the system because they will have to use it every day to perform their jobs. Don't allow your fears of supporting users in this "pilot" test keep you from getting them involved, or you might regret your actions later.

One very valuable tool for testing the capacity and stability of your newly installed Exchange Server is loadsim. Loadsim enables you to simulate the messaging patterns of many users from a few NT workstations. This tool gives you the ability to test how well you planned your message routing and site topology, and to test the impact Exchange will have on your network bandwidth. After you run the loadsim tool a few times, you will have solid performance statistics concerning your network and server hardware that will enable you to eliminate system bottlenecks.

As your site topology and message routing are established, you will want to configure server and link monitors to constantly test site connectivity and server uptime. This way, you can simulate network outages or slow response times to see how your design will react. You can also modify the actions your monitors will take for various problems, and establish which administrators are alerted to different system outages.

While you are testing the validity of your system design, send as many test messages as you can. You should have test accounts on each of the systems to which Exchange is connected to verify that the connectors are working correctly. Send all types of test messages, such as those with large attachments, many attachments, long subject lines, and very complex rich-text formatting. You might discover that messages that worked correctly on your previous system now will not transfer correctly within Exchange. This technique gives you more time to work on fixing these problems early on instead of wrestling with them during your deployment project.

Summary

Exchange Server is a very complex messaging system that requires a structured planning process for proper implementation. Planning for adequate hardware resources to support the organization's messaging needs far into the future will allow for the immediate growth associated with any conversion. The Exchange network requirements affect how your site and routing topology impact the network bandwidth. Careful consideration should be given to determining the needs of your organization's users, support professionals, and management so that they can be matched to Exchange messaging services.

The connectivity options for inter-site connectivity need good planning to match the best connector to the link's support capabilities. Connections to external systems will affect how your message routing topology is determined, creating new challenges for your planning team. The installation of the Exchange Server software is a simple process, assuming that you have done the necessary planning up to this point. After the software is installed, you should validate and verify that the design works as the planning sessions specified to be able to meet the needs of the organization.

The next chapter covers the administration, maintenance, and troubleshooting of the Exchange messaging system. Topics covered include disaster recovery, troubleshooting, configuration of the connectors, assigning permissions, and managing user mailboxes.

Administering Exchange Server and Mail

by Gregory Dodge

IN THIS CHAPTER

22

CHAPTER

Most e-mail engineers regard the flexibility of administration in messaging servers and clients as the most important feature in any product. Rarely do they have to interface with the installation process, and system design tools are normally used only throughout the planning stage of an install. Administration and troubleshooting are daily tasks, which can become mundane at times. User mailboxes need to be deleted and created, distribution lists must be updated, mail delivery problems must be researched, global address lists must be kept up-to-date, system outages must be fixed, and many other routine tasks must be done to keep the system healthy.

Mail systems range from the small workgroup post office to thousands of messaging servers for an entire enterprise—each with different needs for administration and maintenance. As an administrator, you might be responsible for only a few servers with fewer than a hundred users, or a member of a large group of administrators responsible for keeping tens of thousands of users' mail running smoothly for an entire organization. Messaging systems are very dynamic in nature as the needs and structure of an organization grow. Each messaging system is as unique as the company that uses it, but a common set of basic tasks are needed to provide messaging services.

This chapter takes you through the different administrative features of exchange and explains how they can be utilized to keep the system running smoothly. It discusses how the Exchange tools can manage users, servers, distribution lists, connectors, MTAs, public folders, and Groupware applications. It also explores how to set up and use the disaster prevention and recovery tools available throughout the system. Because these systems are built by man, and broken by man, there is a section on what tools are available to troubleshoot system problems. Maintaining secure access to messaging resources is at the top of everyone's list, and this chapter provides the details of how security fits into Exchange administration.

As you read through this chapter, keep this very important thought in mind: there is rarely only one way to perform a specific task or use a feature in Exchange. I will try to point out the different methods available where possible, but you will routinely come up with new methods of your own. This flexibility in choosing the way to get your job done only accentuates the robustness inherent within Exchange Server.

Guided Tour of Administration

The heart of managing any messaging system is the administrative software. It should provide a single view of the messaging resources for your entire organization and enable those resources to be managed from any location. Because it is estimated that over 72 percent of the cost of implementing a client-server messaging system comes from keeping it running, the administrative applications must be robust enough to reduce the time and costs of administration. Exchange Server includes a single-view graphical administrative application that enables you to manage all the various components of Exchange Server from a single interface. From this view, you can manage the following components and objects:

- Mailboxes, recipients, and distribution lists
- Servers, information stores, and associated services
- Connectors, MTAs, and transports
- Link and server monitors
- Directory replication and directory synchronization
- The global address list for an entire organization
- Public, private, and system folders
- Organization and site information
- Electronic forms and Form libraries
- Permissions on all directory objects

The Exchange administration program is started from the icon located in the Microsoft Exchange program group for any Windows NT server or workstation on which it has been installed. The path and filename for the program is <drive>:\exchsrvr\bin\admin.exe if you accepted the defaults for the installation procedure. Remember that Exchange supports various hardware platforms, so don't try to run the alpha version of the application on an Intel machine and vice versa.

The layout of the administration program is simple, but highly informational. When you connect to an Exchange Server at either program startup or by selecting Open from the File menu, a window is opened that displays all the directory information that server is aware of. The leftmost frame contains an organizational view of the Exchange directory hierarchy with the root-level organization, the public folders, the global address list, and each of the Exchange sites that have been replicated, including the local site. The frame on the right contains specific information on the directory object that is selected in the left frame. See Figure 22.1 for an example of the Exchange Administrator user interface.

FIGURE 22.1.

The Exchange Administrator program user interface.

Pull-down menus

Selected object frame

Status bar

Hierarchical directory view

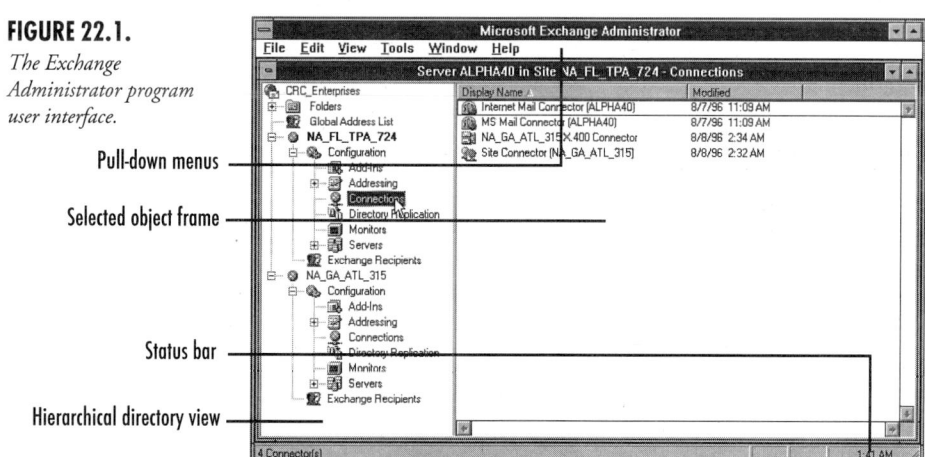

Selecting objects from the left frame exposes the objects relating to the selection in the right frame. If you click on a site object in the left frame, for example, you see the configuration object and all the recipient containers for that site. You can also expand the branch of any object in the left frame that has a plus sign attached to it and see the objects within that branch connected with a dotted line. The local site of the server you are connected to will show up in bold, and replicated sites will be in normal lettering. This method of displaying the Exchange directory enables one to easily traverse the hierarchy to "drill-down" to an object that needs to be managed. Changes can only be made to the site corresponding to the server you have connected to, so you might want to have connections to many servers at once.

Across the top of the interface are the menu selections used to perform various tasks. These menus can be used in combination with the selection of a directory object or used to perform tasks that are not specific to any directory object. Many of the menu selections have associated *hotkeys* that can be used if you prefer not to use the mouse. Although I do not suggest that you learn how to operate this program totally by the keyboard, you might find that many of the keyboard shortcuts are much easier than the corresponding series of mouse clicks. You might be faced with a situation where the mouse has stopped functioning on a server, and you would not want to disconnect hundreds of users from the system just so you can reboot to restore mouse functionality.

For the majority of daily administrative tasks, you use the File menu selection. It includes selections for connecting to Exchange Servers, creating new mailboxes, creating new custom recipients, creating distribution lists, creating other (connector, dirsync, and so forth) objects, displaying the properties for a selected object, and exiting the program. See Figure 22.2 for the File menu selections available.

FIGURE 22.2.

File menu selections.

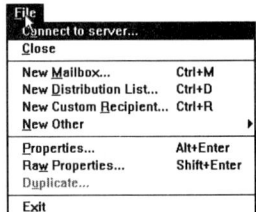

The Edit pull-down menu is used for the various editing features that can be done on certain objects. These objects include recipient containers, recipients, distribution lists, transport stacks, MTAs, and other objects that are not permanent to the administration program. The View pull-down menu is used to change the appearance of the left and right panes, and can be used to expand or contract a single branch or the entire list. This can be very useful for collapsing many branches if you have been searching the tree for a specific object.

Very often overlooked, but very important to keeping the system running, is the Tools menu. It contains the utilities for extracting user accounts, importing and exporting recipients, managing electronic forms, moving or creating mailboxes, and setting program options. As you proceed with a migration or need to change a user's proxy address, these menu selections will be used very often. See Figure 22.3 for the menu selections available under the Tools menu.

FIGURE 22.3.

*Selections available
from the Tools menu.*

The drop-down menus for Window and Help operate just like any standard windows CUA menus. The Window menu enables you to tile, cascade, move, and resize the windows opened for each server connection. The Help menu is designed to give both context-sensitive help and topic search capabilities. The online books for Exchange are used for the help topics and as replacement for the printed manuals.

TIP

The first time you start the administration program, the default values are set for many very important options. You should customize the interface immediately to your needs and make sure that certain custom defaults are configured. To customize the interface, select the Tools root menu, then click on the Options selection. From this page, you configure the default mailbox naming conventions, the Windows NT domain to use for creating new accounts, the different tabs that can be displayed (such as Permissions), and whether NT accounts are deleted when a mailbox is removed. A few minutes should be taken with every new install of the Administrator program to make sure these settings are consistent and meet your requirements. There is nothing more aggravating than to find out that another administrator is creating nonstandard display names or is not able to see the permissions tabs for objects.

Managing User Mail and Mailboxes

How quickly and easily can you create new user mailboxes in your current system? After you create those names, how long does it take for the new account to make it to all the appropriate address lists to enable current users to mail to that person? It takes a considerable amount of your time to perform these tasks, even if you have been doing it for years. Many of the older messaging systems were not designed to handle the fast pace of most companies' business needs. Messaging systems must make speedy mailbox implementation and propagation their primary focus to be able to support the demands of enterprise-level systems.

The user mailbox is the core messaging object that exists in the Exchange directory schema. Exchange has four ways to create user mailboxes and three ways to modify and delete them. The administration program is used for two of the methods, and the NT user manager for domains is the other option. User accounts can also be created using the migration and extraction tools, but they cannot be modified or deleted using these tools. The following examples take you through the best way to use each of these methods.

Let's first examine the most common scenario for creating a new user mailbox. Your company, CRC Enterprises, hires a new employee for the Tampa office in the southeast division. You receive an internal form instructing you to create the appropriate accounts needed for this new user to work, and the form indicates that Bud Johnson will start today. Your company uses both Windows NT and Novell 3.x servers, with a Master domain named CRC_MUD for user accounts and DSMN for managing Novell accounts. You are located in the company's headquarters in Atlanta, which is connected to Tampa by a 256K frame relay connection.

Because you are working from a Windows NT Workstation that does not have the NT Server administration tools installed, you will use the Exchange Administrator program to create the account. You first connect to the server in Tampa, and then expand the site for Tampa named NA_FL_TPA_724. Next, select the recipient container named "Recipients" from under the site, and click on Create New Mailbox from the File menu. This brings up the Mailbox properties sheet, as seen in Figure 22.4.

As you enter his first, middle, and last names, the display name and alias are automatically created as you type. The method used to create the display name and alias is configured under the Options selection from the Tools menu. You then can enter the appropriate extended information, such as address and departmental data. After entering the information for the mailbox names and extended information, click on the Primary NT Account button to set the NT account for his mailbox. Because in this example you do not have account management capabilities, you should select to use an existing account that was previously created by one of the NT account operators. Browse the window to find his appropriate NT account, and click on Add, then on OK to finish your selection.

FIGURE 22.4.

Mailbox General Properties sheet.

TIP

You might not want to get carpal tunnel syndrome from typing all the extended information for every mailbox—so why not use a template. To set a template for accounts created at a specific site, expand the recipient container in that site, and create a mailbox named something like Template. Fill in the appropriate values for any of the common fields, and make any other selections on the other properties pages. You can choose to make this mailbox hidden from the directory on the Advanced page so users will not mail to it. Use this hidden mailbox as the template account for migrations or bulk imports.

To continue to set up Bud's mailbox, you proceed to the Organization Properties page. Here, you select who his manager is and who the people are who report directly to Bud. This information can be used in Groupware applications or to help create an instant view of the organizational chart. You can choose only people who directly report to Bud from the local site, but you can assign Bud as the manager to a user at another site. See Figure 22.5 for Bud's Organization Properties page.

The tab for Phone/Notes is used to enter additional information for Bud, such as his phone, beeper, fax, and cellular phone numbers, and any additional notes for this mailbox. These properties can be very useful for an organization as a replacement for company phone lists. Because Bud has requested that his cellular and beeper numbers not be published, we will leave those fields blank. See Figure 22.6 for Bud's Phone/Notes Properties page.

FIGURE 22.5.

Organization Properties page for a mailbox.

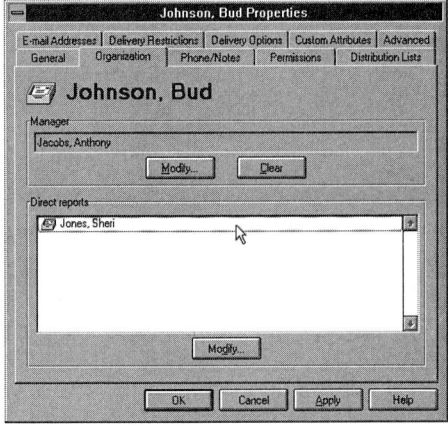

FIGURE 22.6.

Phone/Notes Properties page for a mailbox.

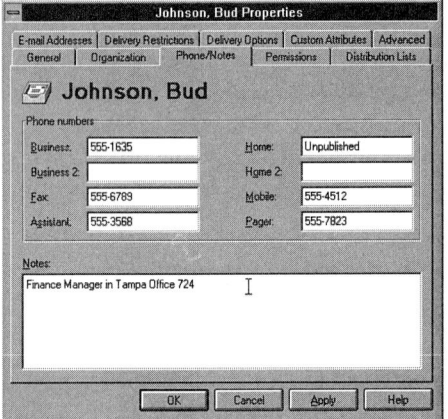

If you checked the "Show Permissions" box in the Options selection from the Tools menu, you will see a Permissions tab for his mailbox. From this page, you can see that the NT account for Bud already has user permissions to his mailbox, and other accounts can administer his mailbox. Here, you can assign other accounts to have Send as or User permissions, but this should be used with caution. If you want another user to be able to send on Bud's behalf or read his mail, use the Delivery Options tab. See Figure 22.7 for an example of the Permissions page for Bud's mailbox.

FIGURE 22.7.

Permissions page for a mailbox.

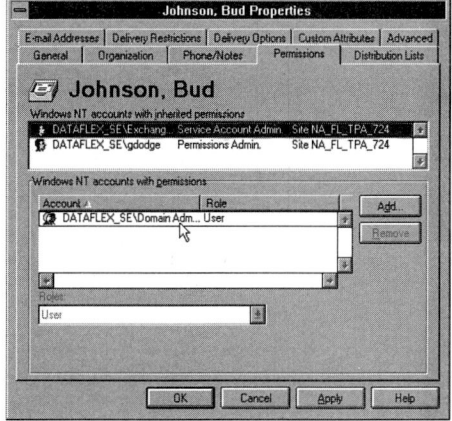

Next, you click on the page titled Distribution Lists to add Bud to the lists he requires. From this page, you can only add Bud to existing distribution lists, so make sure to create them before adding any mailboxes. It is probably easier to add the users to distribution lists as they are created, but this will enable you to add new users to multiple preexisting lists. See Figure 22.8 for an example of the lists of which Bud will be a member.

FIGURE 22.8.

Distribution Lists Properties page for a mailbox.

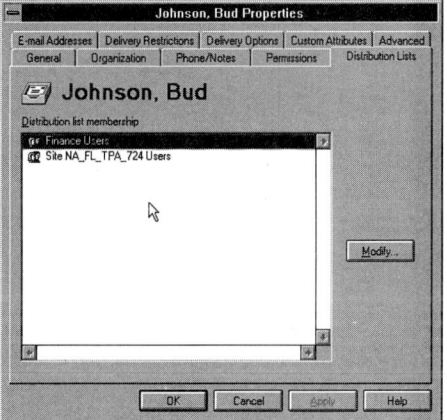

The Delivery Restrictions page is normally not used for individual mailboxes, unless that mailbox needs to interact only with certain recipients, such as for an application. Because Bud does not need any restrictions on his mailbox, you accept the defaults for this page. This Properties page might also be used to restrict who can send mail to the CEO or CFO so it can be screened through their assistants' mailboxes. See Figure 22.9 for the Delivery Restrictions page for Bud's mailbox.

FIGURE 22.9.

Delivery Restrictions page for a mailbox.

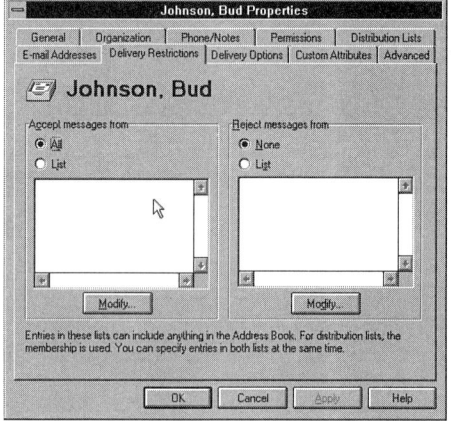

The Delivery Options page is going to be helpful for Bud, because it will enable his assistant to attend to his mail while he is on the road. You click on the Modify button to select his assistant's mailbox for Send On Behalf Of permission. This enables his assistant to send mail for Bud—for example, if he wants to send a message to his team but cannot get to his laptop until the evening. This example does not use the alternate recipient option for Bud's mailbox, but it would be useful if he wanted his assistant to get copies of all the mail sent to him. See Figure 22.10 for the Delivery Options page for Bud's mailbox.

FIGURE 22.10.

Delivery Options page for a mailbox.

The Security tab is only available if you are using the Key Server service for advanced security, and it is covered in the section "Key Management Server" in more detail. The Custom Attributes page is only useful if you have decided to add additional data fields to the Exchange schema. This could contain company-specific information and is customized under the DS site Configuration Custom Properties page. CRC Enterprises has decided to use a few custom attributes to contain employee-specific data to enable cross-referencing to the human resources database. Figure 22.11 is an example of the Custom attributes for Bud's mailbox.

FIGURE 22.11.

Custom Attributes page for a mailbox.

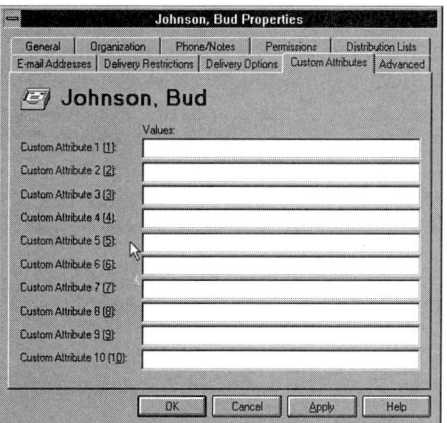

CAUTION

The custom attribute fields can be modified only by the Exchange service account and the account that was used for the exchange install. For this reason, install Exchange Server from an account named E-Mail Administrator or something equivalent, and *never remove that account.* Even though this can be seen as a limitation, it is useful in keeping the custom attribute fields the same throughout the organization. The custom attributes should not be different at each site, because it will confuse users with information that does not seem to belong in a certain custom field.

The Advanced Properties page is very useful in controlling various mailbox capabilities. From here, you can set limits on the size of messages this mailbox can send or receive, as well as override the amount of storage space allocated to this mailbox. You can also control whether this account is replicated to other locations by trust level, or hide the recipient from the address book. Because Bud will be a remote user that will only access his mailbox a few times a week, you increase the amount of space he has on the server and add that he is a remote user to the Administrative Note field. See Figure 22.12 for the Advanced Properties page for Bud's mailbox.

FIGURE 22.12.

Advanced Properties page for a user mailbox.

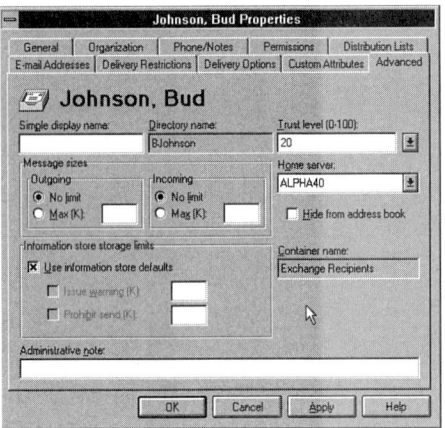

Since you are finished entering the information for Bud's mailbox, click the OK button to save the information and return to the contents window. As you are going through the various tabs when creating a user mailbox, click on the Apply button to save the current data before you go to the next tab. Bud's new mailbox is now ready for him to use, and it instantly showed up on the global address list for the local site. The account information will be replicated to all the other sites based on the replication interval configured at the site, so others in the organization will be able to mail to him as soon as possible. The information in his mailbox can be modified by this method at any time by opening the properties for his mailbox. This can be done by double-clicking on his mailbox or clicking once on his mailbox and pressing the Alt+Enter keys. This concludes this method for creating a new user account.

This method differs in that you are on a workstation that has the NT Server administrative tools and the Exchange administrator program installed. You also have account administrator rights, and you are responsible for creating his NT user account. This procedure is helpful for those administrators already familiar with adding NT user accounts with the user manager, and who might forget to create a mailbox for that user. Remember to install the Exchange administrator program on all machines that will be used for administration, and configure the application options the same. This installs the application extension, MAILUMX.DLL, which adds Exchange functionality to the User Manager for Domains application.

To begin, open the User Manager for Domains application and add an NT user account for Bud with the information required for your company. When you click on the Add button, you are prompted for the Exchange Server to connect to and then see the same Mailbox General Properties page, as in Figure 22.4. From here, use the same procedures outlined previously to enter information for Bud's new mailbox. You will also notice in Figure 22.13 that a new pull-down menu item, Exchange, is available in the user manager interface. This can be used to modify the properties for a mailbox associated with the NT account you have selected.

FIGURE 22.13.

*Creating a mailbox
from the User Manager
for Domains.*

In both of the previous methods, you can delete any user account or associated mailbox from the application interface. If you delete an NT user account from User Manager for Domains, you are prompted to also remove the associated mailbox. If you set the option in the Exchange administrator program for removing NT accounts when mailboxes are deleted, you are also prompted for removal of the NT user account when deleting mailboxes. As you can see from the previous examples, these two methods are not useful if you have a large number of users that need new mailboxes.

To create, modify, or delete a large number of users at an exchange site, you will use the directory import feature found on the Tools menu. This method works with standard comma-delimited files that can be created from many sources, such as your human resources database or one of the Exchange source extraction tools. To create a sample of this type of file, export a few users into an export file from the Administrator program. A list of all the key words used in the header of the file is located in the online help.

For this example, assume that Bud is a member of a large group of new employees that were just hired, and they are currently going through an orientation training class. You need to create accounts and mailboxes for over thirty individuals, making sure that all required fields are filled in for each user. You get a comma-delimited file with information on each of the new employees from the human resources department, but it does not contain data for all the fields you need. The following procedure can be used to get the file imported into Exchange:

1. Open the file in Microsoft Excel or a program that can work with comma-delimited files.
2. Add any additional fields to the top row, making sure to verify spelling.
3. The first column must have the header value Obj-Class with the value of mailbox.
4. The second column should have a header of Mode with the value of Create.
5. Be sure to add columns for the common name, display name, alias, and any other fields you have data for from the HR file.
6. Save the file in comma-delimited format, with the extension CSV.
7. Open the Exchange Administrator and select Directory Import from the Tools menu.
8. Select the appropriate recipients container, a recipient template, and the import file you saved in step 7. Check the Create Windows NT Account checkbox, as seen in Figure 22.14.
9. All other values can be left at the default, so click on the Import button to proceed.

FIGURE 22.14.

Directory Import dialog box.

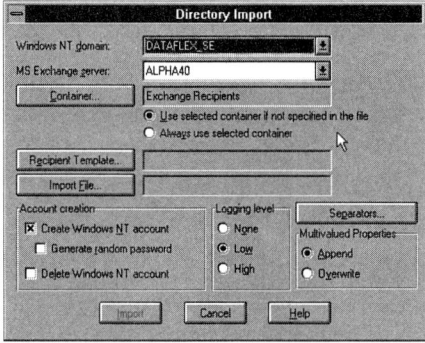

Because you received a very well-populated file from HR, and you used a template account with the other default values filled in, you are now ready to leave early for home with the knowledge that the new users will be able to access their e-mail tomorrow. You can also follow these procedures to modify existing fields within the directory database or delete accounts in batch mode. A good example of modifying current accounts is using this procedure to add values to the Secondary Proxy Addresses field to create aliases for SMTP mail delivery.

> **CAUTION**
>
> If you use Microsoft Excel to manipulate your import and export files, beware of the 256-character limitation for any field. If any of your fields have more than 256 characters (the E-Mail Addresses field, for example), use another program to edit it. Microsoft Access or many third-party editors are better choices because they will not have the same limitation.

In the previous example, you could have also created the import file from other sources. Your current messaging system or NOS already has lots of data that can be used to create Exchange mailboxes. The Exchange Administrator program has extractors on the Tools menu to build import files from current NT domains or NetWare servers. The migration directory on the Exchange Server CD-ROM also contains source extractors for the most popular messaging systems. You can also create your own source extractors to get information out of your current messaging system, or create the import file from databases that contain the information you need.

Managing Servers

The Exchange Server might be the most modified directory object in the schema, after user mailboxes and distribution lists. Servers consist of a set of core services that can be individually configured to override any settings for the site. Each server in the site has the following core components:

- Server Recipients
- Directory Service
- Directory Synchronization
- Message Transfer Agent
- Private Information Store
- Public Information Store
- System Attendant

This section discusses the options available for managing the services and resources available at each Exchange Server. Most of the configuration of the services for each server is done from the Exchange administration program, but management of the services is done through either the server manager or the services icon in Control Panel. Server administration can be broken down into four areas:

- Server services
- Server monitors
- Server properties
- Server information stores

The other two areas for administration of Exchange Servers, the directory service and message transfer agents, are discussed later in this chapter.

Server Services

Because Exchange Server runs exclusively on the Windows NT Server platform, it is composed of various services. Each installation of Exchange Server has the same services installed, even if they are not configured or running on that machine. These services store many of their runtime parameters in the Windows NT registry, and they store any directory-related information in the directory database. See Figure 22.15 for the services installed on every Exchange Server.

FIGURE 22.15.

Exchange Server services.

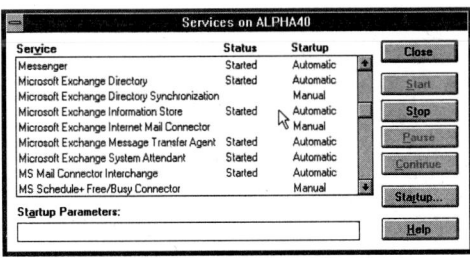

These services are managed normally from the server manager application, but they can also be accessed through the services icon in the control panel. Each service is configured to log on using the service account defined in the server installation. The default startup parameters are for the system attendant, information store, MTA, and directory service to start automatically, with the other services defaulting to manual startup. As you configure each of the services, you need to change the default startup option to allow the service to start automatically, such as the IMC or Directory Replication services. Always check the Event Viewer for messages from these services, depending on the diagnostic level specified for each service.

Some of the services have keys in the Windows NT registry that control the behavior of that service. Modification of these keys should be done with extreme caution, and you should create a emergency recovery disk before you modify anything in the registry. Many of these key values can affect the performance of the services or change the behavior of certain features. Normally, you add or modify these registry values only if instructed by product support or a well-written tech note. You might want to take some time to familiarize yourself with the various values, and they can be found at `HKLM\SYSTEM\CurrentControlSet\Services\MSExchange*`, where * represents a specific service name.

Server Monitors

The server link and service monitors are very powerful proactive troubleshooting tools; every Exchange Server should have at least one of each configured for each server. The Monitors container can be found under the configuration container for a site, and it can be used to monitor one or more servers within that site. You need a machine with the Exchange Administrator program installed to run the monitors from, and it should be running at all times.

The following procedure sets up a link monitor at a site:

1. Click on File, New Other, Link Monitor.
2. On the General Properties page, enter the Display Name for this monitor and the polling interval you need.
3. On the Notification page, select the recipients or distribution lists that will receive the notifications.
4. From the Servers page, select the servers this monitor will use.
5. From the Recipients page, select the recipients that will be used to test the links. You can select recipients that do not actually exist so the Non-Delivery Report (NDR) can be used as the bounce message.
6. On the Bounce page, select the parameters for the times used to test whether a link is down.

The following procedure can be used to set up a server monitor for a site:

1. Click on File, New Other, Server Monitor.
2. On the General Properties page, enter the Display Name for this monitor and the polling interval you need.
3. On the Notification page, select the recipients or distribution lists that will receive the notifications and the notification type.
4. From the Servers page, select the servers this monitor will watch.
5. On the Actions page, specify which actions to take on the first, second, and subsequent hits of stopped services. The actions can be the following: take no action, restart service, or restart computer.
6. On the Clock page, set the properties for clock synchronization and the amount of drift time that will create system alerts.

For each of the monitors you create, give them descriptive directory names that describe what they are monitoring. Create only one or two server monitors in a site, depending on the site topology and network bandwidth available. It is also a good practice to create one link monitor for each link you want to test, to give you more flexibility in the notification process. Although you can overlap monitors from various sites to monitor each other, this can become confusing as your system expands.

Server Properties

Each server within a site has a properties page that can be accessed by clicking on the server and then selecting the Properties option from the File menu (or by pressing Alt+Enter). The properties for each server are Services, Locales, Database Paths, IS Maintenance, and Diagnostic Logging. These options are specific to each server and do not have corresponding global site equivalents.

The server Services page lists all the services running on that server and which of those services will be monitored through a server monitor. Any services installed on the server can be added to the list of monitored services, but you should limit your selections to services that are pertinent to Exchange. You might want to add a service such as RAS or RPC to the list of services to monitor, but would not want a service such as "DDE Server" to be monitored.

The Locales page controls how date, currency, and time values are displayed for the various international languages. Other system settings, such as sort order and language support, are affected by the locales installed. Locales should be installed and configured for all languages the client programs will be using. For instance, if your server will be servicing both U.S. English and Spanish clients, both locales should be installed and configured.

The Database Paths Properties page lists the locations of the various databases and transaction logs for the Exchange components. Although this page enables you to make changes to the locations, you should always use the Exchange Optimizer application to make such a change. If you feel real adventurous and have a confident backup of your system, stop all services before making any changes here.

The IS Maintenance page enables you to determine at what times database maintenance functions will be executed. Because IS maintenance slows systems performance, it should be scheduled for a time when no users or backup processes will be using the server. If you are a 24-hour shop, select an appropriate time outside your backup window that the system can run a little slower. Do make sure that this is configured to run at least once daily, or your Information Stores may get "dirty" over time.

The Diagnostics Logging page for the server enables you to set logging levels for all the components that make up Exchange Server. These logging values can be found on the properties page for each of the individual components, but this is the one place where you can find them all together. If you are troubleshooting the system, this is the first place you should go to control the amount of detail you will see in the Event Viewer.

Server Information Stores

Each Exchange Server has a private message store and a public message store, regardless of the resources configured for the server. Many of the options available for configuration of these components have site-based configuration properties, such as the message store limits and public folder configurations. These properties pages enable further granularity in configuration of these values for each server. This enables you to set up servers differently, such as a dedicated public folder server or an entire server for the finance group.

The private message store properties control the user's private mailbox configurations and enable administrators to easily view the current resource usage at a particular server. Storage limits can be established to issue warnings to users when they reach a certain mailbox size, and prohibit that users send capabilities when they reach a larger value. These settings can be overridden at the individual mailbox level, and override the values established at the site level.

The public folder server page enables an administrator to specify where all the top-level public folders are created for users on this server, enabling the separation of the public and private stores to different servers. This is useful for servers that have a large number of users and need to optimize public folder access for the site.

The Logon and Mailbox Resources Properties pages are useful in seeing how many users are connected to the server in real time and how much space each of them is occupying on the server. This is helpful for troubleshooting user connection problems, because the logon page can be customized for the columns that are displayed. You will probably go to the Mailbox Resources page just before cleaning any user mailboxes to find out who your "worst" users are. These pages can be useful to your tuning process, because it gives real-time data.

Managing Connectors and MTAs

The server and mailboxes are the most frequently modified directory objects, but the connectors and MTAs are the objects that most frequently modify other objects. The MTAs are the backbone of message transfer within the site, and between sites. The connectors are the "translators" that move messages between Exchange and external systems, or between configured Exchange sites. These components are very dynamic in nature, constantly monitoring the routing tables and message delivery statistics to guarantee the shortest message transfer times.

The connector options available within exchange are designed to connect sites for message transfer and directory replication. The capability of performing directory replication between sites and transferring exchange native messages is what separates connectors from standard gateways. Each of the connectors relies on messaging transports to support its services, as well as an MTA to control the flow of those messages. This section describes the administrative interfaces to the various transports, MTAs, and connectors.

MTAs and Transports

Because the Message Transfer Agents are used in intrasite and external communications, there are many places to configure the various parameters that control how they operate. Each MTA has a properties page to control messaging parameters for that individual MTA instance. Each server has a properties page that controls parameters for the MTAs running on that server. Each Exchange site has configuration parameters that will affect any of the MTAs within that site.

The site MTA configuration properties are obtained through the MTA Site Configuration object in the configuration container within a site. The General page has properties for setting enabling message tracking for the site. If you enable message tracking, the MTAs for the site record every message they transfer in the daily tracking logs, enabling administrators to track messages within the site. See Figure 22.16 for an example of the General Properties page for the MTA Site Configuration object.

FIGURE 22.16.

MTA Site Configuration General Properties page.

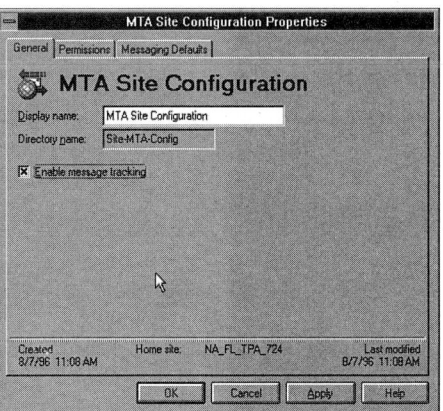

The Messaging Defaults page of the MTA Site Configuration object control the parameters for messaging time-outs for the site. These values include the Return To Sender (RTS) parameters that control how long the MTA tries to send messages. There are also transport-specific values for connection retry and transfer time-outs, to enable some tuning of message transfer within the site. See Figure 22.17 for an example of the Messaging Defaults Properties page for the MTA Site configuration.

FIGURE 22.17.

Messaging Defaults parameters page for MTA Site Configuration.

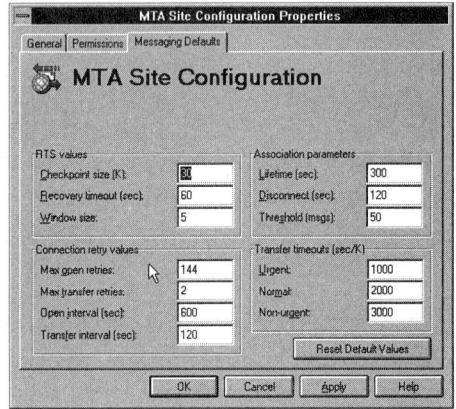

The Server MTA Properties pages control how the MTA on a specific server operates. There is a General, Queues, and Diagnostics Logging Properties page for this object. The General Properties page enables the administrator to set the MTA name, password, and maximum message size when the routing tables are calculated. See Figure 22.18 for the parameters available on the General Properties page.

FIGURE 22.18.

General Properties page for the Server MTA.

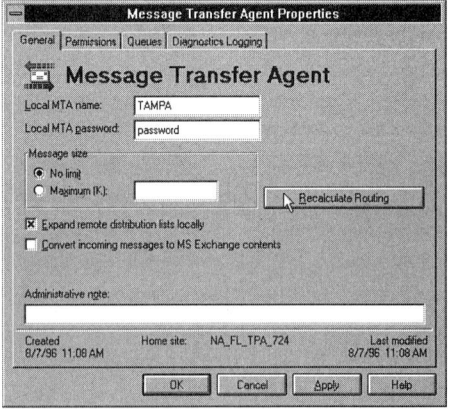

The MTA Queues Properties page is a valuable tool for troubleshooting message delivery. If you suspect that messages are not getting out of the site, check here to make sure the messages are not still in the MTA queues. From the Queues Properties page, you can view detailed information on messages, change the priority of any message, and delete messages destined for any external site or connector. See Figure 22.19 for an example of the Queues Properties page for a server's MTA. The Diagnostics Logging Properties page is a common page for any object and controls the detail level of MTA message logging.

FIGURE 22.19.

Server MTA Queues Properties page.

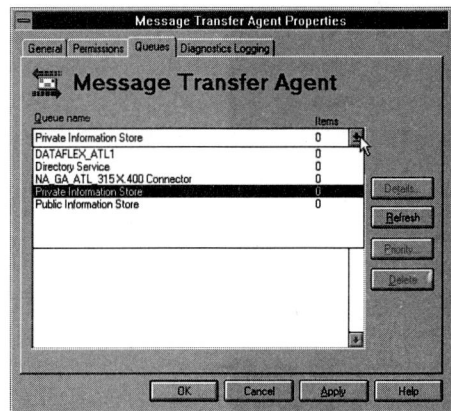

Each MTA for a connector will have properties pages specific to the type of message transport for that connector. These administrative pages are described with the associated connector because each has properties specific to the connector.

Connectors

Exchange has four message transport connectors and one directory transport connector available in the enterprise edition of the server. The message transport connectors can be used to connect exchange sites or link to other messaging systems. The directory transport connector is used exclusively for replicating directory schema information between connected sites. The following are the four message transport connectors:

- Site Connector
- Dynamic RAS Connector
- X.400 Connector
- Internet Mail Connector

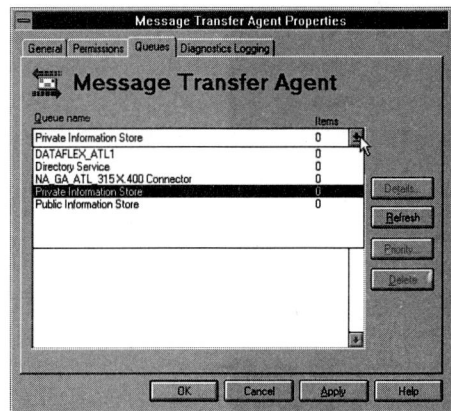

The MS Mail connector is discussed in Chapter 24, "Interfacing with Other Mail Systems," because it is related to interfacing with MS Mail-based systems. The MS Mail connector cannot be used to connect two exchange sites, as is customary with the limitations of the MS Mail protocols.

Site Connector

The Site Connector is created by choosing the File, New Other, Site Connector option. You will be prompted for the name of the site you want to connect to, and the name of any server in that site. You must have rights to the servers in the other site to enable you to configure both sites during the setup. Once created, the Site Connector has four Properties pages for General, Target Servers, Address Space, and Override options.

The General Properties page has the display name and directory name of the Site Connector, which defaults to Site Connector (site name). The target site for this connector is displayed for read-only, but you can modify the cost associated for this connection. You can also specify the messaging bridgehead server in the local site. If you use a local messaging bridgehead server, any messages destined for the remote site will be sent only by the server you name as the bridgehead, which can be helpful in controlling message traffic. See Figure 22.20 for an example of the General Properties page for the Site Connector.

FIGURE 22.20.

General Properties page for the Site Connector.

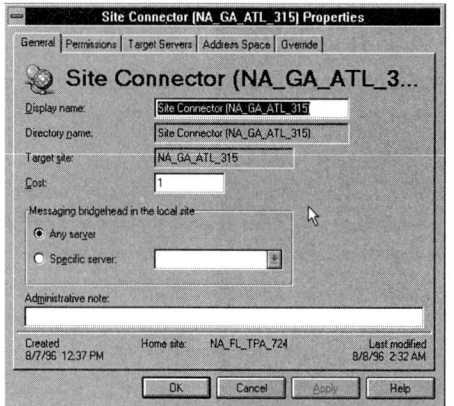

The Target Servers Properties page is used to specify which servers in the remote site can be connected to for message delivery. The server you specified when you set up the Site Connector will already be in the Target Servers list with a cost of one. Other servers in the site can be added to the Target Servers list by clicking on the server name and clicking on the Add button. See Figure 22.21 for an example of the Target Servers Properties page.

FIGURE 22.21.

Target Servers Properties page for the Site Connector.

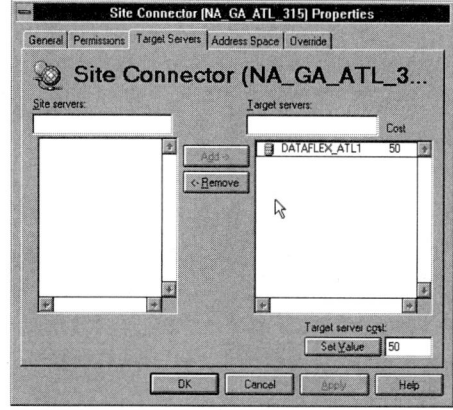

The Address Space Properties page is used to specify address spaces with costs for message routing to the remote site. The X.400 address space is automatically entered when you configure the Site Connector, and is assigned a cost of one. When entering an address space, you need to enter only enough of the address to distinguish which messages will be routed to the remote site. The Address Space Properties page is common to all the connectors, so Figure 22.22 is a standard properties page. The override page is used to specify an NT user account to connect to the other site, and is available in other connectors.

FIGURE 22.22.

Address Space Properties page for the Site Connector.

Dynamic RAS Connector

The Dynamic RAS Connector is created by choosing the File, New Other, Dynamic RAS Connector selection. Before you create a Dynamic RAS Connector, you must create an RAS transport stack. You will be prompted for the name of a server in the remote site, the remote site name, and the RAS phone book entry to use for connection. You should set up and test the RAS phone book entry before setting up this connector, or use the RAS override feature. It is also advisable to set a maximum message size to keep extremely large messages from tying up the connector. See Figure 22.23 for an example of the General Properties page for the RAS Connector.

FIGURE 22.23.

General Properties page for the RAS Connector.

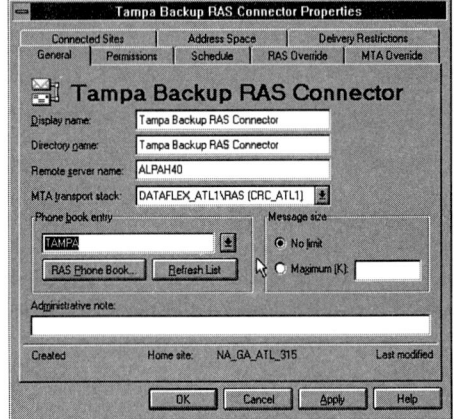

The Permissions and Schedule Properties pages are the same as the others used throughout the other connectors. The Permissions page controls which accounts have associated permissions to the RAS Connector. The Schedule Properties page is used to specify at what times the RAS Connector will make connections, and it can be set for hourly or fifteen-minute intervals. The RAS override page can be used to specify the NT security information and phone numbers to override any values in the RAS phone book entry. See Figure 22.24 for the RAS Override Properties page. The MTA Override Properties page is the same as depicted in Figure 22.17.

FIGURE 22.24.

RAS Override Properties page.

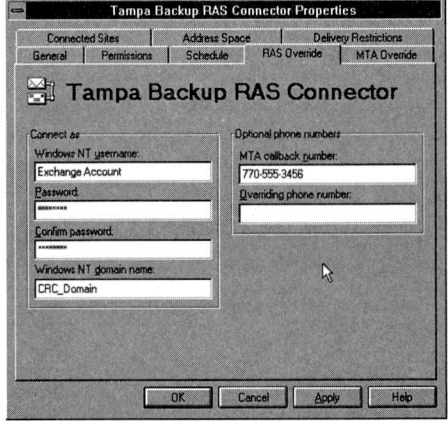

The Delivery Restrictions Properties page for the RAS Connector is the same as in Figure 22.9, and it is not normally used. The Address Space page is used to create routes for message types and associate the appropriate costs. For the RAS Connector, use high costs unless it is the only connection to a site. The Address Space page is the same as depicted in Figure 22.22. The Connected Sites page is common to the RAS, X.400, and Internet Mail Connector, and is used to ensure that directory replication can take place (see Figure 22.25).

FIGURE 22.25.

Common Connected Sites Properties page.

X.400 Connector

Before you can create an X.400 Connector, you must first create an MTA transport stack. To create an MTA transport stack, select File, New Other, MTA Transport Stack and select the appropriate type. You can create MTA transport stacks on X.25, TP4, and TCP/IP, but normally you use TCP/IP. You can optionally also configure the OSI TSP information, if needed for legacy system connections. See Figure 22.26 for an example of the General Properties page for an MTA transport stack.

FIGURE 22.26.

General Properties page for an MTA transport stack.

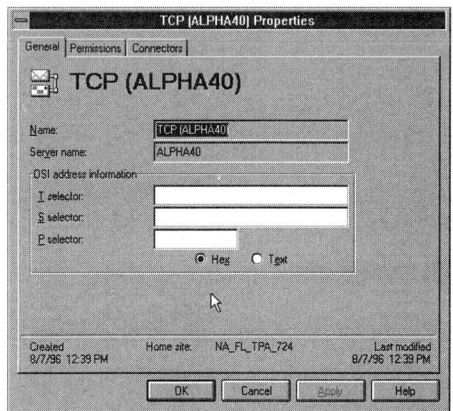

Once you configure the appropriate MTA transport stack, you can create an X.400 Connector by selecting File, New Other, X.400 Connector. You will be prompted for the MTA transport stack to use. Start at the General Properties page, which has information on the display and directory name of the connector, the remote MTA name and password, and an option for word-wrap and remote client MAPI support. See Figure 22.27 for an example of the General Properties page for the X.400 Connector.

FIGURE 22.27.

*General Properties page
for the X.400
Connector.*

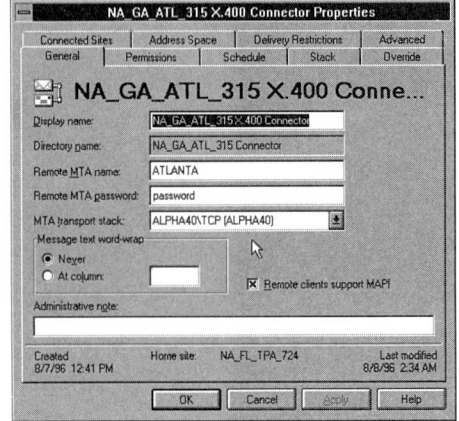

The Schedule Properties page is used to specify the times the X.400 Connector can make connections to the remote MTA, and it allows a remote initiated transfer if both MTAs are configured for the two-way alternate option. The Stack Properties page is similar to the MTA Transport Stack General page, except that you must specify the address or name of the remote MTA. This differs depending on the MTA transport stack, but will normally be the TCP/IP address of the machine that is running the remote MTA.

The Override, Connected Sites, Address Space, and Delivery Restrictions Properties pages are identical to those of previous examples, except that the Override page has the capability of specifying a local MTA name and password. You should refer to previous figures for examples of these pages, because they are configured in the same manner.

The Advanced Properties page for the X.400 Connector has the most critical configuration values for connecting to legacy systems. It enables you to specify the MTA conformance mode, the X.400 link options, message size limitations, the X.400 bodypart to use for message text, and whether to use GDI information from site addressing or specific values. If you are using the X.400 Connector to connect two exchange sites, you will not need to modify these values.

If you are connecting to an X.400 legacy system, you will probably have to modify these values. See Figure 22.28 for an example of the Advanced Properties page for the X.400 Connector.

FIGURE 22.28.

Advanced Properties page for the X.400 Connector.

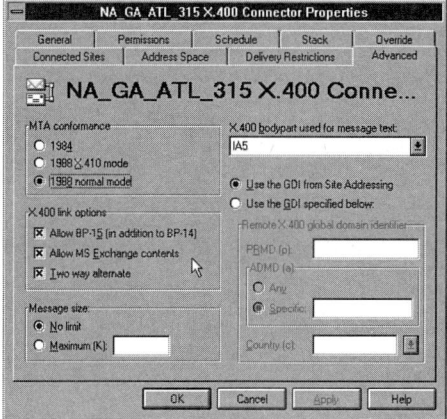

Internet Mail Connector

The Internet Mail Connector already exists in the connections container for the site, and is configured by opening its properties. The first time you open the properties for the IMC, you will see the Internet Mail Properties page as seen in Figure 22.29. Before you can continue, you must select the mailbox to send notifications to by clicking on the Notifications button. From this page you also select the default encoding method for message content and the interoperability options, as seen in Figure 22.30. You can also specify the message content and interoperability options per e-mail domain by clicking on the E-Mail Domain button. This page also has the option of changing the character set translations for MIME and non-MIME attachments.

TIP

Set the default message content to UUENCODE with the rich-text option in interoperability set to Never. This enables your system to interoperate with the majority of systems on the Internet, creating fewer attachment-related problems. You can put e-mail domains that use MIME or that are rich-text-capable in the exception list by specifying Options by e-mail domain. When your list in the e-mail domain gets large, reverse the defaults to make MIME and rich-text the default content types.

FIGURE 22.29.

Internet Mail Properties page for the IMC.

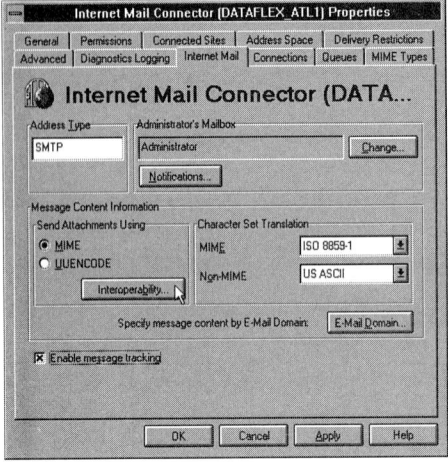

FIGURE 22.30.

Interoperability options for message transfer.

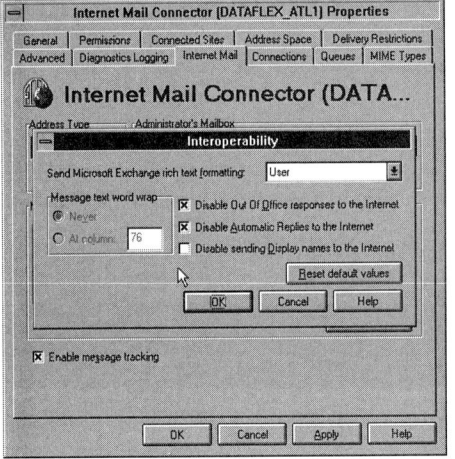

The Connections Properties page enables you to set the IMC transfer mode to handle either inbound, outbound, inbound and outbound, or the "none" transfer mode. This enables you to load balance with multiple IMCs for your enterprise and control where messages flow to your Internet connections. This page also defines whether the IMC uses DNS or forwards all mail to another sendmail host. This is useful if you have a firewall or an existing UNIX sendmail server that needs to handle your message transfer. From this page, you can also specify whether mail is accepted or rejected by the host, the connector retry interval, and message time-out values. See Figure 22.31 for an example of the Connections Properties page for the IMC.

FIGURE 22.31.

Connections Properties page for the Internet Mail Connector.

The pages for Connected Sites, Address Space, Delivery Restrictions, Diagnostic Logging, General, and Queues are similar to the same pages in the other connectors. Because these have already been described and have appropriate figures, please refer to those examples for information on how the IMC will use the similar properties. The Advanced Properties page enables you to set the message parameters for delivery, the maximum transfer times for different priorities of messages, and the message transfer quota size. You can see these parameters in Figure 22.32. The MIME Types Properties page is used to add new MIME content types and extensions to enable proper extension conversion. Refer to Figure 22.33 for an example of the MIME Types Properties page.

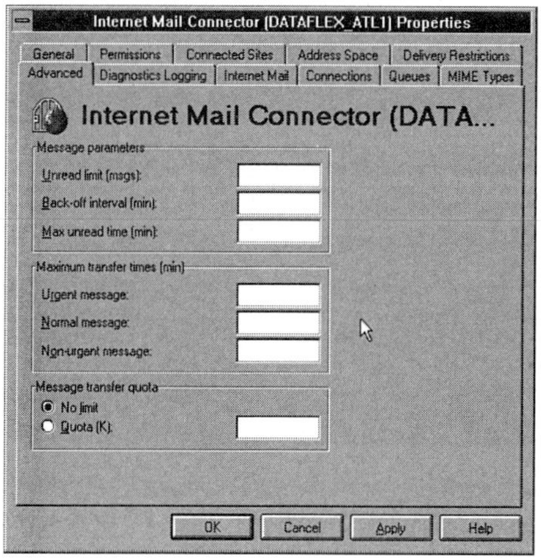

FIGURE 22.32.

Advanced Properties page for the Internet Mail Connector.

FIGURE 22.33.

*MIME Types Properties
page for the Internet
Mail Connector.*

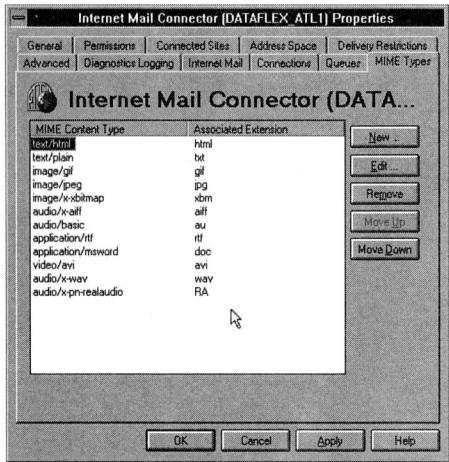

Directory Replication Connector

The MTA relies on the Gateway Address Resolution Table (GWART) to determine the least cost for message routing and the connectors that provide routing for appropriate name spaces. The accuracy of the GWART is dependent on the data from the different connectors and replicated data from other sites. The Directory Replication Connector is responsible for getting that data from other sites to make sure that the MTAs and users have accurate information. The Knowledge Consistency Checker (KCC) is the process that detects new sites and configures replication links to those new sites. This enables one configured directory replication link to gather information about an entire organization without additional administrator intervention.

Setting up a Replication Connector is a simple process, once you have a connector configured to the other site. Make sure to have the Connected Sites page properly configured at each site to facilitate the directory replication. Test the link first by sending a test message to make sure the directory replication messages will make it through.

To set up a Directory Replication Connector, select the File pull-down menu, then New Other, then Directory Replication Connector. You will then be prompted to select which site to set this Replication Connector to. Remember that you only need to replicate to another site replication bridgehead server that has other information for the entire site. The KCC will create replication links to the other sites automatically. Before you set up how your directory is replicated, your planning stage should have identified whether you will use the hub or the cascading routing topology. This will determine which connectors need to have Directory Replication Connector created.

As you can see, the connectors have numerous properties for configuration, but they are very straightforward in the information needed to get them running. As you spend time configuring and managing the connectors within Exchange, you will get more familiar with the locations of the properties you use most. Pretty soon, administration of Exchange Server components will become second nature, and you will wonder how you ever managed your messaging system without them. With such a strong set of administrative tools, the extensibility of the system can only get better in future releases.

Managing E-Forms, Applications, and Public Folders

Microsoft Exchange Server is the e-mail system with integrated Groupware, as Microsoft explains the product. The administration of the Groupware functions built into Exchange involves both the client and administrator programs. Public folders are created and managed from the client desktop, and the administration program is used to replicate the folders throughout the enterprise. Electronic forms are only as good as the ability of users to access them, so you should create forms libraries to use the most common forms. Applications are created and modified within the Electronic Forms designer and placed within public folders through the client application. This section describes the methods used to administer public folders, electronic forms, and applications.

Public Folders

Public folders are created from the client interface by simply selecting the New Folder option from the File menu when selecting the place you want the folder created. They can also be created by copying an existing folder or by using the folder design cue cards available from the Application Design option from the Tools menu. Folders can be created at the root folder level for the organization, or nested within current folders. Once a folder is created at the client, the properties of that folder need to be set to allow proper access and functionality. This involves setting rules for processing messages, setting views for organizing the display fields, setting access privileges, and adding custom forms. The folder properties can be set using the folder design dialog box as pictured in Figure 22.34.

FIGURE 22.34.

*Folder design
dialog box.*

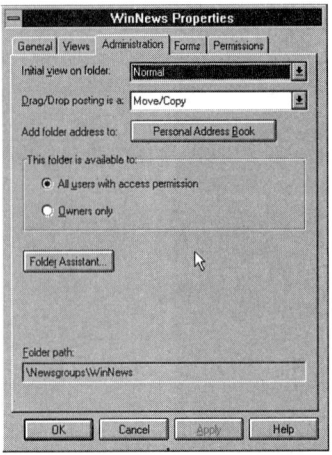

To set the appropriate permissions on the folder from the client interface, the folder owner can use the dialog box in Figure 22.35 to set the user roles and permissions in Table 22.1.

Table 22.1. User roles and associated permissions.

Role	Permissions
Owner	Read items, create items, create subfolders, folder owner, folder contact, edit items (All), delete items (All)
Publishing Author	Read items, create items, create subfolders, edit items (Own), delete items (Own)
Publishing Editor	Read items, create items, create subfolders, edit items (All), delete items (All)
Author	Read items, create items, edit items (Own), delete items (Own)
Reviewer	Read items, edit items (None), delete items (None)
Contributor	Create items, edit items (None), delete items (None)
None	Edit items (None), delete items (None)

To configure public folders from the Exchange Administrator program, select the folder from the organization's public folders container and bring up the folder's properties. This will bring up pages for General, Replicas, Folder Replication Status, Replication Schedule, Permissions, and Advanced. These pages are used to manage where the public folders are located and what servers they are replicated to. The General Properties page specifically enables you to change the folder's name, the alias name, age limits for replicas, and client permissions.

FIGURE 22.35.

Folder roles and permissions.

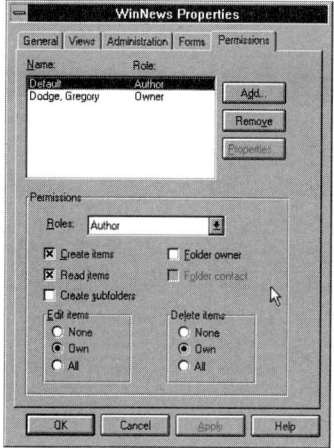

The Replicas Properties page enables the administrator to select which servers have copies of the folder. These servers can be in the same site or located in connected sites. As an administrator, you should take the time to map where certain folders are replicated and how often they are updated. Folder replication can have a large impact on network bandwidth, so try to estimate the amount of data that will change for a folder before deciding where to replicate it. Figure 22.36 shows the Replicas Properties page.

FIGURE 22.36.

Replicas Properties page for a public folder.

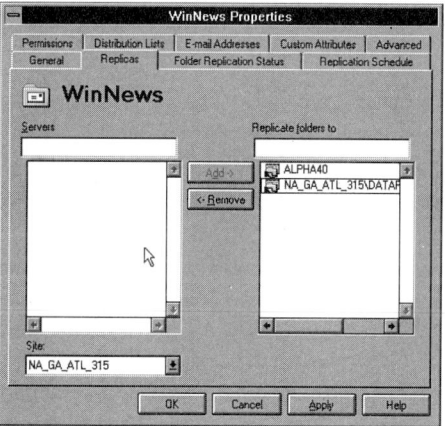

The Folder Replication Status page and the Replication Schedule page are used to monitor and control how the selected folder will replicate. The schedule will control how often the public message store will check this folder for updates and defaults to the schedule set for the public message store for the server. To verify that the folder has been replicated, view the Folder Replication Status page and you will see the status of the replicas of this folder.

The Permissions page for the selected folder will only control the schema security access and has no effect on the user's permissions on the folder. To set the specific folder properties, click on the Client Permissions button located on the General page for the folder. The Advanced tab is used to control the trust level, replication message importance, storage limits, and whether the folder is hidden from the address book. Figure 22.37 is an example of the Advanced Properties page for the public folder.

FIGURE 22.37.

Advanced public folder Properties page.

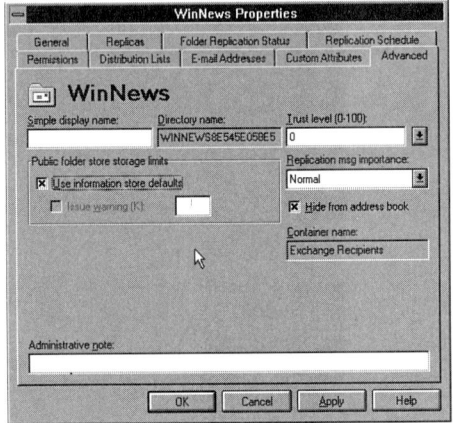

A very important public folder configuration parameter is located in the Information Store Site Configuration Properties page, and it deals with public folder affinity. Public folder affinity is where values are assigned to replicas in other sites to control which replicas of a public folder the local site clients attach to. Sites that do not have affinity will not have any connection attempts for folders from users in this site. When a user attempts to connect to a public folder that is not found in the local site, the connected sites with affinity are searched from the lowest cost to the highest until the folder is found or the list is exhausted. Public folder affinity is useful to guarantee that users will still be able to get to folders if the local public folder is down.

Organizational Forms and Applications

Exchange has a very nontraditional definition of an application, because it is made up of public folders and the electronic forms within them. Public folders have already been defined, but electronic forms are a somewhat different animal. Forms consist of one or more fields that are used to submit and view information in various formats. Forms are associated with a public or private folder, and users compose new forms to enter information into the fields. The electronic forms designer is used to create forms and place them within folders in the organization. An example of the Electronic Forms Designer application interface is seen in Figure 22.38.

FIGURE 22.38.

*Electronic Forms
Designer user interface.*

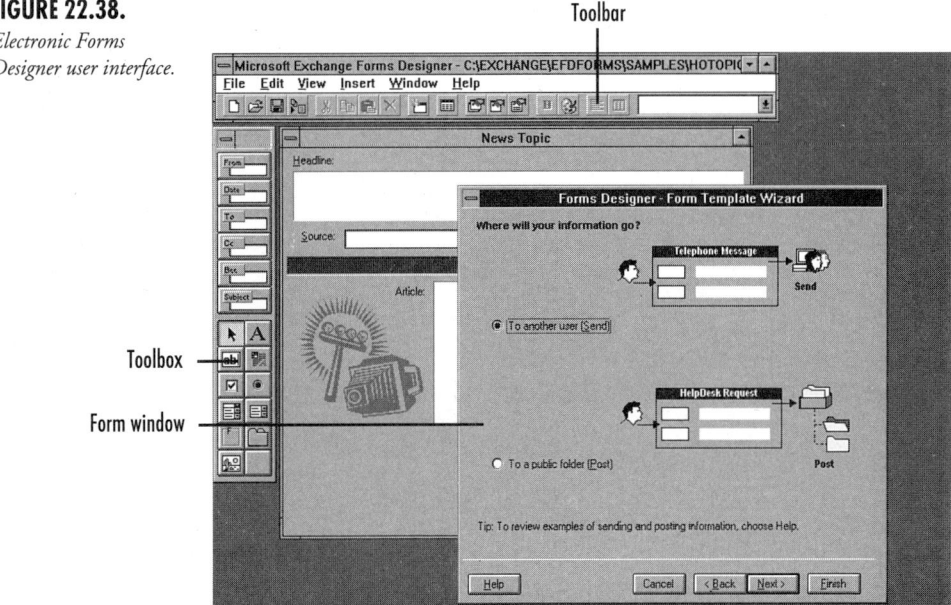

Forms are based on the Visual Basic 4.0 (VB4.0) language, and they can be modified outside the forms designer if needed. Once a form is created, it should be placed within a forms library. There are three types of forms libraries:

- The organizational forms library is a public repository for forms that is available to all users within the organization.

- The personal forms library is a private repository for forms usually located in private folders for private forms.

- A folder library is a repository located in a public folder on a server to be used by anyone who has access to the folder.

Organizational forms libraries are created from the Tools menu and are special folders that can be replicated throughout the entire organization. Public and private libraries are the folders that are created from the client program. Forms are installed in the appropriate library with the Manage Forms button that is available from the client program and the Electronic Forms Designer. Forms are copied to the appropriate library and then made available to the users through the Compose menu or by submitting messages to that folder. Figure 22.39 is an example of the Forms Manager dialog box.

FIGURE 22.39.

Dialog box for managing forms.

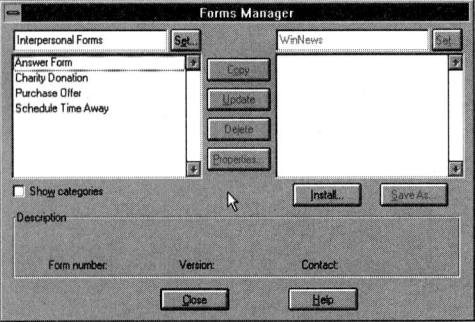

> **TIP**
>
> The organizational forms libraries can be used for many of your send-type forms. Then you can have consistent forms access to users throughout the organization. One such use would be for Human Resources forms, such as vacation requests or time sheets. Make sure that any forms that are installed in an organizational library are the same as any forms installed within folders, or you may have inconsistent forms when users at different sites use them.

Disaster Recovery

Disaster recovery is made possible through the regular backup of the Exchange directory service and information stores with the Windows NT backup program. Exchange installs a new version of NTBACKUP.EXE that is aware of the exchange services and is able to back up and restore these services. See Figure 22.40 for an example of the interface used to back up the Exchange resources.

Other third-party backup programs also have the capability of interfacing with Exchange and backing up the directories and information stores on the servers. Regular nightly backup is needed to assure that you can restore in the case of a catastrophic failure. If you need to restore any part of the system, both the DS and the IS should be restored and a consistency check should be run. The DS/IS consistency check can be performed from the specific server's properties page by clicking on the appropriate button.

FIGURE 22.40.

Windows NT backup interface to Exchange resources.

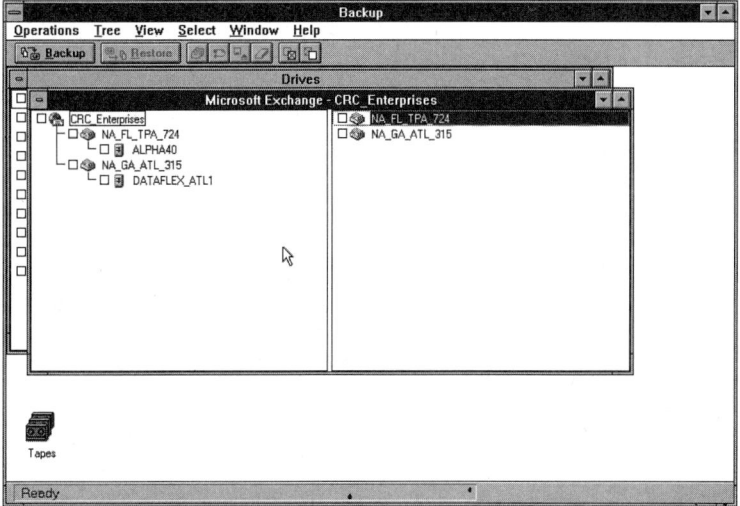

Because Exchange supports restoration only of the entire DS or IS, you need a separate restoration server to be able to retrieve individual mailboxes or folders. This server should have only a copy of Exchange installed and should not be configured to participate in any of your sites within the organization. From this server, you can restore the last backup and then extract the user's mailbox or public folder data to be copied to the production server. Future versions of exchange should enable the restoration of individual mailboxes, folders, and directory information.

TIP

By default, the Exchange backup process is not capable of performing incremental or differential backups, because Exchange Server defaults to having circular logging enabled. This does not enable the log's transactions to be backed up before they are flushed. To disable circular logging, open the properties page for the server on which you want to enable incremental backups. Then uncheck the boxes for circular logging on the DS and the IS. This causes the database logs not to be flushed until the backup process runs, and it should give better performance for high-volume servers. Be sure to disable circular logging when the users are not on the system, because it will stop the directory service and information stores while the change is being made.

Troubleshooting

Troubleshooting a problem with Exchange Server is different for each situation, and this section is only an overview of the tools at your disposal. When looking for an answer to your problem, be sure to use all the resources at your disposal. Many answers to common questions can be bound in Microsoft Technet, which is available on the Microsoft Web site and in CD-ROM format. The Exchange online books are also helpful in finding answers to common configuration and how-to type questions.

When you first determine that you are having a problem with Exchange Server, such as the information store service not starting, try to isolate the nature of the problem with the Event Viewer. All error messages for the Exchange services are placed in the application event log and may have corresponding messages in the system log. The error messages are fairly descriptive and can help point you in the right direction. You may want to increase the level of diagnostics logging for a particular component to give you additional information, and this is available on the Diagnostics Logging Properties page for the component in question.

Always try to stop and restart the service you are having problems with from the service control manager in Control Panel or Server Manager. The services have built-in diagnostic capabilities, and restarting the service will initiate these diagnostic processes. If you are still not successful after trying these steps, take a full system backup of the server. You can then restore to the last-known-good database or configuration. This will correct the majority of system problems, but your specific problem may warrant a call to product support services or a solution provider. Always check with the knowledge base on the Web site or Technet, because you probably do not want to pull your hair out over a problem that someone else has already found and solved.

Security

Secure access to messaging system resources is a top priority for any organization, and Exchange leverages the security built into Windows NT Server. Each object within the directory has both inherited and specific permissions, enabling granularity of security throughout the system. Securing and encrypting messages is also available through the use of the Key Manager service.

NT Integrated security

The Exchange directory databases and information stores have pointers to Windows NT accounts and groups for establishing who has access to what objects. There are three main containers in the hierarchy from which lower objects inherit their permissions: the Organization, the Site, and the configuration container. You can override or add additional permissions to any object from the Permissions Properties page for any object, assuming you have enabled this option from the Options selection under the Tools menu. These permissions are used to grant or deny access to any directory object.

By default, the account used to install Exchange and the service account have admin level permissions to all objects to facilitate Exchange administration. Users get user level permissions to their mailboxes and any public folders they create, and are able to assign the "send on behalf" permission to other users. The "send as" permission can be granted only from the administrator program, and it should be used with caution. Public folders assign access permissions to user mailboxes, which then map to NT accounts. Refer to Figure 22.7 for an example of a Permissions Properties page for a directory object.

TIP

To enhance the security of your system, restrict the logon parameters for the Exchange service account. In User manager for domains, specify the allowed locations for logon under the profile option by entering each server on which this service runs. Use the user rights policy to restrict the capability of the service account logging on interactively, so no person can use the account from the NT user interface.

Key Management Server

Encryption and digital signatures for messages are provided by the Key Management Server included with Exchange. This service is installed separately, and great care should be taken to keep the administration password safe for this service. Once installed, you can use the Advanced Security Properties page for any user mailbox. This creates a security *token* for that user and a somewhat long and cumbersome password that must be given to the user in a secure manner. I suggest that you use voice mail or an equivalent to get users their temporary passwords. They can now enable Advanced Security from the Tools menu, Options selection in the client by clicking on the Setup button and supplying the temporary password you gave to them.

Messages then can be encrypted with standard RSA encoding methods such as CAST-64, DES, or CAST-40 within North America. International versions differ in their encoding methods, governed by laws regarding encryption to other countries. Messages then can be encrypted and signed to other users that are set up for advanced security. If users attempt to send secure messages to recipients that do not have advanced security enabled, they have the option of sending them unsecured or canceling the message.

Additional Tools

Beyond the administration and performance optimizer programs, Exchange includes additional utilities for troubleshooting and performance monitoring. These utilities are installed with the server by default, but do not necessarily have icons created to them.

In the Exchange Server program group created during phase three of the installation process, you will see many performance monitor icons. These are performance monitor charts that enable you to monitor different parts of the Exchange messaging system. There are charts for server health, message queues, server load, number of logged-on users, and various connector status information. These are very helpful tools in analyzing and troubleshooting Exchange Server. You should have a machine running most of these charts somewhere that anyone can check them, because they can be proactive indicators of problems, such as connectors being down or server overload.

The Exchange Server bin directory, \exchsrvr\bin, also contains a few applications that can be used for troubleshooting and testing. The following are the various programs and their usage:

- RESTEST.EXE is used for testing TCP/IP host name resolution to see whether the IMC is able to resolve host and domain names.

- MTACHECK.EXE is used for finding and correcting problems with the MTA database.

- ISINTEG.EXE is used to find and correct corruption in the directory database and the information stores, as well as patching a database that was just restored.

- EDBUTIL.EXE is used for consistency checking and defragmentation of the private and public information store databases.

- RPC Ping server and client are used to test RPC connectivity between a workstation and Exchange Server.

Although this is not a complete list of the utilities available to help you support and trouble-shoot an Exchange Server, these will be very useful for the majority of situations you might be in. There are other utilities, such as client setup editor and loadsim, included with Exchange; They are discussed in Chapters 23, "Mail Clients," and 25, "Exchange Server Performance Tuning and Scaling," respectively. I also suggest that you get a copy of the Windows NT Resource Kit, because it has many utilities, such as PVIEWER.EXE for monitoring processes, that will assist you in diagnosing problems with Exchange. As you already know, utilities are only as good as the vendor that wrote them, and Microsoft has done an adequate job of including many helpful utilities for your time of need. There is a large market for third-party utilities to fill in some of the gaps, so check out the Exchange newsgroups and shareware FTP sites for any additional utilities.

Summary

Because an organization's messaging system is in constant flux, the administrative features must be able to manage this "structured chaos." Exchange Server has a robust administration client that gives you a single view of your entire organization's messaging resources. Managing the objects and resources for sites and servers is made easier with the hierarchical view of the Exchange directory, with properties pages for each object. Administrators just want to be able to do their job quickly and keep their user's messaging flowing to support business processes.

This chapter took you through a guided tour of the administration program used in Exchange and detailed the setup of the various components that make up the system. It explored administration of mailboxes, servers, connectors, MTAs, public folders, and electronic forms and also outlined some disaster recovery options with basic troubleshooting procedures. Security options and other utilities were discussed, with an emphasis being put on how they are used.

The next chapter is on the Exchange client's installation, support, and troubleshooting. Because this is the part your users will interface with daily, it takes special note of the features that will keep your "customers" happy. The client chapter is useful to both end-users and support professionals, because it covers topics important to both. It also assumes that you have an Exchange Server configured and operational, with all appropriate connectors and messaging components.

Mail Clients

by Gregory Dodge

IN THIS CHAPTER

CHAPTER 23

Trying to build a messaging system without any clients is like trying to hold an Olympics without any fans—it might be the best in history, but there would be nobody there to see it. The client application for any messaging system is where the rubber hits the road. The degree of user acceptance is fully dependent on the functionality and ease-of-use of the client interface. If the client application works well, helps in getting the job done, assists in sharing information, and enables users to enhance current business processes, it will be an integral part of a value-added messaging system.

The challenge of any e-mail client is to overcome information overload. As you depend more heavily on any messaging system, the volume and complexity of information increases dramatically. Presenting, managing, and manipulating this information flow is the job of the client interface. The client application should also be able to manage this information in a common format across various platforms. Users are not interested in learning different interfaces for each platform they need to use, and the IS professionals would not be pleased about supporting dissimilar clients.

Exchange client is electronic mail with integrated Groupware, packaged in a single application. It provides a common area to collect, manage, and manipulate electronic messages from various dissimilar systems. It will handle the dirty work of delivering mail to and from various service providers and provide a consistent interface from the Macintosh to the NT platform. End-users can focus on using the messaging and Groupware functions without any worry about how the information is moved throughout the system.

This chapter takes a thorough look at the Exchange client application, Universal Inbox, and Schedule Plus client, providing suggestions for client deployment and troubleshooting. The entire installation process will be explained from beginning to end with suggestions for making the process go smoothly. It will also cover tips and techniques for deploying many clients. Because many of you live and work as I do, roving the countryside attending to business and only going by the office once a month, this chapter discusses the specifics of setting up remote users.

The Universal Inbox

The term Universal Inbox can be found throughout much of Microsoft's marketing literature, but what does it mean? The term "universal" is defined in Funk & Wagnalls Standard Desk Dictionary as "Applicable to everyone or to all cases." Many computer dictionaries define an Inbox as "A container in which new incoming mail, documents, or information is deposited." If you put these two definitions together, you would get a definition of the Universal Inbox as "A container applicable to be used by everyone for all kinds of new incoming mail, documents, and information." This may be a very broad definition, but it does correctly explain the Exchange client's ability to accept messaging information from various services and deposit it into a single container.

The Universal Inbox is just another container within the folder hierarchy in the Exchange client. It is the central repository for all incoming messages, and can exist in any of the various message stores such as a server-based store or a personal store. The location of the Inbox used for message delivery is set by accessing the Delivery Properties page from the Options menu selection available in the Tools pull-down menu in the client. From this page, you set which message store to deliver new messages to, and the selection of a store will automatically create the Inbox, Outbox, Sent Items, and Deleted Items folders. See Figure 23.1 for an example of the Delivery Properties page. From this page, you also set the transport service priority for processing addresses for message delivery.

FIGURE 23.1.

Options Delivery Properties page.

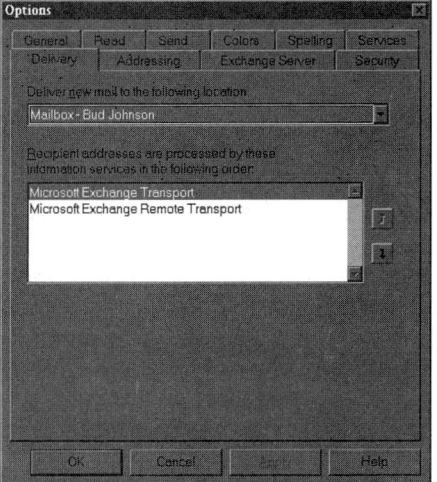

The ability to provide a Universal Inbox for messages is possible because of the various MAPI service providers available for the Exchange client. The MAPI support for the Exchange client includes simple MAPI, CMC, OLE, and extended MAPI, which enables another vendor's application or service to use different interfaces to the Exchange client. These MAPI messaging service providers are responsible for moving messages, providing address books, and storing messages. The three MAPI messaging service providers are defined as the following:

- Messaging transport providers move messages between messaging clients or messaging stores.
- Message store providers supply message storage, organization, and retrieval facilities for a messaging system.
- Address book providers supply message addressing and distribution list facilities to the messaging client.

These messaging services all share a common user interface, the Exchange client. Multiple services of the same type can be installed within the Exchange client, as well as many of different types. For example, you might have a service provider for Exchange Server, a personal message store, CompuServe, and Internet POP3 all installed, and addresses from each of those services would be available. MAPI is able to utilize each of the service providers for message transport and address list access.

An example of a message store is the personal folders service. This service acts as a repository for user mail, and can be used for message delivery to contain the Universal Inbox. The personal folder service will prompt you to specify a filename for storing messages in, and the type of encryption to use for the file. Many of you who support MS Mail 3.x clients today are used to a single file for storing all messages, but Exchange personal stores (*.PST) do not suffer from the compression and corruption problems that were seen in MMF files in MS Mail.

The personal address list service is an example of an address book provider, and is used to store addresses created by the user for any transport service. This service creates a file with the extension of ADB, and I encourage you to use the user's long name if using Windows 95 or NT. Fortunately, this address book does not capture reply-to recipients like the one included in MS Mail, so you may add recipients to your personal address book by right-clicking on their names in the message. The personal address list should be the last address list searched for to resolve names, specified in the Addressing tab in the Options menu. This will ensure that if users have changed their addresses in the global address list, you will not attempt to mail to their old addresses from your personal list. Consistent updating of a personal address list can reduce problems that arise when another user's e-mail address changes.

Different service providers are installed in the Exchange client from the Services Properties page, available from the Control Panel or the Tools, Services option from the client. The default services included with the Exchange 4.0 client are Exchange Server, Microsoft Mail, Personal Folders, and Personal Address Book. Windows 95 clients may also have the Microsoft Fax and MSN services available since they shipped with the operating system. You can add additional services by using the Have Disk option from the Add new service dialog box. See Figure 23.2 for the Services Properties page in the Exchange client.

FIGURE 23.2.

Services Properties page for Configuring Service Providers.

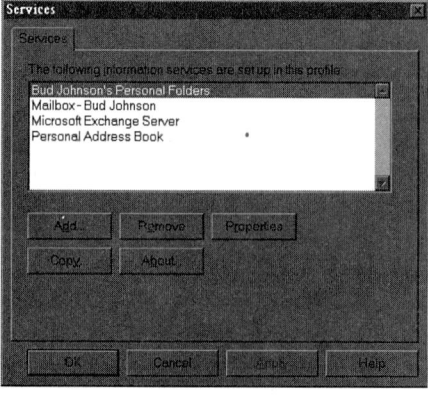

Because service providers are MAPI-based, many third-party vendors have created services to link to their products. A good example of a cross platform provider for Exchange is the Lotus Notes 4.0 mail service that enables Exchange to send and receive mail from the Notes 4.0 client. Service providers are also available for CompuServe, Internet POP3 Mail, cc:Mail, and many others, with new service providers showing up frequently. Many of these providers will only provide the transport and addressing services, because they do not have MAPI interfaces to their own message stores.

TIP

It may be very confusing for your users to figure out which Universal Inbox their mail is being delivered to if they have multiple service providers installed. Inboxes can exist in personal folders, server-based stores, and any service that provides the message storage function. For this reason you should rename the Inbox to something like "Inbox for User Name" where user name is the user's name. This will make it clear which Inbox mail will be delivered to, but still give the users the functionality to switch delivery to another message store of their liking.

Tour of the Exchange Client

This section takes you through the various controls, interfaces, and functions of the Exchange client. Although you may already be familiar with the client interface, you might learn something new this time through. To help us with our tour, Bud Johnson has agreed to let us watch him as he becomes familiar with his new e-mail client. He will first configure the defaults of the client to his liking, and then familiarize himself with sending, receiving, managing, and replying to messages.

Bud is now finished with his new employee orientation and sits down at his desk to begin his first day of work. He begins by logging on to the network, which runs his system login script for NT. The IS staff has set up a process in the login script that determines whether users have their Exchange clients set up by looking for the profile file, and will run the NEWPROF.EXE program to generate Bud a new profile. You will learn about this process in a later section entitled Tools and Utilities, so don't worry about it here. Bud then clicks on the Inbox icon on his Windows 95 desktop to open his Exchange Inbox for the first time.

Because this is the first time Bud has used Exchange, and he is our fictional "ideal" end-user, he decides to open the Microsoft Exchange help topics from the Help pull-down menu before proceeding to dive into the program itself. This has a getting-started section that Bud goes through to familiarize himself with Exchange. He will use the online context-sensitive help throughout his tour for information on performing specific functions. The IS staff has also given Bud a cheatsheet that provides company-specific information about how to operate e-mail's most basic functions.

Bud decides to first configure the various options for the client to customize specific features to the way he likes to do e-mail. From his cheatsheet, he is instructed to open the Tools menu and select Options to bring up a Properties notebook. This displays the General Properties page as seen in Figure 23.3. He decides to have the client play a sound and change the pointer to alert him to new mail messages. He also wants to be warned before permanently deleting items, and does not want his wastebasket to be emptied every time he exits. He is not using multiple profiles, but if he gets a laptop, he will probably use this feature to enable him to connect to the office and his Internet service provider to retrieve mail from each service separately. The rest of the defaults are acceptable concerning tooltips and word selection, because they enable him to better use his mouse.

FIGURE 23.3.

General Properties page for Exchange client options.

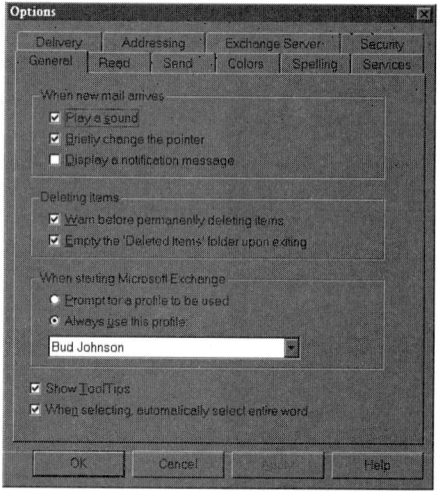

Bud now clicks on the Read tab to display the Read Properties page, as seen in Figure 23.4. Because he normally starts from the top of his received messages, he selects the option to "Open the item below it" to control the behavior when he deletes or moves a mail message. He then checks the three selections for replying or forwarding a message, and clicks the font button to select the font used for the original message body. He then changes his mind, and un-checks the selection for closing the original item when replying or forwarding so that he can keep the original message open to decide what to do with that message.

Moving on to the Send Properties page seen in Figure 23.5, Bud checks the box to make the default to request a receipt when a message has been read. Because this is the default send property, he decides that he can change the sensitivity and importance level on a per-message basis. He also leaves the selection checked for saving sent items in the send mail folder for message history purposes. He should know that this default will increase the amount of space his mailbox takes up on the server. He will receive a warning when he is getting close to the storage limit set by IS, as explained in Chapter 22, "Administering Exchange Server and Mail," concerning storage limits of information stores.

FIGURE 23.4.

Read Properties page.

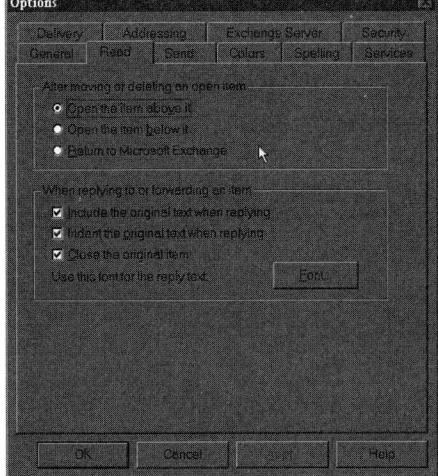

FIGURE 23.5.

Send Properties page.

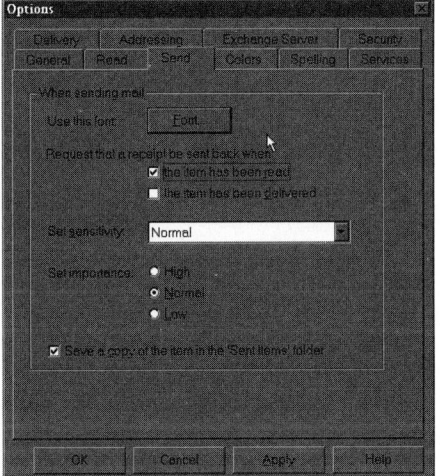

The Colors Properties page defaults are acceptable to Bud, and he decides not to change them at this time. (Bud is not a typical user, because most of the users I have worked with will spend a large amount of time on this page customizing the colors to personalize how they view their e-mail.) The best use for color selections is to change the unread and group label colors, because these are the most noticeable for the user. Changing the readbar or readbar text can create some very interesting results on the "From" line of an open message, but the defaults are much more pleasing to the eye.

Bud now selects the Spelling tab to display the properties options for spell-checking from within the client, as seen in Figure 23.6. He does want his messages to be spell-checked before he sends them, and would like Exchange to make suggestions from the spell-checker dictionary. This keeps Bud from looking bad when he sends that critical e-mail to his boss about his "Goals and plands for teh ew year." He also does not want to take the extra time to spell-check the original contents of a message replied to, so he makes the appropriate selection on this page.

FIGURE 23.6.

Spelling Properties page.

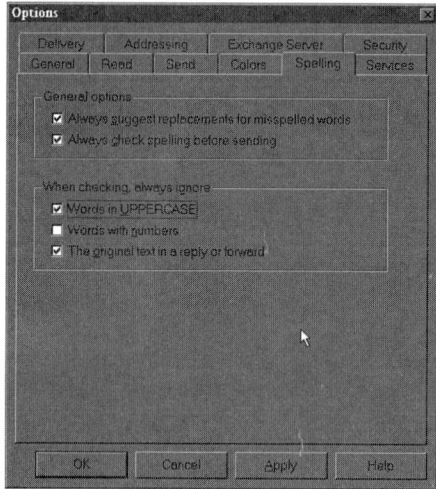

Bud does not know what he needs to configure in the Services Properties page (see Figure 23.7), but he knows from his cheatsheet that it is used for setting various service provider-specific options. If he had his new laptop, he would probably change the properties for Exchange Server service to support remote functionality, as well as create a set of personal folders to store and archive mail. He decides to reconfigure his Personal Address Book to show last names first. This area will be covered in more detail later in this chapter.

FIGURE 23.7.

Services Properties page.

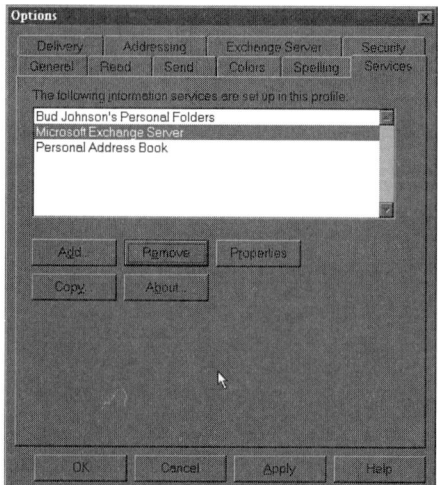

Bud clicks on the Delivery tab to see the properties page for the delivery options (refer to Figure 23.1). From here, he could select an alternate store to deliver mail and create the Universal Inbox, but accepts the default server-based store because it is currently his only option. The default for how recipient addresses are processed is acceptable, and he would only change it when he added another service provider in the future. If he had additional service providers, such as Internet mail or FAX, he would prioritize the transports for the ones he would use the most for outbound mail.

Clicking on the Addressing tab gives Bud the options for processing and storing addresses, as seen in Figure 23.8. Because he will mostly communicate with users internal to the company, he leaves the default for the first address list seen to the global. He also accepts to store personal addresses in his personal address book, but could select another if an additional address service provider was installed. To correspond with the selection for the first address book to show, he selects that the global list will be used before his personal list for checking user names. If he were operating in the field or only sending to a few specific users, he might make his selections favor his personal address lists on this properties page.

FIGURE 23.8.

Addressing Properties page.

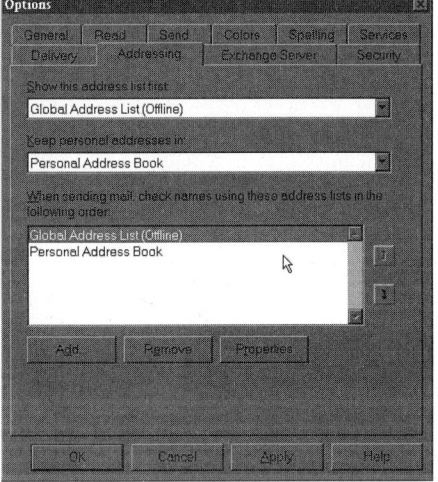

23

MAIL CLIENTS

Bud will be out of the office for the next couple of weeks attending meetings at the company's headquarters, so he needs to allow his administrative assistant to send mail on his behalf while he is out. He clicks the Add button from the Exchange Server Service Properties page to select his assistant for the Send on Behalf permission, as seen in Figure 23.9. The default temporary storage space for forms is acceptable, and he could use the Manage Forms button to add or remove forms from his local machine. The password button could be used to change his Windows NT password, but he will wait until it expires to change it.

FIGURE 23.9.

*Exchange Server
Properties page.*

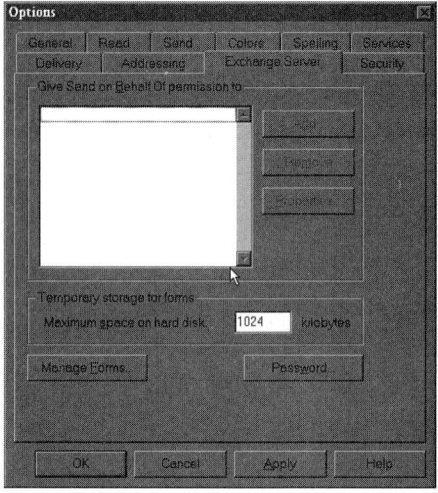

Bud then clicks on the Security tab, which displays a properties page that has most of the selections grayed out, as seen in Figure 23.10. Bud makes a mental note to send a message to the e-mail administrator to set him up for advanced security. This page enables him to configure secure encryption and digital signatures for all outgoing messages, as well as set up and manage advanced security and the private password used for this feature. He decides that he will specify security options for each outgoing message, and only needs to get the administrator to create his unique key from the Key Server add-on service.

FIGURE 23.10.

*Security Properties
page.*

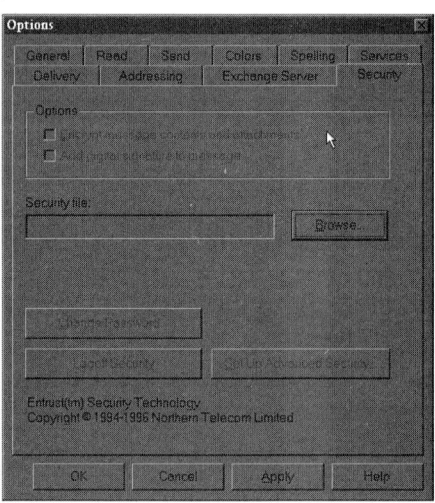

Bud is now finished customizing his options for the client for the standard properties pages. He now wants to customize the way he views his e-mail from within the client. From the View pull-down menu, he finds selections for Personal Views. These are the default views included with the client, but he wants an easy way to compare sent and received times for incoming mail from vendors for time-sensitive material. Routinely, vendors report delays in transfer of mail over the Internet, so Bud wants to be able to easily compare the time the vendors sent the mail, and when the Exchange Server received it.

Bud clicks on the View pull-down menu and then selects the Define Views option, which brings up the Define Views dialog box. He clicks on the New button to define a new view. This brings up the Modify View Properties page seen in Figure 23.11. He clicks the Columns button and selects the Sent, Received, From, Importance, and Subject columns. Then he clicks the Sort button to select the column to sort by the sent time and decides that he does not need to group the messages in the view. He finishes the definition by typing in a name such as "View by Sent and Received Times" for the view and clicks on OK. Now this view is available for his Inbox from the Personal Views selection, and can be used to view information in any of the folders. Folders will remember which view was last assigned to them, and child folders will not inherit the view of parent folders.

FIGURE 23.11.

Modify View definition dialog box.

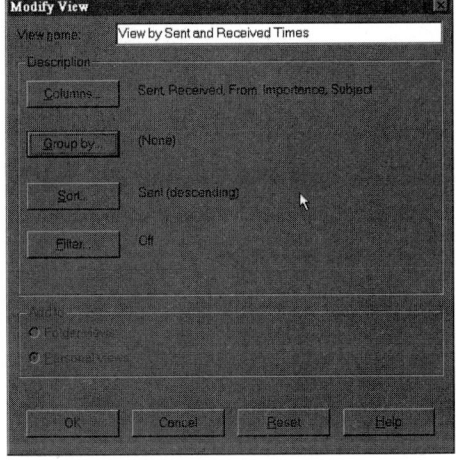

Bud decides that just putting in a new view is not enough; he needs to be able to separate mail from vendors due to the volume of mail he expects to receive from inside the company. He reads on his cheatsheet about the procedures for setting up a private folder with Inbox Assistant rules, and decides that this will get the job done. The cheatsheet reminds him that he must create the folder on his server-based mailbox for the Inbox Assistant to work while he is off-line, and must use properties that Exchange Server can enumerate when he is not connected.

Bud first needs to create a new folder beneath his server-based message store. This is done by selecting the New Folder option from the File pull-down menu, then entering a name for the folder such as Vendor Mail. Then he opens the properties for the newly created folder and defines the views he needs, just as he did for the Inbox. At this time, he does not need any electronic forms, so he is finished setting up the folder. He could have created a local folder for this purpose, but then incoming mail could not be moved to those folders since they are not available when the user is not connected. If he used local personal folders on his hard drive, the Inbox Assistant would only move mail there when that message store was available.

He now needs to set up an Inbox Assistant rule to move incoming mail to the folder just created. This is done by selecting the Inbox Assistant option from the Tools pull-down menu, which brings up the dialog box in Figure 23.12. This configuration screen enables Bud to view, add, edit, remove, and disable the various rules active on his mailbox. He now clicks the Add Rule button to view the configuration screen in Figure 23.13.

FIGURE 23.12.

Rule configuration page for conditions and actions.

FIGURE 23.13.

Options available when viewing a message.

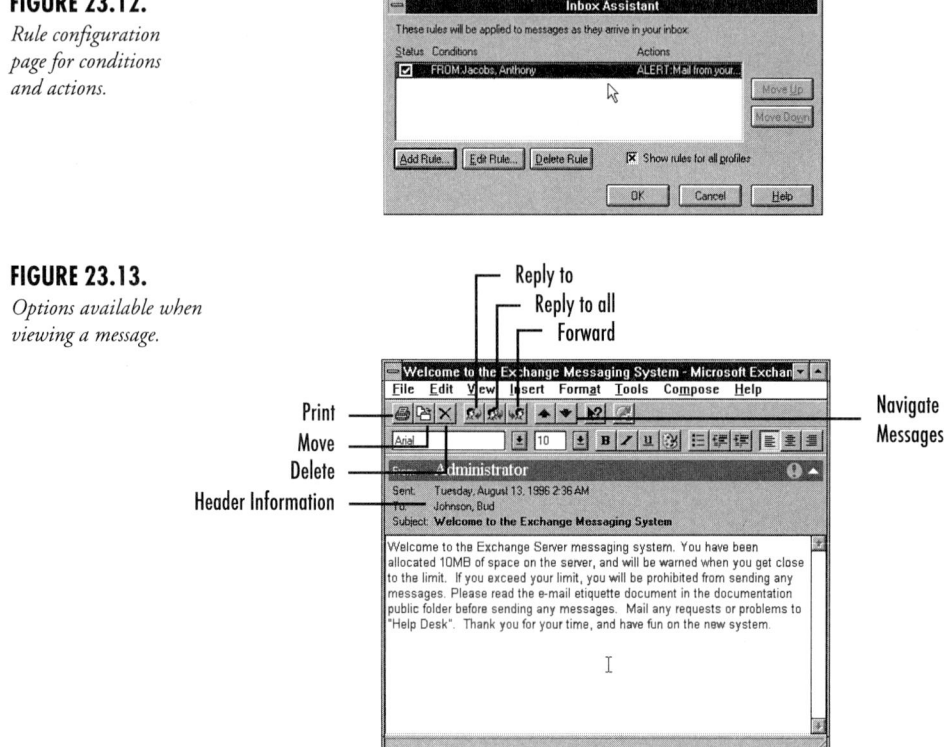

Bud sets the condition for this new rule to select any messages that have senders from the server-based distribution list named "Finance Vendors." He had one of the Exchange administrators create this distribution list and make him the owner so that he could maintain the members. Next, he selects the checkbox to move the messages and then selects the folder created in the previous step. This rule will fire for any incoming mail that is sent from vendors in the distribution list and will move the message to the folder named "Vendor Mail."

TIP

If Bud had selected a public folder to move the messages to in the previous example, the rule would create a deferred action message (DAM) that would only be processed when Bud is logged on. This is because the rule engine is not able to log on as the user, and can only process the move message action if it is in the user's server message store. This deferred action may be acceptable for simple filing, but is not good for critical events. For any critical notification events that need to go to public folders, make the action forward the message to the intended public folder. This will require you to add the folder to your personal address book, since by default for public folders it is to be hidden from the global address book.

Now that Bud has his mail client customized and Inbox Assistants set up to parse incoming mail, he decides to read and send some mail. From the main client window, he can click on his Inbox and view the messages by any of the custom views. The normal view is the best for viewing incoming mail, because it is sorted by date and has many pertinent fields displayed. When viewing a message, the toolbar has icons to Print, Move, Delete, Reply to, and Forward the message, with navigational buttons to move to the previous and next messages. See Figure 23.13 for the options available when viewing a message.

Bud can compose a new message either by selecting the New Message option from the Compose pull-down menu, or by clicking on the icon from the toolbar. This will bring up the New Message window, which displays the most common fields within a message. Bud would like to send a message to a co-worker and a blind carbon copy to his boss, but the field is not available. He only needs to select the Bcc Box option from the View pull-down menu. He also makes the selection to display the toolbar from the View pull-down menu, and chooses not to display the From box because he will not be sending mail on behalf of anybody else. See Figure 23.14 for an example of the New Message composition window.

Bud has finished reading and sending all the messages for today and needs to get ready to catch a two-o'clock plane flight for a two-day trip to headquarters. Because he will be out of the office, he decides to set up an Out of Office Assistant to reply to any messages sent to him. He selects the Out of Office Assistant option from the Tools pull-down menu and sees the configuration window shown in Figure 23.15. He types in text for his auto reply, and then sets up a rule to forward all important mail to his alphanumeric pager through a third-party paging connector, as well as copy his administrator on important messages. After shutting down and logging off, he races to catch his plane.

FIGURE 23.14.

New Message window.

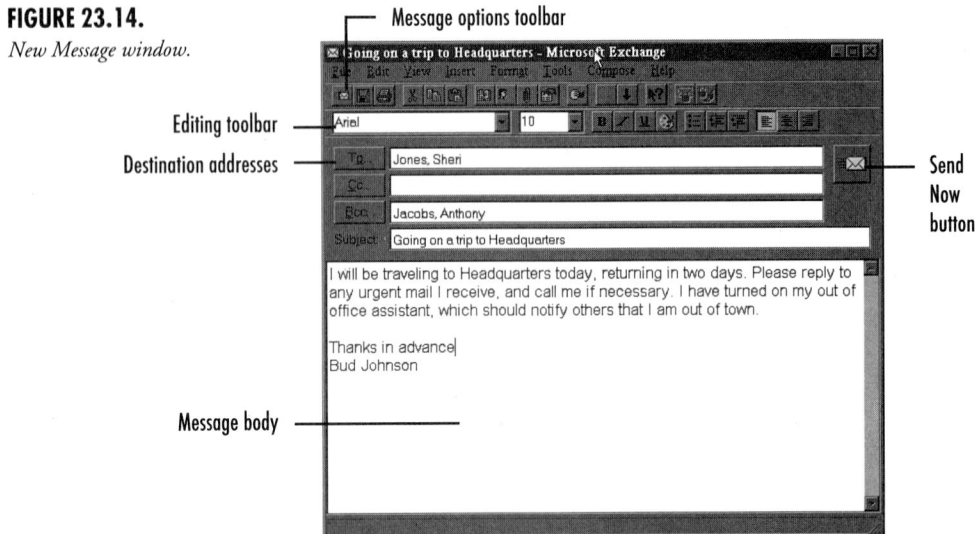

Message options toolbar

Editing toolbar

Destination addresses

Send Now button

Message body

FIGURE 23.15.

Out of Office Assistant configuration page.

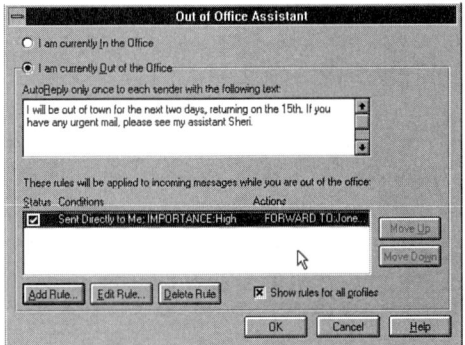

Schedule+

The Exchange client is designed to manage messages, and the Schedule+ client is designed to manage schedules, contacts, and projects. Meetings and appointments are a way of business, and managing them is one of the biggest challenges that face users. Not only is managing your schedule a task, but trying to coordinate the schedules of others can be a nightmare. The pace of business does not allow the time needed for phone tag, so group coordination and project tracking software is needed.

The Schedule+ client is an Exchange MAPI-based application that utilizes the power of the Exchange Server platform to share information about a user's time and tasks. Simple in presentation, the design is built to manage a user's schedule and provide a link to the free and busy times of others. The user interface of the Schedule+ application is designed around a paper planner look, and it is based on earlier versions of the product. See Figure 23.16 for the highlights of the Schedule+ client interface.

FIGURE 23.16.

Schedule+ client interface highlights.

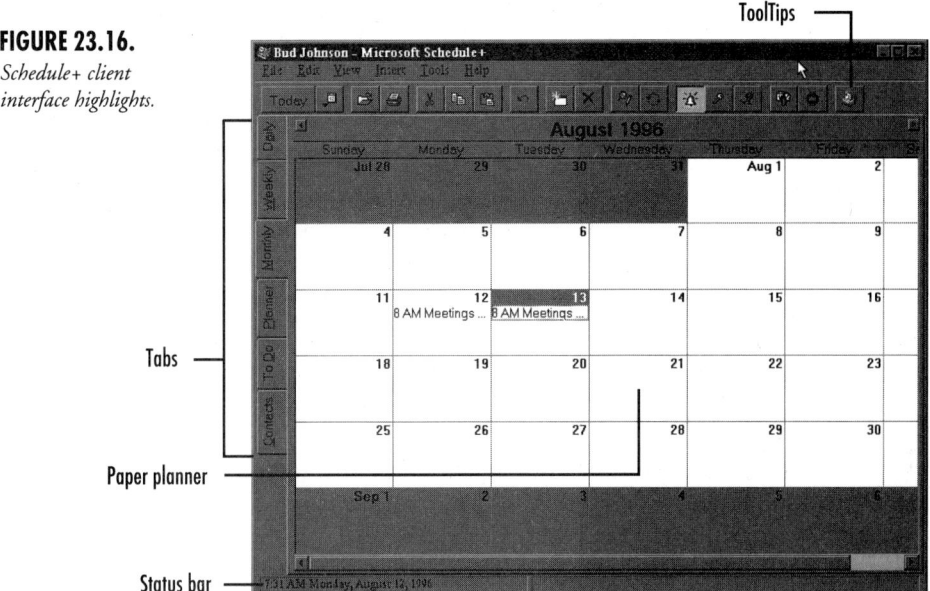

The Schedule+ client uses tabs to navigate between the different client functions. The tab gallery enables the user to customize the tabs that are seen in the main interface window. Selecting any of the tabs will display that information in the main window. The default tabs are for daily, weekly, and monthly calendars, the planner, the To Do list, and contacts. The tabs display information for six different Schedule+ components:

■ Appointments are scheduled activities that occur within a specific time period.

■ Tasks make up a user's To Do list.

■ Projects are groups of tasks or activities with a common goal.

■ Contacts are persons that users keep pertinent information on for future use.

■ Alarms are used to remind the user of an appointment or task milestone.

■ Events are occurrences that do not have a specific occurrence in time planning.

The client can operate in one of two modes, standalone or group-enabled. In the standalone mode, the client can be used to schedule and manage time for a single user, as well as use the contact and planning management functions. When the client first starts up, it is in standalone mode and will prompt users as to whether they want to use an existing file or create a new one. They can use existing Schedule+ files from earlier versions, but they will need to create a new file if they want to import data from another application.

In the group-enabled mode, the user is also prompted to create a new or use an existing file, but the application has determined that a MAPI-based messaging system is available. One of three MAPI messaging systems is needed for this mode: a workgroup post office, an MS Mail or MAPI 1.0 post office, or a Microsoft Exchange Server. In the group-enabled mode, users can invite attendees to appointments, view others' schedules with appropriate permissions, work with custom electronic forms, and send messages. Because the client primarily works from the local file and synchronizes with the server, it is easy on your network bandwidth and works well in remote mode.

To properly support many users' schedules in a large organization, the Schedule+ Free/Busy public folder must be replicated. All the users' free and busy time is stored within the users' information store and a hidden public folder that is created on the first server within a site. The free/busy folder can be accessed by other sites only if RPC connectivity is available; otherwise, the folder must be replicated. The Schedule+ connector can exchange free/busy times with earlier Schedule+ 1.0 distribution programs by a distribution list set up by administrators. This connector is explained further in Chapter 24, "Interfacing with Other Mail Systems."

Users can also access another user's Schedule+ information directly if that other user has given them the appropriate permissions. This can be done by opening another's address book from the File menu or by right-clicking in the planner. This differs from free/busy times in that one user is accessing another user's data directly, and in much more detail.

TIP

The Exchange Schedule+ client is sensitive to scheduling across time zones. In the Time Zone Properties page under Tools, Options, you can set a secondary time zone. This enables the user to select the Second Time Zone option when scheduling an appointment or viewing scheduled data. Any appointment or invitation that crosses a time zone boundary will be automatically converted into the appropriate time for the destination zone. This feature is dependent on the operating system's time zone information being set up correctly, and in the Windows 3.1 platform the Exchange client includes an interface to set up the time zone.

The configuration parameters for the Schedule+ client are found beneath the property pages from the Tools, Options menu selection. These pages include properties for General, Default, Display, Time Zone, and Synchronize options. The General page has options to customize the calendar, archive data periodically, enable a resource account, configure reminders or alarms, and configure meeting request behavior. The Default page contains properties for setting the default values for such things as reminders, priorities, and phone numbers. The Display page affects the fonts and colors for the user interface and controls what items are shown. The Time Zone page enables the user to set the primary and secondary time zones for appointment time management. The Synchronize page controls when to synchronize and whether the application should work primarily from the local file.

Client Installation

Getting your Exchange Server installed and configured is not as time-consuming as the task of deploying the client application to the user desktops. Installing new software on any user's machine can stir up all kinds of problems that are waiting to be brought to light. The setup process for the client software does perform many checks on the system to make sure it is ready for installation, but normal system maintenance is necessary before any software install. Because the Exchange client install process uses the Microsoft ACME setup process, the setup screens are similar for each of the platforms. Before deciding to install the client on a workstation, please refer to the requirements listed in Chapter 21, "Installing Exchange Server and Mail."

Before you perform any install of new software, thoroughly test the machine. This includes running the chkdsk or scandisk programs, defragging the hard drive, deleting temporary files, and tuning the network resources. A little time on the front end of an install can prevent downtime during a deployment that can be caused by general corruption or system problems. Just as your car needs its oil changed and tires rotated, workstations need preventative maintenance performed on a routine basis.

You should also understand the impact this new application will have on the user's workstations. For instance, the Windows 3.x platform has never been known for its capability of multitasking more than a few applications. Do not expect Windows 3.x to allow your users to have the Exchange client, a word processor, terminal emulation, screen saver, spreadsheet application, and a client-server application all running at once. It just exceeds the capacity of the Windows 3.x operating system. Windows NT, Windows 95, and the Macintosh client are much better for multitasking multiple applications, so you may need to put together a plan to upgrade the operating systems on the desktops before deploying the Exchange client.

Another misconception concerning applications is that you can save space and resources by installing a shared network version. Exchange client does support both local and shared network options for the installation, but consider putting the client locally on every desktop. A shared network installation will only eat up your networking resources and prove to be a headache for the administrators in the long run. Maintenance upgrades and service packs can be handled by mailing the users the update program in a scripted format so that users can do the upgrades themselves, thus reducing your support costs. Microsoft Systems Management Server (SMS) is also a good solution for automated deployment of the Exchange client to users' workstations. Consider these options in your implementation plan.

The Installation Process

As with every installation of a new application, you should perform a few dozen installs yourself to get familiar with the process. This section will take you through the install process from beginning to end, and suggest various tips along the way. If you are preparing to deploy many clients, skip to the next two sections before reading this section. They will familiarize you with

23

MAIL CLIENTS

the tools and concepts that should be considered before rolling out many desktops. This section assumes that you are installing a version for the Windows family of operating systems; the MS-DOS and Macintosh setups are not covered.

The client applications are located on a separate CD-ROM included in your Exchange Server package. You should run the setup program located in the specific language directory, such as ENG for English, to create the installation share on the server and move the client software to that share. The share that is created is named Exchange and has subdirectories for each client platform, such as win16, win95, and winnt\i386, winnt\alpha, and winnt\MIPS. Each directory contains the ACME setup program, the setup script, and the CAB files containing the files for installation. You may also opt to install the client from the CD-ROM, but the server-based share is the best method because it gives better speed and customization.

Once you have the installation share created, go to the user's workstation and attach to the Exchange share or the appropriate NetWare volume. Begin the setup program, SETUP.EXE, from the appropriate directory for the installed operating system. There should be no other applications running during the install process because they may hold open critical files, and the system may need to be rebooted after the install. You may want to reboot before the install if any MAPI applications are currently running, or if you suspect that some DLLs may be open that need to be replaced by the install process.

The first dialog box you see will prompt you for the user and organization names. It will attempt to fill in this information from the local configuration data, such as the WIN.INI file or the registry. You may want to enter the user's Exchange alias for the name field since it will be very useful later when the profile is generated. Click on OK and then confirm your entry with another click on OK. The system will now begin to search for installed applications and running applications before proceeding. You might receive an informational message if applications are running that might conflict with the install, so just close them and click on OK to proceed.

If the installation detects an existing version of the Exchange client, it will give you only the options for adding/removing, reinstalling, or removing all the Exchange components from the previous install, as seen in Figure 23.17. If you have an existing version installed, I recommend that you use the Reinstall feature, because it will enable you to verify that the proper components are installed. If you are upgrading from the Windows 95 "Lite" version of the Exchange client that shipped with Windows 95, the installation process advises you that it has found that version and will replace all related files.

Next, you will be prompted for the location to install the client software. The default on the Windows 95 version is "\Program Files\Microsoft Exchange"; the Windows NT and Windows 3.x versions default to "\Exchange". I suggest that you accept the default location unless you have a company standard that specifies that applications are installed in a specific directory. Click on OK to accept the directory location, and the install will proceed to the installation type screen.

FIGURE 23.17.

*Options page displayed
if a previous version
exists.*

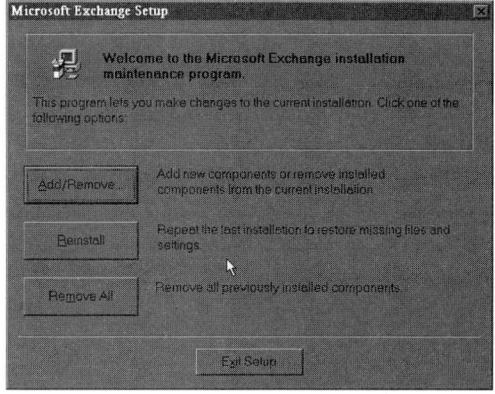

The installation type screen has options for typical, custom, and laptop, as seen in Figure 23.18. You may also have a selection for workstation if you are running from a shared network setup. The typical selection will install the options for a typical user, such as the Exchange client, Schedule Plus, Exchange Server service, and a few of the optional components. The Custom install type enables you or the user to select which components will be installed, and I recommend that you use this one for the first few installs. The Laptop selection will install the minimum files necessary to run the Exchange client, and does not select any of the optional components. The directory where the application will be installed is also listed at the bottom of this screen and can be changed by clicking on the Change Folder button.

FIGURE 23.18.

Installation types.

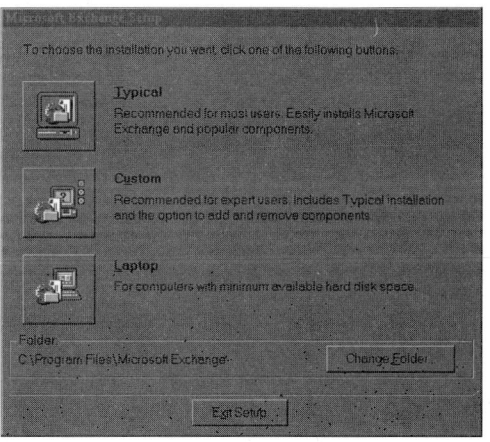

If you select either the typical or laptop installation types, the setup process will proceed to the next step. Let's assume that you selected the custom install type, as you should; you will see the screen shown in Figure 23.19. You can select the Change Option button while highlighting a component to make selections for the components that make up that selection. The Exchange client has additional options for information services, and, by default, the Microsoft Mail service will not be selected unless you modified the setup script. Make your selections and click on the Continue button to proceed.

FIGURE 23.19.

Custom Installation
Options list.

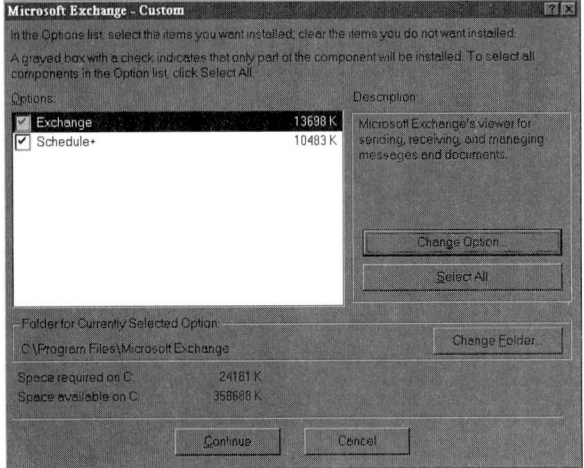

If you are running the Windows 3.*x* or Windows NT version of the setup, you will be prompted for a program group in which to place the icons for the installed applications; accept the default and continue. For Windows 95 the icons for the Inbox and Schedule Plus are placed on the Programs selection from the Start button. The setup process will then check for the necessary disk space for the options selected, and copy the files to your local hard drive based upon those selections. If you have any applications open that the setup process was not able to detect, you may receive an error message that setup cannot write to a file because it is open. Close all open applications and click on the Retry button to proceed.

The end of the installation process will be different for each operating system platform, and it may differ based upon previous installations. For the Windows 16-bit client, you will see the Time Zone setup screen, because this platform does not natively support time zones which the Exchange client requires. The Windows NT version will complete with only an informational message that setup is complete with an OK button. The Windows 95 version will either end at the same informational screen if you already have a default profile, or prompt you for configuration parameters for the Exchange Server service provider for a default profile if one does not exist. You should either configure the properties now or click on Cancel to set them up later. Depending on which system files were replaced, you may be prompted to restart the computer.

Now that the Exchange and Schedule Plus applications are installed, all that remains is to configure the default user profile. To begin this process, click on the Inbox icon, which is located on the desktop for Windows 95 and in an Exchange program group for Win 3.*x* and Windows NT. This will bring up the Inbox Setup Wizard, which will have different service providers listed depending on the platform on which the client is running. See Figure 23.20 for the services Setup Wizard dialog box. You can also select to manually configure the services, although this method is recommended for advanced users.

FIGURE 23.20.

Inbox Setup Wizard services dialog box.

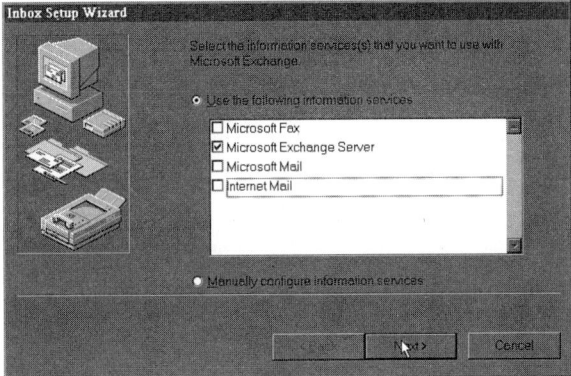

Click on the Next button and you will see the Exchange Server Service properties window. Enter the server name of any Exchange Server within the site, and enter either the display name or alias for the user in the mailbox field. An example of this setup screen can be seen in Figure 23.21 with information for Bud Johnson. It is imperative that you type the name for the mailbox field with the correct spelling and case, because it will be matched up to an entry in the directory on the specified Exchange Server. You can enter the name of any server that has replicated information about the user, because it will be matched to the user's home server by the directory service running on that server.

FIGURE 23.21.

Information services configuration for Inbox Setup Wizard.

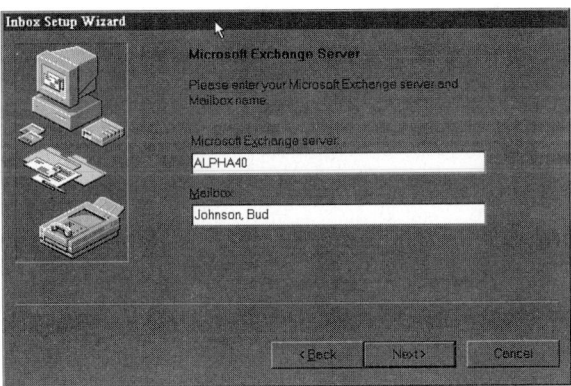

Next, you are prompted to specify whether the user will travel with this computer. If you select the NO option, an off-line message store will not be created and the user must connect to Exchange Server to process messages. The YES option will create a default off-line store named mailbox.ost in the directory that Windows was installed in for synchronization and temporary storage purposes. Make the appropriate selection and click on the Next button to continue.

TIP

If you do not want the off-line store to be created in the directory Windows was installed in, select the NO option. Once you have completed the setup of the default profile, you can open the Exchange Server service properties and click on the "Off-line Folder File Settings" button from the Advanced Properties page, which will prompt you for the location of the off-line store file. You should also name the file specific to the user's name in case other users use this workstation.

You will now see the default filename and location of the user's personal address book, c:\Exchange\mailbox.pab. I suggest that you override the filename and make it specific to the user. In the Windows 3.*x* client, the filename is limited by the 8.3 naming limitation, but for Windows 95, Macintosh, and Windows NT platforms, use the user's full name. This helps keep the personal address book specific to the user, and if other users decide to use the machine, they will not default to the address book of the local user. Click on the Next button and you will see a selection to add the Inbox to the startup group, so make a selection based on company standards or the user's preferences. Click on the Next button, then on the Finish button to complete the process.

The Exchange client should start up and may default to a view that does not include the folders window. Just select the Folders option from the View menu to turn on the folders window. If you did not receive any error messages, you are finished with the installation and configuration of the user's Exchange client. If you received any setup or error messages, proceed to the troubleshooting section later in this chapter.

Tools and Utilities

The installation process outlined previously has many options and configuration parameters that would drive up installation and support costs for a large installation of clients. Microsoft has included a number of tools to assist in standardizing and scripting the installation and configuration processes to keep those costs down. The client setup editor is used to change the default installation options, and it will prove to be a very valuable tool for support professionals. The NEWPROF.EXE utility can generate default user profiles based on a default preferences file (default.prf) that the administrators configured with the client setup editor. These utilities are critical to large deployments of Exchange clients, because they reduce the time it takes to get them installed and enable the users to correctly set up the application for their use.

The client setup editor is an application that is installed and run from any Exchange Server, and it will modify the default profile and set up script information for the Windows-based clients.

Start the application from the program group on Exchange Server; you will see the screen shown in Figure 23.22. You should first select the client installation point from the File pull-down menu by specifying where the client application source files are for a platform. For example, select the win16 directory on the Exchange share to edit the options for the Windows 3.*x* 16-bit client.

FIGURE 23.22.

Dial-Up Networking Properties page.

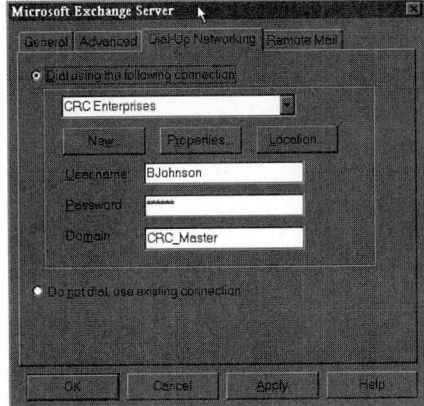

When you select to modify the setup program options from the File menu, a new exchng.stf file is created, and the original is backed up in a directory named BAK. This option enables you to control the following default setup options:

- Installation types presented to the user
- The default installation directory
- The default program manager group name
- The components and information services to install
- The order for protocols for RPC binding

The User Options selection from the File pull-down menu is used to set the default user options stored in the file DEFAULT.PRF. This file is used by the Exchange Inbox Wizard to set the various properties for the configuration pages available under the Tools, Options selection. It sets information for the General, Read, Send, Spelling, and Home Server Properties pages. It can also be used by the NEWPROF.EXE tool to generate a default profile for the user's settings of the Exchange client. The file DEFAULT.PRF is a simple text file and can be edited manually instead of using the setup editor.

The utility NEWPROF.EXE is the automatic profile generator, and can be very helpful if you are responsible for setting up default profiles for many users. Administrators customize the file DEFAULT.PRF via the setup editor, or by hand, and place the file in the server-based install directory used to install the clients. After the client installation, users can run the profile generator from the command line to auto-create their default profiles. A better solution is to set

23

MAIL CLIENTS

up the user's login script to test for the existence of a default profile, and if one is not found, it can launch the NEWPROF.EXE utility to create one. You can also use SMS to launch this process just after the client is installed, and with a little work can send status MIF files back to SMS to report success or failure.

> **TIP**
>
> Where does the utility NEWPROF.EXE get the user's name to set up the default profile? There is a line in the default.prf file for "MailboxName =", but this would require a customized version of the file for every user. Remember that I suggested that you type in the user's name in the name and organization dialog box just as it appears in the directory. This is because the newprof utility will try to use the ACME setup information from the registry or WIN.INI file to retrieve the user's name. You can change the default mailbox name to something like "Lastname, Firstname REPLACEME" so users will not become confused if they cannot connect to their server.

Deployment Concepts

If you are getting ready to deploy an exchange messaging system in your organization, you should consider the time necessary to configure and install the client. A typical installation process is about 30 minutes, with possible additional time necessary for problem management. There are utilities and applications that can assist with deploying the client applications in different levels of automation. These include, but are not limited to, Systems Management Server (SMS) and WINInstall.

SMS is a Microsoft systems management solution that is very strong at managing and tracking software deployment. The Exchange client CD includes package definition files (PDF) that can be imported directly into SMS and used to script the installation of the client software. A better solution is to use a product such as WINInstall to perform the scripting of the installation, and use SMS to deliver it to the user desktops. The WINInstall product has pre- and post-installation options that enable you to automatically run scandisk processes before the installation, and it can also run the NEWPROF.EXE profile generator after the installation to set up the default profile. The combination of these two products will help your Exchange client deployment go much smoother.

I cannot stress enough the importance of making sure your users receive training on the product before you install it on their desktop. E-mail is not like a word processor or spreadsheet application; users depend heavily on messaging and Groupware to get their jobs done. If I had to pick between a thousand users who could not print and a thousand users who could not get into their e-mail, I would always pick the printing situation. If you deploy a new messaging system without properly training the user community, you are asking to drive your support costs higher than by providing simple training. It is also much easier to install and configure an

Exchange client on a user's desktop while the user is attending a two-hour training class, which should pay for itself after only a few installs.

In any large deployment, you should expect new problems to show up, because if it is built by man, it is broke by man. It is nearly impossible to foresee every problem, especially in the larger and more diverse companies. Have a SWAT team on hand to handle the major disturbances, and in their spare time they can work on smaller issues or develop new solutions. Use some of the features within Exchange, such as the help desk application and an anonymous suggestion folder to get feedback from the users. Remember, they are a very important part of making the deployment process successful.

Supporting Mobile Users

Mobile users are an interesting bunch, roving from place to place, always in search of a reliable phone line. Their needs are much different from a LAN-connected user, because they only make periodic connections, and need to have the ability to do their work off-line. They must make slow-link connections by modem to the Exchange Server, and may still require access to LAN resources other than e-mail. The Exchange Server solution has many features designed to specifically support these types of users, such as synchronization, off-line message stores, remote access software, connection scheduling, and selective message retrieval. This section will outline the features and support options for these road warriors.

Exchange Server Remote Support

The most important prerequisite for supporting remote users is the method used to provide remote access. This can range from the RAS included with Windows NT Server to a third-party solution such as Shiva or comparable remote LAN node (RLN) solution. This discussion focuses on the RAS server solution built into the NT Server, and the client remote access software included in the operating system or the Exchange client. If you are already using a third-party solution for RLN support today, you should be able to capitalize on that investment. Many of the remote access vendors have worked out the details of enabling Microsoft's clients to dial in and connect to their solutions. You should consult with your remote access vendor to work out the specifics to enable your Exchange clients to make reliable connections to their products.

The mailboxes that are created for remote users are identical to those of LAN-connected users. The synchronization and off-line access features are built into the client and only require RPC connectivity to Exchange Server to work correctly. You need to set up the off-line address book on Exchange Server so that it is rebuilt on a regular basis. This is done from the Exchange administration program from the Site Directory Configuration object. You set which recipient container, such as the global address list, will be used for the off-line address book, and the times that it is rebuilt. This step is critical to providing reliable address information for the remote users when they are working in off-line mode.

The RAS server need not be installed on the same computer that Exchange Server is running on, although you will get slightly better performance and reliability if they are on the same server. Make sure to allocate an adequate number of modems to support the number of remote users, including those that will not be using the Exchange client. A very rough ratio is to have one modem for every 25 remote users, but this will depend on the frequency and connect times of your particular user community. A typical client makes a connection to upload and download a batch of messages, then reconnects to transfer the responses to those messages fairly quickly. You can use the performance monitor utility included with NT server to monitor how busy your RAS modems are and make adjustments as necessary. Large organizations need many RAS servers located throughout the corporate WAN, because the RAS server supports up to 256 modems and you probably do not want to pay a large phone bill each month.

Exchange Client Remote Support

Each platform that the Exchange client runs on needs remote access client software to be able to connect to the dial-in server. Table 23.1 lists the dial-up networking solutions to support remote Exchange clients.

Table 23.1. Remote networking solutions for the Exchange client platforms.

Client Platform	*Remote Access Solution*
Windows NT client	Microsoft remote access service included in the OS
Windows 95 client	Microsoft dial-up networking included in the OS
Windows 3.x client	Shiva Remote software included with Exchange client
MS-DOS client	Shiva Remote software included with Exchange client
Macintosh	AppleTalk Remote Access (ARA) included with the OS

The Exchange client is integrated with the dial-up networking software to allow scheduled and user-initiated connections. There are two properties pages available in the Windows versions of the Exchange client that enable configuration of remote message transfer. The Dial-Up Networking page, seen in Figure 23.22, enables the creation and selection of a dial-up connection, with fields for the username, password, and NT domain for uninterrupted background connections. The Remote Mail Properties page, seen in Figure 23.23, enables the user to configure the remote mail filters and message retrieval, and schedule periodic connections with or without filters.

The Exchange client has two basic modes of operation: batch mode connections and continuous connection. Users operating in batch mode have a local message store or Inbox, a copy of the off-line global address book, and any synchronized folders. Catch connections can be scheduled and/or user-initiated to initiate two-way mail transfer. The user can initiate remote mail transfer by one of three ways:

■ Choosing the Deliver Now option from the Tools menu while working offline

■ Choosing the Remote Mail option from the Tools menu while working offline

■ Establishing the remote connection manually, and then starting the Exchange client and clicking on the connect button

FIGURE 23.23.

Remote Mail
Properties page.

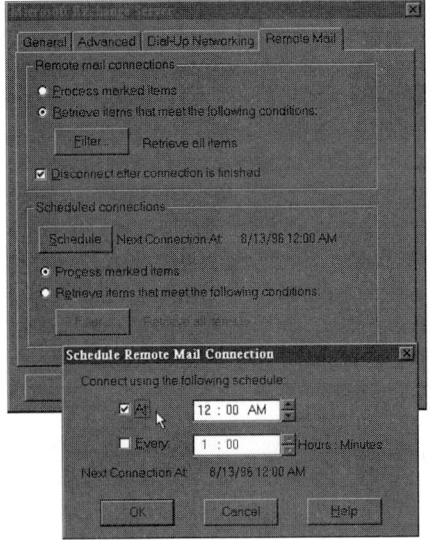

Only the remote mail option enables the user to look over the message headers before selecting messages to download. This screen will also enable the user to request a copy of the message or delete the message from the server. Information about the messages, such as estimated message retrieval time, importance, attachments, and message size, enable the user to make quick decisions on which messages to retrieve in this session. See Figure 23.24 for an example of the remote mail window.

FIGURE 23.24.

Remote Mail window.

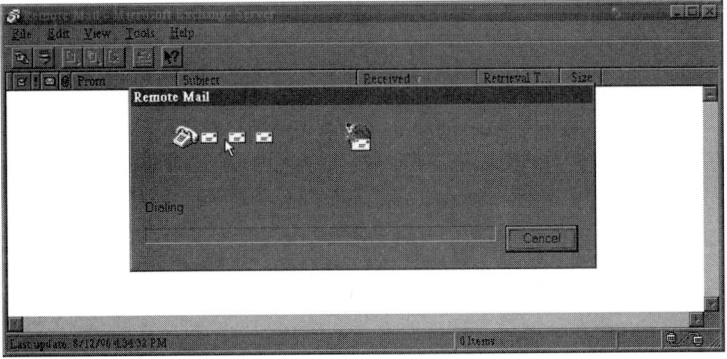

23

MAIL CLIENTS

In a continuous connection, users will still have local message stores and an offline address book, but will establish a connection to the remote network through the dial-in software to operate as if they were LAN-attached. This method enables user access to public folders and the capability of workgroup scheduling, but is the least reliable and efficient. The batch mode of operation is optimized to address the issues associated with slow-links, such as error recovery and bypassing large messages. Because mobile users will eventually come into the office and connect to the LAN directly, they will then be able to access public folders, electronic forms, and Groupware applications.

Troubleshooting Client Issues

The Exchange client software is modular in design, so logic tells us that it should be easier to take apart to troubleshoot problems. You could remove and reconfigure a service provider or change the binding order of the network protocols to track down the source of slow access. Elimination of the client components that are working correctly will help narrow your search for the root cause of a problem. Many client-related problems can be broken down into one or more of these areas:

- Network connectivity
- Security and permissions
- Addressing and message transfer
- System resources
- Software bugs or missing features

Network Connectivity

The connection between the Exchange client and Exchange Server must support synchronous RPC connectivity for messages to flow correctly. Many times, this connectivity will suffer from limitations of the protocols used or physical network outages. Because RPCs are protocol-independent, they can be carried on protocols such as TCP/IP, SPX, Banyan VINES TCP, or NetBEUI and interfaces such as NetBIOS, Named Pipes, and local RPC. The client will search these protocol and interface bindings until it can make a connection with Exchange Server.

The RPC binding order can be established in the client setup editor before you install the clients or modified later in the client's configuration files. For Windows 95 and NT, this value is stored in the registry hive HKLM\Software\Microsoft\Exchange\Exchange Provider \Rpc_Binding_order, and on Windows 16-bit clients, it is in the INI file named Exchange.ini. If you are troubleshooting slow startup problems with a client, remove all unnecessary protocols from this list, making sure to put the actual protocol used to connect to the server at the front of the list.

Each of the Network protocols for RPC connectivity requires that specific features or options be enabled. Use the RPC Ping utility shipped with Exchange Server to test connectivity between the clients and the server. The following are the basic requirements for each protocol for connectivity to the server:

- For TCP/IP connectivity, the client needs to be able to resolve the server's IP address from the name of the server, either by WINS or a local LMHOSTS file. The client must also be able to arp or ping the server properly.

- The Novell native SPX protocol requires that Exchange Server be configured correctly for SAP broadcasts and have a unique internal network number.

- The Microsoft IPX/SPX-compatible protocol requires that routers pass Type 20 IPX packets between subnets, normally disabled by the router administrators.

- The NETBeui protocol will not work in a routed environment, unless broadcasts are forwarded across LAN segments by either a bridge or a router, defeating the purpose of small LAN segments.

Physical network issues can also create problems for the client's connection to the server. Ethernet collision storms or Token Ring purges can disconnect the virtual circuit connection between client and server. Normal levels of physical network problems will not hurt the client's connection, but excessive numbers may delay message transfers. Use a network-based sniffer to track down these types of problems. Normally, if you are having physical problems. the Exchange client will be the last application to show problems, because it is designed to operate over relatively slow-links.

Security and Permissions

Security- and permissions-related problems will be very easy to find, but it might be challenging to find the root cause. Commonly, users will use a co-worker's workstation to access their mailboxes. They will receive error messages that they do not have access to their folders, but because there is no indication as to what user account it is logged on, they may call the help desk. If the workstation is not logged onto the network, the Exchange client will prompt the user for their account information to authenticate to the NT domain.

Frequently, users will set up their workstations for autologon to a domain such as in WFW 3.1 or Windows 95. This may use an account that differs from the owner of a mailbox, and other users will not be able to access their mailboxes. Because they perceive that they are logging onto the network with one account and password, but they are actually using another, it may be a challenge to determine that this is a security problem.

Permissions problems can also arise as users start to use public folders. When you create a public folder, it inherits the client access permissions from the parent folder, but subsequent changes to the parent folder will not change the permissions on the subfolders. This may enable a user to access a folder that they should not be able to or keep them from getting to a public folder of which they seem to be the owner. Remember that permissions to public folders are not recursive, so any changes will need to be done on each individual folder.

Addressing and Message Transfer

Exchange supports various message types, and it may be confusing when those address types are similar for installed service providers. For instance, if a user has two profiles defined, with one having access to an Internet POP3 mail server and the other having access to an Exchange Server, this will load two address types for creating personal address list entries. If the user is connected to the POP3 server and created a new address of type Internet Mail Address, that address type will be unavailable when using the profile that connects only to Exchange Server. If the user attempted to send mail to that personal address when using Exchange Server-only profile, the message will stay in the Outbox when other messages are sent correctly. The user can see an Internet Mail address type available under Exchange Server profile, but this is mutually exclusive to the address created under the Internet Mail service provider.

Message transfer problems are usually caused by permissions or network transport problems, but they can be related to addressing problems. For instance, if you send a piece of Internet mail through the Exchange Server service provider and receive a message back stating No transport provider available, you might be inclined to try to troubleshoot the client. If you trace the message through the system, you will find that it got to the MTA on the Exchange Server that rejected it. This error message means that you forgot to create an address type of SMTP on the Site Addressing Properties page of the IMC, meaning that no transport is able to process that address type.

System Resources

Troubleshooting system resource problems is a very delicate matter, because most users do not like to hear that their workstations are inadequate for running a particular program. Most symptoms of resource-related problems include excessive disk thrashing, low memory messages, extraordinarily long program startup times, and user complaints of systems getting slower over time. At some point, that 486/25 with 4M of RAM and a 120M hard drive will just not be able to run the latest software such as Exchange client.

System resource problems are not limited to just hardware, because software has a limited amount of resources for things such as the system and user memory stack space. This is best represented by a workstation running Windows 3.*x* with 16M of memory reporting that the system is out of memory, even though two applications are running using only 4M of RAM. You can recover system resources by eliminating unnecessary fonts, simplifying your screen saver, turning off those cute sounds, eliminating TSRs, and turning off any features that are not necessary to do business.

The Exchange client requires a good amount of memory to provide MAPI services to itself and other applications, and may require an increase to system memory. For those of you out there that just decided an Exchange deployment is not in your budget because of the memory requirement, quit trying to find a memory scapegoat. It is widely accepted that 12–16M of RAM is the minimum standard for workstations to support today's business applications. Go ahead and make the investment now to support your business requirements in the future. I may seem harsh when presenting the argument for upgrading the workstation's memory; however, I cannot tell you how many times a customer has spent $300–400 in service for me to troubleshoot a system, just to have me come back and tell them to buy a couple hundred dollars of memory to fix the problem.

Software Bugs and Missing Features

Having participated in many beta programs for Microsoft products, I can tell you I have seen my share of weird bugs. When looking into a client problem, do not rule out the possibility that you have found a new bug, or that the user is looking for a feature that is not available. Use another workstation to reproduce the steps to create the problem, and if you can get more than three or four machines to exhibit the problem, you may have discovered a bug. Make sure to call Microsoft product support services if you suspect a software bug, because you will not have to pay for the call if a new bug is documented.

There are many resources available to help you determine whether the problem you are having is a known bug or whether a feature is currently available in the Exchange client. I suggest that you use the Microsoft Technet technical CD-ROM or visit the knowledge base on the Web site for your research. Finding information in the knowledge base on Exchange can be tricky due to the way the search engine finds and lists hits for your searches. For this reason, I suggest that you read Qnote article #140950 for assistance on using specific keywords to narrow your search. The online books included with Exchange Server can also be helpful for finding out whether a specific feature is available.

23

MAIL CLIENTS

Summary

The most important part of a messaging system, from the user's perspective, is the client application. It must enable them to traverse through mountains of messaging data and deliver reliable message handling with stellar performance. The Exchange messaging clients, Universal Inbox and Schedule Plus, are designed to meet these needs. The Universal Inbox enables messages from a multiple of sources to be delivered to a single location, without the user needing to know just how they got there.

This chapter discussed the installation process for the Exchange client and utilities that can help to automate and distribute the client to the user's workstations. The client setup editor and auto profile generator make it easier for administrators to standardize and configure the various Exchange clients. Other systems management and installation applications can be used to deploy the Exchange client, such as SMS and WINInstall.

The Exchange client is designed to let users manage messaging information and collaborate on group projects through public folders and electronic forms. The group scheduling features of the Schedule Plus client enable many users to share information about their meetings and appointments. The Exchange client solution has built-in features to support remote users, such as off-line folders and address books, integration with dial-up remote access client software, remote mail batching and filtering, and selective download of messages by the user or an automated process.

The next chapter explores how the Exchange messaging system integrates with other mail systems. Migration and coexistence issues are discussed in detail, with explanations of the methods used for the most popular e-mail systems. Features of the various tools and system source extractors are explained, with examples of how to use them to migrate.

Interfacing with Other Mail Systems

by Gregory Dodge

IN THIS CHAPTER

CHAPTER 24

How many different e-mail systems make up your company's entire messaging system today? You may have a mixture of LAN- and host-based systems that may or may not be interchanging messages. You might even have just one messaging solution in place that must be able to communicate with systems external to your company, such as the Internet. In any of these scenarios, you should realize the challenges involved in getting these systems to interoperate to meet your company's messaging needs. You only need to review the history of messaging covered in Chapter 20, "Exchange Server and Mail Overview," to realize how your company's messaging system got to where it is today.

Migrating from your current system to Exchange can seem like a scary endeavor. Chances are your current messaging system is capable of providing basic messaging services and may even suit the company's business needs today. Unless your current messaging system is embracing open standards, such as X.400/X.500 or SMTP, its future is very limited. Microsoft listened to its customers concerns and developed very powerful and easy-to-use migration tools. Migration wizards and source extractors are available for Microsoft Mail Server for PC and AppleTalk networks, cc:Mail, DEC All-in-One, IBM PROFS, OfficeVision/VM, and other host-based and LAN-based systems.

This chapter covers the issues facing companies that have decided to migrate to Exchange, and explains how Exchange can interface with current messaging systems. There are many tools and procedures that can help make your migration go smoothly, and you learn about them in this chapter. Because each messaging system is unique, I outline the methods for migration and coexistence separately for each system. Extracting the current messaging information such as mailboxes, address lists, and public data should be easy and practical, enabling you to spend more time running your business and less time managing the keyboard.

This chapter places special consideration on the requirement to keep messaging information flowing smoothly. Keep in mind that the importance of maintaining your messaging system is compounded by the business processes that are utilizing it. Even a few hours of downtime can cost your company money in lost revenue. Your migration plan should recognize the current business processes utilizing your messaging system, and establish how they may be affected. Properly defining and executing your migration plan can help to reduce the risk of lost messaging functionality and business processes.

Migration and Coexistence Issues

Whether you are planning to replace your current e-mail system with Exchange or need to integrate Exchange into your existing messaging environment, you need to come up with a plan to address the many coexistence issues. Each individual e-mail system has a certain way of getting business done and may have certain features that cannot easily be translated to other systems. Users are not concerned with the details involved in moving to a new system, but do not want to experience downtime or lost messaging capabilities. Here are the key issues to keep in mind when planning for migration and coexistence:

■ Messages need to be seamlessly transferred between the systems.

■ Address lists must be kept current and replicated between the systems.

■ Message translation should be kept to a minimum.

■ Limit any situations that might cause changes in external systems.

■ Eliminate any unnecessary messaging data before it is migrated.

■ When a user is migrated, mail should still be accepted at their old address.

To address these issues, your company should put together an implementation team. Depending on the size of your organization, it may be only a few individuals or multiple groups of people. You should include individuals that are supporting the current system, as well as people that understand the network and server systems. You might also have representation from the user community, but be careful that they do not turn your migration plan into a new feature implementation.

Before putting together a plan for migration or integration of Exchange into your current messaging system, your project team must properly define what the current system is doing. In my business, this is called creating a project scope with well defined purposes and objectives. This involves documenting the current messaging services, external connectivity, message volume and routing, group and collaborative functionality, and business processes that depend on the existing system. From this documentation, the team will map out how the functionality of the existing system will match solutions available in Exchange.

The team should also define the various phases and time frames for the project. This will include phases for the initial installation, proof of concept, time of integration and coexistence, migration of messaging resources, and removal of the old system. Larger organizations may select to address the coexistence issues first and migrate the users over a longer period of time. Smaller organizations may have the luxury of skipping coexistence altogether and cut to the new system almost overnight. Your company's strategy will probably fall within these two extremes and should address the goals and objectives defined in the project scope.

Coexistence

Microsoft Exchange Server is designed to coexist with many of the most popular messaging systems and uses open standards to help solve interoperability issues. Before you can begin to migrate user accounts or claim true integration between systems, both systems must be set up to coexist. This is best demonstrated in a multiphased migration strategy, where the two systems will interoperate for an extended period of time. Coexistence is achieved when the following conditions are met:

■ A reliable connection is made between the two systems.

■ The directories on each system contain users and distribution lists from the other systems, which are maintained manually or by an automatic process.

24

INTERFACING WITH OTHER MAIL SYSTEMS

- Mail sent to old addresses must be routed to the new location.
- Message transfer should be secure and reliable.

Connectivity

Connectivity between the two systems for messages is the core component for coexistence. This connection can be through a custom gateway written specifically to link the systems, or through a third entity such as the Internet or a Public X.400 network. Custom-written connection software, such as the one to the MS Mail connector for Exchange, will best support translation of the message properties between the two systems but may not be readily available. Using an open connection such as the Internet or an X.400 backbone to connect the systems may be a better option, but introduces problems with message security and reliability.

The connection between the two systems must be reliable because the systems will need to interoperate for an extended period of time. Carefully plan and monitor the connections you make between the systems to eliminate potential bottlenecks. Add additional connectors with similar costs if message transfer between the systems is expected to be heavy. Tools such as the link monitor can be used to watch the connection, and the administrators should keep an eye on the message queues for the MTA.

Depending on the type of connection you select to link your messaging systems to Exchange, expect that some features will not translate across the gateway. For instance, electronic forms created and mailed in Exchange will not be able to be viewed by users on the connected system. Advanced security features such as encryption and digital signature are not currently supported for non-Exchange recipients. Identify the features on each system that cannot cross the connection, and publish this information to the user community. If a group of users needs a particular feature for business purposes, make sure they are all on the same system.

Directory Exchange

Users on the connected systems will have trouble addressing messages if there are no address lists for them to pick from. The directories on each of the systems that must coexist should have entries for the users on the other systems. This can be done by a manual process initiated by the administrators, or setup for automatic maintenance if the systems share a common directory synchronization protocol.

Special consideration is needed to properly support distribution lists, commonly referred to as groups in other systems. For example, do you want to maintain a list of the finance users on each system, remembering to add a new user to all occurrences of the list? The solution you choose to address this issue is dependent on the way you administer the systems and the flexibility of the directory exchange. The best solution is to move the distribution lists to the Exchange platform, because it supports having custom recipients as members of distribution lists. You can also choose to maintain the lists separately, but if you are planning to migrate it is best to have the distribution lists located on the Exchange Server.

Migration

Migration is the process of moving information from an existing system to Exchange to support user connections to the new server. Exchange includes tools that will assist administrators in performing a migration. These tools leverage the existing information already contained in your current system, reducing the need to retype user information. The migration process should also preserve as much of the user's custom setups as possible.

Even though migrating to an Exchange messaging solution is a straightforward process, your project team will need to address a few issues. They need to plan for training, support, naming conventions, coexistence, and solid contingency procedures. Training for the users should coincide with the migration of their mailboxes, and administrators should be well-versed in the product before you start. The team should take a long look at the current naming conventions and change them to meet the changing needs of the company. Coexistence between the systems is crucial if the migration will happen in multiple phases. You should also have change control and fallback procedures in place should unexpected problems arise.

Establishing a well-thought-out migration plan will pay off during the implementation portion of the migration. Depending on the system you are migrating from, different tools and processes are available to make it progress more easily. There are two basic migration strategies, single-phase and multiphase, that can be modified to meet your company's migration needs. The strategy you use will depend on the size and complexity of your organization, and should leverage the resources you already have within your organization.

Single-Phase Migration

The single-phase migration is often referred to as the "hot cutover." It is best used in smaller organizations that have the resources to support such a conversion. It does require that you have existing Exchange Servers in place, which does not allow for recycling of server hardware. Coexistence issues need not be addressed unless you are using this strategy for branch locations within a larger migration.

An example of a single-phase migration would be if you were moving a single MS Mail post office with less than fifty users to an Exchange Server. You would first deploy the Exchange client to the user's workstations, having it access the current MS Mail post office. Then you could use the migration wizard to migrate the user mailboxes on a Friday night and send out a command to run the NEWPROF.EXE utility to setup the profiles for the users Monday morning. If you have done your planning correctly and all goes well, your company could be converted to Exchange over a single weekend.

Multiple Phases

Multiphased migrations are more in tune with the needs of a larger organization. Due to the size and complexity of their messaging systems, it is neither feasible or cost effective to do a single-phased migration. This migration strategy allows the implementation team to recycle existing hardware and leverage the stability of a known good system for fallback purposes. As explained previously, coexistence between the systems is critical to keeping messages flowing before, during, and after the migration.

An example of a multiphased migration would be for a medium sized organization with ten locations that have MS Mail post offices separated by WAN links. First the company's headquarters, the current routing hub, is integrated with an Exchange Server running the MS Mail connector. User migration can proceed while the server implementation team moves their focus to the branch offices. Exchange Servers are brought online at each of the branch offices, and the mailboxes are migrated individually or by post office depending on the number of users involved. Special planning for message routing and directory synchronization should be done before any of the branch offices are installed.

Microsoft Mail

The Microsoft Mail for PC Networks messaging product line has withstood the test of time, addressing many companies' messaging needs for four years longer than expected. Built upon a courier database developed in the 80s and sporting a flashy but usable client, it has outlived much of the competition of the same period. It's distant cousin, MS Mail for AppleTalk Networks, does have a client-server architecture, but lacks the features necessary for tomorrow's business environment. As we put these faithful companions out to pasture, we can move foreword to an Exchange messaging solution knowing that migration and coexistence issues will be kept at a minimum.

As with any major product upgrade or replacement, moving to the new product should be as painless as possible. The developers of Exchange included some powerful tools and connectors to easily integrate into the MS Mail environment. Customized migration tools and source extractors enable administrators to move users to the Exchange system in only a few clicks of the mouse. A very flexible and feature rich connector is included that will seamlessly integrate Exchange into an existing MS Mail environment. The directory synchronization agent for Exchange will act as both a requester and/or a server to the directory process used to keep addresses updated in MS Mail.

> **TIP**
>
> Before you attempt to setup the MS Mail connector and directory synchronization with your existing MS Mail environment, take some time to verify the health of the system. Run the PODIAG utility on each post office until all errors are corrected. Remove any unnecessary external post office definitions or they will be uploaded into the connector. Use the process of documenting your current configuration to identify things that can be cleaned up, as you do not need to drag any garbage into your brand new Exchange messaging system.

The MS Mail Connector

The Microsoft Mail Connector is specifically designed to link an Exchange Server to a pre-existing Microsoft Mail 3.*x* post office for either PC or AppleTalk networks. Because it was designed from the ground up to be fully compatible with these systems, interoperability issues are kept at a minimum. This connector also allows you to leverage the gateways available for MS Mail, which may provide connectivity not currently available in Exchange. If you have a good understanding of what makes MS Mail tick this section should be very easy to grasp.

Connector Architecture

The MS Mail Connector is made up of four distinct components:

- MS Mail Connector Postoffice (Shadow PO)
- MS Mail Connector Interchange (MSMI)
- MS Mail Connector PC MTA (External MMTA equivalent)
- MS Mail Connector AppleTalk MTA (Includes the Macintosh Gateway Extension)

The connector post office component, commonly referred to as the "shadow post office," has just enough of the database structure to support gateway access components and MTA connections. Used as temporary storage of messages going between Exchange and MS Mail, it does not support native client connections or require any direct administration. The Connector MTAs and the MSMI take care of moving messages in and out of this post office to route them to the appropriate destination.

The MS Mail Connector Interchange is a Windows NT service responsible for moving messages between the Exchange MTA and the connector post office. It takes messages originated by Exchange clients, converts them into MS Mail format, and places them in the connector post office for pickup by the MS Mail MTA. Messages that are received at the connector post office are picked up by the MSMI and converted to the Exchange format so the Exchange MTA can deliver them to the appropriate Exchange recipient. The MSMI also interacts with the AppleTalk MTA by transferring messages to the connection store located on the shadow post office.

The MS Mail Connector PC MTA is a Windows NT service that transfers messages between the connector post office and MS Mail for PC Networks native post offices. This MTA is very similar to the NT MMTA available in version 3.5 of MS Mail, except that is has smarter routing and better reliability. The MS Mail Connector AppleTalk MTA is a service that works with the Macintosh Gateway Extension to transfer mail between Exchange and AppleTalk mail servers. It works just like the MS Mail 3.2 Connection Gateway product used to connect PC mail with AppleTalk mail, sending and receiving messages from the \MACGATE\STORE\PCTOMAC and MACTOPC directories on the shadow post office.

> **CAUTION**
>
> Exchange Server 4.0 shipped with an older version of the gateway extension, version 3.1a. You should update this software component to the 3.1d version located on the disks for the 3.1d version of AppleTalk Server. You should also install and run this extension on the same Macintosh that has the AppleTalk server with the gateway component installed. This will prove to be more reliable and reduce problems related to network connectivity.

Configuration of the MS Mail Connector

The MS Mail Connector object(s) can be found in the connections container located under the configuration object for the site. Each Exchange Server that has an instance of the MS Mail Connector installed will show up here, and can only be configured from this location. Typically, you will only need one MS Mail Connector for each site, but multiple connectors in a site can provide backup routing if the proper costs are associated.

To configure the connector, open the properties for the MS Mail connector to view the following Interchange Properties page in Figure 24.1. If this is the first time you have accessed the connector properties, you will need to click on the Change button next to the Administrator's Mailbox field to select a mailbox to receive administrative messages. From here, you can select the primary language for clients, maximize compatibility of OLE messaging objects and enable message tracking.

The Maximize MS Mail 3.*x* compatibly checkbox will enable creation of two versions of OLE objects to support previous versions of OLE, and will increase the size of messages with embedded objects. You can also enable the MS Mail AppleTalk MTA by clicking on the configure button in the appropriate section of the page, which will only install the service. You will need to setup the Macintosh component separately to complete the configuration for message transfer.

FIGURE 24.1.

Interchange Properties page for the MS Mail Connector.

Select the Local Postoffice Properties page seen in Figure 24.2 to set the address space Exchange will use for Exchange address generation. Enter an appropriate name for the network, post office, and password fields to match the naming conventions you established in your planning sessions. After you change these names, click on the Regenerate button to have the system attendant update the MS proxy addresses for the Exchange recipient objects at the site.

FIGURE 24.2.

Local Postoffice Properties page for the MS Mail Connector.

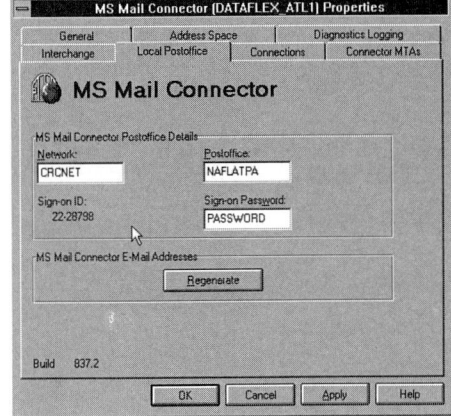

Select the Connections Properties page seen in Figure 24.3 to set up connections to existing MS Mail for PC Networks post offices. You will need to click the Create button for each direct connection to an MS Mail post office, because you will upload routing for all indirect post offices.

FIGURE 24.3.

Connections Properties page for the MS Mail Connector.

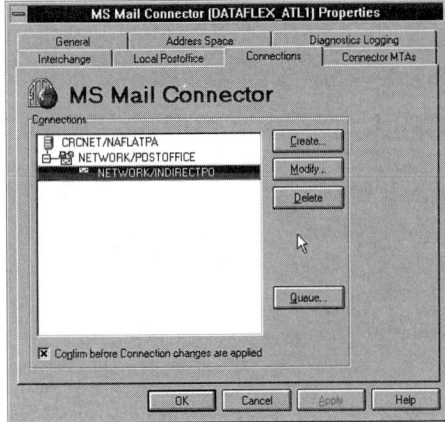

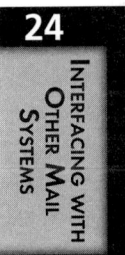

24

INTERFACING WITH
OTHER MAIL
SYSTEMS

Clicking the Create button will bring up the screen in Figure 24.4 to configure a new connection to a post office. For a LAN-connected post office, click the Change button and enter the full UNC path to the post office you want to connect to, such as \\servername\maildata. Enter an account and password if the server you are connecting to will not allow the Exchange service account to make a connection, such as a Novell server or an untrusted NT domain, and click on OK. The information for the post office is automatically filled in, and you should only need to modify the connection attempts to reduce NDRs for slow connections. Click on the update routing button, which brings up the downstream post offices summary page, to automatically upload and configure all post offices that are defined as indirect to this connection.

FIGURE 24.4.

*New Post Office
Connection window.*

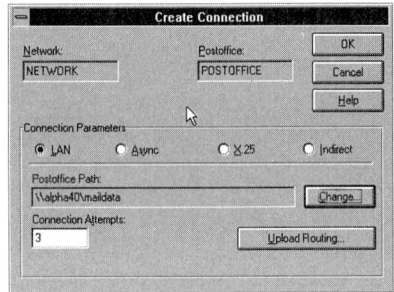

If you choose the Async or X.25 connection type, you will need to enter the network, post office, signon, X.25, and password information manually. You will also not be able to automatically update routing and will need to create connections that are indirect via this post office manually using the same procedure and selecting the Indirect connection type. Make sure to remember to configure an MTA of type Async to handle messages for this connection.

To finish the setup of the MS Mail connector, you create MTAs from the Connector MTAs Properties page displayed in Figure 24.5. Click on the New button to create a new MTA to service connected post offices. Enter an appropriate name for the MTA and set the options according to your needs. When naming MTAs keep in mind that the name you give them will determine where the service will show up in the NT service manager, with ones starting with the letter A at the top and letter Z at the bottom. Create at least one MTA of each type, such as LAN, Async, and X.25, that you need to service connected post offices. Select the MTA you just created and click on the List button to configure which post offices this MTA will service. Remember to use the MS Mail admin program to create a Direct-via-DOS-drive route on each connected post office to the shadow post office, or messages will not be delivered. This concludes the setup of the MS Mail Connector for your Exchange Server.

FIGURE 24.5.

*Connector MTAs
Properties page for the
MS Mail Connector.*

TIP

Do you need to make your Exchange PC MTAs WAN-friendly? When an MTA is WAN-friendly, it will only deliver mail from post office to post office without distributing it to the users or checking for outgoing mail over the WAN link. This configuration requires an MTA locally at each post office on the end of the WAN link to perform the rest of message transfer. This feature is available in the 3.5 MMTA as the Enable WAN Drives option, but is missing from the Properties page of the Connector MTA. The same functionally can be achieved by disabling the mailer from the MTA Properties page, and selecting the Do not pick up mail at this post office selection for the connected post office. This will reduce the load on your WAN link by at least three fold, freeing up valuable bandwidth.

Directory Synchronization

To have Exchange participate in the MS Mail directory synchronization (DirSync) process, you need to set up and configure the Directory Exchange Agent (DXA) on a server within the site that an MS Mail Connector is configured. The DXA can act as both a server and a requester to the MS Mail system, giving administrators added flexibility to control the DirSync process. Your planning sessions will help determine whether you will use the DXA as a server or a requester depending on your migration plan and address list needs. Using the DXA as both a server and a requester can create a multitiered configuration to get around some of the limitations of the MS Mail native process. An example of this multitiered approach is displayed in Figure 24.6.

FIGURE 24.6.

Using the DXA server and requister to create a multitiered DirSync process.

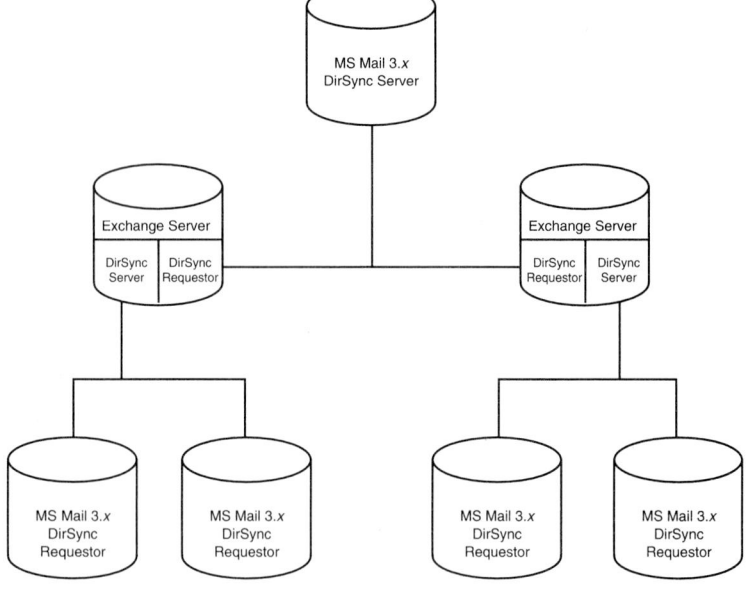

Configuring a DXA Server

To configure the DXA to be a DirSync server to MS Mail, select the New Other option from the File menu in the Exchange administrator, then select the DirSync Server option. This will bring up the General Properties page displayed in Figure 24.7. Click on the DirSync Administrator button to select an account to receive DirSync messages, and check the boxes for copying and forwarding DirSync messages to the administrator as needed. Next, click on the Schedule tab to display the times when the server should send messages to the requesters, referred to in DirSync terminology as the T2 time.

FIGURE 24.7.

General Properties page for a DXA DirSync server.

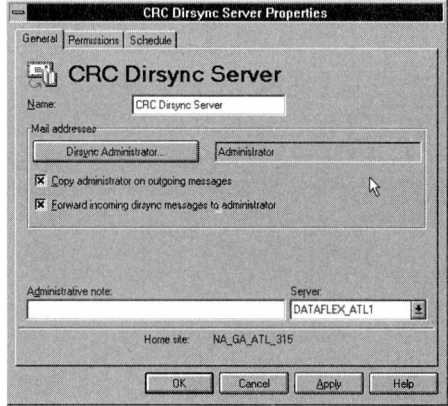

You will now need to create Remote DirSync Requesters for the post offices that will use the server you just configured. Select the New Other option from the File menu in the Exchange Administrator, then select the Remote DirSync Requester option. You will see a list of the MS Mail post offices available through the MS Mail Connector, so select the post office you want to configure. This will bring up the General Properties page for the remote requester as seen in Figure 24.8. The DirSync address field will automatically be filled in, so enter an appropriate password and select which address types are supported on this post office.

FIGURE 24.8.

General Properties page for a remote DirSync requester.

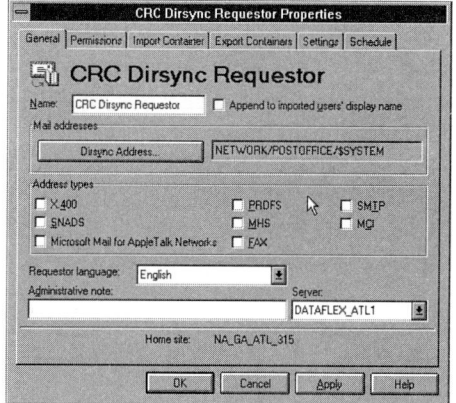

On the Import Container Properties page, you select in which container the addresses from this requester will be stored. I suggest that you create separate recipient containers for each requester post office, which will help with troubleshooting and maintenance. On the Export Containers Properties page, select the containers you would like exported to this requester and the trust level for address filtering. If an Exchange recipient has a trust level higher than the level set here, the information on that account will not be sent. This adds an extra level of configuration to the DirSync process that could be used to keep certain addresses from showing up in the MS Mail global address list. Remember to use the MS Mail admin program to register the address of the DirSync server for each post office you define in this manner. This concludes the setup of the DXA as a DirSync server to MS Mail.

Configuring a DXA Requester

To configure the DXA to be a requester to an existing MS Mail DirSync server, select the New Other option from the File menu in the Exchange Administrator, then select the DirSync Requester option. You will be prompted to select the address of the MS Mail DirSync server from the list of connected post offices. This will bring up the General Properties page displayed in Figure 24.9. You should give the requester an appropriate name and enter the appropriate password for the requester. The Schedule Properties page enables you to configure the send and receive update times, referred to as T1 and T3. Configure the Import and Export Containers Properties pages appropriately. You must also register this newly created requester with the MS Mail DirSync server from the admin program for MS Mail, assigning it the password you entered on the General Properties page.

FIGURE 24.9.

General Properties page for a DXA DirSync requester.

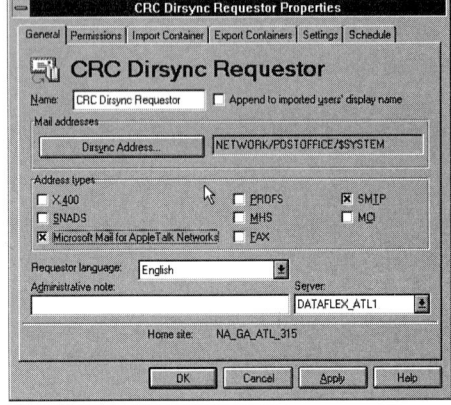

Migration

Migrating from MS Mail to Exchange is a simple process, assuming you have planned accordingly and have set up the systems to coexist. Establishing coexistence involves setting up the MS Mail Connector, configuring the DXA, configuring MS Mail to use Exchange connectors, installing gateway access components on the shadow post office, and planning your routing topology. The degree of coexistence and transfer-of-gateway functionality is fully dependent on your company's willingness to use the various features of Exchange. You may want to leave the existing MS Mail network routing and DirSync configuration intact because it is know to be in working order. If you decide to migrate routing, DirSync, and gateway services to the Exchange platform, you will benefit from the additional control and features inherent to the Exchange messaging solution.

The following list is an example of the suggested twelve steps for migration, but your plan may or may not include all the steps or be in this exact order:

1. Install the first Exchange Server at the site that has the routing hub for the existing MS Mail system, or where you want the hub to be.

2. Configure the MS Mail Connector post office connections and MTAs, uploading the indirect routing for the MS Mail hub post office.

3. Change all connected post offices to only have a direct connection to the shadow post office, redefining the other post offices as indirect via the shadow post office. This will make the Exchange Server the hub for all messaging traffic.

4. Configure the DXA to be either a DirSync server or requester to create custom recipients in the Exchange directory and verify the processing is working correctly.

5. Migrate existing X.400 and SMTP gateways to the Exchange Server, reconfiguring the access components to point to the shadow post office.

6. Test all message routing and functionality.

7. Migrate existing MS Mail groups to Exchange distribution lists.

8. Deploy the Exchange client and have it connect to the MS Mail post offices for now.

9. Use the Migration tool to perform a one-step migration of each MS Mail post office for all the users. You could also migrate each user independently with this tool, but this will require client connectivity to the MS Mail post office until all the users are converted and routing is updated.

10. Update secondary proxy addresses during the client migration.

11. Use link, server, and performance monitors to watch messaging loads before, during, and after the migration to validate your design.

12. Take a two-week vacation, because you've earned it.

TIP

Migrating an existing MS Mail 3.0 SMTP gateway to the Exchange IMC can be a tricky process. You need to make sure that each MS Mail custom recipient in the Exchange directory has a secondary proxy address that matches their original address from the MS Mail SMTP gateway. This address will be *username@po.domain.com*, where *username* is the mailbox of the user, and *po* is the name of the post office. You could export the custom recipients to a file, and use Excel or Access to add the Secondary-Proxy-Addresses field to the file to be re-imported. There is a better option. Use the MIGSMTP utility from the Web site since it will automatically update the MS Mail custom recipients, based on the configuration of the MS Mail SMTP gateway in a very timely manner. You should make sure that the DirSync process is working correctly before using this utility.

Lotus Notes and cc:Mail

Lotus Development Corporation, a subsidiary of IBM, currently offers the Lotus Notes and cc:Mail messaging products. Lotus Notes has evolved over the years from a Groupware application to a full-featured messaging and Groupware solution, and is Exchange's major competition. The cc:Mail product is an SFS-based messaging product that is similar in design to MS Mail, with the message transfer engines located at the client and router applications. Both products have gateways, offered by Lotus and third-party vendors, to connect to external systems via X.400 or SMTP messaging standards. Even though native gateway offerings, such as

LinkAge, are currently available to connect Lotus messaging products directly to Exchange, they can be connected by using open standards such as SMTP or X.400 or through an existing MS Mail to cc:Mail gateway.

Lotus Notes Coexistence

Because Microsoft has not proposed a connectivity option to link Lotus Notes and Exchange, you need to use the X.400 or SMTP connectors. Both systems have native gateways to support these standards, which do support message content and attachment transfer. Managing directory information will be a manual process, involving the export and import of the entire recipients lists for each system. Public folder and Notes database information cannot be natively exchanged between the two systems, unless you use a third-party product such as MESA Jumpstart.

Using the SMTP standard to connect Exchange to Notes has some distinct drawbacks. Messages need to be converted into simple text format, which loses any of the rich text formatting or imbedded objects. File attachments will be handled correctly, and you should configure the connection to use the MIME encoding method for the best performance. You should configure the IMC to never send rich text to the SMTP domain name for the Notes server, and disable any rich-text properties from the Notes side.

Third-party products, such as LinkAge, DiamondNet SoftSwitch, or Control Data Systems Mailhub, can be used to link the two systems via X.400 and support directory exchange for X.500 objects. These solutions are mentioned because they will assist larger organizations in managing the massive volumes of messaging data, using reliable and open standards for coexistence. The project planning team should research the available connectivity solutions to link Notes to Exchange, and select the product that meets the company's long term messaging goals.

Lotus cc:Mail Coexistence and Migration

Integrating an existing cc:Mail messaging system to Exchange Server has many challenges, namely in directory exchange and feature mapping. Microsoft is currently developing a cc:Mail connector to link Exchange to cc:Mail post offices. This product is planned to support the following features:

- Messaging between the cc:Mail and Microsoft Exchange Server environments without the need for SMTP or X.400 gateways
- Bi-directional, incremental directory updates
- An administration interface integrated into the Exchange Administrator program
- Connector setup as a part of Microsoft Exchange Server Setup

This connector will run as a Windows NT service and support intelligent routing and message content conversion for rich text and OLE objects. Messages that are destined for a cc:Mail recipient will be converted to support the features of that platform, removing or modifying parts of the message appropriately. Additionally, it will enable the Exchange Server to participate as a member of the cc:Mail Automated Directory Exchange (ADE) process. This will create custom recipients in the Exchange directory for cc:Mail recipients, and put Exchange mailboxes in the address lists of cc:Mail.

The options for connecting these two systems today utilize the X.400 or SMTP connectors built into Exchange, or existing MS Mail to cc:Mail gateways. These options do require the cc:Mail system to have the appropriate gateway installed, which is available from Lotus or third-party vendors. If you use the X.400- or SMTP-based solution, directory updates to both systems will be a manual process. Many of the gateway products designed to link MS Mail to cc:Mail support the DirSync process, which will enable the Exchange directory to automatically send and receive updates with cc:Mail via DirSync.

The Migration Wizard tool included with the Exchange Server has the ability to extract information about mailboxes, messages, attachments, and public bulletin boards. The source extractor does not support copying public and private mail lists, post office address books, post office remote address lists, or propagation lists. Migration can be a one-step or a two-step migration, depending on whether you need to change directory names. In the two-step migration, you have the ability to edit the migration file before you import it into the Exchange system. The migration process using the Migration Wizard is similar to that for MS Mail, and is discussed later in this chapter.

Host-Based Systems

Many large organizations have lots of time and money invested in host-based messaging systems. Most of these systems were developed in the early to late 1980s and still provide messaging functionality to large numbers of users. As mentioned in Chapter 20, these systems were not known for their interoperability or ease of use, but did meet the needs of an entire organization. As messaging standards evolved, host-based systems began to embrace these standards to facilitate message transfer outside the organization. This section focuses on two of the most popular host-based messaging systems: IBM PROFS/OfficeVision/VM and Digital All-in-One.

As you assemble your migration team, keep in mind the size and complexity of your company's host-based messaging system. You will need to have membership in the group from host administrators, LAN/WAN specialists, desktop support staff, and consultants. The consultants should have practical experience in your host messaging system, as they will need to bring an objective view to the process of downsizing your messaging system. This team will be responsible for the host-based migration utilities and source extractors, as well as for solving any issues relating to the host or migration process.

Exchange Server ships with several applications that will extract and import addresses, mailboxes, messages, shared folders, and scheduling information from your host-based system. The source extractors are used to copy directory, messaging, and scheduling information from your current system into a standard migration file. The Migration Wizard will read the migration file and transfer the information into the Exchange directory and information stores. The administrator program for Exchange will be used to export and import directory files that can be used to manually update both systems. If your host messaging system does not have a source extractor available, you can write one yourself by referring to the Creating a Source Extractor document included on the Exchange Server CD-ROM.

IBM PROFS/OfficeVision/VM

The best method of migration from PROFS (Or OfficeVision/VM) to Exchange is a multiphase migration, but you could perform a single-phased migration if you have a limited number of users. To establish coexistence between the host and Exchange, you need to connect the systems with either Attachmate's ZIP! Office Exchange gateway, MS Mail PROFS gateway, or SMTP. The Attachmate ZIP! Office Exchange gateway has the added benefit of managing the directory syncronization between the two systems.

To begin the migration, you need to install, configure, and run the source extractor on the VM host. This includes transferring the migration software through a 3270 emulator, setting up the accounts to use for the extractor, configuring the host executables, and launching the extractor process. The migration extractor will log on each VM ID and launch a program to extract information to do the following:

- Create mailboxes from the PROFS ID information in the OFSUAD FILE.
- Migrate messages, schedule data, documents, and personal address books from the OFSMCNTL and OFSMLIST files for each PROFS ID to Microsoft Exchange Server migration format files.
- Create recipients using the PROFS ID information.
- Import non-PROFS users from the nickname file into Microsoft Exchange Server as custom recipients with PROFS addresses. Mail sent to these recipients will be passed to the PROFS gateway for delivery.

Once you have used the source extractor to generate standard migration files, run the Migration Wizard to import the information from the migration files into the Exchange directory and information stores. An alternative to migrating the users in phases is to use the PROFS MAPI service provider in Attachmate's ZIP! Office Client Connection product. You could use the source extractor to create the Exchange mailboxes, then link the Exchange client to PROFS and the Exchange Server. When you perform the full migration process for a user, you only need to send out a command to run the NEWPROF utility to remove the PROFS MAPI service provider.

Digital All-in-One

It is also best to use the multiphase migration for moving users from a Digital All-in-One host messaging system to Exchange. You should be running version 2.2 or later of All-in-One to be able to use the source extractor for migration. To connect the Exchange Server and the All-in-One messaging system, you use the X.400 connector or the IMC for the Exchange side, and one of the following for the All-in-One system:

- X.400 with Digital's MRX and Message Router to All-in-One Supports 1984 standards only
- X.400 with Digital's MAILbus Supports 1988 standards
- SMTP with Digital's MAILbus Supports MIME

Before you begin the migration process, you need to get the directories on both systems copied to each other. This can be done with the directory import/export from the administrative client, using Digital's Directory Synchronization Utility. You also can use a third-party program. Plan for naming convention changes, because All-in-One supports accounts of up to 30 characters, but Windows NT accounts are limited to 20 characters.

To install the source extractor on the All-in-One system, create an account named EX_MIGRAGE with the XOWN privilege to run scripts and access the forms libraries. Grant this account the READALL and SYSPRIV privileges, so it can access the users' mailboxes. Transfer the script files and forms from the \MIGRATE\TOOLS\HOST\ALL-IN-1 directory to the All-in-One directory for EX_MIGRATE. For the All-in-One profile for EX_MIGRATE, specify EDT as the default editor, include EXFORMS as a default form library, and include EX_MENU as the initial form. From the $ prompt in the All-in-One directory for EX_MIGRATE, run the command @EX_INST to build the EXFORMS library and rename files.

Log back on as the EX_MIGRATE account, select the MIG command from the menu, and specify the desired parameters. Run the extractor in batches of less than 100 users, and limit the extractor to batches of up to 950 users. Review the log file from the Log menu and then transfer the created migration files to the Exchange Server in binary mode. Now run the Migration Wizard to process the migration files to load the data into the Exchange directory and information stores. The migrated clients should now be able to open the Exchange client and see their messages, folders, and migrated address lists. They will need to send any pending deferred mail from their inbox, and reshare any shared folders by dragging them to the public folder hierarchy.

One thing you should keep in mind when migrating from either of these host systems is the effect the migration process will have on the space messages use. Both PROFS and All-in-One host messaging systems support the single message instance to save space. When you use the source extractor to migrate messaging information, each user will get a copy of that single stored message, increasing the amount of space that will be needed on Exchange. Have the users clean up their mailboxes before you run the extractor, and figure from ten to fifteen percent additional space requirements for migration.

UNIX SMTP and POP3

If your company is currently using a UNIX-based SMTP or Post Office Protocol 3 (POP3) messaging server to provide internal e-mail capabilities, Exchange will easily coexist with these systems. The Internet Mail Connector (IMC) fully supports the RFC #821 and #822 specifications for message transfer to and from SMTP-based systems. This connectivity option also supports UUENCODE and MIME encoding techniques for attachments to messages and extended message bodyparts.

Because these systems do not normally have built-in directories or global address lists, you need to create custom recipients for each of the mailboxes on the foreign system. Many third-party POP3 servers have proprietary methods for providing users with address lists, but normally the users need to know the address of someone they want to send messages to. These systems also lack any Groupware or public folder capabilities, which only simplifies any migration processes.

If you are planning to migrate users from SMTP- or POP3-based systems, the process of connecting the systems and moving user mailboxes will not be very complicated. First, you must decide on which system will be the primary recipient for any external mail from other systems or the Internet. The best choice is to use Exchange to front-end all incoming mail and have Exchange foreword messages to the SMTP host computer. You can configure the default address space in Exchange to be the primary e-mail domain name, and configure the IMC to foreword all mail for the SMTP native users to the IP address of the SMTP host. You should already be running DNS at your site, and can use MX records to make sure all incoming mail is first sent to the Exchange IMC.

You should build custom recipients in a recipients container within the Exchange site with the primary e-mail address set to username@otherhost.domain.com, for example. You can dump the existing list of users from the SMTP host with your favorite UNIX tool, then convert that file to the directory import format for use in the directory import tool from the administration application. Make sure to use the correct type of Remote in the import file, and do not create the Windows NT accounts unless you will need them for other purposes.

Moving users from the SMTP host is not possible with any source extractor or migration tool at this time. Install the Exchange client for the users you wish to migrate, and set up their profile to use the Internet Mail service provider configured for the SMTP host. You should then use the file you exported from the SMTP host to create an import file that can be used to create mailboxes and NT accounts for the users you want to migrate. Once you have created the mailboxes and removed the custom recipients, new messages destined for the users should start being received in the Exchange mailbox. You should then change the users' Exchange client profiles to use only the Exchange service provider, removing the Internet Mail provider connection to the old SMTP system.

If your location has users that are on UNIX-based workstations, the Exchange client is not an option. You will want to leave the SMTP native host in place to support these users, but still use Exchange to front-end all incoming message traffic. The next version of Exchange is slated to support native POP3 connections to Exchange mailboxes. This will enable you to configure UNIX workstations to use the Exchange Server as their e-mail server, with all the benefits of administrating Exchange native mailboxes. The next version should also support LDAP and IMAP4 standards to enable Light Web-based clients to access Exchange native mailboxes and the Exchange directory.

> **TIP**
>
> If your Exchange Server site has more than one server, and requires a connection to the Internet, you have the option of increasing the security for the internal SMTP connections. One IMC can be configured to connect to the Internet, with very little restrictions on what hosts can make connections. The other IMC can be set up with the address space of @host.domain.com to match the internal SMTP host, and restrict access to allow connections only from that host. You should also update your internal DNS record for the internal host with an MX record for better performance.

X.400-Based Systems

Of all the connector options used for coexistence with foreign messaging systems, the X.400 connector is the most robust and reliable. It is hard to find an enterprise level messaging system that does not support native X.400 connectivity, either by design or by gateway options. Exchange Server has gone through extensive conformance and interoperability testing to prove that it subscribes to the standard, and it can communicate with other systems that subscribe to the X.400 recommendations. The following systems have been tested using the OSINET and EUROSINET interoperability test suites for 1984 and 1988 X.400 conformance using the P1, P2, and P22 protocol scenarios:

- DEC MRX (1984)
- Retix Open Server (1984)
- Microsoft Mail 3.2 X.400 Gateway (1984)
- Softswitch Central (1984)
- Isocor Isoplex 800 MTA (1988)
- HP OpenMail (1988)
- Lotus Message Switch (formerly Softswitch EMX) (1988)
- Control Data X.400 Mail system (1988)
- DEC Mailworks (1988)
- INFONET (1988)
- Novell MAWG X.400 Gateway (1988)

24

INTERFACING WITH
OTHER MAIL
SYSTEMS

The Exchange X.400 MTA was tested for conformance with the following network configurations over the three most popular standard OSI transports—TP0/X.25, TP4/CLNP, and TP0/RFC1006 to TCP/IP:

- Digital Equipment Corporation OS TCP/IP and TP4/CLNP
- Hewlett Packard OS TCP/IP, TP4/CLNP, and TP0/X.25
- Retix TP4/CLNP and TP0/X.25
- Isocor TP0/X.25
- Sun Microsystems OSI TP4/CLNP and TP0/RFC1006 to TCP/IP products
- Isocor UNIX version using SCO UNIX TCP/IP & TP0/X.25
- Sprint X.25 Public Services
- AT&T X.25 Public Services

This extensive testing with other vendors' systems does not guarantee complete conformance with the standards, but it is a good indicator of how well the Exchange X.400 connector can "play with others." The capability of Exchange to connect to other vendors systems is very important for larger customers, because they already have these and other systems that use the X.400 standards for interconnectivity. Many of the hub-and-switch technologies used to interconnect the messaging infrastructures of global corporations employ X.400 and X.500 standards to create robust routing backbones and directory services.

The X.400 connector is normally used as a coexistence connector to support a multiphase migration from another messaging system, so it is unlikely that you will need to convert from an X.400 native messaging system. The source extractors for the system you are converting from will extract the messaging information to a common format that can be imported into Exchange by the Migration Wizard. This is why there are no source extraction programs to extract messaging information from X.400-based systems.

The X.400 connector supports sending and receiving messages from other X.400 mail systems operating as a relay MTA. It can also operate as a PRMD-to-PRMD (Private Management Domain) MTA to provide standalone message backbone services for customers that do not want to subscribe to a public X.400 service to connect their systems. This flexibility extends the options companies have to interconnect existing Exchange and foreign X.400 messaging systems.

The Exchange directory service and X.400 name space can include addresses from external X.400 systems to enable customers to mail to recipients on those systems. The directory import tool enables administrators to bulk import X.400 addresses into recipient containers as custom recipients. These addresses are then automatically replicated throughout the Exchange organization by the directory replication process. Users at other Exchange sites will then see those recipients in their global address list and do not need any custom procedures to mail to these recipients. Users also have the option of creating X.400 address recipients in their personal address list as long as they know the address of the person they wish to mail to.

The X.400 connector and MTAs are not limited to just connecting to external systems. Robust message routing and fault-tolerant message transfer can be established between Exchange sites and Exchange organizational messaging systems. You can even connect two MS Mail systems through Exchange if they have the X.400 gateway access components installed. This enables the messaging infrastructure architects to use Exchange to build a corporate backbone without the need for proprietary third-party software solutions.

The X.500 directory schema defines the object properties for all Exchange recipients, which third-party directory services can use to replicate to other systems. Future versions of Exchange will support access and update methods for lookup and modification to the Exchange directory, such as the Lightweight Directory Access Protocol (LDAP) standard. As Exchange is updated and enhanced in new releases, this directory information will be the cornerstone used to build new applications and create a detailed view of the entire organization.

> **CAUTION**
>
> If you use X.400 connectors to connect your sites, make sure to set the conformance options the same for both ends. If you change the conformance options on the Advanced Properties page for the connector only at one site, message transfer will immediately stop between the sites. I suggest that you always create an X.400 connector that will be used exclusively for connections to other Exchange sites, with separate connectors for external or foreign X.400 systems.

Migration and Tools

Earlier sections in this chapter have already covered the various source extraction tools used to create migration files for a two setup migration process. This section covers the use of the Migration Wizard to import those files, as well as the one-step migrations available for MS Mail and Lotus cc:Mail. These tools provide administrators and migration specialists with time- and labor-saving processes that enable them to focus on the migration and coexistence issues, reducing the headaches they may have experienced in previous migrations for other systems.

The Exchange Migration Wizard, MAILMIG.EXE, is installed in the directory \EXCHSRVR\BIN on every server within the organization. It can be copied to an administrative workstation as long as the Exchange administration program is installed and working correctly. It is a Windows NT 32-bit application that does take advantage of some multithreading capabilities. Performance can suffer if it is used to migrate information to a server that is separated from the machine running the program by slow or unreliable links. For performance reasons, run the Migration Wizard from the Exchange Server you are migrating data to. It should generally be run after normal business hours if you are importing large amounts of data. As you use this tool to import new information to your Exchange Servers, you will get a pretty good picture of how well your servers will perform under heavy loads.

Second Half of a Two-Step Migration

Once you are finished with the source extraction process from your existing system, the migration files will need to be processed by the Migration Wizard. The source extractors will create three files: the packing list file, the primary migration file, and the secondary migration file. You should make any directory object naming changes to these files prior to moving to the next step. The following list explains the purpose of each file:

■ The packing list file contains a list of the primary and secondary migration files, as well as the code page of the migrated information.

■ Primary migration files are in comma separated value (CSV) format and contain the changes that need to be made to the directory, mail message headers, and personal address lists. It can also contain pointers to secondary migration files.

■ Secondary migration files contain nondirectory-related pieces of data that do not fit into the primary migration file such as message attachments, binary data, message bodies, and any text that includes carriage returns.

Depending on the amount of information you are migrating, these files can range from a few hundred kilobytes to a few hundred megabytes. They may need to be stored on a system with plenty of temporary drive space, and your migration plan should include procurement of this hard drive space. Before you import the files into your Exchange system, you should run the verification process on the migration files to check them for errors. There is nothing more frustrating than to come into work to find that the import process you started last night hung up on the fifth recipient because of a syntax error. See Figure 24.10 for an example of the import file page and verification options.

FIGURE 24.10.

*Migration Wizard
import file page with
verification option
enabled.*

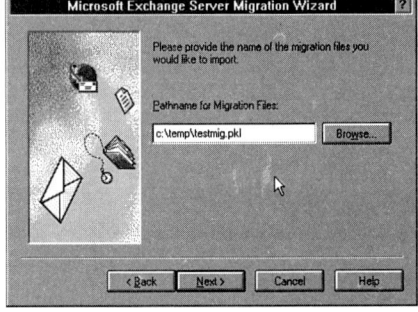

After you have verified the integrity of the three migration import files, you should use the Migration Wizard to start the process. This can take as little as two minutes or two hours, depending on the number of users and the volume of messages. The status screen in Figure 24.11 illustrates the progress and elapsed time for the migration process. It may be informative, but it is as interesting as watching grass grow. This is a good time to review your migration project milestones to make sure you are on target.

FIGURE 24.11.

Migration Wizard status page.

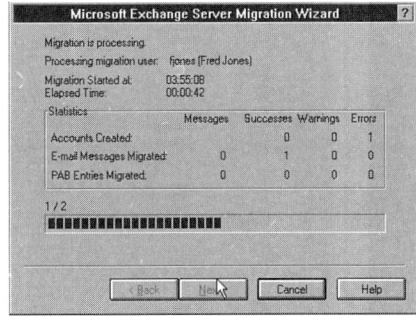

Once the process is complete, review the Migration Wizard error file and the Windows NT event viewer. The wizard error file will contain information from the primary migration file, in the same format, that the process had problems with. It can also contain pointer information from the secondary file that was in error. Edit these entries as needed and run the Migration Wizard on the corrected file to retry those entries. The Windows NT event viewer will have informational and error messages from the Migration Wizard application, or from other processes such as the proxy address generation done by the system attendant. Once the migration is completed without errors, review the mailbox and distribution list objects that were created for accuracy.

MS Mail and cc:Mail Migration

The Migration Wizard will perform the source extraction and import processes for migration of MS Mail and cc:Mail messaging systems. You can perform a one-step migration from the wizard, or do a two-step migration if you need to edit any information before it is imported. The screens and selections for MS Mail and cc:Mail are practically identical, so this section will use a MS Mail migration in the example. If you elect to perform a two-step migration for either of these systems, the three migration files will be created and should be imported as outlined in the previous section.

When you start the Exchange Migration Wizard, you will see the following screen in Figure 24.12. From this page, make the selection for MS Mail for PC Networks and click on the Next button. You will then see information concerning coexistence between the two systems to support the migration process. Click on Next in this window to continue.

FIGURE 24.12.

*Migration Wizard
selection type page.*

You will now see the screen in Figure 24.13, prompting you for the location and security information for an existing post office. Enter the full UNC address of the MS Mail post office, such as \\servername\maildata. Enter the administrator's mailbox and password for the security information, then click on the Next button after you have entered the appropriate information. You will now be prompted to select a one-step or a two-step migration. In this example, you are going to perform a one-step migration, and you make the appropriate selection and click on the Next button.

FIGURE 24.13.

*Migration Wizard post
office and security page.*

NOTE

If you receive an error message that the selected post office is read-only, then users may have the file MASTER.GLB or FLAG.GLB locked. Use server manager to close any connections to either of these files. If you are at the server that has the post office on it, you can issue the command net files ¦ find /I "GLB" to list the user connections to these files. Use the command net files *XXXXXX* /c where *XXXXXX* is the file connection number for the file you want to close. After the MASTER.GLB and FLAG.GLB are closed you can continue with the Migration Wizard by clicking on Next.

The next screen in Figure 24.14 will enable you to select the information to convert. There are selections for the mailboxes, e-mail messages by range, personal e-mail addresses, schedule plus information, and shared folders. You should make appropriate selections for the information you want to migrate. Remember to migrate the shared folder information only once, because you will receive a message in the event viewer if you try to convert the shared folders more than once. Click on the Next button to continue.

FIGURE 24.14.

Migration Wizard items to convert selection page.

The next page you will see will give you a list of the user mailboxes on the selected post office in Figure 24.15. Select the user mailboxes you want to migrate, and if you are going to do the entire post office deselect the admin and any nonuser mailboxes. Click on the Next button to continue.

FIGURE 24.15.

Migration Wizard mailbox selection page.

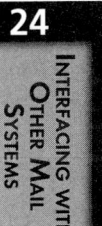

If you selected to migrate shared folder information, you will be prompted to select what type of default access permissions to assign to the public folder that will be created. Be careful if you select the no access selection, because only the folder owner will be able to access and manage the new public folder that will be created. Click on the Next button to continue.

The next selection screen will prompt you for the Exchange Server to use for the migration. Enter the server name of the Exchange Server you want to put the user accounts on and click on the Next button. The next screen, in Figure 24.16, will enable you to select the recipients container and the template mailbox to use for mailbox creation. Choose the recipients container you want the new addresses to appear in, and choose an appropriate template account that has previously been set up. The template account should only include properties that you want all the mailboxes you are migrating to have, so be very careful which one you select. Click on the Next button to continue.

FIGURE 24.16.

Migration Wizard Recipients Container and Template Mailbox page.

The next screen (see Figure 24.17) enables you to select whether you want NT accounts to be created, the passwords to use, and the domain to create them in. If your users already have NT accounts, the migration process will attempt to match an NT account to the mailbox value. If you need NT accounts that will differ from the user mailbox, select to not create accounts. Select also the appropriate Windows NT domain you want the Migration Wizard to use. Click on the Next button to continue.

FIGURE 24.17.

Migration Wizard Windows NT account and Domain page.

The Migration Wizard will now display the status window that will tell you how the migration is proceeding. There is information on the number of accounts, messages, and folders that are being and have been migrated. The number of warnings and errors are also listed. This process will run for as long as there are messages and accounts to be migrated. The length of time it will take is fully dependent on the amount of data to be converted and the connection speed you have to both systems. Remember to avoid running this process across a slow link, because it will take extraordinarily long to complete.

When the process is finished, review the migration log and the NT event viewer application log for errors and warnings. If all has gone well, you have successfully migrated a number of users to Exchange and set up the directory object properties. You will want to review the mailboxes you just migrated to make sure they have the proper primary NT accounts selected and have the users validate that their messages and personal address lists have been properly migrated.

Summary

Many companies have complex messaging systems that are made up of different messaging products. The challenge is to connect these systems to Exchange to establish coexistence for interoperability or support of a migration. Coexistence is a key component for any multiphase migration project to make sure the various systems can interchange messages and directories. Planning your company's migration strategy by utilizing a diverse project team is critical to the success of your endeavor. Users should not experience loss of messaging functionality during the conversion, and directory information must be kept up-to-date on both systems so that users can still find individuals that have and have not been migrated.

Microsoft Exchange includes various tools and connectors to help systems coexist and smooth the migration process. Source extractors are available for the most popular proprietary host- and LAN-based messaging systems, and are used to extract valuable information from your current e-mail system to be loaded into Exchange's directory and information stores. The included Migration Wizard simplifies the process of extracting and propagating the information from the migrated system into the Exchange messaging system. The connector solutions that are used to interconnect Exchange to current messaging systems include the X.400 connector, the Internet mail connector, the MS Mail connector, and various third-party solutions. Exchanging directory information between the systems during coexistence will reduce user addressing problems, and help make the transition much more seamless. Smaller companies may have the luxury of skipping the coexistence phase of a migration and switch to Exchange practically overnight.

Chapter 25, "Exchange Server Performance Tuning and Scaling," covers Exchange Server performance tuning and scaling. I attempt to help you answer the famous question, "How many users can I put on a single Exchange Server?" The chapter also outlines techniques that can be used to tune and monitor your Exchange Servers in a production environment. The need for various utilities and tuning methodologies are balanced against the need to keep your system running reliably. Chapter 25 should be fun for both you and me because it will enable us to get under the hood of Exchange to see just how powerful it really is.

24

INTERFACING WITH OTHER MAIL SYSTEMS

Exchange Server Performance Tuning and Scaling

by Gregory Dodge

IN THIS CHAPTER

An unnamed customer of mine called one day complaining of terrible performance on one of the company's NT servers. When I arrived on-site, the customer explained that the company had just installed a new server and had tuned the system as the white papers had recommended. Unfortunately, users were complaining of delays in running the client-server application that attached to the server. On further examination, it was very clear that the system was severely overloaded and lacked some type of system resource. The paging frequency and low-memory warnings in the Event Viewer showed that the system did not have enough physical memory. It turned out that, in its planning sessions, the customer had made a small miscalculation in determining memory requirements, which gave 32M of RAM rather than the 128M needed. Needless to say, the next system put into production was thoroughly tested and piloted, with simulations of estimated system load after tuning was done.

In my opinion, Exchange Server performance tuning is like selecting a very fine wine and cheese combination: you keep sampling and testing until you find the combination that works exceptionally well together. Selecting the right hardware options to complement your software poses the greatest challenge, because the hardware performance options change almost weekly. Purchasing the right system to meet today's needs must be balanced with the needs for growth and expandability as you add more users and business processes to your messaging system. Underestimating current and future requirements can adversely affect the users' perceptions of the system's capability to meet their ever growing needs.

Every system has some type of bottleneck that limits some aspect of system performance. Hardware tuning involves finding and eliminating these bottlenecks until you reach an acceptable level of performance. Determining where the bottlenecks are in any system requires good tools and structured testing methodologies. Simulating system load in a lab environment is not a good way to find a system's limits; real messaging systems are confined by external forces such as networks and user behavior that can not be simulated in a "clean" lab environment. The planning and pilot phases of any implementation require good benchmarking and logging applications to assist in documenting the actual performance of the system.

This chapter discusses the concepts and methodologies used to tune your Exchange system to an acceptable performance level. You need to have a good grasp of what your current messaging system is doing before you can begin to shop for hardware for your Exchange messaging system. A practical approach to help you select servers and performance options is included, with tips for optimizing network access. The text covers the tools included with the Exchange Server that enable you to gain access to the numerous configuration parameters within the registry and databases. The best way to prove that your design will meet your company's needs is to run a pilot project with a cross-section of your user community, and use simulated clients to determine how well the servers will perform under the estimated load.

Documenting the Current System

The best way to know where you want to go is to fully understand where you have been. Would a doctor prescribe a treatment without first reviewing a patient's medical history? Would an architect draw up plans to remodel a building without viewing the previous plans and performing a site survey? Would you really want to be the customer in either of these scenarios if the proper planning and research were not done? The same importance is put on a proper analysis of your current messaging system and the habits of the end-users. By using the valuable information contained within your current e-mail system, you will be able to design and implement your next-generation messaging system.

The process of documenting your current system involves gathering, parsing, and publishing the information for your planning sessions. The methods you use to gather data from your current messaging system depend on what tools are available. The parsing of the data can be done with many different software analysis tools. The tool could be as complex as a customized application specific to this purpose, or as simple as using office automation products such as Microsoft Excel and Access. To publish and present the data to the project team, you can utilize any of the most popular network modeling tools, or just use your favorite word processor and spreadsheet.

Gathering and Parsing the Data

Within your current messaging infrastructure are valuable messaging statistics just waiting to be uncovered. The way you extract that information might be very formal, or might require some imaginative methods of using features that were not designed to perform data collection. If you currently are not using a messaging system, this section will still be helpful, because you will be able to create virtual data derived from your current messaging needs. You need to collect five main categories of data:

- Message delivery time
- Message layover time
- Average number of messages per connection
- Average size of messages per connection
- Average number of errors or problems per connection

Message Delivery Time

Message delivery time is the total amount of time it takes to move a single message from a sender to the intended recipient, averaged by hour, day, week, or other time frame. This total includes the time it takes for the message to move from the client to the post office, the transfer time from the sender's post office to the recipient's post office, and the time it takes for the recipient to retrieve the message from the destination post office. The time it takes for delivery of any message is affected by its size, complexity, route, and number of conversions. A difference also exists between actual and perceived message transfer times because of the human factor involved.

This is probably the easiest information to extract from your current system. Many of the most popular messaging systems have counters you can use to calculate this data. You should fully enable system logging within the system, as well as turn on any external logging tools. You can parse these logs, depending on the format, to determine the start and end times for each message sent, to determine the delta time of message transfer. This task could be as simple as searching the message headers for the keywords Sent and Received within Excel to use in a formula that calculates the delta time. It could also be as complicated as writing a custom program to parse the logs into a more readable format. You should select which period of time to average the data on and be consistent throughout your analysis.

For example, if you are using an MS Mail messaging system, these logs can be created by the message transfer agents. By enabling the options in the MTA configuration for logging of sent and received messages in verbose format, the files SENT.LOG, RECV.LOG, and SESSION.LOG will be created in the \LOG directory on each post office that MTA services. You can combine this information with the estimated polling frequency of the clients to determine the total time it takes for message transfer. A simple Excel macro, created by an import wizard, can be created to parse these logs and run selected formulas to generate the transfer times.

Message Layover Time

Message layover, or latency, is the amount of time a message is stored at a post office when it is not in transit. Because most systems are based on the store-and-forward delivery model, every message must spend some time in a static state within a post office's area used for "storage" of messages. Calculating this time is more challenging, because you must determine the time the message arrived and the time the message left. Many systems use unique identifiers for each message, which can be used to get the in and out times for each message. You might have to use the subject line combined with the timestamps to uniquely identify each message.

Expanding on our example, you would use the same sent and received logs at each MS Mail post office to calculate the layover time. If a particular message has entries in both the received and the sent logs, the message "hopped" through the post office by an indirect routing method. Excel can also be used to import and parse these logs to compare each message that shows up in the received log that has a match in the sent log, to determine the amount of time the message stayed at the post office.

Average Number of Messages Per Connection

The message volume is the total number of messages sent and received between two distinct points during a specific time period. Most messaging systems have some type of message transfer agent that can be used to get this information. You should identify each point of interest for tracking purposes and calculate the message volume between all these points. As the number of points increases, the number of connections you must track will increase by a factor of the number of points. For instance, if you have 4 destinations, you would have 16 different connections to calculate the message volume for; 5 destinations would give you 25 connections, and 10 would give you 100.

Continuing with the example, MS Mail has a system utility included in the resource kit that performs this function. This utility, called the MS Mail Postoffice Traffic Analyzer, or TRAFFIC.EXE, needs to be run at a dedicated workstation during your collection period. It calculates the number of messages sent to each externally defined post office. You then can export this information into a format that Excel can use to create graphs and calculate the average message volume data you need.

> **TIP**
>
> The preceding example for MS Mail is good at getting message volume information for inter-post office traffic, but it will not get any data on intra-post office messages sent. You can get this data by setting up an automated process to copy the file CONTROL.GLB from the \GLB directory on a post office to a time-stamped file. By comparing values in these files and subtracting the number of messages sent inter-post office, you can get a good estimate of the number of messages and attachments sent within the post office. This procedure is detailed in Microsoft's tech note #Q122852.

Average Size of Messages Per Connection

The average size of messages transferred over a connection is a value in bytes divided by the total number of messages you calculated in the preceding step. You can best determine the average size of messages by analyzing the logs created by your system's message transfer agents. Many systems give you the total amount of data transferred by some time period, and you should use the number of messages transferred during that period to calculate the average size. Some systems also give you the maximum and minimum message sizes, but you should discard these values if they skew your results or have a distinct pattern.

In the MS Mail example, this information is calculated and generated by the message transfer agent and stored in the SESSION.LOG if the option LogMessageVolume is present in the EXTERNAL.INI file. This provides message volume summaries for the number of messages sent and the total number of bytes transmitted and received for a given time period. The default time period is once per day, which should give you a good idea of the average size of the messages sent through this post office.

Average Number of Errors or Problems Per Connection

The average number of errors or problems for a connection is a numerical value of the number of message delivery errors per connection divided by a given time period. This information is almost always logged in any messaging system, because it is used for troubleshooting purposes. It is recommended that you stick to using the actual logs from your system and not attempt to generate this data from your help desk or problem-tracking system. The error logs are an actual representation of the errors for a connection, but your help desk is only human perception of error conditions.

To finish out the MS Mail example, you could extract error information from the SESSION.LOG for each post office and match the instances to identify a problem for a particular connection between two post offices. This task requires some advanced parsing capabilities, which is a good job for PERL (Practical Extraction and Reporting Language). Those of you who are supporting and maintaining Web sites will be very familiar with PERL. You can use PERL to parse each line of the logs, to determine whether the line is relevant through pattern matching, and to keep arrays and totals for significant statistics. You could also use PERL in any of the previous examples, because it is very good at working with these types of files.

Publishing the Information Gathered

Data is truly relevant only if it is organized and presented in a readable and comprehensible manner. The volume of data you parse from your system might complicate your options for tools to present the data. Certain tools have limitations on the amount of data they can handle, so you should be sure that your selection is capable of working with your volume of data. The way these programs present the material also differs, with some choosing a more graphical approach and others using the technical essay format. Choose a program that meets your requirements for presentation and ease of use, because you might not have the time to switch to another program or learn a new program during your documentation phase.

Custom written applications you can use to present your information include such products as Crystal Reports, Visio, and other third-party programs. None of these is specifically targeted at working with the data collected from your system, but they have powerful graphical display or reporting capabilities that can use data from external sources. It is best to load your data into some type of ODBC-compliant database, because these programs can link directly to this type of data source to get their content. Crystal Reports has direct data-extraction options for many of the most popular messaging systems, which reduces the time you need to extract and parse the data. Visio is a better solution for generating diagrams for your post offices and connections, displaying the content in a more visual format.

If you have a very small system or decide that you do not want to learn a program you are not familiar with, you can use office automation products such as the Office95 product suite. Microsoft Access has some very rich importing and reporting capabilities and is best for larger volumes of raw data. Excel is good at importing and parsing various log files and can be used with Access and Word. Word is the application that can pull data from Access and Excel to present it in a technical essay format. The integration between these products, as well as most people's familiarity with them, will prove more useful in small- to medium-sized documentation projects.

Whatever solution you use to present the information obtained from your data collection process, the data should be verified to be accurate and relevant. You can apply some practical knowledge of your system to verify that the data you have collected properly depicts your system. Only you and your technical staff can properly validate the statistics you collected, because it is your job to keep the system running. If you are using this section to plan for a new Exchange messaging system with no current system to replace, you should import your "virtual" data into these same tools and discuss them in your planning sessions.

Hardware Planning

Hardware planning, the process of selecting the fastest "toy" that your budget can afford, can be very complicated and time-consuming. Actually, the process of hardware selection is not so much a search for the most bang for your buck, but a collection of concepts and methodologies that can assist the system designer in meeting practical performance requirements. I don't know many computer engineers, including me, who would not jump at the chance to get their hands on the latest technology. Just buying the "fastest" server on the market, however, does not guarantee that it will meet your performance expectations or requirements.

The hardware industry is constantly in a state of flux, with new and faster hardware options coming out every day. Although you should attempt to keep up-to-date on the hardware industry's newest innovations, don't discount the tried and tested systems that have a well-established history. You might also want to see whether you can utilize your current server hardware to meet your Exchange messaging needs, and with a few upgrades you might be able to get performance numbers to your liking. Keep in mind that your messaging needs of the future will require much more hardware than you need for today, so plan for a system that has scaleability and upgrade options.

Don't kid yourself—Exchange Server is very resource-intensive and will possibly require more hardware than is available in your current system. But you should consider the number of different systems that it can replace while still meeting your company's messaging needs. Many of you are downsizing from a multimillion-dollar mainframe-based messaging system to a server platform that costs only in the thousands of dollars range. There are no cooling towers or lumbering air handlers for these systems, because most will fit under someone's desk.

You can break down the planning for your server hardware requirements into the following five hardware categories:

- Memory
- Storage Subsystem
- Processor Speed and Quantity
- Network Subsystem
- I/O Subsystem

Memory

There is one very solid rule you should keep in mind when looking at memory requirements for NT and Exchange Server: you can never have too much memory. Exchange Server, like any good NT-based application server, is a series of multithreaded processes that allocate and deallocate system memory as needed. Each of these multithreaded processes can utilize any memory that the NT Server software can see, up to maximum hardware limitations somewhere around 1–2G.

If your system does not have enough system memory to meet the requirements of the operating system services running on the server, including Exchange, the system begins to page physical memory to a virtual memory swap file located on the disk subsystem. This action not only creates a resource problem with memory availability, but it also competes with database file operations on the disk subsystem for I/O bandwidth, causing an even greater system slowdown. Running out of physical memory and creating a "disk thrashing" situation is the worst situation you can be in if your server is in production mode.

To determine the amount of memory you should have in your servers, you need to make some decisions about what additional services will run on the server. Following are some examples of server processes that will increase a system's memory requirements:

- Logon and authentication by domain controller services
- Remote access services
- File and printer sharing
- WINS and DHCP servers
- Other network application services such as SQL Server or IIS

Each of these services increases your memory requirements above those of the operating system and Exchange services. As a general rule, you should plan for at least 16M of RAM for the operating system, 16M of RAM for other services such as the ones listed, and at least 16–32M of RAM minimum for the Exchange services. As your number of users increases, the amount of memory for Exchange will increase approximately 100–150K for each connected client, not including background tasks for message transfer and replication processes. Use the guide later in this section to help determine a rough estimate of the amount of memory your system might need.

Storage Subsystem

The Achilles heel of hardware performance is the disk subsystem, because even the fastest SCSI controllers can sustain transfer rates of only 20M per second. Even though network cards can achieve only around 12.5M per second transfer, multiple cards can sustain much higher transfer rates when using PCI technology. Taking into account that the memory and bus are much faster than the disk throughput in most server class hardware, you can see how the disk subsystem can truly be the limiting factor of hardware performance. New RAID controllers can help by writing to many spindles in a RAID5 configuration, spreading the load over many drives working at the same time with a large memory cache to speed the total throughput.

This discussion assumes that the disk subsystem is utilizing SCSI-based technology, because IDE interfaces are currently limited to just under 5M per second of bandwidth. It is also assumed that you will use an EISA or a PCI bus due to serious performance problems with ISA-based systems. Because FAST-WIDE SCSI-2 drives and controllers are readily available, settle only for this type of SCSI technology, unless you are upgrading an existing server that has a non-wide drive built-in controller.

Getting the best performance out of your server's disk subsystem involves planning for adequate drive space and multiple disk channels. Exchange Server requires only approximately 120M of drive space, but your messaging data will use much more. The current release of Exchange supports message store sizes up to 16G, with the directory service also having a maximum of 16G for its database. For this reason, you should plan your drive space accordingly and allocate the right amount of space for each user's mailbox in the Information Store settings at the site on the server. For instance, if 100 users will use an Exchange Server, and your message stores are located on a drive with 4G free space, each user should have not more than 35–40M of space allocated. Single message instance, where a message is stored once in the database with the user's mailboxes just pointing to that message, will reduce the actual amount of space available for each user, but it is better to have some extra room for growth.

Because even the fastest PCI-based hardware caching controllers rarely exceed 25M per second of data transfer bandwidth, you can greatly enhance disk performance by increasing the number of controllers and drives within the system. If you increase the number of SCSI controllers to three, with one being a hardware RAID5 controller, your system performance will be enhanced by the creation of different I/O channels for the Exchange services to use. Optimally, one channel should have a mirrored pair of 1–2G drives for the operating system, Exchange executables, and tracking logs. The next channel should have a 1–2G drive dedicated to the DS and IS transaction logs. The RAID5 controller is used for the public and private message stores and could have 16G or more of storage for each message store. This is an optimal solution for the best level of performance, but you might decide to only use two channels, to keep your costs down.

Raw speed and data-transfer times are not the only factors you should consider when designing your disk subsystem; fault tolerance also plays a very important part. By using the built-in fault tolerance options available in NT Server, you can guard your system against drive failures and improve your system performance, depending on the option you select. Table 25.1 lists the fault tolerance options available in the disk administrator for NT Server, as well as the best way to use each for Exchange Server storage requirements.

25

PERFORMANCE TUNING AND SCALING

Table 25.1. NT Server disk performance options for Exchange Server storage.

Option	Description	Exchange Storage Options
Disk Mirroring	Data is read and written to a pair of identical disks, allowing failure of one	NT operating system, Exchange executables, and tracking logs
Volume Set	A proprietary method of concatenating hard drives to create one virtual drive	Can be used to expand storage for the IS and DS databases, but performance will suffer
Disk Striping	Data is written across two or more drives with no fault tolerance for a drive failure (RAID0)	Used for the personal and private Information Stores with very fast performance
Disk Striping with Parity	Data is written across three or more drives with a parity stripe calculated and written for each data segment, allowing for a single drive failure	Used for the personal and private Information Stores with a good balance between speed and fault tolerance

Although NT Server has these options available for performance and fault tolerance, the best choice for high-speed reliable access is RAID hardware caching controllers. These Fast/Wide SCSI-based controllers have RISC-based processors that perform the striping and parity calculations without putting extra load on the system processor. They also usually support features such as hot-swap and on-the-fly rebuild of replaced drives. If you are building a server that will support more than 500 concurrent users, it will require very fast hardware caching controllers with many hard drives to get acceptable performance.

TIP

One of the best ways to increase the performance of any Exchange Server is to use a dedicated drive for the transaction logs. Both the Directory Service and the Information Store databases use a transaction log to store transactions before they are written to the actual database. When MAPI data is received by the server for storage in the DS or IS databases, it is written from memory to a fast, sequentially organized transaction log file. When the IS database process is not busy, the transaction is written from memory to the database, and a checkpoint is incremented for the transaction log. This technique not only increases performance because it can write to a sequential file very quickly, but also can be used for crash recovery of the databases. If you dedicate a SCSI channel to this purpose, database writes and transaction log transfers will not compete for bandwidth on the same channel. For an extra two to three percent increase in speed, format the dedicated transaction log disk with the FAT file system. The smaller sector size and reduced security storage inherent with FAT will give a slight amount of performance increase on heavily used servers, but will eliminate the advanced security checking and error recovery available in NTFS.

Processor Speed and Quantity

The speed and number of processors will affect the overall performance of your Exchange Server, but you will actually need less processor horsepower that you think. Throughout the history of computer evolution, software performance problems have been fixed with faster and faster processors. This was due in part to operating systems that were not utilizing the advanced features of these new processors. OS/2 and Windows NT were the first operating systems to run on Intel processors that could actually utilize the enhanced performance options available in the fastest processors. Then came SMP and multiprocessor systems to push the performance ceiling even higher, and the advanced operating systems such as NT stepped up to the challenge with multiprocessor support.

The Exchange services fully support and utilize the fastest processors on single- and multiprocessor–based systems. The amount of processor your server will require can differ, depending on the number of users, the types of services, and the number of messages handled. The following Exchange services will increase the need for processor performance:

- Connectors and gateways
- Message transfer agents
- Message attachment encoding for MIME and UUENCODE
- Size of the Information Stores
- Public folder access and replication

25

PERFORMANCE TUNING AND SCALING

In planning for your server hardware, consider purchasing systems that support dual processors or full SMP expandability. Not all Exchange Servers need multiple processors to perform acceptably, but as your system grows and new demands are placed on it for business processes, you will need scaleable processor resources. The general rule for selecting processor type and speed says that Exchange will run on a 486/33 processor with adequate amounts of RAM, but you will get the best bang for your buck if you use Pentium- or Pentium Pro-based systems.

Network Subsystem

All client and interserver connections must be made through the network card and the associated physical network. This can be the one area where system performance suffers because of bottlenecks created by forces outside the server. Networking technologies such as Ethernet and Token Ring are based on shared bus or token passing access methods, and they can run at speeds from 2 megabits to 100 megabits, depending on the cabling and timing specifications. Network cards are the server's link to the physical network, as well as the connection medium for all external connections. Typical Ethernet network cards are capable of supporting the network traffic associated with approximately 250 users simultaneously transferring data, even though many more could be logged on not transferring any data at the same time. You can increase the amount of network bandwidth on your server by installing multiple network cards connected to different physical segments, and use protocols such as IPX/SPX or TCP/IP. Token Ring and FDDI network cards can also be installed in multiple numbers, but these technologies have much higher bandwidth capabilities than Ethernet, so fewer would be needed.

When it comes to Windows NT, the performance of any network card is dependent on the quality of the drivers that support it. Most of the newest cards come with drivers that allow you to set up the options for the card, such as interface, interrupt, and memory address, but the driver should also support high-speed direct transfer modes. Most of the EISA- and PCI-based cards support busmastering to reduce the card's processor utilization. Many Ethernet cards support full-duplex mode connections, and this option is highly recommended if your hubs or switches support this mode. You might need to use standard network benchmarking software to determine the aggregate network bandwidth, and use that information to gauge the requirements for your type of network conditions.

If you decide to use multiple network cards, remember to plan which protocols are bound to which cards. If your network primarily uses the TCP/IP protocol, you must assign a unique address to each card. With the NetBEUI protocol, you can bind it to one or more cards as long as they are not on the same segment and cannot "see" each other. The IPX/SPX-compatible transport can be bound to multiple cards; however, each must have a unique internal IPX network number, and they should be on different network segments. You will get the best performance with multiple network cards if one protocol type is bound to each card, enabling you to isolate network traffic by protocol.

I/O Subsystem

The system backplane and bus make up the I/O subsystem that connects all the system components for data transfer. Older motherboards for 486-class systems did not have very fast backplanes even if they used a PCI or EISA bus for add-in cards. Because the backplane connects all the system components together, you should look for high bandwidth architectures, such as Compaq's Tri-Flex or Intel's Triton or Orion chipsets.

Whether you select an EISA or a PCI bus for your server hardware will depend on your budget and selection of add-in cards. The EISA bus is a proven technology that supports data transfer rates of 33M per second, just above the sustained bandwidth of most disk controllers. PCI, a newer technology that can run as high as 155M per second, is geared toward systems with very fast network controllers and multiple high-speed cards. You will probably want to select a system that uses both technologies to give you a better choice of add-in cards for network and disk controllers. The ISA bus was not mentioned because it should not be an option for your server; it is a desktop-system technology with very poor performance and increased processor utilization under heavy loads.

You might be wondering how you begin the process of selecting which options you will need for your server to support *x* number of users. This question is very subjective because one population of 100 users will use e-mail differently than a separate population of 100 users will. The best way to gain confidence in your selection of server hardware and the number of your company's users it will support is by using the LoadSim utility that comes with the Exchange Server software. This utility is covered in the section Running a Pilot Test later in this chapter, but Table 25.2 gives you a very rough guideline for the hardware options you should use to support various numbers of users.

Your actual hardware configuration will differ from these recommendations, depending on your hardware vendor of choice and your budget for procurement of this system. Two years from the date this book is published, these recommendations will seem ridiculous compared to the hardware technology available at that time. Don't settle for a hardware configuration that you know will not meet your users' messaging needs, because whatever money you saved in hardware costs will be spent in support costs. Use a practical approach to selecting and testing your server hardware—this is your messaging system we are taking about.

25

PERFORMANCE
TUNING AND
SCALING

Table 25.2. Minimum recommended hardware options for concurrent user loads.

Range of Concurrent Users	Processor	Memory	Disk Subsystem	Network Subsystem
0–100	Single Pentium 90MHz	32–48M	Single channel with 1 or 2 drives	Single Ethernet 10BaseT or 16M Token Ring card
100–250	Single Pentium 100MHz with dual processor option	48–64M	Single channel with 3 or more drives	Dual network cards from 10M duplex to 100Tx Ethernet or Token Ring
250–500	Dual Pentium/ Alpha/MIPS 100MHz or higher	64–128M	Dual channel with one software or hardware RAID for the IS	Dual network cards from 10M duplex to 100Tx Ethernet or Token Ring
500–1500	Dual Pentium/ Alpha/MIPS 133MHz or higher	128–256M	Three FAST-WIDE SCSI-2 channels with one being hardware RAID5	Multiple network cards from 10M duplex to 100Tx Duplexed Ethernet or Token Ring optimized for protocols
1500 and up	Two to four Pentium Pro/Alpha/ MIPS 200MHz or higher	256–1024M	Three or more Advanced Hardware Caching Controllers using RAID technologies (PCI)	Multiple network cards from 10M duplex to 100Tx Duplexed Ethernet or Token Ring optimized for protocols

Network Infrastructure

You might have selected the fastest server hardware available to run Exchange on, but if the underlying network is having bandwidth or stability problems, you might have just purchased a very expensive coffee table. Networks can be very complicated in design due to the numerous technologies and connectivity options. A company's network infrastructure can be broken into the local area network (LAN) at a location, and the wide area network (WAN) for connectivity to other LANs. Also, dial-in and remote access are an extension of WAN technologies, but are geared toward supporting remotely connected users.

This discussion uses Ethernet technologies in the examples, but similar concepts can be applied to other network technologies, such as Token Ring and Asynchronous Transfer Mode (ATM). If you currently do not have a LAN or WAN and are planning to design and implement a new one, you should consider the recommendations in this section as a part of your total requirements. Network design should be done by individuals who specialize in this area, to properly meet your company's requirements.

All the data that is transmitted between the users and Exchange Servers is carried over the physical network. Information that is transferred between servers and sites by MTAs is transmitted and received over the same physical network, but is usually is carried across routers or bridges that connect physical LAN segments. Before you begin to map out your Exchange site topology, you need a detailed diagram of your company's entire network for reference. As mentioned earlier in this chapter, you should use these network diagrams to analyze the various connectivity options for optimization of network bandwidth usage.

LAN Performance Considerations

How well is your local area network performing today? Does your network experience frequent transmission delays due to overload or high error rates? Do you currently have network analysis tools available to determine the health of your physical network? You should be able to answer all of these questions before considering ways to optimize and increase performance of your LAN segments. All the computers within a physical location are connected to the network by a network card and physical cable or wire, and they must share network bandwidth with the other network nodes for the transmission and reception of data. A good understanding of your current network performance can help in determining which technologies can be used to increase bandwidth and decrease transmission times.

Ethernet networks use an access method called CSMA/CD, or Carrier-Sense Multiple Access with Collision Detection. Carrier-Sense refers to the process the network card uses to "listen" for a quiet period it can use to send data. Multiple Access refers to many computers sharing the same physical network cable or segment. Collision Detection is the process by which computers detect collisions on the shared wire and wait for a random period before they retransmit their data. Network collisions are normal for any typical Ethernet network, but if experienced in high volumes, they can indicate bad network cards or physical wiring problems. You can use the following guidelines to increase network bandwidth and reduce collisions and retransmissions:

- Reduce the number of computers that share the same physical segment.
- Use routers or bridges to break up a large segment into smaller, more manageable physical segments.
- Install an Ethernet switch to isolate the users' workstations into segments that are separate from the servers without the need for bridging or routing.
- Put servers on Fast Ethernet (100M) or Fiber Distributed Data Interface (FDDI) segments to support the higher volumes of traffic.
- Upgrade your wiring to meet Category 5 wiring specifications.
- Try to limit the volume of broadcasts and multicasts by using TCP/IP with WINS name resolution as your preferred protocol.

Your options for upgrading or enhancing your existing network will depend on the type of hubs and cabling within your network. Network management utilities such as sniffers and network monitors can be used to identify segments that require modifications to increase performance. Microsoft SMS and Windows NT 4.0 have a program called Network Monitor with server-based agents that can be used for this purpose. You should analyze your network during normal business hours to determine performance when the users are connected. You should also separately analyze the network after hours to determine performance when nightly processes such as backup or database maintenance are running when the users are not connected. A six-month history of network statistics in an easy-to-read graph will give you a good idea of your overall performance and help identify times when the network is under a heavy load.

Communications between Exchange clients and servers use synchronous remote procedure calls (RPCs) for all data transfer. RPCs do not require a dedicated amount of network bandwidth, but you will get the best performance when your LAN is operating at less than 25 percent utilization. Because Exchange is based on the client-server architecture with connectivity over RPCs, you should see a decrease in the amount of network utilization compared to your current messaging system. You should also group users who frequently mail to each other on the same Exchange Server, to limit the amount of message transfer between servers or sites.

WAN Performance Considerations

Physical locations that have one or more LANs can be interconnected by WAN connectivity options. The core components of a WAN connection are a bridge or router, DSU/CSU or equivalent, and the physical connection provided by a carrier's network. Due to the options available for WANs today, they are referred to as slow links. Connections range from the slowest speeds of 8K per second to hundreds of megabits per second. Typically, most companies use connection speeds of 56K–1.5Mbit, depending on the bandwidth needs between physical locations.

Tuning the performance of the WAN link involves setting up filters on the bridges or routers to weed out unnecessary protocol traffic between the connected sites. You should take careful consideration when setting up these filters to your specific protocol requirements to allow them to work across the WAN link. If you are using NBT (NetBIOS over TCP/IP) to connect two Exchange sites, make sure that UDP ports 137–139 are not closed to traffic, because they are required for connectivity between the Exchange Servers. The NetBEUI protocol is not even a choice for a WAN, because it is not routable, and it would require a source-route bridge to forward broadcasts across the WAN. The IPX/SPX protocol is not the best choice for WAN links due to the "chattiness" from the Server Advertising Protocol (SAP) broadcasts, but up-dated implementations from Novell can reduce the effect these SAPs have, by decreasing their frequency from one minute to hours or more.

The various Exchange site connectivity options have minimum available bandwidth require-ments for reliable message transfer. The term *available bandwidth* refers to the amount of band-width left available after the requirements of other applications are met. For instance, a 256K frame relay connection might have only 10–15K of bandwidth available after an enterprise database's replication needs are met, whereas a 56K connection might have 40–45K available due to limited inter-site traffic. If you have a WAN connection of less than 56K, you should consider an upgrade of the connection speed. The minimum available bandwidth needs of each connector were outlined in Chapter 24, "Interfacing with Other Mail Systems," but the con-nectors normally require 56–128K of available bandwidth, depending on the message volume expected between the sites.

By examining the network traffic patterns of your WAN, the dollar costs associated with each link, and the estimated message transfer volumes between Exchange sites, you can design your message routing topology to best utilize your network resources. By using a limit on message size for a particular connection, you can eliminate the ability of a single user to effectively take down your WAN by sending a message with an enormous file attachment. By assigning scaled costs to your connections and scheduling connections, you can control the impact that mes-sage transfer will have on a particular WAN link.

Remote Access Performance Considerations

Is the number of employees at your company who work from home or live on the road increas-ing? The nature of business is changing to incorporate "virtual offices" and telecommuting users who might rarely go into the office, but still perform the same job functions. Salespeople are spending more and more time on the road as the size of their sales territories expand. The chal-lenge of providing secure and reliable access to the home office has to be balanced against the current available technologies. Modems have hit a theoretical brick wall when it comes to link speed, and new technologies such as ISDN and cable modems are still finding their place in the industry. Efficient use of these types of connections is the best way to gain better perfor-mance for message transfer.

25

PERFORMANCE
TUNING AND
SCALING

Remote access solutions for connecting users to a branch or central office must support Remote LAN Node (RLN) connections for the Exchange client to operate correctly. Remote control is a completely different concept, and it does not work as well when it comes to the messaging needs of users today. The Exchange client uses the remote access software included within the operating system for Windows 95 and Windows NT and provides a Shiva remote access client for Windows 3.*x* and DOS. These clients can be used to make connections to the Windows NT Remote Access server or a third-party remote access solution, such as Shiva LANRover or 3COM access builder. This discussion uses NT's RAS for performance tuning examples.

Depending on the size and resources of your server hardware, the best performance will be realized if the RAS server is installed on the same physical server as Exchange. This setup gives you the option of limiting the RAS traffic to only that computer, effectively increasing your dial-in security. Also, this reduces the effect that LAN bandwidth problems or error conditions will have on the users who are making remote connections. Because the actual connect speeds with typical compression ratios will not exceed 33.6K, you should be extremely careful about what is transmitted over the modem link. Users can realize better performance by using the remote access features built into the client, allowing them to set up filters for what messages will be downloaded during a session.

You should use high-speed modems combined with advanced serial port I/O port connections to keep the link speed as high as possible. Modems on the server should support at least v.34 and v.42/MNP compression and error control, with similar modems on the client's workstations. Resist the temptation to use the on-board serial ports of the server, and make the investment in a high-speed serial port card such as a Digiboard with an EISA or a PCI interface. As the number of modems on your RAS server increases, you will need to use a high-speed serial port solution that will not use more processor resources. Many third-party solutions work with NT RAS to have a minimal impact on the server's valuable processor resources.

If you have made the switch to ISDN, your users will get much better connection speeds. NT RAS supports ISDN-type connections, and connection speeds can range from 64–128K, depending on the hardware and service you use. You will most probably have to provide solutions for both ISDN and modems, because ISDN is a good solution for someone working out of her home, but it is not practical or available for users with laptops who are constantly on the road. The NetBEUI protocol is the best choice for a protocol if you decide to limit user access to only the Exchange Server, and TCP/IP is the only good solution for connections that need to connect across routers or bridges.

Software Tuning Secrets

This section title, "Software Tuning Secrets," is a little misleading, because we all know that every performance tuning option available in Exchange is published and readily available. Actually, my sarcasm has some merit, because the performance options for Exchange are documented in many white papers and Microsoft technical articles. I will highlight the most common options for tuning performance of Exchange Server services, including the performance optimizer wizard, because it does a very good job at tuning most of the registry parameters for the various services. These "secrets" are well documented by various Microsoft sources, and I will point out specific articles where applicable.

Performance Wizard

Most configuration parameters for tuning and performance of the services within the Exchange Server can be modified with the Exchange Performance Optimizer, also called the performance wizard. Even though many of these parameters are contained within the Windows NT registry, it is best to access and modify them through the performance wizard interface. Any time you add or remove hardware from your Exchange Server or want to modify the parameters used to scale the server, you should immediately run the performance wizard. The first thing you should do after installation is to add the -v option to the icon in the Exchange Server group from Program Manager. This option runs the wizard in verbose mode, allowing greater control over the parameters and values that will be changed, as well as giving you the option to exclude drives from the disk testing process. When you start the performance wizard from the icon in the Exchange program group, you are first asked to confirm that the services will be stopped during the process by clicking Next; then you see the screen shown in Figure 25.1.

FIGURE 25.1.

Performance Optimizer wizard questions and answers screen.

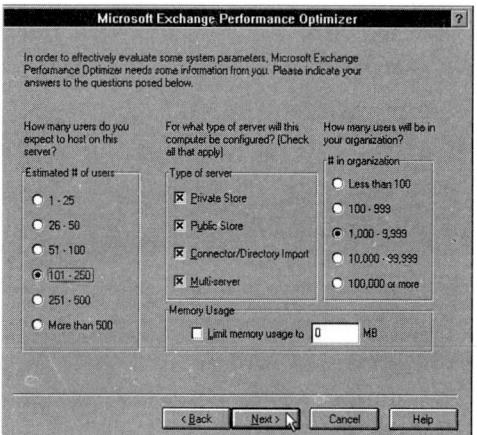

The question concerning the range of users that this server will host should be set to the actual number of users, not the number of concurrent users. This will change the values in the registry for worker threads and maximum concurrent users. Any time you use the wizard to change this value, make sure that you have adequate memory and disk resources to support those users, because the optimizer will notify you if there are inadequate resources to support the number of users you have selected.

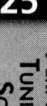

25

PERFORMANCE TUNING AND SCALING

The checkboxes for the types of services this server will provide help determine the parameter changes that should be made on the MTA, connectors, and Information Stores. These are the effects of checking these options:

- *Private Store.* This server will contain a private Information Store for user mailboxes. This changes the values for the IS service threads and database tuning values.

- *Public Store.* This server will contain a public Information Store for public folders and/or replicas of public folders from other servers. This changes the values associated with the public IS database and replication tuning.

- *Connector.* This server will run connector services such as the IMC, MS Mail, or X.400, making it a bridgehead or backbone server. This will tune the MTA and connector thread values to support increased message transfer.

- *Multi-Server.* This server will connect to other servers within the site. Do not deselect this option unless this will be a standalone server, because it will modify parameters for the MTA and connectivity services.

The option to select a range of how many users are in your entire organization will control the parameters associated with the directory service. This will change parameters such as the directory cache buffers and number of threads for the directory service to support directory replication and queries. Changing the range to a higher value will allocate more system resources to the directory service, so you might want to set this value higher than your actual number if you expect more directory lookup and read requests than normal. The last option on this page enables you to limit the amount of memory the Exchange services will see. This option is helpful if you will have other applications such as SQL Server or SMS running at the same time, or if you want to reserve some memory for the disk cache. Click Next to move to the screen for analyzing the hard disks, shown in Figure 25.2.

FIGURE 25.2.

Performance Optimizer wizard disk analysis screen.

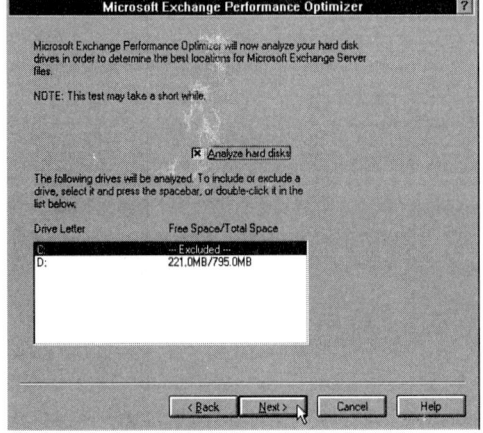

From this screen you can use your mouse or the spacebar to select or deselect the drives you want to test. The wizard then uses a series of reads and writes that emulates the I/O processes of the Exchange databases to determine which drives are the fastest. This process is looking for which drive will be best for the transaction logs, which will be best for the databases, and which will be the best for the MTA and connectors. You then see a list of the statistics gathered from each drive. Click the Next button to get to the screen with suggestions on which drives to move the Exchange database, log, MTA, and connector files to (see Figure 25.3).

FIGURE 25.3.

Performance Optimizer wizard suggested locations for Exchange components.

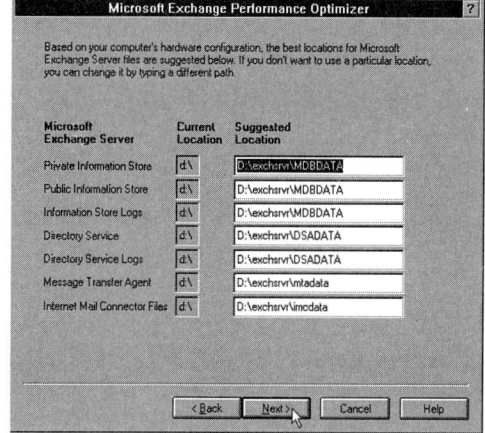

From this screen, you can override any of the suggested locations by changing the path manually, and you might have to carry out this action if you have designated certain drives for the components listed. At this point, I routinely run a full tape backup of the drives, because the Exchange services are stopped and all associated files are closed. I had one system that lost power while moving the files, which forced me to restore everything from the previous night's backup. When you click the Next button, you get a screen that warns you to back up the files, and it has a checkbox selected to move the files automatically. If you uncheck this box, you will need to manually move the components to their appropriate locations before the process is finished. After the files are all moved, you can click the Next button to view the changes to system tuning and registry parameters on the screens shown in Figures 25.4, 25.5, 25.6, and 25.7.

You should review the values on these four screens, but unless specifically instructed, you should not change any of the values. They are calculated using the answers you gave in the previous steps, and are specific to the memory and disk speed of the system. Instead of changing the values from these screens, modify the answers on the first page to have the wizard calculate values closer to what you want. After you have reviewed the four pages of proposed changes to system parameters by clicking the Next button, you are shown the final screen of the performance wizard that saves the system parameters and restarts the Exchange services. This completes the procedure for using the performance tuning wizard that comes with Exchange Server.

25

PERFORMANCE TUNING AND SCALING

FIGURE 25.4.

Performance Optimizer wizard parameter recommendations screen #1.

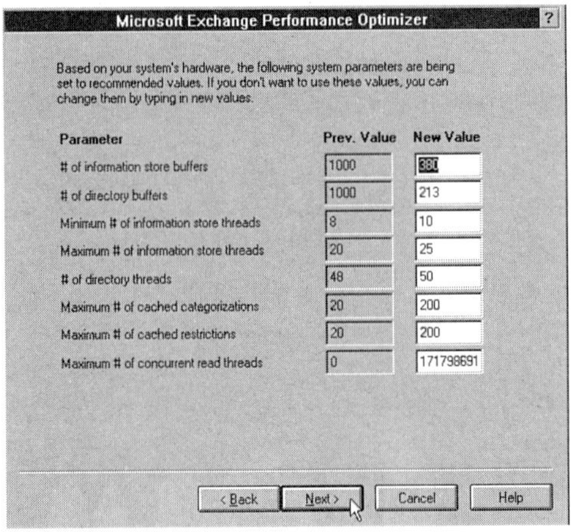

FIGURE 25.5.

Performance Optimizer wizard parameter recommendations screen #2.

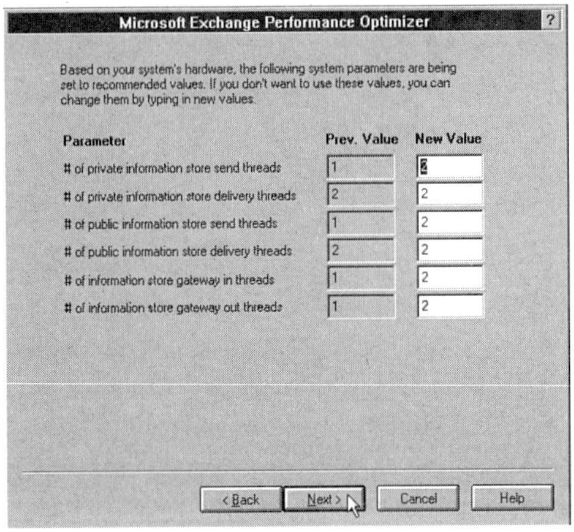

FIGURE 25.6.

Performance Optimizer wizard parameter recommendations screen #3.

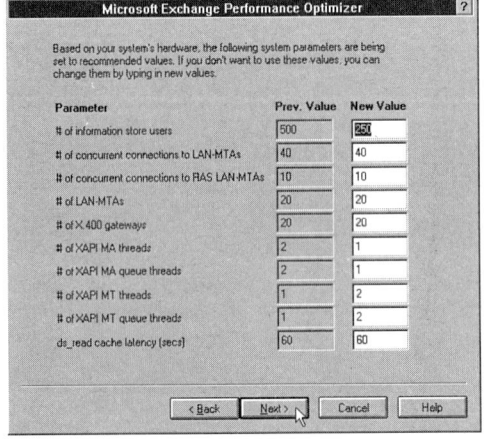

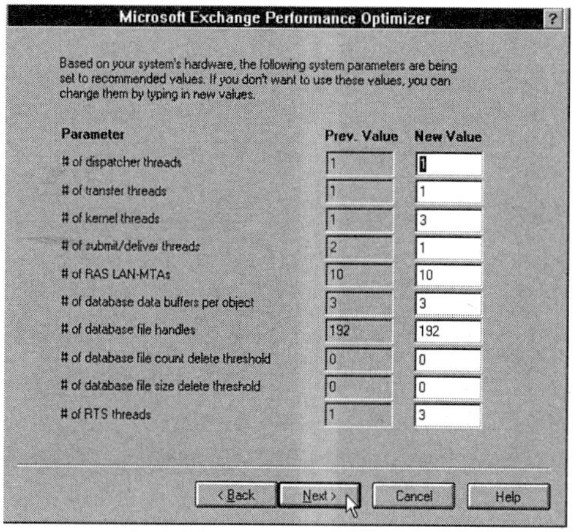

FIGURE 25.7.

Performance Optimizer wizard parameter recommendations screen #4.

Other Performance Tuning Options

The performance tuning wizard is good for scaling the parameters for services to use enough resources to support a specific number of clients, but other changes can affect overall system performance. These changes include, but are not limited to, disabling circular logging for the transaction logs, disabling the loopback messaging for the IMC, and enabling or disabling message tracking.

The circular logging feature for the directory service and Information Store transaction logs is enabled by default. This feature prevents the buildup of transaction log files on the hard drive, but it removes the capability of performing differential or incremental system backups. For systems that will be under a heavy load, this feature also gains some additional performance, because the system does not have to take the time to reset the log files after a predetermined number of checkpoints. If you disable circular logging, make sure that you run a backup program such as NTBACKUP to back up the system each night, resetting the transaction logs automatically. You can disable the circular logging feature from the advanced properties page of any server object by un-checking the appropriate boxes and then allowing the system to stop and restart the DS and IS services. Please note that the users will not be able to access the server temporarily while these changes are being made, so you might want to perform this operation after normal business hours.

The Exchange Internet Mail Connector (IMC) by default checks to see whether a message is being sent to SMTP addresses that reside on the same site as the IMC. It attempts to send those messages to the Internet, which causes the message to be returned to the IMC, creating a loop condition. Because this process requires computing cycles, it is best to disable this process and let the message be delivered or not delivered from within Exchange. To disable loopback messaging, execute the Registry Editor (regedt32.exe) and find the following subkey:

25

PERFORMANCE
TUNING AND
SCALING

```
HKLM\SYSTEM\CurrentControlSet\Services\MSExchangeIMC\Parameter
```

from Registry Editor. Then add the following value:

```
Value Name: DisableLoopbackConnections
Data Type:  REG_DWORD
String:     1 (Default is 0)
```

When done, exit the Registry Editor and stop and restart the IMC to have the change take place. This affects only messages that are addressed to recipients with SMTP domain names that match the address space of the site. If other SMTP-based systems will receive messages for the same domain name configured in Exchange, create custom recipients for each of the recipients on those systems. This operates in a similar manner to an alias file for UNIX sendmail, and requires that SMTP host to have an "A" or "MX" record in DNS.

The message tracking feature is available for the server's MTA, Information Stores, and connector components. The tracking logs enable administrators to use the Track Message feature in the administrator program to trace the route that specific messages take through the site or external connections. You must enable the Track Messages selection for any of these components to allow the message tracking feature to read the tracking file for each server. By enabling this feature, you create a small delay for the time it takes to write the header information to the tracking logs, which might heavily affect performance on systems that are backbone or bridge-head servers. Just be aware of the small performance hit you take by enabling message tracking so that you can disable it if you need to tune a server that is performing poorly.

Running a Pilot Test

Just after you finish your planning and design stages, and just before you move to a production exchange environment, you will want to take some time to develop and run a pilot project. This step enables you to confirm the functionality and design from your planning stage while getting a limited number of users involved in shaping the system to meet your company's messaging needs. You should already have the server hardware in place before you move into a pilot environment so that it will be easier to make the transition into production.

To create a controlled pilot for your Exchange Server messaging system, your project team should implement the following steps in this order:

1. Install, configure, and tune your Exchange Server(s) following the guidelines from your planning sessions.
2. Configure any connections to external systems, to establish coexistence.
3. Set up directory exchange or replication between all messaging systems.
4. Test message connectivity to recipients on each external system, as well as any connected Exchange sites.

5. Set up and test some example public folders, and install test forms for the pilot users to test with. Set up a public folder for users to report problems by using the survey form included in the electronic forms sample application PST file located on the Samples share on the server.

6. Test client connectivity from various locations within the company.

7. Compile a list of users who will best form a cross-section of your user population. Don't include just people you can "trust," because you are looking to find any and all holes in the system now before you let the user population loose on the system.

8. Document and test your migration steps using the pilot group, working out any details or changes into a proven process for the actual migration.

9. Be sure to have definitive start and end dates for the pilot project, because you do not want to hold up implementation unless you have serious issues.

10. Use the LoadSim utility included with Exchange Server to validate system performance when a particular number of workstations are logged on.

11. Require all persons involved in the pilot to routinely provide feedback on the capability of the system to meet the needs of the user community.

The pilot project is the last chance to make any major modifications to the system without affecting a large number of users. Take the time during this process to check and double-check all system functions, and don't be afraid to reverse decisions made during the planning process. Take the recommendations from the users involved in the pilot to your implementation meetings. Have the project team evaluate and vote on which problems will be corrected during the pilot, and which will have to wait until after implementation. A proactive approach to handling the problems that come up during the pilot will help make the implementation of your new messaging system less of a fire-fighting endeavor and more of a successful product deployment.

As mentioned previously in step 10, you should use this opportunity to run the LoadSim utility included with Exchange Server, to validate your system design. At first the LoadSim utility seems complex, but with a little patience and some realistic user loading data, this process should be very useful in analyzing your system's performance. The utility creates a file that you need in order to use directory import to create the simulation accounts, and I suggest that you create them in a separate recipient container for easier cleanup later. You will also define the servers that will participate in the simulation, defining the sites and number of users per server. After you have entered the parameters into the program, you will begin the load simulation to run for a predetermined amount of time, usually 8–24 hours. Remember to have the NT performance monitor logging all the system objects during the simulation so that you can determine system load and response times. Also use the LsLog.exe utility to merge, truncate, and generate the 95th percentile response times and weighted averages (scores) from the raw log files from

25

PERFORMANCE TUNING AND SCALING

each client simulation machine. Refer to the document that comes with LoadSim for guidelines on using and running a simulation in your environment. See Figure 25.8 for an example of the LoadSim application interface.

FIGURE 25.8.

The LoadSim application.

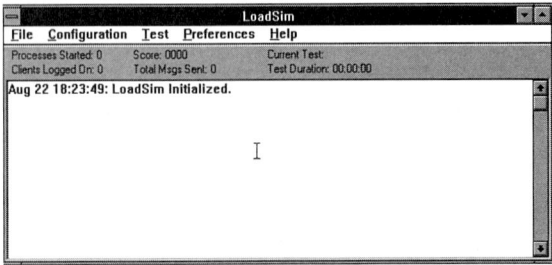

Monitoring

How do you measure the Exchange Server's performance throughout the process of tuning and testing? How will you keep an eye on the operation of the system during the pilot project and implementation phases? Exchange and Windows NT include system utilities to monitor and collect data from the Exchange Server messaging environment. Which monitoring options you use will depend on what portion of the system you are attempting to get information on and what you are going to do with that information after you have it.

The monitoring options for Exchange Servers can be broken into four areas:

- Event viewer
- Performance monitor
- Exchange link monitors
- Exchange Server monitors

The event viewer is very helpful in troubleshooting problems or tracking a process from beginning to end. All error and warning messages are written to the application event log, but you can use the diagnostic logging properties page for many of the directory objects to increase the detail of logging per process. For example, if you were having problems delivering to hosts on the Internet, you would increase the level of diagnostic logging for the message transfer option to get more detailed information on what the IMC is doing during message delivery. The event viewer is the first place to look.

The performance monitor is a helpful tool for charting, logging, reporting, and setting threshold alerts for any of the counters within the Exchange services. The Exchange Server installation process will create icons in the Exchange program group with many useful performance monitor charts to track portions of the Exchange services. One chart monitors server health, and others track things such as number of messages in the MTA queues, MTA delivery times, and IMC statistics. Normally, these performance monitor charts are running on a machine dedicated to monitoring the Exchange messaging system.

An Exchange link monitor is a very useful tool that can be used to determine the speed and reliability of connections to external systems or other Exchange sites. Link monitors bounce messages off of a recipient to determine round-trip message transfer time and link status. You must have an NT workstation or server logged onto the network running a link monitor from the administrator application for this feature to work. This can be the same machine running server monitors or performance monitors, or it can be used during a troubleshooting process to keep tabs on a specific link.

The Exchange Server monitor is used to monitor specific services on an Exchange Server(s), and perform actions that the administrators define when those services stop running. This monitor also requires a dedicated NT workstation or server to be running the administrator program for constant monitoring. When it is determined that a service is no longer running, the monitor can perform different actions on the first, second, and subsequent attempts. The actions it can perform are to take no action and just alert, attempt to restart the service, and even reboot the server if specified by the administrator. Because the server monitor looks at the services running on a specific computer, it can be used to monitor non-Exchange services such as backup software or core NT Server services.

Here are a few notes about link and server monitors for those of you who have very large enterprise messaging systems. Link monitors require no special connectivity between two sites to test the link. As long as a connector is defined and a route to the mailbox is used to bounce messages, the link monitor will perform its duty. The server monitor does require that the machine running the administrator program with the server monitor must have synchronous RPC connectivity to work correctly. This means that if you are in the United States and want to monitor a server in Asia, you need to be able to RPC-ping that server first. There are also practical limitations to the number of servers that can be monitored by a server monitor. Because this type of monitor polls the servers on a routine interval, the more servers you add for it to monitor, the longer the polling period will take, until it begins to miss the window for servers at the end of the list. As a practical design, server monitors should be used for a geographical region or on a per-site basis for better performance and manageability.

Summary

Planning for a messaging system that is scaleable and will deliver performance to meet current and future requirements can be a challenge. The hardware industry is constantly upgrading system options to meet the increased demands placed on servers by new applications and business processes. Messaging systems are unique in their requirements for high I/O bandwidth and scaleable performance options that can expand to meet ever-increasing messaging demands.

As companies move to client-server messaging systems such as Exchange, they are truly realizing the challenges they face in system design and optimization. They must be able to proactively address new requirements as business processes are migrated from legacy systems into a client-server messaging environment.

Designing a hardware solution to support the messaging requirements of the user community requires a careful analysis of the current system. It involves gathering and presenting current statistics on messaging traffic for use in planning sessions to come up with a proposed system design. Your project team should have a good understanding of your company's core messaging requirements, with careful consideration of how network resources will be affected by processes such as message transfer and data replication. In an Exchange messaging system, site and routing topology should be tailored to have a minimal impact on the network infrastructure, and be flexible enough to handle network outages.

After you have a solid system design from your planning sessions, you must validate it to ensure that it will meet your company's messaging requirements. This task involves testing and loading the system with simulated and "real" users in the form of a pilot project. Exchange Server includes utilities such as LoadSim and system monitors to determine how the system will operate under load in a production environment. The pilot project identifies areas that need modification and enables the users to become more involved in evaluating the overall system design to meet their needs. If you follow the recommendations and concepts presented in this chapter, your Exchange messaging system should move smoothly into your production environment to serve your company for years to come.

The next chapter discusses how Exchange Server integrates with the Internet. Topics include using public folders for listservers and newsgroups, SMTP mail integration, and enhancements that will be available in future upgrades. The next version of Exchange will include many features targeted directly at integrating with Internet technologies. By far, the Internet is the hottest thing sweeping the computer industry, and it will continue to drive new business application development into the next century.

Exchange Server and the Internet

by Gregory Dodge

CHAPTER 26

Internet—a word that excites the imagination and conjures up images of millions of users interacting on a vast global network. The Internet we know and love today is vastly different from the Internet of a few years ago. Millions of new users are being added every year, and domain name registrations are topping 50,000 per month. Businesses are now actively embracing the Internet to solve many business requirements, but are leery of the security risks involved in connecting to such a large public network. It is hard to find a company that does not have Internet e-mail connectivity or a home page to establish its presence for marketing purposes and customer relations.

Even though the Internet supports e-mail, this is only a small part of its total offerings. Users can participate in newsgroups, research various topics using vast search engines, download software, and browse the World Wide Web (WWW), all from the comfort of their living room or office cubicle. The sheer volume of information available on the Internet can be overwhelming and confusing at times, but new technologies are being created every day to make the Internet more user friendly. The various search and retrieval services on the Internet are quickly replacing many proprietary methods for information disbursement that companies have used to interact with their customers. Business requirements are driving new technologies that will help make the Internet friendly for doing business.

Messaging and Groupware systems must embrace the Internet if they want to survive in such a dynamic and competitive environment. Microsoft is determined to provide Internet interoperability across its full line of products, and Exchange Server includes connectivity options such as the Internet Mail Connector (IMC) to allow companies to build Internet solutions with minimal time and effort. Future releases of Exchange will extend these capabilities to include support for "light" client access through IMAP4 specifications, newsgroup downloads and hosting from public folders, Web browser access, and directory access through Lightweight Directory Access Protocol (LDAP) specifications.

This chapter covers the options available in Exchange to interoperate with the Internet. It also discusses the procedures used to subscribe a public folder to a listserver to reduce message storage requirements and replicate the information throughout the organization. Security and encryption are very important features for any messaging system connected to the Internet, so this chapter covers the options and features available in the Exchange messaging server to address security issues. It briefly discusses how future releases will add new functionality to Exchange's integration with Internet technologies.

Internet Integration Options

Even though e-mail is a very small part of the services the Internet provides, messaging systems must be able to seamlessly send and receive messages with the millions of other SMTP-based hosts throughout the Internet. Simple Mail Transfer Protocol (SMTP) is the standard method for all message transfer on the Internet, which is defined in RFCs #821 and #822, published in 1982. These RFCs define the handshaking and keywords to use when a host initiates mail transfer using TCP/IP port 25, and the format for the plain-text message body and encoded attachments within e-mail messages. Domain Name Services (DNS) allows hosts to look up and resolve the IP address for the destination host computer, and it can be used for reverse lookups to authenticate another host.

The Internet Mail Connector is the Exchange component used to provide messaging connectivity to the Internet and other SMTP-based messaging systems. It fully supports the SMTP standards for mail transfer, and it encodes and decodes attachments and message body parts using MIME or UUENCODE. The IMC operates as a "smart" host performing lookups in DNS, and can act as a message relay agent for a fully qualified domain name (FQDN) external to Exchange. When determining what type of connectivity your company will need to the Internet, note that the following options are available:

- Microsoft Exchange clients can access their mailboxes on Microsoft Exchange Servers in your site across the Internet, using secure RPC connectivity.

- The Microsoft Exchange IMC can provide general SMTP e-mail connectivity between your messaging system and external SMTP-based messaging systems, such as the Internet.

- You can connect Microsoft Exchange sites within your organization over the Internet using the Microsoft Exchange Internet Mail Connector.

Connecting Exchange Clients over the Internet

Having users access the Exchange Server across an unsecured connection, such as the Internet, could make any network manager's skin crawl. Some options within Exchange, such as encryption and static port assignments, will make this a much more viable solution. If you combine the security and connectivity options in Exchange with a good firewall or proxy solution, or both, this type of connectivity is viable for many businesses' messaging requirements.

The first step in getting the clients to connect to an Exchange Server over the Internet is to set up name resolution. Because the Internet does not incorporate WINS services, and your users will not be able to connect to the WINS servers on your corporate LAN, the clients will need to be set up for DNS or host files. You could choose to hard-code the IP address of the server in the Exchange client profiles for the users, but you might have too much fun changing them all when you decide to change the server's IP address in the future. Name resolution can be performed in one of three ways for the Exchange client:

- Add an entry to the LMHOSTS file of the workstation for the Exchange Server and a domain controller(s); use the #PRE option for speed.

- Put an entry in DNS for the Exchange Server with an FQDN such as exchangesrv.company.com, and make sure that it can be resolved from the Internet.

- Set up a WINS server on the hot side of your firewall, and use this entry as the primary WINS server when clients connect to the Internet.

The solution of using the LMHOSTS file means that the name resolution occurs locally, and it can be maintained by an update process that runs when clients logon to the network in case the addresses change. Placing an entry in DNS enables clients to resolve the address for making the connection, but it exposes your Exchange Server's address, as well as Web indexing software for many search engines, to the world. Putting your own WINS server on the Internet gives you automatic name resolution and registration but opens the NT Server running the services to attack by hackers wanting to test NT's security. Choose the name resolution method that best fits your short-term messaging goals, because future releases of Exchange will support POP3 and "light" client access.

The Exchange Server requires the user to be authenticated by an NT before he can have access to mailbox or messaging resources. This is done through the built-in authentication process for Remote Procedure Calls (RPCs). You can increase the level of security for all information transmitted over the Internet by encrypting the data from the client. To configure an Exchange client to encrypt RPC traffic over dial-up or network connections, follow these steps:

1. From the client, select the Services option from the Tools pull-down menu.
2. Select the Microsoft Exchange Server service provider with the mouse, and click the Properties button.
3. Click the Advanced tab to display the advanced properties page.
4. Select the appropriate checkboxes under the Encrypt Information section for connections to the network and dial-in connections.
5. Click OK twice, and then stop and restart the Exchange client.

Just enabling the client for encryption of all RPC traffic does not give you a completely secure connection. All Exchange clients initially connect to TCP/IP port 135, which is the Windows NT RPC End-Point-Mapper service. This service in turn assigns a dynamic port for the client to use for continued connectivity. This process would create a problem for your firewall's packet filter because such a broad range of ports would need to be opened for Internet access. It would also open a larger security hole that attackers could leverage to compromise mailboxes or messaging resources.

You can configure the Exchange Server to always use a series of static ports, allowing the firewall's packet filter to "close the hole" of ports that attackers could use. You can do this by adding the values of the ports you want to enable as a REG_DWORD value to the following registry keys:

```
HKEY_LOCAL_MACHINE\SYSTEM\CurrentControlSet\Services\MSExchangeDS\Parameters\TCP/IP
➥port
HKEY_LOCAL_MACHINE\SYSTEM\CurrentControlSet\Services\MSExchangeIS\ParametersSystem\TCP/
➥IP port
```

After restarting the Exchange Server, you need to set up the packet filter on the firewall to allow access to the ports listed previously, as well as port 135 for the End-Point-Mapper service. You are not limited to using these features just for Internet-based connections, because they add an extra level of security to your local network. The overhead needed for the encryption process is negligible, and the End-Port-Mapper process will always be used in a dynamic fashion regardless of whether you specify static port assignments. Setting up static RPC ports is also helpful if you use the IMC to connect two Exchange sites over the Internet.

Connecting to the Internet for E-Mail

Connecting Exchange to the Internet for message transfer is the main purpose of the Internet Mail Connector. The IMC is fully compliant with most standards adopted within the Internet community for message transfer. Interoperability options within the IMC properties pages allow customized per-connection configurations to control how and what type of messages are sent. As you configure the IMC, you must consider the least-common-denominator message options for the other domains your users will regularly send messages to. Some of the domains you will exchange messages with will support rich-text and MIME attachment encoding, whereas others will support only basic text and UUENCODE/UUDECODE for message attachments.

The IMC can be configured for two types of outbound delivery: direct to a host through DNS lookup, or via forwarding of all messages to a specific relay host regardless of destination. Inbound messages are automatically accepted by the IMC on port 25, unless specifically set up to allow message reception only with specific hosts. Each IMC instance on a specific server within a site can be set up to handle inbound, outbound, both, or queue messages only. This feature is helpful if you want to control where messages are received from the Internet but want to allow outgoing delivery from multiple Exchange Servers, such as on a per-site basis.

When the IMC is configured for outbound delivery via DNS lookup, it needs access to all hosts on the Internet directly through port 25. It also requires a DNS server to resolve domain names and Mail Exchange (MX) records for Internet-based hosts. This technique allows for non-delivery reports (NDRs) and informational messages, such as retries, to be generated by the IMC rather than another SMTP host. Messages are more easily tracked because the IMC and the host receiving the message are the only parties involved in the message transfer. This can pose a security risk because the address of your Exchange Server must be registered and will be known to anyone on the Internet.

The IMC can also be configured to forward all outgoing messages to a specific host by name or IP address. Any SMTP-type messages that need to be transferred outside the Exchange site are relayed to this sendmail relay host. This allows the use of a firewall to perform the actual message delivery process, removing the burden of the DNS lookup and message transfer from the Exchange Server. The host or firewall specified as the SMTP relay host needs adequate storage for outbound messages, reliable and secure connection to the Internet, and the capability to perform DNS lookups for external domains and hosts. This will prove to be the most secure type of outbound mail transfer because only the firewall will be exposed to the Internet on outbound deliveries, and it should be used for any inbound deliveries as well. For inbound deliveries an alias table will need to be maintained on the firewall or sendmail host, and the Exchange recipients will need Secondary Proxy Addresses for inbound delivery.

Inbound message transfer can be handled directly by the Exchange IMC, or by another host with a list of aliases for the recipients on Exchange. The IMC accepts any allowed inbound message transfer request and can also perform the relay functionality if it is the primary domain contact with custom recipients for other local SMTP host mailboxes. Using another sendmail host, such as a firewall or UNIX server, with a list of aliases to Exchange recipients is the best configuration for Internet connectivity. In this configuration the firewall accepts the incoming messages and forwards them to the Exchange Server through a lookup in an alias table maintained locally. If you do not want the maintenance headache of an alias file or the additional security of a firewall, you can make the Exchange Server the primary contact for the domain with custom recipients for aliasing to other sendmail hosts.

As previously mentioned, you should configure the default interoperability options to cover the broadest number of hosts that messages might be transferred to. UUENCODE is the best option for the default outbound attachment encoding method, because most hosts accept this type of transfer if they are RFC #822-compliant. As you determine e-mail domains that support MIME or have Exchange recipients, you can specify overrides for these domains in the Specify Message Content By E-Mail Domain option on the Internet Mail property page for the IMC. The interoperability button is available for the default, and per-domain connections allow configuration of message word wrap, rich text, automatic replies, and out-of-office responses. The word wrap option is only available when MIME is selected, and will control at which character place a line will be wrapped. Since rich text is normally only supported by Exchange clients, this option should be disabled for any domain that does not have Exchange recipients to eliminate the winmail.dat file being transmitted. The out-of-office and automatic replies can be disabled for SMTP recipients so that persons outside your organization will not accidentally receive confidential information from an Inbox Rule or know that an employee is on vacation.

TIP

Have you noticed that messages sent to people over the Internet have a file named winmail.dat attached? This file is created by a user sending a message to a recipient who has the Send in Exchange Format option checked in her personal address book. It contains rich-text formatting and attachments for use by a client that can support rich-text formatting. This option sounds great, but it will prove to be useful only if the recipient is using Exchange or MS-Mail. As an administrator, you should disable all Rich Text functionality for all default connections through the interoperability options in the IMC. Then use the Specify Message Content By E-Mail Domain option on the Internet Mail property page to "register" domains that have Exchange or MS-Mail recipients. When the list of Exchange-enabled e-mail domains gets too large to manage, set the interoperability defaults to support rich text, switching those domains that do not support rich text set to disabled by specific e-mail domain name.

Connecting Exchange Sites over the Internet

Does your WAN budget have fewer digits than a three-toed sloth? Are you searching for an inexpensive way to connect your home office to a branch location? Are you willing to trust your messaging data to a public network that has no guaranteed delivery? If you answered yes to all three questions, you will probably want to connect your Exchange sites over the Internet with the Internet Mail Connector. This functionality is available because the IMC has the capability to handle the special "EX" address type that is necessary for the directory replication connector.

You might be wondering how much security is available in this type of connection. The IMC, as well as SMTP hosts, does not encrypt the messages as they are transmitted from host to host. The message header information is transmitted in free-form text; the message body might or might not be encoded with MIME or UUDENCOE, but is still in the form of ASCII characters. To ensure that messages are securely transmitted between users at each site, you should install and configure advanced security. This task involves a simple installation of the Key Server component, and then a two-step procedure to set up the private encryption keys for each user. The end-users need to complete the setup of advanced security to make this a viable option. Users must then set their default send options to always send messages in encrypted format to ensure that messages sent to IMC-connected sites will be encrypted and secure.

> **NOTE**
>
> Many of you just read the preceding section and probably decided not to connect your company's sites over the Internet because of the security concerns. Windows NT 4.0 will be available in stores by the time you read this, and it includes a Point-To-Point Tunneling Protocol (PPTP) that enables a network manager to create virtual private networks over unsecure public networks. This new option in NT 4.0 makes connecting two sites over the Internet via the IMC much more appealing, because all traffic is encrypted over the PPTP virtual network.

These are the steps to connect two Exchange sites over the Internet using the Internet Mail Connector:

1. Set up the IMC to connect to the Internet and test e-mail and DNS name resolution functionality. Make sure that you can send messages between the sites using the FDQN for a test user account, such as `testuser@sitea.company.com` to `testuser@siteb.company.com`.

2. On `sitea` open the properties for the IMC, and click the Connected Sites tab to bring up the Connected Sites properties page.

3. Click the New button, and you should be prompted for the organization and site name on a general properties page. The organization field is already filled in with your

current organization name, which is required for two sites to connect. Enter the name of the site you want to make a connection to, keeping in mind that these names are case sensitive and must be spelled correctly.

4. Click the Routing Address tab to enter the type of SMTP, enter the routing address of `@siteb.company.com`, and assign an appropriate cost to the connection. Click the OK button to save. Multiple IMCs can be used with various costs if you have multiple connections to the Internet or would like fault tolerance.

5. Next, set up a directory replication connector for the site you just connected to replicate the directories from this site.

6. Perform steps 2 through 5 for `siteb` to complete the connection between the two sites.

After directory replication has completed, users at `sitea` should see users from `siteb` in their global address list and vice versa. When users at `sitea` send messages to users at `siteb`, the messages are routed through the IMC at `sitea`, transmitted through a series of SMTP hosts over the Internet, received at the IMC at `siteb`, and delivered to the intended recipients. Seems simple enough, unless the messages transmitted between the two sites are caught in a "traffic jam" or just end up as road kill on the information superhighway.

Using Exchange Public Folders for Listserver Messages

If you had some information that a group of people would be interested in, how would you go about getting that information to them? We are all familiar with the current tactics used by the marketing departments of many companies: junk mail. We have gotten on the mailing lists of these companies and had our names and addresses sold and resold to hundreds of companies. Wouldn't it be nice if you could control who had your address and what information they sent to you? Luckily, the Internet has just this feature, called listservers, and so far it has not had a major insurgence of electronic junk mail.

Mailing lists are the electronic version of a well-maintained "little black book." Listservers maintain a mailing list of the users who have subscribed to receive information about a common interest. When someone sends a message in a specific format to the listserver address, it records her e-mail address in the master list. When the listserver owner mails a message to the mailing list, all the subscribed users receive a copy of the message. The list owner is also responsible for keeping the listserver in running order and must intervene when problems occur.

Subscribing and unsubscribing to a listserver is as simple as sending a message to an address with the word SUBSCRIBE or UNSUBSCRIBE within the message body. Usually, one address is used for subscriptions, and another is used to post messages to all the members of the list after those messages have been screened by the list owner. After a user has subscribed to a listserver, he receives in his mailbox any messages sent to the mailing list. This functionality works well if the number of users within your company is small, but it increases messaging traffic on your IMC every time a new message is sent to the list if a large number of "subscribed" users exist within your company.

There is a better way to coordinate and manage listserver message traffic: by subscribing a public folder to the mailing list. This technique reduces the traffic from the listserver to just a single message any time a new mailing is sent to the list. The messages then can be organized by various folder views and replicated throughout your organization for use by users at other sites. These are the advantages of using a public folder instead of receiving the messages at individual mailboxes:

- Users in your organization can "join" or browse the messages from a listserver by adding the public folder to their favorites folder on their server-based mailbox. This method enables them to read the messages at any time, instead of wading through many messages in their personal mailbox.

- Messages from the list are delivered to a public folder rather than a user's inbox. Many users subscribe to more than one list, which can flood their inbox with a large volume of messages if the listservers are very active. Users might try to use inbox rules to organize the incoming messages into a series of folders, but most users do not have the time to read all messages, and many messages are subsequently deleted.

- Valuable storage space and messaging traffic bandwidth are used more efficiently. One message sent from a listserver to 100 users has 100 instances of the message. A listserver message sent to a public folder has only one instance with 100 users pointing to that message, or multiple instances if the folder is replicated throughout the organization.

- The public folder can be set up to send an "update" message to a distribution list to alert specific users that new messages have been received. This informational message is stored as a single message instance on each server, still saving valuable storage space.

Because some users might want to be able to post new messages to the list, you need to set the proper folder permissions to allow the users to send-on-behalf of the public folder. Then users can use the From field when composing a message to set the sender address to that of the public folder. The easiest way to configure this functionality is to create a group on the NT domain for the user accounts, and then give this group the Send as permission for the public folder. This action is not necessary if the mailing list is deemed open (will accept messages from anyone) or if the users will not be posting any messages to the listserver.

Subscribing a Public Folder to a Mailing List

The process of subscribing a public folder to the mailing list of a listserver is relatively simple. Because every object in the Exchange directory has proxy addresses for the default address types, all public folders will have a valid SMTP address that can be mailed to over the Internet. To subscribe a public folder to a listserver, perform the following steps:

1. From the Exchange client create the public folder with a descriptive name the users will associate with the listserver that messages will be received from.

2. Set the proper permissions for the folder by using the Permissions page of the folder properties. The default permissions must include the capability to create items or an NDR report will be sent to the message originator every time a new message arrives. This is not the way to win friends and influence people in the Internet community.

3. Create a default view for the folder that will organize the messages by conversation topic. Create any additional views that will be helpful to the users, such as views by send date or message size.

4. Originate the message that will subscribe the public folder to the list. Some listservers allow a message from any address with the command subscribe *list e-mail address*, in which *list* is the list name and *e-mail address* is the SMTP address of the public folder. To get the SMTP address of the public folder, open the properties pages for the folder, and click the Add to Personal Address Book button on the administration page.

Some listservers require that the subscription message originate from the user who is subscribing to the list. This limitation is designed to keep your buddies from subscribing your account to all sorts of weird listservers as a joke, which would require you to take the time to unsubscribe from each listserver manually. This task requires the administrator or folder owner to send a subscription message on behalf of the public folder. The following steps lead you through subscribing a public folder to this type of listserver:

1. Open the folder properties from the administrator program, click the Permissions tab, and give the NT user account you will use the Send as permission.

2. Start the Exchange client and log on to a mailbox that has the NT account from step 1 as its primary account. To make sure that you have the proper permissions to the folder, open its properties pages and you should see all the folder tabs.

3. Capture the SMTP address of the public folder by opening the properties for the folder in the Exchange client and clicking the Add to Personal Address Book button on the administration page.

4. Compose a new message from the Exchange client, and enable the From field by selecting the From option from the View menu.

5. Click the From button and select the public folder address from your personal address list. Enter the subscription address on the To field in SMTP format, such as listserv@domain.com.

6. Enter the subscription command for the listserver in the message body. This is usually something like SUBSCRIBE *LIST NAME*.

7. Send the message to the listserver by clicking the Send Now button. The message delivery can be tracked via the Track Message feature in the administrator program. Most listservers send a confirmation message that should show up in the public folder to verify that it is subscribed.

The public folder should now start receiving new messages sent to the mailing list. Test the folder views to make sure that they are working correctly and that they will provide users with valuable sorting and viewing capabilities. You might also want to limit the number of messages within this folder by setting an age limit from the Age Limits properties page of the public Information Store on each server. You should also check the storage limits for this folder from its advanced properties page to make sure that the listserver will not receive NDR messages when the folder is over its limit.

The folder should be frequently checked to ensure that it is still receiving updates because some listservers require frequent subscriptions to keep the e-mail address in the list. You should notice a renewal-type message in the folder indicating that it is time to resubscribe the folder to the mailing list. Also, the folder owner should browse the content frequently to look for messages that might be objectionable to the users. When you decide to remove the public folder, be sure to unsubscribe it from the list first. Otherwise, nondelivery reports will be returned for every new message sent to the folder, requiring administrator intervention to unsubscribe the folder from the mailing list.

Exchange Server and Internet Security

Internet security is first and foremost on the minds of administrators when it comes to connecting their company to the public network. This type of connection can open their business data to attacks from various types of individuals, often collectively called hackers. The term *hacker,* however, should be reserved for individuals who find new ways to circumvent security measures to obtain a "trophy," proving to their friends that they were able to obtain access to a specific network or computer. Hackers normally are not trying to damage anything, but they might inadvertently cause problems in their search for the trophy. Attackers are much more dangerous, because they are trying to steal information or destroy computer resources. You must take measures to protect your Exchange messaging system from these types of individuals, because you risk losing confidential data or suffering unnecessary downtime.

These are the types of attacks you should protect your network and messaging systems from:

- E-mail spoofing of messages in which an attacker can make it appear as if a message came from someone else. This technique can be used to trick users into revealing sensitive data or to spread false information.

- Theft or corruption of data through the use of "sniffing" software to intercept messages in transit. The attacker can use this method to obtain sensitive documents to be used for illegal or immoral purposes.

- E-mail spamming of your messaging system. The invader overwhelms the servers with thousands of messages, using valuable processor and bandwidth resources.

- Spreading viruses within e-mail messages. Users might unexpectedly infect their machines with viruses by clicking on attachments to messages. This has become a serious problem with the addition of macro viruses that live in documents, such as the word prank macro virus that has been wreaking havoc even within Microsoft's messaging system.

- Exploiting weaknesses within the network operating system to gain access to services and resources that will give the attacker valuable information. This will be their "ticket" into the system later, when you might not be watching.

Attackers are dreaming up new ways to infiltrate your messaging system and network every day. As messaging technology advances, so do the methods used to break into these new systems. I like to use the "car alarm" approach to ward off potential attackers. If you put enough security measures on your system to increase the risk that intruders will be found, they will pass over your system for a less risky target. If there is one thing hackers and attackers fear the most, it is being identified for all to see. Many Web sites publish the names of attackers and information about them that administrators can use to help protect their networks.

Even though administrators fear the problems associated with external attacks on their messaging systems, most problems are created by the inadvertent actions of users. A user could accidentally send a sensitive document to a distribution list that has a similar spelling to a user's name, or could send a very large message to the Everyone distribution list, tying up valuable resources. You can protect against these types of problems by using the option to restrict who can mail to distribution lists, and by establishing maximum message sizes for MTAs and connectors.

Security Measures in Windows NT

Windows NT Server is built on a very solid security platform currently listed in the NCSC's C2 Evaluated Products list. Exchange Server leverages the security features of the NT Server product to provide secure access to all messaging resources. Each object in the directory has properties that map to accounts in the NT security database. This tight integration allows Exchange to do what it does best, messaging, and NT to do what it does best, security. A user must have the proper security clearance before accessing objects such as mailboxes and public folders.

Windows NT Logon Security

The heart of the advanced security within NT is the challenge/response method of authentication. When the user logs on to the network or accesses a mailbox resource, the server issues a challenge request to the client. The client networking software then sends a response to the server with the password as the encryption key. The server then decrypts the response to validate that the client knows the correct password. Because the password is never transmitted over the network in an un-encrypted format, it is nearly impossible for an attacker to get a password through packet sniffing.

NT Server also uses a distributed accounts database that is replicated from the Primary Domain Controller (PDC) to all Backup Domain Controllers (BDCs) so that account information is easily accessed from remote sites. When an administrator changes information for a particular user account, that information is automatically replicated from the PDC to all BDCs in two-minute intervals. If an unauthenticated user attempts to access a mailbox on the Exchange Server, she is automatically prompted to supply her domain logon account and password. This challenge can be processed by a BDC, eliminating the need to communicate with a PDC that might be a few network hops away.

Windows NT RPC

Windows NT provides RPC services to support the security needs of Exchange Server, as well as the NT administrative tools such as Server Manager and User Manager for domains. The RPC service within NT uses the RC4 40-bit encryption algorithm from RSA Data Security, Inc., to encrypt traffic sent over networks. Because RPC allows an application to execute remote procedures on the server, it is very important that a high level of secure access be maintained. The RPC services support the challenge/response authentication method to eliminate the capability of a program to spawn a remote process via RPC if the user is not authenticated by an NT domain.

Microsoft Exchange Server Advanced Security

The capability to securely encrypt and digitally "sign" messages is definitely required when sensitive or private information is sent to any recipient. This is the only way to guarantee that the message can be seen only by the intended recipient, and it enables the user receiving the message to validate the sender. Microsoft Exchange Server includes an advanced security option, the key management server, that provides this level of security to end-users and administrators.

After the key management server service is installed, the advanced Security properties page becomes available for all the mailboxes within the site. The security administrator is someone who knows the advanced security password chosen when the key server was initially installed. That person has the ability to create new public and private keys for users from the Security properties page of any mailbox. This creates a security "token" that the administrator must give to the user to enter when setting up security within the client. The administrator should use a secure method to get the user his unique security token, such as via voice mail or by delivering it in person. When the user sets up advanced security from the Exchange client, he must supply a password that is used to encrypt the security file and must supply it each time advanced security options are used.

Within an organization one primary key server maintains the security database, and secondary servers are located at each of the other connected Exchange sites. The secondary key server forwards any security requests to the primary key server, which is the first key management server installed within the organization. Management of the key server involves enabling security for mailboxes, revoking security certificates, recovering security keys, and forgetting the remembered password. Users must renew their security once every year, and they are prompted when this time is near expiration.

For bulk encryption of message content, the key management server supports both the DES and the CAST algorithms with 56- and 64-bit key lengths in the United States and Canada only. CAST encryption with 40-bit keys is available worldwide due to U.S. government regulations on the export of encryption technologies. The key server automatically encrypts messages sent to international versions of Exchange using 40-bit encryption keys. Digital signatures and bulk encryption key exchange uses 512-bit public keys using encryption from RSA Data Security, Inc. All the advanced security options available with key management server are based on the X.509 standard certificate format, which allows for more security options in future versions of Exchange.

If a user attempts to send a signed message to a recipient who is not on a Microsoft Exchange Server, or who is in another Exchange organization, the message can be read but is not verifiable. Sealed or encrypted messages can be received only by recipients who are also enabled for advanced security. The Exchange client prompts users when they attempt to send an encrypted message to an unsecure recipient, and it gives them the options of sending the message unencrypted or canceling the message. I suggest that administrators create a security request form that users can mail to a public folder for requests to have advanced security enabled, thus providing a history of requests that can be used to track which users are using this level of security.

Microsoft Exchange Server Internet Mail Connector Security Options

The Exchange Internet Mail Connector has options that can increase the security of SMTP-based messaging and provide limits on the capability to attack your messaging system either directly or inadvertently. These options should be used with care, because they can create message delivery problems if not properly understood. Most of these features are best used when connecting your company's Exchange messaging system to the Internet, but they could also be used in a private network.

Accept/Reject by IP Address

After an initial installation, the Exchange IMC is configured to accept incoming SMTP connections from any host or IP address. If you are using a firewall or sendmail relay host, you might want to configure the IMC to allow only connections from those hosts. This option is configured on the Connections property page for the IMC and is enabled by selection of the Accept or Reject by Host option. You must click the Specify Hosts button to specify which hosts can or cannot make connections to this server. If you want to reject messages only from specific hosts, ones that are not reliable or might be rogue, use this same option to reject by IP address or host name.

Message Size Limit

By establishing message size limits on the messages on incoming and outgoing connections, administrators can prevent users and attackers from tying up the system with large message attachments. This technique might seem useful for incoming message transfer, but it is also practical for any outgoing messages. Because all message attachments must be encoded before they are transmitted, a large message could tie up your server for hours. There are also practical size limitations for Internet-based mail because the Internet is not designed for bulk file transfer. If your users need to transmit or receive large files, they should use FTP instead because it is built to handle these types of bulk transfers. This option also protects against external attack in which an attacker might send a large message to tie up the system to keep administrators busy while they look for security holes.

Disabling Auto-Replies to the Internet

The Exchange client has the capability to create auto-replies with inbox rules or the out-of-office assistant. Most companies do not want this type of information to leave the confines of the corporate messaging system, because it could provide an attacker with an account to hack that they know will not be used for a specific amount of time. Inbox rules to forward messages to external recipients also might inadvertently transmit confidential information that can be intercepted on the Internet. Even worse, what if an auto-reply was accidentally sent to a mailing list? Auto-replies are disabled from the interoperability button on the Internet Mail properties page for the IMC and can be configured for all default connections or on a per-domain basis.

Delivery Restrictions

Many corporations want the capability to control which users have access to Internet mail for security or tracking purposes. By using the Delivery Restrictions properties page for the IMC, administrators can specify which users or distribution lists have permission to send mail through the IMC. The best way to configure this option is to create a distribution list named Internet Mail Users to add members whom you want to be able to send Internet mail. This option can also be used to deny messages from specific recipients, such as known attackers/hackers or junk mail listservers. Use this option with care; all administrators should be aware that this option is being used so that they do not attempt to troubleshoot problems that are actually delivery restrictions.

Microsoft Exchange Client Security Features

Most users are unaware of the security risks associated with Internet-based messaging, and they might inadvertently send sensitive data to an attacker if they do not verify the address of the person they are replying to. The Exchange client always displays the "friendly" name and e-mail address of any sender in the message header section of the view message window. Users can also examine the headers of any message by selecting the Message Properties from the File menu, then clicking the Headers tab for display. You should publish a security document to all your users, advising them of the security risks and the steps they can take to protect their messages from attackers and hackers. I like to configure a public folder to publish all the company's messaging policies and set up a rule to remind users to review the documents regularly.

Future Enhancements

Exchange Server is a very robust and secure messaging system, with many options for connectivity to the Internet. The current version does fall short in a few key areas, mostly dealing with enhanced Internet services and access by "light" clients. By the time this book is published, the beta of Exchange 4.1 should be well underway. This updated version promises to bring new features to the table, especially in the area of Internet value-added services. The following bulleted items outline those new features. This text is taken from the document "Microsoft Exchange Server Features Native Internet Protocol Support," available on Microsoft's Web site at the URL www.microsoft.com/exchange:

- Using POP3 clients to access the mail services of Microsoft Exchange Server. POP3 is a basic client-server protocol for extracting messages from a mail drop. With POP3 support on Microsoft Exchange Server, any commonly available POP3 client, such as Eudora, Pegasus Mail, or the Microsoft Exchange Inbox with Internet Mail Service Provider, can be used to access mail.

- Using Web browsers to access Microsoft Exchange Server. The World Wide Web is a dramatically growing phenomenon on the Internet, and Web browsers have already become ubiquitous. Many large organizations are implementing Webs on intranets to distribute corporate information internally. Users running Microsoft Internet Explorer, Netscape Navigator, Mosaic, and so on will have live read/write access to Microsoft Exchange Servers. They will be able to send/receive mail, browse the directory, access private and public folders, and even have some access to Schedule+ calendars without requiring any additional software.

- Accessing the Microsoft Exchange Server directory using LDAP-compliant e-mail clients and Web browsers. LDAP is a Lightweight Directory Access Protocol used to access X.500 directories. Users will be able to choose from a wide variety of "light" e-mail clients and Web browsers to access directory information in Microsoft Exchange Server. In addition, LDAP support in Microsoft Exchange will potentially enable directory synchronization with other LDAP-compliant systems for increased interoperability.

- Making Internet newsgroup data available to Microsoft Exchange Server users. NNTP News feeds can be downloaded to Microsoft Exchange public folders. The capabilities of public folders can then be leveraged to replicate and control access to the information within an organization. Items within a newsgroup are assembled by conversation topic, which is the view preferred by most discussion groups. Users can then utilize Microsoft Exchange client software to read the articles and post replies that can be sent back to the Internet newsgroups.

- Using NNTP (newsreader) clients to access Microsoft Exchange Server. NNTP clients will be able to access information stored in Microsoft Exchange Server public folders.

- Using IMAP4-compliant clients and Web browsers to access Microsoft Exchange Server. IMAP is an emerging Internet standard mailbox access protocol. It enables synchronized online/offline mailbox access by "light" clients.

I took these descriptions directly from Microsoft's publicly published document on the Web because I would not want to misquote any of the features slated for a version of Exchange that will ship in the near future. I also am currently under a standard nondisclosure agreement that restricts me from discussing features of a beta product. Many critics have claimed that products from Microsoft suffer from "feature creep," which might be true for previous product offerings. Exchange Server has provided almost all the features promised in early 1991, which might explain why the product took longer to develop than originally planned. The next version will bring tight integration with these new Internet-based services to put even more information at the user's fingertips.

Summary

The Internet seems to ignore the laws concerning calendar time, with minutes spanning years of technological advancement. The constant change within this electronic world creates many challenges for businesses that are trying to develop solutions to solve common business needs. Connection costs and security risks might keep some companies away initially, but eventually they must get connected just to match their competition. Electronic mail is the core service offered by the Internet, but many value-added services such as search engines, newsgroups, and Web browsers are extending its value to users and companies. The massive volume of information contained within the Internet makes it a very valuable source for information storage and retrieval.

Exchange Server has tight Internet integration options to enable it to transfer messages to any of the almost 30 million recipients who connect regularly. The Internet Mail Connector is the core Exchange component that uses standards such as SMTP and MIME to transfer messages to any of the millions of hosts on the Internet. Security options enable the IMC to communicate only with a restricted list of hosts, allowing it to seamlessly fit into any firewall solution your company might have. The Exchange client supports complete encryption of all data sent over an RPC connection, and it has advanced security options that enable users to digitally sign and encrypt confidential messages.

Even though the current version of Exchange Server supports the core messaging protocols for Internet-based mail, the next version will add features for services such as POP3 and IMAP4 access for light clients. New protocol support for NNTP News feeds and HTML publishing will extend the functionality of public folders, allowing data exchange with newsgroups and Web clients. These new features will allow Exchange to take the meaning of Groupware to the next level, enabling users on an Exchange messaging system to collaborate with the millions of users on the Internet.

## CHAPTER 27

The Exchange Forms Designer

by Diane Andrews and Rick Andrews

IN THIS CHAPTER

Most organizations (if not all) use custom forms in some way to communicate, move, tabulate, survey, and record information in the workplace, whether the workplace is an in-home small business or a worldwide enterprise. Often, you or another individual within the company is responsible for creating some of these forms because your company has specific needs that require customized forms (that is, forms that are not readily available from a supplier). Creating these forms the "old-fashioned" way meant simply drawing boxes on a piece of paper (with text identifying each box's purpose) in an organized collection, printing multiple copies of these forms, and making them available to others in your workplace.

Microsoft Exchange Forms Designer (EFD), a new application that comes with Microsoft Exchange, provides a way to create electronic forms (forms that are sent electronically across the computer network) to replace the old fashioned forms to which you are accustomed. The Forms Designer does the same things for electronic forms that your pencil, typewriter, and printer does for paper forms. In this chapter, you use EFD to create an expense report form that you can use in your company. The techniques demonstrated in this chapter will be applicable to any type of EFD you will want to design.

What Is EFD?

The Exchange Forms Designer (EFD) is a tool that enables you to easily create custom e-mail forms for your organization without writing a single line of code; you don't have to be a programmer to design Exchange forms! EFD provides a simple, easy-to-use, drag-and-drop interface that enables you to visually create your forms. A simple wizard gets you started, and EFD then makes it easy for you to design the form and install it into Exchange, making it available to everyone in your organization.

If you want to add functionality to your Exchange form that is beyond what is provided in EFD, EFD creates forms that are extensible. This means that after you create a fully working Exchange form application with EFD, you can go further and make custom modifications to it using the Microsoft Visual Basic programming language. After you design your form with EFD, EFD produces the Visual Basic source code that builds the form. You can ignore this source code and let EFD do everything for you automatically. However, if you are a programmer, or someone interested in programming, you can view the source code to study the internals of e-mail messaging in Microsoft Windows, modify the source code, and rebuild and install the form with added functionality or special customization. Note that the subject of extending your Exchange forms with Visual Basic is covered lightly at the end of this chapter in the section, related topics Extending the Expense Report Form with Visual Basic, but is not considered within the scope of the topic discussed here. This chapter primarily focuses on developing forms without programming. For more information on extending forms, read the *Application Designer's Guide* that came with your Microsoft Exchange Forms Designer.

27

What Are Exchange Forms?

To many, it is not obvious what exactly an Exchange form is. Assuming that you are familiar with what a standard e-mail message is (see Figure 27.1), start by recognizing your standard e-mail message as nothing more than a simple form that contains only envelope fields (the place where you enter To:, Cc:, Subject:, and so on) and a single message body field (the place where you type or read your actual message).

Forms can be made up of several windows, and forms you design with EFD will generally have more than one. For example, a standard e-mail message you could create in EFD might have a Compose window, a Read window, a Forward window, and a Reply window. Each window represents a different view of the form for each context in which the form will be used (for example, a Reply window appears when you want to reply to an e-mail message; that is, you use this window to type in your reply). Together, the windows define the form.

FIGURE 27.1.

A standard e-mail form.

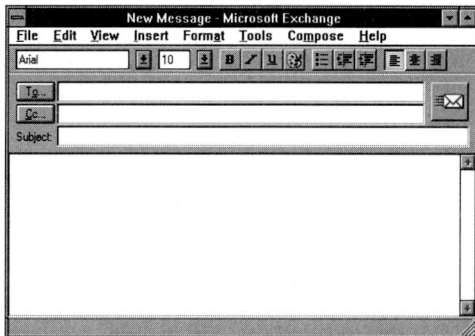

All you are doing with EFD is creating more functional forms that, besides the basic envelope and message body fields, might have listboxes from which users make selections, multiple text fields into which they enter data, or even picture boxes so you can decorate your form with pictures.

Exchange Forms in the Workplace

How do forms fit into the workplace? As the Exchange administrator, it will probably be your responsibility to address this problem in your organization. Generally, whenever you need to obtain information in an organized fashion, you should use forms. Several very useful forms ship with the sample applications that come with EFD. You'll also find several forms from independent Exchange form developers; some of these might be perfect for your organization. Because designing forms is so easy with EFD, you'll probably find that several people in your own organization will design them when the need arises (or even just for fun). But often, it will be up to you to determine what forms are needed and then to design them.

You can design a form for practically every type of activity in your organization—a form that enables employees to check out books from the company library; perform a company-wide inventory of computer equipment at everyone's workstation; conduct surveys, employment reviews, or job interviews; or to disperse reports to all the employees. And you aren't limited to just your local workplace. If your business has people at remote locations, they can access the forms created by EFD, too. All they need is the Exchange Client running on their computer and a way to connect to the Exchange server (by WAN, modem, or ISDN).

After you've created a form, EFD makes it easy for you to install the form into the Exchange Server so that all the Exchange users in your organization can send and receive the forms.

Administrator's Roles

As the Exchange administrator, you will have certain roles to perform to incorporate EFD into your company. This section summarizes what these roles are. For more information, refer to your Exchange Server documentation.

Install EFD

You will need to install the EFD software before you can begin to design Exchange forms. You find the installation files for EFD on the same distribution CD and subdirectory as the Exchange client software, under EFDSETUP. Note that EFD setup cannot be completed unless you already have an Exchange client installed.

From the \EFDSETUP subdirectory of the Exchange Client CD, run setup.exe. Choose the Typical setup option to install all of EFD's available features. This will include the installation of some of the sample applications that come with Exchange. These sample application files will be installed under \EFDFORMS\SAMPLES.

> **TIP**
>
> Opening these sample application files in EFD and examining them is an excellent way to familiarize yourself with how EFD can be used.

Other people in your organization who will be designing forms will also need to have EFD installed. We suggest you create a share point (a shared directory) on your Exchange server from which others can install EFD. To do so, simply copy the entire EFDSETUP directory from your CD to this share point.

Set Up the Organization Forms Library

In order to make forms available for Exchange users, you must place the forms into a forms library that is available to your Exchange users. The Organization Forms library is such a library. Examples of other forms libraries are Personal Forms Library, Public Folder Library, and Personal Folder Library, but these are not necessarily available to all users. For example, forms installed into your Personal Forms Library are accessible only to you.

> **NOTE**
>
> A library is located in Exchange where you put your forms so users can access them. You can choose to have one library where all your company's forms are located or you can make separate libraries to organize your forms according to topic, security access, departments, and so on.

Establish an Organization Forms Library

You use the Microsoft Exchange Administrator to establish an organization forms library. (We assume use of the default name of Organization Forms, but you can modify this name as you wish when you create the library.)

To create an Organization Forms Library, follow these steps:

1. Start the Exchange Administrator program.
2. Select Forms Administrator from the Tools menu. The Organization Forms Library Administrator dialog box will appear.
3. Click New. The Create New Forms Library dialog box will appear.
4. Select the appropriate language from the Language list.
5. Click OK.

The Organization Forms library you just established is now visible in the Organization Forms Library Administrator dialog box. Leave this dialog box open; next, you'll need to set permissions to use the Organization Forms library.

Set Permissions to Install Forms in the Organization Forms Library

The permission level for the Organization Forms library is set to Reviewer by default. A user with Reviewer permission can read only existing items—similar to having read-only access to a file on your hard drive or on a network share.

As the administrator, you will need to give yourself Owner permissions to the Organization Forms library so that you can fully administer your company's forms.

To do so, follow these steps:

1. Open the Organization Forms Library dialog box (see previous section) if it is not already open.
2. Select Organization Forms.
3. Click Permissions. The Forms Library Permissions dialog box will appear.
4. Click Add. The Add Users dialog box will appear.
5. Locate your Exchange Client user name in the list on the left.
6. Add your user name to the list on the right.
7. Click OK. You'll return to the Forms Library Permissions dialog box.
8. Select your name.
9. Set the Roles (under Permissions) to Owner.
10. Click OK.

You will now be able to perform every available administration task on the Organization Forms library, including the installation of forms.

Creating and Providing Exchange Forms

As the Exchange administrator, you might be responsible for providing forms to your Exchange users that they can use in their daily work to improve communication and efficiency in the workplace. Your first thought might be to create these forms yourself. However, you should be aware that there are other resources available from which you can obtain forms that can do the job you need. Besides creating the forms yourself, you might want to consider looking for other solutions, such as the Exchange Application Farm (see the section Other Sources of Information at the end of this chapter) page on the Web. The Exchange Application Farm is a place where you can find and contribute application forms for others to share. Other sites where you can locate consultants who develop Exchange form applications should be available.

Create Folders

As the administrator, you will probably want to create public folders for some of your forms. Forms in public folders can provide information updates to the entire organization quickly and in one central location. You can build custom views for the public folders in the Exchange Viewer and enable users to see important information at a glance. When users post forms to a specially designed public folder, they can use the Exchange Viewer to quickly view the information from the forms.

Basic Design Process

The following is a quick overview of the entire design process involved in building a custom form with EFD. Later, in the section A Sample Expense Report, you build a sample expense report Exchange application that takes you through this design process in more detail.

Planning a Form

As with any design process, the first thing you need to do is plan. Make sure you know what you want before you get started. What does the form need to do? What problem is it trying to solve? Where is this form supposed to go, to other users or a public folder? Do you want the recipient(s) to see the information in the form differently than the way the sender sees it? You should answer questions like these before you begin creating the form.

Use the Wizard to Create a Skeleton Form

Without EFD, creating forms can be extremely complicated if you are not a skilled developer familiar with Exchange messaging concepts. For this reason, EFD begins with a Wizard to help you establish the basics of your form. The Wizard asks you a series of questions about the type of form application you want to create and then it creates a skeleton "working" form ready for you to customize. It does the hard part and leaves the easy, fun part for you.

Add Fields to the Form

The next step is an easy drag-and-drop operation. You choose fields, such as Entry fields, ListBox fields, and OptionButton fields, from the ToolBox window of EFD, add them to the window of your form, and position them as you want. Fields are the main elements that make up a form. They are used to display information and get input.

Set Properties for Fields, Windows, and Forms

Just about everything in EFD has properties (for example, Font size, Background color, and Window name) to set. There are properties specific to the form, properties specific for each window, and properties specific for each field. In most cases, you should be able to use most of the default property settings that were initialized when you first created the object (form, window, or field). But you will need to change some properties to fit the requirements of your individual form. You use the Property Inspector and the Field Appearance Palette to change most of the properties that need changing. The Property Inspector and Field Appearance Palette are discussed later in the sections, Property Inspector and The Field Appearance Palette.

Finishing Up

After you have designed your form you'll want to install it into the Exchange Server so your organization can use it. You do this by selecting Install from the File menu or by clicking the

Install toolbar button. Either action launches a four-step process that results in the final form. (By the way, unless you are a programmer who wants to extend the form with custom programming, you probably won't care much about these steps; the important thing to know is that when these steps are completed, your form will be installed and ready to use.)

1. **Save Form to .EFP file.** The file type used by EFD is called EFP. Your Exchange Forms Project (EFP) file is a database containing all the information needed to define the form's structure and functionality. Perform this step only if you have not manually saved your project by using the Save command in the File menu or clicking the Save toolbar button.

2. **Generate VB Source Code.** EFD next uses the information in the EFP file to generate Microsoft Visual Basic (VB) source code that implements the runtime version of your form. Until now, you've been dealing with the design-time version of the form. The *design-time* version of the form is what you use in EFD when you are designing the form. The *runtime* version is what your users will actually send, receive, post, and reply to on the Exchange network. The EFP file contains the information for both the design-time and runtime versions of the form.

3. **Compile VB Source Code.** Next, EFD compiles the VB source code into an EXE file that can be executed by Exchange. Note that you will not be able to easily run this EXE as a stand-alone application because it expects to receive commands (events) from Exchange that tell it what to do. Without these messages, no window will ever appear.

4. **Install Form.** Finally, the form is installed into the Exchange server and is available for use. Don't forget to test it thoroughly before everyone on Exchange starts using it.

That's the whole process from beginning to end. To summarize, you start by planning the form you want to design. You then use the EFD Forms Wizard to create a basic form to get you started. Next, you add fields and then set properties to customize the form to fit your design needs. Finally, you instruct EFD to generate and install your form.

We are now going to take a close look at EFD and look at the tools and methods it provides to make designing forms easier.

A Quick Tour of EFD

This section takes you through a quick tour of the features and tools in EFD that you'll use to design forms.

The Basic Windows of EFD

There are several important windows in EFD that you will use while you design your form. This section lightly touches on each one to give you a feel for the overall structure of EFD.

The Layout Window

The layout window is where you actually place the fields you want on your form. It represents a window of the final form itself, but at this point it has no functionality other than enabling you to place and position fields. Figure 27.2 shows the layout window with some fields already on it.

FIGURE 27.2.

The EFD layout window.

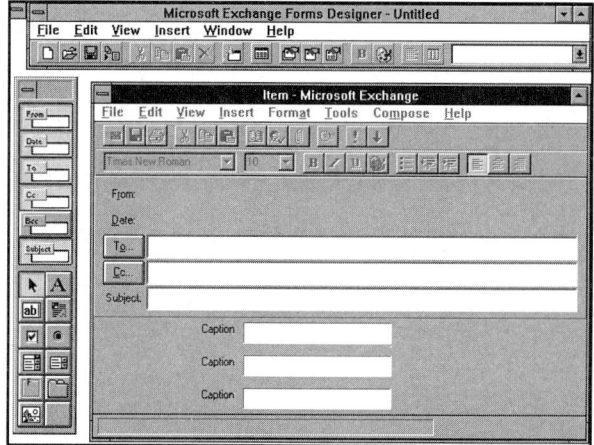

Note that there are several parts to the layout window. The *canvas* is where most of the design activity will take place. The canvas represents the body of your form. You choose fields from the toolbox and place them on the canvas. The *envelope* area is where your envelope fields go. Envelope fields are the From, Date, To, Cc, Bcc, and Subject fields that appear in an e-mail message so the user can enter and/or read header information regarding the message and its recipient(s). The *menu, toolbar,* and *status bar* on the canvas are non-functional, except that you can change the menu captions. These pieces are here mainly for cosmetic reasons to give you a feel for the final look of your form. Collectively, the envelope area, menu, toolbar, and status bar are referred to as the *header,* distinguished from the canvas. As you'll see later, you can hide the header to give you more room for working on the canvas.

The Menu Bar

The menu bar, not to be confused with the non-functional menu on the layout window, includes a toolbar and is where you can process commands that affect the layout window and other windows. (See Figure 27.3.)

The Toolbox

The toolbox is where you select fields to place on the canvas. It has two parts. The top part contains buttons from which you choose envelope fields, and the bottom part is where you choose body fields to place on the canvas (see Figure 27.4).

FIGURE 27.3.

The menu bar.

Menu bar

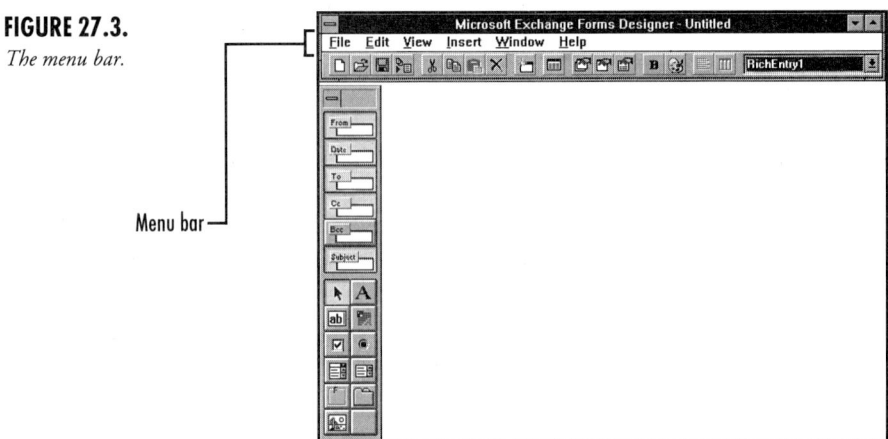

FIGURE 27.4.

The toolbox.

Toolbox

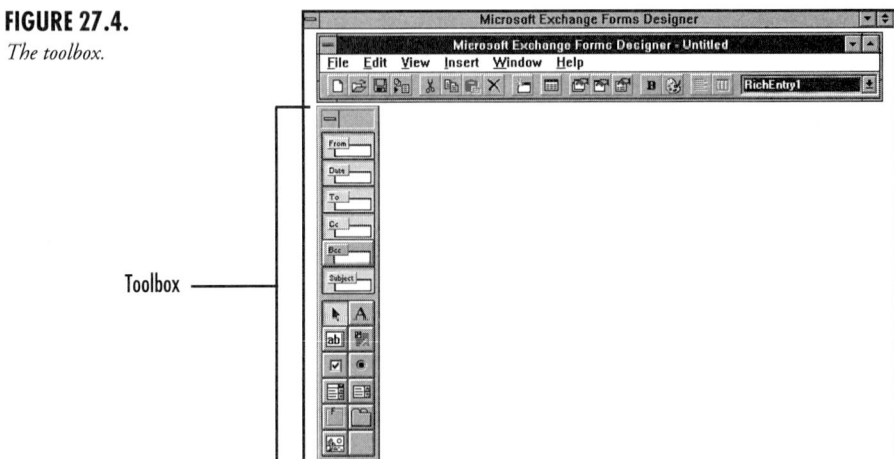

The Envelope Fields

You place envelope fields on the canvas by clicking the button of the envelope field you want. Clicking it again removes the envelope field. You cannot position these fields; they can only be turned on and off. Envelope fields are often referred to as header fields.

Body Fields

You add the body fields to the canvas by clicking the desired field in the toolbox and then clicking on the canvas. A field with default size is placed where you click the canvas. The individual fields are discussed shortly in the section The Body Fields of EFD. Body fields are often referred to as canvas fields.

TIP

If you hold down the Ctrl key when you click the body field on the toolbox, that field becomes "sticky" and you can place several copies of this field on the canvas by repeatedly clicking on the canvas. Clicking anywhere outside the canvas or back on the toolbox causes this sticky mode to end and return to normal.

Property Inspector

Each field you place on the layout window has several properties that you can customize. For example, you can change the caption, back color, size, and location of most fields. You also can set properties for each window that makes up your form, and for the form itself. You set and view these properties using the property inspector (PI); it can be displayed from the View menu. There are three types of property inspectors; one for form properties (the Form PI), one for window properties (the Window PI), and one for field properties (the Field PI). Only one can be shown at a time.

All three PIs are made up of tabbed dialog boxes and are described in the following sections.

The Form PI

You set and view properties for your overall form in the Form PI.

On the General tab of the Form PI, you can change properties such as the name of your form and the icons associated with it.

On the Events tab, you can specify or view the action that will take place or the window to show when the user performs certain events (for example, clicking the Reply or Print button). These settings are called the form's Events Properties.

NOTE

Events Properties refers to a collection of properties that define how the form will react when certain events occur. For example, when Exchange tells you that a Print event occurred (for example, the user clicked the Print button on the toolbar), you will probably want to set the Print event's properties to print the active window. Figure 27.5 shows the General tab of the Form PI.

FIGURE 27.5.

The Form PI showing
the General tab.

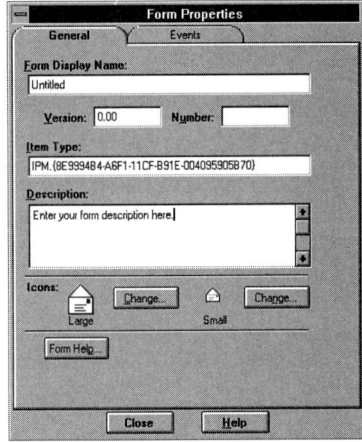

The Window PI

You set properties specific to each window in your form in the Window PI. You'll probably want to provide different windows that the users see when they are, for example, composing a new form to send as opposed to reading a form they just received. EFD enables you to create several windows for various purposes, and each has its own individual properties. Examples of window properties are the window caption, background color, and menu captions. Figure 27.6 shows the Menus tab of the Window PI.

FIGURE 27.6.

The Window PI
showing the Menus tab.

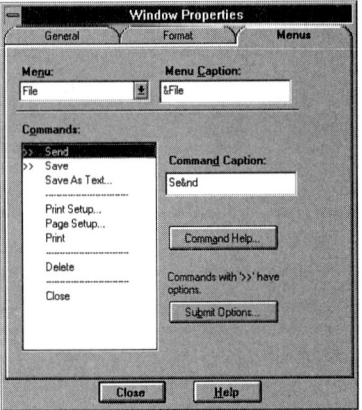

The Field PI

Each field you place on the canvas in turn has its own properties to set or view. If you click on different fields of the canvas while the Field PI is displayed, the Field PI changes to reflect the properties of the selected field. As you change field types, the settings available also change to those appropriate for the selected field's type. For example, a CheckBox field will have a property setting for declaring whether the checkbox should be initially checked or unchecked; such a property wouldn't make sense for an Entry field that shows only text. The CheckBox and Entry fields are described later in the sections The CheckBox Field and The Entry Field, respectively. Figure 27.7 shows the Format tab of the Field PI.

FIGURE 27.7.

*The Field PI showing
the Format tab.*

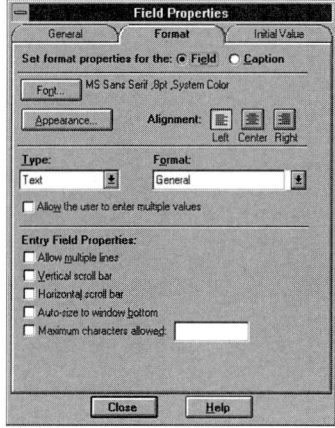

The Field Appearance Palette

Not all field properties can be set by the PI (for example, 3D and border properties can't be set using the PI). The Field Appearance Palette enables you to set the background and foreground colors of each field and modify their 3D or flat appearance. For example, you can show an entry field that has a very wide border with a raised 3D look to give it special emphasis. Giving it red text on a green background might be just what you want for the company's Christmas forms. Figure 27.8 shows the Field Appearance Palette. Note that the two rows of small boxes labeled Fore Color and Back Color each display a set of colors you can change for these properties.

FIGURE 27.8.

*The Field Appearance
Palette.*

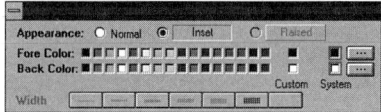

The Body Fields of EFD

There are ten different field types, plus variations of some of the types, which you can place on the canvas (body) part of the form. Figure 27.4, earlier in this chapter, shows which toolbox button creates each of these fields. Figure 27.9 shows an example of each field, including some variations, after the field has been placed on the canvas. They will look different in the final runtime form (for example, the listbox will probably be populated with items you specified in its properties), but their sizes and positions will remain the same in most cases. Note that some fields, such as the ComboBox field, can take on different appearances depending on their properties. Also, some fields (the Frame, PictureBox, and Tab fields) are known as container fields. A container field is a special type of field that can contain other fields. This is described in more detail in the section The Frame Field.

FIGURE 27.9.

EFD field types.

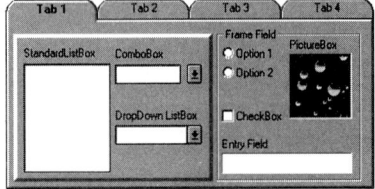

The Label Field

The Label field is a simple field for displaying read-only text on the canvas. The text will word-wrap if there is more text than will fit within the width of the field.

The Entry Field

The Entry field is a field in which the user can enter text. You will often use the Entry field when you want to require the user to enter formatted data, such as dates, currency, or numbers. You can also use it for entering plain text, but the RichEntry field (described next) is better suited for this purpose.

The RichEntry Field

You also use the RichEntry field to enter text, but unlike the Entry field, the user can change the font, color, size, and so on of individual characters within the field at runtime; text that can be changed like this is commonly referred to as rich text. You can also embed OLE objects, such as Excel spreadsheets, within the body of the RichEntry field at runtime. Note that at design time, the Entry field and RichEntry field appear identical. For this reason, only one is shown in Figure 27.9.

The CheckBox Field

The CheckBox field enables you to prompt the reader for simple yes/no input. It's a great field to use for surveys.

The OptionButton Field

The OptionButton field is also commonly used in surveys. Option buttons, unlike checkboxes, operate together in groups. When you place an option button on the canvas, it is automatically contained within a Frame field (see The Frame Field, later in this chapter). The OptionButton field cannot exist outside a Frame field. If you try to move it out of the Frame field and place it directly on the canvas, another Frame field will automatically be created to contain it. You can place multiple OptionButton fields within the same Frame field, and that is exactly what you want to do. When you have multiple option buttons within the same Frame field only one can be selected at a time. Whenever you select another option button, the one currently selected becomes unselected.

> **TIP**
>
> If you want to make the option buttons appear as if they are not within a frame, you can set the properties of the containing frame to have no border or caption and a background color that matches the background color of the canvas (or the frame's container). This gives the appearance that the frame is invisible. The option buttons are still in a frame, but the frame appears invisible. To do this, follow these steps:
>
> 1. Place your option button on the canvas.
> 2. Display the Field Appearance Palette (Ctrl+A).
> 3. Select the first option button labeled None to make the option button non-3D.
> 4. Select the Frame field that contains the new OptionButton field.
> 5. Change the Frame Style to Panel in the Field PI's Format tab.
> 6. Display the Field Appearance Palette while the Frame field is still selected.
> 7. Click the blank button on the far right in the row of buttons labeled Width (refer to Figure 27.8).
>
> Your Frame field's background color will change to match the background color of the canvas (or container). If you later change the background color of the canvas (or container), the background color of the frame will also change to match, thus keeping it virtually invisible. It will not appear invisible, though, if you put a picture behind it.

The ComboBox Field

The ComboBox field gives you a field that can contain a list of items from which the user can select and/or enter his or her own new item. Note that when the user enters a new item, it is not added to the list, but it does remain in the entry part of the ComboBox. Whatever item the user selects or adds is displayed as the active item to the recipient of the form.

When first dropped on the canvas, the ComboBox has the Dropdown ComboBox style. You can change it, though, to a Standard List or Dropdown List field by changing its style property in the Field PI. The listbox and drop-down listbox styles enable you to add items to their respective lists at design time, but at runtime the users cannot type in their own choices as they can with the ComboBox style. Again, the selected item in the list remains the selected item when the recipient receives the form. Each style of the ComboBox field can be seen in Figure 27.9.

The ListBox Field

The ListBox field is exactly the same as the ComboBox field except that when it is dropped on the canvas it is initialized with the ListBox style instead of the ComboBox style. See The ComboBox Field earlier for more information.

The Frame Field

The Frame field is the first of the container fields. *Container fields* are fields in which you can place other fields. For example, Figure 27.9 shows a frame field containing two OptionButton fields, a CheckBox field, an Entry field, and a PictureBox field (described later in the section The PictureBox Field). These fields aren't merely positioned in front of the Frame field, they are actually contained by it. If you reposition the Frame field, all of its contained fields will move along with it.

The Frame field can take on one of two styles, Standard and Panel, when you set its Frame Style property in the Field PI. In Figure 27.9, the frame on the right is the Standard style. To the left of the Standard style Frame field is a Panel style Frame field containing the three styles of the ComboBox (or ListBox) field. You can change the look of the Panel style to be either raised or inset 3D, or you can make it appear invisible by giving it no border at all using the Field Appearance Palette. When you remove the border from the Panel style, it takes on a new feature; its background color will now always match the background color of either its container or the canvas if it's not in another container.

Note that container fields can be contained within other container fields. This is called *nesting*.

> **NOTE**
>
> Nesting means that you place a field within another field. It is said that one field is nested within the other. Only container fields can nest other fields. Sometimes, the container field is referred to as the Parent and the nested field is referred to as the Child.

The Tab Field

When there is not enough room on the canvas to hold all the fields you need for your form, or you want to organize the fields on your form into logical groupings, the Tab field comes to the rescue. Like the Frame field, the Tab field is a container field, but with multiple containers. Only one container can be seen at a time, but you can easily switch from one to the other by clicking the tabs at the top of the field. By setting properties in the PI, you can change the number of tabs in your Tab field. You can change the captions of the individual tabs by clicking the selected tab's caption and typing in a new one.

> **NOTE**
>
> You can have only one Tab field per window of your form.

The PictureBox Field

The PictureBox field enables you to display a bitmap, icon, or metafile on your form. By setting properties in the Field PI, you can configure the PictureBox field to automatically size itself to the size of the picture or to stretch the picture to fit the size of the control. Like the Frame and Tab fields, the PictureBox field is also a container field in which you can nest other fields.

The Form Template Wizard

The Form Template Wizard is similar to other wizards you might have used with other software applications. By answering the Wizard's questions, you can create a template in which the number of windows, default envelope fields, form types, and form event properties are already defined. You then add fields and customize the properties for your fields, windows, and the form.

Form Types Created by the Wizard

There are two basic form types created by EFD's Wizard: forms to send information and forms to post information. As the names imply, a *Send* form is used to send information from point A to point B, and a *Post* form is used to post information in a specific location (most commonly in a public folder). See Figure 27.10 for an example of the Form Template Wizard.

FIGURE 27.10.

The "Where will your information go?" screen of the Wizard.

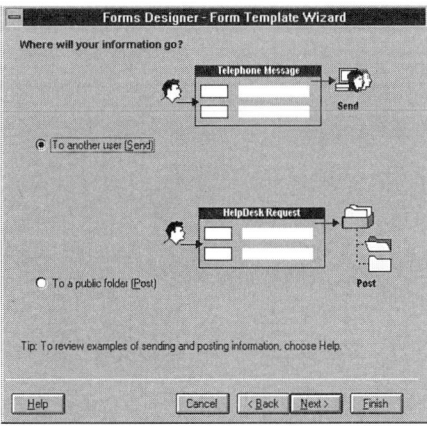

These two basic form types each fall into two categories: a Send category and a Reply category. Send and Post forms used for sending information are very straightforward to design and use. Send and Post Reply forms, though, are a bit more complicated, because to use them you must integrate them with another form—that is, the form to which you are replying. You must modify the other form's event properties to make this connection. The primary difference between the Send and Reply forms is the types and handling of envelope fields. A Reply form will automatically initialize some of its envelope fields. For example, it will automatically address the reply to the sender of the original message. A Send form's envelope fields will automatically be blank. (Note that you can change any of the settings using the Field and Form Property Inspectors—the settings discussed here refer to Wizard default settings.) Figure 27.11 shows the Wizard screen where you tell EFD whether your form will be used to send a new message or send a response.

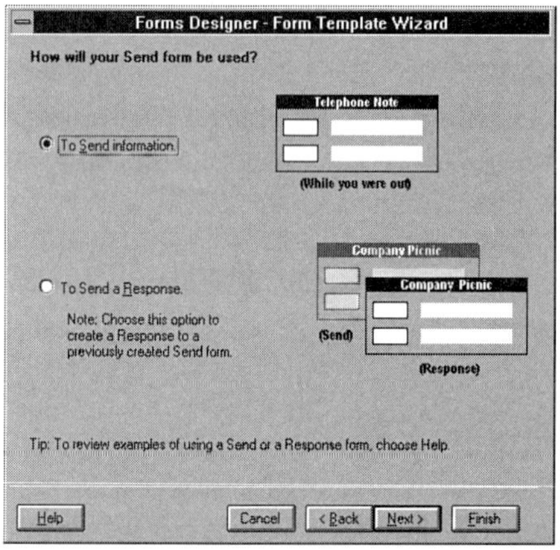

FIGURE 27.11.

The "How will your Send form be used?" screen of the Wizard.

After you become familiar with using EFD and setting form properties, Reply forms will not seem as complex. For more information on using Reply forms, refer to the *Application Designer's Guide* or EFD's online help.

Window Types Created by the Wizard

The Form Template Wizard can create a one-window form or a two-window form for both the Send and Post forms. With a one-window form you get a single window that is used for both composing and reading a note. With a two-window form you get separate windows for composing and reading. You use the Compose window to compose the information to be sent or posted. You use the Read window to view the information after it has been sent or posted. The Read window also has additional fields (such as From) that are initialized with information from the Compose window. Figure 27.12 shows the Wizard screen in which you specify whether you want a one-window or a two-window form.

FIGURE 27.12.

The Wizard screen that asks, "Do you want one window or two windows in your form?"

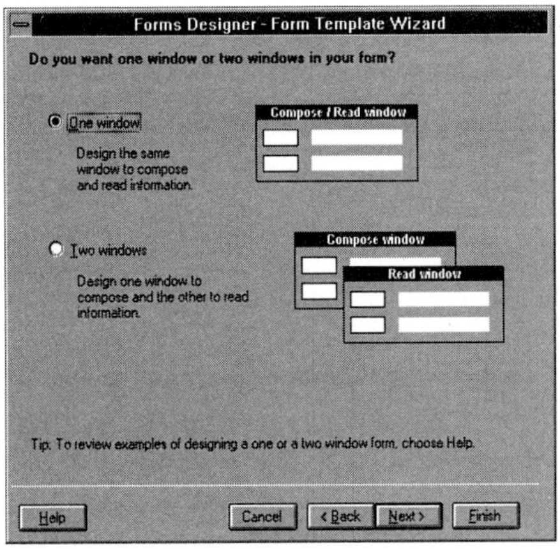

If you ask the Wizard for a form with two windows, the Wizard will create windows named Compose and Read, respectively.

If you ask for a one-window form, it will be named simply Window1. Again, the same window is used for both composing and reading.

There are several occasions in which a two-window form is advantageous, if not necessary. For example, the Expense Report form (which you will design later in this chapter) has a specific need for two windows. You need to allow the employee to enter expense items in the form, but you must not allow the employee's manager to alter it. To meet this need, use two windows; in the Compose window, all fields on the form can be written to, but in the Read window, the window read by the manager, the expense item fields have been "locked" from use (made read-only). This easily shows the same information to both users without allowing the manager to modify the pertinent data.

Another occasion on which a two-window form would be appropriate is for an information-gathering form used over and over by a specific department. For example, perhaps your Human Resources department sends out a form to every new employee requesting routine data such as his or her name, address, phone number, and so on. The Compose window might need only the To: and Subject: envelope fields. The Read window, though, would look like a standard data entry form, with field names and places for the employee to type in the required data. Rather than show all the empty data fields to Human Resources over and over, you can simply show them a small form with To: and Subject: fields.

Any time your form's composer and your form's reader don't need to see the same information, a two-window form might be in order.

Summary of Form Types Created by the Wizard

To summarize, depending on your answers to the Wizard's questions, the Wizard will produce one of the following eight types of forms:

- A one-window Send note: A form for sending and receiving messages between users using the same window. The sender sees the same window the recipient sees.

- A two-window Send note: Same as the one-window Send note except that the sender composes the note in a different window than the reader will read it in.

- A one-window Post note: Same as the one-window Send note except that the destination of the form is a public folder. Users reading the note in the public folder see the same window in which the sender composed the note.

- A two-window Post note: Same as the one-window Post note except that the sender composes the note in a different window than the reader will read it in (in the public folder).

- A one-window send-response note: A form for replying (responding) to a Send note a user received. The person replying and the reply's recipient see the same window.

- A two-window send-response note: Same as the one-window Send-response note except that the person replying composes the reply in a different window than the recipient of the reply reads it in.

- A one-window post-response note: A form for replying (responding) to a Post note a user read in a public folder. The reply becomes another post in the public folder. The form with which the person replying creates their reply is the same as the one someone else will use to read the reply in the public folder.

- A two-window post-response note: Same as the one-window post-response note except that the person replying composes the reply in a different window than the recipient of the reply reads it (in the public folder).

General Usage

As the last part of the quick tour of EFD, make a simple form and install it. You'll make a simple Send note, similar to the standard message window in which you currently compose mail with Exchange. This will simply be a form with the standard envelope fields and a RichEntry field. The following are the steps you should take:

1. Start EFD.

2. Use the Wizard to make a simple one-window Send note. Simply clicking Next and then Finish will do this for you. Because you used the Wizard, the envelope fields are already added to your form.

3. Add a RichEntry field to the canvas of the form. Just click the RichEntry button on EFD's toolbox, and then click on the canvas. A RichEntry field with default size and properties will appear on the canvas. Figure 27.13 shows the canvas after the RichEntry field is added.

FIGURE 27.13.

Placing the RichEntry field onto the canvas.

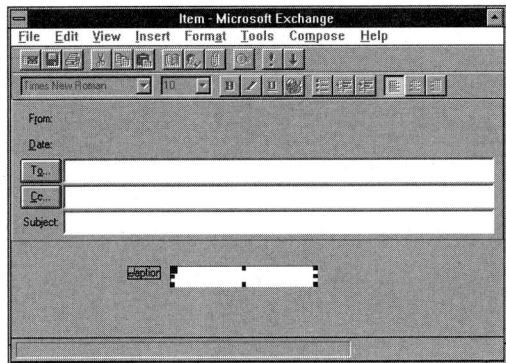

4. Position the main part of the RichEntry field in the upper-left corner of the canvas. To do so, simply click the main part of the field (most field types in EFD have two parts: the main part and the caption) and drag it to the upper-left corner while you hold the mouse button down. Let the caption move off the screen to the left; it isn't important for this form. (Alternatively, you could set the Left and Top properties of the field in the Field PI to get more precise placement; close is good enough for now.)

Notice that the field has stretch handles (boxes in the corners of the field—refer to Figure 27.13) that you can use to size it. Because you are making a Message Body field you will later set properties so it will size itself at runtime to fill the window, so don't worry about sizing it now. If you want, you can try out the sizing handles to get a feel for how they work. The large box in the upper-left corner does not size the field; instead, it gives you a way to move the main part of the field independent of its caption. Figure 27.14 shows the RichEntry field after you've moved it to the upper-left corner of the canvas.

FIGURE 27.14.

The RichEntry field moved to the upper-left corner of the canvas.

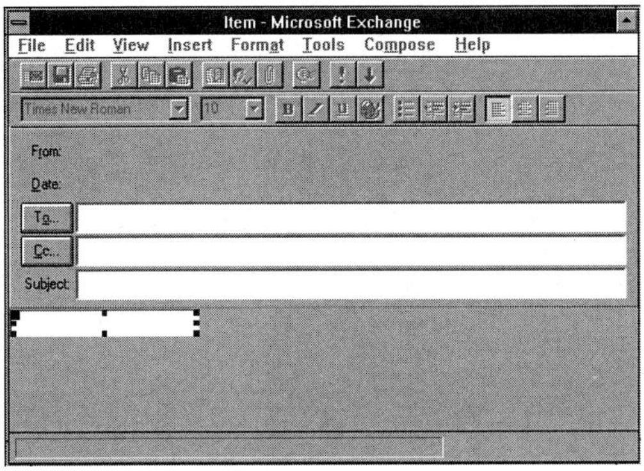

5. Press F4 to display the Field PI. Make sure the RichEntry field is still selected.

6. Select the Format tab.

7. Check the Vertical scroll bar and Auto-size to window bottom checkboxes. The Vertical scroll bar checkbox will cause a vertical scrollbar to appear in the runtime form whenever more lines of text are entered into the window than will fit. Auto-size to window bottom will cause the RichEntry field to grow (to the right and down) when the window is resized so it always uses as much space as is available. Note that only one RichEntry field on any one window can have the auto-size property set. You'll get an error if you try to set it on a second one.

8. Select Form Properties from the View menu to display the Form PI. Make sure it is on the General tab.

9. Enter My First Form in the Form Display Name field. When you want to open the runtime form later, this is the name that will appear in the list of available forms.

10. Enter One-Window Send Note in the Description field. When you want to open the runtime form later, this is the description that will appear when you select this form from the list of available forms.

11. Click Save from the File menu and save your form as myform.efp.

12. Click Install from the File menu to install the form into Exchange.

    In a few moments, the Set Library To dialog box will appear (see Figure 27.15). This is where you specify where you want your form installed. For this exercise, just install it to your Personal Forms Library. This makes the form available only to you, which is great for testing your form. If you have set up other libraries on Exchange (see the section Set Up Organization Forms Library, earlier in this chapter) you could select those instead. For now, though, stick with the Personal Forms Library.

FIGURE 27.15.

The Set Library To
dialog box.

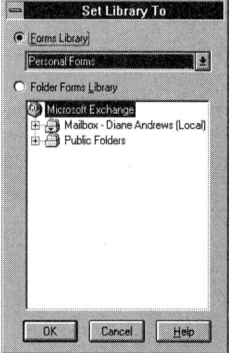

13. Click OK in the Set Library To dialog box after verifying that the Forms Library option button is selected and that Personal Forms is selected in the drop-down listbox.

14. Click OK when the Form Properties dialog box appears. You already set the important properties shown here in steps 9 and 10. The form will finish installing and focus will return to EFD when it's complete.

   You are now ready to test the runtime form.

15. Start up the Microsoft Exchange client.

16. Select New Form from the Compose menu in Exchange.

17. Select Personal Forms from the listbox at the top of the New Form dialog box. You should see your form My First Form in the list of available forms that appears (see Figure 27.16).

FIGURE 27.16.

The New Form dialog box.

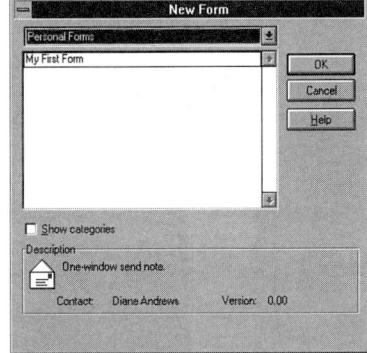

18. Select My First Form from the list and click OK.

In a moment, your runtime form should appear. Notice that the RichEntry field (the Body field) you added to the form now fills up the entire canvas. This is the result of checking the Auto-size to window bottom property. Notice how much Figure 27.17 looks like the standard e-mail note shown in Figure 27.1.

FIGURE 27.17.

The runtime form showing the RichEntry field filling the canvas.

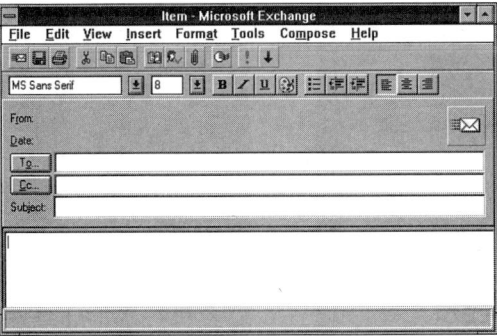

Enter some text in the body field (because it's a RichText field, try using various font styles, sizes, colors, and so on) and send the form to yourself. Open it up when it appears in your inbox.

That completes the quick tour of EFD. Without going into great detail you have seen all the elements for designing forms with the Microsoft Exchange Forms Designer. You are now ready to jump in and build a more complex form, the Expense Report form, which should be useful within your organization.

> **TIP**
>
> The form you just created does not enable you to insert files into the body of the message. You can add this capability easily in EFD by going to the Field PI's General tab (when the RichEntry field is selected on the canvas) and selecting MAPI_Body_Custom from the Reference Name drop-down listbox. That's all you need to do. When you reinstall the form (see the following tip) it will now enable you to insert files into the body field.

A Sample Expense Report

In this section you will design, install, and integrate three forms that will work together as an expense report Exchange application. Your objective is to create a method for employees to create expense reports electronically and submit them to their managers for approval. The managers will need the capability to either approve the expense reports for payment and forward them to another department for processing or to decline approval and return the expense report to the employee with comments explaining why the report was declined. To implement this, you will design and build the following three forms:

1. Expense Report Form. This will be a two-window Send note. The employee will use the Compose window (see Figure 27.18) to enter expenses and the manager will use the Read window (see Figure 27.19) to review the expenses. All the expense fields will be locked (read-only) in the Read window but not in the Compose window; therefore, a two-window Send note is required.

2. Approve Form. This will be a one-window response note. Assuming the manager approves the expense report, this form will appear pre-addressed to the Accounting department marked as approved. The Accounting department will read the same form that the manager sends. See Figure 27.20 for an example of the Approve form's window.

FIGURE 27.18.

The Compose window of the Expense Report form.

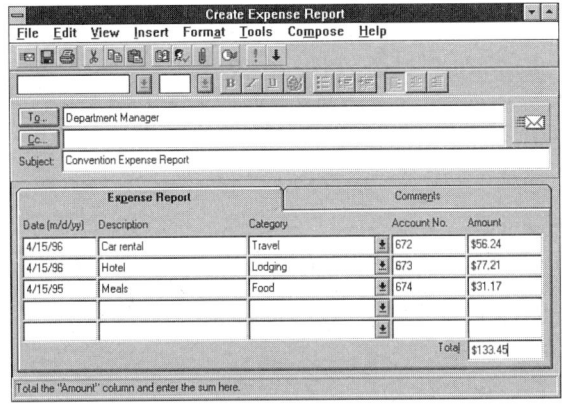

FIGURE 27.19.

The Read window of the Expense Report form.

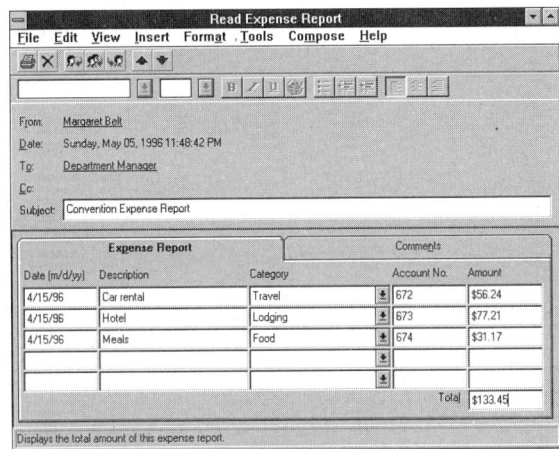

FIGURE 27.20.

The Approve form's window.

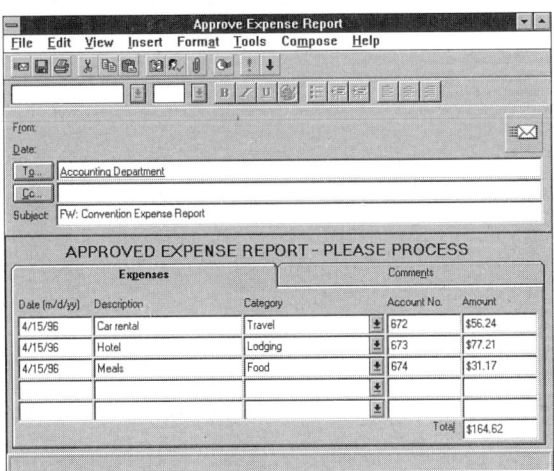

27

THE EXCHANGE
FORMS DESIGNER

3. Decline Form. This will be a two-window response note. If there is a problem with the expense report submitted by the employee, the manager will decline it. When doing so, this form's Compose window will appear (see Figure 27.21) and the manager will enter comments explaining the reason for the decline. The manager will send it back to the employee, who will read the comments in the Read window (see Figure 27.22). The difference in the two windows, and thus the reason for a two-window form, will be the menu choices available in each case.

FIGURE 27.21.

The Compose window for the Decline form.

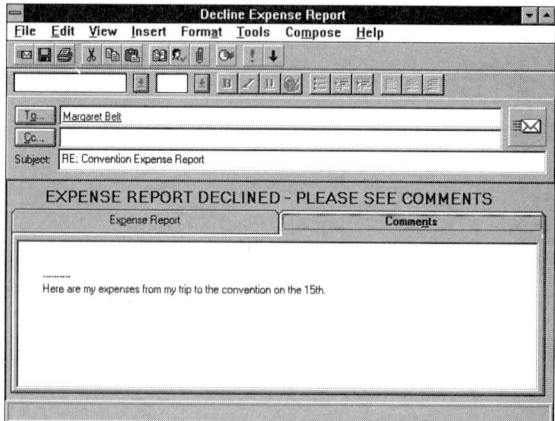

FIGURE 27.22.

The Read window for the Decline form showing the Comments tab with comments thread.

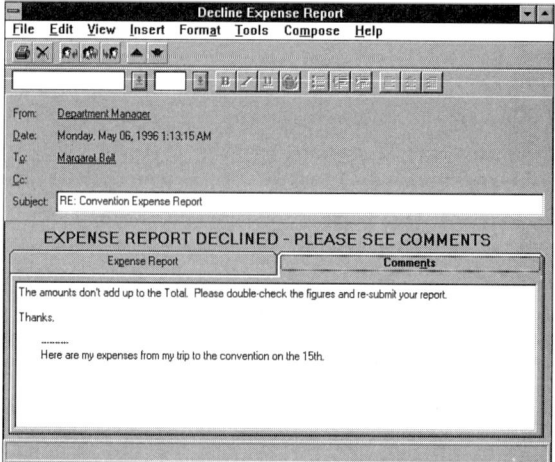

You design these three forms entirely within the EFD environment—there will be no programming required. Later, you'll add a custom feature to the form to learn how to make programming changes to the form if you want.

First, you will build the three forms one at a time, and then integrate them. In the following sections you will find a major section for each form that is broken down into steps for you to follow.

Expense Report Form

The Expense Report form is the form in which the employee will enter expenses. First you'll build the form, and then you'll install it. You'll then test the runtime form to verify that it works properly on its own before you proceed with building the other two forms.

Building the Form

As you learned earlier, when you build a form with EFD, you will do the following:

1. Use the Wizard to create a two-window send form.

2. Design the Compose Window.

3. Design the Read Window.

4. Set Form Properties.

Step 1: Use the Wizard to Create a Two-Window Send Form

Start EFD. In the opening window, select Form Template Wizard, and then click Next. Continue through the Wizard and answer its questions according to Table 27.1.

Table 27.1. Creating a two-window Send form.

When asked this:	Choose this, and then click Next
Where will your information go?	To another user (Send)
How will your Send form be used?	To Send information
Do you want one window or two windows in your form?	Two windows

The Wizard will now prompt you for a form name and description. Enter Expense Report as the form name. Enter Expense Report Form as the form description.

NOTE

The Form Display Name represents how your form will be identified to the users of Exchange. After your form is installed in the Organization Forms Library, the form name will be visible in the New Form dialog box whenever a user selects New Form from the Exchange Viewer's Compose menu.

> The Description tells the users about your form. It is also visible in the New Form dialog box and other places in Exchange. It is good practice to include a short but clear description of your form's purpose in its Description field so that users can easily tell from the New Form dialog box what your form can do for them.

Click Next, and then click Finish. The Wizard will now create and display the form you requested.

Before proceeding, save your work. From EFD's File menu, select Save. In the Save As dialog box, enter `EXPENSE.EFP` as the filename. Click OK. Your form is now saved as `...\EFDFORMS\EXPENSE.EFP`.

Step 2: Design the Compose Window

To design the Compose window, you will go through the steps described in the following sections:

1. Add Tab and Expense Report Fields
2. Set Field Properties of Tab and Expense Report Fields
3. Add Comments Field to Tab Field
4. Set Field Properties of Comments Field
5. Set Properties for the Window

Add Tab and Expense Report Fields

Using the method discussed earlier in the General Usage section, add the fields shown in Table 27.2 to the canvas in the following order: start with the Tab field, and place the remaining fields inside of Tab 1 of the Tab field (make sure that Tab 1 is the current tab page). After all the fields have been added to the canvas, put them in the proper position by setting their properties in the Field PI.

Table 27.2. Adding fields to the expense report Compose window.

Field Name	Number of Fields
Tab field	1
Label field	5
Entry field	21
ComboBox field	5

Set Field Properties of Tab and Expense Report Fields

The next step is to set the field's properties. To set a field's properties, you must first select the field. Because there are a large number of fields in this window of the form, it will be difficult to select a field by clicking on it as you did before. Instead, select the field in the Fields drop-down listbox (located at the far right side of EFD's menu window). After the field is selected, the Field PI will show its properties so you can change them.

The following list shows the fields whose properties need setting and the order in which we will proceed.

1. Tab field
2. Label fields for the column headings
3. Entry fields for the date column
4. Entry fields for the Description column
5. ComboBox fields for the Category column
6. Entry fields for the Account No. column
7. Entry fields for the Amount column
8. Total field

Tab field

Select the Tab field, and then press F4 to load the Field PI (or select Field Properties from the View menu). By default, the General properties tab of the Field PI is loaded. Set the General properties shown in Table 27.3 for the Tab field. If Table 27.3 does not specify a property setting, leave the default setting alone.

Table 27.3. Setting the General properties for the Tab field.

General Property	Value
Left	75
Top	90
Width	8670
Height	2820

> **NOTE**
>
> Instead of setting the Left, Top, Width, and Height properties in the PI you could instead drag the field to its location with your mouse. Entering the property values in the PI, though, allows for better precision, so use this method to build the expense report.

Click the Format tab on the Field PI. The expense report form uses only two tabs, so you need to remove Tab 3 and Tab 4 from the Tab field. Locate the Pages list (in the middle of the Format tab of the Field PI). Select Tab 3 and click the Remove button. Repeat the process for Tab 4. This should leave only Tab 1 and Tab 2.

Set the Format properties shown in Table 27.4 for the Tab field. If Table 27.4 does not specify a property setting, leave the default setting alone.

Table 27.4. Setting Format properties for the Tab field.

Format Property	Value
Tabs per row	2
Tab 1 caption	Ex&penses
Tab 2 caption	Comme&nts

> **TIP**
>
> For detailed information on any of the available field properties, select the property and press F1 to display EFD's online help, or refer to the *Application Designer's Guide*.

To change the tab captions, double-click the tab name in the Pages field of the Format tab. A dialog box in which you can change the caption will appear. Alternatively, you can edit the caption directly in-place on the tab itself by moving the mouse cursor over the tab and clicking it when the mouse cursor changes to an I-beam.

> **TIP**
>
> Notice that the ampersand (&) character becomes an underline of the following character when you accept your entry. The underlined character is now a hot key, which enables the user to reach either tab page simply by pressing Alt+P (to reach the Expenses tab page) or Alt+N (to reach the Comments tab page).

Label fields for the column headings

Now you set the properties for the Label fields. You will use the Label fields for the column headings in the expense report. Start by selecting Label1; this will be the heading for the column in which the employee enters the date of the expense. Note that when you select Label1, the Field PI automatically updates to display its properties. Click the General tab of the Field PI. Set the General properties for Label1 as shown in Table 27.5.

Table 27.5. Setting General properties for Label1.

Property	Value
Reference Name	LabelDate
Left	60
Top	35
Width	1200
Height	300

> **NOTE**
>
> The reference name is just a name you give to the field that identifies it to you later. You could leave it with its default name, but it will make your design easier if you give it a meaningful name. Later you will be copying information from fields in one form to fields in another form; you will use the reference name to identify the fields you are copying from and to.

Click the Initial Value tab of the Field PI and enter the following in the Initial Text field:

`Date (m/d/yy)`

This will be the text of the heading for the date column.

Set field properties for Label2 through Label5. Go back to the General tab of the Field PI, and for each field use the same values as those used for Label1, substituting the Reference Name and Left values as shown in Table 27.6. (Remember, to select a field, choose it from the drop-down listbox on the right side of EFD's menu bar.)

Table 27.6. Setting General properties for Label2 through Label5.

Label Number	Property/Value
Label2	Reference Name = LabelDescription
	Left = 1290
Label3	Reference Name = LabelCategory
	Left = 3720
Label4	Reference Name = LabelAccountNo
	Left = 6045
Label5	Reference Name = LabelAmount
	Left = 7275

Click the Initial Value tab of the Field PI. Enter `Initial Text` for Label2 through Label5 as shown in Table 27.7. Recall that these will be the column headings for the expense report.

Table 27.7. Setting initial values for Label2 through Label5.

Label Reference Name	*Initial Text*
LabelDescription	Description
LabelCategory	Category
LabelAccountNo	Account No.
LabelAmount	Amount

Entry fields for the date column

Users will enter the date of the expense in the date column. For example, `1/1/96`.

Locate Entry1 in the Fields drop-down listbox on EFD's menu bar. Set General properties for Entry1 as shown in Table 27.8.

Table 27.8. Setting field General properties for the Entry1 field.

General Tab Property	*Value*
Reference Name	`Date1`
Left	`60`
Top	`335`
Width	`1200`
Height	`300`

You also need to set properties for Field Help. Click the Field Help button on the General tab of the Field PI to display the Field Help for Users dialog box. In the Status Bar field, enter the following:

```
Enter the expense date in the following format: m/d/yy.
```

NOTE

Field Help is displayed when the user of the runtime form presses F1 from within a field. Instructions on what type of information goes in a field and how to enter it can be put into Field Help. When you enter status bar text for your fields, the text is visible on the runtime form's status bar whenever the field has focus.

Set field Format properties for Entry1 as shown in Table 27.9.

Table 27.9. Setting field Format properties for the Entry1 field.

Format Tab Property	Value
Type	Date
Format	System Default (Short)

> **NOTE**
>
> The Type and Format properties are available for the Entry and Label fields. These properties control what kind of data can be used by the field. There are six different types: Text, Integer, Date, Time, Currency, and Floating Point. For each type except Text there are several predefined formats from which you can select. The Text field type enables you to enter any kind of data. The Date field, like that used here, enables the user to enter only dates. If the field contains data that does not correspond with its Type/Format properties, Exchange will not enable the message to be sent until the data is corrected.

> **NOTE**
>
> Some Format properties are available only for the field itself, and not for the field's caption. You control which properties are visible by selecting Field or Caption at the top of the Format tab.

Set field properties for Entry2 through Entry5. For each field, use the same values as those used for Entry1, substituting the Reference Name and Top values as shown in Table 27.10.

Table 27.10. Setting the field properties for Entry2 through Entry5.

Field Number	Property/Value
Entry2	Reference Name = Date2
	Top = 665
Entry3	Reference Name = Date3
	Top = 995

continues

Table 27.10. continued

Field Number	Property/Value
Entry4	Reference Name = Date4
	Top = 1325
Entry5	Reference Name = Date5
	Top = 1655

Entry fields for the Description column

In the Description column the user will be able to enter a brief description of the expense. For example, "Lunch meeting with Sam to discuss budget issues."

Set the properties for Entry6 as shown in Table 27.11.

Table 27.11. Setting properties for Entry6.

General Property	Value
Reference Name	Description1
Left	1290
Top	335
Width	2400
Height	300
Status Bar	Enter a brief description of the expense item.
Field Help—QuickHelp caption	Description
Field Help—QuickHelp body text	Enter a brief description of the expense item. Example: Lunch meeting with Sam to discuss budget issues.

Remember, to set Field Help properties, you must first click the Field Help button on the General tab of the Field PI.

Set field properties for Entry7 through Entry10. For each field, use the same values as those used for Entry6, substituting the Reference Name and Top values as shown in Table 27.12.

Table 27.12. Setting properties for Entry7 through Entry10.

Field Number	Property/Value
Entry7	Reference Name = `Description2`
	Top = `665`
Entry8	Reference Name = `Description3`
	Top = `995`
Entry9	Reference Name = `Description4`
	Top = `1325`
Entry10	Reference Name = `Description5`
	Top = `1655`

ComboBox fields for the Category column

Expenses generally fall into categories such as Meals and Lodging. The Category column is where the user will select under which category each expense belongs. At times, an expense will not fit into one of the predefined categories and the user will need to enter a new category. The ComboBox field is perfect for this type of situation, so for this exercise use ComboBox fields for the Category column.

Set properties for ComboBox1 as shown in Table 27.13.

Table 27.13. Setting properties for ComboBox1.

General Property	Value
Reference Name	`Category1`
Left	`3720`
Top	`335`
Width	`2295`
Field Help—Status Bar	`Select an expense category from the list.`
Field Help—QuickHelp caption	`Category`
Field Help—QuickHelp body text	`Select an expense category from the list.`
	`To see the list of available choices, click`
	`on the arrow located at the right-hand side`
	`of the Category field.`

Note that you did not set the Height property for ComboBox1. This is because ComboBox fields have a fixed size.

Set field Initial Value properties for ComboBox1 as shown in Table 27.14.

Table 27.14. Setting field Initial Value properties for the ComboBox1 field.

Initial Value Tab Property	*Value*
List values	Entertainment
	Food
	Lodging
	Office Supplies
	Other
	Telephone
	Training
	Travel

NOTE

Initial Value properties set and display the initial entry contained in the field when the form is first displayed at runtime. In the case of the Category combobox, you are setting the initial value to the different available expense categories. Other fields also have initial value properties. For example, you use the Initial Value tab to give an entry field an initial value that the user can type over if they choose to.

Set field properties for ComboBox2 through ComboBox5. For each field, use the same values as those used for ComboBox1, including the Initial Value properties, substituting the Reference Name and Top values as shown in Table 27.15.

Table 27.15. Setting properties for Category2 through Category5.

Field Number	*Property/Value*
ComboBox2	Reference Name = Category2
	Top = 665
ComboBox3	Reference Name = Category3
	Top = 995
ComboBox4	Reference Name = Category4
	Top = 1325
ComboBox5	Reference Name = Category5
	Top = 1655

Entry fields for the Account No. column

You might want to have an account number for the employee's use in entering their expense item. For example, 001 could be food, 002 could be supplies, and so on.

Set properties for the Entry11 field as shown in Table 27.16.

Table 27.16. Setting properties for Entry11.

General Property	Value
Reference Name	AccountNo1
Left	6045
Top	335
Width	1200
Height	300
Field Help—Status Bar	Enter the expense account number.
Field Help—No Help	Selected
Format Tab Property	Value
Type	Integer
Format	0

Set field properties for Entry12 through Entry15. For each field, use the same values as those used for Entry11, substituting the Reference Name and Top values as shown in Table 27.17.

Table 27.17. Setting properties for Entry12 through Entry15.

Field Number	Property/Value
Entry12	Reference Name = AccountNo2
	Top = 665
Entry13	Reference Name = AccountNo3
	Top = 995
Entry14	Reference Name = AccountNo4
	Top = 1325
Entry15	Reference Name = AccountNo5
	Top = 1655

Entry fields for the Amount column

Employees will need to enter the amount of each expense item in the amount column.

Set properties for Entry16 as shown in Table 27.18.

Table 27.18. Setting properties for Entry16.

General Property	Value
Reference Name	Amount1
Left	7275
Top	335
Width	1200
Height	300
Field Help—Status Bar	Enter the expense amount in dollars and cents (for example, 10.95).
Field Help—No Help	Selected
Format Tab Property	Value
Type	Currency
Format	General

Set field properties for Entry17 through Entry20. For each field, use the same values as those used for Entry16, substituting the Reference Name and Top values as shown in Table 27.19.

Table 27.19. Setting properties for Entry17 through Entry20.

Field Number	Property/Value
Entry17	Reference Name = Amount2
	Top = 665
Entry18	Reference Name = Amount3
	Top = 995
Entry19	Reference Name = Amount4
	Top = 1325
Entry20	Reference Name = Amount25
	Top = 1655

Total field

The employee enters in the Total field the total of all amounts in the Amount column.

Set properties for Entry21 as shown in Table 27.20.

Table 27.20. Setting properties for Entry21.

General Property	Value
Reference Name	Total
Left	7275
Top	1985
Width	1200
Height	300
Required	Checked
Field Caption	Tota&l
Field Help—Status Bar	Total the Amount column and enter the sum here.
Field Help—No Help	Selected
Format Tab Property	Value
Type	Currency
Format	General

> **NOTE**
>
> Required is a property that specifies that the user must enter something. He or she won't be able to send the form without doing so. In this case, you are specifying that the user must total his or her expense report before sending it. How many times have you turned in an expense report without a total and had the form sent back to you without payment because of the missing total?

The Expense Report tab page is now complete.

Add Comments Field to Tab Field

Click on the Comments tab page, and then use the toolbar to add a RichEntry field to the Comments tab. This field will give the form's users a place in which to enter their comments.

Set Field Properties of Comments Field

Set field properties for the RichEntry field as shown in Table 27.21.

Table 27.21. Setting field properties for the RichEntry field.

General Property	Value
Reference Name	`MAPI_Body_Custom` (set this by selecting it in the Reference Name listbox by clicking on the arrow at the right side of the field)
Left	`45`
Top	`30`
Width	`8475`
Height	`2310`
Field Caption—Position	None
Field Help—Status Bar	`Use this field to add your comments.`
Field Help—No Help	`Selected`
Format Tab property	`Value`
Vertical Scroll Bar	`Checked`

NOTE

Recall that MAPI_Body_Custom is a special reference name available only for the RichEntry field that, when set, enables the user to attach files to the field in the runtime form. To learn more about the MAPI_Body_Custom field, put the focus in the Reference Name field of the Field PI and press F1.

You are now finished setting field properties for the Compose window. From EFD's File menu, select Save to save your changes before proceeding.

TIP

After you become more familiar with using EFD, you might find it easier to use the Clipboard to copy and paste similar fields when you are adding several fields of the same type. For example, you could have copied the first row of entry fields (Date1 through Amount1) to the Clipboard, and then pasted four copies onto the Expense Report tab to make the other four rows. Most of the properties will be copied with the fields, but you will still have to reposition the fields and enter a new Reference Name for each one.

Setting Window Properties

To set Window properties, display the Window PI by pressing Ctrl+W (or select Window Properties from the View menu). By default, the General properties tab of the Window PI is loaded. Set the Compose window's General properties as shown in Table 27.22. If Table 27.22 does not specify a property setting, leave the default setting alone.

Table 27.22. Setting General properties for the Compose window.

Property	Value
Window Name	Compose
Window Caption	Create Expense Report
Field Tab Order	(see Setting Field Tab Order on the General Tab, later in the chapter)
Window Help—caption	Expense Report
Window Help—body field	Use this form to prepare an expense report for manager's review.

> **NOTE**
>
> The Window Name identifies the window to EFD and to Exchange. EFD uses the Window Name for setting the form's Events properties (discussed later in this chapter under Set the Form's Events Properties) to the correct window. Exchange uses the Window Name to determine which window the Exchange client will display at runtime.
>
> The Window Caption will be displayed as the runtime form's caption to users who are creating an expense report (they will be viewing the Compose window of the form).
>
> Setting Window Help properties enables you to display instructions to the runtime user on how to use the current window of the form.

Setting Field Tab Order on the General tab

The Field Tab Order section of the Window PI enables you to add your fields to the form's tab order (the order in which the cursor moves through fields each time you press the Tab key). By default, EFD always includes the envelope fields (that is, the To and Subject fields) first in the form's tab order. Generally, the envelope fields should always remain at the top of the window's tab order. To add a field from the Available Fields list to the Fields in Tab Order list, first click the field you want to add in the left column, and then click the (>>) button to move the field to the right column (it will be placed after the field currently selected in the right column). Finally, use the Up and Down arrows to position the field in the proper order, the top field being number one in the tab order.

Add the Compose window's fields to the form's Tab Order in the following order:

1. Click Date1 in the left column, and then click MAPI_Subject in the right column (note that MAPI_Subject is the default reference name for the envelope subject field).

2. Click the >> button.

3. Add Description1 from the left column to the right column (to follow Date1). Then add Category1, AccountNo1, and Amount1.

4. Repeat this process for Date2 through Amount2. Continue adding the next three rows of fields from the Compose window, finishing with the Total field as the last field in the tab order.

Setting properties on the Format tab

To set properties on the Format tab, click the Format tab of the Window PI. Set Format properties for the Compose window as shown in Table 27.23.

Table 27.23. Setting Format properties for the Compose window.

Property	Value
Maximize Button	Checked
Minimize Button	Checked
Toolbar	Checked
Status Bar	Checked
Formatting Toolbar	Checked
Window Icon	C:\EXCHANGE\EFDFORMS\ICONS\NOTE2L.ICO
Window Sizing Options	Fixed Size

NOTE

The minimize and maximize properties control whether your runtime form can be minimized or maximized. Note that maximizing a runtime form does not have any effect on the size or location of the form's fields—keep this in mind when you are deciding whether to include a maximize button on your form. If the form is minimized, the Window icon will be the visible representation of your form on the user's desktop.

The toolbar properties control whether your runtime form will display the specified toolbars. Typically, forms should always have a toolbar. You use the Formatting toolbar to format the contents of the RichEntry field. The status bar displays status-bar text for fields and menu command items.

EFD uses the Window icon to represent the minimized window on the user's desktop (note that the path specified in Table 27.23 assumes you installed EFD in the default location; if you installed it elsewhere, you will need to modify this property setting accordingly).

You use the Background property to control the background color of the window.

The Window Sizing Options control whether your window can be sized with the mouse (by using the mouse to drag the window borders to a desired size). This property is separate from the Maximize and Minimize properties (that is, a Fixed Size window can still be maximized or minimized if these properties are checked in the Format page of the Window PI).

Congratulations! You've just finished the toughest part of the Expense Report Exchange Application. From EFD's File menu, select Save to save your changes before proceeding.

Step 3: Design the Read Window

You are now ready to design the Read window.

From EFD's Window menu, select Read. EFD will load the Expense Report form's Read window. The Read window will be seen by recipients of the expense report (when an employee sends an expense report to his or her manager for approval, the manager will see the form's Read window when he or she opens the item in his or her Exchange inbox).

Insert the Tab Field from the Compose Window

The Read window is going to look just like the Compose window, except that most of the fields will be locked (read-only). Because the Read and Compose windows are so similar, make things easy by copying the fields from the Compose window using EFD's Insert Fields feature.

1. Select Field from EFD's Insert menu. The Fields from Expense Report dialog box will be displayed.
2. Select Tab, and then click the Insert button. EFD will place a copy of the Tab field and its contained fields in the center of the Read window (you might need to resize the Read window so that the entire tab is visible).
3. Click the Close button.

Modify Field Properties

Because you used the Insert Fields feature, most of the field properties are already set appropriately for the Read window. However, you will need to do the following:

1. Reposition the Tab field.
2. Set the Locked property on all the Entry fields and ComboBox fields on the Expense Report tab.
3. Modify the Field Help to make it relevant.

Click on the Tab field and press F4 to load the Field PI. In the General tab of the Field PI, set the tab's Left property to 75, and the Top property to 90.

After the employee completes and sends his or her expense report, you (the form designer) need to make the form do the right thing with the employee's information. In this case, you need to make sure that the expense report items cannot be modified after the employee has sent the form. You can do this by setting a single property for every Entry field and ComboBox field on the Read window (Date1 through Date5, Description1 through Description5, Category1 through Category5, AccountNo1 through AccountNo5, Amount1 through Amount5, and Total). Each of these fields on the Read window must be set to Locked (read-only). This will ensure that the employee's expense items cannot be modified after the employee sends the form. Go ahead now and set the Locked property for these fields. You'll find it on the General tab of the Field PI.

Now that the Entry and ComboBox fields are locked, you need to modify the help text. Because the viewer of the Read window cannot make entries to these fields, change their help text to describe what the field contains (for example, change "Enter the date of the expense item" to something like "Displays the date of the expense item"). Go ahead now and modify the help text for each of the fields on the Expense Report tab page. Recall that you set the Field Help properties by clicking the Field Help button on the Field PI's General tab.

The Comments tab and its contained field (the MAPI_Body_Custom RichEntry field) require no changes. The manager will be allowed to enter comments into this field, just as the employee can.

Set Window Properties

You should set the Read window's Window properties identical to those for the Compose window, with two exceptions: the window Name should be Read and the window Caption should be changed to Read Expense Report. Refer to Table 27.22 and 27.23 to set the Read window's remaining properties. Go ahead and set these properties now.

You are finished setting the Read window's properties. From EFD's File menu, select Save to save your changes before proceeding.

Step 4: Set Form Properties

The last thing you need to do before this form is finished is set the Form properties themselves. There are two types of properties you will be setting:

1. General Properties
2. Events Properties

Set the Form's General Properties

To set the form's General properties, display the Form PI by pressing Ctrl+F (or select Form Properties from the View menu). By default, the General properties tab of the Form PI is loaded. Notice that the form name and description you entered when you first started with the Wizard are displayed in the Form PI.

Enter values for the rest of the form's General properties as specified in Table 27.24.

Table 27.24. Setting the Expense Report form's General properties.

Property	Value
Version	1.00
Item Type	IPM.Send.ExpenseReport
Large Icon	C:\EXCHANGE\EFDFORMS\ICONS\NOTE2L.ICO
Small Icon	C:\EXCHANGE\EFDFORMS\ICONS\NOTE2S.ICO
Form Help—Caption	Expense Report
Form Help—body text	Use this form to send an Expense Report to your manager for approval.

27

THE EXCHANGE
FORMS DESIGNER

NOTE

Use the Version property to track changes to your .EFP file. When you add new features or revise existing ones, update your Version property accordingly. (Usually, if you make minor modifications to an existing form design, the Version number will become 1.1. If you make major modifications, or if you redesign the form, the Version number will become 2.0.)

Exchange uses the form's Item Type to locate the form in the Forms Library. For example, when you ask Exchange to load the Expense Report form later in this chapter in the section Test the Form, Exchange will search through the Forms Library for a form with the item type IPM.Send.ExpenseReport (the Expense Report form's item type). It is very important that this item type be unique to all other forms that might be used in your system. You don't need to enter a value here if you prefer not to. EFD automatically generates one for you that is guaranteed to be unique. The advantage to creating your own is you can give it a name that is meaningful and easier to refer to. Later, when you integrate the three forms, you will use the item type to identify each one.

The form's large and small icons are visible to the user in different Exchange locations. The large icon is displayed in various Exchange dialog boxes, such as the New Form dialog box and the Forms Manager dialog box. The small icon is visible in the Item Type column in the Exchange Viewer. Several pairs of matched large and small icons are shipped with EFD, and they reside in the `C:\EXCHANGE\EFDFORMS\ICONS` directory, but you can use any icons you want to with your forms. Note that the small icon consists of approximately the upper-left 16×16 pixels of a regular icon. Anything beyond this area in the small icon property will not be visible in the Viewer.

Use Form Help to tell the user about your form. Forms can also work with external help files. For specific instructions on implementing Form Help, refer to the *Application Designer's Guide* or EFD's online help.

Set the Form's Events Properties

You will use the Expense Report form's Events properties to integrate the form with the Approve and Decline forms, which you will design later in this chapter in the sections The Approve Form and The Decline Form. Wait until then to set these properties.

NOTE

All of the functions that users can perform with a form are *events*. Examples are Printing, Saving, Replying, and Forwarding. Notice that these are some of the same items that appear in the form's Compose menu and File menu. You use the Compose menu to create new messages and to respond to messages you receive. The Events properties are probably the most complex properties of forms, and will typically be modified only by advanced users of EFD. Note that the Wizard automatically sets the Events properties of each form it creates. When you design the Decline Form later in this chapter, you will be shown exactly how to set the form's Events properties so that Exchange will know when to display each of the form's windows to the user.

For more detailed information on setting form Events properties, click the Help button on the Form Properties dialog box, or refer to the *Application Designer's Guide*.

Install the Form into Your Personal Forms Library

Before you can use the form in Exchange, you need to create a runtime version of the form. You do this by "installing" the form into Exchange.

Select Install from EFD's File menu. EFD will now generate VB source code, create an executable file (.EXE) for your form, and install the .EXE into Exchange. At the end of this process, you will be prompted to select the forms library into which you want to install the form. For now, select Personal Forms, and click OK. (Later, after the application is complete and tested, you'll move it into the Organization Forms Library.)

> **TIP**
>
> After you install your form into a Forms library, you should test it to verify that it behaves as you intended before making it available to Exchange users. A good practice to follow is to install your form into your Personal Forms library and test the form's behavior locally (send the form to yourself and use it as you expect users to). After you have verified that it is ready for general use, copy the form to the Organization Forms library.

The Form Properties dialog box will appear next; enter yourself as the contact name (the name of the person who should be contacted with questions about the form). Note that all the other properties were set during the design process. Click OK to complete the installation of the expense report form into your Personal Forms library.

Test the Form

Your first form is complete. Test it now and verify that it works as expected.

From the Exchange Compose menu, select New Form. In the New Form dialog box, locate Expense Report in your Personal Forms library. Select the form and click OK. When the form is loaded, try using the form as you would expect users to, and verify that all the fields function as intended. Verify the status bar text for the different fields by putting focus on the field and observing the status bar of the form. Try sending the form without totaling the items. The form should not enable you to send without completing the Total field. Verify that you can enter data in all of the fields of the Compose window. Send the form to yourself and verify that you can see all of the information in the Read window. Verify that you cannot modify the Expense Report items in the Read window. Verify that you can enter comments in both the Compose window and the Read window.

If you find errors, go back to EFD and make the necessary corrections. Then choose Install from EFD's File menu, and repeat the code generation and form installation process. Re-test to verify that any problems were corrected.

The Approve Form

When a manager receives an expense report, he or she will either approve it for payment and forward the report for processing or decline approval and return the report to the employee for correction. In order to preserve the employee's original information and transfer it from the Expense Report form to the Approve form, use the fields you've already created in the Expense Report form to build the Approve form.

An important difference between the Approve form and the Expense Report form is that the Approve form will have only one window. It has only one window because after the expense report is approved, nothing changes from what the manager sees and what the Accounting department sees. Recall that you use two windows if the form's sender and the form's recipient need to see different information (for example, in the case of the Expense Report form, the expense item fields are locked in the Read window, but not in the Compose window); in this case they are seeing the same information (the fields are locked for both the sender and the recipient), therefore you need only one window.

Building the Form

To build the form, you will do the following:

1. Use the Wizard to create a one-window Send form.
2. Design the Window.
3. Set Form Properties.

Step 1: Use the Wizard to Create a One-Window Send Form

Use the Wizard and answer its questions according to Table 27.25.

Table 27.25. Creating a one-window Send form.

When Asked This:	*Choose This, and Then Click Next*
Where will your information go?	To another user (Send)
How will your Send form be used?	To Send information
Do you want one window or two windows in your form?	One window

Enter `Approve Expense Report` as the form name, and enter `Form for approving Expense Report` as the form description. Click Next, and then click Finish. The Wizard will now create and display the form.

Now save your form as `APPROVE.EFP`.

Step 2: Design the Window

To design the window, you will do the following:

- ■ Insert the Tab field from the Expense Report form's Read window.
- ■ Modify the Tab field properties.
- ■ Add Label field.
- ■ Set Label field properties.
- ■ Set the window properties.

Insert the Tab Field from the Expense Report Form's Read Window

To insert the Tab field from the Expense Report form's Read window, you will again (as you did for the Expense Report form's Read window) copy the fields you have already created using the Insert Field feature. You are inserting the fields from the Read window because these fields have already been set to locked, which is what you want for the Approve form.

Follow these instructions to insert the fields:

1. Select Field from EFD's Insert menu. The Fields from... dialog box is displayed.
2. In the Fields from... dialog box, click the Browse button. The Select Project dialog box is displayed.
3. In the Select Project dialog box, locate your EXPENSE.EFP file. Select it, and click OK.
4. In the Window list, choose Read. In the Fields list, scroll down to locate Tab, select it, click the Insert button, and then click Close. EFD will insert a copy of the Tab field onto the Approve form's canvas. You are now ready to modify the fields to suit the purpose of the Approve form.

Modify the Tab Field Properties

Position the Tab field by setting its Left property to 75, and its Top property to 420.

Add Label Field

Next, add a Label field directly to the canvas (not to the Tab field, as you did for the Expense Report form).

Set Label Field Properties

Set field properties for the Label field according to Table 27.26, Table 27.27, and Table 27.28.

Table 27.26. Setting field general properties for new label field.

General Property	Value
Reference Name	LabelApprove
Left	75
Top	90
Width	8370
Height	300

Table 27.27. Setting field format properties for new label field.

Format Property	Value
Font	12 pt, Bold
Alignment	Center

> **NOTE**
>
> Clicking the Font button on the Format tab displays the Font dialog box, which is used to set font attributes for the entire Label field (you can't mix fonts or font attributes in the same Label field).
>
> The alignment buttons enable you to left-, center-, or right-justify the field's text.

Table 27.28. Setting field initial value properties for new label field.

Initial Value Property	Value
Initial Text	APPROVED EXPENSE REPORT - PLEASE PROCESS

You are now finished modifying the field properties. Save your changes before proceeding.

Set Window Properties

To set the window properties, select Window Properties from the View menu. Set the window's General properties as shown in Table 27.29. If Table 27.29 does not specify a property setting, leave the default setting alone.

Table 27.29. Setting the window's General properties.

Property	Value
Window Caption	Approve Expense Report
Field Tab Order	(see earlier in the section Setting Field Tab Order on the General tab for the Expense Report form)
Window Help—caption	Approve Expense Report
Window Help—body field	This Expense Report has been approved for payment by the employee's manager.

Set the window's Format properties as shown in Table 27.30.

Table 27.30. Setting the window's Format properties.

Property	Value
Window Icon	`C:\EXCHANGE\EFDFORMS\ICONS\PENL.ICO`
Window Sizing Options	`Fixed Size`

For descriptions of the different window properties, refer to the subsection Setting Window Properties in the section Expense Report Form earlier in this chapter.

Save your changes before proceeding.

Step 3: Set Form Properties

The last thing you need to do before this form is finished is set the Form properties themselves. There are two types of properties you will be setting:

1. General Properties
2. Events Properties

Set the Form's General Properties

To set the form's General properties, select Form Properties from the View menu. Enter values for the form's General properties as described in Table 27.31.

Table 27.31. Setting the Approve form's General properties.

Property	Value
Version	`1.00`
Item Type	`IPM.Approve.ExpenseReport`
Large Icon	`C:\EXCHANGE\EFDFORMS\ICONS\PENL.ICO`
Small Icon	`C:\EXCHANGE \EFDFORMS\ICONS\PENS.ICO`
Form Help—caption	`Approve Expense Report`
Form Help—body text	`This form is used for approving payment of expense reports.`

You are now ready to set the form's Event properties. Save your changes before proceeding.

Set the Form's Event Properties

There is only one Events property that needs to be modified for the Approve form. Because this form is used only to forward an approved expense report form for processing, this form will never be opened as an original form; therefore, the user does not need to see it in the Forms Library. Set the form's Viewer Menu Command property to Hidden. This will prevent it from showing in the New Forms dialog box.

To set the Hidden property, follow these steps:

1. Go to the Events tab in the Form PI.
2. Select Hidden from the Viewer Menu Command drop-down list.

Save your changes before proceeding.

Install the Form into Your Personal Forms Library

As you did with the Expense Report form earlier in this chapter, you will need to install the Approve form into Exchange before you can use the runtime form. Do this by selecting Install from EFD's file menu.

Because this form was designed specifically to work with the Expense Report form, there is no way to properly test it until you integrate the forms. Therefore, don't test this form now. Later in this section, after you install the Decline form into your Personal Forms library, you will test all three forms together to verify that they behave as expected.

The Decline Form

If a manager chooses to decline approval of an expense report form for any reason, he or she will use the Decline form to return the expense report to the employee who submitted it. Use the fields you've already created in the Approve form to build the Decline form. This will enable you to continue transferring the employee's original information as you send the expense report and its related forms through Exchange.

Now that you've created two forms, you've gained a lot of expertise in using EFD. To give you more exposure to working with EFD, for the Decline form you will rely less on the Wizard, and instead, set more of the event-handling properties yourself.

Building the Form

To build the form, you will do the following:

1. Use the Wizard to create a simple blank form.
2. Design the Compose Window.
3. Create the Read Window.
4. Set Form Properties.

Step 1: Use the Wizard to Create a Simple Blank Form

This time, start EFD, click Next, and then click Finish. This will create a blank form.

Save your form as DECLINE.EFP.

Step 2: Design the Compose Window

To design the window, you will do the following:

- Insert the Tab field from the Expense Report form's Read window.
- Modify the Tab and Label field properties.
- Set the window properties.

Insert the Tab Field from the Expense Report Form's Read Window

From EFD's Insert menu, select Field. In the Fields from... dialog box, click the Browse button. In the Select Project dialog box, locate your EXPENSE.EFP file. Select it, and click OK. Select Read from the Window drop-down list. In the Fields list, scroll down to locate Tab, select it, and click the Insert button. EFD will insert a copy of the Tab field onto the Decline form's canvas. Click Close. You are now ready to modify the fields of the Decline form.

Modify the Tab and Label Field Properties

In the Field listbox on EFD's main window, locate LabelApprove. Select it in the listbox and press F4 to display the Field PI (or select Field Properties from EFD's View menu). Modify field properties according to Table 27.32 and Table 27.33.

Table 27.32. Modifying field general properties for the Label field.

General Property	Value
Reference Name	LabelDecline
Left	75
Top	90

Table 27.33. Modifying field initial value properties for the Label field.

Initial Value Property	Value
Initial Text	EXPENSE REPORT DECLINED - PLEASE SEE COMMENTS

Reposition the Tab field by setting its Left property to 75 and its Top property to 420.

You are now finished modifying the field properties. Save your changes before proceeding.

Set the Window Properties

To set the window properties, select Window Properties from the View menu. Set the window's General properties as shown in Table 27.34. If Table 27.34 does not specify a property setting, leave the default setting alone.

Table 27.34. Setting the window's General properties.

Property	Value
Window Name	Compose
Window Caption	Decline Expense Report
Field Tab Order	(see earlier in the section Setting Field Tab Order on the General tab for the Expense Report form)
Window Help—caption	Decline Expense Report
Window Help—body field	Use this form to return an Expense Report to the originating employee for corrections. Explain your reason for not approving this report in the Comments tab.

Set the window's Format properties as shown in Table 27.35.

Table 27.35. Setting the window's Format properties.

Property	Value
Window Icon	C:\EXCHANGE\EFDFORMS\ICONS\NOTE1L.ICO
Window Sizing Options	Fixed Size

For descriptions of the different window properties, refer to the subsection Setting Window Properties in the section Expense Report Form earlier in this chapter.

You are now ready to create the Decline form's Read window. Save your changes before proceeding.

Step 3: Create the Read Window

Earlier, when you created the Expense Report form, you used the Wizard to create a two-window Send form. When the Wizard created the form for you, it automatically set all the necessary Event properties so that Exchange would know which of your form's windows to display for specific events. This time, you will create the second window for your Decline form by copying it from the existing Compose window and then manually set all of the form's Event properties to control which window Exchange displays for the different form events.

To create the Read window, you will do the following:

- Copy the Compose window.
- Modify the window properties.

Copy the Compose Window

To copy the Compose window to create a new window, follow these steps:

1. Select New Window from EFD's Edit menu. The Create New Window dialog box will appear.
2. Change the Window Name to Read.
3. Select Copy of: to make a copy of the Compose window.
4. Click OK.

EFD will create the new window, and the window will automatically have the same fields and window properties as those in the Compose window except for the window name, which you just set to Read.

There is no need to modify field properties—the properties copied from the Compose window meet the needs of the Read window as is.

Modify the Window Properties

To modify the window properties, select Window Properties from the View menu. Modify the window's General properties as shown in Table 27.36.

Table 27.36. Modifying the Read window's General properties.

Property	Value
Window Help—body field	`This Expense Report has been returned to you by your manager. Please refer to the Comments section of the form for details.`

Copying the Compose window to create the Read window preserved all of the window properties that you already set, including the Field Tab Order. As you can see, using the New Window dialog box with the Copy of feature selected can save a great deal of design time in this type of form (a form that uses the same fields, layout, names, and so on, in more than one window).

Save your changes before proceeding.

Step 4: Set Form Properties

The last thing you need to do before this form is finished is set the Form properties themselves. There are two types of properties you will be setting:

1. General Properties
2. Events Properties

Set the Form's General Properties

To set the form's General properties, select Form Properties from the View menu. Enter values for the form's General properties as described in Table 27.37.

Table 27.37. Setting form properties for the Decline form.

General Property	Value
Form Display Name	Decline Expense Report
Version	1.00
Item Type	IPM.Decline.ExpenseReport
Description	Used to decline approval of a submitted Expense Report form.
Large Icon	C:\EXCHANGE\EFDFORMS\ICONS\NOTE1L.ICO
Small Icon	C:\EXCHANGE \EFDFORMS\ICONS\ NOTE1S.ICO
Form Help—caption	Decline Expense Report
Form Help—body text	Use this form to return an Expense Report to the originating employee for corrections or changes.

Save your changes before proceeding.

Set the Form's Events Properties

You will need to manually set the form's Events properties so that Exchange will display the appropriate window for each of the form's events. You will also set the Hidden property for the form like you did with the Approve form.

When the Wizard creates a form, it automatically sets the form's Events properties appropriately. For example, all events that involve an "unsubmitted" item are set to the Compose window, and all events that involve a "submitted" item are set to the Read window.

> **NOTE**
>
> *Submitted* and *unsubmitted* might be new terms to you. Until a Send form has been sent, or until a Post form has been posted, the item is considered unsubmitted, meaning that it has not been given to Exchange for processing and delivery. After a form has been sent or posted, it becomes a submitted item—an item that has gone through Exchange and been processed and delivered. The events for a single-window form will be set either to Window1 or to Unsupported (meaning that the event is not available to the user).

Select Form Properties from EFD's View menu. Enter values for the form's Events properties as described in Table 27.38. To set Events properties on the Events tab of the Form PI, do the following:

1. Select the event shown in the left column of Table 27.38 from the For This Event: drop-down list.
2. Select the Pass To Window: option.
3. Choose the property in the right column of Table 27.38 from the drop-down list associated with the Pass To Window: option.

Table 27.38. Setting the Decline form's Events properties.

Event	Pass to Window Property/Value
Create new item	Compose
Open unsubmitted item	Compose
Open submitted item	Read
Print unsubmitted item	Compose
Print submitted item	Read
Save unsubmitted item as text	Compose
Save submitted item as text	Read

Select the Create new item event again and set the Viewer Menu Command property to Hidden.

Save your changes before proceeding.

Install the Form into Your Personal Forms Library

As you did with the Expense Report and Approve forms earlier in this chapter, you will need to install the Decline form into Exchange before you can use the runtime form. Do this by selecting Install from EFD's file menu.

Because the Decline form (like the Approve form) was designed specifically to work with the Expense Report form, there is no way to properly test it until you integrate the forms, which you will do next. Then you will test all three forms together to verify that they behave as expected.

Integrating the Expense Report, Approve, and Decline Forms

To make the three forms you have created work together in Exchange, you need to customize some of the properties for the forms' Events properties. The changes you are about to make will tell Exchange what forms to display for which events. This is how you will give the manager Approve and Decline options for the employee's expense report. You will also provide an option for the employee to make corrections to a declined expense report and resubmit it for approval.

To modify the Expense Report and Decline forms you will first open each form separately in EFD and then make the necessary modifications.

The Approve form requires no further modifications to work with the Expense Report form because after the manager sends it to the Accounting department, its task is finished.

Customizing the Expense Report Form

You will now customize the Expense Report form to include Approve Expense Report and Decline Expense Report menu items on the Exchange Client Viewer's Compose menu and on the Read window's Compose menu. To do this, you will set properties for Custom Response events for the Expense Report form.

Custom Response events are special events that you can define in addition to the standard, default events. You will usually use Custom Response events to enable the user to open other custom forms (EFD forms) from your current form's menu, as you will do here.

The Custom Response properties will be set in two places:

- The Form PI's Events tab is where you set menu items that are shown on the Exchange Viewer's Compose menu.
- The Window PI's Menus tab is where you set menu items that are shown on the form window's Compose menu.

This can be a little confusing. It is important to understand that each Custom Response menu item (as well as each default Response menu item) is displayed in two places.

- On the Exchange Viewer menu
- On the form window's menu

You need to change each of these places separately (changing one does not change the other).

To begin customizing the Expense Report form, select Open from EFD's File menu. Use the Open dialog box to locate and open your EXPENSE.EFP file.

To add the Approve Expense Report menu item to the Exchange Viewer's Compose menu and prepare it for integration, do the following:

1. Select Form Properties from EFD's View menu, and go to the Events page of the Form PI.
2. Select Custom Response 1 in the For This Event: list.
3. Change the Viewer Menu Command: to `Approve &Expense Report`. (Note that the Viewer Menu Command refers to the Exchange Client Viewer.)
4. Select the Create Response option.
5. Set Response Form's Item Type: to `IPM.Approve.ExpenseReport` (`IPM.Reply.Approve` is the Approve form's item type; this is how you tie the two forms together). You can do this either by typing the item type directly into the field or clicking the Browse button, and then using the Select Form's Item Type dialog box to locate and select the DECLINE.EFP file.
6. Set Response Style: to Forward.
7. Check Initialize new items when created.
8. Click the Options button. The Response Form Initial Values dialog box will appear.
9. In the Response Form Initial Values dialog box, add all of the fields in the Field: list to the Fields copied: list. (See the following note.)
10. Check both the Add response item to conversation thread and Initialize To, CC, and Subject values in response item checkboxes. The first checkbox will cause new comments to be added to the previous comments on the Comments tab. The second checkbox will make sure the envelope fields are initialized when a person is approving or declining the form.
11. Click OK.

> **NOTE**
>
> Adding the fields to the Fields copied: list in step 9 is how your field values get copied from one form to the next. That is, this is how the expense items the employee entered in the original expense report show up in the same places in the Approve and Decline forms; otherwise, the fields would all be blank. This works because the Field Reference Names are identical in both forms.

To add the Decline Expense Report menu item to the Exchange Viewer's Compose menu and prepare it for integration, do the following:

1. Select Form Properties from EFD's View menu, and go to the Events page of the Form PI.
2. Select Custom Response 2 in the For This Event: list.
3. Change the Viewer Menu Command: to `&Decline Expense Report`.
4. Select the Create Response option.
5. Set Response Form's Item Type: to `IPM.Decline.ExpenseReport` (the Decline form's item type).
6. Set Response Style: to Reply.
7. Check Initialize new items when created.
8. Click the Options button. The Response Form Initial Values dialog box will appear.
9. In the Response Form Initial Values dialog box, add all of the fields in the Field: list to the Fields copied: list.
10. Check both the Add response item to conversation thread and Initialize To, CC, and Subject values in response item checkboxes.
11. Click OK.

To add the Approve Expense Report and Decline Expense Report menu items to the Read window's Compose menu, do the following:

1. Select Read from EFD's Window menu. The Read window will be displayed.
2. Press Ctrl+W to display the Read window's Window PI, and go to the Menus tab.
3. Select Compose in the Menu list.
4. Select Custom Response 1 in the Commands list.
5. Change the Command Caption for Custom Response 1 to `Approve &Expense Report`.
6. Select Custom Response 2 in the Commands list.
7. Change the Command Caption for Custom Response 2 to `&Decline Expense Report`.
8. Close the Window PI.

> **NOTE**
>
> The Menus tab of the Window PI is where you set properties for all of the window's menu items (that is, you can change the command name of a menu item or add status bar text). Note that these properties are preset by default, and you will usually not make changes to the settings. In the case of your Expense Report Exchange Application, though, you will need to make some minor modifications, as shown in the preceding steps.

The Menu list contains all of the menu items that make up a window's menu bar. The Menu Caption property applies to the menu bar item currently selected in the Menu list.

The Commands list contains all of the individual menu options for the currently selected Menu list item. The Command Caption property applies to the individual menu option currently selected in the Commands list. Note that on a Windows menu, the items typically on the menu bar (File, Edit, View, and so on) are the menu items and the items that appear in the submenu when you click one of these menu items are the menu commands.

For more information on window menu properties, refer to the *Application Designer's Guide*, or EFD's online help.

27

THE EXCHANGE
FORMS DESIGNER

In order to incorporate the preceding changes into the runtime form, you will need to reinstall the form into your Personal Forms library. Select Install from EFD's File menu to reinstall the form.

The Expense Report form is now integrated with the Approve and Decline forms.

Customizing the Decline Form

Now you will add a Correct Expense Report option to the Decline form, which will enable employees to make corrections to their expense reports. This option will simply open a new Expense Report form and copy the field values from the Decline form to the new Expense Report form. This will effectively give the employees their original expense items, which can now be modified as necessary.

As you did for the Expense Report form, you will now set the necessary properties for the Decline form to add this new option to the Exchange Client Viewer's Compose menu and to the Read window's Compose menu.

To begin customizing the Decline form, select Open from EFD's File menu. Use the Open dialog box to locate and open your DECLINE.EFP file.

To add the Correct Expense Report menu item to the Exchange Viewer's Compose menu and prepare it for integration, do the following:

1. Select Form Properties from EFD's View menu, and go to the Events page of the Form PI.
2. Select Custom Response 1 in the For This Event: list.
3. Change the Viewer Menu Command: to &Correct Expense Report.
4. Select the Create Response option.
5. Set Response Form's Item Type: to IPM.Send.ExpenseReport (IPM.Send.ExpenseReport is the Expense Report form's item type; this is how you tie the two forms together).
6. Set Response Style: to None.

7. Check Initialize new items when created.

8. Click the Options button. The Response Form Initial Values dialog box will appear.

9. In the Response Form Initial Values dialog box, add all of the fields in the Field: list to the Fields copied: list.

10. Check the Add response item to conversation thread checkbox.

11. Click OK.

To add the Correct Expense Report menu item to the Read window's Compose menu, do the following:

1. Select Read from EFD's Window menu. The Read window will be displayed.

2. Press Ctrl+W to display the Read window's Window PI, and go to the Menus page.

3. Select Compose in the Menu list.

4. Select Custom Response 1 in the Commands list.

5. Change the Command Caption for Custom Response 1 to &Correct Expense Report.

6. Close the Window PI.

Again, as with the Expense Report, in order to incorporate these changes into the runtime form, you will need to reinstall the form into your Personal Forms Library. Select Install from EFD's File menu to reinstall the form.

Testing the Integration of the Forms

Now open the runtime Expense Report form and use it as you would expect users to. This is how you test the runtime form to verify that it behaves as you intended.

To open the runtime Expense Report form, follow these steps:

1. Start your Exchange Client.

2. Select New Form from the Compose menu. The New Form dialog box will appear.

3. Select Personal Forms from the drop-down list at the very top of the New Form dialog box.

4. Select Expense Report and click OK.

When the Create Expense Report window is displayed, complete at least the first row of expense items, enter the total of the amount column, enter comments on the Comments tab, and send it to yourself.

When the Expense Report form arrives in your inbox, open it as you would any other mail message. From the Read Expense Report window's Compose menu, select Decline Expense Report. When the Decline Expense Report window is displayed, verify that the To: field already contains your address, and that the Subject: field reads RE: followed by the subject you entered for the Expense Report. Verify that the expense items and total that you entered in the

Expense Report are visible in the Decline Expense Report window. Verify that your comments are contained in the Comments field. Enter new comments into the Comments field, and then send the form.

Open the Decline form in your inbox. Verify that the expense report items are still intact, and that the original comments, along with the additions you made, are still intact. From the form's Compose menu, select Correct Expense Report. Verify that the expense items and comments are intact. Make modifications to the Expense Report, including adding more comments, and send the form to yourself.

When the corrected Expense Report arrives in your inbox, open it and verify that your changes are visible. From the form's Compose menu, select Approve Expense Report. When the Approve form is displayed, again verify that all information has been preserved as expected. The Approve form's To: field should be empty, and the Subject: field should read FW: followed by the subject from your corrected Expense Report. Address the form to yourself, send it, and then open the item when it arrives in your inbox and verify that all information is intact and that you cannot modify any of the fields on the Expense Report tab.

If you find any problems, go back to EFD to make the necessary corrections, and then reinstall the forms and repeat the testing process.

After the forms pass the testing process, you are ready to make them available to the users of Exchange.

Placing the Forms in the Organization Forms Library

To make the forms automatically available to all the Exchange users, you will need to place them in the Organization Forms library. Because the forms currently reside in your Personal Forms library, you can simply copy them to the Organization Forms library.

From the Exchange Tools menu, select Options. From the Options dialog box, select the Exchange Server tab. Under Exchange Server, click Manage Forms. In the Forms Manager dialog box, you should see a list of organization forms on the left and a list of personal forms on the right. Under Personal Forms, select the three forms (Approve Expense Report, Decline Expense Report, and Expense Report), and then click Copy. The Forms Manager will copy the three forms to the Organization Forms library.

The forms are now installed in the Organization Forms library, and the Expense Report form will be visible to Exchange users and available for their use. Because the Approve and Decline forms are hidden, they will not be visible to Exchange users, but Exchange will display them whenever the appropriate menu items are selected from the Expense Report form's compose menu.

You're finished! Your Expense Report Exchange Application can now be used by everyone in your organization.

Advanced Topics

This section looks at what else you can do with your forms beyond what is provided by EFD. Three topics are covered here:

1. Making the Expense Report a Public Folder Application
2. Creating an Expense Report View in Microsoft Exchange
3. Extending the Expense Report Form with Visual Basic

Making the Expense Report a Public Folder Application

The Approve form you made as part of the Expense Report Exchange application will lend itself nicely to a public folder application because by putting the approved expense reports into a public folder, the Accounting department, the manager, and the employee can easily review them. Furthermore, after they are in a public folder, you can create a custom view for that folder so all the expense reports will be listed with the fields of interest shown as columns in the viewer.

In this section you create a public folder called Expense Reports, add the folder to your personal address book, and then set the initial value of the Approve form's To: envelope field to the folder's address. You also create a custom view in the public folder for viewing the Approve form items.

Note that this topic will require that you have public folders set up on your Exchange Server and that you have a personal address book (PAB) on your client.

Prepare the Folder In Microsoft Exchange

You must first create a public folder. In the left column of your Exchange client, locate Public Folders. Open the public folders, and select All Public Folders. From the File menu, select New Folder. In the New Folder dialog box, enter Expense Reports, and click OK.

> **TIP**
>
> To keep other users from accessing this folder until you are finished setting it up and testing the forms, set the Default Permission Role to None. To do so, display the Properties dialog box for the folder by selecting the folder and clicking the right mouse button. In the Permissions tab, change the Default Role to None by selecting Default in the list box and then selecting None in the drop-down list labeled Roles.

Modify the Form In EFD

To modify the form in EFD, you must first set the Initial Value property of the Approve form's To: field. To complete this step, you need to add the Expense Reports public folder (which you just created) to your personal address book (PAB). This will ensure that the folder's address is available to you from the Approve form's Form PI.

To add the Expense Reports folder to your PAB, first click the Expense Reports folder with the right mouse button and select Properties. Click the Administration tab in the Properties dialog box and click on the Personal Address Book button to add the folder address to your PAB. Click OK to close the Properties dialog box.

Start EFD and open APPROVE.EFP. Select the To: field in the Approve form's window and press F4 to display the Field PI. Go to the Initial Value tab and click the To button. In the Address Book dialog box that appears, select Personal Address Book in the Show Names from the: list. Select the Expense Reports folder on the left and click the To...-> button to add the folder to the Message Recipients list on the right. Click OK.

Click the Subject field on the Approve form. Set the Subject field's initial value to Approved Expense Report.

Setting these initial values automatically addresses your Approve form to the Expense Reports public folder and enters the subject text Approved Expense Report whenever a user selects Approve Expense Report from the Expense Report form's Read window.

Save your changes before proceeding.

You next must install the form into a public folder. As part of converting the Expense Report and its related forms to a Public Folder application, you should first remove the forms from the Organization Forms library. This will ensure that Exchange users are not creating their expense reports with the wrong forms and using an outdated process. You will use the Exchange Client's Forms Manager dialog box to copy the forms to the Public Folder library, and then delete the forms from the Organization Forms library.

To do this, select Options from the Exchange Tools menu. In the Options dialog box, go to the Exchange Server tab, and click Manage Forms. In the Forms Manager dialog box, set one side (either side is OK) of the dialog box to Organization Forms Library, and the other side to the Expense Reports Public Folder. Select the Expense Report and Decline forms in the Organization Forms list and click Copy. Exchange will copy the forms to the Expense Reports folder. (You don't copy the Approve form because you have to install the revised form into the public folder.) Now select the Expense Report, Approve, and Decline forms again in the Organization Forms library, and click Delete. The forms will be deleted from the Organization Forms library. Close the Forms Manager dialog box, and then close the Options dialog box.

Now install the revised Approve form into the Expense Reports public folder. From EFD's File menu select Install. When prompted to Set Forms Library, set it to the Expense Reports public folder.

The Expense Report forms, including your newly modified Approve form, are now installed in the Expense Reports public folder. Whenever an Expense Report is approved, the Approved form will automatically be sent to the Expense Reports public folder.

Creating an Expense Report View in Microsoft Exchange

You will now create a custom view for the Expense Reports folder. By creating custom views, you can control and arrange the information displayed in the Viewer so that Exchange users immediately see the relevant data whenever they open the Expense Reports folder. Creating custom views is an excellent way to make it easy for users to get the information they need from public folders. This can greatly increase the usability of your folders and encourage user participation.

Preparing the Form in EFD

To prepare a form to be used in a custom view, set the Microsoft Exchange Column Name property in EFD's Field PI for each field of your form that you want shown as a column name in the view. When you designed the Expense Report forms, you already prepared the forms for public folder views when you set the field captions (changing the field caption automatically changes the Microsoft Exchange column name to match, unless you manually change the Microsoft Exchange Column Name property).

Defining the View in the Public Folder

Follow these steps to define the view in the public folder:

1. From your Exchange Client, right-click the Expense Reports public folder.
2. Select Properties from the menu list.
3. In the Properties dialog box, go to the Views tab. Select Folder views, and click New.
4. Enter By Expense Report as the View name. Click the Columns button.
5. Remove the following fields from the Show the following list (on the right) by selecting the item and clicking the Remove button: Importance, Attachment, Subject, and Size.
6. In the Available columns list, locate Total, and add it to the Show the following list.
7. Click OK to accept your changes.
8. Click OK to close the New View dialog box, and again to close the Expense Report Properties dialog box.

You will now see the column names you just set in the right side of the Viewer. When new Approved Expense Report messages are sent to the folder, they will automatically be displayed by the columns you just set in your By Expense Report view.

Testing the Folder Application

To test the Folder application, select the Expense Reports folder and click the Compose menu. At the bottom of the Compose menu, you will see New Expense Report. When forms are installed into public folders, they are automatically added to the folder's Compose menu (and their name is automatically preceded by New). Select New Expense Report to open a new form. Complete the form and send it to yourself. Open the item in your inbox, and select Approve Expense Report from its Compose menu. When the Approve form is displayed, verify that it is already addressed to the Expense Reports public folder and that the subject line reads Approved Expense Report. Send the form. When it arrives in the Expense Reports public folder, verify that it is displayed correctly in the Viewer.

After you are satisfied that the Expense Report public folder application is working properly, you need to change the default permission role so that Exchange users can access the folder and use its forms. From your Exchange client, select the Expense Reports folder and click the right mouse button. Select Properties from the menu list. In the Properties dialog box, go to the Permissions tab. Change the Default Role to Author.

The Expense Reports public folder is now ready for use.

Extending the Expense Report Form with Visual Basic

After you've designed and installed your form using EFD, you can use Visual Basic for Microsoft Exchange Server to customize your form even further. To do this step you must be familiar with programming in the Visual Basic programming language. Depending on what you want to customize, you might also need to be familiar with the Microsoft Message API (MAPI) to extend your form. Both of these subjects are beyond the scope of this book, but you can learn more about Visual Basic and MAPI by referring to the *Application Designer's Guide* and the Visual Basic documentation.

The following is just a brief example of how to extend your form with Visual Basic. In this example, you will add a CommandButton control to the sample Expense Report form you made earlier in this chapter. When you click this button it will add up the expenses in the last column and insert the total in the bottom right cell of the expense report.

> **CAUTION**
>
> If you modify the form's code using Visual Basic, you will not be able to load the form back into EFD to make modifications without losing the changes you made by hand. We suggest you make a copy of your hand code before making additional changes to your form in EFD. This will make it easy to insert your code back in afterward.

Load Source Code into Visual Basic

When you installed EFD onto your system, you also installed a special version of Visual Basic for EFD called Visual Basic for Microsoft Exchange Server. It should have been installed into the Exchange\EFDFORMS\VB directory. Start up this version of VB.

The first thing you want to do is load the VB project that EFD automatically generated when you clicked File.Install on EFD's menu bar. EFD created a subdirectory below the directory in which your EFP file was saved. This directory, Expense.vb, contains the VB source code that EFD generated. In this directory, you'll find the Expense Report form's project file, Expense.vbp. Load that file into VB as you would load any other Visual Basic project file.

Replace the Total Label with the Total Command Button

Display the Compose Window's VB form, which is named COMPOSE.FRM. This form should look a lot like the form you created in EFD except that things have been moved around a bit. The first thing you'll want to do is temporarily reposition the canvas a bit to make your work easier.

Select the control named Canvas_Ctrl in the VB properties window. Canvas_Ctrl is the control that EFD generated for your canvas. Notice that it is a standard VB picture box control.

Note that the Top property of Canvas_Ctrl is currently set to –30. Change that to –1000 to move the interesting part of the canvas up into better view. Remember the original setting of –30 because you'll want to move it back later.

Step 1: Add the Total Command Button to the Form

Select a command button control from VB's toolbox and place it in the same location as the Label control whose caption is Total. For simplicity here, just place the command button on top of the label to hide it. You could choose to remove the Label control altogether, but then you'd have to also remove any code that references it. Position the command button as shown in Figure 27.23. Name the command button control cmdTotal. Give it the caption Tota&l.

FIGURE 27.23.

Adding the Total button to the runtime form in Visual Basic.

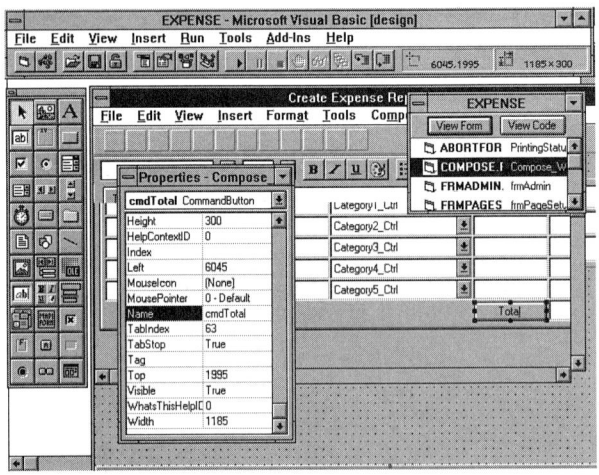

Set the Top property of Canvas_Ctrl back to –30.

Step 2: Write Code for the Total Command Button

Add the following code to the cmdTotal_Click event in COMPOSE.FRM. This is the only code you need to add to allow your expense form to total the expenses.

```
Private Sub cmdTotal_Click()
Dim curTotal As Currency

    curTotal = _
    CCur(IIf(Amount1_Ctrl.Text = vbNullString, 0, Amount1_Ctrl.Text)) + _
    CCur(IIf(Amount2_Ctrl.Text = vbNullString, 0, Amount2_Ctrl.Text)) + _
    CCur(IIf(Amount3_Ctrl.Text = vbNullString, 0, Amount3_Ctrl.Text)) + _
    CCur(IIf(Amount4_Ctrl.Text = vbNullString, 0, Amount4_Ctrl.Text)) + _
    CCur(IIf(Amount5_Ctrl.Text = vbNullString, 0, Amount5_Ctrl.Text))

    Total_Ctrl.Text = Format(curTotal, "Currency")
End Sub
```

TIP

If you are making a lot of hand-coded changes to your EFD generated code, we suggest you add separate forms, classes, and/or modules, as appropriate, to the EFD generated project instead of adding your code to the existing forms, classes, and/or modules. By doing this you can separate your hand code from the generated code. This will make maintenance of your code more manageable, plus it will make it easier for you to regenerate your code with EFD without losing your hand coded changes.

Build the New Compose Form EXE

Now build a new EXE to replace the one generated by EFD; choose Make EXE File from VB's File menu. Do not change the name of the EXE from the one that appears. The name was randomly generated by EFD, and changing it will cause problems when you install the form.

Now exit VB. You are finished with the hand coding. Don't forget to save your changes if you want to keep them.

NOTE

Note that if you made a mistake when you enter the code or something goes wrong at this stage and your form doesn't work when you install it, you can simply start over by regenerating the code again from EFD. Of course, you will have to enter your hand-coded changes again from scratch.

Install the Form into the Expense Report Public Folder

For the purposes of this example, assume that the Expense Report form is currently installed into the Expense Report public folder. If it is in the Organization Forms library, you need to make the appropriate changes when you are following the instructions.

1. From the Exchange Client's Tools menu, select Options.
2. In the Options dialog box, click the Exchange Server tab.
3. On the Exchange Server tab, click Manage Forms.
4. In the Forms Manager dialog box, set the right-hand forms list to the Expense Report public folder (click the Set button, then in the Set Library To dialog box, choose the Expense Report public folder under Forms Library).
5. On the Forms Manager dialog box, click the Install button.
6. In the Open dialog box's Directories list, locate and select the Expense.vb directory. A file named Expense.cfg will appear in the File Name list.
7. Select the Expense.cfg file and click OK.
8. Make any desired modifications in the Form Properties dialog box (for example, enter your name as Contact Name), and then click OK.

The Forms Manager will install the form into the Expense Report public folder.

> **NOTE**
>
> If you want to add a new control when you are customizing code and you want the contents of that control to show in the Viewer, you will need to make appropriate changes to the .CFG file. The .CFG file is a text file that you can edit using any text editor. For information on making changes to the .CFG file, see the *Application Designer's Guide*.

Test the Form

When you test the form, select New Expense Report from the Expense Report public folder's Compose menu. Complete two or more lines of expense items, and then click the Total button. Verify that the Total field receives a value, and that the value is the sum of all amounts in the Amount column. Send the form to yourself. Open the Expense Report in your inbox and verify that the Total value is intact.

Related Topics

This section looks at additional resources that may be helpful to you for using EFD and designing custom forms. Two topics are covered here:

1. Microsoft Exchange Sample Applications
2. Other Sources of Information

Microsoft Exchange Sample Applications

The Exchange product comes with a collection of sample applications. These samples demonstrate how to use EFD to provide real-world solutions.

You find the sample applications on the Exchange server (in the same location as the Exchange clients), under the SAMPAPPS subdirectory. Within the SAMPAPPS directory, you will find several subdirectories, a readme.wri file, and a sampapps.pst file. The readme.wri file contains detailed instructions for setting up the sample applications in Exchange Server's public folders. The sampapps.pst file is a preconstructed folder that contains all of the installed sample application folders, forms, and sample items that demonstrate how to use the individual forms and folder applications. The sample application folders come with predefined custom views (when applicable).

Within each of the subdirectories under \SAMPAPPS, you will find .efp files, readme.wri files, and any Visual Basic hand code (if applicable) for that particular sample application. The readme.wri files contain detailed information about the samples, including how to use the forms and how to set up the folders.

You can open the .EFP files in EFD, where you can examine the properties to see how the forms are designed. You can also modify the forms to customize them for use within your organization. For additional information about any given form's design, consult the form's Designer Notes from within EFD (open the .EFP file in EFD, and then press Ctrl+F1 to display Designer Notes, or select Designer Notes from EFD's Help menu).

Other Sources of Information

There are several other locations you might want to look for additional information on designing forms with Microsoft Exchange Forms Designer. Some are listed in the following sections.

Online Help

EFD comes with extensive context-sensitive online help. Most of your questions should be easily answered by simply pressing the F1 key.

Application Designer's Guide

The *Application Designer's Guide* is the printed documentation that comes with EFD. It goes into much more detail than this chapter can, particularly with respect to extending forms and working with MAPI.

27

THE EXCHANGE
FORMS DESIGNER

MAPI Documentation

If you really want to get down to the level of basic Messaging API coding, you'll want to study MAPI. You can get more information on MAPI from Microsoft and you can find it on the Microsoft Developer's Network (MSDN). To find out how to subscribe to MSDN, check out `http://www.microsoft.com/msdn` on the Web.

Microsoft Web Site

Microsoft maintains a Web site specifically devoted to Microsoft Exchange. You should check this site frequently for additional information and new developments regarding Microsoft Exchange and EFD. As additional software and tools become available, you will probably find information about them here. You can find the Web site at the following:

`http://www.microsoft.com/exchange`

Microsoft Application Farm

The Application Farm is another Web page maintained by Microsoft. It is a place to look for a variety of sample applications for Microsoft Exchange. You can find the Web site at the following:

`http://www.microsoft.com/technet/boes/bo/mailexch/exch/tools/appfarm/appfarm1.htm`

Exchange Newsgroups

Microsoft maintains a peer-to-peer newsgroup on the Internet specifically designed for discussing Exchange. It's called `microsoft.public.exchange.applications` and can be accessed on the `msnews.microsoft.com` server. Here you can ask questions and discuss topics related to EFD with other EFD users. Check `http://www.microsoft.com/exchange` for information on how to get to this newsgroup.

Summary

In this chapter, you learned how to create Microsoft Exchange forms using the Microsoft Exchange Forms Designer. This chapter covered how to use the EFD Wizard to start your form, how to customize the form by adding windows and fields and setting their properties, how to join forms together into an Exchange application, how to install your completed form into the Exchange Server, and finally, advanced topics on extending the capabilities of EFD.

V

PART

SQL Server

CHAPTER 28

SQL Server 6.5 Overview

by Vipul Minocha

IN THIS CHAPTER

Microsoft SQL Server 6.5 is a highly scalable and high-performance relational database management system. SQL Server 6.5 is the latest release from Microsoft and replaces Microsoft SQL Server 6.0 in BackOffice. SQL Server can manage a large amount of data in a multiuser distributed client-server environment. It offers a high degree of data availability, concurrency, and integrity while delivering high performance.

Distributed Client-Server Computing

Most of the applications developed in the past were host-based, where mainframes had all the processing power. All aspects of an application (application logic, business rules, data integrity, security, and so forth) were implemented on the central host to which terminals were connected. These terminals did not have any processing power and were used for display purposes only. Figure 28.1 shows a typical mainframe-based environment.

FIGURE 28.1.

Host-based environment.

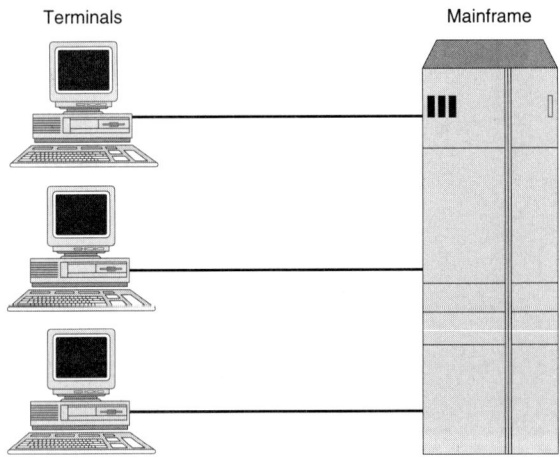

Terminals   Mainframe

There are advantages to host-based computing, the most important being that all aspects of the computing environment are centralized. Because all components of the application exist on the central host, it is simpler to implement security and provide maintenance. The major disadvantage of host-based computing is the high cost of operation and maintenance.

Faster networks and inexpensive personal computers have made it possible to develop applications that provide a flexible and adaptable development environment resulting in tremendous cost savings. Client-server is a networked computing environment (see Figure 28.2) where a client submits a request over the network that is processed by the server. The processing power is distributed between the client and the server. The client side of application focuses more on the user interface and application logic. Typically, clients are not responsible for doing any data manipulation. The server, on the other hand, can handle application logic, perform data manipulation, and enforce data integrity, business rules, and security. Unlike terminals in host-based computing, clients in a client-server environment have processing power and memory.

Therefore, some of the business rules can be implemented on the client so that the server resources can be utilized more efficiently.

FIGURE 28.2.

Client-server environment.

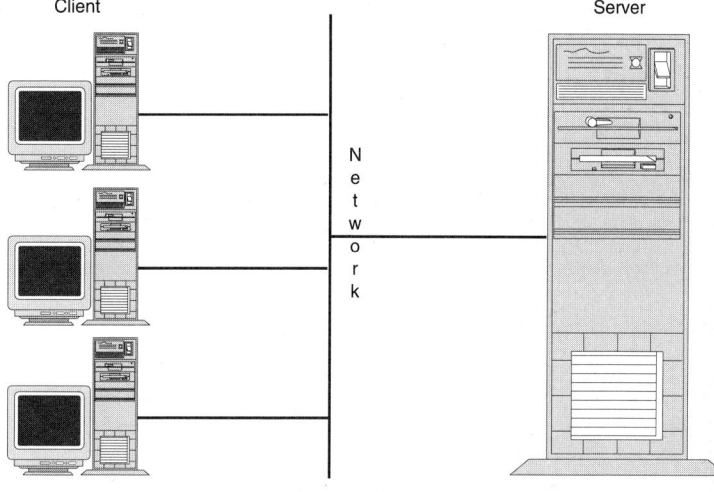

> **NOTE**
>
> It is important to balance the load between the client and the server so that resources on both sides are used optimally. Application and database design have become important aspects of client-server computing. For example, a poorly designed application can create a network bottleneck by retrieving hundreds of rows from the database, even though only a few rows are necessary for the front-end application.

Features

SQL Server is designed to understand Structured Query Language (SQL), which was developed by IBM for relational databases. Most of the relational database vendors provide SQL as a query language to perform data manipulation in the database. The American National Standard Institution (ANSI) has set standards for SQL. Various DBMS vendors comply with either ANSI 89 or ANSI 92 standards of SQL. The SQL Server query language called T-SQL (Transact-SQL) is an enhanced version of ANSI SQL and complies with ANSI 92 standards. The following are three components of ANSI SQL:

- Data Definition Language (DDL), required to create database objects
- Data Manipulation Language (DML), required to modify (insert, delete, update) data
- Data Control Language (DCL), required to control security access on various database objects

T-SQL fulfills all the ANSI requirements listed. T-SQL is a very powerful language and provides many 3-GL-like extensions (such as BEGIN-END and IF-ELSE WHILE constructs) to ANSI SQL. SQL Server processes T-SQL commands sent by the clients and, if required, sends the result back to them.

SQL Server Databases

A database is a collection of tables containing related information. This information can be user data as well as data required by the DBMS to perform its regular functions. A SQL Server consists of multiple databases, as shown in Figure 28.3. Some of the databases are user databases and some are system databases required by SQL Server to perform its own operation. SQL Server can hold up to 32,767 databases.

FIGURE 28.3.

Databases in SQL Server.

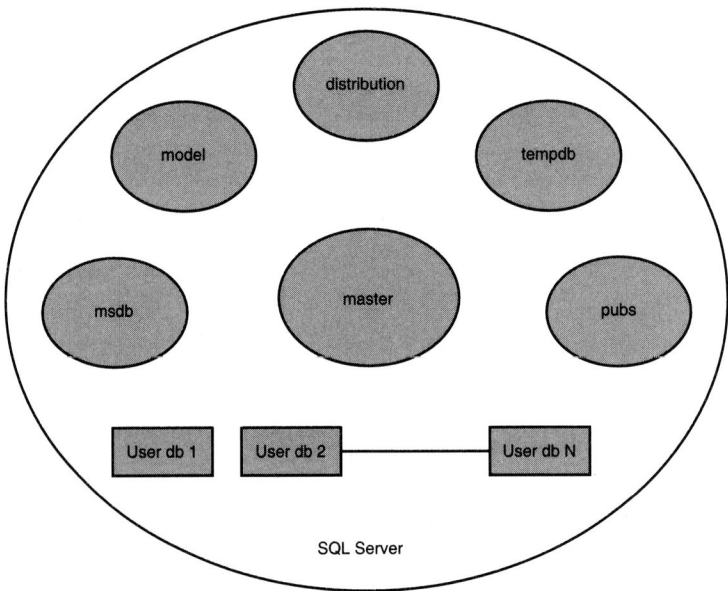

SQL Server consists of the following databases:

- The master database controls the SQL Server operations. It checks for user access to SQL Server and holds critical information regarding user accounts, database storage allocations, SQL Server configurable parameters, system stored procedures, and so forth. The master database is created at the time of SQL Server installation.

- The model database provides a template for a user database. It contains all the system tables required by a user database. System tables are tables used to store information about an individual database. For example, system table sysobjects keeps information about all the user tables of a database. Names of most of the system tables begin with sys. When a new user database is created, all the tables are copied from the model database. The model database is created as a part of SQL Server installation.

■ The tempdb database provides a scratchpad area to hold temporary objects. tempdb is a shared area used by all the users of SQL Server to create temporary objects and hold intermediate data results. This database is also used by SQL Server to create internal worktables and for data sorting for its own use (for example, worktables created by the GROUP BY and ORDER BY clauses). tempdb is created as a part of SQL Server installation, but can be extended in size by the database administrator, depending on the nature of the applications running on SQL Server.

■ The msdb database is used by the scheduler component (SQL Executive) of SQL Server. SQL Server provides the facility to schedule tasks. The various types of tasks that can be scheduled are command file execution (cmd or exe files, or operating system commands), T-SQL statements (including stored procedures), execution, and data replication-related tasks. For example, certain routine tasks such as database backups can be scheduled through SQL Executive. All task schedules, alert notifications, event handling information, and history of the task scheduled are stored in the msdb database. This database is created as a part of SQL Server installation.

■ The distribution database is required to provide replication functionality in SQL Server. This database is not created as a part of default SQL Server installation. This database is created when you want to provide replication functionality. The database name does not have to be "distribution." The database administrator can choose a different name. The distribution database receives data from the publishing server and holds the data until it is moved to the subscribing servers. This database is used as a placeholder for all transactions that are waiting to be replicated on the destination databases.

■ The pubs database is a demo database created when SQL Server is installed. This database is not required for the working of SQL Server, but is provided mainly as a sample database for educational purposes.

■ User-defined databases, consisting of a number of tables holding important information, are created to support development, testing, or production environments for business applications.

28

SQL SERVER 6.5 OVERVIEW

NOTE

The master database is critical to the operation of SQL Server. A disk failure may result in a damaged or corrupt master database on a server, rendering all the other databases useless on that server. Therefore, it is quite important to have an up-to-date backup copy of the master database to deal with such disasters.

SQL Server Database Objects

A database is a collection of tables holding related information. A table consists of columns containing rows of data. There are other objects in a database besides tables. These objects don't hold any data, but they provide assistance in implementing business rules, data and referential integrity, business logic, and so forth. Examples of some of these objects are stored procedures, triggers, rules, and defaults. All these objects occupy space in a database and are referred to by a name.

> **NOTE**
>
> Even though all the objects are referred to by a name, SQL Server assigns a unique integer ID to all the objects, and internally uses these IDs to access these objects.

Tables

A table consists of rows and columns. A table is created by using the CREATE TABLE T-SQL construct. Each column in a table is required to have a name and a corresponding datatype and, optionally, other attributes. The following example creates a table called employee:

```
create table employee (
    empid int,
    emp_lname char(55),
    emp_mname char(2) NULL,
    emp_fname char(20),
    salary money
)
```

SQL Server enables the use of predefined system datatypes or user-defined datatypes that can be attached to a column property. Each column of the table may have other optional attributes associated with it. In the previous example, column emp_mname has an attribute NULL attached to it, signifying that if a record is inserted without specifying a middle name, the employee's middle name is stored as NULL (unknown value).

> **NOTE**
>
> A NULL value does not mean spaces or no value. A NULL value means that the value is unknown. In the previous example, each record having a NULL value in the emp_mname column does not signifiy that an employee does not have a middle name; it means that the middle name is unknown or not available.

Datatypes

Datatypes are essential for defining a column property of a table. A datatype specifies the characteristics of a column in terms of size and storage. Datatypes are also used for stored procedure parameters and T-SQL local variables. SQL Server provides two kinds of datatypes:

- *Server-supplied datatypes.* SQL Server provides a comprehensive set of datatypes, including `int`, `char`, `varchar`, `money`, `float`, `datetime`, `bit`, and `text`.
- *User-defined datatypes.* SQL Server enables users to create their own datatypes, which are based on SQL server-supplied datatypes. These datatypes can be used in place of system datatypes.

User-defined datatypes bring consistency among the columns that are used across various tables in a database. User-defined datatypes are created by using the `sp_addtype` system stored procedure. In the following example, a user-defined datatype `udd_empid` is created and bound to the column `empid` of the `employee` table:

```
sp_addtype udd_empid , " int "

create table employee (
    empid udd_empid ,
    emp_lname char(55),
    emp_mname char(2) NULL,
    emp_fname char(20) ,
    salary money
)
```

A user-defined datatype should be created before it can be attached to a column of a table.

Rules and Check Constraint

Rules and check constraints are used as methods of enforcing a set of data values on a particular column of a table or a user-defined datatype. A rule is a SQL Server database object that is created and attached to a column of a table or a user-defined datatype. Rules can be used to validate a specific value or a range of values entered for a column. A rule on a column of a table is activated when data is inserted or updated into a table. SQL Server raises an error if the value entered in the column violates the rule defined on it. A rule can be bound to a column or a user-defined datatype by using the `sp_bindrule` system stored procedure. In the following example, `rul_salary` rule is created and bound to the column `empid` to ensure that `empid` is always a positive number but less than or equal to `100000`:

```
create rule rul_empid
as
@empid  between  1 and 100000

Exec sp_bindrule rul_empid, "employee.empid"
```

A rule definition can be bound to many columns in various tables in a database.

An alternate method of enforcing a business rule is to use a check constraint when creating a table. A check constraint is similar to a rule, except that it is defined on a column during a CREATE TABLE statement. A check constraint can coexist with a rule; however, it does not make much sense to use both rules and check constraint to enforce a business rule. The following example shows how to create a check constraint on a table:

```
create table employee (
    empid int constraint gt_zero check (empid between 1 and 100000 ),
    emp_lname char(55),
    emp_mname char(2) NULL,
    emp_fname char(20) ,
    salary money
)
```

Defaults

A default is a method of inserting a specific value into a column when no value is explicitly specified as part of an INSERT statement. There are two methods of creating defaults in SQL Server. The first method is to use a CREATE DEFAULT clause followed by executing the sp_bindefault stored procedure, which binds the default to the column of a table. The second method is to create a default on a column directly by using a DEFAULT clause in a CREATE TABLE statement. The following two examples illustrate both methods of creating defaults:

```
create default mname_def as "M"
exec sp_bindefault mname_def , "employee.mname"

create table employee (
    empid int,
    emp_lname char(55),
    emp_mname char(2) constraint mname_def DEFAULT "M",
    emp_fname char(20) ,
    salary money
)
```

A default can also be bound to a user-defined datatype.

CAUTION

Be very careful when using default values for a column of a table if there is also a rule defined on it. Default values should not violate the rule definition. For example, if a rule on the salary column of the employee table allows values between $50000 and $150000 and the default value for the salary column is $25000, an INSERT statement to the employee table with no salary value causes SQL Server to raise an error, because the default on the salary column violates the rule.

Stored Procedures

One of the most powerful features of SQL Server is stored procedures. A stored procedure is a collection of SQL statements that is pre-parsed and stored on the SQL Server. Each stored procedure is given a name and is referenced by that name. A query contained in the definition of a stored procedure can be executed by sending an EXECUTE (or EXEC) command followed by the name of the stored procedure to SQL Server. A stored procedure can be called from another stored procedure. Stored procedures can accept parameter values and return parameter values to the calling procedure along with the return status indicating success or failure of the execution. There are a number of advantages to using stored procedures:

■ *Improved performance.* When a T-SQL query reaches SQL Server, it is parsed and compiled before it can be executed. Because stored procedures are pre-parsed, the optimizer does not have to parse it again before executing it.

■ *Reduced network traffic.* Because only the name of the stored procedure is sent across the network instead of an entire batch of SQL statements, there is less traffic on the network.

■ *Efficient application design.* Because stored procedures can accept parameters and can be called from other stored procedures, it is possible to write common application logic and business rules using stored procedures.

■ *Enhanced security.* By granting execute permissions on stored procedures and not on the underlying tables, the users do not need any direct access to underlying database tables. Data manipulation on the tables can be done entirely by using stored procedures.

SQL Server also comes with a number of system stored procedures. System stored procedures are created in the master database at the time of SQL Server installation. A number of stored procedures are provided to display useful information about database objects. Some of the system procedures are provided for the system administrator (sa) to perform routine administrative tasks, such as adding/dropping users, creating/dropping database backup devices, and so forth. Most of these stored procedures have names beginning with sp_. The sp_helpdb system stored procedure, for example, displays information about a specific database or all databases on a SQL Server.

Extended Stored Procedures

SQL Server also provides the capability of performing actions outside the SQL Server environment by executing extended stored procedures. Extended stored procedures help application developers perform various tasks that typically fall under the realm of an operating system. Extended stored procedures are functions stored in a dynamic link library (DLL) loaded as a part of the SQL Server process. In the following example, a file is copied from one directory into another by using an extended stored procedure called xp_cmdshell:

```
Exec master..xp_cmdshell "copy c:\sourcedir\filename c:\destinationdir\filename"
```

All the extended stored procedures have names beginning with xp_. In addition to all the extended stored procedures provided as a part of SQL Server, application developers can create their own extended stored procedures by using Microsoft Open Data Services (ODS). Open Data Services are discussed later in this chapter under the heading Architecture.

Views

Views in SQL Server are like virtual tables. They provide a snapshot of data from one or more underlying database tables. To an end-user, a view looks like a regular table. A logical representation of the view is shown in Figure 28.4. SQL Server cannot restrict access to only certain rows of a table (that is, a user can either select all the rows or no rows at all from a table). By using views, you restrict direct access to the database tables by providing a horizontal and vertical snapshot of the data from underlying tables. Views help simplify data representation and provide logical data independence. Because SQL Server enables permissions to be granted on the view and not the underlying tables, the end-users need not know about the underlying data structures from which a view is created. Views can also be used as security mechanisms for data. Data modification to a table can also be done through a view. SQL Server places a few restrictions, however, on doing data modifications on underlying tables through views.

FIGURE 28.4.

Using views in SQL Server.

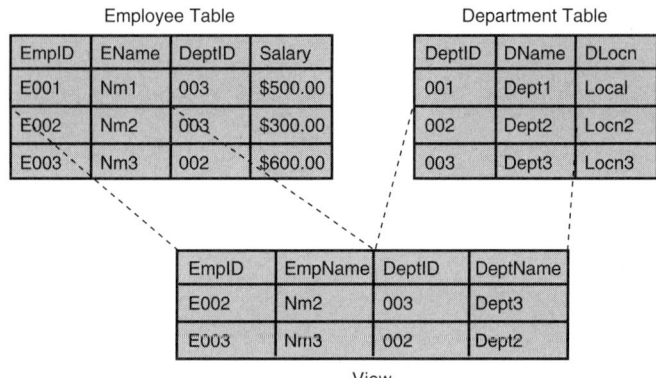

Triggers

Triggers are database objects created to maintain referential integrity of the database. A trigger is like a stored procedure except that a trigger gets fired automatically whenever data modification takes place on the table on which a trigger is created. SQL Server allows three kinds of triggers that can be attached to a table:

- The UPDATE trigger gets activated as a result of an update statement on the table. A trigger can be written to get activated unconditionally or only when specific columns get updated.
- The DELETE trigger gets activated as a result of a delete statement on the table.
- The INSERT trigger gets activated as a result of an insert statement on the table.

Triggers are also used to implement complex business rules. Triggers are sometimes used to record certain events. For example, an update trigger on an employee table can record the user ID of the person performing updates on the salary column. Because triggers are directly attached to the table, they cannot be executed manually or called from a stored procedure.

SQL Server also provides declarative referential integrity (DRI) using CREATE TABLE and ALTER TABLE T-SQL statements. DRI complies with ANSI standards.

> **NOTE**
>
> In general, it is a good idea to use declarative referential integrity using CREATE TABLE and ALTER TABLE clauses, because such queries are portable across various DBMS. However, some complex tasks such as CASCADE DELETES, determination of before and after values of records in a DELETE statement, cannot be done using DRI. Such tasks can be done easily within a trigger.

Indexes

SQL Server provides indexes for faster access to the data and to enforce uniqueness of the data in the database tables. Creating an index on a table improves query search performance. SQL Server provides two types of indexes: *clustered index* and *nonclustered index*. Both these indexes are B-Tree structures and require separate storage space in the database. You can create indexes on tables either by using the create index statement or by using the UNIQUE or PRIMARY KEY integrity constraints of the create table clause of T-SQL. In a clustered index, the data in the table is physically sorted based on the columns that constitute a key. In a nonclustered index, data is inserted at the end of the table, and there are indexed pointers to each row of the table. SQL Server enables only one clustered index per table and up to 249 nonclustered indexes. Because data is physically sorted in case of a clustered index, searches on a clustered index are almost always faster than on a nonclustered one. Although indexes speed up search operations, inserts, deletes, and updates may be slow, because each of these operations may result in modifying the B-Tree index structure for the table. In general, the following guidelines should help you decide whether to use an index:

- Columns that are often specified in the order by clause should be indexed so that SQL Server makes use of the indexed order. This eliminates an additional step of sorting the data after retrieval.

- Columns that are often searched for a range of values are good candidates for a clustered index. Once the first value in the range is located, subsequent values are guaranteed to be physically adjacent rows.

- Columns that are frequently used in table joins should be indexed, because SQL Server can locate rows faster if the columns are in sorted order.

- It does not make much sense to create an index on a column that has a low distribution value. For example, creating an index on a column named sex is not going to bring any benefits, because there are only two possible values: male and female.

Indexes are mostly transparent to the users. Query optimizer decides whether to use an index on a table for a particular query. If there is more than one index on a table, query optimizer chooses the index that is most effective in terms of number of I/Os. However, SQL Server allows an application developer to pass hints to the query optimizer to use a specific index in a query.

Cursors

SQL Server cursors enable row-by-row operation on a given result set from a SELECT statement. A cursor is similar to a file pointer to a particular record in a file consisting of numerous records. Cursors enable users to traverse the query results one row at a time. They are useful in situations where each row of the result set needs to be examined individually. In order to make use of the cursor functionality of SQL Server, the following steps are required in T-SQL:

1. Declare a cursor.
2. Open the cursor.
3. Fetch data using the cursor.
4. Modify data through the cursor, if necessary.
5. Close the cursor.
6. Deallocate the cursor.

SQL Server cursor declaration is like a SELECT statement with a declaration of a cursor by name. By examining the declaration structure, SQL Server compiles the SQL query. Opening the cursor results in the execution of SQL contained in the cursor declaration, and the cursor pointer is positioned on the first row of the result set. The data fetch stage involves retrieving data from the result set one row at a time. With each data fetch, the cursor pointer moves down to the next row of the result set. Fetches are allowed until the cursor pointer reaches the end of the result set. Data modification is possible through cursors, although SQL Server places a few restrictions on doing so (for example, an UPDATE statement on a table that uses the WHERE CURRENT OF T-SQL construct can modify the row on which the cursor is currently positioned). Once the user finishes using the result set, the cursor is closed. SQL Server then releases all the resources required for the cursor operation, except for the compiled query plan. A user can reopen a cursor after closing it without having to redeclare the cursor. If a cursor definition is not required anymore, the cursor can be deallocated. SQL Server then removes the query plan for the cursor and releases the data structures associated with the cursor.

SQL Server offers rich cursor functionality. Cursors can be created and used from within stored procedures, triggers, and batch SQL scripts. Using SQL Server cursor functionality, it is possible to directly access the first and last row, fetching forward and backward using absolute or relative cursor positions in the result set.

Concurrency and Locking

In a multiuser environment, it is important to prevent transactions from interfering with each other while preserving data integrity. SQL Server 6.5 uses various kinds of locks, depending on the type of transaction. SQL Server allocates space in 2K pages. Default locking granularity of SQL Server is a page. SQL Server uses the following three types of locking schemes:

- *Shared locks* are used for operations, such as a SELECT statement, that are read-only in nature. If a shared lock is applied on a page, another transaction can also acquire a shared lock on the same page. Once the read operation is finished on the page, SQL Server releases the lock from that page. SQL Server also provides a feature called HOLDLOCK in which locks are not released after the read operation is finished, but are held for the entire duration of the transaction.

- *Exclusive locks* are acquired by SQL Server for data manipulation statements such as delete, insert, and update. If such a transaction is in progress, no other transaction can acquire any other kind of lock. Lock on a particular page is released after the transaction is complete.

- *Update locks* are acquired by a transaction with an intent to modify a page that is currently locked by another transaction. This lock escalates to an exclusive lock once the page becomes available, and the lock exists for the duration of the transaction.

Page level locking can become a bottleneck in situations where multiple users are trying to insert records on the same page. To overcome such performance issues, SQL Server 6.5 now has a new feature called Insert row-level locking (IRL). IRL can be enabled for some or all the tables of a database by using the sp_tableoption stored procedure, enabling users to lock a specific row during insert, instead of the whole page.

Query Optimizer

Microsoft SQL Server comes with an intelligent cost-based query optimizer, which determines the most efficient path to the data in various tables involved in a join, instead of a predefined rule. A cost-based optimizer does not depend on the way a query is stated (order of tables in the FROM clause of a query, for example). The following is the sequence of events that take place once a query reaches SQL Server:

1. SQL Server parses the query to check for any syntax errors and existence of objects defined in the query. It then converts these object names to internal integer IDs. This process is also called *normalization* of a query.

2. The query optimizer analyzes various access methods for each table in the query, determines the cost of each, and finally decides on the one that is least expensive in terms of the response time.

A significant factor in deciding cost is the number of physical I/Os that are required to get the desired results. It is always the intent of an optimizer to reduce the number of physical I/Os for a query. The following are some of the parameters SQL Server analyzes before making a query plan:

1. Key distribution values of indexes involved in the join. SQL Server keeps the distribution of key values in the sysindexes system catalog table.

2. Estimated number of physical I/Os from the disk and logical I/Os from the cache to access data.

3. Number of records in each table. If possible, the optimizer makes an attempt to avoid multiple scans on large tables.

4. Search criteria defined in the WHERE clause of the query. This determines which indexes will be used to access the data.

5. Whether a query includes any aggregate functions (such as MIN or MAX). If there is an index on such tables, data can be retrieved directly from index pages instead of data pages, resulting in fewer page scans.

6. Optimizer hints in the FROM clause. Sometimes it is possible for an optimizer to select a query plan that is not very efficient. In such cases, an application developer can pass hints to the query optimizer to use specific indexes defined in the FROM clause of a query.

By analyzing these parameters, SQL Server quickly builds several plans for query execution and chooses the one that it thinks is the most efficient. Query plans for triggers and stored procedures are created when they are executed for the first time. These plans stay in the SQL Server cache and are reused upon subsequent execution of the stored procedures and triggers. However, query plans are not sharable; that is, if two users invoke the same stored procedure *simultaneously*, two query plans will be created—one for each user. SQL Server also provides a number of SQL commands and trace calls to analyze query behavior.

> **NOTE**
>
> When a stored procedure (or a trigger) is compiled, the text of the stored procedure is stored in the syscomments system catalog of the database in which the procedure is created. The parsed and compiled query tree is stored in the sysprocedures system table.

SQL Mail

Microsoft SQL Server comes with built-in extended stored procedures that perform mail-related functions. SQL Mail features enable users to send queries through the mail that can be executed by SQL Server. SQL Server, in turn, can send the results back through the mail. SQL Mail should be started before you can use the mail features in SQL Server. SQL Mail can be started and stopped by using the xp_startmail and xp_stopmail extended stored procedures, respectively. SQL Server also provides a graphical user interface to configure, start, and stop

SQL Mail. Mail is sent using the `xp_sendmail` extended stored procedure. This stored procedure can be used to send ordinary messages, query results, blind copy, mail attachments, and so forth. SQL Mail can be used to send alerts or to notify users after the completion of a scheduled task. The following example sends the output of the system stored procedure `sp_helpdb` on the Internet to a user called `netuser`:

```
exec master..xp_sendmail @recipients = 'netuser1@noname.com',
@query = 'sp_helpdb master',
@copy_recipients = 'netuser2@noname.com',
@subject = 'master database information'
```

It is possible to send or read mail from within triggers and stored procedures. SQL Mail is compatible with Microsoft Exchange Mail or any other MAPI provider. For SQL Server to work with Exchange Mail, it is necessary to set up a domain user account for Exchange. This account is used by SQL Server.

Distributed Transactions

In a distributed client-server environment, sometimes it is necessary to run transactions across multiple servers. It is important to maintain the integrity and consistency of the data on each server; that is, if a transaction fails on one of the servers, the entire transaction should be rolled back. SQL Server provides a two-phase commit protocol that preserves data consistency across several SQL Servers. A two-phase commit protocol represents the tight consistency model of SQL Server, where it is ensured that a transaction across servers is treated as a single unit of work. Two-phase commit is implemented programatically. Microsoft DB Library Toolkit provides a number of C library calls to implement two-phase commit. Distributed transactions can also be achieved by using the Microsoft Distributed Transaction Coordinator (MSDTC), which also uses a two-phase commit protocol and runs as a service under Windows NT. This service must be started by using the SQL Enterprise Manager utility from the SQL Server 6.5 program group. By using the SQL Enterprise Manager graphical tool, it is possible to configure MSDTC and review and control the state of each transaction participating in a distributed transactional environment.

Replication

Replication is data duplication from one database to one or more databases on the same or different servers. SQL Server replication is based on the loose consistency model. This means that there is a certain amount of time lag before data gets replicated from source to destination. Data can be replicated either on a scheduled basis or on a number-of-transaction basis. Both these parameters can be configured by the database administrator at the time of setting up replication. The source database, which sends the data, is called *publisher,* and the destination database, which requests the data, is called *subscriber.* Each table that is participating in replication is called an *article.* A collection of articles is known as a *publication.* It is not necessary to publish all the rows and all the columns of a table (article). SQL Server replication enables horizontal and vertical partitioning of the data from an article—that is, you can publish selected columns and selected rows from a table. All the publishing databases on a server use a distribution database, which acts like a placeholder for all the publications that need to be published. Once the data reaches the subscriber, it may be deleted from the distribution database. The distribution database can reside on the same server as the publication database (see Figure 28.5) or on a remote server (see Figure 28.6). SQL Server replication comes with a graphical user interface to set up and manage replication among various servers. SQL Server databases can also participate in two-way replication, in which the database that is publishing the data can also subscribe to data from various servers. Version 6.5 is also capable of providing replication to ODBC subscribers other than SQL Server, such as Oracle.

FIGURE 28.5.

Local publishing, local distribution.

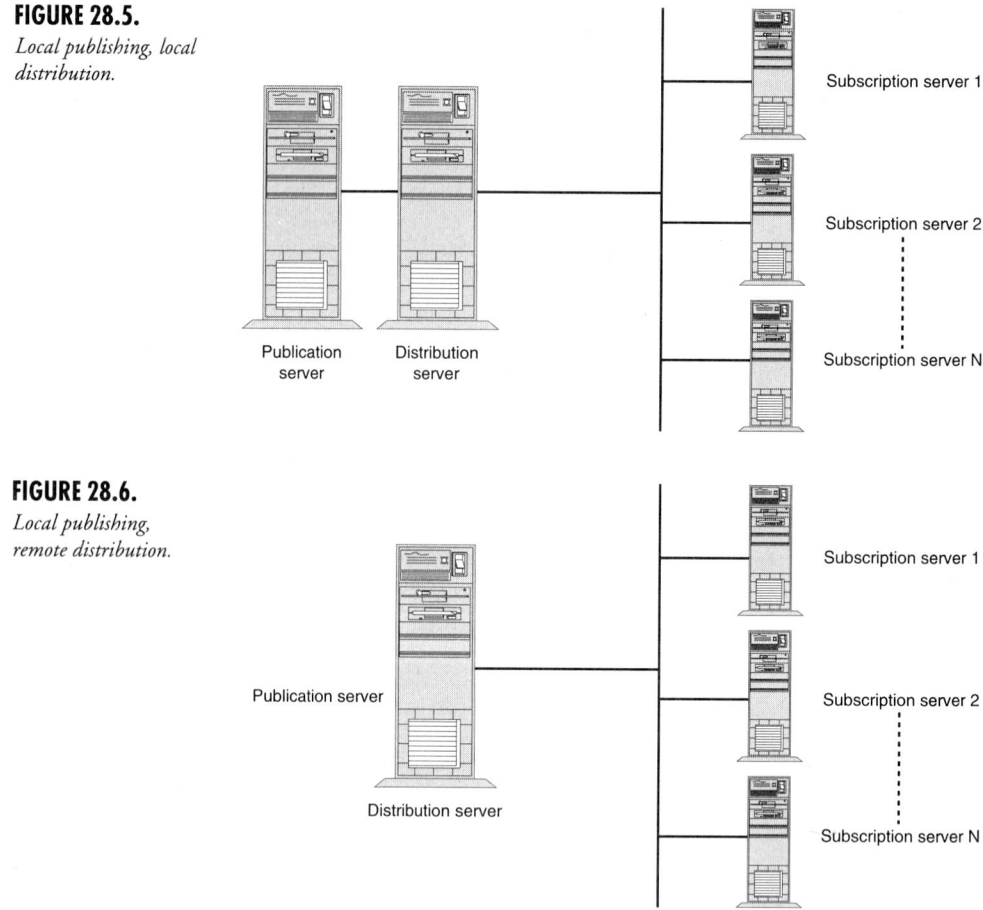

FIGURE 28.6.

Local publishing, remote distribution.

Network Protocols

SQL Server is designed to handle communication from clients using various network protocols. SQL Server includes several Net Libraries that are used to communicate with the clients. At the time of SQL Server installation, you can specify the network protocols SQL Server should listen on. Currently, Multi-protocol, NWLink IPX/SPX, TCP/IP sockets, Banyan VINES, Apple Talk ADSP, DECnet, and Named Pipes are supported. By default, SQL Server listens only on the named pipes protocol. The default pipe name for SQL Server is \\pipe\sql\query. TCP/IP sockets and Named Pipes are the two most popular protocols used by SQL Server. UNIX clients can access SQL Server by using TCP/IP sockets.

SQL Server and the Internet

With the growing popularity of the Internet, many organizations have recognized the benefits of extending the enterprise to the Internet and letting people use existing business applications over the Internet without sacrificing reliability and compromising on security. SQL Server allows users to access databases over the Internet. For an application to access SQL Server, both the client and the server must be directly on the Internet. Applications can connect to SQL Server either by using the absolute IP address of the server or through Domain Name Service (DNS). To access SQL Server through the Internet, the only currently supported protocol is TCP/IP.

Using Microsoft SQL Server it is possible to publish data in the database in the form of a standard Hypertext Markup Language (HTML) file. SQL Server comes with a graphical user interface called SQL Server WEB Assistant, which can be used to publish data on the Web server. These HTML files can also be created by using SQL Server supplied stored procedures. These files can be viewed by any Internet browser, such as Netscape or Microsoft Internet Explorer. SQL Server allows creation of HTML files from within triggers. It is possible, therefore, to update these files dynamically whenever the data changes. HTML files can also be updated on a scheduled basis by using the SQL Server scheduler.

Architecture

SQL Server is an advanced and highly scalable relational database management system. SQL Server software makes available a suite of products that provide a foundation for implementing a complete business solution in a client-server environment. These products include the SQL Server database engine, a number of tools, and a set of application programming interfaces (APIs) to support development environment. The SQL Server product family is designed with a layered approach in mind. Each layer provides a programmable functionality to extend SQL Server capabilities and also to develop client applications. Each layer builds on top of another (see Figure 28.7) and makes use of the services provided by the inner layer. This, in turn, provides services to the outer layer through a set of function calls. The following are the various layers of the SQL Server product family:

- SQL Server Database Engine
- SQL Distributed Management Framework
- SQL Server Application Programming Interface
- Tools and Utility programs

FIGURE 28.7.

SQL Server product philosophy.

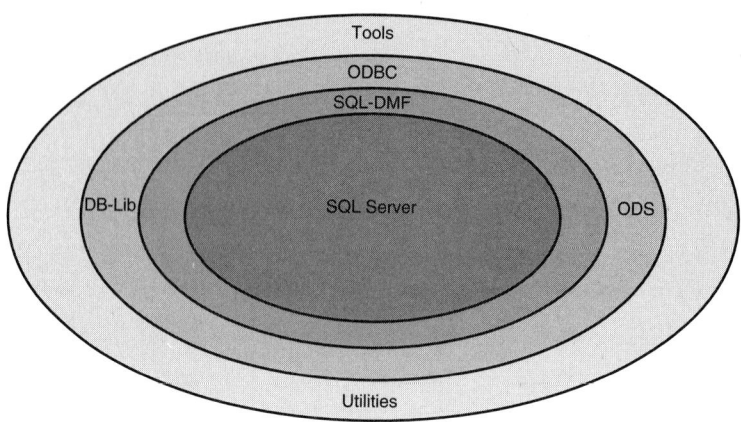

SQL Server Database Engine

The SQL Server database engine is the innermost layer, providing all DBMS-related functions. It is designed to work in a distributed client-server environment. SQL Server runs as a service on Windows NT. Unlike many other relational databases that either simulate thread code in the database engine or use shared memory for user connections, SQL Server is integrated closely with Windows NT to make use of native operating system threads (see Figure 28.8). Use of Windows NT threads results in better performance and stability of SQL Server. The following are some of the benefits of using native threads:

■ Because SQL Server does not have to simulate any threads in the database engine, system overhead and complexity are significantly reduced.

■ Because SQL Server executes each task on a separate thread, in case of a protection fault on one of the threads, the problematic user connection can be killed without affecting the SQL Server process as a whole, resulting in better stability and reliability of the system.

■ As operating system threading performance improves (for example, when the operating system version upgrades to a higher version), SQL Server automatically gets the performance boost.

SQL Server supports Symmetric Multiprocessing (SMP). SMP hardware is a server that has more than one CPU, and each CPU can handle a load (I/Os, interrupts, and so forth) independent of other CPUs. SMP support enables SQL Server to run multiple tasks, simultaneously resulting in excellent load balancing. SQL Server is designed in such a way that applications and end-users see a single database process, leaving the number of processors completely transparent to the end-user.

FIGURE 28.8.

Threading in SQL Server.

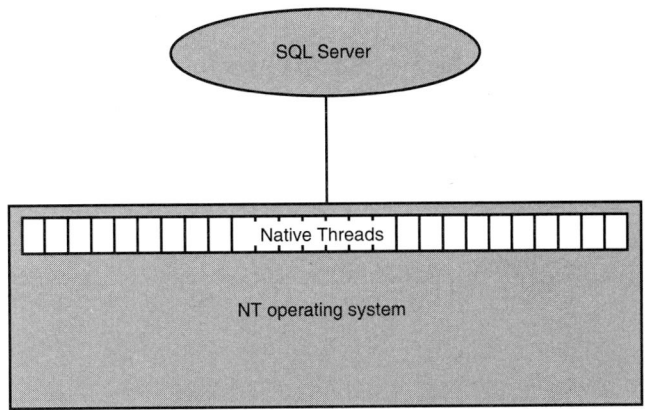

SQL Distributed Management Framework

Sitting on top of the SQL Server layer is the SQL Server management layer. This layer is also known as SQL Distributed Management Framework (SQL-DMF). SQL-DMF provides a set of services and objects through which it is possible to access the SQL Server database engine. Using the components of SQL-DMF, it is possible to develop management tools that are specific to the requirements of an enterprise. Because SQL-DMF is a programmable interface, it is possible to write sophisticated database management tools. For example, by using SQL-DMF object interfaces, an automated database backup tool can be written that will allow consistency checks on a database on a flexible schedule, perform database backups, raise alerts (mail and/or page) in case of failures, and send backup reports to relevant people.

SQL Server Application Programming Interface

This layer provides a set of application programming interfaces (APIs) access to the SQL Server database engine, and consists of the following components:

- Open Client DB-Library
- Open Database Connectivity (ODBC)
- Open Data Services (ODS)

Open Client DB-Library is a set of C API calls that are used in writing client applications. These libraries include routines that send T-SQL requests to the server and process the results of the queries. Using these libraries, it is possible to write customized applications with comprehensive error handling features. An example of a DB-Library application is ISQL/w, which is supplied with SQL Server software.

ODBC is also an API used in developing client applications. The main difference between ODBC and Open Client DB-Library is that applications written using DB-Library calls are specifically written for SQL Server, whereas the applications using ODBC are written to be independent of the database running at the backend.

Microsoft ODS provides a set of C API calls for server-based applications. An example of these applications is extended stored procedures. These applications are added to SQL Server to enhance the functionality of SQL Server. Typically, these applications are written to provide non-SQL-related features and to create gateways between SQL Server and non-SQL-Server-based applications. Applications written using ODS can accept connections from Open Client DB-Library and ODBC clients.

Tools and Utility Programs

The outermost layer is the application layer. All the third-party software and tools that interact with the SQL Server database engine are written using Open Client DB-Library or ODBC APIs. Examples of such applications are MS Query, MS Access, ISQL/w, and so forth.

SQL Server Tools and Utilities

The SQL Server product comes with a number of graphical tools and command-line utilities. These tools and utilities are installed on the server machine at the time of SQL Server installation. These tools and utilities help in performing various tasks. These tasks may range from something very simple, such as adding a user to a database, to more complex tasks, such as setting up replication. Some of the graphical tools available with the SQL Server product family are described in the following sections.

SQL Enterprise Manager

SQL Enterprise Manager is possibly the most important tool for the database administrator. This tool enables enterprise-wide management of SQL Servers. SQL Enterprise Manager is a 32-bit application; therefore, it can run on either Windows NT or Windows 95 clients. Here are some of the major functionalities provided by SQL Enterprise Manager:

- Register multiple SQL servers.
- Start, stop, and configure SQL Server.
- Start, stop, and configure SQL Mail.
- Start and stop SQL Executive, a scheduler for SQL Server.
- Set up and review tasks scheduled by SQL Executive.
- Set up alerts for various SQL Server events.
- Create and drop backup devices for SQL Server databases.
- Create and drop databases and modify database attributes on SQL Server.
- Back up and restore databases.
- Manage SQL Server user logins and security.
- Create, drop, and modify SQL Server objects.

■ Transfer database objects and data from another server, which may or may not be a SQL Server.

■ Set up replication.

A typical screen of SQL Enterprise Manager is shown in Figure 28.9.

FIGURE 28.9.

Managing Servers using SQL Enterprise Manager.

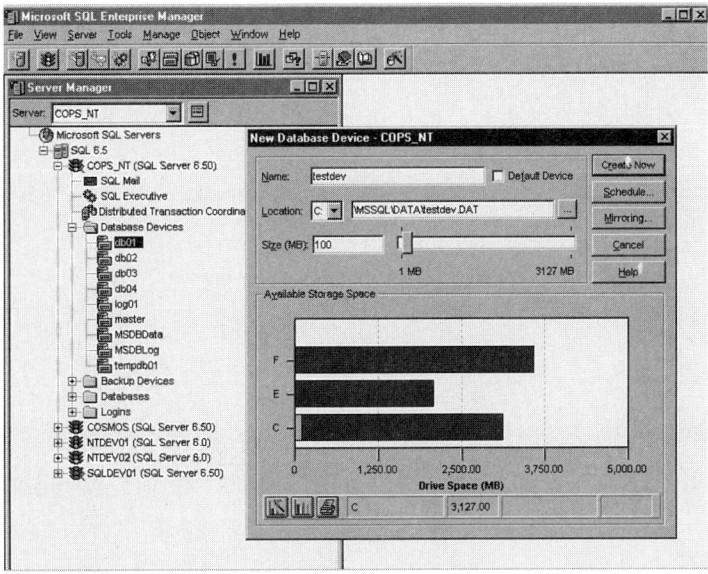

SQL Performance Monitor

SQL Performance Monitor integrates SQL Server with Windows NT Performance Monitor. SQL Server performance counters can then be collected by running this tool or the Windows NT Performance Monitor. This tool provides valuable performance statistics regarding a number of SQL Server performance counters, such as processor time, cache hit ratio, I/O batch size, disk transfer/sec, I/O lazy writes/sec, and so forth. Performance Monitor objects are discussed in Chapter 4, "Monitoring Environment," under the section Understanding SQL Server Performance Counters.

SQL Security Manager

SQL Server provides three types of security modes:

■ Standard Security, in which SQL Server handles and validates user connections directly from the clients, bypassing Windows NT security. Users that only want to access SQL Server on a machine are not required to have an account on Windows NT.

- Integrated Security allows SQL Server user logins to be integrated with Windows NT security. A user can maintain one login ID for both Windows NT and SQL Server. This security method allows SQL Server to make use of Windows NT security features and create a more secured environment.

- Mixed Security allows login IDs to be validated either by standard or integrated security modes.

The SQL security manager tool is used to manage login accounts for SQL Servers that are using Windows NT Integrated Security.

ISQL/w

ISQL is a graphical query tool that enables a user to send queries to SQL Server. From a single ISQL session, a user can open multiple connections to one or more SQL Servers. Some of the capabilities of ISQL include reading queries from and writing queries to an operating system ASCII file, saving query results, formatting query results, and analyzing a query plan by using the showplan and statistics io options. A graphical display of ISQL/w is shown in Figure 28.10.

FIGURE 28.10.

Using the ISQL/w query tool.

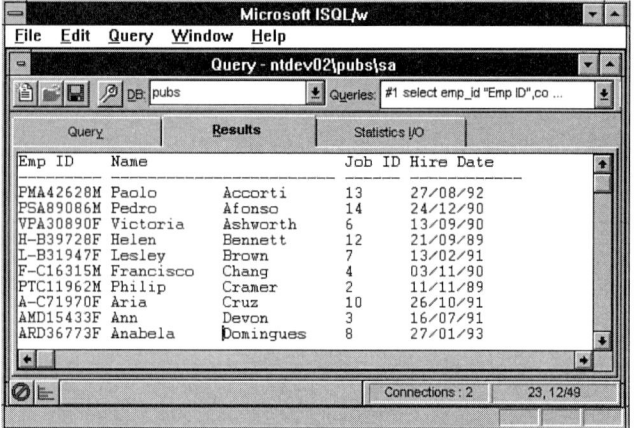

SQL Client Configuration Utility

SQL Client Configuration Utility enables a client to set the default net-library. Network libraries are DLLs that perform network operations (such as passing network packets) between the client and SQL Server. A client uses a specific Net-Library to connect to SQL Server, depending upon the network protocol. For example, to connect to a SQL Server from a client using Named Pipes network protocol, DBNMPNTW.DLL network library is required. If one is using TCP/IP network protocol, the network library required to connect to SQL Server is DBMSSOCN.DLL. For a client to connect to SQL Server using a specific Net-Library, SQL Server must be configured to listen on that protocol. This tool also displays the current version number and timestamp of the Net-Library being used on the server or the client. The Client Configuration Utility also helps in creating multiple alias names for a particular SQL Server.

SQL Service Manager

SQL Service Manager is used to stop, pause, and start SQL Server, SQL Executive, and MSDTC services. These functions can also be performed using SQL Enterprise Manager. A graphical display of the SQL Service Manager is shown in Figure 28.11.

FIGURE 28.11.

Using the SQL Service Manager.

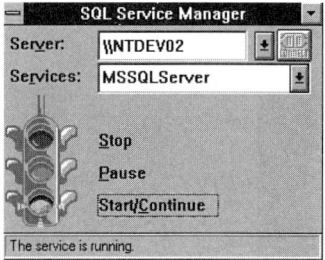

SQL Setup

SQL Setup is provided to reconfigure SQL Server. Database administrators use this tool to change network support options, install new languages, upgrade or remove SQL Server, and set SQL Server options. Some of these options include defining the location of the SQL Server errorlog, location of the master database device, whether to start SQL Server and Executive at machine boot time, defining a profile name for Microsoft Exchange, and so forth.

SQL Server Web Assistant

SQL Server Web Assistant is a graphical tool that enables publication of SQL Server data from SQL queries or stored procedures into HTML files. These files can be placed on a Web server and be browsed using a standard browser. Using this tool, it is possible to define a frequency at which these Web pages can be updated.

SQL Trace

SQL Trace is an administrative tool that provides an online display of all or specific SQL statements going to a specific SQL Server. It also captures connects and disconnects to a SQL Server. This tool enables a database administrator to create filters based on login name, application name, and host name. Output from SQL Trace can be viewed on the screen online or can be saved to a file. Multiple filters can be created against a single server and can be active at the same time. Filters can be paused, stopped, deleted, and saved for future references. SQL Trace is discussed in Chapter 4 under the topic Using SQL Trace.

Command-Line Utilities

BCP stands for bulk-copy program. This utility is used to transfer data between SQL Server and an operating system file. The file format (for example field terminator, record terminator, and so forth) can be specified by the user. The most frequent use of BCP is to import data from another data source. BCP can be used to import data into a SQL Server database from a file created using an Excel spreadsheet. BCP can also be used to export data. BCP can create an operating system file from a SQL Server database table, for example. Other products (such as a spreadsheet program or another DBMS import utility) can then import the data from the file created by BCP. This utility provides a number of optional parameters that can be passed during data import or export. These options include number of rows to transfer, starting record number, last record number, network packet size, and maximum number of errors before BCP aborts. The SQL Server BCP utility also enables users to export data from a VIEW, which is a very helpful feature when one wants to export selective data from various tables. A user has to be a valid user of the database in order to import/export data from a database.

ISQL is a command-line interface to send queries to SQL Server. It is also possible to send a batch of queries using ISQL. This utility provides many optional parameters that can be passed on the command line. These include name of input file containing SQL commands, name of output file where query results will be redirected, print statistics, column formatting, and so forth. A valid database login ID is required for a user to use this utility.

MAKEPIPE AND READPIPE utilities are provided with SQL Server to test network connectivity using Named Pipe protocol. Typically, the MAKEPIPE utility is run on the server, where it opens a pipe and waits for a client to connect to it. The READPIPE utility is run on a client to make sure that it is able to communicate on the pipe connection created by MAKEPIPE.

Summary

Earlier versions of Microsoft SQL Server were primarily used by businesses to support department-level applications. With SQL Server 6.5—which includes features such as built-in replication, SQL Mail, Distributed Transaction Coordinator, versatile and easy-to-use administrative tools, and extremely rich T-SQL query language—Microsoft offers a low-cost and high-performance database engine capable of handling mission-critical applications at the enterprise level. In the next chapter, you examine the step-by-step procedure for installing SQL Server 6.5 on Windows NT.

Installing SQL Server

by Vipul Minocha

IN THIS CHAPTER

CHAPTER 29

This chapter introduces you to SQL Server installation procedures, including the steps that should be taken before and after installation so that the installation process is smooth and uninterrupted.

System Requirements

SQL Server software is available in two configurations: Server Software and Workstation Software. Both configurations provide the same SQL Server features. There are some differences between the two, however:

■ A workstation's software is licensed for a single user, and only 15 concurrent connections are allowed to the database. Server software may be licensed for an unlimited number of users and connections.

■ A workstation's software is less expensive than the server software.

■ Once you have installed the workstation software, it is not possible to upgrade it to the server software.

SQL Server does not require many resources to run. If more resources (such as number of CPUs, memory, and so forth) are assigned to SQL Server, however, better performance gains are achieved. The following are the minimum requirements necessary for a successful installation of SQL Server:

■ *Operating System.* Microsoft SQL Server 6.5 runs only under Windows NT version 3.51. It will be supported on Windows NT version 4.0 when it becomes commercially available.

■ *Processor Architecture.* SQL Server can run successfully on a hardware platform that is based on Intel 32-Bit, MIPS and DEC Alpha processors. The minimum processor architecture requirement for Intel-based machines is 80486.

■ *Disk Space.* The installation procedure copies SQL Server software in the installation directory specified during SQL Server setup. It also creates the MASTER device on which various system databases (master, model, tempdb, and so forth) are created. The minimum disk space requirement for SQL Server software is 56M. This does not include space required by online books and the master device. SQL Server online books take 1M to 15M of disk space depending on whether books are run from CD or the hard drive. The minimum disk space required for the MASTER device is 25M.

■ *Memory.* SQL Server can be installed on a machine running with 16M of memory. However, if the server is going to participate in data replication, the machine must have at least 32M of memory, of which at least 16M should be assigned to SQL Server.

■ *Network Software.* No special network software is required for SQL Server to run. SQL Server makes use of the operating system network services.

> **TIP**
>
> Faster processors and more memory are two of the most important factors governing the performance of a system. If more memory is allocated to SQL Server, it can cache large amounts of data, and many requests for data can be satisfied from memory rather than doing physical I/Os. CPU-bound queries (such as queries performing complex mathematical computations) are greatly benefited by faster processors.

Planning and Things to Consider

In order to have a reliable, stable, and high-performance database engine, it is important that each step of SQL Server installation is carefully planned with good understanding of the operating environment (hardware resources, network type, and so forth). The SQL Server SETUP program prompts you to enter values for a number of parameters during the course of installation. Before you start the installation, it is generally a good idea to have a list of these parameters and their values ready. This list contains information such as SQL Server software location, location of the MASTER device, character set information, user account name under which SQL Executive will run, and so forth. Having this list ready before the setup saves a lot of time during SQL Server installation This list can also be used as a reference for future SQL Server installations. The following sections explain the factors that should be considered and planned before you start installation of SQL Server.

Select a File System

SQL Server can run with both FAT and NTFS file systems. There are no significant performance improvements by choosing one over the other. In a mainly read-only environment, however, NTFS is normally faster because it does transaction logging. The NTFS file system also provides better security (C2 level) and recoverability. The FAT file system may be faster in write operations because it does not perform any transaction logging. Given these facts, you should choose a file system that best suits your needs. From the security and recoverability points of view, it is prudent to have your production environment running on the NTFS file system.

Create SQL Executive User Accounts

An individual who is responsible for installing SQL Server should have Administrative privileges on the machine.

SQL Server's scheduler component, SQL Executive, runs as a service under Windows NT. This service can run either under LocalSystem or under a user account. If the service runs under a LocalSystem account, SQL Executive will not be able to perform various jobs, such as task scheduling and data replication. Assigning a user account allows the service to do network connectivity. Windows NT will not allow a service that is running under the Local System account to communicate with other servers on the network. Therefore, if you need to schedule tasks through SQL Executive or set up data replication, be sure that SQL Executive service runs under a user account. This user account can be created on the machine on which SQL Server will be installed or at a domain level.

> **TIP**
>
> The user account for SQL Executive should be a part of Administrative group and should be created with Log on as a Service privilege. It is generally a good idea to create a user account at the domain level; if you have multiple SQL Servers, they can all share the same account name. It is also convenient from a maintenance point of view to select the password never expires option at the time of creating the user account.

Verify Network Functionality

SQL Server can use a number of network protocols to communicate with the clients. Verify that the network is configured properly and that you can ping to the machine from a client, using either an absolute IP address or a friendly name using DNS. You should also choose the network protocols that will be used by SQL Server. If you are using TCP/IP protocol, for example, make sure that the socket number that will be used by SQL Server is not in use by any other application on the same machine.

Select Software Location

SQL Server software takes up 55–60M of disk space (not including the space used by the MASTER device and online books). Therefore, you should have enough disk space available on the drive on which you plan to install SQL Server. The SETUP program creates all the necessary directory structures for SQL Server software during the installation.

Select Master Device Size

During SQL Server installation, master, model, and tempdb databases are created on the MASTER device. The MASTER device is a file created during SQL server installation and is critical to the operation of SQL Server. Choose the location of the MASTER device carefully, preferably on a drive that is mirrored. Many third-party products install their stored procedure in the master database. If you plan to use such tools, you should estimate size of the MASTER device accordingly.

Select Default Character Set

SQL Server supports character sets for many languages. Each character set is given a standard code called code page. For example, the ISO character set is called code page 8859-1. SQL Server's default character set is ISO. If your application can include words and letters from different languages, you must choose an appropriate character set.

If North American and European characters are used in an application, for example, you should use the 850 Multilingual character set. The following character sets are available with SQL Server:

- ISO (code page 8859-1) is the default character set, which complies with ANSI and Windows NT character sets.

- Multilingual (code page 850) includes characters for most European, North American, and South American countries.

- US English (code page 437) includes characters from US English, along with some extended graphical characters.

- Japanese (code page 932) includes the Japanese character set.

- Chinese includes two character sets: Simplified Chinese character set (code page 936) for Chinese and Singapore character sets, and Traditional character set (code page 950) for Chinese, Taiwan, and Hong Kong character sets.

- Korean (code page 949) includes characters for the Korean language.

- Central European (code page 1250) includes characters for Central European countries.

- Cyrillic (code page 1251) includes the Cyrillic character set.

- Greek (code page 1253) includes the Greek character set.

- Turkish (code page 1254) includes the Turkish character set.

- Hebrew (code page 1255) includes the Hebrew character set.

- Arabic (code page 1256) includes the Arabic character set.

- Baltic (code page 1257) includes the Baltic character set.

Select Default Sort Order

Sort order is the collate sequence in which data is presented to the user (for example, `display Tom before tom` or `display Tom afer tom`). A number of T-SQL commands (such as `ORDER BY`, `GROUP BY`, and so forth) are affected by the way a sort order is defined on a SQL Server. SQL Server's default sort order is dictionary order with case-insensitive. A dictionary order is one in which data is displayed to the user based on dictionary collate sequence. Case-insensitive sort order signifies that SQL Server does not distinguish between an uppercase or lowercase letter. Therefore, such a SQL Server will treat a column value of tom, TOM, and tOM identically during comparisons (in a WHERE clause). When the data is displayed using ORDER BY, it is displayed in the dictionary order with no preference for an upper- and lowercase letter. Depending on the nature of your application, you must choose an appropriate sort order. SQL Server provides a number of sort order options. Some of the most commonly used sort orders are as follows:

- *Dictionary order, case-insensitive* is the default sort order. SQL Server does not differentiate between uppercase and lowercase letters, and data sorting result is intermixed.

- *Binary order* sorts data according to the numeric ASCII values of characters—that is, all uppercase letters are sorted before lowercase letters. This sort order provides the fastest data sorting. Because uppercase letters are always sorted before lowercase, it is not a very commonly used sort order for business applications.

- *Dictionary order, case-sensitive* differentiates between uppercase and lowercase letters and sorts data in dictionary order.

- *Dictionary order, case-insensitive, uppercase preference* does not differentiate between uppercase and lowercases letters, and uppercase letters are sorted before lowercase letters.

- *Dictionary order, case-insensitive, accent-insensitive* does not differentiate between uppercase and lowercase letters, including the ones that have diacritical marks (for example, e = è = E), and data sorting result is intermixed.

> **TIP**
>
> If the language installed on SQL Server is Code page 850 (Multilingual character set), which includes a number of characters with accents (diacritical marks such as è, é, ê, ë, and so forth), dictionary order, case-insensitive, accent-insensitive sort order is more useful than dictionary order, case-insensitive sort order from an application perspective.

Step-by-Step Installation Procedure

SQL Server installation includes installing SQL Server software in a designated directory and creating MASTER device and system databases, tools and utilities, and so forth. After a successful SQL Server installation, the installation procedure creates a program group called Microsoft SQL Server 6.5, as shown in Figure 29.1. The default directory of SQL Server software is C:\MSSQL. The SQL Server installation procedure creates the following directories under the installation directory:

- Root directory is C:\MSSQL (or the directory location you selected in the earlier section, Planning and Things to Consider).

■ Subdirectories are the following:

BIN is the location for executables and DLLs for Windows and DOS-based clients.

BINN is the location for executables and DLLs for Windows NT-based clients.

CHARSETS is the location for character set and sort order files required to define the character set for SQL Server.

DATA is the default location of database device files. By default, the MASTER device (master.dat) gets created in this directory during installation.

INSTALL is the location for various script files required during SQL Server installation and output files created during various steps of the installation.

LOG is the default location of the SQL Server error log file. Most of the SQL Server messages, depending on the criticality of the errors, are stored in this file.

REPLDATA is the location used during the data replication for storing data definitions and the data for various tables participating in replication.

SQLOLE is the location for sample files for SQL-DMO (SQL distributed Management Objects), which can be used to write applications for managing SQL Server.

SNMP keeps a copy of MSSQL.MIB file, which is used by an SNMP (Simple Network Management Protocol) application to monitor SQL Server.

SYMBOLS is the location for files used mainly for debugging purposes to generate stack traces and so forth.

FIGURE 29.1.

Installing SQL Server tools and utilities.

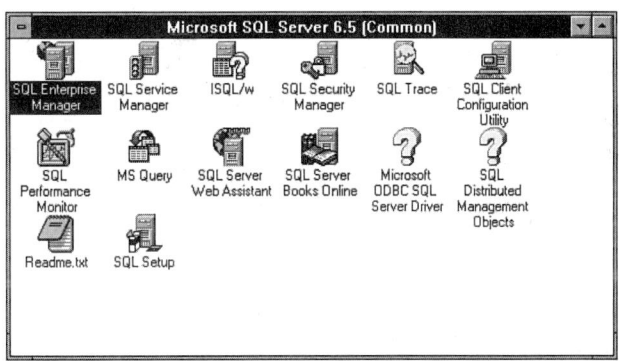

Administrative privileges are required by the user on the machine on which SQL Server is going to be installed. The SETUP program enables you to install SQL Server on a local machine or on a remote machine. Most of the steps are common to both types of installations. For remote installation of SQL Server, there are some additional steps required that are discussed in a later section.

29

INSTALLING SQL SERVER

Local Installation

The following steps are required to install SQL Server on a machine running Windows NT.

Step 1: Running Setup

You can install SQL Server either from the CD or from a network drive containing SQL Server software by running the SETUP.EXE program. Based on the platform type, the SETUP program is executed from the following locations:

- \I386, for Intel-based platforms
- \ALPHA, for DEC Alpha-based platforms
- \MIPS, for MIPS-based computers

Once you run the SETUP program, you are presented with the screen shown in Figure 29.2. This screen basically greets you with a message indicating the version number of SQL Server you are about to install.

FIGURE 29.2.

Starting SQL Server installation.

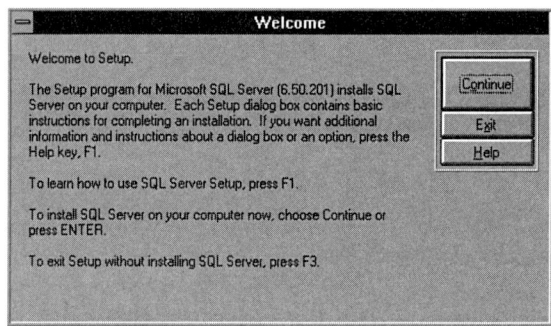

You can always use online help by clicking on the Help button (or by pressing F1). Click on the Continue button to go to step 2.

Step 2: Providing Licensing Information

This step requires you to enter your name (see Figure 29.3) or the name of the person responsible for managing this SQL Server in the Name textbox. This is a mandatory field. Although entries in the Company and Product ID fields are optional, it is a good idea to provide these values from product support standpoint. Product ID can be located on the software distribution CD. Enter the relevant information and click on the Continue button to go to the next step.

FIGURE 29.3.

Providing name, organization, and product ID information.

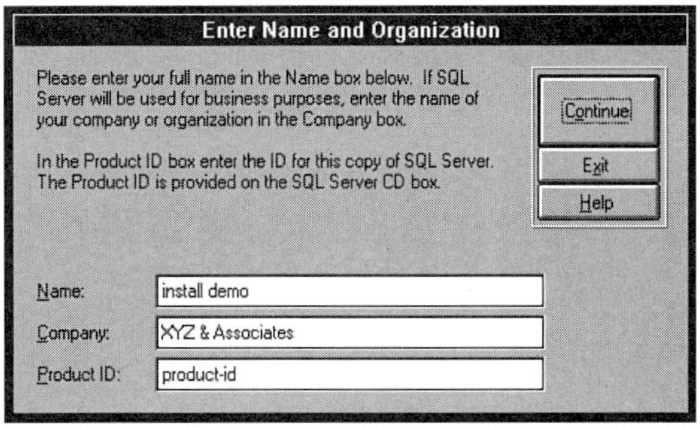

Step 3: Choosing Install Options

This screen presents various installation options (see Figure 29.4). For a new installation the following three options are activated:

1. The Install SQL Server and Utilities radio button is activated by default for a new installation.

2. Upgrade SQL Server is usually selected for upgrading a previously installed SQL Server to the new release.

3. Install Utilities Only is selected when you want to install SQL Server tools and utilities only (such as ISQL/w, Enterprise Manager, SQL Server Web Assistant, and so forth). Choosing this option will not install SQL Server on the machine.

The other options (Change Network Support, Add Language, Rebuild Master Database, Set Server Options, Set Security Options, and Remove SQL Server) are activated when SQL Server is already installed on the server. For example, Change Network Support option is required when you want to add another network protocol or modify values of the existing ones (for example, changing the socket number for TCP/IP protocol from the current value to a new value). To continue installation of SQL Server, click on the Continue button.

FIGURE 29.4.

Choosing SQL Server installation options.

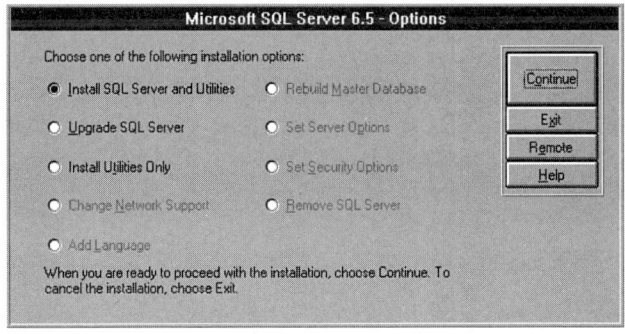

Step 4: Selecting Licensing Mode

At the time of purchase of SQL Server, your company must have agreed to either per-server or per-seat licensing mode (see Figure 29.5). The per-server licensing mode requires that each client license access only a specific SQL Server, and there is a limit on the number of concurrent connections to SQL Server. The per-seat license mode requires that each client connecting to SQL Server has a client access license. A client access license is not tied to any SQL Server. Based on the licensing agreement, you must choose a valid licensing mode. Choosing either of the two options does not change the installation procedure in any way. Select the valid licensing mode and click on the Continue button to go to the next step. It is important to remember that if you choose per-seat mode, you can't change back to per-server licensing mode. Therefore, if you are not sure about the licensing mode, choose per-server mode to continue with installation of SQL Server.

FIGURE 29.5.

Selecting licensing mode.

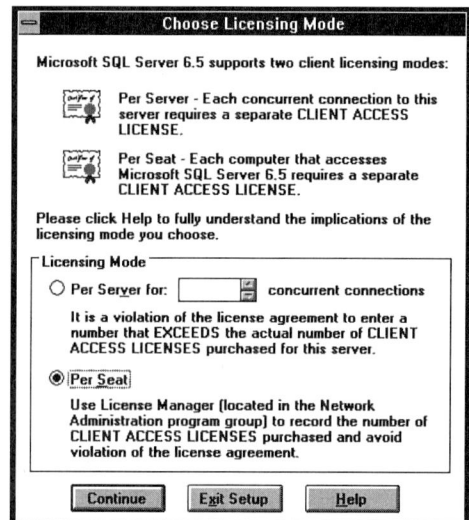

Step 5: Confirming Licensing Agreement

Before you can proceed with the actual installation, you must comply with the licensing agreement. If you agree with the licensing agreement, check the box that says 'I agree that:', and click on the OK button (see Figure 29.6); otherwise, click on the Cancel button and go back to the previous screen to choose the correct licensing mode.

FIGURE 29.6.

Confirming licensing agreement.

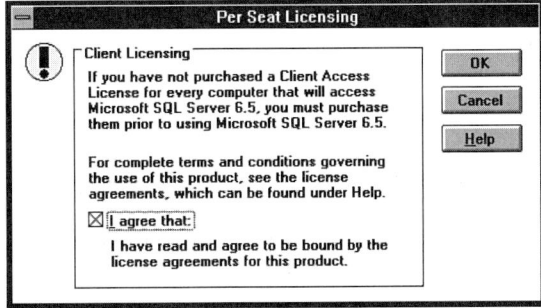

Step 6: Designating SQL Software Location

This is the first real step toward the installation of SQL Server. This dialog box prompts you for the drive and the directory location where the SQL Server software will be copied (see Figure 29.7). The default drive for the installation is C, and the default directory is \MSSQL. SQL Server software requires about 56M of disk space for the software, 25M for the MASTER device, and 1–15M for online books, depending on whether online books are installed on the hard drive or run from the CD ROM drive. Choose a different drive letter if there is not enough space on the C drive or if you wish to install the software on a different drive. There is seldom a reason to change the directory name for a new installation. If you want to continue installation with the default selection, click on the Continue button; otherwise, enter the valid drive letter and/or the directory name and then click on the Continue button.

FIGURE 29.7.

Designating SQL Server software location.

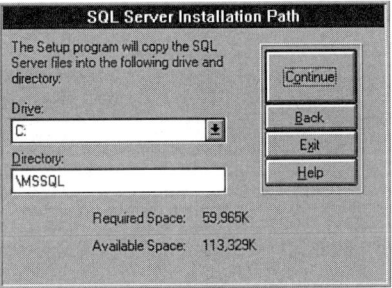

Step 7: Choosing Location for the MASTER Device

The MASTER device is a physical file on which master, model, msdb, and tempdb databases are created during the installation process. The dialog box shown in Figure 29.8 displays default values for the drive (C:), location (\MSSQL\DATA), filename (master.dat), and size (25M) for the MASTER device. If you want to continue with the default values, click on the Continue button; otherwise, select the desired drive letter, directory location, name of the MASTER device file, and size of the MASTER device; then click on the Continue button to go to the next step of installation. SETUP program creates the directory path if the specified directory does not exist. It is also important to note that the name of the MASTER device can have a maximum of eight characters with a three-character file extension.

FIGURE 29.8.

Choosing MASTER device location.

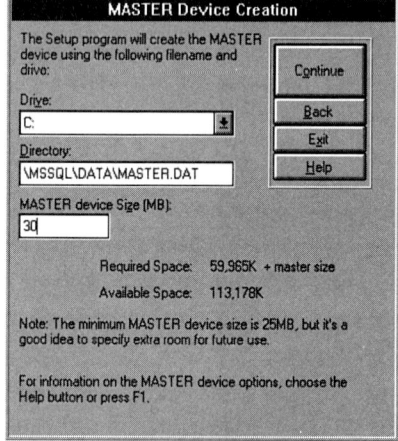

TIP

Some third-party tools create stored procedures in the master database. Therefore, to provide space for growth of objects in the master database, it is advisable to create the size of the MASTER device greater than the default value (25M). If you do not wish to increase the size of the MASTER device at the time of installation, it is possible to increase the size at a later stage using the DISK RESIZE T-SQL command.

Step 8: Selecting Auto Start Options

This step (see Figure 29.9) enables you to decide whether you want SQL Server and SQL Executive to start automatically after the machine reboots. It is a good idea to select these options, especially in case of a production environment where you want SQL Server and the SQL Executive to come up as soon as possible to minimize downtime.

NOTE

SQL Server also provides the facility to execute one or more stored procedures at the time when SQL Server is started. These stored procedures are executed after all the databases have been recovered. Execution of these stored procedures can be very useful in performing certain housekeeping tasks and for notification purposes. Startup procedures cannot accept parameters and run under the login ID of sa.

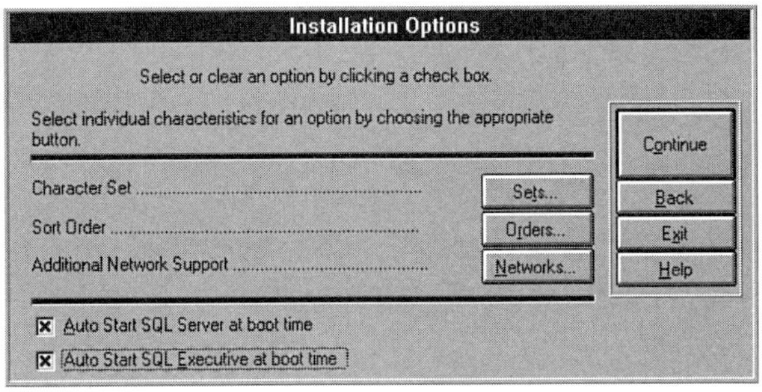

FIGURE 29.9.

Selecting autostart options.

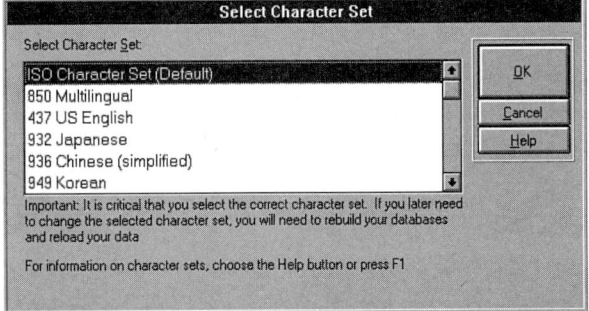

Step 9: Choosing a Character Set

This step involves choosing a language character set for the SQL Server. Click on the Sets button (see Figure 29.10) to choose the character set you want to install on your server. The default character set is ISO, which is compatible with ANSI and Windows NT character sets. After selecting an appropriate character set, click on the OK button to continue with the installation.

FIGURE 29.10.

Choosing a character set.

Step 10: Installing Sort Order

Click on the Orders button (see Figure 29.11) to choose the sort order you want to install on your server. SQL Server provides a number of sort options. The default Sort order for SQL Server is dictionary order, case-insensitive. After selecting the sort order of your choice, click on the OK button to continue with the installation.

29

INSTALLING SQL
SERVER

FIGURE 29.11.

Installing sort order.

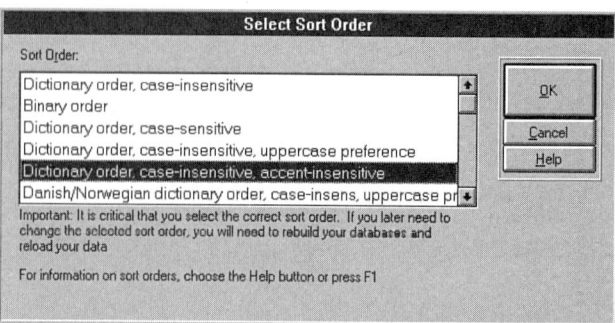

WARNING

Be very careful when selecting a sort order or a character set for the SQL Server. Once a character set or a sort order is installed on a server, the only way to change it is by rebuilding the master database. Database backups taken from one SQL Server with a particular character set/sort order are not compatible with those taken from a SQL Server running with another character set/sort order. If the character set/sort order is changed on a SQL Server, database dumps prior to the change are not recognized by the SQL Server with the new character set/sort order. Therefore, it will not be possible for you to load the databases from the previous backups. To avoid such a situation, it is important that, before you change the character set or sort order, you save all the database object definitions (such as table, trigger, procedure, and so forth) and transfer the data to operating system files. After the new language or new sort order is installed on the server, you recreate your databases using these files and reload the data.

NOTE

It is important to note that character set and sort order options are available at the SQL Server level, and all the databases on that particular server use the same character set and sort order.

Step 11: Selecting Network Support

By default, SQL Server listens on the Named Pipes network protocol. The default pipe name for SQL Server is \\pipe\sql\query. However, using the dialog box shown in Figure 29.11, it is possible to install various other Net-Libraries for SQL Server. Using these libraries, SQL Server can listen on multiple protocols at the same time. Click on the Networks button to choose network protcols for SQL Server. Figure 29.12 shows Named Pipes and TCP/IP network protocols being selected. Choose the protocols based on your environment, and click on the OK button to continue with the installation.

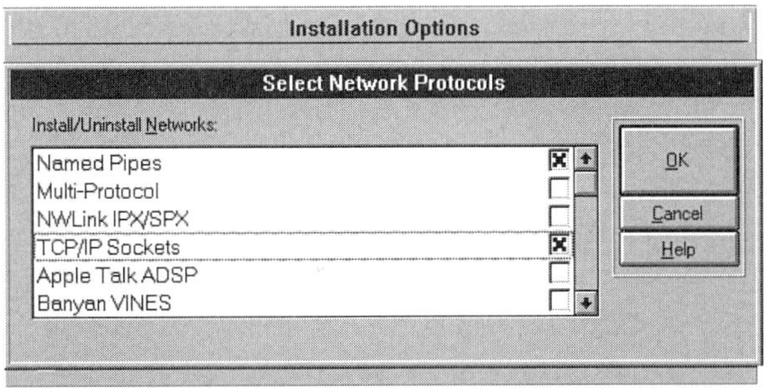

FIGURE 29.12.

Selecting network protocols.

WARNING

It is important that you do *not* deselect the Named Pipes protocol option during the installation, because the SETUP program uses the Named Pipes protocol for SQL Server installation. It is generally not a good idea to disable Named Pipes, because SQL Executive connects to SQL Server through this protocol. Although there is seldom a reason to change the name of a pipe, you can do so after the successful installation of SQL Server. You are then required to configure SQL Executive to connect to SQL Server using the new value of the pipe.

Step 12: Review Changes

At this time, you have already selected a character set, sort order, and network protocols for SQL Server installation. If you need to change any of these options, you can go back to the previous steps and make necessary changes. If there are no changes to be made, click on the Continue button to proceed with the installation.

Step 13: Setting Up a SQL Executive Account

SQL Executive runs as a service under Windows NT. This service can run under Windows NT either by using a system account or a user account name. A system account is a LocalSystem account on NT. If a LocalSystem account is used, certain scheduled and data replication tasks will not work. However, this can be a useful option in cases where you have not defined a user account for SQL Executive service. Until you create a user account, you can leave SQL Executive running under LocalSystem account and then change it at a later stage to run under a user account. A user account can be a local account or a domain account. It is necessary for the user account to be a part of the Administrator group on the machine on which SQL Server is running. This dialog box (see Figure 29.13) prompts you to enter the name of user account and the password. Alternatively, you can choose the Install to log on as LocalSystem account radio button, if you want SQL Executive to run under LocalSystem account. Click on Continue after providing the relevant information on the dialog box.

FIGURE 29.13.

*Providing SQL
Executive user account
name.*

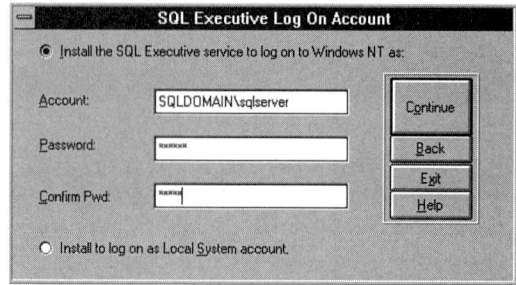

Step 14: Providing Network Information

This dialog box (see Figure 29.14) appears only if you select a network protocol other than the Named Pipes protocol in step 11 (for example, TCP/IP network protocol). This screen prompts you to enter additional information required by the network protocol you selected for SQL Server. If you had selected, for example, TCP/IP as a network protocol for SQL Server, this screen prompts you for the TCP/IP socket number. Enter the relevant information on this screen and click on Continue to finish the installation.

FIGURE 29.14.

*Providing network
information.*

NOTE

TCP/IP socket number 1433 is officially assigned for MS SQL Server by Internet Assigned Number Authority. However, you should still make sure that there is no other application on the machine using this socket number. SQL Server will fail to listen on the TCP/IP port if there is another application using the same TCP/IP socket number. You can run the netstat command from the command prompt to check the TCP/IP ports that are currently in use. It is generally a good idea to use a standard socket number for SQL Server throughout the enterprise to maintain consistency.

After step 14, the SETUP program copies the software in the designated directories, creates the MASTER device, creates master, model, and tempdb databases, installs ODBC drivers, and installs tools and utilities. Status of each of these actions is provided on the screen such as the one shown in Figure 29.15.

Figure 29.16 indicates the success of the installation by displaying the SQL Server version number and a prompt that enables you to exit to Windows NT.

FIGURE 29.15.

SQL Server installation progress information.

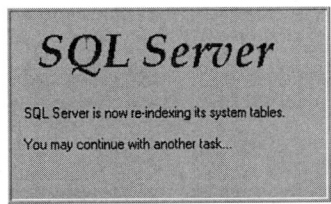

FIGURE 29.16.

SQL Server installation completion information.

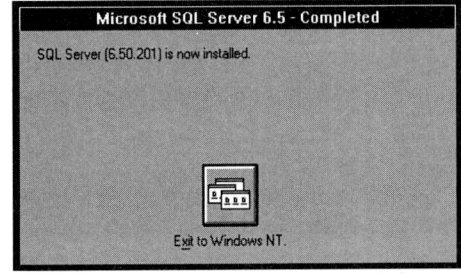

Step 15: Starting SQL Server and SQL Executive

After completion of installation, reboot the machine on which SQL Server is installed. SQL Server and SQL Executive should start automatically if the auto startup options were selected during the installation procedure. If not, SQL Server and SQL Executive can be started by using the SQL Server Manager tool.

Remote Installation

It is also possible to install SQL Server on a remote machine. Remote installation of SQL Server is quite similar to a local installation. The only difference is that with remote installation, you are required to provide the name of SQL Server installation drive, the drive on which Windows NT is installed, and the location for the MASTER device (see Figure 29.17). To perform remote installation, follow steps 1 and 2 of local installation. Click on the Remote button to continue with remote installation. Select the Remote Installation checkbox to indicate that you want to perform remote installation of SQL Server. Enter the name of the remote server in the Remote Server Name textbox. Provide the drive letter information for SQL Server installation drive, Windows NT installation drive, and the MASTER device. Click on OK to continue with the remote installation. From this point onward, all the steps are similar to local installation.

29

INSTALLING SQL SERVER

FIGURE 29.17.

Providing information for remote installation.

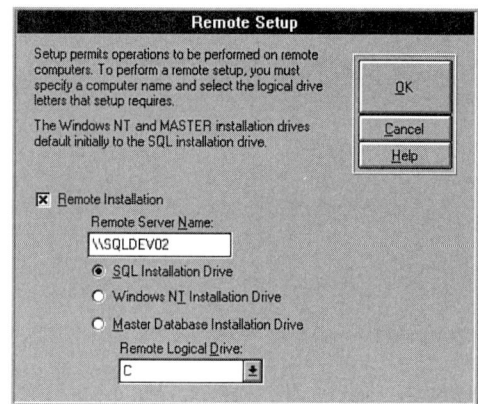

Unattended Installation

In a large organization, it may be required to install multiple SQL Servers with identical configurations. In such cases, it could be very time-consuming to install all the SQL Servers interactively by using the SETUP graphical user interface. Unattended installation is a more efficient method of installing SQL Servers, where one does not need to provide any input to the user prompts. Unattended installation is accomplished by using the SETUP program and providing the name of an input file that contains all installation parameters in a specified format. The command syntax for unattended installation is the following:

```
SETUP /t IniFilePath = "initialization file name"
```

Here is the text of a typical initialization file:

```
[License]
FullName=Test User
OrgName=XYZ Co.
ProductID=!@#$
Mode=1

[SQLPath]
SQLPath=\MSSQL
LogicalSQLDrive=C:

[MasterPath]
MasterSize=30
LogicalDBDrive=C:
MasterDBPath=\MSSQL\DATA
MasterDBFileName=MASTER.DAT

[NewOptions]
AutoServerService=CHECKED
AutoExecutiveService=CHECKED
BooksOnline=1
```

```
[CharSet]
CharSet=cp 850
[SortOrder]
SortFileName=noaccent.850
SortConfigValue=44

[Network]
NetLibList={"SSNMPN60"}
ServerNMPipe=\\.\pipe\sql\query

[LogonAccount]
LocalSystem=NOTCHECKED
Username=devdomain\sqlserver
Password=*******
```

> **WARNING**
>
> The password for the user account for SQL Executive is written in the initialization file in plain text. Because this user account has administrative privileges, it is important to keep this file in location with appropriate security access.

> **NOTE**
>
> SQL Server has a generic login called sa (system administrator). This login is responsible for managing SQL Server. An sa login is required to initialize the database device, create databases, create SQL Server logins, and so forth. Any person who knows the sa password can log on to SQL Server with all the privileges on the system. When SQL Server is installed for the first time, there is no password assigned to sa. Therefore, it is important to change it as soon as possible after the installation.

Issues and Cautions

The SETUP program provides a friendly and reliable graphical user interface to install SQL Server. Typically, you will not have any problems during the installation process. However, there are certain issues that can result in installation failures. Insufficient disk space, probably, is the most common cause of installation failure. Be sure that you have enough disk space for SQL Server software, MASTER device, and online books. SQL Server SETUP program also writes messages to a number of output files during various steps of the installation. All these files have .OUT extensions, and the default location of these files is C:\MSSQL\INSTALL, unless a different root directory was specified during SQL Server installation. In that case, the location of the files are DRIVE:\ROOTDIR\INSTALL. You can view the most recently created .OUT file to identify the cause of the failed installation. The SETUP program also writes

29

INSTALLING SQL
SERVER

all the messages to an errorlog file. Default location of the errorlog file is C:\MSSQL\ LOG\ERRORLOG, unless the default software location was changed during the installation process. The SQL Server SETUP program also writes to the Windows NT event log. You can view the SQL Server errorlog by using a text editor. The Windows NT event log can be viewed by using the Event Viewer graphical tool. By looking at these errorlogs, you can get some information about the cause of installation failure.

Configuration Tasks After Setup Is Complete

SQL Server is a highly configurable database engine. There are a number of configuration parameters that can be set by the database administrator for optimal performance of SQL Server. The SETUP program installs SQL Server with reasonable default values for these configuration parameters. However, there are certain parameters, such as memory, user connections, number of devices, open databases, and so forth, where the choice made by the SETUP program may not be suitable for a specific environment. Therefore, after the installation, it is important to configure these parameters. Some of the advanced configuration parameters are discussed at length in Chapter 31, "SQL Server Monitoring and Tuning." Use the following steps to configure a SQL Server after a successful installation, by using the SQL Enterprise Manager graphical administration tool:

1. Create SQL Server Group with SQL Enterprise Manager.

   SQL Enterprise Manager allows you to logically group SQL Servers. A group with name SQL 6.5 is created by default. To create a server group, invoke SQL Enterprise Manager from the SQL Server 6.5 program manager group. From the Server menu, select Server Groups. Enter the name of the group you want to create in the textbox and click on the Add button.

2. Register SQL Server with SQL Enterprise Manager.

   Click on the Server group in which you want to register a SQL Server. From the Server menu of SQL Enterprise Manager, select Register Server. Enter the name of the machine on which SQL Server is running in the Server textbox. Enter the login ID sa in the Login Id textbox and click on the Register button.

3. Change the sa password.

   To change the password from SQL Enterprise Manager, select the server name in the main window (also known as the Server Manager window). From the Manage menu, select the logins option. From the drop-down list box Login Name, select sa. Enter a new password in the Password textbox and click on the Modify button. Another dialog box is presented asking for the confirmation of the new password. Enter the new password again and click on the OK button. The new password will take effect the next time someone tries to log in as sa.

> **NOTE**
>
> Passwords for all SQL Server logins can also be changed using the sp_password system stored procedure from an ISQL session.

4. Change the SQL Server configuration parameters.

   SQL Server provides a number of configurable parameters that can be set for an optimal value for a particular environment by the administrator. These configuration parameters range from very basic to advanced. Some basic parameters that should be changed just after the installation are locks, memory, open databases, open objects and user connections. Memory in SQL Server is expressed in terms of 2K pages (for example, a memory value of 8192 means 8192 x 2K = 16M). Choose a value for these parameters that is appropriate for your environment. For example, if the machine on which SQL Server is running has 256M of RAM, and if SQL Server is the only application running on that server, it is appropriate to assign 200M to 225M to SQL Server. These parameters can be changed either by executing the sp_configure system stored procedure through an ISQL session (see Figure 29.18) or by using the SQL Enterprise Manager. To change SQL Server configuration parameters using SQL Enterprise Manager, click the right mouse button on the server name to bring up a pop-up menu and choose configure (or choose SQL Server, Configure from the Server menu). Choose the Configuration tab and enter the appropriate values in the appropriate fields (see Figure 29.19).

FIGURE 29.18.

Setting up SQL Server configuration parameters using ISQL/w.

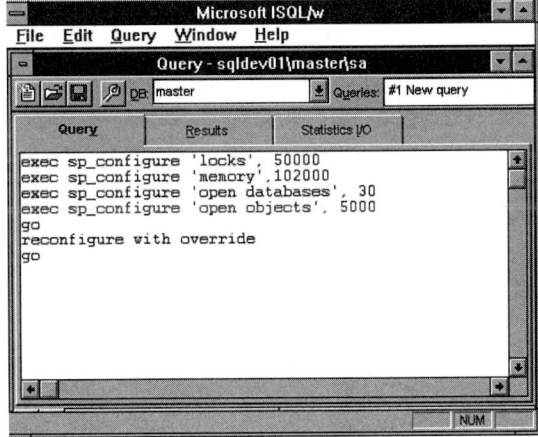

FIGURE 29.19.

Setting up SQL Server configuration parameters using SQL Enterprise Manager.

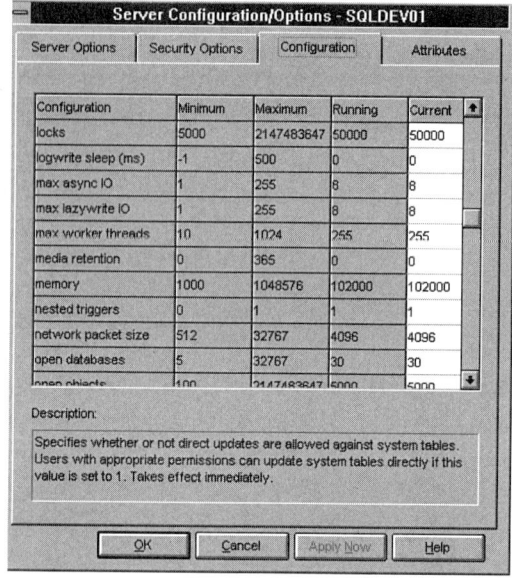

> **TIP**
>
> Some of the parameters are dynamic in nature and take effect immediately (such as `allow updates`). Some take effect upon the next start of SQL Server (such as memory, user connections, and so forth).

5. Expand the tempdb database.

   Database tempdb is created during installation of SQL Server. The initial size of tempdb is 2M, and all of it resides on the MASTER device. tempdb is actively used by end-users for creating temporary objects and by SQL Server for sorting purposes and for creating its internal work tables (created by the GROUP BY clause). In most of the cases, 2M is not sufficient space for the end-user applications and should be increased in size. It is preferred that tempdb be created on its own device, which is not shared by another database for performance reasons. A device for tempdb can be created by SQL Enterprise Manager or by using a DISK INIT T-SQL command. Subsequently, the database can be altered in size by the graphical tool or by using ALTER DATABASE T-SQL command. You can choose the size of the tempdb database based on the nature of the applications running on SQL Server.

6. Back up the master database.

   The master database holds critical information about user accounts, database storage allocations, SQL Server configurable parameters, system stored procedures, and so forth in various system catalog tables. Therefore, it is quite important to back up the master database immediately after any changes are made that affect it. After the installation, you should create a dump device for the master database, either by using SQL Enterprise Manager or by using the sp_addumpdevice system stored procedure. The database can then be backed up on the backup device, either by using Enterprise Manager or by using the DUMP DATABASE T-SQL command.

Verifying Successful Installation

A SQL Server installation can be verified by trying to connect to the SQL Server from a client—such as ISQL/w on all the active network protocols (the protocls SQL Server is listening on). The following steps help determine whether the installation is successful:

1. Make sure SQL Server is running.
2. Connect to SQL Server from a client on the same machine using ISQL/w.
3. Connect to SQL Server from a client on a network using ISQL/w.
4. Make sure SQL Executive is running.
5. Schedule a task through SQL Enterprise Manager and verify the results after the task is executed.

If you are able to perform all these tasks, you have successfully installed a SQL Server.

Summary

Installing SQL Server on a Windows NT machine is a relatively simple task. Careful planning will always result in a SQL Server installation that is high-performance, reliable, and does not require frequent configuration changes. If you have many SQL Servers to install, it is beneficial to have an initialization file and run the unattended setup. In the next chapter, you explore the roles and responsibilities of a database administrator and effective database administration techniques.

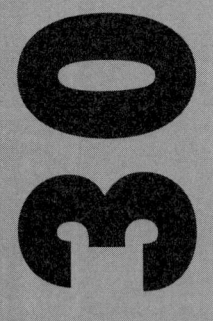

SQL Server Administration

by Vipul Minocha

IN THIS CHAPTER

CHAPTER

30

After SQL Server has been successfully installed on a server, the system administrator undertakes various responsibilities to manage it. Some of these responsibilities include creating database devices, managing space on existing devices, creating databases and monitoring space usage, creating segments, creating backup devices, backing up and restoring databases, creating SQL Server logins, managing security, configuring SQL Server for optimal performance, designing databases, performance, and tuning, and diagnosing SQL Server problems. Depending on the size of the applications and the number of SQL Servers in an organization, one or more system administrators might be assigned to perform these functions. SQL Server provides a special login called sa (System Administrator). This login is responsible for managing SQL Server. Anyone who can connect to SQL Server using the sa login and password can perform system administrative tasks.

> **NOTE**
>
> SQL Server provides a graphical tool, called SQL Enterprise Manager, that enables system administrators to manage multiple SQL Servers in an organization. Although graphical tools are convenient for performing day-to-day operations, they do not provide any details on how a particular task is executed at SQL Server. For this reason, this chapter focuses on the commands that are used to accomplish such tasks (such as creating devices, databases, segments, and so on). You can send all these commands to SQL Server by using a query tool such as ISQL/W.

Creating Devices

SQL Server supports multiple databases, both system and user. Before a user database can be created on a SQL Server, it is necessary to initialize database devices on which the various user databases can be created. A database device can hold one or more databases, depending on the space available on the device.

Initializing Database Devices

A database device is a file on an operating system, and it must be initialized before it can be used for creating databases on it. A database device on a SQL Server is created (or initialized) by use of the DISK INIT T-SQL. command. After a device has been successfully initialized, multiple databases can be created on that particular device. This is the syntax of the DISK INIT command:

```
DISK INIT    NAME = "logical name of the device",
        PHYSNAME = "physical name ",
        VDEVNO = device number,
        SIZE = size of device on 2K blocks
        [, VSTART = virtual address]
```

All the parameters of the DISK INIT command are described here:

- *NAME (mandatory parameter)*. This is the logical name of the device. A logical name is a method of mapping a physical filename to a more meaningful name. After a device has been initialized, it is always referred to and accessed by its logical name. The logical name of the device is meaningful only within SQL Server; it has no significance outside SQL Server. This name should conform to SQL Server naming rules (for example, the name cannot exceed 30 characters and cannot have embedded spaces in it).

- *PHYSNAME (mandatory parameter)*. This is the actual physical location of the file. This should be a valid path and must conform to operating system rules for file naming conventions. The account name under which SQL Server is running should have permission to create this file. SQL Server does not enable you to create a database device across the network.

- *VDEVNO (mandatory parameter)*. This parameter stands for virtual device number. Each database device is assigned a unique VDEVNO ranging from 0 to 255. Because device number 0 is reserved for the MASTER device, the legal values for this parameter are 1 through 255. When you create a device, you must provide a VDEVNO number that is not in use. To find out the virtual device numbers that are in use, execute the sp_helpdevice system stored procedure.

- *SIZE (mandatory parameter)*. This parameter specifies the size of the device in terms of 2K blocks. For example, a value of 8192 for this parameter creates a 16M device (8192*2K). The minimum size of a device is 1M.

- *VSTART (optional parameter)*. This parameter specifies the starting virtual page number in a device. It is usually not specified during DISK INIT. If specified, however, it should be set to 0.

Only an sa can issue a DISK INIT command, and permissions cannot be granted on this command to other users. The following example creates a logical device called test_dev that is 64M in size:

```
DISK INIT   NAME = "test_dev",
        PHYSNAME = "c:\dbdata\test_dev.dat ",
        VDEVNO = 2
        SIZE = 32768
```

> **TIP**
>
> As a result of the DISK INIT command, a row is inserted into the sysdevices system table in the master database. Information such as logical name, physical name, type of device (database or backup), status (default, mirrored), and size is stored in this table.

30

SQL SERVER ADMINISTRATION

Designating Default Devices

SQL Server enables you to designate database devices as default devices. By designating default devices, you do not have to provide the names of database devices at the time of database creation. In such cases, space for a database is allocated from the default devices. The devices are used in the order of their logical names; that is, when space on the first device is consumed, the next device is used for further allocation. A device can be designated as a default device by use of the `sp_diskdefault` system stored procedure. The syntax for `sp_diskdefault` is as follows:

```
sp_diskdefault "logical name" , <defaulton ¦ defaultoff>
```

When a device is created using the DISK INIT command, the device is created with the `defaultoff` option. The following example sets device `test_dev` as a default device:

```
Exec sp_diskdefault "test_dev", defaulton
```

> **TIP**
>
> The `status` column of the `sysdevices` table is a bitmapped field that is used by SQL Server to indicate various attributes of a device. These attributes include default disk, mirror enabled, serial writes, and so on. Therefore, when you execute `sp_diskdefault` to turn default on for a device, SQL Server updates the bitmap of the status column in `sysdevices` and sets it to 1.
>
> After a new installation of SQL Server, MASTER is the only device that's available on the server. The SETUP program designates MASTER as the default device. You should remove MASTER from the list of default devices by executing this command:
>
> ```
> Exec sp_diskdefault "master", defaultoff
> ```

Mirroring Database Devices

Disk mirroring provides fault tolerance in the event of a disk failure. This enables the secondary (mirrored) device to become active, in case of a primary device failure, until the faulty device is fixed and reinstalled. Fault tolerance to a system can be provided at various levels by using

- Hardware-based RAID (Redundant Array of Inexpensive Disks)
- Windows NT-based RAID
- SQL Server-based disk mirroring

Hardware-based RAID provides the most reliable and configurable fault tolerance. In the event of a disk crash, the system continues to run because the mirror device takes over. RAID-based disk controllers recognize the new drive after the faulty drive is replaced, bringing the system back to the level of tolerance where it was before the disk failure. Hardware-based fault tolerance does not cause any performance degradation to the system because it is handled at the controller level and is completely transparent to the operating system and the applications. Hardware-based fault tolerance, however, suffers from a cost disadvantage. Check your hardware installation guide to see whether your hardware supports fault tolerance.

Windows NT-based fault tolerance can be done only on Windows NT Server. Windows NT-based fault tolerance allows logical drives to be mirrored. In the event of media failure, the system continues to run, but unlike with hardware-based fault tolerance, you must shut down the system to repair the drive that failed. Operating system-based fault tolerance is less expensive than hardware-based tolerance, but it adds more overhead to system processors and can contribute to performance degradation, especially for applications that are CPU intensive.

Fault tolerance is supported by SQL Server also for database devices. SQL Server T-SQL commands enable you to mirror, unmirror, and remirror a database device. In case of a device failure, the mirror device takes over and the system continues to run. The syntax for mirroring a database device is as shown here:

```
DISK MIRROR   NAME = "logical device name",
        MIRROR = "physical name of the mirror file",
        [, WRITES SERIAL ¦ NOSERIAL  ]
```

Only an sa can run this command, and permissions cannot be granted to other users to run this command. Mirroring is enabled after successful execution of the DISK MIRROR command. All the parameters of the DISK MIRROR command are described here:

- *NAME (mandatory parameter).* This is the logical name of the device you want to mirror. This device should have been previously created using the DISK INIT command.

- *MIRROR (mandatory parameter).* This should be the complete and valid pathname of the mirror device file. This file cannot be an existing file on the operating system.

- *WRITES (optional parameter).* The SERIAL parameter specifies whether writes to the mirrored device take place after writes to the database device are finished. The NOSERIAL parameter specifies whether writes can take place simultaneously on both the devices. The default for disk mirroring is SERIAL.

The following example creates a mirror device called test_dev.mir for a database device called test_dev:

```
DISK MIRROR   NAME = "test_dev",
        MIRROR = "e:\dbmirror\test_dev.mir"

Creating the physical file for the mirror...
Starting Dynamic Mirroring of 32768 pages for logical device 'test_dev'.
 512 pages mirrored...
 1024 pages mirrored...
 1536 pages mirrored...
.....
.....
.....
 31744 pages mirrored...
 32256 pages mirrored...
 32768 pages mirrored...
```

30

SQL SERVER ADMINISTRATION

TIP

When you issue the DISK MIRROR command, SQL Server updates the mirrorname column of sysdevices for the logical device specified in the command. It also updates the status column to indicate that mirroring is enabled. For the example given previously, this is the entry in the sysdevices table:

```
SELECT * FROM master..sysdevices
WHERE  name = "test_dev"


low         high       status  cntrltype  name      phyname
mirrorname
stripeset
  ----------------------------   -------------------------------   --------
  -------------------------------------------------------------------------
  -------------------------------------------------------------------------
  -------------------------------------------------------------------------
  ------------------------------------------------
33554432    33587199   738     0          test_dev  c:dbdata\test_dev.dat
e:\dbmirror\test_dev.mir
(null)


(1 row(s) affected)
```

After a device is mirrored, it is possible to unmirror it without shutting down SQL Server. SQL Server provides disk unmirroring options such as unmirror the primary device (permanently or temporarily) and unmirror the mirror device (permanently or temporarily). The T-SQL command DISK UNMIRROR causes mirroring to be disabled for a database device. This is the complete syntax for this command:

```
DISK UNMIRROR    NAME = "logical device name"
        [, SIDE = PRIMARY ¦ SECONDARY ]
        [, MODE = RETAIN ¦  REMOVE ]
```

Only an sa can run this command, and permissions cannot be granted to other users to run this command. Mirroring is disabled after successful execution of the DISK UNMIRROR command. All the parameters of this command are described here:

■ *NAME (mandatory parameter)*. This is the logical name of the device you want to unmirror. This device should have been previously created using the DISK INIT command.

■ *SIDE (optional parameter)*. This option specifies whether the database device (primary side) or its mirror (secondary side) should be disabled. The default is the mirror device.

■ *MODE (optional parameter)*. This option specifies whether unmirroring is permanent (remove) or temporary (retain). The default is retain.

The following example temporarily disables the secondary side of the test_dev device:

```
DISK  UNMIRROR NAME = "test_dev",
           SIDE = "SECONDARY",
           MODE = "RETAIN"
```

If a device is unmirrored permanently, you must reissue the DISK MIRROR command to enable fault tolerance. If, however, the mirroring is disabled temporarily, you can remirror the device by using the DISK REMIRROR command. The complete syntax of this command is shown here:

```
DISK REMIRROR  NAME = "logcal device name"
```

The NAME parameter is the logical device name for which mirroring was previously turned off using the DISK UNMIRROR command. The following example shows you how to reactivate fault tolerance for the test_dev device:

```
DISK REMIRROR NAME = "test_dev"

Starting Dynamic Mirroring of 32768 pages for logical device 'test_dev'.
512 pages mirrored...
1024 pages mirrored...
1536 pages mirrored...
.....
.....
......
 31232 pages mirrored...
 31744 pages mirrored...
 32256 pages mirrored...
 32768 pages mirrored...
```

> **TIP**
>
> You can mirror the MASTER device by using the DISK MIRROR command. It is also possible to specify a mirror device for the MASTER device at the time of SQL Server startup by supplying the -r mirror filename option. In the event of loss of the MASTER device, SQL Server can be started with this filename and the -d option.
>
> From a flexibility, recoverability, and performance point of view, fault tolerance is best provided at the hardware level or by the operating system. Using SQL Server for fault tolerance is not advisable. In fact, future releases of SQL Server might not support disk mirroring.

Resizing Database Devices

After a device has been created using the DISK INIT T-SQL command, it is possible to increase the size of a device by using the DISK RESIZE command. After a device has been created, it is not possible to reduce the size of the device. Only an sa can run this command. The syntax of this command is as shown here:

30

SQL SERVER ADMINISTRATION

```
DISK RESIZE     NAME = "logical device name",
        SIZE =  new size in 2KB Pages
```

The following example increases the size of the device test_dev to 80M:

```
DISK RESIZE NAME = "test_dev",
        SIZE = 40960
```

If you specify a size that is smaller than the existing device size, SQL Server returns an error and the command fails.

Creating Backup Devices

Databases are backed up on dump devices. These devices are used to restore databases in the event of database corruption or device failure. SQL Server database dump devices are different from the database devices. You cannot create a database on a dump device, and it is not possible to dump a database on a database device. But as with database devices, you create dump devices by providing a logical name and a physical location of the backup file. SQL Server dump devices are created using the sp_addumpdevice system stored procedure. A dump device is not tied to a database. SQL Server enables you to perform backups on disk files, tapes, and disks. Unlike database devices, a dump device file can be a file on a network. This is the syntax of sp_addumpdevice:

```
sp_addumpdevice {"disk" ¦ "tape" ¦ "diskette" }, "logical_name", "physical_name",
        [, {{cntrltype [, noskip ¦ skip [, media_capacity]]} ¦ {@devstatus =
{noskip ¦ skip}}}]
```

All the parameters of this procedure are described here:

- *"disk" ¦ "tape" ¦ "diskette" (mandatory parameter)*. This parameter specifies the backup media for the database.

- *logical_name (mandatory parameter)*. This is the logical name of the dump device. A logical name is a method of mapping a physical filename to a more meaningful name. After a dump device is created, it is always referred to and accessed by its logical name.

- *physical_name (mandatory parameter)*. This is the actual physical location of the file. SQL Server does not verify the validity of the path.

- *cntrltype (optional parameter)*. This is used for backward compatibility with previous versions of SQL Server.

- *noskip ¦ skip (optional parameter)*. This parameter is specified for the tape dump devices. This parameter is used to read (noskip) or ignore (skip) ANSI labels on a tape.

- *media_capacity (optional parameter)*. This is used for backward compatibility with previous versions of SQL Server.

- *@devstatus (optional parameter)*. This parameter is also used to specify noskip or skip.

The following example creates two disk dump devices, one on a local hard drive (testdb_1_dump) and one on the network (testdb_n_dump):

```
Exec sp_addumpdevice "disk", "testdb_l_dump", "d:\dump00\dbdumps\testdb.dmp"
Exec sp_addumpdevice "disk", "testdb_n_dump",
➥"\\backupserver\e$\dump00\dbdumps\testdb.dmp"

'Disk' device added.
'Disk' device added.
```

When you execute the sp_addumpdevice procedure, SQL Server does not create the physical dump device file and also does not validate the path. Dump file path validity and appropriate permissions are checked at the time of backup.

Getting Information on Devices

The system stored procedure sp_helpdevice provides information about a specific device when a device name is passed as a parameter. If no parameters are passed to sp_helpdevice, it displays information about all the devices on SQL Server. The following example displays information about the device test_dev:

```
Exec sp_helpdevice "test_dev:"

device_name                     physical_name
➥description
status cntrltype device_number low          high
------------------------------- -------------------------------------------------- -----
------------------------------- -------------------------------------------------- -----
------------------------------- -------------------------------------------------- -----
------------------------------- -------------------------------------------------- --
------ ---------- ---------------------
test_dev                        c:\dbdata\test_dev.dat
➥special, MIRROR ENABLED, mirrored on 'e:\dbmirror\test_dev.mir', serial writes,
➥reads mirrored, physical disk, 64 MB
738    0        2              33554432     33587199
```

Dropping Devices

A database or a dump device can be dropped by using the sp_dropdevice system stored procedure. The two parameters to this procedure are the logical device name (mandatory parameter) and DELFILE (optional parameter). A database device cannot be dropped if a database is created on it. Without the optional DELFILE, the sp_dropdevice stored procedure simply removes a row from the sysdevices table of the master database and frees up the virtual device number. It does not delete the physical file. As a result, you cannot create another database device with the same physical filename (however, you can create one with same logical name but with a different physical name). To delete the physical file associated with the logical name, either supply the DELFILE parameter when executing sp_dropdevice or delete the file from the operating system command line after executing sp_dropdevice. The following example shows how to drop a SQL Server device:

```
Exec sp_dropdevice "test_dev",  DELFILE

File: 'c:\dbdata\test_dev.dat' closed.
Device dropped.
```

30

SQL SERVER
ADMINISTRATION

```
(0 row(s) affected)
```

```
Physical file deleted.
```

Creating Databases

SQL Server can hold up to 32,767 databases, including system databases. A database is a collection of objects such as tables, triggers, stored procedures, views, and rules that take up space in a database. Users of a database perform various kinds of operations to select and modify data using various T-SQL commands such as SELECT, DELETE, UPDATE, and INSERT. SQL Server provides a mechanism by which all data modifications are first written to a part of the database called Transaction Log and then written to the actual tables. This technique of writing first to the transaction log is also called a write-ahead scheme and is used for recovering transactions in the event of a SQL Server crash or shutdown. When a SQL Server is started after a crash or a shutdown, the transaction log of the database is used to roll forward or roll back changes that took place before the crash or shutdown. All the committed changes that exist in the transaction log but not in the data tables are written (rolled forward) to the relevant tables. All uncommitted transactions at the time of the crash/shutdown are undone (rolled back). This method of recovery is performed on all the databases of SQL Server after the restart. Therefore, it is obvious that the transaction log plays an important role for up-to-the-minute recovery of transactions. At the time of database creation, you can specify the names of devices on which database objects and data will reside and the names of devices on which a transaction log will be created. A database is created on the database devices by using the CREATE DATABASE T-SQL command. The relationship between a database and a device is many-to-many; that is, a single database can span multiple devices, and a single device can hold multiple databases. The complete syntax of CREATE DATABASE is shown here:

```
CREATE DATABASE database_name
[ON {DEFAULT ¦ device_name} [= size]
    [, device_name [= size]]....]
[LOG ON device_name [= size]
    [, device_name [= size]]....]
[FOR LOAD]
```

Typically, databases on a SQL Server are created by an sa. It is possible, however, to grant CREATE DATABASE permissions to other users. All the parameters of this command are explained here:

- *database_name (mandatory parameter).* This is the name by which a database will be recognized within a SQL Server. The name of the database can have a maximum of 30 characters.

- ON *(optional parameter).* This parameter is supplied if you do not want to use a default database or default size.

- *device_name (optional parameter).* This parameter is required to specify the database device on which you want to create your database. You can specify multiple device names if you want to spread the database across multiple devices.

- `size` *(optional parameter)*. This parameter is used to specify the size of the database or the transaction log as a whole or on a particular database device.

- `LOG ON` *(optional parameter)*. This parameter is used to specify a device for the transaction log of a database. It is very important to create a transaction log on a device that is different from the database device from a recovery point of view. SQL Server provides the facility to back up the entire database using the `DUMP DATABASE` command. It also allows incremental changes on a database (changes that are stored in the transaction log) to be backed up by use of the `DUMP TRANSACTION` command. If the `LOG ON` option is not used during the `CREATE DATABASE` command, the space allocated for a database will be shared by the data and the transaction log, and it will not be possible to back up the transaction log (and hence the incremental changes). In such cases if you lose your database in the event of a disk crash, you can recover the database only up to the last database backup. If, however, a transaction log is created on its own device, it is possible to back up incremental changes. In case of a disk crash, you can load the database from the previous database backup and apply the incremental transaction log backups to bring the database up to the point of the last transaction dump.

- `FOR LOAD` *(optional parameter)*. This parameter is used to create database space that will act like a placeholder. A database created by using this option can be used *only* to load a database from a database backup with the `LOAD DATABASE` command. After a database is loaded, it can be accessed like an ordinary database. When a database is created without the `FOR LOAD` option, SQL Server initializes all the allocation pages on the database devices with zeroes. If you specify the `FOR LOAD` option, SQL Server simply allocates the space for the database and does not initialize allocation pages with zeroes. Therefore, a database is created faster with this option as compared to normal database creation.

When you create a database, SQL Server copies all the system tables from the `model` database into the new template. These catalog tables are essential for the internal working of SQL Server. For this reason, a newly created database cannot be smaller than the `model` database. One of the configuration parameters of SQL Server is `database size`, which represents the minimum size of the database. The default value for this parameter is 2M. If you do not specify any size information during `CREATE DATABASE`, SQL Server creates the database of the size of the `model` database or the `database size` SQL Server configuration parameter—whichever is larger. You can set the `database size` configuration parameter value by executing the `sp_configure` system stored procedure or by using SQL Enterprise Manager. In its simplest form, a database can be created as shown here:

```
CREATE DATABASE TESTDB
```

This example creates a database of 2M on the first default database device. If no default devices are available or if the space is less than 2M, SQL returns an error. The following example creates the database TESTDB (500M data, 100M log) on two devices, DB01 and DB02 (250M each), and places the transaction log on LOG01 (100M):

30

SQL SERVER ADMINISTRATION

```
CREATE DATABASE TESTDB ON
    DB01=250 , DB02 =250
    LOG ON LOG01 = 100
```

TIP

Following are some of the things you should know about the CREATE DATABASE command:

- If not enough space is available on a particular device, SQL Server does not give an error, but instead allocates whatever space is available on the device.

- If you don't provide the LOG ON option during the CREATE DATABASE command, it is still possible to create a log device for the database later by executing the sp_logdevice stored procedure.

- When you create a database, the system tables affected in the master database are sysdatabases and sysusages. The table sysdatabases stores the information about the database name, creation date, owner, database options (read-only, single-user, and so on). The table sysusages maps database allocation to various devices.

Changing the Ownership of a Database

Each database on a SQL Server is assigned an owner. This login is recognized by a special name within that particular database: DBO (database owner). This login, being the owner of the database, has all the privileges within that database. The login ID that creates the database (usually the sa) automatically becomes the owner of the database. In a multiserver, multidatabase environment, sometimes it is necessary to assign database ownership to individual logins to distribute database responsibilities to individuals and reduce workload on the system administrator. This way, the system administrator can focus more on server-related issues (such as device creation and configuration). A database ownership is changed by executing the sp_changedbowner system stored procedure. This procedure must be executed by the sa from within the context of a database. A database context is similar to a working directory on an operating system. A user on a SQL Server can be a valid user of multiple databases and at any given time must be working in a particular database. This is accomplished via the USE T-SQL command. This command enables a user to switch from the current working database to another (provided that the user is a valid user in the other database). Therefore, to change the ownership of a database, the sa must take these steps:

1. Switch to the database by executing the USE T-SQL command.

2. Execute the sp_changedbowner login_name command. The login name must exist on SQL Server.

The following example changes the ownership of the database TESTDB to the SQL Server login TESTDB_ADM:

```
USE TESTDB
go
Exec sp_changedbowner TESTDB_ADM
go
```

There can be only one owner (DBO) of a database. It is possible, however, to impersonate a database owner's privileges within a database by executing the `sp_addalias` system stored procedure. This way, individual logins can maintain their identity and have the DBO privileges at the same time. Aliases are created in a database by which one or more database users can be mapped to a particular user, thereby inheriting all the privileges held by that user. This technique enables a database user to impersonate another database user. Aliases are generally created to impersonate a DBO so that multiple user IDs can perform the function of a DBO. The syntax of this stored procedure is

```
sp_addalias login_name, name_in_database
```

in which `login_name` is the login ID you want to map, and `name_in_database` is the user name to which you want to map. It is important to note that the `login_name` cannot be an existing user of the database. The following example maps the SQL Server login Johnm to DBO:

```
USE TESTDB
go
Exec sp_addalias Johnm, "dbo"

Alias user added.
```

Changing Database Options

SQL Server enables you to set certain database options for an individual database. These options can be turned on or off by the DBO or the system administrator. All these options are set by execution of the `sp_dboption` system stored procedure. The complete syntax of this procedure is as follows:

```
sp_dboption [ database_name, option_name, { TRUE ¦ FALSE }]
```

If you execute this stored procedure without providing any parameters, it displays all the options that can be set using this procedure. All the parameters of this command are explained here:

■ `database_name` *(optional parameter)*. This parameter is used to specify the name of the database for which you want to set database options. If you execute this procedure without providing the `option_name` parameter value, this procedure displays the options that are currently set for the database.

- `option_name`. This parameter is used to specify a particular option you want to set for a database. These are some of the commonly used options:

  `ANSI null default`: At the time of table creation, if you don't specify NULL or NOT NULL as a column property, SQL Server defaults to NOT NULL. The ANSI standard is that if you don't specify the NULL property of a column during CREATE TABLE, the default should be NULL. SQL Server provides compatibility with ANSI standards by enabling you to set this flag to TRUE.

  `DBO use only`: This option is used to prevent access to the database by ordinary users of the database. If this option is set to TRUE, only an sa or a DBO can use the database. This is a useful option if you want to perform some maintenance on the database and don't want interference from the user transactions.

  `no chkpt. on recovery`: If this option is set to TRUE, no CHECKPOINT record is added to the database after SQL Server startup. CHECKPOINT is an internal SQL Server process that is activated automatically by SQL Server to write completed transactions from memory to the disk. This method provides faster recovery when a SQL Server is restarted after a crash or shutdown. After the recovery (that is, rolling forward/rolling back transactions), SQL Server by default writes a checkpoint record to record the time stamp. The default for this option is TRUE. It is required to be turned off if you are loading transaction log backups from another server.

  `offline`: This option is used to make a database unavailable.

  `published`:This option must be set to TRUE if data is published from the database for performing data replication.

  `read only`: If this option is set to TRUE, no data modifications (such as DELETE, INSERT, and UPDATE) are allowed inside a database.

  `select into/bulkcopy`: This option is required to be set to TRUE if you want to import data (using the bcp utility) into tables that have indexes and triggers on them.

  `single user`: If this option is set to TRUE, only one user can access the database at any given time. Even an sa or a DBO cannot access the database if the database is being used by another user.

  `subscribed`: This option must be set to TRUE if a database is subscribing data from a publishing database.

  `trunc. log on chkpt`: If this option is set to TRUE, the CHECKPOINT process forces all the committed transactions to the database device and then removes all these transactions from the transaction log without making a backup copy of the transaction log. This is a useful option in a test environment, where full recovery is not an issue. This option should be turned off for production databases to ensure full recoverability.

The following example sets the `trunc. log on chkpt` and `select into/bulkcopy` options on for database TESTDB:

```
Exec sp_dboption "tempdb", "trunc. log on chkpt", TRUE
Exec sp_dboption "tempdb", "select into", TRUE

CHECKPOINTing database that was changed.
CHECKPOINTing database that was changed.
```

The following example displays the options that have been set on the database TESTDB:

```
Exec sp_dboption "TESTDB"

The following options are set:
-----------------------------------
select into/bulkcopy
trunc. log on chkpt.
```

> **TIP**
>
> If you want to set certain options on all the database, set those options on the model database. When a new database is created, it will inherit all the options from the model database. The following example sets the `trunc. log on chkpt` option to TRUE for the model database:
>
> ```
> Exec sp_dboption "model", "trunc. log on chkpt", TRUE
> ```
>
> After this command has been executed, the `trunc. log on chkpt` option will be set to TRUE.

Renaming a Database

SQL Server provides the `sp_renamedb` system stored procedure to rename an existing database. A database must be brought into single-user mode before it can be renamed. The following example renames a database called TESTDB to DEVDB:

```
Exec sp_dboption 'TESTDB', 'single user', true
go
Exec sp_renamedb 'TESTDB', 'DEVDB
go
Exec sp_dboption 'DEVDB', 'single user', false
go

CHECKPOINTing database that was changed.
DBCC execution completed. If DBCC printed error messages, see your System
➡Administrator.
Database is renamed and in single-user mode.
System Administrator (sa) must reset it to multi-user mode with sp_dboption
CHECKPOINTing database that was changed.
DBCC execution completed. If DBCC printed error messages, see your System
➡Administrator.
```

30

SQL SERVER
ADMINISTRATION

Changing the Size of a Database

Each database on SQL Server is created with a fixed amount of space. As objects are created in a database and data is added, the amount of free space decreases. For a database to stay active, it is important that there always be enough room to grow. A database size can be increased with the ALTER DATABASE command. This command is similar to the CREATE DATABASE command. This command can be run by the sa or by the database owner (DBO), provided that the DBO has CREATE DATABASE permissions. Following is the complete syntax of this command:

```
ALTER DATABASE database_name
[ON} {DEFAULT ¦ database_device } [=size],
[, database_device } [=size...]
FOR LOAD
```

The minimum size by which a database can be expanded is 1M. The following example increases the size of the database TESTDB by 100M on device DB03.

```
ALTER DATABASE TESTDB ON DB03 =100
```

SQL Server enables you to reclaim database space if it has been over-allocated. The SQL Server T-SQL command DBCC SHRINKDB enables you to reclaim only unused database space. The syntax of this command is as follows:

```
DBCC SHRINKDB (database_name [, new_size [, 'MASTEROVERRIDE']])
```

Before this command can be executed, the database must be brought into single-user mode with sp_dboption. The *new_size* parameter is specified in terms of 2K pages. If you are not sure how much to specify as the new size, run this command without specifying the *new_size* value, and SQL Server returns the minimum size the database can be reduced to. The following example reduces the size of TESTDB to 160M.

```
exec sp_dboption 'TESTDB', 'single user', TRUE
go
USE TESTDB
go
DBCC SHRINKDB("TESTDB,81920)
go

CHECKPOINTing database that was changed.
DBCC execution completed. If DBCC printed error messages, see your System
➥Administrator.
```

Getting Information About Databases

The system stored procedure sp_helpdb provides information about a specific database when a database name is passed as a parameter. If no parameters were passed to sp_helpdb, it displays information about all the databases on SQL Server. The following example displays information about the TESTDB database:

```
Exec sp_helpdb "TESTDB"

name                    db_size      owner                      dbid   created
----------------------- ------------ -------------------------- ------ -----------
------------------------------------------------------------------------------------
------------------------------------------------------------------------------------
TESTDB              400.00 MB TESTDB_ADM      8        Mar  8 1996 select into/
bulkcopy, trunc. log on chkpt., ANSI null default

device_fragments            size         usage
--------------------------- ------------ -------------------
DB01                         250.00 MB data only
DB01                         250.00 MB data only
DB03                         100.00 MB data only
LOG01                        100.00 MB log only
```

To find out the space used within a database, execute the sp_spaceused stored procedure. This procedure reports space usage at the table level or for the entire database. This procedure reports space usage for the current database. The following example shows the space usage of the database TESTDB:

```
USE TESTDB
go

Exec sp_spaceused
go

database_name                    database_size      unallocated space
-------------------------------- ------------------ ------------------
TESTDB                               700.00 MB         567.63 MB

reserved            data               index_size          unused
----------------    ----------------   ----------------    ----------------
135552 KB           56810 KB           63670 KB            15072 KB
```

Dropping Databases

If a database is not required any longer, it can be dropped with the DROP DATABASE T-SQL command. When a database is dropped, all the objects and data contained in it are removed, and allocation on various devices is released. The syntax for this command is as follows:

```
DROP DATABASE database_name [, database name ]
```

The following example drops the database TESTDB:

```
DROP DATABASE TESTDB
```

This command can be run only by the sa or by the database owner. It is not possible to drop a database if it is in use.

Using Segments

When a database is initially created on SQL Server with the CREATE DATABASE command, all the space allocated to the database is shared by all the objects of the database, and there is no way to allocate space to specific database objects. A segment is a mechanism by which one can manage the growth of database objects on particular device segments. This helps in better placement of data and improved performance. When you first create a database, SQL Server creates three segments in the database:

- *System Segment* is used to store system catalog tables. By default, this segment spans across all the devices on which a database is created.

- *Default Segment* is used to store tables and indexes. By default, this segment spans across all the devices on which a database is created.

- *Log Segment* is used to store the transaction log. By default, this segment spans across all the devices specified in the LOG ON clause of CREATE DATABASE or in the sp_logdevice stored procedure. If the transaction log is not on a separate device, it shares the database space with the other two segments.

Adding Segments

SQL Server enables you to create user-defined segments in a database. These segments are a subset of the space allocated to a database. At the time of table creation and index creation, you can specify the segments on which these objects should be created. After an object is defined on a particular segment, it cannot grow beyond the segment boundary. If a segment gets full, however, it is possible to extend the size of a segment. You create segments in a database by executing the sp_addsegment system stored procedure from the database in which you want to define the segment. The syntax of this stored procedure is

```
sp_addsegment segment_name, logical_device_name
```

in which *segment_name* is the name of the segment you want to create, and *logical_device_name* is the name of the device on which the database is created.

The following example creates the table_seg segment on DB01 and the index_seg segment on DB02 for the database TESTDB:

```
USE TESTDB
go

Exec sp_addsegment table_seg, DB01
Exec sp_addsegment index_seg, DB02
```

Any object that gets created on segment table_seg can use all the DB01 space that is assigned for the database. It is important to note that table_seg cannot use all the space on device DB01, but only the space allocated to the database TESTDB. The following example creates the table test_table on table_seg and a nonclustered index on index_seg:

```
create table test_table ( col1 int, col2 int ) on  table_seg
create unique nonclustered index nc1 on test_table ( col1 ) on index_seg.
```

By creating `test_table` on `table_seg` and a nonclustered index on `index_seg`, you can control the placement of the data and index segment on different devices, and the growth of one does not interfere with that of the other. Also, the devices DB01 and DB02 are on two different controllers, so there is a big performance improvement because the I/O is now split across controllers. A logical diagram of the use of segments in a database is shown in Figure 30.1.

FIGURE 30.1.

Using database segments.

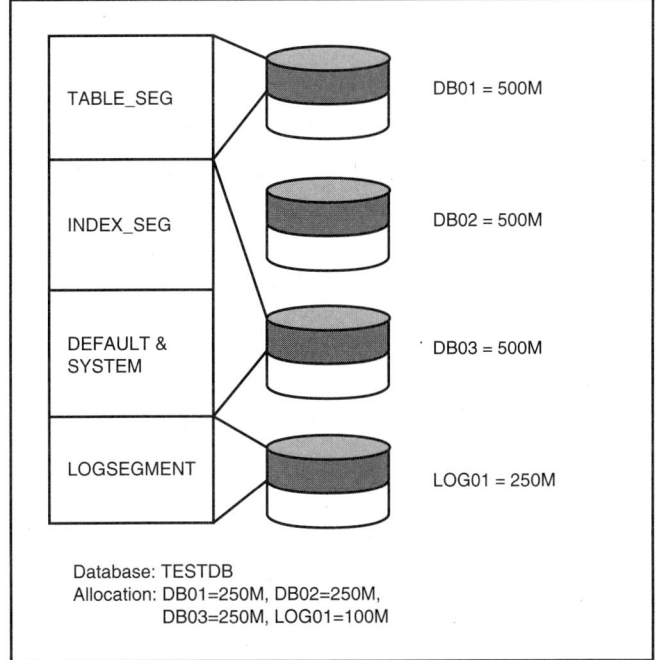

TABLE_SEG — DB01 = 500M

INDEX_SEG — DB02 = 500M

DEFAULT & SYSTEM — DB03 = 500M

LOGSEGMENT — LOG01 = 250M

Database: TESTDB
Allocation: DB01=250M, DB02=250M,
DB03=250M, LOG01=100M

> **TIP**
>
> If you create a table on one segment and its clustered index on another segment, the entire data moves to the segment on which the clustered index is defined. The reason is that in case of a clustered index on a table, data is physically sorted on the key, and the bottom of the index page is the table data; therefore, you cannot isolate the data from the index.

Extending Segments

As objects are created in database segments and data is added, the amount of free space decreases. For a database to stay active, it is important that there be enough space for objects to grow. It is possible to extend a segment on devices on which the database is created. A segment can be extended with the `sp_extendsegment` system stored procedure. The syntax for this stored procedure is

```
sp_extendsegment segment_name, logical_device_name
```

in which *segment_name* is the name of the segment you want to extend, and *logical_device_name* is the name of the device on which the database has been created.

The following example extends the `table_seg` segment on DB03 for the database TESTDB:

```
USE TESTDB
go

Exec sp_extendsegment table_seg, DB01
```

If the database size is increased on a particular device, the segment defined on that device automatically gets expanded to make use of the additional space.

Getting Information About Segments

The system stored procedure `sp_helpsegment` provides information about the objects in a segment when a segment name is passed as a parameter. If no parameter is passed to `sp_helpsegment`, it simply lists all the segments on a database. The following example displays information about the `table_seg` segment of the TESTDB database:

```
USE TESTDB
go

Exec sp_helpsegment "table_seg"

segment name                                   status
-------  ------------------------------------  ------
3           table_seg                             0
device                           size
------------------------------   ------------------------
DB01                             250MB
DB03                  100MB
table_name                       index_name                          indid
------------------------------   ----------------------------------  ------
test_table                       idx1                                      0
```

Dropping Segments

A segment can be dropped if no objects are defined on it. SQL Server returns an error if you try to drop a segment that is being used. If there are objects on a database, you need to reassign them to a different segment before you can drop a segment. You can drop a segment by executing the `sp_dropsegment` system stored procedure. A segment can be dropped from a specific device, or it can be dropped completely. The syntax of `sp_dropsegment` stored procedure is as follows:

```
sp_dropsegment database_name, [device_name]
```

The following example drops the `table_seg` segment from the DB03 database device for the database TESTDB:

```
USE TESTDB
go

Exec sp_dropsegment "table_seg", "DB03"
go

DBCC execution completed. If DBCC printed error messages, see your System
➥Administrator.
Segment reference to device dropped.
```

The system stored procedure `sp_helpdb` also provides information about the segments on a database.

> **TIP**
>
> Segments are particularly useful when you want to split a large table across multiple devices. This technique can help improve performance of the system because I/Os on the large table can now be split across multiple drives. Although the use of segments can provide better overall system performance, segments add more complexity and reduce overall manageability of the database. Hardware-based RAID can also distribute load across various disks and might provide better performance than the use of segments alone.

Managing Security

In a business environment, it is important to protect business-critical information stored in a database. SQL Server can prevent unauthorized access to data at the following levels:

- *Server Level.* At this level SQL Server authenticates whether a connection request should be granted or denied based on the user ID and password information.
- *Database Level.* At this level SQL Server verifies whether a particular login is a valid user of the database.
- *Object Level.* At this level SQL Server verifies permissions on the objects a user is trying to access.

Managing Security at the Server Level

This is the first step of user authentication in which SQL Server determines whether a login is a valid SQL Server login. SQL Server security can be configured to handle user connections in one of the following ways:

- Standard security
- Integrated security
- Mixed security

Standard Security

In this security mode, SQL Server validates the user logins directly. To access a SQL Server, a user must supply a user ID and a password. This security mode does not require any user account on Windows NT. This is the default security mode for SQL Server. User logins are created on SQL Server with the `sp_addlogin` system stored procedure. Following is the syntax for this procedure:

```
sp_addlogin login_id, [password, [,defdb [ ,deflanguage ]]]
```

All the parameters of `sp_addlogin` are explained here:

- `login_id` *(mandatory parameter)*. This is the name of the user you want to create an account.
- `password` *(optional parameter)*. This is the password for the `login_id` that will be used to authenticate for connection to SQL Server. You are not required to provide a password to this procedure, although omitting it is not recommended.
- `defdb` *(optional parameter)*. A valid user of SQL Server can use multiple databases. This parameter enables you to define a default database for a user. If this parameter is not specified, a user is connected to the master database.
- `deflanguage` *(optional parameter)*. This is the default language for a user connection. If this is not specified, the language used by SQL Server is chosen. The following example creates a login called testuser with a default database of TESTDB:

```
EXEC sp_addlogin "testuser", "123user", TESTDB

New login created.
```

> **NOTE**
>
> Creating a login with a default database does not make a login a valid user of the database. After a login has been created on SQL Server, it is necessary to add this login to all the databases this login should be allowed to access. You accomplish this task by executing the sp_adduser system stored procedure from within a database. The stored procedure sp_adduser is discussed later in this chapter.

Integrated Security

In this security mode a user should have a Windows NT account, and login authentication is done by the operating system. After a login is verified by Windows NT, SQL Server does not validate the login, and a user can access SQL Server. Integrated security has advantages over standard security because it provides better security (C2 compliance, password expiration and aging, and so on) and better manageability at the enterprise level (accounts can be created at machine level or at domain level). The disadvantages are that integrated security works only with the Named Pipes protocol and the Multi-protocol, and each user who uses integrated security to log on to SQL Server is mapped to a default login of SQL Server (or as an sa, if the user has administrative privileges). Because all users are mapped to one login of SQL Server, all the users of SQL Server have the same permissions within a database.

Mixed Security

This mode of security combines the standard security and integrated security methods. In this mode, if a login request is first matched against an account name on Windows NT and if a match is found, integrated security rules are applied. Otherwise, SQL Server validates the login ID using standard security mode by validating the user name and password.

> **TIP**
>
> Mixed security is very useful if you forget the sa password. Because standard security does not let you connect to SQL Server without a valid password, you can still connect to SQL Server by using your network account name, and if the account name is a part of the administrative group, SQL Server lets you connect as an sa. After you are connected, you can change the sa password by using the sp_password system stored procedure.

Managing Security at the Database Level

To access a database, a user needs to be assigned to the database. A user can be a user in multiple databases. Before a user can be added to a database, the user should already have a login created (the sa must have created the login by using the sp_addlogin procedure) on SQL Server.

Adding Groups

SQL Server also enables you to create groups within a database. A group is a logical way of defining a collection of users. Groups in SQL Server provide a convenient method of managing object permissions. After a group is created, it is possible to grant and revoke object permissions to the group, and all the users who exist in the group automatically inherit the permissions assigned to the group. In SQL Server, a user can belong to only one group. A group in a database can be created with the sp_addgroup system stored procedure. The syntax is as follows:

```
sp_addgroup  "group_name"
```

Either the DBO or the sa can run this command. The following example creates three groups called readonly, readwrite, and developer in the database TESTDB:

```
USE TESTDB
go
```

30

SQL SERVER ADMINISTRATION

```
Exec sp_addgroup readonly
Exec sp_addgroup readwrite
Exec sp_addgroup developer
go

New group added.
New group added.
New group added.
```

It is not necessary for a user to be a part of any user-defined group. Each database of SQL Server has a built-in group called `public`. All the users of a database by default are a part of this group.

Adding Users

All users in a SQL Server database, by default, belong to the group `public`. Users can be added to a database with the `sp_adduser` system stored procedure. The syntax for this command is as follows:

```
sp_adduser user_name, [name_in_database, [, group_name]
```

All the parameters of this procedure are described here:

- ▪ *user_name (mandatory parameter).* This is the name that was used at the time of creation of the login; that is, it is the name used in the `sp_addlogin` command.

- ▪ *name_in_database (optional parameter).* If this parameter is not specified, the user of the database is given the same name as the user's login name on SQL Server. By using this parameter, you can specify a name in the database that is different from the login name (that is, the name required to connect to SQL Server).

- ▪ *group_name (optional parameter).* This is the name of the group the user is assigned to. The group name must already exist in the database before a user can be assigned to it.

This stored procedure can be executed only by the DBO or the sa. The following example creates a user called Tom who has a SQL Server login name of testuser and assigns it to the readonly group in the database TESTDB:

```
USE TESTDB
go

Exec sp_adduser testuser, Tom, readonly
go
```

Getting User and Group Information

Information on the users and groups of a database can be obtained via the `sp_helpuser` and `sp_helpgroup` system stored procedures. Both of these stored procedures accept user name/group name as input parameters. If no input parameters are provided, they display information about all the users/groups of the database. The following example provides information about the user Tom in the database TESTDB:

```
USE TESTDB
go

Exec sp_helpuser "Tom"
go
```

UserName	GroupName	LoginName	DefDBName	UserID	SUserID
Tom	readonly	testuser	TESTDB	3	11

Dropping Aliases, Users, Groups, and Logins

You can drop an alias user from a database by executing the sp_dropalias stored procedure by passing the login_id to the procedure. You cannot drop an alias if objects are owned by the user in the database. Therefore, to drop an alias you must drop the objects owned by the user.

You can drop a user from a database by executing the sp_dropuser stored procedure by passing the user name to the procedure. You cannot drop a user if objects are owned by the user in the database. Therefore, to drop a user you must drop the objects owned by the user.

You can drop a group from a database by executing the sp_dropgroup stored procedure by passing the group name to the procedure. You cannot drop a group if users are assigned to it. Therefore, before you can drop a group, you can either drop users from the database by executing sp_dropuser or assign them to a different group by executing the sp_changegroup system stored procedure.

You can drop a login from a SQL Server by executing the sp_droplogin system stored procedure by passing the login name to the procedure. You cannot drop a login if it is created as a user in a database. Therefore, to drop a login you must drop the user from the databases where it exists.

The following examples demonstrate how the previously listed actions can be accomplished:

```
USE TESTDB
go
Exec sp_dropalias John
Exec sp_dropgroup developer
Exec sp_dropuser Tom
Exec sp_droplogin testuser
go

Alias user dropped.
Group has been dropped.
User has been dropped from current database.
Login dropped.
```

> **NOTE**
>
> SQL Server enables a user on one SQL Server to execute a stored procedure on another SQL Server. To provide this functionality, all the steps similar to the ones mentioned

previously (such as create login and add user) are taken at the remote server. The various stored procedures used to accomplish this are sp_addserver, sp_addremote_login, and sp_remoteoption.

Managing Security at the Object Level

A database is a collection of objects (such as tables, views, and procedures). It is important to allow and restrict access on these objects to various users of the database, depending on the privileges of a user, as governed by the business. Users within a database are assigned permissions. Some logins of SQL Server have more privileges than others. A user connection to a SQL Server can be at one of the following privilege levels:

- *System Administrator (sa).* This login ID is at the highest permission level. Anyone who has access to the sa password has all the privileges within SQL Server. This login owns everything in a SQL Server, directly or indirectly (through permission levels). There are certain commands that only an sa can run (such as DISK INIT and DISK MIRROR).

- *Database Owner (DBO).* This is a special login that owns a particular database and is a superuser within that database. This login owns everything within the database, directly or indirectly (through permission levels). There are certain commands that only a DBO can run within a database (such as LOAD DATABASE and DROP DATABASE). DBO is the login that grants (or revokes) permissions (such as CREATE TABLE and CREATE PROCEDURE) to the ordinary users of the database.

- *Other Users.* These are the regular logins of the database; they work with the privileges assigned to them by the DBO. Based on the privileges assigned to them, individual users can create objects in the database, and they can select or modify data in tables owned by them or other users (including the DBO). A user who creates an object has all permissions on it. For others to access that object, they are required to have permissions for performing various operations on the object. There are two T-SQL commands to control permissions on an object: GRANT and REVOKE. Both these commands specify the privilege list, the object name, and the user or group to which a privilege is applicable. The following example creates a table called test_table and grants all permissions to the readwrite group, revokes all the permission from a user called Tom, and grants SELECT access to the readonly group:

```
USE TESTDB
go

CREATE TABLE test_table ( col1 int, col2 int )
go

GRANT ALL ON test_table to readwrite
REVOKE ALL ON test_table from Tom
GRANT SELECT ON test_table to public
go
```

> **TIP**
>
> Unless specific permissions are granted, even the DBO (and the sa) don't have any permissions on an object created by a user. The workaround for this situation is that a DBO impersonates the user by the SETUSER T-SQL command and then grants permissions to himself.

SQL Server also enables system administrators to grant permissions to run certain T-SQL administrative commands, such as CREATE DATABASE and DUMP DATABASE, to some users of SQL Server.

One of ways you can provide security on table data is by using views in a database. Views provide a snapshot of data from one or more underlying database tables. To an end-user, a view looks like a regular table. By using views, you can restrict direct access to the database tables by providing a horizontal (that is, specific rows) and vertical (that is, specific columns) snapshot of the data from underlying tables. Therefore, views help simplify data representation and provide logical data independence. Because permissions are required to be granted on the view and not on the underlying tables, the end-users need not know about the underlying table structures and data from which the view was created. Thus, views provide excellent data security.

Enhanced data security can be achieved via SQL Server stored procedures. A user who has permissions to execute a stored procedure does not require any permissions on the underlying tables used within the procedure. Therefore, by granting execute permissions on stored procedures and revoking all permissions on the underlying tables, you can prevent any direct access to the database tables. This way, all data manipulation on the tables can be done entirely with stored procedures.

Backup and Recovery

Database backups are required to recover from failures such as widespread database corruption or media failure. SQL Server provides various T-SQL commands to back up data in a database. One of the features of SQL Server backups is that users can access the database while backups are being performed. This method of backing up, called dynamic dumps, is quite useful in a 7×24 environment, in which it is not feasible to secure any downtime. Because backups are very I/O intensive, they do affect system performance; therefore, it is important to perform database backups during a time of low activity on the server. Backups are generally performed by the sa or DBO, but it is possible to grant access to back up a database to a user of the database. SQL Server enables you to perform data backups at the following levels:

- Back up an individual table
- Back up an entire database
- Back up incremental changes (backup transaction log) of a database

Backing Up and Restoring Tables

Table-level backups are useful in situations in which most of the tables in a database are static in nature. In such cases backing up a few active tables of the database can save time compared with backing up the entire database. The T-SQL command to back up a table is this:

```
DUMP TABLE [ [database_name].owner.]table_name
TO dump_device, [dump_device2 [, dump_device3.....]]
WITH options
```

All the parameters of this command are explained here:

- `database_name` *(optional parameter)*. You can specify the name of the database in which the table exists. If you don't specify a database name, it is assumed that the table is being backed up from the current database.

- `table_name` *(mandatory parameter)*. This parameter specifies the name of the table that needs to be backed up.

- `dump_device` *(mandatory parameter)*. This parameter specifies the logical name of the dump device.

- `dump_device2, dump_device3...` *(optional parameters)*. Additional dump devices can be specified if you want to stripe dumps across various devices. This is a useful feature for large databases. It results in improved performance because the I/Os are split across various devices. This feature, however, also results in additional maintenance, because you need to keep track of all the devices a database was dumped on.

- `options` *(optional parameters)*. This parameter specifies various dump options such as `init` (overwrite a previous dump file), `noinit` (add to existing dump file), and `stats` (show percentage of dump completed).

> **TIP**
>
> It is also possible to dump a table without specifying a logical dump device name. You can specify the absolute path by specifying `disk="path"` in the DUMP TABLE command.

The following example dumps the `employee` table to a disk file:

```
DUMP TABLE TESTDB..employee TO disk="c:\temp\employee.dmp" with INIT, STATS=10

Msg 3211, Level 10, State 5
10 percent dumped
Msg 3211, Level 10, State 5
20 percent dumped
Msg 3211, Level 10, State 2
100 percent dumped
Msg 4035, Level 10, State 1
Database 'TESTDB' table 'employee' (24 pages) dumped to file <1> on device
➥'c:\temp\employee.dmp'.
```

A table can be restored with the LOAD TABLE command. The syntax is similar to that of the DUMP TABLE command. The following example restores new_employee, which has the same structure as the employee table, from a previously taken dump:

```
LOAD TABLE TESTDB..new_employee FROM disk="c:\temp\employee.dmp" with  STATS=10

Msg 4039, Level 10, State 1
Warning, file <1> on device 'c:\temp\employee.dmp' was dumped from database
➥'TESTDB'.
Msg 3211, Level 10, State 6
10 percent loaded
Msg 3211, Level 10, State 6
20 percent loaded
Msg 3211, Level 10, State 6
30 percent loaded
Msg 3211, Level 10, State 6
40 percent loaded
Msg 3211, Level 10, State 6
50 percent loaded
Msg 3211, Level 10, State 6
60 percent loaded
Msg 3211, Level 10, State 6
70 percent loaded
Msg 3211, Level 10, State 6
80 percent loaded
Msg 3211, Level 10, State 6
90 percent loaded
Msg 3211, Level 10, State 6
100 percent loaded
```

Backing Up and Restoring Databases

Database dumps are performed to back up the entire contents of a database. Database backups are done with the DUMP DATABASE T-SQL command. This command copies all the object definitions, including SQL Server internal objects, and the data in the dump device files. Database dump files are used to recover databases in case one of the devices (on which the database is created) crashes. A database dump file can also be used to restore a database on another server, provided that the character set and sort order are compatible. For example, you might set up a database on a test server and want to keep it in sync with a database on a production server. Each night after the database backups are performed on the production server, you can take that dump file and load it on the test server. The syntax of DUMP DATABASE is similar to that of the DUMP TABLE command. The following example dumps the TESTDB database to a logical device called testdb_dump:

```
DUMP DATABASE TESTDB TO testdb_dump WITH INIT, STATS=50

Msg 3211, Level 10, State 2
50 percent dumped
Msg 3211, Level 10, State 2
100 percent dumped
Msg 4035, Level 10, State 1
Database 'TESTDB' (324 pages) dumped to file <1> on device 'testdb_dump'
```

A database can be restored with the LOAD DATABASE command. To load a database, you need to take into account the following rules:

- The target database should not be in use by anyone.
- You must be a DBO (or an sa).
- The target database should be created before it can be loaded.
- The target database should be at least as big as the database for which the dump was initially taken.
- The character set and sort order of the server where the database is loaded should be the same as the server from which the database dump was initially taken.

The following example loads the database TESTDB from the logical dump device testdb_dump:

```
LOAD DATABASE TESTDB FROM testdb_dump WITH STATS=30

30 percent loaded
Msg 3211, Level 10, State 2
60 percent loaded
Msg 3211, Level 10, State 2
90 percent loaded
Msg 3211, Level 10, State 2
100 percent loaded
```

Incremental Backup and Recovery

SQL Server enables you to back up incremental changes in a database by providing the DUMP TRANSACTION T-SQL command. By doing incremental backups, you can ensure full recoverability of the database. The syntax of DUMP TRANSACTION is similar to that of DUMP TABLE and DUMP DATABASE. This is the complete syntax of this command:

```
DUMP TRANSACTION {database_name ¦ local_variable_name}
TO dump_device [, dump_device2 [, dump_device3...]]
[WITH { TRUNCATE_ONLY ¦ NO_LOG ¦ NO_TRUNCATE }
options
```

When you dump the transaction log, it backs up all the committed changes that took place since the last transaction log dump. After the successful dump, SQL Server clears those transactions from the transaction log. In some cases (such as test or development environments), if you don't want to make a backup copy of the transaction log of a database, and you only want to clear out the transaction log, you should use the dump option of TRUNCATE_ONLY. When you are using this option, it is not necessary to specify a dump device. The transaction log of database is created with finite space, and it can fill up completely over a period as a result of data modifications taking place in the database. If the transaction log becomes completely full, you cannot back up the transaction log on a device or use the TRUNCATE_ONLY option. You must use the NO_LOG option to clear out all the committed transactions from the transaction log. This option removes all committed transactions without creating a backup copy. Therefore, it is quite important to back up your databases using the DUMP DATABASE command if you have used the TRUNCATE_ONLY or NO_LOG option to create space in the transaction log.

In the event of a database device failure, you can still back up the transaction log to a dump device by using the DUMP TRANSACTION command with the NO_TRUNCATE option. The following example illustrates a typical sequence of database backups. The database dumps are taken each day at 6:00 a.m., and incremental transaction log backups are taken every hour (that is, 7:00 a.m., 8:00 a.m., and so on).

```
6:00 AM:
    DUMP DATABASE TESTDB TO testdb_dump with init.
7:00 AM
    DUMP TRANSACTION TESTDB TO disk="e:\tranlog\testdb_tran_1" with init
8:00AM
    DUMP TRANSACTION TESTDB TO disk="e:\tranlog\testdb_tran_2" with init
```

Assume that the database in the preceding example is created on the logical device DB01 and has a transaction log created on LOG01, and assume that a disk crash occurs at 8:30 a.m. These are the three possible failure scenarios:

- Scenario 1: Device DB01 crashes, but LOG01 is still intact.
- Scenario 2: Device LOG01 crashes, but DB01 is still accessible.
- Scenario 3: Both DB01 and LOG01 crash.

In scenario 1, because LOG01 is accessible, you can still back up all the changes that took place between 8:00 a.m. and 8:30 a.m. by dumping the transaction log with the NO_TRUNCATE option. To bring the system back up to the point of failure, you can now load the database dump (6:00 a.m.) and the transaction log dumps (7:00 a.m., 8:00 a.m., and 8:30 a.m.).

In scenario 2, failure on the transaction log device renders the database useless (even though DB01 is still active). Therefore, in this case you can recover the system only up to 8:00 a.m., and all the changes made after that are lost. For this reason, it is strongly recommended that you mirror the transaction log device of the database.

In scenario 3, because both of the devices have failed, you can bring the system back up to 8 a.m., and all the changes made after that are lost.

Recovering the Master Database

It is quite important to keep an up-to-date backup copy of the master database. Recovery of the master database is different from that of other databases. For the master database, data and transaction logs are on the same device. Therefore, it is not possible to back up incremental changes. To recover the master database, you must go back to the latest copy of the master database dump. Any changes made to the master database after the dump cannot be recovered. To recover a master database, you must take the following steps:

1. Shut down SQL Server (if it has not already crashed), and run SQL SETUP from the SQL Server 6.5 program group. Continue to the Microsoft SQL Server 6.5 options screen, and select Rebuild Master. The next few screens prompt you to select the character set, sort order, and location of the SQL Server installation directory. It is important that you choose the original character set and sort order; otherwise, you will not be able to load the master database dump file.

2. After a successful master database rebuild, shut down the SQL Server and start it in single-user mode from the command line. For example, if the MASTER device location is c:\mssql\data\master.dat, you can start SQL Server in single-user mode by typing this:

```
c:\mssql\binn\sqlservr /dc:\mssql\data\master.dat /m
```

3. Connect to SQL Server as an sa. After the master rebuild, the password is set to NULL. Create a dump device that points to the location of the master dump file you want to restore. Load the master database using the LOAD DATABASE command. After the successful load, SQL Server shuts itself down. Now you can start SQL Server from the command line (without supplying the /m option) or by using the SQL Service Manager graphical tool.

Summary

SQL Server provides various T-SQL commands and system stored procedures to perform administrative tasks. Certain tasks such as database backups and transaction log dumps are executed more frequently. It is important that database and transaction logs be backed up regularly to provide full recovery in the event of a disk crash. Based on the activity on your system, you can schedule backups for tables, databases, and transaction logs.

SQL Server Monitoring and Tuning

by Vipul Minocha

IN THIS CHAPTER

Today's distributed client-server applications demand a high performance and robust computing environment. To efficiently and reliably fulfill such requirements, it is important that all components of the application should be optimized in the best possible way. This chapter covers topics that deal with tuning SQL Server configuration parameters and monitoring techniques.

Defining Performance

In a typical client-server–based application, end-user requests in the form of T-SQL queries are sent over the network to the SQL Server. The SQL Server executes these requests and, if necessary, sends the results back to the client. Time taken from request initiation to completion is known as the *response time* for the request. Measurement of response time defines the performance of the system. If the response time is within "acceptable" limits, performance is considered to be good. Measurement of performance is somewhat discretionary and is generally based upon the perception of the end-users and nature of the business application. For example, a two-second response for a request from an inquiry screen for a customer support application may be considered good. It may be regarded as extremely slow, even hazardous, however, in a real-time application for steel industry, where speed of the trolley carrying molten steel must be calculated in a matter of a subsecond. For these reasons, performance of a system is best defined by the users and the designers of the system, because they know the functionality of the various modules of the system and the acceptable response time for each of the modules.

There are various components in a client-server–based application that can have a significant effect on the performance of a system. These components are as follows:

- Client component
- Network component
- Hardware component
- SQL Server component

Each of the preceding components, individually or collectively, can contribute to poor performance of the system. Capacity planning is a very important step in designing an application. You should carefully evaluate and choose these components so that they are most effective in your computing environment.

Client Component

Many of the GUI-based applications are memory-intensive. If there is not enough memory on the client hardware, it will affect the performance of the application adversely. An application that is CPU-intensive (performing large data sorts, for example) on the front-end will also suffer from performance degradation because of a slower processor. Therefore, at the time of designing the front-end application, estimate the amount of resources, such as memory, CPU, and so forth, that will be required to run the application smoothly. Compare your estimate with the resources that are currently available so that you can do a hardware upgrade, if necessary.

Network Component

A network bottleneck is usually caused by available network bandwidth, network traffic, and the speed of the network. A poorly designed application can create a network bottleneck by retrieving hundreds of rows from the database, even though only a few rows are necessary for the front-end application. Some of the network-related bottlenecks can be eliminated by efficient application and database design and by using database objects such as stored procedures, rules, triggers, and so on. Other options include the use of a faster network, keeping the machine in a subnet with less traffic, and adding network redundancy.

Hardware Component

Various subsystems of a server's hardware can also contribute to poor performance. Some of these subsystems are processors, disk subsystems, and physical memory on the machine. A system that usually suffers from performance problems at the hardware level may exhibit that one subsystem is idle while the other one has a high percentage of utilization. For a poorly performing application, low CPU utilization may indicate that the processor may be waiting on a disk subsystem to finish I/Os. Alternatively, if CPU utilization is constantly at a high number (usually ninety percent is considered high), that could indicate that the congestion is at CPU level. When the CPU is overworked, there may be a need for faster or additional processors (or both) on the system. Total physical memory on the machine is one of the important factors governing the performance of a system. Insufficient memory on a server will cause more I/Os from the disk. Because accessing a disk is much slower than accessing the memory, a large number of physical I/Os can lead to performance degradation. If more memory is installed on a server, it can cache a large amount of data, and many requests for data can be satisfied from memory rather than doing physical I/Os.

SQL Server Component

All the previously mentioned components (client hardware, network, and server hardware) are essential for a well-performing system. They also add to the overall cost of the system, and therefore investment on these components is limited by the budget constraints. No matter how many resources you provide on the client—the network and the hardware—there is no substitute for an efficient database design, well-written queries, and a well-configured SQL Server. You can gain a tremendous amount of performance by using normalization and denormalization techniques (when necessary). You can also configure the SQL Server to provide excellent performance and throughput without compromising the data integrity. The SQL Server provides a number of parameters that can be configured to provide optimal performance for a particular environment. Next, you will learn about the topics that pertain to configuring, tuning, and monitoring the SQL Server.

Configuring the SQL Server

The SQL Server provides a number of parameters that can be set by the system administrator (sa) to maximize performance of a system. These parameters can be set using the sp_configure system-stored procedure. This stored procedure can be executed using a query tool such as ISQL/w. The syntax of this procedure is

```
sp_configure [ parameter_name [, parameter_value ]]
```

where *parameter_name* is the name of the configuration parameter you want to set and *parameter_value* is the value for the parameter. Both the parameters are optional. All the users have permissions to run this stored procedure, but only an sa (system administrator) can set the value of a parameter. If you execute this procedure without specifying any parameters, the SQL Server returns the current configuration values of the SQL Server. The following example displays the output of the sp_configure stored procedure executed without any parameters:

```
Exec sp_configure
go

name                    minimum         maximum     config_value      run_value
--------------------    ----------      ----------- -------------     -----------
affinity mask                   0                   2147483647      0               0
allow updates           0               1               0               0
backup buffer size      1               10              1               1
backup threads          0               32          5                   5
cursor threshold        -1              2147483647      -1              -1
database size           1               10000           2               2
default language        0               9999            0               0
default sortorder id    0               255             50          50
fill factor             0               100             0               0
free buffers            20              524288          6400            6400
hash buckets            4999            265003      7993            7993
language in cache       3               100             3               3
LE threshold maximum    2               500000          500             500
LE threshold minimum    2               500000          20              20
LE threshold percent    1               100             0               0
locks                   5000            2147483647      15000           15000
logwrite sleep (ms)     -1              500             0               0
max async IO            1               255             25              25
max lazywrite IO        1               255             8               8
max text repl size              0               2147483647      65536           6
max worker threads      10              1024            255             255
media retention         0               365             0               0
memory                  1000            1048576         128000          128000
nested triggers         0               1               1               1
network packet size     512             32767           4096            4096
open databases          5               32767           20              20
open objects            100             2147483647      5000            5000
priority boost          0               1               1           1
procedure cache         1               99              30              30
RA cache hit limit      1               255             4               4
```

name	minimum	maximum	config_value	run_value
RA cache miss limit	1	255	3	3
RA delay	0	500	15	15
RA pre-fetches	1	1000	3	3
RA slots per thread	1	255	5	5
RA worker threads	0	255	3	3
recovery flags	0	1	0	0
recovery interval	1	32767	5	5
remote access	0	1	1	1
remote login timeout	0	2147483647	5	5
remote query timeout	0	2147483647	0	0
remote login timeout	0	2147483647	5	5
remote proc	0	1	0	0
resource timeout	5	2147483647	10	10
set working set size	0	1	0	0
show advanced option	0	1	1	1
SMP concurrency	-1	64	0	0
sort pages	64	511	64	64
spin counter	1	2147483647	10000	10000
tempdb in ram (MB)	0	2044	0	0
user connections	5	32767	125	125
user options	0	4095	0	0

```
(1 row(s) affected)
```

If you specify only the parameter name, the SQL Server returns the current configuration of that particular parameter. Parameters set by `sp_configure` take effect at the SQL Server level. You can assign a new parameter value by specifying both parameter name and parameter value to the `sp_configure` stored procedure. There are two types of parameters: dynamic and static. Dynamic parameters take effect immediately after executing the `sp_configure` stored procedure, followed by running the RECONFIGURE T-SQL command. Some of the dynamic parameters include `network packet size`, `backup buffer size`, `free buffers`, and so on. Static parameters require the SQL Server to be restarted and take effect upon the next start of the SQL Server.

If `sp_configure` is run without any parameters, the output consists of the following five columns:

- `name`: This is the name of the parameter that should be passed to `sp_configure` in order to set the parameter value.

- `minimum`: This is the minimum legal value allowed for this parameter by the SQL Server. If you pass a value less than the minimum value, the SQL Server will not set the new value and instead will return an error.

- `maximum`: This is the maximum legal value allowed for this parameter by the SQL Server. If you pass a value greater than the maximum value, SQL Server will not set the new value and instead return an error.

- `config_value`: As mentioned before, some parameters (static parameters) take effect after the SQL Server restarts. The new value of such parameters is shown in this column.

■ run_value: This column displays the parameter values that are being used by the SQL Server. Therefore, if you changed a static parameter value, the values shown in the config_value column will be different from the run_value column. At the time of the SQL Server reboot, the config_value value for all the parameters is copied into run_value. Therefore, immediately after the SQL Server reboots, both these columns should display the same parameter values.

TIP

The SQL Server internally maintains two tables: syscurconfigs and sysconfigures. The syscurconfigs table contains current configuration values of SQL Server parameters. These parameter values are shown under the run_value column when you execute sp_configure without parameters. The sysconfigures table stores new values about the parameters that are set using sp_configure. These parameter values are shown under the config_value column when you execute sp_configure without parameters. Dynamic parameter values are written to both these tables. At the time of the SQL Server reboot, the SQL Server copies information from the sysconfigures table and applies them to the syscurconfigs table.

SQL Server configuration parameter values can also be set by using the SQL Enterprise Manager graphical administrative tool. It makes no difference whether you use sp_configure or SQL Enterprise Manager to set parameter values. To get to the SQL Server configuration screen of SQL Enterprise Manager, select the SQL Server you want to configure (assuming you have registered the server), click the right mouse button, and choose the Configuration option from the pop-up menu. The SQL Enterprise Manager configuration screen is shown in Figure 31.1.

FIGURE 31.1.

Configuring the SQL Server using SQL Enterprise Manager.

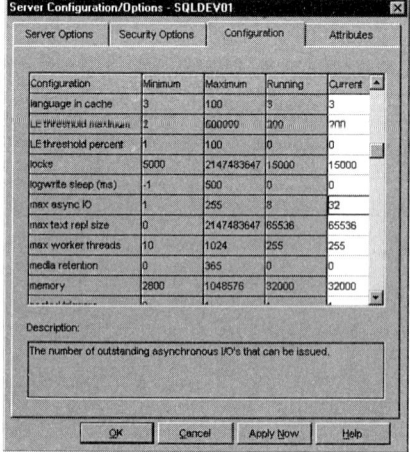

Tuning SQL Server Parameters

At the time of SQL Server installation, the SETUP program takes reasonable default values for all the SQL Server configuration parameters. However, there are certain parameters, such as memory, user connections, number of devices, open databases, and so on, where the choice made by the SETUP program may not be suitable for a specific environment. The system administrator should change these parameter values accordingly. SQL Server configuration parameters are divided into two broad categories: basic and advanced. When a SQL Server is installed, the output of sp_configure will list only the basic configurable parameters. There is a SQL Server option called the show advanced options parameter. If this option is set to 1, executing sp_configure (with no parameters) will list all the configuration parameters. You can set this option on by executing the following:

```
Exec sp_configure 'show advanced option' , 1
go
Reconfigure
go
```

CHECKPOINT and LAZY WRITER Processes

Before we describe the parameters that have a significant impact on SQL Server performance, it will be worthwhile to discuss two SQL Server internal processes—CHECKPOINT and LAZY WRITER. During startup, the SQL Server acquires a certain amount of memory (see the memory configuration parameter later in this chapter) from the operating system. A part of SQL Server memory is used for data caching by creating buffer pools of 2K pages. When a transaction is committed, modified information is stored in the data cache buffers and also written to the disk device(s) on which the transaction log has been created. These modifications may not be written to the database device(s) on which tables reside. This improves the performance of the system because the SQL Server does not have to perform physical writes to the database device(s) for individual transactions. The disadvantage of this scheme is that if the SQL Server crashes, it may take a long time to recover, because the transactions that have been written on the transaction log device may not have been written to the database device. When the SQL Server is restarted, all the changes written to the transaction log will have to be rolled forward (that is, written to the database device on which data resides), which can be a time-consuming process. Therefore, to reduce recovery time, the SQL Server has a CHECKPOINT process. This process wakes up automatically at regular intervals (approximately once a minute) and forces all the committed changes from data cache (called *dirty pages*) to be written to the database devices. This way, the SQL Server ensures that committed transactions are also written to the database device, and, in case of SQL Server crash, recovery will be faster because there are fewer transactions to be applied to the actual tables.

It is also important to remember that there are only a limited number of buffers available for the SQL Server. The CHECKPOINT process forces dirty pages to be written to the disk, but does not free up any buffers. That's where the LAZY WRITER process comes into the picture. This process makes sure that there are always a certain number of buffers available to the SQL Server. This process wakes up automatically, writes the oldest used buffer pages (least recently used pages) to the disk, and frees a number of buffers until the number of free buffers is above a specified threshold.

Changing `affinity mask`

The SQL Server supports Symmetric Multiprocessing (SMP). SMP hardware is a server that has more than one CPU, and each CPU can handle a load (for example, I/Os, interrupts, and so on) independent of other CPUs. An SMP support means that a thread is not tied to a particular processor of the machine and may therefore execute on a different processor each time. SMP support allows the SQL Server to run multiple tasks simultaneously, resulting in excellent load balancing. If there are other applications running on the machine besides the SQL Server, however, or there is a very high load on the SQL Server, it may be desirable to bind thread affinity to processors. The `affinity mask` parameter is a bitmapped field where individual bits specify a processor on the machine. Therefore, on a four-processor server, if you want the SQL Server to use processor 0 and processor 1, use the bitmap 00000011 (decimal 3, that is) and execute the following:

```
Exec sp_configure 'affinity mask', 3
go
Reconfigure
go
```

Default for this parameter is 0. That is, there is no affinity between a thread and a processor. This is not a dynamic option, so in order for this parameter to take effect, you must recycle the SQL Server.

Allocating `free buffers`

You can maximize the performance of the SQL Server by caching as much data as possible in the SQL Server data cache so that the SQL Server does not have to do physical I/Os. Usually, however, database sizes are much bigger than the amount of data cache available to the SQL Server. In such cases, there will always be situations when the data requested is not found in cache and has to be fetched from the disk. To deal with such situations, the SQL Server maintains a number of free buffers. These free buffers are provided by the LAZY WRITER process. This number can be set by setting the `free buffers` configuration parameter. The default value of this parameter is five percent of the total memory allocated to the SQL Server. When the number of free buffers on the SQL Server falls below this parameter value, the LAZY WRITER process writes dirty pages to the disk and adds those pages to the free buffer list until the number of free buffers is greater than or equal to the `free buffers` parameter value. This parameter is specified in terms of 2K pages. This parameter should be set to a higher value (around 10 to 15 percent) in an environment that is highly I/O-intensive and in which data requests are generally not met by the SQL Server cache.

SQL Server Monitoring and Tuning

CHAPTER 31

777

31

SQL SERVER
MONITORING AND
TUNING

Controlling Lock Escalation Behavior

SQL Server default locking granularity is page level. When a query requests a large amount of data that spans across multiple pages, the SQL Server places locks on those pages. The type of locks depends upon the nature of transaction. For a SELECT statement, the lock mode is SHARED; for an UPDATE statement, it is EXCLUSIVE. For a particular T-SQL statement, if the SQL Server has accumulated locks on 200 pages, it escalates the page-level lock to table level lock. This lock escalation behavior is efficient for tables that have fewer records. If a database contains a number of tables that contain millions of records, lock escalation to table level after two hundred page reads is not very efficient, because in a multiuser environment, by holding a lock on the entire table, data concurrency is drastically reduced. This leads to performance problems. To avoid such situations, the SQL Server provides the following three parameters by which you can control the lock escalation behavior:

- ■ LE threshold maximum: This parameter signifies the maximum number of locks held by a statement before a lock can be escalated to a table-level lock. The default value for this parameter is 200 pages. Set it to a high value if your environment has many tables, with each holding a large number of records.

- ■ LE threshold minimum: This parameter signifies the minimum number of locks held by a statement before a lock can be escalated to a table-level lock. The default value for this parameter is 20 pages. This parameter is useful in an environment where you have a number of tables that hold fewer records.

- ■ LE threshold percent: The SQL Server also enables you to specify a percentage value for lock escalation. If this percentage value is exceeded, the SQL Server escalates the lock to table level. The default for this parameter is 0, which means that locks on a table will escalate to table level if the number of locks held on the table exceeds the LE Threshold minimum parameter.

All the preceding parameters are dynamic in nature and take effect immediately. The following example sets the LE Threshold maximum parameter value to 500 pages:

```
Exec sp_configure "LE threshold maximum", 500
go
Reconfigure
```

Changing `logwrite sleep`

logwrite sleep specifies the time (in milliseconds) that the SQL Server should wait before writing a buffer to the transaction log device. The default for this parameter is 0. This means that after a committed transaction, if other users are ready to commit their transactions, the log writer will wait for them. Otherwise, buffers are immediately flushed to the log device. Setting this value to a higher number is useful in an environment where there is high activity on a database and transactions are short. Setting this parameter to a higher value allows more transactions to be saved in the buffers with fewer physical writes to the log device.

Setting max async IO

max async IO defines the number of asynchronous threads that can be issued for batch write requests such as checkpoint and bcp. You should increase this parameter value if there are multiple controllers on the system or hardware-based RAID for disk striping is being used. Because more threads will be used to perform write operations, the system performance improves by using the faster writes. The default value for this parameter is 8. Increasing this parameter is quite useful in an environment that is write-intensive and in which the disk subsystem is capable of sustaining high write volume. The SQL Server should be recycled for this parameter to take effect.

Setting max lazywrite IO

max lazywrite IO is similar to the max async IO configuration parameter. However, the difference is that max lazywrite IO controls the total number of asynchronous IOs that can be issued by the LAZY WRITER process. You may want to increase this value if the load is heavy and there are multiple controllers on your system. The default for this parameter is 8. This parameter cannot have a value greater than the max async IO parameter value.

max worker threads

The SQL Server is integrated closely with Windows NT to make use of native operating system threads. Use of Windows NT threads results in better performance and stability of the SQL Server. The SQL Server can listen on multiple network protocols at the same time. One or more threads are used by the SQL Server for each network protocol that the SQL Server listens on. Threads are also used by the CHECKPOINT and LAZY WRITER processes. The worker threads parameter defines the number of threads that can used for handling SQL Server connections. The default value for this parameter is 255. If the number of connections is less than this parameter value, each thread handles a user connection. If the number of connections is more than the worker thread configuration value, connections are handled by the next available thread. There is seldom a reason to increase this value. Threads can cause overhead on the system processors. Therefore, lowering this value can sometimes improve the performance of the system. For a system with a few hundred user connections, a reasonable number for this parameter is around 125. You may want to experiment with various values to find out the appropriate value for the max worker threads parameter. This is a dynamic parameter and takes effect immediately. The following example sets the max worker threads value to 100:

```
Exec sp_configure 'max worker threads', 100
go
Reconfigure
go
```

SQL Server Monitoring and Tuning

CHAPTER 31

779

31

SQL SERVER
MONITORING AND
TUNING

memory

memory defines the amount of memory (in terms of 2K pages) available to the SQL Server. SQL Server memory is primarily used for data caching. By caching data, a number of requests for data can be satisfied from memory rather than doing physical I/Os—resulting in better overall performance of the system. To calculate the amount of memory that should be assigned to the SQL Server, execute the following steps:

1. Calculate the total physical memory on the machine.

2. Subtract the memory required by the operating system from the total physical memory.

3. Subtract the memory used by other applications from the value in the preceding step.

Memory allocated to the SQL Server is mainly used by SQL Server code, internal static structures, and configuration parameters (such as user connections, locks, open databases, and so on). The rest of the memory is shared by the data cache and the procedure cache. Procedure caches are a part of memory area where the SQL Server stores plans for the stored procedures, triggers, and queries. Query compilation also takes place in the procedure cache. The procedure cache is configured as a percentage of the memory area shared by the data cache and the procedure cache. It is a SQL Server configurable parameter with a default value of 30 percent. To view memory usage on your system, run the T-SQL command DBCC MEMUSAGE. A partial output of this command follows:

```
DBCC MEMUSAGE
go

Memory Usage:
                        Meg.        2K Blks        Bytes

Configured Memory:    250.0000       128000      262144000
Code size:              1.7166          879        1800000
Static Structures:      0.5066          260         531200
Locks:                  0.7439          381         780000
Open Objects:           1.0681          547        1120000
Open Databases:         0.0096            5          10020
User Context Areas:     3.3721         1727        3535882
Page Cache:           169.7083        86891      177952032
Proc Headers:           4.0889         2094        4287568
Proc Cache Bufs:       68.6426        35145       71976960
```

The following example sets the SQL Server memory to 160M (81920 2K pages):

```
Exec sp_configure 'memory', 81920
Reconfigure
```

This is not a dynamic option. Therefore, a SQL Server restart is necessary for this parameter to take effect.

Setting network packet size

network packet size is a dynamic parameter and specifies the default network packet size for the SQL Server. Setting this parameter to a larger value can improve performance of the tasks that involve larger amounts of data transfer, such as bcp. SQL Server default network packet size is 4096. You should set it to an appropriate value depending upon your network configuration and application environment.

> **TIP**
>
> You can also specify the network packet size from the client. Setting network packet size from a client is quite useful when default SQL Server packet size is adequate for general application needs, but a larger packet size is required for some specific operations (such as bcp).

Setting SQL Server priority boost

priority boost signifies the process priority of the SQL Server on a Windows NT operating system. The default value is 0, indicating that the SQL Server will run on the same priority level as other applications on the machine. By setting this value to 1, the SQL Server runs under the real-time priority class under Windows NT. This causes SQL Server threads to be executed before any other application that is running with normal priority. If the SQL Server is the only application running on the machine, setting this parameter value to 1 may provide significant performance improvement. The SQL Server is required to be started for this parameter to take effect.

Changing the Size of the Procedure Cache

The procedure cache is a part of the SQL Server memory area where the SQL Server stores query plans (the mechanism to access the data in the least costly way) for the stored procedures, triggers, rules, defaults, queries, and so forth. Query compilations also take place in the procedure cache. The SQL Server query plan is *always* stored in cache (a query plan is never stored on the disk; only the compiled code is kept on the disk). If you have a large enough procedure cache, subsequent execution of the same procedure results in the usage of the same query plan and thus faster execution of stored procedures. Because procedure cache is only a finite space in memory, a previously stored query plan gets thrown out (on the Least Recently Used, or LRU, algorithm) of the procedure cache to make room for a new query plan. Procedure cache is configured as a percentage of the memory area shared by the data cache and the procedure cache. It is a SQL Server configurable parameter with a default value of 30 percent. If an application uses a large number of stored procedures and triggers, it may be useful to increase this value. To find out an appropriate size for procedure cache, use the DBCC MEMUSAGE T-SQL

SQL Server Monitoring and Tuning

CHAPTER 31

781

31

SQL SERVER
MONITORING AND
TUNING

command. This command displays 20 of the largest stored procedures in the procedure cache. Execute the main (and big) stored procedures on the SQL Server and find out how many can fit in cache with the existing configuration. If you don't find most of the desired stored procedures in cache, you may want to increase the size of procedure cache. If you find all of them, consider reducing the size. Some iterations of these steps will help you determine the optimal size of the procedure cache. The following is a partial output of a DBCC MEMUSAGE command:

```
DBCC MEMUSAGE
go

Procedure Cache, Top 20:


Procedure Name: proc_get_emp_info
Database Id: 6
Object Id: 137278234
Version: 1
Uid: 1
Type: stored procedure
Number of trees: 0
Size of trees: 0.000000 Mb, 0.000000 bytes, 0 pages
Number of plans: 2
Size of plans: 0.042969 Mb, 45056.000000 bytes, 24 pages
```

Changing the Read-Ahead Configuration

There are a number of situations where the data retrieval from a database is sequential (SELECT lname, fname from employee), especially when doing table scans on large tables. The SQL Server can detect such queries and issue background threads that read the data that is not yet requested but is expected at a later stage in the query. This read-ahead feature provides the capability to scan data in parallel. There are a number of configuration options that enable you to control this behavior in a way that best suits your environment. All these parameters are dynamic in nature. That is, the new value takes effect immediately. The following are the SQL Server read-ahead configuration parameters:

- ■ RA cache hit limit. If the data requested by the query is found each time in the data cache, after a certain number of hits on the data cache, the SQL Server cancels read-ahead for the query. This parameter controls this behavior of the read-ahead thread.

- ■ RA cache miss limit. This parameter forces the read-ahead manager to pre-fetch data, if the data requested by the query is still not found in the cache after RA cache miss limit number of attempts.

- ■ RA delay. This is the time in milliseconds that the read-ahead manager takes before it initiates a read-ahead thread.

- ■ RA pre-fetches. The read-ahead manager pre-fetches data in terms of extents. An extent on the SQL Server consists of 8 2K pages. This parameter specifies the number of extents that the read-ahead manager will read in one attempt.

■ RA slots per thread. This parameter signifies concurrent read-ahead requests on each background thread. The default value for this parameter is 5. For large databases and systems with multiple disk controllers, a higher value for this parameter may result in better performance for queries doing sequential data scans.

■ RA worker threads. This parameter designates the total number of threads to be used for queries that require read-ahead. You can disable read-ahead capabilities of the SQL Server by changing the RA worker threads value to 0.

Changing recovery interval

This parameter defines the frequency of checkpoints on a SQL Server. If this value is low, the SQL Server will issue checkpoints more frequently. In the event of SQL Server crash, recovery will be much faster simply because there are fewer records to roll forward or roll back. Because CHECKPOINT is very I/O-intensive (the checkpoint writes all committed changes to the disk), setting the value too low may therefore have an adverse effect on the performance of the system. On the other hand, setting it too high will cause longer recovery time for the SQL Server in case of a crash. You should determine this value based upon the frequency of transactions in your environment and the amount of downtime that you can afford. The default value for this parameter is five minutes, signifying that the maximum allowable time for a database to recover is five minutes. The following example sets this interval to five minutes (that is, more checkpoints will be issued):

```
Exec sp_configure 'recovery interval, 3
go
Reconfigure
```

This is a dynamic option and takes effect immediately.

> **NOTE**
>
> Unless there is very high write activity on the SQL Server, there is seldom reason to change the default value for the recovery interval configuration parameter.

Defining the Number of sort pages

The sort pages parameter specifies a maximum number of pages allotted for sorting for each SQL Server connection. The default value for this parameter is 64 2K pages. You may want to increase this value if your application environment employs queries that involve sorting large numbers of records.

Creating tempdb in RAM

The SQL Server database provides a scratchpad area to hold temporary objects. This database is a shared area used by all the users of the SQL Server to create temporary objects and hold intermediate data results. This database is also used by the SQL Server to create internal work tables and for data sorting (work tables created by the GROUP BY and ORDER BY clauses, for example) for its own use. tempdb is created as a part of the SQL Server installation. During installation of the SQL Server, tempdb is created on the MASTER device with a size of 2M. For most of the applications, this is not sufficient. Database tempdb can be expanded either on a database device or in RAM. If the queries on a system use tempdb extensively, it may be advantageous to put tempdb in RAM. This parameter enables you to specify the size (in megabytes) of tempdb in RAM. This size is not taken from SQL Server memory, but is taken from the operating system. Make sure that you have enough memory for the SQL Server and tempdb if you are using this option. You need to restart the SQL Server after changing this parameter. It makes sense to use this option if you have a large amount of physical memory on the machine. As a general rule, you should not put tempdb in RAM at the expense of SQL Server memory. Usually, you are better off assigning memory to the SQL Server, where you gain performance improvement by caching the data.

> **TIP**
>
> It is important to realize that when you put tempdb in RAM, you are allocating memory that could have been used by the SQL Server to cache data. Because of this, sometimes setting this option ON may adversely impact the performance of the system. The tempdb in RAM option is useful in cases where you have a large amount of physical memory on the machine and there is sufficient amount of memory available for the SQL Server data cache and the procedure cache.

Setting user connections

The user connections parameter enables you to specify the total number of connections the SQL Server can handle simultaneously. Each user connection uses approximately 40K of memory. Setting it too high is a waste of SQL Server memory. If it is set too low, after a configured number of connections have been established, any additional login requests will be denied by the SQL Server. Therefore, configure this parameter optimally based on your environment. You must restart the SQL Server after changing this parameter. The following example changes this parameter to a value of 50:

```
Exec sp_configure 'user connections', 50
```

Integrating the SQL Server with Windows NT Performance Monitor

Using Windows NT Performance Monitor, it is possible to monitor SQL Server performance counters. The SQL Server installation program (SETUP.EXE by default) enables integration of SQL Server statistics with the Performance Monitor. There are two modes by which SQL Server statistics can be collected:

- *Direct Response Mode.* This is the default statistics collection method. This method of data collection is fast because statistics are compiled independent of the display of the statistics. Therefore, you see information that is "almost" up-to-date.

- *On Demand Mode.* In this mode, the Performance Monitor demands data from the SQL Server and then displays it. This method of data collection is slower than the direct response mode, but provides up-to-date statistical information. When using the mode, make sure that the collection interval is not very small. Otherwise, you may flood the SQL Server with requests, which will affect the performance of overall system significantly.

To select these modes and to turn off integration of the SQL Server with Performance Monitor, run SQL SETUP from the SQL Server 6.5 program group and on the Microsoft SQL Server 6.5 Options dialog box (see Figure 31.2). Select the Set Server Options radio button and click the Continue button. On the next screen (see Figure 31.3) choose the mode you want. To turn off monitoring, deselect the SQL PerfMon Integration checkbox and click the Change Options button to activate/deactivate required modes.

> **TIP**
>
> It is generally a good idea to monitor the SQL Server in direct response mode. However, if you are looking for certain counters online during a specified time frame, you may want to use 'on demand mode'. After you are finished and would like to perform unattended monitoring (that is, you are redirecting output to a log file), switch back to direct response mode.

FIGURE 31.2.

Selecting SQL Server options.

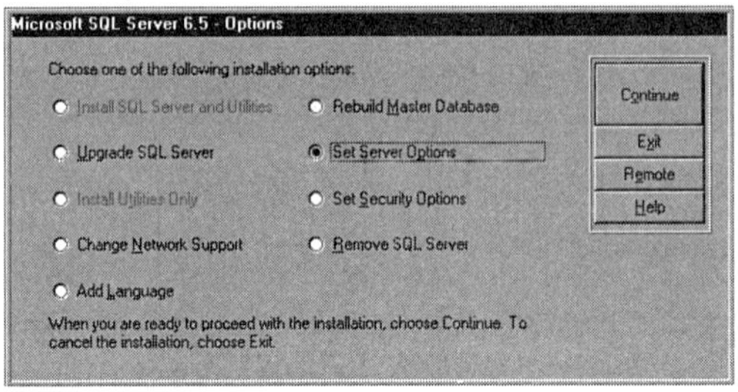

FIGURE 31.3.

Choosing monitoring mode.

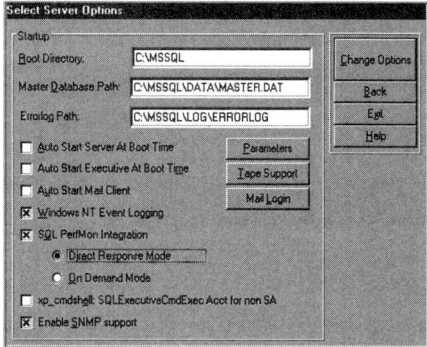

Understanding SQL Server Performance Counters

Performance counters will help you detect bottlenecks on the system. This section explains some useful performance counters of the SQL Server object. We assume that you are familiar with Windows NT Performance Monitor. To invoke Performance Monitor, run SQL Performance Monitor from the SQL Server 6.5 program group and select the machine you want to monitor. In this section, you explore various performance counters for the following Performance Monitor objects:

- Processor
- PhysicalDisk
- SQLServer
- SQLServer-Procedure Cache

Object: Processor

There are a number of counters that are quite helpful in detecting bottlenecks at the processor level. Some of the counters include percent of processor time, percent of privilege time, percent of user time, and so forth. Depending upon the usage of each counter, you can determine the types of activities taking place on a system.

Counter: Processor Time

If the SQL Server is the only main process on the machine, this counter represents the time the CPU is busy executing a SQL Server request. If the process utilization is constantly at a very high percentage across all the CPUs (above 90 percent), you may have a processor bottleneck. The first step to fix this situation is to tune the queries on the system that are CPU-intensive (such as the ones doing complex calculations, using the ORDER BY clause). Adding additional CPUs or faster CPUs will also improve performance of the system.

Counter: % Privilege Time

This counter represents the percentage of time a processor is spending executing Windows NT kernel instructions. This also includes processor time that is spent executing device driver instructions and SQL Server I/O requests. If the percent of privilege time is very high, that will indicate that the larger amount of I/O activity is taking place on the system. If you observe this counter at a very high number constantly (50–60 percent), adding more physical memory to the system and assigning it to the SQL Server may help reduce it. Processor time can be very high if your disk subsystem is very slow.

Counter: % User Time

This counter represents the percentage of time a processor is spending servicing application requests. Usually, if this is a high number (between 60–80 percent), that is not necessarily indicative of a problem on the system. If the percent of user time is above 90 percent, however, that indicates that the SQL Server application is very CPU-intensive. To reduce the percent of user time, you should take a good look at complex queries of the system. Adding additional or faster CPUs may also help remove the performance bottleneck from the system.

Object: PhysicalDisk

Performance counters defined under this object category help determine whether there is a bottleneck on the disk subsystem. Some of these counters include Disk Reads/sec, Disk Writes/sec, Avg. Disk sec/Read, and Avg. Disk sec/Write. By measuring these counters, you can detect whether there is a disk that has higher utilization than others, indicating a load balancing problem on the system.

Counter: % Disk Time

This counter provides an overall picture of how busy a disk drive is while servicing read and write requests. For an appropriately configured system, you should have almost equal activity on all the disks. If one drive is far more active than others, you should investigate how your databases are spread out on the disk. For good load balancing, you should spread out the database, transaction log, nonclustered index, and tempdb on different devices. If all the drives are always at very high utilization, that could indicate that either the overall disk subsystem is slow or there is not enough memory on the system.

Counters: Disk Writes/sec and Disk Reads/sec

These two counters together provide information about the throughput of the disk subsystem. If you are using hardware-based disk mirroring, these counter values are required to be adjusted based on the RAID level being utilized on your hardware. For example, if the devices are mirrored, there will be a write operation on the primary device and then a write on the mirror device. Therefore, in order to calculate actual throughput of the system, multiply the counter value by the total number of write operations (based on the RAID level). Typically, you expect to see better throughput for the devices on which the transaction log is placed, because it is always a sequential write. Numbers will be slightly lower in cases of database devices, because requests for data are usually random in nature.

Counters: Avg. Disk sec/Read, Avg. Disk sec/Write

These two counters provide useful information about individual reads and writes on a disk. For example, Avg. Disk sec/Write signifies the number of seconds it takes to complete a write operation. A high number for these counters indicates that the system is very I/O-intensive and the I/O request queue will be quite large. To remedy this situation, it is advisable to add faster drives to the system.

Object: The SQL Server

The SQL Server is well-integrated with Windows NT Performance Monitor. It provides valuable information through various counters that help facilitate monitoring of the SQL Server and detect bottlenecks on the system. Some of the most commonly used counters are described in the following paragraphs.

Counter: Cache—Number of Free Buffers

The number of free buffers on the SQL Server is maintained by the LAZY WRITER process. This process makes sure that buffers are always available in the free pool area (as defined by the `free buffers` configuration parameter). If this counter displays a value that is continually far less than the `free buffers` configuration parameter value or if this value is steadily reducing, it means that LAZY WRITER is not able to keep up with the demand for the free buffers. Increasing the value of the `free buffers` configuration parameter is not going to help, because that fixes the problem only temporarily. Increasing the value of the `max lazywrite IO` configuration parameter may help improve the situation. Adding additional and faster drives will also result in improved I/O throughput.

Counter: Cache Hit Ratio

This counter defines a percentage of time that a requested database is found in the SQL Server cache. Cache hit ratio is dependent upon the size of memory available to the SQL Server and the size of the database. For better performance, you should have a high ratio of memory and database size.

Counters: I/O Batch Average Size and I/O Batch Writes/sec

These counters define the I/O performance of the system for batch processes (such as the CHECKPOINT process, bulk-copy, and so forth). In a typical application environment, CHECKPOINT is mainly responsible for issuing batch I/O requests. If the batch size is very large, you may want to increase the frequency of the CHECKPOINT process by setting the recovery interval configuration parameter value to a lower value.

Counter: I/O Lazy Writes/sec

This counter signifies the number of buffer pages written to the disk per second by the LAZY WRITER process in order to maintain the number of free buffers above the threshold. This counter should be measured with the cache—number of free buffers counter. Even with a high value for I/O Lazy writes/sec counter value, cache—number of free buffers counter may still be continuously falling. This indicates that the `free buffers` configuration parameter value should be set to a higher value.

Counter: I/O Log Writes/sec

This counter indicates the number of writes per second on the transaction log device. Because writes to the transaction log device are always sequential, you should expect to see a high value for this counter. A consistent low value for I/O Log writes/sec indicates a slow disk subsystem. In this situation, adding faster drives can make a significant difference on performance.

Counters: I/O Outstanding Reads, I/O Outstanding Writes

These counters are useful for monitoring physical reads and writes that are pending. I/O Outstanding Reads and I/O Outstanding Writes provide the most definitive information if there is a bottleneck at the disk subsystem. A large number of outstanding reads or writes on a system indicates that there is a need for faster disks on the system. Spreading your data across multiple drives may also improve performance of the system.

Counters: I/O Page Reads/sec, I/O Page Writes/sec

These two counters are used to monitor physical reads and writes of the SQL Server. These counters don't represent batch reads and writes (such as CHECKPOINT, LAZY WRITER, and so forth). For a SQL Server configured with large amount of memory, you should see little I/O activity on the system, except immediately after SQL Server restart when there is no data in the SQL Server data cache. Reducing the number of physical writes to the database device makes a significant impact on the performance.

Counter: I/O Trans. per Log Record

This counter provides measurement of transactions in a log record before being flushed to the disk. This counter monitors the SQL Server logwrite sleep configuration parameter. The logwrite sleep parameter specifies the time (in milliseconds) the SQL Server should wait before writing a buffer to the transaction log device. The default for this parameter is 0. That means that if other users are ready to commit their transactions, the log write will wait for them; otherwise, buffers are immediately flushed to the log device. If this counter displays a low value, you may want to set the logwrite sleep parameter to a higher value. Setting this parameter to a higher value enables more transactions to be saved in the buffers with fewer physical writes to the log device. This counter provides very useful information in an environment where there is high activity on a server.

Counter: I/O transactions/sec

This counter is somewhat of a misnomer because it does not provide information about transactions per second. This counter monitors the total number of command batches (a batch may contain multiple SQL statements) executed per second. This is a useful counter to measure overall performance of the system. A low value for this counter signifies poor performance of a system. If that is the case in your environment, you should investigate all parts of the system, such as database design, processing power, disk subsystem, and so forth.

Counter: Max tempdb Space Used (MB)

This counter monitors the maximum space consumed in tempdb during the time frame in which you are monitoring the SQL Server. This counter is quite useful for determining the size of tempdb. You may want to turn this counter on during peak activity for a few hours. If tempdb usage is quite heavy and a larger amount of space is being consumed, you may want to consider splitting tempdb across multiple disks.

Counter: Max Users Connected

This counter monitors the maximum number of concurrent connections to the SQL Server during the monitoring window. This counter is quite helpful in determining the peak activity hours for the application. You may want to schedule some of the time-consuming batch processes during the window when there are fewer user connections on the system. In an environment where the number of users is gradually increasing, this counter can also help you determine whether the SQL Server is configured for the appropriate number of user connections. If the counter value is very close to the user connections configuration parameter, you should increase the number of connections for the SQL Server.

Counters: Network Reads/sec, Network Writes/sec

These two counters indicate network traffic to and from the SQL Server. A high value for these counters means that the network traffic is quite high. High traffic on a network can lead to poor overall performance of the system. If the Network Reads/sec counter is high, you may want to evaluate queries and, if possible, convert those to stored procedures. On the other hand, if Network Writes/sec is high, that means that the SQL Server is returning a large number of data sets. A poorly designed application can create a network bottleneck by retrieving hundreds of rows from the database, even though only a few rows are necessary for the front-end application.

Object: SQLServer-Procedure Cache

Procedure cache is a part of the SQL Server memory area where the SQL Server builds and stores query plans for the stored procedures, triggers, rules, views, defaults, and queries. The SQL Server procedure cache is a finite space of buffer pool. This pool consists of the following:

- Buffers for procedures that are currently executing
- Buffers for procedures currently not active, but which have been used in the past
- Buffers that are available

There are a number of counters available for this object on the SQL Server 6.5 that can tell you what percentage of procedure cache is in use by each of these buffers. Some of the main counters are described in the following sections.

Counter: Max Procedure Cache Active %

This counter monitors the maximum percentage use of procedure cache by the procedures that were active during the monitoring window. If this limit is very close to the total procedure cache, it is necessary to increase procedure cache.

SQL Server Monitoring and Tuning

CHAPTER 31

791

31

SQL SERVER
MONITORING AND
TUNING

Counter: Procedure Cache Active %

This counter monitors the percentage of procedure cache that is currently being used by the procedures that are currently running. If this limit is very close to the total procedure cache, there may not be enough space for a new procedure in procedure cache while the other procedures are still executing. In this situation, either you wait until some of the procedures finish their execution or increase total procedure cache.

Counter: Procedure Cache Used %

This counter monitors the percentage of procedure cache that is currently being used by the procedures. Procedures using procedure cache may not be currently running. If this limit is very close to the total procedure cache, there may not be enough space for a new procedure in procedure cache while the other procedures are still executing. In this situation, either you wait until some of the procedures finish their execution or increase total procedure cache.

Counter: Procedure Cache Size %

This counter provides the size of the procedure cache in terms of 2K pages.

Using SQL Trace

Microsoft SQL Server 6.5 provides a graphical utility called SQL Trace. SQL Trace enables the users to monitor T-SQL commands and remote procedure calls (RPCs) going to a SQL Server. To invoke this tool, run SQL Trace from the SQL Server 6.5 program group. SQL Trace enables you to define filters where you can monitor T-SQL commands. Information that can be entered for a filter is shown in Figure 31.4. By using SQL Trace, you can monitor the following:

- Commands sent by all or specific logins (it is also possible to use wildcard characters to filter certain logins)
- All or specific applications
- All or specific clients of the SQL Server
- Connects and disconnects to the SQL Server
- T-SQL commands or SQL commands with specific patterns (it is also possible to use wildcard characters to filter T-SQL commands)
- All or specific remote procedures calls
- Queries that are aborted by the clients

FIGURE 31.4.

Creating a New Filter.

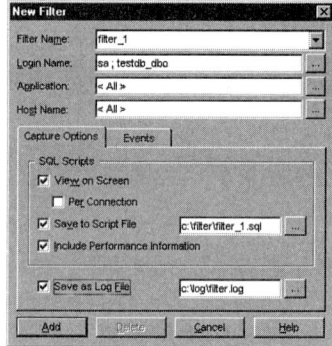

Once a filter is created, you can run it, pause it, delete it, or save it for future use. Figure 31.5 shows the screen output of a typical filter. Using SQL Trace, it is possible to run multiple filters against a SQL Server. Output of these filters can be viewed on the screen or directed to a log file. It is also possible to store the output in a script file, which will have only T-SQL commands in it. This tool can also generate some basic information pertaining to performance such as CPU usage, disk utilization, and so on.

SQL Trace is just a graphical front-end that is built around an extended stored procedure called xp_sqltrace. This extended stored procedure takes a number of input parameters and can redirect the output to the client or to a file (if specified as an input parameter).

FIGURE 31.5.

Monitoring the SQL Server using SQL Trace.

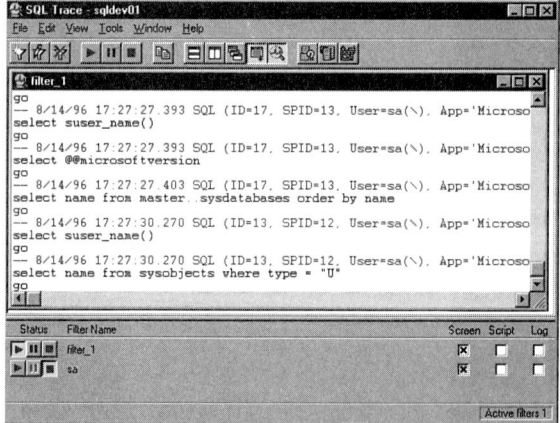

Summary

For a system to have an acceptable performance, various components of the system should be optimized to yield high performance. These components include client hardware, server hardware, network configuration, database design, and the SQL Server. The SQL Server provides numerous parameters that can be configured to tune the SQL Server to provide excellent performance and throughput. The SQL Server is well-integrated with Windows NT Performance Monitor and provides a number of counters that help determine bottlenecks in your system. By removing these bottlenecks, you can ensure high performance for the application.

SQL Server Database Design and Planning

by Vipul Minocha

IN THIS CHAPTER

CHAPTER

32

A good database design is fundamental to the success of any application. Database design primarily consists of two parts: logical design and physical design. Logical database design follows certain rules and results in a structure that can be translated into a physical model. A logical data model does not depend on the relational database engine you intend to use. A physical database design makes extensive use of the features of the underlying database engine to yield high performance for the application. SQL Server database engine features have been discussed in previous chapters. The topics described in this chapter include some of the rules for logical database design, indexing techniques, and their implementation in SQL Server.

What Is Normalization?

A database is a collection of related information. Data is stored in database tables consisting of rows and columns. Usually, a database includes numerous tables, each keeping relevant information. One might ask, Why keep data in so many tables, and why not have just one large table that has all the columns? This question can be answered by keeping two facts in perspective:

- You want to store data on the disk in a way that is most efficient in disk space usage.
- You want to present data to the user with the fastest response time.

To an organization, it is important to have a system that can be implemented with low cost and that yields high performance. Unfortunately, one goal is usually achieved at the expense of the other. Typically, you can achieve performance improvements by keeping redundant and duplicate data in the system. Normalization is a technique of spreading data across multiple tables so that relevant data information is kept together based on certain guidelines. Normalization results in controlled redundancy of data and therefore provides a good balance between disk space usage and performance. There are five rules of normalization. Most database designers, however, follow the first three rules. The rules of normalization can be explained effectively by taking a real-life example. Consider the following scenario:

ABC Corp is a software development company developing multiple software packages. An employee within ABC Corp is known by a unique employee id, but in general employees are recognized by their first names. Human Resources personnel keep track of some important attributes of an employee, such as exempt or nonexempt, salary, bonus, and gross salary. ABC Corp assigns a unique project ID for each project that is currently under development. Each project has a start date and an end date. Employees usually work on multiple projects and come and go as governed by the project requirements.

The goal for ABC Corp is to design a database that keeps track of all the employees working on various projects. From the scenario just explained, you can see the two main database entities here: Employee and Project. Each entity has some attributes associated with it that describe the entity. An attribute that uniquely defines an entity is called the primary key. For example, `employee id` is the primary key for the Employee entity because it uniquely identifies an employee. Some of the attributes are explained in the following table:

Attribute Name	Abbreviated Name
Employee Entity	
employee id	emp_id
employee name	name
salary	salary
bonus	bonus
gross salary	gros_sal
exempt	exempt
Project Entity	
project id	proj_id
project name	p_name
project start date	p_start
project end date	p_end
employee project start date	e_p_start
employee project end date	e_p_end

Abbreviated attribute names will be used in the examples throughout this chapter. Now, to design a database, the simplest method is to create an `employee_project` table with all the columns in it. The primary key for this table is a composite key of `emp_id` + `proj_id`. Table 32.1 depicts a completely denormalized `employee_project` table containing a few records.

Table 32.1. Creating a denormalized employee_project table. The primary key is emp_id + proj_id.

emp_id	name	exempt	salary	bonus	gros_sal	proj_id	p_name	p_start	p_end	e_p_start
100	Jeff	Y	50000	1000	51000	P100	internet	1/1/95	1/1/97	3/3/96
100	Jeff	Y	50000	1000	51000	P200	admin	1/1/96	1/1/98	4/4/96
200	Sam	N	60000	0000	60000	P100	internet	1/1/95	1/1/97	2/2/95
300	Sue	Y	70000	1000	71000	P300	intranet	1/1/96	1/1/97	1/1/96
400	Dave	Y	50000	2000	52000	P300	intranet	1/1/96	1/1/97	1/1/96
500	John	N	80000	5000	85000	P300	intranet	1/1/96	1/1/97	3/18/96
500	John	N	80000	5000	85000	P100	internet	1/1/95	1/1/97	1/1/96

The following section describes the three rules of normalization.

The First Rule of Normalization

The first rule of normalization requires removal of repeating data values and specifies that no two rows should be identical.

In the example shown in Table 32.1, for each employee the columns name, salary, bonus, and gros_sal are being repeated in each row of the table. To conform with the first rule of normalization, these values should be removed and stored separately along with the emp_id column. Therefore, you create a new table called employee_profile consisting of the columns that were being repeated. The resulting structures of the employee_profile and employee_project tables are shown in Tables 32.2 and 32.3.

Table 32.2. The employee_profile table in first normal form. The primary key is emp_id.

emp_id	name	exempt	salary	bonus	gros_sal
100	Jeff	Y	50000	1000	51000
200	Sam	N	60000	0000	60000
300	Sue	Y	70000	1000	71000
400	Dave	Y	50000	2000	52000
500	John	N	80000	5000	85000

Table 32.3. The employee_project table. The primary key is emp_id + proj_id.

emp_id	proj_id	p_name	p_start	p_end	e_p_start
100	P100	internet	1/1/95	1/1/97	3/3/96
100	P200	admin	1/1/96	1/1/98	4/4/96
200	P100	internet	1/1/95	1/1/97	2/2/95
300	P300	intranet	1/1/96	1/1/97	1/1/96
400	P300	intranet	1/1/96	1/1/97	1/1/96
500	P300	intranet	1/1/96	1/1/97	3/18/96
500	P100	internet	1/1/96	1/1/95	1/1/96

The benefits gained here are obvious. The employee_project table is much smaller now. SQL Server can now pack more rows per data page. A fewer number of I/Os will be required to read pages, and more information can be cached in SQL Server memory.

The Second Rule of Normalization

An entity is in second normal form if it conforms to the first normal form and all nonkey attributes are fully dependent on the *entire* primary key. If the primary key consists of multiple attributes, the nonkey attributes should depend on the entire key and not just a part of the key. All nonkey attributes that are dependent on a part of the key should be removed and stored separately along with the attributes they are dependent on.

Take the example shown in Table 32.3. The primary key for the employee_project table is a composite key consisting of the emp_id and proj_id columns. To conform with the second normal form, all the nonkey attributes (such as p_start and p_end) should completely depend on the primary key (emp_id + proj_id). However, attributes such as project name (p_name), project start date (p_start), and project end date (p_end) are dependent only on the proj_id attribute and not on the emp_id. This is a violation of the second normal form. Therefore, these attributes need to be removed from the employee_project table and stored in a different table called project_profile. This is shown in Table 32.4 and Table 32.5.

Table 32.4. The project_profile table in second normal form. The primary key is proj_id.

proj_id	p_name	p_start	p_end
P100	internet	1/1/95	1/1/97
P200	admin	1/1/96	1/1/98
P300	intranet	1/1/96	1/1/97

Table 32.5. The employee_project table. The primary key is emp_id + proj_id.

emp_id	proj_id	e_p_start
100	P100	3/3/96
100	P200	4/4/96
200	P100	2/2/95
300	P300	1/1/96
400	P300	1/1/96
500	P300	3/18/96
500	P100	1/1/96

The Third Rule of Normalization

An entity is in third normal form if it already conforms to the first two normal forms and no nonkey attribute is dependent on any other nonkey attributes. All such attributes are required to be removed from the table.

For example, the attribute gros_sal in Table 32.2 is calculated as follows:

```
gros_sal  = salary + bonus
```

The attribute gros_sal is a dependent on two other nonkey attributes: salary and bonus. This is a violation of the third normal form. Because gros_sal is a computed field and can always be calculated using the other two (salary and bonus) fields, it should be removed from the table. The resultant table structure is shown in Table 32.6.

Table 32.6. The employee_profile table in third normal form. The primary key is emp_id.

emp_id	name	exempt	salary	bonus
100	Jeff	Y	50000	1000
200	Sam	N	60000	0000
300	Sue	Y	70000	1000
400	Dave	Y	50000	2000
500	John	N	80000	5000

As you can see, by following the rules of normalization, one large table (employee_project) has been broken into three smaller tables (employee_profile, project_profile, and employee_project). The following section explains the benefits of normalization.

Why Normalize?

After you have designed your database to be in the third normal form, you can create physical tables in the database. As a result of normalization, because data is split into multiple tables with fewer columns, you can store more data (that is, more rows) on each page of the database. Some of the advantages of using normalization are listed here:

- Because information is logically kept together, normalization provides a better overall understanding of the system.
- A database in its third normal form has far less data than the one without normalization. This can result in substantial cost savings in terms of disk space usage.
- Index creation and data sorts are faster because of smaller tables.
- More rows per page means that fewer I/Os are performed and more data can be cached in memory.

- SQL Server allows only one clustered index per table. Using normalization rules, you would typically have multiple smaller tables; therefore, you can create more clustered indexes.

- Because the amount of redundant data is reduced, it is faster and easier to maintain data integrity.

Denormalizing a Database

After a database has been normalized to third normal form, sometimes it is necessary to back-track from normalization for performance reasons. This step of rolling back from normalization is called denormalization. The sole purpose of denormalizing a database is to improve performance. One of the major benefits of normalization techniques is the reduction of redundant data. This results in efficient usage of disk storage space. But at the same time, because data is now split into multiple tables, joins are required across tables to retrieve information that resides in various tables. This method results in slower performance for queries. Continuing with the scenario of ABC Corp, assume that you want to find out the names of all the employees who are working on a project with project ID P100. For a normalized database (Tables 32.5 and 32.6), you can get the desired results to be returned from the query by *joining* the `employee_profile` and `employee_project` tables. The query example is shown here:

```
SELECT     name
FROM       employee_profile, employee_project
WHERE      employee_profile.emp_id = employee_project.emp_id
AND        employee_project.proj_id = "P100"
```

If the database was denormalized (see Table 32.1), you could have gotten the same results *without* the joins. The query example is as shown here:

```
SELECT     name
FROM       employee_project
WHERE      proj_id = "P100"
```

In the first example, storage efficiency is achieved at the cost of performance. In the second example, better performance is achieved at the cost of higher usage of disk space. You can see that there is a trade-off between performance and cost. Therefore, to build a system with low cost and high performance, you must first normalize your database; then if you experience any performance bottlenecks, you should consider denormalizing the database.

Criteria for Denormalization

Before you denormalize a database, consider the following points:

- Be sure to have a good overall understanding of the logical design of the system. This knowledge helps in determining how the other parts of the application are going to be affected when you change one part of the system.

- Try not to denormalize the entire database. Instead, focus on specific queries that are executed more frequently and that are suffering from performance problems. Determine the expected response time for each such query.

- Understand the volume of data and type of queries (such as select, delete, insert, update) that will be run against specific tables.

- Determine whether there is a need for derived columns. Derived columns are ones that are computed from other columns.

- Understand data integrity issues. One must realize that with denormalization, more redundant data will be included. Therefore, maintaining data integrity will be more difficult, and data modifications might be slower.

- Understand storage technique for the data. Usage of segments can also improve performance without having to denormalize database tables.

TIP

If you are experiencing application-wide performance problems, denormalizing should not be the first step you take to try to fix the problem. Before you denormalize your database, make sure that other components of the system (such as hardware, network, and SQL Server) are configured optimally.

Methods of Denormalization

Various methods can be employed to denormalize a database table. One or more of these methods can be used to achieve the desired performance goals. Some of the most common methods for denormalization are discussed in the following paragraphs.

Horizontal Partitioning

In this method of denormalization, a large table is split into multiple smaller tables based on specific criteria. Each resultant table has the same data structure (that is, the same column names and column properties) as the parent table but contains mutually exclusive data. This method is commonly used for tables that contain an extremely large number of rows. Queries on such large tables are sometimes quite slow because of the large amount of data being scanned. Horizontal splitting of the data can be explained by taking the example of the `employee_profile` table. Assume that most of the queries on the `employee_profile` table pertain to exempt employees (Table 32.6) and that many rows in the table have employees of both types (exempt and nonexempt). This table can be split into two tables, based on whether an employee is an exempt or a nonexempt employee. Tables 32.7 and 32.8 depict two tables, `exempt_emp_profile` and `nonexempt_emp_profile`, that are a result of a horizontal split of the `employee_profile` table.

Table 32.7. Horizontal partitioning: the `exempt_emp_profile` table.

emp_id	name	exempt	salary	bonus
100	Jeff	Y	50000	1000
300	Sue	Y	70000	1000
400	Dave	Y	50000	2000

Table 32.8. Horizontal partitioning: the `nonexempt_emp_profile` table.

emp_id	name	exempt	salary	bonus
200	Sam	N	60000	0000
500	John	N	80000	5000

> **TIP**
>
> Horizontal partitioning is quite useful when a large amount of historical information is kept along with the currently active data. If historical information is used only occasionally, it can be placed in multiple tables (for example, one table for each month), and active data can be stored in a separate table. Programming with tables that are horizontally split, however, can sometimes become very complicated.

Vertical Partitioning

A database in SQL Server consists of multiple 2K pages. The number of rows on a page depends on the width of the table (plus some overhead). This means that the wider the table, the fewer the number of rows per page. Significant performance gains can be achieved by reducing the number of I/Os on a table. Vertical splitting is a method of reducing the width of a table by splitting the table into two or more tables: all frequently used columns are kept together in one table, and the others are kept in another table. This method results in a reduction of table width. Therefore, more rows can be accommodated per page, a fewer number of I/Os will be generated, and more data can be cached in SQL Server memory. Take the example of the `employee_profile` table. If `name` and `salary` are the only two columns that are accessed frequently, the `employee_profile` table can be partitioned vertically as shown in Tables 32.9 and 32.10.

Table 32.9. Vertical partitioning: the `primary_employee_profile` table.

emp_id	name	salary
100	Jeff	50000
200	Sam	60000
300	Sue	70000
400	Dave	50000
500	John	80000

Table 32.10. Vertical partitioning: the `secondary_employee_profile` table.

emp_id	name	exempt	salary	bonus
100	Jeff	Y	50000	1000
200	Sam	N	60000	0000
300	Sue	Y	70000	1000
400	Dave	Y	50000	2000
500	John	N	80000	5000

Adding Redundant and Computed Columns

Joins are usually expensive in terms of CPU usage and from an I/O point of view. Performance gains can be achieved by reducing the number of joins in a query. You can do this by keeping some redundant information in a table so that you can avoid joins in some frequently executed queries. Assume that you want to find out the names of all the employees who are working on a project with project ID P100. For a normalized database (Table 32.5 and 32.6), you can get the desired results to be returned from the query by *joining* the `employee_profile` and `employee_project` tables. The query is shown here:

```
SELECT     name
FROM       employee_profile, employee_project
WHERE      employee_profile.emp_id = employee_project.emp_id
AND        employee_project.proj_id = "P100"
```

Now if you denormalize the `employee_project` table and add an additional column, `name`, to the table (see Table 32.11), you eliminate the need for a join in the query. Although Table 32.11 is in violation of the first normal form, it gives better performance because of the absence of a join. The query is as shown here:

```
SELECT     name
FROM       employee_project
WHERE      proj_id = "P100"
```

Table 32.11. Adding a redundant column to the `employee_project` table. Denormalization with a violation of the first normal form.

emp_id	name	proj_id	e_p_start
100	Jeff	P100	3/3/96
100	Jeff	P200	4/4/96
200	Sam	P100	2/2/95
300	Sue	P300	1/1/96
400	Dave	P300	1/1/96
500	John	P300	3/18/96
500	John	P100	1/1/96

Some queries compute aggregate values derived from one or more columns of a table. Computation of aggregate values (such as mathematical calculations) can be highly CPU intensive. If such computations are frequent enough, they can impact performance adversely. One of the techniques for dealing with such situations is to create an additional column that stores the derived value. For the `employee_profile` table (Table 32.6), if the gross salary (`salary + bonus`) is being calculated quite often, it might be more beneficial to add a column called `gross_salary` to the `employee_profile` table. A trigger can be created on this table that can maintain the value in the `gross_salary` column. Although this is a violation of the third normal form, it might provide significant performance improvements in an application that uses several derived columns. Table 32.12 illustrates this method of denormalizing the database.

Table 32.12. Adding a redundant column to a table.

emp_id	name	exempt	salary	bonus	gross_salary
100	Jeff	Y	50000	1000	51000
200	Sam	N	60000	0000	60000
300	Sue	Y	70000	1000	71000
400	Dave	Y	50000	2000	52000
500	John	N	80000	5000	85000

Using Indexes

SQL Server provides indexes for faster access to the data and to enforce the uniqueness of the data in the database tables. Creating indexes on a table improves the query search performance. Indexes are one of the most important aspects of database design. They are essential for faster retrieval of data from various tables. You create indexes on a table by specifying column names that constitute a key. SQL Server provides two types of indexes: clustered index and nonclustered index. Both of these indexes are B-Tree structures and require *separate* storage space in the database. You can create indexes on tables either by using the CREATE INDEX statement or by using the UNIQUE or PRIMARY KEY integrity constraint of the CREATE TABLE clause of T-SQL. SQL Server allows only one clustered index per table (soon I will explain why) and up to 249 nonclustered indexes. Before I get into the specifics of each type of index, it is important that you understand the storage and data-access techniques of SQL Server.

SQL Server Data Access Technique

A SQL Server database is created with the following logical storage hierarchy:

- Page (consists of 2K)
- Extent (consists of eight 2K pages)
- Allocation unit (consists of 32 extents)

Pages

A page is the minimum allocation unit in a SQL Server database. The size of each page is 2048 bytes (2K). Pages allocated to a table are maintained in the form of a double link list; that is, each page has a pointer to the next as well as the previous page in the link. SQL Server stores the following information on each page of a database:

- Page Header (32 bytes per page): The header information of each page keeps information about the current, next, and previous pages for the table within an extent.

- Meta-Data Information (54 bytes per page): Each row on the data page has some overhead associated with it. These bytes don't store any table data. Information stored in these bytes is used by SQL Server to retrieve row atributes such as total number of columns in a row, row location on page, row number and so forth. Following are some of the attributes associated with a row:

  Column Information (1 byte): Usually, there are columns in a table that allow null or have variable-length data types (for example, varchar). This byte stores the number of columns that either allow nulls or have variable-length data types. The value stored in this byte is 0 if the table has no variable-length or null columns.

  Row ID (1 byte): Each row in a page is assigned a unique row number. This byte stores the row number of the row. Because this is a 1-byte field, the maximum row number is 256. Therefore, the maximum number of rows per page is 256.

Row Offset Table (2 bytes): Because columns of a table might consist of variable-length data types or allow nulls, row length is not expected to be fixed. Therefore, it is necessary to store the starting position of each row on the page. This is accomplished by the use of a row offset table. The starting position of each row is stored in the row offset table. The row offset table is located at the end of the page, and it requires two bytes for each row on the page. It starts at the last byte of the page and grows backward as rows are added to the page.

Variable Length Column Information(5 bytes): This overhead is incurred only for the tables that allow nulls for the column property or have variable-length data types. These bytes store information such as row size and the starting location of each variable-length column.

- Data Rows (1962 bytes): The total space left for the data row on a page is 2048 − (32 + 54) = 1962. This is the maximum space available for data rows. All the rows on a page are arranged sequentially. The number of rows per page will depend on the width of the table. A data row for a table *must* fit within a page. Therefore, the total width (the sum of all column data type storage lengths) of the table cannot exceed 1962 bytes. Each row on a page also has some overhead associated with it, as detailed in the following list:

  - *Column Information (1 byte).* Usually, there are columns in a table that allow null or have variable-length datatypes (varchar, for example). This byte stores the number of columns that either allow nulls or have variable-length datatypes. The value stored in this byte will be zero if there are no variable length or null columns in a table.

  - *Row ID (1 byte).* Each row in a page is assigned a unique row number. This byte stores that row number. Because this is 1-byte field, it is obvious that the maximum row number can be 256. Therefore, the maximum number of rows per page is 256.

  - *Row Offset Table (2 bytes).* Because columns of a table may consist of variable-length datatypes or allow nulls, row length is not expected to be fixed. Therefore, it is necessary to store the starting position of each row on the page. This is accomplished by using the row offset table. The starting position of each row is stored in the row offset table, which is located at the end of the page and requires 2 bytes for each row on the page. It starts at the last byte of the page and grows backward as rows are added to the page.

  - *Additional overhead (5 bytes).* This overhead is incurred only for the tables that allow nulls for the column property or have variable-length datatypes. These bytes store information such as row size, starting location of each variable-length column, and so forth.

32

SQL Server
Database Design
and Planning

Figure 32.1 shows a typical page structure in SQL Server.

> **NOTE**
>
> Because each row must fit completely on a page, if a table has row width greater than 981 bytes (1962 divided by 2), the remaining space on the page is rendered useless because no other row can fit into the rest of the space.

FIGURE 32.1.

Page structure in a
SQL Server database.

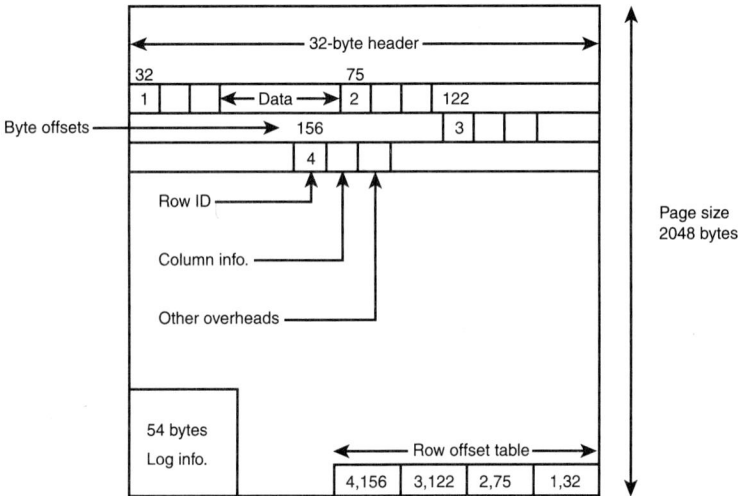

Extents

An extent in SQL Server is a block of eight contiguous 2K pages (16K). Extents are used for space allocation for tables in a database. Space is always allocated to tables one extent at a time. A new extent is allocated to a table at the time of table creation or when a previously allocated extent becomes full. An extent is deallocated from a table when all the pages on that extent don't contain any data. Each extent within an allocation unit is a doubly linked list; that is, each extent has pointers to the previous and the next extent in the link list. Page links are maintained only within an extent, and links to other pages on a different extent are maintained through extent level links. Figure 32.2 shows a typical extent structure.

FIGURE 32.2.

Extents in a SQL Server database.

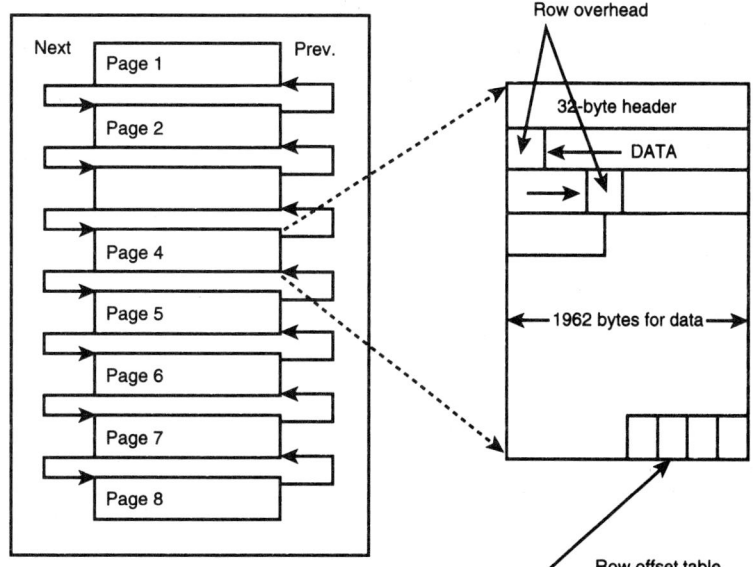

Allocation Units

When a new database is created with the CREATE DATABASE T-SQL command, SQL Server internally divides the total space into multiples of 256 2K page blocks. Each such block is called an allocation unit. Each allocation unit is divided into 32 extents, each extent consisting of eight contiguous pages. An allocation unit keeps track of space usage within an allocation unit. Each allocation unit is a doubly linked list; that is, each allocation unit has pointers to the previous and the next allocation unit in the linked list. The first page of each allocation unit keeps information about the next and previous allocation unit pointers. This first page of each allocation unit keeps track of free extents within an allocation unit. It also keeps track of the extents that have been allocated to a specific table. A representation of the storage scheme of an allocation unit is shown in Figure 32.3.

Because space allocation for tables is always in terms of extents, no two tables can share an extent within an allocation unit. Multiple tables can, however, share the same allocation unit. A table can span multiple allocation units, depending on the number of rows in the table. If a table has no indexes, data is always added at end of the last page of the table. For performance reasons, SQL Server tries to allocate data for a table in contiguous extents in the current allocation unit. If no contiguous extents are available, it tries to allocate an extent within the same allocation unit. If no extents are available within the allocation unit, it tries to allocate an extent on allocation units on which the table already has extents.

FIGURE 32.3.

Allocation units in SQL Server.

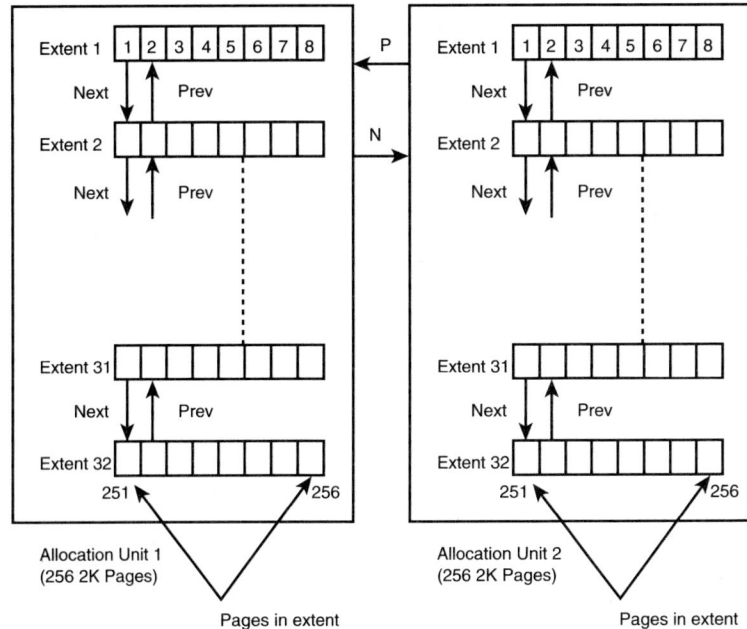

In the example shown in Figure 32.4, Table A and Table B are using separate extents on Allocation Unit 1. Table A also has an extent allocation on Allocation Unit 2. The first page of each table stores information about all the allocation units the table is split across. In the example shown in Figure 32.4, the first page of Table A keeps pointers to Allocation Units 1 and 2. For Table B, the pointers are only to Allocation Unit 1. The first page of each allocation unit stores the information about the extents that have been allocated to various tables. The location of the first page for each table is stored in the sysindexes system table. Now you'll see what happens if a user requests some data from Table A that resides on Page 5 of Extent 18 on Allocation Unit 2 (see Figure 32.4). SQL Server fetches the starting data page number of Table A from the sysindexes system table. Because the first page of a table has pointers to all the allocation units on which table data is present, this page has pointers to Allocation Units 1 and 2. The first page of Allocation Unit 1 points to Extent 2 and Extent 31. SQL Server reads all the pages on both the extents, then continues on to Allocation Unit 2, which points to Extent 18 for Table A. SQL Server starts reading pages in Extent 18 until it reaches Page 5, where it finds the requested data.

FIGURE 32.4.

Locating table data in SQL Server.

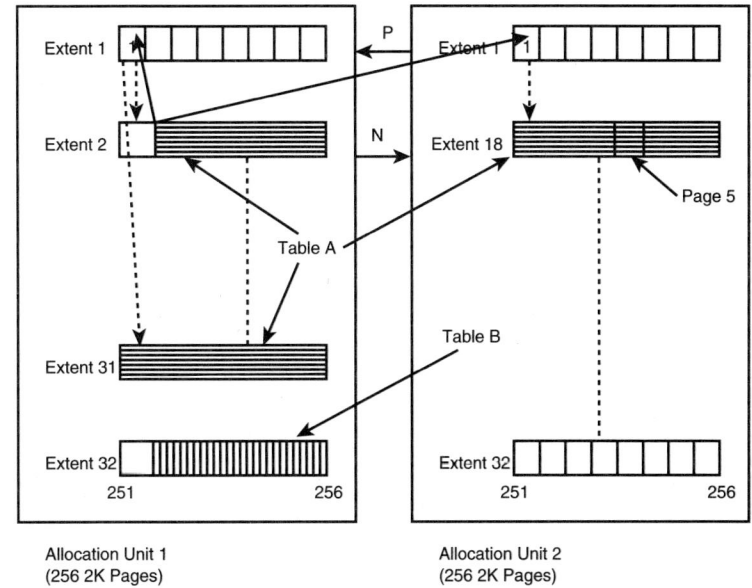

Allocation Unit 1
(256 2K Pages)

Allocation Unit 2
(256 2K Pages)

This whole process of reading all the pages in a table is called a table scan. Table scans are very slow, because SQL Server starts reading from the first page and continues reading until it finds the desired result set. For tables that have many records and joins that are complex and involve such tables, the table scan will be very slow and unacceptable. That's why indexes are created on tables—to eliminate table scans and access the data directly rather than sequentially. Indexes in SQL Server are created as B-Tree structures, and they provide more direct access to the data. Similar to data pages, index pages are also stored in 2K pages. Unlike data pages, index pages store values of indexed columns and pointers to the data. The following paragraphs explain the B-Tree structure.

B-Tree Structure

There are various methods of index storage structures. SQL Server indexes are stored as B-Tree (Balanced Tree) structures. As the name suggests, indexes are stored in the form of a balanced tree with multiple levels. Indexes use separate storage space on SQL Server. There are three levels of a B-Tree:

- Root Level
- Leaf Level
- Intermediate Level

Root Level

The root level is the highest level of an index. Usually, index pages contain more rows than the data pages simply because index pages store only the key column values and pointers to the data pages. Depending on the number of rows in a table, the root level points either to the data page or to a lower level that is an intermediate level. There is only one page at the root level.

Leaf Level

Leaf level is the lowest level of an index. This level stores the pointer values that point directly to the data page. There might be multiple pages at the leaf level, depending on the number of rows in a table.

Intermediate Level

All the levels between the root level and the leaf level are termed as intermediate level. The number of intermediate levels depends on the total number of records in a table and the size of the key. A larger key and a larger number of records results in a greater number of intermediate levels. These levels are numbered in increasing order from leaf level (which is also called Level 0) to the root level.

An example is necessary here to demonstrate how indexes are maintained. Assume that the table `employee` is indexed on a column called `empid`. Also assume that the data page can store three rows per page and the index page can store five rows per page (in reality, there will be many more rows on data and index pages). In the beginning, let's say that the `employee` table contains five records, as shown in Figure 32.5.

In the example shown in Figure 32.5, there is only one level of index: the leaf level. Now if three more records are inserted in this table, one data page is added to accommodate the new rows, and two additional index pages are required to maintain the B-Tree. This structure is depicted in Figure 32.6.

You can see from Figure 32.6 that there is an extra level of index pages to support data in the table. As more data gets added to this table, more index pages are utilized, and more intermediate levels are created. If you create an additional index on the same table, a separate B-Tree is created to maintain that index.

As mentioned before, SQL Server provides two types of indexes: clustered and nonclustered. They are both stored as B-Tree structures. Both of the indexes are covered in the following paragraphs.

FIGURE 32.5.

Basic B-Tree structure.

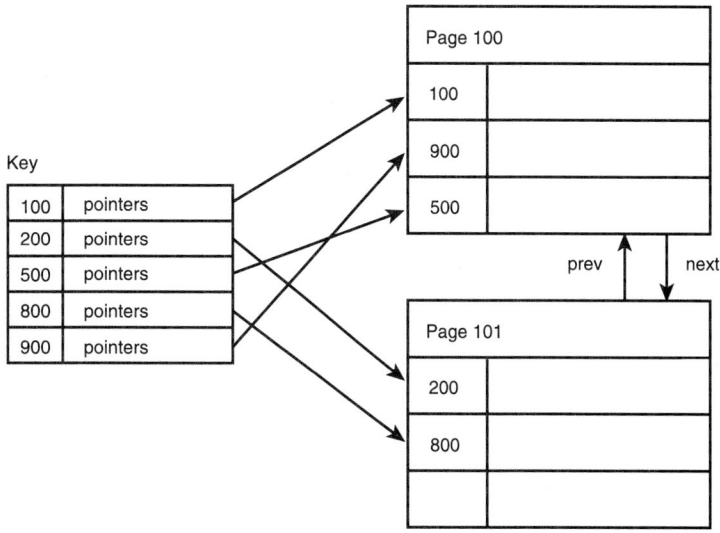

FIGURE 32.6.

*B-Tree structure after
the data insert.*

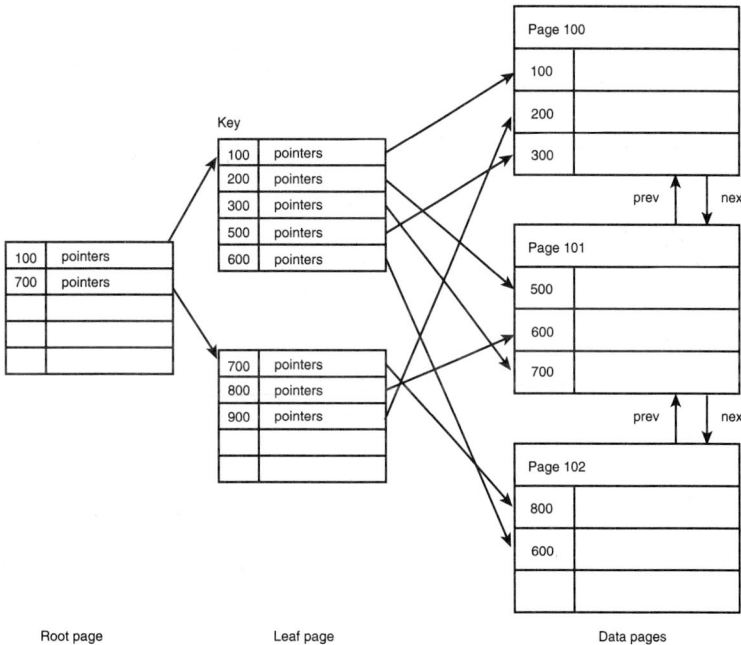

Clustered Index

A clustered index enables you to create an index in which the physical order of the rows on data pages is the same as the physical order of the keys on index pages. That means data is physically sorted on the pages in the order of the indexed keys. Therefore, if you create a clustered index on empid, the B-Tree shown in Figure 32.6 will look like the one shown in Figure 32.7.

FIGURE 32.7.

Clustered indexes in SQL Server.

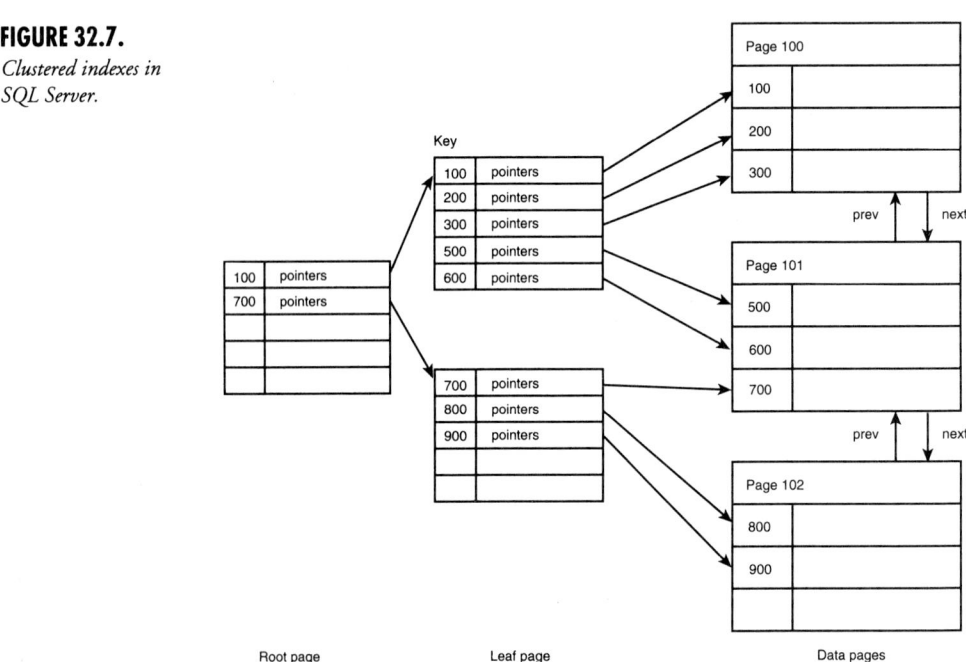

Root page   Leaf page   Data pages

If you notice closely, the key values on the data pages and the leaf pages are identical. Therefore, to eliminate redundancy, leaf pages are substituted by the data pages. That means that the bottom of the leaf page is actually a data page and there is one fewer level for indexing. This is shown in Figure 32.8.

Because there can be only one physical order of the key, you can have only one clustered index per table. Also note that the pointers in a clustered index do not point directly to data rows, but to the page on which the rows reside. It's now time to examine the effect of various data manipulation statements on a table with a clustered index on it.

FIGURE 32.8.

B-Tree structure for clustered indexes.

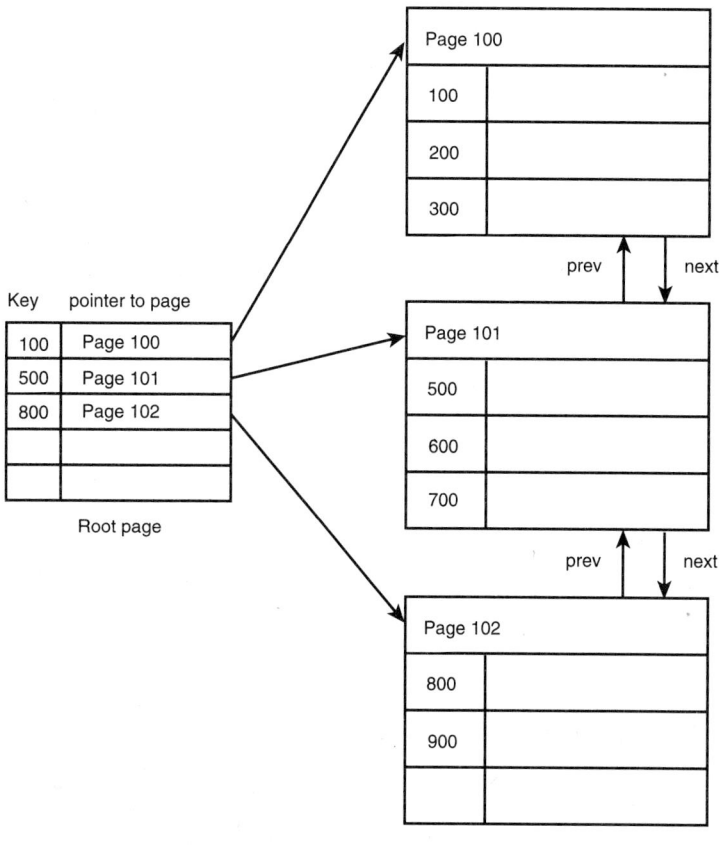

Data Manipulation with Clustered Indexes

When a row is inserted into a table, because data is physically sorted on the pages, some rows move down to accommodate the new row. A row is added at the end of the page only when the key value is greater than the previous maximum value for the key. For example, in Figure 32.8 if you insert a record with empid = 750, then to accommodate this row, rows with empid = 800 and 900 move down one position. SQL Server also modifies the B-Tree structure to accommodate this insert. The result is shown in Figure 32.9.

A delete operation is just the opposite of the insert statement. For example, if you delete a row from the table shown in Figure 32.9 in which empid = 750, then rows with empid = 800 and 900 move up one row and the B-Tree is now modified to point to the page with empid = 800.

An update statement is essentially a delete followed by an insert statement. Therefore, if you update empid 750 with 850, there is physical movement of the rows for the delete statement and then for the insert statement.

FIGURE 32.9.

Insert operation with a clustered index.

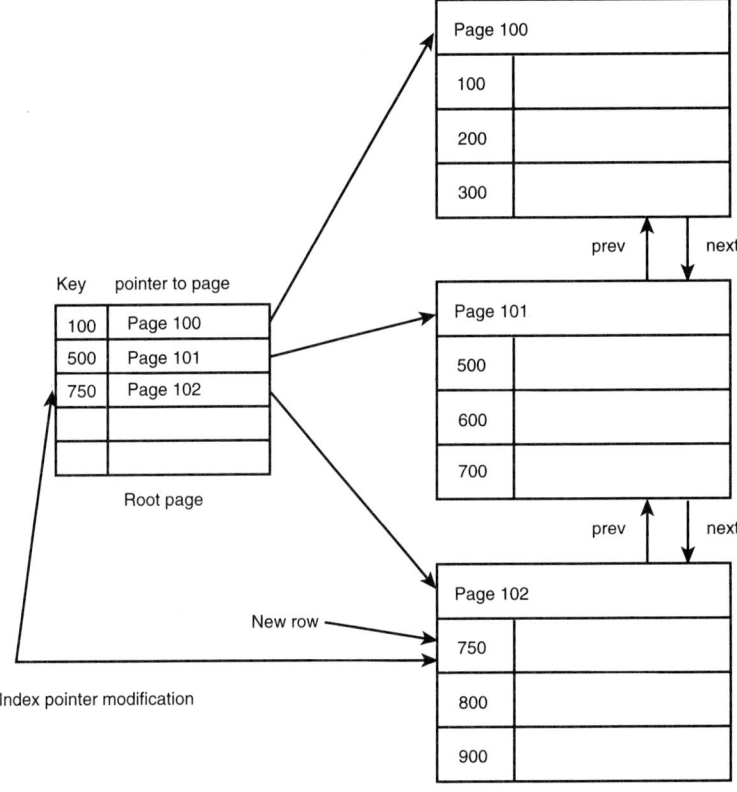

Leaf/data pages

TIP

SQL Server enables you to write queries in such a way that an update can be performed "in place." That means there is no physical movement of the row. To perform an update in place, you must follow certain rules, including the following ones:

- A query cannot update the columns participating in the clustered index.
- The table can't have an update trigger defined on it.
- The table must not be used for data replication.

An update in place results in better performance of the query due to the lack of physical movement of the row and the lower amount of data logging by SQL Server. For a complete list of rules for an update in place, refer to the SQL Server documentation.

If you refer to Figure 32.9, you will notice that all the data pages are completely full and there is no place to add a new row. In such cases if an insert takes place, SQL Server adds a new page to the link list from the extent and splits the information 50-50 on the old page and the new page. Figure 32.10 shows an example of page splitting in which a new record is inserted with `empid = 950`.

FIGURE 32.10.

Page splitting in SQL Server.

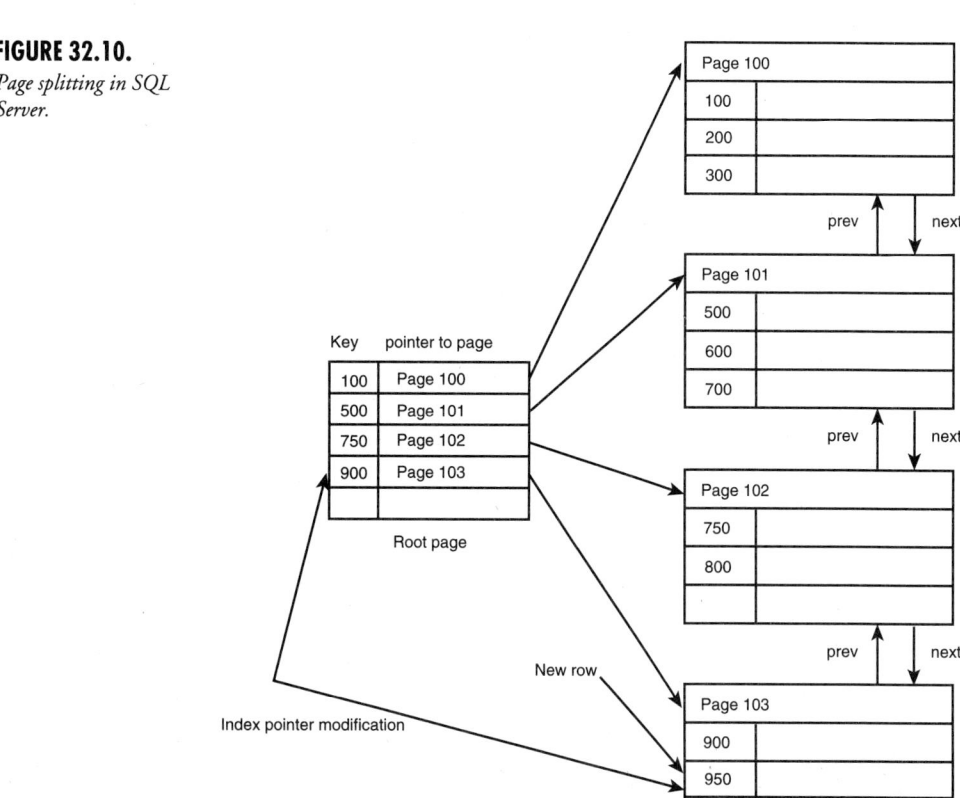

Nonclustered Index

Nonclustered indexes are also B-Tree structures. A nonclustered index differs from a clustered index in the following ways:

- Data is not physically sorted on the pages in the order of the key. Therefore, data is always inserted at the end of the last data page in the link list.

- Unlike with a clustered index, the leaf page of a nonclustered index is not a data page. The leaf page of a nonclustered index stores the key value, page number, and ROWID of the row to provide direct access to the row. ROWIDs point to the offset table on the page, which in turn points to the data for the row.

- You can create up to 249 nonclustered indexes on a table. Each index is a separate B-Tree structure and requires storage space in the database.

A typical B-Tree structure for a nonclustered index looks as shown in Figure 32.11. Because there is an additional level of indexing, a nonclustered index requires extra storage space.

FIGURE 32.11.

B-Tree structure for a nonclustered index.

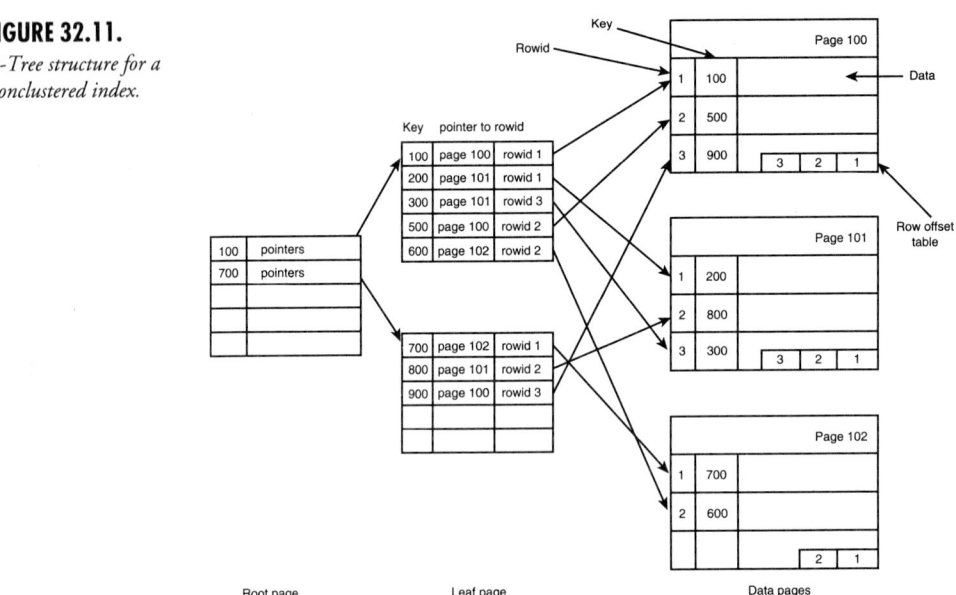

Data Manipulation with Nonclustered Indexes

When a row is inserted into a table with a nonclustered index, data is always added at the end of the page. But index pages are always kept in the sorted order. The row ID of a row is a pointer to an offset table on each data page. The offset table stores the starting location of data for each row on the page. The starting position of the offset table is always at the last byte of the page. The offset table grows backward when records are inserted on a page using a 2-byte pointer for each row. The advantage of using ROWID and the offset table is that when data gets inserted or deleted from a page, existing ROWIDs and corresponding index pointers for other rows remain unaffected. For an insert statement, a new ROWID is assigned for the row, and changes are made to the offset table to point to the location of data. Figure 32.12 illustrates a scenario in which a record with empid = 750 is inserted into the table. You will notice that the record is added at the end of the data page with a new ROWID, and unlike with clustered indexes, there is no physical movement of the rest of the records.

As a result of the delete operation, the row is deleted from the data page, and all the rows below the deleted one move up. The ROWID for the other records remains unaffected. The offset table is modified to reflect the new location of the data for the records that physically moved on the page. Now for index pages, the B-Tree is modified to remove the reference for the deleted row. Because the leaf page stores the ROWID of the rows, other entries in the B-Tree remain unaffected by the delete operation. Figure 32.13 illustrates a scenario in which a record with empid = 700 is deleted from the table. You will notice that the ROWIDs for the other records remain unchanged.

FIGURE 32.12.

Insert operation with a nonclustered index.

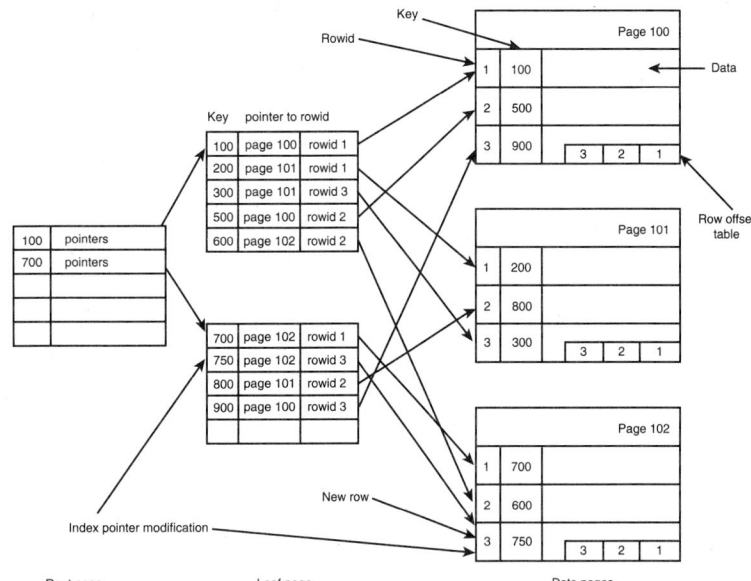

FIGURE 32.13.

Delete operation with a nonclustered index.

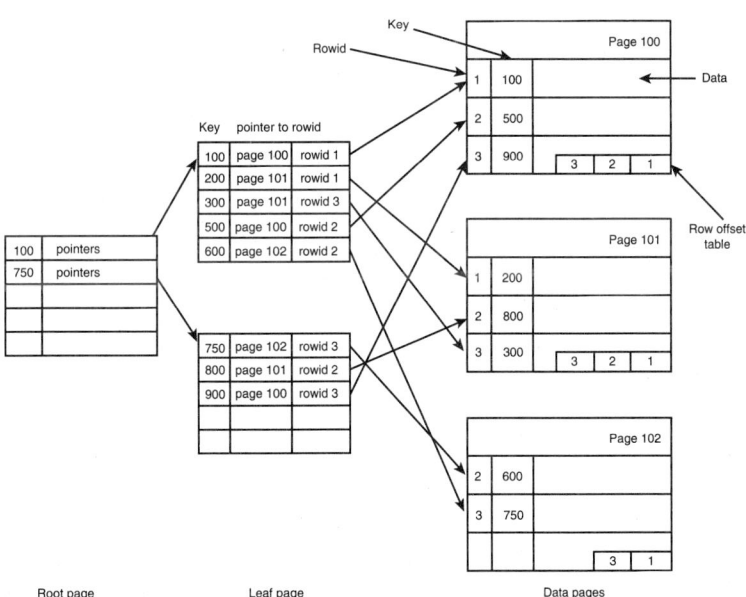

The Advantages of Indexes

Indexes are primarily used for faster retrieval of data. Creating appropriate indexes for a database is one of the most important aspects of database design. Although indexes speed up search operations, the inserts, deletes, and updates might be slow, because each of these operations might result in modifying the B-Tree index structure for the table. An index created without any consideration for performance usually results in slower data modification statements. Therefore, it is very important to carefully choose indexes in a database and measure the overall performance impact on the system.

SQL Server indexes are mostly transparent to the users. SQL Server's cost-based query optimizer decides whether to use an index on a table for a particular query. If more than one index is on a table, the query optimizer chooses the index that is most effective in terms of the number of I/Os. SQL Server does, however, allow an application developer to pass hints to the query optimizer to use a specific index in a query. The following broad guidelines might help you decide whether to use an index:

- Columns that are often specified in the ORDER BY clause should be indexed so that SQL Server makes use of the indexed order and eliminates an additional step of sorting the data after retrieval.

- Columns that are often searched for a range of values are good candidates for a clustered index. This is true because after the first value in the range is located, subsequent values are guaranteed to be physically adjacent rows.

- Columns that are frequently used in table joins should be indexed simply because SQL Server can locate rows faster if the columns are in sorted order.

- Creating an index on a column that has a low distribution value does not make much sense. For example, creating an index on a column named sex will not bring any benefits because only two values are possible: male and female.

- Because data is physically sorted in case of a clustered index, searches on a clustered index are almost always faster than those on a nonclustered one. But data modification statements on a table with a clustered index might be slower compared with those on a nonclustered index.

Things to Consider when Planning a Database

Database planning is one of the most complex parts of application design. The following paragraphs describe the steps necessary to ensure that you have a robust and high-performance database application.

Database Design

A good database design is fundamental to the success of any application environment. Database design can be split into two parts:

- Logical design
- Physical design

Logical Design

Logical design is the first step when you start planning your application. This step involves collecting user requirements. Database designers take these specifications and identify entities, attributes, relationship between entities (one to many, many to many, and such), primary keys, and so on. Based on this information, an entity relationship model is built for the system. An entity relationship diagram should satisfy at least the first three rules of normalization. After this step, you are ready to translate your logical model into a physical one.

Physical Design

When the logical design is complete and conforms to the rules of normalization, entities become tables and attributes become columns in a table. This step involves the following actions:

- Identifying tables, columns, and column properties (nullable, data types, rules, defaults, and so on)
- Identifying primary keys and other useful access paths (indexes) to data
- Estimating the size of each table and of the total database
- Determining the size of the transaction log
- Identifying whether segments are useful for the application
- Planning for placement of data, segments, indexes, and logs on various devices to reduce I/O contention and to provide maximum performance and full recoverability in the event of a disk failure
- Creating devices, databases, and database objects on SQL Server with the previously listed facts in mind
- Adding logins and users and enforcing security

There also are some additional steps one should plan for. Although these steps are not related to the physical design of the database, they are important to provide maximum uptime for a database. These are the necessary actions:

- Creating database backup devices
- Creating a comprehensive backup and recovery plan
- Creating schedules for routine tasks such as running DBCC (for verifying data integrity), UPDATE STATISTICS (for better performance), and so on

Planning Client Configuration

It is always important to know what kind of resources will be required to run an application smoothly. An end-user application might suffer from performance problems if not enough memory is available on the client or if the hardware is slow. You should also determine whether the end-users will be running any other resource-intensive applications on the client along with this application. Therefore, at the time of designing the frontend application, estimate the amount of resources (memory, CPU, disk space) that will be required in order to run the application smoothly.

Planning Server Configuration

In a client-server environment, the server usually does most of the work. Therefore, it is important that the hardware is configured to provide an excellent price/performance ratio. The following sections discuss various components of the server configuration.

Hardware Components

This step deals with defining hardware resources for the machine on which SQL Server will be installed. These are some of the important subsystems of server hardware that can make a significant impact on performance:

- System processors
- Disk subsystem
- Physical memory

It is very important that sufficient resources always be available on the server hardware. All the previously listed parts of hardware work together. A system that suffers from performance problems at the hardware level might indicate that one subsystem is idle while another one has a very high percentage of utilization. For example, low CPU utilization might indicate that the processor is waiting on the disk subsystem to finish I/Os.

System Processors

To provide a sufficient number of processors on the machine, determine the following items of information:

- The number of concurrent users on the SQL Server
- The types of transactions (I/O bound or CPU bound)
- The expected throughput and response time
- The need for SMP hardware

SQL Server supports Symmetric Multiprocessing (SMP). SMP hardware has more than one CPU, and each CPU can handle a load independent of other CPUs. For SMP hardware, a SQL Server thread is not tied to a particular processor of the machine and might therefore execute on a different processor each time. This allows SQL Server to run multiple tasks simultaneously, resulting in excellent load balancing.

Disk Subsystem

Choosing the right kind of disk subsystem is an important aspect of application design. This step allows you to determine these facts:

- The number of controllers on the hardware to split I/O work to yield high throughput
- The number of disk drives to effectively meet capacity utilization
- The level of fault tolerance

The placement of data on devices makes a significant impact on the performance of the system. It is quite important that you keep a transaction log on a separate disk (and mirror it, if possible) to provide full recovery in the event of a disk crash. Keeping nonclustered indexes on one device and data on another device (by using SQL Server segments) usually results in good performance of the system. If the database and transaction logs are to be backed up on disk drives, you should consider that fact also in your capacity planning. You should also forecast the growth of the database and acquire disk space accordingly.

Memory

Memory dedicated to SQL Server is primarily used to cache data and procedures. SQL Server also provides the capability to keep `tempdb` in RAM. The total physical memory on the machine is of one of the important factors governing the performance of SQL Server. Insufficient memory on SQL Server causes more I/Os from the disk. Because accessing a disk is much slower than accessing the memory, a large number of physical I/Os can lead to performance degradation. If more memory is installed on a server, it can cache a large amount of data, and many requests for data can be satisfied from memory rather than via physical I/Os. SQL Server can use a maximum of 2G memory on a machine. The amount of memory installed on a machine is primarily determined by the size of the database.

Network Configuration

It is important to choose an appropriate network protocol. For Microsoft SQL Server, the Named Pipes protocol delivers the highest performance. TCP/IP, however, is the most widely used protocol for SQL Server. Using TCP/IP protocols, UNIX clients can also communicate with SQL Server. SQL Server can listen on several protocols simultaneously. Because listening to multiple protocols can add to overheads, choose the ones that are appropriate for your network environment, and disable the others from SQL Server.

A network bottleneck is usually caused by available network bandwidth, network traffic, and the speed of the network. A poorly designed application can create a network bottleneck by retrieving hundreds of rows from the database, even though only a few rows are necessary for the frontend application. Some of the network-related bottlenecks can be eliminated by efficient application and database design and by using database objects such as stored procedures, rules, and triggers. Other options include using a faster network, keeping the machine in a subnet with less traffic, and adding network redundancy.

SQL Server Configuration

All the previously mentioned components (client hardware, network, server hardware) are essential for a well-performing system. But they also add to the overall cost of the system, and investment on these components is therefore limited by the budget constraints. No matter how many resources you provide on the client, the network, and the hardware, there is no substitute for an efficient database design, well-written queries, and a well-configured SQL Server. A database administrator can configure SQL Server to provide excellent performance and throughput without compromising the data integrity. SQL Server provides various parameters that can be configured to provide optimal performance for a particular environment.

Denormalization

To improve performance, sometimes it is necessary to backtrack from a fully normalized database. These are the various methods of using denormalization techniques:

- Horizontal partitioning of data
- Vertical partitioning of data
- Adding redundant and computed columns

These methods of denormalization were discussed earlier in this chapter, in the section Methods of Denormalization. Choose the method that provides the best performance improvement for your application design.

Summary

A good database design should conform to the third normal form. A logical model with the third normal form can be easily translated into a physical model. Denormalization techniques can be utilized for performance reasons. You should, however, have very good understanding of the logical and physical model of the system before making an attempt at denormalizing data. The next chapter explores the areas where SQL Server can be used.

CHAPTER

33

Using SQL Server in Commercial and Local Applications

by Vipul Minocha

IN THIS CHAPTER

Microsoft SQL Server has shown tremendous growth in the past few years. SQL Server 6.5 is truly an industry-level, high-performance relational database engine that has set various benchmark results on Windows NT. Low cost and a large number of useful features have made SQL Server an attractive choice for all kinds of applications, ranging from departmental-level applications to data warehousing solutions. In this chapter, you will read about some of the areas where SQL Server can be used effectively.

Data Warehousing Applications

Data warehousing is a collection of a large amount of information (usually over 20G) stored in the database. Data warehousing systems are designed to provide a strategic viewpoint of the entire enterprise data. Data stored in the database can come from different data sources, including many of the legacy systems. Data warehousing systems are quite different from online transaction processing (OLTP) applications. In an online application, data viewed and modified by the end-users is current, databases are usually not all that large, and there might be a lot of write activity on the databases. On the other hand, data warehousing applications are mainly decision support systems (DSS) with a very high volume of data. Data stored in a warehousing system is usually not online, but is refreshed at regular intervals, depending on the requirements of an organization. Activity on a database is mostly read-only. Users of a data warehousing application use the system to analyze current business methodologies and use that information to chart out a strategy that is critical to the success of the core business of the enterprise.

The airline industry is a good example of a data warehousing solution. Historically, airline reservation and flight information systems are implemented on mainframes. As with any other industry, the goal of an airline is to maximize revenue while keeping the cost low. The airline can achieve this objective by keeping fares higher (to maximize revenue) on the busy flights and lowering fares (to increase capacity utilization) for the less-busy flight legs. For an airline analyst, it is critical to create a balance between airfare and capacity utilization (for example, very high fares might result in lower capacity utilization). To maximize revenue, it is important that airline analysts can accurately calculate capacity utilization for each leg of the flight and forecast the fare. To achieve this, a data warehouse can be created where relevant information can be summarized and downloaded from the mainframes and stored in a SQL Server database. Analysts can then use various cost models and perform ad hoc queries against databases to build an optimal model that will result in higher revenue generation and better capacity utilization for each flight.

Building a data warehouse is a complex task. Various factors govern the success of a warehousing solution. Some of these factors are discussed in the following sections.

Data Volume

Data warehousing solutions manage huge amounts of information, potentially up to hundreds of gigabytes of data. SQL Server is capable of handling a large volume of data and provides effective solutions to complex business problems with great efficiency. In a warehousing system it might be necessary to spread data across multiple databases on the same server. SQL Server can handle up to 32,767 user databases to provide such capability.

Cost of Implementation

To an organization, cost is always an important factor in implementing a large system. SQL Server 6.5 provides one of the best price/performance ratios on Windows NT. Unlike many other relational database vendors, Microsoft SQL Server comes with built-in data-replication capabilities. Because replication features come free with SQL Server, no additional costs are involved in implementing a distributed data warehousing solution using DBMS-provided replication techniques.

Data Access Performance

One of the biggest challenges of a warehouse application is providing fast response time for the end-user queries. Ad hoc queries can specify a different search criteria each time, and a database engine must respond within an acceptable response time. Following are some of the features of SQL Server that can provide fast response time for the queries:

■ *Indexes:* Indexes are created on a table for faster retrieval of data. SQL Server enables you to create 1 *clustered* index and up to 249 *nonclustered* indexes on each table. Therefore, by anticipating the majority of end-user ad hoc queries and choosing indexes judiciously, you can achieve significant performance improvements.

■ *SMP Support:* SQL Server supports Symmetric Multiprocessing (SMP). SMP support allows SQL Server to run multiple tasks simultaneously on different threads, resulting in excellent load balancing and throughput.

■ *Parallel Data Scans:* In a warehousing system, a user might request information from the database in various ways. In some situations the data requested by the end-user is sequential in nature, especially when the user is retrieving a large amount of information from the database tables. SQL Server can detect such queries and issue background threads that read the data that is not yet requested but is expected at a later stage in the query. This read-ahead feature provides the capability of scanning data in parallel. Various SQL Server configuration parameters enable you to control read-ahead behavior of SQL Server in a way that best suits a specific environment.

Reduced Query Complexity

SQL Server 6.5 provides various aggregate functions and T-SQL operators. Many complex queries using multiple steps can be substituted by simpler queries using such operators. A number of queries in a data warehousing application compute multidimensional aggregates (called super aggregates) by using multistep queries. SQL Server 6.5 provides two T-SQL operators, called CUBE and ROLLUP, that are used with the GROUP BY clause to simplify such queries.

Enterprise-Wide Applications

Many organizations are moving forward with SQL Server to deploy enterprise-wide, mission-critical applications. SQL Server can support a large number of concurrent users and high transactional volume with excellent performance, without compromising data integrity. Microsoft SQL Server complies with American National Standard Institute (ANSI) SQL-92 standards. SQL Server provides a powerful T-SQL query language with an intelligent cost-based optimizer, as well as configurable parameters that can be tuned to yield high performance. SQL Server's versatile locking strategy provides high data concurrency and data integrity. One of the new locking features in SQL Server is Insert Row-Level Locking (IRL), which enables you to enable row-level locking for data inserts. This feature provides performance improvements in a high-load environment.

An enterprise-wide distributed client-server computing environment demands a highly reliable database administration. An application that is global in nature can run on multiple SQL Servers housing multiple databases. All of these servers can be placed in separate geographical locations and can be interchanging information. Managing these SQL Servers individually can be a nightmare for database administrators. SQL Server comes with a friendly graphical user interface, called SQL Enterprise Manager, that allows a centralized administration of enterprise-wide SQL Servers.

Departmental Applications

Low cost and high performance have made it possible for organizations to adopt SQL Server for departmental-level applications. SQL Server is now widely used in places that are traditionally mainframe-oriented but have started to migrate some of the application functionality to the client-server environment. Many banking applications fall into this category. Usually, customer financial information is kept on the mainframes. However, some customer transactions (such as loans) can be done by individual branches of a bank on a local SQL Server database. At the end of the day, this information can be exported out of the SQL Server database and sent to the mainframe for consolidation.

Internet and Intranet Applications

With the growing popularity of the Internet and intranets, many organizations have recognized the benefits of extending the enterprise to the Internet and letting people use existing business applications over the Internet, without sacrificing reliability or compromising on security. SQL Server enables users to access databases over the Internet. For an application to access SQL Server, both the client and the server must be directly on the Internet. Using Microsoft SQL Server, it is possible to publish data in the database in the form of a standard Hypertext Markup Language (HTML) file. SQL Server comes with a graphical user interface called SQL Server Web Assistant that can be used to publish data on the Web server. These HTML files can also be created by use of SQL Server–supplied stored procedures. These files can be viewed by any Internet browser, such as Netscape or Microsoft Internet Explorer. Data can be published on a scheduled basis or upon data change (through SQL Server triggers). The following section takes you through the creation of a simple application. This exercise demonstrates how to build an application using SQL Server Web Assistant to publish data in a database on the Web.

Using SQL Server Web Assistant

Following are the step-by-step instructions for generating an HTML file from the data of a SQL Server database.

Step 1: Invoke SQL Server Web Assistant

Run SQL Server Web Assistant from the SQL Server 6.5 program group. Enter the name of the SQL Server you want to publish data from, along with the SQL Server login ID and password (see Figure 33.1). It is also possible to connect to SQL Server using Windows Integrated Security.

FIGURE 33.1.

Starting SQL Server Web Assistant.

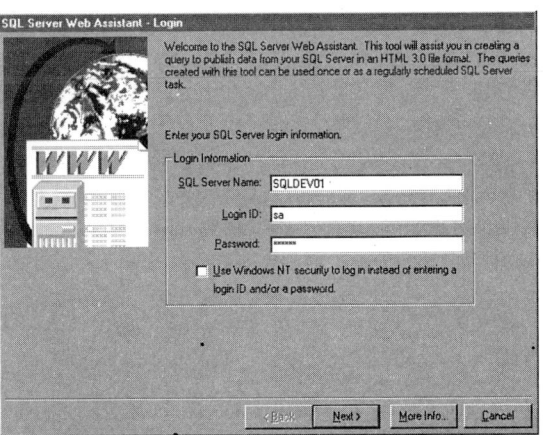

33

COMMERCIAL AND LOCAL APPLICATIONS

Step 2: Build a Query

This step enables you to build a query in one of the following three ways:

- Build a query using the point-and-click method
- Write your own query
- Specify a stored procedure name

Figure 33.2 shows the screen where you can write your own queries. This feature is useful when you want to display data from a complex join.

FIGURE 33.2.

Building a query for data publication.

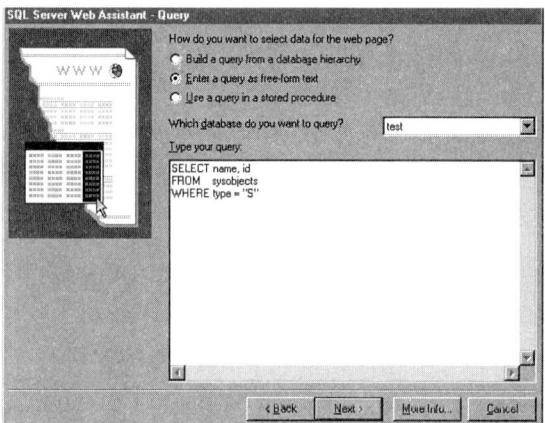

Step 3: Define a Schedule

This step enables you to specify the timeframe when you want to create the Web page. Choose an appropriate schedule from the drop-down listbox, as shown in Figure 33.3.

FIGURE 33.3.

Specifying the HTML file update schedule.

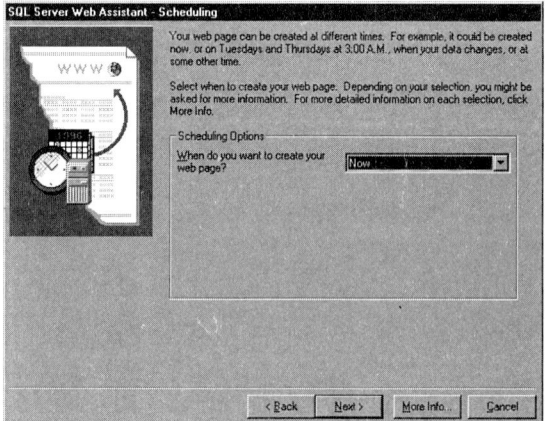

Step 4: Specify the HTML File Options

In this step you can define the location of the HTML file. You can also create a URL to refer to an Internet location. Figure 33.4 shows the dialog box where you can enter the relevant information.

FIGURE 33.4.

Specifying the HTML file location.

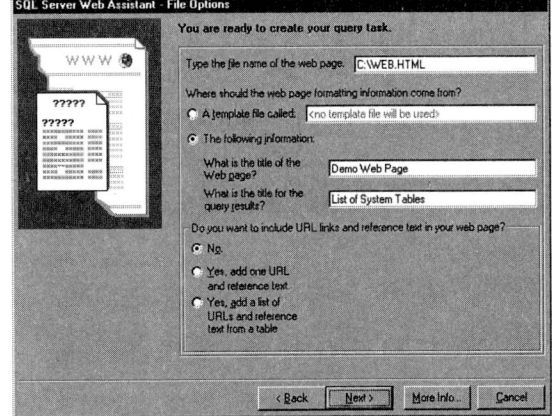

Step 5: Choose an HTML File Format

This step lets you choose a very basic display format for the HTML file. Choose an appropriate format (see Figure 33.5) and click the Finish button to create an HTML file.

FIGURE 33.5.

Defining the HTML file format.

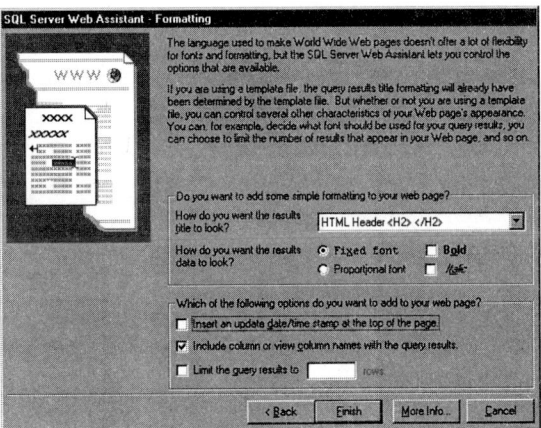

Step 6: View the Data

The data is published in the HTML file you specified in step 4, and you now can view it using any standard browser. Figure 33.6 displays the HTML file using the Netscape browser.

FIGURE 33.6.

Viewing the HTML file through a browser.

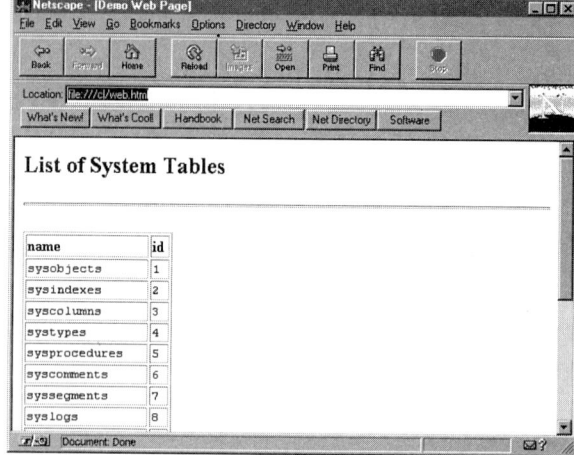

Developing Monitoring and Management Tools

Software vendors develop tools for SQL Server using SQL Server C DB-Library Open Client Library or ODBC calls. Some of these tools provide a friendly development and debugging environment for software developers. Others provide a helpful user interface for managing and monitoring SQL Server databases. Microsoft's supplied graphical tool called SQL Enterprise Manager is an example of such a tool.

SQL Server in a Heterogeneous Distributed Environment

In a distributed client-server environment, sometimes it is necessary to run transactions across multiple servers. It is important to maintain the integrity and consistency of the data on each server—that is, if a transaction fails on one of the servers, the entire transaction should be rolled back. SQL Server provides a two-phase commit protocol that preserves data consistency across several SQL Servers. Distributed transactions can also be managed with Microsoft Distributed Transaction Coordinator (MSDTC), which uses a two-phase commit protocol and runs as a service under Windows NT. Using MSDTC, it is possible to review and control the state of each transaction participating in a distributed transactional environment.

SQL Server 6.5 also includes built-in data-replication capabilities. Replication is data duplication from one database to one or more databases on the same or different servers. SQL Server enables you to replicate data either on a scheduled basis or on a number-of-transactions basis. SQL Server replication can be managed with the easy-to-use SQL Enterprise Manager. SQL Server databases can also participate in two-way replication. In a two-way replication, the database that is publishing the data can also subscribe to data from various servers. SQL Server is also capable of handling data replication from ODBC subscribers other than SQL Server, such as Oracle and Sybase.

Summary

Microsoft SQL Server 6.5 provides robust, efficient, and effective solutions for complex business problems in the Windows NT environment. A host of features, such as the powerful T-SQL language, an intelligent cost-based optimizer, built-in replication, a versatile locking strategy, and a distributed transaction control mechanism, makes Microsoft SQL Server 6.5 ideal for all kinds of client-server computing environments. SQL Server also provides tools for database administrators for centralized management of SQL Server.

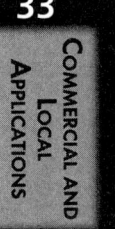

33

COMMERCIAL AND
LOCAL
APPLICATIONS

VI
PART

Systems Management Server

SMS Overview

by Richard Neff

Microsoft's Systems Management Server (SMS) is an extremely powerful product to help network administrators control an organization's entire network. SMS is designed to help administer large enterprise-wide networks, but is flexible enough to maintain even small networks. It is extremely versatile, being able to handle networks with a wide variety of configurations.

However, with this power SMS requires careful planning and an understanding of the network's configuration to be the most effective. Planning how your SMS sites are arranged helps to implement an effective SMS strategy. SMS takes advantage of features found in Windows NT and uses another BackOffice product, SQL Server, for its record keeping. SMS can be used on a single server in an organization, or SMS tasks can be divided between different servers.

In this chapter, you will learn the following:

■ The different features of Microsoft Systems Management Server

■ The SMS site functions and hierarchy and the basics of planning the right site hierarchy for your organization

■ The different types of servers used by SMS to administer a network

■ The different server components of SMS and their functions

■ The different client components of SMS and their functions

The Network Administrator's Struggle for Control

When corporations first started using computers, those computers were typically mainframe computers. These large machines were housed in special rooms, and terminals scattered throughout the office were connected to these mainframes. The actual processing of the mainframe was handled by the central computer, not the terminals. All administrative control was also handled at the central computer.

Later, personal computers were introduced and adopted by companies. Initially, most PCs were not connected to each other, but now, networks have been created to connect the individual personal computers in an office together. A personal computer network, however, is managed differently from a mainframe configuration. Each personal computer has the ability to process and store user information. Furthermore, users can often share individual resources, such as printers and directories, on that machine.

Personal computers and additional hardware are often purchased from different manufacturers and can have many different operating systems. The modern network administrator has to deal with a large number of personal computer types, computer peripherals, and operating systems. Additionally, the network administrator has to do a lot of record keeping of how the networked systems are configured. A dramatic change from the older mainframe-computing scenario!

Fortunately, Microsoft Systems Management Server is designed to help a network administrator take back some control over the network. SMS is flexible enough to help administration of different-sized networks, from small networks all the way to enterprise networks. SMS can also view and access Novell NetWare and LAN Manager servers incorporated with a Windows NT network. SMS can take advantage of wide-area network links and remote access links to further extend the management reach of the network administrator.

SMS Features

SMS provides a large array of features to help the network administrator control the network. SMS is also very versatile in its configuration to better serve the needs of different network designs. It takes advantage of Windows NT and BackOffice features, such as using SQL Server as its information store. SMS tasks can also be distributed on other servers in the network to reduce the load on one server. Conversely, SMS can run on a single server for smaller network environments.

SMS provides some of the following features to help network administrators control the network:

- Hardware inventory
- Software inventory
- Software distribution
- Network application management
- Network performance analysis
- Network configuration information
- Remote client troubleshooting and support

The primary program the administrator will use is the SMS Administrator program, which provides the user interface between the administrator and the SMS services. Figure 34.1 shows the SMS Administrator program running on a Windows NT computer.

Hardware Inventory

One of the most daunting tasks for a network administrator is trying to keep up with each user's computer configuration. Although a network administrator may easily remember that Bill in Accounting has an Intel 486 machine and Jill in Engineering has a Pentium, the IRQ settings for the network adapter in either computer are a bit harder to remember. Even on small networks, most administrators usually write down important hardware settings. In environments with very large networks, hardware record keeping is vital.

FIGURE 34.1.

The SMS Administrator.

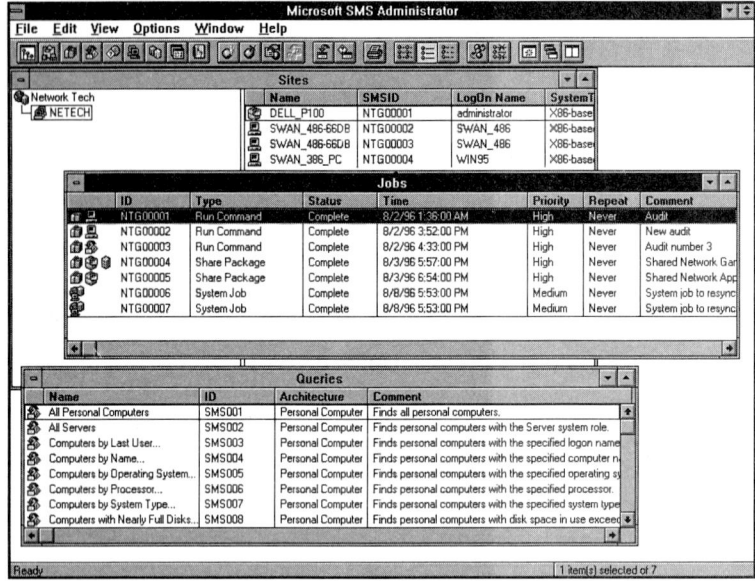

SMS makes the important job of hardware record keeping a lot easier. When a computer joins an SMS site, hardware information is recorded about that computer. SMS stores a wide variety of hardware information, including items such as the following:

- The Central Processing Unit (CPU) type of the computer
- The amount of physical memory
- The type and size of hard disk drives and other storage devices on the system
- The video adapter
- The network adapter
- The mouse and keyboard type
- The operating system

Systems Management Server also enables custom information to be added to the inventory list. SMS does this by using the Desktop Management Task Force's (DMTF) file format known as a Management Information File (MIF). An MIF is simply an ASCII text file with a standardized structure and format. SMS uses graphical forms to fill in the necessary information into the MIF file. SMS also provides a MIF form creator to enable the administrator to create user MIF forms.

MIF forms enable users the ability to fill in custom information when their machine is inventoried by the SMS server. This custom information can include information such as the building where the computer is located, the phone extension of the computer user, or the department of the computer user. Forms can also have text, number, or list fields to store custom information. SMS provides a sample MIF form for use with SMS.

The user fills out the form, and the data is collected on the next hardware inventory. If SMS collects data from the login script, the next hardware inventory will be run the next time the hardware inventory agent is run, usually by a login script when the user logs in to the network. Otherwise, the user may have to run the hardware inventory manually. Figure 34.2 shows a MIF form displayed on a client computer.

FIGURE 34.2.

The MIF form displayed on a client computer.

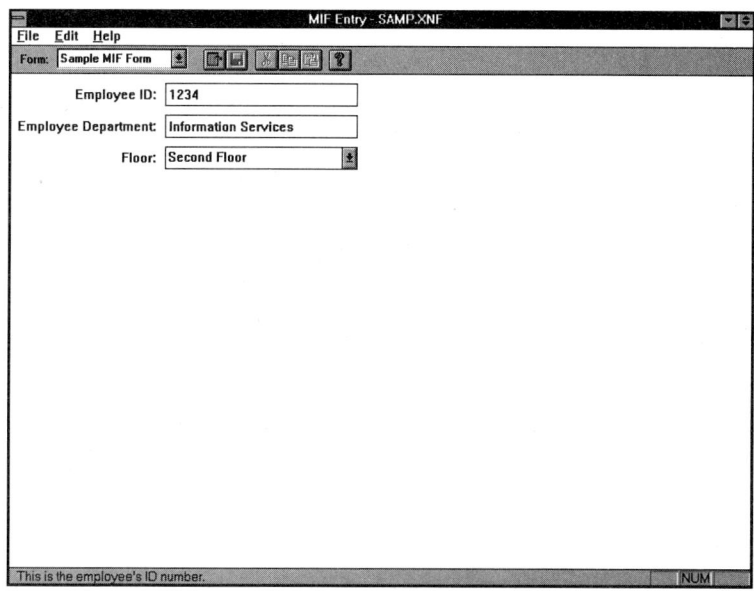

The SMS Administrator program is used to view MIF form data. The MIF form information for that user is shown in the computer properties of the SMS Sites window. This example shows a sample MIF form with information. Figure 34.3 shows the MIF form information displayed in the SMS Administrator program.

SMS provides a default MIF form with the SMS program. This form, the User Information MIF form, is automatically collected with the inventory when a computer first connects to an SMS site. This form contains the following information: name, e-mail address, phone number, department, building, and office. The User Information form can be used without modification, or it can be modified using the SMS MIF Form Generator.

Software Inventory

SMS enables the network administrator to inventory software on network machines by a method called *auditing*. SMS auditing can be used to find individual files based on criteria set by the SMS administrator. This is useful in trying to find how many users have a particular file on their system, such as WINWORD.EXE. SMS contains a predefined *package rule file*, also known as a RUL, that audits many popular types of user applications. You can also create a custom package rule file to inventory other software applications. A package is then created to run on workstations on the network and report back the audited information. The SMS Administrator program then shows the software audit in the properties for that computer.

FIGURE 34.3.

The MTF Form displayed on a client computer.

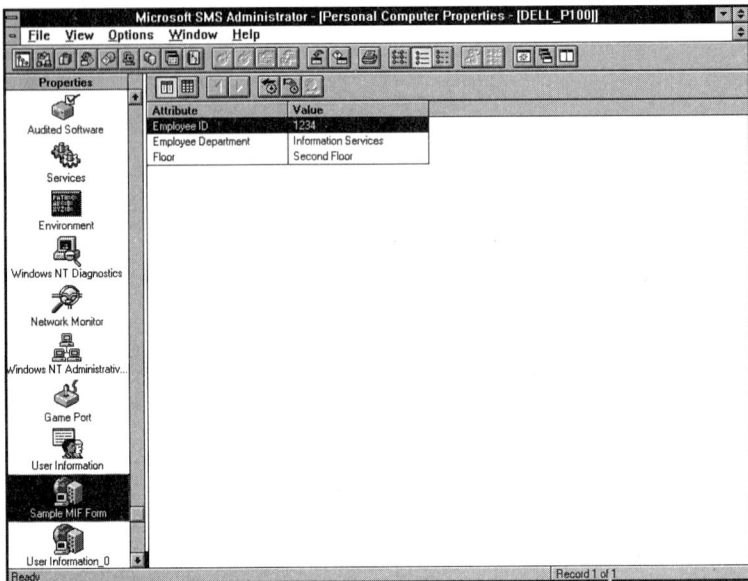

When software auditing is used, the computer's property sheet will show the software that was found. This is a useful feature for determining how many copies of a particular program are stored throughout the network. When software auditing is used, the computer's property sheet shows the software that was found.

Figure 34.4 shows the SMS Administrator program with audited software information.

> **NOTE**
>
> Although an inventory of software can be performed by SMS, it should not be confused with *software metering*. Software metering refers to a type of process on a server that actively monitors how many users are currently using a program. This type of process is used to help large sites to properly use license agreements of a software package. The SMS software inventory records only actual files on a computer; it does *not* check actual usage.

FIGURE 34.4.

The SMS Administrator program with audited software information.

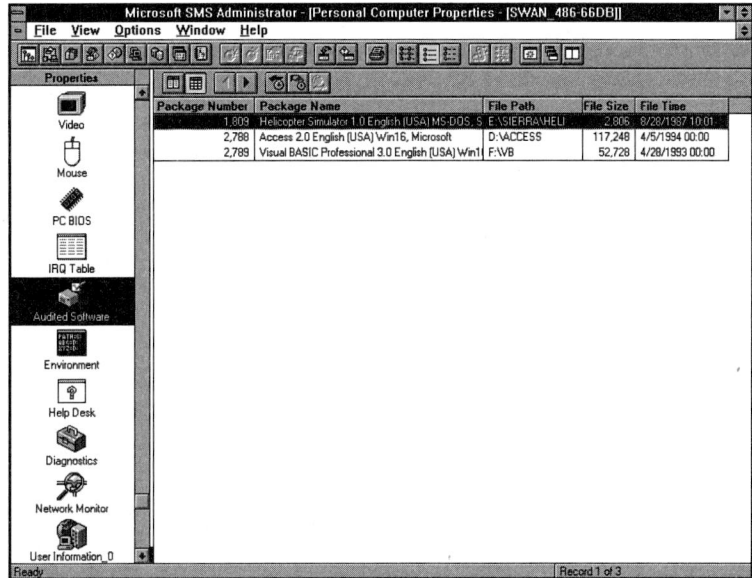

Software Distribution

Another strong feature of Systems Management Server is the ability to distribute software across the network. The software distribution feature of SMS is very versatile, allowing automated setup options and both mandatory and expiring distributions. Previously, most administrators had two options for installing software on networked computers: take the application's disks or CD-ROM to each individual machine and run the setup program, or create a network share and instruct the user to install the program off the share. The first method was very time-consuming, and the second relied on the expertise of the user to configure the software correctly.

Systems Management Server's ability to deliver software across the network and allowing automated setups help the software-distribution process become more efficient. As with other features of SMS, larger organizations or organizations with remote computers may find this ability more useful. SMS can be used to distribute both optional and mandatory software packages. Mandatory packages are useful when a network administrator wants all the network users to install a software program. SMS also can set expiration dates for software distributed over the network. This means that if the software distributed by SMS is not installed by a certain date, the software is no longer available for installation.

34

SMS OVERVIEW

> **CAUTION**
>
> SMS makes software distribution very convenient, but always be sure when using SMS to distribute software, that you understand and comply with the license agreement of the software. Many companies, including Microsoft, are very specific about licensing agreements and will enforce them.

Application Management

One of the advantages of using a networked personal computer is the ability to run programs either from the personal computer or over the network from a server. Running programs from a central server provides many advantages to a company. When a new version of an application is released, it can be installed once on a server and all of the clients using that program can run the updated version. Also, the storage and processing requirements for client machines are not as large as clients that do not run programs from the server. However, some of this advantage is offset by the increased storage and processing requirements of the server running these applications.

SMS provides the ability to better manage network-based applications. Typically, the network administrator or the computer user had to manually connect to the share to run the program. SMS allows the automatic installation of shared programs over the network, similar to the distribution of other software. Program group control is also available for controlling the program groups used for network applications. This feature is available only for computers that use Program Manager, such as Windows 3.1 machines.

Network Analysis

Another important aspect of maintaining a network is understanding how data moves between network nodes and ensuring that the network traffic load does not become too large. SMS uses a program called Network Monitor that enables a network administrator to watch data traffic on the network. The SMS Network Monitor captures all of the frames, also known as packets, on the network. The captured frames are graphically displayed on the Network Monitor screen. You can filter frames to narrow the information to specific data. You can also transmit frames from the Network Monitor computer for diagnostic testing of the network. Triggers based on buffer space or pattern matching can also be defined.

SMS also enables you to watch the network information between the SMS computer and another network computer, using the computer's property window in the SMS Administrator program. This is the standard Network Monitor program with a filter applied to monitor the network traffic of only that particular computer. All of the features and items found in the Network Monitor program are available when it is used from the SMS Administrator program to view a specific computer.

The SMS Network Monitor provides detailed information about the network and its performance. Network Monitor captures all of the frames transmitted on the network so the administrator can monitor the data flow of the network. Figure 34.5 shows an example of network monitoring under SMS.

FIGURE 34.5.

An example of network monitoring under SMS.

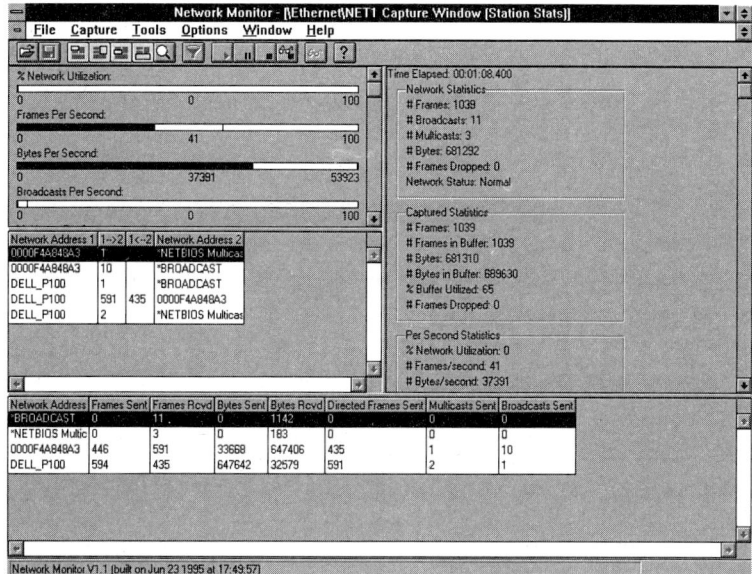

Remote Help Features

Of course, the primary purpose of a computer network is to give users the tools to help them accomplish their everyday tasks. With any type of machine, problems do occur. Most users on the network aren't knowledgeable of the internal workings of computer hardware and software and require assistance in fixing these computer problems. The situation is sometimes further complicated by the user not knowing how to effectively describe the problem to the administrator.

Systems Management Server provides the administrator with utilities designed to help a user by allowing remote administration of a network computer. Administrators can see exactly what is occurring on the screens of users' computers and can perform all the on-screen tasks as if they were sitting directly at those computers. Although this feature may not be as useful for a network contained in a single building, it is handy for administrators who have to handle network users on the opposite end of the country!

The Remote Control feature of SMS is a powerful tool for providing support to network users. Especially in geographically dispersed network configurations, the Remote Control feature saves

34

SMS OVERVIEW

time and trouble for an administrator who would otherwise have to be physically at that workstation. Figure 34.6 shows an example of the SMS Remote Control function being used to remotely view and control a client on the network.

FIGURE 34.6.

An example of the SMS Remote Control function being used to remotely view and control a client on the network.

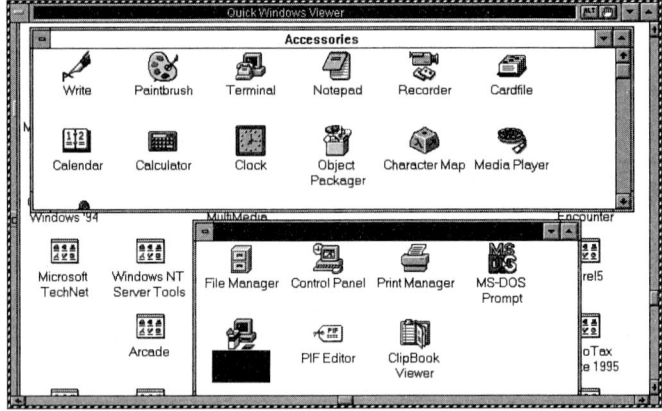

On-screen viewing of a network computer isn't the only remote help feature found in SMS. An administrator can also do a remote reboot of a computer or execute a program on the remote machine. An SMS administrator can also view dynamic configuration and memory information that isn't stored in the SMS database of a remote computer. All of these remote functions enable the SMS administrator to provide better support to remote network users.

Third-Party Programs

Many third-party programs exist that integrate and extend the features found in Microsoft SMS. Some examples include the following:

- Intel LANDesk Manager
- DEC POLYCENTER Assetworks
- Seagate Technologies WinINSTALL

Many of these products add support for vendor-specific platforms, whereas others extend the ability of SMS by incorporating new features for systems SMS already supports. With these packages, you can build on SMS's already strong management functions.

Basic Overview of SMS Sites

SMS uses a site-based organizational structure. An SMS site is used to organize the different networks of an organization into logical units. This structure is known as a *site hierarchy*. SMS uses the site hierarchy to better help the network administrators manage the different networks they control. Understanding the SMS site structure and how it relates to Windows NT domains and your network configuration is important to a successful implementation of SMS.

What Is an SMS Site?

An SMS site is simply an organizational structure using logical groupings of computers and networks. For instance, a company that has many small regional offices of less than 20 computers may want to put those regional offices into a single site so one central administrator can remotely handle network functions from one location. Also, a very large company with large offices worldwide may want to organize each office into a single site so a network administrator can handle the individual network needs of that office.

SMS sites are based primarily on how the network is to be managed. SMS has two distinct types of sites: *primary sites* and *secondary sites*. A primary site has its own SQL Server database, in which all information about that site is stored. A secondary site does not have its own SQL database, but rather it is linked with a primary site that records information about the secondary site. A primary site is designed to administer itself and any secondary sites that report SMS information to its SQL database. A secondary site does not have the SMS administration tools available; it is managed by the primary site to which it reports.

Primary sites also can be linked to other primary sites. For example, a primary site in a regional office, with its own network administrator, can be linked to a primary site at the corporate headquarters. This enables a site to be managed by both a network administrator at that site or a network administrator in the parent site. In this type of site configuration, the topmost site in the SMS site hierarchy is called the *central site*.

With the different levels in the SMS site structure, an organization has a lot of flexibility in organizing the site structure. Two companies with very similar network organizations may use two completely different types of site layouts. Determining the SMS sites depends on the administrative needs of a company for its network structure.

SMS Sites Versus Windows NT Domains

Windows NT Server uses domains to logically group network computers together. SMS sites also logically group network computers together; however, SMS sites do not always correspond with the Windows NT domain structure. It is possible to have many different Windows NT domains in a single site. Conversely, it is possible to have many SMS sites in a single Windows NT domain.

Most administrators new to SMS may at first find this very confusing, but the SMS site structure is based on different requirements than the Windows NT domain structure. The Windows NT domain structure is based on the needs of resource-sharing for network users, whereas the SMS site structure is based on the needs of administrators to manage the network. The

34

SMS OVERVIEW

requirements for Windows NT domains and SMS sites vary from organization to organization, so the two may not match each other. However, some organizations may have Windows NT domains and SMS sites arranged in the same structure.

Planning Is the Key

With the number of different site configurations available, how does an organization decide how to set up an SMS site structure? Understanding the current network configuration and planning how to manage that network is the key. SMS is designed to be flexible in its configuration, but when implemented, constant changing of that structure is not recommended. Be sure to plan how the network is to be managed, the number of resources available at each planned site, and the command structure of the organization.

Be sure to think about how your network is currently configured, and also what future changes will occur to the network. Although you probably can not foresee all the future changes, having an idea will help to ensure that the SMS structure can grow without causing problems. Computer networks change and grow as new technology is introduced or a company expands its operations.

Take a look at some examples of SMS site structures. The first example is the simplest. There is a single Windows NT Domain for an office of 35 networked computers. A single Windows NT Server provides all of the network services. The SQL Server and SMS are installed on the single Windows NT Server, and only one site is used. It is a primary site because it uses the SQL Server, and it is also the central site. A network administrator, or group of network administrators, controls all of the network-management functions.

The second example includes an office in New York, another in Chicago, and a third in Los Angeles. Each office uses its own Windows NT domain. For example, the New York office has a single domain called the New_York domain. Each domain trusts the other two, enabling user accounts to access resources on each domain. Each office has a SQL Server and a network administrator, so the company has decided to make the SMS site structure follow the Windows NT domain structure. For example, the New York office is set up as the New York site. Each site is a primary site using its respective SQL Server.

Another organization has a single office, but is very large. Each department uses a Windows NT domain to help control departmental computing resources. Even though there are multiple domains, there is a central staff of network administrators for the entire company. In this case, the company has decided to set up a single SMS site to handle the entire organization to allow the network administrators better control of the network.

The final example is a company that has a single Windows NT domain with multiple SMS sites. A Chicago-based company is located in a single building, but on different floors. A single Windows NT domain is used for the resource sharing and user administration of the company. However, a network administrator is available on each floor. The company decides to divide the SMS site structure for each floor. Each network administrator has a single site to control within a single domain. Communication can occur between sites, so the different network administrators can have access to those other sites.

Different Types of SMS Servers

As mentioned previously, SMS utilizes both Windows NT Server and SQL Server for its proper operation. For networks that have multiple sites, there may be different types of SMS servers. Furthermore, for networks that have a lot of users or heavy network traffic, individual functions of SMS can be divided among computers, known as *helper servers*. SMS requires or uses the following types of servers:

- Windows NT Server
- SQL Server
- SMS Primary Site Servers
- SMS Secondary Site Servers (optional)
- Logon Servers
- Distribution Servers
- Helper Servers (optional)

> **NOTE**
>
> When discussing servers, many people may be confused about the difference between software servers and actual physical server machines. A physical computer can be a file and print server, an authentication server, SQL Server, and a primary or secondary SMS site server. In certain instances, software servers may be divided among many different computers. The term *server* is used in this chapter to describe an individual software system, not a physical machine.

The Role of the SQL Server

As mentioned previously, SMS requires a SQL Server to store the acquired information into a database. A dedicated SMS database is created in SQL Server when SMS is installed. The central site and all primary sites require a SQL database in each site. Secondary SMS sites do not have a SQL database at that site, rather the parent site stores the information.

The SQL Server used in a site may be dedicated to SMS information or it may be used for the sites other client-server database needs. SMS usually does not place very heavy demands on SQL Server, so the SQL Server is often available for other database tasks. A SQL Server must be installed and configured before SMS is installed. The SQL Server may either be located on the same physical computer as the SMS computer or they may be two different machines on the network.

Primary Site Server

Primary site servers are usually the most common site servers in an SMS configuration. In every organization using SMS, at least one primary site server is required. The primary site server has its own SQL Server database and SMS administration tools. Primary sites are installed using the distribution media—typically a CD-ROM or server-based network installation.

A primary site can have either primary or secondary sites below it. A primary site that contains sites below it can also administer those sites. If a primary site is the highest level of the site hierarchy, then it is known as the *central site server.*

Secondary Site Server

Secondary site servers are used when a site is to be controlled by a parent primary site. No SQL Server is used at that site, and no SMS administration tools are installed there. Secondary sites can be installed directly by the primary site server, without the need for the distribution media. A secondary site may not have any other sites below it.

Logon Servers

A logon server is a server that processes user logon requests and stores the user login scripts. It is added to the SMS site through the SMS Administrator program. It holds temporary SMS inventory data obtained through the client inventory agent. The data is then transferred to the SMS server to be stored in the SQL database. Logon servers may also act as distribution servers and may either be the same computer as the SMS server or other computers on the network.

Distribution Servers

A distribution server is used to send packages from the SMS server to client computers on the network. A distribution servers receives packages from the SMS server, then sends the packages to the appropriate clients. It also acts as a location for shared network applications. Distribution servers can also be logon servers.

Helper Servers

Most of the components of SMS are Windows NT Services. In large networks, a single SMS server may become overburdened. To help reduce this load, helper servers may be used to handle certain SMS tasks. Helper servers help move information between sites and are also known as *senders.* Three types of senders are supported: LAN senders, RAS senders, and SNA senders. Helper servers must also be logon servers.

Server Components

The majority of SMS functionality takes place at the site server. SMS uses Windows NT Services for the background work and the SMS Administrator program for interaction with the network administrator. Other SMS programs (such as the SMS Security Manager, MIF Form Creator, and Network Monitor) provide other server-based components to help the administrator.

SMS Services and Service Manager

Almost all of the functions provided by SMS are handled through Windows NT services. These services automatically run in the background performing the information-gathering and software-distribution functions of SMS. Because they run in the background, other processing can be done on the Windows NT server while these functions are being performed. SMS runs some of the following services in the background:

- SMS Executive (made up of additional components)
- SMS Site Hierarchy Manager
- SMS Site Configuration Manager
- Package Command Manager
- Inventory Agent
- SMS SNA Receiver (when using SNA)

These services are displayed from the Windows NT Control Panel using the Services item. As noted, the SMS Executive is composed of many different components. These individual components can be viewed from a program known as the SMS Service Manager.

The SMS Service Manager enables you to see the SMS services being run on a site, logon, or helper server (see Figure 34.7). You can also stop or pause any services that are currently running. Conversely, you can start or continue any services that have been stopped or paused. You may also start or stop tracing options for a particular service and set the location of the trace log filename. The SMS Service Manager can view services on either the local computer or any other SMS computer on the network. The SMS Service Manager enables you to view the available SMS services being run on the Windows NT machine. It also enables you to start, stop, and pause an SMS service. Tracing options can be turned on or off as well.

The SMS Administrator Program

The primary tool used by a network administrator to schedule SMS tasks is the SMS Administrator program. This program does not actually do the distribution work of SMS, which is handled by the SMS services, but rather allows an administrator to view the information collected by SMS and to create and schedule distribution packages and jobs. The SMS Administrator program also enables the administrator to schedule queries and alerts and to see the results of each.

FIGURE 34.7.

*The SMS Service
Manager.*

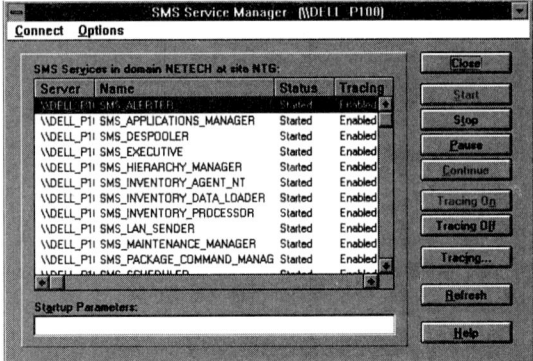

The SMS Administrator also handles some of the SMS site-creation tasks, including the creation of secondary sites. The Sites window is used with the New command to create secondary sites. The Site Properties page shows information about the selected site configuration and enables the administrator to make changes to the site. The Site Properties page also enables computers to be added to the site and enables the selection of a parent primary site for the selected site.

The SMS Administrator program enables a network administrator to view the collected SMS information, perform queries to find certain network information, create software distribution packages, and schedule SMS jobs. Figure 34.8 shows the SMS Administrator program with a sample site listed.

FIGURE 34.8.

*The SMS Administra-
tor program with a
sample site listed.*

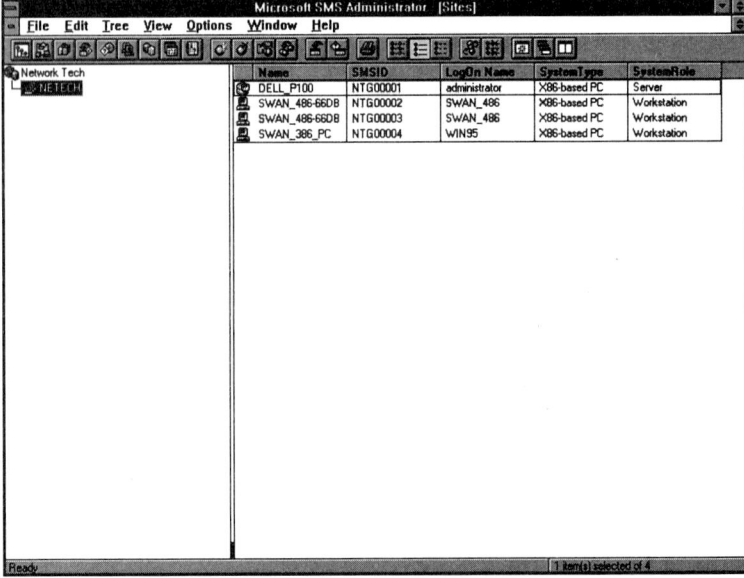

Packages and Jobs

SMS distributes software to network computers by using packages and jobs. An SMS package defines the properties of the software. Packages can have three distinct purposes. You can define a package to obtain inventory information, install software on a client machine, or to install a shared network application. Packages can be manually created by the administrator or predefined *package definition files*, also known as PDFs, can be used. The SMS program contains predefined PDF files for the installation of a wide variety of existing programs. Some examples include the following:

- MS-DOS 5.0, 6.0, and 6.22
- Windows 3.1 and 3.11/Windows for Workgroups 3.11
- Windows NT 3.5 and 3.51 (both Server and Workstation)
- Windows 95
- Microsoft Office 4.2 (both Standard and Professional)
- Microsoft Office 95 (both Standard and Professional)
- Microsoft Access 2.0
- Microsoft Excel 5.0
- Microsoft PowerPoint 4.0
- Microsoft Project 4.0
- Microsoft Word for Windows 6.0

Many of Microsoft's new products also may have .PDF files on the distribution media for that program. For example, .PDF files are available on the Windows 95 and Windows 4.0 CD-ROMs for distributing those applications using SMS. These .PDF files contain the information about the application's configuration. .PDF files simply provide the information rather than require the administrator to input the information manually. Using .PDF file to better understand package creation is a good way to learn how to create SMS packages.

> **TIP**
>
> The Microsoft World Wide Web site periodically updates PDF files for releases of new products. You can access the Microsoft Web site at: http://www.microsoft.com.

An SMS job actually handles the delivery of the SMS package across the network. An SMS job controls items such as the delivery time, which computers will receive the package, and which distribution servers to use. Jobs can be can be made available to users, be made mandatory, or expire after a certain date.

34

SMS OVERVIEW

Jobs run as a background task on Windows NT machines and, therefore, take some time to be distributed throughout the network. The speed of the links between the SMS server and the final destination path also affect the speed in which jobs deliver their packages. Jobs can also have three different priorities: high, medium, and low. By default, most SMS jobs are given a low priority and may take a while to deliver packages to their destination.

Program Groups

On computers that have Program Manager running, standardized program groups can be created for network applications. These program groups contain any network-based programs the administrator wants to add. This way, Windows 3.1 clients and Windows NT 3.5x clients can have a program group automatically created for them containing the specified network applications. This feature helps to ensure a consistent grouping of network applications throughout the organization.

Queries

Queries enable the network administrator to search and find computers on the network that meet certain criteria. For instance, a network administrator may want to distribute software across the network to client machines. However, the program can run only on computers with 8M or more of physical memory. Rather than send the software to all of the computers on the network, it is more practical to send the software only to machines with 8M or more of RAM installed. The administrator can query all the computers in the SMS database for those machines and send the software only to them.

The queries can be stored for future use, making them available even when the network changes. An SMS group type, known as a *machine group*, can be created based on query results. This makes it easier to view and distribute packages to those machines. By using queries and machine groups together, the administrator is able to quickly access the machines that meet certain specifications.

> **TIP**
>
> Queries are ideal before installing new software on network workstations. You can use a query to find out which computers on the network have the required processor, memory, and storage space for an application. The results of this query can be saved into an SMS machine group and distributed directly to this group.

Alerts

One of the key requirements for keeping a network running smoothly is detecting potential problems. SMS alerts make this job easier by providing warnings about potential trouble spots. Alerts use queries to find certain information; when the alert detects a certain condition, an alert event is triggered. When an alert event occurs, it can be set to perform any of the following actions:

- Send a message to any network user or computer
- Execute a program or command
- Put an event into the SMS event log

Any item that can be used in a query can be used for an SMS alert. However, many items that can be used in a query are not appropriate for alerts. One query that is predefined in SMS is querying machines for nearly full disk space. This query is well suited for an alert.

Network Monitoring

Many times the network administrator will have to check the performance of the network infrastructure. SMS provides monitoring features to help the administrator view the data traffic on the network or between two stations. The SMS Network Monitor, found in the Systems Management Server group, enables the administrator to view all of the packets moving across the network. The Network Monitor shows a multipaned display containing a variety of network information. It shows items such as the percentage of network utilization, the frames per second, the network address packet senders, the type of packet being sent, and the total statistics for the network. You can also view network information in a report view after the session has been captured.

The Network Monitor program provides other features like filtering. Filtering enables the administrator to determine which type of packets should be monitored. The Network Monitor also allows triggers, based on either buffer space or pattern matching, that can stop the capture or run a command-line program. You can also select which network to monitor if multiple types of network connections are available, such as a remote access connection to an Ethernet network.

The Network Monitor item located in the SMS Administrator uses a filter to view information about only a particular computer. It provides the same display and features as the Network Monitor item in the Systems Management Server group, but it provides network information about the selected machine. This is useful if you want to see how a particular computer is utilizing the network and don't want to manually create a filter.

> **NOTE**
>
> Before the SMS Administrator can monitor network connections, the Network Monitor Agent has to be installed from the Windows NT Control Panel. When SMS is installed, it checks to see whether it has been configured. If it hasn't, then it gives the user the option of installing it. However, the user installing the software can still choose not to install the Network Monitor Agent. When this occurs, the Network Monitor Agent has to be added in the Network item in Control Panel. If you are using version 1.0 or 1.1 of SMS, the network adapter must be able to operate in a mode known as promiscuous mode. This does not apply to SMS version 1.2. Check the documentation or contact the manufacturer to determine whether your network adapter can support this mode.

Client Components

The other component to SMS is the client component. Certain programs are installed when a computer connects to an SMS server. These components handle the actual information about the computer and send a file with the information to the SMS server. Also, client software is installed to enable the user to run SMS packages that are sent from the SMS server. Finally, help desk functions are available to operating systems in which the SMS administrator can connect to the client computer when trying to troubleshoot computer problems.

SMS can support the following operating systems on client computers:

- Windows NT Server
- Windows NT Workstation
- Windows 95 (requires SMS version 1.1 or later)
- Windows for Workgroups 3.11
- Windows 3.1 or 3.11
- MS-DOS 5.*x* or 6.*x*
- IBM OS/2
- Apple Macintosh

Inventory Agent

The client inventory agent collects hardware and other inventory information when the client connects to the network. The data is stored in a file and transmitted to the SMS server. The SMS server processes the information and sends the data to the SQL database. Inventory agents are typically run from a user's login script, or they can be run as part of the manual installation of a client to an SMS site.

Package Command Manager

The Package Command Manager is the client program that handles the receipt and execution of SMS packages. The Package Command Manager receives SMS packages sent from a distribution server. The packages can then be executed by the Package Command Manager. If the package is an optional package, the user can run it manually. If the package is a mandatory package, the Package Command Manager will display a message indicating that the package is mandatory when the mandatory date is reached. It will also give the user the option to run the package immediately or wait five minutes for the user to save any work before the package runs.

The Package Command Manager also keeps track of executed packages run on the client machine. Keeping track of these packages enables the package to be reinstalled in case the original installation becomes corrupted. Package Command Manager also enables packages to be archived for later use. Folders are used to store the pending, archived, and executed packages. After a package is executed, it automatically is moved from the Pending folder to the Executed folder.

The Package Command Manager receives incoming SMS packages and allows the user to execute the SMS package. Figure 34.9 shows an example of the SMS Package Command Manager on a client computer.

FIGURE 34.9.

An example of the SMS Package Command Manager on a client computer.

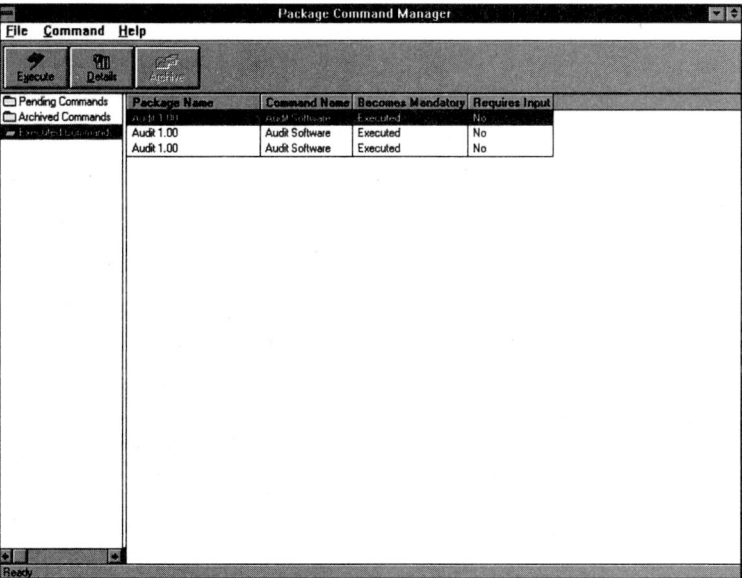

34

SMS OVERVIEW

Program Group Control

The Program Groups window enables you to standarize the program groups for network applications. This allows for a consistent user interface when accessing applications run from a network server. When a user logs in to the network SMS verifies the existance and format of the program group and, if needed, makes any changes to the groups listed in the Program Groups window of the SMS Administrator program.

Program groups enable the SMS administrator to create a standard program group that all network users have for shared network applications. Figure 34.10 shows the properties of a program group created in the SMS Administrator program.

FIGURE 34.10.

The properties of a program group created in the SMS Administrator program.

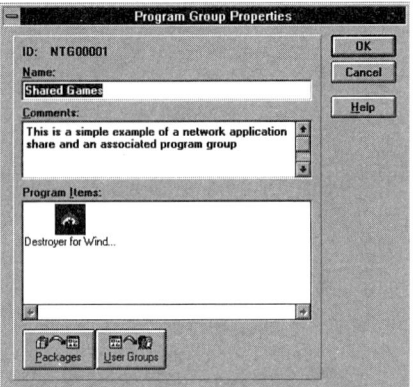

Program group control is only available for clients that use Program Manager. Therefore, it is not able to control groups for Windows 95, MS-DOS, IBM OS/2, or Apple Macintosh computers.

Help Desk Options

Probably some of the strongest tools that SMS provides for client troubleshooting and maintenance are the help desk options. The help desk options enable the SMS administrator to control certain parts of the client machine via the SMS Administrator program. This is especially useful if the client is geographically separate from the rest of the network. The network administrator uses the SMS to find the computer and send a message to the client asking for permission to access that computer. After the client gives permission to access the computer, the administrator can then access the machine as if he or she were sitting directly in front of it.

Help desk options are not available for all of the supported SMS clients. Only MS-DOS, Windows 3.1, Windows for Workgroups 3.11, and Windows 95 computers can be accessed through the SMS help desk options. SMS cannot be used to access Apple Macintosh, or OS/2 computers. SMS version 1.2 allows help desk options to be used to remotely control

Windows NT clients. Versions 1.0 and 1.1 of SMS do not allow Windows NT computers to be remotely controlled. However, those versions allow access to certain administrative tools and the Windows NT diagnostic tool on Windows NT clients.

The Help Desk item in the SMS Administrator program enables the administrator to access a client workstation and perform certain tasks over the network. This enables the administrator the ability to provide assistance to a user without physically being at the client computer. Figure 34.11 shows the help desk options located in the SMS Administrator program.

FIGURE 34.11.

The help desk options located in the SMS Administrator program.

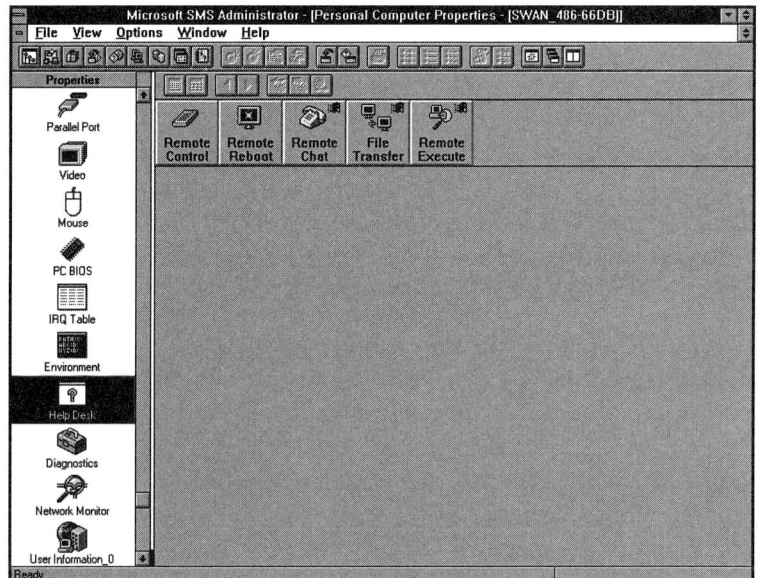

SMS enables the following functions to be performed using the help desk utilities:

- *Remote Reboot.* This enables the reboot (software, not hardware) of a remote machine. This is useful for rebooting the system if changes have been made—for example, when you install a program and the computer needs to be restarted for the changes to take effect.

- *Remote Program Execution.* This enables a program located on the client machine to be run. The SMS administrator types the command-line parameters of the program to be run, and it is executed on the client machine. This is useful when the administrator wants to run a diagnostics program found on the client computer.

- *Remote Control.* This function will display a window on the SMS Administrator screen showing the current display of the remote computer. The administrator can interact with the display, including mouse actions. If the remote display is at a higher resolution than the SMS computer, scrollbars appear to enable navigation through the

34

SMS OVERVIEW

display. The Remote Control function allows a client computer to be controlled by an administrator. The administrator can control the computer in the same manner as a user sitting in front of the machine. In Figure 34.12, the display resolution of the remote computer is greater than the display of the SMS computer, so scrollbars are added to give the administrator full access to the screen.

FIGURE 34.12.

An example of a remote computer being controlled by the SMS Remote Control function.

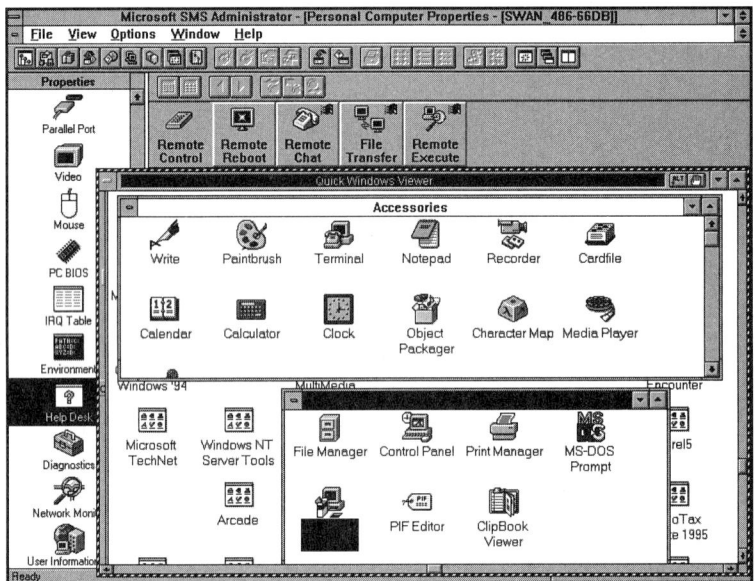

- *Remote Chat.* This gives the SMS administrator and the user of the remote computer the ability to communicate by typing data on the screen (see Figure 34.13). This is extremely helpful for remote users working from home or a hotel where only one phone line is available and being used for the SMS Help Desk functions.

- *Remote File Transfer.* If the administrator needs to send a file from the SMS computer to the remote computer, the Remote File Transfer is used. Likewise, files can be retrieved from the remote computer and stored on the SMS computer. This function enables file transfer between the two computers. Keep in mind, however, that if the link between the two computers is a slow link, such as a modem, large file transfers may take an extremely long time.

- *Remote Diagnostic Information.* Diagnostic information about the remote machine can be viewed through the SMS Administrator program. In Figure 34.14, you can see the CMOS information about a remote network computer: CMOS settings, Windows resources, device drivers, and DOS memory information. This provides current information that is usually not stored in the SMS database due to the changing nature of this information. However, it may be useful when trying to troubleshoot problems.

FIGURE 34.13.

An example of the Remote Chat function.

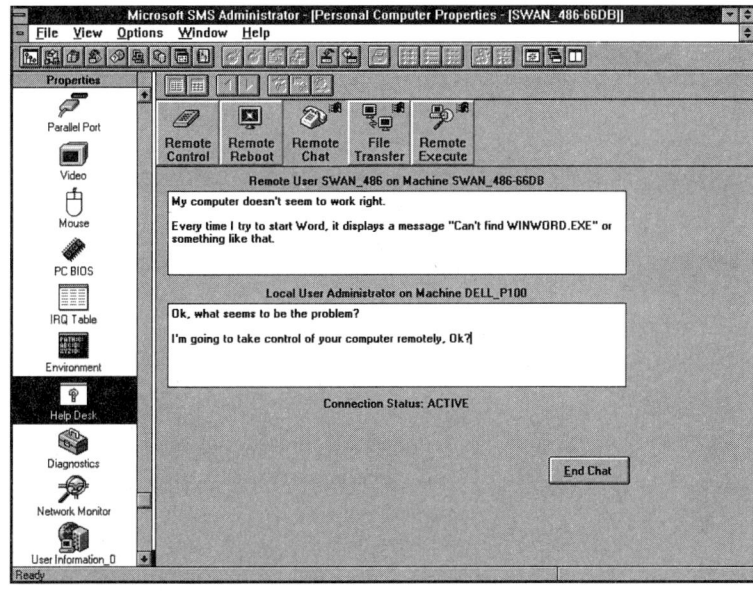

FIGURE 34.14.

An example of the Remote Diagnostic Information function when used for a remote machine.

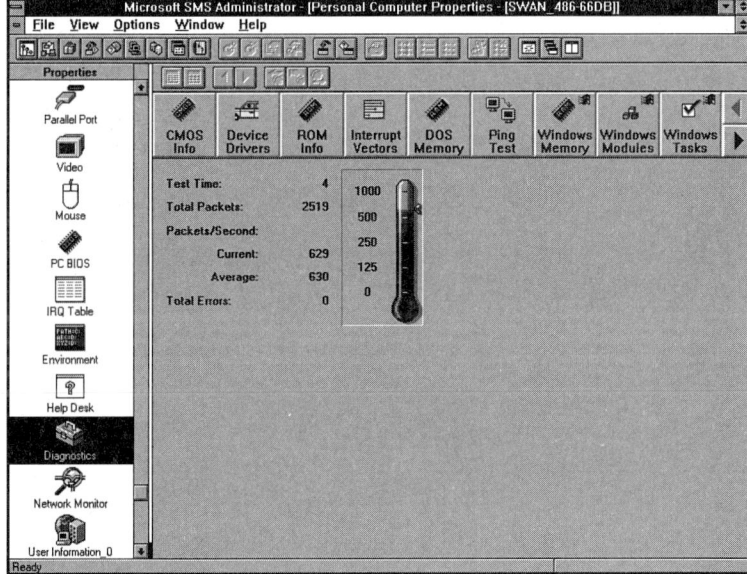

34

SMS OVERVIEW

> **NOTE**
>
> With the powerful nature of the SMS remote control abilities, many network administrators will obviously be concerned about misuse or security problems with someone taking control of another computer. The SMS client must be running the Remote Control client program before the computer can be accessed. Also, before anyone else can control the computer, a dialog will be displayed to the client asking whether remote control access is allowed. This helps to prevent unauthorized remote control access of client computers.

Summary

Microsoft Systems Management Server provides a wealth of tools to help a network administrator take control of a network. Whether it is a small network with only a few computers or a large network that is geographically dispersed, SMS is flexible and powerful enough to ease the burden of some of the network administrator's most important jobs. SMS builds on Windows NT's management features, and it utilizes another component of the BackOffice package: SQL Server.

With the right planning and site layout, SMS can be used to properly manage multiple networks with many network administrators. SMS provides strong client support, allowing remote control and other supporting functions to MS-DOS, Windows 3.1, and Windows 95 computers. The features of SMS are very powerful, and the next few chapters explore these features even further.

Installing SMS

by Ahsan Farooqi

IN THIS CHAPTER

CHAPTER 35

Before you begin to install and configure the Systems Management Server, you should understand the concepts and terminology that SMS uses. SMS uses the same items that you have probably used before, but defined differently. Let's review those terms.

Sites are a group of computers that you may want to manage as a separate group. Each site is its own entity within the SMS and is distinguished with its unique three-character site code. Each site also requires a Site Server where you install the SMS software and Services. This server has the primary responsibility for managing the site. Within each site are one or more domains.

A domain is also a group of computers. This group consists of the type of computers that are to be managed or inventoried (as you will later find out). This is a somewhat misunderstood term and needs to be defined properly. In doing so, I would like to draw upon your NT knowledge to define domains.

The Networking Environment includes NT or LAN Manager domains, as well as Novell or NetWare Servers, or NetWare Networks as they may be known to some of you CNEs out there. A domain in the NT environment is one wherein a group of computers share a common user database to provide networking security and networking functions. If the SMS is installed on the NT Domain Controller, that domain automatically becomes part of the SMS site. In SMS terms, it is the site's domain. You can add domains to sites or assign a site to part of a domain, thereby gathering a group on computers in multiple NT domains to be a part of the SMS site. In Novell networks, there is no concept of a domain, and users log on to the server themselves and are not managed centrally. For NetWare networks, artificial domains can be created, and Novell servers and client computers can be added to the domain. This can all be done by the SMS itself through the SMS Administrator. You administer a site through an SMS Administrator utility, and you administer an NT Domain through NT utilities such as User Manager for Domains or Server Manager.

SMS has four types of servers; all these servers operate within a site:

- Site server
- Distribution server
- Logon server
- Helper server

Because the site server is the NT Domain Controller on which the SMS is originally installed, it is the server where everything to do with SMS is installed—the file and print services of SMS, for example. The distribution servers are distribution points for the software for clients. The distribution servers also play an important role in software sharing and in company rollouts of new software. If a company decided to go with Windows 95 as its operating system on every desktop for every employee, for example, the entire procedure could be done using SMS and its distribution server. (For further information, refer to my *SMS Survival Guide* by Sams Publishing.) The helpers do just what their name says—they help in network administration of SMS Services and administration. These servers are designed to ease the load of some SMS Services to other controllers.

Clients are the computers that are going to be managed by SMS Server. These clients are the following

- MS-DOS
- Windows 3.*x*
- Windows 95
- Windows NT (new to SMS version 1.2 for remote control)

Microsoft's Systems Management Server provides centralized administration of computers in an enterprise network. The SMS has four major functions:

- Distributing and installing software
- Collecting hardware and software inventory
- Sharing network applications
- Troubleshooting hardware and software problems

Distributing and installing software is a function of the Systems Management Server and gives the administrator the ability to install software unattended. It also helps in planning operating systems rollout of the organization.

Collecting hardware and software inventory information is also a function of the Systems Management Server and is the one that is arguably the one most used. It is a collection of Systems Management Server methods and processes for organizing and querying inventory data.

Sharing network application is a unique function that operates on a user's membership in a user group to generate program groups for network applications.

Troubleshooting hardware and software problems is the function of a group of network utilities that help in monitoring and troubleshooting network problems. Examples of such utilities are the Network Monitor diagnostic utility and the Help Desk utility, which enables remote control of Windows for Workgroups and MS-DOS–based clients.

> **NOTE**
>
> In SMS version 1.2, the Help Desk utility is scheduled to include remote control of Windows 95 and Windows NT clients. As yet, these clients are not supported only in the Help Desk environment.

In Systems Management Server, automatic inventory collection is enabled at the site server. The SMS can be configured to automatically scan the hardware and software information on all computers managed by SMS as users log on the network. This information is called inventory and is stored in a Microsoft SQL Server database at the site server. This database can then be queried by the administrator for specific information, including which computer has a certain software installed or the number of computers in the network with Pentium processors.

This process can be started either from the SMS Server or the client.

> **NOTE**
>
> One important use of the inventory collection function is that it can also be used to collect files such as CONFIG.SYS from inventoried computers. This enables the network administrator to troubleshoot the client computer rights from one location.

Shared Application Management is used to distribute and install Network Applications to distribution servers. These applications can then be used by SMS clients. When an application is set up on the network, groups can be specified that have certain rights to use or administer the network. The servers to be used as distribution points can also be specified. The desktop on the clients is automatically built, and the client or user can start to use the application. Upon execution, the application is run from the distribution server. If the distribution server is down or not available, the client continues to run the application from other distribution servers if specified. This process is transparent to the user. The shared applications are supported for the Windows 3.*x*, Windows 95, and Windows NT operating systems.

The software management server uses packages and jobs to distribute and install software. The package consists of software and instructions for distributing and installing software, or for carrying out a command. A package contains one or more of the following:

- Commercial software
- Custom upgrades
- Any executable file of a batch file

A package therefore includes multiple sets of instructions for a particular software to be installed. It also contains installation instructions or deinstallation instructions, as the case may be. A job specifies which client receives and which clients do not receive the package. SMS also enables the administrator to appoint which servers will serve as the distribution servers for the software or the entire network.

The diagnostic utilities are there to troubleshoot and support not only Systems Management Server but also the entire network.

Preinstallation Considerations

Some preinstallation considerations include recognizing that SMS is not just software that can be installed by itself. It works only on the Windows NT Server operating system, which must be installed as a Domain Controller—either a Primary or Backup Domain Controller. For this to take place, the NT Server 3.51 must meet the hardware compatibility list.

Systems Management Server and the SQL Server

The SMS stores information it collects from the network in a database that can then be queried. SQL Server for Microsoft Windows NT is the only database supported by the Systems Management Server. SMS version 1.1 supports either SQL Server 4.21a or 6.0. Although SMS is a SQL Server client, no client licenses are required. If the SQL Server is configured with its own standard security, you must have a SQL login ID to create and access an SMS database one. For this, a new SQL account can be created, or the existing SQL sa account can also be used. However, if SQL is configured for integrated accounts security, Windows NT accounts can be used.

Creating Devices on the SQL Server for an SMS Database

Creating devices on the SQL Server for an SMS database varies depending upon whether the SQL Server is the same computer that has the Systems Management Server software installed as well. A SQL device is nothing more than preallocated space on the hard disk. SMS requires two devices: one for the site database and the other for the transaction log. The latter is used to recover the SMS Server in case of system failure and to store before and after images of data changed in the database.

If the Systems Management Server and SQL are installed on the same computer, the SMS Setup program can create the database and the log devices.

If the two server softwares are on two separate computers, SMS Setup requires that SQL devices have already been created on the SQL Server. The SQL administrator is responsible for this task. It can be achieved using the SQL Enterprise Manager.

> **NOTE**
>
> Although new devices are not required, they are highly recommended. You can specify existing SQL devices on the SQL Server machine, but during installation, the SMS Setup program *deletes* any and all databases existing on those devices before creating the database required for the SMS usage. It does so because SMS uses all the space available in the SQL devices assigned to the SMS software.

SQL Configurations

The following options are recommended for configuration of the SQL Server to be used with Systems Management Server.

- *User connections.* SMS requires five connections during operation; however, it uses a *minimum* of 20 user connections during installation. Therefore, SQL Server must allow for up to 25 simultaneous user connections for smooth operation.

- *Open objects.* The default value of the SQL Server is 500 objects (files and so forth). It is recommended that you increase this value on the SQL Server to 5,000 for usage with SMS.

- *Memory.* The bottom line is: the more the merrier. The SQL Server will take as much RAM as is available without any concern for the pocket of the user or organization. You must meet minimum installation requirements and anything beyond is a result of your generosity or to your advantage.

- *Size of devices in megabytes.* Size should be approximately 10K per machine in the organization, and 10 percent of the database should be the log size. For example, if you are storing inventory collection of your company and there are 50,000 computers in the organization, the device size for the database is 10K per machine (or 500M minimum), and the log device is 10 percent of 500M (about 50M for the SMS log).

- *Temporary database size.* Size should be 2K per machine with a minimum of 10M.

In addition to these parameters, if the SQL and the SMS Servers are not the same computer, the administrator must take care to synchronize the clocks of these two computers. The Systems Management Server uses the clock of the SQL Server to schedule tasks. This could become very troublesome if the computers are not synchronized. For some computer installations, this is not an issue.

SMS Service Account

Systems Management Server is installed on the Windows NT Domain Controller machine as a set of services running in the background. Therefore, it requires a Windows NT account that enables it to run in this fashion. This account is referred to as the SMS Services Account. The Services account must have the Log on as a Service user right and must also have administrative privileges.

Hardware and Software Requirements

The following are minimum requirements. By this, I mean they are bare essentials. Remember—the more the merrier.

Hardware

- Must meet Windows NT Hardware Compatibility List.

- 32M of RAM; 64 is recommended although servers with 128M of RAM are a common site for SMS.

- 100M of hard disk space (NTFS); this is for the SMS software only. I recommend at least 200M of free hard disk space for SMS software only.

Software

- Windows NT Server 3.5*x* (Domain Controller only—that is, a PDC or BDC).
- SQL Server for Windows NT 4.21 or 6.0 for SMS version 1.1; for version 1.2 (soon to be released), SMS works only with SQL Server for NT 6.0 or 6.5—that is, SQL 6.*x*.

> **NOTE**
>
> SMS is compatible only with the Windows NT Server 3.5*x* operating system and Microsoft SQL Server database program and nothing else.

Installing SMS

For installing SMS, you should run the SETUP.BAT from the SMSSETUP directory on the Systems Management Server CD-ROM. This program automatically detects the type of hardware platform (Intel, MIPS, DEC ALPHA) and installs the appropriate version (see Figure 35.1).

This program has two modes: Default and Custom.

FIGURE 35.1.

This screen shows the various Systems Management Server software installation options that are available.

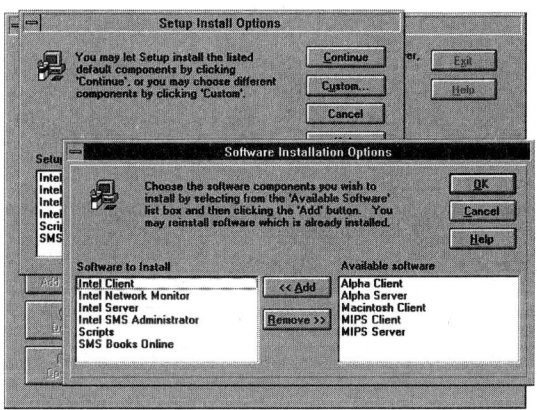

Default is synonymous with the Express mode of Microsoft products and installs Systems Management Server with typical defaults for the most common Windows NT environment. The Custom mode enables the administrator to install optional products, such as BOOKS ONLINE, as well as to include and exclude optional components, such as Network Monitor and the platform upon which the SMS is being installed. The platform includes Intel and MIPS (Motorola-based CPUs).

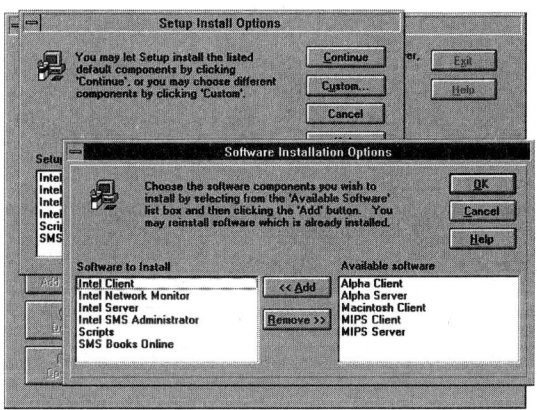

35

INSTALLING SMS

Configuring the SMS Database

After the SMS installation, the screen in Figure 35.2 appears. The SQL Server should already be installed and the SMS Setup program needs the information about what type of account to log in as and the database name to create. It also requires the device name on which to create the SMS database.

FIGURE 35.2.

The SMS Setup program requiring information about the SQL Server account and the name of the database device to create.

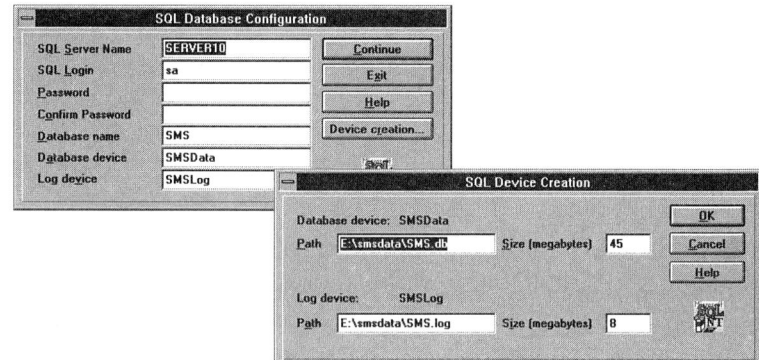

Configuring the Primary Site Server

After the SQL information has been supplied and verified by SMS Setup, the Primary Site Configuration screen appears (see Figure 35.3). This screen requires a three-character site code to identify this site. This must be unique in the entire organization within the SMS hierarchy. This is followed by a site name, which is a name used to refer to this site. Think of it as an alias for the site number.

FIGURE 35.3.

Primary Site Configuration Information for the Systems Management Server. This requires the Service Account for SMS logon.

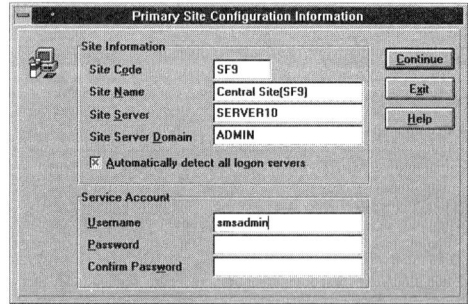

SMS Services

SMS is installed on the Windows NT computer as Services. The following Service monitors the SMS database for configuration changes and updates SMS with the completed changes:

SMS_HIERARCHY_MANAGER

This Service is important because it implements configuration changes and installs secondary sites:

`SMS_SITE_CONFIG_MANAGER`

The following manages a number of SMS processes, which are sometimes referred to as Services. These SMS Services are not managed by the Windows NT Service Manager or by Windows NT in any fashion:

`SMS_EXECUTIVE`

This is the primary service agent responsible for collecting inventory at the Site Server:

`SMS_INVENTORY_AGENT_NT`

These Services can be viewed from the Control Panel and can be configured or even stopped and started as desired.

Installing Clients to the SMS Site

Generally, a client computer is added to a site through inventory collection. This is done in four steps. First, the administrator puts the information about the client to be installed in a package. This package is then put on the distribution server. As the client logs on, the SMS client is installed on its machine and the inventory is collected and passed to the logon on servers. This is then processed into the database, and the administrator can query the database for further review. The SMS clients use an SMS.INI file to configure themselves. This file is installed on all clients during the client software installation program.

Events and Logs

SMS is designed to report events and logs back to the administrator. This reporting is done to both the SMS database as well as to Windows NT logs. When an application is reporting a significant event or an error, it gets written in two places:

- The Windows NT event log, so the administrator can view the process in the Event Viewer
- The events table in the SMS database, which can be viewed from the Events windows in the SMS Administrator

Troubleshooting Installation and Configuration

The majority of the time, SMS Setup failure is due to SQL Server, disk, or security problems. During installation, while SMSSETUP is running, events are written in C:\SMSMSETUP.LOG. This can be viewed to find out where the failure occurred during SMS Setup.

Secondary Site Installation

This section describes a basic process of secondary site installation. Briefly, the secondary sites do not have or maintain their own SQL Server database. The secondary sites also use the SMS Administrator program to install secondary sites instead of the Setup program on the SMS CD-ROM. These are also the primary differences between the primary site and the secondary site.

The basic steps are as follows:

1. Start SMS and log on to the primary site that is to become the parent of the secondary site.

> **NOTE**
>
> Because the secondary sites have no database, they must report their inventory collections and other services backups to the primary site, also known as their parent site, which does have a database.

2. Select the Sites window.
3. From the SMS Administrator's File menu, choose New.
4. The New Secondary Site dialog box appears (see Figure 35.4).

FIGURE 35.4.

New Secondary Site installation screen requiring information for installation of the secondary site.

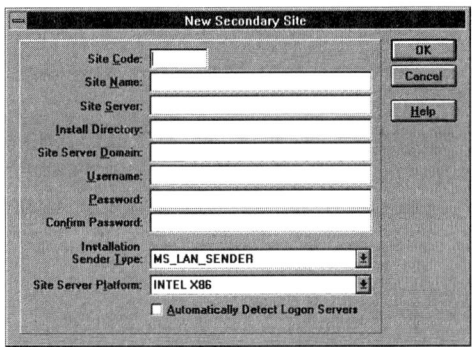

As shown in the figure, the New Secondary Site dialog box requires specific information about the new site. The following are required:1

■ Site Code—A three-character unique code chosen for this site.

■ Site Name—A name to be displayed for this site in the SMS Administrator program. Must be unique as well. Human beings generally do well with names, but the computer programs including the Systems Management Server work well with codes and numbers—in this case, Site Code.

- Site Server—The computer name of the server where you are installing the secondary site.

- Install Directory—The specific location for the drive and directory where the SMS files will go.

- Site Server Domain—An existing domain where the site server will be installed.

- Username—The SMS Service user account created during initial installation of SMS.

- Password—The password of the SMS Service Account.

- Installation Sender Type—The type of sender the sites communicate with. This is discussed in detail in Chapter 37, "Planning and Managing a LAN with SMS." Other senders can also be added after installation. The default is the MS_LAN_SENDER.

- Site Server Platform—The architecture of the site server computer. The default platform is the Intel X86.

- Automatically Detect Logon Servers—If selected, it automatically detects and adds all the logon servers that are detected in the secondary site to that primary site.

Secondary Site Process

You just learned how to install secondary sites. You have yet to explore how it is actually done through the two sites. The concepts of the process are described in this section. Use Figure 35.5 as a guide.

FIGURE 35.5.

Steps outlining the installation of the secondary sites.

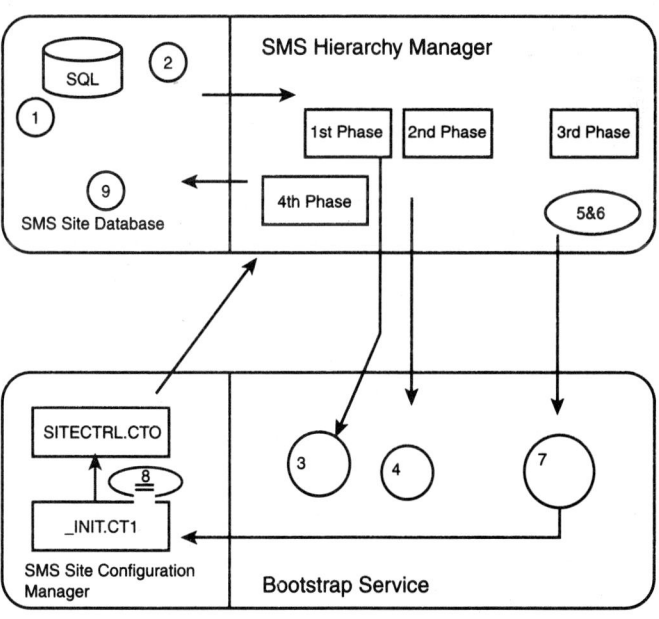

Let's trace through the steps in Figure 35.5 to better understand the process.

Step 1. In this step, you complete the New Secondary Site dialog box, which updates the SQL database in the primary site of the SMS system.

Step 2. The SMS Hierarchy Manager (a Service) checks on the SQL database and finds a new site configuration. In this step, the Hierarchy Manager updates the site's information so that it can communicate with the secondary site. All this takes place on the primary site.

Step 3. Part of this step is performed on the primary site and is referred to as Phase 1. In this, the Hierarchy Manager in the primary site creates a job to create the SMS installation directory (also specified in the New Secondary Site dialog box) and starts the BOOTSTRAP program in the secondary site. This eventually enables the sites to communicate.

Step 4. Now that the BOOTSTRAP is installed so that the communication is established, you have most of your job done. Once the BOOTSTRAP program is installed, the Hierarchy Manager creates the SMS site package containing the files necessary to install the secondary site. The site package is created using the information in the SYSTEM.MAP file.

Step 5. This and the next step are usually done together at the primary site by the Hierarchy Manager. In this step, the Hierarchy Manager creates a second job to send and install the site package. This is labeled Site Install Job. This process is Phase 2 of the entire process.

Step 6. This step follows step 5 very quickly. Here, the Hierarchy Manager creates a third job to send the secondary configuration file. The job is labeled Site Control Job. The configuration file is created by SMS with the name of _INIT.CT1. This is called Phase 3 of the secondary site installation process.

Step 7. In this step, most of the work is done by the BOOTSTRAP program in the secondary site. The BOOTSTRAP program receives the configuration file, verifies the packages, decompresses the packages, and creates the SMS directories as specified in the dialog box (as that same information was put in to the package in step 4). Finally, the BOOTSTRAP program starts the Site Configuration Manager before stopping itself. The work for the BOOTSTRAP program is now over.

Step 8. The Site Configuration Manager uses the _INIT.ct1 configuration file to complete the installation and start the SMS Services on the new site. A new file is created with the extension of CT2, which is returned to the primary site for confirmation.

Step 9. At the primary site, the SMS Hierarchy Manager receives the CT2 file and sees it as a confirmation of this entire process. Thus, it now knows that the information that was updated in the SQL database through the New Secondary Site dialog box has been processed correctly. It reads the information of the CT2 file and updates the SQL database on the primary site permanently (until another change is requested).

> **NOTE**
>
> The same procedure is followed if a change is requested in the SQL database regarding its own primary site or the newly installed secondary site. For example, after installation, if any change in the configuration of the secondary site needs to be done, it will go through the same process. The administrator will make the desired request in the SQL database, which then follows the nine steps until the CT2 file is received back at the primary site. Then it makes the requested change in the SQL database permanent.

Summary

The initial installation verifies that the server to be used as the site server is a Windows NT primary or backup Domain Controller. It is important to synchronize the time on all the servers and the clients to ensure that the times set by the SMS are identical on all computers.

When you install the secondary site, the information is stored in SMS's SQL database. The Hierarchy Manager reads this information and creates a package and a job to send and install the BOOTSTRAP program. When the BOOTSTRAP program is running, the Hierarchy Manager then creates another job to send the site files and the job control file CT1 to the secondary site. The secondary site server BOOTSTRAP program receives the package, verifies it, decompresses it, and installs the Site Server Manager to complete the installation. Upon completion, the Site Configuration Manager creates a site control file, CT2, that the primary site Hierarchy Manager uses to update the Systems Management Server's SQL database.

The Automatically Detect Logon Server option in the New Secondary Site dialog box, when checked, causes the SMS site to include all the servers detected as logon servers. If unchecked, it includes only the site server as the logon server.

SMS Administration

by Richard Neff

CHAPTER 36

Systems Management Server is a very powerful program that enables a network administrator to take control over the network. The majority of SMS management is handled through a program known as the SMS Administrator. The SMS Administrator program enables you to perform tasks such as queries of the network computers, distribution of software, and diagnostic tasks.

The SMS Administrator Program

The primary tool used to control SMS is the SMS Administrator program. The SMS Administrator program provides the central interface for the definition of SMS tasks to be carried out by the various SMS services. The information in the SMS database can be viewed from the SMS Administrator program in a logical, tree-like hierarchy. Many different window types can be displayed to handle different SMS functions.

The SMS Administrator program is located in the Systems Management Server program group.

Before you start the SMS Administrator program, know the name of the SQL Server where the SMS database is located. Be sure to know the name of that database, named SMS by default. You also need to know the SQL account name and password to connect to the SQL database. The default account called sa is created when SQL Server is installed and, by default, it has no password. However, in many instances the account may be renamed or assigned a password.

When you start the SMS Administrator, the SMS title screen is shown, then the window shown in Figure 36.1. If this is the first time you are using the SMS Administrator, all the fields will be blank. You need to fill in the SQL Server name, the SMS database name, the account name, and the account password. If you have used the SMS Administrator previously, all the fields except the password field will be shown. After the fields have been entered, click the OK button or press Enter.

FIGURE 36.1.

The initial sign-in screen of the SMS Administrator program.

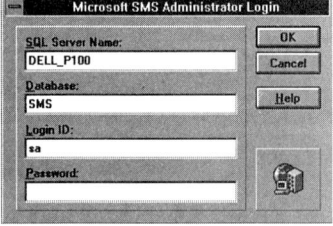

After you successfully complete the login window, the SMS Administrator is started. If this is the first time you have started the SMS Administrator, a window will be displayed listing the different windows you can open. This list contains the following possible windows:

- The Sites window enables you to view the current site and any sites that are child sites.

- The Jobs window displays all the jobs on the current SMS site and their current status.

- The Packages window shows all the packages that have been created and enables editing of existing packages and creation of new ones.

- The Queries window lists all the SMS queries that have been defined. SMS provides some predefined queries by default.

- The Alerts window shows all the alerts currently defined on the SMS system.

- The Machine Groups window displays all the various machine groups that have been created.

- The Site Groups window displays any site groups that have been created and enables new groups to be added.

- The Program Groups window shows the various program group configurations that have been defined for shared network packages.

- The Events window has a similar format to the Windows NT Event viewer; however, this contains information specific to SMS.

- The SQL Server Messages window shows any messages from the SQL Server that are created by actions of the SMS Administrator program.

You can select one window or multiple windows to be opened by holding down the Ctrl key and clicking the desired window with the left mouse button. A description is also displayed at the bottom of the window to provide more information about the selected item.

The optional Open SMS Window box opens when the SMS Administrator starts (see Figure 36.2). You can open any of the listed windows from this box. You also have the option of not displaying the window when the SMS Administrator starts.

FIGURE 36.2.

The optional Open SMS Window screen that is displayed when the SMS Administrator first starts.

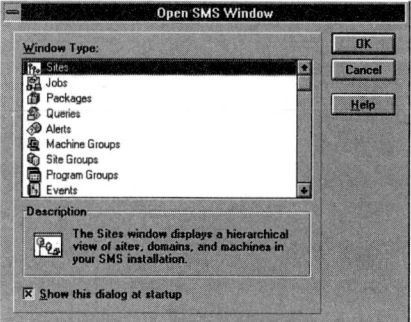

At the bottom of the window, a checkbox is available to select whether to display the Open SMS Window dialog when the SMS Administrator is started. If you prefer not to display this window when the SMS Administrator program starts, clear the checkbox. If you clear the checkbox, you can display the Open SMS Window dialog by selecting File, Open from the SMS Administrator menu.

Once you choose the OK button of the Open SMS Window screen, or have turned off the startup display of the Open SMS Window screen, the SMS Administrator window is shown. The SMS Administrator displays a menu, toolbar, and any function windows you have selected. A majority of the SMS Administrator functions are easily available on the toolbar.

The SMS Administrator has a toolbar used to open all the available windows (see Figure 36.3). It also contains other key functions of the SMS Administrator for easy access.

FIGURE 36.3.

The SMS Administrator toolbar, with the function of each icon.

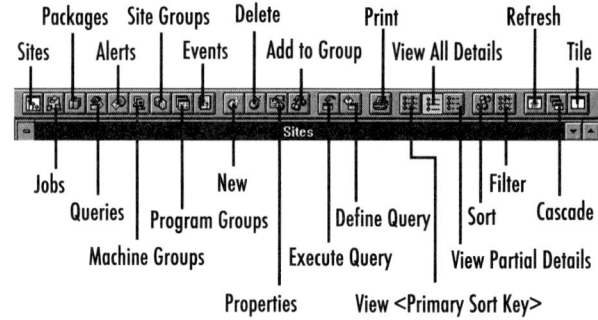

The following icons are available on the SMS Administrator toolbar:

- Sites displays the Sites window.
- Jobs displays the Jobs window.
- Packages displays the Packages window.
- Queries displays the Queries window.
- Alerts displays the Alerts window.
- Machine Groups displays the Machine Groups window.
- Site Groups displays the Site Groups window.
- Program Groups displays the Program Groups window.
- Events displays the SMS Events window.
- New creates a new item for the active window. A window is active if the title bar of that window is blue. If the title bar is gray, it is in the background. If no window is open, this icon is disabled until a window is opened.

- Delete removes an item from the active window. As with the New icon, if no windows are displayed, the icon is grayed out.

- Properties displays the Properties window for the currently selected item. The type of information displayed depends on the item that is selected. Once again, this item is available only when a window is displayed.

- Add to Group adds an item to a group. This function varies according to the window that is currently active and the type of item highlighted. This icon is available only when the following windows are active: Sites, Package, Machine Groups, or Site Groups.

- Execute Query displays a dialog to enable the administrator to either execute an existing query or define and execute an ad hoc query.

- Define Query Results Format enables the display of query results to be changed and defined.

- Print displays a dialog to enable the administrator to print the entire contents or selected items in the active window.

- View <Primary Sort Key> displays the items in the active window based on the primary sort key if one is defined.

- View All Details views all details of items listed in the active window.

- View Partial Details shows a dialog to display selected details of items in the active window.

- Sort displays a dialog to enable the administrator to define and sort the list on both primary and secondary keys.

- Filter displays a dialog to enable the administrator to define and filter the list of items in the active window.

- Refresh refreshes the items in the active window with the current values.

- Cascade places all open windows on top of each other with the active window on top. The other windows are arranged so the title bars are visible.

- Tile Vertically tiles all open windows so that the administrator can see their contents.

The windows that can be opened from the toolbar are the same as the windows in the Open SMS Window dialog. The toolbar, however, provides a more convenient way of opening windows after the SMS Administrator program is started.

The SMS Administrator program saves the positions of all open windows when the user exits the program. When the SMS Administrator program is restarted, all the windows that were open at the close of the last session are opened and located in the same position. This gives the administrator easier access to the more commonly used windows.

Viewing the Site Inventory

The first thing a network administrator probably wants to see is the current inventory of the computers on the network. The Sites window displays the different computers and their properties of all the computers that have been added to the SMS inventory. The Sites window displays items in a hierarchical fashion. You can double-click on the sites, domains, and computers you want to expand.

The left side of the Sites window shows the different SMS sites in an organization. If a site is double-clicked to expand the site tree, domains in that site will be displayed. When the domain is highlighted, the right side of the window will display all of the computers inventoried in that domain. Servers will be differentiated by a different icon than client computers.

The SMS site window displays information about the SMS site structure (see Figure 36.4). From this window you can also view specific information about servers and workstations in the site or perform other administrative site functions.

FIGURE 36.4.

An example of the Sites window with a sample site displayed.

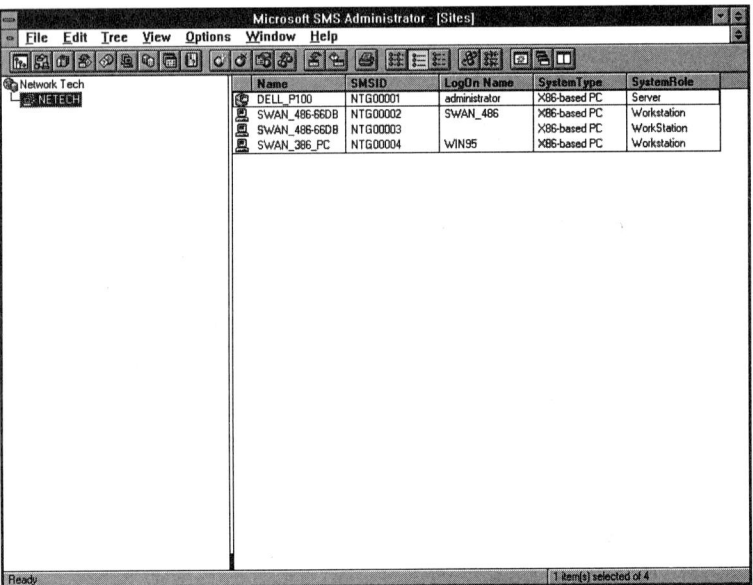

You can view the properties of a single computer in the right side of the Sites window by selecting that computer and either double-clicking that computer, selecting File, Properties from the menu, or clicking on the Properties icon in the toolbar. A Personal Computer Properties window, similar to Figure 36.5, will be displayed.

FIGURE 36.5.

The Personal Computer Properties window of a selected computer shows all the information about that computer in the SMS database.

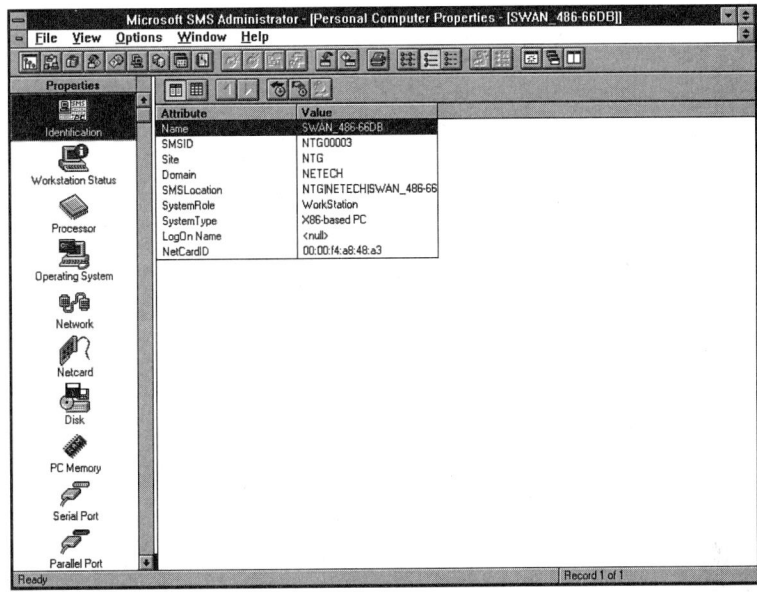

Defining and Running Queries

Queries are used to find computers on the network that meet certain criteria. A query is useful to network administrators when they want to find out things such as the following:

- Which computers have enough physical memory to run a particular application?
- How many machines have hard disks that are almost full?
- How many computers on the network have Intel Pentium Processors and who uses them?

Queries are a fast way to know exactly how the computers on the network are configured. Queries are often used before installing applications over the network to help ensure that the machines receiving the application meet the needed hardware requirements of that application.

To run an SMS query in order to find computers meeting certain criteria, use the following steps:

1. Start the SMS Administrator program. This is located in the Systems Management Server group. In order to start the administrator program, you will be prompted for the SMS Administrator account name, password, and database. The Microsoft SMS Administrator program is displayed.

2. Now it is time to define the criteria items to be used in the query. These items include the processor type, memory, hard disk space, and so forth. To create a new query, open the Queries window by clicking on the Queries icon (the fourth on the toolbar). This will display the Queries window with any queries that have been defined.

3. While the Queries window is selected, select File from the menu, then New. The Query Properties window will appear, similar to Figure 36.6, which will enable you to create a new query.

FIGURE 36.6.

The Query Properties window enables you to create new queries.

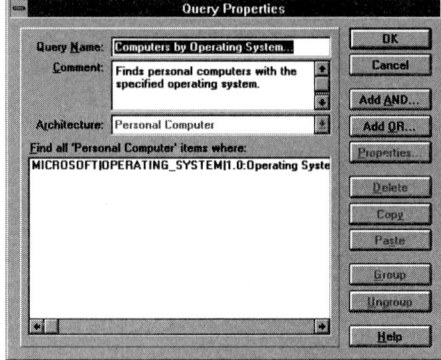

4. In the Query Name box, type a name for the Query. The name Computers Able to Run Windows NT, for example, is appropriate if you want to find computers able to run Windows NT. You may also type a comment in the Comment box to further describe the function of the Query.

5. In the Architecture box, be sure Personal Computer is displayed. To the right, the Add AND... and Add OR... buttons can be found. These buttons are used to select the criteria for the query. Click on the Add AND... button to enter the first item in the query. The Query Expressions Properties window is displayed (see Figure 36.7).

FIGURE 36.7.

The Query Expression Properties window enables you to select the conditional items used in the query.

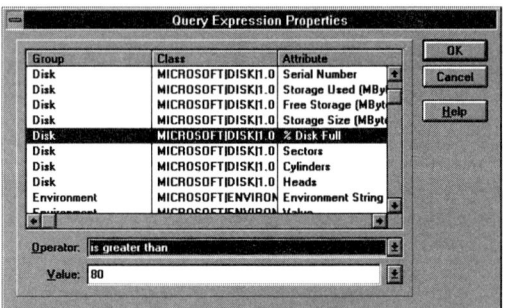

6. In the Query Expressions Properties window, you can choose the different items to search. For example, to find computers that have Pentium processors, select Processor in the group column. In the Operator box, select is. In the Value box, select Intel Pentium from the drop-down list. In most instances, you will want to use the greater than or equal to item in the Operator box.

7. Continue to add items using the Add AND... and Add OR... buttons until you have all the items that you want to search for. After you select all the items, click on the OK button.

8. To perform a query, choose File from the menu, then Execute Query. The Execute Query icon can also be selected. The Execute Query window will be displayed, shown in Figure 36.8. You can select the query to run. The default query to run is the highlighted query in the Query window. You can also select the query from the Query window and drag it to the site to run the query in the Sites window.

FIGURE 36.8.

The Execute Query window enables you to select the query to run.

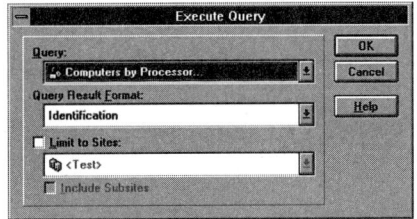

9. After the query is started, the Query Results window will be displayed. As SMS finds computers that match the query criteria, the computers will be added to the list. Keep in mind that on large networks, the queries may take some time.

Creating Machine Groups

Machine Groups can be created in SMS to better organize the different types of computers found on the network. Machine groups are often used to group computers together that have similar features. For example, a network administrator my want to put all the computers that run Windows NT into one machine group, while putting all the other computers running Windows 95 into another. In this instance, it becomes easier to send applications that are specific to Windows NT to the correct computers.

Machine groups are not limited to grouping machines with different operating systems, however. They can be used to group any type of computers. Machine groups can be created from query results or computers can be manually added to a machine group. Creating a machine group from a query is usually the simplest way to group machines that have a particular item in common. Manually creating a group is useful when the administrator wants to control which machines are in the group.

To put the computers found in a query into an SMS machine group, use the following steps:

1. Start the SMS Administrator program. Provide the SMS Administrator account name, password, and database. See the section titled The SMS Administrator Program for more information on starting SMS. The Microsoft SMS Administrator program is displayed.

2. Create a new query, or select an existing query and execute that query. A Query Results window will be displayed. For more information on creating and executing queries, see the previous section titled Defining and Running Queries.

3. Open the Machine Groups window by clicking on the Machine Groups icon on the toolbar. A Machine Groups window will be displayed. If there were any machine groups previously defined, they will be displayed in this window. (Note: Do *not* close the Query Results window!)

4. To add a machine group, choose File, New while the Machine Groups window is active. The Machine Group Properties window will be displayed, shown in Figure 36.9. Type the name of the new machine group you want to create in the Name: box. You can also type an optional comment about the machine group.

FIGURE 36.9.

The Machine Group Properties window enables you to type a name for a new machine group.

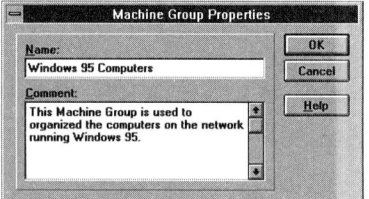

5. Select the computers in the Query Results window from the query you just ran. Hold down the left mouse button and drag the computers from the Query Results window to the Machine Groups window. The Add to Machine Group window, shown in Figure 36.10, will be displayed.

FIGURE 36.10.

The Add to Machine Group window enables you to select the computers to add to the machine group or change the machine group.

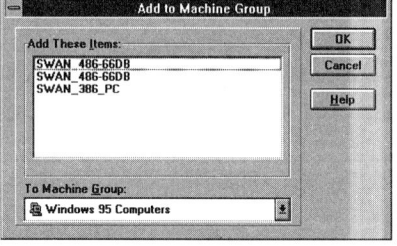

6. The Add to Machine Group window will list the computers to add to the machine group in the first listbox. The To Machine Group drop-down list enables you to select the machine group where the computers will be added.

7. Be sure that the machine group that you just created is selected in the To Machine Group list, and click on the OK button.

To manually create a machine group or to manually add items to an existing machine group, use the following steps:

1. If it is not running, start the SMS Administrator program.

2. Open the Machine Groups window by using the Machine Groups icon on the toolbar or from the Open SMS Windows dialog.

3. To create a new machine group, click on the New icon on the toolbar or select File, New item from the menu. A Machine group Properties box will appear, enabling you to type a name for the machine group and a comment for that group. Click on the OK button to add the machine group to the window.

4. To add computers to a machine group, open the Sites window or Query Results window and highlight the computers you want to add. Click on the Add to Group icon on the toolbar or select File, Add to Group from the menu. The Add to Machine Group window will be displayed. An example of this window is shown in Figure 36.11.

FIGURE 36.11.

The Add to Machine Group window enables you to add computers to a selected machine group.

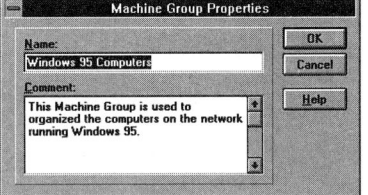

5. The Add These Items: box lists all the highlighted computers. Highlight any or all of the computers listed in the Add These Items: box and choose the machine group from the To Machine Group: drop-down list.

6. Click on the OK button to add the computers to the machine group.

You can also drag and drop computers to the Machine Group window from the Sites window, with a procedure similar to the steps outlined for creating a machine group from queries.

Creating Packages

The SMS software distribution function is divided into two parts: packages and jobs. Packages are used to define the various installation options about the application. Jobs handle the actual delivery of the software to the appropriate machines.

> **NOTE**
>
> Many SMS users may at first wonder why the software distribution feature is broken into the two phases of packages and jobs. The two-step distribution concept enables a package to be created and later distributed to different groups. This is extremely useful when using a pilot program before implementing a software application company-wide. The package can be created once and then sent to the pilot site immediately; then the same package, with or without modification, can be used to send the application to the entire company at a later date.

Packages must be defined to inform the SMS process how to install or run the distributed programs. You can have three types of packages:

- Run on workstation packages are typically used to install applications on a client computer. These applications, once installed, are run from the local client machine and may not require the use of a network server for proper installation. Creating these types of packages are discussed later.

- Shared network applications packages enable an application to be installed on a server and shared for network clients to use it. The clients don't store the program files, but rather run them directly from the server. See the section titled Using Program Groups and Shared Packages for more information about shared network application packages.

- Inventory packages are similar to running a software audit on client computers, except the package inventory is placed in a different property item on the computer properties. Inventory packages are ideal for finding a few specific files, and software audits are better for many different applications.

This section focuses on the run on workstation type of packages. These packages are usually the most common type used by network administrators. Shared network application packages are discussed later in the section titled Using Program Groups and Shared Packages.

To create an SMS package to install an application, use the following steps:

1. If it is not already started, start the SMS Administrator program. The Microsoft SMS Administrator program is displayed.

2. Open the Packages window by clicking on the Packages icon. This is the third icon from the left side of the toolbar.

3. While the Packages window is active, select File, then New from the main menu. This will display the Package Properties window, shown in Figure 36.12.

36

FIGURE 36.12.

The Package Properties window enables you to configure the SMS package.

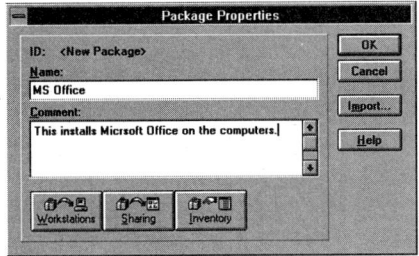

4. The Package Properties window enables you to define the package to install the application. In the Name: box, type a descriptive name for the package. Optionally, you may also type comments for the package in the Comment: box.

5. On the bottom of the Package Properties window, there are three buttons: Workstations, Sharing, and Inventory. A majority of SMS packages are used to install applications on a client computer's hard disk, so let's concentrate on this type of package in this section. (For more information on shared packages, see the section titled Using Program Groups and Shared Packages, later in this chapter.) Click on the Workstations button. The Setup Package for Workstations window appears. An example of the Setup Package for Workstations window is shown in Figure 36.13.

FIGURE 36.13.

The Setup Package for Workstations window enables you to select items such as the source directory where the installation files are stored.

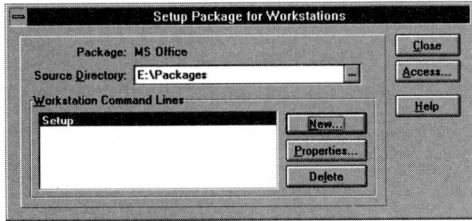

6. In the Source Directory box, type the directory where the package files can be found. You may also click on the Browse button to search the directory tree for the desired directory. The directory that is selected must be shared using the Windows NT File Manager before client computers can use this package.

7. At the Bottom of the Setup Package for Workstations window, you will see a box titled Workstation Command Lines. Because we're creating a new package, there should be no command-line options in the box. Beside the box, click on the New... button to create a new command-line option. The Command Line Properties window is displayed, shown in Figure 36.14.

FIGURE 36.14.

The Command Line Properties window enables you to enter the command to run with the appropriate parameters for the SMS package.

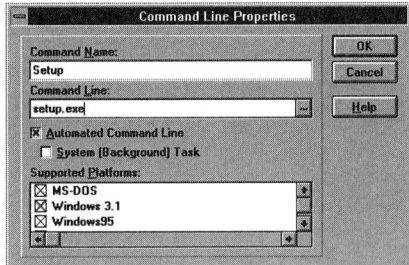

8. Under Command Name: give the command a descriptive name. This is *not* the command to be used. In the Command Line: box, type the command and any parameters to be used with that command. If you want the package not to prompt the user for input, check the Automated Command Line box. This is used for unattended installations. If you need the user to input information, be sure that the Automated Command Line checkbox is cleared. Be sure to check the computer types to run this package in the Supported Platforms list. When you are finished entering the appropriate information, click on the OK button.

Running Jobs

Once a package is created, a job is created to distribute the package across the network. A job determines the distribution servers and client computers where the package will be delivered. Once the job is sent, you can also monitor the job status to verify that the package was correctly sent.

To create an SMS job to deliver a package, use the following steps:

1. If it is not running, start the SMS Administrator program.

2. Verify that the package you want to send exists. If a package has not been created, create the SMS package. For more information on creating SMS packages, see the previous section titled Creating Packages.

3. Open the Jobs window by clicking on the Jobs icon, which is the second icon from the left on the SMS toolbar. You can also open the Jobs window by selecting Jobs from the Open SMS Windows dialog box.

4. While the Jobs window is active, choose File, New. This will open the Job Properties window. The Job Properties window is displayed in Figure 36.15.

5. The Comment box in the Job Properties window is optional. If you want, you can type a descriptive comment for the job. The Job Type is a drop-down list. To install an application of the hard disk of a workstation, be sure that the Run Command on Workstation option is selected. If you want to run a job to set up a shared application, see the section titled Using Program Groups and Shared Packages later in this chapter.

FIGURE 36.15.

The Job Properties window enables you to enter the settings for an SMS job.

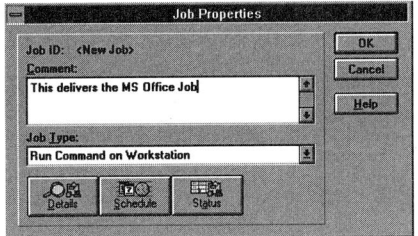

6. You should also see three buttons located at the bottom of the window: Details, Schedule, and Status. To configure a new job, click on the Details button. The Details button will display the Job Details window, shown in Figure 36.16. With this window, you can select the package to run, which computers to send the job to, and whether the job is mandatory.

FIGURE 36.16.

The Job Details window enables you to set many job options.

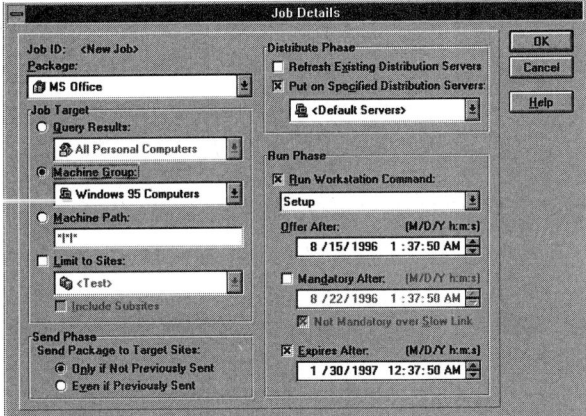

7. Choose the package you created in the earlier procedure from the Package drop-down list.

8. In the Job Target box, you can choose which machines will receive the SMS package. Usually, choosing a machine group is the easiest method of distributing the package to the correct computers.

9. There are other options in the Job Details window. In the Send Phase box, you can choose whether to send the package only if it has not been sent before or even if it has. In the Distribute Phase box, you can determine which SMS site servers to use to distribute the package. In the Run Phase box, you can set when the package is available to clients, whether it is a mandatory package, and when the job expires. In most instances, you will probably want to leave the default settings unchanged. After you finish making selections in the Job Details window, click on the OK button until you return to the main SMS Administrator screen.

The job will be handled by the SMS services and distributed to the necessary distribution servers and then to the client computers. However, this may take a little while, and the status of the job will be marked as Pending. While the job is pending, the job can be modified if needed. However, when the job status becomes Active, the job can no longer be modified. Once the job status changes to Active, the SMS job can be can be monitored.

To monitor an active job, use the following steps:

1. If it is not running, start the SMS Administrator program.

2. Open the Jobs window by clicking on the Jobs icon, which is the second icon from the left on the SMS toolbar.

3. In the Jobs window, select a job that displays Active in the Status column that you want to monitor. Choose File, Properties from the menu, or double-click on the job. The Job Properties window will be displayed.

4. In the Job Properties window, click on the Status button at the bottom of the screen. The Job Status window will be displayed. An example of the Job Properties window is displayed in Figure 36.17.

FIGURE 36.17.

The Job Status window enables you to see the overall status of an active job.

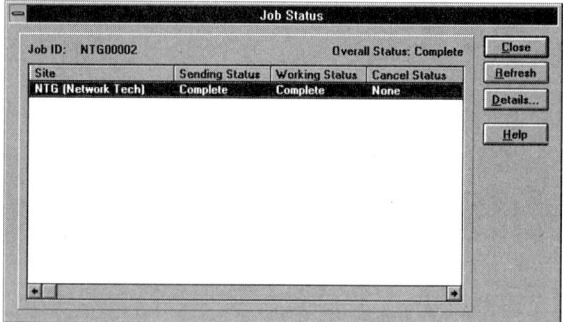

5. If the job has had a chance to propagate across the network, you can click on the Details... button on the right side of the window. Clicking on the Details... button displays the Job Status Details window. The Job Status Details window is displayed in Figure 36.18.

6. You can click on the Refresh button to recheck the status if the Job Status Details window has been open for a while. When you are finished viewing the details, click on the Close button.

7. Once the Sending Status column displays Complete, the job has been sent. The Working Status column displays the working status of the job, and if the job has been canceled, the Cancel Status column will be used. Otherwise, the Cancel Status column will display None. When you finish checking the status, click on the Close button.

FIGURE 36.18.

The Job Status Details window shows a listing of how the job is spreading across the network.

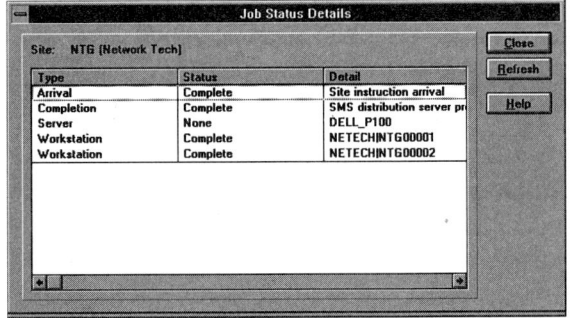

Defining Alerts

Alerts are useful for warning the network administrator of certain conditions. One of the more commonly used examples of an alert is to check for computers that have a low amount of disk space. SMS already has a query defined for checking disk space of inventoried computers, so the administrator simply has to define the query and the threshold for how much available disk space is considered as low. Alerts can be logged in the Windows NT Event Log, trigger a program execution, or send a message directly to a user or computer on the network.

To create an SMS alert, use the following steps:

1. If it is not running, start the SMS Administrator program. Be sure you have created a query for use by the alert. For more information on creating queries, see the previous section titled Defining and Running Queries.

2. Open the Alerts window by selecting the Alerts icon on the SMS Administrator toolbar or by selecting the Alerts item on the Open SMS Window list. The Alerts window will be displayed with any SMS alerts that have been created.

3. Create a new alert by selecting File, New from the menu while the Alerts window is highlighted, or click on the New icon from the toolbar when the Alerts window is selected. An Alert Properties window is displayed (see Figure 36.19 for an example).

FIGURE 36.19.

The Alert Properties window enables you to create an alert and define the conditions for that alert.

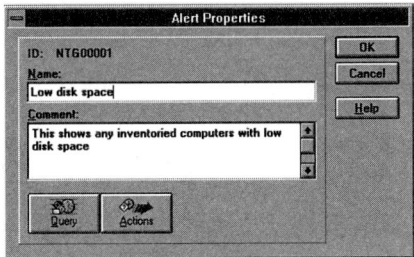

4. In the Alert Properties window, type the name and a comment for the alert. Two buttons are displayed at the bottom of the Alert Properties window: Query and Actions.

5. Click on the Query button to select the query options for the alert. This will display the Alert Query window, shown in Figure 36.20. This window enables you to select which query to use for the alert from a drop-down list of existing queries. The Alert Query window also enables you to limit the query to certain sites, define the repeat interval for the query in minutes, and specify what conditions are needed to generate the alert.

FIGURE 36.20.

The Alert Query window enables you to select the query to use for the alert.

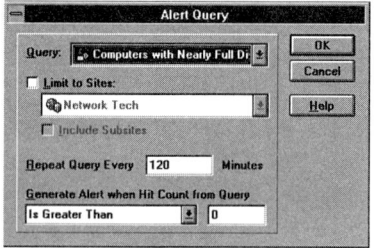

6. When you finish defining the options in the Alert Query window, click on the OK button. If more information is needed about the query options, a warning dialog will be displayed and a Resolve Query window will be displayed (see Figure 36.21). Type any required information in the resolve window and click on the OK button.

FIGURE 36.21.

The Resolve Query dialog is shown only when SMS needs more information about the query items for the alert.

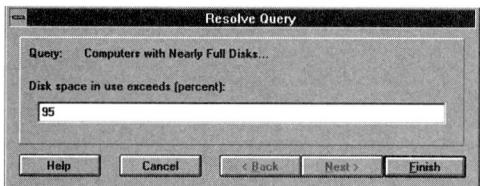

7. After returning to the Alert Properties window, click on the Actions button. This displays the Alert Actions window. Here, you can select to log the event in the event log, execute a program using the command line, or notify a user account or computer on the network. After selecting the appropriate options, click on the OK button.

8. In the Alert Properties, click on the OK button to add the query to the Alert window. When the OK button is pressed, SMS gives the alert a unique ID used to identify the alert in the event log.

Using Program Groups and Shared Packages

In order to use Program Groups, you have to have network applications using a shared SMS package. Program Groups create a standardized group or folder for shared network applications created by SMS. SMS versions 1.0 and 1.1 support only program groups for Windows 3.1, Windows for Workgroups, and Windows NT computers. Version 1.2 of SMS enables program groups to be created for Windows 95 clients.

To create a shared SMS package, use the following steps:

1. If it is not already started, start the SMS Administrator program. The Microsoft SMS Administrator program is displayed.

2. Open the Packages window by clicking on the Packages icon or by selecting Packages from the Open SMS Windows dialog box. This icon is the third icon from the left of the toolbar.

3. While the Packages window is active, select File, then New from the main menu. This will display the Package Properties window shown in Figure 36.22.

FIGURE 36.22.

The Package Properties window enables you to configure the SMS package.

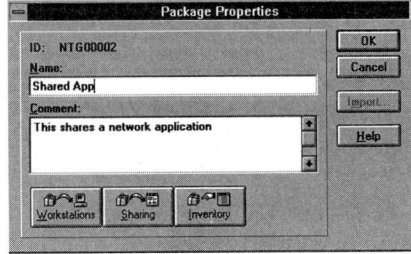

4. The Package Properties window enables you to define the package to install Windows NT. In the Name: box, type a descriptive name for the package. Optionally, you may also type comments for the package in the Comment: box.

5. On the bottom of the Package Properties window, there are three buttons: Workstations, Sharing, and Inventory. Because you want to create a shared package, click on the Sharing button. The Setup Package for Sharing window appears. An example of the Setup Package for Sharing window is shown in Figure 36.23.

FIGURE 36.23.

The Setup Package for Sharing window enables you to select items such as the source directory and the share name.

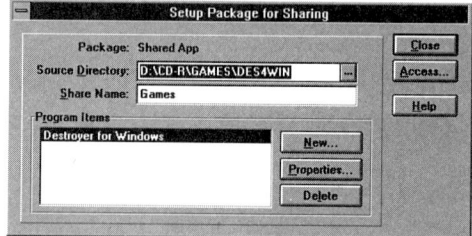

6. In the Source Directory box, type the directory where the package files can be found. You may also click on the Browse button to search the directory tree for the desired directory. Type a share name for the directory in the Share Name: box.

7. At the Bottom of the Setup Package for Workstations window, you will see a box titled Program Items. Because you are creating a new package, there should be no command-line options in the box. Beside the box, click on the New... button to create a new command-line option. The Program Item Properties window is displayed, shown in Figure 36.24.

FIGURE 36.24.

The Program Item Properties window enables you to enter the appropriate share parameters for a shared network application.

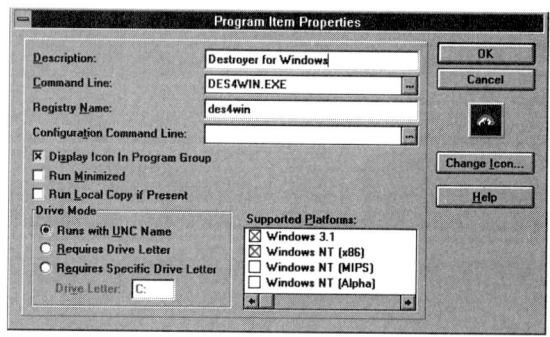

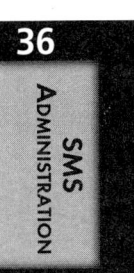

8. In the Program Item Properties window, type a description for the application in the Description: box. In the Command Line: box, you can either type in the command name to start the shared application, or you can browse for the file by clicking on the button at the end of the box. The Registry Name: box is used for shared applications that will be run on computers that use a Registry. The name that is put in this box will be used as a subtree for the application's registry information. You can specify other options, such as running a local copy if it is available. Be sure to select the operating system that is going to be used to run the shared network package. When you finish entering the appropriate information, click on the OK button.

You will have to create and run a job to distribute the shared package. This is similar to creating a job to deliver a run on workstation type of package, but some of the windows will be different for the shared job.

To create an SMS job to deliver the SMS package, use the following steps:

1. If it is not running, start the SMS Administrator program.

2. Open the Jobs window by clicking on the Jobs icon, which is the second icon from the left on the SMS toolbar.

3. While the Jobs window is active, choose File, New. This will open the Job Properties window. The Job Properties window is displayed in Figure 36.25.

FIGURE 36.25.

The Job Properties window enables you to enter the settings for an SMS job.

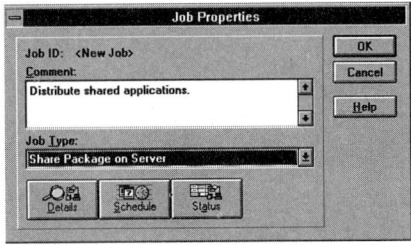

4. The Comment box in the Job Properties window is optional. If you want, you can type a descriptive comment for the job. The Job Type is a drop-down list. Select the Share Package on Server item from the Job Type drop-down list.

5. You should also see three buttons located at the bottom of the window: Details, Schedule, and Status. To configure a new job for the shared application, click on the Details button. The Details button will display the Job Details window for a shared application, shown in Figure 36.26. With this window, you can select the package to run and which computers will receive the job. Note that the window is different for shared network packages than for workstation packages.

FIGURE 36.26.

*The Job Details
window enables you to
set many job options.*

6. Choose the package you created in the earlier procedure from the Package drop-down list.

7. In the Job Target box, you can choose to limit to a site or to send the job to all sites on the network.

8. There are other options in the Job Details window. In the Send Phase box, you can choose whether to send the package only if it has not be sent before or even if it has been sent before. In the Distribute Phase box, you can determine which SMS site servers to use to distribute the package. After you finish making selections in the Job Details window, click on the OK button until you return to the main SMS Administrator screen.

Once the shared network application is distributed using SMS, you can use the SMS Program Group window to create a program group on client machines containing the shared packages.

To create a program group for shared network applications, use the following steps:

1. If it is not running, start the SMS Administrator program.

2. Open the Program Group window from the Program Group icon on the toolbar or from the Open SMS Windows dialog.

3. Create a new item by clicking on the New icon on the toolbar or by selecting File, New from the menu. The Program Group Properties window is displayed, enabling you to configure options about the shared program group, such as which shared packages are to be contained in the group (see Figure 36.27).

4. In the Program Group Properties window, type the name of the program group in the Name: box. This name will be displayed at the bottom of the program group on all client computers using this group. You also may type an optional comment in the Comments: box.

FIGURE 36.27.

*The Program Group
Properties window
enables you to configure
options about the
shared program group.*

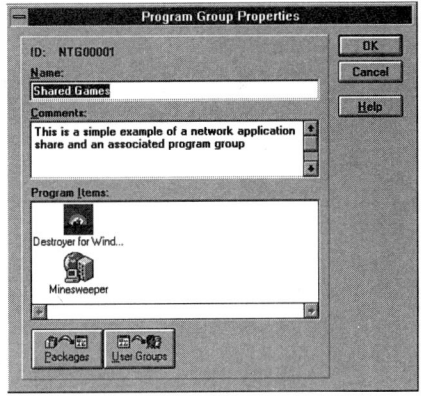

5. Click on the Packages button to add or remove the shared SMS packages that have been created. Once you have selected the shared packages you want to be placed in the program group, click on the OK button.

6. Click on the User Groups button to configure the groups that have access to this program group. The User Groups button enables you to add or remove Windows NT user groups that can access the program group. When you are finished, click on the OK button.

7. Click on the OK button in the Program Group Properties window to add the program group to the window.

Viewing SMS Events

SMS has an event log, just like Windows NT does, to record specific SMS events and errors. You can view this information from the Events window. To view the entries in the SMS event log, use the following steps:

1. If it is not running, start the SMS Administrator program.

2. Select the Events icon in the SMS Administrator toolbar; or, in the Open SMS Window dialog, select the Events item in the list.

3. The SMS Events window will be displayed. At the top of the window, the number of events in the log and a timestamp, with the last recorded date and time, will be shown. Below these items, a listing of the various SMS events will be shown with the date and time of the occurrence, the machine name where the event occurred, and an event ID and type. Figure 36.28 shows an example of the Event window.

FIGURE 36.28.

The Event window lists all the events that have been recorded in the SMS event log.

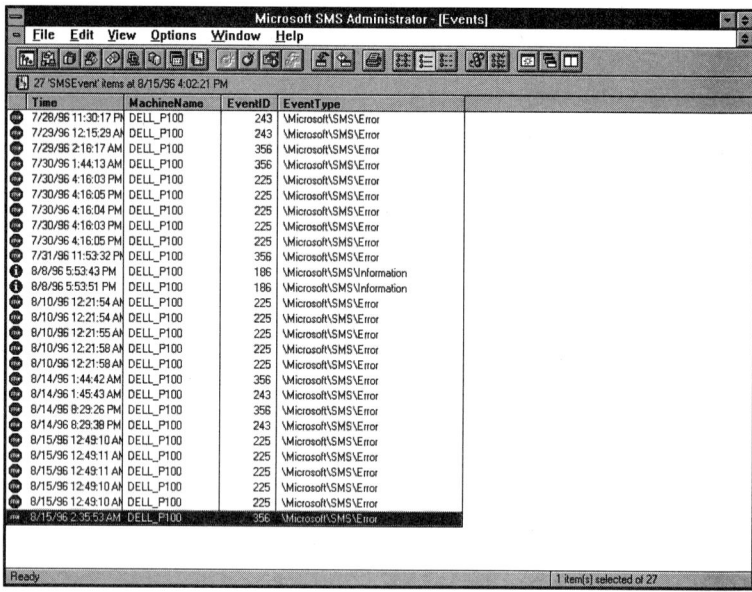

4. If you need more information about a particular event in the SMS log, you can double-click on the entry in the list to display more information. You can also select File, Properties when the event is highlighted to display the same information. The Event Detail window is displayed, shown in Figure 36.29. A description of the event, and possibly what caused it, is displayed at the bottom of the window.

FIGURE 36.29.

The Event Detail window provides more information about an SMS event.

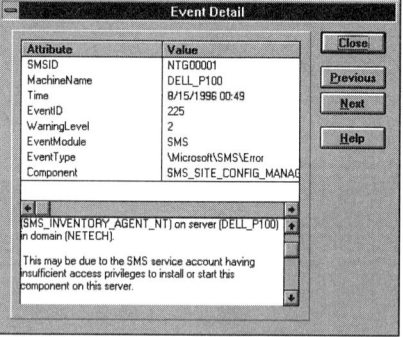

5. The Event Detail window displays more information about the event, including a more lengthy description of the event and what caused it. From this window, you can view the next event by clicking on the Next button or the previous event by clicking on the Previous button. To close the window, select the Close button.

SMS Help Desk Options

One of the most powerful features of SMS is the capability of using remote help desk options for certain computers in the SMS Site. These options enable a variety of functions, such as remote control of a computer, remote reboot of a computer, and transfer of files between the SMS computer and a remote computer, and so on. Not all operating systems support the SMS help desk options, however. Computers with the following operating systems can use the remote help desk features:

- MS-DOS
- Windows 3.1 and Windows for Workgroups 3.11
- Windows 95 (requires SMS version 1.1)
- Windows NT (requires SMS version 1.2)

Although Windows NT computers cannot use the help desk options, in SMS versions 1.1 and 1.2, the SMS Administrator program enables the administrator to view diagnostic information of a remote Windows NT machine. It also enables the User Manager and other options to be controlled via the SMS Administrator program.

> **NOTE**
>
> All the SMS Help Desk and Diagnostic options require the Remote Control Agent to be running when the computer is being accessed. The Remote Control Agent is found in the SMS Client program group or folder. The options for remote access must be configured in the Help Desk Options program on the client machine. This is designed as a security measure to ensure that unauthorized personnel are not able to take control of another computer. Be sure to contact the user before performing any remote Help Desk or Diagnostic functions.

Because the SMS help desk options are very powerful, the potential for abuse by unauthorized personnel exists. To help prevent this situation, the SMS Remote Control Agent has to be running on the client computer before an administrator can access the machine. The Remote Control Agent also has to be configured to enable the remote functions to work. To set the configuration for remote administration, the Help Desk Options program is used. The Help Desk Options program is displayed in Figure 36.30.

The Help Desk Options program simply enables the user to select which remote options are available to the SMS Administrator. The options are selected or deselected by using checkboxes. If an item is checked, that function is available to the administrator for the remote computer. The button sets on the side—Current and Default—are used to set options for either the current session or the default options set. The Status: item at the top of the window displays the current set being used.

FIGURE 36.30.

The Help Desk Options window enables the remote user to determine which remote functions are available to the administrator trying to access that computer.

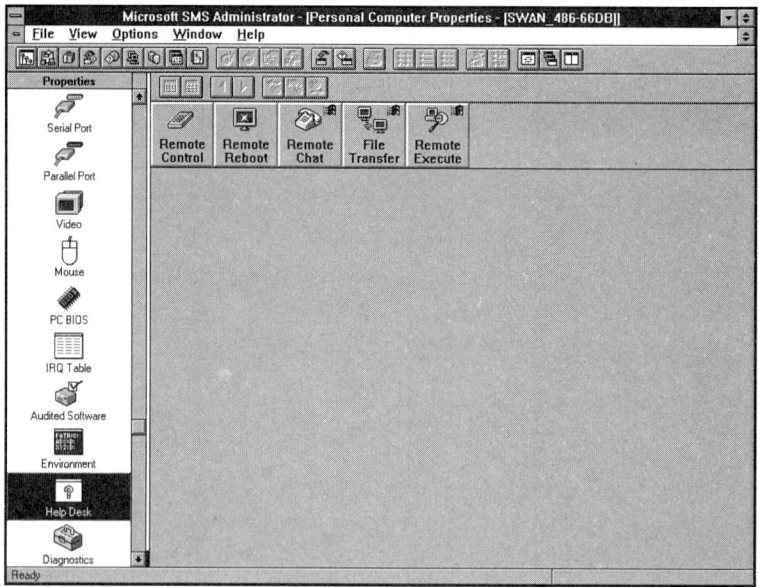

The window is broken into two sections: Remote Viewer Options and Local Options. Remote Viewer Options contain items that can be performed on the machine from the SMS computer. Local Options contain items that provide signals to inform the user that the computer is being remotely accessed. The Local Options group also contains an item turning off the explicit permission of the user before the machine is accessed remotely.

Performing a Remote Reboot

CAUTION

Use the Remote Reboot option with extreme care! Inform the user before the reboot to save any data, and close all applications to ensure that no unsaved data is lost.

To reboot a remote computer, use the following steps:

1. If it is not running, start the SMS Administrator program.
2. Open the Sites window by clicking on the Sites icon on the SMS Administrator toolbar, or by choosing File, Open and selecting Sites from the Open SMS Window dialog.

3. On the left of the Sites window, highlight and expand the site where the computer you want to remotely reboot is located. Once the site is expanded, select the domain of the desired computer. Once this is selected, the right side of the Sites window will list the computers in the SMS inventory.

4. On the right side of the Sites window, double-click on the computer you want to remotely access. The Personal Computer Properties window for that computer will be displayed. You can also open the Personal Computer Properties window by highlighting the desired computer and selecting File, Properties from the menu.

5. The user of the remote computer will have to be sure that the Remote Control Agent is running on the computer before the Help Desk options are available. Once the agent program is started on the remote computer, click on the Help Desk item in the Properties listing.

6. Select Remote Reboot from the items on the top right of the window. Once this is selected, the remote computer will display a dialog asking users if they want to allow remote access of the computer. The user must click on the Yes button.

7. Once the Yes button is selected by the remote user, a confirmation dialog box will be displayed, similar to the one shown in Figure 36.31. If you are sure you want to reboot the remote computer, click on the Yes button.

FIGURE 36.31.

A Remote Reboot confirmation box is displayed before the remote reboot is performed, to ensure that an accidental reboot isn't performed.

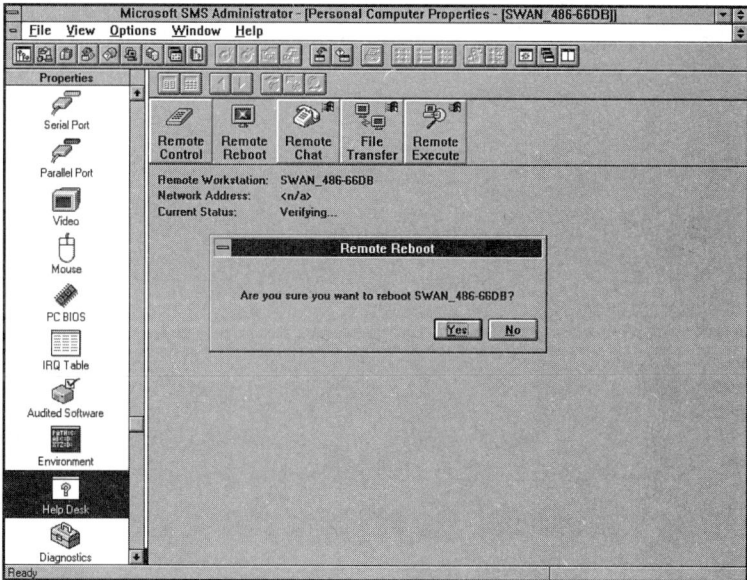

8. Once the Yes button is selected, the remote computer will reboot. The message Request Acknowledged will be displayed in the Current Status field of the SMS Administrator window.

Remotely Executing a Program

To remotely execute a program, use the following steps:

1. If it is not running, start the SMS Administrator program.

2. Open the Sites window by clicking on the Sites icon on the SMS Administrator toolbar, or by choosing File, Open and selecting Sites from the Open SMS Window dialog.

3. On the left of the Sites window, highlight and expand the site where the computer you want to remotely execute a command is located. Once the site is expanded, select the domain of the desired computer. Once this is selected, the right side of the Sites window will list the computers in the SMS inventory.

4. On the right side of the Sites window, double-click on the computer you want to remotely access. The Personal Computer Properties window for that computer will be displayed. You can also open the Personal Computer Properties window by highlighting the desired computer and selecting File, Properties from the menu.

5. In the Properties listing of the window, scroll down until you find the Help Desk item. Before selecting it, however, make sure the user of the remote computer is running the Remote Control Agent on that machine. The client Remote Control Agent is found in the SMS Client program group or folder. If this program is not running, the SMS Administrator program will not find the computer and you cannot use the Help Desk options.

6. After the user has started the Remote Control Agent, click on the Help Desk item in the Properties listing. The SMS Administrator program then tries to establish a remote session with the client computer. If it connects correctly, the icons on the right side of the window change from a grayed-out state to an active state. If it fails, an error message will be displayed on the screen.

7. When a correct connection is established, users of the client machine will be asked whether they want to allow remote control of the computer. They *must* click on the Yes button in order for the process to continue! This is designed as a security measure in SMS to prevent unauthorized users from remotely controlling a computer. Be sure to contact the user prior to remote administration to ensure the proper responses.

8. After the user has allowed remote control over the computer, the Run Program at the User's Workstation window will be displayed. This window is shown in Figure 36.32.

FIGURE 36.32.

*The Run Program at
User's Workstation
window enables a
command to be typed
and executed on a
remote computer in the
SMS Site.*

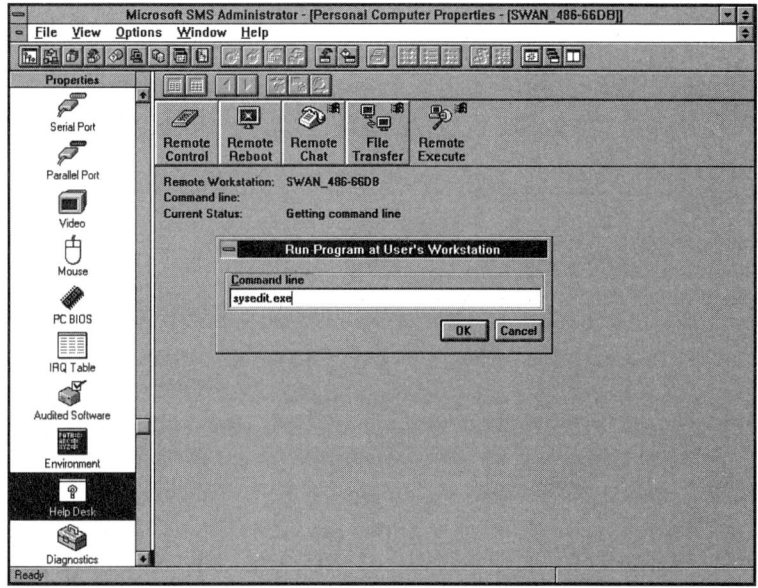

9. Type the command and any required parameters in the Run Program at User's Workstation window. After you type the command, press Enter or click on OK. The command will be executed on the remote computer.

10. After the command is successfully executed, the message Executed is listed in the Current Status field.

Taking Remote Control over a Network Computer

To use the Remote Control feature to control a client machine from the SMS Administrator computer, use the following steps:

1. If it is not running, start the SMS Administrator program.

2. Open the Sites window by clicking on the Sites icon on the SMS Administrator toolbar, or by choosing File, Open and selecting Sites from the Open SMS Window dialog.

3. On the left of the Sites window, highlight and expand the site where the computer you want to remotely control is located. Once the site is expanded, select the domain of the desired computer. Once this is selected, the right side of the Sites window will list the computers in the SMS inventory.

4. On the right side of the Sites window, double-click on the computer you want to remotely access. The Personal Computer Properties window for that computer will be displayed. You can also open the Personal Computer Properties window by highlighting the desired computer and selecting File, Properties from the menu.

5. In the Properties listing of the window, find the Help Desk item. Before selecting it, make sure the user of the remote computer is running the Remote Control Agent on the client machine. If it is not running, the SMS Administrator program will not find the computer and you cannot use the Help Desk options.

6. After the user starts the Remote Control Agent, click on the Help Desk item in the Properties listing. The SMS computer and the remote computer will make contact, and the icons at the top of the SMS window will become active.

7. Click on the Remote Control icon in the Help Desk toolbar. Once this item is selected, the user of the remote computer will be prompted to allow remote access. The user should click on the Yes button for the remote control function to work.

8. A window with a yellow and black border will appear on the SMS computer containing a portion of the display from the client computer. If the display size is smaller than the actual screen size of the computer being controlled, scrollbars will appear. From this window, the administrator is able to act as if sitting directly in front of that computer. The mouse and the keyboard can be used to control both the SMS computer and the remote computer. An example of the remote control window is shown in Figure 36.33.

FIGURE 36.33.

The remote control window displays the screen of the client computer.

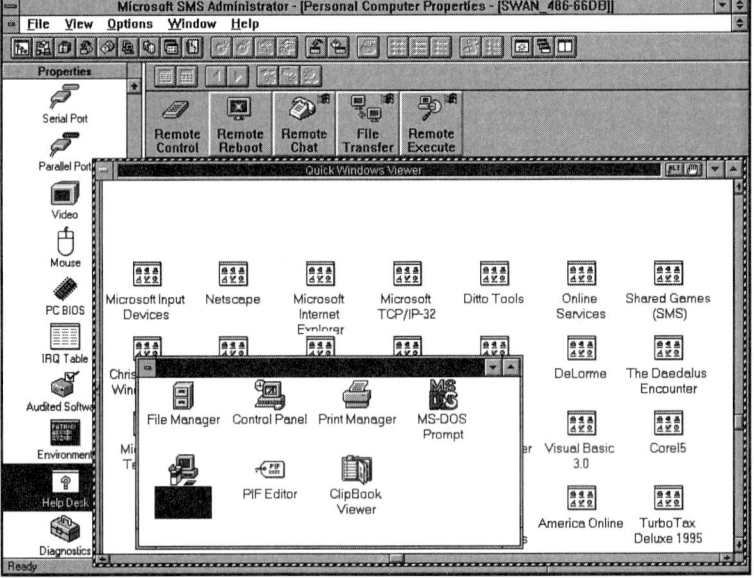

9. When you finish with the remote control session, you can close it by selecting another Help Desk Option or by selecting another item in the Properties list.

Using Remote Chat

To open a remote chat session between the SMS Administrator computer and a remote client on the network, use the following steps:

1. If it is not running, start the SMS Administrator program.

2. Open the Sites window by clicking on the Sites icon on the SMS Administrator toolbar, or by choosing File, Open and selecting Sites from the Open SMS Window dialog.

3. On the left side of the Sites window, highlight and expand the site where the computer you want to establish a chat session on is located. Once the site is expanded, select the domain of the desired computer. Once this is selected, the right side of the Sites window will list the computers in the SMS inventory.

4. On the right side of the Sites window, double-click on the computer on which you want to start a remote chat session. The Personal Computer Properties window for that computer will be displayed. You can also open the Personal Computer Properties window by highlighting the desired computer and selecting File, Properties from the menu.

5. Assuming the user has the Remote Control Agent running on the client machine, click on the Help Desk item in the Properties listing. Once the remote computer is connected, the Remote Chat item will be available.

6. Click on the Remote Chat item in the top right side of the window. This sends a request to the client machine asking for permission to access the client remotely.

7. The remote user needs to select the Yes button to allow the rest of the operation to be completed. After the Yes button has been selected, a window similar to Figure 36.34 will appear on both the SMS Administrator computer and the remote computer. The top text box on the SMS Administrator computer shows the user name and the computer name of the remote workstation. This text box displays any text that the remote user types. The bottom text box enables the administrator to type text back to the client computer.

8. To close the chat session, either computer may close the chat window or the administrator of the SMS computer may choose another Help Desk option.

FIGURE 36.34.

The Remote Chat window enables the SMS administrator and a remote user to communicate with each other.

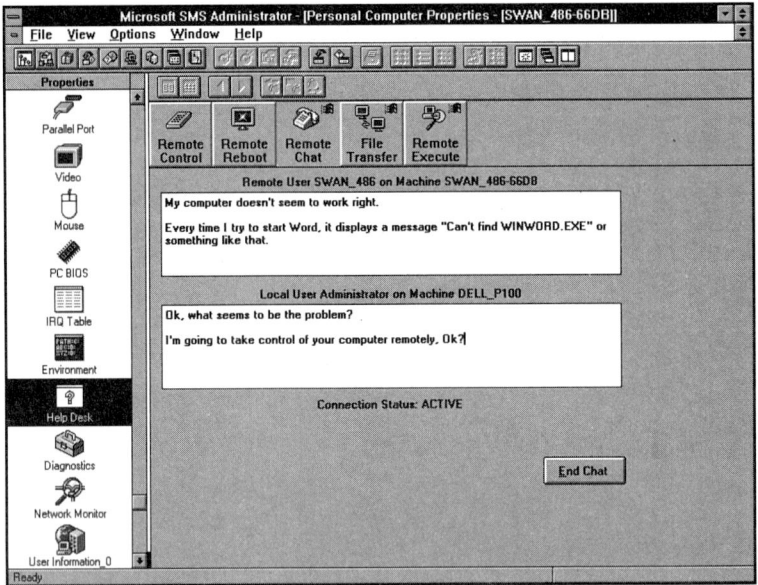

Transferring Files Between an SMS Server and a Remote Client

To transfer files between the SMS server and a remote client on the network, use the following steps:

1. If it is not running, start the SMS Administrator program.

2. Open the Sites window by clicking on the Sites icon on the SMS Administrator toolbar, or by choosing File, Open and selecting Sites from the Open SMS Window dialog.

3. On the left side of the Sites window, highlight and expand the site where the desired computer is located. Once the site is expanded, select the domain of the desired computer. Once this is selected, the right side of the Sites window will list the computers in the SMS inventory.

4. On the right side of the Sites window, double-click on the computer you want to remotely access. The Personal Computer Properties window for that computer will be displayed. You can also open the Personal Computer Properties window by highlighting the desired computer and selecting File, Properties from the menu.

5. In the Properties listing of the window, find the Help Desk item. Before selecting it, make sure the user of the remote computer is running the Remote Control Agent on the client machine. If it is not running, the SMS Administrator program will not find the computer and you cannot use the Help Desk options.

6. After the user starts the Remote Control Agent, click on the Help Desk item in the Properties listing. The SMS computer and the remote computer will make contact and the icons at the top of the SMS window will become active.

7. Click on the File Transfer icon in the Help Desk toolbar. Once this item is selected, the user of the remote computer will be prompted to allow remote access. The user should click on the Yes button for the file transfer process to continue.

8. Once the File Transfer icon is selected, a window similar to Figure 36.35 will be displayed. This window displays four listboxes containing individual files or drive/directory listings. The left box contains files in the current directory of the local SMS computer. The next box displays all the available drives and directories on the local SMS computer. The third box contains the drives and directories of the remote client computer. The last box displays the files of the current directory in the remote client computer. You can use the Copy>> or Copy<< buttons to transfer files between the two computers.

FIGURE 36.35.

The Remote File Transfer window enables the SMS administrator to transfer files to and from the local SMS computer to and from the remote client computer on the network.

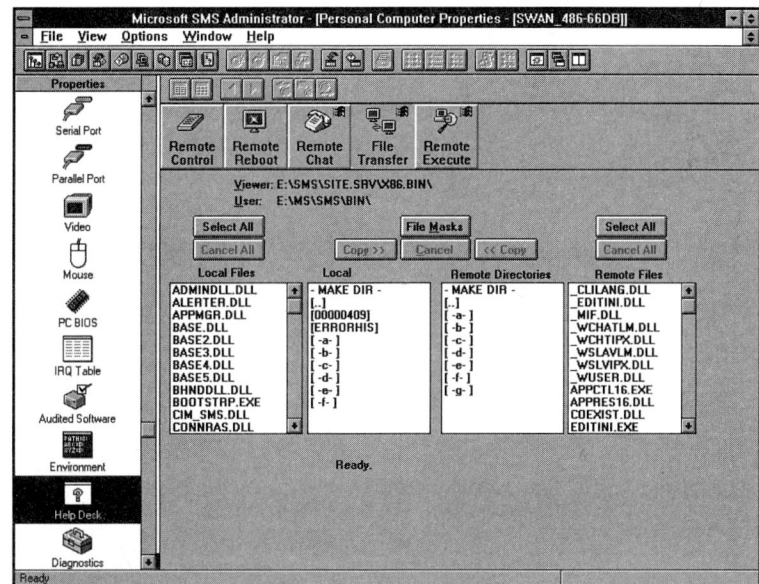

Viewing Remote Diagnostic Information

To view remote diagnostic information for a remote computer, use the following steps:

1. If it is not running, start the SMS Administrator program.

2. Open the Sites window by clicking on the Sites icon on the SMS Administrator toolbar, or by choosing File, Open and selecting Sites from the Open SMS Window dialog.

3. On the left side of the Sites window, highlight and expand the site where the computer you want to view diagnostic information for is located. Once the site is expanded, select the domain of the desired computer. Once this is selected, the right side of the Sites window will list the computers in the SMS inventory.

4. On the right side of the Sites window, double-click on the computer on which you want to view remote diagnostic information. The Personal Computer Properties window for that computer will be displayed. You can also open the Personal Computer Properties window by highlighting the desired computer and selecting File, Properties from the menu.

5. Be sure the client computer has the Remote Control Agent running and click on the Diagnostics item in the Properties list. Once the item is selected, SMS will try to find the remote computer on the network. Once it is found, the toolbar at the top of the window will turn from a grayed-out state to an active state.

6. Once the toolbar is active, click on the desired diagnostic information you want to view. When the item is selected, the remote computer will prompt the user at that machine to verify permission for remote access. The user should select the Yes button for the process to continue.

7. Once the user allows remote access, the diagnostic information will be displayed. Figure 36.36 shows an example of a Ping Test that checks to see whether packets transmitted from the SMS computer make a complete trip to and from the remote computer.

FIGURE 36.36.

The Ping Test is one example of the remote diagnostic information available in the Diagnostics item.

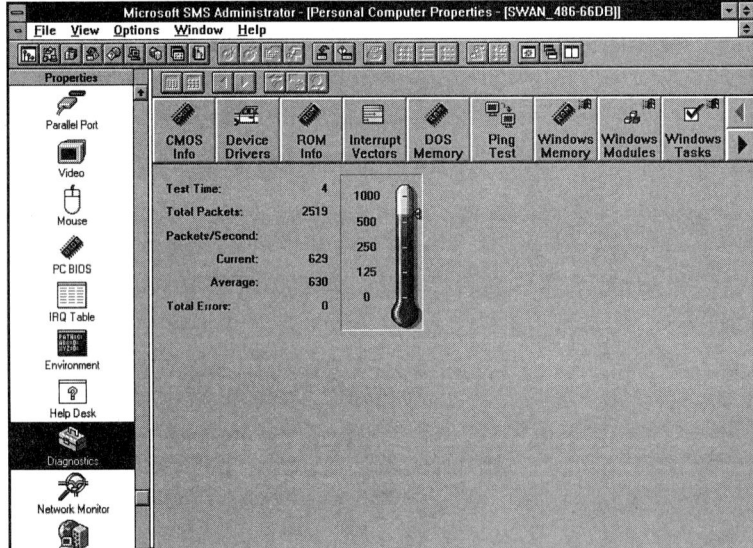

8. To exit the Diagnostics display, click on another item in the Properties list.

Summary

The SMS Administrator program provides a wealth of useful tools to help a network administrator manage the network. This chapter covered how to use a number of these tools. However, due to space limitations, not all the features of the SMS Administrator were introduced. As you work with the SMS Administrator program and explore its capabilities, you will probably find it a very useful tool for network administration.

Planning and Managing a LAN with SMS

by Ahsan Farooqi

IN THIS CHAPTER

Thus far, the majority of this book has been about the communication within a site. In this chapter, you learn how to communicate between sites in Systems Management Server. Site-to-site communication plays an important role in a regular daily setup of SMS and is usually involved in tasks from inventory collection to setting up a secondary site. In both cases, the Scheduler, the Senders, and the Despooler play significant roles in transferring data from one site to another.

As you can see in Figure 37.1, the Scheduler initiates most data transfers by activating jobs from the SMS database (see step 1). Next, the Scheduler prepares packages and instructions for sending and produces send requests. The Scheduler has full control over where these files are placed and usually places the files in appropriate sender boxes. The third step in the figure shows that each sender monitors its own outbox and provides data transfer to another site. Finally, when the data is received, the Despooler decompresses it and carries out any associated instructions.

FIGURE 37.1.

Overall flow of the way communication takes place between sites.

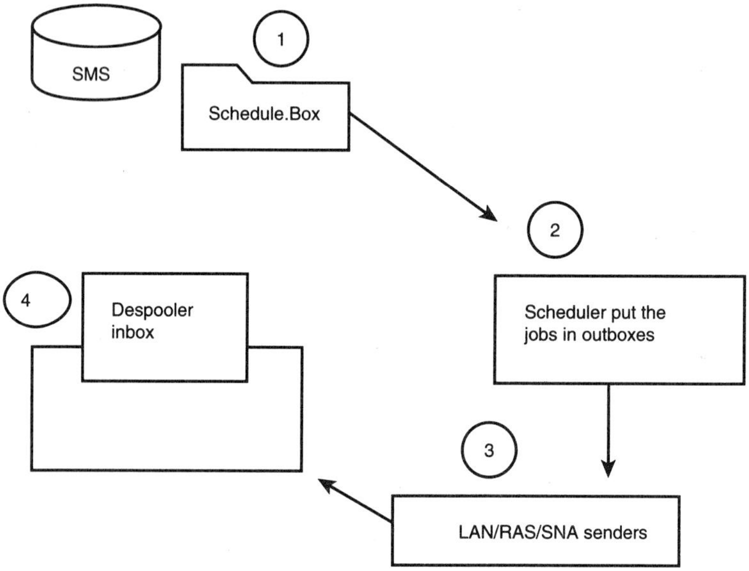

The Despooler and the Scheduler are not discussed in this chapter because I assume you have already studied them. This chapter concentrates on *senders* and their role in site-to-site communication, as well as how the senders work with the Scheduler Service.

Introduction to Senders

Think of a sender as a kind of a robust copy program. This program is designed to send data over a variety of network connections and to handle interruptions and data transfer errors. The information is transferred by the sender to locations that can still be specified. Systems

Management Server provides senders for local area networks (LAN), Remote Access Service (RAS), SNA architecture, and communication mechanisms. There is room for third-party vendors to extend the System Management Server (SMS) with their own senders, such as MAPI. An example of a third-party vendor is a MAPI sender.

Different Types of Senders

Information between sites can generally flow through three types of senders (see Figure 37.2):

- RAS
- LAN
- SNA

FIGURE 37.2.

The LAN/WAN, RAS, and SNA senders that are included with the Systems Management Server.

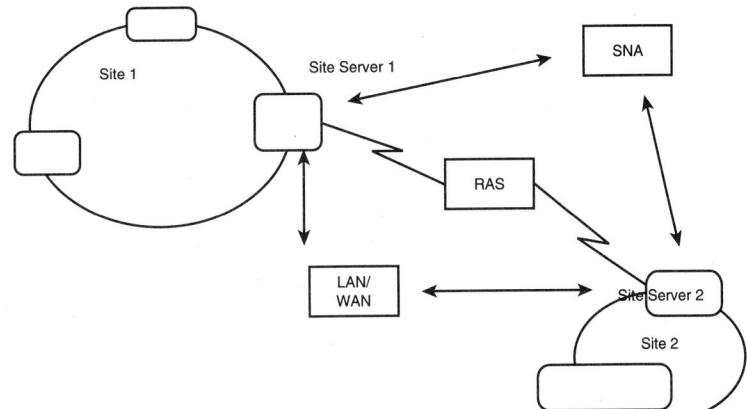

RAS

RAS senders use only Windows NT Remote Access connections to send data between two sites. Once connected, the data can only use three types of connections:

- *Normal phone lines (ASYNC).* This type of connection is called an ASYNC, for asynchronous, connection.

■ *Integrated Services Digital Network (ISDN).* These use a special type of modem but are twice as fast as the fastest 28.8K/sec transfer-rate modems currently available. The ISDN speeds start at 56K/sec transfer rate.

■ *X.25 lines.* These are special lines that require special X.25 cards in the Site Servers for communication to take place.

For all the preceding methods to be available, RAS must be started on Windows NT.

LAN

The LAN sender is the default sender that is installed when the site is first installed. Any job that is not to go over the network to another site (that is, any job that is not part of site-to-site communications and has a destination of local site) uses this sender. The LAN sender uses the Windows NT redirector-server (that is, it uses the Windows NT workstation and Server services) to send traffic over a LAN or wide area network (WAN).

SNA

Two sites communicating over SNA senders use the SNA's Advanced Peer-to-Peer (APPC) or Advanced Program-to-Program (APPC) to communicate. The communication takes place between the two sites' servers, each acting as a SNA LU 6.2 (Logical Unit) node, and each must have the required Systems Management Server (SMS) software installed. The Microsoft SNA Server must be installed in order to use the SNA sender.

Site Communication

This section discusses the methodology of site communication and the actual sending of the data, as well adding senders and configuring outboxes and bandwidth. You explore the topics in the following order:

■ Sending data

■ Checking sender status

■ Adding senders

■ Configuring sender outboxes

■ Controlling sender bandwidth

■ Interacting with Scheduler

Data Sending

In site-to-site communication, each of the six senders (three on each side) performs three tasks:

■ Monitoring the outbox

- Moving data to destination site
- Updating status with Scheduler

Monitoring the Outbox

The outbox of each sender is monitored by the SMS_EXECUTIVE service. This occurs for each installed sender. For every installed sender, a thread called the sender dispatcher thread within the SMS_EXECUTIVE is used for monitoring the outbox associated with that particular sender. The outbox is monitored for send requests. The instructions for senders are placed in the outbox by the Scheduler Service. These instructions are placed as Send Request Files (with the SRQ extension). Monitoring the outbox includes any file changes in the SITE.SRV\SENDER.BOX\REQUESTS\outbox directory. The sender wakes up at the interval specified in the Polling Interval in the registry. This is determined by the Services Response time that in turn is set in the Services dialog box displayed from Site Properties. Upon monitoring its outbox if the sender finds an SRQ file, it creates another thread to service the send request placed in the outbox by the Scheduler. This is displayed in Figure 37.3.

FIGURE 37.3.

Senders move the file from one site to another.

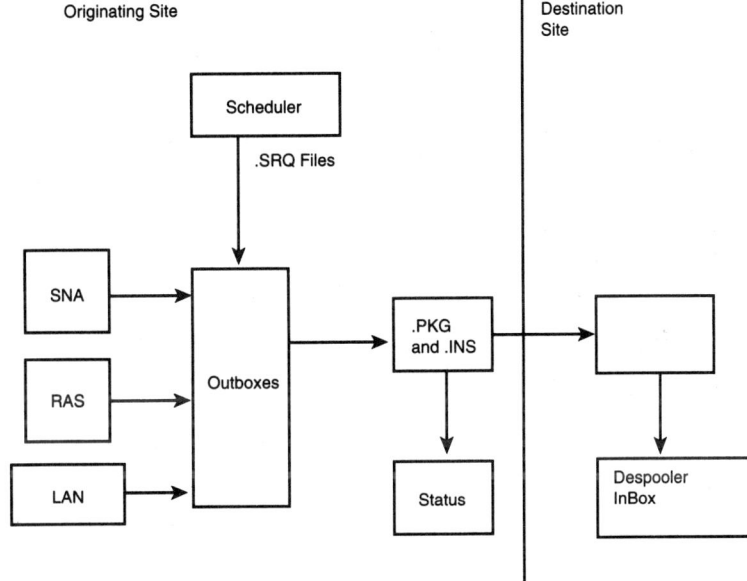

Moving Data to the Destination Site

The sender moves the data. The data moved is *not* SRQ files. The SRQ files are only a send request put in the outbox by the Scheduler. The data is moved to the site or between sites, packages, and jobs. Usually, the data moved is in the form of PKG or INS files. The data is moved from the location of the SITE.SRV\SENDER.BOX\TOSEND directory of the sender site to the SITE.SRV\DESPOOLER.BOX\RECEIVE directory in the destination site. The sender uses standard I/O file requests to move data to the destination site. No SMS processes are required at the destination site to receive the data, because the Windows NT Server service receives the data. The data is then placed in the remote receive box. Data is transferred in blocks. The type of sender used (LAN, RAS, SNA) determines the size of these blocks. The default sender, the LAN sender, has a block size of 256K blocks at a time. At every successful send of every block, the status file is updated. If, however, the block transmission failed, the sender will retransmit the block starting from the last successful send. During the transmission, the file's extensions are changed to prevent the Despooler service from starting to process the data before it is fully received. The PKG files become PCK, and the INS files become TMP.

Updating Status with Scheduler

The final piece of the puzzle in data sending is to update the status of the files or data transmitted with the Scheduler. As the processing of the SRQ file begins, this file is renamed to a status file with an SRS extension. This file is constantly being updated by the Scheduler. The update occurs after each block transmission to the destination site. This is a successful transmission. If an error is encountered in the transmission, an error status is placed in the SRS file. Upon completing the transmission, the file is updated with a Complete status and is then deleted by the Scheduler.

Sender Status

The previous sections lead to this general summary: A pending request is SRQ, and a working or in-process request is SRS. Either or both of these request files are composed of different sections that describe details at various levels of the request:

- Send Request Data
- Sender/Scheduler
- Cancel
- Action Code
- Address
- Package File
- Instruction File

All of preceding can be displayed with a utility that is provided on the SMS Server CD-ROM: DUMPSEND.EXE.

Send Request Data

The Send Request Data record has various fields:

- Priority
- Destination Site

■ Job

■ Job Request

■ Outbox

The range of priority is 1, 2, and 3 for high, medium, and low, respectively. The other two fields are important because the Destination Site is a three-letter site code assigned by the SMS Administrator during installation and the JOB ID number in the SMS Server software.

Sender/Scheduler

Both the Sender and the Scheduler service use or update the Sender/Scheduler record. In fact, it is updated by the sender and used by Scheduler to determine the status of the send request.

The fields or sections are as follows:

■ First sender started at

■ Sender started at

■ Sender ended at

■ Sender gate heartbeat at

■ Scheduler to restart at

■ Total bytes to send

■ Total bytes left to send

■ Sync point is

■ File type is 0 = none, 1 = Instruction, 2 = Package File

■ Number of connections = number of attempts

■ Sender ID

Cancel

Cancel has only one field: MODE.

It can read Canceled or Not Canceled. If the send request is canceled, this section is changed from Not Canceled to Canceled.

Action Code

Action Code also has only one major heading: Code.

The Scheduler sets the action code to instruct the sender how to handle the send request. There are three requests:

■ SREQ_ACTION_NONE(0) means normal processing.

■ SREQ_ACTION_RETRY(1) means failed requests are retried.

■ SREQ_ACTION_DELETE(2) is for canceled requests or completed requests.

Address

Address has just one field: Address.

This specifies a universal naming convention (UNC) addressing scheme or RAS phone book entry. The SNA pathname can also be used. The UNC goes hand-in-hand with the Default LAN Sender.

Package File

The package file contains a new heading: File. This is merely a UNC pathname to the package file to be sent.

Assume that an Windows NT-based computer that is a Site Server has a computer name of Test1 and the package file is called TESTPACK.PKG. Assume also that the file is located in the SITE.SRV directory and OUTBOX subdirectory. A UNC for the location of the package file will read as follows:

```
\\Test1\SITE.SRV\OUTBOX\TESTPACK.PKG
```

Instruction File

Instruction File has one field: File. This contains the UNC pathname for the instruction file to be sent.

Adding Senders

You learned earlier that, by default, only the LAN sender is installed. For the Site Server to communicate over a different type of communication medium such as RAS or SNA, additional senders need to be installed or added (see Figure 37.4).

This section briefly mentions how to pass senders in SMS (see Figure 37.5). To communicate with another site using a sender other than the default [LAN] sender, you must first install the sender at each site. This requires a series of steps:

1. Choose Sender from Site properties. The sender dialog box appears.
2. Choose Proposed Properties.
3. Choose Create. A sender Properties dialog box appears.
4. Choose the appropriate sender from this list:
    MS_LAN_SENDER
    MS_ASYNC_RAS_SENDER
    MS_X25_RAS_SENDER

MS_ISDN_RAS_SENDER

MS_INTER_SNA_SENDER

MS_BATCH_SNA_SENDER

5. Type the name of the server in the Server box.

6. Type the letter of the Systems Management Server drive in the Drive box.

FIGURE 37.4.

The hierarchy of communicating between sites in an SMS environment.

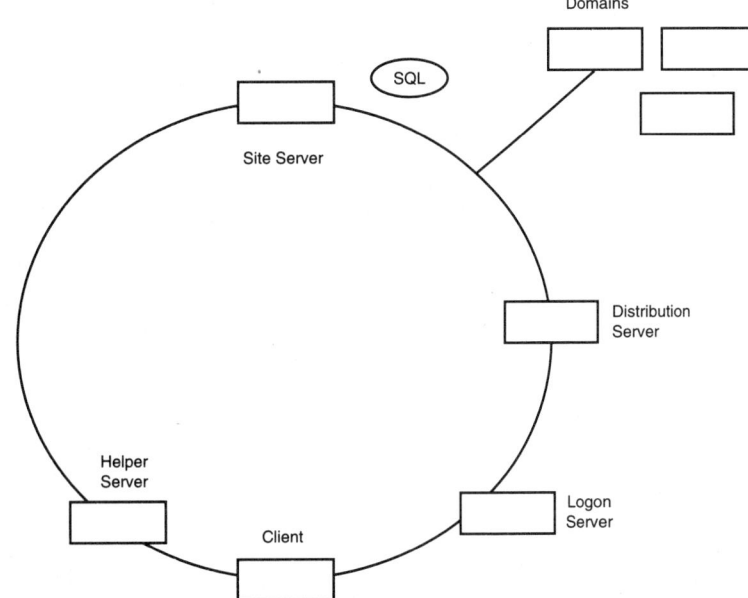

FIGURE 37.5.

The steps necessary to add a sender in an SMS environment.

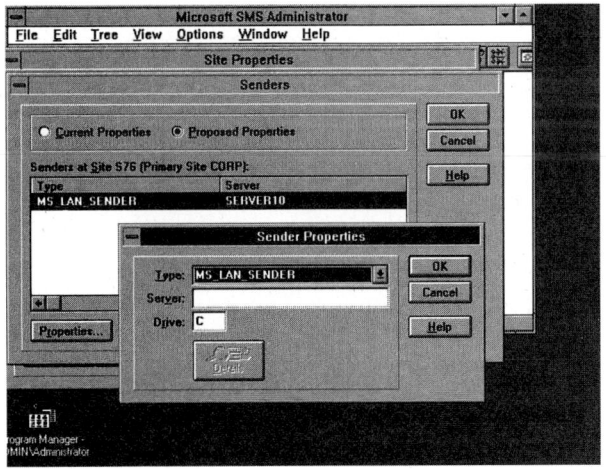

Configuring Sender Outboxes

Sender outboxes are a means of controlling how the Scheduler uses the senders. Therefore, it is an integral part of tuning the site-to-site communication mechanisms (see Figure 37.6). The outboxes are no more than subdirectories in the SITE.SRV\SENDER.BOX\REQUESTS directory.

FIGURE 37.6.

The configuration screen in the SMS when configuring outboxes.

Each outbox has the following properties to be configured:

- Priority
- Backup
- Closed

To configure outboxes, choose Outboxes from the Site Properties dialog box, select an outbox, then choose Schedule.

Priority

Priority has three levels of adjustment: low, medium, and high. This priority can be adjusted for each outbox and can also be adjusted for the same box at different times of the day. The Scheduler Service places the job in the outbox only if the job's priority is higher or equal to that of the outbox for that particular instant or time of the day.

Backup

If an outbox is configured as a backup, a job that has failed during the regular start from the original outbox can be retried from the backup outbox. Remember, each sender (RAS, LAN, SNA) has its own outboxes, so you can use one outbox as its own media sender and the other as a sender's backup. This works only if the destination site or the remote site also has a backup outbox.

Closed

The outbox can be closed and used during different times of the day. If the outbox closes while a request is in progress, the job is *paused* and later *resumed* when the outbox is available.

Controlling Sender Bandwidth

The utility that enables you to control the sender bandwidth is the SMS Sender Manager. This utility is located on the PSSTOOLS directory on the SMS Server CD-ROM and enables the administrator of the SMS management system to control the bandwidth usage either by site or by sender. The site controlling is done by address rather by site name. In this section, you look at control of the bandwidth usage by the sender. Different rates can be set for each sender. The options are as follows:

- Rate Limits
- Concurrent Sessions
- Retry Settings

Rate Limits

The rate can be set for each hour of the day and therefore is extremely important in regulating network traffic. This option controls the packets sent each hour. Using this, you can also set the Maximum Transfer Rate and choose Set Limit.

Concurrent Sessions

Using Concurrent Sessions, you can set the total number of concurrent sessions per site as well as the number of concurrent sessions.

Retry Settings

Retry Settings merely sets the frequency of the sender retries.

Interaction with Scheduler

The Scheduler selects a sender to send data to a remote site or a destination site. If multiple jobs are waiting to send data, the Scheduler automatically orders the jobs in a queue for servicing. This order is created or based upon two conditions: the priority of the job and the job start time. The senders are then scheduled to send the jobs' data in that order. In short, the Scheduler not only queues the jobs in short time order but also selects the sender that will send the job across to the destination site in the shortest time.

Implementing the LAN Sender

The LAN sender is the default sender loaded when the SMS is first installed. The configuration of site-to-site communication using the LAN sender is a three-step process (see Figure 37.7). This sender can easily be thought of as an enhanced version of the COPY application.

FIGURE 37.7.

The steps taken to configure a LAN Sender Address.

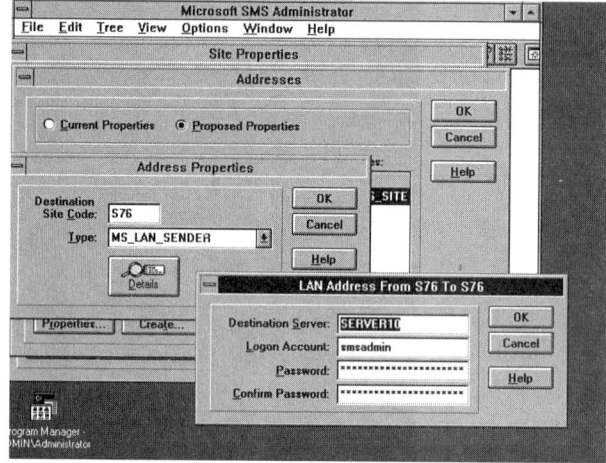

The LAN sender uses general Windows NT components to communicate with the destination site. Loopback functions are used to send the job to itself. In self-promoting jobs, the LAN sender does not use Windows NT components. Because the LAN sender works on a block at a time, it automatically knows where to start should the communication fail, which makes it an enhanced copy program—one that is smarter and one that does not work on sectors, but rather on blocks at a time. The three steps are as follows:

1. Configure the physical network (that is, with TCP/IP IPX/SPX or NetBEUI protocols). If using NetBEUI and going over a WAN link, you must use a bridge and not a router because NetBEUI is a non-routable protocol.

2. Install the Site Servers (the LAN sender is automatically installed as the default sender).

3. Configure the address between sites.

Implementing the RAS Sender

As with the LAN sender, implementing the RAS sender is also done in three steps, but they are quite different because the protocol they use is different (see Figure 37.8):

1. Install and configure the RAS server at each site. This does *not necessarily* have to be the Site Server.

2. Install the RAS sender at each site. It is important to note here that the RAS server must be installed on the Windows NT Domain Controller. If it is installed on a computer that is not the Site Server, the computer on which the RAS sender is installed becomes the helper computer in the SMS environment. Then the RAS sender server also can have either the server or client RAS or RAS software installed. If the client RAS software is installed, although it has the RAS sender on it, this computer does not receive incoming traffic. RAS clients do not receive calls. The RAS server with the RAS sender is a better combination to choose.

3. Configure an address, using the RAS sender to the destination site.

FIGURE 37.8.

The steps taken to configure a RAS Sender Address.

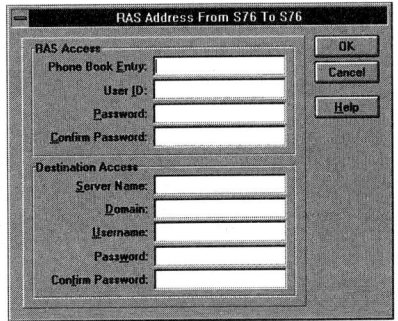

RAS Sender Architecture

The RAS sender is similar to the LAN sender in its architecture, because it also uses the Windows NT network components to move data. The RAS sender resides in the application layer, and from there it makes requests to the lower layers to complete the connection to the destination site. In short, the RAS sender does its work on top of the RAS mechanism.

Implementing the SNA Sender

Configuring the SNA sender is achieved in four steps (I assume that the reader is knowledgeable about SNA architecture). Therefore, try to integrate the Systems Management Server into an existing architecture (see Figure 37.9). Here are the steps:

1. Install Microsoft SNA Server on a computer at each site. This is a must for the SNA sender to work. The computer on which the SNA Server is installed does not necessarily have to be a Site Server.

2. Configure the SNA Link services between sites. These services include SDLC, X.25, and 802.2. The link services control hardware-to-software communications in the SAN architecture.

3. Install the SNA client software on the Site Server in order to receive packages over the SNA.

4. Install and configure the SNA sender on the Site Server. Then create an address at each site to use the SAN sender and the link.

FIGURE 37.9.

The steps taken to configure the SNA Sender Address.

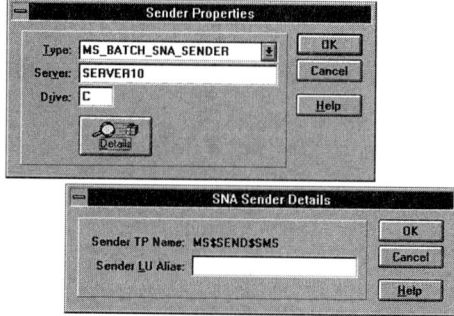

Sender Troubleshooting

If the data is not flowing properly between sites, it could initially mean a few possibilities:

- Data is not arriving at the sender.
- Data is not processed properly by the destination site.
- Data is not being transmitted correctly by the sender.

The way to approach this is in the following order:

1. First check the Scheduler service as it controls the sender. Check to see whether the monitoring of the outboxes is appropriate. Check also to see whether the Scheduler is receiving the jobs.

2. After full verification of the Scheduler, the second area is the sender. Check to see whether the appropriate sender is installed and configured for the destination site.

3. Finally, the Despooler service at the destination site should be checked for proper processing.

Planning the SMS Site

A Systems Management Site is composed of a Site Server and a SQL Server database for Windows NT. This is required for the primary site only, a Site Server domain, and additional domains, as well as logon servers, distribution servers, helper servers, and client computers. The key to efficiency of network management lies in properly selecting a site development plan for your organization. This is discussed in Chapter 35, "Installing SMS," in more detail.

Planning Within a Site

Planning within a site is also important because a user must determine which servers to use as logon servers, which computers as a distribution server, and which ones as helper servers. You should also evaluate the following and incorporate it in the final decision:

- The amount of hard disk space needed to support the MSSQL database
- The amount of hard disk space required to support the Systems Management Server Services and applications
- The amount of hard disk space needed for software packages
- The amount of memory needed
- The load on the Server processor

The preceding parameters should not only be thought of just during the planning stage and during installation, but also be kept in mind for future growth of the corporate network—which usually grows both in size and complexity. Keep in mind that the SMS domain and the NT domain are two different logics. That is, an NT Domain can be an SMS domain. This is the reason you need Windows NT Server as a Domain Controller and install SMS Server on it. The SMS Domain that you set up during installation can easily make use of and work within the Windows NT Domain. SMS Server can include a Novell Server, however, and thus operate at a different Domain Boundary. This boundary is not recognized by Windows NT Domain Controller; hence, every machine within the SMS boundary is not able to function in the Windows NT Domain Security environment.

Summary

It is extremely important for the network administrator to seriously plan the implementation and managing strategies of the SMS architecture. One small mistake could turn out to be extremely costly in troubleshooting. Furthermore, if SMS is to be implemented, the network architecture of the existing backbone may also have to be altered to account for the difference in the Windows NT domain environment and the SMS domain environment. The bandwidth usage suddenly becomes an important issue as yet another server will take up part of the bandwidth.

VII
PART

IN THIS PART

SNA Server

SNA Server Overview

by John Fronckowiak

IN THIS CHAPTER

Using advanced client-server architecture, Microsoft SNA Server offloads the communications processing from host computers and desktop PCs. Each PC uses standard networking protocols, such as TCP/IP, IPX/SPX, NetBEUI, Banyan VINES, or AppleTalk to connect to one or more SNA Servers (see Figure 38.1). The SNA Servers connect to IBM mainframes and AS/400s using the SNA networking protocol. The SNA Server version 2.11 supports up to 2,000 clients and 10,000 host sessions (version 3.0 supports 5,000 users and 15,000 host sessions, see The SNA Server 3.0 Features section later in this chapter) and offers advanced tools for easy system setup and centralized administration. It supports all standard PCs and network operating systems, LAN protocols, SNA host connections, and host types. Client computers and administrator workstations can connect to SNA Servers across LAN (local area network) and WAN (wide area network) bridges, routers, and over dial-up lines. The SNA Server, an integral component of Microsoft BackOffice, takes full advantage of the Windows NT Server operating system to deliver power, scalability, and security. Combined with the industry-standard SNA APIs, this foundation makes the SNA Server the most flexible platform for integrating PC and host environments.

FIGURE 38.1.

The SNA Server environment overview.

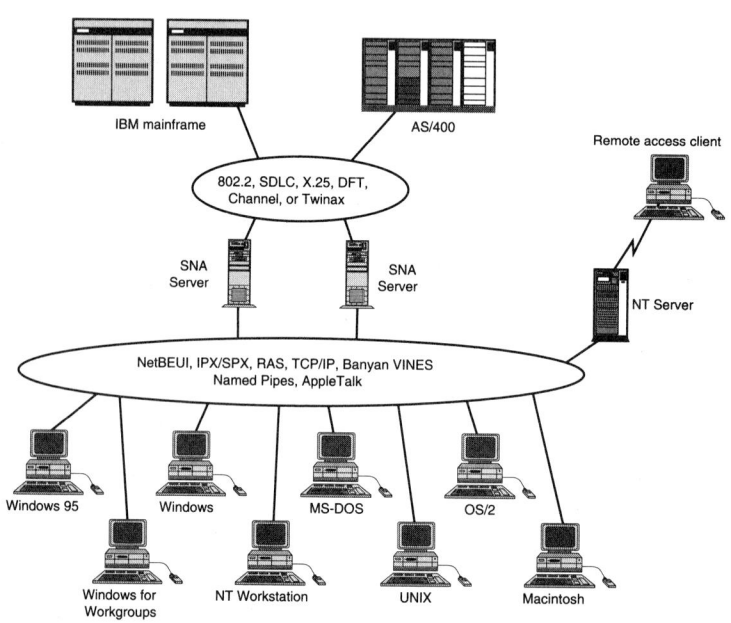

The SNA Server also includes ODBC (Open Database Connectivity) drivers for access to DRDA (Distributed Relational Database Architecture) databases. The ODBC drivers support connectivity to the following IBM host databases: DB2 for MVS, SQL/DS for VM, and DBS/400 for OS/400. With AFTP (Advanced File Transfer Protocol) services, files can also be downloaded from the host using FTP (File Transfer Protocol) commands. AFTP enables large file transfers between host and Windows NT-based systems to be performed quickly using native SNA protocols, eliminating the need to install the CPU-intensive TCP/IP stack for the host. Also, the SNA Server acts as a proxy, which enables users on the Internet to access host information.

Microsoft SNA Server includes a full SDK with library and header files and sample applications. It provides extensive support for industry-standard client and server protocols as well as APIs, making it an ideal tool for integrating diverse enterprise systems. All SNA Server APIs (APPC, CPI-C, LUA, and CSV) are fully compatible with the WOSA (Windows Open System Architecture) SNA API standard.

The SNA Server enables enterprises to utilize legacy mission-critical applications and data available on IBM mainframes and AS/400s by distributing these over the local area network to host PCs, while still providing reliable, fast, and secure access. Although many organizations are moving to LAN-based PC client-server models, the generally accepted practice of running these mission-critical applications on IBM hosts is not likely to change soon. The ability of the Microsoft SNA Server to integrate these mainframe applications and data into the corporate LAN in a fast, secure, reliable way, along with its centralized enterprise-wide management capabilities, make it an integral component of corporate computing environments.

IBM Network Architecture (Mainframe and AS/400)

In the early seventies, IBM discovered that enterprise customers required highly reliable and redundant communications networks to distribute mission-critical applications. In response, IBM developed Systems Network Architecture (SNA). SNA may be unique in trying to identify literally everything that could possibly go wrong in order to specify the proper response. Certain types of expected errors, such as a phone line or modem failure, are handled automatically. Other errors—software problems, configuration tables, and so on—are isolated, logged, and reported for analysis and response. This SNA design worked well as long as communications equipment was properly installed and managed by a competent staff. It was less useful in LAN environments, in which any PC easily connects and joins the LAN.

An SNA network is comprised of host systems (mainframes or AS/400s), terminals (or PCs of clients running terminal emulation software), printers, communication controllers, and cluster controllers. Terminals and printers connect to cluster controllers. Cluster controllers connect directly to the host or communications controller. The terminals, printers, communication controllers, and cluster controllers are generally referred to as nodes. Nodes are endpoints or linkages in the network. There are different types of nodes:

- *Type 2 nodes* are generally endpoints, such as PCs running terminal emulation software, terminals, and printers.

- *Type 4 nodes* are communication controllers. Communication controllers link remote terminals to host systems. They service terminals connected to them by transmitting and receiving host data, detect and correct errors, and serve as concentrators for groups of terminals.

■ *Type 5 nodes* control and manage the network.

Linking SNA Networks

SNA requires a reliable network. When a packet of data moves between nodes, it must be checked for errors and either accepted or retransmitted. Only after it has been accepted will it be sent on to the next node. To achieve this reliability, SNA depends on the connection-oriented protocols of High Level Datalink Control (HDLC). HDLC is an international standard developed in the seventies to provide simple, reliable modem communications. Because it is an international standard, it has a very broad definition.

The HDLC definition leaves open many facets of the communications process. Communication can be full or half duplex. If a sequence of data packets is transmitted and one is found to be in error, the receiving node can request that the individual packet or the entire packet sequence be resent.

IBM refined this ambiguous international HDLC standard. Instead of allowing multiple choices to resolve a problem, IBM modified the standard for their own devices, which required a specific response to be generated in a situation where the international standard would allow multiple responses. Even though IBM-specific devices generate specific responses, they will permit devices created by other vendors to generate responses valid in the international standard. IBM took the HDLC standard and resolved the uncertainties within it. It called this new protocol subset Synchronous Data Link Control (SDLC).

SDLC

In the early seventies, most large U.S. corporate networks were developed using modems, leased phone lines, SDLC, and SNA. SDLC is based on the Normal Response Mode subset of HDLC. When the host system sends a sequence of packets to a 3270 control unit, it pauses and waits for confirmation. The 3270 acknowledges that the data packets were received correctly, or it requests retransmission of the data packets starting with the packet discovered to be in error. The host node and the control unit "talk" to each other in short packet bursts—the host node sending data packets to the control unit, and the control unit acknowledging packets or requesting retransmission. SDLC is a very linear protocol, with events happening in sequence and producing immediate results. Figure 38.2 shows a typical use of an SDLC connection with the SNA Server.

FIGURE 38.2.
*View of the SNA Server
utilizing an SDLC
link.*

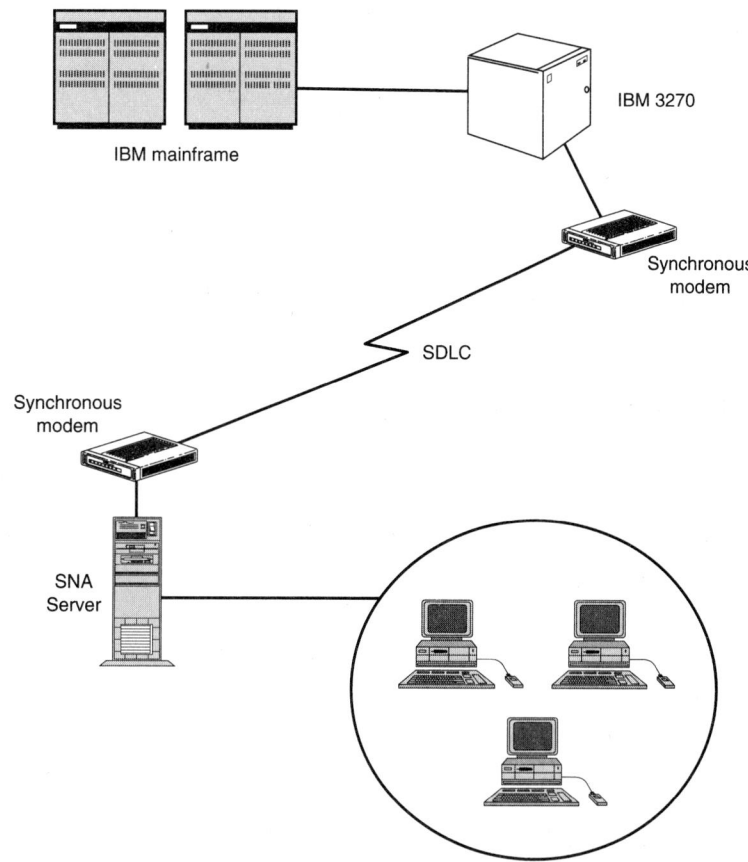

38

SNA SERVER
OVERVIEW

X.25

X.25 is similar to the SDLC protocol. X.25 is a service provided by the phone company to accept and route individual data packets. In an X.25 packet-switching network, the network determines the most efficient means of transmitting packets from the transmitter to receiver. The phone company charges by the packet for use. As with SDLC, X.25 is based on HDLC, but X.25 is based on a more complex subset called LAP-B (Link Access Protocol—Balanced). The Balanced mode is in contrast to the SDLC Normal Response Mode. Both ends of an X.25 connection can send data simultaneously. Error correction and detection is still supported, although it is a more complex process. Figure 38.3 shows a typical use of an X.25 connection with the SNA Server.

FIGURE 38.3.

*A view of the SNA
Server utilizing an
X.25 link.*

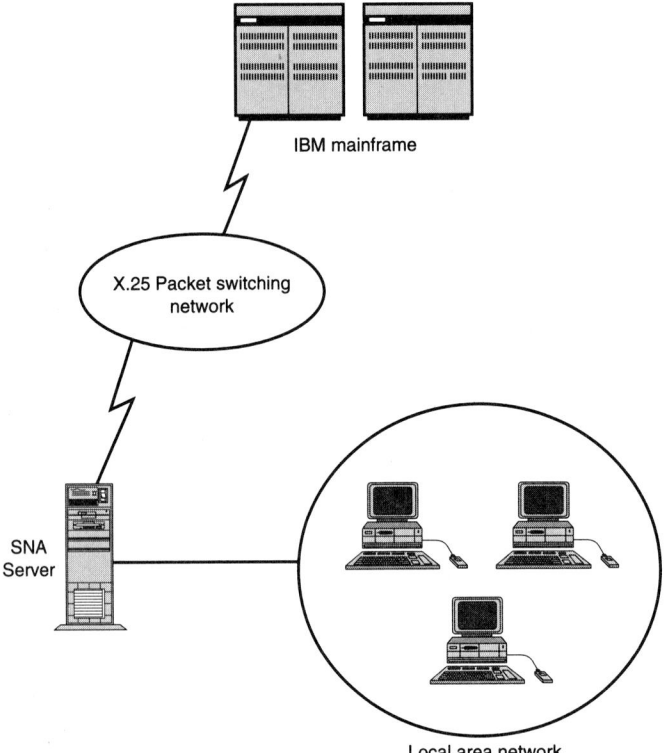

IBM mainframe

X.25 Packet switching
network

SNA
Server

Local area network

DLC/802.2

SDLC reflected the technology of the early seventies, before the invention of the microprocessor. The IEEE began work to standardize LAN communications utilizing the microprocessor. Because of the processing power available, the IEEE adopted the most complex subset of the HDLC standard, called Asynchronous Balance Mode. IBM introduced its Token Ring technology after the IEEE 802 standards were released and integrated these standards into Token Ring communications.

In an HDLC or IEEE 802 connection, data is transferred as numbered units called I-frames. When a connection is established, both ends negotiate on the number of I-frames (called the window) that they can transfer between each other before requiring data acknowledgment. In each I-frame that is sent, and in a separate control packet (Receiver Ready or RR) which is sent if there is no pending data, each end transmits which packet it expects to receive next. By doing so, it implicitly acknowledges that all packets before that number have been received correctly. Each end should be able to receive the number of I-frames negotiated upon when the session was established, but if problems occur that stem the flow of packets (for example, a buffer overflow), a Receiver Not Ready (RNR) message is sent from the receiver to the packet transmitter. Using just I-frames and the RR and RNR packets, it is possible to detect and correct communications errors. Other control packets can be used to increase efficiency, but they are not required in the 802.2 standard. Figure 38.4 shows a typical use of a DLC/802.2 connection with the SNA Server.

FIGURE 38.4.

A view of the SNA Server utilizing a DLC/802.2 link.

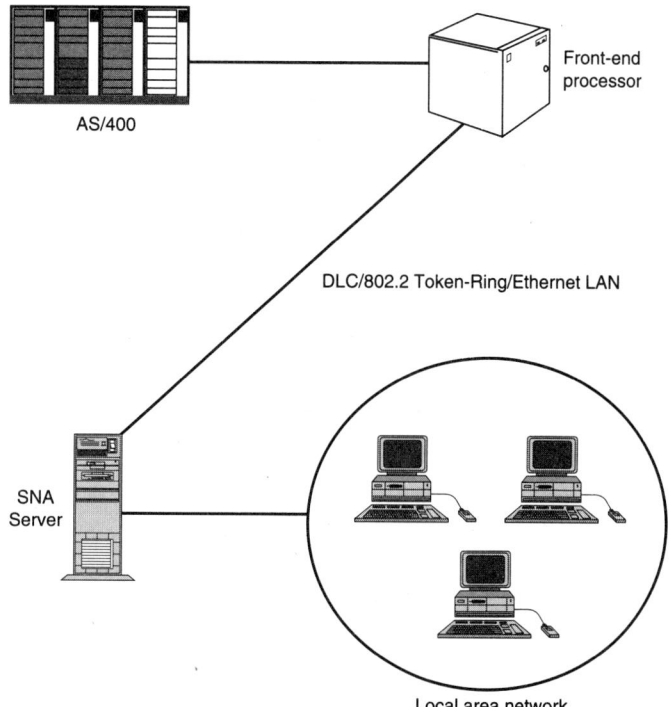

DLC/802.2 Token-Ring/Ethernet LAN

Front-end processor

AS/400

SNA Server

Local area network

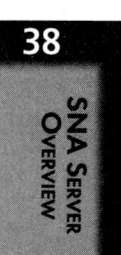

DFT/Twinax

The DFT (Distributed Function Terminal)/Twinax networking protocol provides a connection between the communications controller and the host system over more modern coaxial or twisted-pair cables. The host system and communications controller are directly connected to each other using a high-speed data link. The DFT protocol can support multiple user sessions. Figure 38.5 shows a typical use of an DFT/Twinax connection with the SNA Server.

Sessions

When running an application, a user creates a *session*. A session is a channel to a network-addressable unit. An SNA network is comprised of logical and physical units. The resources associated with logical and physical units are discussed below.

FIGURE 38.5.

*A view of the SNA
Server utilizing a DFT/
Twinax connection.*

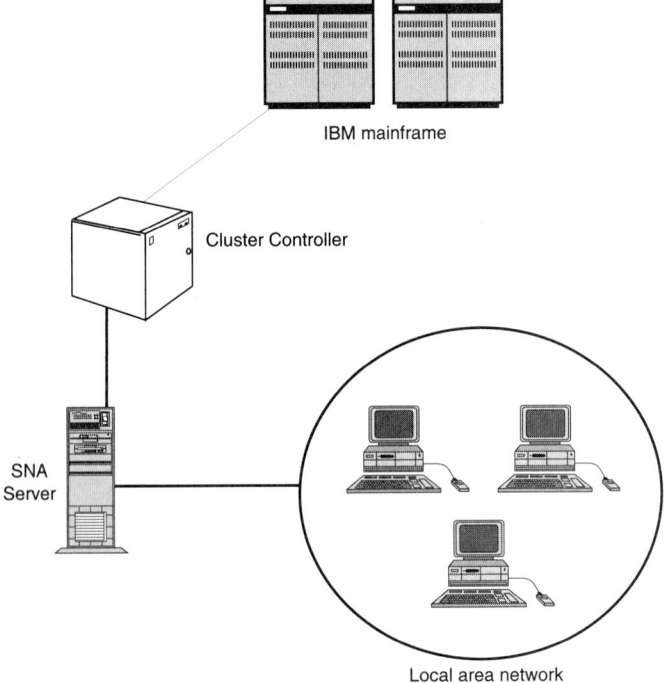

IBM mainframe

Cluster Controller

SNA
Server

Local area network

Logical Units (LUs) are sessions. The following types of SNA network resources can be accessed
through these sessions:

- *Type 1* provides interactive batch transfers.
- *Type 2*, the IBM 3270 display terminal.
- *Type 3*, the IBM 3270 printer.
- *Type 6.2*, program-to-program communication.
- *Type 7*, IBM midrange computer sessions.

Physical Units (PUs) remain in the node that communicates with the host. They manage and
control the communication link. There are three types:

- *Type 2* resides in cluster controllers.
- *Type 4* resides in front-end processors.
- *Type 5* resides in host communication software.

Here are the two main software modules in an SNA network:

- *Systems Services Control Point (SSCP)* runs in the host and controls all the resources
  within the host's domain. The host system runs the Virtual Telecommunications
  Access Method (VTAM), which contains the SSCP.

■ *Network Control Program (NCP)* runs in the communication controller. It manages the communications with the host, including routing, session management, buffering, and error detection and correction.

Two forms of SNA were developed: subareas, managed by mainframes, and APPN (Advanced Peer-To-Peer Networking), based on networks of minicomputers. In the original design of SNA, a network is built out of expensive, dedicated-switching minicomputers managed by a central mainframe. The dedicated minicomputers run a special system called NCP. No user programs run on these machines. Each NCP manages communications on behalf of all the terminals, workstations, and PCs connected to it. Traffic is routed between the NCP machines and eventually into the central mainframe. The mainframe runs an IBM product called VTAM, which controls the network.

The rapid growth in minicomputers, workstations, and personal computers forced IBM to develop a second kind of SNA. Customers were building networks using AS/400 minicomputers that had no mainframe or VTAM to provide control. The new SNA is called APPN (Advanced Peer-to-Peer Networking). APPN and subarea SNA have entirely different strategies for routing and network management. Their only common characteristic is support for applications or devices using the APPC (LU 6.2) protocol. SNA is generally viewed as a single networking architecture, although it would more accurately be described as two complementary architectures that can exchange data.

Subarea SNA

The more traditional SNA networking model is based upon a hierarchical approach, organized into subareas. The host system (a PU 5) is at the top of the hierarchy. The host system runs the VTAM, which manages the networking the sessions connected to the host. There is only one PU 5-type device in the hierarchy or domain. Connected to the host system is the front-end processor (a PU 4). The front-end processor is an intelligent device that manages connections between the host system, devices, users, and applications connected to it. The cluster controller (a PU 2) connects to the front-end processor, and manages the users and devices connected to it, in a specific area. Different types of LUs connect to the cluster controller—for example, LU 2 3270 terminals and LU 3 3270 printers. A typical subarea SNA configuration is shown in Figure 38.6.

The SNA Server functions as an interconnecting network gateway in the subarea SNA model. The SNA gateway connects to the LU 1, 2, and 3 terminal and printer emulators running on the LAN PCs using standard LAN protocols (NetBEUI, IPX/SPX, TCP/IP, Banyan VINES, or AppleTalk). Also, the SNA Server connects to the SNA network by emulating a cluster controller (a PU 2). The SNA Server is generally connected to the front-end processor utilizing the SDLC, X.25, or DLC/802.2 protocols. The SNA Server connects to the front-end processor and manages all the LU device emulators running on the LAN. A typical subarea SNA model utilizing the SNA Server is shown in Figure 38.7.

FIGURE 38.6.

Typical subarea SNA network configuration.

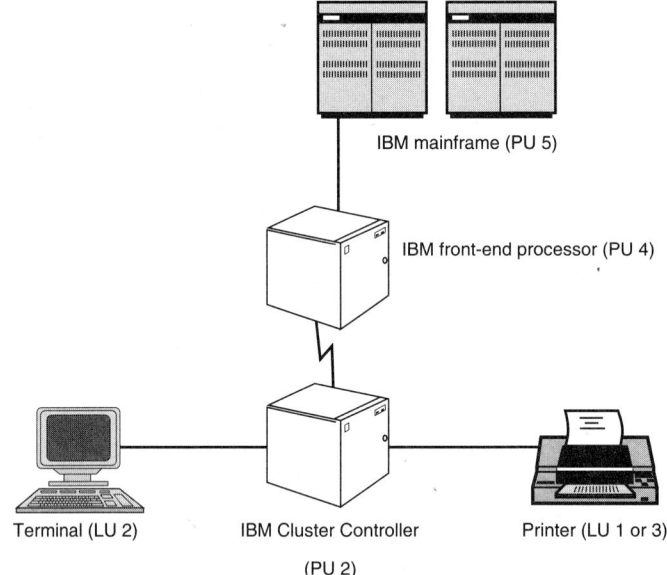

IBM mainframe (PU 5)

IBM front-end processor (PU 4)

Terminal (LU 2) IBM Cluster Controller Printer (LU 1 or 3)

(PU 2)

FIGURE 38.7.

A view of the SNA Server in the Subarea SNA configuration.

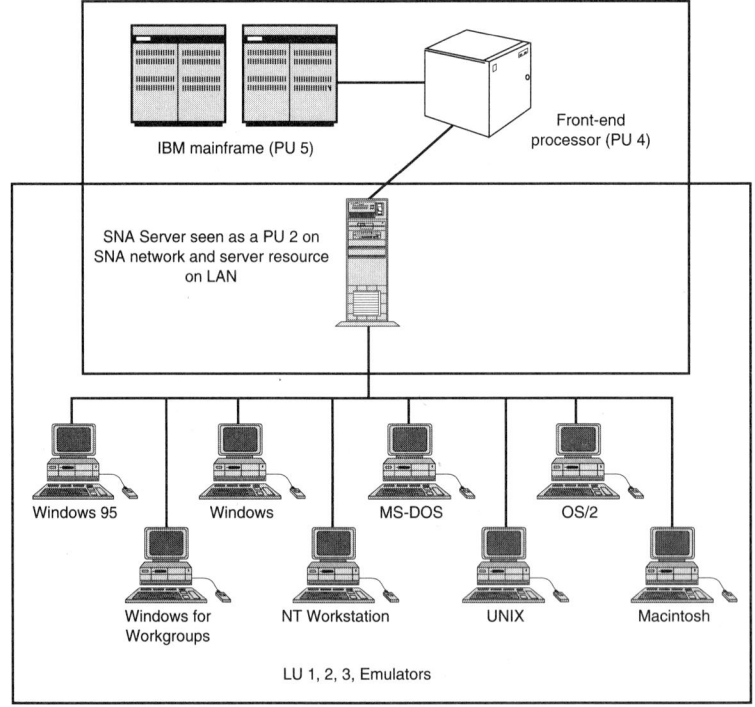

IBM mainframe (PU 5) Front-end processor (PU 4)

SNA Server seen as a PU 2 on SNA network and server resource on LAN

Windows 95 Windows MS-DOS OS/2

Windows for Workgroups NT Workstation UNIX Macintosh

LU 1, 2, 3, Emulators

Peer-To-Peer/APPN SNA Model

The rapid growth of personal computers and workstations created an evolution in SNA networking. The peer-to-peer SNA model was created to support the AS/400 minicomputer environment. The AS/400 environment had no mainframe or VTAM to rely upon to provide control. Whereas the traditional SNA networking model can be viewed as an organized hierarchy, where increasingly intelligent devices connect to the host, in the APPN model each computer (PU 2.1) provides its own functionality to communicate on the network. The APPN model is more similar to traditional LAN-based networking models. The host systems in the APPN model are usually AS/400s (PU 2.1). The AS/400s provide their own functionality to manage the LU connections to them. Normally, PCs (LU 6.2) emulating terminals and printers are connected to the AS/400s over the LAN. APPN also allows two applications to appear as LU 6.2 devices on the network, and communicate with each other using the Advanced Program-to-Program Communication (APPC) protocols. A typical APPN SNA model is shown in Figure 38.8.

FIGURE 38.8.

*A typical peer-to-peer/
APPN SNA network
configuration.*

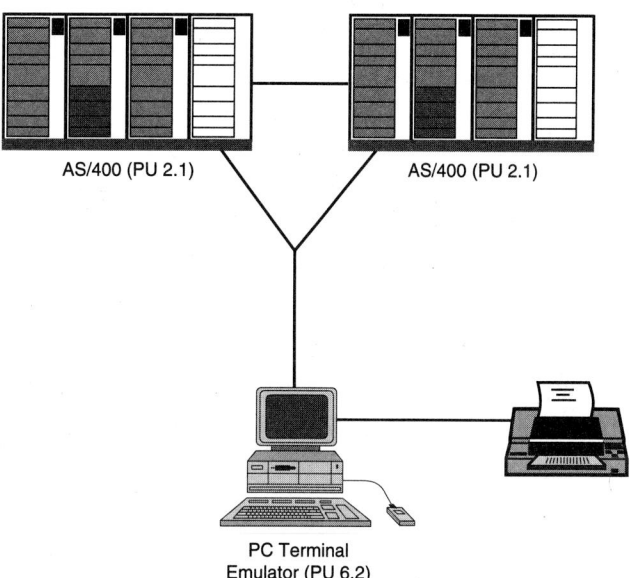

AS/400 (PU 2.1) AS/400 (PU 2.1)

PC Terminal
Emulator (PU 6.2)

As in the subarea SNA networking model, the SNA Server functions as an interconnecting network gateway. The SNA Server emulates a PU2.1 type device on the SNA Network, which manages the LU 6.2 sessions running on the PCs connected to the LAN. The SNA Server emulates an APPN Low-Entry Network node. The SNA Server is generally connected to the AS/400 utilizing the DFT/Twinax protocol. A typical APPN SNA model that utilizes an SNA Server is shown in Figure 38.9.

38

SNA SERVER
OVERVIEW

FIGURE 38.9.

An SNA Server in the peer-to-peer/APPN SNA configuration.

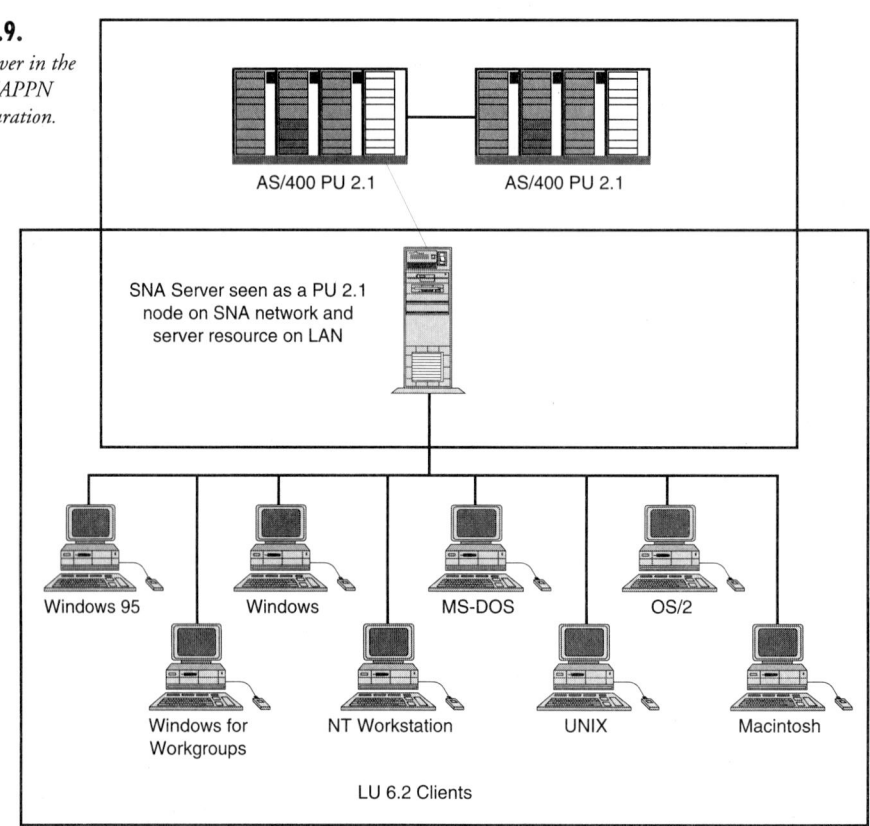

AS/400 PU 2.1   AS/400 PU 2.1

SNA Server seen as a PU 2.1 node on SNA network and server resource on LAN

Windows 95   Windows   MS-DOS   OS/2

Windows for Workgroups   NT Workstation   UNIX   Macintosh

LU 6.2 Clients

Services Provided by the SNA Server

The SNA Server manages connectivity to the host systems and provides mechanisms to ensure their reliability. Two or more SNA Servers can be configured to handle multiple-user connections to a host. These SNA Servers can work together to balance the load between the PC terminals and the host. Also, multiple servers can provide redundancy to eliminate a single point of failure.

Detailed Features of the SNA Server

SNA Server offers a standard Windows interface, centralized monitoring and control, administrative tools, integration with Windows NT, security, reliability, capacity, enterprise configuration flexibility, a variety of host connectivity options, complete SNA LU and PU support, host data access tools, client-server APIs, and remote access services. In the following sections, these features are described in detail.

Standard Windows Interface

The SNA Server utilizes the standardized Windows interface to facilitate installation, configuration, and management. The SNA Server Setup enables the user to configure SNA link services for installed adapters, specify the server role, and select LAN client-server protocols. The SNA Server Setup also provides an option to completely remove the SNA Server from the system.

The Admin utility provides an easy-to-use interface to manage Servers and Connections, LU Pools, and Users and Groups. The Admin utility enables a user to filter and adjust displayed information to suit his or her needs. The Admin utility supports standard drag-and-drop functionality to facilitate LU pool setup and user and group assignment. All information displayed by the Admin utility is dynamically updated.

Centralized Monitoring and Control

Close integration with Windows NT Server permits monitoring and control of the SNA Server from a centralized location. The SNA Server provides a complete set of utilities to assist in the management of the SNA Server. The Admin utility can be run on NT Server or Workstation, and it provides the capabilities for day-to-day management of the SNA Server. Integration with the IBM mainframe, host-based NetView application also permits communication with the SNA Server from the host system. Linking SNA Servers with the Windows NT Server performance monitor creates a graphical interface for monitoring and troubleshooting SNA Server performance. The SNA Server can facilitate the centralized monitoring and control of the following SNA Server functions:

- *LU and User Management.* The Admin utility permits management of users, user groups, and assignment of sessions for users given access to SNA Server resources. Admin also permits LU and LU poll assignment to users and user groups. C2-level security to SNA Server resources is provided through Windows NT Server user-management features.

- *Configuration Management.* The Admin utility enables multiple system configurations to be defined, saved, and edited. In a multiple SNA Server environment, the primary SNA Server keeps the master configuration files, which are automatically migrated to backup servers. This promotes the SNA Server's resource reliability; in the event that the primary SNA Server goes down, sessions are automatically rerouted to backup servers, even during the middle of an active session. Because SNA Servers in a single domain are aware of each other, they can distribute new sessions to servers with more available resources to help balance the load.

- *Troubleshooting.* The SNA Server provides extensive troubleshooting capabilities. The SNA Server provides the SNA Trace tool; support for 3270 terminal emulator Response Time Monitor; support for NetView, NVRunCmd, and NVAlert utilities; and integration with Window NT Server's Event Viewer and Performance Monitor.

■ *Connection Management.* The Admin utility shows the status of the SNA Server and connection status (active, inactive, stopping, or pending). Connections can be created, removed, or stopped. Connections can be started manually, at server startup, or on demand. On-demand activation can be useful for activating backup SNA Server connections.

■ *Link Management.* Utilizing SNA Server setup, new SNA link services can be installed, configured, or removed. Mappings between NT device-driver names and their associated Windows NT device drivers can be viewed. Individual device drivers can be activated and deactivated in the Devices applet of the Control Panel.

■ *Batch Mode Configuration.* The SNA Server provides a command-line utility SNACFG to automate the configuration of the SNA Server. The command-line interface can also print a text version of the current SNA Server configuration.

■ *Remote Access Administration.* The SNA Server Admin utility can be utilized over a Remote Access Service (RAS) link to facilitate centralized management of distributed SNA Servers. Only one domain can be administered at a time; the Select Domain command can be used to connect to different remote domains.

Administration Tools

The SNA Server provides a number of tools to simplify administration. These utilities are closely integrated with Windows NT and can provide information regarding the events that occurred leading up to a difficulty. These tools and utilities are as follows:

■ The Admin utility can provide information regarding Server status (inactive, pending, active, or stopping), Connection status (inactive, pending, active, or stopping), and LU status (active or inactive, associated user, computer name).

■ The SNA Trace utility can dynamically collect information on the activity of the SNA Server. The Trace utility can be started and stopped independently of the SNA Server. The information gathered by the trace utility can be effective in improving performance and diagnosing configuration problems.

■ The SNA Server provides the ability for remote diagnosis. Microsoft support can log into the server and utilize the available diagnostic tools (such as the Event Viewer or Trace Tool). The remote diagnostic facilities can help resolve problems faster, without personnel having to be on site.

■ The Response Time Monitor (RTM) is an IBM NetView tool that can monitor how long it takes the host to respond to a 3270 session request. The Admin utility can configure how often the RTM data should be updated. RTM is available only on supported emulators. The 3270 applet that is part of the SNA Server supports RTM data collection. RTM data can be utilized with Windows NT Server Performance Monitor.

■ The SNA Server integrates with IBM's NetView network-management system, which runs on an IBM host system. NetView can help an administrator manage operations, diagnose network problems, and enhance system performance. With the NVAlert utility, alerts generated by the SNA Server can be passed along to the host systems. Alerts such as a full disk or inability to open a file can be processed.

■ SNA Server integration with Netview's NVRunCmd enables an administrator seated at a NetView monitoring console to enter Windows NT commands to be carried out at a remote Windows NT SNA Server. In conjunction with the NVAlert utility, NVRunCmd is very useful in monitoring and quickly responding to reported problems. For example, if a disk-full alert is sent to a NetView operator, he or she could take the appropriate measures to free up disk space on the remote SNA Server.

Integration With Windows NT

The SNA Server is tightly integrated with Windows NT Server. Windows NT Server provides consistent and user-friendly tools for the administration and management of the SNA Server in a secure and reliable environment. The utilities and applets available from Windows NT for the SNA Server are as follows:

■ *Control Panel.* The Windows NT Server Control Panel provides SNA Server integration through a number of applets. The Services applet provides the ability to start, stop, and pause various SNA Server services. The Network applet provides the ability to install and configure network cards. Windows NT Server enables you to have one card running multiple protocol stacks or individual protocol stacks running on multiple cards. The Devices applet provides the ability to start, stop, and report the status of system drivers, network protocols, and adapter drivers. The Server applet provides the ability to monitor who is connected to the server and which shared resources they are utilizing.

■ *Performance Monitor.* The Windows NT Performance Monitor provides the ability to monitor the real-time performance of the SNA Server in a graphical representation. Charts, triggers, tables of values, and logs can be generated. The Performance Monitor can track throughput and transmission volume for connections, LUs, and adapters— and, if supported by the terminal emulator client, response times measured by NetView RTM.

■ *Event Viewer.* The Event Viewer can log and track significant events that occur on the Windows NT Server and the SNA Server. The Event Viewer can notify administrators of important events with pop-up messages and/or send information to a log file. The severity of errors that are recorded can be adjusted. The size of the log file can also be controlled. The Event View can filter recorded events by event types, date and time, source, category, user, computer, or event ID. Event logs can also be exported as comma-delimited files for analysis in a spreadsheet.

- *User Manager.* The User Manager creates and manages Windows NT Server user accounts and group accounts within a domain. The SNA Server utilizes these user accounts to manage access to SNA services. Any account created by the SNA Server or Windows NT Server is available for use by the other. This creates a single user-information repository that is efficient and secure.

- *Server Management.* Windows NT Server user accounts can be grouped into domains. The primary domain server keeps the user-account database. Users can log into other systems in the domain that have copies of the primary server user database. A single account provides access to all services within the domain (including files, directories, servers, and printers), providing an effective way to manage enterprise wide access.

Security, Reliability, and Capacity

The SNA Server provides a highly secure environment for SNA access. Through the use of hot backup and load balancing, the SNA Server also provides a highly reliable environment necessary for mission-critical SNA access in the largest of enterprises.

- *Security.* Through the security measures designed to meet U.S. government C2-level compliance, via Windows NT Server domain logins, the SNA Server guards the most critical corporate data by effectively preventing unauthorized access to the Windows NT Server and SNA Server. The sharing of the user database between the Windows NT Server and the SNA Server provides an effective, centrally managed mechanism to control access to SNA resources. The Admin utility can allow read-only, read-write, full-control, and no access. Full auditing measures are also supported through the use of the Windows NT event log.

- *Reliability.* The high reliability of the SNA Server is provided through the hot-backup and load-balancing capabilities. The hot-backup utility assures users continual access to their sessions if the SNA Server goes down. This is assured through multiple servers in a domain, or through multiple connections to an SNA Server. Through LU pooling, LUs (from one or more servers) are grouped together. If a data link fails, the SNA Server can reroute sessions to other functioning LUs in the pool. If an entire server fails in a multiserver domain, the session can automatically be redirected to other functioning servers in the LU pool. In a multiserver domain, load balancing routes new LU sessions to the server in the domain that is the least busy, ensuring maximum response time.

- *Capacity.* The SNA Server can support up to 250 simultaneous PU connections, up to 2,000 clients per server, up to 10,000 LU sessions per server, and up to 50 SNA Servers in a domain for load balancing and hot backup. This makes the SNA Server the highest capacity SNA gateway available on a PC platform.

Enterprise Configuration Flexibility

The SNA Server can be located in two distinct enterprise locations. They can be located in branch offices (closer to the users) or in a centralized location (closer to the host system).

■ *Branch Configuration.* In the Branch Configuration (see Figure 38.10), the SNA Server is located in a branch office, close to the actual end users. The Branch Configuration is a better choice when utilized over low-bandwidth WAN links. The Branch Configuration minimizes the WAN traffic and also increases user responsiveness through local-connection management. The SNA Server's remote-administration capabilities provide an effective means of managing the remotely located SNA Servers.

FIGURE 38.10.

SNA Server Branch Configuration.

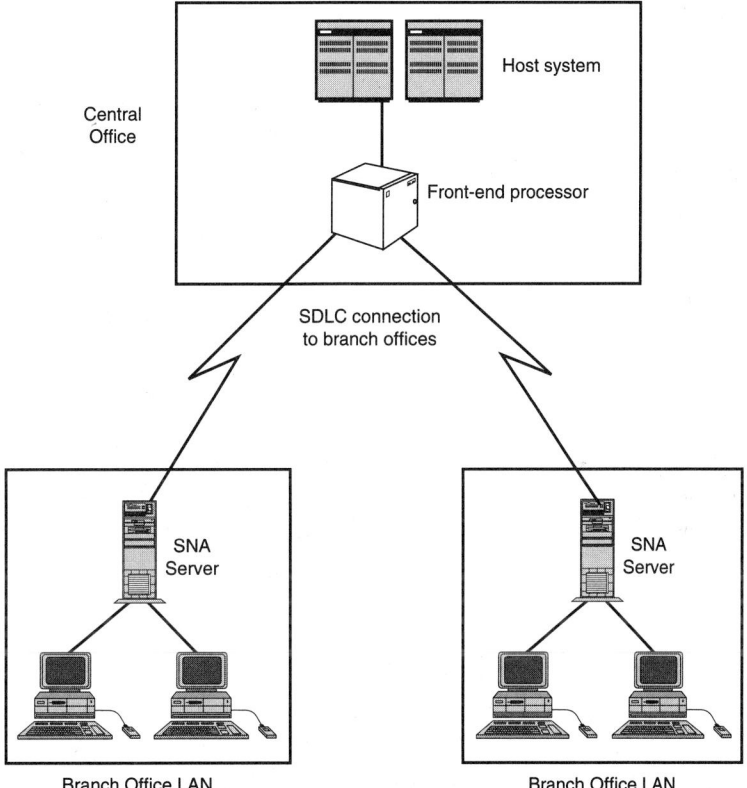

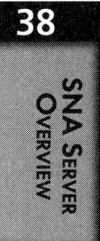

■ *Centralized Configuration.* In the Centralized Configuration (see Figure 38.11), the SNA Server is placed in a centralized location close to the host system, maximizing security and reliability. The Centralized Configuration simplifies the load-balancing and hot-backup setup. Centralized Configurations are a better choice when a high-bandwidth WAN is available, or if enterprise operations are confined to a single location. A single, routable protocol (such as IPX or TCP/IP) can be utilized over the WAN to provide SNA Server access.

FIGURE 38.11.

SNA Server Central-ized Configuration.

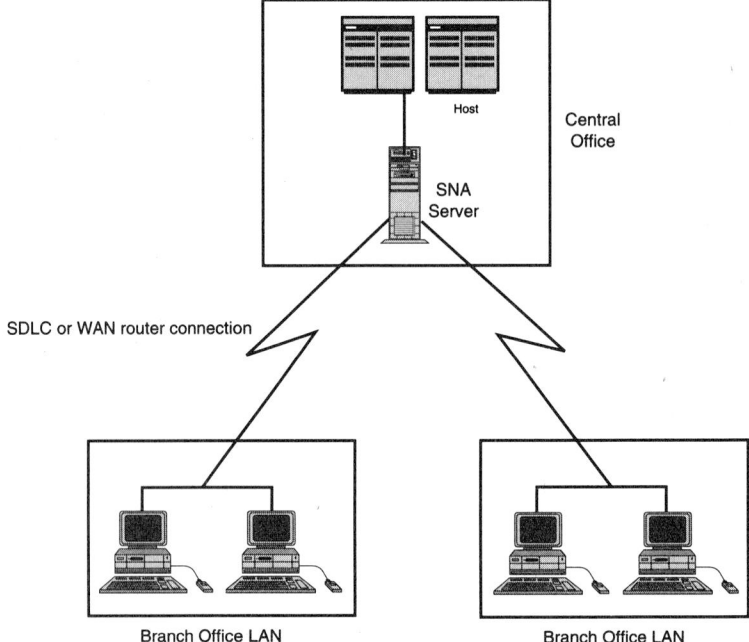

■ *Distributed Deployment Configuration.* The Distributed Deployment Configuration (see Figure 38.12) combines the strengths of the Branch and Centralized Configurations. In this configuration, branch-based SNA gateways connect to the host through centralized SNA gateways. The connection between the branch-based and centralized SNA gateway is via native LAN protocols such as TCP/IP. The SNA Server introduced the first architecture designed to meet TCP/IP and SNA Inter-networking requirements. SOGA (SNA Open Gateway Architecture) is a scaleable framework for SNA enterprise gateways that offers multiple options to integrate branch offices via routed LAN internetworks with host computers.

Many organizations utilizing IBM mainframes or AS/400s are in the process of moving from a hierarchical SNA network to an interconnected, TCP/IP-based LAN. Continued access to applications and data from these legacy host systems is a necessary requirement during this migration process. The maintenance of separate SNA and TCP/IP networks can be cost prohibitive and problematic. Installing a TCP/IP protocol stack on the host system can be viewed as another alternative, but this can also be cost prohibitive, difficult to manage, and it can degrade system performance.

The SNA Server is a split-stack SNA gateway, enabling access to host SNA data and applications for PCs on the LAN. WAN bandwidth capacities have become a factor, due to the overhead generated by the client-server traffic of the SNA gateway. The SNA Server is the first gateway solution that can deploy split-stack gateway clients (where multiple protocol drivers need to be loaded into memory) in remote branch offices while maintaining the advantages of a centralized configuration.

FIGURE 38.12.

SNA Server Distributed Deployment Configuration.

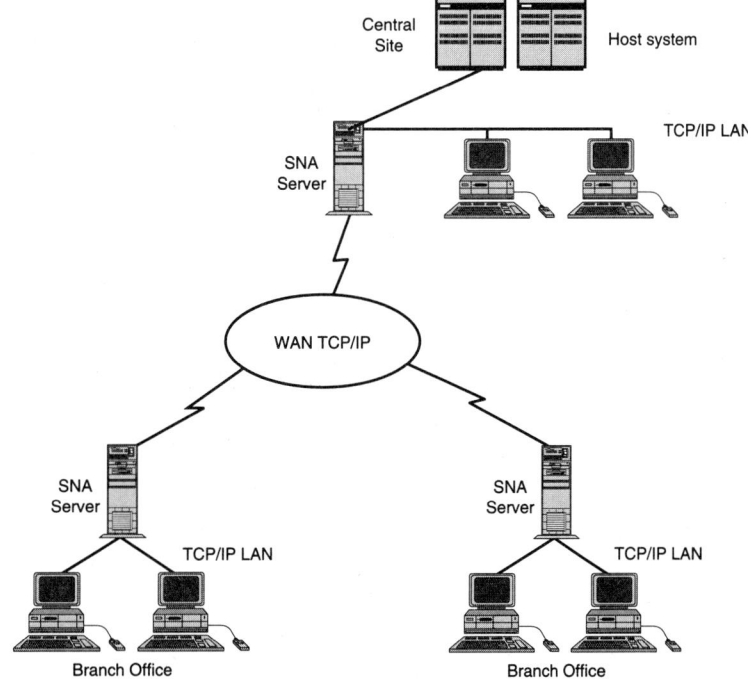

Host-Connectivity Options

The SNA Server provides a number of host-connectivity options and support drivers (called link services). Each single link can support only a single adapter; each link can support multiple sessions. The following connection types are supported by the SNA Server:

- 802.2
- SDLC (Synchronous Data Link Control)
- X.25
- DFT (Distributed Function Terminal)
- Channel
- Twinax

Complete SNA LU and PU Support

The SNA Server supports the following Logical Units: LU 0, LU 1, LU 2, LU 3, and LU 6.2. The SNA Server supports the following Physical Units: PU 2.0, PU 2.1, APPN LEN Node, and Downstream PU (DSPU).

38

SNA SERVER
OVERVIEW

Host Data-Access Tools

The SNA Server includes ODBC/DRDA (Open Database Connectivity/Distributed Relational Database Architecture) drivers for Windows and Windows NT clients. The ODBC driver enables database connectivity for applications such as Microsoft Excel and Microsoft Access to IBM-host databases, without the need for an expensive host-based database gateway. The ODBC drivers support DB2 for MVS, SQL/DS for VM, and DBS/400 for AS/400. The ODBC/DRDA drivers provide an efficient and cost-effective means for accessing host-based databases. Any Windows-application development tools that support ODBC connectivity (such as Microsoft Visual Basic) can access host-based databases from custom-created applications.

Client-Server Application-Development APIs

The SNA Server comes with a full SDK for building client-server solutions. The SNA Server supports the WOSA-compliant (Windows Open Systems Architecture) standard APIs for Windows and OS/2-based standards for OS/2. The SNA Server also supports IBM's standard API for AS/400 systems, as well as the new EHNAPPC API. This provides a mechanism to write Windows-based applications that integrate with the AS/400 data and applications.

Remote Access Service

Remote Access Service (RAS) enables clients in remote locations to access SNA Server and Windows NT services.

RAS servers can be accessed from the SNA Server or any Windows NT Server in the domain, providing a remote connection to the SNA Network or LAN. All SNA Server functions are supported over RAS connections. Windows NT logon and domain security, data encryption, and callback options are supported for RAS connections, ensuring secured remote access.

SNA Remote Access Service is a feature that allows administrators to create virtual LAN connections between Windows NT systems across an existing SNA network. This is accomplished by using SNA's LU6.2 transport mechanism with the RAS architecture, enabling enterprises to leverage existing equipment to facilitate the SNA Server and host management. SNA Remote Access Services supports IPX, TCP/IP (PPP), and NetBEUI from Windows NT and Windows NT Workstation clients.

Integration with Other BackOffice Components

The SNA Server provides integration with other BackOffice components to deliver enterprise-wide connectivity solutions.

Windows NT Server

Integration with Windows NT Server is provided through the following services:

- SNA Remote Access Service creates a virtual WAN over SNA networks to link two or more Windows NT Server LANs.
- The SNA Server's NetView Services enable host administrators to execute any NT command line from an IBM NetView console, make it possible to forward any Windows NT event-log message to NetView, and permit LAN administrators to view NetView performance data on any Windows NT Performance Monitor.

SQL Server

Integration with SQL Server is provided through the following services:

- ODBC/DRDA driver integrates host data from DB2, SQL/DS, and DB2/400 with Microsoft SQL Server.
- You no longer need expensive, single-purpose SQL-to-host database gateways to access host databases.

Systems Management Server

Integration with Systems Management Server is provided through the following services:

- SNA Remote Access Service supports all functions of SMS, including remote control of remote workstations over SNA networks.
- The systems administrator can utilize SMS software distribution, remote control, and other management capabilities even if the network is a host-based SNA network.

Mail and Exchange

Integration with MS Mail and Exchange Server is provided through the following services:

- SNA Remote Access Service enables postoffice-to-postoffice connectivity over SNA networks.
- PROFS and SNADS gateways (third-party products) link host e-mail and scheduling to the Microsoft Mail and Exchange Servers.

Service Pack for the SNA Server Version 2.11

In January 1996, Microsoft released a service upgrade to the SNA Server. Service Pack 1 for the SNA Server 2.11 included the following features:

38

SNA SERVER
OVERVIEW

- Distributed Gateway Service. Distributed deployment improves host response times and saves WAN bandwidth compared to the centralized model, while making host access more reliable and simplifying network management compared to the branch-based model.

- Support for TN3270E clients.

- FTP-AFTP gateway. The Service Pack includes a new server-based function to convert FTP file-transfer requests into AFTP.

- AFTP API support. The Service Pack adds a new API to automate AFTP file transfers programmatically.

- Support for ESCON channel attachment.

- Windows 95 client for the SNA Server.

- Support for SQL/DS and stored procedures in the ODBC/DRDA driver.

- Drivers for several new SDLC and X.25 adapters.

Service Pack 1 for the SNA Server is available to download at `ftp://ftp.microsoft.com/bussys/winnt/sna-public/fixes/sna211/` or on disk from Microsoft. The Intel version of the service pack is in the directory USSP1/WINNT/I386/, the filename is 211SP1IS.EXE.

To extract the Service Pack, copy the file to an empty directory on your hard drive and issue the command:

```
211SP1IS.EXE -d PATH
```

where *PATH* is the destination directory for the service pack. If you wish to extract the service pack to the current directory, leave *PATH* blank.

After the service pack has been decompressed, stop all SNA Server services running on the machine (including SnaBase, TN3270, APPC transaction programs, and so forth) and run the UPDATE.EXE program to install the updated SNA Server 2.11 server files.

The SNA Server Version 3.0 Features

With the release of Windows NT Server version 4.0, the SNA Server 3.0 will be available soon afterwards. The new version will feature the following:

- *SNA Print Service.* This feature provides server-based 3270 and 5250 print emulation, allowing mainframe and AS/400 applications to print to any LAN printer supported by Windows NT Server or Novell NetWare. Host printing supports both LU1 and LU3 devices. AS/400 printing supports SCS line printing and pass-through support for host-based 3812 graphics-printing emulation. Printer-emulation sessions no longer need to be configured separately. Centralized control and greater sharing of printer resources is achieved.

■ *Increased Capacity.* The SNA Server 3.0 now supports up to 5,000 users and up to 15,000 host sessions. Fewer centralized SNA Servers are required to support the entire enterprise. This higher capacity has become possible due to the channel-attachment solutions recently made available for the SNA Server, which offer throughput several times that of a Token Ring connection to the host.

■ *Single Sign-On To AS/400s And Mainframes.* Integrated password synchronization and single sign-on covers the primary IBM mainframe operating system, OS/390 (previously MVS), the AS/400 operating system OS/400, and all desktop operating systems that are integrated with Windows NT Server security: Windows NT Workstation, Windows 95, Windows for Workgroups, Windows 3.*x*, MS-DOS, Macintosh, and OS/2. The unified sign-on feature of Windows NT Server permits client users to log in once to gain access to all files, printers, databases, messaging systems, and other applications running on the Windows NT Server-based network. Password synchronization with AS/400 and other mainstream mainframe security systems make it possible to utilize one password for host and LAN access. User passwords are kept synchronized regardless of which environment—the host or the Windows NT Server-based computer—initiates the change.

■ *Data Encryption.* Encryption of all data passed between the SNA Server and the client using the RSA RC4 data-encryption standard is now provided. Due to the SNA Server's client-server architecture, existing 3270/5250 emulators and applications written to the SNA Server's APIs will automatically provide encrypted sessions. This feature may be disabled on a user-by-user basis. Data encryption is also supported in the Distributed Configuration of SNA Open Gateway Architecture (SOGA), providing secure SNA Server-to-SNA Server communications across the Internet, Intranet and WANs. The centralized SNA Server can be placed next to the host in a secure room, providing host-to-client encryption of all client sessions without affecting host performance.

■ *Shared Folders Service.* Similar to the Gateway Service for NetWare in Windows NT Server, Shared Folders Service permits PCs with no SNA client software installed to access "shared folders" files on an AS/400. The Shared Folders Service makes AS/400 files available to users as just an additional drive on the Windows NT Server. Windows NT Server security systems can be used to set permissions on the shared folders.

■ *TN5250 Service.* The TN5250 Service enables any TN5250 emulator to connect to an AS/400 through the SNA Server without requiring a TCP/IP protocol stack on the AS/400. This frees up significant host processing power. The TN5250 Service also provides support for UNIX and Macintosh clients that were previously unable to connect to an AS/400 through the SNA Server.

■ *Support For TN3287 Clients In TN3270E Service.* Adds support for the TN3287 print-emulation capability implemented in some TN3270 emulators.

38

SNA SERVER
OVERVIEW

- *Syncpoint Support For APPC.* The SNA Server 3.0's Software Development Kit (SDK) includes the addition of Syncpoint level 2 support in the WinAPPC API. The APPC Syncpoint API provides the coordination necessary to implement robust, cross-platform distributed-transaction processing in conjunction with host-based databases (for example, DB2) and transaction-resource managers (for example, CICS).

- *SNA Explorer.* SNA Explorer is a new, integrated administration tool. SNA Explorer is consistent with the look and feel of the Windows 95 Explorer, and it functions as the single point of control for configuring and managing all SNA Servers, host connections, sessions, users, security, auditing, and other functions in the same domain. SNA Explorer combines the administration of the SNA Server, TN3270 Service, TN5250 Service, SNA Print Service, Shared Folders Service, and Host Security into a single application.

- *Improved Setup Programs.* The SNA Server's client and server setup programs have been redesigned to be consistent with other Microsoft BackOffice and Office applications. The setup program supports the automatic upgrade of the SNA Server 2.1 and 2.11 to the SNA Server 3.0. Microsoft Systems Management Server can be utilized to complete unattended and remote installations of the SNA Server and clients.

Summary

It is estimated that more than 80 percent of all information on enterprise computer systems is available only through an IBM SNA network. Enterprise efficiency and competitiveness require that people using desktop PCs be able to access enterprise data applications effectively and efficiently. The SNA Server gives PC users reliable, fast, and inexpensive access to host data and applications, preserves the security and control of host systems, and frees up host and PC resources for what each does best.

The SNA Server reduces the need for client workstations to run dual protocol stacks to participate in the enterprise LAN and SNA Network. This increases client workstation support and stability. Hot backup and LU pooling help assure consistently reliable access to host systems and data.

The SNA Server provides a number of tools to ease the administration of the SNA Network resources. All host changes can be tracked centrally at the SNA Server. The SNA Server provides integrated security for access to SNA Network resources, through the use of the combined Windows NT Server and SNA Server security mechanisms. Performance and event-monitoring utilities are provided, making it easier to diagnose SNA Network problems and the events that lead up to them.

The SNA Server can reduce the amount of network-definition work on host systems. Large numbers of users can be supported through a single PU controller. This can greatly minimize the number of times VTAM regenerations need to be run, which reduces host system downtime, frees up staff time, and reduces potential errors. The SNA Server also decreases host memory requirements and frees up host processing power for running applications. The SNA Server can also decrease network traffic. The host system no longer needs to poll each client terminal emulator connected to it. The host system just needs to maintain connectivity to the SNA Server, increasing network performance and reducing session time-outs. Through the use of hot backups, LU pooling, and load balancing, the SNA Server assures reliable access to enterprise host systems and data.

Installing SNA Server

by John Fronckowiak

IN THIS CHAPTER

CHAPTER

39

This chapter covers the step by step installation of SNA Server and clients, including the systems requirements and detailed setup and configuration of the DLC 802.2, SDLC, IBM X.25, and DFT link services, and clients on different host operating systems. A step by step guide to verifying a successful SNA Server installation through the use of the DEMO Link Services appears at the end of this chapter.

System Requirements

The following sections detail the system requirements for SNA Server and client installation.

SNA Server Requirements

The following sections explore the system requirements needed to install the SNA Server version 2.11.

LAN Network Protocol and Adapter

The first requirement is one or more network adapters supported by Windows NT Advanced Server version 3.1 or Windows NT Server version 3.51 installed with support for one or more of the following network protocols:

- Microsoft networking (included with Windows NT)
- NWLink or equivalent IPX/SPX services
- Microsoft TCP/IP or equivalent Win32 Windows Sockets version 1.1
- Banyan Enterprise Client version 5.52 for Windows NT
- Services for Macintosh

Memory Requirements

A minimum of 20M of total system RAM is required. This is 4M more than required by Windows NT Server. This extra memory is recommended to support optimal performance under peak loads.

Hard Disk Requirements

A minimum of 11M free hard-disk space is required to install the SNA Server version 2.11.

SNA Communications Adapter

The following is a partial list of SNA communications adapters supported:

- Any Windows NT NDIS-compliant Token Ring or Ethernet device driver, using Windows NT 802.2 DLC transport protocol
- Attachmate SDLC

- Barr Systems T1-SYNC (for SDLC)
- DCA IRMA (for DFT)
- DCA ISCA (for SDLC and X.25)
- Microgate MGx, Microgate DSA, Microgate USA (for SDLC and X.25)
- IBM SDLC
- IBM MCPA
- IBM MPA/A
- IBM DFT
- IBM 3270 Connection A,B
- IBM 3278/9 Advanced Emulation adapter
- Any driver developed through the SNADIS interface

Client Requirements

SNA Server supports clients running under Windows NT Server and Workstation, Windows 95, Windows 3.*x*, MS-DOS, OS/2, and Macintosh operating systems. The system requirements for each of these operating systems are detailed in this section.

SNA Server Clients for Windows NT

The operating system versions, networking protocols, network adapters, memory, and hard disk requirements for a Windows NT client installation are detailed in this section.

Operating System

Operating systems required include Windows NT Advanced Server version 3.1, Windows NT version 3.1, Windows NT Server version 3.51, or Windows NT Workstation version 3.51.

LAN Network Protocol and Adapter

Another requirement is one or more network adapters, supported by Windows NT installed with support for one or more of the following network protocols:

- Microsoft networking (included with Windows NT)
- NWLink or equivalent IPX/SPX services
- Microsoft TCP/IP or equivalent Win32 Windows Sockets version 1.1
- Banyan Enterprise Client version 5.52 for Windows NT
- Services for Macintosh

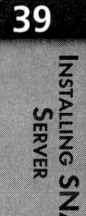

39

INSTALLING SNA
SERVER

Memory Requirements

A minimum of 14M of total system RAM is required. This is 2M more than the minimum required by Windows NT and Windows NT Workstation.

Hard Disk Requirements

A minimum of 7M free hard disk space is also required.

SNA Server Clients for Windows 95

The operating system versions, networking protocols, network adapters, memory, and hard disk requirements for a Windows 95 client installation are detailed in this section.

Operating System

Operating systems required include Windows 95, Windows NT Server 3.51, or Windows NT Workstation 3.51.

LAN Network Protocol and Adapter

Another requirement is a network adapter supported by Windows 95, Windows NT Server version 3.51, or Windows NT Workstation 3.51, installed with support for one or more of the following network protocols:

- Microsoft networking (included with Windows NT and Windows 95)
- NWLink or equivalent IPX/SPX services
- Microsoft TCP/IP or equivalent Win32 Windows Sockets version 1.1
- Banyan Enterprise Client version 5.52

Memory Requirements

For Windows NT, a minimum of 14M of total system RAM is required. For Windows 95, a minimum of 8M of total system RAM is required.

Hard Disk Requirements

4 M free hard-disk space.

SNA Server Clients for Windows Version 3.x

The operating system versions, networking protocols, network adapters, memory, and hard disk requirements for a Windows version 3.x client installation are detailed in this section.

Operating System

Operating systems required include Windows for Workgroups or Windows 3.x.

LAN Network Protocol and Adapter

Another requirement is one or more network adapters supported by Windows for Workgroups or Windows 3.*x*, installed with support for one or more of the following network protocols:

- The network software included in Windows for Workgroups
- LAN Manager version 2.*x*
- Novell NetWare (IPX.COM) version 3.10 or later, or any ODI driver
- Microsoft TCP/IP or equivalent Windows Sockets version 1.1
- Banyan VINES version 5.52

Memory Requirements

A minimum of 4M of total system RAM is required. The following are the memory requirements of each of these applications:

Client Application	RAM Required
3270 Applet	525K
5250 Applet	490K
3270 and 5250 Applet both loaded simultaneously	830K
Base support for ISV 5250 emulator	185K
Base support for ISV 3270 emulator	185K
Base support for APPC, CPI-C, LUA, or CSV application	185K

The base support does not include the actual memory required by the emulation application.

Hard Disk Requirements

A minimum of 4M free hard disk space is also required.

SNA Server Clients for MS-DOS

The operating system versions, networking protocols, network adapters, memory, and hard disk requirements for an MS-DOS client installation are detailed in this section.

Operating System

The MS-DOS operating system version 3.2 or later is required.

LAN Network Protocol and Adapter

Another requirement is a LAN Manager version 2.*x*, Novell NetWare (IPX.COM) version 3.10 or later, or Banyan VINES version 5.52 and supported network adapter.

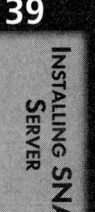

39

INSTALLING SNA
SERVER

Memory Required

A minimum of 640K RAM is required. Actual RAM occupancy is shown in the following table:

Client Application	RAM Required
Base support for IBM PC Support functions	100K
Base support for ISV 3270 emulator	50K
Base support for APPC, LUA-RUI, or CSV application	50K

The base support does not include the actual memory required by the emulation application.

Hard Disk Requirements

A minimum of 2.2M free hard disk space is also required.

SNA Server Clients Running OS/2

The operating system versions, networking protocols, network adapters, memory, and hard disk requirements for an OS/2 client installation are detailed in this section.

Operating System

An OS/2 operating system version 1.21 or later, with a network adapter installed, is required.

Memory Required

A minimum of 8M of total system RAM is recommended.

Hard Disk Requirements

A minimum of 1M free hard disk space is also required.

SNA Server Clients on Macintosh Computers

The operating system versions, networking protocols, network adapters, memory, and hard disk requirements for a Macintosh client installation are detailed in this section.

Operating System

A System 6.0.2 or later and Finder version 6.0 or later is required (System 7.0 and Finder 7.0 can be used).

Networking Protocol

Another requirement is a standard Macintosh platform with AppleTalk access.

Other

A Macintosh terminal emulation software is required.

Planning

Before beginning the SNA Server installation, a few planning steps should be executed. A set of planning forms, provided with the SNA Server documentation, should be completed to assist in organizing your installation. The SNA Server domain configuration should be determined, and the role of this server should be selected. Other security and auditing issues should also be taken into account before installation. These planning issues are discussed in more detail in this section.

Filling Out Planning Forms

In the Microsoft SNA Server Version 2.11 Administration Guide, a set of planning forms are provided. These forms are useful for organizing the information necessary to install and configure SNA Server. Information from the host system administrator, LAN administrator, and client workstations is required to complete the planning forms. The planning forms are also available on the Microsoft Web Site at `http://www.microsoft.com/sna/prepform.htm`. The following forms are available:

- Server Resources Planning
- Server Information
- Initial Connections Settings
- 802.2 Settings
- SDLC Settings
- X.25 Settings
- Channel Settings
- 3270 RTM Settings
- Users and Groups
- 3270 LUs (Individual)
- 3270 LUs (Ranges)
- 3270 LU Pools
- Local APPC LUs
- Remote APPC LUs
- Mode Properties for LU-LU Pairs
- CPI-C Properties

SNA Server Domains

When planning an SNA Server installation, you need to decide whether the enterprise SNA Servers should be centralized in one location or distributed in branch offices. The necessary tools to effectively manage SNA Servers are provided for both configurations. The advantages of the centralized configuration are that all the SNA Servers are located in one place, easing administration. The advantages of the distributed configuration are that it uses smaller domains, which can be easier to configure, and requires smaller servers. A complete discussion of SNA Server Domain Configurations is provided in Chapter 38, "SNA Server Overview."

Server Role

The SNA Server can be designated to function in one of three different types of roles. This should be determined before installation begins.

Primary Configuration Server

The Primary SNA Server contains the domain-wide configuration file. This configuration file contains the SNA Server resources for the domain, including SNA servers in the domain, link services, LUs, 3270 users, and so forth. Only one primary server can operate in a domain. The primary server is usually the first SNA Server installed.

Backup Configuration Server

A Backup SNA Server is a server on which the configuration file is replicated by the Primary SNA Server. More than one backup server can be configured in a domain. If the Primary SNA Server cannot function, SNA Server will utilize the backup configuration file. Using the configuration file on the Backup Server, servers and connections can be started and stopped, but the configuration cannot be modified or saved. Up to 49 backup servers can be installed in a single domain.

Member Server (No Configuration)

A Member Server does not have the configuration file or a backup of the configuration file. A Member Server applies the Primary Server's configuration file as changes are made.

Security

To provide the highest level of security for Windows NT and SNA Servers in a domain, access to the SNA Server configuration file must be controlled. To control user access to files, SNA Server should be installed on a Windows NT File System (NTFS) partition. Only through utilizing NTFS can permission be assigned on a file-by-file basis. This is the most effective way to control access to the SNA Server configuration file.

Windows NT Server and SNA Server share the same user database. When a change is made to either user database, it is reflected in both. A user must successfully be logged into the Windows NT domain to gain access to SNA Server and its resources. A user or user group must be assigned to an LU to access host system resources.

Auditing

The Event Monitor in Windows NT Server enables various SNA Server events to be logged and monitored, creating an effective audit trail. Events to be monitored can be specified, and the date and time they occur will automatically be logged. The Event Viewer can filter out which events to view and specific dates and times. The event audit trail can be an effective security monitoring tool. Careful consideration of which events will be monitored should be taken. Event logging takes a small amount of system resources to accomplish, and if too many events are logged, the event log file can quickly become large.

Installation Procedure

Step-by-step procedures to install the SNA Server are detailed in this section, including the configuration of the DLC 802.2, SDLC, IBM X.25, and DFT link services.

Setup

The SNA Server Setup application is used to install the SNA Server. Because the SNA Server Setup requires the capability of accessing the Windows NT Registry, you need to be logged in as the Administrator before beginning.

From the File Manager, select the CD from which you are installing SNA Server. Then run the SETUP.BAT file located in the root directory of the SNA Server CD. The SETUP.BAT file will initiate the appropriate installation for the hardware platform you are using. You will need to wait a few moments while your system configuration is determined. As the setup application proceeds, a number of dialog boxes will be displayed.

A Welcome To SNA Server dialog box will be displayed. Click on the Continue button to begin the installation process or click on the Exit button to abort the installation process. You will then be asked to choose your licensing mode: Per-Server or Per-Seat. In the Per-Server licensing mode, each concurrent connection to the SNA Server requires a separate Client Access License. In the Per-Seat licensing mode each computer that accesses the SNA Server requires a separate Client Access License. After specifying the License mode, click on Continue to proceed with the installation. You then must agree to the Client Licensing mode you have selected to continue.

A standard Software Licensing dialog box is displayed. This dialog box is used to enter identifying information for you and your company. Enter your name, company name (optional), and product ID, which is located on the inside back cover of the installation guide. Click on Continue to proceed with the installation. After reviewing the information you have entered, you may click on on the Back button to return to editing your information, or the Ok button to proceed.

The Installation Path dialog is displayed next. The default installation path is C:\SNA. You may edit the installation. If you edit the installation path, be sure to use an empty directory so that the SNA Server will not accidentally write over any files required by another application. Click on the Continue button to proceed.

Select Client-Server Protocols

The system is then checked for available client-server networking protocols. If more than one client-server networking protocol is installed on the system, the Select Client/Server Protocols dialog box in Figure 39.1 is displayed; otherwise, the installation will proceed to the next step of selecting the SNA Server Role.

FIGURE 39.1.

The Select Client/Server Protocols dialog box displays the available client-server networking protocols that have been automatically detected.

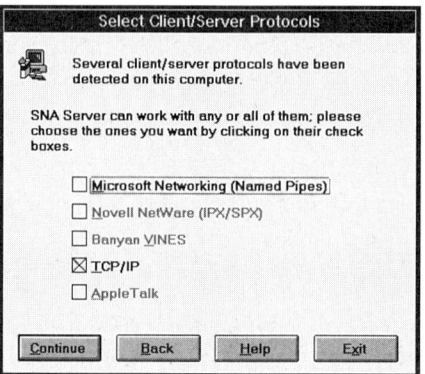

Only the protocols that are not grayed out are installed and available for selection. The protocols that have been detected will automatically be checked. You can select and deselect which protocols you want the SNA Server to utilize.

> **NOTE**
>
> For peak efficiency, select only one protocol for broadcasts between SNA servers. For peak efficiency in domains where SNA server adapters can use multiple protocols and broadcasts will not be routed over IP routers, for Server Broadcasts, select one (and only one) of the following protocols: IPX/SPX, Banyan VINES, or TCP/IP.

If you do not select the Microsoft Networking (Named Pipes) protocol, you must specify the name of the network domain in which your SNA Server will participate. The Network Domain Name dialog box in Figure 39.2 will be displayed. Enter the domain name and click on Continue to proceed.

FIGURE 39.2.

The Network Domain Name dialog box is used to specify the domain in which the SNA Server will participate.

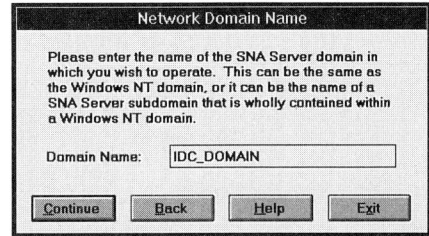

If the TCP/IP networking protocol is selected, the domain name can be specified in three ways:

- The domain name used in the Windows NT domain.
- The host name with the TCP domain name—for example, `drwho.gallifrey.com`. If this form is used, the Domain Name System (DNS) resolver must be configured to map the name to an IP address.
- The actual IP address—for example, `192.46.12.1`.

If the Banyan VINES protocol is selected, the StreetTalk Group Name dialog box is displayed. SNA Server Setup creates a StreetTalk name by combining information stored on the Banyan VINES network with information you type into the Setup dialog boxes. If you leave the Group Name entry blank, Setup uses the group name of the user currently logged on in the Banyan VINES network. You must ensure that the group name of the user logged on in the Banyan VINES network during installation of the SNA Server is always the same group name, regardless of whether client or server software is being installed.

Select Server Role

Once the client-server networking protocols have been selected, the role for the SNA Server must be designated. The Change SNA Server Role dialog box in Figure 39.3 is displayed. The SNA Server roles are described in the Planning And Things To Consider section earlier in this chapter.

By default, the Primary Configuration Server is selected. Click on the Backup or Member Server option if you want to change the server's role. An SNA Server can be designated to only one role.

FIGURE 39.3.

The Change SNA Server Role dialog box designates the configuration role for the SNA Server.

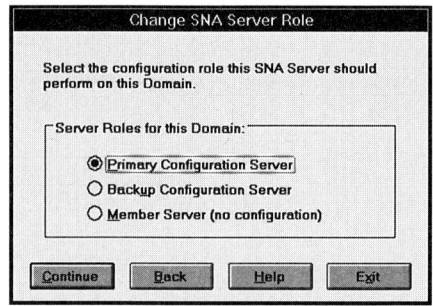

> **NOTE**
>
> When a primary server or backup server is installed, the path of NAROOT\SYSTEM\CONFIG (where *SNAROOT* is the installation directory specified) is automatically shared as \\servername\COMCFG. This enables the SNA Server to access the configuration file on the primary or backup servers.
>
> To control user access to files, the SNA Server should be installed on a Windows NT File System (NTFS) partition. NTFS will allow permissions to be set on the SNA Server configuration files. If you are installing a primary server or backup server, it is important that NTFS be used. You can exit the SNA Server Setup and run the CONVERT utility to convert FAT or HPFS partitions to NTFS. See your Windows NT Server manuals for more information on the CONVERT utility.

Once the server role is designated, click on Continue to proceed. The Review Settings dialog box is displayed next. Click on the Review button to review and edit your installation directory and server role designations. To install the online documentation, click on the Install On-Line Documentation checkbox. Online documentation will require 14M additional free disk space. Click on Continue to proceed with copying the appropriate SNA Server files. Once the application files have been installed, if online documentation was selected to be installed, the On-Line Documentation Destination Path dialog box appears. By default, the online documentation is installed in the help subdirectory of your initial installation path. Click on Continue to proceed with installing the online documentation.

Install Link Services

Link services define the protocols used to connect the SNA Server with the communications adapter. The Link Service Installation dialog box in Figure 39.4 displays Available Link Services. You may click on Continue to complete the SNA Server installation without installing any link services. You need to run the SNA Server Setup application to install a link service before connections can be configured.

FIGURE 39.4.

The Link Service Installation dialog box displays the list of Available Link Services to install and configure.

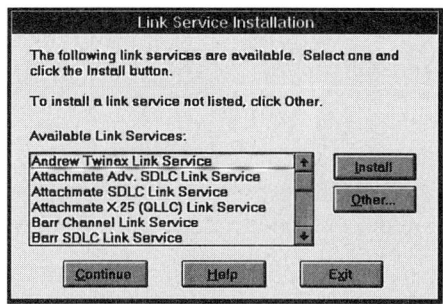

Select the desired link service to install and configure from the list of Available Link Services. Click on the Install button to begin the link service configuration. A dialog box appropriate to the type of link service being installed will be displayed for configuration. The defaults can be accepted or modified for your needs. Click on the Continue button to begin copying the appropriate link service support files.

When installing different link service adapters, if more than one adapter is installed in the server, the extras must be configured to work together so that there are no interrupt, port address, or direct memory access (DMA) conflicts. When you install a new adapter in your computer, you may need to study the configuration of the new and old adapters to make sure there are no conflicts.

If the DLC 802.2 link service is selected for installation, the SNA Server Setup application checks to ensure that the DLC networking protocol has been installed through the Windows NT Server setup. The SNA Server Setup will assist you in the installation of the DLC protocol, but to do so requires that you have the Windows NT Server setup disks available.

If a link service that you want to install is not listed in the Available Link Services list, the new link service can be installed using the link service installation disk. Clicking on the Other button requires that a path be specified for the new link services drivers. Once the new drivers are located, the link service configuration proceeds in a similar manner to any of the Available Link Services procedures.

Configure Link Services

Once a link service is selected, it must be configured. An installed and configured link service is required before configuration of the SNA Server can proceed. There are four basic types of link services. A detailed guide to installing and configuring these basic link services follows.

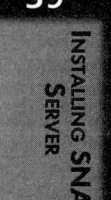

DLC 802.2

To configure a DLC 802.2 link service, follow these steps:

1. Select the 802.2 DLC Link Service from the Available Link Services list. If the DLC protocol has not been installed by the Windows NT Server setup, you will be prompted to do so now. This will require the Windows NT Server Setup disks. Once the DLC protocol has been verified to be installed, the DLC 802.2 Link Service Setup dialog box in Figure 39.5 appears.

FIGURE 39.5.

The DLC 802.2 Link Service Setup dialog box.

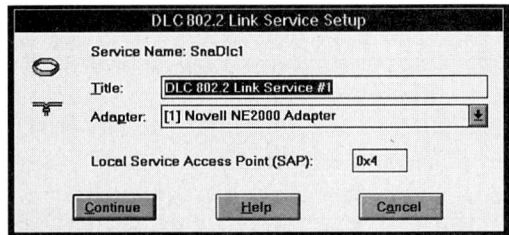

2. The default title for the DLC 802.2 Link Service is displayed in the Title edit box. This title can be modified if desired; up to 40 characters can be used to specify the title.

3. The Adapter box is used to select the adapter card being used. The drop-down box displays the list of available adapter cards. Select the desired adapter card to configure for this link service.

4. The Local Service Access Point (SAP) box, contains the local SAP code, which is used in accessing certain services on an 802.2 connection in an SNA Network. The default SAP value for the SNA Server is 4; this number must be divisible by four and ranges from 4 through 252. The SAP value should be verified with the host administrator.

5. Click on the Continue button to copy the necessary Link Service files. Once complete, the Link Service Configuration dialog box in Figure 39.6 is displayed, showing the new Link Service.

FIGURE 39.6.

The Link Service Configuration dialog box, showing the newly configured DLC 802.2 link service.

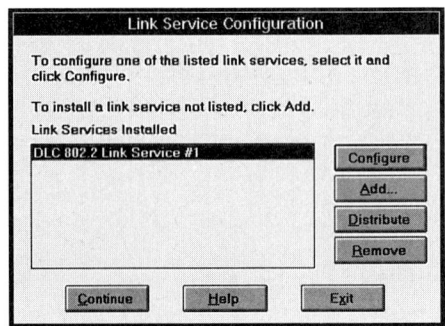

6. Additional link services can be added by clicking on the Add button. The highlighted Link Service can be reconfigured by clicking on the Configure button or removed by clicking on the Remove button. (When removing a link service, a Link Service Removal box will appear; click on Continue to remove the link service.)

7. To normally complete the SNA Server installation, click on the Continue button.

Installing SNA Servers on Ethernet LAN with Routers

If the SNA Server will communicate with remote hosts, peers, or downstream systems via routers, the FrameType entry may require adjustment in the Windows NT Registry. FrameType specifies the type of frames the DLC link service sends over the LAN. These frame types must match the frame type used by the routers. The FrameType entry is found in the registry at

```
HKEY_LOCAL_MACHINE
SYSTEM
  CurrentControlSet
    Services
      DLCLinkServiceName
        Parameters
          ExtraParameters
            FrameType
```

The values for FrameType and their corresponding effects are detailed in the following table.

Frame Type Value	Effect
0	This is the default. Uses the frame type specified for the adapter in the registry entry for the DLC protocol: HKEY_LOCAL_MACHINE\SYSTEM\CurrentControlSet\ Services\DLC\Parameters\AdapterName\UseDixOverEthernet. The default for UseDixOverEthernet is 0, resulting in an 802.3 frame.
1	Uses the frame type automatically determined by the DLC protocol during XID exchange.
2	Uses standard 802.3 format.
3	Uses 802.2 packets prefixed by DIX headers using EtherType value 0x80D5.

SDLC

To configure an SDLC link service, follow these steps:

1. Select the SDLC Link Service you want to install and configure from the list of Available Link Services. Click on the Install button to proceed.

2. If one or more dialog boxes appear, asking you to enter information for IRQ, DMA, and other settings for the specific communications adapter you have selected, complete the dialog boxes and click on the Continue button to proceed. Once these dialog

39

INSTALLING SNA SERVER

boxes have been completed, the SDLC Link Service Setup dialog box shown in Figure 39.7 will appear.

FIGURE 39.7.

The IBM SDLC Link Service Setup dialog box. The configuration for an IBM SDLC communications adapter is displayed.

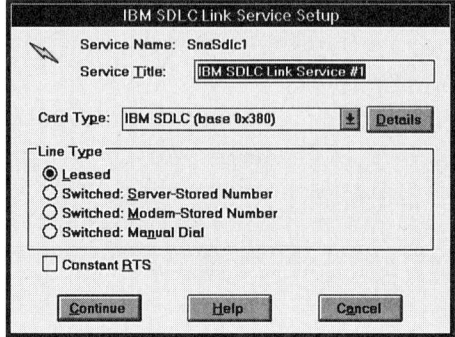

3. The default title for the SDLC Link Service is displayed in the Title edit box. This title can be modified if desired; up to 40 characters can be used to specify the title.

4. Depending on the communications adapter selected, the Card Type drop-down box may appear. Select the communications adapter card you will be using from this list.

> **TIP**
>
> If you are using an IBM SDLC adapter or an IBM MCPA adapter, and you need to use a transmission speed faster than 9600 baud, you must select half-duplex in the SNA Server Admin configuration. These adapter cards do not have a coprocessor and are unable to handle full-duplex at these higher baud rates.

5. Depending on the SDLC communications adapter you have selected, the Details or Adapter Details button will be visible. Consult the documentation specific to your communications adapter for information regarding changing specific settings for your card. Clicking on the Details or Adapter Details button will display the specific settings.

6. In the Line Type group box, you may select one of four different options for the telecommunications line that will be connected:

Line Type	Choose If
Leased	If you are using a leased line, select this option.
Switched: Server-Stored Number	If the communications adapter has a built-in serial (COM) port to which the synchronous modem attaches, select this option.

Switched: Modem-Stored Number   If the communications adapter can store a phone number and pass it along to the synchronous modem when the Data Terminal Ready (DTR) is raised, select this option.

Switched: Manual Dial   If the phone will be manually dialed when prompted by the SNA Server, select this option.

Server-Stored Numbers

If the Switched: Server-Stored Number line type is selected for the SDLC link service being installed, the synchronous modem must be set up so that the following are true:

- It will not dial when the DTR signal is raised.
- It will set Clear to Send (CTS) and Data Set Ready (DSR) to on when ready to accept dial commands.
- It will set DSR to off after accepting a dial command.
- It will set DSR to on again only when the dialed connection is made.
- It will change to synchronous mode after the dial-up has completed.
- It will change back to dial-command mode if Data Terminal Ready (DTR) is dropped and raised again.

A dialing attempt by the SNA Server will be assumed to have failed if the DSR stays on after the dial string has been sent or the connection time-out expires before DSR comes on to indicate that the call is connected.

7. Click on the Constant RTS checkbox, if Constant Request To Send (RTS) is required. Constant RTS puts the SDLC adapter in a state in which it is constantly ready to send data. This is required if a full-duplex line will be used. It cannot be used in a multidrop configuration. If Constant RTS is not used, the SDLC adapter must raise the RTS signal and wait for the remote end to raise the CTS (Clear To Send) signal before data can be sent. Keeping the RTS signal raised precludes this wait time.

NOTE

To achieve higher throughput, select the Constant RTS whenever possible. It is required on a full-duplex line. It cannot be selected in a multidrop configuration.

8. Depending on the SDLC communications adapter selected, other options may be displayed. Provide the necessary information by consulting the reference material provided with the SDLC adapter.

9. The Dialer Settings button may be displayed, depending on the SDLC communications adapter selected. If the Dialer Settings button is clicked, the following configuration settings may be provided:

COM Port: Select the COM port used by the SDLC adapter. If you are adding a new COM port, the Windows NT COM Port configuration dialog box is displayed. The range for the comport is None through 254. The default value is None.

Baud Rate: Select the transmission baud rate for the SDLC adapter. The range is 75 through 115200, with the default 9600.

Incoming String: Specify the string to be sent to the modem when an incoming call is detected. If the modem accepts standard AT commands, the default string AT&F&C1&S1&D3&Q1Q1S0=1 will be appropriate under most operating conditions.

Outgoing String: Specify the string to be sent to the modem when an outgoing call is detected. If the modem accepts standard AT commands, the default string AT&F&C1&S1&D3&Q1Q1S0=0DT will be appropriate under most operating conditions.

Modem Command Strings

When the SNA Server prepares to send a dial string to the modem, it utilizes the outgoing command string configured in the Dialer Settings dialog box. It appends the phone number to be dialed to this string. If the standard AT command set is used, the default outgoing command string is AT&F&C1&S1&D3&Q1Q1S0=0DT. This string will be appropriate under most operating conditions. The components of the command strings are described as follows:

AT: Standard modem command prefix

&F: Resets the modem to the factory defaults

&C1:   Causes the modem to track the status of the Carrier Detect (CD) line

&S1:   Causes the modem to raise the Data Set Ready (DSR) line after it has dialed

&D3:   Causes the modem to reset when the Data Transmit Ready (DTR) line drops

&Q1:   Causes the modem to come up in command mode and switch to synchronous mode when it has dialed (on some modems, this may be &M1 instead)

Q1:   Disables modem result codes

S0=0:   Disables auto-answer mode

DT: Causes the number following it to be dialed, using tone dialing (substitute DP for pulse dialing)

The incoming command string is used when an incoming call is detected. The default incoming command string is AT&F&C1&S1&D3&Q1Q1S0=1. The only difference from the default outgoing command string is the S0=1, which causes the modem to answer the phone after one ring.

10. Click on the Continue button to copy the necessary Link Service files. Once complete, the Link Service Configuration dialog box in Figure 39.8 is displayed, showing the new Link Service.

FIGURE 39.8.

The Link Service Configuration dialog box, showing the newly configured SDLC link service.

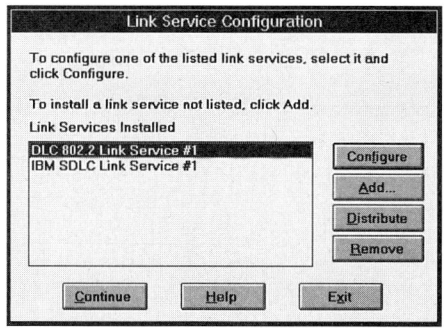

11. Additional link services can be added by clicking on the Add button. The highlighted Link Service can be reconfigured by clicking on the Configure button, or removed by clicking on the Remove button. (When removing a link service a Link Service Removal box will appear; click on Continue to remove the link service.)

12. To normally complete the SNA Server installation, click on the Continue button.

X.25

To configure an X.25 link service, follow these steps:

1. Select the X.25 Link Service you want to install and configure from the list of Available Link Services. Click on the Install button to proceed. The X.25 Link Service Setup dialog box will be displayed; if the IBM X.25 link service is selected, the IBM X.25 Link Service Setup dialog box shown in Figure 39.9 will be displayed.

FIGURE 39.9.

The IBM X.25 Link Service Setup dialog box.

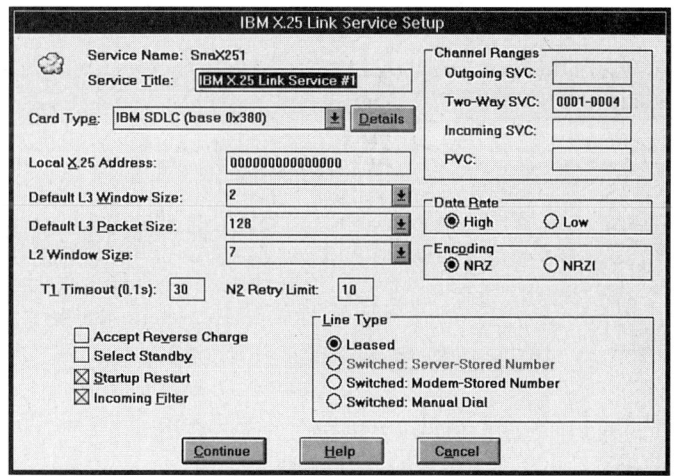

2. The default title for the IBM X.25 Link Service is displayed in the Title edit box. This title can be modified if desired; up to 40 characters can be used to specify the title.

39

INSTALLING SNA SERVER

3. Depending on the communications adapter selected, the Card Type drop-down box may appear. Select the communication adapter card you will be using from this list.

> **TIP**
>
> If you are using an IBM SDLC adapter or an IBM MCPA adapter and you need to use a transmission speed faster than 9600 baud, you must select half-duplex in the SNA Server Admin configuration. These adapter cards do not have a coprocessor, and are unable to handle full-duplex at these higher baud rates.

4. Depending on the X.25 communications adapter you have selected, the Details or Adapter Details button will be visible. Consult the documentation specific to your communications adapter for information regarding changing specific settings for your card. Clicking on the Details or Adapter Details button will display the specific settings.

5. Enter the Local X.25 Address in the corresponding edit box. A Local X.25 Address contains 15 decimal digits, with no spaces separating the digits. The ending 3 digits of the address are used for routing between stations with the same 12-digit address. No default value is provided.

6. Enter the Default L3 Window Size in the corresponding edit box. The default L3 window size specifies the maximum number of packets that can be sent or received before an acknowledgment is required. The window size only applies to a switched virtual circuit (SVC). The range is 1 through 7. The default value is 2.

7. Enter the Default L3 Packet Size in the corresponding edit box. The default L3 packet size is the maximum size of the data packets that can be sent or received. This value can be overridden in the User Data or Facility Data fields in the X.25 Setup dialog box in the SNA Server Admin. Packet sizes allowed are 64, 125, 256, 512. The default value is 128.

8. Enter the L2 Window Size in the corresponding edit box. The L2 window size specifies the number of frames that the SNA Server can send without waiting for acknowledgment. The range is 1 through 7. The default value is 7.

9. Enter the T1 Timeout in tenths of a second in the corresponding edit box. The T1 timeout specifies the amount of time the SNA Server should wait for the receiving station to respond to a transmission before resending. A time greater than needed for relaying frames between the SNA Server and the remote system should be specified. The range is 1 through 100 tenths of a second. The default value is 30.

10. Enter the N2 Retry Limit in the corresponding edit box. The N2 retry limit specifies the number of times to attempt to resend data. The range is 1 through 100. The default value is 10.

11. Select the Accept Reverse Charge checkbox if the SNA Server should accept an incoming call, if a reverse charge (the receiving end is charged for the call) is specified in the call packet. This option is turned off by default.

12. Select the Select Standby checkbox if the modem standby line should be set to on. The standby line (commonly a switched line) is sometimes included on lease line modems. The standby line serves as a backup if the primary leased line fails. This option is turned off by default.

13. Select the Startup Restart checkbox if a restart is necessary every time the link is activated. This option is turned on by default.

14. Select the Incoming Filter checkbox if X.25 addresses should be filtered out if they are not local. This option is turned on by default.

15. Enter the Outgoing SVC channels in the corresponding edit box. The Outgoing SVC is the range of channels on the switched virtual circuit (SVC) that is used for outgoing calls. The range of Outgoing SVC channels must follow the channel number rules listed next, and be greater than any PVC, Incoming SVC, or Two-Way SVC channels specified for this link. No default value is provided.

    When entering channel numbers in the X.25 Link Service Configuration dialog box, remember these rules:

    - Channel numbers must be from 1 through 4096.
    - The format of channel numbers is *n - n* (0008 - 00012 is a valid entry, for example).
    - For a particular Switched Virtual Circuit (SVC) or Permanent Virtual Circuit (PVC), there is no requirement for the number of channels used, but the total number of channels must be greater than 1 but less than 16.
    - The range of channel numbers must be unique for each type of circuit. There cannot be any overlap of channel numbers.
    - At least an Incoming SVC or Two-Way SVC channel is required to answer incoming calls.
    - If more than one type of channel needs to be configured, channel numbers should be assigned in ascending order. PVCs are not required to start at channel 1, but they must have the lowest value. Outgoing SVCs are not required to end at 4096, but they must have the highest value.
    - Channel ranges must match the X.25 carrier configuration.

16. Enter the Two-Way SVC channels in the corresponding edit box. The Two-Way SVC is the range of channels on the switched virtual (SV) circuit that is used for both incoming and outgoing calls. The range of Two-Way SVC channels must follow the channel number rules listed previously, be greater than any Incoming SVC, and less than any Outgoing SVC channels specified for this link. The default value is 0001 - 0004.

39

INSTALLING SNA
SERVER

17. Enter the Incoming SVC channels in the corresponding edit box. The Incoming SVC is the range of channels on the switched virtual circuit (SVC) that is used for incoming calls. The range of Incoming SVC channels must follow the channel number rules listed previously, be greater than any PVC, and less than any Two-Way SVC channels specified for this link. No default value is provided.

18. Enter PVC channels in the corresponding edit box. The PVC is the range of channels on the permanent virtual circuit (PVC) used by the server on the X.25 network. The range of PVC channels must follow the channel number rules listed previously and be less than any Incoming SVC, Two-way SVC, or Outgoing SVC channels specified for this link. No default value is provided.

19. Select the communications Data Rate in the corresponding selection box. This specifies the data rate between the modem and communications adapter if applicable. Select Low if low-quality data lines hamper communications.

20. Select the scheme for encoding when transmitting and receiving data. Both the local and remote system *must* use the same encoding scheme. Select NRC for NonReturn To Zero and NRZI for NonReturn to Zero Inverted.

21. In the Line Type group box, select one of four different options for the telecommunications line that will be connected:

    Leased: If you are using a leased line, select this option.

    Switched: Server-Stored Number. If the communications adapter has a built-in serial (COM) port to which the synchronous modem attaches, select this option. See the Server Stored numbers topic under the preceding Configuring the SDLC Link Adapter section for more information.

    Switched: Modem-Stored Number. If the communications adapter can store a phone number and pass it along to the synchronous modem when the Data Terminal Ready (DTR) is raised, select this option.

    Switched: Manual Dial. If the phone will be manually dialed when prompted by the SNA Server, select this option.

22. Depending on the X.25 communications adapter selected, other options may be displayed. Provide the necessary information by consulting the reference material provided with the X.25 adapter.

23. The Dialer Settings button may be displayed, depending on the SDLC communications adapter selected. If the Dialer Settings button is clicked, the following configuration settings may be provided:

    COM Port: Select the COM port used by the SDLC adapter. If you are adding a new COM port, the Windows NT COM Port configuration dialog box is displayed. The range for the comport is None through 254. The default value is None.

    Baud Rate: Select the transmission baud rate for the SDLC adapter. The range is 75 through 115200, with the default 9600.

Incoming String: Specify the string to be sent to the modem when an incoming call is detected. If the modem accepts standard AT commands, the default string AT&F&C1&S1&D3&Q1Q1S0=1 will be appropriate under most operating conditions. See the Modem Command Strings section in the preceding Configure the SDLC Link Adapter section for more information.

Outgoing String: Specify the string to be sent to the modem when an outgoing call is detected. If the modem accepts standard AT commands, the default string AT&F&C1&S1&D3&Q1Q1S0=0DT will be appropriate under most operating conditions. See the Modem Command Strings section in the preceding Configure the SDLC Link Adapter section for more information.

24. Click on the Continue button to copy the necessary Link Service files. Once complete, the Link Service Configuration dialog box in Figure 39.10 is displayed, showing the new Link Service.

FIGURE 39.10.

The Link Service Configuration dialog box, showing the newly configured X.25 link service.

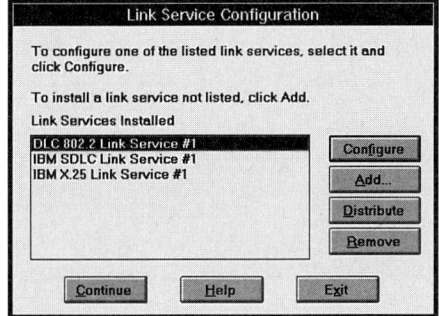

25. Additional link services can be added by clicking on the Add button. The highlighted Link Service can be reconfigured by clicking on the Configure button or removed by clicking on the Remove button. (When removing a link service, a Link Service Removal box will appear. Click on Continue to remove the link service.)

26. To normally complete the SNA Server installation, click on the Continue button.

DFT

To configure a DFT link service, follow these steps:

1. Select the DFT Link Service you want to install and configure from the list of Available Link Services. Click on the Install button to proceed. The DFT Link Service Setup dialog box will be displayed. If the IBM DFT link services is selected, the IBM DFT Link Service Setup dialog box shown in Figure 39.11 will be displayed.

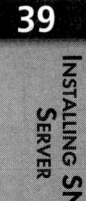

FIGURE 39.11.

The IBM DFT Link Service Configuration dialog box.

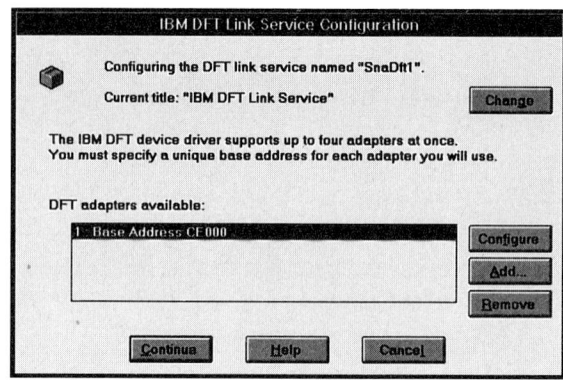

2. The default title for the IBM DFT Link Service is displayed. This title can be modified if desired; up to 40 characters can be used to specify the title by clicking on the Change button.

3. The default base address may be accepted. To change the default base address, click on the Configure button; the Adapter Base Address dialog box in Figure 39.12 will be displayed.

   Enter the new Base Address in the corresponding edit box and click on the Continue button to proceed. The address must be entered as a hexadecimal value, in the range A0000 to FF000.

FIGURE 39.12.

The Adapter Base Address dialog box.

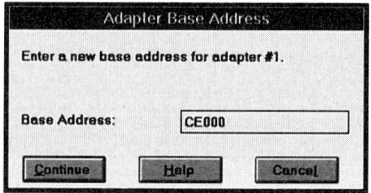

4. To add additional DFT adapter cards, click on the Add button. The Adapter Base Address dialog box in Figure 39.12 will again be displayed. Enter the new base address and click on Continue to save the new adapter address. Up to four adapter cards can be specified.

5. To remove a DFT adapter card, highlight the adapter address you want to remove in the DFT adapter available list and click on the Remove button.

6. Click on the Continue button to copy the necessary Link Service files. Once complete, the Link Service Configuration dialog box in Figure 39.13 is displayed, showing the new Link Service.

FIGURE 39.13.
The Link Service Configuration dialog box, showing the newly configured DFT link service.

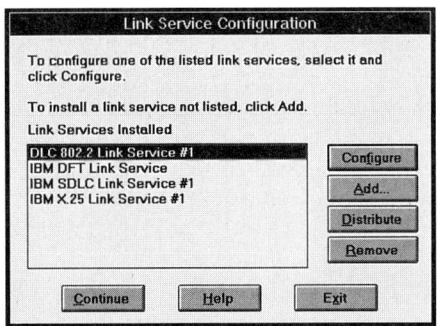

7. Additional link services can be added by clicking on the Add button. The highlighted Link Service can be reconfigured by clicking on the Configure button or removed by clicking on the Remove button. (When removing a link service, a Link Service Removal box will appear; click on Continue to remove the link service.)

8. To normally complete the SNA Server installation, click on the Continue button.

Finishing SNA Server Installation

After the SNA Server Setup is completed, the Finished dialog box in Figure 39.14 will appear. A number of configuration tasks still needs to be accomplished by using the SNA Server Admin application. The Admin application can be launched by clicking on the Admin button, or click on the Exit button to end the SNA Server Setup.

FIGURE 39.14.
The Microsoft SNA Server Setup Finished dialog box.

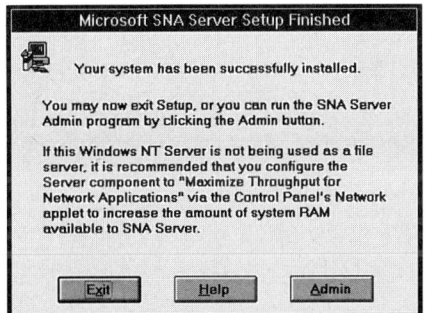

Using Setup After Installation

After installation is complete, the Server Role can be changed, link services can be linked or removed, a link service configuration can be modified, client-server protocol selections can be modified, or the SNA Server can be removed by accessing the SNA Server Setup application from the Microsoft SNA Server Program Manager group.

39

INSTALLING SNA SERVER

> **NOTE**
>
> Do not use the Network Option of the Windows NT Control Panel to remove Link Services drivers; this may cause unexpected system events. To correct such a situation, remove and reinstall the SNA Server, using SNA Server Setup.

Removing the SNA Server

The SNA Server can be removed at any time. It must be stopped if it is running before it is removed.

To remove the SNA Server, follow these steps:

1. Stop all the SNA Server components.
2. Run the SNA Server Setup application.
3. Click on the Continue button to display the Setup Options dialog box.
4. Click on the Remove button and confirm the removal of the SNA Server.

Changing the SNA Server Role

To change the server role, follow these steps:

1. Run the SNA Server Setup application.
2. Click on the Continue button to display the Setup Options dialog box.
3. Click on the Role button to display the SNA Server role dialog box. See the Server Role section earlier in the chapter for more information on changing the Server Role.

Adding Link Services

To add a Link Service, follow these steps:

1. Run the SNA Server Setup application.
2. Click on the Continue button to display the Setup Options dialog box.
3. Click on the Link button to display the Link Configuration dialog box. See the Configure Link Services section earlier in the chapter for more information on configuring link services.

Removing Link Services

To remove a Link Service, follow these steps:

1. Run the SNA Server Setup application.
2. Click on the Continue button to display the Setup Options dialog box.

3. Click on the Link button to display the Link Configuration dialog box. Highlight the link service to be removed and click on the Remove button. Confirm the Link Service Removal to complete the link removal.

Reconfiguring Link Services

To reconfigure a Link Service, follow these steps:

1. Run the SNA Server Setup application.
2. Click on the Continue button to display the Setup Options dialog box.
3. Click on the Link button to display the Link Configuration dialog box. Highlight the link service to be reconfigured and click on the Reconfigure button. See the Configure Link Services section earlier in the chapter for more information on configuring link services.

Changing Client-Server Protocols

To change client-server protocol selections, follow these steps:

1. Run the SNA Server Setup application.
2. Click on the Continue button to display the Setup Options dialog box.
3. Click on the Protocols button to display the Select Client Server Protocols dialog box. See the Select Client Server Protocols section earlier in the chapter for more information on changing the Client Server Protocols.

Issues and Cautions

Once SNA Server installation is complete, there are a few issues and cautions that should be considered. These include backing up your configuration files, what to do if you change the name of your server, how to automatically start the SNA Server at boot up, and how to maximize your Windows NT performance through configuration tuning. These issues are detailed in this section.

Backing Up Configuration Files

Once the SNA Server configuration is complete, and whenever a configuration change is made, the SNA Server configuration file should be backed up. The configuration file is stored on the Primary SNA Server. The configuration file COM.CFG is stored in the *{SNAROOT}* \SYSTEM\CONFIG (where *{SNAROOT}* is the installation directory specified) directory.

To back up the configuration file, in the SNA Admin application, choose the File menu option, and then choose Backup. All backup configuration files have an extension of SNA.

39

INSTALLING SNA
SERVER

Server Name Change

If the name of the Windows NT Server that the SNA Server is running on is changed, the SNA Server configuration file must be updated to reflect this change. To update the Windows NT Server name, in the SNA Admin application, select File menu option, then Server Properties. After changing the server name, save the updated configuration file.

Automatically Starting the SNA Server from the Control Panel

To automatically start the SNA Server when the Windows NT system is started, the SNA Server service must be set to run automatically. Use the Service application to change the SNA Server startup method to Automatic.

Windows NT Server Configuration

To optimize performance of the SNA Server, the Windows NT Server should be set to maximize throughput for network applications. This should only be done if the server is not also used as a file server. From the Network applet in Control Panel, select Server from the Installed Network Software list, click on the Configure button, select Maximize Throughput For Network Applications, then Click on Ok to save the new system configuration.

Configuration Tasks After Setup Is Complete

This section presents step-by-step procedures for client setup and modification.

Client Setup

Before you begin to use the SNA Server, client emulators need to be configured. When installing the client emulators supplied with the SNA Server, you need to supply certain information:

■ Whether the client workstation is in a local (the same domain as the SNA Server) or remote (a domain different from the SNA Server) domain. If the client is in a remote domain, one or two remote SNA Server names must be supplied.

■ When installing an MS-DOS, the network card interrupt must be supplied.

■ If the client is not using Named Pipes (Microsoft Networking), the domain name must be supplied. If the client is using Banyan VINES, the Banyan StreetTalk group name must be supplied.

Client installation can be performed over the network or by using floppy disks. To perform the client installation over the network, the client installation files should be placed in a shared directory on the server. To make the client installation files available on the network, follow these steps:

1. From the server you want to make the client installation files available from, create

and share a directory. See your Windows NT Server documentation for more information on creating and sharing a directory.

2. If your SNA Server installation is on a CD, continue with the next step. If your SNA Server installation disks are floppies, create another subdirectory, in the directory that you just created, for each client you need to install:

Client OS	Create This Subdirectory
Windows NT	winnt
Windows 95	win95
Windows 3.*x*	win3x
MS-DOS	msdos
OS/2	os2

Place your floppy disk in the appropriate drive. Type the corresponding command for the client you need to install (where *d:* is replaced with the appropriate floppy drive letter, *servername* is the name of your server, and *sharename* is the name of the directory you created in step 1). For each of the installation disks for that client, repeat the process of inserting the disk and typing the command:

Client OS	Command
Windows NT	xcopy *d:* *servername**sharename*\winnt /s /e
Windows 95	xcopy *d:* *servername**sharename*\win95/s /e
Windows 3.x	xcopy *d:* *servername**sharename*\win3x /s /e
MS-DOS	xcopy *d:* *servername**sharename*\msdos /s /e
OS/2	xcopy *d:* *servername**sharename*\os2 /s /e

3. If your SNA Server installation disk is on a CD, at the command prompt, type the following command, where *d:* is replaced with the appropriate CD drive letter, *servername* is the name of your server, and *sharename* is the name of the directory you created in step 1:

```
xcopy d:\clients \\servername\sharename /s /e
```

To create floppy installation disks from the SNA Server CD, follow these steps:

1. The correct number of formatted blank disks is required for each client:

Client OS	Number Of Disks Required
Windows NT	3
Windows 95	7
Windows 3.*x*	2
MS-DOS	2
OS/2	1

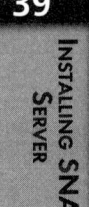

2. Place the SNA Server CD into the CD-ROM drive.

3. From the File Manager or command prompt, change to the CD drive.

4. Change to the \I386\DISKS directory on the CD if you are installing the Windows NT, Windows 3.*x*, MS-DOS, or OS/2 client.

5. Insert a floppy disk into the appropriate drive.

6. Copy all files and subdirectories from the appropriate directory on the CD to the floppy disk:

Client OS	Directories To Copy From
Windows NT	DISK1
Windows 3.*x*	WIN3X_1
MS-DOS	MSDOS_1
OS/2	OS2

7. For the following clients, repeat this process until all directories have been copied onto separate floppies:

Windows NT:	DISK2 and DISK3 directories
Windows 3.*x*:	WIN3X_2 directory
MS-DOS:	MSDOS_2 directory

To install the client applications on a Windows NT computer, follow these steps:

1. Access the shared client installation directory or place the client installation floppy in the floppy drive. Then run the command *d*:\setup (if you are installing from a floppy drive) or *d*:\winnt\setup (if you are installing from a network share), where *d*: is the drive letter of the appropriate drive. An introductory Setup dialog box will appear.

2. Click on the Continue button to proceed. If you are installing from floppy disks, the Server/Client Selection dialog box will appear; click on the Client button.

3. Accept or modify the default installation path, then click on Continue to proceed.

4. If more than one client-server protocol is detected, select one or several of the checkboxes for Microsoft Networking, Novell Netware, Banyan VINES, and TCP/IP. Unavailable protocols will be grayed out. Otherwise, proceed to step 6.

5. If Microsoft Networking was not selected, the Network Domain Name dialog box will appear. Type the domain name and click on Continue to proceed.

6. If the TCP/IP networking protocol is selected, the domain name can be specified in three different ways:

   ■ The domain name used in the Windows NT domain.

   ■ The host name with the TCP domain name—for example, drwho.gallifrey.com. If this form is used, the Domain Name System (DNS) resolver must be configured to map the name to an IP address.

   ■ The actual IP address—for example, 192.46.12.1.

7. If the BANYAN Vines protocol is selected, the StreetTalk Group Name dialog box is displayed. SNA Client Setup creates a StreetTalk name by combining information stored on the Banyan VINES network with information you type into the Setup dialog boxes. If you leave the Group Name entry blank, Setup uses the group name of the user currently logged on in the Banyan VINES network. You must ensure that the group name of the user logged on in the Banyan VINES network during installation of the SNA Server is always the same group name, regardless of whether client or server software is being installed.

8. Specify the client mode:

   Local: If the client is located in the same network domain as the Primary SNA Server (the server that contains the configuration file), click on the Continue button.

   Remote: If the client is *not* located in the same domain as the Primary SNA Server, click on the Remote button and click on the Continue button. In the Remote SNA Server Names dialog box, type the name of the Primary SNA Server in the Primary edit box. Optionally, type the name of a Backup SNA Server in the Backup edit box. Once the client is connected to an SNA Server, it automatically learns the names of all the other servers in the domain. Click on Continue to proceed.

   The Optional Administration Program dialog box will be displayed.

9. If you don't want to install the SNA Server Admin application, click on the Continue button. To install the SNA Server Admin application, select the Install Administration Program checkbox. Click on Continue to proceed.

10. The Review Settings dialog box will appear. Click on the Review button to review the configuration or the Continue button to begin file installation. If you are installing from floppy disks, insert the appropriate floppy disks as required.

11. When the Client Setup Finished dialog box appears, click on the Exit button to end.

To install the client applications on a Windows 95 computer, follow these steps:

1. Access the shared client installation directory, or place the client installation floppy in the floppy drive. Then run the command *d*:\setup (if you are installing from a floppy drive) or *d*:\winnt\setup (if you are installing from a network share), where *d*: is the drive letter of the appropriate drive. An introductory Setup dialog box will appear.

2. Click on the Continue button to proceed.

3. In the Name and Organization Information dialog box, enter your name and organization name. Click on OK to proceed, and OK again to confirm your name and organization name.

4. Click on Continue to accept the default folder for installation, or click on Change Folder to select a new folder for installation. Click on OK to proceed.

5. Click on the Complete button to install all client components and applications, or click on the Customized button to select which components and applications you

want to install. If you select Customized, place a checkmark by the components and applications you want to install, and then click on Continue to proceed.

6. Enter the name of the Program Group you want the applications to be installed into, or accept the default Program Group name.

7. Click on Yes to agree to the Licensing Agreement.

8. If more than one client-server protocol is detected, select one or several of the checkboxes for Microsoft Networking, Novell Netware, Banyan VINES, and TCP/IP. Unavailable protocols will be grayed out. Otherwise, proceed to step 10.

9. If Microsoft Networking was not selected, the Network Domain Name dialog box will appear. Type the domain name and click on Continue to proceed.

   If the TCP/IP networking protocol is selected, the domain name can be specified in three different ways:

   ■ The domain name used in the Windows NT domain.

   ■ The host name with the TCP domain name—for example, `drwho.gallifrey.com`. If this form is used, the Domain Name System (DNS) resolver must be configured to map the name to an IP address.

   ■ The actual IP address—for example, `192.46.12.1`.

   If the BANYAN Vines protocol is selected, the StreetTalk Group Name dialog box is displayed. SNA Server Setup creates a StreetTalk name by combining information stored on the Banyan VINES network with information you type into the Setup dialog boxes. If you leave the Group Name entry blank, Setup uses the group name of the user currently logged on in the Banyan VINES network. You must ensure that the group name of the user logged on in the Banyan VINES network during installation of the SNA Server is always the same group name, regardless of whether client or server software is being installed.

10. Specify the client mode:

    Local: If the client is located in the same network domain as the Primary SNA Server (the server that contains the configuration file), click on the Continue button.

    Remote: If the client is *not* located in the same domain as the Primary SNA Server, click on the Remote button and click on the Continue button. In the Remote SNA Server Names dialog box, type the name of the Primary SNA Server in the Primary edit box. Optionally, type the name of a Backup SNA Server in the Backup edit box. Once the client is connected to an SNA Server, it automatically learns the names of all the other servers in the domain. Click on Continue to proceed.

11. When the Windows 95 Client for the SNA Server Setup dialog box appears, click on the OK button to end.

To install the client applications on a Windows 3.*x* computer, follow these steps:

1. Access the shared client installation directory, or place the client installation floppy in the floppy drive. Then run the command *d*:\setup (if you are installing from a floppy drive) or *d*:\winnt\setup (if you are installing from a network share), where *d*: is the drive letter of the appropriate drive. An introductory Setup dialog box will appear.

2. Accept or modify the default installation path, then click on Continue to proceed.

3. If more than one client-server protocol is detected, select one or several of the checkboxes for Microsoft Networking, Novell Netware, Banyan VINES, and TCP/IP. Unavailable protocols will be grayed out. Otherwise, proceed to step 6.

4. If Microsoft Networking was not selected, the Network Domain Name dialog box will appear. Type the domain name and click on Continue to proceed.

   If the TCP/IP networking protocol is selected, the domain name can be specified in three different ways:

   ■ The domain name used in the Windows NT domain.

   ■ The host name with the TCP domain name—for example, drwho.gallifrey.com. If this form is used, the Domain Name System (DNS) resolver must be configured to map the name to an IP address.

   ■ The actual IP address—for example, 192.46.12.1.

5. If the BANYAN Vines protocol is selected, the StreetTalk Group Name dialog box is displayed. SNA Server Setup creates a StreetTalk name by combining information stored on the Banyan VINES network with information you type into the Setup dialog boxes. If you leave the Group Name entry blank, Setup uses the group name of the user currently logged on in the Banyan VINES network. You must ensure that the group name of the user logged on in the Banyan VINES network during installation of the SNA Server is always the same group name, regardless of whether client or server software is being installed.

6. Specify the client mode:

   Local: If the client is located in the same network domain as the Primary SNA Server (the server that contains the configuration file), click on the Continue button.

   Remote: If the client is *not* located in the same domain as the Primary SNA Server, click on the Remote button and click on the Continue button. In the Remote SNA Server Names dialog box, type the name of the Primary SNA Server in the Primary edit box. Optionally, type the name of a Backup SNA Server in the Backup edit box. Once the client is connected to an SNA Server, it automatically learns the names of all the other servers in the domain. Click on Continue to proceed.

7. Click on the Continue button to begin file installation. If you are installing from floppy disks, insert the appropriate floppy disks as required.

8. When the Client Setup Finished dialog box appears, click on the Exit button to end.

To install the client applications on an MS-DOS computer, follow these steps:

1. Access the shared client installation directory, or place the client installation floppy in the floppy drive. Then run the command *d*:\setup (if you are installing from a floppy drive) or *d*:\winnt\setup (if you are installing from a network share), where *d*: is the drive letter of the appropriate drive. An introductory screen will appear.

2. From the introductory screen, press Enter to proceed.

3. Accept or modify the Home Directory path and press Enter to proceed.

4. If more than one client-server protocol is detected, select one or several of the checkboxes for Microsoft Networking, Novell NetWare, and Banyan VINES. Otherwise, proceed to step 6.

5. If the BANYAN Vines protocol is selected, the StreetTalk Group Name dialog box is displayed. SNA Server Setup creates a StreetTalk name by combining information stored on the Banyan VINES network with information you type into the Setup dialog boxes. If you leave the Group Name entry blank, Setup uses the group name of the user currently logged on in the Banyan VINES network. You must ensure that the group name of the user logged on in the Banyan VINES network during installation of the SNA Server is always the same group name, regardless of whether client or server software is being installed.

6. Specify the location of the SNA servers in the domain:

   No Remote Operation: If this client is located in the same network domain as the Primary SNA server, select No Remote Operation, and press Enter to proceed.

   Remote Operation: If this client is not located in the same domain as the Primary SNA server, select Remote Operation and press Enter. In the Primary Remote Server screen, enter the name of the first SNA Server the client should attempt to connect to and press Enter to proceed. Optionally, in the Backup Remote Server Name screen, type the name of the second SNA server that the client should attempt to connect to. Once a connection to a server is established, the client learns all the other servers in the domain. Press Enter to proceed.

7. The Operating Environment screen appears next. To install the MS-DOS client, press Enter. To install the MS-DOS client for a Windows 3.*x* system, select the MS-DOS Client on a Windows 3.*x* system option and press Enter to proceed. An MS-DOS–based client can run as an MS-DOS application or as a character application under Windows 3.*x*. If Windows 3.*x* Enhanced Mode is running, the Background option must be enabled.

8. The LAN Adapter Interrupt Level screen is displayed. Select the correct interrupt value from the available list.

9. The Number of SNA Servers screen is displayed. Modify or accept the number of SNA Servers. Connecting to fewer servers reduces memory utilization.

10. The Backup Extension screen is displayed. Specify the file extension to be used when the SNA Server makes backup copies of AUTOEXEC.BAT and of any other INI files that may be changed. Press Enter to accept the default extension OLD or correct the extension and press Enter.

11. The Confirm Setup Execution screen is displayed. To review your selections, press Enter; otherwise, select Execute Setup and press Enter to proceed with file installation.

12. When file installation is complete, the Setup Completed Successfully screen appears; press Enter to end the installation.

13. Reboot your computer to complete the installation.

> **NOTE**
>
> If you are using a 5250 emulator on an APPC network, you may be required to install the SNA Server Router to allow the client to communicate through the SNA Server (using IPX/SPX, NetBEUI, or any other LAN/WAN protocol) instead of directly with the AS/400 (using DFT).

Modifying a Client

Once a client has been installed, you may need to modify setup options. For example, you may need to change the server the client tries to connect to first, or change the client operation from local to remote. Run the Setup application accordingly for the client platform. The Setup application first determines whether any components are already installed. You will be walked through the installation process as usual, and will be able to make any necessary changes.

Verifying Successful SNA Server Installation

The SNA Server provides the capability of setting up a demonstration link, to test and evaluate the SNA Server without the need for a live host or a specialized communications adapter. The demo link setup can also be used to verify a successful SNA Server installation. To install a 3270 Continuous Demo Link, follow these steps.

1. Using the steps outlined in the Using Setup After Installation section, install a new Link Service. The Link Service Configuration dialog box will be displayed. Click on Add to install a new link service.

2. From the Link Service Installation dialog box (shown in Figure 39.15), select the DEMO SDLC Link Service link and click on Install to install and configure this link.

39

INSTALLING SNA
SERVER

FIGURE 39.15.

*The Link Service
Configuration
dialog box.*

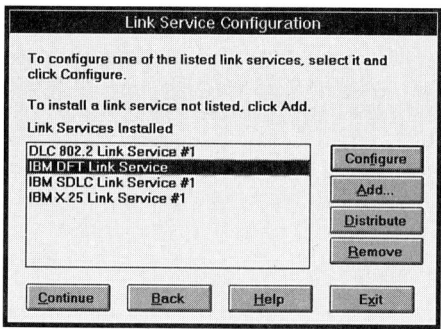

3. The DEMO SDLC Link Service Setup dialog box in Figure 39.16 will be displayed. Click on Add to install an additional link. Accept the default Service Title and make sure the script file 3270 Continuous Demo is selected in the script file combobox. This script will emulate the 3270 Flash test application. The Flash application continuously sends screens of data to the 3270 terminal emulator. Click on Continue to proceed with the Demo Link installation.

FIGURE 39.16.

*The DEMO SDLC
Link Service Setup
dialog box.*

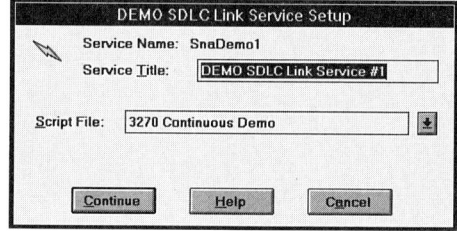

4. The Link Service Installation dialog box will again be displayed; click on Continue, and click on Continue again to complete the Link Service setup.

5. Click on the Admin button or click on the Exit button, and from the Program Manager, select and run the SNA Server Admin application. The SNA Server Admin application in Figure 39.17 will be displayed.

6. Select the Servers and Connections window.

7. Select the SDLC1 service.

8. Select Services, then Properties.

9. The Connection Properties dialog box in Figure 39.18 will be displayed. The Link Service should be SnaDemo1, the Remote end should be Host System, and Activation should be On Demand.

FIGURE 39.17.

The SNA Server Admin Application.

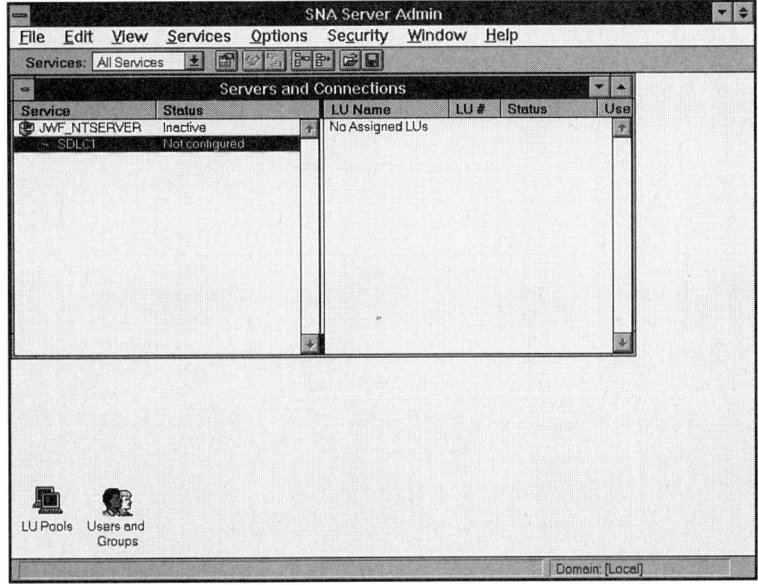

FIGURE 39.18.

The Connection Properties dialog box.

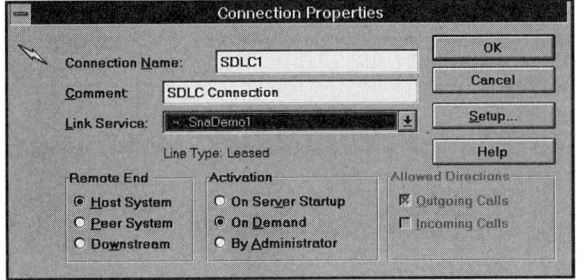

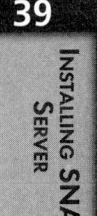

10. Click on the Setup button to display the SDLC Setup dialog box. Click on OK to close the SDLC Setup dialog box (these steps *must* be performed to configure the Demo Link) correctly.

11. Click on OK to close the Connection Properties dialog box.

12. Select the Servers and Connections windows again. Select the Services, Assign LUs menu items. You should see the Insert LU dialog box in Figure 39.19.

FIGURE 39.19.

The Insert LU dialog box.

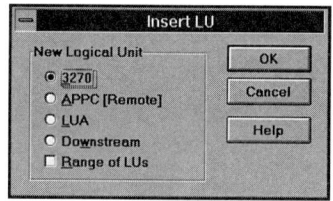

13. Select 3270 as the New Logical Unit. Click on OK to proceed.

14. The New 3270 LU Properties dialog box in Figure 39.20 will be displayed.

FIGURE 39.20.

The New 3270 LU Properties dialog box.

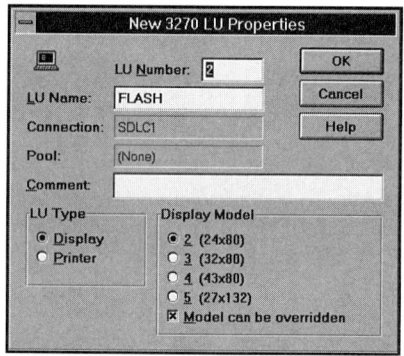

15. The LU Number must be 2. Enter FLASH for the LU Name. Select Display for the LU Type. Select Model 2 as the Display Model type. Click on OK to proceed.

16. Select the Users and Groups window.

17. Select the Users, New User menu items. The Add Users and Groups dialog box in Figure 39.21 will be displayed.

FIGURE 39.21.

The Add Users and Groups dialog box.

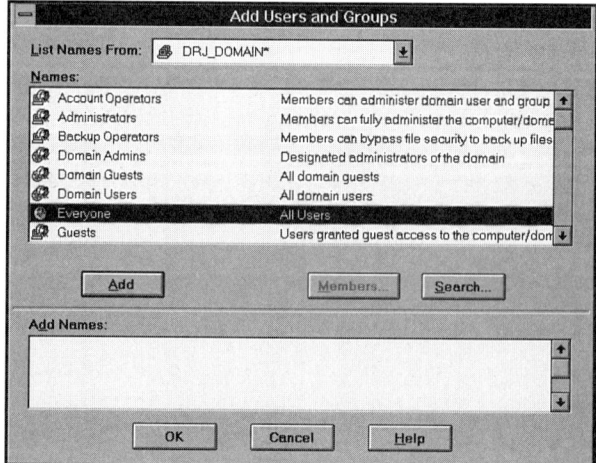

18. Select a user or group of users to assign rights to host LUs from this SNA Server—for example, select Everyone. Click on the Add button to Add the new user or group to the Add Names list. Click on OK to save your selection and proceed.

19. Highlight the new user or group and select the Users, Assign LUs menu items. The Assign User/LU Pool Sessions dialog box in Figure 39.22 is displayed.

FIGURE 39.22.

The Assign User LU/Pool Sessions dialog box.

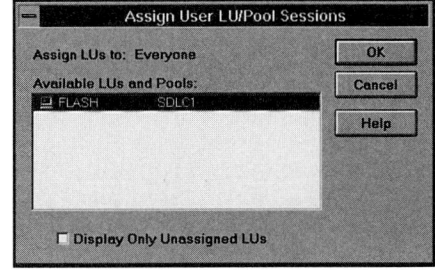

20. Select the available LU to assign to the selected user. Click on OK to close the Assign User/LU Pool Sessions dialog box.

21. Select the Services and Connections window. Select the Service, Start Services menu items.

22. Start the 3270 Applet from the Microsoft SNA Server group window.

23. Select the Session, Session Configuration menu items. Choose the FLASH session and click on OK to proceed.

24. Select the Session, Connect menu items. The host SSCP screen should appear. Type VM and press Enter. A host login screen will appear. Type USER for the userid and press the Tab key; type PASS for the password and press the Enter key. A VM ready prompt will be displayed; type FLASH and press Enter to begin the 3270 Continuous Demo.

25. Select the Session, Disconnect menu items to end the demo.

Summary

This chapter covered the planning and steps necessary to install the SNA Server and clients on multiple platforms. Once the SNA Server Setup is complete, the Admin application is used to configure Link Services, Connections, LUs and LU Pools, and Users. The Admin application is also used in the day-to-day management of the SNA Server.

39

INSTALLING SNA SERVER

Managing Your SNA Server Gateway

by Arthur Knowles

IN THIS CHAPTER

Managing your SNA Server gateway consists of three basic precepts: configuring and maintaining your network, configuring SNA Server, and troubleshooting. The first part deals with specifying your network transport protocols, configuring your routers to pass the appropriate network packets, and maintaining the rest of your physical network. These are readily understood functions of a network Administrator, however, and are not the focus of this chapter. Instead, this chapter is concerned primarily with configuring SNA Server with the SNA Server Administrator and performing basic troubleshooting with the SNA Trace utility.

> **NOTE**
>
> The actual name for the tool is really SNA Server Admin, which can be found in your Microsoft SNA Server Program Manager group. Rather than call it this, however, I prefer to call it the SNA Server Administrator because this more fully describes its function. For the rest of the chapter, this is how I refer to it.

Using SNA Server Administrator

The SNA Server Administrator is your primary interface to managing your SNA Server domains. The majority of this chapter focuses on how to use the SNA Server Administrator to perform the following tasks:

- Configuring the link services. Because the first thing you must do after installing SNA Server is configure a link service so that SNA Server can provide a connection to your SNA-compatible mainframe, it makes sense to start the discussion here as well.

- Managing users and groups. After you configure the link service, you need to specify who can use your SNA Server connection. This is where group and user management comes into play.

- Managing logical unit pools. An LU pool is a means of grouping several LUs into a single entity or pool that you can manage. If you are looking for additional means to improve response time, balance the load on SNA Server, and provide additional fault tolerance, then this section can help you achieve your goals.

- Managing SNA services, security, and SNA Administrator access. Managing the SNA Server services usually is limited to starting and stopping the various services involved. This chapter discusses these services, along with the means to automate the startup sequence, but the more important aspect is learning how to restrict access to the SNA Server Administration features. After all, you do not want to allow just anybody to play with your SNA Server installation.

Configuring a Link Service

The first time you open the SNA Server Administrator, it displays the Servers and Connections window, which lists only the servers, because you haven't created any connections yet (see Figure 40.1). A connection is the basic building block you use to define a linkage between your SNA-compatible mainframe and your SNA Server clients. This process is what the SNA Server Setup program describes as a link service and is what is discussed here. It is not really a difficult process if you have some help from your technical support personnel. If you do not have this help and do not know what addresses, node identification strings, or other salient reference numbers have been assigned for your use, then you can pretty much forget about a working SNA Server configuration. This means that you will need help from your mainframe MIS department and service provider for an X.25/QLLC connection in order to supply the required information.

FIGURE 40.1.

Administering your SNA Server domain with the SNA Server Administrator.

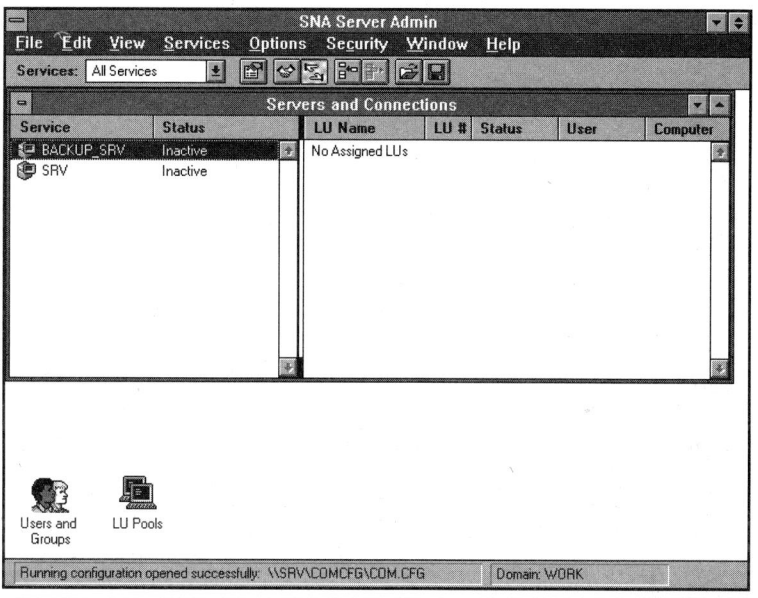

The idea of this discussion is to walk you through the actual process of creating a connection and assigning logical units so that you will understand what information you need to successfully complete your SNA Server configuration. This chapter begins with assigning the properties to your SNA Server that will be used for APPC or AS/400 connections. Then, you'll step through the process of creating connections. Finally, you'll learn how to assign logical units to a connection. Because this discussion includes all the various types of connections and logical units, you might want to skip the parts that do not concern you at this time.

Assigning Server Properties

If your SNA Server installation will be supporting incoming calls; advanced peer-to-peer communications (APPC), which also includes 5250 terminal emulation; or an AS/400 connection, then you must configure the server properties to identify your installation. This is accomplished by selecting the server in the Servers and Connections window and then choosing Services, Properties from the menu. The Server Properties dialog box appears, in which you can assign a comment, network name, and control point name (see Figure 40.2).

FIGURE 40.2.

Assigning server properties to uniquely identify your SNA Server installation.

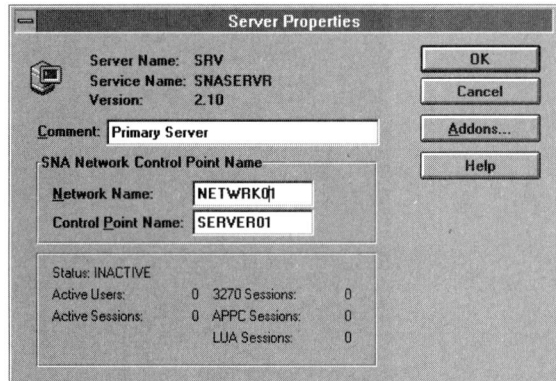

TIP

Alternatively, you can select the server and press Alt+Enter or just double-click on a server to display the Server Properties dialog box.

The comment can contain up to 25 characters, and is used to aid you in identifying your installation when you have more than one SNA Server in your domain. The network name and control point name are the identifiers, which uniquely identify your SNA Server installation on the network. These names are required only for systems using Format 3 XIDs, and define one point of the connection mechanism between SNA Server (the local node) and your SNA-compatible mainframe (the remote node). The remote node names are defined as you create your connections. These values should be supplied by your MIS department, and they vary, depending on how your server is connected to your mainframe.

For an AS/400, the values in the Server Properties dialog box follow:

- Network Name: This name will be the RMTNETID value on the AS/400.
- Control Point Name: This name will be the RMTCPNAME in the host controller description.

For a VTAM or NCP connection, you will use these values:

- Network Name: This name will be the NETID value in the VTAM Start command for the local SSCP. The SSCP is the VTAM connection where SNA Server is attached.

- Control Point Name: This name will be the CPNAME in the Physical Unit (PU) definition for the VTAM or Network Control Point (NCP).

NOTE

The network name and control point name can contain from one to eight alphanumeric characters. They can include the special characters $, #, and @. The first character must be alphabetic. All lowercase characters are converted to uppercase characters. You cannot use just one name; if you supply one of these names, you must supply both these names.

TIP

Click the Addons button to display the SNA Server Additions dialog box. By default, this dialog box includes only the SNA Server Trace options, which you can select to configure the Trace utility. If you have added any third-party software, however, you might be able to configure it here as well.

Creating a Connection

A connection can be considered as the means SNA Server uses to communicate with your SNA-compatible mainframe. It is not used directly by your SNA Server clients. Instead, your SNA Server clients use a logical unit (terminal) that has been assigned to a specific connection. Your clients do not need to know what type of connection they are using, but as the SNA Administrator, you do.

SNA Server supports six types of connections:

- A Data Link Control (DLC) 802.2 connection: This is a network-adapter-to-network-adapter connection that uses the DLC transport protocol. It can be used on Ethernet or token ring–based networks.

- A Distributed Function Terminal (DFT) connection: This type of connection is used to connect SNA Server to a 3270 control unit on your host SNA-compatible mainframe over a coaxial cable connection.

- A Synchronous Data Link Control (SDLC) connection: This is a modem-adapter-to-modem-adapter connection that uses the DLC transport protocol. It is a direct (SDLC-to-SDLC), low-speed connection that uses leased or switched phone lines to connect the two adapters.

40

MANAGING YOUR
SNA SERVER
GATEWAY

- An X.25/QLLC connection: This is a packet-switching-network-adapter-to-packet-switching-network-adapter connection that uses the Qualified Logical Link Control protocol. It is most commonly used to provide low-speed interstate or international connections through a host packet-switched network. Its primary usefulness stems from local access numbers to a packet-based connection point, which then can be used to connect to your mainframe.

- A Channel connection: This type of connection is used to directly connect to a channel attachment on your SNA-compatible mainframe.

- A TwinAx connection: This type of connection is used to directly connect to your AS/400 mainframe over a TwinAx connection.

SNA Server has some limitations that you should be aware of that may determine how many SNA Server installations you require and how many adapters per server you need to meet your requirements. Table 40.1 summarizes these limitations.

Table 40.1. SNA server connection and session limitations.

Software/ Hardware	Total Connections	Total Sessions	Note
SNA Server	250	10,000	This includes a maximum of 2,000 clients. A single downstream connection is equivalent to a single client when determining the total number of clients per SNA Server installation.
802.2	250	254	
DFT	1	5	Although you can use up to four DFT adapters in a single system, they must all be controlled by a single link service. This can provide you with up to four connections with 20 sessions.
SDLC	1	254	
X.25/QLLC	250	254	If your adapter does not include a coprocessor, you cannot support a duplex transmission with a DTE speed higher than 9600bps.
Channel	250	254	
TwinAx	1	20	

NOTE

The total number of sessions applies to 3270, LUA, and dependent APPC LU-LU sessions. For independent APPC LU sessions, the maximum is 10,000 sessions.

NOTE

You cannot use multiple 802.2, X.25/QLLC, or channel adapters to increase the number of supported connections.

To create a new connection, follow these steps:

1. Select the server where you want the connection to be created in the Servers and Connections window. Then choose New Connection from the Services menu or use the shortcut key F2. The Insert Connection dialog box appears.

2. Select the connection to create. This can be 802.2, SDLC, DFT, X.25, Channel, or TwinAx. Then click the OK button.

3. In the Connection Properties dialog box, enter the relevant information for your connection type, as described in the following sections.

4. Click the OK button to accept the connection definition or press Cancel to abort.

NOTE

The following sections assume that you have already made your choice in the Connection Details dialog box and that the Connection Properties dialog box for your connection type is active.

Creating a DLC 802.2 Connection

Creating a DLC 802.2 connection consists of three parts: defining the connection, assigning the basic settings for the connection, and assigning the advanced settings for the connection. To define the connection, follow these steps:

1. When the Connection Properties dialog box appears, enter a name for the connection in the Connection Name field (see Figure 40.3). The connection name can be from one to eight alphanumeric characters. The name can include the special characters $, #, and @. All lowercase characters are converted to uppercase characters. The name must be unique and cannot be the reserved name SNASERVR.

40

MANAGING YOUR
SNA SERVER
GATEWAY

FIGURE 40.3.

Assigning connection properties for an 802.2 connection.

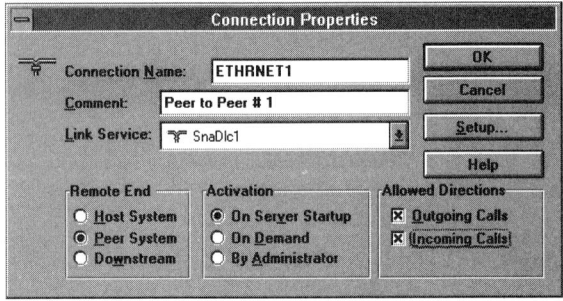

2. In the Comment field, enter a description for the connection. The description can be a maximum of 25 characters.

3. In the Link Service field, choose the service the connection will use to communicate with an SNA adapter.

> **NOTE**
>
> If no entry is available, you need to use the SNA Server Setup program to install a link service.

4. In the Remote End section, choose the type of remote system for the connection to use. This can be one of the following:

   ■ Host System: This type of remote system is usually a mainframe that controls all interactions between the mainframe and any clients that connect to it. This type should be used for dependent APPC, 3270, and LUA logical units.

   ■ Peer System: This type of remote system usually is used for mainframes, minicomputers, and clients that communicate with each other as equal partners (independent APPC). The most common reason to use this type is for an AS/400 connection or when setting up a peer-to-peer connection to be used with Systems Management Server.

   ■ Downstream: This type of remote system is used by clients, such as the IBM Communications Manager/2, that do not support the SNA Server client-server interface, but that still can access host connections provided by SNA Server.

> **NOTE**
>
> When using a Downstream type, be sure to configure the Max BTU setting, as described later in this section, to a value supported by the downstream client.

5. Choose an entry in the Activation section to specify when to make the connection available. This can be one of the following:

   ■ On Server Startup: Specifies that the connection will be activated (made available to clients) when SNA Server starts.

   ■ On Demand: Specifies that the connection will be activated on an as-required basis and deactivated when no longer required.

   ■ By Administrator: Specifies that an Administrator must manually activate or deactivate a connection. This option only applies to outgoing connections. If a connection has been configured to accept incoming calls, the connection begins to listen to calls as soon as SNA Server starts.

6. Next, choose the type of connection support to implement in the Allowed Directions section. This can be Incoming Calls, Outgoing Calls, or both. The default is Outgoing Calls.

7. You now have defined the connection, but you are not finished yet. At this point, you must click the Setup button to configure the basic properties for the connection. This displays the 802.2 Setup dialog box, as shown in Figure 40.4.

FIGURE 40.4.

Configuring the basic properties for an 802.2 connection.

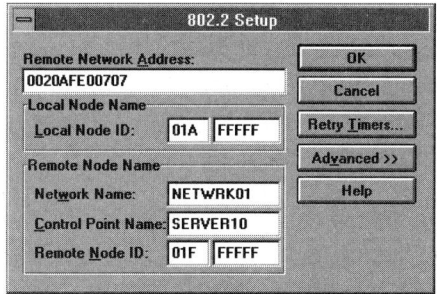

You can configure the following fields in the 802.2 Setup dialog box:

   ■ Remote Network Address: This 12-digit hexadecimal address specifies the network address of the remote (the system to which you will connect) host, peer, or downstream system. This is one of those times when you need to contact your MIS department in order to find out the correct address. To aid you in this effort, here are a few tips that might help you in identifying your requirements:

   For a connection to a 3174, you can use the `configuration response 900` value in the customization program.

   For a connection to a 3720, 3725, or 3745 front-end processor (FEP), you can use the MACADDR= value in the NCP configuration.

For a connection to an IBM 3970 mainframe, you can use the MACADDR= value in the VTAM PORT definition.

For a connection to another SNA Server installation, use the network adapter address. This can be determined by executing the NET CONFIG SERVER command from a command prompt and using the 12-digit value in the Server Is Active On entry.

> **TIP**
>
> If the server on which SNA Server is installed uses DHCP, then another way to find the network address is to use the DHCP Manager. Just select the primary server and then choose Scope, Active Leases. Then, in the Active Leases dialog box, select the server in the Client field and click the Properties button. The network address will be listed in the Unique Identifier field.

- Local Node ID: This is an eight-digit hexadecimal that uniquely defines the local system to the remote system. The first three digits are commonly referred to as the block number, and the final five digits are referred to as the node number. Here are a couple of rules for their usage:

    The first three digits cannot be 000 or FFF, because these are reserved values.

    In order for a remote or downstream connection to use this connection, you must inform the local Administrator of your local node identifier.

    In order to use a host connection, you must use the IDBLK value for the block number and the IDNUM value for the node number in the VTAM PU definition.

    The same local node identifier must be used for all connections on your SNA Server installation.

- Network Name: If connecting to a host system that uses a remote network name, this entry should be the NETID value in the VTAM start command for the local SSCP (the VTAM connection where SNA Server is attached). If connecting to an AS/400, this value will be the Network Name of the AS/400 (the RMTNETID value on the AS/400).

- Control Point Name: If connecting to a host system using a remote control point name, this value will be the SSCPNAME value in the VTAM start command of the remote SSCP. For an AS/400, enter the name of the AS/400.

- Remote Node ID: This entry is a unique identifier of the remote node. It must be supplied by your MIS department for a host connection or by the local Administrator for a downstream connection. The first three digits cannot be 000 or FFF because these are reserved values.

> **NOTE**
>
> The network name and control point name can be from one to eight alphanumeric characters. They can include the special characters $, #, and @. The first character must be alphabetic. All lowercase characters are converted to uppercase characters. You cannot use just one name; if you supply one of these names, you must supply both these names.

8. To specify how often to retry a connection operation, click the Retry Timers button. This displays a dialog box in which you can specify the following choices:

   ■ Maximum Number of Attempts: Specifies how many times SNA Server will attempt to make a connection. When the maximum value is reached, an entry is made into the event log, and no further attempts are made to connect. The range is from 1 to no limit, and the default is no limit.

   ■ Delay After Failed Attempts: Specifies how long to wait, in seconds, between connection attempts. The range is from 5 to 255, with a default of 10.

9. If required, you can configure additional characteristics for the connection by clicking the Advanced button. This expands the dialog box to offer you the following fields:

   ■ XID Type: Specifies the type of identifying information SNA Server will send. A Format 0 XID sends only the node ID and should be used only for systems that do not support a Format 3 XID. A Format 3 XID sends up to 100 bytes of identifying information, including the local node ID and control point name.

> **NOTE**
>
> If you will be using independent APPC LUs on the connection, you must specify a Format 3 XID.

   ■ Remote SAP Address: Specifies the remote system access point (SAP) address. This is a two-digit hexadecimal value in multiples of four. The default value of 04 should suffice for most installations. If you will be using a 3174 controller for your connection, however, this value should be the same as the `configuration response 900` of the controller's customization program. Or, if you will be using an IBM 9370 host, use the value in the SAPADDR= value specified in the VTAM PU definition.

   ■ Retry Limit: Determines how many times the local system will resend a frame when no response from the remote system is received. The range is from 0 to 255, with a default of 10.

■ Max BTU Length: Defines the size of the basic transmission unit (BTU), also referred to as an I-frame, that can be sent in a single Data Link Control (DLC) frame. The range is from 265 to 16393, and the default is determined by your adapter.

> **NOTE**
>
> The maximum BTU length should be less than the MAXDATA= value in the VTAM PU definition for a host connection. For a 4Mb token ring adapter, the value should be equal to or less than 4195; for a 16Mb token ring adapter, the value should be equal to or less than 16393; and for an Ethernet adapter, the value should be equal to or less than 1493.

■ XID Retries: Specifies how often the local system should resend an identifier (XID) message when no response is received from the remote system. The range is from 0 to 30, with a default of 3.

■ Response (t1) Timeout: Specifies the time that the local system will wait for a response from a remote system before retransmitting. The value specified should be greater than the total time it takes for the data to be relayed between the local system, the remote system, and the network.

> **TIP**
>
> If you choose the default value for Response Timeout, the system maintains two separate time-out values: one for a remote system on the local network and the other for a remote system on a remote network. If you do not use the default value, the value you choose is used both for local and remote networks. The default for a local network is 400 milliseconds and 2 seconds for a remote network.

■ Receive ACK (t2) Timeout: Specifies the maximum time a local system can delay before sending an acknowledgment to the remote system. The value specified should be less than the response time-out so that the system takes less time to acknowledge a received transmission than it requires to seek a response to a transmission.

> **TIP**
>
> If you choose the default value for Receive ACK Timeout, the system maintains two separate time-out values: one for a remote system on the local network and the other for a remote system on a remote network. If you do not use the default value, the value you choose is used both for local and remote networks. The default for a local network is 80 milliseconds, and the default for a remote network is 800 milliseconds.

- Inactivity (ti) Timeout: Specifies the maximum time a link can be inactive before SNA Server assumes that the link is malfunctioning and deactivates it.

> **TIP**
>
> If you choose the default value for Inactivity Timeout, the system maintains two separate time-out values: one for a remote system on the local network and one for a remote system on a remote network. If you do not use the default value, the value you choose is used both for local and remote networks. The default for a local network is 5 seconds, and the default for a remote network is 25 seconds.

- Receive ACK Threshold: Determines the maximum number of frames that can be received before the local system must send a response. The value ranges from 1 to 127, with a default of 2.
- Unacknowledged Send Limit: This entry, often referred to as the window send size, specifies the maximum number of frames the local system can send without receiving an acknowledgment from the remote system. The range is from 1 to 127, with a default of 8.

> **TIP**
>
> Receive ACK Threshold should be less than Unacknowledged Send Limit so that the local system acknowledges received transmissions more frequently than it requires responses from the remote system to sent transmissions.

> **TIP**
>
> If you increase Unacknowledged Send Limit and Receive ACK Threshold, you may achieve greater throughput. You should attempt this only on connections with low error conditions, however, or you may actually decrease throughput.

10. Click the OK button to accept your connection definition.

Creating a DFT Connection

Creating a DFT connection is much easier than creating some other types of connections. All it requires is the basic definition, which can be accomplished by following these steps:

40

MANAGING YOUR
SNA SERVER
GATEWAY

1. When the Connection Properties dialog box is displayed, enter a name for the connection in the Connection Name field. The connection name can be from one to eight alphanumeric characters. The name can include the special characters $, #, and @. All lowercase characters are converted to uppercase characters. The name must be unique, and cannot be the reserved name SNASERVR.

2. In the Comment field, enter a description for the connection. The description can be a maximum of 25 characters.

3. In the Link Service drop-down list, choose the service the connection will use to communicate with an SNA adapter.

> **NOTE**
>
> Even though you can use up to four DFT adapters, you must use only one link service for all of them. If no entry is available, you need to use the SNA Server Setup program to install a link service.

4. Specify when to make the connection available by choosing an entry in the Activation section. This can be one of the following:

   - On Server Startup: Specifies that the connection will be activated (made available to clients) when SNA Server starts.

   - On Demand: Specifies that the connection will be activated on an as-required basis and then deactivated when no longer required.

   - By Administrator: Specifies that an Administrator must manually activate or deactivate a connection. This option applies only to outgoing connections. If a connection has been configured to accept incoming calls, then the connection begins to listen to calls as soon as SNA Server starts.

> **NOTE**
>
> The Remote End section is preset to Host System, and the Allowed Directions section is preset to Outgoing Calls.

5. Click the OK button to accept your connection definition.

Creating an SDLC Connection

Creating an SDLC connection also consists of three parts: the first defines the connection, the second assigns the basic settings, and the third assigns the advanced settings for the connection. To create your SDLC connection, follow these steps:

1. When the Connection Properties dialog box is displayed, enter a name for the connection in the Connection Name field. The connection name can be from one to eight alphanumeric characters. The name can include the special characters $, #, and @. All lowercase characters are converted to uppercase characters. The name must be unique and cannot be the reserved name SNASERVR.

2. In the Comment field, enter a description for the connection. The description can be a maximum of 25 characters.

3. In the Link Service drop-down listbox, choose the service the connection will use to communicate with an SNA adapter.

> **NOTE**
>
> If no entry is available, you need to use the SNA Server Setup program to install a link service.

4. In the Remote End section, choose the type of remote system the connection will use. This can be one of the following:

   - Host System: This type of remote system is usually a mainframe that controls all interactions between the mainframe and any clients that connect to it. This type should be used for dependent APPC, 3270, and LUA logical units.

   - Peer System: This type of remote system is usually used for mainframes, minicomputers, and clients that communicate with each other as equal partners (independent APPC). The most common reason to use this type is for an AS/400 connection or for a peer-to-peer connection for Systems Management Server.

   - Downstream: This type of remote system is used by clients, such as the IBM Communications Manager/2, that do not support the SNA Server client-server interface, but that can still access host connections provided by SNA Server.

> **NOTE**
>
> When using a Downstream system type, be sure to configure the Max BTU setting, as described later in this section, to a value supported by the downstream client.

5. Specify when to make the connection available, by choosing an entry in the Activation group. This can be one of the following:

- On Server Startup: Specifies that the connection will be activated (made available to clients) when SNA Server starts. This is a good choice for connections that use a leased line.

- On Demand: Specifies that the connection will be activated on an as-required basis and then deactivated when no longer required. This is a good choice for connections that use switched lines.

- By Administrator: Specifies that an Administrator must manually activate or deactivate a connection. This option applies only to outgoing connections. If a connection has been configured to accept incoming calls, the connection begins to listen to calls as soon as SNA Server starts.

6. Next, choose the type of connection support to implement in the Allowed Directions group. This can be Incoming Calls, Outgoing Calls, or both. The default is Outgoing Calls.

> **NOTE**
>
> When using multiple SDLC connections for incoming calls, all these connections must use the same encoding (NRZ or NRZI) setting. A DFT connection can be configured only for outgoing calls.

7. At this point, you have defined the connection; however, before you can use the connection, you must click the Setup button to configure the basic properties for the connection. This displays the SDLC Setup dialog box, and if you choose the Advanced button (as you have here) the dialog box expands, as shown in Figure 40.5.

FIGURE 40.5.

Configuring the basic and advanced properties for an SDLC connection.

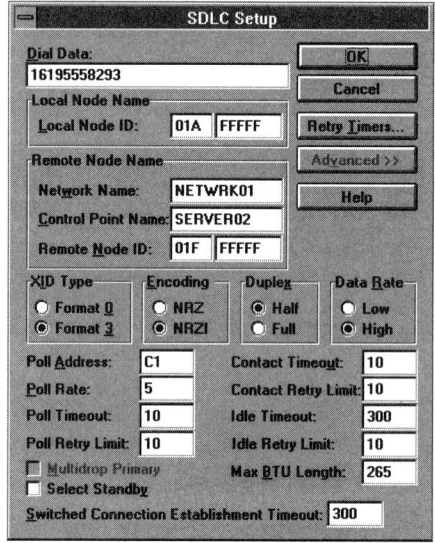

You can configure the following fields in this expanded SDLC Setup dialog box:

■ Dial Data: Specifies a phone number, from 1 to 40 digits, that will be used for SDLC adapters on a switched phone line.

> **NOTE**
>
> If the SDLC adapter has a built-in communications port, the number is a phone number that is sent directly to the adapter. If the adapter is configured for a manually dialed number, the number entered here is specified in the pop-up message box that appears whenever the adapter is used for an outgoing call.

■ Local Node ID: This is an eight-digit hexadecimal that uniquely defines the local system to the remote system. The first three digits are commonly referred to as the block number, and the final five digits are referred to as the node number. Here are a couple of rules for their usage:

The first three digits cannot be 000 or FFF, because these are reserved values.

In order for a remote or downstream connection to use this connection, you must inform the local Administrator of your local node identifier.

In order to use a host connection, you must use the IDBLK value for the block number and the IDNUM value for the node number in the VTAM PU definition.

The same local node identifier must be used for all connections on your SNA Server installation.

■ Network Name: If connecting to a host system that uses a remote network name, this entry should be the NETID value in the VTAM Start command for the local SSCP (the VTAM connection where SNA Server is attached). If connecting to an AS/400, this value is the Network Name of the AS/400 (the RMTNETID value on the AS/400).

■ Control Point Name: If connecting to a host system using a remote control point name, this value is the SSCPNAME value in the VTAM Start command of the remote SSCP. For an AS/400, enter the name of the AS/400.

■ Remote Node ID: This entry is a unique identifier of the remote node. It must be supplied by your MIS department for a host connection or by the local Administrator for a downstream connection. The first three digits cannot be 000 or FFF, because these are reserved values.

NOTE

The network name and control point name can be from one to eight alphanumeric characters. They can include the special characters $, #, and @. The first character must be alphabetic. All lowercase characters are converted to uppercase characters. You cannot use just one name; if you supply one of these names, you must supply both these names.

- XID Type: Specifies the type of identifying information that SNA Server will send. A Format 0 XID sends only the node ID and should be used only for systems that do not support a Format 3 XID. A Format 3 XID sends up to 100 bytes of identifying information, including the local node ID and the control point name.

NOTE

If you will be using independent APPC LUs on the connection, you must specify a Format 3 XID.

- Encoding: Specifies the encoding scheme the modem will use. This can be NRZ (Nonreturn to Zero) or NRZI (Nonreturn to Zero Inverted). The default is NRZI.

NOTE

Both modems (the local and remote modems) must use the same encoding schemes. For connection to a host system, the encoding scheme is specified in the LINE/GROUP definition in VTAM. This value should be specified by your MIS Administrator.

- Duplex: This entry is based on your modem configuration. It will be Half or Full, depending on the feature set of your modem. You should refer to your SDLC adapter documentation to determine whether it supports half or full duplex.

NOTE

If Full is specified, then your SDLC configuration must have the Constant RTS option set.

TIP

If your adapter lacks a coprocessor and you want to use a transmission speed higher than 9600bps, choose Half.

- Data Rate: This entry specifies the rate at which SNA Server can communicate with the SDLC adapter. You should refer to your adapter documentation to determine whether it supports a high data rate for optimum performance. If you have communications problems, then choose the low setting.

NOTE

The Data Rate option can be considered as the DTE rate when compared to a modem. And just like a modem, the maximum DTE rate is determined based on your UART. Even though the UART can handle higher data rates (19200bps for an 8250, 38400bps for a 16450, and 57600bps–115200bps for a 16550), if you specify a rate that is too high for your processor to handle, you will encounter data errors (dropouts), which will require retransmissions.

- Poll Address: This two-digit hexadecimal address should be supplied by your MIS Administrator for a host connection. It will be the ADDR= value of the VTAM definition. For a peer connection, this value can be anything but the reserved values 00 and FF, because these peers will negotiate an acceptable value.
- Poll Rate: For peer or downstream services, this value determines the pool rate. The default is 5, with a range of 1 to 50.
- Poll Timeout: For a peer or downstream connection, this value specifies the time, in tenths of a second, for the local system to pause before polling again. The range is from 1 to 300, with a default of 10.

CAUTION

If you set the Poll Timeout value too low, it may cause link failures.

- Poll Retry Limit: For a peer or downstream connection, this entry determines how many times the local system will poll the remote system when no response is received. The range is from 1 to 255, with a default of 10.
- Contact Timeout: Specifies the time, in tenths of a second, that the local system will pause between connection attempts. The range is from 5 to 300, with a default of 10.

40

MANAGING YOUR
SNA SERVER
GATEWAY

> **NOTE**
>
> The Contact Timeout value is not used for incoming calls.

- Contact Retry Limit: Specifies how many times the local system should attempt to make a connection to the remote system. The default is 10, with a range of 1 to 10.

> **NOTE**
>
> The Contact Retry Limit value is not used for incoming calls.

- Idle Timeout: For a host or peer connection, this entry specifies the time, in tenths of a second, that the local system will wait for a response from the remote system before resending the data. The range is from 1 to 300, with a default of 10.

> **NOTE**
>
> If the Idle Timeout value is too small, you may experience link failures.

- Idle Retry Limit: For a host or peer connection, this value determines the number of times the local system will attempt to send data to a remote system if no response is received. The range is from 1 to 255, with a default of 10.
- Max BTU Length: Defines the size of the basic transmission unit (BTU), also referred to as an I-frame, that can be sent in a single Data Link Control (DLC) frame. The range is from 265 to 16393, and the default is 265 for an SDLC connection.

> **NOTE**
>
> The maximum BTU length should be less than the MAXDATA= value in the VTAM PU definition for a host connection. For a downstream service, this value should be equal to or less than the maximum value supported by the downstream service. For specific values, you should refer to your documentation or just use the default value.

- Multidrop Primary: If you are using a leased SDLC line to a downstream connection and the local system is the primary station for a multidrop connection, this option should be enabled.

- Select Standby: If your modem supports a standby line (refer to your documentation if you are unsure) and it is enabled, this option should be enabled as well. The default is disabled.

- Switched Connection Establishment Timeout: If you are using a switched SDLC line, this value defines the maximum time, in seconds, to wait for a connection to be established. The range is from 10 to 500, with a default of 300.

8. To specify how often to retry a connection operation, click the Retry Timers button. This displays a dialog box where you can specify the following choices:

    - Maximum Number of Attempts: Specifies how many times SNA Server will attempt to make a connection. When the maximum value is reached, an entry is made into the event log, and no further attempts are made to connect. The range is from 1 to no limit, and the default is no limit.

    - Delay After Failed Attempts: Specifies how long to wait, in seconds, between connection attempts. The range is from 5 to 255, with a default of 10.

9. Click the OK button to accept your connection definition.

Creating an X.25/QLLC Connection

Creating an X.25/QLLC connection is similar to creating an SDLC connection because it also consists of three parts: defining the connection, assigning the basic settings, and assigning the advanced settings for the connection. To create an X.25/QLLC connection, follow these steps:

1. When the Connection Properties dialog box is displayed, enter a name for the connection in the Connection Name field. The connection name can be from one to eight alphanumeric characters. The name can include the special characters $, #, and @. All lowercase characters are converted to uppercase characters. The name must be unique and cannot be the reserved name SNASERVR.

2. In the Comment field, enter a description for the connection. The description can be a maximum of 25 characters.

3. In the Link Service drop-down listbox, choose the service the connection will use to communicate with an SNA adapter.

40

MANAGING YOUR
SNA SERVER
GATEWAY

> **NOTE**
>
> If no entry is available, you need to use the SNA Server Setup program to install a link service.

4. Choose the type of remote system the connection will use in the Remote End group. This can be one of the following:

   ■ Host System: This type of remote system is usually a mainframe that controls all interactions between the mainframe and any clients that connect to it. This type should be used for dependent APPC, 3270, and LUA logical units.

   ■ Peer System: This type of remote system is usually used for mainframes, minicomputers, and clients that communicate with each other as equal partners (independent APPC). The most common reason to use this type is for an AS/400 connection or for a peer-to-peer connection for Systems Management Server.

   ■ Downstream: This type of remote system is used by clients, such as the IBM Communications Manager/2, that do not support the SNA Server client-server interface, but that can still access host connections provided by SNA Server.

> **NOTE**
>
> When using a downstream system type, be sure to configure the Max BTU setting, as described later in this section, to a value supported by the downstream client.

5. Specify when to make the connection available, by choosing an entry in the Activation group. This can be one of the following:

   ■ On Server Startup: Specifies that the connection will be activated (made available to clients) when SNA Server starts. This is a good choice for connections that use a leased line.

   ■ On Demand: Specifies that the connection will be activated on an as-required basis and then deactivated when no longer required. This is a good choice for connections that use switched lines.

   ■ By Administrator: Specifies that an Administrator must manually activate or deactivate a connection. This option applies only to outgoing connections. If a connection has been configured to accept incoming calls, then the connection begins to listen to calls as soon as SNA Server starts.

6. Choose the type of connection support to implement in the Allowed Directions group. This can be Incoming Calls, Outgoing Calls, or both. The default is Outgoing Calls.

7. Select the type of virtual circuit that will be used in the Virtual Circuit Type field. This can be one of the following:

   ■ Switched (SVC): This type of virtual circuit is the default, and is called and cleared dynamically rather than being constantly active. A destination address is supplied when the circuit is called.

   ■ Permanent (PVC): This type of virtual circuit is constantly active with a preset destination address.

8. At this point, you have defined the connection; however, before you can use the connection, you must click the Setup button to configure the basic properties for the connection. This displays the X.25 Setup dialog box, and if you click the Advanced button, the dialog box expands.

   You can configure the following fields in the expanded X.25 Setup dialog box:

   ■ Remote X.25 Address: This entry consists of from 12 to 15 hexadecimal digits (the final three digits are used for routing between installations with the same first 12-digit address) and should be specified by the Administrator of the remote system. If you are connecting to a host using VTAM, the DIALNO= parameter in the VTAM PORT definition should be used.

   ■ Local Node ID: This is an eight-digit hexadecimal that uniquely defines the local system to the remote system. The first three digits commonly are referred to as the block number, and the final five digits are referred to as the node number. Here are a couple of rules for their usage:

   The first three digits cannot be 000 or FFF, because these are reserved values.

   In order for a remote or downstream connection to use this connection, you must inform the local Administrator of your local node identifier.

   In order to use a host connection, you must use the IDBLK value for the block number and the IDNUM value for the node number in the VTAM PU definition.

   The same local node identifier must be used for all connections on your SNA Server installation.

   ■ Network Name: If connecting to a host system that uses a remote network name, this entry should be the NETID value in the VTAM `start` command for the local SSCP (the VTAM connection where SNA Server is attached). If connecting to an AS/400, this value is the network name of the AS/400 (the RMTNETID value on the AS/400).

■ Control Point Name: If you are connecting to a host system using a remote control point name, this value is the SSCPNAME value in the VTAM start command of the remote SSCP. For an AS/400, enter the name of the AS/400.

■ Remote Node ID: This entry is a unique identifier of the remote node. It must be supplied by your MIS department for a host connection or by the local Administrator for a downstream connection. The first three digits cannot be 000 or FFF, because these are reserved values.

NOTE

The network name and control point name can be from one to eight alphanumeric characters. They can include the special characters $, #, and @. The first character must be alphabetic. All lowercase characters are converted to uppercase characters. You cannot use just one name; if you supply one of these names, you must supply both these names.

■ XID Type: Specifies the type of identifying information that SNA Server will send. A Format 0 XID only sends the node ID and should be used only for systems that do not support a Format 3 XID. A Format 3 XID sends up to 100 bytes of identifying information, including the local node ID and control point name.

NOTE

If you will be using independent APPC LUs on the connection, you must specify a Format 3 XID.

■ Max BTU Length: Defines the size of the basic transmission unit (BTU), also referred to as an I-frame, that can be sent in a single Data Link Control (DLC) frame. The range is from 265 to 16393, and the default is 1033 for an X.25/QLLC connection.

NOTE

The maximum BTU length should be less than the MAXDATA= value in the VTAM PU definition for a host connection. For a downstream service, this value should be equal to or less than the maximum value supported by the downstream service. For specific values, you should refer to your documentation or just use the default value.

- PVC Alias: Specifies the PVC channel. The range is from 1 to the configured number of channels. The default is 1.
- Packet Size: For a PVC, this entry specifies the maximum number of data bytes to be sent in a frame. The range is 64 to 1024 in 64-unit increments with a default of 128. This entry should be specified by your network service provider.
- Window Size: For a PVC, this entry specifies the maximum number of frames that can be sent without receiving a response from the remote system. This entry should be obtained from the Administrator of the remote system.
- Facility Data: For an SVC, this entry specifies the codes for any facility data required by your network service provider or Administrator of the remote system. The data can be a maximum of 126 hexadecimal characters (63 hexadecimal bytes) in length.

NOTE

Facility data is a coded string that is used primarily to request nonstandard functions from your X.25 network.

- User Data: For an SVC, this entry specifies the codes for any user data required by your network service provider. It can be a maximum of 32 characters and must be an even number of characters.

NOTE

User data is a coded string used primarily to specify the protocol to be used. For SNA, this value must be C3, which specifies the QLLC protocol.

9. To specify how often to retry a connection operation, click the Retry Timers button. This displays a dialog box where you can specify the following choices:
   - Maximum Number of Attempts: Specifies how many times SNA Server will attempt to make a connection. When the maximum value is reached, an entry is made into the event log, and no further attempts are made to connect. The range is from 1 to no limit, and the default is no limit.
   - Delay After Failed Attempts: Specifies how long to wait, in seconds, between connection attempts. The range is from 5 to 255, with a default of 10.
10. Click the OK button to accept your connection definition.

Creating a Channel Connection

Creating a channel connection also consists of three parts, but there is less information to supply. The first part follows the standard to define the connection, the second assigns the basic settings, and the third assigns the advanced settings for the connection.

To define the connection, follow these steps:

1. When the Connection Properties dialog box is displayed, enter a name for the connection in the Connection Name field. The connection name can be from one to eight alphanumeric characters. The name can include the special characters $, #, and @. All lowercase characters are converted to uppercase characters. The name must be unique and cannot be the reserved name SNASERVR.

2. In the Comment field, enter a description for the connection. The description can be a maximum of 25 characters.

3. In the Link Service drop-down listbox, choose the service the connection will use to communicate with an SNA adapter.

> **NOTE**
>
> If no entry is available, you need to use the SNA Server Setup program to install a link service.

4. Specify when to make the connection available, by choosing an entry in the Activation group. This can be one of the following:

   - On Server Startup: Specifies that the connection will be activated (made available to clients) when SNA Server starts. This is the preferred setting for a channel attachment.

   - On Demand: Specifies that the connection will be activated on an as-required basis and then deactivated when no longer required.

   - By Administrator: Specifies that an Administrator must manually activate or deactivate a connection. This option only applies to outgoing connections. If a connection has been configured to accept incoming calls, then the connection begins to listen to calls as soon as SNA Server starts.

> **NOTE**
>
> The remote system will be preset to Host System, and the Allowed Directions group will be preset to Outgoing Calls.

5. At this point, you have defined the connection; however, before you can use the connection, you must click the Setup button to configure the basic properties for the connection. This displays the Channel Attached Setup dialog box, and if you click the Advanced button (as you have here) the dialog box expands, as shown in Figure 40.6.

FIGURE 40.6.

Configuring the basic and advanced properties for a channel connection.

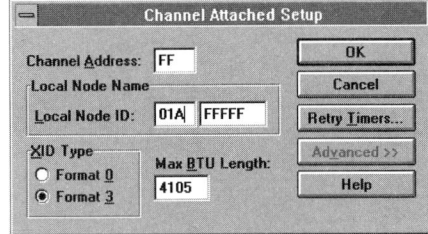

You can configure the following fields in this dialog box:

- Channel Address: This hexadecimal entry uniquely identifies the channel. The range is from 00 to FF, with a default of FF.

- Local Node ID: This is an eight-digit hexadecimal that uniquely defines the local system to the remote system. The first three digits commonly are referred to as the block number, and the final five digits are referred to as the node number. Here are a couple of rules for their usage:

  The first three digits cannot be 000 or FFF, because these are reserved values.

  In order for a remote or downstream connection to use this connection, you must inform the local Administrator of your local node identifier.

  In order to use a host connection, you must use the IDBLK value for the block number and the IDNUM value for the node number in the VTAM PU definition.

  The same local node identifier must be used for all connections on your SNA Server installation.

- XID Type: Specifies the type of identifying information SNA Server will send. Format 0 XID sends only the node ID and should be used only for systems that do not support a Format 3 XID. Format 3 XID sends up to 100 bytes of identifying information, including the local node ID and control point name.

NOTE

If you will be using independent APPC LUs on the connection, you must specify Format 3 XID.

■ Max BTU Length: Defines the size of the basic transmission unit (BTU), also referred to as an I-frame, that can be sent in a single Data Link Control (DLC) frame. The range is from 265 to 16393, and the default is 4105 for a channel connection.

> **NOTE**
>
> The maximum BTU length should be less than the MAXDATA= value in the VTAM PU definition for a host connection. For a downstream service, this value should be equal to or less than the maximum value supported by the downstream service. For specific values, you should refer to your documentation or just use the default value.

6. To specify how often to retry a connection operation, click the Retry Timers button to display a dialog box where you can specify the following choices:

   ■ Maximum Number of Attempts: Specifies how many times SNA Server will attempt to make a connection. When the maximum value is reached, an entry is made into the event log and no further attempts are made to connect. The range is from 1 to no limit, and the default is no limit.

   ■ Delay After Failed Attempts: Specifies how long to wait, in seconds, between connection attempts. The range is from 5 to 255, with a default of 10.

7. Click the OK button to accept your connection definition.

Creating a TwinAx Connection

Creating a TwinAx connection is just like creating a DFT connection in that it requires only the basic definition. You can accomplish this by following these steps:

1. When the Connection Properties dialog box is displayed, enter a name for the connection in the Connection Name field. The connection name can be from one to eight alphanumeric characters. The name can include the special characters $, #, and @. All lowercase characters are converted to uppercase characters. The name must be unique and cannot be the reserved name SNASERVR.

2. In the Comment field, enter a description for the connection. The description can be a maximum of 25 characters.

3. In the Link Service drop-down listbox, choose the service the connection will use to communicate with an SNA adapter.

> **NOTE**
>
> If no entry is available, you need to use the SNA Server Setup program to install a link service.

4. Specify when to make the connection available, by choosing an entry in the Activation group. This can be one of the following:

   ■ On Server Startup: Specifies that the connection will be activated (made available to clients) when SNA Server starts. This is the preferred choice for a TwinAx connection.

   ■ On Demand: Specifies that the connection will be activated on an as-required basis and then deactivated when no longer required.

   ■ By Administrator: Specifies that an Administrator must manually activate or deactivate a connection. This option applies only to outgoing connections. If a connection has been configured to accept incoming calls, the connection begins to listen to calls as soon as SNA Server starts.

> **NOTE**
>
> The remote system is preset to Peer System, and the Allowed Directions group is preset to Outgoing Calls.

5. Click the OK button to accept your connection definition.

Assigning a Logical Unit (LU) to a Connection

Before your clients can actually connect to your SNA-compatible mainframe, you must assign the logical units (LUs) to a connection. This is performed by selecting the connection in the Servers and Connections window and then choosing Services, Assign LU. The Insert LU dialog box appears, where you can select from one of the following:

   ■ 3270: Supports users of 3270 emulation software to access an SNA-compatible mainframe. You can define the LU to support a 3270 terminal or a compatible printer.

   ■ APPC (Remote): Supports advanced program-to-program communications (transaction program (TP) to transaction program (TP) communications), which use the LU 6.2 protocol. It is most frequently used to support SNA-to-SNA communications or 5250 terminal emulation.

   ■ LUA: Supports Logical Unit Application (LUA) client-to-host communications.

   ■ Downstream: Supports applications that do not support the SNA Server client server interface, but that still can access host services provided by SNA Server.

After you select the appropriate LU type and click the OK button, a New LU Properties dialog box is displayed, where you can define the LU. Each LU has a slightly different dialog box, which is described in the following sections.

40

MANAGING YOUR
SNA SERVER
GATEWAY

Creating a 3270 Logical Unit (LU)

To create a 3270 LU, fill out the following fields in the New 3270 LU Properties dialog box:

- For a DFT connection, enter the number for the DFT adapter that will be used in the Port Number field. This value can range from 1 to 4.

- For a DFT connection, enter the logical terminal number, as specified in the 3174 FEP, in the LT Number field. This value can range from 1 to 5 and most likely will require help from your MIS Administrator to determine.

- For a DLC 802.2, SDLC, or X.25/QLLC connection, enter a number in the LU Number field to identify the LU. This number should be assigned by the MIS Administrator. It should match the LOCADDR= parameter in the VTAM or NCP Gen on the host system. This value can range from 1 to 254.

- Specify a unique name for the logical unit in the LU Name field. The name can be from one to eight alphanumeric characters. The name can include the special characters $, #, and @. All lowercase characters are converted to uppercase characters.

- Specify a description for the LU in the Comment field. This entry can be a maximum of 25 characters.

- Choose the type of LU in the LU Type field. This will be 3270 for a 3270 terminal emulation, or printer for printer emulation.

- If this LU is a 3270 terminal emulation, choose the default display mode in the Display Model field. If you want to allow your users to choose a different display model, enable the Model Can Be Overridden checkbox.

- Click the OK button.

TIP

If you have several 3270 LUs to create, you can use a shortcut. Along with selecting the 3270 entry in the Insert LU dialog box, enable the Range of LUs checkbox. Then, in the Add LU Range dialog box, enter a name in the Base LU Name field (such as TERM), the starting number in the First LU Number field (01, for example), and the total number of LUs to create in the Number of LUs field (10, for example).

Then click the OK button. This displays the 3270 LU Range Properties dialog box, where you should specify a description for the LUs in the Comment field, choose an LU type, and—if the LU type is a 3270 terminal emulation—choose a display mode as well. After you click the OK button, several LUs are created on the selected connection (in this example, these are TERM01 through TERM09).

Creating an Advanced Program-to-Program (APPC) Logical Unit (LU)

There are two types of APPC LUs you can create: an independent APPC LU, which can communicate directly with a peer system and support multiple parallel sessions, or a dependent APPC LU, which requires the support of a host configuration in order to communicate with a transaction program. When creating an APPC LU, keep in mind that you have to create a local and a remote APPC in order to create a link between two transaction programs. The local APPC is created on a server, and the remote APPC is created on a connection.

You should follow a couple of rules for a successful configuration.

For an independent APPC LU, follow these rules:

- If your local system will be communicating with a host system transaction program, the host system must use VTAM version 3, release 2, or higher. The host also must use NCP version 5, release 3, or higher. The LOCADDR= parameter should be set to 0 in the VTAM, NCP, and CIS parameters on the host system.
- You must use Format 3 XIDs.

For a dependent APPC LU, follow these rules:

- The connection should be configured with a remote end of host, rather than a peer.
- If using a version of VTAM earlier than version 3, this is the only type of APPC LU you can use to communicate with transaction programs on the host system.
- The host system should have the LOCADDR= parameter set to 1 or greater in the NCP Gen.

To create a local APPC LU, fill out the following fields in the New APPC LU Properties dialog box:

- First, determine whether you will create a dependent or independent LU in the LU 6.2 type field.

> **NOTE**
>
> If you will be using a remote APPC LU on a DFT connection, you must configure the local APPC LU for a dependent connection.

- Enter a name in the LU Alias field that will be used by local transaction program (TP) applications. The name can be from one to eight characters and can include the special characters %, $, #, and @. The name must be unique on the connection and cannot match an LU on the server.
- Enter the name in the Network Name field. The name can be from one to eight alphanumeric characters. They can include the special characters $, #, and @. The first character must be alphabetic. All lowercase characters are converted to uppercase characters.

NOTE

This name should be obtained from the Administrator of the host or peer APPC LU. For a host connection, the name should be the NETID value in the VTAM Start command for the VTAM system. If the server will communicate with several hosts over several connections, use the subarea name.

NOTE

For an independent APPC LU, the network name is required. For a dependent APPC LU, the network name is not required, but is recommended, because it is used only by local applications.

■ Enter a name in the LU Name field to identify the LU. The name can be from one to eight alphanumeric characters. They can include the special characters $, #, and @. The first character must be alphabetic. All lowercase characters are converted to uppercase characters.

■ Enter a number in the LU Number field if this APPC LU will be a dependent APPC LU. This number should be obtained from your host system Administrator and is usually the LOCADDR= value in the LU definition in VTAM or NCP. The range is from 1 to 254.

■ Enter a description for the APPC LU in the Comment field.

■ To enable automatic partnering of APPC LU, set the Enable Automatic Partnering checkbox. This creates LU-LU pairs for all APPC LUs that have the automatic partnering option enabled.

NOTE

To specify partners manually, click the Partners button and add the specific partners to create your LU-LU pairs.

■ If you want to specify a default LU for use by transaction programs that do not specify a local LU, enable the Member of Default Outgoing Local APPC LU Pool checkbox.

■ To specify a default remote APPC LU to be used by transaction programs that specify a local LU that SNA Server does not recognize, select it from the Implicit Incoming Remote LU listbox.

■ To specify the number of seconds SNA Server waits for an invokable transaction program to respond to a start request, enter a value in the Timeout for Starting Invokable TPs field. This value can range from 1 to 3600, with a default of 60.

■ Click the OK button.

To create a remote APPC LU, fill out the following fields in the New APPC LU Properties dialog box:

■ Enter a name in the LU Alias field that will be used by local transaction program (TP) applications. The name can be from one to eight characters and can include the special characters %, $, #, and @. The name must be unique on the connection and cannot match an LU on the server.

■ Enter the name of the server in the Network Name field. The name can be from one to eight alphanumeric characters. They can include the special characters $, #, and @. The first character must be alphabetic. All lowercase characters are converted to uppercase characters.

■ Enter a name in the LU Name field that identifies the APPC LU. The name can be from one to eight characters and can include the special characters %, $, #, and @. The name must be unique on the connection and cannot match an LU on the server, although it can match the LU Alias name.

■ If the APPC LU will be used for a dependent APPC LU, enter a name in the Uninterpreted LU Name field for the remote LU. Generally, this name is the name of the remote LU on the host system, as defined in the SSCP (such as TSO). The name can include the special characters ., #, @, and $.

■ Enter a description for the APPC LU in the Comment field.

■ If the APPC LU will be used for an independent APPC LU, enable the Supports Parallel Sessions checkbox. If the APPC LU will be used for a dependent APPC LU, clear the checkbox.

■ To enable automatic partnering of APPC LU, set the Enable Automatic Partnering checkbox. This will create LU-LU pairs for all APPC LUs that have the automatic partnering option enabled.

> **NOTE**
>
> To specify partners manually, click the Partners button and add the specific partners to create your LU-LU pairs.

- Choose a mode from the Implicit Incoming Mode listbox to preselect a default mode for sessions from remote APPC LUs that specify a mode not understood by SNA Server. This can be one of the following:

  #BATCH: A batch session.

  #BATCHSC: A batch session that uses minimal security.

  BLANK: A session that uses a default mode name specified as eight blank characters in EBCDIC format in BIND.

  #INTER: An interactive session.

  #INTERSC: An interactive session with minimal security.

  QPCSUPP: A session with an AS/400 minicomputer.

- To modify the security for the APPC LU, click the Security button. Then you can specify one of the following:

  No Session Level Security: The default, which requires no security key.

  Security Key in Hex: A maximum of 16 hexadecimal characters.

  Security Key in Characters: A maximum of eight characters. The key can include the special characters ., #, @, and $.

NOTE

If you specify a security key, the session will not be activated unless both APPC LUs have keys that match.

- Click the OK button.

Creating a Logical Unit Application (LUA)

To create an LUA LU, fill out the following fields in the New LUA Properties dialog box:

- Enter a number in the LU Number field if this APPC LU will be a dependent APPC LU. This number should be obtained from your host system Administrator and is usually the LOCADDR= value in the LU definition in VTAM or NCP. The range is from 1 to 254.

- Enter a name in the LU Name field to identify the LU. The name can be from one to eight alphanumeric characters. They can include the special characters $, #, and @. The first character must be alphabetic. All lowercase characters are converted to uppercase characters.

- Enter a description for the LU in the Comment field.

- Enable the High Priority LU checkbox to give this LU higher precedence over lower priority LUs.
- Click the OK button.

Creating a Downstream Logical Unit (LU)

To create a downstream LU, fill out the following fields in the New Downstream LU Properties dialog box:

- Enter a number in the LU Number field if this APPC LU will be a dependent APPC LU. This number should be obtained from your host system Administrator and is usually the LOCADDR= value in the LU definition in VTAM or NCP. The range is from 1 to 254.
- Enter a name in the LU Name field to identify the LU. The name can be from one to eight alphanumeric characters. They can include the special characters $, #, and @. The first character must be alphabetic. All lowercase characters will be converted to uppercase characters.
- Enter a description for the LU in the Comment field.
- Click the OK button.

Managing Your Users

Before your users can actually use a connection or logical unit, they must be granted permission to do so. This can be accomplished at the group level or at the user level. As with most other issues relating to security, this is much easier to perform at the group level. The basic series of steps follows:

- Use User Manager for Domains to create a new group. In actuality, you will want to create several groups. You might want to segment these groups by department boundaries or specific hardware (such as terminals and printers). As usual, you can create both local and global groups to make your management tasks easier.
- Use User Manager for Domains to create new user accounts as required.
- Use User Manager for Domains to assign your users to the appropriate groups.
- Finally, use SNA Server Administrator to assign users or groups to logical units.

This last step is the focus of this discussion, and you will be happy to know that it follows the same basic principles as assigning permissions to any other object (such as a directory or file).

The basic steps follow:

1. Open the Users and Groups window.
2. Choose New User from the Users menu to display the Add Users and Groups dialog box.

3. If the default domain, which is where the current SNA Server installation resides, is not the domain in which the group or user accounts reside, choose another from the List Names From field.

4. In the Names field, select the groups or users and click the Add button.

5. Click the OK button. This adds the groups or users to the Users and Groups window in the left window.

6. Select the group or user and choose Assign LUs from the Users menu to display the Assign User LU/Pool Sessions dialog box.

7. In the Available LU and Pools field, select the LUs and pools to assign to the account and click the OK button.

NOTE

Before you can assign permission to an LU or LU pool, you must create one. Creating an LU is discussed in the previous sections, and creating an LU pool is discussed in the following section.

Using Logical Unit (LU) Pools

An LU pool is a collection of logical units grouped into a single entity. It is similar to a group account in that it contains multiple user accounts grouped into a single entity. Both offer easier management of resources, but LU pools offer additional benefits as well:

- Efficient resource management: Most installations find that not every user is accessing the same resource at the same time. So it is possible to support 50 users with only 25 LUs if you group all the LUs into a single pool and assign all 50 users to this LU pool. As long as you do not have more than 25 simultaneous users, you'll never run out of LUs.

- Fault tolerance: An LU pool can contain LUs from more than one SNA Server. As long as one server is available with LUs in this pool, your users can continue to access them without interruption. This can be very useful when you need to perform maintenance or in case of a server failure.

- Load balancing: You can use an LU pool to balance the load on a particular server, which increases perceived user performance. When you use an LU pool with LUs from multiple servers, the individual load is balanced among these servers based on the number of connected users.

You can create a 3270 terminal/printer, LUA, or downstream pool by opening the LU Pools window and then choosing Pools, New Pool to display the New Pool dialog box. Then enter a unique name for the pool in the Pool Name field, enter a description in the Comment field, and choose the type of pool to create in the LU Type field. If you specified 3270 for the LU type, choose a display mode in the 3270 Display Mode field. Then just click the OK button.

After you create the pool, you have to assign logical units to it. Select the pool and choose Pools, Assign LUs to display the Assign Pool LUs dialog box. This is just a matter of selecting the individual LUs in the Available LUs field and clicking the OK button to assign the LUs to the pool.

> **TIP**
>
> Don't forget that before your users can actually use the LU pool, you must assign the appropriate permissions, as described in the preceding section.

By default, the SNA Server Services are configured to be inactive at system startup. This means that before your users can use an LU, you have to start the appropriate server or individual connection. This is accomplished by choosing the server or connection in the Servers and Connections window and choosing Services, Start Service. Stopping a server or connection follows the same methodology, but you should choose Services, Stop Service instead.

Any connection configured with On Server Startup activation will be automatically activated when you start the appropriate server. Connections that use the On Demand activation setting are activated as required when a user attempts a connection. Any connection configured with the By Administrator activation requires manually starting or stopping the connection, as specified earlier.

> **TIP**
>
> You can provide additional fault tolerance and ease of administration by configuring SNA Server to start up when NT Server starts. Just set the SnaServer service to automatic, rather than manual, in the Control Panel Services applet. You can do the same for the NVAlert and NVRunCmd (NetView Alert and Run Command services). Do not configure the SnaNtMn service to Automatic, however, or it will fail to start. SNA Server automatically starts this service for any connection that is configured to use it.

Configuring SNA Administrator

Configuring SNA Server consists of only two choices. You can configure the display options by choosing Options, Preferences, which is pretty self-explanatory, or Options|Server Broadcasts, which requires a bit of discussion. This choice displays the Server Broadcasts dialog box, as shown in Figure 40.7.

40

MANAGING YOUR
SNA SERVER
GATEWAY

FIGURE 40.7.

*Configuring SNA
Server broadcasts.*

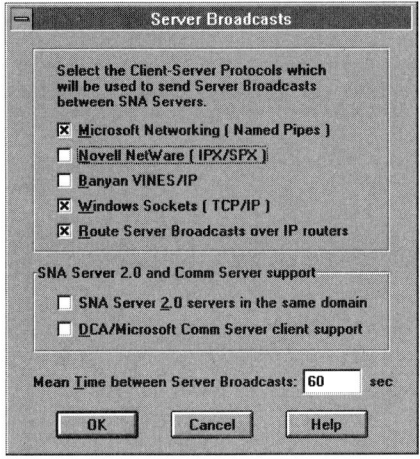

In the Select the Client-Server Protocols which will be used to send Server Broadcasts between SNA Servers section, you can choose from the protocols you have installed and configured SNA Server to use. For efficiency, use a single protocol for server broadcasts if you can. If all your installations support TCP/IP, for example, use just TCP/IP. But if you have some servers configured for TCP/IP and some for IPX/SPX, be sure to enable both these protocols so that the installations can communicate between themselves. If you will be using non-TCP/IP protocols over a WAN, you should enable the Route Server Broadcasts over IP Routers checkbox. If you do not, the server broadcasts will fail to propagate across the routers.

TIP

Before you do decide to enable the Route Server Broadcasts over IP Routers, check with your network administrators (if your company has a separate network administration group), as this option, relies on the TCP/IP capability to encapsulate NetBIOS requests. Sometimes, this may not be considered the best option, because it can utilize a high percentage of network bandwidth. Your network administrators may have a better alternative.

In the SNA Server 2.0 and Comm Server support group, you should disable the SNA Server 2.0 servers in the same domain checkbox unless you have SNA Server 2.0 installations in the same domain. This option can seriously degrade SNA Server 2.*x* performance, because it requires server broadcasts be sent once a minute. It also uses a significant portion of your network bandwidth that could be used for more productive requirements. If you have any DCA/Microsoft clients, you should enable the DCA/Microsoft Comm Server client support checkbox. You also should make sure that you have enabled Microsoft Networking as an available transport protocol, because these applications require NetBEUI.

If you are not supporting SNA Server 2.0 installations, you can specify how often SNA Server broadcasts set the time, in seconds, in the Mean Time between Server Broadcasts field. This value ranges from 45 to 65535, with a default of 60. The default is a good choice because broadcast messages are not guaranteed to be received by the client, and this will compensate for lost messages. If your network is not error prone, however, and your servers are not overburdened, then you can increase this value and lower the network bandwidth requirement.

Securing SNA Server

Now that you have spent so much time configuring SNA Server, you should spend a little more time to protect your investment. This is very important and should not be overlooked in your effort to provide a service to your network clients. Spend just a little more time to restrict the modifications that are possible to just a few Administrators by following these steps:

1. Choose Permissions from the Security menu to display the SNA Domain Permissions dialog box.
2. Click the Remove button to remove the default Everyone group (which has full control of SNA Server Administrator).
3. Click the Add button to display the Add Users and Groups dialog box.
4. Choose the group you want to allow full administration of your SNA Server domain (such as Domain Admins) in the Names field. If you want to choose a user account instead of a group account, first click the Show Users button. If the user or group is not in the current domain, choose the correct domain from the List Names From drop-down listbox.

> **NOTE**
>
> If you have not already created a group for SNA Server administration, it is a good idea to do so in User Manager for Domains. This group can be assigned permission to administer SNA Server and to limit the damage that could be caused by unfamiliar domain Administrators (Domain Admins).

5. Choose the access control setting of Full Control in the Type of Access drop-down listbox, and click the OK button.
6. Click the OK button once again, and you have secured access to your SNA Server domain.

> **TIP**
>
> You can further restrict access to groups or users by selecting them and assigning a different type of access. This could be No Access, which prevents them from using SNA Server Administrator; Read, which provides the capability to see the configuration but not change it; Read/Write, which provides the capability to read and modify the configuration but not change permissions; and Full Control, which provides complete access.

> **TIP**
>
> It is a good idea to use the Security, Auditing option to enable auditing of your SNA Server configuration if you will be providing access to several users. In this way, you can determine who did what in case of a user error—not so much to assign blame, but instead to determine who needs additional tutoring in their duties.

Using the SNA Trace Utility

If you are encountering problems with SNA Server, you might want to look into the SNA Server Trace utility. This utility is located in your Microsoft SNA Server Program Manager group. It provides two basic options for you:

- It can be used to send trace messages to the event log, which makes them easier to read.
- It can send detailed trace messages to trace files (*.TRC) in the TRACES directory of your SNA Server root installation directory (generally, C:\SNA\TRACES).

To use the SNA Server Trace utility, follow these steps:

1. Launch the SNA Server Trace utility. The SNA Server Trace Options dialog box appears, as shown in Figure 40.8.
2. In the Service Name drop-down listbox, specify the service to trace.
3. In the Message Traces group, choose what messages to trace. This varies based on the selected service and may be any of the following:
   - Admin Messages: Messages between SNA Server Administrator, SnaBase, and SnaServer (PU 2.1 node).
   - 3270 Messages: Messages between 3270 applications.
   - Data Link Control: Messages between SnaServer (PU 2.1 node) and the link services.
   - SNA Formats: DLC messages in SNA Server formats.

■ LU 6.2 Messages: Messages between SnaServer (PU 2.1 node) and the APPC dynamic link library.

■ Level 2 Messages: Messages specific to the ISO Level 2 model.

FIGURE 40.8.

The SNA Server Trace Options dialog box.

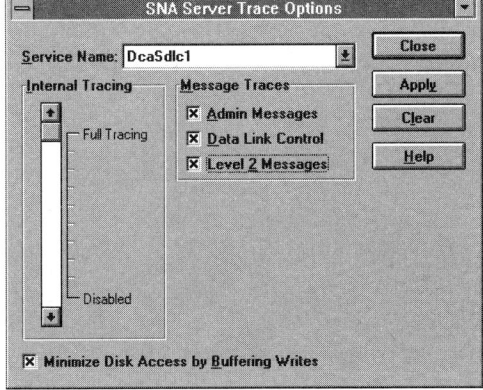

4. If you have specified the SNA applications as the selected service, you can trace API messages, which can be any of the following:

■ APPC API: Activity between APPC applications and the APP dynamic link library.

■ CPI-API: Activity between the CPI-C applications and the CPI-C dynamic link library.

■ LUA API: Activity between the LUA applications and the LUA dynamic link library.

■ CSV API: Activity between the CSV applications and the CSV dynamic link library.

5. If you have a support provider on the line, such as Microsoft Product Service Support, you may need to enable the Internal Tracing option by moving the slider to the requested level. This is not normally useful to Administrators.

6. To enhance performance, leave the Minimize Disk Access by Buffering Writes checkbox enabled, but if you are attempting to determine the cause of a system crash, disable this option so that the trace logs will be more current (if the system crashes, information in the buffer will be lost).

7. Repeat these steps for each service to trace.

8. Click the Apply button and then click the Close button.

40

MANAGING YOUR
SNA SERVER
GATEWAY

> **NOTE**
>
> Although the trace files might be helpful in some situations, you most likely will require some help from a network guru in order to interpret the data. Most times the information obtained from the trace utility is only used by Microsoft technical support personnel to resolve an otherwise unresolvable problem.

Summary

In this chapter, you explored some of the basic requirements for configuring your SNA Server installations to support your clients' access to your SNA-compatible mainframe. The key feature to remember is that before you can use a link service, you must define the connection, set up the connection, and then configure any advanced properties. After the connection is created, you must assign logical units. And, finally, you must assign permissions to groups or users to access the logical units. Permissions should be based on groups rather than individual users.

You can use Logical Unit pools to offer increased resource efficiency, fault tolerance, and increased performance. And before you walk away from your SNA installation, be sure to safeguard it by assigning specific security to determine just who can use the SNA Server Administrator to configure the installation.

In the next chapter, you will look into optimizing your SNA Server installation. Some of the topics you will consider include how to choose the right server platform and server models. You'll also learn how to configure your base Windows NT Server platform, and then you will look into specific SNA Server configuration choices to improve performance.

Optimizing SNA Server

by Arthur Knowles

IN THIS CHAPTER

CHAPTER 41

After SNA Server is up and running, you naturally will consider how you can make it perform better. Then again, you might not. A lot depends on your network clients' requirements. Because you are a busy network Administrator (aren't we all?) and your job is to serve your network clients as best you can, it follows that their needs will determine your goals. You might be thinking that if your network clients are happy, then why should you make any changes. After all, the number one rule of a network Administrator is "Don't fix what isn't broken," right? This type of philosophy is a defensive one, however, and it means that you are always playing catch-up while you try to put out the immediate fires. I prefer to choose a proactive methodology and to solve potential problems before they become noticeable to my network clients. This has proven to be a good methodology because it provides a basis for a smooth-running network, and it is really nice to be able to tell your colleagues at your weekly meetings that everything is under control and working fine.

Of course, you cannot do this properly unless you also understand the limitations imposed upon you by your choice of a hardware platform and server configuration. You also need to understand the limitations of SNA Server and, in particular, how you can tell when SNA Server is bogging down and what you can do to improve the situation. This chapter examines these topics. It starts with a look at how you can optimize your server platform within these limitations, and then moves on to how you can optimize SNA Server performance. The key to this entire discussion is the choices you make, the choices you have already made, or the choices that have already been made for you concerning your SNA Server implementation.

Examining Server Optimization

When you build a house to live in, the first item on the agenda is to build a solid foundation. This foundation then supports the framework that carries the load for your house. If the foundation is poorly built, then the framework that supports the house may collapse. This leaves you sleeping in the rain, if you are lucky enough to survive the collapse. When you look at the BackOffice components, you can think of Windows NT Server as the foundation and various operating modes as rooms within the house. You can consider the individual BackOffice components—which include Mail/Exchange, SQL Server, Systems Management Server, and SNA Server—as the furnishings within the rooms. Each piece of furniture places a load on the room's floor, which in turn places a load on the framework and foundation of the house. It takes careful planning to make sure the framework or foundation is not overloaded. So, in keeping with this architectural analogy, the first concern in getting SNA Server to perform well is to choose a foundation or, in your case, to pick a server platform. After you decide this, it is time to build your rooms by choosing the right server model to implement.

Choosing the Right Server Platform

As much as I would like to give you a single recommendation for the foundation to build your house on, in all honesty, I can't do this. Not because I don't want to, but because the technology changes too rapidly. The platform that is fastest today might not be the fastest tomorrow.

If you are looking for the fastest possible computer to use for SNA Server, I suggest that you rely on your vendor to show you proof of the platform's performance, and then shop around a bit more to see whether the vendor's claims are legitimate. Your choice for a platform that will support SNA Server today falls into two camps. There is the Intel and compatible group, and then there is the RISC group, which includes the MIPS, PowerPC, and Alpha processors.

There are really only two problems with the RISC choice, but if you can overcome them, then these platforms can serve you well. The first problem is device drivers. Without the proper device driver, your peripherals will not work with Windows NT or SNA Server. This is likely to be a short-term problem because device drivers are being ported to these platforms. The more serious problem is your choice of peripherals to support SNA Server. If you are planning to use an SDLC or X.25/QLLC adapter, you probably will not have much of a problem. On the other hand, if you are looking to use a DFT, TwinAx, or Channel adapter, you probably will find that a device driver is lacking or that your hardware platform cannot support it. Most DFT adapters require interrupt 2 in order to function properly, for example, and the current RISC platforms do not support peripherals that require this interrupt.

These problems do not occur on the Intel processor platforms, which is one reason why I tend to lean toward their recommendation. I do suggest that you be careful, though, in choosing a compatible Pentium processor from AMD or Cyrix—not because these processors do not perform their function, but because Windows NT was not specifically designed for them. In most cases, these compatible processors work fine for Windows 3.x, OS/2, or UNIX, but I have seen a few quirks with Windows 95 and would not be surprised to see them with Windows NT as well.

> **NOTE**
>
> The new Pentium Pro recently introduced by Intel is a very fast processor. For 32-bit code, it performs as well or exceeds many of the RISC platforms. And because the BackOffice components are 32-bit code, it should make a good high-end server platform for NT and SNA Server.

Regardless of your processor choice for your server platform, you should consider a few tips to improve performance:

- Choose a multiprocessing platform or one that can be expanded to support multiple processors. SNA Server, like most of the rest of the BackOffice components, is very processor intensive. An additional CPU can offer performance benefits.

- Choose the fastest possible I/O expansion bus. The PCI bus is one of the best out there, and it makes a good backbone for your disk subsystem, video subsystem, and network subsystem. But these three choices often fill up the available PCI bus slots, leaving you with ISA slots for the rest of your peripherals. You can do better by choosing EISA as your secondary bus. This gives you compatibility with existing ISA components, yet enables you to use 32-bit bus mastering peripherals as well.

■ Choose the fastest possible network adapter. There are two reasons to use the fastest network adapter possible on your server. First, SNA Server uses a Windows NT Server domain controller to authenticate users prior to giving them access to an SNA Server session. Second, SNA-to-SNA (or APPN/APPC) connections can be improved. Both of these can generate a lot of traffic on the network, so if all your servers are on a high-speed backbone, they can take advantage of this to improve the authentication and SNA Server performance.

■ Choose a fast disk subsystem. If you designate your server just for SNA Server and supply enough physical RAM to prevent paging, then your disk subsystem is not as critical. If you do not have sufficient RAM to prevent paging, however, or you use your server for other needs besides SNA Server, then a fast disk subsystem becomes critical. A fast wide SCSI subsystem is a good choice and is preferred over EIDE/IDE subsystems.

■ Don't skimp on system memory. Nothing is more critical to your performance than physical memory. You should have at least 32M, and if you can, use 64M or more of RAM. The exact amount you need varies based on the load you place on SNA Server.

Choosing the Right Server Model

When you install SNA Server, you can use a primary domain controller, a backup domain controller, or a server as the base platform. Each of these has performance trade-offs, as summarized in Table 41.1, that you should consider before you install SNA Server. In any case, if you limit your server for use only by SNA Server, rather than using it for more than one BackOffice component, you will achieve better overall performance.

Table 41.1. Server model performance trade-offs.

Windows NT Server Model	Pro	Con
Primary domain controller	Useful for organizations with a limited number of servers. Increases SNA Server authentication performance, thereby lowering network traffic slightly.	Decreases general performance of the server, impacts user/group replication, lowers its capability to authenticate users, and decreases overall SNA Server performance.

Windows NT Server Model	Pro	Con
Backup domain controller	Provides increased SNA Server user authentication performance. Lowers network authentication traffic. Best used for periodic connections.	Decreases general performance of the server, lowers its capability to authenticate users, and decreases overall SNA Server performance.
Server	Provides the most processor time for SNA Server and can increase performance. Best used for consistent SNA Server connections.	Requires a primary or backup domain controller to authenticate SNA Server users, which increases network traffic.

As you can see from Table 41.1, the best platform for SNA Server is Windows NT Server operating in server mode, dedicated specifically to SNA Server. This mode does not perform any network authentication or maintain an account database, so it is a superior base platform because it can provide more processor time to SNA Server. Because it does not include a user database, however, all user authentication must be performed by a primary or backup domain controller. This increases the network traffic for each SNA Server session. This is not a problem if all your servers are on a high-speed network backbone and if your primary or backup domain controllers can handle the increased authentication load. For these reasons, this platform serves best for long-term SNA Server sessions.

For short-term sessions, in which a user logs on and off rapidly from SNA Server and his mainframe connection, the best platform is a backup domain controller dedicated to SNA Server. This decreases the user wait time to be authenticated for the SNA Server session and decreases the network traffic for user authentication. Due to the increased load SNA Server places on the backup domain controller, however, its capability to authenticate other network users may be diminished. This may increase the wait time for your network clients to be authenticated, and therefore require you to add an additional backup domain controller to compensate.

The worst possible choice is to use your primary domain controller as your SNA Server platform. A primary domain controller is the heart of your network. It is responsible for maintaining your entire user account database. Any account administration occurs on this copy of the database. Any changes must be replicated from the primary domain controller to your backup domain controllers. Any increased processor load, such as by SNA Server or other BackOffice components, impacts your entire network—and, generally, not for the better. There are really only three reasons why I would recommend this. First, if you have no other choice. Second, if you are building a development platform for testing custom code. And finally, if you have a network with less than 50 users, it offers acceptable performance.

Configuring Your Server as a Base Platform for SNA Server

The final step in configuring your base platform is to tune the basic network configuration and to set your process priorities. These steps should be completed before using Performance Monitor to tweak the best possible performance. The first step in this process is to choose a network model to increase SNA Server's network throughput. This is accomplished by configuring the Server service in the Control Panel Network applet.

You can follow these steps:

1. Open the Control Panel Network applet. The Network Settings dialog box appears.
2. In the Installed Network Software field, double-click on the Server entry. Or, highlight the server entry and click the Configure button to display the Server dialog box.
3. Select the Maximize Throughput for Network Applications radio button. This allocates additional nonpageable memory for use as network buffers and increases the performance of your client/server application.
4. Click the OK button. Then click the OK button in the Network Settings dialog box. Do not restart your computer as prompted at this time.

After you configure the network to increase the throughput of your client/server applications, it is time to set your process priorities. This can be accomplished by following these steps:

1. Open the Control Panel System applet. The System dialog box appears.
2. Click the Tasking button to display the Tasking dialog box.
3. Select the Foreground and Background Applications Equally Responsive radio button. This provides equal processor time to all processes in the system.

TIP

By setting all processes to be equally responsive, you increase the performance of all background processes at the expense of foreground applications. This can make the computer difficult to use for centralized administration. If you will be using this computer for additional tasks, select the Foreground Application More Responsive Than Background option. This still increases the performance of your background applications, of which SNA Server is one, and increases the performance of your foreground application to a point where it is usable.

4. Click the OK button, and then click the OK button in the System dialog box. Restart your computer as prompted in order for the changes to be put into effect.

Tuning SNA Server

Tuning SNA Server for maximum performance with the Performance Monitor is not an easy task. Before you even begin this process, optimize your base platform. Then you can work at tuning for optimum SNA Server performance. Keep in mind, though, that performance tuning is always going to uncover another bottleneck whenever you solve a bottleneck. If you add another processor to increase processor performance, for example, then most likely, you will find that the disk subsystem becomes a bottleneck. In the next section, you will look at the SNA Server performance object counter, which you can use to determine the load on your server in an effort to tweak the maximum possible performance.

You should keep some additional concerns in mind:

■ Processor activity: Windows NT Server requires more processor power than other network file servers. And each additional service you add to this base increases the load on the processor. You should monitor your processor activity to make sure that it stays below 80 percent usage. Slight peaks of 100 percent are okay; however, a constant usage of 80 percent or higher is an indication that more processing power is required for optimum performance.

■ Memory activity: If you are paging to disk at all, then you do not have sufficient memory for maximum performance. This is not a problem unless you are attempting to get the best possible performance from SNA Server. If you do want the best, however, then you should never even see the disk light in an active state. With sufficient physical memory, SNA Server and any required supporting services and buffers can be completely resident in system memory.

NOTE

Keep in mind that each process, or thread, requires additional system resources. Each SNA Server connection requires additional resources as well. So as additional connections come online, additional resources are required to maintain the same level of performance. If you are paging to disk, then you are wasting processor cycles that could be used to service your client requests. If maximum throughput is your goal, then no other single component can increase your performance as much as adding sufficient memory to keep all your processes resident in physical memory.

- Disk activity: If you do not have sufficient physical RAM, then your disk subsystem becomes a bottleneck as your server pages to/from your paging file. A slow disk subsystem can drag your system to its knees.

- Network activity: Considering that all of your SNA Server clients pass data through one network card, and then SNA Server passes this data through your SNA network adapter card, you can understand that your network adapter's capability to pass data is going to impact your SNA Server performance. You should monitor your network activity to see how much of your bandwidth is in use and prepare to split your network into additional segments if required. You will look into this subject a bit more in the following section.

> **TIP**
>
> In order to properly maintain your SNA Server installations you'll also need to be kept in the loop regarding modifications to the network topology. What I mean here is that if your mainframe administrators plan to make any changes, they should notify you first. You should also be informed of any software additions—such as those planned by your SNA application development group—or any modifications planned for your SNA clients—such as a new version of their connectivity software.

Load Balancing SNA Server

Load balancing is a means of splitting the load on a particular service or peripheral. This section focuses primarily on network activity. This includes both your network adapters and your SNA adapters. Both these impact your ability to service your SNA Server clients. The things to look out for follow:

- Network bandwidth: If your network is using 50 percent of your network bandwidth on an Ethernet network, you should consider splitting the network into multiple segments. If you do not split the segment, you most likely will encounter additional network collisions. This increases the error rate and decreases network throughput.

> **TIP**
>
> If you are using TCP/IP as your primary network protocol and reach 50 percent network bandwidth utilization, then you can use two network adapters on your server, with each adapter having a different TCP/IP address, and split the single segment into two separate segments. You can even use Windows NT's capability to internally route the two physical segments to create a single logical segment.

■ SNA bandwidth: Your capacity to transfer data to and from your SNA-compatible mainframe is limited by the bandwidth of your SNA Server adapter and the performance capabilities of your SNA-compatible mainframe. When your adapter becomes the limiting factor, you can add adapters to increase the data-carrying capacity. If your SNA-compatible mainframe is a bottleneck, then adding additional adapters will not help. Your only choice in this matter is to add additional mainframe capacity through additional hardware on your mainframe.

■ Network protocols: Although you can bind all your network protocols to a single network adapter, you will realize increased performance by using a single adapter per protocol.

Using the SNA Server Performance Monitor Counters

As with most products that you add to Windows NT Server, SNA Server also includes performance object counters you can use to determine its activity. Table 41.2 summarizes the available object counters you can use to monitor the activity of your SNA Server installation. You must realize that performance is relative to your hardware platform, however. To determine your capacity, you should start by monitoring your system in an idle state to gain a feel for its base capacity. Then, as time goes by, and you add users to your system, you can determine SNA Server's capability to handle the additional load.

Table 41.2. SNA Server performance monitor object types and object counters.

Performance Object	*Object Counters*	*Description*
SNA Adapter SnaAdapterName	Adapter Failures	Number of times since startup that a network adapter has encountered an error condition.
SNA Adapter SnaAdapterName	Connection Failures	Number of times since startup that a connection has encountered an error condition.
SNA Adapter SnaAdapterName Received/Sec	Data Bytes	Number of data bytes received per second.
SNA Adapter SnaAdapterName Transmitted/Sec	Data Bytes	Number of data bytes transmitted per second.

continues

Table 41.2. continued

Performance Object	Object Counters	Description
SNA Adapter SnaAdapterName	Frames Received/Sec	Number of data frames received per second. A frame is an information structure recognized by one of the various protocols related to SNA. Frames contain multiple bytes of data.
SNA Adapter SnaAdapterName Transmitted/Sec	Frames	Number of data frames transmitted per second.
SNA Adapter SnaAdapterName	Successful Connects	Number of times since startup that a successful connection has been made.
SNA Adapter SnaAdapterName	Throughput Bytes/ Sec	Total number of bytes flowing through the SNA Server per second. This includes both incoming and outgoing bytes, and is a good indicator of how heavily your SNA Server is loaded.

Performance Object	Object Counters	Description
SNA Adapter SnaAdapterName Frames/Sec	Throughput	Total number of data frames flowing through the SNA Server per second. This includes both incoming and outgoing frames, and is a good indicator of how heavily your SNA Server is loaded.
SNA Logical Unit Sessions Received/Sec	Data Bytes	Number of data bytes received per second.
SNA Logical Unit Sessions Transmitted/Sec	Data Bytes	Number of data bytes transmitted per second.
SNA Logical Unit Sessions	Throughput Bytes/ Sec	Total number of bytes flowing through the SNA Server per second. This includes both incoming and outgoing bytes, and is a good indicator of how heavily your SNA Server is loaded.

NOTE

SnaAdapterName is used as a generic name to replace the specific SNA Server adapter. If you have installed an SNA Server SDLC adapter, for example, then the name you see in the Performance Monitor object type is SnaSdlc1.

TIP

Instead of being concerned with byte-oriented counters when looking to optimize performance for your SNA Server clients, use the frame-oriented counters. Most SNA Server traffic is frame-based, rather than byte-based, and these counters give you a more realistic performance curve to use.

Summary

This chapter's primary concern was to help you optimize SNA Server's performance. First, you need to choose the right platform to build the foundation for your SNA Server installation. The best overall choice you can make for maximum performance and compatibility with existing SNA adapters is to choose a multiprocessor-capable platform with an Intel processor (preferably a Pentium or Pentium Pro). Then choose the right server mode. If your domain controllers can handle the additional authentication requirements, then you should install SNA Server on a Windows NT Server platform operating in server mode. Otherwise, use a backup domain controller dedicated to SNA Server.

After you pick the best possible platform, you can turn your eye toward configuring the software. Configure your server to optimize your network throughput and set your process priorities so that your foreground and background processes receive equal processor time.

When considering hardware upgrades, adding physical RAM is the best solution to increasing overall system-related performance. Then consider using multiple network adapters to increase your network capacity and using multiple SNA adapters to increase your SNA data-carrying capacity.

When looking to use Performance Monitor to fine-tune your SNA Server installation, rely on the frame-based performance object counters for the most realistic view of SNA Server performance.

VIII
PART

Integrating BackOffice

Interfacing Applications to Exchange Server

by Stephen Gutknecht

IN THIS CHAPTER

This chapter covers application integration with Exchange Server. Sample programs demonstrate how to link Microsoft Office to the Exchange Server client, and there is a Visual Basic 4.0 example of how to interface with Schedule+. General information is provided about the Exchange SDK and the MAPI programming architecture.

Extending Exchange

Exchange Server can be extended at the server to provide additional gateways or to assist with administrative tasks. The programming is not easy, but the potential exists to write programs that automate or extend the functionality of the management tools for the directory and message stores.

Users can be assisted by automating applications. An Exchange developer or administrator may be asked to extend or optimize a form application developed by a user. The Forms Designer is included with Exchange Server, allowing users to create simple front-ends to the mail. Visual Basic OLE Automation library for Exchange allows relatively uncomplicated interfacing from Excel, Word, or other tools based on Visual Basic interfaces.

Exchange Software Developer's Kit

Microsoft uses the term Software Developer's Kit, often abbreviated as SDK, to describe the samples and documentation for a particular product. In some cases, special tools such as debug builds of the programs are included in the kit.

The Exchange SDK is part of the BackOffice SDK. This is available on Microsoft Developer's Network (MSDN) Level II or higher. MSDN is a subscription service of CD-ROM programming tools for all of Microsoft's products.

Gateway Developer's Kit

As part of the Exchange SDK, Microsoft includes the Gateway Developer's Kit. The Gateway Developer's Kit allows developers to interface Exchange with other mail systems. Gateway services have special abilities that allow them to transparently interface with systems that may not be so transparent.

Because of these abilities, security is an important consideration. As a mail message is converted from a gateway, the message recipients may be mapped to Exchange directory entries. Ultimately, the user may not want to know that a message came from a foreign system, but the gateway designer needs to consider the power of this capability. An example how this can be done is the properties page of the message; with Exchange Server 4.0, a message received from the Internet Mail Connector will have a property page showing the SMTP message header.

Consideration should also be given to the interface for controlling the gateway. Ideally, a gateway service would read configuration data from the Directory. An Exchange Administration extension could be created to allow the administrator to update and view these settings.

Considerations must be made to account for the various system processor platforms that Windows NT and Exchange Server support. Microsoft has defined a structure to allow the Administration program to detect updated extension files; these add-on modules are registered in the Directory, and the Exchange Administrator program uses this information to locate the server with the most current DLL.

Introduction to MAPI

For programmers who wish to link custom or off-the-shelf applications to Exchange Server, MAPI is the solution. MAPI, Messaging Application Programming Interface, is the programming interface that Microsoft has defined for electronic mail systems.

Exchange Server Public Folders can be used as a database. Although not relational like a SQL Server database, there are some properties in common. Multiple users can read the same data at the same time, plus the data can be searched (or queried). However, a Public Folder would not be suitable for situations where many small transactions take place or records are frequently updated.

Where Public Folders may have their most potential is with multiuser documents. In many cases, a document may be maintained for record purposes or future updates. Consider the case of a law firm where boilerplate documents covering various legal situations may be used for long periods of time.

Lotus Notes has been successfully used for many such applications. Replication technology, the ability to maintain updates to a number of servers inexpensively, has also been leveraged for such applications. At least in current release, Notes has more capability to automate the entry and processing of these documents. Notes applications are typically written using Lotus 1-2-3–like @ commands, not a traditional language like BASIC. Microsoft is working to bring such automation tools to Exchange.

Many customers are anxious to see Microsoft link ActiveX, VBScript, and possibly Java Script (Visual J++) added to Exchange. None of these have been committed, but these technologies are clearly part of Microsoft's total BackOffice and (Desktop) Office product strategies.

Exchange Application Types

Terminology exists to describe the various roles that a application will serve. In the Exchange Software Developer's Kit, Microsoft defines three categories of Exchange Server applications:

- *Client Application* uses the services of a server running Exchange Server, but executes on the user's workstation. This workstation could be running any of the available client operating systems.

■ *Server Application* interacts with the Exchange Server services such as the Information Stores or the Directory. A Server Application can be used to provide tools for administrators or users, but they are not associated with any user.

■ *Combined Client and Server Application* is a true customer client-server application that uses back-end server services to support one or more users. Components are installed on both the server and user workstations.

Understanding the unique requirements of each type of application can assist in understanding the technical development needs. For example, a Client Application would interface with the user on a daily basis, so clear screen design and ease of use are high priorities. The Server Application must concern itself with scale, because multiple users access it at once. Consider also the message traffic; a search engine that searches the Information Store at the server is going to produce less traffic than one that pulls from a client workstation.

Client Messaging Applications

The case could be made that almost any client Windows program could interface with Exchange Server. In place of saving or printing a data file, it could be mailed directly to another user. In other cases, a custom work environment may want to have a complete interface for reading and sending mail. In most documentation, Microsoft organizes client applications into one of the following three categories:

■ Messaging-aware applications

■ Messaging-enabled applications

■ Messaging-based applications (workflow)

A messaging-aware application does not require the services of a messaging system, but includes messaging options as an additional feature. For example, a word processing application that includes a Send command in its File menu to enable documents to be sent is considered messaging-aware. Components of Microsoft Office, such as Word and Excel, support this feature.

> **TIP**
>
> Office 95 for Windows 95 and NT has been updated. Make sure users have Office 95A or Office 95B, especially for Exchange messaging-enabled features for public folders. Microsoft offers these as updates to corporate customers on Select CD-ROM sets.

A messaging-enabled application requires the services of a messaging system and typically runs on a network or an online service. An example of a messaging-enabled application is Microsoft Mail.

A more advanced client application is the messaging-based workgroup application. The workgroup application requires full access to a wide range of messaging system services, including storage, addressing, and transport services. These applications are designed to operate over a network without users having to manage the applications' network interaction. Examples of such applications include work flow automation programs and bulletin board services.

Client Programming Interfaces

Client application developers can choose to use one or more of the MAPI client interfaces: Simple MAPI, CMC, MAPI, and the OLE Messaging Library. Consider the following factors before making a decision:

- Programming languages supported
- Time and skill level required to develop the application
- System Resource constraints
- Type of client application

The language in which your client application is written is an important issue. If you are modifying an existing application, you must use a client interface that supports your application's language. If you are writing a new client application, the choice of language depends on your experience with the supported languages and any requirements for interoperability that might exist with other components. All the client interfaces work with C and C++, whereas Visual Basic developers are limited to using the OLE Messaging Library and Simple MAPI.

The amount of time you need to create or modify your client application is also a consideration. A simple API such as Simple MAPI or CMC is more appropriate if you have limited time. Resource constraints might also be an issue. To successfully develop a client application, you should have experience with messaging and the appropriate programming language.

Messaging-enabled and messaging-aware client applications have different requirements than messaging-based applications. Messaging-enabled and messaging-aware applications have fewer and simpler messaging features to implement. Messaging-based applications have more complex messaging requirements because they have more direct contact with and control over the underlying messaging system services like address books, message stores, and transports. These applications often implement a wide variety of messaging features, such as rules processing, automatic forwarding, and support for Rich Text Format. Shared group applications like schedulers and calendars, work flow and message management applications, electronic mail clients, and rules-based inbox managers are examples of messaging-based applications. Complex messaging-based applications like these require the MAPI client interface.

The OLE Messaging Library is a good choice for applications that require a moderate amount of messaging support. The OLE Messaging Library is an object-oriented API used primarily by Visual Basic and Visual C/C++ client application developers. It provides programmable objects that publish properties and methods which can then be managed by Visual Basic and Visual Basic for Applications programs or other OLE Automation controllers. The OLE Messaging Library is based on the capabilities provided by OLE Automation. In terms of messaging functionality, it offers more than CMC and Simple MAPI offer, but less than MAPI offers.

Simple MAPI or CMC is the best choice for messaging-enabled and messaging-aware applications. These interfaces provide a fast and easy way to build basic applications from scratch or add messaging functionality to existing applications.

Mail Client MAPI Extensions

Microsoft offers the Client Extensions Programmer's Reference, a section of the MAPI SDK documentation. The purpose of such extensions is to allow new functions to be added to the Exchange Client. Microsoft defines four types of Microsoft Exchange Client extensions:

■ *Command Extensions.* Examples include custom Spelling, Thesaurus, and Grammar commands to assist the user. Other, more Exchange-centric examples include Public Folder commands that provide folder-sensitive menu items or toolbar buttons. Finally, Message Class commands can override the default behavior of Microsoft Exchange commands.

■ *Event Extensions.* These enable a programmer to extend or override behavior on events such as the arrival of new messages, reading and composing messages, opening of attachments to a message, and interaction with the folders and messages. Cited examples include an Attachment virus detection program that intercepts the opening of attachments.

■ *Property Sheet Extension.* Custom property tabs can be added to the Microsoft Exchange configuration screens or specific message form classes. An example of custom form classes could be a workflow application with a property page that identifies specific information about the task start time and person who initiated the task. For configuration tabs, one might be added to configure system file paths and other settings required to interface with an outside program.

■ *Advanced Criteria Extensions.* A programmer can add additional search criteria for custom properties of a public folder.

The MAPI SDK includes examples of these extensions. Fundamentally, as these are written to MAPI, they can work with mail products other than Exchange. Also consider that the Exchange Client could be used to drive other information services such as the Internet (POP3 client), MSN, CompuServe, and Microsoft Mail 3.*x* servers.

Programming Environment

Microsoft offers several methods of encapsulating MAPI programming. The MAPI Software Developer's Kit, MAPISDK, documents and details these methods. Raw MAPI programming is the lowest level of access, the OLE Messaging interfaces are easiest to use. Selecting the correct programming interface will be a key to success when extending Exchange functionality.

Visual Basic

Visual Basic 4.0 includes a MAPI sample in the VB directory \SAMPLE\MAPI\VBMAIL.VBP project file. The sample is a minimal client for composing and reading e-mail. It works with either the Microsoft Mail 3.x or Exchange client.

MSMAPI16.OCX and MSMAPI32.OCX are the two Visual Basic library files—the first for 16-bit environments, the second for 32-bit environments.

Visual Basic encapsulates MAPI into two main objects. The first of these objects is named MAPISession; it has properties and several action codes. This object encapsulates the underlying MAPI connection.

The second object is MAPIMessages. This is the primary interface for manipulating, creating, and sending messages.

Electronic Forms Designer

Exchange includes an Electronic Forms Designer, a tool that Microsoft promises end-users can access without programming experience. The Forms Designer installs with a separate SETUP program. The program code is on the Clients CD-ROM, included with Exchange Server.

The Forms Designer works in two stages. A program is used to draw the forms using a drag-and-drop interface. This creates an EFP file that is used to store the design of the form. Once ready, the user selects Install from the File menu of the Forms Designer. This initiates a process that generates source code and a project for Visual Basic 4.0. Visual Basic is then automatically launched to compile the source code. Once the program is compiled into an executable program (EXE), the Forms Designer will prompt which library to install the forms.

Typically a library will be an Exchange Server public folder specific to the application being developed. Exchange maintains a hidden folder for system-wide registered forms. In addition, forms can be installed to local Personal Folders or to a private mailbox folder.

> **NOTE**
>
> The Visual Basic included with Exchange Server is licensed only for use with Exchange Server. It identifies itself as "Visual Basic for Exchange Server." For programmers wanting to develop MAPI or OLE Messaging applications, it is recommended that the full Visual Basic 4.0 Professional system be acquired.

It is important to understand the implications of Exchange Server's use of executable programs, EXE files, for electronic forms. When a user activates a form, Exchange checks if the EXE is already present on the local system. If this is a new or updated form program, Exchange will download the program to the local system. The client will then invoke the program. (See Figure 42.1.)

> **NOTE**
>
> The Visual Basic included with Exchange Server is 16-bit. It is not a feature of the current product to create 32-bit source code.

FIGURE 42.1.

Forms Designer shown with sample Help Desk application.

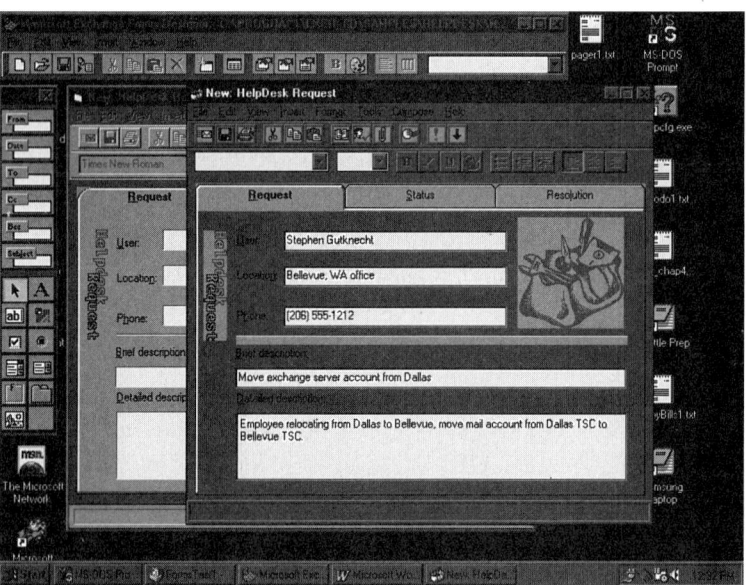

Simple MAPI

In simplified terms, Simple MAPI is the least-common denominator of Message Application Programming Interfaces. Most third-party messaging products (not from Microsoft) have implemented Simple MAPI in their client programs.

In general, when working with Exchange, Simple MAPI is best passed up in favor of Extended MAPI. However, there are some reasons that a programmer may consider working with Extended MAPI:

- It is the older, more established environment. There are existing Simple MAPI code libraries, books, and expertise.

- There is a need to develop an application that is targeting a messaging system that does not support Extended MAPI 1.0.

■ The application will be used during a migration from MS Mail 3.*x* to Exchange Server where both clients need similar custom programs.

Extended MAPI

Sometimes known as MAPI 1.0, Extended MAPI is the full iteration of the API. The Windows Messaging System and Exchange Server clients are examples of products that fully support Extended MAPI.

Extended MAPI differs from Simple MAPI in that it is built around the Common Object Model (COM). COM is what Microsoft has evolved to from Object Linking and Embedding (OLE).

OLE Messaging Library

The Microsoft OLE Messaging Library is an alternate programming interface for Extended MAPI. Microsoft's emphasis on the COM design encourages this more generic encapsulation of the underlying Extended MAPI programming routines. ActiveX, most typically associated with Microsoft's Internet/intranet initiative, is also fundamentally based on COM.

The file OLEMSG.HLP, installed along with the Exchange Electronic Forms Designer, documents the programming interfaces to OLE Message Automation. The MAPI SDK documentation also includes this information.

The Microsoft OLE Messaging Library is designed to handle the most common tasks for client developers using Visual Basic and Visual C++. To use the library, MAPI must be installed and accessed via a tool that supports OLE Automation. The following Microsoft applications support OLE Automation:

■ Microsoft Visual Basic version 4.0

■ Microsoft Visual Basic for Applications

■ Microsoft Access version 2.0 or later

■ Microsoft Excel version 5.0 or later

■ Microsoft Word version 6.0 or later

■ Microsoft Project version 4.0 or Later

■ Microsoft Visual C++ version 1.5 or later

Schedule+

Exchange Server includes Schedule+, a tool for tracking personal schedules, coordinating appointments, and controlling access to resources such as meeting tools. From a programming perspective, Schedule+ is another Extended MAPI application. In fact, Schedule+ has a OLE Automation interface for similar purposes.

Microsoft's Schedule+ Programmer's Reference is designed for use with the Microsoft Schedule+ OLE Automation. This allows the customization of menus and extension with programming tools such as Visual Basic or Visual C++.

> **TIP**
>
> A help file, OLEMSG.hlp, is included with the Exchange Server 4.0 Electronic Forms Designer. This help file covers both Exchange and Schedule+ OLE Automation programming interfaces.

> **NOTE**
>
> Before rolling out a MAPI application, consider that Extended MAPI is delivered in various flavors. Windows 95 originally came with what was called the Exchange 4.0 client, now renamed to the Windows Messaging System. Updates are available for this; it is recommended that all MAPI application clients have a consistent (and the most recent) environment. Consider also that Windows 3.x, Windows 95, and Windows NT versions of MAPI may have different patch levels.

Server-Side Extensions

Exchange can be extended at the server side. The Exchange Administrator program is an example of an application that access the Directory, Public, and Private information stores.

Mailbox monitors, what Microsoft calls Mailbox Agents, can be created to provide an interface between a program and Exchange. A special system mailbox could be created, for example, to manage Distribution Lists. A program could be written that monitors this mailbox, enabling mail messages to manipulate the directory. A message could be sent with the name of the Distribution List and the members to add and remove members. Although this specific example is not included, see the Microsoft Exchange SDK Sample Mailbox Agent (SMBA) for details of the programming logic.

Running as a Service

The most desirable way of running a server-side client may be as a Windows NT service. This allows the program to start without user intervention when the system is started. The program can also be managed (stop/start) remotely using standard Windows NT tools such as Server Manager.

There are some considerations about the use of MAPI programs as a service. In particular, care must be taken to ensure that the program does not require access to the screen or a response from the user. Because it must run as a background program, error messages should be written to a file or the standard Windows NT Event Viewer.

MAPI programs also have special requirements for profiles. Depending on which Windows NT user account is used to execute the service, efforts must be made to dynamically create the profile. If the MAPI program does not interact with other installed services, the service can be installed to run with a defied user account. The user then needs to log in as that account to create the profile, which could then be used by the background program.

If the program needs to interact with other services, however, it may need to run with the System service account. An example of such a program is one that links Microsoft's Internet Information Server (IIS) to MAPI routines. The System service account has special considerations; it can not be logged into interactively, so a profile can not be created by the user before the MAPI program is started. To work around this, the profile should be created by the program as it starts. The MAPI function `HrCreateMailboxAgentProfile` can be used for this purpose. This issue is covered in more detail, with examples, in Microsoft's Exchange SDK.

Sample Excel and Word Macro Programs

This section combines BackOffice with the "Front" Office. Microsoft Word, Excel, and Project all have applications that may require linkage to Exchange electronic forms or mail messages.

To run any of the samples presented, it is assumed that the Exchange Client is the MAPI provider. A working profile should also be configured and working. For best operations, it is suggested that a profile be used that contains only the Exchange Server information service. Other services may introduce unanticipated problems.

> **NOTE**
>
> The samples presented in this chapter have only been tested with Exchange Client 4.0 Service Pack 2 on Windows 95 Service Pack 1 and Windows NT 4.0. They may not function correctly with Information Services other than Exchange Server.

OLE Automation is the preferred programming interface for Visual Basic for Applications. Using the OLE Messaging interface, applications can quickly be constructed that transfer data to or from Exchange.

Address Book Macro in Excel

This section presents a sample program written in Visual Basic for Applications. The sample program uses an Excel spreadsheet as a database of message recipients.

The scenario used in the example is a tax office sending out a brief reminder of taxes owed. Suppose that a small sweepstakes recently took place with cash prizes. To facilitate reporting, the tax office is provided a list of prize amounts and contact information for the prize winners.

In an effort to be proactive, the tax office wants to send out mail messages to the prize winners. Using last year's tax rate as an example, the tax office wants to remind the prize winner that they should save some of their money for the purposes of paying at tax time.

Spreadsheet Layout

The spreadsheet itself is rather simple (see Figure 42.2). The sheet with the data is named MailList1. The first row is a description of the fields, and the second is a colored (empty) separator row. The data starts on the third row.

Column A is a record number; this is not used by the program—it helps to troubleshoot the process. Column B and Column C are the first and last name of the recipient, respectively. Column D is the e-mail address. The example uses SMTP address types. Others could be used, but the program as written uses SMTP.

Column F contains the prize amount in dollars. Column G shows the tax rate, represented as a percentage, the data presumed to be based on the tax office's own records. Column K contains a simple formula that multiplies the prize amount (Column F) by the tax rate (Column G).

FIGURE 42.2.

Sample dataset for the Excel-to-OLE messaging example.

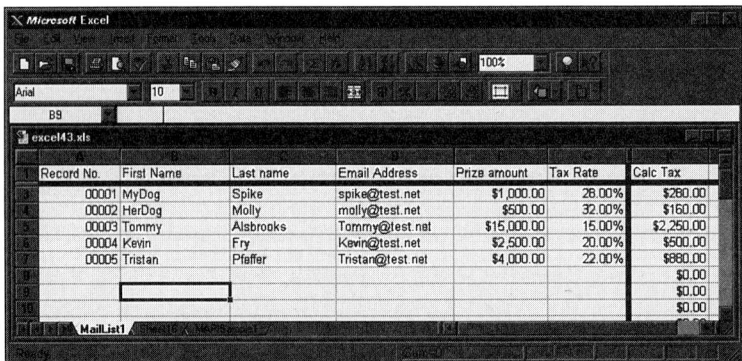

Three additional columns are unused in the sample. Column E contains the number of copies of the message to be sent, but the program does not incorporate this logic. Column I records when the message was sent, and Column J whether there were any errors in sending. The logic for this is also not included in the sample program.

Cell Formatting

The cell columns are formatted for the appropriate values. For example, Column F is formatted with a currency property to display the dollar sign ($) and proper decimal places. This is significant, because the Visual Basic for Applications program logic uses this formatting for the message content.

Linking to Other Tables

Obviously, this example is a simple one. A more realistic one would be that the social security number of the prize winner is used to look up a second table that shows the individual's last year earnings and associated tax rate. It would also be sensible to include those figures in the message as a method of documenting to the prize winner how the numbers were calculated.

Examining the Program Logic

The program is implemented as a single function for simplicity. A subroutine called `MAPI_Ole_Sample1` invokes the function named `Mail_TaxNotice1`.

The first line of code sets the spreadsheet to the MailList1 sheet. The variable `CurrentRow` is initiated to two, skipping over the two header lines of the sample spreadsheet. The active cell is set to the first in the spreadsheet, and the `CurrentRow` variable will be used as an offset to access data for the remainder of the program:

```
Sheets("MailList1").Select
CurrentRow = 2
Range("A1").Select
```

Starting the Session and Message

OLE Message treats session handles as objects. A mail message consists of a MAPI Session, a logon instance, and an address instance. Here is an overview of a session:

```
Open MAPI Session
Logon
Create Address Object
Create Message Object
Send message with connected address
Logoff
```

The next line of program code initiates an OLE Automation connection to the OLE Messaging interface:

```
Set MAPISession = CreateObject("MAPI.Session")
```

The variable `MAPISession` will serve as a handle to the session. The session is then logged on:

```
MAPISession.Logon
```

Because no parameters are passed, the user is prompted for required information. Assuming the Exchange Client is the MAPI provider, the logon will prompt for the profile to use. Assuming the logon is successful, the program initiates the main data processing loop.

The loop itself is a while/wend loop that cycles until an empty cell in the A column is found. Assuming a row is to be processed, a new message object is started. The `Message` object variable will contain a handle to the message:

```
Set Message = MAPISession.Outbox.Messages.Add
```

The message subject starts with the recipient's first name. This is accessed from the first column in the row and appended with the string ", you are a prize winner!". At this point, it is stored in a local string, not yet associated to the mail message being generated:

```
MessageSubject = ActiveCell.Offset(CurrentRow, 1).Value & ", you are a prize
➥winner!"
```

In the example, the body of the message is stored in a single string variable, named MessageBody. The first line addresses the person by first name in the format "Dear FirstName,". Chr$(13) is added to indicate that a carriage return (the Enter key) needs to be placed; two are added to provide one blank line:

```
MessageBody = "Dear " & ActiveCell.Offset(CurrentRow, 1).Value & ":" & Chr$(13) &
Chr$(13)
```

The message content starts with a simple introduction:

```
MessageBody = MessageBody &
   ➥"Congratulations!  We have been informed that you have recently received a
➥prize!"
   ➥& Chr$(13)
MessageBody = MessageBody & "This is a reminder that taxes are due on your "
```

The amount of the prize is taken from column five of the spreadsheet. The ActiveCell.Offset.Text method returns the cell as formatted by Excel on-screen; this is significant, because it will include the dollar sign ($) and so forth in proper format. If ActiveCell.Offset.Value or ActiveCell.Offset.Formula had been used, it would have lost the formatting properties:

```
MessageBody = MessageBody & ActiveCell.Offset(CurrentRow, 5).Text
   & " prize amount.  As your current tax rate is "
```

In similar fashion, the formatted percentage rate in column six of the spreadsheet is added to the growing message:

```
MessageBody = MessageBody & ActiveCell.Offset(CurrentRow, 6).Text
   & ", it is estimated that you will owe "
```

The formula in column ten is used to derive the calculated estimate of owed taxes:

```
MessageBody = MessageBody & ActiveCell.Offset(CurrentRow, 10).Text & "." + Chr$(13)
+ Chr$(13)
MessageBody = MessageBody & "Thank you!" & Chr$(13)
```

Addressing the Message

The string variable MessageTo is used to hold the working address for the recipient of the message. A one-off address is formatted so that the display name of the user will match the First and Last name fields in the data, but the address will be formatted with SMTP. Other address types could be used, including those that require Ambiguous Name Resolution, but that requires modification to these lines of code:

```
MessageTo = ActiveCell.Offset(CurrentRow, 1).Text & " " &
ActiveCell.Offset(CurrentRow, 2).Text
MessageTo = MessageTo & "[smtp:" & ActiveCell.Offset(CurrentRow, 3).Text & "]"
```

> **NOTE**
>
> Ambiguous Name Resolution is the term used to describe the process of matching the TO: of a message to the Global Address List or Personal Address List.

> **NOTE**
>
> A one-off address is the term used to describe an address used in a message that is not selected from the Global Address Book or Personal Address Book. This is the same as when a user free-form types an address.

A new Address Recipient Object is created to tie the message to the recipient. The type used in the program is called a "One-off recipient," a dynamically created address. This is similar to the user free-form typing on the TO: line instead of selecting from the Global Address List (GAL). The `MessageTo` variable is put in the `.Name` field of the object:

```
Set OneOffRecip = Message.Recipients.Add
OneOffRecip.Name = MessageTo
OneOffRecip.Type = mapiTo
OneOffRecip.Resolve
```

The message object is provided with the previously generated strings for the body and subject of the message:

```
Message.Subject = MessageSubject
Message.Text = MessageBody
```

The `Update` and `Send` methods of the message are called to initiate the actual sending of the message. The `showDialog:=False` property on `Message.Send` instructs MAPI to not pop up the actual screen showing the message:

```
Message.Update
Message.Send showDialog:=False
```

Next, the `CurrentRow` is incremented to move to the next row of spreadsheet data. The whole process of composing and addressing the message starts on the next line. (See Figures 42.3 and 42.4.)

Word, Project, and Other Applications

Project and Word are two other applications that benefit from linkage to Exchange electronic mail—for example, a Word document that sends personalized letters to employees in a distribution list, addressing them by first and last name. The Exchange Address Book contains a wealth of fields that could be exploited for such purposes.

FIGURE 42.3.

Exchange Client message queue shown in the outbox.

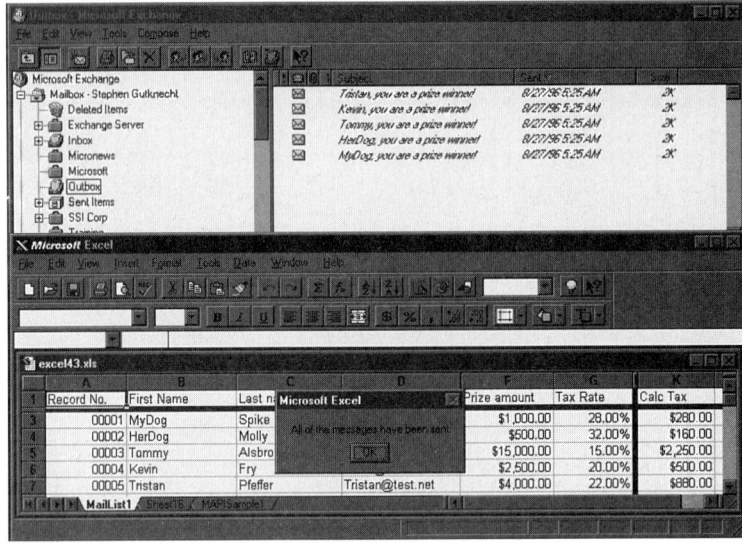

FIGURE 42.4.

Capture of the message.

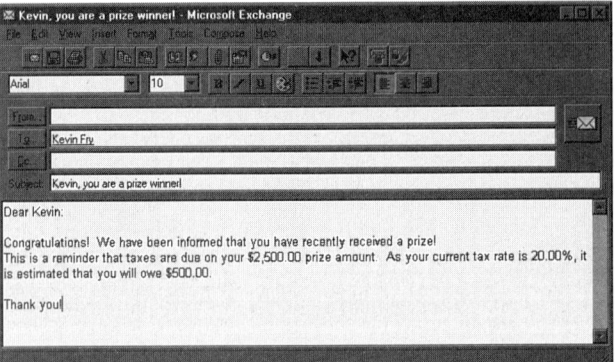

TIP

Microsoft's Knowledge Base (KB) Technote Q121424 has information on linking Visual Basic for Applications to MAPI. This can be accessed on the Microsoft TechNet CD-ROM or the Internet at http://www.microsoft.com/kb URL.

TIP

Microsoft offers a Microsoft Word Developer's Kit that includes a wrapper for MAPI. Complete C source code is included for the wrapper. If direct access is required to MAPI, without using OLE Automation, this could serve as an example. This is distributed in the form of a book with disk by Microsoft Press.

OLE Automation Schedule+ to Create Tasks

As mentioned earlier, Schedule+ has MAPI and OLE Automation interfaces. As with the Exchange Server client, OLE Automation is the easiest method for developing with Visual Basic. Figure 42.5 shows a Visual Basic form that was custom-developed to drive Schedule+.

Although this example does not use Exchange directly, it does show how programming logic could be applied to link Schedule+ to other applications. A practical application could be to link tasks and appointments to a project plan in Microsoft Project, Excel, or a custom Visual Basic program.

42

INTERFACING APPLICATIONS TO EXCHANGE SERVER

FIGURE 42.5.

Main screen of the Schedule+ sample application.

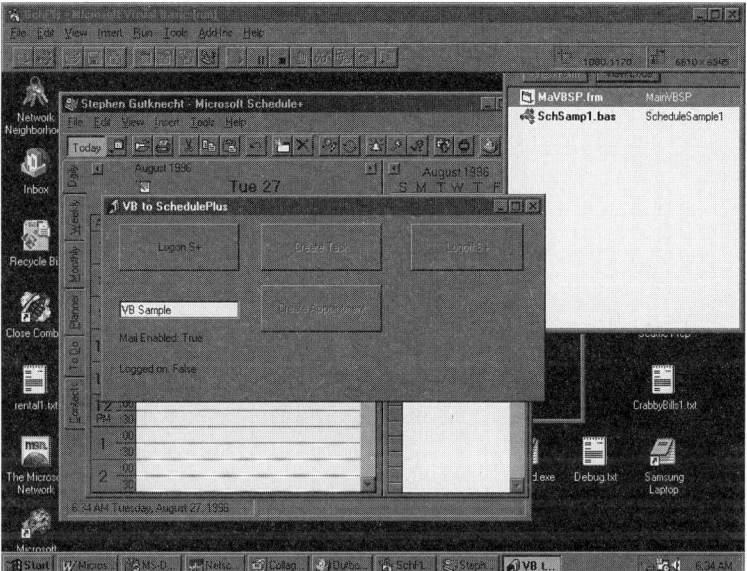

TIP

Schedule+ 7.0 is actually available in two flavors. One is included with Office 95 and is identified as Schedule+ 7.0 in the Help About. The second one is included with Exchange Server client and is identified as Schedule+ 7.0a in the Help About. Make sure the client has the appropriate Exchange-aware version to ensure proper compatibility with the programs.

Program Review

The program main form, titled MainVBSP.frm, contains four buttons. The first of these buttons, labeled Logon S+, initiates the MAPI session. The second button, labeled Create Task, initiates the creation of Schedule+ to-do entry. The third button, Create Appointment, initiates the creation of a sample appointment. The final button, Logoff S+, closes the MAPI session.

Initial Button State

The properties of the buttons are set in such a way that only the Logon S+ button is enabled when the form is first started. This ensures that a logoff is always proceeded by a logon, and that the test routines are not executed without being logged on to the MAPI provider (Exchange).

Logging On

When the Logon S+ button is pressed, the following code is activated (tied to the button event). `LogonSchedule` is a call to a subroutine that will initiate the MAPI logon. The Logon S+ button is then disabled, the Logoff S+ button is enabled, and the two sample activity buttons are enabled:

```
LogonSchedule
ButtonLogon.Enabled = 0
ButtonLogoff.Enabled = 1
ButtonCreateTask.Enabled = 1
ButtonCreateAppointment.Enabled = 1
```

The `LogonSchedule` subroutine actually performs the MAPI logon. A global variable `GLB_MAPISession` will point to the MAPI logon. The following code establishes that session and sets the global variable:

```
Set GLB_MAPISession = CreateObject("MAPI.Session")
GLB_MAPISession.Logon
```

The following code actually links to the schedule itself. `GLB_AppSchedulePlus` global variable will be set to the schedule:

```
Set GLB_AppSchedulePlus = CreateObject("SchedulePlus.Application")
Set GLB_UserSchedule = GLB_AppSchedulePlus.ScheduleLogged
```

Sample Task on To Do List

The button labeled Create Task will use the active MAPI and Schedule+ sessions to create an appointment on the To Do list of Schedule+. The button calls the routine `VBSampleTask` that performs the procedure.

A new Table object is created of type `SingleTasks` to define the structure. Next, a task item is created from this structure. The task will be tracked by the variable `TaskItem`:

```
Set objTable = GLB_UserSchedule.SingleTasks
Set TaskItem = objTable.New
```

The variables `DateToday` and `DateEnd` are created to define the end date of the task. Schedule+ typically tracks tasks by their end date. The routine `LConvertTo32bitDate` is described in the OLE Messaging help file; it is required due to the unique way that Schedule+ encodes dates (different from the Visual Basic data type):

```
DateToday = DateAdd("d", 1, Now)
DateEnd = LConvertTo32bitDate(DateAdd("d", 1, DateToday))
```

The `TaskItem` is then populated with the sample data:

```
TaskItem.SetProperties _
    Text:=MainVBSP.TextSample1.Text & ": " & Now(), _
    Notes:="Sample task from _BackOffice Unleashed_", _
    EndDate:=DateEnd
```

The object is released to initiate the actual transaction:

```
Set TaskItem = Nothing
Set objTable = Nothing
```

Looking at the Schedule+ application main view, a new to-do event should now appear. Figure 42.6 shows the details of this event.

FIGURE 42.6.

Details of the Task created by the sample Visual Basic program.

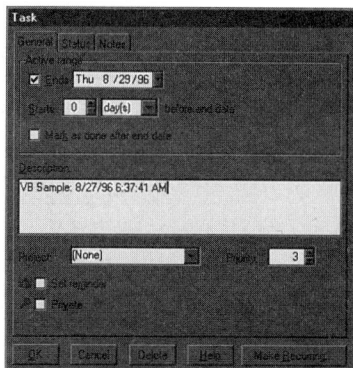

Sample Appointment

Pressing the Create Appointment button initiates the subroutine `VBSampleAppointment`. Using the already-open MAPI and Schedule+ sessions, a new appointment will be created.

> **TIP**
>
> The appointment created is flagged as "`tentative`". This allows the users who receive the appointment a chance to confirm that they are actually accepting the appointment.

The subroutine first creates a table object of the new `SingleAppointments` object:

```
Set objTable = GLB_UserSchedule.SingleAppointments
```

The start and end appointment dates are set. The date will be set to start in one minute (from execution time) and end in two hours:

```
AppointmentStart = DateAdd("n", 1, Now)
AppointmentEnd = DateAdd("h", 2, AppointmentStart)
```

A new instance of the `SingleAppointments` object is created. The properties of the appointment are set to sample entries:

```
Set AppointmentItem = objTable.New
AppointmentItem.SetProperties _
  Text:="Work with BackOffice Unleashed", _
  Notes:="Spend Two Hours working with OLE/MAPI samples to construct super app!", _
  Start:=AppointmentStart, _
  End:=AppointmentEnd, _
  CreatorName:="VB Sample Program"
```

The object is released to initiate the actual creation of the object:

```
Set AppointmentItem = Nothing
Set objTable = Nothing
```

Figure 42.7 shows the appointment in the Schedule+ main screen; Figure 42.8 shows the details of the appointment.

FIGURE 42.7.

*Main Schedule+ screen
showing new
appointment.*

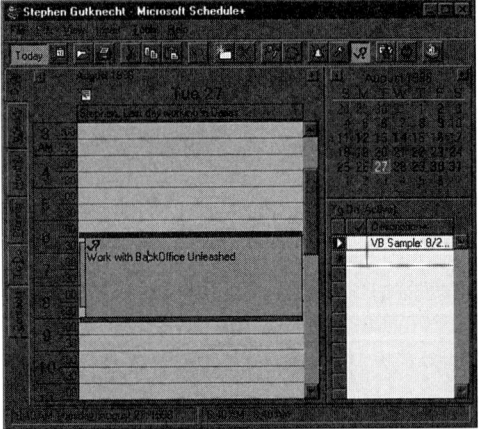

Logoff of Session

The Logoff S+ button will close the links to Schedule+ and MAPI. The buttons are restored to their previous states, as they were when the program first started. The MAPI session is closed, closing the link to the Schedule+ program.

FIGURE 42.8.

Details of new appointment.

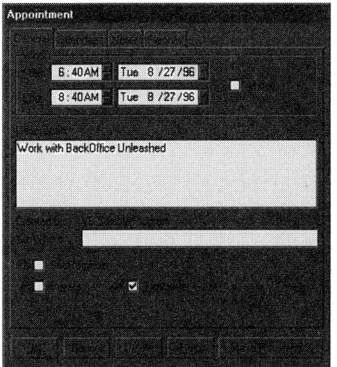

Sample Custom Forms Applications

Microsoft has included several excellent form samples. Using the Electronic Forms Designer, these can quickly be compiled and installed.

As mentioned previously, the forms are saved as Visual Basic projects. These can be manually edited with the 16-bit version of Visual Basic.

Performance of Exchange Forms

As mentioned earlier, the Exchange Forms Designer generates 16-bit Visual Basic EXE program files.

> **NOTE**
>
> Windows NT on Alpha, MIPS, Power PC, and other RISC platforms do not have a compiler to generate forms. Because the forms are 16-bit EXE programs, they can run in x86 emulation mode of Windows NT. However, the forms themselves need to be authored and/or compiled on an Intel i386-compatible machine.

Many users have complained about the time it takes to open and process even simple forms using Exchange. If there is an opportunity to assist these users, one of the easiest tips is to hide and unhide the form instead of closing and opening between processing. Exchange and Visual Basic, especially on Windows NT or Windows 95 where they run with Win16 emulation, can take time to load and start. By keeping the form process and associated resources in memory, almost all of the performance bottlenecks are eliminated.

Samples Included with Visual Basic 4.0

Microsoft's Visual Basic 4.0, when installed, includes a MAPI sample in the \SAMPLE\MAPI\VBMAIL.VBP project file. The sample is a minimal client for composing and reading e-mail. It works with either the Microsoft Mail 3.*x* or Exchange client.

MSMAPI16.OCX and MSMAPI32.OCX are the two Visual Basic library files—the first for 16-bit environments, the second for 32-bit environments.

Visual Basic encapsulates MAPI into two main objects. The first of these objects is named MAPISession; it has properties and several action codes. The second object is MAPIMessages.

Internet Explorer to Exchange

Microsoft's ActiveX architecture can be linked to OLE Automation interfaces, such as the OLE Messaging architecture used in the earlier Visual Basic and Visual Basic for Applications samples.

There also seems to be considerable interest in linking the Internet Information Server (IIS) to Exchange Public Folders or Exchange mail. Microsoft is working on integrating such features into the next update of Exchange.

> **NOTE**
>
> See Chapter 20, "Exchange Server and Mail Overview," for information on Exchange Server and the forthcoming Internet Web Connector.

Additional Information

Programming in any environment benefits from good sample programs and documentation. Exchange Server is no exception.

C++ is the dominant tool Microsoft and third-party vendors use to develop the Exchange Client.

Visual Basic seems best suited for "glue logic" when combining Exchange Server with other applications. Especially when working with Microsoft Office and Microsoft Project, OLE Automation programming interfaces and Visual Basic for Applications is an effective solution.

As mentioned earlier in the chapter, the Win32 and BackOffice SDK can be acquired by subscribing to Microsoft's Developer's Network (MSDN). Here are some of the resources of interest to an Exchange developer:

- Microsoft Win32 SDK; MAPI SDK
- Microsoft BackOffice SDK; Exchange SDK

- Microsoft Visual Basic Programming System for Windows
- Microsoft OLE Messaging Library Programmer's Reference
- Microsoft Exchange Application Designer's Guide
- MAPI Programmer's Reference

Internet Resources

The Internet is obviously a valuable resource for program samples, API documentation, and advice from other developers.

MAPI-L Mailing List

A mailing list for discussion of MAPI programming can be accessed using Internet electronic mail. Send a message to `"LISTSERV@PEACH.EASE.LSOFT.COM"` with the message text `"SUBSCRIBE MAPI-L"`. The mail list server at LSOFT.COM will automatically respond to the request with a mail message providing further instructions.

> **NOTE**
>
> When sending a subscribe command for an Internet Mailing list, make sure automatic signature features are turned off. The automated list processor programs parse all the incoming lines of a message; the only entry should be the `"SUBSCRIBE MAPI-L"` command.

Microsoft's World Wide Web Site

With the fast pace of Exchange and Internet development, electronic communications is often the fastest and most efficient means of communicating information. Microsoft has several Web pages of interest to developers of Exchange.

Microsoft has a series of pages devoted to Exchange Server, including sample applications and product announcements. The site can be found at

`http://www.microsoft.com/Exchange`

In addition, a MAPI home page has been established. This is the source for the most recent MAPI SDK and other valuable documentation. The site can be found at

`http://www.microsoft.com/win32dev/mapi/`

Look also at Microsoft Developer's Network resources at

`http://www.microsoft.com/msdn`

Information on these pages enables a developer to get the programming tools described in this chapter.

Summary

This chapter introduced the interfaces, tools, and possibilities of Exchange and MAPI programming. However, this is just a starting point. The samples shown can get a programmer started, but much more can be done.

Although this chapter concentrated on client-side OLE Automation, Extended MAPI programming opens a wider range of possibilities. To exploit these more advanced routines, expect to spend more time learning the programming. C++ is by far the preferred language.

Interfacing Applications to IIS

by Martin Larsson

IN THIS CHAPTER

This chapter explains how to interface with the Microsoft Internet Information Server. There are two different perspectives on interfacing:

- Browser interface
- Extensions and interfaces to the server software

The first deals with how various browsers handle the information provided by IIS. Most of this is general and works with other Web servers as well. The second is used to provide dynamic Web pages by executing a program on the server. Both perspectives are described in this chapter. The main focus is on extensions and interfaces to the actual server software. The chapter also provides general overviews of alternatives, mainly options for executing code on the client.

ISAPI, CGI, and Visual Basic Scripting Interface

If you want to create dynamic Web pages, you have to execute code somewhere. This could be on the server or on the client machine.

Client-Side Code

To execute code on the client machine, you can embed some form of a script in the HTML document. This could be JavaScript or VBScript. Currently, only Microsoft Internet Explorer 3 supports both (actually, IE 3 supports JScript, a 100% JavaScript-compatible scripting language). Netscape Navigator 2 and 3 support JavaScript. Both scripting languages are embedded as plain text, so anyone can see, copy, modify, and use the code. Another drawback is that you are quite limited in what you can do with these scripting languages. To remedy this, Java and ActiveX controls can be used. Java applets and ActiveX controls are not included in an HTML document, but rather referenced from it. Net browser sees the reference and opens a second connection to the server to fetch the code. The code is then run on the client machine.

Although running code on the client machine is very tempting, it has its drawbacks:

- Not all browsers support the necessary language(s).
- Code has to be downloaded; this takes time and bores customers.
- Proprietary code is distributed.
- The security issues are not resolved, so users might be weary.

Server-Side Code

The alternative is to run the code on the server. This supports all browsers, even the ones not created yet. With careful planning, even people running Lynx will be able to get exciting output from your site! What you lose is interactivity. Nothing happens in the users' browsers until they submit or request additional information from the server.

To provide input to server-side code, you'll usually use HTML forms, although this is not strictly necessary. The following are the three main jobs for server-side code:

■ Perform some kind of advanced calculation (such as a nontrivial tax calculation).

■ Enable users to search a database.

■ Enable users to buy or order merchandise.

To perform a calculation, the user enters the needed information into a form and sends it to the server. The server executes the needed code and then returns the result to the user, possibly with graphics, links, suggestions, and so on. You will typically develop custom code for this type of task.

If you want users to search a database, you might not need any initial input, but you are producing an HTML document to send back. Applications like this are ideal jobs for IDC (Internet Database Connector).

To sell merchandise on the Internet, you typically bring up a fairly large form where the user inputs name, address, card number, and so on. When the order is processed, a page containing a "Thank you for your order" usually is sufficient. This page does not need to be dynamic, but can often be created once and for all. There are several commercially available solutions for providing a "shopping basket" type of ordering. Alternatively, you can build your own using IDC, custom-code, or both.

The following sections describe what interfaces IIS supports to enable you to create exciting, dynamic Web pages of the three types. The sample program provided later in this chapter searches and displays posts I've saved from various newsgroups. The database here is simply a directory with text files.

CGI

If you want to perform a nontrivial calculation, and do not want to give away the code, you have to use some form of server-executable code. There are several ways to execute code on the server. Common to them all is that some HTML document references the executable, either directly or via a <form> tag. By locating the executable in a special directory (typically named Scripts or Bin), the server executes it rather than sending it to the client.

The most used server-side interface to Web servers is the Common Gateway Interface (CGI). To comply with the interface, the Web server software first fills environment variables with various information such as the following:

■ The IP address of the connected user

■ The user name, if provided

■ The referring page (how did we get here)

- The current path
- The query string

Then the server executes the referenced executable. This executable is called a script for historical reasons. When the web was young, CGI apps were usually written in one of UNIX's many scripting languages such as Perl. It is therefore common to call the application a CGI script, even if it's written in C or Pascal. The script reads the environment variables, as well as additional information from standard input, does its thing, and writes the resulting HTML document to standard output. The Web server sends this back to the client.

The main advantage of CGI is that most Web servers support it. Because of this, a script written in Perl for a UNIX server will likely run without modification on a Windows NT–based server. Another advantage is that since a CGI script is a separate application, it can be written in any language. A third advantage is that each instance of the CGI application is running in its own address space, so if one of them goes wild, none of the others are affected, and the server continues to work normally. Finally, all resources used are freed by the OS when the script terminates.

The various ups and downs of creating CGI scripts is a huge topic which will not be covered here. Sams Publishing has several books on this topic, among others, *CGI Developer's Guide* by Eugene Eric Kim.

IIS supports running CGI scripts directly by adding elements to the registry. You can associate an application with an extension the usual way. For instance, you tell Windows to always open files with extension TXT with Notepad. Similarly, you can tell Windows that all files with extension PL should be executed with Perl.EXE. Another possibility is to add a REG_SZ entry to the following registry key:

```
HKEY_LOCAL_MACHINE\SYSTEM
  \CurrentControlSet
    \Services
      \W3SVC
        \Parameters
          \ScriptMap
```

The main drawback of CGI is that each user needs a new process to be executing on the server. This can eat a lot of resources. If you have a heavy-traffic server (such as Alta Vista or Microsoft's home page), it is likely that the server will kneel and die. Because of this, Microsoft created an alternative, ISAPI.

ISAPI Extension DLL

To overcome the problems of CGI, IIS supports extensions in a DLL. The server needs to load the DLL only once, but can start many threads within that DLL. This way the startup time is minimized, and the resource use is lowered.

> **TIP**
>
> Because the DLL is loaded only once, the Web server must be stopped to be able to overwrite the DLL. This can be quite a hassle when developing and testing. To avoid this, set the following registry key to 0:
>
> ```
> HKEY_LOCAL_MACHINE\SYSTEM
>   \CurrentControlSet
>     \Services
>       \W3SVC
>         \Parameters
>           \CacheExtensions
> ```

There are two types of ISAPI DLL's. The first is called an *extension DLL*. The other is called a *filter DLL*. Extension DLLs are called by IIS whenever an HTML page references it. They therefore sit between IIS and the resources on the server. Filter DLLs, on the other hand, are called at every client connection. They are located between the client and IIS, and can filter out and add information.

For an extension DLL to adhere to the ISAPI specification, it must export two functions, `GetExtensionVersion()` and `HttpExtensionProc()`. The first provides version control, and the last does all the actual work. The two functions are prototyped as follows in Borland Delphi 2:

```
function GetExtensionVersion(var Ver: THSE_VERSION_INFO) : BOOL; stdcall;
function HttpExtensionProc(var ECB: TEXTENSION_CONTROL_BLOCK) : DWORD; stdcall;
```

When IIS calls `GetExtensionVersion()`, it expects the DLL to set the two fields of the `THSE_VERSION_INFO` structure. A typical `GetExtensionVersion()` looks like this:

```
function GetExtensionVersion(
        var Ver : THSE_VERSION_INFO
        )        : BOOL; stdcall
begin
  Ver.dwExtensionVersion := MAKELONG(HSE_VERSION_MINOR,
                                     HSE_VERSION_MAJOR);

  StrLCopy(Ver.lpszExtensionDesc, 'My Extension DLL',
        HSE_MAX_EXT_DLL_NAME_LEN);

  Result := True;
end; { GetExtensionVersion }
```

This tells IIS what version of the ISAPI specification the DLL was compiled for and gives the DLL a descriptive name. The name is not currently used for anything but could probably be used for logging purposes.

`HttpExtensionProc()` is a bit more interesting. It takes only one argument, but that is a pointer to a large structure, the `TEXTENSION_CONTROL_BLOCK`. This is defined as follows:

```
TEXTENSION_CONTROL_BLOCK = packed record
    cbSize: DWORD;                      // size of this struct.
    dwVersion: DWORD;                   // version info of this spec
    ConnID: HCONN;                      // Context number not to be modified!
    dwHttpStatusCode: DWORD;            // HTTP Status code
            // null terminated log info specific to this Extension DLL
    lpszLogData: array [0..HSE_LOG_BUFFER_LEN-1] of Char;
    lpszMethod: PChar;                  // REQUEST_METHOD
    lpszQueryString: PChar;             // QUERY_STRING
    lpszPathInfo: PChar;                // PATH_INFO
    lpszPathTranslated: PChar;          // PATH_TRANSLATED
    cbTotalBytes: DWORD;                // Total bytes indicated from client
    cbAvailable: DWORD;                 // Available number of bytes
    lpbData: Pointer;                   // pointer to cbAvailable bytes
    lpszContentType: PChar;             // Content type of client data

    GetServerVariable: TGetServerVariableProc;
    WriteClient: TWriteClientProc;
    ReadClient: TReadClientProc;
    ServerSupportFunction: TServerSupportFunctionProc;
  end;
```

The most important fields are lpszMethod, lpszQueryString, cbTotalBytes, cbAvailable, and lpbData. lpszMethod can be either POST or GET. POST can send more data, but GET is easier to handle. If the lpszMethod is POST, cbTotalBytes bytes has been sent from the client. Of these, cbAvailable are currently stored in an area pointed to by lpbData. To get more data, ReadClient must be used. If the lpszMethod is GET, all available data is contained in the 0 terminated lpszQueryString. (When I use the term "query string," it will refer to either lpszQueryString or ldbData, depending on the method.)

The query string contains all input from the form on the Web page. The entries are separated by an ampersand. Each entry contains the name of the variable, an equals sign, and the value. Because the parameters were originally passed on the command line to CGI scripts, all spaces are replaced with a plus sign. The query string is also limited to 7-bit ASCII, so all other characters as well as the special ones (=, &, +, and %) are translated into a hexadecimal representation. This starts with a % and is followed by two characters denoting the hexadecimal value of the actual character. To use the query string in any useful manner, it must be decoded.

An example will clarify. Consider a form with two input variables, Var1 and Var2. Suppose the user writes I am with you in Var1 and 100% in Var2. The query string will look like this:

Var1=I+am+with+you&Var2=100%25

> **NOTE**
>
> Here are some notes on decoding the query string:
>
> 1. If a variable does not contain any data, the browser may or may not include the variable in the query string. When it is included, the equals sign is followed directly with an ampersand or the end of the string.

2. The last variable does not have an ampersand at the end.
3. Some browsers attach an extra CRLF to the query string. This is nonstandard.

The four last fields in the `TEXTENSION_CONTROL_BLOCK` are functions used to communicate with IIS and the client:

- `GetServerVariable()` enables you to query for other variables not provided in one of the other fields. It is, for instance, possible to query for the referring page, the name of the user's browser, and so on.

- `ReadClient()` enables you to get more information from a `POST` operation.

- `WriteClient()` enables you to write to the user's browser. Everything you pass to `WriteClient()` will show up at the user's browser.

- `ServerSupportFunction()` is a general purpose function for setting various status information and so on.

ISAPI Filter DLLs

A filter DLL is located between the Web server and the client. All data flowing between the two can be routed through the filter. It can then translate, modify, add, and remove information as it sees fit.

The ISAPI filter specification is very similar to the extension specification. A filter DLL exports two functions: `GetFilterVersion()` and `HttpFilterProc()`. Contrary to the `GetExtensionVersion()` function, the `GetFilterVersion()` does more important things than just return the supported version and a description. The prototype looks like this in C/C++:

```
BOOL WINAPI GetFilterVersion(HTTP_FILTER_VERSION * pVer);
```

`HTTP_FILTER_VERSION` looks like this:

```
typedef struct _HTTP_FILTER_VERSION
{
    DWORD  dwServerFilterVersion;  /* Version of the spec the  *
                                    *     server is using      */
    DWORD  dwFilterVersion;        /* Fields specified by the  *
                                    *     client               */
    CHAR   lpszFilterDesc[SF_MAX_FILTER_DESC_LEN];
    DWORD  dwFlags;
} HTTP_FILTER_VERSION;
```

The `dwFilterVersion` and `lpszFilterDesc` is set as in the extension DLL. `dwFlags` is a combination of flags indicating what the filter wants to see and at what priority the filter should run. Usually the default priority by specifying `SF_NOTIFY_ORDER_DEFAULT` is sufficient. Table 43.1 shows the different notifications a filter can hook.

43

INTERFACING APPLICATIONS TO IIS

Table 43.1. ISAPI filter notifications.

Notification Flag	Description
SF_NOTIFY_SECURE_PORT	Notify application only for sessions over a secure port.
SF_NOTIFY_NONSECURE_PORT	Notify application only for sessions over a nonsecure port.
SF_NOTIFY_READ_RAW_DATA	Allow the DLL to see the raw data. The data returned will contain both headers and data.
SF_NOTIFY_PREPROC_HEADERS	The server has preprocessed the headers.
SF_NOTIFY_AUTHENTICATION	The server is authenticating the client.
SF_NOTIFY_URL_MAP	The server is mapping a logical URL to a physical path.
SF_NOTIFY_SEND_RAW_DATA	The server is sending raw data back to the client.
SF_NOTIFY_LOG	The server is writing information to the server log.
SF_NOTIFY_END_OF_NET_SESSION	The session with the client is ending.

When a filter hooks any of these, it will be called each time the server gets an event that matches. It is therefore often useful to hook SF_NOTIFY_URL_MAP. This will let you tag connections to files you will modify. If you write a filter for macro substitution, for instance, you have to make sure you're not modifying files the users are downloading.

When one of the hooked events occurs, HttpFilterProc() is called. Its function has the following prototype:

```
DWORD WINAPI HttpFilterProc(
    HTTP_FILTER_CONTEXT *     pfc,
    DWORD                     NotificationType,
    VOID *                    pvNotification
    );
```

The filter context uniquely identifies this communication with the client. It has the following attributes:

```
typedef struct _HTTP_FILTER_CONTEXT
{
    DWORD        cbSize;
    DWORD        Revision;      /* Structure revision level. */
```

```
    PVOID           ServerContext;
    DWORD           ulReserved;
    BOOL            fIsSecurePort;  /* TRUE if this request is    *
                                    * coming over a secure port */
    PVOID           pFilterContext;/* A context that can be used *
                                    * by the filter             */
    BOOL (WINAPI * GetServerVariable) (
        struct _HTTP_FILTER_CONTEXT * pfc,
        LPSTR                         lpszVariableName,
        LPVOID                        lpvBuffer,
        LPDWORD                       lpdwSize
        );
    BOOL (WINAPI * AddResponseHeaders) (
        struct _HTTP_FILTER_CONTEXT * pfc,
        LPSTR                         lpszHeaders,
        DWORD                         dwReserved
        );
    BOOL (WINAPI * WriteClient)  (
        struct _HTTP_FILTER_CONTEXT * pfc,
        LPVOID                        Buffer,
        LPDWORD                       lpdwBytes,
        DWORD                         dwReserved
        );
    VOID * (WINAPI * AllocMem) (
        struct _HTTP_FILTER_CONTEXT * pfc,
        DWORD                         cbSize,
        DWORD                         dwReserved
        );
    BOOL (WINAPI * ServerSupportFunction) (
        struct _HTTP_FILTER_CONTEXT * pfc,
        enum SF_REQ_TYPE              sfReq,
        PVOID                         pData,
        DWORD                         ul1,
        DWORD                         ul2
        );
} HTTP_FILTER_CONTEXT, *PHTTP_FILTER_CONTEXT;
```

As you can see, the filter can use many of the functions the extension DLL can. ReadClient() is not supported, but you can get all data from the client by hooking SF_NOTIFY_READ_RAW_DATA. AllocMem() can be used in conjunction with the pFilterContext field. Together they provide for connection-local memory. Any memory allocated by AllocMem() will automatically be released when the connection terminates. However, it is not very efficient. If you want high speed, you can allocate memory any way you want, and then free it during the SF_NOTIFY_END_OF_NET_SESSION event.

The NotificationType parameter is one of the flags in Table 43.1. If you have selected multiple flags, HttpFilterProc() will be called multiple times for each client connection.

pvNotification contains the data specific to the connection and the event. Table 43.2 summarizes the actual type of pvNotification for the different events.

Table 43.2. ISAPI filter events.

Event Type	pvNotification *Points To*
SF_NOTIFY_READ_RAW_DATA	HTTP_FILTER_RAW_DATA
SF_NOTIFY_SEND_RAW_DATA	HTTP_FILTER_RAW_DATA
SF_NOTIFY_PREPROC_HEADERS	HTTP_FILTER_PREPROC_HEADERS
SF_NOTIFY_AUTHENTICATION	HTTP_FILTER_AUTHENT
SF_NOTIFY_URL_MAP	HTTP_FILTER_URL_MAP
SF_NOTIFY_LOG	HTTP_FILTER_LOG

Once you determine that you want to do something with an event, you are free to modify the data to be sent or read. You can also write additional information to the user. Because IIS only supports the simple file-include part of Server Side Includes (SSI), you could write a filter that adds the missing functionality.

Problems with ISAPI DLLs

Unfortunately, using a DLL isn't all sweet. Because the DLL is only loaded once, any resource leakage in it will accumulate and eventually bring down the server. When you create a DLL to provide dynamic Web pages, you usually use code written by others. This could be a graphics library, or the compiler's runtime library. Because you often don't have control over these, resource leaks can be impossible to fix. The only solution is to stop IIS regularly and then re-start it. Windows NT frees all resources when a process is stopped.

> **TIP**
>
> Using the standard Windows NT scheduler, you can automatically start and stop the Web server service at regular intervals. This reduces the chances for violent crashes.

In addition to leakage problems, you get concurrency problems. This means, among other things, that you have to make sure global variables will not be read and written by different threads at the same time, and the code has to be thread safe. Again, because you usually don't have control over all the source, maintaining thread safety can be very difficult.

Because Windows NT will not allow 32-bit code to execute 16-bit code, all ISAPI DLLs have to be 32-bit. Sometimes this is not an option. You might be depending on some old code that won't easily recompile, or maybe a third-party component that's not currently available in a 32-bit version. One solution to this is to run the 16-bit application as a CGI script. Another solution is to run the 16-bit code as a separate application and use the WM_COPYDATA message to transfer data.

Httpodbc.dll reads this file and hooks up to the doc_archive database using guest as the login name and secret as the password. The SQL statement is then executed, and a result table is returned. Using the returned table and the referenced HTX file, a Web page is created.

A Sample HTX File

The following is the HTX file that matches the IDC file. It looks very much like a normal HTML file except for some special <%xxx%> tags. These tags either expand to the content of a column in the result table, or are special macro markers for Httpodbc.dll. For instance, in the following code, the <%begindetail%> and <%enddetail%> tags signify that the text between them should be output once for each row in the table. <%file%>, on the other hand, expands to the content of the column named file in the current row:

```
<html>
<head></head>
<body>

<h1>Found documents</h1>

<table border="1">
  <tr>
    <th>ID</th>
    <th>Issue</A></th>
    <th>Creation data</th>
    <th>Project</th>
  </tr>

<%begindetail%>
  <tr>
    <td><%ID%></td>
    <td><a href="/documents/<%file%>"><%issue%></a></td>
    <td><%db_createdate%></td>
    <td><%Prosjekt%></td>
  </tr>
<%enddetail%>
</table>

</body>
</html>
```

The HTX files support nested <%if%>, <%else%>, and <%endif%> tags. IIS 1.0 didn't support nested <%if%> constructs, but IIS 2.0 does. Armed with this, you can do different things, depending on various results in the table.

Problems with ODBC

Although using IDC is very nice, it has some serious drawbacks. One of the problems is that many ODBC drivers are not threadsafe. Currently, only the driver for MS SQL Server works reliably on a Web server. This should be fixed quickly, but make sure your ODBC driver works.

Testing it is very simple. Just bring up two instances of your favorite browser and request the IDC document from the server in both windows simultaneously. If the server crashes, you need to change your ODBC driver.

Another problem with IDC is that error messages from the database turn up on the users' monitors. The only way to avoid that is to write an ISAPI filter DLL that modifies the output stream. Doing so is fairly simple, but it requires knowledge of either C/C++ or Borland Delphi. One of the sample DLLs in this chapter looks for errors from IIS and displays a nicer version. It should be fairly straightforward to modify it to look for database errors instead.

Active Web Concepts and Extensions

You have already explored in detail some possibilities for creating HTML documents on the fly. To create truly interactive Web pages, however, requires code to run on the client machine. There are a lot of ways to do this. This section touches lightly on the various concepts.

The simplest way to create a Web page with some movement on it is to use animated GIFs. An animated GIF is simply a series of pictures shown in quick succession. Running over the Internet is very slow, but once all the images are in the browser's cache, speed is acceptable. Because the pictures are shown in a constant loop, they quickly become boring and soon after that annoying. If you change them often enough, they might be worth it.

Another option is to use scripting languages such as JavaScript and VBScript. Although they are limited in functionality, they still can verify input. Combined with code on the server it could be a winning combination. The main advantage with a script is that it is embedded in the HTML document and is therefore very fast to download.

A third option is to use plug-ins. A plug-in is an extension of the user's browser. Usually, it knows how to decode one or several special file formats (or MIME formats to be correct). For instance, a plug-in can understand the Virtual Reality Markup Language (VRML). With it, the browser can render 3D worlds on the user's screen. Other plug-ins support real-time audio transmissions, such as radio, over the Internet. Plug-ins can usually be used to view many different sites, so although it might take a user quite some time to download a specific plug-in, once it is there it is instantly useful in many places.

A fourth option is to execute code that is visually separate from the browser, but still controlled by it. Examples of this are Java applets and ActiveX controls. These extensions create and use their own windows. They receive user input, deal with it, and/or communicate with their originating server to create a really active Web presence. At this point, there's not much difference from downloading and running programs the way you are used to through anonymous FTP. The extensions are normally only usable for the given site, and they do take quite some time to download.

The last option is to abandon the limitations of the browser entirely and run everything over the Internet, much like you run programs on a LAN today. This has actually been suggested as the future of computing by Oracle, IBM, and others. Current bandwidth prohibits this, however.

Adaptive Web Programming for Various Browsers

One of the big problems with creating a Web presence today is the enormous number of different browsers available. Although there actually exists standards for HTML documents (three versions), few browsers implement the entire standard and most add some features of their own. This creates a nightmare for Web designers and programmers. One possibility is to use the least common denominator. This means no graphics, no tables, and no fun. An alternative is to target only the newest browsers. Unfortunately, this is rarely an option because most users don't want to spend the time and money to download 8M executables over a 14,400 modem—especially not in countries where local calls are not free.

The solution, then, is to provide both. That creates the extra headache of keeping two separate versions of the documents updated, but it often is the only solution. The good news is that tags not supported in a browser are supposed to be ignored. This means that you can create an entrance that lets the people with the fancy browsers automatically get the fancy layout, while the rest get something decent.

One common way to separate the pages is to make one version with tables and simple graphics, and the other version support frames, JavaScript/VBScript, Java, ActiveX, animated GIFs, and so on. The reason for separating at frames versus no-frames is that most browsers support tables and graphics. The ones who don't can still display a usable result by using some simple HTML tricks. However, frame-enabled pages look really silly with browsers that don't support them.

Using HTML

Text-mode browsers generally support only the HTML 1.0 specification. Liberal use of the `alt` parameter on `<img>` tags enables these browsers to display something meaningful. Browsers for seeing-impaired people also have something to say if the `alt` parameter is used.

To create a table that displays acceptably on most browsers, including Lynx, add a `<br>` tag as the last tag in each `<td>` element. Add a `<p>` tag after the table, also. A typical table then looks like this:

```
<table>
  <tr>
    <td>Row 1, Column 1<br></td>
    <td>Row 1, Column 2<br></td>
  </tr>
  <tr>
    <td>Row 2, Column 1<br></td>
    <td>Row 2, Column 2<br></td>
  </tr>
  <!-- And so on -->
</table>
<p>
```

This will not disturb browsers that support tables, because they try to limit the size of each cell. A <br> won't matter in that case.

To differentiate between frames and no-frames browsers, use the following HTML document:

```
<html>
<head>
<title>A Frame Selector</title>
</head>
<frameset rows="100%,*">
<noframes>
<body>
This will only be read by browsers that have no idea about frames.
You can put an entire page here, or just a note stating that the
users should upgrade their browsers. Just telling the users to
upgrade will probably not gain you many friends, but at least you
don't have to maintain two separate versions of the same
information.
</body>
</noframes>
<frame src="framed.htm">
<frame src="dummy.htm" scrolling="NO" noresize>
</frameset>
</html>
```

The reason this works is that browsers that do not support frames will ignore the <frameset> and <noframes> tags. This brings them to the <body> tag, which they handle as usual. When they are finished with the </body> tag, they will ignore the rest of the file, except the very last tag.

Frame-enabled browsers, on the other hand, will understand all tags and create two frames—one that uses the entire screen, and one that uses the rest. The last will, of course, be invisible. All the fancy formatting, such as animated GIFs, JavaScript, and real frames, is then placed in the framed.htm file.

Using ISAPI

One of the functions available to ISAPI extension and filter DLLs is GetServerVariable(). If you pass ALL_HTTP to this function, it will return a newline-separated list of additional variables. One of these is HTTP_USERAGENT, an identifier of the user's browser. You can use this to target each different version of browser specifically. Doing so can be necessary, because each browser has its own set of features and bugs. It is, however, a large undertaking, because there are an incredible number of different browsers. Each time a new one comes along, you have to update the code. Using plain HTML, as shown previously, should get you by in most cases.

Java and J++ Alternatives

While the incredible explosion of the usage of the Internet totally surprised most of the existing software houses, the popularity of Java was more expected. But Java is still one of the most hyped-up and confusing parts of the Internet hoopla. There are Java applications, Java applets, and JavaScript. In addition, Microsoft has introduced ActiveX controls. This has been looked upon as evidence that Microsoft doesn't support Java. While describing all these technologies in detail is way beyond the scope of this chapter (and this book as well), a basic knowledge is very useful when considering the options to make attractive Web pages. I'll therefore provide an overview of the involved technologies here.

Java

Java is a general-purpose multiplatform programming language based on C++. The language is developed and owned by Sun Microsystems, Inc. The main purpose of Java is to be able to create efficient programs with an attractive GUI that can be downloaded over a network (such as the Internet) and executed. All potentially difficult issues of C++ programming have been left out. Multiple inheritance and pointers are among the things that were discarded. Other useful features were added, such as garbage collection and the capability of supporting multiple interfaces in a single object. This creates a compact language that is easy to write code in and easy to compile. Microsoft claims its Visual J++ compiles at speeds up to one million lines per minute.

A Java compiler does not create a binary executable. Instead, the source code is compiled to a byte code that is interpreted on the target platform. This means that a Java application can be compiled on a NeXT machine running NeXTStep and executed under Windows NT on a PowerPC machine. This makes Java applications very attractive for distributed computing in a heterogeneous network environment.

Of course, executing through an interpreter is slow, because each instruction has to be decoded each time. The answer is JIT, a Just In Time compiler. JIT simply compiles the code to native machine code before the execution of the Java application starts. After that, the Java application runs at full speed.

A reduced version of Java applications, known as Java applets, can be run with both MS IE 3 and Netscape Navigator 2 and 3. The Java applets can create a separate GUI for your Web pages, with buttons, windows, animation and the like. Someone has already created a multiplayer version of Tetris using Java at

```
http://ariel.cobite.com/ultram/tetris/tetris.html
```

One of the biggest problems when defining what Java applets could do was to ensure that downloaded code was safe to execute—no matter where it came from or what evil intentions the original author had. To make sure violent code is not allowed to run, Java applets are, among other things, prohibited from writing to disk and communicating with other servers than the one they were downloaded from. They are also verified thoroughly before being allowed to run. Unfortunately, if there are bugs in the verifier, the system breaks down. The latest version of JavaScript can control Java applets, so they work in conjunction.

JavaScript is defined by Netscape. It is based on Java, but much of the original language has been removed to make JavaScript a lightweight scripting language. JavaScript supports most of the operators of Java, but has only a very limited number of datatypes. It is not possible to define new datatypes as is possible in Java.

J++

Visual J++ is Microsoft's development platform for Java applets. It is based on Microsoft's Visual C++ Developer Studio. J++ is Java with some added class libraries to make it possible to integrate Java, ActiveX controls, and VBScript. Among the extensions is that Microsoft's Virtual Java Machine, the interpreter that runs Java code, automatically creates COM objects of all Java objects. The result is that all available COM objects are used in the Java program looking like native Java classes. This makes it possible to integrate Java and ActiveX without any additional coding.

Visual J++ is currently in beta. Its main competitors are Symantec Café and Borland Latte. Café 1.0 was released in March 1996. Café 1.5 is currently in beta. All three are supposed to be released during the fall of 1996.

ActiveX

ActiveX controls, the concept formerly known as OLE Controls, is a specification for COM-based controls that can be transferred and executed over the Internet. Currently, the only implementation is on Windows, but there are supposedly UNIX versions and a Mac version in the works. ActiveX controls are allowed to do anything they want, including deleting files and formatting your hard drive. Instead of limiting the capabilities of the controls, and therefore their usefulness, Microsoft decided to include a verification system with the ActiveX specification. When you hit a Web page that references an ActiveX control, the author of the control is identified. If you trust the author, the control is downloaded and checked to make sure it has not been tampered with. Finally, it is executed. This is very similar to how shrinkwrapped applications work today. You don't worry about Microsoft Office destroying your hard disk, because you know who made it and you trust them.

Microsoft claims that ActiveX controls are not direct competitors to Java applets, but rather that they supplement each other. The evidence of this is most apparent in the different constraints they live under. Java applets are prohibited from doing anything that could potentially damage the client machine. ActiveX controls, on the other hand, do not have any limits of operation. This makes them more dangerous to use, but not worse than the shareware and freeware utilities we use every day.

I suspect Java applets will be used for smaller tasks that enhance the Web experience. ActiveX controls will be used for small distributed and client-server applictaions. Finally, Java applications will be used as a multi-platform alternative to C++.

Sample Programs

The first of the two sample programs in this chapter is an extension DLL. I read several newsgroups regularly. Because my current work involves Borland Delphi, I spend most of my Internet-time with the Delphi groups. Often, someone writes an article I find valuable enough to save. Usually it's about something I know I will be using in the near future. The number of saved articles quickly grew, and it became hard to find what I was looking for. Because we are running Microsoft IIS at work, I wrote a little DLL using Borland Delphi 2 to help me organize my articles.

Figure 43.1 shows what the input form looks like. The user can type words here that should be included and/or excluded from the search. Words separated by space are OR-ed. Clicking on the Search Now! button in the example brings up all articles containing the word `dynamic` or the word `array`. The example is available from my Web page at `http://www.delfidata.no/users/~martin` by following the Delphi link.

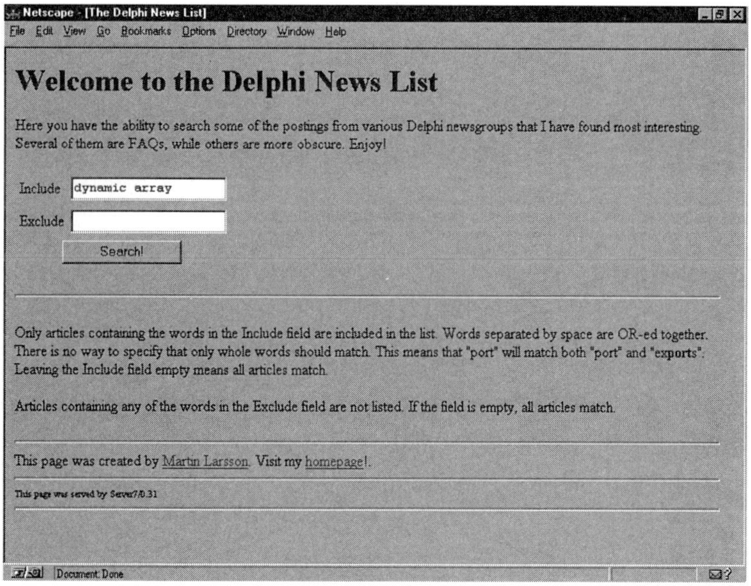

FIGURE 43.1.
Input form for the sample ISAPI DLL.

The second sample is a simple filter DLL that shows a nice message if a user requests a nonexisting URL. ISS normally shows a rather ugly `HTTP/1.0 404 Object Not Found` message. The DLL adds a nicer message and enables the user to link back to the referring page. Figure 43.2 shows what the user will see when they follow an outdated link.

FIGURE 43.2.

A user follows an outdated link.

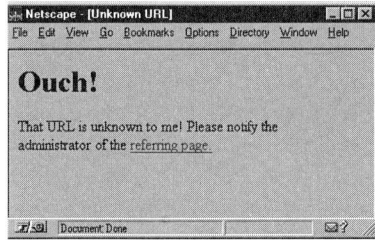

The Extension DLL

The sample extension DLL is very simple. It searches for all files with a TXT extension in a given directory. Each file is then loaded into memory and checked for the `Include` and `Exclude` parameters from the Web page. If the file is accepted, the `subject` and `from` fields of the posting are extracted and listed on the page. Figure 43.3 shows the result of the query in Figure 43.1.

FIGURE 43.3.

Example of search results.

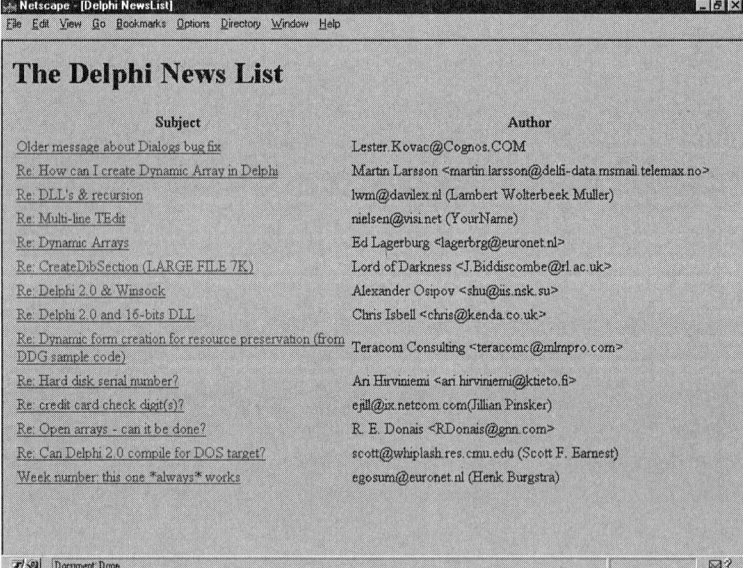

The DLL is composed of the following files:

- *News.List.DPR.* This is the project file. It defines the interface of the DLL and support for a test version in a standard EXE file.
- *Main.PAS.* This file implements the two functions required by ISAPI: GetExtensionVersion() and HttpExtensionProc().
- *NLExt.PAS.* In this file, a class TNLExt is defined. This does all the actual work of reading the directory, checking the files, and updating the client's Web browser.
- *ISAPILib.PAS.* Here, a general purpose THTTPExt class is defined. It encapsulates the TEXTENSION_CONTROL_BLOCK structure. In addition, it defines several functions to make it easier to write to Web clients. This class can be extended ad infinitum to make it very easy to create ISAPI DLLs.
- *Tester.PAS.* Debugging an ISAPI DLL is very difficult. The Web server is usually a separate machine from the place where you do development. In addition, debugging a service with a low-level debugger, using remote debugging or attaching to a running process isn't really my idea of fun. Therefore, I created a skeleton test application that sets up the TEXTENSION_CONTROL_BLOCK structure and calls HttpExtensionProc().

All the code for the sample is included at the end of the chapter. In the following paragraphs, you look at the most important areas of the DLL and explore possible enhancements and possibilities.

The Main Code

The GetExtensionVersion() function isn't very interesting. It doesn't do much other than telling IIS what version of the ISAPI specification the DLL supports. HttpExtensionProc(), on the other hand, is where all the action occurs. It looks like this:

```
function HttpExtensionProc(
          var ECB : TEXTENSION_CONTROL_BLOCK
          )            : DWORD; stdcall;
var
hMutex : THandle;
begin
  hMutex := CreateMutex(nil, False, 'NewsListMutex');
  WaitForSingleObject(hMutex, INFINITE);

  with TNLExt.Create(ECB) do begin
    DoIt;
    Result := ReturnValue;
    Free;
  end;

  ReleaseMutex(hMutex);
  CloseHandle(hMutex);
end; { HttpExtensionProc }
```

As you can see, it is very simple, but it does nonetheless perform some crucial operations. First of all, it threadsafes the DLL. This is done in a rude manner, namely by limiting the number of threads that can execute at any time to one. If two users try to access this DLL at the same time, one has to wait for the other to finish. This is not as bad as it sounds, because the DLL only takes a couple of seconds to run.

Using a mutex is a bit of an overkill here; a critical section object should be sufficient because you only need to control threads in a process and not different processes. However, critical section objects require initialization and finalization calls to be performed once. Usually, this happens in the DllEntryPoint() function when it receives DLL_PROCESS_ATTACH and DLL_PROCESS_DETACH. I put all the synchronization code here to keep the code simpler.

Between the WaitForSingleObject() and ReleaseMutex() calls, I created an object of type TNLExt. This object encapsulates the process of listing the news postings to the user.

TNLExt.DoIt is also a simple function, which looks like this:

```
procedure TNLExt.DoIt;
begin
  try
    with httpConnection do begin
      StdHeader('Delphi NewsList');
      StdBody;
      Paragraph;
      Header(1, 'The Delphi News List');
    end;
    ListFiles;
  except
    on E : Exception do
      httpConnection.Error('Exception ' + E.ClassName + #13 +
                            E.Message);
  end;
end; { TNLExt.DoIt }
```

httpConnection is an object of class THTTPExt. This class encapsulates the TEXTENSION_CONTROL_BLOCK and adds methods to make it easier to send text to the user's browser. WriteClient clutters the code, but procedures such as OutLine(), StdHeader(), Header(), and so on make the code easier to read and write. The five functions of the THTTPExt class used here do the following:

1. StdHeader() sends a note to the browser that it should expect text to follow. It also adds <html>, <head>, and <title> tags. The title is the string passed as a parameter.

2. StdBody() just outputs a <body> tag. It could be extended to include background picture and color information.

3. Paragraph() outputs a <p> tag.

4. Header() creates a header tag at the given level and outputs the text. In the previous code, the output would be <h1>The Delphi News List</h1>.

ListFiles does all the actual work of searching through the directory, checking the files, and adding the ones that match the search criteria to a table. The code for that is not very Web specific, so I'll just refer to the complete listing at the end. A commented version of all the code is available on my home page.

The exception handling ensures that errors in the extension DLL don't affect the Web server. Here, I'm just outputting the exception class and the message to the Web page to aid my debugging efforts. In a production environment, Error() would probably write the string parameter to a log file and display a general error message to the user.

> **TIP**
>
> When creating HTML documents dynamically, there is nothing stopping you from outputting the entire document as one line. However, this is extremely hard to read when you need to debug your DLL. Using indentation and line breaks liberally does wonders for readability and debugging.

Managing the Connection

There are two main objects dealing with the Web page in the NewsList.DLL: TNLExt and THTTPExt. They divide the work of getting a result to the user evenly. TNLExt decides the content and the layout of the page, and THTTPExt controls the actual sending of data and the physical layout to make the document readable in a text editor as well as a word processor.

The constructor of TNLExt looks like this:

```
constructor TNLExt.Create(var ECB : TEXTENSION_CONTROL_BLOCK);
var
  sIniFile  : string;
  tini      : TIniFile;
begin
  inherited Create;

  SetLength(sIniFile, 250);
  GetModuleFilename(hInstance, PChar(sIniFile), Length(sIniFile));
  sIniFile := Copy(sIniFile, 1, Pos('.', sIniFile)) + 'ini';
  tini := TIniFile.Create(sIniFile);
  sInsideSearchDir  := tini.ReadString('Inside',
                                       'SearchDir',
                                       '.');
  sOutsideSearchDir := tini.ReadString('Outside',
                                        'SearchDir',
                                        '.');
  if sInsideSearchDir[Length(sInsideSearchDir)] <> '\' then begin
    sInsideSearchDir := sInsideSearchDir + '\';
  end;
```

```
    if sOutsideSearchDir[Length(sOutsideSearchDir)] <> '/' then begin
      sOutsideSearchDir := sOutsideSearchDir + '/';
    end;
    tini.Free;

  httpConnection := THTTPExt.Create(ECB);
end; { TNLExt.Create }

destructor TNLExt.Destroy;
begin
  httpConnection.Free;

  inherited Destroy;
end; { TNLExt.Destroy }
```

Even though it is rather long, it performs only two tasks. The first is to read an INI file to determine where it should look for news postings, and how to link to them. The second is to create the THTTPExt object used for this connection. A typical INI file looks like this:

```
[Inside]
SearchDir=L:\~martin\delphi\

[Outside]
SearchDir=/users/~martin/delphi
```

This tells NewsList.DLL that it should search for postings in L:\~martin\delphi\. If a file called Posting.TXT should be included in the Web page, it should be referred to as /users/~martin/delphi/Posting.TXT. This is a relative path that will expand to http://www.delfidata.no/users/~martin/delphi/Posting.TXT in my case. Putting this information in an INI file is only one option, but it is very convenient because it's easy to modify if the DLL needs to be moved.

The constructor of THTTPExt looks like this:

```
constructor THTTPExt.Create(var ECB : TEXTENSION_CONTROL_BLOCK);
begin
  inherited Create;

  fECB := ECB;
  fECB.dwHttpStatusCode := 200;      // Success!
  fECB.lpszLogData[0] := #0;         // No log data by default.
  fdwReturn := HSE_STATUS_SUCCESS;
  fsQueryString := GetQueryString;
end; { THTTPExt.Create }
```

This initializes the connection to assume it will succeed. I believe it is better to send some nice information to the users explaining that something went wrong rather than return a failure and let their browsers handle it. Usually, error messages from browsers are big and ugly and not very helpful.

GetQueryString() simply creates a copy of lpszQueryString or lpbData, depending on whether lpszMethod is POST or GET. This frees the remanding code from checking lpszMethod all the time; it can simply use fsQueryString or (preferably) the Query property.

When the DLL is done, the TNLExt object is freed. The destructor of TNLExt frees the THTTPExt object. During its constructor, the closing </body> and </html> tags are transmitted. You could also add a standard footer here, if you want.

Getting the Value of the Variables

As described earlier, the query string contains all variables from the Web page. To be compatible with the largest number of servers, the string is encoded to exclude spaces and characters with the high-bit set. A typical query string for the NewsList.DLL is Include=dynamic+array&Exclude=. This lists all articles containing either the word dynamic or the word array or both. THTTPExt contains a function called GetQueryVariable(). This function takes two parameters: the name of the variable, and a default value if the variable isn't found. Typical defaults are an empty string and a string containing 0. Here is the code for GetQueryVariable():

```
function THTTPExt.GetQueryVariable(
        const sVarName : string;
        const sDefault : string
        )              : string;
var
  ns      : integer;
  nStart  : integer;
  bDone   : boolean;
begin
  {
    Find sVarName in Query.
  }
  nStart := Pos(LowerCase(sVarName), LowerCase(Query));
  if nStart = 0 then begin
    Result := sDefault;
  end
  else begin
    {
      Convert to 'normal' format.
    }
    Result := '';
    {
      Skip the varname and the '=' sign.
    }
    ns := nStart + Length(sVarName) + 1;
    bDone := False;
    while not bDone and (ns <= Length(Query)) do begin
      case Query[ns] of
        '+' :
          Result := Result + ' ';
        '%' : begin
          Inc(ns);
          Result := Result +
                  Char(StrToInt('$' + Copy(Query, ns, 2)));
```

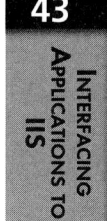

43

INTERFACING
APPLICATIONS TO
IIS

```
      Inc(ns);
    end;
    '&' :
      bDone := True;
    else begin
      Result := Result + Query[ns];
    end;
  end;
  Inc(ns);
end;
  end;
end; { THTTPExt.GetQueryVariable }
```

The algorithm for this function is very simple. First, I search the query string for the variable name. If it is not found, the default string is returned. Otherwise, the value is copied, character-by-character, from the query string to the returned string. Of special note here is the conversion of a character from a %XX form to a normal character, and the termination at the end of the query string or when an ampersand is found.

This DLL manages a very simple database, but there's nothing preventing you from using a similar approach to dynamically publish Microsoft Word documents, for instance. One possibility is to add a real database that contains keywords, an abstract, the author name, and the title. Depending on your documentation guidelines, this information might already be available, so transferring it to the database could be as simple as moving the document to the right directory. A conversion utility can wait for new documents and use Word's Automation Server capabilities to extract information to put in the database.

The DLL also does a very simple search. When the number of articles increase, the search time increases. An option is to generate a database of all words longer than five characters, as well as capitalized words because they are usually acronyms. This can also be done automatically.

The Filter DLL

The filter DLL is very simple. It hooks SF_NOTIFY_SEND_RAW_DATA and looks for the ugly error message from IIS. If it is found, the DLL replaces it with a more understandable one.

The complete listing is as follows:

```c
#define WIN32_LEAN_AND_MEAN
#include <windows.h>
#include <httpfilt.h>
#include <alloc.h>

char    *szErrorString = "HTTP/1.0 404 Object Not Found";
char    *szMsgStart =
        "<html>\
         <head>\
           <title>Unknown URL</title>\
         </head>\
```

```
            <body>\
              <h1>Ouch!</h1>\
              <p>\
              That URL is unknown to me! \
              Please notify the administrator \
              of the "; /* referring page */
char    *szMsgEnd =
          "</body>\
           </html>";

BOOL WINAPI __stdcall __export GetFilterVersion(
    HTTP_FILTER_VERSION *pVer)
{
    pVer->dwFlags = SF_NOTIFY_SEND_RAW_DATA |
                    SF_NOTIFY_ORDER_DEFAULT;

    pVer->dwFilterVersion = MAKELONG(0, 1);

    strcpy(pVer->lpszFilterDesc, "Invalid URL Catcher");

    return TRUE;
}

DWORD WINAPI __stdcall __export HttpFilterProc(
    HTTP_FILTER_CONTEXT     *pfc,
    DWORD                   NotificationType,
    VOID                    *pvData)
{
    PHTTP_FILTER_RAW_DATA    pRawData;
    LPSTR                    lpszData;
    DWORD                    dwLength;
    char                     szBuffer[1024];
    char                     *sz;

    switch (NotificationType)
    {
        case SF_NOTIFY_SEND_RAW_DATA:
            pRawData = pvData;
            lpszData = (LPSTR) calloc(pRawData->cbInBuffer + 1,
                                      sizeof(char));
            memcpy(lpszData, pRawData->pvInData,
                   pRawData->cbInBuffer);
            if (strstr(lpszData, szErrorString))
            {
                *((char *) pRawData->pvInData) = '\0';
                pRawData->cbInBuffer = 0;

                dwLength = strlen(szMsgStart);
                pfc->WriteClient(pfc, szMsgStart, &dwLength, 0);

                dwLength = sizeof(szBuffer);
                pfc->GetServerVariable(pfc, "ALL_HTTP", szBuffer,
                                       &dwLength);
                sz = strstr(szBuffer, "HTTP_REFERER");
```

```
                if (sz)
                {
                    sz += strlen("HTTP_REFERER") + 1;
                    strtok(sz, "\r\n");
                    sz = strdup(sz);
                    wsprintf(szBuffer, "<a href=%s>\
                                        referring page.</a>",
                                        sz);
                    free(sz);
                }
                else
                {
                    strcpy(szBuffer, "referring page.");
                }
                dwLength = strlen(szBuffer);
                pfc->WriteClient(pfc, szBuffer, &dwLength, 0);

                dwLength = strlen(szMsgEnd);
                pfc->WriteClient(pfc, szMsgEnd, &dwLength, 0);

                return SF_STATUS_REQ_FINISHED_KEEP_CONN;
            }
            free(lpszData);
            break;

        default:
            break;
    }

    return SF_STATUS_REQ_NEXT_NOTIFICATION;
}
```

That's all! However simple it seems, there are some things to look out for. First, if you don't set the `pvInData` and `cbInBuffer` fields to `0`, IIS shows its ugly error message anyway. Second, the search string should be unique. The previous code will terminate any request that contains the original error message. One optimization would be to check either more of the message, or to verify that the entire message is very short.

Third, the referring page will be set only if there is a referring page. If the user types the URL directly, there will be nowhere to link. Fourth, you should normally return `SF_STATUS_REQ_NEXT_NOTIFICATION` to inform IIS that the other filters that are installed can get a hand on the data. However, this is not what we want in this case. Therefore, the filter returns `SF_STATUS_REQ_FINISHED_KEEP_CONN` when it has shown the alternative error message.

TIP

Here are a couple of tips for developing filters:

■ Make sure the compiler is set to align record fields at 4-byte boundaries (double word). Without this, IIS will simply never call your `HttpFilterProc()`.

■ If you are using any DLLs, make sure that they are present on the Web server. Most C/C++ compilers put the RTL in a DLL by default. If a DLL is missing, IIS will not load your filter.

Complete Source Code Listing

The file HTTPExt.PAS can be found at `http://www.borland.com/techsupport/delphi/devcorner/internet/internet.html` as httpext.zip. The other files needed for compiling and running the project are listed here. Tester.PAS is needed only for testing. It contains a stub that sets up the TEXTENSION_CONTROL_BLOCK structure and calls HttpExtensionProc(). Currently, it supports only WriteClient().

NewsList.DPR

```
{ $DEFINE EXEFILE}
{$IFDEF EXEFILE}
program NewsList;

(*
  This code is based on code donated to the public domain by
  Martin Larsson, http://www.delfidata.no/users/~martin.
*)

uses
  Main in 'Main.pas',
  HTTPExt in 'Httpext.pas',
  ISAPILib in ISAPILib.pas
  Tester in 'Tester.PAS',
  NLExt in 'NLExt.pas';

begin
  Test;

{$ELSE}

library NewsList;

uses
  Main in 'Main.pas',
  HTTPExt in 'Httpext.pas',
  NLExt in 'NLExt.pas',
  ISAPILib in ISAPILib.pas;

exports
  GetExtensionVersion,
```

```
    HttpExtensionProc;

begin

{$ENDIF}

end.
```

Main.PAS

```
unit Main;

(*
  This code is based on code donated to the public domain by
  Martin Larsson, http://www.delfidata.no/users/~martin.
*)

interface

uses
  HTTPExt, Windows;

function GetExtensionVersion(
          var Ver : THSE_VERSION_INFO
          )        : BOOL; stdcall;
function HttpExtensionProc(
          var ECB : TEXTENSION_CONTROL_BLOCK
          )        : DWORD; stdcall;

implementation

uses
  NLExt, SysUtils, Dialogs;

function GetExtensionVersion(
          var Ver : THSE_VERSION_INFO
          )        : BOOL; stdcall
begin
  Ver.dwExtensionVersion := MAKELONG(HSE_VERSION_MINOR,
                                     HSE_VERSION_MAJOR);

  StrLCopy(Ver.lpszExtensionDesc, 'Delphi NewsList',
          HSE_MAX_EXT_DLL_NAME_LEN);

  Result := True;
end; { GetExtensionVersion }

function HttpExtensionProc(
          var ECB : TEXTENSION_CONTROL_BLOCK
          )        : DWORD; stdcall;
var
hMutex : THandle;
begin
```

```
    hMutex := CreateMutex(nil, False, 'NewsListMutex');
    WaitForSingleObject(hMutex, INFINITE);

    with TNLExt.Create(ECB) do begin
      DoIt;
      Result := ReturnValue;
      Free;
  end;

    ReleaseMutex(hMutex);
    CloseHandle(hMutex);
  end; { HttpExtensionProc }

  end.
```

NLExt.PAS

```
unit NLExt;

(*
  This code is based on code donated to the public domain by
  Martin Larsson, http://www.delfidata.no/users/~martin.
*)

interface

uses
  ISAPILib, HTTPExt, Windows;

type
  TNLExt = class(TObject)
    private
      httpConnection    : THTTPExt;
      sInsideSearchDir  : string;
      sOutsideSearchDir : string;

      procedure ListFiles;
      function Line(s : string; nStart : integer) : string;
      procedure GetSubjectAndAuthor(
                const sEntireFile   : string;
                var sSubject, sAuthor : string);
      function GetReturnValue : DWORD;
      function GetEntireFile(sName : string) : string;
      function IncludeFile(sEntireFile : string) : boolean;
    public
      constructor Create(var ECB : TEXTENSION_CONTROL_BLOCK);
      destructor Destroy; override;
      procedure DoIt;

      property ReturnValue : DWORD read GetReturnValue;
  end;

implementation
```

```
uses
  IniFiles, SysUtils, Classes;

constructor TNLExt.Create(var ECB : TEXTENSION_CONTROL_BLOCK);
var
  sIniFile  : string;
  tini      : TIniFile;
begin
  inherited Create;

  SetLength(sIniFile, 250);
  GetModuleFilename(hInstance, PChar(sIniFile), Length(sIniFile));
  sIniFile := Copy(sIniFile, 1, Pos('.', sIniFile)) + 'ini';
  tini := TIniFile.Create(sIniFile);
  sInsideSearchDir  := tini.ReadString('Inside',
                                       'SearchDir',
                                       '.');
  sOutsideSearchDir := tini.ReadString('Outside',
                                       'SearchDir',
                                       '.');
  if sInsideSearchDir[Length(sInsideSearchDir)] <> '\' then begin
    sInsideSearchDir := sInsideSearchDir + '\';
  end;
  if sOutsideSearchDir[Length(sOutsideSearchDir)] <> '/' then begin
    sOutsideSearchDir := sOutsideSearchDir + '/';
  end;
  tini.Free;

  httpConnection := THTTPExt.Create(ECB);
end; { TNLExt.Create }

destructor TNLExt.Destroy;
begin
  httpConnection.Free;

  inherited Destroy;
end; { TNLExt.Destroy }

function TNLExt.GetReturnValue : DWORD;
begin
  Result := httpConnection.ReturnValue;
end; { TNLExt.GetReturnValue }

procedure TNLExt.DoIt;
begin
  try
    with httpConnection do begin
      StdHeader('Delphi NewsList');
      StdBody;
      Paragraph;
      Header(1, 'The Delphi News List');
    end;
    ListFiles;
  except
    on E : Exception do
      httpConnection.Error('Exception ' + E.ClassName + #13 +
                           E.Message);
```

```pascal
    end;
end; { TNLExt.DoIt }

function TNLExt.IncludeFile(sEntireFile : string) : boolean;
var
  sInclude  : string;
  sExclude  : string;
  n, nLast  : integer;
begin
  Result := False;
  sInclude := httpConnection.GetQueryVariable('Include', '');
  sInclude := Trim(sInclude);
  n := Pos('  ', sInclude);
  while n <> 0 do begin
    Delete(sInclude, n, 1);
    n := Pos('  ', sInclude);
  end;

  if Length(sInclude) > 0 then begin
    sInclude := AnsiLowerCase(sInclude);
    nLast := 1;
    n := Pos(' ', sInclude);
    while not Result and (n <> 0) do begin
      Result := Pos(Copy(sInclude, nLast, n - 1),
                        sEntireFile) <> 0;
      nLast := n + 1;
      n := Pos(' ', Copy(sInclude, nLast, Length(sInclude)));
    end;
    if not Result then begin
      sInclude := Copy(sInclude, nLast, Length(sInclude));
      Result := Pos(sInclude, sEntireFile) <> 0;
    end;
  end
  else begin
    Result := True;
  end;

  sExclude := httpConnection.GetQueryVariable('Exclude', '');
  sExclude := AnsiLowerCase(sExclude);
  sExclude := Trim(sExclude);
  n := Pos('  ', sExclude);
  while n <> 0 do begin
    Delete(sExclude, n, 1);
    n := Pos('  ', sExclude);
  end;

  nLast := 1;
  n := Pos(' ', sExclude);
  while Result and (n <> 0) do begin
    Result := Pos(Copy(sExclude, nLast, n - 1), sEntireFile) = 0;
    nLast := n + 1;
    n := Pos(' ', Copy(sExclude, nLast, Length(sExclude)));
  end;
  if Result then begin
    sExclude := Copy(sExclude, nLast, Length(sExclude));
```

43

```
      Result := Pos(sExclude, sEntireFile) = 0;
    end;
end; { TNLExt.IncludeFile }

procedure TNLExt.ListFiles;
var
  sSubject    : string;
  sAuthor     : string;
  tsr         : TSearchRec;
  nFinding    : integer;
  sEntireFile : string;

begin
  with httpConnection do begin
    TableStart;
    nFinding := FindFirst(sInsideSearchDir + '*.txt',
                          faAnyFile, tsr);
    try
      RowStart;
      TableHeading('Subject');
      TableHeading('Author');
      RowEnd;
      while nFinding = 0 do begin
        sEntireFile := GetEntireFile(sInsideSearchDir + tsr.Name);
        sSubject := tsr.Name;
        sAuthor := 'Unknown';
        GetSubjectAndAuthor(sEntireFile, sSubject, sAuthor);
        if IncludeFile(AnsiLowerCase(sEntireFile)) then begin
          RowStart;
          Column(MakeLink(sSubject, sOutsideSearchDir + tsr.Name));
          Column(sAuthor);
          RowEnd;
        end;
        nFinding := FindNext(tsr);
      end;
    finally
      FindClose(tsr);
    end;
    TableEnd;
  end;
end; { TNLExt.ListFiles }

function TNLExt.Line(s : string; nStart : integer) : string;
begin
  Result := '';
  while not (s[nStart] in [#10, #13]) do begin
    case s[nStart] of
      '>' :
        Result := Result + '&gt;';
      '<' :
        Result := Result + '&lt;';
      else
        Result := Result + s[nStart];
    end;
    Inc(nStart);
```

```
   end;
end; { TNLExt.Line }

procedure TNLExt.GetSubjectAndAuthor(
         const sEntireFile     : string;
         var sSubject, sAuthor : string);
var
  nPos         : integer;
begin
  nPos := Pos('From:', sEntireFile);

  if nPos <> 0 then begin
    sAuthor := Line(sEntireFile, nPos + 6);
  end;

  nPos := Pos('Subject:', sEntireFile);

  if nPos <> 0 then begin
    sSubject := Line(sEntireFile, nPos + 9);
  end;
end; { TNLExt.GetSubjectAndAuthor }

function TNLExt.GetEntireFile(sName : string) : string;
var
  tfs          : TFileStream;
begin
  tfs := TFileStream.Create(sName, fmShareDenyWrite);
  try
    SetLength(Result, tfs.Size + 1);
    Result[tfs.Size + 1] := #0;
    tfs.ReadBuffer(PChar(Result)^, tfs.Size);
  finally
    tfs.Free;
  end;
end;

end.
```

ISAPILib.PAS

```
unit ISAPILib;

(*
  This code is based on code donated to the public domain by
  Martin Larsson, http://www.delfidata.no/users/~martin.
*)

interface

uses
  HTTPExt, Windows;

type
  THTTPExt = class(TObject)
    private
      fECB          : TEXTENSION_CONTROL_BLOCK;
      fdwReturn     : DWORD;
      fsQueryString : string;
```

```pascal
      function GetQueryString : string;
    public
      constructor Create(var ECB : TEXTENSION_CONTROL_BLOCK);
      destructor Destroy; override;

      procedure OutStr(s : string);
      procedure Error(s : string);
      procedure OutLine(s : string);
      procedure StdHeader(sTitle : string);
      procedure StdBody;
      procedure Paragraph;
      procedure Header(nLevel : integer; s : String);
      procedure TableStart;
      procedure TableEnd;
      procedure RowStart;
      procedure RowEnd;
      procedure Column(sText : string);
      procedure TableHeading(sText : string);
      procedure Link(sText, sLocation : string);
      function MakeLink(sText, sLocation : string) : string;
      function GetQueryVariable(
                const sVarName : string;
                const sDefault : string
                )              : string;

      property ReturnValue : DWORD read fdwReturn;
      property Query : string read fsQueryString;
    end;

const
  sNewLine = #13 + #10;

implementation

uses
  SysUtils;

constructor THTTPExt.Create(var ECB : TEXTENSION_CONTROL_BLOCK);
begin
  inherited Create;

  fECB := ECB;
  fECB.dwHttpStatusCode := 200;      // Success!
  fECB.lpszLogData[0] := #0;         // No log data by default.
  fdwReturn := HSE_STATUS_SUCCESS;
  fsQueryString := GetQueryString;
end; { THTTPExt.Create }

destructor THTTPExt.Destroy;
begin
  OutLine('</body>');
  OutLine('</html>');

  inherited Destroy;
```

```
end; { THTTPExt.Destroy }

procedure THTTPExt.OutStr(s : string);
var
  dw   : DWORD;
begin
  dw := Length(s);
  fECB.WriteClient(fECB.ConnID, PChar(s), dw, 0);
end; { THTTPExt.OutStr }

procedure THTTPExt.Error(s : string);
var
  dw   : DWORD;
begin
  dw := Length(s);
  fECB.WriteClient(fECB.ConnID, PChar(s), dw, 0);
end; { THTTPExt.Error }

procedure THTTPExt.OutLine(s : string);
begin
  OutStr(s + sNewLine);
end; { THTTPExt.OutLine }

procedure THTTPExt.StdHeader(sTitle : string);
var
  s       : string;
  dwSize  : DWORD;
  dwType  : DWORD;
begin
  s := '';
  dwSize := 0;
  dwType := 0;
  fECB.ServerSupportFunction(
        fECB.ConnID,
        HSE_REQ_SEND_RESPONSE_HEADER,
        PChar(s), dwSize, dwType);
  OutLine('<html>');
  OutLine('<head>');
  OutLine('  <title>');
  OutLine('    ' + sTitle);
  OutLine('  </title>');
  OutLine('</head>');
end; { THTTPExt.StdHeader }

procedure THTTPExt.StdBody;
begin
  OutLine('<body>');
end; { THTTPExt.StdBody }

procedure THTTPExt.Paragraph;
begin
  OutLine('<p>');
end; { THTTPExt.Paragraph }

procedure THTTPExt.Header(nLevel : integer; s : String);
```

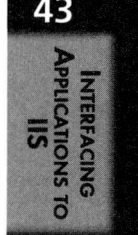

43

INTERFACING
APPLICATIONS TO
IIS

```
var
  sHeader : string;
begin
  sHeader := 'h' + IntToStr(nLevel);
  OutLine('<' + sHeader + '>' + s + '</' + sHeader + '>');
end; { THTTPExt.Header }

procedure THTTPExt.TableStart;
begin
  OutLine('<table>');
end; { THTTPExt.TableStart }

procedure THTTPExt.TableEnd;
begin
  OutLine('</table>');
end; { THTTPExt.TableEnd }

procedure THTTPExt.RowStart;
begin
  OutLine('  <tr>');
end; { THTTPExt.TableStart }

procedure THTTPExt.RowEnd;
begin
  OutLine('  </tr>');
end; { THTTPExt.TableEnd }

procedure THTTPExt.Column(sText : string);
begin
  OutLine('    <td>');
  OutLine('      ' + sText);
  OutLine('    </td>');
end; { THTTPExt.Column }

procedure THTTPExt.TableHeading(sText : string);
begin
  OutLine('    <th>');
  OutLine('      ' + sText);
  OutLine('    </th>');
end; { THTTPExt.Column }


procedure THTTPExt.Link(sText, sLocation : string);
begin
  OutLine(MakeLink(sText, sLocation));
end; { THTTPExt.Link }

function THTTPExt.MakeLink(sText, sLocation : string) : string;
begin
  Result := '<a href="' + sLocation + '">' + sText + '</a>';
end; { THTTPExt.MakeLine }

function THTTPExt.GetQueryVariable(
          const sVarName  : string;
```

```
              const sDefault  : string
              )                : string;
var
  ns      : integer;
  nStart  : integer;
  bDone   : boolean;
begin
  {
    Find sVarName in Query.
  }
  nStart := Pos(LowerCase(sVarName), LowerCase(Query));
  if nStart = 0 then begin
    Result := sDefault;
  end
  else begin
    {
      Convert to 'normal' format.
    }
    Result := '';
    {
      Skip the varname and the '=' sign.
    }
    ns := nStart + Length(sVarName) + 1;
    bDone := False;
    while not bDone and (ns <= Length(Query)) do begin
      case Query[ns] of
        '+' :
          Result := Result + ' ';
        '%' : begin
          Inc(ns);
          Result := Result +
                    Char(StrToInt('$' + Copy(Query, ns, 2)));
          Inc(ns);
        end;
        '&' :
          bDone := True;
        else begin
          Result := Result + Query[ns];
        end;
      end;
      Inc(ns);
    end;
  end;
end; { THTTPExt.GetQueryVariable }

function THTTPExt.GetQueryString : string;
var
  pc  : PChar;
begin
  if CompareText(string(fECB.lpszMethod), 'POST') = 0 then begin
    SetLength(Result, fECB.cbAvailable);
    StrLCopy(PChar(Result), fECB.lpbData, fECB.cbAvailable);
  end
  else begin
    pc := AllocMem(StrLen(fECB.lpszQueryString) + 1);
    StrCopy(pc, fECB.lpszQueryString);
```

```
      Result := StrPas(fECB.lpszQueryString);
      FreeMem(pc, StrLen(fECB.lpszQueryString) + 1);
    end;
    if Result[Length(Result) - 1] = #13 then begin
      Delete(Result, Length(Result) - 1, 2);
    end;
  end; { THTTPExt.GetQueryString }

end.
```

Tester.PAS

```
unit Tester;

(*
  This code is based on code donated to the public domain by
  Martin Larsson, http://www.delfidata.no/users/~martin.
*)

interface

uses
  HTTPExt, Windows;

procedure Test;
function GetServerVariable(
        hConn         : HCONN;
        VariableName  : PChar;
        Buffer        : Pointer;
        var Size      : DWORD
        )             : BOOL; stdcall;

function WriteClient(
        ConnID        : HCONN;
        Buffer        : Pointer;
        var Bytes     : DWORD;
        dwReserved    : DWORD
        )             : BOOL; stdcall;

function ReadClient(
        ConnID    : HCONN;
        Buffer    : Pointer;
        var Size  : DWORD
        )         : BOOL; stdcall;

function ServerSupportFunction(
        hConn         : HCONN;
        HSERRequest   : DWORD;
        Buffer        : Pointer;
        var Size      : DWORD;
        var DataType  : DWORD
        )             : BOOL; stdcall;
```

```
implementation

uses
  Main, Classes, SysUtils;

const
  sFilename = 'e:\arbeid\test.htm';
  sQuery    = 'Include=%25&Exclude=';

procedure Test;
var
  tecb  : TEXTENSION_CONTROL_BLOCK;
begin
  FillChar(tecb, sizeof(TEXTENSION_CONTROL_BLOCK), 0);
  tecb.cbSize := sizeof(TEXTENSION_CONTROL_BLOCK);
  tecb.WriteClient := WriteClient;
  tecb.ReadClient := ReadClient;
  tecb.GetServerVariable := GetServerVariable;
  tecb.ServerSupportFunction := ServerSupportFunction;

  tecb.lpszMethod := 'GET';
  if CompareText(tecb.lpszMethod, 'POST') = 0 then begin
    GetMem(tecb.lpbData, Length(sQuery) + 1);
    StrPCopy(tecb.lpbData, sQuery);
    tecb.cbAvailable := Length(sQuery);
  end
  else begin
    GetMem(tecb.lpszQueryString, Length(sQuery) + 1);
    StrPCopy(tecb.lpszQueryString, sQuery);
  end;

  HttpExtensionProc(tecb);
end; { Test }

function GetServerVariable(
         hConn        : HCONN;
         VariableName : PChar;
         Buffer       : Pointer;
         var Size     : DWORD
         )            : BOOL; stdcall;
begin
  Result := True;
end; { GetServerVariableProc }

function WriteClient(
         ConnID      : HCONN;
         Buffer      : Pointer;
         var Bytes   : DWORD;
         dwReserved  : DWORD
         )           : BOOL; stdcall;
```

```pascal
var
  tfs : TFileStream;
begin
  tfs := nil;
  try
    tfs := TFileStream.Create(sFilename, fmOpenWrite);
    tfs.Seek(0, soFromEnd);
  except
    on EFOpenError do begin
      tfs.Free;
      tfs := TFileStream.Create(sFilename,
                                fmOpenWrite or fmCreate);
    end;
  end;
  tfs.WriteBuffer(Buffer^, Bytes);
  tfs.Free;
  Result := True;
end; { WriteClientProc }

function ReadClient(
         ConnID    : HCONN;
         Buffer    : Pointer;
         var Size  : DWORD
         )         : BOOL; stdcall;
begin
  Result := True;
end; { ReadClientProc }

function ServerSupportFunction(
         hConn       : HCONN;
         HSERRequest : DWORD;
         Buffer      : Pointer;
         var Size    : DWORD;
         var DataType : DWORD
         )           : BOOL; stdcall;
begin
  Result := True;
end; { ServerSupportFunctionProc }

initialization
  DeleteFile(sFilename);

end.
```

Summary

In this chapter, we looked at the various interfaces to Microsoft's Internet Information Server. There are several ways to couple your code up with IIS. The simplest is to use one of the various scripting languages such as JavaScript and VBScript. To increase interactivity and versatility, Java applets and ActiveX controls can be used. These techniques are not specific to IIS, but rather demand support on the client side.

If you don't want to limit your audience by requiring specific capabilities in the browser, you must run code on the server. IIS supports the standard CGI interface, so most existing CGI script will run unmodified. To overcome the limitations of CGI, IIS offers the ability to write special DLLs that run within the IIS memory space. These DLLs follow the ISAPI specification for extensions or filters. ISAPI extension DLLs are the direct alternative to CGI scripts, and are usually used for forms processing and calculations. Filters, on the other hand, operate between the server and the client. This means they have the ability to perform macro-expansion, on-the-fly document conversion among other things.

When all you want to do is to interact directly with a database, you can use the high-level database interface, the Internet Database Connector (IDC). This is actually supported through a standard IIS extension DLL. Through IDC, you can connect to any database through ODBC and SQL.

IDC and ISAPI filters and extension DLLs were covered in detail, but we also touched upon Java, JavaScript, ActiveX controls, and CGI.

Hopefully, the information contained in this chapter will enable you to add the dynamics to your Web pages that makes them interesting to visit over and over again.

43

INTERFACING
APPLICATIONS TO
IIS

Interfacing Applications to and Extending SMS

by Paul Thomsen

IN THIS CHAPTER

CHAPTER 44

Microsoft's Systems Management Server (SMS) is a solution to one of the large general problems facing organizations today—managing large numbers of computers, especially personal computers. SMS is also an excellent architecture on which to build solutions to specific problems. Sometimes these solutions require extending SMS, and other times they involve using other applications interfaced to SMS. This chapter discusses a variety of approaches to programming such solutions with SMS.

SMS is composed of various elements, but central to most of them is the SMS database, stored by Microsoft's SQL Server. This chapter starts by exploring this database and how a particularly appropriate tool for accessing the database, Microsoft Access, interfaces with SMS. You will then look at how you can extend the SMS database to include additional information that a typical organization might require. Microsoft Word will then be used to bridge the gap between all this technical data and the various worlds of your users. The chapter finishes by reviewing some less commonly used programming interfaces to SMS.

The SMS Database

SQL Server includes a variety of tools that prove very useful for exploring the databases it stores, presuming you have the privilege to do so. The most appropriate starting point for SQL Server version 6.5 is the SQL Enterprise Manager. You may need to register the server where your SMS database resides, by taking the Server menu's Register Server item. Once you have your server listed in the Server Manager window, you can dig down to the databases on that server and look at the SMS database. For now you are particularly interested in the Objects, Tables subtree. You probably have over 50 tables listed, a rather intimidating prospect. However, you'll soon make sense of these tables.

> **TIP**
>
> If a list of all columns in the tables is desired, the SQL Enterprise Manager's SQL Query Tool (under the Tools menu) can be used to execute the following SQL statement:
>
> ```
> SELECT sysobjects.name Table_Name, syscolumns.name Column_Name from syscolumns,
> sysobjects where syscolumns.id=sysobjects.id and syscolumns.id>100
> ```

The Machine Data Table

Technical specialists looking to gain the greatest benefit from SMS will have two primary expectations for the SMS database. The first is to extract data, usually for reporting. The second is to store additional data, in order to serve needs specific to their organizations. From these points of view, the center of the SMS database design is the MachineDataTable table. This table contains pointers to all the data for every machine (computers and other devices you keep track of SMS with). Every machine has a unique identification number (dwMachineID) and is categorized as being part of an architecture. The architecture for our purposes will usually be 5, which the ArchitectureMap table refers to as "Personal Computer." Every machine will have multiple records within the MachineDataTable, one for each pointer to data stored in other tables. You can tell which table these records point to by referring to the GroupKey column. The numeric GroupKey values can be used with the ArchitectureKey to look up a descriptive name for the group in the GroupMap table.

SMS's machine data is stored in a series of tables appropriate to each group of machine characteristics. There are tables for disk, IRQ, network card, operating system, memory, and similar information. Most of these categories have two tables, one for common data and another for specific data. For instance, you may have many PCs that have NTFS-formatted SCSI fixed drives, CD-ROMs, FAT16-formatted DoubleSpace drives, and so on. You will have only one, however, that has a drive with a serial number of A049-6B6D and 370M used of 532M. The former kind of data goes in the common tables, and the latter goes in the specific tables, thus maximizing the efficiency with which information is stored. In this case, the common data goes into a table called Disk_COMM and the specific data goes into a table called Disk_SPEC.

Going back to the MachineDataTable, you can use the GroupKey and ArchitectureKey to look in the GroupMap table and figure out the table names for the common and specific tables. You can then use MachineDataTable's SpecificKey to find the data in the specific table and the CommonKey to find the data in the common table. In some cases, a machine may have several instances of a specific group, and the InstanceKey distinguishes between these. A good example, again, is disks—each PC will probably have a floppy drive, hard disk, and a CD-ROM, each of which is an instance of a disk.

Figure 44.1 graphically represents the relationships just described. You can see samples of the actual data contained in the tables by starting the SQL Enterprise Manager's SQL Query Tool (under the Tools menu) and then entering a query of `Select * From MachineDataTable`, for example (note that case is not significant). Then click on the Execute Query button (the one with a green right arrowhead icon).

> **NOTE**
>
> For many of the machine data groups (disk, operating system, and so forth), previous data is kept for each machine as new, changed data is recorded by SMS. The pointers to this information are kept in the MachineDataHistoryTable, which has an identical layout to the MachineDataTable and is used in the same way. In order to determine which groups have historical data, you can refer to the GroupMap table, HistoryFlag column.

Views

Understanding the SMS database is important, enabling you to explore the database and find information you need. However, producing reports using the database as it is would be very tricky. Microsoft has addressed this issue by providing the SMSVIEW.EXE program, which can be found in the site's executables directory, most commonly called \SMS\SITE.SRV\X86.BIN. If you execute this program, SQL Server is provided with views that will probably be more useful for producing reports. You have to provide logon information to access the database, but otherwise SMSVIEW will automatically execute without intervention, pausing only to announce success or failure. If you want, it can be run from the command line, by providing the logon information on switches. As an example, SMSVIEW /s:*NT4_Server* /l:sa /p: /d:SMS runs SMSVIEW on the SMS database on the NT4_Server, using the sa logon and no password.

Views are literally just views on the database—they do not contain data and thus do not consume any disk space. SMSView creates views that essentially flatten and amalgamate the machine detail tables. As an example of an SMSView view, for disks there is a view called vDisk, which contains both specific and common data on all disks for all machines. The only information missing is machine identification details, which are available in the Identification_SPEC table.

> ## WARNING
>
> Microsoft reserves the right to change the layout of the SMS database. The views are likely to remain stable, but if you work with the tables then you should be prepared to adjust your code when new versions (especially major versions) appear.

FIGURE 44.1.

Relationships among the SMS machine detail tables.

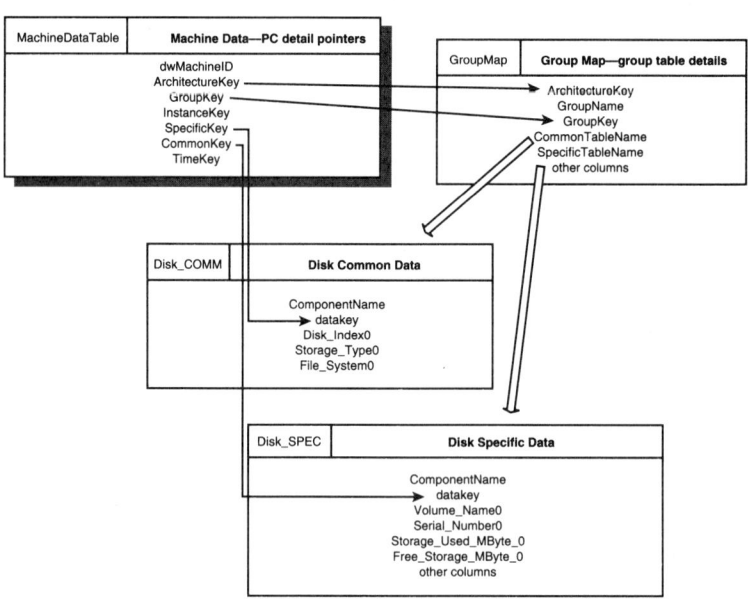

Other group tables are available for environment, identification, IRQ, mouse, network card, network, operating system, parallel port, BIOS, memory processor, serial port, services, user information, and video information

Other Tables

Beyond the machine-related tables, the SMS database contains tables for the other architecture elements, the things that can be used or controlled by the SMS Administrator and Security programs, and the inevitable overhead details.

The tables for the other architecture elements are the following: Jobs and JobDetails for jobs; Packages, PackageLocations, PackageDistributions, Platforms, and WCLs for packages; SMSEvent for events; SNMP_Traps and SNMP_Varbinds for SNMP traps; and UserGroups for user groups.

The tables for other items that the SMS Administrator program can manipulate or use are the following: Alerts and AlertRecipients for alerts; MachineGroups and MachineGroupDetails for machine groups; ProgramGroups, ProgramGroupProgramItems, ProgramGroupUserGroups, and ProgramItems for program groups; Queries, QueryExpressions, QueryFormatDefaults, and QueryFormats for queries; and SiteGroups and SiteGroupDetails for site groups.

The tables for things that the SMS Security program can manipulate are stored in the SecurityObjAccessList, SecurityObjAssocation, SecurityObjects, and SecurityUserTemplates tables.

With any complex system there are various minor details and interior elements that the system must keep track of. For SMS, these are kept in the AttributeMap, DeletedMachines, Domains, DomainTypes, PropertyDisplayGroups, PropertyDisplayPanes, PropertyDisplayUsage, Requests, SchedulerSafeDelete, ServerShares, SetupInfo, SiteControl, SiteUses, SiteWork, SMSData, SqlStoreTable, SyncModification, and WorkstationStatus tables. The SMSData table is particularly central to many other tables in that it contains the next values for many keys, as well as other data.

Interfacing Microsoft Access with SMS

Microsoft Access is often thought of as a small database system (like SQL Server but less serious) that has some easy-to-use programming features included. This is true, but don't forget that other databases can serve up the database functionality, and Access can be used to easily access that data (thus the name). In this case, the Access database is just used to store queries, reports, and so on. Using Access with SMS's SQL Server database is a good example.

Using ODBC

When installing Access for Windows 95, the custom install should be chosen, and it should be ensured that the SQL Server ODBC driver was installed as part of the Data Access options. If so, using the 32-bit ODBC control panel, a data source can be added for the SMS database. It will use the SQL Server driver, of course. The Data Source Name can be anything, but let's call it SMS. The Server will be the computer name of the SMS SQL Server, and under Options you can specify the Database Name as SMS.

Using Access, a new blank Access database can be opened and the SMS database can be linked in, using the File, Get External Data, Link Tables… options. In the Link dialog box, the ODBC Databases option should be chosen from the Files of type drop-down listbox. The SQL Data Sources dialog box will appear, and the SMS database defined in the ODBC control panel can be selected. You will then be able to link in the tables you need (you may wish to link in all of them, for future needs). For most tables, you have to clarify for Access what the key is; this is usually fairly simple, because the column name will end in the word "key" and be appropriate for that table.

Access Options

At this point, Access knows where the data is and how to look it up, but it's not clear to Access how the tables relate to each other. If information is needed from two tables, how does Access ensure that the same machine is referred to by the selected records in each table? This is where relationships come in, and these are defined using the Relationships menu item under the Tools menu. The relationships are specified by choosing the appropriate tables and then dragging the field that relates to a corresponding field in the other table onto it. The end result will be something like what we see in Figure 44.2.

FIGURE 44.2.

*Setting up the table
relationships in Access.*

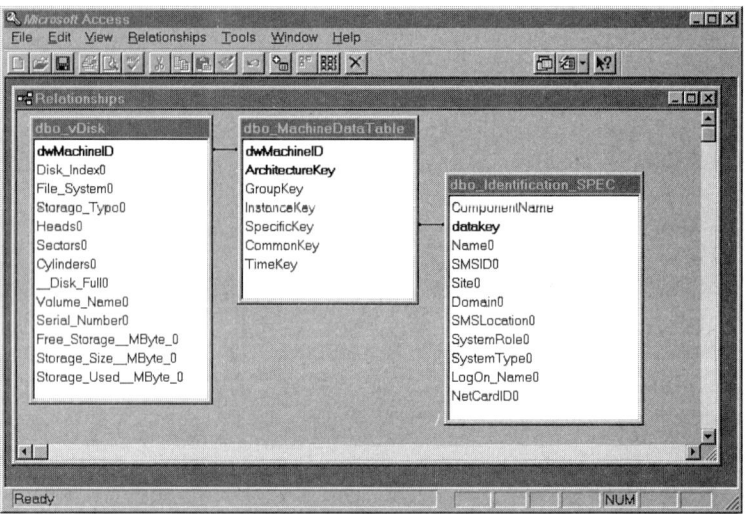

Creating a query to collect the data needed for a report is fairly straightforward using Access. A new query based on the Simple Query Wizard can be created within minutes. The appropriate fields (columns) from the desired tables must be chosen with the wizard. Typically, these will be from the SMS view tables, such as dbo_vDisk, and dbo_Identification_SPEC. The wizard can then finish up and will present the basic query results. It may be necessary to use the Design View for the query and specify additional details—for example, if multiple tables are used then the relationship might involve the MachineDataTable. For each machine in the MachineDataTable, however, there are multiple records—at least one for each group for which the machine has data. Thus, it would be necessary to specify which record should be used to establish the relationship, based on the appropriate GroupKey value. The Design View can also be used to specify some formatting details, calculations, and so forth.

An even more attractive and powerful Access report can be created by generating a new report using the report wizard and choosing the query as the source of the data. All the fields could be selected and various formatting options chosen.

Sample Access Interface to SMS: A Disk Usage Report

A common use for the data collected by SMS is to report on who has what—for instance, who has what disks, and how full they are.

As per the previous discussion, Access must be set up to link in the SMS data via ODBC, with the appropriate relationships among tables. Then a query can be created using the Simple Query Wizard. The Disk_Index0, File_System0, Storage_Type0, Free_Storage__Mbyte_0, and Storage_Size__Mbyte_0 fields from the dbo_vDisk table will be selected, along with GroupKey from the dbo_MachineDataTable and Name0 from dbo_Identification_Spec. This will be a detail query, called Disk Query, and it will be necessary to modify the query design after you finish with the wizard.

In the Design View, you can specify that you don't want to show the GroupKey, but you want it to have a value of 1 as the criteria so that you select the Identification table record when making the relationship between the vDisk and Identification_SPEC tables (via the MachineDataTable). You also specify that you don't want to see records where the Disk_Index0 is equal to A, because you presume every machine has a diskette drive (whose characteristics you already know). By inserting columns, cutting, and pasting, the fields can be moved into a reasonable order. You can also specify that the query results should be sorted by the Name0 and then Disk_Index0 fields. More descriptive names can be given by right-clicking on each column and giving it a description in its Properties dialog box. A percentage of disk space free column can be added with the Expression Builder, which can be invoked by right mouse-clicking on the Field row of a new column and taking the Build... option (and yes, there is a percent free column in the vDisk table already, but for the purposes of demonstration, let's create our own expression). The expression can be given a format property of percent to make it more readable. The Design View should look like Figure 44.3.

The SQL view will be much like the following:

```
SELECT DISTINCT dbo_Identification_SPEC.Name0, dbo_vDisk.Disk_Index0,
➥dbo_vDisk.Storage_Type0, dbo_vDisk.File_System0, dbo_vDisk.Storage_Size__MByte_0,
➥ dbo_vDisk.Free_Storage__MByte_0, [Free_Storage__MByte_0]/[Storage_Size__MByte_0]
➥ AS Expr1
FROM (dbo_vDisk INNER JOIN dbo_MachineDataTable ON dbo_vDisk.dwMachineID =
➥dbo_MachineDataTable.dwMachineID)
```

44

INTERFACING TO
AND EXTENDING
SMS

```
INNER JOIN dbo_Identification_SPEC ON dbo_MachineDataTable.SpecificKey =
➥ dbo_Identification_SPEC.datakey
WHERE (((dbo_vDisk.Disk_Index0)<>"A") AND ((dbo_MachineDataTable.GroupKey)=1))
ORDER BY dbo_Identification_SPEC.Name0, dbo_vDisk.Disk_Index0;
```

The query in the end will be in the form of Table 44.1—column widths may need adjustment, and the data will vary, of course.

Table 44.1. The start of the output from the sample query.

Computer Name	Disk	Disk Type	Type	Size	Free	% Free
ABOYD	C	Fixed Disk, CMOS Type 65	FAT16	602	365	60.63%
AFULTON	C	Fixed Disk, CMOS Type 0	FAT16	1215	469	38.60%
AHALVERSON	B	Floppy Drive, 5.25 1.2M				

FIGURE 44.3.

Design view of a query in Access.

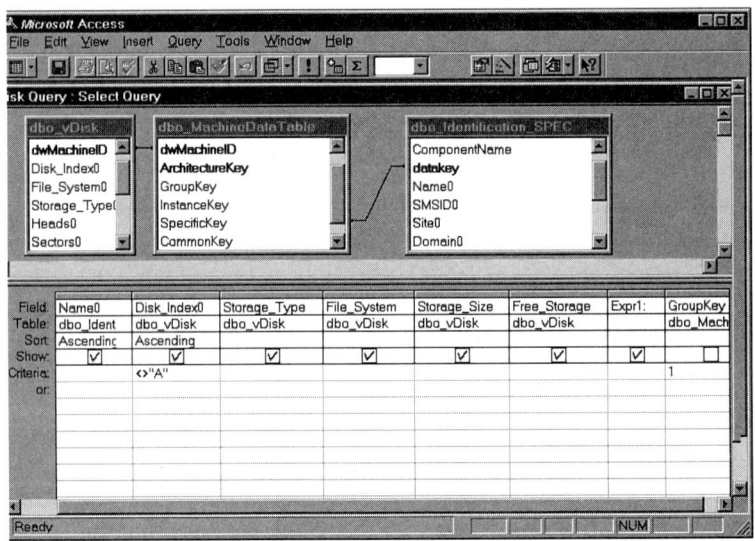

A report preview based on this query (but with different data) can look like Figure 44.4.

FIGURE 44.4.

Report based on the sample Access query.

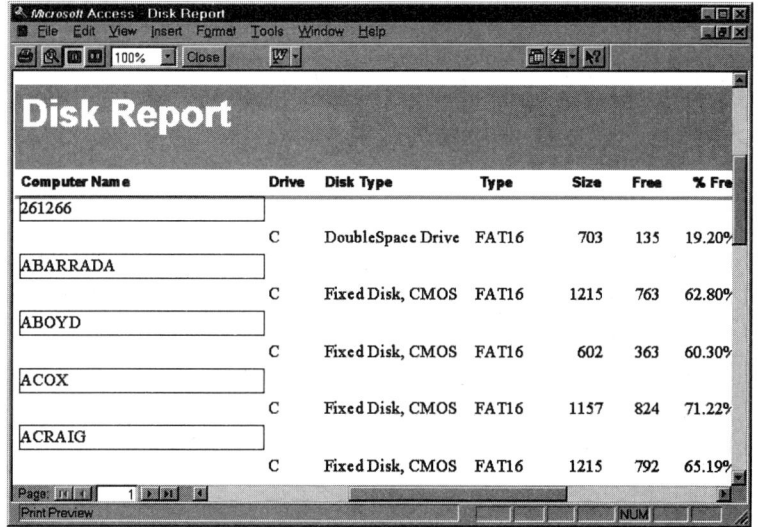

Extending the SMS Database

As we have seen, the SMS database is a wealth of information, but nonetheless it's not omniscient—it doesn't know everything about everything. Additional details that may be required can be collected and stored in the SMS database, and they can then be reported on or manipulated along with all the other information. The data that becomes the machine details in the SMS database starts out at the clients, where it is collected by the software and hardware inventories. The inventories write their findings to Management Information Format (MIF) files, in the \MS\SMS\NOIDMIF's directory. This data is then collected and eventually stored in the SMS database. Every SMS administrator should be comfortable with this process, which is well detailed in Appendix C, "SMS System Flow," of the *SMS v1.1 Administrator's Guide.* Other programs can also write MIF files to this directory, enabling collection of additional needed data.

Management Information Format Files

Management Information Format files are ASCII text files with fairly straightforward formats. Listing 44.1 is a typical MIF.

Listing 44.1. A representative Management Information Format (MIF) file.

```
Start Component
  Name = "Data"
  Start Group
    Name = "Data Information"
    ID = 1
```

continues

44

INTERFACING TO AND EXTENDING SMS

Listing 44.1. continued

```
    Class = "Your Organization Name¦Data Information¦1.0"
    Start Attribute
      Name = "Files"
      ID = 1
      Type = String(5)
      Storage = Specific
      Value = "23"
    End Attribute
    Start Attribute
      Name = "Word Documents"
      ID = 2
      Type = String(5)
      Storage = Specific
      Value = "15"
    End Attribute
  End Group
End Component
```

The formatting of this MIF should be fairly intuitive. The Name just after Start Group is the group name, as it will appear in the Personal Computer Properties window of the SMS Administrator program. This will also become the table name in the SMS database, except that spaces will be replaced with underscores, and _COMM and _SPEC will be suffixed to the common and specific tables, respectively. The attributes are then the columns of the table. The Name after Start Attribute is the column name. The IDs must be unique and increment appropriately. The Type can either be Counter or String, and if it's a string, the maximum field length must be specified in parentheses and must not exceed 255. Counters are 32-bit integers. Storage specifies whether the value ends up in the common or specific tables. Value is the data to be recorded; strings must be within quotation marks.

Other parts of the syntax may be less intuitive. Class is the source of the data, as in who provided it, from which process, and which version. This is useful for analysis down the line if MIFs are found at a stage where the source is not obvious. In addition to ID, groups can also have a Key. This is necessary in those situations where there may be multiple instances of the group for a machine (disk drives being the example discussed earlier in this chapter).

An unsupported tool is provided by Microsoft to check for MIF file syntax validity. It can be found in the \PSSTools directory tree of the SMS CD-ROM and is called MIFCHECK.EXE. If there are any doubts about the syntax of a MIF, this tool should be used to check for problems.

NOTE

MIFs can include many other details, useful in only the most advanced situations, which space does not allow discussion of here (see the BackOffice SDK discussion at the end of this chapter). In particular, MIFs can include details about architectures other than PCs, including completely new architectures. In these cases, the MIFs have to go in the IDMIFS directory of the client PCs. With no-ID MIFs, the architecture defaults to the current architecture. With ID MIFs, the architecture must be specified. If it is a new architecture, that architecture is automatically added in the SMS database.

Adding Groups

Adding groups to the inventory for an architecture is very simple. When the first MIF for that group is collected, the Inventory Data Loader will create the appropriate data structures to support that group—namely, specific and/or common tables and an entry in the GroupMap table. Once the group is added, any further MIFs for that group must be compatible with the first MIF's definition. For instance, if the first MIF defines the datatype as a string of 10 characters, all further MIFs must also provide strings. If they're longer than 10 characters, they will be trimmed to 10 characters.

Once the group is added, it will be displayed with the default icon. This may be acceptable, but if you want to use a more appropriate icon, one must be provided in a Dynamic Link Library (DLL), with appropriate changes to ensure it can be found by the SMS Administrator program when it is started. The icon can be created as a 32-pixel-by-32-pixel icon using an appropriate program, such as Visual C++'s Microsoft Developer Studio, or Visual Basic's IMAGEDIT.EXE. Then, a stub C program (see Listing 44.2) and resource definition files (see Listing 44.3) must be created and compiled to produce the DLL. Finally, the appropriate registry keys must be adjusted so that the DLL can be found.

Listing 44.2. A stub DLL source program for the resource DLL.

```
// resdll.c - defines the minimal DLL entry point
#include <windows.h>

// stub resource DLL entry point
BOOL WINAPI DllEntryPoint(HINSTANCE hinstDLL, DWORD fdwReason, LPVOID lpvReser_
{
    // Nothing to initialize.
    return TRUE;
}
```

Listing 44.3. The resource compiler source file for a resource DLL.

```
// resdll.rc - defines a resource for an SMS resource DLL.
#include <windows.h>

// a Program Display Group icon (as seen in Machine Property windows)
PDG_Personal_Computer_Disk ICON test.ico
```

44

Interfacing to and Extending SMS

The files are then compiled with the following commands, presuming Microsoft's Visual C++ is appropriately installed:

```
cl -DLL -c resdll.c
rc docs.rc
link -DLL resdll.obj docs.res
```

It's necessary to run REGEDT32 to set up the registry so that the SMS Administrator will find this resource DLL—that is, on Windows NT 3.*x*. Use REGEDIT on Windows 95. You can use either REGEDT32 or REGEDIT on Windows NT 4.*x*. Then, under the HKEY_LOCAL_MACHINE hive, find SOFTWARE\Microsoft\SMS and add a new key (use Edit, Add Key) with a keyname of ResDLLs, no class name. With this new key selected, add a value with a value name of Installed and data type of REG_MULTI_SZ. With the Multi-String Editor dialog box, you can enter as many lines as there are DLLs to register. Each one must be given a unique name, such as ResDLL1. Then it will be necessary to add keys for each of the DLL names, spelled exactly the same as in the Multi-String Editor dialog box, and with no class. Finally, with each key selected in turn, these keys must have values added with the value name of PathName and Data Type of REG_SZ. The string for each will be the full path where the resource DLL file exists, such as C:\SMSADMIN\RESDLL.DLL.

> **NOTE**
>
> If you want this special icon loaded only for yourself, when registering the key be sure to do it under the HKEY_CURRENT_USER hive while you're logged in.

Collecting User Documents Information

Organizations spend a lot of money providing their staffs with computers, trusting that they are providing a useful tool to the workers. The computers may be used for a variety of tasks, such as client-server applications, but one of the primary uses will probably be office systems, as provided by Microsoft Office. The organization may want to collect information on how many documents users are producing with Office—not to monitor productivity necessarily, but to see how valuable Office is to the organization. This information could be critical to making decisions relating to training, upgrades, standardization, and so on.

With the popularity of Microsoft Office within large organizations, it is reasonable to expect that users will keep their documents within the My Documents directory tree, as recommended by Microsoft. If so, the batch procedure in Listing 44.4 quickly provides totals of the various kinds of directories.

Listing 44.4. Batch file to do the directory listings for the sample program.

```
@ECHO OFF

rem Get lists of the appropriate files, in all subdirectories, wide format
rem (thus quicker to read), don't stop after each set of 24 lines, and
rem don't include commas in the totals (easier to parse)
DIR "C:\MY DOCUMENTS\*.DO?" /S /W /-P /-C > WORD_DIR.TXT
DIR "C:\MY DOCUMENTS\*.XL?" /S /W /-P /-C > EXCL_DIR.TXT
DIR "C:\MY DOCUMENTS\*.*"   /S /W /-P /-C > ALLD_DIR.TXT

rem turn the lists into a MIF
SMS_DOCS

rem erase the temporary files
ERASE WORD_DIR.TXT
ERASE EXCL_DIR.TXT
ERASE ALLD_DIR.TXT
```

Listing 44.5 is a program that analyzes the directory listings and produces a MIF file. The program can be compiled with the command CL SMS_DOCS.C.

Listing 44.5. C program to analyze directory listings and create a MIF file.

```c
/* SMS_DOCS.c   - Office document count .MIF file creation program (for use on SMS
PC clients)
            - Paul Thomsen, August 20th, 1996
            - the idea is that we want to collect a count of all Word, Excel and
              similar documents under the C:\My Documents directory tree. Then we
              also want to store this info in SMS, with all the similar data
*/

#include <stdio.h>
#include <string.h>
#include <time.h>

FILE *mif;      // the mif file (the output)
FILE *tempnes;  // the directory listing file (the input)
char input_buffer[100];

void get_numbers( char filename[40] );
void create_mif();
void read_line();
void write_line();

int files, sizes;

void main()
{
    mif = fopen( "C:\\MS\\SMS\\NOIDMIFS\\SMS_DOCS.MIF", "w" );
    create_mif();
    fclose( mif );
}
```

continues

Listing 44.5. continued

```
void create_mif()
{

    int total_files=0, total_sizes=0;
    char temp_buffer[100];

    // start the file
    write_line( "Start Component\n" );
    write_line( "  Name = \"MS Office Documents\"\n" );
    write_line( "  Start Group\n" );
    write_line( "    Name = \"MS Office Documents\"\n" );
    write_line( "    ID = 1\n" );
    write_line( "    Class = \"your organization¦MS Office Documents¦1.0\"\n" );
    write_line( "    Start Attribute\n" );
    write_line( "      Name = \"Word Files\"\n" );
    write_line( "      ID = 1\n" );
    write_line( "      Type = Counter\n" );
    write_line( "      Storage = Specific\n" );

    get_numbers( "WORD_DIR.TXT" );
    sprintf( temp_buffer, "      Value = %i\n", files );
    write_line( temp_buffer );
    total_files += files;

    // finish this value and start the next one
    write_line( "    End Attribute\n" );
    write_line( "    Start Attribute\n" );
    write_line( "      Name = \"Word File Sizes\"\n" );
    write_line( "      ID = 2\n" );
    write_line( "      Type = Counter\n" );
    write_line( "      Storage = Specific\n" );

    sprintf( temp_buffer, "      Value = %i\n", sizes );
    write_line( temp_buffer );
    total_sizes += sizes;

    // finish this value and start the next one
    write_line( "    End Attribute\n" );
    write_line( "    Start Attribute\n" );
    write_line( "      Name = \"Excel Files\"\n" );
    write_line( "      ID = 3\n" );
    write_line( "      Type = Counter\n" );
    write_line( "      Storage = Specific\n" );

    get_numbers( "EXCL_DIR.TXT" );
    sprintf( temp_buffer, "      Value = %i\n", files );
    write_line( temp_buffer );
    total_files += files;

    // finish this value and start the next one
    write_line( "    End Attribute\n" );
    write_line( "    Start Attribute\n" );
    write_line( "      Name = \"Excel File Sizes\"\n" );
    write_line( "      ID = 4\n" );
    write_line( "      Type = Counter\n" );
    write_line( "      Storage = Specific\n" );
```

```
        sprintf( temp_buffer, "       Value = %i\n", sizes );
        write_line( temp_buffer );
        total_sizes += sizes;

        // finish this value and start the next one
        write_line( "      End Attribute\n" );
        write_line( "      Start Attribute\n" );
        write_line( "        Name = \"Other Files\"\n" );
        write_line( "        ID = 5\n" );
        write_line( "        Type = Counter\n" );
        write_line( "        Storage = Specific\n" );

        get_numbers( "ALLD_DIR.TXT" );
        sprintf( temp_buffer, "       Value = %i\n", files - total_files );
        write_line( temp_buffer );

        // finish this value and start the next one
        write_line( "      End Attribute\n" );
        write_line( "      Start Attribute\n" );
        write_line( "        Name = \"Other File Sizes\"\n" );
        write_line( "        ID = 6\n" );
        write_line( "        Type = Counter\n" );
        write_line( "        Storage = Specific\n" );

        sprintf( temp_buffer, "       Value = %i\n", sizes - total_sizes );
        write_line( temp_buffer );

        // finish this value and the file
        write_line( "      End Attribute\n" );
        write_line( "   End Group\n" );
        write_line( "End Component\n" );
}

void get_numbers( char filename[40] )
{
    char number[15];

    files = 0;
    sizes = 0;

    if ( ( tempnes = fopen( filename, "r" ) ) == NULL )
        printf( "Couldn't open the %s directory listing\n", filename );

    // and if successful then do what we need to and close the file
    else {

        // get to the grand totals - while string not found and not end of file
        while ( ( strncmp( "   Total Files Listed:", input_buffer, 24 )!=0 )
                                    && ( feof( tempnes )==0 ) )
            read_line();

        // get the actual totals file
        if ( feof( tempnes )==0 ) {
            read_line();
            strncpy( number, input_buffer+6, 10 );
            number[11]=0;
            // printf( "number: %s\n", number );
            files = atoi( number );
```

continues

Listing 44.5. continued

```
                strncpy( number, input_buffer+29, 10 );
                number[11]=0;
                // printf( "number: %s\n", number );
                sizes = atoi( number );
            }

            fclose( tempnes );

        }
    }

void read_line()
{
    char character=0;
    int i=0;

    // make sure the buffer is a null string before we start
    input_buffer[0]=0;

    // fill the buffer until end of file or end of line
    while ( !feof( tempnes ) && ( character != 10 ) ) {
        character = fgetc( tempnes );
        input_buffer[ i++ ] = character;
    }

    // make sure we know where the end of this line was
    input_buffer[i]=0;

    // for testing
    // printf( "reading: %s", input_buffer );
}

void write_line( char buffer[100] )
{
    int i=0;

    while ( buffer[i] != 0 )
        fputc( buffer[ i++ ], mif );

    // for testing
    // printf( "writing: %s", buffer );
}
```

A typical MIF file produced by the SMS_DOCS program is provided in Listing 44.6.

Listing 44.6. Output from the SMS_DOCS program.

```
Start Component
  Name = "MS Office Documents"
  Start Group
    Name = "MS Office Documents"
```

```
        ID = 1
        Class = "your organization¦MS Office Documents¦1.0"
        Start Attribute
          Name = "Word Files"
          ID = 1
          Type = Counter
          Storage = Specific
          Value = 31
        End Attribute
        Start Attribute
          Name = "Word File Sizes"
          ID = 2
          Type = Counter
          Storage = Specific
          Value = 803804
        End Attribute
        Start Attribute
          Name = "Excel Files"
          ID = 3
          Type = Counter
          Storage = Specific
          Value = 29
        End Attribute
        Start Attribute
          Name = "Excel File Sizes"
          ID = 4
          Type = Counter
          Storage = Specific
          Value = 295332
        End Attribute
        Start Attribute
          Name = "Other Files"
          ID = 5
          Type = Counter
          Storage = Specific
          Value = 129
        End Attribute
        Start Attribute
          Name = "Other File Sizes"
          ID = 6
          Type = Counter
          Storage = Specific
          Value = 4555055
        End Attribute
      End Group
End Component
```

A resource icon is also supplied with the sample program, in the ICON subdirectory (details the same as in the previous discussion). Figure 44.5 shows the data collected by the SMS_DOCS program when viewed with the SMS Administrator (once it has had a chance to go through the inventory collection system).

FIGURE 44.5.

Information about Office documents, as collected by the SMS_DOCS program.

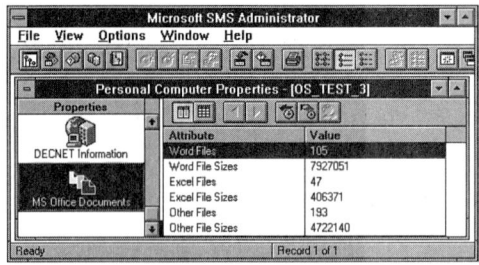

Interfacing Microsoft Word with SMS

Intuitively, one might think that word processing has little to do with managing PCs. Traditionally, this may have been true, but with a little imagination, SMS administrators can get Word to do a lot of their legwork for them. The most significant Word feature is mail merging, which can automatically produce paper or electronic mail based on data that SMS has collected, notifying users of various things SMS administrators think are important. If SMS administrators also have the Office Developers Kit (ODK), they can write programs in Word Basic to further enhance their SMS reporting.

SMS administrators might use Microsoft Word with SMS to notify users who have certain software packages that training is soon going to be available. They might advise users who have more than 90 percent of their disks full that their disks are getting full, and thus it would be advisable to review their disk usage. SMS administrators might also include various common solutions to the problem. If users are found using nonstandard (or banned) software, administrators can send a stern message to them. By using Word, such tasks can be accomplished with a minimum of coding, and the message can include formatting, graphics, and effects to communicate the message and intent most effectively.

Mail Merging

The important aspect of Word mail merging for the SMS Administrator is that it can use SQL statements to collect the data to be merged with the document. The Word mail merge feature is based on the Microsoft Query engine, so the SQL syntax must be legal for Microsoft Query. Microsoft Query should be used to generate the SQL commands to collect the data and to test it to ensure that the correct data is collected.

Programming a mail merge-based report should start with creating a new template. A new document can then be created, based on this template, that contains the message to be sent to the users, complete with whatever formatting may be desired. Some of the text will vary from user to user, such as user name, software used, disk capacity, or whatever else the requirement may be. The points where the variable text (fields) will go should be left blank and bookmarks must be placed there. This is done by selecting the Bookmark item under the Edit menu. A bookmark can be added wherever the cursor is currently sitting. The Go To button of this dialog box can also be used to find the bookmarks later and to ensure they exist in the correct places.

Programming in Microsoft Word is done with Word Basic in routines called macros. The macros can be created by selecting Tools, Macro from the menu. For simplicity, the program should be split into two routines—one to ask the user where the database is and how to log into it, and another to actually do the work.

The first routine should probably be automatically executed when the master document is opened, and thus must be called AutoOpen. It should display a dialog box asking for the ODBC data source, the SQL Server user identification, and the corresponding password. See the Using ODBC section earlier in this chapter for a discussion of setting up an ODBC data source.

The code that actually does the work should start with a `MailMergeMainDocumentType 0` statement in order to tell the mail merge to activate the loaded (and currently visible) document. The collection of the data is done with a `MailMergeOpenDataSource` command, with the significant switch being `.SQLStatement`, which is the SQL command generated and tested in Microsoft Query. It is then necessary to ensure that the main document is ready for mail merging, with a `MailMergeEditMainDocument` command. Associating the collected data with the bookmarks previously set up can be done by first going to the bookmarks with an `EditBookmark .name=name of bookmark`, `.SortBy=-1`, `.Goto` command, and then inserting the field name with `InsertMergeField .MergeField=column name`, `.WordField=-1`. Finally, the merging of data and document is done and printed by executing `MailMergeToPrinter`.

> **TIP**
>
> One common problem is that SQL statements can be very lengthy, but Word Basic has limits on how long strings (which contain the SQL statements) can be. This is solved by using additional `.SQLStatement` switches on the `MailMergeOpenDataSource` command, such as `.SQLStatement1`. The strings in the `.SQLStatement` switches must still be valid SQL commands, when they are concatenated.

44

INTERFACING TO AND EXTENDING SMS

Mail merging can also send the generated documents to the user via MAPI-based mail, such as Microsoft Exchange or Microsoft Mail. The SQL statement used to collect the data in the `MailMergeOpenDataSource` command should be extended to include fields from the SMS database that contain the e-mail address of the users. The `MailMerge` command can be used to send the documents via e-mail, and it has additional switches to associate the appropriate column with the e-mail address. Check out the ODK for details on this and other mail merge features.

With the template (and its macros) and the main document saved, the program is ready to run. The simplest way is to open the main document, which will activate the initial routine, prompting the administrator for login details. With these entered, the link will be made, the data collected, and the print initiated. This process may take a minute or so, depending on the data being collected and the size of the database being scanned. For development and testing purposes, it may not be desirable to repeatedly close and open the document in order to initiate the program, so the Run button from the Macro dialog box (Tools, Macro) or from the macro toolbar can be used.

Accessing SMS from Word Basic

Word Basic, which is much like Visual Basic, is a powerful, easy-to-program language. With the powerful benefits of mail merging and word processing, as just discussed, SMS administrators may want to do significant programming using it. The only significant problem they will discover is accessing the SQL Server database where the SMS data resides. Word Basic doesn't have commands (other than mail merging) to do this. This problem is rectified with a dynamic link library (DLL) called WBODBC.WLL (WLLs are Word DLLs).

WBODBC.WLL is an unsupported library distributed with the Office Development Kit, and is documented in an appendix of the ODK's documentation. There is also a copy of this program included with the BackOffice SDK; however, that version is a 16-bit version, and thus only works with Word for Windows, in the Windows 3.*x* environment.

WBODBC.WLL provides functions to do various things with ODBC databases, such as open and close links, submit queries, retrieve the associated data, figure out how much data is available, and so forth. With Word Basic, the programmer can then list data collected in dialog boxes, allowing the user to review it or make selections.

Sample Word Interface to SMS

This program will demonstrate how to use Microsoft Word's mail merging feature to prepare documents to advise users who are running low on disk space. As an example main document we'll use the following letter:

```
Dear ,

        A review of records finds that your personal computer's C: disk
drive is % full. This could soon lead to problems when your disk does
fill up. You may not be able to create or save documents that you are
working on, or you may not be able to install new programs that you
may require.

        We would like to suggest, when you get a few minutes, that you
review what is on your hard disk to see whether anything can be
removed. Common possibilities are old programs or old documents. If
you are uncertain as to which files to remove then please don't
hesitate to contact the helpdesk.

        Thank you for your attention to this matter.
```

Notice that there is no word after Dear, and the percent sign has no number before it. These are where the SMS data will be substituted, so there are bookmarks at each of these points, called Username and Percent, respectively.

The AutoOpen macro prompts the user for login information (see Listing 44.7):

Listing 44.7. AutoOpen macro for sample Word interface.

```
'mail merging using SMS dat

Sub MAIN

    UID$ = "sa"
    PWD$ = ""
    DSN$ = "SMS"

    Begin Dialog UserDialog 660, 216, "Connection Information"
        Text 12, 46, 196, 13, "ODBC Connection Name: ", .Text5
        TextBox 218, 44, 160, 18, .DSN$
        Text 14, 9, 447, 13, "Fill in the following information and press OK when
        ➥finished", .Text6
        Text 14, 76, 113, 13, "SQL Logon ID:", .Text7
        TextBox 217, 75, 160, 18, .UID$
        Text 14, 106, 73, 13, "Password", .Text8
        TextBox 217, 106, 160, 18, .PWD$
        OKButton 529, 23, 88, 21
        CancelButton 529, 47, 88, 21
    End Dialog

Dim GetUserInfo As UserDialog
    GetUserInfo.UID$ = UID$
    GetUserInfo.PWD$ = PWD$
    GetUserInfo.DSN$ = DSN$

    If Dialog(GetUserInfo, - 1) = 0 Then
        MsgBox("Operation Canceled")
    Else
        UID$ = GetUserInfo.UID$
        PWD$ = GetUserInfo.PWD$
        DSN$ = GetUserInfo.DSN$

        ODBCstr$ = "DSN=" + DSN$ + ";UID=" + UID$ + ";PWD=" + PWD$ +
        ➥";DATABASE=SMS"

        Call SMS.MAIN(ODBCstr$)

    End If

End Sub
```

44

Listing 44.8 is the SMS macro, called at the end of AutoOpen.

Listing 44.8. The SMS macro.

```
Sub MAIN(ODBCstr$)

MailMergeMainDocumentType 0

'the Microsoft Query style SQL statement to get the data
statement$ = "SELECT Name0,__Disk_Full0 FROM
➥Disk_COMM,Disk_SPEC,MachineDataTable,vIdentification WHERE
```

continues

Listing 44.8. continued

```
SpecificKey=Disk_SPEC.datakey AND CommonKey=Disk_COMM.datakey AND
MachineDataTable.dwMachineID=vIdentification.dwMachineID"
'continuation of statement$
statement1$ = " And Disk_Index0='C' AND __Disk_Full0>90 AND GroupKey=8"

'get the data for the mail merge
MailMergeOpenDataSource .Name = "", .ConfirmConversions = 0, .ReadOnly = 0,
.LinkToSource = 0, .AddToMru = 0, .PasswordDoc = "", .PasswordDot = "", .Revert =
0, .WritePasswordDoc = "", .WritePasswordDot = "", .Connection = ODBCstr$ +
";APP=Microsoft Query", .SQLStatement = statement$, .SQLStatement1 = statement1$

'indicate where the data should go in the document
MailMergeEditMainDocument
EditBookmark .Name = "Username", .SortBy = 0, .Goto
InsertMergeField .MergeField = "Name0", .WordField = - 1
EditBookmark .Name = "Percent", .SortBy = 0, .Goto
InsertMergeField .MergeField = "__Disk_Full0", .WordField = - 1

'do it!
MailMergeToPrinter

End Sub
```

The attentive reader will notice the use of MachineDataTable in addition to the SMSVIEW views in the SQL statement. This was done because the SMSVIEWS use double outer joins, which Microsoft Query does not have good facilities to handle (the HAVING clause does help in many cases). It is tricky to ensure that inappropriate records are not collected. Partially bypassing the views can avoid this problem. Microsoft Access has a more sophisticated SQL syntax and thus doesn't have this problem.

When the main document is opened, AutoOpen gets the login information from the user, and then calls the SMS macro, producing letters such as the following for all the users that have more than 90 percent of their C: drives full:

```
Dear JGilbert,

        A review of records finds that your personal computer's C: disk
drive is 95% full. This could soon lead to problems when your disk
does fill up. You may not be able to create or save documents that you
are working on, or you may not be able to install new programs that
you may require.

        We would like to suggest, when you get a few minutes, that you
review what is on your hard disk to see whether anything can be
removed. Common possibilities are old programs or old documents. If
you are uncertain as to which files to remove then please don't
hesitate to contact the helpdesk.

        Thank you for your attention to this matter.
```

Other SMS Programming Interfaces

SMS offers several other programming interfaces that may be of interest to you. They provide some powerful options; however, they are much more complicated to implement than those you have looked at so far. They also rely upon the BackOffice Software Developers Kit (discussed in the Summary of this chapter) due to the requirement for headers, libraries, and so forth. The BackOffice SDK includes fairly good documentation on these programming interfaces. Given these factors, you should check this out if you require these options. Only a brief description is provided here.

SMS API

There is a powerful application programming interface for SMS that provides the opportunity to view and manipulate data objects in much the way that SMS itself manipulates them. The programmer can manipulate jobs and packages, as well as work with architectures, security details, and all the other data objects of SMS.

The SMS API requires learning the terminology of SMS's internals and how they relate to each other. Programs can be developed in C or Visual Basic. Approximately eight sample programs are supplied, many of which are potentially useful or interesting in themselves. You may want to explore this area of SMS programming even if you have no particular applications currently in mind.

Packages

Preparing packages to install programs is usually fairly straightforward, as any experienced SMS administrator will know. The SMS Administrator provides a nice facility to create packages and set appropriate options. There are also additional package options available—you may have observed this from more advanced packages provided by Microsoft or other vendors.

The BackOffice SDK does include a discussion of creating packages to do installations. This mostly involves details relating to package definition files and the considerations under which these files are used.

Extending the Network Monitor

The network monitor is a powerful utility, useful for resolving some kinds of computer management problems, but it is not strongly related to SMS. The SMS Administrator can be used to initiate the network monitor for a particular computer, but otherwise the two are separate products. Recognizing these factors, Microsoft has now made the network monitor available with Windows NT 4.0.

The BackOffice SDK provides the resources necessary to extend the Network Monitor, regardless of whether it is used with SMS. The extensions enable the Network Monitor to understand

44

INTERFACING TO
AND EXTENDING
SMS

protocols that Microsoft has not yet provided parsers for (an example of which is DECnet). A new parser can be used by creating and registering a DLL, which is called at predefined functions and which should use various functions and data structures that Network Monitor provides. Note that DLLs are normally created in the C programming language.

Summary

This chapter provided you with many details on programming solutions with SMS. With a good understanding of the SMS database, interfacing SMS with Word or Access provides the programmer with powerful yet easy-to-use facilities to use the data collected by SMS. The SMS administrator can also readily extend the SMS database to collect other data that may be required. Other programming options enable the programmer to extend the network monitor, use packages more effectively, or manipulate SMS objects.

Combined with reviewing the sample code provided on this book's CD-ROM, you should be able to work out any details needed to implement your own solutions. Microsoft's BackOffice Software Developers Kit (SDK) is an excellent source for a more in-depth discussion of these topics. The BackOffice SDK (at least the SMS-related materials) are good for reference purposes, but often presume details that may not be obvious to the novice SMS programmer. *Microsoft BackOffice 2 Unleashed* is a good source to start on this advanced topic, and the BackOffice SDK can be used to build on that knowledge. The BackOffice SDK has been included with the Microsoft Developers Network subscriptions on occasion and is also an important part of the Microsoft Solutions Developers Kit. See `http://www.microsoft.com/catalog/products/msdk/default.htm` for more details.

IX
PART

Finishing Touches

BackOffice Logo Requirements

by Joe Greene

IN THIS CHAPTER

Logo requirements? This sounds like something that should be in a marketing book rather than a technical computer book. One of the things that I have often observed in the computer industry is that many of the growing software firms out there are composed of a group of techies who get together with a good idea, a little money, and a lot of energy. They tend not to have huge marketing or legal departments, so they make their own decisions on licensing agreements, product literature, and other such issues. I thought that these people would benefit from a brief discussion of the BackOffice logo program that Microsoft runs.

Even if you are a regular user, developer, or system administrator, you might want to understand a little more about what the logo means. You see hundreds of product logos every year as you read materials and install new software. Most are designed strictly for their artistic and marketing appeal. They want to make you run right out and buy the product. There are several key differences with the BackOffice logo program that actually provide benefits to the consumer rather than to the sales organization.

This chapter is designed to cover what is required to get the BackOffice logo. It also focuses on what benefits this logo can provide to the developers, resellers, and consumers.

Value of Certification

With the rapid pace of change in the computer industry, a problem arose for the larger companies such as Microsoft and Novell. People started making products that claimed to work perfectly with Windows or Netware. Many of these did work well; however, a number did not. Perhaps they worked correctly with an old version of Netware or Windows, but caused serious problems with the current versions. This led to a lot of fussing over whether the problem was with the operating system or with the third-party product.

No one was really happy with this situation. The operating system vendors were made to look bad because products were difficult to integrate. Application vendors were under pressure to say that they were compatible with the operating system, because all their competitors were making the same claim. Information systems shops had to perform a lot of inhouse testing to see whether a product actually lived up to its claims. It was tough because there was no one definition of what "compatible" actually meant.

The larger companies came up with a brilliant use of the trademark laws to settle this issue. Anyone can write applications to run on these operating systems. Anyone can say the words "works with Windows NT." Microsoft has implemented a trademark logo, however, that has some graphics and the words "Designed for Microsoft BackOffice." It has gone out to the users and said that it has successfully tested the products that are licensed to use this logo. Users want tested products, so this is a big selling point for products. Because the logo is trademarked, you cannot display this logo unless you let Microsoft test the product.

The concept of Microsoft logo testing is easy enough to understand. Vendors send a copy of their product to Microsoft. The folks in Redmond put the product through a standard series of tests against a published list of requirements. If everything works well, the product is authorized to use the logo, which is shown in Figure 45.1.

FIGURE 45.1.

The Designed for Microsoft BackOffice logo.

Designed for

Microsoft®
BackOffice™

It is important to understand what this list of requirements is in order to understand the value of the logo program. If these tests merely showed that the application could execute in some form under the Windows NT operating system, they would be pretty meaningless. There is a big difference between having an application capable of running and having it run well and fit in with other applications. Most of the requirements for the BackOffice logo are actually focused on using the standard technologies, discussed earlier in this book, that build a tightly integrated environment.

This logo certification process was actually a bit of a fuss when it came to the Windows 95 operating system. Windows 95 implemented a number of changes to the standard Windows client interface. Microsoft had issued the Windows logo for years based on the technologies of the older Windows 3.1 product. It had to face the fact that many application developers did not want to spend the time to implement all the new technologies, such as 32-bit operations and the registry that are a part of the Windows 95 environment. If this wasn't a part of the certification process, however, you would have a number of applications that executed under Windows 95, but did not implement the advanced features that Microsoft spent so much time implementing and that increased user productivity. Microsoft decided to make these technologies part of the requirement for the logo in this environment, although it gave developers a little time to implement the new technologies.

BackOffice takes a similar position when it comes to its technologies. One of the key requirements for a server application to get BackOffice certification, for example, is that it run as a Windows NT service. This actually requires a bit of work by the software developers, who have to deal with the fact that services run in a much different environment than regular user processes. If the server applications did not run as services, however, you would not be able to use standard Windows NT commands to start and stop the server application. This is just one example of how developers are asked to put up with a little pain to make applications more standard and easy to use.

What are the benefits of this program for application developers and those of us who consume the products that wear this logo? My list of advantages includes the following:

■ These products have been tested to function with the latest versions of the BackOffice family. Note that this is not a quality assurance test from Microsoft that every function on every menu will work as advertised. Instead, Microsoft tests the key interface technologies that relate to the application's capability of working in the BackOffice environment.

- These products incorporate the key technologies on which Microsoft is betting its future. A lot of engineers sit around and argue about which object model is the best. Microsoft builds operating systems that outsell the competition. If you want to use and develop products that work in this environment and with other products designed for this environment, you have to use the technologies that are standards in this environment. A lot of DOS developers built their own printer schemes and security schemes, but in the end everyone flocked to products that implemented the new Windows standards because they were common across a wide range of applications.

- These vendors have shown a fair commitment to standards that exist in the BackOffice environment. It takes time to implement all these standard technologies. This time translates into development costs, which can be substantial—especially for smaller companies. This willingness to spend the time and money is a good sign that this vendor does not have the mindset of some of the early PC companies (and mainframe companies) who firmly believed in standards, as long as the standards were the ones that they made up.

- These products incorporate key interoperability features that make integrating them into a BackOffice environment easier. Many of the requirements relate to the product's capability of interfacing with the applicable components of BackOffice, especially those of the Windows NT operating system. Interoperability makes the programmer's and user's jobs so much easier.

- These products incorporate technologies that make them easier to maintain. Another significant feature of these standards is that they emphasize using standard operating system utilities (such as the Windows NT unified logon) as opposed to having vendors make up their own administrative schemes. Other requirements facilitate remote administration of the system, which means that the poor system administrators no longer have to sit at the console in the data center or communications closet, neither of which is as comfortable or productive as their desks.

- The logo reduces the research burden for overloaded information systems organizations. It would be nice if you could run a thorough, full-scale test of every application that you bring into your environment. However, in the real world, most of us have limited time and budget for these purposes. Therefore, every bit of third-party data, such as the logo certification, can be helpful in making your product decisions.

Perhaps many of us get a little nervous every time we see license agreements and all those legal terms. We see all the trademarks and know that there are a bevy of lawyers just waiting to enforce potential violations. Many will remember how Apple computer started suing people, saying that the image of a garbage can was Apple's and that no one else could use it. (I'm not sure what the trash pickup services would have done.) In this case, however, all the legal controls do have a purpose. They designate products that meet a certain set of published criteria that you can review. If you want products that meet these standards, you look for the logo. If you do not care about these standards, you are free to buy whatever product you like.

The Certification Process

This section documents the current certification process for those of you who are developers considering trying to get the logo and for regular users who are curious about what this logo really means. I want to emphasize that I am documenting the current process as of this writing, as downloaded from the Microsoft Web. Microsoft reserves the right to change the process as BackOffice and operating systems evolve. Certainly the requirements continue to evolve as more BackOffice products and application programming interfaces come into being. If you want to apply for the logo, go straight to the Microsoft Web page, then to the BackOffice page, and look for the current logo requirements and applications.

With that legalistic caveat out of the way, let's plunge right into the certification process as it currently exists. When you visit the Microsoft Web page and go to the current page on the BackOffice logo program (see Figure 45.2), you will notice that there are several tracks of certification. The current tracks are as follows:

- *Reseller.* This final track is designed to help people who are not making the products, but want to use the logo when selling products that have been certified for the logo. This is a set of guidelines as to what is legal and what is not with which the reseller needs to comply.

- *Publisher.* This track is designed for authors and publishers who want to place the logos on their publications. There is no formal set of requirements here; rather, it takes the form of a survey (to determine applicability) and license agreement.

- *ISV.* ISV stands for independent software vendor. This is the track that you pursue if you have an application that is designed to work in the BackOffice environment and you want to obtain the right to use the logo.

- *OEM.* OEM stands for original equipment manufacturer. This is the track that you pursue if you have a piece of hardware that you want to have certified as working in the BackOffice environment.

The process for each of these tracks is slightly different. Let's start first with the reseller track because it is the simplest. Resellers do not have to license the BackOffice logo for themselves. Instead, they have to follow the guidelines provided by Microsoft for the use of the logo. Basically, this boils down to using it only to market products that are in the BackOffice family or have been licensed to use the logo by the independent software vendor. Microsoft also asks that you get the artwork directly from Microsoft so that it is sure that it has not been altered in any way. You can get this artwork by sending an e-mail message to Microsoft.

The next track that you might consider is that for publishers. This is actually not very hard, because you have only three pieces of paper to submit. The first is a survey that Microsoft uses to determine the applicability of this publication for the logo and also captures key contact information. (I suppose it would look stupid to have a BackOffice logo on a book about Oracle.) The next piece of paper is a formal license agreement that commits the publisher to using the logo properly. The final requirement is that Microsoft wants a copy of the table of contents or an introductory chapter. You send these materials to Microsoft and it gets back to you within three weeks or so.

FIGURE 45.2.

Designed for BackOffice logo program Web page.

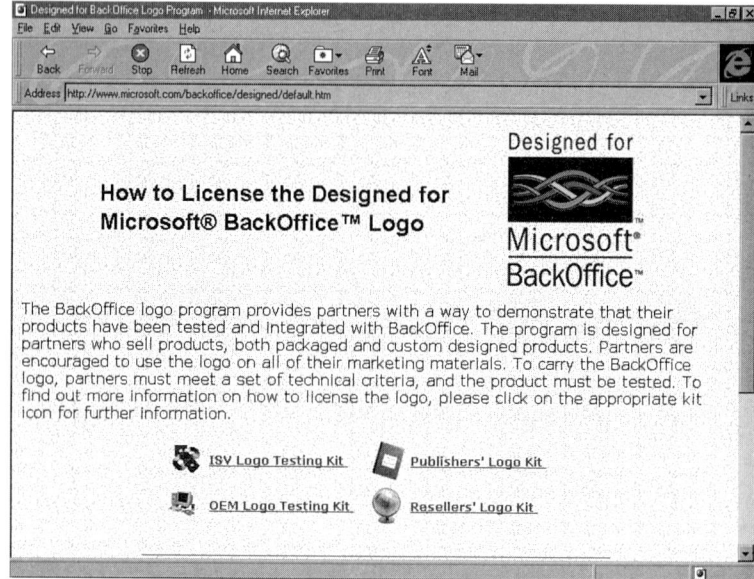

Now you come to some of the more challenging certification processes (which are not really all that difficult). The first one that I want to cover is the five-step certification process for independent software developers:

1. Fill out the software testing questionnaire.
2. Fill out the license agreement.
3. Pay the the testing fees.
4. Send a completed package with the materials mentioned and a copy of your software.
5. Microsoft conducts the test and sends you the results.

The first two steps are basic paperwork. The license agreement is pretty simple to understand and is designed to legally bind you to using the logo properly. The survey is designed to provide Microsoft with the information that it needs to contact you and know what features need to be tested (for example, applicants do not necessarily need to be able to execute jobs on the mainframe as a part of their applications).

The testing fees are the next step in the process. They are not really all that high (ranging from $400 to $3,600 at the current time). Microsoft probably wants to keep people who are not really serious about marketing major commercial applications from sending in products. Imagine if it had to certify every little tool that midnight programmers came up with.) The key here is to look up what the current fees are (server applications are different from client applications, and you have to pay more for non-English products). Then send the money.

In the fourth part of this process, you send Microsoft a copy of your software product. It may require you to send specialized hardware (for example, a mainframe connection if you are testing a package that works with a corresponding product on a mainframe). Typically, however, all it needs is your software. It will test only release versions or final beta versions. It expects that they be fully functional and that no features that affect logo certification will be added after the test process.

After Microsoft has all the information, it conducts the tests. If it finds that you are a wonderful addition to the logo program, it sends you information about using the logo. If you have problems, it will also contact you within 10 days (that is the current schedule as of this writing—again check the Microsoft Web page for current schedules). It does conduct random re-tests of products to verify that the final versions still meet the logo requirements.

The process is similar for the Original Equipment Manufacturers, but is slightly more controlled. The six-step OEM logo certification process is designed for companies that manufacture entire computer systems as opposed to the folks who just make tape drives:

1. Complete the Windows NT Hardware Compatibility Test.
2. Schedule a test appointment.
3. Complete the hardware test questionnaire.
4. Complete the logo license agreement.
5. Pay the testing fee.
6. Send the system to Microsoft.
7. Microsoft completes the testing.

An interesting prerequisite to this test process is that your system has to have completed the Windows NT Hardware Compatibility Test. This makes sense because all BackOffice components are based on NT. It does enable vendors to complete a lower level of certification if all they want to do is state that they can run NT. The requirements for BackOffice in terms of system configuration are much greater (and therefore the systems are more expensive) than those of the NT certification.

A major difference in the OEM certification process is that you have to schedule an appointment to get your system tested. You can request your appointment via e-mail. Microsoft suggests that you allow 45 days for testing at the current time, so do not wait until the week before you release the new server line on which you want to place the logo.

The next two steps involve filling out the applicable questionnaires and license agreements. As with the ISV program, the questions are relatively straight forward. I like the fact that these are more direct, short answers as opposed to essay questions.

After you finish with the paperwork, your next task is to write a check for the testing and send a system to Microsoft for the actual testing. Again, there are requirements that you have to pay careful attention to that ensure that Microsoft is testing a representative sample of your product. If you offer multiple configurations, you have to send copies of those configurations to Microsoft. If you ship systems that do not contain certain standard components (you let users choose their video cards, for example), Microsoft will include standard cards to fill these configurations. If everything goes well, you will receive the kit that contains the logo and all the stuff that your graphics and marketing departments have been screaming for in a relatively short period of time.

I'm not going to leave this section without once again repeating my caveat. The process that I described is the process as it currently exists. Microsoft will probably have to evolve this process as it evolves the BackOffice product family. You really need to check the Microsoft Web page for the current logo requirements when you are about to start the certification process.

Requirements for Certification

So far, you have explored the benefits of the logo program and the basic steps that vendors have to go through to obtain certification. It is useful at this point to go over some of the current requirements for the logo. These requirements will also continue to change, but they give you a feel for what the logo means. As with the certification process, the requirements are divided into four tracks.

The first set of requirements applies to the resellers of BackOffice products:

- The logo may be used in advertising, displays, and other materials that help sell BackOffice components and products licensed to use the BackOffice logo.

- You have to use the logo exactly as it is supplied to you (you cannot cut up pieces or add your own words).

- You need to obtain the artwork (free) from Microsoft directly, rather than getting it from the product vendors.

- You cannot imply that Microsoft is providing endorsements.

- You cannot imply that you are affiliated with or part of Microsoft as part of this logo program.

The next set of requirements applies to the publishers who wish to use the BackOffice logo:

- This is not exactly clear in the program materials, but the implication is that the publication has to contain information on products that work with the BackOffice suite.

The third set of requirements is used to certify software applications produced by ISVs:

■ Server applications must run as a service.

■ Server applications must support both IPX/SPX and TCP/IP. They must support RPC, OLE, named pipes, or Winsock.

■ Server applications must use the unified logon that is the basis of Windows NT security.

■ Server applications must be installable using SMS.

■ If your server application works with Internet Information Server, you must support the ISAPI programming interface.

■ Client applications must meet the requirements for SNA Server, Exchange Server (or Mail), Systems Management Server, SQL Server, or Internet Information Server.

■ Client applications must have a 16-bit Windows architecture.

■ Client applications must use the application programming interfaces for the products with which they interface (MAPI for messaging, for example).

■ SNA client applications must use the WOSA APIs, SNA Server client APIs, and SNA Server compatibility APIs.

■ Messaging client applications must use MAPI, OLE/Messaging, or OLE/Scheduling.

■ SQL Server client applications must use ODBC, DBLib, or embedded SQL to interface with an SQL Server database.

■ SMS client applications must use SMS APIs or ODBC. They must also provide an MIF file.

■ Internet Information Server client applications must support keep-alive processing and NT challenge response.

The final set of requirements is used to certify servers produced by OEMs. The servers must

■ Be on the Windows NT Hardware Compatibility List

■ Have a Pentium-90 (or equivalent RISC processor) or better processor

■ Have a minimum of 32M of RAM per processor

■ Be expandable to 128M of RAM per system

■ Support a 32-bit bus

■ Have 256K or greater of level-2 CPU cache memory

■ Support at least VGA video resolutions

■ Have only components that pass the Windows NT Hardware Compatibility Testing program

■ Have only components that have Windows NT drivers

■ Have, certified by you, the configuration or configurations that you will be delivering (you cannot just certify your high-end machine), including all configuration utilities.

45

BACK**O**FFICE
LOGO
REQUIREMENTS

Summary

This chapter provided you with an appreciation of what the BackOffice logo program is. You learned the basics of the certification process and the current list of requirements to help give you an appreciation of what this process means to you. This chapter also presented a few reasons why you might want to consider looking for this logo when shopping for components to add to your server. The Microsoft BackOffice Web page contains a link to the current program requirements if you are curious.

Resources for BackOffice

by Joe Greene

CHAPTER 46

BackOffice is a broad product line that is getting broader every day. New products and upgrades are going to continue at a furious pace. Add to that service packs, upgrades to drivers, and new drivers and you have quite a task just to keep up with the pace of technology. There is no easy solution to this problem, because it is somewhat analogous to drinking from a fire hose. There are some resources, however, that can help you with the task of keeping up.

This chapter covers some of my favorite sources of information. Because you all have slightly different sets of needs and different ways that you like to get information, a broad sampling of sources is in order.

Information Needs for Administrators and Users

It might be useful to go over some of the information needs that I have run across working with BackOffice servers. Figure 46.1 illustrates some of the basic question areas that might come up. Some of the areas where you might need additional information include the following:

- Detailed information about new products that have been introduced
- Information on service packs and what they can do for your operating system
- Detailed information about the architecture of the products that you have installed
- Detailed operational information for the products that you are supporting
- Problem solving and bug fixes
- Information on interfacing your applications with BackOffice servers
- Information about hardware that is on the market that you might use in an upgrade
- Information about vendor product directions
- List of jobs for experts in the Windows NT and BackOffice environments

FIGURE 46.1.

Basic BackOffice information areas.

Publications

The first tool that you can use in your quest for knowledge includes traditional print publications. This book is one example of such a printed resource. You might consider books that provide more detailed information on specific topics, such as Windows NT Server or SQL Server database administration. It always amazes me when I go to my favorite local bookstore and find how large the section on computer books is and how it always seems to be packed. It's a tribute to the pace of change in the computer industry. If you are not working almost every day to keep up, you are going to fall way behind and forever be confined to modestly paying jobs working on "legacy" systems.

Other good books on the BackOffice family of products can be found in the catalogue in the back of this book or on the Sams Publishing Web site at `http://www.mcp.com/sams/`.

Books have the advantage of being able to provide a lot of detail. Authors and editors spend a lot of time preparing the various sections, graphics, and all the other details. Magazines have the advantage of being quick to produce, however. They are distributed on a routine basis (weekly, monthly, and so forth) and therefore are a great resource for the latest breaking information. They also include some insightful articles and interesting commentary. These magazines vary in focus from those that try to cover the computer industry in general to those that focus on a very specific product (BackOffice, for example). Although I am not here to make any endorsements, here are some of the more popular and topical magazines for your consideration:

- *PCWeek*
- *DBMS*
- *Microsoft Systems Journal*
- *Windows NT Magazine*
- *BackOffice Magazine*
- *Newsletters from the Cobb Group*
- *Information Week*

Microsoft Informational CDs

One of the things that you might notice when you purchase computer software these days is that you do not get a lot of books with the products. Although this makes for a great market for books such as this one, it also leaves some holes in the area of detailed technical information that were typically included in the reference documents of yesteryear. It just seems to cost too much to put out these long-winded technical volumes to everyone when very few people actually get down to this low level of technical detail. One of the common solutions to this information need is to publish CD-ROMs on a routine basis that delve into the more arcane subjects related to a computer product.

Figure 46.2 shows the information from one such CD-ROM product. It comes from the Visual C++ CD that Microsoft sends quarterly to developers who have subscribed to the Microsoft Developers Network. Here you will find all sorts of technical details about the products. The example that I chose focuses on the section on using ODBC with the Visual C++ tool, as in the case of an application that you were interfacing with a SQL Server database.

FIGURE 46.2.

Sample documentation CD-ROM.

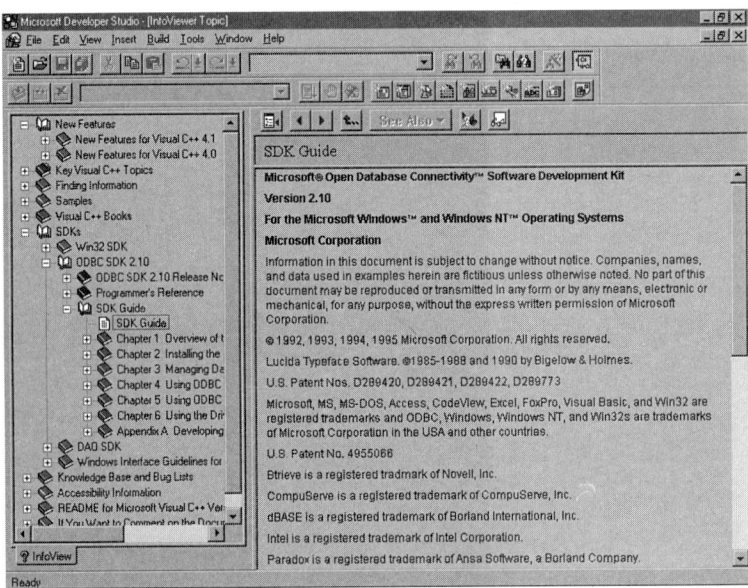

Another subscription product that might be of interest to the more general BackOffice community would be the Technet CD subscription program. The focus here is on the Microsoft products and technologies (that is, COM and DCOM). It is a good resource both for learning the technologies and also for troubleshooting when problems arise. This program uses a tree and book view display similar to that shown in Figure 46.2. I have even installed this product in the CD drive on a server for use by the entire network. CD drives are getting relatively cheap these days, and it is a great way to distribute only the most current information.

The World Wide Web

My favorite source of information is the World Wide Web. Why am I so enthusiastic about this medium when it comes to system support? Not too many years ago, I was quite proud of the set of files that I maintained with vendor product documentation. I religiously sent for information on magazine reader service cards for products that I might need to integrate into one of my projects. My goal was to be able to pull out the product literature when we had to prepare that quick turn-around proposal and then merely confirm pricing.

This system did work, but it became a burden to maintain. I spent a lot of time filing the information that I received. I organized my information by vendor. Sometimes, however, I wished that I had the information by product category (tape drives, for example), because I had trouble remembering what some of the smaller vendors actually sold. I also had trouble keeping track of when I received all the information. It seemed as if I had to work hard to keep refreshing the literature, especially in light of the rapid change in products and pricing that goes on in the computer industry (who would buy a 386/33 PC for $2,500 today!).

One of the first serious uses of the Web by businesses, especially those in the computer industry, was marketing. They realized that with the way they changed their product lines and pricing, it was almost impossible to keep their clients up-to-date. They also had the advantage that computer techies were among the first users of the Web, so they could reasonably argue that their Web pages were reaching the buying audience. Anyway, it is a great way of doing business when researching and integrating computer systems. If you assume that vendors keep their Web pages up-to-date, which I have found to be the case, you are guaranteed to get the latest information whenever you need it. You do not have to listen to salespeople trying to make a sale or answer all the calls to see whether you are going to buy anything after you receive the literature.

What is my process for finding information using the Web? For many vendors, I already know their Web addresses (URLs in Internet parlance). For example, `www.microsoft.com`, `www.oracle.com`, and `www.intel.com` are pretty easy to remember (`www` in front and `com` on the back). I will usually try to see whether the company has a Web site that fits this pattern when I am trying to look up information. If I do not succeed in finding the simple pattern (because the parent company has a name that is different from the common product name or someone else got that Internet name first), I will try one of the Internet search engines to find the appropriate page. Some of the common search engines can be found at the following addresses:

- `www.yahoo.com`
- `www.webcrawler.com`
- `www.lycos.com`

These engines typically have a box in which you would enter the search criteria. Suppose, for example, that I wanted to find the address for Hewlett-Packard printers. I would type **Hewlett-Packard** as my search criteria and then touch the search button. I would then get a number of matching responses back in a display similar to Figure 46.3. The nice feature about this result is that the underlined lines are actually links to the pages themselves. You can just click on the underlined text to go to the Web site that is described. It is a very easy way to navigate to an unknown location.

Once you find the address of the site that you want, you will typically be taken to the main page for the company. After that, you have the opportunity to follow links to other pages at the site that are of interest to you. You can find general Microsoft information, information about various products, and other literature. Figure 46.4 shows a sample of one of the pages in the BackOffice section of Microsoft's Web site. As you can see, there is a wealth of information available.

FIGURE 46.3.

Sample search engine results page.

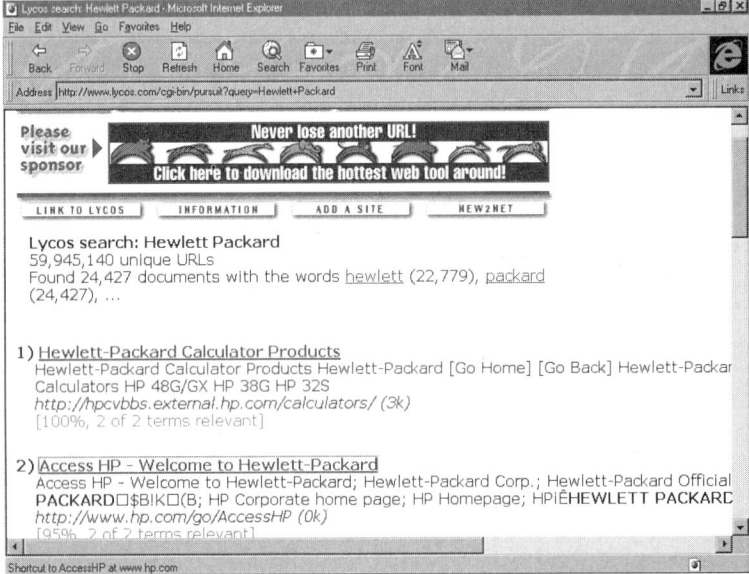

FIGURE 46.4.

Sample BackOffice Web page.

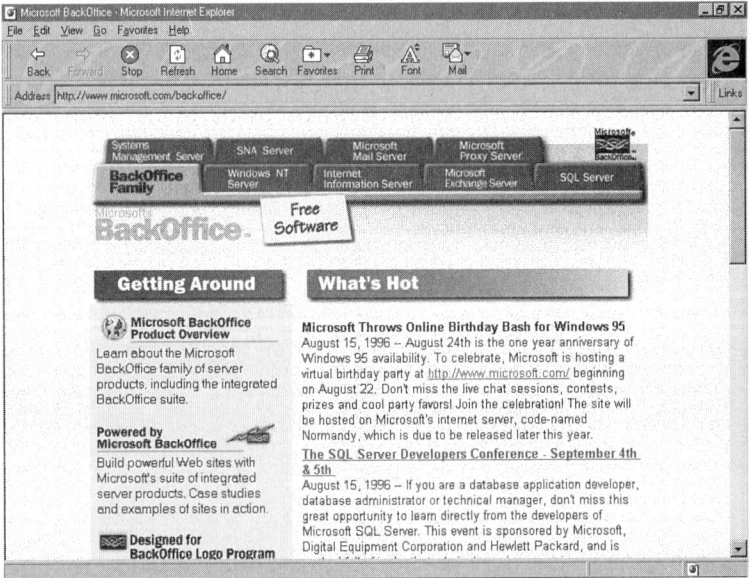

Another good use of the Web is to download the latest drivers and other products. Figure 46.5 shows a sample page on the Microsoft site and some of the new products and drivers for existing products that you can download. Examples here include an evaluation version of the latest release of SQL Server, the initial release of the Internet Information Server (for NT 3.51 systems that did not have IIS bundled with them as NT 4.0 systems do), and a set of ODBC drivers. Again, once you learn the easy point-and-click interface of the Web, you can navigate to other sites and pages. You can also download software with a single click. It can be a very powerful tool, because there is already a great deal of product support on the Web and it continues to increase.

FIGURE 46.5.

Sample page on the Microsoft site showing new products and drivers that you can download.

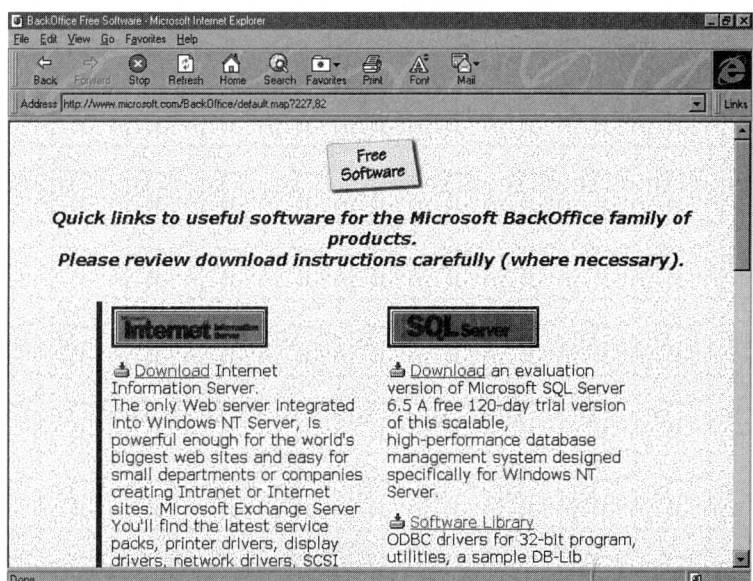

A final note is that many third-party vendors provide a good deal of support through the Web similar to the Microsoft examples that have been covered so far. Obviously, some are better than others. However, even on the poorer sites you can usually get basic product information and numbers to call if you have questions that are not answered on the Web site. You never know until you try. Heck, I even downloaded a specific MPEG driver for an IBM notebook for the Windows 95 operating system in a matter of minutes that helped me get a system out in the field in an afternoon. Imagine how long it would have taken if I'd had to send for the disk.

Newsgroups

Web pages are a really great source of information. However, they tend to be a one-way communications vehicle. The provider determines the content and you review it. There is often far more content than you would want to see, so you can usually find what you want. What do you do when you have a really unusual or specific problem, however?

One answer to this dilemma is the Internet Newsgroups. There are an enormous number of newsgroups out there with topics ranging from beer making to social commentary (there are a lot of commentary pages for frustrated individuals). Anyway, this is an interactive medium where you post a question or comment in a newsgroup that is devoted to the subject matter that you want to discuss. The goal here is to get a review of what you write by a large number of people, some of whom are experts and others who are amateurs. In most cases, you can find someone who has the same or a similar problem and can provide you with some insight into your situation.

Figure 46.6 shows a partial listing of the newsgroups that might be of interest to BackOffice users. Best of all, most newsgroup readers will provide you with a list of newsgroups that are available on your news server. You do not have to look at the list provided in a book that was published several months or years ago. Go out and look at the list in the `comp.os` and `comp.database` sections to see what is currently available. Newsgroups often split up to reduce the number of messages that a given individual has to monitor. Other times, new ones are formed and old ones die out. Check what is currently available using your browser (which is what I was doing in Figure 46.6).

FIGURE 46.6.

Some newsgroups of interest to BackOffice users.

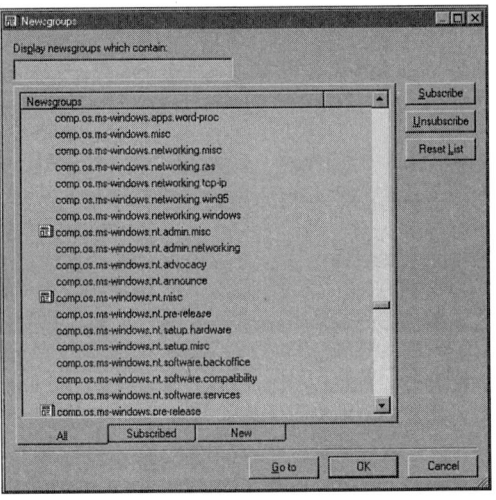

A few words of caution are in order about newsgroup postings. This is an interesting world subculture where you get some of the best minds in the business. You also get a lot of lonely people and some people that are downright arrogant. Here are some suggestions for those of you who are new to newsgroups:

- Carefully evaluate the responses that you receive to questions. Usually, you will get someone with a high level of experience who can really save you a lot of time. Occasionally, you will get people who just want to see their names on a list of postings. If a response does not make sense to you and is not corroborated by other responses, you might want to just ignore it.

■ Be careful about using inflammatory tones in your postings. There are a number of people out there who are just looking for something to gripe about, and this will distract people from the business at hand (answering your question).

■ You might want to study the etiquette of the Net before you deviate from simple technical question and response postings. There are a lot of people who are sensitive about job postings (even though you see them all of the time in the technical newsgroups for products that are in demand) and topics that do not relate to the designated subject matter of the newsgroup. It's a good idea to read the newsgroup for a while to see what is generally accepted and what is not.

Newsgroups can be a very powerful tool. They can give you access to other people out there who are doing work similar to your own. Many of these people might have seen the problem before and may have actually solved it. An amazing number of people will take time to help someone whom they do not even know in response to a posting on the newsgroup. (I like that flavor of community that is found on the Net.) Perhaps you have more in common with a BackOffice administrator in a foreign country than you do with the politicians who are running your own country. . .

Users Groups

A local alternative for those who are not connected to the Internet or who like interpersonal communications is a local users group for NT and/or BackOffice users. What users groups are available in your area? The best way to find out would be to call your local Microsoft representatives or monitor the newsgroups and list servers to see whether there are any in your area. If you know of several people who do work similar to your own, you might want to form your own users group, local contacts who may be willing to have you call them for advice when you are in real trouble.

Microsoft NT and BackOffice users groups are relatively new and rare. Here are a few ideas from the local Oracle users group that I belong to—it shows what a group that has been around for a little while can do:

■ Have speakers from the product vendors come in to discuss new products. You would be amazed at the number of sales and technical people who will even fly in from out of town if you tell them that you have a fair-sized group of people who actually work in the environment of interest.

■ Provide sessions where members bring up problems that they are challenged with and see whether others have any suggestions for these problems.

■ Have members present their evaluations of new products that might be of interest to other members. This is often better than having vendor representatives come in, because your members will often give you more candid opinions about the products.

■ Have members provide feedback on all those major conferences that you would like to attend, but there is no budget or time.

Listservers

Finally, there is an Internet tool that lets you routinely receive electronic mail on a given subject. You send an e-mail to the appropriate listserver administrator who then adds your name to his or her distribution list (this is usually an automated process where you type the word subscribe in the text or heading of your message and it figures out your e-mail address). You then continue to receive mailings until you tell them to stop your subscription. In effect, these listservers are the equivalent of electronic magazines that get delivered to your electronic mail inbox as opposed to your paper mailbox.

Where do you find out the listservers that are available? You will often find articles discussing them in the appropriate Internet newsgroups. You can also find references to a number of them on various Web pages while you are surfing around. There are several newsgroups on Windows NT and BackOffice that are provided by Microsoft. To subscribe, go to the Microsoft home page and surf around until you find them (they are relatively easy to find once you get the knack of surfing the Web; they move around as the Web pages are designed, so polish up your surfing skills).

Summary

This chapter provided you with a start on finding resources that will help you administer and use your BackOffice environment to its maximum potential. The use of Internet resources was stressed in this discussion because that is a current emphasis of Microsoft. It enables you to get up-to-date information and software whenever you need them. Traditional printed materials (such as this book) provide you with insight and information about the products. Most of the people that I have come across (even computer types) tend to prefer printed material for commentary, general discussions, and step-by-step instructions. The electronic forms of media tend to be better when you need up-to-date information, software to download, or answers to a very specific technical question. Try out these various information sources when you have the time so that you know exactly where to go and how to use these tools when problems arise and you are desperate for information.

The Future of BackOffice

by Joe Greene

IN THIS CHAPTER

So far, this book has been devoted to technical facts and step-by-step procedures. Before you leave this book, let's have a little bit of fun speculating on where the BackOffice family is going to be a few years from now. Actually, there is some good that comes of all this speculation. If you read enough speculations about where the industry is going, you can get a feel for common themes. More often than not, these common ideas lead to products that will be on the market down the road.

This chapter is divided into three basic sections. In the first section I reiterate my beliefs on the market-driven nature of the BackOffice product family to set the stage for my later work at the crystal ball. Next, you learn some of the things that I have gleaned from watching the videotapes and reviewing the presentation slides from the 1996 Microsoft Professional Developer's Conference. Finally, the third section in this chapter presents some impressions that I have obtained from recent product announcements and position papers from both Microsoft and the other major players in this field.

Market Drives

Many vendors—some of who are no longer around—have complained that the Microsoft marketing machine is an unstoppable force. They credit all of Microsoft's success to this marketing machine. Perhaps this is just an excuse for their own lack of success. Although it is true that Microsoft does have a marketing flair, it is also good at anticipating what the market is going to demand and having products ready (or at least close to ready) when they are needed.

A few examples seem to be in order here. When Windows first came out, many vendors ignored the success of the Macintosh environment and stuck with their good old DOS products where the development costs had already been paid and they were in the mode of raking in the profits. They felt that users were weak when they asked for a convenient user interface and strong standards for interacting with the computer. This incorrect reading of the market cost many of the early PC industry giants their dominance in the industry, if their companies survived at all.

Microsoft was also one of the first companies to sense the desire among users for a tightly integrated office automation environment. Although other companies were content to be the dominant force in a particular market (spreadsheets or PC databases), Microsoft built up a suite of products that were eventually integrated to enable users to easily move data from one application into another. It also provided common tools and interfaces between the products to make them easier to use. The market preferred this integrated approach to processing over a series of individual products that might have been stronger in certain specialty areas. This correct reading of the market's desires led to Microsoft's dominance in the office automation world where it had lagged behind for many years.

With BackOffice, Microsoft is turning its attention to the server market, as shown in Figure 47.1. This is a market that is ripe for integration and simplification. The market leaders are fragmented. They provide a number of proprietary solutions designed for certain niche tasks.

It is the responsibility of the local information systems shops to integrate applications that run on Novell servers and several flavors of UNIX with the processing capabilities of the mainframe. There are a number of specialty-product vendors, each of which has its own set of requirements and system of doing business. This is not a pleasant situation for many information systems shops that are under pressure to do more with less resources. Several vendors have seen this situation—the real question is which one or ones will get to market with viable solutions.

FIGURE 47.1.

Factors in the server marketplace.

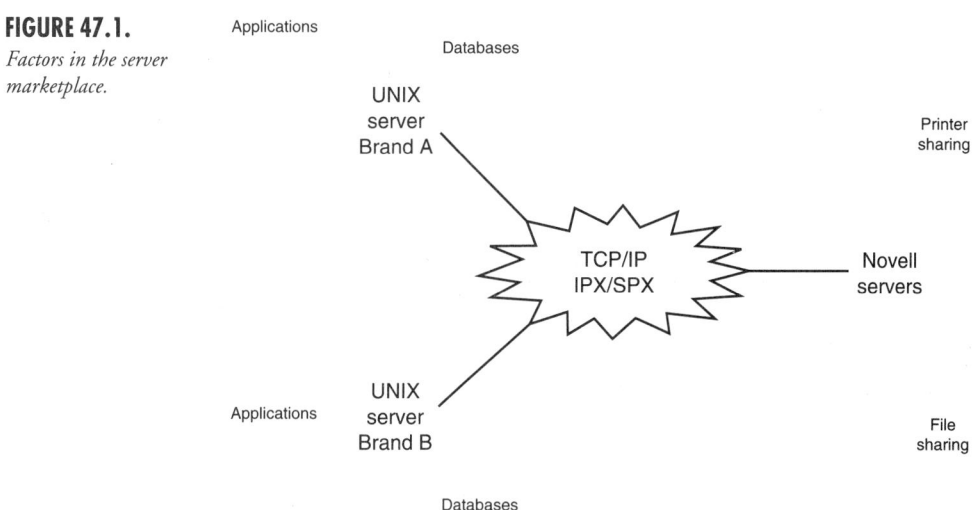

BackOffice is Microsoft's solution to this situation. Microsoft read this situation several years ago and started to work on solutions. It has had to make changes along the way. The rapid growth of the Internet technologies has caused it to place additional emphasis on ensuring that their solutions use these standards. It also has the advantage of being large and successful enough to be able to devote massive resources to their projects. Most of the software companies that have long success records have regularly devoted large portions of their profits to research and development that fuels future growth. Those that try to build a product and then collect the profits are now chapters in the history books.

Anyway, the key point is that if you want to see where Microsoft is headed, look at where the industry is going. You could argue that Microsoft has a strong influence on where the computer industry is headed. There are many cases, however, where Microsoft has realized that it was not heading in the right direction and took action to correct its course. Examples of this include the small Internet-related companies such as Vermeer that Microsoft purchased when it realized that it was lacking in certain product areas, such as Web page authoring tools.

47

THE FUTURE OF
BACKOFFICE

Predictions from 1996 Professional Developer Conference

The strongest theme that I gathered from my review of the materials from this conference was Microsoft's strong commitment to being a provider of Internet-based solutions, as witnessed in most of the talks by high-level officials. It was also reflected in many of the lower-level detailed talks that were designed to actually show how to implement solutions. Specifically, the following key elements struck me as important:

- The BackOffice product family was going to contain products that met all the major Internet product needs.

- Specific emphasis was placed on developing tools that facilitated commerce over the Internet.

- Tools that enabled the Web to integrate with database management systems were deemed necessary to enable Web pages to be based on dynamic user needs as opposed to being static-based on what the authors came up with.

- Tools that enabled developers to build programming constructs into the Internet environment were also a major emphasis. These tools enable developers to build custom applications to meet specific product needs.

- Commitments were made to place many of the common services that are needed in an Internet environment into the operating systems themselves. This includes support for the TCP/IP protocol, Web servers, FTP servers, and domain name servers in the case of server operating systems.

- Commitments were also made to build Internet information access tools directly into the operating system or make them available for free through the Internet. The prime example of this is the Internet Explorer Web browser, which now includes newsgroup reader and Internet mail services in addition to its traditional Web and FTP browser capabilities.

- The operating system will evolve to incorporate some of the object-oriented file technologies that have been under development by Microsoft under various code names such as Cairo.

Another common theme that struck me in these presentations was the desire to provide a complete product family. Perhaps drawing from their successes in the office automation world, Microsoft seems committed to build a suite of products that are designed to work together and meet all of the common Internet server needs. Many of these products are built directly into the Windows NT Server operating system. The rest will be provided by one or more of the BackOffice products. These products feature tight integration with one another and the Windows NT Server operating system.

A theme that ran through many of the discussions was that of building intranets (see Figure 47.2). Many of the services that people envision for the Internet of the future are just not practical today. People want to exchange large amounts of information, such as full motion video presentations and audio files. The support infrastructure of the Internet, and even most local communications lines, is just not big enough to transfer significant volumes of this information. That volume of information, however, can be transmitted over many of the existing Ethernet local area networks. This will be especially true as more organizations upgrade to the 100 Mbps networks that are starting to become commercially available.

FIGURE 47.2.

Advantages of intranets.

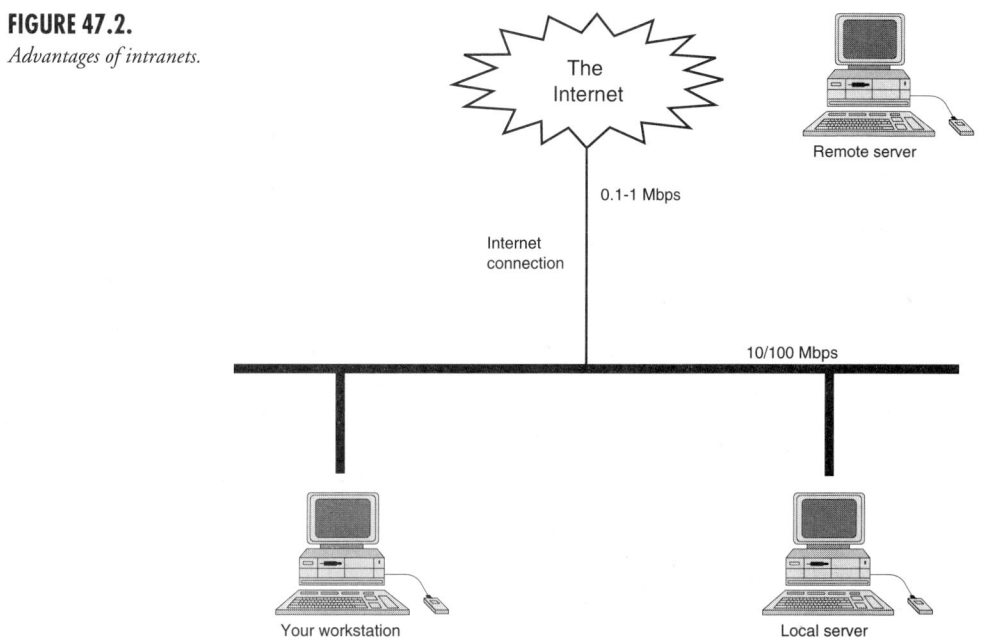

Also, there are many organizations that are just not ready to put their entire company on the Internet. They may be willing to keep a Web server for product information, but they have too much in the way of sensitive material to risk on the Internet. Perhaps they just want to use the powerful yet friendly tools that have been developed for the Internet to provide access to their own internal information. Microsoft seems to be well positioned to move into this market. Its capabilities of supporting a less-expensive server environment than many UNIX-based Internet tools and using more powerful development tools (such as ISAPI and Java) enable you to develop full Internet-based applications for the first time. Although it is true that you can find Java in other environments, many of the early Java applications have been interesting toys and not fully database-integrated business applications.

A final theme that I would like to mention in this section is that of building a complete package for Internet Service Providers (ISPs). Currently, most of the vendors who offer Internet services to other companies and individuals use UNIX computers. The ISPs then integrate a series of products that they feel has the best cost/performance benefits to build a suite of services to offer to their clients. The ISP is usually responsible for working out conflicts between the products and keeping the environment running smoothly on their chosen flavor of UNIX. What Microsoft seems to be targeting here is the use of the BackOffice products that it has developed to sell to these integrators. They offer the benefits of tight integration, easier administration, and the capability of using potentially less expensive hardware platforms. You may have read about this product under the Normandy code name.

Recent Product Announcements

Everyone that I talked to seemed almost overwhelmed by the volume of product announcements and new application programming interfaces that were discussed at the Professional Developers Conference. Since this conference, however, the pace of announcements has not seemed to slack up. Specific initiatives that have caught my interest include the following:

- *Activating Web pages.* This is a series of ActiveX technologies that enable applications to be downloaded and run by Web browsers as they are needed. This is, in effect, a technology that enables you to download miniature applications when needed as opposed to loading a large application suite.

- *Activating Web servers.* This is a series of programming technologies that enables your server to adapt the pages it displays based on previous input by the user or information retrieved from a database. You also have the option of performing some of the work done by active clients on the server if you desire more control or want to support less powerful clients.

- *Internet security and Internet commerce products.* A number of Internet security and Internet commerce products have been released for beta testing. These technologies would turn the Internet into a business technology that would convert Internet servers from a marketing expense into a source of revenue.

- *Group conferencing technologies.* Several group conferencing technologies have been released in beta format that could enable the Internet and other corporate networks to be used for meetings by groups that are geographically separated.

- *Integration of newsgroup server technology into Exchange Server.* Early testing of the last common Internet technology that is missing from the BackOffice family—the integration of newsgroup server technology into Exchange Server.

Next, there seems to be a strong direction towards supporting as many technologies as possible. This is exemplified by the support of Java (in the J++ version of the language), ISAPI interfaces to C++, Visual Basic Web scripting, ActiveX components, and a number of other technologies. Perhaps Microsoft concluded that no one can accurately see exactly where the market is going. Therefore, it is trying to provide a range of products and see which one consumers prefer.

Finally, Microsoft is moving to merge the Web technologies directly into the operating system itself. Just as Network Neighborhood and Explorer enable you to actively scan and work with documents on your current local area network with the same ease that you work with documents on your own computer, they will be modified to enable you to access documents on the Internet or intranet. This is a good feature because most users do not really care where a document is or what format it is stored in—they just want access to the data. They also tend to not want to have to learn a number of different interfaces to find that information.

Summary

This chapter was not designed to be a long, exhaustive analysis of where Microsoft is heading with the BackOffice family. A lot will be determined based on how users accept some of the Internet products that are being put forth today. Especially in the area of tools to develop applications based on the Web technologies, there are a number of tools that are being offered in parallel with one another to see what people will choose. Microsoft also seems to be working to build a complete server product line of supporting tools. I have seen no indications that it plans on releasing a series of vertical applications (that is, Oracle's manufacturing suite), but then again only time will tell.

INDEX

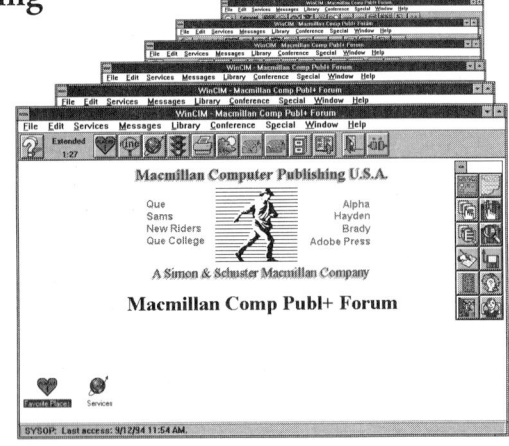

Windows NT 4 Server Unleashed

Jason Garms

The Windows NT Server has been gaining tremendous market share over Novell, and the new upgrade—which includes a Windows 95 interface—is sure to add momentum to its market drive. To that end, *Windows NT 4.0 Server Unleashed* is written to meet that growing market. It provides information on disk and file management, integrated networking, BackOffice integration, and TCP/IP protocols. CD-ROM includes source code from the book and valuable utilities. Focuses on using Windows NT as an Internet server. Covers security issues and Macintosh support.

$59.99 USA/$84.95 CDN   *User Level: Accomplished - Expert*
ISBN: 0-672-30933-5   *1,100 pages*

Windows NT 4 Workstation Unleashed

Sean Mathias, et al.

NT Workstation is expected to become the platform of choice for corporate America! This new edition focuses on NT Workstation's new and improved features as a high-end graphics workstation and scaleable development platform. Provides in-depth advice on installing, configuring, and managing Windows NT Workstation. Features comprehensive, detailed advice for NT. CD-ROM includes Windows NT utilities, demos, and more. Covers version 4.

$49.99 USA/$70.95 CDN   *User Level: Accomplished - Expert*
ISBN: 0-672-30972-6   *800 pages*

Microsoft Internet Information
Server 2 Unleashed

Art Knowles, et al.

The power of the Microsoft Internet Information Server 2 is meticulously detailed in this 800+ page volume. Readers will learn how to create and maintain a Web server, integrate IIS with BackOffice, and create interactive databases that can be used on the Internet or a corporate intranet. Readers learn how to set up and run IIS. Teaches advanced security techniques and how to configure the server. CD-ROM includes source code from the book and powerful utilities. Covers Microsoft Internet Information Server.

$49.99 USA/$70.95 CDN   *User Level: Accomplished - Expert*
ISBN: 1-57521-109-2   *896 pages*

Microsoft Exchange Server Survival Guide

Greg Todd

Readers will learn the difference between Exchange and other groupware, such as Lotus Notes, and everything about the Exchange Server, including troubleshooting, development, and how to interact with other BackOffice components. Teaches how to prepare, plan, and install the Exchange Server. Explores ways to migrate from other mail apps, such as Microsoft Mail and cc:Mail. Covers Microsoft Exchange.

$49.99 USA/$70.95 CDN   *User Level: New - Advanced*
ISBN: 0-672-30890-8   *800 pages*

Programming Windows NT 4 Unleashed

David Hamilton, Mickey Williams, and Griffith Kadnier

Readers get a clear understanding of the modes of operation and architecture for Windows NT. Everything—including execution models, processes, threads, DLLs, memory, controls, security, and more—is covered with precise detail. CD-ROM contains source code and complete sample programs from the book. Teaches OLE, DDE, Drag and Drop, OCX development, and the component gallery. Explores Microsoft BackOffice programming.

$59.99 USA/$84.95 CDN　　　*User Level: Accomplished - Expert*
ISBN: 0-672-30905-X　　　*1,200 pages*

Windows NT 4 Web Development

Sanjaya Hettihewa

Windows NT and Microsoft's newly developed Internet Information Server is making it easier and more cost-effective to set up, manage, and administer a good Web site. Because the Windows NT environment is relatively new, there are few books on the market that adequately discuss its full potential. *Windows NT 4 Web Development* addresses that potential by providing information on all key aspects of server setup, maintenance, design, and implementation. CD-ROM contains valuable source code and powerful utilities. Teaches how to incorporate new technologies into your Web site. Covers Java, JavaScript, Internet Studio, and Visual Basic Script. Covers Windows NT.

$59.99 USA/$84.95 CDN　　　*User Level: Accomplished - Expert*
ISBN: 1-57521-089-4　　　*744 pages*

Microsoft BackOffice 2.0 Administrator's Survival Guide, Second Edition

Arthur Knowles

This all-in-one reference describes how to make the components of BackOffice version 2 work best together and with other networks. BackOffice is Microsoft's complete reference for networking, database, and system management products. Contains the fundamental concepts required for daily maintenance, troubleshooting, and problem solving. CD-ROM includes product demos, commercial and shareware utilities, and technical notes from Microsoft vendor technical support personnel. Covers version 2.0.

$59.99 USA/$84.95 CDN　　　*User Level: Accomplished*
ISBN: 0-672-30977-7　　　*1,200 pages*

Apache Server Survival Guide

Manuel Alberto Ricart

As one of the most popular servers on the Internet, Apache Server is an inexpensive, secure alternative to other Web servers! This book is an excellent resource that addresses diverse networking and configuration issues. Provides all the knowledge needed to build and manage an Apache Web site. CD-ROM includes source code from the book, utilities, and demos. Covers the latest version.

$49.99 USA/$70.95 CDN　　　*User Level: Accomplished*
ISBN: 1-57521-175-0　　　*700 pages*

Add to Your Sams Library Today with the Best Books for Programming, Operating Systems, and New Technologies

The easiest way to order is to pick up the phone and call
1-800-428-5331
between 9:00 a.m. and 5:00 p.m. EST.
For faster service please have your credit card available.

ISBN	Quantity	Description of Item	Unit Cost	Total Cost
0-672-30933-5		Windows NT 4 Server Unleashed (Book/CD-ROM)	$59.99	
0-672-30972-6		Windows NT 4 Workstation Unleashed (Book/CD-ROM)	$49.99	
1-57521-109-2		Microsoft Internet Information Server 2 Unleashed (Book/CD-ROM)	$49.99	
0-672-30890-8		Microsoft Exchange Server Survival Guide (Book/CD-ROM)	$49.99	
0-672-30905-X		Programming Windows NT 4 Unleashed (Book/CD-ROM)	$59.99	
1-57521-089-4		Windows NT 4 Web Development (Book/CD-ROM)	$59.99	
0-672-30977-7		Microsoft BackOffice 2 Administrator's Survival Guide, Second Edition (Book/CD-ROM)	$59.99	
1-57521-175-0		Apache Server Survival Guide (Book/CD-ROM)	$49.99	

❑ 3 ½" Disk

❑ 5 ¼" Disk

Shipping and Handling: See information below.

TOTAL

Shipping and Handling: $4.00 for the first book, and $1.75 for each additional book. Floppy disk: add $1.75 for shipping and handling. If you need to have it NOW, we can ship product to you in 24 hours for an additional charge of approximately $18.00, and you will receive your item overnight or in two days. Overseas shipping and handling adds $2.00 per book and $8.00 for up to three disks. Prices subject to change. Call for availability and pricing information on latest editions.

201 W. 103rd Street, Indianapolis, Indiana 46290

1-800-428-5331 — Orders   1-800-835-3202 — FAX   1-800-858-7674 — Customer Service

Book ISBN 0-672-30816-9

What's on the Disc

The companion CD-ROM contains all the authors' source code and samples from the book and many third-party software products.

Windows 95 Installation Instructions

1. Insert the CD-ROM disc into your CD-ROM drive.
2. From the Windows 95 desktop, double-click on the My Computer icon.
3. Double-click on the icon representing your CD-ROM drive.
4. Double-click on the icon titled SETUP.EXE to run the installation program.

Installation creates a program group named MS BackOffice 2 Unleashed. This group contains icons to browse the CD-ROM.

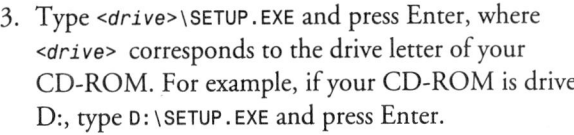

> **NOTE**
>
> If Windows 95 is installed on your computer, and you have the AutoPlay feature enabled, the SETUP.EXE program starts automatically when you insert the disc into your CD-ROM drive.

Windows NT Installation Instructions

1. Insert the CD-ROM disc into your CD-ROM drive.
2. From File Manager or Program Manager, choose Run from the File menu.
3. Type `<drive>\SETUP.EXE` and press Enter, where `<drive>` corresponds to the drive letter of your CD-ROM. For example, if your CD-ROM is drive D:, type `D:\SETUP.EXE` and press Enter.

Installation creates a program group named MS BackOffice 2 Unleashed. This group contains icons to browse the CD-ROM.